THE LAW OF TRUSTS

THE LAW OF TRUSTS
Fourth Edition

AUSTIN WAKEMAN SCOTT
Late Dane Professor of Law, Emeritus
Harvard University

WILLIAM FRANKLIN FRATCHER
R. B. Price Distinguished Professor of Law, Emeritus
University of Missouri

VOLUME IVA

LITTLE, BROWN AND COMPANY
Boston   Toronto

Library of Congress Catalog Card No. 86-81171

ISBN 0-316-29231-1

Fourth Printing

The Law of Trusts was first published in 1939 in four volumes; the
second edition, in five volumes, was published in 1956; and the
third edition, in six volumes, was published in 1967.

MV NY

Published simultaneously in Canada
by Little, Brown & Company (Canada) Limited

Printed in the United States of America

SUMMARY OF CONTENTS

VOLUMES V & VA

VOLUMES VI & VIA

Contents
Table of Cases
Table of Statutes
Table of Uniform Acts
Table of Restatements of the Law
Bibliography
Index

CONTENTS

The complete Table of Contents to the Fourth Edition appears in Volume VI, Fourth Edition.

VOLUME IVA

Contents

Contents

THE LAW OF TRUSTS

════ CHAPTER 11 ════

CHARITABLE TRUSTS

Charitable Trusts

TOPIC 4.   THE ADMINISTRATION OF CHARITABLE TRUSTS

TOPIC 1.   GENERAL PRINCIPLES

§348.   *Definition of Charitable Trust*

For some reason best known perhaps to the psychologists, most legal writers and many courts, when they deal with charitable trusts and particularly when they attempt to define them, are likely to become somewhat lyrical. Even lawyers, otherwise hardheaded, are likely to become poetic. Thus Mr. Horace Binney, the noted lawyer of Philadelphia, in his successful attempt to induce the Supreme Court of the United States to uphold the trust created by the famous merchant prince of the early nineteenth century, Mr. Stephen Girard, who left his wealth for the foundation of a school for orphan children, gave full range to his poetic imagination when he offered to the Court the following definition: "whatever is given for the love of God, or for the love of your neighbor, in the catholic and universal sense — given from these motives, and to these ends — free from the stain or taint of every consideration that is personal, private or selfish."[1] Although this striking statement may appeal to the ear, it is wholly unsound as a definition of a charitable trust. It is not the motive inducing the giver to make his gift that makes the gift charitable. So far as the love of God as a motivating force is concerned it is not essential. Indeed, Mr. Daniel Webster, who was engaged by the heirs of Girard to overthrow his will, and who was to receive $25,000 if successful (at least that is what John Quincy Adams in his diary says that he had heard), laid great stress on the fact that Mr. Girard, so far from showing the love of God, exhibited quite a different feeling when he provided in his will that no minister of any sect whatsoever should ever perform any duty in the institution or should be admitted for any purpose, even as a visitor, within its premises. Mr. Webster said of Mr. Girard's scheme for helping the orphan children to obtain an education: "The plan is unblessed in design and

§348.   [1]See Girard Will Case (1854) 52, containing the arguments of the defendants' counsel in Vidal v. Girard's Exrs., 2 How. 127, 11 L. Ed. 205 (U.S. 1844). The definition is quoted in Price v. Maxwell, 28 Pa. 23, 35 (1857).

See Reiling, Federal Taxation: What Is a Charitable Organization?, 44 A.B.A.J. 525 (1958); Rickett, Charitable Giving in English and Roman Law: A Comparison of Method, [1979] Cambridge L.J. 118.

unwise in purpose. If the court should set it aside, and I be instrumental in contributing to that result, it will be the crowning mercy of my professional life."[2] This crowning mercy and the contingent fee (if the gossip that Mr. Adams heard was based on fact) were denied to Mr. Webster. The Court was not concerned with Mr. Girard's theological orthodoxy. It was not even concerned with the question whether his motive in establishing the institution was to help his neighbors or to spite his heirs, although in fact there is no doubt that Mr. Girard was motivated by an intense desire to serve the community by giving proper secular instruction to orphan children, permitting them to obtain their religious instruction elsewhere. It is the purpose to which the property is to be devoted that determines whether the trust is charitable, not the motives of the testator in giving it. The Court had no difficulty in holding that the establishment of a school for orphan children is a charitable purpose. The real difficulty in deciding the case lay in the fact that in Pennsylvania the English Statute of Charitable Uses, passed in the reign of Queen Elizabeth, had not been adopted. Mr. Binney succeeded in inducing the Court to uphold the trust by his historical researches, which convinced the Court that charitable trusts were enforced in England long before the statute was enacted. This was not an easy task since in an earlier case the Court had held that charitable trusts are not valid in a jurisdiction in which the statute is not in force.[3]

A more cold-blooded definition or description of a charitable trust is given in the Restatement of Trusts. It is there stated that "A charitable trust is a fiduciary relationship with respect to property arising as a result of a manifestation of an intention to create it, and subjecting the person by whom the property is held to equitable duties to deal with the property for a charitable purpose."[4]

---

[2]Vidal v. Girard's Exrs., 2 How. 127, 183, 11 L. Ed. 205 (U.S. 1844).

[3]Trustees of the Philadelphia Baptist Assn. v. Hart's Exrs., 4 Wheat. 1, 4 L. Ed. 499 (U.S. 1819).

[4]The definition is quoted with approval in the following cases:

Federal: Agudas Chasidei Chabad of United States v. Gourary, 650 F. Supp. 1463 (E.D.N.Y. 1987), citing text.

Kansas: In re Estate of Freshour, 185 Kan. 434, 345 P.2d 689, 81 A.L.R.2d 806 (1959) (quoting Restatement of Trusts §348).

A charitable trust, like a private trust, is a fiduciary relationship. The relationship in the case of a private trust is between the trustee and the beneficiaries. In the case of a charitable trust there is ordinarily no definite beneficiary, but the trust is enforceable at the suit of the Attorney General or other public officer.[5] The trustee of a charitable trust is subject to duties as fiduciary similar to those to which the trustee of a private trust is subject, such as the duty of loyalty and the duty not to delegate. Thus a trustee of a charitable trust, like a trustee of a private trust, violates his duty if he permits his self-interest to conflict with his duties as trustee, as, for example, where he sells trust property to himself individually, or purchases his individual property for the trust. It is difficult, if not impossible, in dealing with charitable trusts to employ the terminology of the late Professor Hohfeld, who insisted that all legal relations are relations between persons, and that where one person is under a duty the duty is always owing to another person who has a correlative right. A trustee of a charitable trust is clearly under a duty properly to administer the trust, but it is difficult to see who has the correlative right. The duty can be enforced, as has been stated, in a proceeding brought by the Attorney General, but the duty is not owing to him. It can hardly be said that the duty is owing to the state. Certainly the state as such is not the beneficiary of a charitable trust, except in rare cases; and it has been held that the legislature has no power to destroy or to vary the terms of a valid charitable trust. The truth seems to be that the trustee of a charitable trust owes duties, but the duties are not owing to any person or persons in particular, although they are enforceable at the suit of a public officer for the benefit of the community.

A charitable trust is a relationship "with respect to property." Neither a charitable trust nor a private trust can be created unless there is some property that is the subject of the trust.

Maine: Fitzgerald v. Baxter State Park Auth., 385 A.2d 189 (Me. 1978).

Massachusetts: Hillman v. Roman Catholic Bishop of Fall River, 24 Mass. App. 241, 508 N.E.2d 118 (1987), citing text.

Minnesota: In re Estate of Quinlan, 233 Minn. 35, 45 N.W.2d 807 (1951).

New York: Matter of Morgan, 200 Misc. 645, 107 N.Y.S.2d 180 (1951) (citing the text and quoting Restatement of Trusts §348).

[5]See §391.

The property may, of course, be an interest in a tangible thing, it may be a chose in action, it may be an equitable interest. The principles in regard to what property may be the subject of a charitable trust are the same as the principles applicable to private trusts. It is a relationship "arising as a result of a manifestation of an intention to create it." A charitable trust, like an express private trust, and unlike a constructive trust, is created because a person having power to create it has manifested by his words or conduct an intention to create it.[6] It is a relationship "subjecting the person by whom the property is held to equitable duties." The duties of the trustee of a charitable trust, like those of the trustee of a private trust, are enforceable in a court of chancery or in a court having the powers of a court of chancery. In many states the same court has the powers of a court of law and a court of chancery. In some states courts of probate to some extent have the powers of a court of chancery.

The trustees of a charitable trust are under a duty "to deal with the property for a charitable purpose." In the case of a private trust it is the duty of the trustees to deal with the property for the benefit of the designated beneficiary or beneficiaries. In the case of a private trust, property is devoted to the use of specified persons who are designated as beneficiaries of the trust. In the case of a charitable trust, property is devoted to the accomplishment of purposes that are beneficial or may be supposed to be beneficial to the community. This, indeed, is the fundamental distinction between private trusts and charitable trusts.

We shall more fully consider hereafter questions as to the meaning and scope of charitable purposes.[7]

§348.1. Charitable corporations. The owner of property may devote it to charitable purposes not only by transferring it to trustees in trust for such purposes, but also by transferring it to a charitable corporation.[1] A gift to a charitable

---

[6]United States v. Moon, 718 F.2d 1210 (2d Cir. 1983), *cert. denied,* 466 U.S. 971, 104 S. Ct. 2344, 80 L. Ed. 2d 818 (1984), citing text.

[7]See §§368-377.

§348.1. [1]See Fratcher, Bequests for Purposes, 56 Iowa L. Rev. 773, 797-800 (1971); Note, Permissible Purposes for Nonprofit Corporations, 51 Colum. L. Rev. 889 (1951).

corporation may be made without any restrictions, in which case it may be used by the corporation in such manner as it sees fit for the accomplishment of any of the purposes for which it exists; or the gift may be restricted to the accomplishment of one of the purposes for which the corporation exists; or it may be provided that the corporation may devote the income to any of its purposes or to a particular purpose, but shall not expend the principal. In any event it may be asked whether a gift to a charitable corporation creates a charitable trust.

Certainly many of the principles applicable to charitable trusts are applicable to charitable corporations. In both cases the Attorney General can maintain a suit to prevent a diversion of the property to purposes other than those for which it was given;[2] and in both cases the doctrine of cy pres is applica-

---

As to the distinction between dispositions to a charitable corporation, or an unincorporated charitable association, or a charitable trust, see Fisch, Choosing the Charitable Entity, 114 Trusts & Estates 874 (1975).

As to the dispositions to an unincorporated charitable association, see §397.2.

See also Rickett, Charitable Giving in English and Roman Law: A Comparison of Method, [1979] Cambridge L.J. 118, 122-129; Warburton, Charitable Companies [1984] Conveyancer 112.

[2]*England:* Attorney-General v. Coopers' Co., 19 Ves. 187 (1812); Liverpool and District Hospital for Diseases of the Heart v. Attorney-General, [1981] 1 All E.R. 994 (Ch. Div.) (National Health Service had taken over the functions of the charitable corporation and its own memorandum of association provided for judicial application cy pres if the corporation could not function).

California: Younger v. Wisdom Soc., 121 Cal. App. 3d 683, 175 Cal. Rptr. 542 (1981) (charitable corporation).

Pennsylvania: Musical Fund Soc. of Philadelphia, 73 D.&C.2d 115 (Pa. 1975).

Texas: Blocker v. State of Texas, 718 S.W.2d 409 (Tex. App. 1986).

See Bradshaw v. American Advent Christian Home and Orphanage, 145 Fla. 270, 199 So. 329 (1940); Smith v. Livermore, 298 Mass. 223, 10 N.E.2d 117 (1937), noted in 23 Iowa L. Rev. 274, 13 Notre Dame Law. 313; State ex rel. Hunter v. Home Savings & Loan Assoc., 137 Neb. 231, 288 N.W. 691 (1939) (citing Restatement of Trusts §391); St. Joseph's Hosp. v. Bennett, 281 N.Y. 115, 22 N.E.2d 305, 130 A.L.R. 1092 (1939); Elliott v. Teachers College, 177 Misc. 746, 31 N.Y.S.2d 796 (1941), *aff'd,* 264 A.D. 839, 35 N.Y.S.2d 761 (1942), *aff'd mem.,* 290 N.Y. 747, 50 N.E.2d 97 (1943); Matter of Callahan, 85 N.Y.S.2d 95 (1948); Matter of Lane, 203 Misc. 661, 119 N.Y.S.2d 17 (1953).

In Massachusetts Charitable Mechanic Assn. v. Beede, 320 Mass. 601, 70

ble.[3] On the other hand, some of the rules that are applicable

N.E.2d 825 (1947), the court said that a charitable corporation cannot bind itself by setting up a trust of its general funds limiting the use of those funds to particular charitable purposes.

In Samuels v. Attorney General, 373 Mass. 844, 370 N.E.2d 698 (1977), where a fraternal organization voted to set aside a fund for the relief of indigent members, it was held that it could not thereafter use the fund for its general purposes. The court cited the text and the Restatement of Trusts, §348, Comment *f.*

In National Found. v. First Natl. Bank, 288 F.2d 831 (4th Cir. 1961), where a national foundation had a local chapter, it was held that contributions were not limited to the purposes of the local chapter.

[3]*England:* Liverpool and District Hospital for Diseases of the Heart v. Attorney-General, [1981] 1 All E.R. 994 (Ch. Div.), *supra,* note 2; In re Woodhauer, Decd.; Lloyds Bank Ltd. v. London College of Music, [1981] 1 W.L.R. 493 (Ch. Div.) (bequest to two musical colleges to establish scholarships for "absolute orphans"; colleges would not accept restriction to orphans because the government paid the expenses of orphans; restriction deleted).

Federal: Stevens Bros. Found., Inc. v. Commissioner, 324 F.2d 633 (8th Cir. 1963) (citing the text), *cert. denied,* 376 U.S. 969.

Hawaii: See Hite v. Queen's Hosp., 36 Haw. 250 (1942).

Massachusetts: See Smith v. Livermore, 298 Mass. 223, 10 N.E.2d 117 (1937).

New York: Sherman v. Richmond Hose Co., 230 N.Y. 462, 130 N.E. 613 (1921).

See Matter of Brundrett, 87 N.Y.S.2d 851 (1940), noted in 23 Iowa L. Rev. 274, 13 Notre Dame Law. 313.

Texas: Blocker v. State of Texas, 718 S.W.2d 409 (Tex. App. 1986).

By Minnesota Stat. Ann., §501.79, as amended by Laws 1976, c. 161, it is provided that "no notice need be provided to the attorney general of a charitable devise under a will for which no charitable trust is created."

By New York Estates, Powers and Trusts Law, §8-1.1, as amended by Laws 1971, c. 1058, and Laws 1985, c. 492, it is provided that the Supreme Court and the Surrogate's Court shall have control over gifts, grants, legacies, and devises made for a religious, charitable, educational, or benevolent purpose to a corporation or an unincorporated association, and the jurisdiction of the court to prevent failure of such a gift, grant, legacy, or devise and give effect to the general purpose thereof is not defeated by the fact that the donee, grantee, legatee, or devisee does not exist or lacks capacity to take at the time the gift, grant, legacy, or devise would otherwise become effective, whether or not the gift, grant, legacy, or devise creates an express trust for such purpose.

See Matter of Will of Kraetzer, 119 Misc. 2d 436, 462 N.Y.S.2d 1009 (Sur. 1983).

Where there are bequests to charitable corporations, the Attorney General is a necessary party to an accounting by the executor. Matter of Lown, 59 Misc. 2d 987, 301 N.Y.S.2d 746 (1969).

to the one are not applicable to the other. The circumstances under which and the proceedings by which creditors can reach the property are different; for example, if a charitable corporation incurs a liability in contract or in tort, an action at law will lie against the corporation, whereas it is only in equity, if at all, that a creditor can reach trust property.[4]

It is not infrequently stated in the cases that a charitable corporation does not hold on a charitable trust property conveyed or bequeathed to it.[5] In fully as many cases, however, it

[4]As to the delegation by charitable institutions, see §379; as to investments by charitable institutions, see §389; as to gifts to charitable institutions, see §397.3.

[5]*Federal:* Art Students' League of N.Y. v. Hinkley, 31 F.2d 469 (D. Md. 1929), *aff'd sub nom.* Hinkley v. Art Students' League, 37 F.2d 225 (4th Cir. 1930).

California: City of Hermosa Beach v. Superior Court, 231 Cal. App. 2d 295, 41 Cal. Rptr. 796 (1964).

Colorado: Gately v. El Paso County Bar Assoc., 137 Colo. 599, 328 P.2d 381 (1958).

Connecticut: Town of Winchester v. Cox, 129 Conn. 106, 26 A.2d 592 (1942); New York East Annual Conference of Methodist Church v. Seymour, 151 Conn. 517, 199 A.2d 701 (1964) (citing the text).

Delaware: Denckla v. Independence Found., 41 Del. Ch. 247, 193 A.2d 538 (1963) (citing the text and Restatement of Trusts §348, Comment *f*); Hanover Street Presbyterian Church v. Buckson, 42 Del. Ch. 292, 210 A.2d 190 (1965); Executive Council of Protestant Episcopal Church v. Moss, 43 Del. Ch. 379, 231 A.2d 463 (1967) (New York law).

Florida: In re Thourez' Estate, 166 So.2d 476 (Fla. App. 1964).

Indiana: Stockton v. Northwestern Branch of Women's Foreign Missionary Soc., 127 Ind. App. 193, 133 N.E.2d 875 (1955).

Maryland: Waters v. Order of the Holy Cross, 155 Md. 146, 142 A. 297 (1928); Sands v. Church of Ascension and Prince of Peace, 181 Md. 536, 30 A.2d 771 (1943), noted in 8 Lawyer 14, 42 Mich. L. Rev. 198; McMahon v. Consistory of St. Paul's Reformed Church, 196 Md. 125, 75 A.2d 122 (1950); Mayor & Aldermen v. West Annapolis Fire & Improvement Co., 264 Md. 729, 288 A.2d 151 (1972).

Massachusetts: Greek Orthodox Community v. Malicourtis, 267 Mass. 472, 166 N.E. 863 (1929); Massachusetts Charitable Mechanic Assn. v. Beede, 320 Mass. 601, 70 N.E.2d 825 (1947) (citing the text).

Nebraska: Clarke v. Sisters of Soc. of the Holy Child Jesus, 82 Neb. 85, 117 N.W. 107 (1908); State ex rel. Hunter v. Home Savings & Loan Assn., 137 Neb. 231, 288 N.W. 691 (1939) (quoting Restatement of Trusts, Introductory Note, p. 1093); Rohlff v. German Old People's Home, 143 Neb. 636, 10 N.W.2d 686 (1943).

is stated that a charitable corporation holds its property in

---

New Jersey: Leeds v. Harrison, 15 N.J. Super. 82, 83 A.2d 45 (1951), *rev'd on other grounds,* 9 N.J. 202, 87 A.2d 713 (1952) (citing the text), noted in 40 Geo. L.J. 122, 100 U. Pa. L. Rev. 457; Paterson v. Paterson General Hosp., 97 N.J. Super. 514, 235 A.2d 487 (1967) (citing the text); Midlantic Natl. Bank v. Frank G. Thompson Found., 170 N.J. Super. 128, 405 A.2d 866 (1979) (citing the text and Restatement of Trusts, §341, Comment *f*).

New York: Wetmore v. Parker, 52 N.Y. 450 (1873); Bird v. Merklee, 144 N.Y. 544, 39 N.E. 645, 27 L.R.A. 423 (1895); Matter of Hart, 205 A.D. 703, 200 N.Y.S. 63 (1923); Corporation of Chamber of Commerce v. Bennett, 143 Misc. 513, 257 N.Y.S. 2 (1932); Matter of Oliver, 42 N.Y.S.2d 865 (1943); Matter of Fowler, 43 N.Y.S.2d 94 (1943), *aff'd mem.,* 268 A.D. 788, 50 N.Y.S.2d 174 (1944), *leave to appeal denied,* 293 N.Y. 934, 57 N.E.2d 752 (1944); Matter of Callahan, 85 N.Y.S.2d 95 (1948); Matter of Jolson, 202 Misc. 907, 114 N.Y.S.2d 135 (1952); Matter of Lane, 203 Misc. 661, 119 N.Y.S.2d 17 (1953); Cadman Memorial Congregational Soc. v. Kenyon, 306 N.Y. 151, 116 N.E.2d 481 (1953); Matter of James, 130 N.Y.S.2d 693 (1954), *aff'd mem.,* 284 A.D. 936, 135 N.Y.S.2d 781 (1954), *aff'd mem.,* 309 N.Y. 659, 128 N.E.2d 316 (1955); Matter of Bergen, 22 Misc. 2d 762, 193 N.Y.S.2d 817 (1959) (though bequest "in trust").

By New York Not-for-Profit Corporation Law, §513, as amended by Laws 1978, c. 690, it is provided that a charitable corporation shall hold full ownership rights in property given to it in trust for, or with a direction to apply the same to, any purposes specified in its certificate of incorporation, and shall not be deemed a trustee of an express trust of such assets.

North Carolina: Young Women's Christian Assn. v. Morgan, 281 N.C. 485, 189 S.E.2d 169 (1972) (citing Restatement of Trusts §348).

Ohio: In re Estate of Bicknell, 108 Ohio App. 51, 160 N.E.2d 550 (1958) (citing Restatement of Trusts §99).

Oregon: Hall v. Dolph, 184 Or. 319, 198 P.2d 272 (1948).

Pennsylvania: Craig Estate, 356 Pa. 564, 52 P.2d 650 (1947).

Rhode Island: Israel v. National Board of Y.M.C.A., 117 R.I. 614, 369 A.2d 646 (1977).

South Dakota: In re Havesgaard's Estate, 59 S.D. 26, 238 N.W. 130 (1931).

Tennessee: Moore v. Neely, 212 Tenn. 496, 370 S.W.2d 537 (1963).

In Spoerl Estate, 5 D.&C.2d 130 (Pa. 1955), it was held that a pecuniary legacy to a charitable corporation to be used as an addition to its endowment fund was not "a pecuniary legacy bequeathed in trust," and therefore interest was not payable from the death of the testator under Fiduciaries Act of 1949, 20 Pa. Stat. §320.753. The court cited Restatement of Trusts, Introductory Note to Chapter 11.

In Grace v. Grace Inst., 19 N.Y.2d 307, 226 N.E.2d 531, 279 N.Y.S.2d 721 (1967), it was held that the rules as to the removal of a trustee of a charitable corporation were applicable rather than those applicable to a charitable trust.

In Perpetual Exrs. and Trustees Assn. v. Puke, [1974] Vict. Rep. 788 (Australia), a testator bequeathed the residue in trust for his wife for her life,

trust.[6] It is sometimes said that a charitable corporation holds

---

and on her death in trust for a corporation for its general purposes. It was held that the disposition was valid whether or not the corporation was a charitable institution, and that it did not hold the property in trust.

See Hodgson and McNeely, Trusteeship and the Charitable Corporation, 4 Philanthropist 26 (1984).

[6]*England:* The Abbey, Malvern v. Minister of Town and Country Planning, [1951] 2 All E.R. 154.

Federal: Werlein v. New Orleans, 177 U.S. 390, 20 S. Ct. 682, 44 L. Ed. 817 (1900); King v. Richardson, 136 F.2d 849 (4th Cir. 1943), *cert. denied sub nom.* Richardson v. King, 320 U.S. 777 (1943).

California: In re Los Angeles County Pioneer Socy., 40 Cal. 2d 852, 257 P.2d 1 (1953); American Center for Education, Inc. v. Cavnar, 80 Cal. App. 3d 476, 145 Cal. Rptr. 736 (1978) (citing the text).

Connecticut: Ministers & Missionaries Benefit Bd. v. Meriden Trust & Safe Deposit Co., 139 Conn. 435, 94 A.2d 917 (1953).

Florida: Jordan v. Landis, 128 Fla. 604, 175 So. 241 (1937), *semble.*

Maine: First Universalist Socty. of Bath v. Swett, 148 Me. 142, 90 A.2d 812 (1952), noted in 5 Baylor L. Rev. 205.

Massachusetts: Smith v. Livermore, 298 Mass. 223, 10 N.E.2d 117 (1937), noted in 23 Iowa L. Rev. 274, 13 Notre Dame Law. 313; Wellesley College v. Attorney General, 313 Mass. 722, 49 N.E.2d 220 (1943).

Michigan: Detroit Osteopathic Hosp. v. Johnson, 290 Mich. 283, 287 N.W. 466 (1939), noted in 38 Mich. L. Rev. 406, 19 Mich. S.B.J. 42.

Minnesota: In re Estate of Quinlan, 233 Minn. 35, 45 N.W.2d 807 (1951); Schaeffer v. Newberry, 235 Minn. 282, 50 N.W.2d 477 (1951) (citing Restatement of Trusts §348); In re Americana Found., 145 Mich. App. 735, 378 N.W.2d 586 (1985).

New Jersey: Fidelity Union Trust Co. v. Ackerman, 18 N.J. Super, 314, 87 A.2d 47 (1952); Montclair Natl. Bank & Trust Co. v. Seton Hall College of Medicine & Dentistry, 90 N.J. Super. 419, 217 A.2d 897 (1966) (citing the text), *rev'd,* 96 N.J. Super. 428, 233 A.2d 195 (1967).

Mississippi: Mississippi Children's Home Socy. v. City of Jackson, 230 Miss. 546, 93 So. 2d 483 (1957) (citing the text).

Missouri: Voelker v. St. Louis Mercantile Library Assn., 359 S.W.2d 689 (Mo. 1962) (citing the text and Restatement of Trusts, §348, Comment *f*).

Nebraska: Stork v. Evangelical Lutheran Synod, 129 Neb. 311, 261 N.W. 552 (1935); In re Estate of Harrington, 151 Neb. 81, 36 N.W.2d 577 (1949); In re Estate of Halstead, 154 Neb. 31, 46 N.W.2d 779 (1951) (tax case); Board of Trustees of York College v. Cheney, 158 Neb. 292, 63 N.W.2d 177 (1954) (citing Restatement of Trusts §348).

New York: Matter of Brundrett, 87 N.Y.S.2d 851 (1940).

Pennsylvania: Abel v. Girard Trust Co., 365 Pa. 44, 73 A.2d 682 (1950) (citing the text and Restatement of Trusts, §348), noted in 24 Temp. L.Q. 373; Loechel v. Columbia Borough School Dist., 369 Pa. 132, 85 A.2d 81 (1952), s.c. *sub nom.* Glatfelder Trust Deed Case (Appeal of School Dist. of Borough

property in trust if the property is to be used only for a particular charitable purpose or if only the income is to be used.[7]

---

of Columbia), 372 Pa. 502, 94 A.2d 723 (1953); Bangor Park Assn. Case, 370 Pa. 442, 88 A.2d 769 (1952); Mary J. Drexel Home Petition, 13 D.&C.2d 371 (Pa. 1957).

Rhode Island: Thomas v. General Bd. of Church of Nazarene, 76 R.I. 197, 68 A.2d 66 (1949).

Texas: Blocker v. State of Texas, 718 S.W.2d 409 (Tex. App. 1986).

Virginia: Wellford v. Powell, 197 Va. 685, 90 S.E.2d 791 (1956).

Wisconsin: Estate of Rowell, 248 Wis. 520, 22 N.W.2d 604 (1946) (quoting Restatement of Trusts, §348).

Wyoming: Town of Cody v. Buffalo Bill Memorial Assn., 64 Wyo. 468, 196 P.2d 369 (1948) (citing the text and Restatement of Trusts, p. 1093).

Canada: In re MacKay Estate, [1948] S.C.R. 500 (Canada).

See Daughters of the American Revolution of Kansas, Topeka Chapter v. Washburn College, 160 Kan. 583, 164 P.2d 128 (1945), in which the court said it was unnecessary to consider whether a trust was created by a gift to a college for a scholarship.

In Fidelity Union Trust Co. v. Ackerman, 18 N.J. Super. 314, 87 A.2d 47 (1952), where property was bequeathed to a trust company to divide among certain charitable institutions, which were to use the property for specific charitable purposes, it was said that the trust company was a trustee and the institutions were subtrustees.

In Clark v. Portland Burying Ground Assn., 151 Conn. 527, 200 A.2d 468 (1964), where a testatrix made a bequest to an incorporated cemetery association for the perpetual care of a cemetery lot, the court said that the disposition was valid insofar as the amount bequeathed was reasonable, although the purpose was not charitable and that it was immaterial whether the corporation was technically a trustee, citing the text and Restatement of Trusts, §348, Comment *f.*

See Taylor, A New Chapter in the New York Law of Charitable Corporations, 25 Cornell L.Q. 382 (1940); Lincoln, Gifts to Charitable Corporations, 25 Va. L. Rev. 764 (1939); Blackwell, The Charitable Corporation and the Charitable Trust, 24 Wash. U.L.Q. 1 (1938); Note, Gifts to Charitable Corporations, 26 S. Cal. L. Rev. 80 (1952).

As to the duty of a charitable corporation with respect to the investment of funds held by it, see §389.

As to the delegation of duties by trustees or directors of charitable institutions, see §379. See Haskell, The University as Trustee, 17 Ga. L. Rev. 1 (1982).

[7]Knights of Equity Memorial Scholarships Commn. v. University of Detroit, 359 Mich. 235, 102 N.W.2d 463 (1960) (citing the text); Lehigh University v. Hower, 159 Pa. Super. 84, 46 A.2d 516 (1946).

In Girard Will Case, 386 Pa. 548, 127 A.2d 287 (1956), *aff'g* 4 D. & C. 2d 671 (Pa. 1955), it was held that where property was given to a city to establish

A charitable corporation certainly does not hold its property beneficially in the same sense in which an individual or noncharitable corporation holds it beneficially, since in the case of a charitable corporation the Attorney General can maintain a suit to prevent a diversion of the property from the purposes for which it was given.[8] In states like New York, that formerly did not permit charitable trusts, a conveyance inter vivos or a devise or bequest to a charitable corporation was valid, unless forbidden by statute, even though by the terms of the instrument of conveyance or will it was provided that the corporation should use the property only for a particular one of its purposes, and even though it was provided that the principal should be held in perpetuity and only the income expended.[9] It has, in-

---

a school for poor male white orphan children, it held the property not in its municipal capacity but in trust, and that therefore segregation was not prohibited by the Fourteenth Amendment to the Constitution of the United States. The judgment was reversed by the Supreme Court of the United States in Pennsylvania v. Board of Directors of City Trusts, 353 U.S. 230, 989, 77 S. Ct. 806, 1281, 1 L. Ed. 2d 792, 1146 (1957). Thereafter the Orphans' Court removed the Board of Directors of City Trusts as trustee and appointed individual trustees, and its action was approved by the Supreme Court of Pennsylvania. In re Girard College Trusteeship, 391 Pa. 434, 138 A.2d 844 (1958), *cert. denied and appeal dismissed,* 357 U.S. 570 (1958), noted in 20 Ohio St. L.J. 132. See §96.4, nn. 7-10.

In Commonwealth v. Brown, 392 F.2d 120, 25 A.L.R.3d 724 (3d Cir. 1968), *cert. denied,* 391 U.S. 921 (1968), it was held that the change of trustees was a state involvement, and that Girard College must admit Negro children.

As to the effect of racial and religious restrictions, see §399.4.

[8]In Lefkowitz v. Lebensfeld, 68 A.D.2d 488, 417 N.Y.S.2d 715 (1979), *aff'd,* 51 N.Y.2d 442, 415 N.E.2d 919, 434 N.Y.S.2d 929 (1980), it was held that the Attorney General had no standing to compel a charitable corporation, to which stock had been given without designation of a particular charitable purpose, to sue the corporation whose stock it held to compel it to pay dividends. One justice dissented.

[9]*Maryland:* Waters v. Order of the Holy Cross, 155 Md. 146, 142 A. 297 (1928).

New York: Wetmore v. Parker, 52 N.Y. 450 (1873); Bird v. Merklee, 144 N.Y. 544, 39 N.E. 645, 27 L.R.A. 423 (1895).

See Howard, Charitable Trusts in Maryland, 1 Md. L. Rev. 105, 113 (1937).

In Petition of Simpson, 89 N.H. 550, 3 A.2d 97 (1938), where a bequest was made to a town "to be forever held in trust, the income from the same may be used as may be deemed for the best interests of" the town, it was held

deed, occasionally been said that where property is conveyed to a charitable corporation, a provision restricting the use of the property to one of the purposes of the corporation, or a provision that only the income of the property shall be used, is invalid on the ground that the absolute owner of property cannot be restricted in its use.[10]

By the weight of authority and on principle, however, such restrictions are valid, as they would be if the property were given to individual trustees for charitable purposes.[11] Thus in the

---

that the income should not be paid over for such purposes as the voters should determine.

[10]*New York:* Corporation of Chamber of Commerce v. Bennett, 143 Misc. 513, 257 N.Y.S. 2 (1932); Matter of Lawless, 194 Misc. 844, 87 N.Y.S.2d 386 (1949), *aff'd mem.,* 277 A.D. 1045, 100 N.Y.S.2d 537 (1950).

Canada: In re Marshall, [1945] 1 D.L.R. 271 (Ont.).

[11]*England:* In re Brunner's Declaration of Trust, [1941] 2 All E.R. 745, noted in 6 Convey. (N.S.) 51.

Arizona: Dunaway v. First Presbyterian Church, 103 Ariz. 349, 442 P.2d 93 (1968); In re Estate of Criswell, 20 Ariz. App. 147, 510 P.2d 1062 (1973), *semble.*

California: Solheim Lutheran Home v. County of Los Angeles, 152 Cal. App. 2d 775, 313 P.2d 185 (1957); Brown v. Memorial Natl. Home Found., 162 Cal. App. 2d 513, 329 P.2d 118, 75 A.L.R.2d 427 (1955), *cert. denied,* 358 U.S. 943 (1959); California Corporations Code, §9143, added by Laws 1982, c. 242, provides that when a corporation receives property for a specific purpose from a person directly affiliated with the corporation and uses it for other purposes the contributor or any officer, director, member or former member may sue. The directors or members may, however, ratify the use made of the property if it has become impracticable or impossible or contrary to the policies or best interests of the corporation to use the property for the specific purpose.

Colorado: Galiger v. Armstrong, 114 Colo. 397, 165 P.2d 1019 (1946).

Illinois: City of Aurora v. Young Men's Christian Assn., 9 Ill. 2d 286, 137 N.E.2d 347 (1956).

Indiana: Bible Inst. Colportage Assn. v. St. Joseph Bank & Trust Co., 118 Ind. App. 592, 75 N.E.2d 666 (1947) (quoting Restatement of Trusts §348).

Kentucky: City of Danville v. Caldwell, 311 S.W.2d 561 (Ky. 1958).

Maine: First Universalist Socy. of Bath v. Swett, 148 Me. 142, 90 A.2d 812 (1952), noted in 5 Baylor L. Rev. 205.

Maryland: Van Reuth v. Mayor & City Council of Baltimore, 165 Md. 651, 170 A. 199 (1933), noted in 19 Iowa L. Rev. 574; Mayor & City Council of Baltimore v. Peabody Inst., 175 Md. 186, 200 A. 375 (1938); Gray v. Harriet Lane Home for Invalid Children, 192 Md. 251, 64 A.2d 102 (1949).

Massachusetts: See Smith v. Livermore, 298 Mass. 223, 10 N.E.2d 117

(1937), noted in 23 Iowa L. Rev. 274, 13 Notre Dame Law. 313; Franklin Found. v. Collector-Treasurer of Boston, 344 Mass. 573, 183 N.E.2d 710 (1962) (gift to capital of school cannot be used to acquire additional site); Franklin Found. v. City of Boston, 336 Mass. 39, 142 N.E.2d 367 (1957) (gift to capital of a school cannot be used to pay current expenses), noted in 37 B.U.L. Rev. 504; Nickols v. Commissioners of Middlesex County, 341 Mass. 13, 166 N.E.2d 911 (1960) (conveyance of Walden Pond reservation to the Commonwealth).

See Attorney General v. President & Fellows of Harvard College, 350 Mass. 125, 213 N.E.2d 840 (1966).

Montana: Hames v. City of Polson, 123 Mont. 469, 215 P.2d 950 (1950).

Nebraska: Rohlff v. German Old People's Home, 143 Neb. 636, 10 N.W.2d 686 (1943); School Dist. No. 70, Red Willow County v. Wood, 144 Neb. 241, 13 N.W.2d 153 (1944).

New Jersey: Rowe v. Davis, 138 N.J. Eq. 122, 47 A.2d 36 (1946); Trustees of Alexander Linn Hosp. Assn. v. Richman, 46 N.J. Super. 594, 135 A.2d 221 (1957).

New York: St. Joseph's Hosp. v. Bennett, 281 N.Y. 115, 22 N.E.2d 305, 130 A.L.R. 1092 (1939), *rev'g* 256 A.D. 120, 8 N.Y.S.2d 922 (1939), noted in 19 B.U.L. Rev. 655, 18 Chi.-Kent L. Rev. 325, 40 Colum. L. Rev. 550, 53 Harv. L. Rev. 327, 23 Minn. L. Rev. 670, 17 N.Y.U. L.Q. Rev. 275; Matter of Oliver, 42 N.Y.S.2d 865 (1943); Matter of Allen, 45 N.Y.S.2d 699 (1943); Matter of Lachat, 184 Misc. 486, 52 N.Y.S.2d 445 (1944); Matter of Eaton, 62 N.Y.S.2d 348 (1946); Matter of Pelton, 190 Misc. 624, 74 N.Y.S.2d 743 (1947); Matter of MacFarland, 95 N.Y.S.2d 258 (1950); Matter of Martin, 96 N.Y.S.2d 842 (1950); Matter of Jolson, 202 Misc. 907, 114 N.Y.S.2d 135 (1952); Matter of Wells, 204 Misc. 975, 126 N.Y.S.2d 441 (1953); Matter of Mauser, 151 N.Y.S.2d 993 (1956); Matter of Mott, 9 Misc. 2d 1018, 171 N.Y.S.2d 403 (1958); Matter of McCarthy, 75 Misc. 2d 193, 347 N.Y.S.2d 490 (1973); County of Suffolk v. Greater New York Councils, Boy Scouts of Am., 51 N.Y.2d 830, 413 N.E.2d 363, 433 N.Y.S.2d 424 (1980); Matter of Estate of Brown, 109 A.D.2d 950, 486 N.Y.S.2d 446 (1985).

See Elliott v. Teachers College, 177 Misc. 746, 31 N.Y.S.2d 796 (1941), *aff'd,* 264 A.D. 839, 35 N.Y.S.2d 761 (1942), *aff'd mem.,* 290 N.Y. 747, 50 N.E.2d 97 (1943).

North Carolina: Wilson v. First Presbyterian Church, 284 N.C. 284, 200 S.E.2d 769 (1973) (to a church to erect a building).

Ohio: Ohio Socy. for Crippled Children v. McElroy, 175 Ohio St. 49, 191 N.E.2d 543, 100 A.L.R.2d 1202 (1963) (citing the text).

Pennsylvania: Craig Estate, 356 Pa. 564, 52 A.2d 650 (1947); Lehigh University v. Hower, 159 Pa. Super. 84, 46 A.2d 516 (1946); Loechel v. Columbia Borough School Dist., 369 Pa. 132, 85 A.2d 81 (1952), s.c. *sub nom.* Glatfelder Trust Deed Case (Appeal of School Dist. of Borough of Columbia), 372 Pa. 502, 94 A.2d 723 (1953); Cowperthwaite Trust (No. 2), 15 Fiduciary Reporter 638 (Pa. 1965) (oral direction); Petition of Acchione, 425 Pa. 23, 227 A.2d 816 (1967).

See Alumnae Assn. of William Penn High School for Girls v. University of Pa., 306 Pa. 283, 159 A. 449 (1932).

See 15 Pa. Cons. Stat., §7549, as to property held by a nonprofit corporation for charitable purposes.

Wisconsin: In re Berry's Estate, 29 Wis. 2d 506, 139 N.W.2d 72 (1966) (*semble,* citing the text).

Canada: Toronto Gen. Trusts Corp. v. Congregation of St. Andrew's Wesley Church, [1946] 3 D.L.R. 571 (B.C.).

In First Methodist Church of Vineland v. Pennock, 130 N.J. Eq. 452, 22 A.2d 889 (1941), where land was devised to a church with directions to use the income to feed and clothe the poor, it was held that the church held the land in trust and could not sell it.

If the donor uses precatory language and does not manifest an intention to impose a binding restriction on the use of the property, the corporation is not bound thereby. Matter of James, 130 N.Y.S.2d 693 (1954), *aff'd mem.*, 284 A.D. 936, 135 N.Y.S.2d 781 (1954), *aff'd mem.*, 309 N.Y. 659, 128 N.E.2d 316 (1955). Compare §351.

In City of Gering v. Jones, 175 Neb. 626, 122 N.W.2d 503 (1963), where land was conveyed to a city to be used for the benefit of its citizens, it was said that the conveyance was not in trust and it was held that the city had power to sell the land.

In Queen of Angels Hosp. v. Younger, 66 Cal. App. 3d 359, 136 Cal. Rptr. 36 (1977), it was held that where a corporation was created to conduct a hospital, it had no power to lease the premises and to apply the rentals to conducting clinics, even though that might be a better purpose.

See Note, Nature of estate created by, and enforceability of, provision in devise or bequest to charitable, religious, or educational corporation as to particular purpose of the corporation for which it shall be used, 130 A.L.R. 1101 (1941); Note, Charitable gifts; definiteness, 163 A.L.R. 784, 798 (1946); Note, Validity and effect of provision or condition against alienation in gift for charitable trust or to charitable corporation, 100 A.L.R.2d 1208 (1965).

Where a municipal corporation holds land for a particular purpose, the courts often speak as though the power to use the land for other purposes depends on whether it holds the land in trust. But even though it does not hold the land upon a technical trust, it may be under a duty to use the land for the designated purpose.

Thus if a gift is made to a city subject to restrictions as to its use (as for example for park purposes), the city is bound by the restrictions. Lancaster v. City of Columbia, 333 F. Supp. 1012, 1024 (N.D. Miss. 1971); City of Reno v. Goldwater, 92 Nev. 698, 558 P.2d 532 (1976).

In Brisbane City Council v. Attorney-General, [1979] A.C. 411, [1978] 3 W.L.R. 299, 3 All E.R. 30 (P.C.), land was conveyed to a city for "showground, park and recreation purposes." It was held that the city held upon a charitable trust, and the city could not sell the land to a corporation to be used as a shopping center.

In In re City of Altoona, 479 Pa. 252, 388 A.2d 313 (1978), where abutting owners dedicated a road to a city, it was held that when the road was abandoned by the city it reverted to the donors, and could not be used by the city for other purposes.

In Ward v. City of Baltimore, 267 Md. 576, 298 A.2d 382 (1973), 60 A.L.R.3d 571, where land was devised to a city to be sold and the proceeds invested in a public park, without further restrictions, it was held that the city could properly construct a highway through the park.

In War Memorial Library v. Franklin Special School Dist., 514 S.W.2d 874 (Tenn. App. 1974), where land was conveyed to a town in trust for school purposes, it was held that the town could not convey it to a library corporation, since this was not a school purpose.

In Old Colony Trust Co. v. Board of Governors, 355 Mass. 776, 247 N.E.2d 583 (1969), it was held that a bequest to a hospital owned by a city was not a gift to the city (as was claimed by the Internal Revenue Service), but was a bequest upon trust for charitable hospital purposes in the area of the city. The federal courts later held that the bequest was exempt. Old Colony Trust Co. v. United States, 438 F.2d 684 (1st Cir. 1971).

In Ink v. City of Canton, 4 Ohio St. 2d 51, 33 Ohio Ops. 2d 427, 212 N.E.2d 574 (1965), where land was given to a city for a park, and it was provided in the gift that it would revert if not so used, and part of the land was taken by the state on eminent domain, it was held that the proceeds should revert unless used for park purposes.

In Foote Memorial Hosp. v. Kelley, 390 Mich. 193, 211 N.W.2d 649 (1973), a woman conveyed land in 1916 to a city with a provision that it should be used for no other purpose than that of a city hospital, and in case of violation of this command it should revert to her, her heirs, and assigns. It was proposed, under authority of a statute, to use the land for other purposes. The Attorney General objected on the ground that the city held the land in trust for hospital purposes. It was held that a condition and not a trust was created, and that only the heirs of the settlor had any remedy.

In Greenville Borough Petition, 11 D.&C.2d 50 (Pa. 1957), where land was given to a city for a park and it became unsuitable for the purpose, it was held that it might be sold and the proceeds used for the upkeep of public parks.

The court may, however, permit the land to be sold or to be used for other purposes under the rules as to deviation (see §381), or the rules of cy pres (see §§399 to 399.5).

But the application of the cy pres power is for the courts and not for the legislature. See Opinion of the Justices to the House of Representatives, 374 Mass. 843, 371 N.E.2d 1349 (1978), cited in Supp. §399.5, n. 8.

There is a question as to who can enforce the restriction, whether the Attorney General, or any taxpayer, or owners of adjoining property.

In City of Wilmington v. Lord, 378 A.2d 635 (Del. 1977), where land was given to a city to be used for public park purposes, it was held that taxpayers had standing to sue to prevent the erection of a water tank on the land, and that such erection should be enjoined.

In Fitzgerald v. Baxter State Park Auth., 385 A.2d 189 (Me. 1978), land was conveyed to the state of Maine as a state park. The state by legislation designated the defendant Park Authority to carry out the terms of the trust.

The plaintiffs, as Maine citizens, domiciliaries, voters, and property holders, brought a class suit against the Park Authority to enjoin a deviation from the terms of the trust. The Attorney General was a member of the Park Authority and was therefore precluded from suing, and was named co-defendant. The court held that the plaintiffs had standing to sue. It said that it expressed no opinion whether the plaintiffs would have standing as having a special interest, if the Attorney General were not precluded. The court cited the text, §391.

See Parsons v. Walker, 28 Ill. App. 3d 517, 328 N.E.2d 920 (1975) (gift to a state university for a park; held citizens had standing to enjoin deviation).

See Citizens for Washington Square v. City of Davenport, 277 N.W.2d 882 (Iowa 1979), where the suit was brought by an organization formed to promote the historic preservation of a park. It was held that it had standing to set aside a conveyance by the city of land given to it for park purposes.

Where the restriction is not imposed by a donor of the land but the land is dedicated to the purpose by the city itself, there is a question whether the city can use the land for other purposes. So where it is given by the state, there is a question how far the state can later permit the land to be used for other purposes.

In Reichelderfer v. Quinn, 287 U.S. 315, 53 S. Ct. 177, 77 L. Ed. 331 (1932), where by Act of Congress land was conveyed to the District of Columbia to be perpetually dedicated as a public park for the benefit of the people of the United States, it was held that the Congress might thereafter permit the erection of a fire engine house in the park and that the Court should not enjoin this at the suit of neighboring owners. The Court said that "It has often been decided that when lands are acquired by a governmental body in fee and dedicated by statute to park purposes, it is within the legislative power to change the use." The Court distinguishes a case where the land was given to a municipality for a particular purpose, or where the municipality, not the legislature, authorized the deviation.

In McLeod v. Town of Amherst, 44 D.L.R.3d 723 (N.S. 1974), *aff'g* 39 D.L.R.3d 146 (N.S. 1973), a grantor conveyed land to a town to have and to hold for use as a public or community beach and for other recreational purposes. It was held that no condition or trust was created, and the town could sell the land.

In Dunphy v. Commonwealth, 368 Mass. 376, 331 N.E.2d 883 (1975), a man in 1917 conveyed land to a town "to be kept and used as a Public Park in perpetuity" as a memorial to and to be named for his father. The town accepted. In 1971 the town voted to permit the erection and maintenance of an artificial ice skating rink on the land and the legislature passed a statute authorizing the town to convey the land to the Commonwealth as a site for a rink. It was so conveyed. In a suit brought by residents of the town and relatives of the grantor to set aside the conveyance, it was held for the plaintiffs. The court said that the land was held upon a charitable trust, and that the legislature had no power to authorize the use for other purposes. See also Opinion of the Justices, 309 Mass. 979, 338 N.E.2d 806 (1975).

In Grant v. Koenig, 39 A.D.2d 1000, 333 N.Y.S.2d 591 (1972), *aff'g* 67 Misc. 2d 1028, 325 N.Y.S.2d 428 (1971), land was conveyed to a city to be used

leading case of *St. Joseph's Hospital v. Bennett*[12] a testator bequeathed a share of the residue of his estate to St. Joseph's Hospital, a charitable corporation, "to be held as an endowment fund and the income used for the ordinary expenses of maintenance." The hospital brought an action for a declaratory judgment, seeking authorization to apply the fund in partial payment of a mortgage debt, or in its judgment to use the principal of the fund for objects within its corporate powers other than meeting the ordinary expenses of maintenance. The Attorney General

---

as a public park, with a provision that if such use were discontinued the land should revert to the settlor or his heirs. It was held that with the cooperation of the heirs the land could be sold.

In Housing & Redev. Auth. v. Stock Yards Corp., 309 Minn. 331, 244 N.W.2d 275 (1976), it was held that a provision for municipal purposes, and another provision for park purposes, were precatory.

In Funk v. Library Bd., 44 Ill. App. 3d 180, 2 Ill. Dec. 633, 357 N.E.2d 853 (1976), where a testator devised land to a municipal library board to establish a library, it was held that he did not intend to create a trust or to impose a condition, and that the board was not under a duty to continue the library.

In State v. Rand, 366 A.2d 183 (Me. 1976), a woman in 1903 conveyed to the city of Portland a parcel of land for a public park in memory of her parents. She provided that the conveyance was on condition that it should revert to her if it was not improved within two years. The city accepted the gift and made the improvements within two years. It maintained the park for over 50 years, but then it was taken by eminent domain for a road. The question arose as to the disposition of the proceeds. It was held that the conveyance was in trust, and that the city did not take a determinable fee simple, and therefore there was no reverter. It was further held that the doctrine of cy près was applicable and that the city should use the proceeds in acquiring a nearby lot as a park. The court cited the text.

In Knightstown Lake Property v. Big Blue River, 383 N.E.2d 361 (Ind. App. 1978), the grantors of a subdivision set aside certain areas for the benefit of all lot owners, and of a municipal corporation if it was created. The corporation was not created. The areas were taken by eminent domain. It was held that the lot owners were entitled to the proceeds.

See Tennessee Laws 1974, c. 602, as to funds contributed by nongovernmental sources to the University of Tennessee.

As to municipal corporations as trustees, see §96.4.

[12]281 N.Y. 115, 22 N.E.2d 305, 130 A.L.R. 1092 (1939), *rev'g* 256 A.D. 120, 8 N.Y.S.2d 922 (1939) (citing the Restatement of Trusts, c. 11, Introductory Note), noted in 19 B.U.L. Rev. 655, 18 Chi.-Kent L. Rev. 325, 40 Colum. L. Rev. 550, 53 Harv. L. Rev. 327, 23 Minn. L. Rev. 670, 17 N.Y.U. L.Q. Rev. 275.

opposed the application on the ground that the bequest was a gift in trust. The Supreme Court held that the bequest did not create a trust but an absolute gift, and that the plaintiff need not maintain the gift intact as an endowment fund, but that it could use the income and principal for any of its corporate purposes, and in particular toward the discharge of the mortgage on its property. The judgment was affirmed by the Appellate Division. The Court of Appeals reversed the judgment, two judges dissenting. The court said that the clearly expressed directions of the testator must be obeyed. It said that no trust arises in a technical sense because the trustee and beneficiary are one, and that a charitable corporation is not bound by all the rules that apply to a technical trustee. But the court said, "It may not, however, receive a gift made for one purpose and use it for another, unless the court applying the cy pres doctrine so commands." In another case in New York[13] it was held by the Appellate Division, reversing the Supreme Court, that a hospital should not be permitted to use the principal of its endowment funds to pay current expenses, although its income was insufficient, since it could curtail its operations. On the other hand, it was held[14] that where a testator left a large sum to a hospital as an endowment, the income to be used for its general purposes, it should be permitted to use the principal where it appeared that otherwise the hospital would be forced to close its doors. Where the creator of the trust does not intend to impose a legal restriction on his gift to a charitable corporation, as for instance where his language is construed as being purely precatory, the corporation may use the property for any of its purposes.[15]

[13]Application of Brooklyn Children's Aid Socy., 269 A.D. 789, 55 N.Y.S.2d 323 (1945).

See Lutheran Hosp. of Manhattan v. Goldstein, 182 Misc. 913, 46 N.Y.S.2d 705 (1944).

[14]Knickerbocker Hosp. v. Goldstein, 181 Misc. 540, 41 N.Y.S.2d 32 (1943).

[15]*Kansas:* Zabel v. Stewart, 153 Kan. 272, 109 P.2d 177 (1941).

Maryland: Sands v. Church of Ascension & Prince of Peace, 181 Md. 536, 30 A.2d 771 (1943), noted in 42 Mich. L. Rev. 198.

Missouri: Pilgrim Evangelical Lutheran Church of the Unaltered Augsburg Confession v. Lutheran Church-Missouri Synod Found., 661 S.W.2d 833 (Mo. App. 1983), *transfer to S. Ct. denied* (1984), citing text.

The truth is that it cannot be stated dogmatically that a charitable corporation either is or is not a trustee. The question is in each case whether a rule that is applicable to trustees is applicable to charitable corporations, with respect to unrestricted or restricted property. Ordinarily the rules that are applicable to charitable trusts are applicable to charitable corporations, as we have seen, although some are not. It is probably more misleading to say that a charitable corporation is not a trustee than to say that it is, but the statement that it is a trustee must be taken with some qualifications. Thus where property is left by will to a charitable corporation, whether it may be used for the general purposes of the corporation or

---

New York: County of Suffolk v. Greater N.Y. Councils, Boy Scouts of Am., 51 N.Y.2d 830, 413 N.E.2d 363, 433 N.Y.S.2d 424 (1980).

North Carolina: Young Women's Christian Assn. v. Morgan, 281 N.C. 485, 189 S.E.2d 169 (1972) (citing Restatement of Trusts §348).

Pennsylvania: City of Lebanon v. Schaffer, 58 D.&C. 368 (Pa. 1946).

In Roman Catholic Archiepiscopal Corp. v. Ryan, 12 D.L.R.2d 23 (B.C. 1958), *rev'g* In re Delaney, 10 D.L.R.2d 213 (1957), the testator left a share of the residue of his estate to the Roman Catholic Archiepiscopal Corporation of Winnipeg for the benefit of a particular church or otherwise as the corporation should think fit. The lower court held that the gift failed because it was not limited to charitable purposes. The upper court reversed, holding that it was a gift to the corporation for its general purposes.

In Alumnae Assn. of Newport Hosp. School of Nursing v. De Simone, 106 R.I. 196, 258 A.2d 80 (1969), where a testatrix left $60,000 to an alumnae association to be used to provide scholarships, it was held that the principal could be used. The court said that it was immaterial whether the legacy is considered as a gift to a charitable corporation or a gift in trust, since the testatrix did not manifest an intention that income only be used.

In Lefkowitz v. Cornell Univ., 35 A.D.2d 166, 316 N.Y.S.2d 264 (1970), *aff'd mem.,* 28 N.Y.2d 876, 271 N.E.2d 552, 332 N.Y.S.2d 717 (1971), *rev'g* 62 Misc. 2d 95, 308 N.Y.S.2d 85, where an aeronautical laboratory was conveyed to Cornell University for the advancement of science and education, it was held that the University could sell the laboratory and use the proceeds for the advancement of science and education. The court said that there was no other restriction on the gift. The gift was a gift to a charitable corporation, and not a gift in trust.

In Hull v. Calvert, 475 S.W.2d 907 (Tex. 1972), it was held that the University of Texas could accept a large tract of land although the deed provided that it should never be a part of the permanent University fund and should not be subject to legislative control.

whether the devise or bequest is subject to restrictions as to its use, and the property is conveyed by the executor to the corporation, the corporation is not thereafter bound to account as if it were a testamentary trustee.[16] The situation is quite different

[16]American Inst. of Architects v. Attorney Gen., 332 Mass. 619, 127 N.E.2d 161 (1955) (citing the text). In that case a Massachusetts testatrix gave the residue of her estate to The American Institute of Architects, a charitable corporation of New York, upon trust to maintain scholarships for advanced study by deserving architects and students of architecture. It was held that the corporation did not hold the property upon a technical trust and was not subject to appointment and qualification as a trustee by the Massachusetts Probate Court. See In re Berry's Estate, 29 Wis. 2d 506, 139 N.W.2d 72 (1966) (citing the text).

In Portsmouth Hosp. v. Attorney Gen., 104 N.H. 51, 178 A.2d 516 (1962), a testator left property in trust to pay the income to his sisters and after their deaths to erect and maintain an annex to an incorporated hospital. It was held that after the death of the sisters the trustees should transfer the trust property to the hospital to be administered by it. The court further held that the hospital was not required to qualify as trustee in the Probate Court. The court cited the text and Restatement of Trusts, §348, Comment f.

In In re Myra Found. 112 N.W.2d 552 (N.D. 1961), a testator left his estate to trustees as a charitable foundation. He provided that they should have power to organize a corporation. They organized such a corporation before probate was completed. The court held that the trust ceased on the formation of the corporation, that the executors should transfer the property to the corporation, and that the corporation was not subject to the supervision of the court as it would be if it were a charitable trust. The court cited Restatement of Trusts, §348, Comment f.

In Edgeter v. Kemper, 73 Ohio Abs. 297, 136 N.E.2d 630 (1955), where money was bequeathed to the United States as a permanent fund for the benefit of indigent American Indians, it was held that the disposition was valid, and that the United States should not be required to account to the Probate Court.

In In re Estate of Bicknell, 108 Ohio App. 51, 160 N.E.2d 550 (1958), where a legacy was given to a Massachusetts college by the will of a person domiciled in Ohio in trust to preserve the principal and use the income for furnishing and refurbishing its buildings, it was held that the legacy should be paid to the college, and that no trustee should be appointed. The court said that because the college had the whole legal and beneficial interest, no trust was created.

In Wanamaker Trust, 7 Fiduciary Rep. 486 (Pa. 1957), the Orphans' Court directed that funds for an endowment of an incorporated school should be paid to that school as trustee, so that the Orphans' Court might retain jurisdiction.

In re Proctor, 140 Vt. 6, 433 A.2d 300 (1981), involved a bequest to a trust

from that which arises where property is left by will to individual trustees, or to a trust company, charged with a duty to make the property productive and to pay the income to a charitable corporation.[17]

The distinction between the situation that arises where property is held by trustees for charitable purposes and that which arises where property is given to a charitable corporation is brought out in a case decided by the Circuit Court of Appeals for the First Circuit.[18] A testator left the residue of his estate to his executors to manage the estate for 25 years and accumulate the income and at the expiration of that period to form a corporation to maintain a hospital. The court held that a valid charitable trust was created. Putnam, J., said:

> We should observe that the corporation contemplated by the will was not to hold in trust, in the technical sense of the word, the property which it might receive. It was to hold it for its own purposes in the usual way in which charitable institutions hold their assets. Such a holding is sometimes called a quasi trust, and an institution like the one in question is subject to visitation by

company upon trust to pay certain sums to a village for specified school purposes. It was held that, while a probate court with jurisdiction over testamentary trusts could compel the trust company to account, it lacked jurisdiction to compel the village to account.

But in Estate of Vanderbilt, 109 Misc. 2d 914, 441 N.Y.S.2d 153 (Surr. 1981), it was held that a charitable corporation could sue the attorney general for allowance of its accounts.

By Kansas Stat. Ann. §59-1105, it is provided that charitable corporations acting as trustees of funds bequeathed for educational purposes need not report to the court unless ordered by it to do so.

As to statutes providing for the supervision of charitable trusts and institutions by the office of the Attorney General, see §391, note 21.

[17]See §367A.

[18]Brigham v. Peter Bent Brigham Hosp., 134 F. 513, 517 (1st Cir. 1904).

See Bradshaw v. American Advent Christian Home & Orphanage, 145 Fla. 270, 199 So. 329 (1940).

In Animal Rescue League v. Assessors of Bourne, 310 Mass. 330, 37 N.E.2d 1019, 138 A.L.R. 110 (1941), noted in 22 B.U.L. Rev. 346, where land was devised to a charitable corporation with directions to use it for charitable purposes not wholly within the corporate purposes, it was held that the land was subject to taxation because it was held in trust and, under the statute, charitable corporations were exempt only when they were owners of the land.

See Haskell, The University as Trustee, 17 Ga. L. Rev. 1 (1982).

the state; but the holding does not constitute a true trust. On the transfer of the property devised by the fourteenth paragraph to a corporation as was anticipated, all technical trusts cease. Meanwhile, as we shall see, if the gift in dispute vested, the legal fee, wherever it remained, was held on a true trust to such an extent that if, on the organization of the corporation in accordance with the provisions of the will, the title did not at once vest in it under the statutes of uses, which statutes still have force in the United States when the fee is held on a mere passive trust, of which Sawyer v. Skowhegan, 57 Me. 500, is a striking illustration, the equity courts would compel a conveyance from whomsoever held the fee.[19]

We shall consider hereafter the power of trustees for charitable purposes to convey the trust property to a charitable corporation organized by them to receive it, or to an existing charitable corporation.[20]

[19]See Note, The Charitable Corporation, 64 Harv. L. Rev. 1168 (1951).

The question whether an organization is charitable may arise where it seeks to be recognized as a charitable institution. Thus in the New York Judiciary Law, §495, as amended by Laws 1979, c. 706, it is provided that a corporation or voluntary association shall not practice law, but that this shall not apply to "organizations organized for benevolent or charitable purposes, or for the purpose of assisting persons without means in the pursuit of any civil remedy, whose existence, organization or incorporation may be approved by the appellate division of the supreme court." In Application of Thom, 33 N.Y.2d 601, 301 N.E.2d 542, 347 N.Y.S.2d 569 (1973), rev'g 40 A.D.2d 787, 337 N.Y.S.2d 588 (1972), it was held that it was improper for the Appellate Division to deny the application of an organization to provide free legal assistance to homosexuals on the ground that the purpose was not charitable, and the matter was remitted to the Appellate Division. Three judges were of the opinion that the Appellate Division had not abused its discretionary power.

The New York Law Revision Commission has recommended that the reference to charitable and benevolent organizations should be omitted. McKinney, 1979 Session Laws of New York, p. 1445.

So also in England where charitable trusts are registered, the question may arise whether an organization is entitled to be registered. See Construction Indus. Training Bd. v. Attorney-General, [1972] 2 All E.R. 1339.

In People ex rel. Dunbar v. Trinidad State Junior College, 184 Colo. 305, 520 P.2d 736 (1974), a polytechnic college though not conducted for profit was not an "eleemosynary" institution under a statute regulating proprietary schools.

[20]See §385A.

We shall also consider hereafter statutory provisions as to nonprofit corporations.[21]

§348.2. **History of charitable trusts in England.** Charitable trusts were enforced in England long before the seventeenth century. Prior to the time when the chancellor first began in the fifteenth century to enforce uses and trusts, gifts for charitable purposes, whether inter vivos or testamentary, were protected to a certain extent by the courts of law. The principal charities were those of a religious nature. A gift for charitable purposes usually took the form of a gift to a religious corporation. The corporation would hold the property by the tenure known as frankalmoign. These religious corporations included religious persons as well as religious institutions. The parson of a parish was regarded as a corporation although he had not been expressly so made either by royal charter or by act of Parliament. Other religious persons or associations were also regarded as corporations by prescription. During this period various statutes were passed to prevent what was from the point of view of the overlord and of the Crown a growing evil, namely the accumulation of land in the hands of religious bodies. To permit land to be held in mortmain was to deprive the overlord and the king of many of the feudal rights that they would have enjoyed if the land had been held by private persons. Accordingly, statutes were enacted providing that lands held by religious bodies should be forfeited to the overlord; and if he failed to enter, then to his overlord, and finally to the Crown.[1] It is to be noticed that these statutes did not prevent a conveyance of land to the corporation; they merely provided for a forfeiture of the land so conveyed. Such forfeiture, however, did not take place if the overlord granted to the corporation a license in mortmain. It finally came to be held that a license from the Crown was sufficient to prevent a forfeiture.

Although a conveyance to a religious corporation was one

---

[21]See §379, as to delegation by charitable institutions; §389, as to investments by charitable institutions; §397.3, as to gifts to charitable institutions.

§348.2. [1]Stat. 9 Hen. III, c. 36 (1225); Stat. 7 Edw. I, st. 2 (1279); Stat. 13 Edw. I, c. 32 (1285); Stat. 18 Edw. III, st. 3, c. 3 (1344).

method of devoting property to charitable purposes, there was another method available. It was possible to convey property to individuals to the use of religious organizations. Maitland was of the opinion that the first occasion on which land was held to the use of others, other than where the uses were merely for a temporary purpose, was where land was conveyed to the use of the Franciscan friars.[2] The friars came to England early in the thirteenth century. They were sworn to poverty, not only individually but, unlike other orders, collectively. It became customary, however, to convey land to the use of the friars. Since the obligations of the feoffee to uses were merely honorary obligations unenforceable in the courts, it was not felt that there was any violation of the principle that they should own no property. After the enactment of the early statutes of mortmain forbidding religious corporations to hold land, it became not uncommon to convey land to private persons to the use of religious bodies. Although uses were not enforced by the chancellor until the beginning of the fifteenth century, nevertheless Parliament again interposed. In 1391 the mortmain statutes were extended to cover cases where land was conveyed to individuals to the use of religious corporations.[3]

The next period in the development of charitable trusts begins with the time when in the early part of the fifteenth century the chancellor first began to issue subpoenas for the enforcement of uses. This period ends with the enactment of the Statute of Charitable Uses[4] in 1601, which provided a new method for the enforcement of charitable trusts. Unfortunately, the records of the Court of Chancery during this period are fragmentary. A few chancery decisions are to be found reported with the decisions of the common-law courts in the Year-books. The early chancery reports are meager. They are so meager, in fact, that it was at one time thought that charitable trusts were not enforced until after the enactment of the Statute of Charitable Uses in 1601. However, we now have sources of information other than the printed reports showing beyond peradventure

[2]Maitland, Equity 25 (1936).
[3]Stat. 15 Rich. II, c. 5 (1391).
[4]Stat. 43 Eliz. I, c. 4 (1601).

that charitable trusts were enforced in the Court of Chancery long before the seventeenth century.

In the first place, there are the three large volumes called "Calendars of the Proceedings in Chancery in the Reign of Queen Elizabeth," which were published by the Record Commission in England in the years 1827 to 1832. These records were compiled from original bills and answers in chancery preserved in the Tower of London. They are prepared in tabular form showing the names of the parties, the object of the suit, a description of the premises, and the name of the county. They do not show what decree was made, nor do they give in detail the allegations of the parties. They do show, however, the character of the litigation. They show that suits in chancery to enforce charitable trusts were not infrequent during the reign of Queen Elizabeth. It was chiefly by means of cases abstracted from these Calendars that Horace Binney succeeded in convincing the Supreme Court of the United States in the famous case of *Vidal v. Girard's Executors*[5] that charitable trusts were enforced in England prior to the enactment of the Statute of Charitable Uses in 1601.

Again, there is a veritable mine of information as to the early law of charitable trusts to be found in the thirty-seven volumes of Reports of the Commissioners of Charities, a board appointed by Parliament in 1818 to inquire into existing charities. The board was continued from time to time and finished its labors in 1837. It made an examination into charitable foundations throughout England and Wales. In many cases questions concerning the charities investigated had been raised in the Court of Chancery and decrees had been rendered. Copies of the decrees were often preserved in the archives of the charity. Scattered throughout these volumes, therefore, are many valuable decisions as to the early law of charitable trusts. This material has been in part made accessible by Professor Theodore W. Dwight of the Columbia Law School, who made a most elaborate argument before the Court of Appeals of New York in the *Rose Will Case.* He prepared an appendix to his argument, which has been printed under the title of Dwight's Charity Cases. Profes-

[5] 2 How. 127, 11 L. Ed. 205 (U.S. 1844).

sor Dwight estimated that the Reports show that more than 5000 charitable trusts that were still subsisting when the Reports were issued had been created prior to the Statute of Charitable Uses.

From these sources, therefore, and from the results of further historical research,[6] it clearly appears that long before the enactment of the Statute of Charitable Uses the Court of Chancery had enforced charitable trusts. The purposes for which these trusts were created were in general the same as the purposes mentioned in the preamble to the statute. They include trusts for the benefit of the poor, trusts to provide chaplains or preachers, trusts for the repair of churches, for the support of schoolmasters, for the repair of highways and bridges, and the like. The suits were usually brought by inhabitants of a town or parish on behalf of themselves and other inhabitants or parishioners. Sometimes they were brought by churchwardens and sometimes in the name of the poor of a town or parish. In a few of the cases they were brought by the Attorney-General.

In 1601, the forty-third year of the reign of Elizabeth, Parliament enacted the Statute of Charitable Uses. In the preamble to the statute there is an enumeration of charitable purposes that will be discussed hereafter.[7] The statute conferred authority upon the chancellor to appoint commissioners from time to time to inquire into any abuses of charitable bequests or donations.[8] The commissioners were empowered to impanel juries,

---

[6]See Helmholz, The Early Enforcement of Uses, 79 Colum. L. Rev. 1503 (1979); DeVine, Ecclesiastical Antecedents to Secular Jurisdiction over the Feoffment to the Uses to Be Declared by Testamentary Instructions, 30 Am. J. Legal Hist. 296 (1986).

See also Duke, Law of Charitable Uses (1676); Shelford, Law of Mortmain (1836); Maitland, The Origin of Uses, 8 Harv. L. Rev. 127 (1894); Bourchier & Chilcott, The Law of Mortmain (1905); Brown, Ecclesiastical Origin of the Use, 10 Notre Dame Law. 353 (1935); Barton, The Medieval Use, 81 Law Q. Rev. 562, 565 (1965); Tudor, On Charities 200-201 (6th ed. 1967); Jones, History of the Law of Charity, 1532-1827 (1969); Fratcher, Trust, §§7, 59, 6 International Encyclopedia of Comparative Law, c. 11 (1974).

[7]See §368.

[8]After reciting in the preamble the various purposes for which property had been given and stating that the property so given had frequently been misapplied, the statute provides: "Be it enacted by authority of this present parliament, That it shall and may be lawful to and for the Lord Chancellor

to summon and hear witnesses, and to make decrees that should be valid until undone or altered by the chancellor. It was further provided that persons aggrieved by the decrees of the commissioners might make complaint to the chancellor for redress, and that the chancellor might thereupon make such decrees as "should be thought to stand in equity and good conscience according to the true intent and meaning of the donors and founders." The statute thus provided a new remedy for the enforcement of charitable trusts. This new remedy, however, did not supersede or displace the already existing remedy by an original proceeding in the Court of Chancery. Apparently this new procedure was extensively employed for a time, but gradually it fell into disuse.[9] The gradual decline in the use of the remedy provided by the statute appears from a list of the proceedings of commissioners appointed under the statute, which was published by the Public Record Office in 1899. The statute was finally repealed, except for the preamble, in 1888.[10] The remedy provided by the statute has not had much influence on the development of the law of charitable trusts. The preamble, however, has played a great part in shaping the law, both in England and in the United States. It is to the preamble that the courts have turned to determine whether a purpose is charitable.

... from time to time to award commissions under the Great Seal of England, ... to the bishop of every several diocese ... and to other persons of good and sound behaviour, authorizing them ... to enquire ... of all and singular such gifts, ... and of the abuses, breaches of trusts, ... or misgovernment of any lands, ... goods, chattels, money or stocks of money, heretofore given, ... or which hereafter shall be given, ... for any of the charitable and godly uses before rehearsed: ... and upon such enquiry ... set down such orders, judgments and decrees, as the said lands, ... goods, chattels, money and stocks of money, may be duly and faithfully employed, to and for such of the charitable uses and intents before rehearsed respectively, for which they were given ... by the donors and founders thereof: which orders, judgments and decrees, not being contrary or repugnant to the orders, statutes or decrees of the donors or founders, shall by the authority of this present parliament stand firm and good, ... and shall be executed accordingly, until the same shall be undone or altered by the Lord Chancellor ... upon complaint by any party grieved to be made to them. ..."

[9]As to the practice relating to Commissioners appointed under the Statute of Charitable Uses, see Herne, The Statute of Charitable Uses (1660, 1663).

[10]Mortmain and Charitable Uses Act, 1888, 51 & 52 Vict., c. 42.

As the remedy provided by the Statute of Charitable Uses became obsolete, the task of enforcing charitable trusts fell upon the Attorney-General. He might act upon his own initiative, or he might proceed at the relation of others. In certain cases persons having an interest in the enforcement of a charitable trust might bring a suit in chancery.[11] The result was that charitable trusts were left very largely without supervision. Great abuses naturally resulted. In the early part of the nineteenth century, as has been stated, a parliamentary commission, under the leadership of Lord Brougham, was appointed and spent many years in investigating the administration of charitable trusts in England. The reports of this commission, contained in some sixty volumes, disclosed a state of affairs that showed the need of some form of public supervision. Accordingly, Parliament provided for the appointment of a permanent Charity Commission, which has general oversight of charitable trusts,[12] except those created for educational purposes, supervision of which was entrusted to the Board of Education.[13]

§348.3.   **Charitable trusts in the United States.**   In most of the states the courts have had no difficulty in accepting the English law of charitable trusts. It is true that none of the states has accepted the whole of the English law; for example, as we shall see, none of the states has accepted the old doctrine relating to the prerogative cy pres, since this was an arbitrary doctrine and was not applicable to conditions in the United States.[1] In most of the states, however, there has been no difficulty in holding that charitable trusts are valid. The requirement in the case of private trusts that there should be definite beneficiaries is not applicable to charitable trusts. It is, indeed, of the essence of a charitable trust that the beneficiaries should not be definite.

[11]See §391.

[12]Charitable Trusts Act, 1853, 16 & 17 Vict., c. 33.

[13]Board of Education Act, 1899, 62 & 63 Vict., c. 33.

By the Education Act, 1944, 7 & 8 Geo. VI, c. 31, this jurisdiction is conferred upon the Ministry of Education.

For an extensive study of charitable trusts in England, see the Report of the Committee on the Law and Practice Relating to Charitable Trusts (Cmd. 8710). This is a parliamentary report issued in 1952 by the so-called "Nathan Committee." See 16 Mod. L. Rev. 343 (1953).

See Charities Act, 1960, 8 & 9 Eliz. II, c. 58.; Charities Act 1985, c. 20.

§348.3.   [1]See §399.1.

In a few states, however, the courts held that charitable trusts were invalid. It was so held in New York,[2] Michigan,[3] Minnesota,[4] Maryland,[5] Virginia,[6] West Virginia,[7] and Wiscon-

[2]Owens v. Missionary Socy., 14 N.Y. 380, 67 Am. Dec. 160 (1856); Downing v. Marshall, 23 N.Y. 366, 80 Am. Dec. 290 (1861); Levy v. Levy, 33 N.Y. 97 (1865); Bascom v. Albertson, 34 N.Y. 584 (1866); Adams v. Perry, 43 N.Y. 487 (1871); White v. Howard, 46 N.Y. 144 (1871); Holmes v. Mead, 52 N.Y. 332 (1873); Prichard v. Thompson, 95 N.Y. 76, 47 Am. Rep. 9 (1884); Cottman v. Grace, 112 N.Y. 299, 19 N.E. 839, 3 L.R.A. 145 (1889); Read v. Williams, 125 N.Y. 560, 26 N.E. 730, 21 Am. St. Rep. 748 (1891); Fosdick v. Hempstead, 125 N.Y. 581, 26 N.E. 801, 11 L.R.A. 715 (1891); Tilden v. Green, 130 N.Y. 29, 28 N.E. 880, 14 L.R.A. 33, 27 Am. St. Rep. 487 (1891).

See Scott, Charitable Trusts in New York, 26 N.Y.U.L. Rev. 251 (1951); Katz, Sullivan, & Beach, Legal Change and Legal Autonomy: Charitable Trusts in New York, 1777-1893, 3 Law & Hist. Rev. 51 (1985).

[3]Methodist Church of Newark v. Clark, 41 Mich. 730, 3 N.W. 207 (1879); Wheelock v. American Tract Socy., 109 Mich. 141, 66 N.W. 955, 63 Am. St. Rep. 578 (1896).

See Fratcher, Perpetuities and Other Restraints, 239-240, 422-423 (1954).

[4]Little v. Willford, 31 Minn. 173, 17 N.W. 282 (1883); Atwater v. Russell, 49 Minn. 57, 51 N.W. 629 (1892); Watkins v. Bigelow, 93 Minn. 210, 100 N.W. 1104 (1904).

[5]Gambell v. Trippe, 75 Md. 252, 23 A. 461, 32 Am. St. Rep. 388, 15 L.R.A. 235 (1892); Trinity M.E. Church v. Baker, 91 Md. 539, 46 A. 1020 (1900); Salem Church of United Brethren v. Numsen, 191 Md. 43, 59 A.2d 757, 4 A.L.R.2d 117 (1948).

See Howard, Charitable Trusts in Maryland, 1 Md. L. Rev. 105 (1937).

In Beach v. Gilbert, 77 App. D.C. 117, 133 F.2d 50 (1943), aff'g Gilbert v. Beach, 42 F. Supp. 168 (D.D.C. 1941), where a testator domiciled in the District of Columbia left property in trust for his widow for life and on her death to pay the income to a committee in Maryland to apply it for the benefit of the poor, and charitable trusts were not permitted in Maryland until the enactment of a statute between the death of the testator and the death of his widow, it was held that the charitable trust was valid.

[6]Gallego's Exrs. v. Attorney Gen., 3 Leigh 450, 24 Am. Dec. 650 (Va. 1832); Stonestreet v. Doyle, 75 Va. 356, 40 Am. Rep. 731 (1881); Fifield v. Van Wyck, 94 Va. 557, 27 S.E. 446, 64 Am. St. Rep. 745 (1897); Moore v. Perkins, 169 Va. 175, 192 S.E. 806 (1937); Maguire v. Loyd, 193 Va. 138, 67 S.E.2d 885 (1952); Norfolk Presbytery v. Bollinger, 214 Va. 500, 201 S.E.2d 752 (1974) (except to the extent permitted by statute).

See 1 Va. L. Reg. (N.S.) 161 (1915).

[7]Bible Socy. v. Pendleton, 7 W. Va. 79 (1873); Pack v. Shanklin, 43 W. Va. 304, 27 S.E. 389 (1897).

But see Hays v. Harris, 73 W. Va. 17, 80 S.E. 827 (1912); Beatty v. Union Trust & Deposit Co., 123 W. Va. 144, 13 S.E.2d 760 (1941).

sin.[8] In these states, however, it is now provided by statute that charitable trusts shall be valid.[9] In these states, until the law was changed by statute, the only method of devoting property to charitable purposes was to give it to a charitable corporation, either one already in existence[10] or one to be organized.[11]

[8]Ruth v. Oberbrunner, 40 Wis. 238 (1876).

[9]*Maryland:* Ann. Code, Estates and Trusts Article, §14-301. See also §11-102.

Michigan: Stat. Ann., §26.1191.

Minnesota: Stat. Ann., §501.12.

New York: Estates, Powers and Trusts Law, §8-1.1, as amended by Laws 1971, c. 1058, and Laws 1985, c. 492, originally enacted in 1893.

Virginia: Code 1950, §55-26.1, as inserted by Laws 1976, c. 546.

West Virginia: Code §§35-2-1, 35-2-2.

Wisconsin: Stat., §701.10.

For statutes in other states expressly permitting charitable trusts, see:

California: Prob. Code, §27.

Colorado: Rev. Stat. 1963, §153-16-1.

Connecticut: Gen. Stat., §45-80, as amended by Laws 1980, c. 80-476, §224.

Georgia: Code 1981, §§53-2-99, 53-12-70, 53-12-73, 53-12-75.

Kentucky: Rev. Stat. Ann., §381.260, as amended by Laws 1980, c. 123.

Louisiana: Rev. Stat. Ann., §9:2271; as to granting a servitude in immovables for charitable purposes, see Rev. Stat. Ann., §9:1252.

Mississippi: Code 1972, §§39-9-1 to 39-9-13.

Montana: Code Ann. 1983, §§72-27-101, 72-27-102, assume the validity of charitable trusts.

Nebraska: Rev. Stat. 1943, §30-239.

North Carolina: Gen. Stat., §§36A-43, 36A-46.

South Carolina: Code Ann., §§21-27-50, 21-29-20.

Tennessee: Code Ann., §35-1-114, as enacted by Laws 1986, c. 566.

Wyoming: Stat. §§34-93 to 34-96.

See Note, Charitable gifts; definiteness, 163 A.L.R. 784, 789, 796 (1946); Note, Charitable Trusts in Texas, 3 Sw. L.J. 168 (1949); Note, The Charitable Trusts Doctrine in Montana, 11 Mont. L. Rev. 96 (1950).

See Note, The Enforcement of Charitable Trusts in America: A History of Evolving Attitudes, 54 Va. L. Rev. 436 (1968).

[10]*Maryland:* Trinity M.E. Church v. Baker, 91 Md. 539, 46 A. 1020 (1900); Holloway v. Mission Helpers, 119 Md. 667, 87 A. 269 (1913); Novak v. Orphans' Home, 123 Md. 161, 90 A. 997, Ann. Cas. 1915C 1067 (1914).

Minnesota: Young Men's Christian Assn. v. Horn, 120 Minn. 404, 139 N.W. 805 (1913); Schaeffer v. Newberry, 235 Minn. 282, 50 N.W.2d 477 (1951).

New York: Wetmore v. Parker, 52 N.Y. 450 (1873); Bird v. Merklee, 144 N.Y. 544, 39 N.E. 645, 27 L.R.A. 423 (1895).

Virginia: Protestant Episcopal Socy. v. Churchman's Reps., 80 Va. 718

The principal reason for refusing to uphold charitable trusts in these states was that the Statute of Charitable Uses was not in force in the state, either because a statute of the state so provided, or because it was omitted from the enumeration of English statutes that were accepted, or because it was held not to be applicable to American conditions. The truth is, of course, that although the charitable purposes enumerated in the preamble of the statute are as applicable to American conditions as to those in England, the remedy afforded by the statute for the enforcement of charitable trusts was not applicable to our conditions and was never applied in any of the states. The remedy, as we have seen, was through the appointment of commissioners by the chancellor under the Great Seal. The real mistake made by the courts of these states was in holding that the law of charitable trusts had its origin in and was dependent upon the enactment of the Statute of Charitable Uses. The mistake at first was excusable in view of the paucity of available historical material. The records that were available did not clearly show that charitable trusts were enforced in England prior to the enactment of the statute in 1601. The courts were compelled to rely on secondary authorities, and the authorities to which they resorted were the ill-considered dicta of English judges. It is astonishing how frequently courts rely on the words of other courts not merely as indications of the law but as proof of facts. The words that fall from judges are seldom a sound foundation for historical research. It was this historical error that led the Supreme Court of the United States to hold invalid a charitable disposition made by a testator who was domiciled in Virginia. This was in the case of *Trustees of Philadelphia Baptist Association v. Hart's Executors*, [12] decided in 1819, Chief Justice Marshall deliv-

---

(1885); Jordan's Admr. v. Richmond Home for Ladies, 106 Va. 710, 56 S.E. 730 (1907).

West Virginia: Osenton v. Elliott, 73 W. Va. 519, 81 S.E. 837 (1914).

But in jurisdictions where charitable trusts failed unless there was a definite beneficiary, a bequest or devise to a corporation for other than its corporate purposes was invalid. Fosdick v. Hempstead, 125 N.Y. 581, 26 N.E. 801, 11 L.R.A. 715 (1891); Trinity M.E. Church v. Baker, 91 Md. 539, 46 A. 1020 (1900).

[11] See §401.8.

[12] 4 Wheat. 1, 4 L. Ed. 499 (U.S. 1819).

ering the opinion. In that case a testator by his will executed in 1790 made a bequest to an unincorporated religious association as a fund for the education of youths of the Baptist denomination who should appear promising for the ministry. In 1792 the legislature of Virginia repealed all English statutes including the Statute of Charitable Uses. The testator died in 1795. Suit was instituted in the Circuit Court of the United States for the District of Virginia by the association, which had been incorporated after the testator's death, and by the individuals who were members of the association at the time of his death, against the executors of the testator to enforce the charitable trust. The question of the validity of the trust was certified to the Supreme Court. The Court held that the trust was invalid. Chief Justice Marshall expressed the opinion that a private trust is invalid unless there is a definite beneficiary; and that although in England a charitable trust without definite beneficiaries is valid, yet this exception is due to the operation of the Statute of Charitable Uses, or Statute of Elizabeth, as it is frequently called, and that with the repeal of that statute in Virginia the law of charitable trusts was repealed in that state.

The question of the dependency of the law of charitable trusts on the Statute of Charitable Uses was again raised in the Supreme Court of the United States in 1844 in the case of *Vidal v. Girard's Executors.* [13] In that case a testator, domiciled in Pennsylvania, left his fortune to the city of Philadelphia in trust to establish a school or college for the education of white orphan children. Suit was brought in the Circuit Court of the United States for the Eastern District of Pennsylvania by the heirs of the testator to set aside the bequest. The Circuit Court dismissed the complaint, and on appeal its decree was affirmed. It had previously been held by the courts of Pennsylvania that the Statute of Elizabeth was not in force in that state. The Supreme Court held that the trust was valid. The Court found that it was clearly proved by the early records that had recently been published that charitable trusts were enforced in England before the enactment of the Statute of Elizabeth, and the fact that that statute was not in force in Pennsylvania was immaterial. Indeed,

[13] 2 How. 127, 11 L. Ed. 205 (U.S. 1844).

the Pennsylvania courts had already come to the same conclusion.[14]

Although the Supreme Court of the United States as well as the courts of Pennsylvania recognized that the validity of charitable trusts did not depend on whether the Statute of Elizabeth was in force, the courts in a few other states continued to hold charitable trusts invalid until they were permitted by statute. In New York, although at first charitable trusts were upheld,[15] the courts later held them invalid.[16] In *Bascom v. Albertson*[17] the court gave three grounds for invalidating charitable trusts. In the first place there was the fact that the Statute of Elizabeth had been repealed in New York. As we have seen, this reason is unsound and is based on lack of knowledge of the actual development of charitable trusts in England prior to the statute. In the second place, the Revised Statutes of New York, adopted in 1828, provided that an express trust might be created only for four purposes, and these purposes did not include charitable purposes.[18] It is doubtful, however, whether the commissioners who drafted the statutes or the legislature that enacted them intended to deal with any but private trusts. In the third place, the court expressed the opinion that it was a better policy to limit gifts for charitable purposes to gifts made to charitable corporations. There were various restrictions on the making of gifts to charitable corporations imposed by statute, and the court felt that if property could be given to trustees for charitable purposes as to which there were no statutory restrictions, the policy of the restrictive statutes might be evaded. Moreover, the court felt that the legislature could exercise its

[14]Witman v. Lex, 17 S.&R. 88, 17 Am. Dec. 644 (Pa. 1827); Zimmerman v. Anders, 6 W.&S. 218, 40 Am. Dec. 552 (Pa. 1843).

See Magill v. Brown, Fed. Cas. No. 8952 (C.C.E.D. Pa. 1833).

To the same effect, see Frost Natl. Bank v. Boyd, 188 S.W.2d 199 (Tex. Civ. App. 1945) (citing Restatement of Trusts, §§348, 368), *aff'd sub nom.* Boyd v. Frost Natl. Bank, 145 Tex. 206, 196 S.W.2d 497, 168 A.L.R. 1326 (1946), noted in 25 Tex. L. Rev. 434.

[15]Williams v. Williams, 8 N.Y. 525 (1853).

[16]See note 2, *supra*.

[17]34 N.Y. 584, 615 (1866).

[18]N.Y. Rev. Stat., 1830, Pt. 2, c. 1, tit. 2.

discretion in permitting or refusing to permit incorporation, whereas if charitable trusts were upheld, this would give "to every private citizen the right to create a perpetuity for such purpose as to him may seem good, and to endue it with more than corporate powers and more than corporate immunity." Later, when Governor Tilden's great legacy to found a public library in New York failed, the legislature passed a statute, known as the Tilden Act, which provided that charitable trusts should thereafter be valid.[19]

Today all of the states recognize the validity of charitable trusts. If the trust is properly created, if there is no violation of any statutory restriction on the creation of the trust, if the purposes are recognized as charitable, and if the purposes are sufficiently definite, the trust will be upheld if it is possible to perform it. The states differ to some extent on the question whether it is necessary that the charitable purpose be clearly defined by the settlor or whether it is sufficient that the property is to be devoted generally to charitable purposes. The states differ also as to the extent to which they will go under the doctrine of cy pres to prevent the failure of the trust where it is impossible to perform it exactly as the settlor intended. These differences will be considered in their appropriate places.

§348.4. Effects of charitable dispositions. There are numerous cases in which the courts have held that a particular disposition is or is not one for charitable purposes. It is important, however, to bear in mind in each case the precise question which the court is called upon to determine. In many of the cases the question is whether the disposition is valid. Ordinarily, no difficulty arises where there is a direct gift or bequest to a corporation, whether the corporation is a charitable organization or not. Where the gift or bequest is one in trust, however, and especially where the trust is to continue for an indefinite period, the validity of the disposition ordinarily depends on the question whether the trust is charitable or not. It is this question with which we shall deal rather extensively hereafter. Where the disposition, whether it is made to a corporation or is made to

---

[19]Laws 1893, c. 701, now Estates, Powers and Trusts Law, §8-1.1, as amended by Laws 1971, c. 1058, and Laws 1985, c. 492.

trustees, is valid, another question frequently arises, namely whether a tax is due to the government. The question may be one of liability for an estate or inheritance tax, or an income tax, or a property tax. Statutes frequently provide for exemption from such taxes in the case of a charitable organization or charitable trust. Ordinarily, if the purpose is so far charitable that the disposition is valid as a charitable disposition, it is also entitled to the exemption provided for by statute. It is to be borne in mind, however, that the statutes differ in their language, and do not necessarily exempt all charitable organizations or trusts.[1] A

§348.4. [1]The statutes as to exemption from taxation in the case of charities are, generally, somewhat randomly worded. They ordinarily include general purposes as well as specific provisions relating to certain charities that would have fallen naturally under the more general words. Thus by the Internal Revenue Code, 26 U.S.C. §501(c)(3), it is provided that there shall be an exemption from taxation in case of "corporations, and any community chest, fund or foundation, organized and operated exclusively for religious, charitable, scientific, testing for public safety, literary, or educational purposes, [or to foster national or international amateur sports competition (but only if no part of its activities involve the provision of athletic facilities or equipment)], or for the prevention of cruelty to children or animals, no part of the net earnings of which inures to the benefit of any private shareholder or individual, no substantial part of the activities of which is carrying on propaganda, or otherwise attempting, to influence legislation, [except as otherwise provided in subsection (h)], and which does not participate in, or intervene in (including the publishing or distributing of statements), any political campaign on behalf of any candidate for public office." The provisions in square brackets were inserted by the Tax Reform Act of 1976. See also the provisions in 26 U.S.C. §170, as to deductions from income taxes for charitable dispositions; and §§2055 and 2522(a)(2), as to deduction in estate and gift taxes of charitable dispositions.

First, it is to be noticed that there is no express provision relating to the relief of poverty. Certainly, such a purpose is to be included in the word "charitable," but it seems clear that this word is not limited to relief of poverty. It would include other purposes that are recognized as charitable, such as the promotion of health as well as religious and educational purposes, although these latter purposes are expressly, though unnecessarily, stated.

In a case decided by the Judicial Committee of the Privy Council, Ashfield Mun. Council v. Joyce, [1976] 3 W.L.R. 617 (P.C.), it was held that under a tax statute of New South Wales the term "charity" or "public charity" presumptively was not limited to relief of poverty but included other purposes legally recognized as charitable.

Second, it is to be noted that in the federal statute there is the provision that no part of the net earnings shall inure to the benefit of any private

decision that in the case of a gift or bequest in trust there is no

---

shareholder or individual. This is true also as to the validity of a charitable disposition. See §375.

Third, there is the provision that no substantial part of the activities shall be the carrying on of propaganda to influence legislation. This is not a requirement for the validity of a charitable disposition. See §§374.4, 374.5.

Fourth, there is the provision as to political campaigns. A trust for such a purpose is not a charitable trust. See §374.6.

See Lyles & Blum, Development of the Federal Tax Treatment of Charities, 39 Law & Contemp. Probs. 6 (1975); Stone, The Charitable Foundation: Its Governance, 39 Law & Contemp. Probs. 57 (1975); Bittker & Rahdert, The Exemption of Nonprofit Organizations from Federal Income Taxation, 85 Yale L.J. 299 (1976); Lipton, Significant Private Foundations and the Need for Public Selection of Their Trustees, 64 Va. L. Rev. 779 (1978); Ginsberg, The Real Property Tax Exemption of Nonprofit Organizations: A Perspective, 53 Temple L.Q. 291 (1980).

As to the English law, see Gravells, Public Purpose Trusts, 40 Mod. L. Rev. 397 (1977); Watkin, Charity: The Purport of "Purpose," [1978] Conv. 297.

It is to be noted that even if the purposes are such as to make a trust charitable, it may not be exempt from taxes during a period in which the property is not actually used for such purposes. See, for example, Pentecostal Church v. Hughlett, 601 S.W.2d 666 (Mo. App. 1980); Home of Sages v. Tishelman, 100 Misc. 2d 911, 120 N.Y.S.2d 343 (1979), aff'd, 81 A.D.2d 886, 441 N.Y.S.2d 413 (1981); Trustees of Vermont Wild Land Found. v. Town of Pillsford, 137 Vt. 439, 407 A.2d 174 (1979).

In Merged Area (Education) VII v. Board of Review, 326 N.W.2d 310 (Iowa 1982), it was held that, although a nonprofit school of technology would be a charitable organization for the purpose of determining the validity and effect of a testamentary disposition to it, it did not fall within the charitable organization exception to the property tax because another section of the statute specifically provided a property tax exemption for school corporations.

It was held in Inland Revenue Commrs. v. Helen Slater Charitable Trust, Ltd., [1981] 3 All E.R. 98 (C.A.), that a charitable corporation could take income and capital transfer tax deductions for amounts given to another charitable corporation although the latter did not spend the money for charitable purposes within the tax year.

There are also cases that hold that to be exempt from taxes, a trust must be for "public" purposes, even though the beneficiaries are of a sufficiently broad class as to make the trust charitable. See §368.

See Pedrick, "And Then to Charity:" Charitable Remainder Trusts and the Federal Estate Tax, 17 U. Miami Inst. Est. Plan. ¶¶300-08 (1983).

In Westport Bank & Trust Co. v. Fable, 126 Conn. 665, 13 A.2d 862 (1940), in upholding a general bequest for charitable and educational purposes, Maltbie, C.J., said that "it may be well to point out that a trust may be

exemption from a tax is not necessarily a decision that it is not

---

charitable even though it is taxable, for the Legislature can tax all charitable trusts or such only of them as are characterized by distinguishing elements."

In Presbyterian Center, Inc. v. Henson, 221 Ga. 750, 146 S.E.2d 903 (1966), it was held that a religious corporation, although charitable, was not exempt from tax as a purely public charity.

In Croton Community Nursery School v. Coulter, 121 N.Y.S.2d 755 (1953), it was held that a private nursery school operating under a charter received from the state Board of Regents was not exempt from taxation.

In Graphic Arts Educ. Found. v. State, 240 Minn. 143, 59 N.W.2d 841 (1953), it was held that a nonprofit trade school was not exempt from taxation as a "seminary of learning."

In In re Estate of Julian, 93 Ohio App. 221, 113 N.E.2d 129 (1952), it was held that a bequest to the Roman Catholic archdiocese of Cincinnati, an unincorporated religious society, and to the Archbishop of Cincinnati, as trustees for the furtherance of such "charitable, benevolent, scientific and educational works and activities of said archdiocese as may be designated by said Archbishop of Cincinnati," was not exempt as a "public charity" from the inheritance tax.

In In re Estate of Salisbury, 90 Ohio App. 17, 101 N.E.2d 304 (1951), *appeal dismissed,* 155 Ohio St. 615, 99 N.E.2d 671 (1951), where property was bequeathed to the endowment fund of a church, the income to be used solely for the charitable purposes of the church, it was held that the bequest was not exempt from inheritance tax, since it was not restricted to public charitable purposes.

In Cleveland Bible College v. Board of Tax Appeals, 151 Ohio St. 258, 85 N.E.2d 284 (1949), it was held that a Bible college was exempt from taxation because students other than Christians could be admitted to the college.

In Beerman Found. v. Board of Tax Appeals, 152 Ohio St. 179, 87 N.E.2d 474 (1949), a nonprofit corporation renting apartments to disabled war veterans at a rental below cost was held not to be exempt from property tax.

See Hill School Tax Exemption Case, 370 Pa. 21, 87 A.2d 259 (1952), in which the court held that a nonprofit preparatory school was exempt from taxation as a "purely public charity"; West Indies Mission Appeal (In re Assessment for the Year 1952), 180 Pa. Super. 216, 119 A.2d 550 (1956).

In Oregon Methodist Homes v. State Tax Commn. (Horn), 226 Or. 298, 360 P.2d 293 (1961), it was held that a home for the aged, although a nonprofit corporation, was not exempt from taxation, since residents all paid fees.

In Second Church of Christ Scientist of Philadelphia v. City of Philadelphia, 398 Pa. 65, 157 A.2d 54, 75 A.L.R.2d 1103 (1960), it was held that a parking lot of a church was subject to taxation, since it was not used for religious purposes.

In People v. Haring, 8 N.Y.2d 350, 170 N.E.2d 677 (1960), *rev'g* 10 A.D.2d 167, 198 N.Y.S.2d 135 (1960), the court held exempt from real estate tax a

a charitable trust for other purposes. So also it is held in some states that a charitable organization is exempt from liability in tort at least under certain circumstances. A decision that a particular organization is not exempt from such liabilities is not necessarily a decision that it is not a charitable organization.

By the federal Tax Reform Act of 1969, charitable trusts and foundations are made subject to taxation unless they comply with the provisions of the Act as to self-dealing, current distribution of income, excessive business holdings, and improper investments and expenditures.[2]

---

farm on which produce was raised for feeding the employees of a religious organization, although a small surplus of the produce was sold. The court said that the primary purpose was the feeding of students, teachers, workers, and members of the religious body and the sale of the surplus was incidental and insubstantial.

See Bell, Pennsylvania's Transfer Inheritance Tax on Charitable Bequests, 60 Dick. L. Rev. 75 (1955); Lowndes, Tax Advantages of Charitable Gifts, 46 Va. L. Rev. 394 (1960); Sugarman & Pomeroy, Business Income of Exempt Organizations, 46 id. 424 (1960); Clark, The Limitation on Political Activities, 46 id. 439 (1960).

See Note, When is corporation, community chest, fund, foundation, or club "organized and operated exclusively" for charitable or other exempt purposes under Internal Revenue Code, 69 A.L.R.2d 871 (1960).

See Note, Charitable, educational or religious tax exemption of property held in trust for tax-exempt organization, 94 A.L.R.2d 626 (1964).

As to the validity of trusts for the benefit of limited classes of persons, see §375.2.

See Note, Exemption of charitable organization from taxation or special assessment, 34 A.L.R. 634 (1925), 62 id. 328 (1929), 108 id. 284 (1937).

See Note, Nonprofit hospitals or other charitable institutions as within contemplation of Federal or state legislation regarding relation of employers and employees, 132 A.L.R. 1153 (1941); Note, Construction and application of provision of social security or unemployment compensation acts relating to exemption of corporations or institutions of a religious, charitable or educational character, 155 id. 369 (1945); Note, Nonprofit charitable institutions as within operation of labor statutes, 26 A.L.R.2d 1020 (1952).

See Note, Estate Tax Deductions for Gifts to Charity — The Certainty Requirement, 13 Geo. Wash. L. Rev. 198 (1945); Note, Exemption of Educational, Philanthropic and Religious Institutions from State Real Property Taxes, 64 Harv. L. Rev. 288 (1951); Note, Taxation of Charities in Massachusetts, 31 B.U.L. Rev. 200 (1951); Note, Charitable and Religious Tax Exemptions in Ohio, 20 U. Cin. L. Rev. 266 (1951).

[2]Act of December 30, 1969, Pub. L. 91-172, as amended, 26 U.S.C. §§4940-4948.

In several cases it was thereafter held that trusts and foundations were to be administered in accordance with the requirements of the Act, even though there were no such requirements in the terms of the trust; or that the court would authorize a modification of the terms of the trust so as to include such requirements.[3]

[3]*Connecticut:* MacCurdy-Salisbury Educ. Fund v. Killian, 30 Conn. 203, 309 A.2d 11 (1973) (citing the text).

Illinois: Matter of Estate of Bishop, 127 Ill. App. 3d 165, 82 Ill. Dec. 244, 468 N.E.2d 506 (1984) (decree in suit in which income and remainder beneficiaries filed appearances reducing income payable to 5 percent of value of trust assets in order to qualify trust as a charitable remainder trust under the Federal Tax Reform Act of 1969 not subject to collateral attack despite failure of income beneficiaries to consent to amendment; Ill. Rev. Stat. 1981, c. 148, ¶51(2), requiring such consent, applies only when the trustee amends the trust without court proceedings); Flanagan State Bank v. Bromenn Healthcare, 140 Ill. App. 3d 137, 94 Ill. Dec. 303, 487 N.E.2d 1180 (1986).

Maine: Canal Natl. Bank v. Old Folks' Home Assn., 347 A.2d 428 (Me. 1975).

New Jersey: See Stat., §§3B:11-8 to 3B:11-15, effective 1 May 1982 — Charitable Trust Law of 1971 — split interest and private foundation trusts.

New York: Matter of Barkey, 65 Misc. 2d 738, 318 N.Y.S.2d 843 (1971); Matter of Klosk, 65 Misc. 2d 1005, 319 N.Y.S.2d 685 (1971); Matter of Roche, 69 Misc. 2d 481, 330 N.Y.S.2d 441 (1972); Matter of Presley, 76 Misc. 2d 462, 351 N.Y.S.2d 305 (1973); Matter of Larus, 78 Misc. 2d 122, 356 N.Y.S.2d 395 (1974), *semble;* Matter of Stalp, 79 Misc. 2d 412, 359 N.Y.S.2d 749 (1974); Matter of Hammer, 81 Misc. 2d 25, 362 N.Y.S.2d 753 (1974); In re Will of Danforth, 81 Misc. 2d 452, 366 N.Y.S.2d 329 (1975); Matter of Newell, 81 Misc. 2d 1050, 367 N.Y.S.2d 703 (1975); Will of Atlas, 86 Misc. 2d 387, 380 N.Y.S.2d 1012 (1976); Matter of Otto, 86 Misc. 2d 20, 381 N.Y.S.2d 617 (1976); Matter of Rayvid, 88 Misc. 2d 372, 388 N.Y.S.2d 211 (1976); Matter of Webster, 90 Misc. 2d 939, 396 N.Y.S.2d 592 (1977); Matter of Witz, 95 Misc. 2d 36, 406 N.Y.S.2d 671 (1978).

But in Matter of Reinhardt, 81 Misc. 2d 184, 366 N.Y.S.2d 87 (1975), reformation was refused because this would be detrimental to individual beneficiaries.

North Carolina: Davison v. Duke Univ., 282 N.C. 676, 194 S.E.2d 761, 57 A.L.R.3d 1008 (1973).

See N.C. Gen. Stat., §36A-53(b), as enacted by Laws 1979, c. 772.

Pennsylvania: W. W. Smith Found., Petitioner, 52 D.&C.2d 203 (Pa. 1970); Mode Estate, 54 D.&C.2d 550 (Pa. 1972) (although a statute made reform of the terms of the trust unnecessary); Hering Trust, 55 D.&C.2d 326 (Pa. 1972); Arner Estate, 65 D.&C.2d 421 (Pa. 1974).

But in Finley Trust, 60 D.&C.2d 38 (Pa. 1972), the court refused to modify

TOPIC 2.   CREATION OF CHARITABLE TRUSTS

§349.   *Methods of Creating a Charitable Trust*

A charitable trust may be created by any of the methods used in creating a private trust.[1] Thus the owner of property can create a charitable trust, either by conveying it inter vivos to

---

by eliminating a provision for accumulation, because this would substantially impair the purposes of the trust.

In Estate of Mabury, 54 Cal. App. 3d 969, 127 Cal. Rptr. 233 (1976), the court refused to allow present payment of interest to the charitable beneficiaries, contrary to the terms of the trust, in order to avoid taxation under the Tax Reform Act of 1967, because it was uncertain whether the Act applied to the trust. The court said that that question should first be decided by the federal courts, and that if the federal courts should hold that the Act was applicable, it would then consider whether it would permit such payments under the doctrine of cy pres or deviation.

In Wierman Trust, 68 D.&C.2d 525 (Pa. 1975), the court refused to allow the transfer of property held for a charitable purpose to a foundation in order to avoid a tax.

In Shriners Hosp. v. Maryland Natl. Bank, 270 Md. 564, 312 A.2d 546 (1973), it was held that a modification of the terms of the trust could be permitted only if all of the income beneficiaries consented.

In almost all of the states statutes have been enacted making provision for charitable trusts and foundations so as to avoid tax liabilities under the Tax Reform Act of 1969.

In several states there are statutes making similar provisions as to charitable remainders.

See the broad provisions applicable to private foundation trusts and split interest trusts in Florida Stat. Ann., §§737.501 to 737.512.

We are not here concerned with the exemption from taxation under the Tax Reform Act of 1969 of a gift for charitable purposes in which the donor reserves a life interest in the form of a charitable remainder unitrust, a pooled income fund trust, or a charitable remainder annuity trust. See Teikehl, Charitable Remainder Unitrusts under the Tax Reform Act, 111 Trusts & Estates, 858 (1972). See also 114 Trusts & Estates, 862, 870 (1975).

As to the consequences of the Tax Reform Act of 1969, see 39 Law & Contemp. Probs., 232, 255 (1975); Schmolka, Income Taxation of Charitable Remainder Trusts and Decedents' Estates: Sixty-Six Years of Astigmatism, 40 Tax L. Rev. 1-351 (1984).

§349.   [1]See Scarney v. Clarke, 282 Mich. 56, 275 N.W. 765 (1937) (citing Restatement of Trusts §349), noted in 18 Mich. S.B.J. 44.

See §17.

another person as trustee, or by devising or bequeathing it upon a charitable trust. As we shall see, however, there are by statute in some states restrictions on the power of a testator to create a charitable trust by will that are not applicable to the creation of private trusts.[2] So also the owner of property can create a charitable trust by declaring himself trustee of the property for a charitable purpose.[3] Where a person has a general power of appointment by deed or by will, he can create a charitable trust through the exercise of the power. Where the power has been defectively exercised, the donee failing to comply fully with the requirements of the instrument creating the power in regard to its exercise, it has been held that equity will disregard the defect, or, as it is said, will aid the defective exercise of a power of appointment in favor of a charity.[4] So also a charitable trust, like a private trust, can be created by a binding promise made by one person to another as trustee. The latter then holds in trust his rights as promisee. In such a case there is not merely a promise to create a trust in the future, but the immediate creation of a trust of a right of action. No trust arises, however, if the promise is not binding, as where it is made gratuitously and not under seal; and in some states a gratuitous promise under seal is no longer binding.

[2]See §362.

[3]*California:* American Bible Socy. v. Mortgage Guar. Co., 217 Cal. 9, 17 P.2d 105 (1932).

New York: Robb v. Washington & Jefferson College, 185 N.Y. 485, 78 N.E. 359 (1906); Marshall v. Franklin Socy., 131 Misc. 611, 228 N.Y.S. 270 (1928), *aff'd,* 224 A.D. 834, 231 N.Y.S. 812 (1928).

Pennsylvania: Dickerson's Appeal, 115 Pa. 198, 8 A. 64, 2 Am. St. Rep. 547 (1887).

[4]See Innes v. Sayer, 7 Hare 377 (1849), *aff'd,* 3 Mac. &G. 606 (1851). But see In re Carey, [1901] 1 I.R. 81.

The principle as to the aiding by equity of the defective execution of a power is thus stated in the Restatement of Property §347: "Failure of an appointment to satisfy formal requirements imposed by the donor does not cause the appointment to be ineffective in equity if (a) the appointment approximates the manner of appointment prescribed by the donor; and (b) the appointee is a wife, child, adopted child or creditor of the donee, or a charity, or a person who has paid value for the appointment." See Restatement (Second) of Property (Donative Transfers) §18.3(2)(d).

In a number of states statutes have been enacted regulating the solicitation of funds for charitable purposes.[5]

[5]*Federal:* Pilsen Neighbors Community Council v. Burris, 672 F. Supp. 295 (N.D. Ill. 1987) (Illinois statute).

Arkansas: Stat. 1947, §§64-1610 to 64-1615, as amended by Laws 1979, c. 400.

California: Business and Professional Code, §§17510 to 17510.7, as enacted by Laws 1973, c. 1113; §17510.3, as amended by Laws 1986, c. 138.

See Eye Dog Found. v. State Bd., 63 Cal. 2d 21, 432 P.2d 717 (1967) (holding constitutional solicitation statute as to dogs for the blind).

Connecticut: Gen. Stat. 1958, §§17-21e to 17-21r, as amended by Laws 1967, c. 690, by Laws 1973, c. 73-568, by Laws 1976, c. 76-406, and by Laws 1978, c. 78-205; Laws 1986, c. 86-369.

District of Columbia: Code Ann. 1981, §§2-701 to 2-714.

Florida: Stat. Ann., §§496.02 to 496.13, as amended by Laws 1967, c. 67-205, by Laws 1974, c. 74-332, and by Laws 1976, c. 76-162.

Wickman v. Firestone, 500 So. 2d 740 (Fla. App. 1987) (Florida statute constitutional).

Georgia: Code 1981, §§43-17-1 to 43-17-10, 43-17-18.

Hawaii: Rev. Stat., §§467B-1 to 467B-11, as amended by Laws 1971, c. 162, and by Laws 1978, c. 182.

Illinois: Rev. Stat., c. 23, §§5101 to 5114, as amended by Laws 1969, c. 76-1928, Laws 1972, c. 77-2357, and Laws 1975, c. 79-137.

In People v. Caldwell, 8 Ill. App. 3d 485, 290 N.E.2d 279, 76 A.L.R.3d 918 (1972), it was held that the statute was not unconstitutional.

Kansas: Stat. Ann., §17-1740.

Kentucky: Rev. Stat. Ann., §§367.650 to 367.670.

Maine: Rev. Stat. Ann., tit. 22, §3155, as inserted by Laws 1973, c. 436.

Maryland: Ann. Code, art. 41, §§103B to 103D, as amended by Laws 1966, c. 639, Laws 1967, c. 44, and Laws 1978, c. 149.

In Secretary of State of Md. v. J. H. Munson Co., 467 U.S. 947, 104 S. Ct. 2839, 81 L. Ed. 2d 786 (1984), a statute prohibiting charitable organizations from paying expenses of more than a quarter of the amount raised was held unconstitutional. A city ordinance with similar provisions was held unconstitutional in People v. American Youth Sports Found., 194 Cal. App. 3d 6, 239 Cal. Rptr. 621 (Cal. Super. 1987).

Massachusetts: Ann. Laws, c. 68, §§17 to 31.

Bellotti v. Telco Communications, 650 F. Supp. 149 (D. Mass. 1986), *aff'd sub nom.* Shannon v. Telco Communications, 824 F.2d 150 (1st Cir. 1987) (statute prohibiting professional solicitor from receiving as compensation more than 25 percent of charitable contributions is unconstitutional).

Michigan: Comp. Laws Ann., §§400.271 to 400.294.

Minnesota: Stat. Ann., §§309.50 to 309.61, as amended by Laws 1967, p. 2314, and by Laws 1969, c. 112. Heritage Publishing Co. v. Fishman, 634 F. Supp. 1489 (D. Minn. 1986) (statute partially unconstitutional).

New Hampshire: Rev. Stat. Ann., §§31:91, 320:20.

§350. Capacity of the Settlor

The principles as to the capacity of a person to create a trust, whether inter vivos or by will, are applicable to charitable

---

New Jersey: Rev. Stat., c. 469, §§45:17A-1 to 45:17A-17 (Charitable Fund Raising Act of 1971), Laws 1971, as amended by Laws 1975, c. 279.

New York: Executive Law, §§171 to 176, as amended by Laws 1986, cc. 440, 441.

In Sport Celebrities v. Maull, 56 A.D.2d 849, 392 N.Y.S.2d 315 (1977), it was held that only the Attorney General had power to bring a proceeding to enjoin violations of the statute.

As to what constitutes a charity for the purposes of the statute, see Matter of Green v. Javits (Application of Green), 7 Misc.2d 312, 166 N.Y.S.2d 198 (1957), *aff'd mem. sub nom.* Matter of Green v. Lefkowitz, 4 A.D.2d 869, 947, 167 N.Y.S.2d 431 (1957), *leave to appeal denied,* 4 N.Y.2d 704, 148 N.E.2d 308 (1958).

North Carolina: Gen Stat., §§108-75.1 et seq. National Fed. of the Blind of North Carolina v. Riley, 635 F. Supp. 256 (E.D.N.C. 1986) (statute partially unconstitutional).

In Heritage Village Church & Missionary Fellowship v. State, 299 N.C. 399, 263 S.E.2d 726 (1980), *aff'g* 40 N.C. App. 429, 253 S.E.2d 473 (1979), the statute as worded was held unconstitutional as applied to religious organizations.

North Dakota: Cent. Code, §§50-22-02.1, 50-22-04.1, 50-22-01, 50-22-02, 50-22-05.

Oklahoma: Stat. Ann., tit. 18, §§552.1 to 552.18, as amended by Laws 1976, c. 200, and by Laws 1978, c. 244.

Oregon: Rev. Stat., §§128.801 to 128.898, the Oregon Charitable Solicitation Act, enacted by Laws 1985, cc. 729, 730.

Pennsylvania: 10 Pa. Stat., §§161.1 to 161.18, enacted by Laws 1986, c. 36.

See Commonwealth v. Schren, 26 D.&C.2d 275 (Pa. 1961).

See Commonwealth v. National Fed. of the Blind, 471 Pa. 529, 370 A.2d 732 (1977), applying the act to out-of-state charities soliciting by mail sent to residents of the state.

See Rehabilitation Center & Workshop v. Commonwealth, 43 Pa. Commw. 295, 405 A.2d 980 (Pa. 1979), where the state Commission on Charitable Organizations denied renewal of certification because of violation of the statute.

Rhode Island: Gen. Laws 1956, §§5-53-1 to 5-53-14, as enacted by Laws 1976, c. 189.

South Carolina: Code Ann., §§33-55-10 to 33-55-190.

Tennessee: Code Ann., §§48-2201 to 48-2218.

Virginia: Code 1950, §§57-48 to 57-69.

Washington: Rev. Code, §19.09.020, as amended by Laws 1977, c. 222.

as well as to private trusts.[1] There are in some states statutory provisions restricting the power of the owner of property to create a trust for charitable purposes by will,[2] but these statutes have nothing to do with the lack of capacity of the particular testator.

The question has arisen whether a business corporation can properly make contributions for charitable purposes or whether the making of such contributions is ultra vires. It is frequently provided by statute that such contributions may be made, subject to such restrictions as are imposed by the statute. In a case in New Jersey where a contribution was made by a manufacturing corporation to Princeton University and objection was made by a shareholder of the corporation, it was held that the New Jersey statute was not unconstitutional as impairing the obligation of contracts or as a denial of due process of law.[3] The decision has met with general approval.[4]

West Virginia: Code, §§29-19-1 to 29-19-15, as enacted by Laws 1977, c. 64, and amended by Laws 1979, c. 13.

Wisconsin: Stat., §175.13, as amended by Laws 1969, c. 330.

In Holloway v. Brown, 62 Ohio St. 2d 65, 403 N.E.2d 191 (1980), it was held that a city ordinance restricting solicitations for charity was not unconstitutional.

On the question of unconstitutionality of statutes or ordinances restricting solicitations for charity under the First or Fourteenth Amendments, see Village of Schaumburg v. Citizens for a Better Envt., 444 U.S. 620, 100 S. Ct. 826, 63 L. Ed. 2d 273 (1980), and the cases there cited.

See Quandt, The Regulation of Charitable Fundraising and Spending Activities, 1975 Wis. L. Rev. 1158.

See Note, Criminal offenses under statutes and ordinances regulating charitable solicitations, 75 A.L.R.3d 924 (1977).

§350. [1]See §§18-22.

[2]See §362.

[3]A. P. Smith Mfg. Co. v. Barlow, 26 N.J. Super. 106, 97 A.2d 186 (1953), *aff'd,* 13 N.J. 145, 98 A.2d 581, 39 A.L.R.2d 1179 (1953), noted in 67 Harv. L. Rev. 343.

[4]See 29 Ind. L.J. 295 (1954); 8 Rutgers L. Rev. 327 (1954); 102 U. Pa. L. Rev. 243 (1953).

See Note, Power of a business corporation to donate to a charitable or similar institution, 39 A.L.R.2d 1192 (1955).

See also Andrews, Corporate Giving (1952, Russell Sage Found.).

See La. Rev. Stat. Ann., §9:2271.1, as added by Laws 1954, c. 638.

§351. *Intention to Create a Trust*

A charitable trust, like an express private trust, is created only if the settlor properly manifests an intention to create it.[1] The settlor need not, however, use any particular language in showing his intention to create a charitable trust; he need not use the word "trust" or "trustee." It is sufficient if he shows an intention that the property should be held subject to a legal obligation to devote it to purposes that are charitable.[2]

Where the settlor uses language expressive of a desire

---

§351. [1]*Federal:* See National Found. v. First Natl. Bank, 288 F.2d 831 (4th Cir. 1961) (citing Restatement of Trusts (Second) §351); United States v. Moon, 718 F.2d 1210 (2d Cir. 1983), *cert. denied,* 104 S. Ct. 2344, 80 L. Ed. 2d 818, (1984), citing Restatement (Second) of Trusts §351.

Arizona: Lacer v. Navajo County, 141 Ariz. 396, 687 P.2d 404 (Ariz. App. 1983).

Arkansas: Cammack v. Chalmers, 284 Ark. 161, 680 S.W.2d 689 (1984) (conveyance to state university, which contracted to use the land as a campus).

California: Lodi v. Lodi, 173 Cal. App. 3d 628, 219 Cal. Rptr. 116 (1985).

Illinois: Matter of Estate of Offerman, 153 Ill. App. 3d 299, 106 Ill. Dec. 107, 505 N.E.2d 413 (1987), citing Restatement (Second) of Trusts §351.

Iowa: In re Will of Faber, 259 Iowa 1, 141 N.W.2d 554 (1966) (quoting the text).

Massachusetts: Board of Selectmen of Provincetown v. Attorney Gen., 15 Mass. App. 639, 447 N.E.2d 677 (1983), citing Restatement (Second) of Trusts §351; Hillman v. Roman Catholic Bishop of Fall River, 24 Mass. App. 241, 508 N.E. 2d 118 (1987), citing Restatement (Second) of Trusts §351.

Michigan: See Knights of Equity Memorial Scholarships Commn. v. University of Detroit, 359 Mich. 235, 102 N.W.2d 463 (1960) (citing the text).

Minnesota: See In re Estate of Quinlan, 233 Minn. 35, 45 N.W.2d 807 (1951) (citing the text).

North Carolina: Wilson v. First Presbyterian Church, 284 N.C. 284, 200 S.E.2d 769 (1973) (to a church to erect a building; citing the text).

Pennsylvania: See Loechel v. Columbia Borough School Dist., 369 Pa. 132, 85 A.2d 81 (1952) (citing the text and Restatement of Trusts §351); McClain Estate, 435 Pa. 408, 257 A.2d 245 (1969) (to be used for scholarships as directed by a named person; held valid charitable trust).

Texas: Trustees of Casa View Assembly of God Church v. Williams, 414 S.W.2d 697 (Tex. Civ. App. 1967) (deed of land to pastor on which to build a parsonage; held no trust).

See §25.4.

[2]*Louisiana:* Succession of Mizell, 468 So. 2d 1371 (La. App.), 475 So. 2d 765 (La.), 477 So. 2d 94 (1985) (devise to church created trust for charity).

rather than of a command, precatory rather than mandatory language, it is a question of interpretation whether his intention is to leave the donee or legatee free to decline to carry out the designated charitable purpose, or to impose a binding obligation on him to devote the property to the designated purpose. The question is the same as in the case of private trusts. Thus in *Estate of Hamilton*[3] a testator bequeathed the residue of his estate to the Right Reverend William J. Walsh, Archbishop of Dublin, adding, "and I request that masses be offered for the repose of my soul" and the souls of certain relatives. The lower court held that the residuary bequest was to the archbishop individually without any trust, but the Supreme Court held that a charitable trust was created.[4] The Court held that in spite of the precatory character of the language used by the testator, he intended to impose a duty on the archbishop to apply the property to the designated purpose. In other cases also it has been held that in spite of the precatory language used the testator intended to impose a legal obligation on the legatee to apply the property to charitable purposes, and a valid charitable trust was created.[5] On the other hand, the testator may manifest an inten-

[3]181 Cal. 758, 186 P. 587 (1919).

In Matter of Geller, 201 Misc. 381, 111 N.Y.S.2d 464 (1952), where a woman left money to the alumnae association of a nursing school with a request that it be used for its pension fund, it was held that a charitable trust was created, although some of the other purposes of the association were not charitable.

[4]On the question whether a trust for masses is a charitable trust, see §371.5.

[5]*California:* Estate of Hood, 57 Cal. App. 2d 782, 135 P.2d 383 (1943).

Illinois: In re Estate of Schaaf, 19 Ill. App. 3d 662, 312 N.E.2d 348 (1974).

Louisiana: Oroszy v. Burkard, 158 So. 2d 405 (La. 1963).

Massachusetts: Schouler, Petitioner, 134 Mass. 426 (1883); Weber v. Bryant, 161 Mass. 400, 37 N.E. 203 (1894); Temple v. Russell, 251 Mass. 231, 146 N.E. 679, 49 A.L.R. 1 (1925); Nickols v. Commissioners of Middlesex County, 341 Mass. 13, 166 N.E.2d 911 (1960); Trustees of First Methodist Church v. Attorney Gen., 359 Mass. 658, 270 N.E.2d 905 (1971) (to the treasurers of six church committees, with a request to use for homes for the needy).

New Hampshire: Trustees of Pembroke Acad. v. Epsom School Dist., 75 N.H. 408, 75 A. 100, 37 L.R.A. (N.S.) 646 (1910).

New York: Matter of Murray, 198 Misc. 45, 99 N.Y.S.2d 32 (1948); Matter of Falvey, 15 A.D.2d 415, 224 N.Y.S.2d 899, 5 A.L.R.3d 458 (1962), *aff'd mem.*, 12 N.Y.2d 759, 186 N.E.2d 563 (1962).

tion not to impose a legal obligation on the legatee, but to leave him free to apply the legacy to the designated purpose or to keep it for his own benefit. In such a case the legatee takes the legacy beneficially and the expression of the testator's wish has no legal effect except to promote litigation.[6] Thus in *Bacon v. Ransom*[7] a testatrix left the residue of her estate in equal shares to Susan B. Anthony and Lucy Stone Blackwell, absolutely, but requested that they use the fund to further the cause of women's rights, stating that neither should be under any legal responsibility. The court held that the legatees took the residue free of trust; and that although the promotion of women's suffrage is not a charitable purpose in Massachusetts,[8] so that a trust for that purpose would fail, the bequest of the residue was not

---

Oregon: Wemme v. First Church of Christ, Scientist, 110 Or. 179, 219 P. 618, 223 P. 250 (1924).

Scotland: Magistrates of Dundee v. Morris, 3 Macq. 134, 156 (1858).

[6]*Federal:* Norris v. Commissioner, 134 F.2d 796, 149 A.L.R. 1324 (7th Cir. 1943) (citing the text and quoting Restatement of Trusts §351), *cert. denied,* 320 U.S. 756 (1943).

California: Estate of Purcell, 167 Cal. 176, 138 P. 704 (1914); Estate of Davis, 74 Cal. App. 2d 357, 168 P.2d 789 (1946).

Massachusetts: Dickson v. United States, 125 Mass. 311, 28 Am. Rep. 230 (1878); Poor v. Bradbury, 196 Mass. 207, 81 N.E. 882 (1907).

See MacDonald v. Board of Street Commrs. of Boston, 268 Mass. 288, 167 N.E. 417 (1929).

New York: Matter of O'Regan, 62 Misc. 592, 117 N.Y.S. 96 (1909); Matter of Cushman, 82 N.Y.S.2d 714 (1948); Matter of Saulpaugh, 15 Misc. 2d 856, 180 N.Y.S.2d 623 (1958); County of Suffolk v. Greater N.Y. Councils, Boy Scouts of Am., 51 N.Y.2d 830, 413 N.E.2d 363, 433 N.Y.S.2d 42 (1980).

Pennsylvania: Second Reformed Presbyterian Church v. Disbrow, 52 Pa. 219 (1866).

Rhode Island: See Champlin v. Powers, 80 R.I. 30, 90 A.2d 787, 33 A.L.R. 2d 1176 (1952).

West Virginia: Baker v. Baker, 53 W. Va. 165, 44 S.E. 174 (1903).

In In re Estate of Corbett, 430 Pa. 54, 241 A.2d 524 (1968), a testator left the residue to two sisters and a brother "who are instructed as to my charitable wishes." All three predeceased the testator, one leaving a son. It was held that no trust was created, and that under an antilapse statute the son was beneficially entitled to the residue. The court cited Restatement of Trusts §§25, 351.

[7]139 Mass. 117, 29 N.E. 473 (1885).

[8]See Jackson v. Phillips, 14 Allen 539 (Mass. 1867); Bowditch v. Attorney Gen., 241 Mass. 168, 134 N.E. 796, 28 A.L.R. 713 (1922).

See §374.6.

invalid as an attempt to evade the policy of the law. In *Matter of Hayes*[9] a testatrix left a legacy to Arthur Garfield Hays "to use at his discretion in promoting the ends of justice." The court held that the testatrix manifested an intention not to impose a legal duty on the legatee to use the legacy to promote the ends of justice, but to leave it to his discretion whether to use it in this manner or not, and that he was entitled to the legacy beneficially. In *Beals v. Villard*[10] a testator left a legacy to Oswald Garrison Villard "believing that whatever property comes into [his] hands . . . will enable him to devote himself more effectively to the service of humanity." It was held that the testator did not intend to impose a legal obligation on the legatee to apply the property to the service of humanity, but intended to make a beneficial gift to the legatee. In each of these last two cases the court was of the opinion that if there had been an intention to create a trust, the trust would have failed because the purposes were indefinite and not limited to charity, and the legatees would have been compelled to hold the property upon a resulting trust. Since in each case there was a beneficial gift to the legatee, however, he was free to do as he liked with the property bequeathed to him.

As in the case of private trusts, a charitable trust can be created by words of condition.[11] Thus it has frequently been held that where property is devised or bequeathed "upon condition" that it be applied to certain charitable purposes, a charitable trust is created.[12] On the other hand, in some cases the court

---

[9]263 N.Y. 219, 188 N.E. 716 (1934), 264 N.Y. 459, 191 N.E. 513 (1934), noted in 19 Iowa L. Rev. 574, 9 Notre Dame Law. 473, 8 St. John's L. Rev. 308, 43 Yale L.J. 146.

[10]268 Mass. 129, 167 N.E. 264 (1929), noted in 14 Minn. L. Rev. 310.

[11]*Minnesota:* See Schaeffer v. Newberry, 235 Minn. 282, 50 N.W.2d 477 (1951) (citing Restatement of Trusts §11; §351, Comments *d, e*).

Pennsylvania: Abel v. Girard Trust Co., 365 Pa. 44, 73 A.2d 682 (1950) (quoting Restatement of Trusts §351, Comment *e*), noted in 24 Temp. U.L.Q. 373; Bangor Park Assn. Case, 370 Pa. 442, 88 A.2d 769 (1952).

See §§11, 401.2.

In Hill v. Townson Realty, 221 Md. 389, 157 A.2d 796 (1960), where a deed to two individuals stated that it was the intent of the parties that the land be maintained as a cemetery, it was held that neither a condition nor a trust nor a covenant was created.

[12]*England:* Attorney-General v. Leigh, 3 P. Wms. 146n (1732); Attorney-General v. Christ's Hosp., 3 Bro. C.C. 165 (1790); Poor v. Mial, 6 Madd. 32

has found an intention to impose a condition rather than to create a trust.[13] The question in each case is whether the testator intended to provide that if the property were not used for the designated charitable purposes it should revert to his estate, or whether he intended to impose an obligation on the trustees to devote it to those purposes. Since a forfeiture operates harshly, the inclination of the courts is to construe words of condition as intended to impose an obligation rather than to impose a true

---

(1821); Merchant Taylors' Co. v. Attorney-General, L.R. 6 Ch. App. 512 (1871); Attorney-General v. Wax Chandlers' Co., L.R. 6 H.L. 1 (1873); Goodman v. Mayor of Saltash, 7 App. Cas. 633 (1882); In re Christchurch Inclosure Act, 38 Ch. D. 520 (1888), *aff'd sub nom.* Attorney-General v. Meyrick, [1893] A.C. 1.

Federal: Stanley v. Colt, 5 Wall. 119, 18 L. Ed. 502 (U.S. 1866); Jones v. Habersham, 107 U.S. 174, 2 S. Ct. 336, 27 L. Ed. 401 (1882).

Massachusetts: Sohier v. Trinity Church, 109 Mass. 1 (1871); Amory v. Trustees of Amherst College, 229 Mass. 374, 383, 118 N.E. 933 (1918).

New Hampshire: Rolfe & Rumford Asylum v. Lefebre, 69 N.H. 238, 45 A. 1087 (1897); Ashuelot Natl. Bank v. Keene, 74 N.H. 148, 65 A. 826, 9 L.R.A. (N.S.) 758 (1907).

New Jersey: Mills v. Davison, 54 N.J. Eq. 659, 35 A. 1072, 35 L.R.A. 113, 55 Am. St. Rep. 594 (1896); MacKenzie v. Trustees of Presbytery, 67 N.J. Eq. 652, 61 A. 1027, 3 L.R.A. (N.S.) 227 (1905).

New York: Van De Bogert v. Reformed Dutch Church, 219 A.D. 220, 220 N.Y.S. 58 (1927).

Rhode Island: Greene v. O'Connor, 18 R.I. 56, 25 A. 692, 19 L.R.A. 262 (1892); City of Providence v. Payne, 47 R.I. 444, 134 A. 276 (1926).

In Hagaman v. Board of Educ., 117 N.J. Super. 446, 285 A.2d 63 (1971), *aff'g* 112 N.J. Super. 221, 270 A.2d 736 (1970), it was held that a provision in a deed of land to the Board of Education of a township that the land is conveyed solely for the erection and maintenance of a public school, did not create a condition forfeiting the land if it was later not so used (citing the text and Restatement of Trusts §351).

See also Wilbur v. University of Vt., 129 Vt. 33, 270 A.2d 889 (1970).

[13]*Maryland:* Bennett v. Baltimore Humane Impartial Socy., 91 Md. 10, 45 A. 888 (1900).

Nebraska: Clarke v. Sisters of Socy. of the Holy Child Jesus, 82 Neb. 85, 117 N.W. 107 (1908); In re Estate of Douglass, 94 Neb. 280, 143 N.W. 299, Ann. Cas. 1914D 447 (1913).

New York: Upington v. Corrigan, 151 N.Y. 143, 45 N.E. 359, 37 L.R.A. 794 (1896); Norton v. Valentine, 151 A.D. 392, 135 N.Y.S. 1084 (1912); Trustees of Calvary Presbyterian Church v. Putnam, 221 A.D. 502, 224 N.Y.S. 651 (1927), *aff'd,* 249 N.Y. 111, 162 N.E. 601 (1928) (release by heirs), noted in 76 U. Pa. L. Rev. 752, 37 Yale L.J. 530.

Canada: In re McMaster Univ. Lands, 3 D.L.R.2d 95 (Ont. 1956).

condition. Although words of condition are somewhat inept if no condition is intended, it is very common to use words of condition when the intention is simply to impose an obligation.

The settlor may manifest an intention to create a charitable trust although he does not expressly state that the property given by him is to be applied to charitable purposes. Thus where a testator leaves property to a designated person who is the holder of an office in a charitable institution, he may thereby manifest an intention that the property should be applied to the purposes of the institution rather than that the legatee should take it for his own benefit. In *In re Delany* [14] a testator bequeathed property to three persons "Nazareth House, Hammersmith, or their successors." These persons were officials of a religious community known as the Poor Sisters of Nazareth, a community of Roman Catholic ladies, who devoted themselves to assisting the poor. The court held that the legacy was not intended as a gift to the legatees for their own benefit but as a gift in trust for the purposes of the community. So also in *In re Garrard,* [15] where property was bequeathed to the vicar and churchwardens of a church for the time being to be applied by them in such manner as they should in their sole discretion think fit, it was held that the intention of the testator was that the property should be applied for religious purposes and that the legacy was not a beneficial gift to the legatees.[16] Similarly, in *In re Flinn,* [17] where a testatrix left the residue of her estate to a Roman Catholic archbishop for the time being "to be used by him for such

[14][1902] 2 Ch. 642.

See also Lucey v. Catholic Orphanage of Prince Albert, [1951] S.C.R. 690 (Can.), where a legacy was held to lapse because given to a priest personally and not for charitable purposes; Kohn v. Pearson, 282 Ark. 418, 670 S.W.2d 795 (1984) (conveyance to individuals described as "Committee for Church House site").

[15][1907] 1 Ch. 382.

[16]See §371.3.

[17][1948] Ch. 241, noted in 11 Mod. L. Rev. 343.

In Wilson v. Toronto Gen. Trusts Corp., [1954] 3 D.L.R. 136 (Sask.), the testator left the residue of his estate in trust to pay the net income to the Board of Governors of a university, to provide scholarships or for such other purposes as the Board might determine with the consent of the trustee. It was held that the property could be applied only to educational purposes and that the trust was therefore valid.

purposes as he shall in his absolute discretion think fit," it was held that the bequest was not a beneficial gift to the archbishop but was a gift upon a valid trust for ecclesiastical purposes.

A different result was reached, however, in *In re Spensley's Will Trusts*. [18] In that case a testator devised a house in England to the National Trust for the use of the High Commissioner of Australia in England to use as a country residence, and it was provided that if the government of Australia should at any time renounce the legacy the house was to be used preferably for some purpose in connection with Australia as the National Trust and the testator's sister, if living, might determine. The government of Australia renounced the legacy. It was held that the alternative disposition failed. The court held that, although the National Trust was a charitable corporation, its authority to dispose of the property was not limited to charitable purposes.

§352. *Consideration*

A charitable trust, like a private trust, can be created gratuitously; indeed, the settlor seldom receives consideration for the creation of such a trust. Thus if the owner of property transfers it to trustees for charitable purposes, it is of course entirely immaterial that the transfer is gratuitous. Similarly, where the owner of property declares that he holds it upon trust for a charitable purpose, a valid charitable trust is created although he receives no consideration for the declaration of trust. On the other hand, if he does not show an intention to create a present trust but merely promises to create a trust in the future, no trust is presently created, and the promise to create the trust is not binding unless the promisor receives consideration for his promise or, in states in which a promise under seal is binding, he executes an instrument under seal. As in the case of private trusts,[1] a promise to give property for a charitable purpose is not binding unless the requirements for the creation of a contract are complied with. As to what those requirements are in the case of charitable subscriptions, the cases are not altogether in agree-

---

[18][1954] Ch. 233, *rev'g* [1952] Ch. 886, noted in 70 L.Q. Rev. 149.
§352. [1]See §30.

ment. Ordinarily, it would seem, a charitable subscription is a mere gratuitous promise and is unenforceable because of the lack of consideration.[2] In the United States, however, charitable subscriptions have frequently been enforced where expenditures have been made in reliance on the subscriptions, or where the promise of each subscriber is treated as given in consideration of the promises of the other subscribers, or where the promise to apply the property to the designated charitable purpose is treated as consideration for the subscription.[3]

In the Restatement (Second) of Contracts §90(2), it is stated that a charitable subscription is binding without proof that the promise induced action or forbearance by the donee.[4]

In *Maryland National Bank v. United Jewish Appeal Federation*[5] a decedent had made a pledge to a charitable corporation of $200,000. He paid part but died before paying the balance of $133,000. The court held that his estate was not liable for the balance. The court applied the provision of the original Restatement of Contracts §90, which allowed recovery on a gratuitous promise only if there was action or forebearance by the donee. It refused to apply the provision of the Restatement (Second) of Contracts §90 (not yet finally adopted), which did away with the requirement of action or forebearance in the case of a charitable subscription.[6]

---

[2]*England:* In re Hudson, 54 L.J. Ch. 811 (1885), [1885] W.N. 100.

Massachusetts: Boutell v. Cowdin, 9 Mass. 254 (1812); Trustees of Bridgewater Academy v. Gilbert, 2 Pick. 579, 13 Am. Dec. 457 (Mass. 1824); Cottage St. M.E. Church v. Kendall, 121 Mass. 528, 23 Am. Rep. 286 (1877).

Canada: See also Dalhousie College v. Boutilier, [1934] S.C.R. 642, 95 A.L.R. 1298 (Can.), noted in 1 Alberta L.Q. 115.

[3]Robinson v. Nutt, 185 Mass. 345, 70 N.E. 198 (1904).

In Faith Lutheran Retirement Home v. Veis, 156 Mont. 38, 473 P.2d 503 (1979), a written provision to pay $10,000 to a charitable home was held to be enforceable.

For a discussion of the validity of such subscription agreements, see 1 Williston, Contracts §116 (rev. ed. 1936); 1A Corbin, Contracts, §198.

See also 95 A.L.R. 1305 (1935); 18 Calif. L. Rev. 314 (1930); 12 Cornell L.Q. 467 (1927); 13 id. 270 (1928); 34 Yale L.J. 99 (1924).

[4]See §30, *supra.*

See Note, Enforceability of subscription under conditional charitable pledge, 97 A.L.R.3d 1054 (1980).

[5]286 Md. 274, 407 A.2d 1130 (1979).

[6]As to the effect of the Statute of Frauds in the case of a gratuitous promise to convey land, see §§50, 466.1.

§353. Necessity of Transfer

Where an owner of property makes a gift inter vivos of the property upon a charitable trust, but the gift is incomplete because of his failure to make delivery of the property or of a deed of gift of the property, a charitable trust is not created, but the title to the property remains in the donor who holds it free of trust.[1] The principle is the same as that which is applicable to a gift upon a private trust.[2] But where the owner of property conveys it to another upon a charitable trust and the conveyance is ineffective only because the grantee is incapable of taking title to the property, it has been held that the charitable trust does not fail.[3] There is some authority, however, to the effect that where a conveyance of land is made to an unincorporated charitable organization, and the deed is ineffective because of the lack of capacity of the grantee to take title to land, the gift fails. Thus in *Heiligenstein v. Schlotterbeck*[4] it was held that a deed of land to a church, an unincorporated religious society, was invalid because of the incapacity of the transferee to take title to the property. It was subsequently held in *Wittmeier v. Heiligenstein*[5] that where the deed to the church included a provision that the church should make certain payments to a third person, and the donor subsequently died, a valid trust in favor of the third person was created, which did not fail for want of a trustee, and that although the title was not transferred by the donor a trust would

§353. [1]Welch v. Henshaw, 170 Mass. 409, 49 N.E. 659, 64 Am. St. Rep. 309 (1898).

As to what is a sufficient delivery of manuscripts to a public library, see Matter of Kallman, 103 Misc. 2d 339, 425 N.Y.S.2d 938 (1980).

[2]See §32.

But the gift may be enforceable, as in the case of a private trust, when the donee has changed his position in reliance on the incomplete gift. Thus in Hebrew Univ. Assn. v. Nye, 26 Conn. 342, 223 A.2d 397 (1966), it was held that even if a gift of a collection of books to a university was incomplete, where the university set aside a room for the books as the donor had reason to know there was yet sufficient reliance to make the gift enforceable. And, as we have seen, the Restatement (Second) of Contracts takes the position that in the case of a charity such reliance is not required in the case of a gratuitous promise; and the same reasons are applicable to an imperfect gift.

[3]Stowell v. Prentiss, 323 Ill. 309, 154 N.E. 120, 50 A.L.R. 584 (1926), noted in 31 Law Notes 133.

[4]300 Ill. 206, 133 N.E. 188 (1921).

[5]308 Ill. 434, 139 N.E. 871 (1923).

be imposed on the property in the hands of her heirs. It has been held that where a conveyance upon a charitable trust is ineffective to transfer the title to the property because no trustee is named in the instrument of conveyance, nevertheless the charitable trust does not fail.[6] Similarly, where a conveyance for charitable purposes is ineffective to transfer the title to the property because of a defect in the deed of conveyance, it has been held that the court will decree reformation of the deed so that the charitable trust will not fail.[7]

Where a devise or bequest is made for charitable purposes, the trust does not fail because no trustee is named or the trustee named is incapable of taking or holding title to the property or is incapable of administering the trust. In such a case the court can appoint a trustee. The result is the same as in the case of private trusts.[8] Thus where the trustee named predeceases the testator, or is unable or unwilling to act, or no trustee is named, the intended charitable trust does not fail.[9]

Where the settlor, however, manifests an intention that the intended charitable trust shall not arise or shall not continue unless the person named by him as trustee is able and willing to act as trustee, or if the purposes of the trust cannot be carried out unless he acts as trustee, the intended charitable trust fails if the person named as trustee is unable or unwilling to act.[10]

§354. Notice to and Acceptance by Trustee

As in the case of private trusts,[1] notice to the trustee of the transfer of the property to him is not a necessary element in the

---

[6]Dominy v. Stanley, 162 Ga. 211, 133 S.E. 245 (1926); Bailey v. Kilburn, 10 Met. 176, 43 Am. Dec. 423 (Mass. 1845).

[7]*England:* Emanuel College v. Evans, 1 Ch. Rep. 16 (1625).

Illinois: Price v. School Directors, 58 Ill. 452 (1871); Stowell v. Prentiss, 323 Ill. 309, 154 N.E. 120, 50 A.L.R. 584 (1926), noted in 31 Law Notes 133.

New Jersey: Visitors M.E. Church v. Town, 47 N.J. Eq. 400, 20 A. 488 (1890).

See 69 A.L.R. 423, 434 (1930).

[8]See §33.

[9]See §397.

[10]See §397.

§354. [1]See §§35, 102.

creation of the trust, nor is acceptance by the trustee essential. It is possible to vest the title to the property in a person without his knowledge or consent, as by delivering the property or by delivering the instrument of conveyance to a third person. In such a case, however, the transferee can disclaim or renounce, with the effect that the title to the property is divested; and such disclaimer has the effect of relieving him of all liability, since it operates retroactively and so far as he is concerned produces the same effect as though the title had never vested in him. Where the transfer is made to him as trustee, however, the trust is not extinguished, but the court will appoint a new trustee and compel the settlor to convey the property to the new trustee or will by its decree vest the title to the property in the new trustee.[2] The acceptance of the position as trustee is not a necessary element in the creation of the trust, but none of the duties of a trustee will be imposed on the person named as trustee unless he accepts. A refusal by the person named as trustee to accept a conveyance of property to him in trust may prevent the creation of a trust by making the conveyance incomplete for want of delivery. Thus if the owner of property offers to deliver it to another as trustee, or offers to deliver a deed of conveyance in trust to him, and he declines to accept, the intended transfer is incomplete for want of delivery, and no trust is created.

Where the settlor manifests an intention that an intended charitable trust shall not arise unless the person named by him as trustee is willing to act as trustee, or if the purposes of the trust cannot be carried out unless he acts as trustee, the intended charitable trust fails if he refuses to accept the trust.[3]

§355. The Parol Evidence Rule

The parol evidence rule in its application to the creation of a private trust has already been stated.[1] The same principles are applicable to charitable trusts. Where property is transferred by a written instrument declaring that the property is to be held

[2] See §397.
[3] See §397.
§355. [1] See §38.

upon a particular charitable trust, extrinsic evidence is not admissible to show the intention of the donor that it should be held upon a different charitable trust. But if the terms of the instrument are ambiguous or incomplete, extrinsic evidence is admissible to show the intended purposes.[2] Extrinsic evidence is also admissible to show that there are grounds for reformation or rescission of the instrument, on account of fraud, duress, or mistake.

§356. The Statute of Frauds

In states in which there is a statute providing that all declarations or creations of trusts of land shall be manifested and proved by some writing, or that a trust of land can be created only by a written instrument, the statute is applicable to charitable trusts as well as to private trusts.[1] In the absence of any statute requiring a writing, a charitable trust as well as a private trust can be created and enforced although no writing is signed by the settlor or by the trustee. This matter has already been considered in its relation to private trusts.[2]

§357. The Statute of Wills

A charitable trust, like a private trust, cannot be created by a testamentary disposition unless the requirements of the Statute of Wills are complied with. The questions of what is a testamentary disposition, and what is a sufficient compliance with the requirements of the Statute of Wills, are the same in the case of charitable trusts as in the case of private trusts.[1] In the following sections these questions are considered with reference to charitable trusts.

[2]Richards v. Wilson, 185 Ind. 335, 112 N.E. 780 (1916).

In Kerney v. Kahn, 46 N.J. 535, 218 A.2d 403 (1966), where a charitable foundation was organized to assist charitable institutions in the city of Trenton, it was held that there was no limitation to Roman Catholic charities.

§356. [1]See Union Trust & Sav. Bank of Pasadena v. Ishkanian, 45 Cal. App. 347, 187 P. 757 (1919).

[2]See §§39-52.1.

§357. [1]See §53.

§358. Creation of Charitable Trust by Will

A charitable trust can, of course, be created by will, where the will states the purposes to which the property devised or bequeathed is to be devoted. It happens not infrequently, however, that a testator leaves property upon an intended charitable trust, indicating in the will that the trust is for charitable purposes, but not indicating in the will the precise character of the purposes. The fact that the precise character of the charitable purposes is not stated in the will is not necessarily fatal. Thus a charitable trust is valid although by the will the trustee is authorized to apply the trust property to any charitable purpose that he may select. Such a trust is upheld if the trustee is able and willing to make the selection;[1] and the trust does not fail even if he is unable or unwilling to do so, unless the selection by the named trustee was an essential part of the testator's scheme.[2] So also it is held that a charitable trust is created where the testator leaves the property "for charity," without indicating further the character of the purposes.[3]

The question with which we are at present concerned arises where the testator indicates in the will that the property devised or bequeathed by him is to be applied to charitable purposes, but states that the character of the purposes is to be ascertained from matters extrinsic to the will. He may state that the purposes are to be ascertained from a written instrument, which may or may not be already in existence at the time of the execution of the will; or from oral directions given by him to the person named as trustee; or from other circumstances.

In spite of the fact that the particular purposes are to be ascertained by resort to matters outside the will, the intended charitable trust does not fail

    (1)   if the doctrine of incorporation by reference is in force in the jurisdiction and is applicable; or

    (2)   if the purposes of the charitable trust can be ascertained from facts that have significance apart from

---

§358. [1]See §396.

See Fratcher, Powers of Appointment to Unspecified Charities, 32 Mo. L. Rev. 443 (1967).

[2]See §397.

[3]Ibid.

their effect on the disposition of the property devised or bequeathed in the will; or

(3) if the particular purposes are not an essential part of his scheme.

So also, as we shall see, the intended charitable trust may be enforced where the devisee or legatee agreed with the testator to apply the property to the intended charitable purposes.[4] In this case, although the charitable trust is not enforceable as such, a constructive trust for the intended purposes may be imposed.

The question whether an unattested instrument can be incorporated in a will by reference in the will to the instrument is one on which there is a conflict of authority. Where incorporation by reference is permitted, the instrument to be incorporated must be in existence at the time when the will is executed and must be referred to in the will as in existence.[5]

Even though the doctrine of incorporation by reference is not accepted or is not applicable, a testamentary gift for charitable purposes does not necessarily fail although the purposes are not declared in the will. The disposition is valid if the purposes can be ascertained from facts of independent significance, facts that have significance apart from their effect on the disposition in the will. This is true, as we have seen, in the case of private trusts.[6] It is equally true in the case of charitable trusts.

Where a charitable trust has been created inter vivos by the testator, or has been created by others, and the testator desires to leave property by will to be held upon the same charitable trust, the question arises whether it is necessary for him to spell out the terms of the trust in the will, or whether it is sufficient for him to refer in the will to the charitable trust that has already been created. It is held that it is not essential that the terms of the trust should be spelled out in the will.[7] This is clearly so, of

[4]See §359.
[5]See §54.1.
[6]See §54.2.
[7]*Massachusetts:* Dexter v. Gardner, 7 Allen 243 (Mass. 1863).

New York: Matter of Feehan, 135 Misc. 903, 241 N.Y.S. 669 (1929); Matter of Tiffany, 157 Misc. 873, 285 N.Y.S. 971 (1935).

Ohio: Linney v. Cleveland Trust Co., 30 Ohio App. 345, 165 N.E. 101 (1928), noted in 13 Minn. L. Rev. 749, 38 Yale L.J. 1144.

Canada: In re Johnson, 30 D.L.R.2d 474 (B.C. 1961).

course, where the bequest is to an incorporated charitable institution.[8] Even though the bequest is not to a charitable corporation but to the trustees under an existing charitable trust, the bequest is valid although the charitable purposes are not stated in the will.[9] It is immaterial whether in the will there is an express reference to the instrument under which the inter vivos trust was created. If, indeed, there is a reference to the instrument, it might be held to be incorporated by reference in the will. But even if the instrument is not so incorporated, or even if the doctrine of incorporation by reference is rejected in the state, the bequest is nevertheless valid. The existence of the charitable trust already created is a fact of independent significance, a fact of significance apart from its effect on the disposition in the will. A disposition by will in favor of an already existing charity is valid even though the charitable purposes may have been altered between the time of the execution of the will and the time of the testator's death, provided that the testator manifested an intention that the property should be devoted to the purposes to be served by the charity from time to time and not merely to the purposes to which the charity was devoted at the time when he executed his will.[10]

[8]Matter of Feehan, 135 Misc. 903, 241 N.Y.S. 669 (1929).

[9]*Massachusetts:* Dexter v. Gardner, 7 Allen 243 (Mass. 1863); Old Colony Trust Co. v. Forsyth Dental Infirmary for Children, 271 Mass. 511, 171 N.E. 734, 70 A.L.R. 633 (1930).

New York: Matter of Tiffany, 157 Misc. 873, 285 N.Y.S. 971 (1935).

Ohio: Linney v. Cleveland Trust Co., 30 Ohio App. 345, 165 N.E. 101 (1928), noted in 13 Minn. L. Rev. 749, 38 Yale L.J. 1144.

See Note, Validity of testamentary gift to existing nonreligious, noneducational, or noncharitable trust, 8 A.L.R.2d 614 (1949). See §54.3.

[10]In Matter of Nurse, 35 N.Y.2d 381, 321 N.E.2d 537, 362 N.Y.S.2d 458 (1974), a physician created an inter vivos trust for the operation of a laboratory for experimental surgery at the Harlem Hospital in New York. Thereafter he executed a will leaving the residue of his estate to be added to the funds of the inter vivos trust. Before he died it was seen that it was impractical to maintain such a laboratory, and on application to the court it was held, with the consent of the settlor, that the funds of the inter vivos trust should be paid to the city of New York to be used by it for lecturers to be chosen by the Director of Surgery of the Hospital, for which black surgeons should be eligible, and for a fellowship to be granted to a black surgeon. On the settlor's death, the question arose as to the disposition of the residue under his will. It was held that it should be added to the inter vivos trust as it was at the time of his death. The court held that the inter vivos trust had been amended under

In *Matter of Tiffany,* [11] Mr. Tiffany by trust deed transferred land and personal property to trustees in trust to found an institution for education in art to be known as the Louis Comfort Tiffany Foundation. He reserved the right during his lifetime to modify the terms of the trust and reserved the absolute dominion over the income during his life. Additional gifts were received by the trustees from two other persons. By his will he left property to "the Louis Comfort Tiffany Foundation, an educational institution organized and existing under the laws of the State of New York, or to its Trustees." It was held that the legacy was valid. It was immaterial that the purposes of the trust were not stated in the will. The court said that the will must be read and construed in connection with the trust deed creating the charitable foundation. The legacy was to the trustees of the foundation as such to apply the income to the purposes of the foundation expressed in the trust instrument. It was immaterial that the doctrine of incorporation by reference is not accepted in New York.

These principles are applicable with respect to bequests of property to be held upon the so-called community trusts, which have been created in a number of cities. These trusts are created by the execution of a somewhat elaborate and detailed trust instrument under which the trustees named, certain trust institutions, undertake to hold property in trust for charitable purposes. It is usually provided that the purposes shall be determined from time to time by a selected group of citizens who are to act as a distribution committee. One of the purposes of the creation of these trusts is to provide flexibility; instead of determining at the outset the precise charitable purposes, the committee is to determine from time to time what needs are greatest in the community and provide for the meeting of these needs. The community trust is ordinarily started with small contributions and members of the community are invited to make further contributions by will or otherwise. The question then arises whether it is sufficient to make a bequest to the trustees of the community trust without spelling out in the will the terms

---

the cy pres doctrine, and had not been terminated. Two of the judges dissented, holding that the residue should go as on intestacy.

[11]157 Misc. 873, 285 N.Y.S. 971 (1935).

of the trust. It is clear on principle that this is sufficient. In some cases, where there is a reference in the will to the trust instrument under which the community trust is created, the bequest can be upheld under the doctrine of incorporation by reference. But even if that doctrine is not accepted or if it is not applicable because there is no specific reference to the trust instrument, the bequest is nevertheless valid, since the existence of the trust is a fact of independent significance. The same principles are applicable as in the case of private trusts.[12] In *Linney v. Cleveland Trust Co.*[13] a testator left the residue of his estate to the Cleveland Trust Company as trustee "for the charitable uses and purposes set forth in a resolution adopted by the board of directors of the Cleveland Trust Co., on the second day of January, 1914, providing for a community charitable trust, designated in said resolution as The Cleveland Foundation." He directed that the property be disbursed as provided in the said resolution "reference to which is hereby made, as fully and with like effect as if herein set forth at length." It was held that the bequest was valid. The court went primarily on the ground that the resolution was incorporated by reference in the will. It would seem, however, that even in states that reject the doctrine of incorporation by reference the decision could be upheld on the ground that the purposes of the trust appeared from facts that had significance apart from their effect on the disposition made by the will. The testator was simply adding property to an already existing trust. In *Jeffreys v. International Trust Co.*[14] a testator left his estate "to the Denver Foundation for the benefit of needy Denver people." The Denver Foundation was a community trust created by a resolution and declaration of trust executed by several trust companies of Denver. The testator named one of the trust companies as executor but did not name a trustee. The court held that the trust did not fail.

In some states statutes have been enacted which expressly provide that bequests for such community trusts shall be valid although the purposes of the trust are not stated in the

[12] See §§54-54.4.

[13] 30 Ohio App. 345, 165 N.E. 101 (1928), noted in 13 Minn. L. Rev. 749, 38 Yale L.J. 1144.

[14] 97 Colo. 188, 48 P.2d 1019 (1935), noted in 14 Tenn. L. Rev. 118.

will.[15] The enactment of these statutes was no doubt due to the existence of lingering doubts as to the validity of bequests to a community trust where the terms of the trust were not spelled out in the will. It would seem, however, that these statutes are declaratory of the common law. Although the statutes refer only to community trusts, the same principles are applicable in the absence of a statute to other charitable trusts. It is to be hoped that the fact that the statutes apply only to community trusts will not lead the courts to throw doubt on the validity of bequests in favor of other charitable trusts although the terms of the trust are not stated in the will.

On the other hand, if the purposes of the charitable trust cannot be ascertained from the will itself or from an instrument properly incorporated in the will or from facts that have significance apart from their effect on the disposition of the property, the intended charitable trust fails. This is true where it is impossible to ascertain what charitable purposes the testator had in mind, as, for example, where he bequeaths property in trust for such charitable purposes as he may designate in a codicil and he never executes a codicil. It is true also where the purposes can be ascertained only from an unattested memorandum not incorporated in the will by reference as, for example, where he makes a bequest for such charitable purposes as he may designate in a letter to be found with his will. Even if such a letter is found it is not admissible to determine the intended purposes, since it is not properly incorporated in the will and is not a fact of independent significance.[16]

---

[15]*Colorado:* Rev. Stat. 1963, §153-16-2, as amended by Laws 1973, c. 450.

Connecticut: Gen. Stat., §45-81, as amended by Laws 1980, c. 80-476, §225.

New York: Estates, Powers and Trusts Law, §8-1.1, amended by Laws 1971, c. 1058, and Laws 1985, c. 492.

Virginia: Code 1950, §55-32.

Wyoming: Stat. Ann., §§34-93 to 34-96.

See also the statutes cited in §54.3, permitting pour over by will into other trusts, which make no distinction between private and charitable trusts.

See Hair, The Community Trust Regulations — What Does it All Mean?, 14 New Eng. L. Rev. 755-782 (1979).

[16]*England:* See In re Jones, [1942] Ch. 328, noted in 7 Convey. (N.S.) 45, 59 L.Q. Rev. 23, cited in §54.3, n. 16.

Massachusetts: Thayer v. Wellington, 9 Allen 283, 85 Am. Dec. 753 (Mass. 1864).

Where the particular purposes of the testator cannot be ascertained in fact, or cannot be ascertained without resorting to evidence that is inadmissible, whether the intended charitable trust fails depends on whether the particular purposes are an essential part of the testator's scheme. Where they are an essential part of the scheme, the trust will fail. Thus in *Aston v. Wood*[17] a testator made a bequest of a sum of money to trustees "the money to be appropriated according to statement appended." After his death a statement was found among his papers appropriating the named sum to certain charitable purposes, but the statement was not appended to the will and was refused probate. The court held that the intended charitable trust failed. In *Wilcox v. Attorney General*[18] a testatrix left the residue of her estate to a trustee "to carry out certain other purposes of mine mentioned to him and to Abbie C. Anthony . . . and relating to certain benevolent and charitable institutions and associations." The court held that the intended trust failed. The court said:

> But while a general purpose to devote the residue to charity is evident, the objects finally to be selected are not designated, and can be ascertained only upon resort to the verbal communications made to the trustee and to Abbie C. Anthony. If these

---

Canada: In re Mihalopulos, 5 D.L.R.2d 628 (Alta., 1956).

See §395.

In Matter of Rosenstock, 192 Misc. 936, 82 N.Y.S.2d 428 (1948), a testatrix left money to trustees to be paid to such institution for needy persons as the trustees should select. Shortly after executing her will she signed an unattested memorandum that was found on her death attached to the will, directing the trustees to pay the money to a particular institution. It was held that the trustees could properly consider the memorandum in the exercise of the discretion conferred on them by the will, but were not bound by it.

In Baxley v. Birmingham Trust Natl. Bank, 334 So. 2d 848 (Ala. 1976) (quoting the text) a testatrix, who had a general power of appointment, appointed to "The Allan-Bryant Educational Foundation," and directed that if this corporation was not in existence on her death, her executor should create it in accordance with the terms that she had given to a certain law firm. The corporation was not created prior to her death. It was held (one judge dissenting) that the disposition failed because it could not be supported either on the ground of incorporation by reference or of resorting to facts of independent significance. But query.

[17]L.R. 6 Eq. 419 (1868).

[18]207 Mass. 198, 199, 93 N.E. 599, Ann. Cas. 1912A 833 (1911).

instructions had been in writing, a reference to the instrument would have incorporated it with the will, but as a testamentary disposition of property cannot be made partly under the statute of wills, and partly by parol, the trust is so indefinite that it cannot be executed.[19]

In *Smith v. Smith*[20] a testator bequeathed property to nine persons as a board of trustees in trust to establish a school for apprentices and young mechanics on plans to be thereafter described by him or, if he should die before perfecting such plans, on plans that he had from time to time described to some of the trustees. He died without having described plans for the school, although he had indicated to some of the trustees his general ideas with reference to the school. The court held that the testator did not intend that the legacy should take effect except in accordance with his plans, and since he had never expressed his plans in a duly attested will, the whole trust failed.

On the other hand, where the particular purposes are not an essential part of the testator's scheme, the charitable trust does not fail even though the particular purposes cannot be ascertained in fact or cannot be ascertained without resorting to evidence that is inadmissible. Thus in *Noice v. Schnell*[21] a testator disposed of the residue of his property to trustees in trust "to maintain and develop in accordance with my known wishes, the Palisades along the Hudson, in the borough of Englewood Cliffs and vicinity." He further stated that he was formulating more definitely plans for the development and maintenance of the Palisades and had requested two persons to submit a plan to him. He provided that if such plan were submitted and received his approval, his trustees should carry out such plan; but that if such plan did not receive his approval, the trustees should use the trust fund for the development and maintenance of the

---

[19]In some states, however, the communication of the testator's intention to the trustee and his agreement to carry out that intention is a sufficient ground for imposing a constructive trust for the intended purpose. See §359.

[20]54 N.J. Eq. 1, 32 A. 1069 (1895), *aff'd mem.,* 55 N.J. Eq. 821, 41 A. 1116 (1896).

[21]101 N.J. Eq. 252, 137 A. 582, 52 A.L.R. 965 (1927), *cert. denied sub nom.* Allison v. Schnell, 276 U.S. 625 (1928), noted in 32 Law Notes 33.

See also McMenomy v. Williford, 526 S.W.2d 880 (Mo. App. 1975), where a testator referred to a list of suggestions to be filed with her will).

Palisades in accordance with his wishes as expressed to them. It appeared that no plan had been submitted to the testator and that he had never communicated any plan to the trustees. The court held that a valid charitable trust was created. The general purpose of the testator sufficiently appeared in the will, and the existence of a plan was not an essential part of his purpose. The court distinguished *Smith v. Smith* on the ground that in that case the intention of the testator was to create a charitable trust of a limited and special character and the will failed to show that character. In *Sherman v. Congregational Home Missionary Society*[22] a testator devised land "as a Rest Home for worthy working girls, or Old Ladies' Home, the plan to be hereafter devised or left in care of said executor." It was held that a valid charitable trust was created. There was a general charitable intent although the particular manner of carrying it into effect was left undetermined. Even though the clause should be construed as meaning that a plan was to be left by the testatrix with her executor and no plan was prepared by her, this does not override the general charitable intent.[23]

§359. Secret Charitable Trusts

Where a testator devises or bequeaths property to a person in reliance on his agreement to hold the property upon a charitable trust, the devisee or legatee cannot keep the property nor will he hold it upon a resulting trust for the estate of the testator but he holds it upon a constructive trust for the charitable purposes for which he agreed to hold it. The principle is the same

[22]176 Mass. 349, 57 N.E. 702 (1900).

[23]In Souhegan Natl. Bank v. Kenison, 92 N.H. 117, 26 A.2d 26 (1942), a testator left the residue in trust for charitable purposes "in accordance with a suggestive memorandum which I have prepared and hereby make a part of this will," and no memorandum was prepared then or later. It was held that the trust was valid, since the word "suggestive" showed that the memorandum was not intended to be mandatory.

In Estate of Moffett, 138 N.Y.S.2d 774 (1955), a testator left his estate to named persons "knowing full well that each will distribute the funds to Catholic institutions for the charitable purposes upon which we have agreed." It was held that a valid charitable trust was created.

as in the case of private trusts.[1] This is well-settled law by the great weight of authority where the devise or bequest is absolute on the face of the will, but is induced by the promise of the devisee or legatee to hold the property upon trust. Thus where a testator devises or bequeaths property to a person without mention in the will of any intended trust, but the devisee or legatee agreed with the testator either before or after the execution of the will that he would hold the property for certain charitable purposes, he will not be permitted to keep the property for himself, but will be compelled to hold it upon a constructive trust for the intended purposes.[2] If he is unwilling to carry out the intended purposes he can be compelled to convey the property to a trustee appointed by the court to administer the trust.

It is immaterial whether the agreement made by the legatee to hold the property for charitable purposes was made before or after the execution of the will. It is also immaterial whether his agreement to apply the bequest to the charitable purposes was made in express words or was to be inferred from his conduct. On the other hand, if no agreement, express or implied, was made by the legatee and no agreement was made on his behalf, he is permitted to keep the legacy although the testator intended that he should apply it to charitable purposes. If, for example, the testator did not communicate to the legatee his intention that the legacy should be held in trust, and no one agreed on his behalf that he would hold it in trust, he takes it free of trust.[3]

Where the intention to create a trust appears on the face of the will, but the terms of the trust can be ascertained only from the oral agreement of the legatee, there is a difference of opinion on the question whether a constructive trust will be imposed for the purpose of carrying out the intended trust, or whether a resulting trust arises in favor of the estate of the testator. In England and in a few American cases it is held that a constructive

----

§359. [1]See §§55-55.9.

[2]O'Brien v. Tyssen, 28 Ch. D. 372 (1884); In re Wedgwood, [1915] 1 Ch. 113.

For cases involving private trusts as well as charitable trusts, see §55.1, nn. 3, 4.

[3]See §55.5.

trust arises, and that the legatee can be compelled to apply the property for the purposes for which he agreed with the testator to hold it.[4] In *In re Williams*[5] a testatrix left all her property to her husband "absolutely, knowing that he is fully aware of my intention that at his death all my possessions are to be sold and given to All Souls Church." She appointed her husband executor, and provided that if he should be incapacitated from acting as such and be prevented from making a fresh will, she wished that a certain solicitor should act as her executor and also for her husband in seeing that their mutual wishes respecting their properties passing at the death of both of them to All Souls Church should be carried out. Her husband made his will on the same day and left all his property to her. She died and four years later he died without having altered his will. Suit was brought by the personal representatives of the wife and husband, making the church and the Attorney-General and the husband's next of kin defendants, to determine who was entitled to the property. Evidence was given by two solicitors that they were present when the wife executed her will and that the husband was aware of the terms of the will and did not disapprove. It was held that the church was entitled to the wife's estate. The court said that the language of the will was probably sufficient to create an enforceable express trust, but that even if it were not the agreement by the husband expressed by his conduct was a sufficient ground for imposing a constructive trust in favor of the church.

In a majority of the American cases, however, it is held that where the intention to create a trust appears on the face of the will, but the terms of the trust can be ascertained only from an oral agreement between the testator and the legatee, a constructive trust will not be enforced for the purpose of carrying out the intended trust, but a resulting trust arises in favor of the estate of the testator.[6] Thus in *Olliffe v. Wells*[7] a testatrix left the residue

[4]In re Williams, [1933] Ch. 244; Cagney v. O'Brien, 83 Ill. 72 (1876); Hughes v. Bent, 118 Ky. 609, 81 S.W. 931 (1904).

[5][1933] Ch. 244.

[6]Olliffe v. Wells, 130 Mass. 221 (1881); Wilcox v. Attorney Gen., 207 Mass. 198, 93 N.E. 599, Ann. Cas. 1912A 833 (1911); Smith v. Smith, 54 N.J. Eq. 1, 32 A. 1069 (1895), aff'd, 55 N.J. Eq. 821, 41 A. 1116 (1896).

For cases involving private trusts as well as charitable trusts, see §55.8.

[7]130 Mass. 221 (1881).

of her estate to the defendant "to distribute the same in such manner as in his discretion shall appear best calculated to carry out wishes which I have expressed to him or may express to him." It appeared that the testatrix had orally directed the defendant to distribute the property for certain charitable purposes. The court held that the intended trust failed and that the next of kin were entitled to the property.

As we have seen in the case of private trusts, it is difficult to see why the legatee should not be compelled to apply the property to the purposes agreed on where the will states that there has been such an agreement, if he can be so compelled to apply it where the will makes no mention of such an agreement. In either case much may be said for the view that it violates the purpose of the Statute of Wills to compel or to permit the legatee to apply the property to purposes not designated in the will; but if he can be so compelled to apply it where the agreement is not mentioned in the will, it would seem that a fortiori he should be compelled to do so where the will mentions the fact that such an agreement has been made.

It is to be remembered that where the oral directions of the testator are applicable only to the particular purposes to which the property is to be applied, and those purposes are not an essential part of the testator's scheme, the trust will not fail even though evidence as to the directions is inadmissible.[8]

Where the testator manifests an intention not to impose a legal obligation on the devisee or legatee, but to leave him free to carry out the intended purpose or not as he sees fit, no trust or constructive trust arises, but he is entitled to the property beneficially. Thus in *Sparks v. De La Guerra*,[9] where a testator bequeathed property to his executors to dispose of "according to the directions which I have given to them, of the fulfillment whereof they shall have to give account to God alone," it was held that there was no intention to impose any legal obligation upon them, and they were beneficially entitled to the property.

The effect of an agreement by a devisee or legatee to apply the property to charitable purposes in a state in which statutes impose restrictions on the power of a testator to devise or be-

[8]See §358.
[9]18 Cal. 676 (1861).

queath property for charitable purposes is dealt with hereafter.[10]

§360. Disposition Inter Vivos Where Death of Settlor Is a Condition Precedent

Where a person makes a conveyance of property upon a
charitable trust, or declares himself trustee for charitable purposes, the intended charitable trust may fail because the disposition is not effective during his lifetime, and is therefore a
testamentary disposition. The situation is the same as in the case
of a private trust.[1] The intended charitable trust fails where
there is no compliance with the requirements of the Statute of
Wills, if the conveyance is incomplete at the settlor's death, or
if the trust property or the purposes of the trust are not designated until the settlor's death. On the other hand, a disposition
is not testamentary and is not invalid because of failure to comply with the requirements of the Statute of Wills merely because
the charitable trust is not to take effect in enjoyment until the
settlor's death, if it is effectively created prior to his death. Thus
where the owner of property transfers it in trust to pay the
income to him for life and on his death to hold the property for
charitable purposes, a charitable trust is created immediately,
and is not invalid because of failure to comply with the requirements of the Statute of Wills.

§361. Disposition Inter Vivos Where Settlor Reserves Power to Revoke, Modify, or Control

Where a charitable trust is declared during the lifetime of
the settlor, the disposition is not testamentary merely because
he reserves a beneficial interest in the trust property for his life,
or because he reserves in addition a power to revoke or modify

---

[10]See §362.
§360. [1]Welch v. Henshaw, 170 Mass. 409, 49 N.E. 659, 64 Am. St. Rep.
309 (1898).
See §§56-56.7.

the trust. The principle is the same as that applicable to private trusts.[1] In *Stone v. Hackett*[2] the owner of shares of stock delivered them with blank assignments endorsed thereon to another in trust to pay the income to the settlor for life and on his death to transfer the shares to certain charitable organizations, the settlor reserving power to modify or revoke the trust. After the death of the settlor his widow claimed the shares, contending that the trust was invalid as a testamentary disposition. The court held that a valid trust was created. In *City Bank Farmers Trust Co. v. Charity Organization Society*[3] a man transferred property to a trust company in trust to pay the income to himself for life and on his death to pay the income to certain charitable organizations. He reserved power to revoke the trust and provided that the trustee should not make investments except with his consent. After his death his daughter sought to set aside the trust as testamentary. It was held that a valid trust was created. In *Kings County Trust Co. v. Domestic & Foreign Missionary Society*[4] a man made a transfer of property in trust to pay the income to himself and to his wife for their lives and on the death of the survivor for designated charities. It was further provided that the trustee might pay as much of the principal as should be necessary for the support of himself or his wife, but only on the recommendation of two named persons. It was further provided that their funeral expenses should be paid out of principal or income. The settlor reserved power to revoke the trust. After the death of his wife the settlor married the plaintiff and subsequently died. The plaintiff claimed that the trust was invalid as a testamentary disposition. The court held that the trust was valid.

In the Restatement (Second) of Trusts §361, it is stated that

Where a charitable trust is declared during the life of the settlor, the disposition is not testamentary and invalid for failure to comply with the requirements of the Statute of Wills merely because

§361.   [1]See §57.
[2]12 Gray 227 (Mass. 1858).
[3]238 A.D. 720, 265 N.Y.S. 267 (1933), *aff'd mem.*, 264 N.Y. 441, 191 N.E. 504 (1934).
[4]N.Y.L.J., June 26, 1933, p. 3819.

the settlor reserved a beneficial life interest or because he reserved in addition a power to revoke the trust in whole or in part, and a power to modify the trust, and a power to control the trustee as to the administration of the trust.[5]

Where the owner of property, instead of transferring the property to another in trust, declares himself trustee for charitable purposes, and reserves a beneficial life interest and a power to revoke or modify the trust, the disposition is not invalid as a testamentary disposition.[6] But if he reserves in addition power to deal with the property as he likes as long as he lives, the disposition is testamentary and is invalid if not executed with the formalities necessary for a will.[7]

As in the case of private trusts, however, where a person makes a deposit in a savings account in a bank in his own name as trustee, the inference is that a trust is created but with full power in the depositor to withdraw the whole or any part of the deposit and to deal with it as he sees fit, and it is held that the trust is not invalid as a testamentary disposition.[8] This rule as to the so-called "tentative trust" of a savings deposit has been applied where the deposit is made in the name of the depositor as trustee for a charitable purpose. Thus where a person deposits money in a savings account in his own name as trustee for a charity, the inference is that as long as he lives he may withdraw the money and use it for his own purposes but that if he dies without withdrawing it or otherwise revoking the trust, the trust is enforceable.[9] On the other hand, evidence may be introduced

---

[5]This supersedes the statement in the original Restatement of Trusts §361.

For a similar provision as to private trusts, see §§57-57.6.

[6]Robb v. Washington & Jefferson College, 185 N.Y. 485, 78 N.E. 359 (1906).

[7]See §57.6.

[8]See §§58-58.6.

[9]American Bible Socy. v. Mortgage Guar. Co., 217 Cal. 9, 17 P.2d 105 (1932); Matter of Koster, 119 N.Y.S.2d 2 (1952); Estate of Hall v. Father Flanagan's Boys' Home, 30 Colo. App. 296, 491 P.2d 614 (1971) (citing the text).

See Board of Domestic Missions of the Reformed Church v. Mechanics' Sav. Bank, 40 A.D. 120, 54 N.Y.S. 28 (1899).

to show that he intended to create an irrevocable trust.[10] So also the evidence may show that he had no intention of creating a trust.[11]

The question of the validity of a trust created inter vivos in which the settlor reserves power to revoke or modify the trust in states in which statutes impose restrictions on the power of a testator to devise or bequeath property for charitable purposes is dealt with hereafter.[12]

§362. Restrictions on the Creation of Charitable Trusts

Unless a statute provides otherwise, the owner of property can create a charitable trust as freely as he can create a private trust. This is true with respect to testamentary dispositions as well as dispositions inter vivos. By statute in some states, however, restrictions have been placed on the power to create charitable trusts that are not applicable to the creation of private trusts. There are two grounds of policy underlying these statutes. The first ground is that it is against public policy that a large part of the wealth of the community, particularly in the case of land, should be taken out of commerce and devoted to charitable purposes. The second ground is that it is against public policy to permit a person on his death to give to charity property that he is unwilling to give to charity while he lives; a policy against the disinheriting of heirs in favor of charity by

---

In Howard Sav. Inst. v. Baronych, 8 N.J. Super. 599, 73 A.2d 853 (1950), where a testator made a deposit in a savings bank in his own name as trustee for a charity and retained complete control over the account, his executor on his death was held to be entitled to the deposit, the court holding that no trust was created.

In Spivey v. Methodist Home, 226 Ga. 100, 172 S.E.2d 673 (1970), where money was deposited in the name of the depositor "or" a charitable institution, the institution was held entitled to the deposit on her death; but it was not entitled to a deposit in the name of the institution "by" the depositor.

[10]Marshall v. Franklin Soc., 131 Misc. 611, 228 N.Y.S. 270 (1928), *aff'd*, 224 A.D. 834, 231 N.Y.S. 812 (1928).

[11]Sinnett v. Herbert, 12 Eq. 201 (1871), L.R. 7 Ch. App. 232 (1873).

[12]See §362.6.

deathbed dispositions or by dispositions of too large a proportion of the testator's estate.

In the legislation in England and in the United States imposing restrictions upon dispositions for charitable purposes it is not always clear which of these two grounds of policy is the basis of the legislation. Ordinarily to a certain extent the legislation has been dictated by mixed motives. Undoubtedly, however, in the earlier statutes the primary purpose was to prevent property, particularly land, from being taken out of commerce, and the purpose of the later statutes is perhaps primarily to protect the family from being disinherited.

Whether the interests of the community call for such restrictions must depend in large part upon the circumstances of time and place, and there may well be differences of opinion on the questions of policy involved. The accumulation of a considerable portion of the wealth of the community in the hands of charitable institutions may be an evil which requires some form of regulation.[1] So too there may well be differences of opinion

---

§362. [1]In another place the present editor has said, following suggestions of the late Professor F. H. Lawson of Oxford University, that charitable corporations and charitable trusts are subject to the same changes in legislative, judicial, and public attitudes toward charity. Until recent years charitable dispositions have been discouraged or prevented by mortmain legislation designed partially to keep property subject to feudal dues and public taxation and partially to protect the families of potential donors from disinheritance. The fact that most feudal dues attached on the death of the owner of land, which never occurs if it is held for charity, was important in shaping mortmain legislation in England. So was the fact that there was virtually complete freedom of testation in England, enabling a wealthy man to leave his wife and children in want. A third important consideration in both England and this country is that property devoted to charity is not available as risk capital. English courts were less favorable to charity after the Industrial Revolution of the eighteenth century created a shortage of risk capital for business and industrial ventures. American courts were inclined to disfavor charity during the nineteenth century, when risk capital for railroads, mining, industry, and the like was much needed. The repeal of mortmain legislation in the twentieth century, and the increased favor shown by American courts in recent years, together with legislation making charitable donations advantageous for tax reasons, may reflect a diminished need for risk capital. It may also reflect the development of schemes for protecting surviving spouses and other dependents by family maintenance and forced share legislation instead of by restrict-

on the question as to how far restrictions are necessary to protect the family from disinheritance. There has been of late years an increasing tendency on the part of legislatures to protect the widows of testators by providing that they shall take a distributive share in their husbands' estates of which they cannot be deprived by will. On the other hand, no need has apparently been felt to protect the children of the testator from being disinherited, except in a state like Louisiana where the conceptions of the French law have prevailed. In several states, however, as we shall see, it has been felt that there is a need to protect the children and other relatives against testamentary dispositions in favor of charity. It is felt that although the children and other relatives can compete on an equality with other legatees, they cannot so compete with the desire of the testator to end his life with a generous gesture. Sir Francis Bacon said: "Defer not charities till death, for, certainly, if a man weigh it rightly, he that doth so is rather liberal of another man's than of his own." Bacon himself bequeathed his property to found lectureships in the universities, but died insolvent.

An analysis of the statutes imposing restrictions on dispositions for charitable purposes shows how the problem has been attacked by various methods from time to time. Sometimes the statutes are aimed at the taking or holding of property by corporations; sometimes they impose restrictions on the creation of charitable trusts. Sometimes the restrictions are applicable only to dispositions of real property; sometimes they are applicable also to personal property. Sometimes the restrictions are applicable only to testamentary dispositions; sometimes they are applicable also to dispositions inter vivos.

§362.1.   Restrictions in England on the holding of land by corporations.   There are two methods of appropriating property to charitable purposes. It may be given to a charitable corporation for its general purposes or for some particular purpose. It may be given to one or more persons to hold in trust

---

ing charitable dispositions. The growth of income taxation is probably a factor. See Fratcher, Trust, §59, 6 International Encyclopedia of Comparative Law, c. 11 (1974).

for charitable purposes. Even before private trusts or charitable trusts were enforced by the chancellor in the fifteenth century, there was legislation restricting the power of corporations to take or hold land. In examining this legislation one must bear in mind the distinction between restrictions on the power of corporations to take land and restrictions on their power to hold it, between restrictions on dispositions inter vivos and testamentary dispositions. Under the feudal system it was possible for the owner of an estate in land to transfer it inter vivos, by feoffment or otherwise, to a corporation, and it was possible for the corporation to continue to hold the land. It was clear, however, that it was contrary to the policy underlying the feudal system that any considerable portion of the land of England should come into the dead hands of corporations. The result would be to deprive the overlord, including the king himself as lord paramount, of the benefits accruing from human tenants, who would live and marry and have children and die. The result might be to endanger the defense of the realm, which was based on the relation of landlord and tenant. So much of the land of England was coming into the hands of corporate bodies, especially the church, that the legislature felt it necessary to intervene to prevent the holding of land by the dead hand. Accordingly, Parliament enacted a series of mortmain acts, beginning with Magna Carta, Stat. 9 Hen. III, c. 36, which was followed by other statutes enacted from time to time to carry out the purpose. These statutes did not prevent the owner of an estate from transferring it to a corporation, but they deprived the corporation of the right to hold the land. Under these statutes the transferor or his heirs had no power to set aside the transfer, but the overlord could take the land from the corporation. The restriction was not on the power of the corporation to take but on its power to retain the land. The overlord might, however, give the corporation a license in mortmain authorizing it to retain the land, and later this power to issue licenses in mortmain passed to the Crown. This restriction on the power to hold land was applicable to private corporations as well as to charitable corporations, but in the earlier law most corporations were either ecclesiastical or political organizations, or what are now known as charitable corporations. The English law as to the holding of land by corporations was thereafter regulated by the Mortmain and Charitable Uses Act, 1888,[1] until that Act was repealed by the Charities Act, 1960.[2]

§362.2. Restrictions in England on devises of land to corporations. A second restriction imposed on the making of dispositions in favor of corporations relates to testamentary dispositions. At common law the owner of an estate in land could not devise it, except in London and some other towns by local custom. The policy against testamentary dispositions of land was evaded during the latter part of the fifteenth century and the earlier part of the sixteenth century through the device of a feoffment to uses. Finally, however, in the middle of the six-

---

§362.1. [1]Stat. 51 & 52 Vict., c. 42, Part I.

In Attorney-General v. Parsons, [1956] A.C. 421, noted in 19 Mod. L. Rev. 294, where a term for years was assigned to a corporation that was not entitled to hold it, it was held that the title did not automatically vest in the Crown under the Mortmain and Charitable Uses Act, 1888, so as to make the Crown liable on covenants in the lease; it would not vest in the Crown until the Crown took steps to enforce a forfeiture.

See Settled Land Act, 1925, 15 Geo. V, c. 18, §29; Education Act, 1944, 7 & 8 Geo. VI, c. 31, §87; Companies Act, 1948, 11 & 12 Geo. VI, c. 38, §14.

See Report of the Committee on the Law and Practice Relating to Charitable Trusts (Cmd. 8710) (1952), c. 7. That report makes the following recommendations:

"Charitable trusts are subject to three different sets of restrictions regarding land. The first of these, embodied in the Charitable Trusts Acts jurisdiction, is designed to enable trustees to carry out such dealings in land as may be beneficial to the trust, but always subject to the consent of the Commissioners or the Ministry. We make two minor suggestions relating to these provisions, but in general we consider them well conceived and recommend their continuance.

"The last two sets of restrictions, mortmain and charitable uses, have a long history behind them and now apply, in a highly illogical manner, only to trusts for certain purposes, many types of trusts having from time to time been exempted from them. They are in any case an anachronism in the conditions of the twentieth century and we recommend their repeal. The recording of assurances under section 29(4) of the Settled Land Act, 1925, or under section 87(2) of the Education Act, 1944, should also be repealed; its incidental practical advantage, in supplying a record of land given to charity, goes by the board, since such records will be built up as a result of the provisions for the recording of trusts recommended in Chapter 4."

[2]8 & 9 Eliz. II, c. 58, §38.

teenth century the Statute of Wills[1] was enacted, permitting devises of land. The statute, however, expressly excepted devises to corporations, to "bodies politic or corporate." The owner of land, therefore, could not make a testamentary disposition in favor of a corporation, whether charitable or otherwise. At the beginning of the seventeenth century, however, the Statute of Charitable Uses was enacted, to which we have already referred.[2] That statute, after enumerating in its preamble various charitable purposes and stating that property given by the donors for such purposes had been frequently misapplied, provided for the appointment of commissioners to inquire into such breaches of trust. Although the statute contained no provision with respect to the creation of charitable trusts, the courts held that because it showed an intention on the part of Parliament to encourage charitable trusts it had the effect of rendering valid, in equity at least, devises to charitable corporations. Again, however, in the eighteenth century Parliament was impelled to intervene, and enacted the Georgian Statute of Mortmain,[3] which forbade devises of land to any person or corporation for charitable uses. Of this statute we shall have more to say hereafter, since it was the first statute to restrict the owner of land in the creation of charitable trusts, the earlier legislation being aimed at the taking or holding of land by corporations, whether charitable or otherwise. In the Wills Act,[4] enacted in 1837, there was no provision excepting devises to corporations, but the restriction imposed by the Georgian Statute of Mortmain on devises for charitable purposes, whether to a corporation or to trustees, was left untouched.

§362.3. Restrictions in England on devises for charitable purposes. The first attempt by statute in England to restrict the creation of trusts for charitable purposes, and not

---

§362.2. [1]Stat. 32 Hen. VIII, c. 1 (1540), as explained in Stat. 34 Hen. VIII, c. 5 (1542).

See Jones, History of the Law of Charity, 1532-1827 (1969); Oosterhoff, The Law of Mortmain: An Historical and Comparative Review, 27 U. Toronto L.J. 257 (1977).

[2]See §348.2. See also §368.1.

[3]Stat. 9 Geo. II, c. 36 (1736).

[4]Stat. 7 Will. IV and 1 Vict., c. 26 (1837).

merely to restrict the taking or holding of land by corporations, was by the enactment of the Georgian Statute of Mortmain.[1] This statute provided that no lands or personalty to be laid out in the purchase of land should be given to any person or corporation in trust for or for the benefit of any charitable uses, except

> by deed indented, sealed and delivered in the presence of two or more credible witnesses twelve calendar months at least before the death of such donor or grantor (including the days of the execution and death) and be inrolled in his Majesty's high court of Chancery, within six calendar months next after the execution thereof; . . . and unless the same be made to take effect in possession for the charitable use intended, immediately from the making thereof, and be without any power of revocation, reservation, trust, condition, limitation, clause, or agreement whatsoever, for the benefit of the donor or grantor, or of any person or persons claiming under him.

Although the purpose of the statute, as recited in its preamble, was to restrict "dispositions made by languishing or dying persons, or by other persons, to uses called charitable uses, to take place after their deaths, to the disherison of their lawful heirs," the purpose of the statute must have been, in part at least, to prevent the taking of land out of commerce, and not merely to protect the heir of the settlor, because the statute applied to testamentary dispositions of money to be laid out in the purchase of land, although it did not apply to personal property bequeathed as such for charitable purposes. This statute continued in force until it was repealed in the latter part of the nineteenth century by the Mortmain and Charitable Uses Act of 1891.[2] By this Act it was provided that land may be given by will to or for the benefit of any charitable use, but it was required that the land be sold within one year from the death of the testator unless the High Court or a judge thereof or the Charity Commissioners extend the time or sanction the retention of the land when it is required for actual occupation for the purposes

§362.3. [1]Stat. 9 Geo. II, c. 36 (1736).
[2]Stat. 54 & 55 Vict., c. 73 (1891).
For a late case applying the Georgian Statute of Mortmain, the testator having died in 1878, see Fyfe v. Garden, [1946] 1 All E.R. 366, *rev'g* Re Nicol, [1944] 2 All E.R. 181, noted in 9 Convey. (N.S.) 87.

of the charity and not as an investment. This Act, however, left unchanged the restrictions on the holding of land by corporations, which restrictions applied to charitable as well as other corporations.[3] But the Act was repealed by the Charities Act, 1960.[4]

§362.4. Statutory restrictions in the United States. In some states there are no restrictions on dispositions, whether inter vivos or testamentary, for charitable purposes. In other states there are various kinds of restrictions imposed by statute, some of them dealing with devises or bequests for charitable purposes, some of them dealing with the power of charitable corporations to take or hold property.

Restrictions as to time of execution of will and as to amount devised or bequeathed. In some states there are statutory restrictions on the power of a testator to devise or bequeath property for charitable purposes. The purpose of these statutes is clearly to limit the power of the testator to disinherit members of his family. The statutes are of two kinds. In one type it is provided that no devise or bequest for a charitable purpose shall be good if the

[3]See §362.1.

See Walford, Charities and Conveyancing, 9 Convey. (N.S.) 130, 191 (1945).

By the Education Act, 1944, 7 & 8 Geo. VI, c. 31, §87, it is provided that the Mortmain and Charitable Uses Act, 1888, the Mortmain and Charitable Uses Act, 1891, and the Mortmain and Charitable Uses Act Amendment Act, 1892, imposing restrictions on assurances of land and personal estate to corporations and to charitable uses, shall not apply if the land or the income thereof is to be used for educational purposes, provided notice is given within six months to the Minister of Education or provided the Minister extends such six months' period of notice. See In re No. 12, Regent Street, Oxford, [1948] Ch. 735.

In Ireland by the Charitable Donations and Bequests Act, 1844, 7 & 8 Vict., c. 97, §16, devises of land for charitable purposes are invalid unless the will is executed at least three months before the death of the testator. See In re Nolan, [1939] I.R. 388; In re Elwood, [1944] I.R. 344; In re Morrissey, [1944] I.R. 361, noted in 78 Ir. L.T. 281, 287.

In In re Scarlett, [1958] No. Ir. L.R. 28, it was held that the Irish statute was not applicable where the testator had made a contract to sell the land prior to his death.

[4]8 & 9 Eliz. II, c. 58, §38.

will is executed within a certain time before the death of the testator, such as a month or three months or a year.[1] In some

---

§362.4. [1]*California:* Prob. Code, §§40 to 43, repealed by Laws 1971, c. 1395.

District of Columbia: Code 1967, §18-302. The question of constitutionality arose in Estate of French, 365 A.2d 621 (D.C. Cir. 1976). Section 18-302 provided that a devise or bequest for religious purposes was not valid unless the will was executed at least 30 days before the testator's death. A testatrix made bequests to two churches and died within 30 days. It was held that the statute was unconstitutional, as in violation of the First and Fifth Amendments to the Constitution, and that the bequests were valid.

Florida: Stat. Ann. §732.803, as amended by Laws 1975, c. 75-220 and by Laws 1977, c. 77-87. This statute was held valid in Arthritis Found. v. Beisse, 456 So. 2d 954 (Fla. App. 1984), *review denied,* 467 So. 2d 999 (Fla. 1985).

Georgia: Code 1981, §53-2-10.

Idaho: Code, §15-2-615, as amended by Laws 1978, c. 286 (120 days before death unless caused by accident).

Mississippi: Code 1972, §91-5-31.

See Crook v. Commercial Nat. Bank & Trust Co., 375 So. 2d 1006 (Miss. 1979).

Montana: Code Ann., §72-11-334. This was held to be repealed by the adoption of the Uniform Probate Code. See Estate of Holmes, 183 Mont. 290, 599 P.2d 344 (1979); Estate of Kinyon, 189 Mont. 76, 615 P.2d 174 (1980). Code §72-11-334 was repealed by Laws 1981, c. 575.

Ohio: Rev. Code Ann., §2107.06 (six months).

Pennsylvania: 20 Pa. Cons. Stat. §2507(1), repealed by Laws 1976, c. 135. See also 20 Pa. Cons. Stat. §6118, as inserted by Laws 1974, c. 293, but repealed by Laws 1976, c. 135.

In Chapman Estate, 39 D.&C.2d 701 (Pa. 1966), it was held that the statute was applicable although the testator left no relatives and that the Commonwealth was entitled to the property.

In Cavill Estate, 459 Pa. 411, 329 A.2d 503 (1974), noted in 37 Pittsb. L. Rev. 169, it was held that the statute (20 Pa. Cons. Stat., §2507) was unconstitutional as denying equal protection of the laws, two justices dissenting. See also Riley Estate, 459 Pa. 428, 329 A.2d 511 (1974), *cert. denied,* 421 U.S. 971 (1975).

In Decker v. American Univ., 236 Iowa 895, 20 N.W.2d 466 (1945), it was held that such a statute is not unconstitutional as discriminating against charitable corporations.

See Note, The Status of Charitable Trusts in California, 18 Hastings L.J. 450 (1967); Report of Committee on Succession, Restrictions on Charitable Gifts, 5 Real Prop., Prob. & Tr. J. 290 (1970); Des Jardins, Mortmain Statutes: Questions of Constitutionality, 52 Notre Dame Law. 638 (1977).

of these states the statute is applicable only if the testator leaves certain near relatives. The other type limits the proportion of the testator's estate that can be devised or bequeathed by him for charitable purposes, if he leaves certain near relatives such

---

In Gredler Estate, 361 Pa. 384, 65 A.2d 404 (1949), noted in 63 Harv. L. Rev. 697, 48 Mich. L. Rev. 246, and in Heim's Estate, 50 D.&C. 239 (Pa. 1944), it was held that a statute invalidating bequests to charity by a will executed within thirty days of death does not apply where an agreement was made between husband and wife that the survivor will bequeath the property to charity, and the property was so bequeathed by the survivor in pursuance of the agreement.

See Fisch, Restrictions on Charitable Giving, 10 N.Y.L.F. 307 (1964); Joslin, "Mortmain" in Canada and the United States: A Comparative Study, 29 Can. B. Rev. 621 (1951).

See Note, What institutions or gifts are within statutes declaring invalid bequests for charitable, benevolent, religious, or similar purposes, if made within a specified period before testator's death, or prohibiting, or limiting amount of, such bequests, 111 A.L.R. 525 (1937); Note, Waiver, or failure to invoke protection, of statute regarding amount, or time of making, of bequest to religious, charitable, or other specified classes of institutions, 154 id. 682 (1945).

The mortmain provisions of the Constitution of Mississippi, §§269, 270, have been amended by repealing §269 and amending §270 so as to provide that no person leaving a spouse or child, or descendants of a child, shall bequeath or devise more than one third of his estate to any charitable, religious, educational, or civil institutions, and the will must be executed at least ninety days before the death of the testator. See Miss. Laws 1940, cc. 325, 326. By Laws 1940, c. 318, a similar provision is inserted in Miss. Code 1930, §3565 (now Miss. Code 1972, §91-5-31), in which it is also provided that land devised to such an institution may be held for a period not longer than ten years, and that if it is not sold within such period it shall revert to the heirs of the testator. See Old Ladies' Home Assn. v. Grubbs' Estate, 191 Miss. 250, 199 So. 287, 2 So. 2d 593 (1941); Bell v. Mississippi Orphans Home, 192 Miss. 205, 5 So. 2d 214 (1941); Mississippi College v. May, 235 Miss. 200, 108 So. 2d 703 (1959), s.c. 241 Miss. 359, 128 So. 2d 557 (1961).

In Roenick v. Dollar Sav. & Trust Co., 87 Ohio Abs. 289, 179 N.E.2d 379 (1960), the testator left the residue of his estate in trust for the support of his grandson until he should reach the age of forty, when the property was to be transferred to him provided that he pay certain sums to certain charitable institutions. The testator died within a year. It was held that the provision for the charities failed, since the testator could not avoid the statute by imposing such a condition. It was further held that the grandson took free of the condition rather than that the amounts specified for the charities should pass as intestate property.

as a wife or children or parents.[2] It is to be noticed that these

[2]*California:* Prob. Code, §§40 to 43, repealed by Laws 1971, c. 1395.

In Estate of Bunn, 100 Cal. App. 2d 228, 223 P.2d 320 (1950), it was held that the husband's right to take against the will is personal and cannot be exercised by his executor or administrator.

See In re Estate of Reardon, 243 Cal. App. 2d 221, 52 Cal. Rptr. 68 (1966).

Georgia: Code 1981, §53-2-10.

In Hood v. First Natl. Bank, 219 Ga. 283, 133 S.E.2d 19 (1963), it was held that the statute did not invalidate a bequest of more than one third of his estate if the will was executed more than 90 days before his death, although he left a wife or child. Accord, Baker v. Citizens & So. Natl. Bank, 240 Ga. 549, 242 S.E.2d 39 (1978).

Idaho: Code 1947, §14-326 (unless descendants receive $100,000).

Iowa: Prob. Code, §266.

Iowa Code, §633.3 (superseded by Prob. Code, §266) provided that no devise or bequest to a nonprofit corporation or to a trustee for such corporation shall be valid in excess of one fourth of the testator's estate if he leaves certain relatives. In Palmer v. Evans, 255 Iowa 1176, 124 N.W.2d 856 (1963), it was held that this restriction is not applicable where the devise or bequest is not to or for the use of a corporation, that it does not apply to charitable trusts, and that it does not apply where the testator directs that a corporation be created by the trustee to carry out his charitable purpose.

Mississippi: Constitution, §270; Code 1972, §91-5-31.

See Crook v. Commercial Natl. Bank & Trust Co., 375 So. 2d 1006 (Miss. 1979).

New York: Estates, Powers and Trusts Law, §5-3.3. as inserted by Laws 1967, c. 683, and by Laws 1973, c. 45. Repealed by New York Laws 1981, c. 461.

In Matter of Webster, 178 Misc. 342, 345, 33 N.Y.S.2d 862, 865 (1942), a wife by will bequeathed to charity more than the amount permitted by statute. Her husband murdered her and immediately committed suicide. It was held that his representatives could not object to the disposition, since quite apart from the fact that he murdered her (see §492.2) his right was personal.

See Matter of Brest, 76 Misc. 2d 570, 350 N.Y.S.2d 37 (1973), holding that cousins of the testator could not contest the charitable disposition under the present statute.

In Matter of Klitenik, 53 Misc. 2d 955, 280 N.Y.S.2d 488 (1967), it was held that the statute (D.E.L. §17, cited in this note) was not applicable to a bequest without restrictions to a municipal corporation. The bequest was to the city of New York.

Ohio: Rev. Code Ann., §2107.06, repealed effective August 1, 1985, and held unconstitutional in Shriners' Hosp. for Crippled Children v. Hester, 23 Ohio St. 3d 198, 492 N.E.2d 153 (1986).

Virgin Islands: Code Ann., tit. 15, §9.

statutes in some respects go further than the Georgian Statute of Mortmain, but in other respects they do not go so far. Thus they are applicable to personalty as well as to realty, unlike the Georgian Statute, which was limited to land or personalty to be laid out in the purchase of land. They were enacted for the purpose of protecting the family of the testator, and not for the purpose of preventing the taking of land out of commerce. In other respects these statutes do not go as far as the Georgian Statute. Under the first type testamentary dispositions are not forbidden if the testator does not in fact die shortly after the execution of the will, whereas under the Georgian Statute devises for charitable purposes were forbidden even though the testator might live for many years after the execution of the will. Under the second type the testator is permitted to devise or bequeath a portion of his property for charitable purposes, whether his estate consists of land or personalty.[3]

Where the statute, whether requiring that the will making gifts to charity be executed more than a certain time prior to the testator's death or limiting the amount of the testator's estate that can be given to charity, is applicable only where the testator leaves certain near relatives, the question arises as to a waiver by such relatives. Clearly enough, if they all join in such waiver after the death of the testator, the charitable disposition is valid

---

[3]As to a method of determining the amount that may be given to charity where the property is left in trust for life beneficiaries with remainder to charity, see Matter of Mayers, 189 Misc. 700, 73 N.Y.S.2d 715 (1947), *aff'd mem.*, 274 A.D. 918, 84 N.Y.S.2d 895 (1948), *aff'd*, 299 N.Y. 388, 87 N.E.2d 422, 11 A.L.R.2d 1136 (1949), noted in 15 Albany L. Rev. 100, 1 Syracuse L. Rev. 321; Matter of Williams, 195 Misc. 461, 90 N.Y.S.2d 727 (1949); Matter of Chamot, 201 Misc. 374, 111 N.Y.S.2d 299 (1951); Matter of Walsh, 34 Misc. 2d 388, 228 N.Y.S.2d 75 (1962).

In Matter of Rothko, 98 Misc. 2d 718, 414 N.Y.S.2d 444 (1979), it was held that under the New York statute where there was a postponement of distribution caused by the improper conduct of the executors, the charitable institutions were entitled to one half of the value of the estate at the time of distribution, which was much greater than at the time of the testator's death.

See Note, Valuation of estate for purposes of statutes limiting proportion that may be devised or bequeathed for charitable purposes; problems of computation, 11 A.L.R.2d 1142 (1950).

because the restriction is imposed only for their benefit.[4] On the

[4]As to the effect of a waiver by the relatives of objection to the charitable bequest, see *Florida:* Taylor v. Payne, 154 Fla. 359, 17 So.2d 615, 154 A.L.R. 677 (1944); *appeal dismissed,* 323 U.S. 666, 65 S. Ct. 49, 89 L. Ed. 541 (1944), *reh'g denied,* 323 U.S. 813, 65 S. Ct. 113, 89 L. Ed. 647 (1944).

New York: Trustees of Amherst College v. Ritch, 151 N.Y. 282, 45 N.E. 876, 37 L.R.A. 305 (1897), *reargument denied,* 152 N.Y. 627, 641, 46 N.E. 1152 (1897); Matter of Hills, 264 N.Y. 349, 191 N.E. 12, 93 A.L.R. 1380 (1934) (wife insane); Matter of Kruger, 23 A.D.2d 667, 257 N.Y.S.2d 232 (1965), *semble, aff'd mem.,* 17 N.Y.2d 495, 214 N.E.2d 377 (1966).

Ohio: Deeds v. Deeds, 58 Ohio Abs. 129, 94 N.E.2d 232 (1950), noted in 20 U. Cin. L. Rev. 308; Ireland v. Cleveland Trust Co., 80 Ohio Abs. 94, 157 N.E.2d 396 (1958) (quoting text); Central Natl. Bank of Cleveland v. Morris, 10 Ohio App. 2d 225, 39 Ohio Op. 2d 433, 227 N.E.2d 418 (1967), *aff'g* 9 Ohio Misc. 167, 8 Ohio App. 2d 58, 31 Ohio Op. 2d 537, 220 N.E.2d 674 (1967); see §362.5, nn. 3, 4.

As to the effect of such a waiver on the deduction of the charitable bequest for the purposes of the federal estate tax, see First Natl. Bank of Atlanta v. Commissioner, 36 B.T.A. 491 (1937), *aff'd,* 102 F.2d 129 (5th Cir. 1939); Estate of Blossom, 45 B.T.A. 691 (1941); Estate of Carey, 9 T.C. 1047, 1054 (1947).

See Estate of Adams, 164 Cal. App. 2d 698, 331 P.2d 149 (1958), as to the effect of a waiver on a state inheritance tax.

In Kirkbride v. Hickok, 155 Ohio St. 293, 98 N.E.2d 815 (1951), noted in 65 Harv. L. Rev. 1074, a testator left property in trust to pay the income to his children for twenty years and then to pay the principal to certain charities. It was held that the children by accepting the income under the trust did not waive the right to have the charitable bequests held invalid on the ground that the testator died within a year after the execution of the will.

Under the former New York statute (Estates, Powers and Trusts Law, §5-3.3) the bequest to charity was valid unless contested by one who stood to benefit from its invalidity. See Matter of Cairo, 35 A.D.2d 76, 312 N.Y.S.2d 925 (1970), *aff'd mem.,* 29 N.Y.2d 527, 272 N.E.2d 574, 324 N.Y.S.2d 81 (1971); Estate of Rothko, 71 Misc. 2d 74, 335 N.Y.S.2d 666 (1972), *aff'd mem.,* 40 A.D.2d 965, 338 N.Y.S.2d 854 (1972); Matter of Alexander, 90 Misc. 2d 482, 395 N.Y.S.2d 598 (1977).

The question in these cases was as to the effect of provisions in the will showing an intent to exclude the persons who would otherwise be entitled to contest the charitable disposition.

In Matter of Eckart, 39 N.Y.2d 493, 348 N.E.2d 905, 384 N.Y.S.2d 429 (1976), *rev'g* 48 A.D.2d 61, 368 N.Y.S.2d 28 (1975), it was held that where a testatrix left $50 each to a son and daughter and for good reasons left them no more, they could not contest the charitable disposition. See also Matter of Newkirk, 86 Misc. 2d 930, 383 N.Y.S.2d 466 (1974). See also Matter of Willey, 85 Misc. 2d 380, 380 N.Y.S.2d 940 (1976).

other hand, it has been held that a consent given prior to the testator's death is not effective. Thus in *Matter of Watson*[5] a testatrix bequeathed more than half of her property to charity. After the execution of the will her children agreed with her that, if any portion of the estate was not effectually disposed of by the will, they would give the property to the designated charities. It was held that the children were entitled to the excess over one half of her estate and were not bound to give it to the charities.

A further question arises whether a testator can avoid the statutory restriction by making a gift over to a nonrelative. If only the designated relatives can object to the gift to charity, and if in the event of the invalidity of the charitable gift they would not take, it has been held that they cannot object to the charitable gift; and the nonrelative cannot object because the statutory restriction is not imposed for his benefit. Hence no one can object. This is the result that was reached in California.[6]

By the Pennsylvania Wills Act of 1947 (20 Pa. Stat., §180.7(1)) it was provided that any bequest or devise for charitable purposes in a will executed within thirty days of the death of the testator shall be invalid "unless all who would benefit by its invalidity agree that it shall be valid." 20 Pa. Stat., §180.7 was superseded by 20 Pa. Cons. Stat., §2507(1), which was repealed by Laws 1976, c. 135.

[5]177 Misc. 308, 30 N.Y.S.2d 577 (1941).

[6]In California by Prob. Code, §41, repealed by Laws 1971, c. 1395, it was provided that where devises or bequests to charity exceed one-third of the testator's estate, they shall not be valid as to the excess against his spouse, brother, sister, nephew, niece, descendant, or ancestor, who would otherwise have taken the excess; but that this shall not be deemed to vest any property devised or bequeathed to charity in any person who is not a relative of the testator or in any such relative unless such relative takes the property under a substitutional or residuary bequest or devise or under the laws of succession.

Hence if there was a gift over to a nonrelative on the failure of the charitable bequests, the charitable bequests were valid although they exceeded one-third of the testator's estate and he left relatives within the designated classes. See Estate of Davis, 74 Cal. App. 2d 357, 168 P.2d 789 (1946); Estate of Haines, 76 Cal. App. 2d 673, 173 P.2d 693 (1946); Estate of Randall, 86 Cal. App. 2d 422, 194 P.2d 709 (1948); Estate of Davison, 96 Cal. App. 2d 263, 215 P.2d 504 (1950); Estate of Leymel, 103 Cal. App. 2d 778, 230 P.2d 48 (1951); Estate of Neubauer, 315 P.2d 494 (Cal. App. 1957), *modified,* 49 Cal. 2d 741, 321 P.2d 741 (1958); see In re Estate of Coburn, 20 Cal. App. 3d 368, 97 Cal. Rptr. 597 (1971).

In In re Estate of Taylor, 33 Cal. App. 3d 44, 108 Cal. Rptr. 778 (1973), it was held that although California Probate Code, §41, was not repealed prior

A similar result was reached in Ohio.[7]

Where a statute invalidates a bequest for charitable purposes if the will is executed within a certain time before the

to the testator's death, the charitable bequest was valid where no claim was made by the heir before the repeal.

Estate of Sanderson, 58 Cal. 2d 522, 375 P.2d 37 (1962); Estate of Robison, 242 Cal. App. 2d 19, 51 Cal. Rptr. 751 (1966) (gift over to a college to which the statutory limitation did not apply, although the college later assigned its interest to the charities); In re Estate of Goyette, 258 Cal. App. 2d 768, 66 Cal. Rptr. 103 (1968).

See Joslin, Restrictions on the Testamentary Gift to Charities in California, 25 S. Cal. L. Rev. 419 (1952); Doggett, Restrictions on Testamentary Gifts to Charity Under the California Probate Code, U.C.L.A. Intra. L. Rev. 3 (1953).

In Estate of Munson, 164 Cal. App. 2d 146, 330 P.2d 302 (1958), where a testator left all his property to charitable corporations and provided that if any of his heirs should become entitled to any part of his estate they should each receive $10, it was held that the charitable disposition was valid only as to one third of his estate and that his heirs were entitled to the other two thirds as on intestacy.

In Estate of Thomason, 245 Cal. App. 2d 793, 54 Cal. Rptr. 229 (1966), where property was bequeathed for cancer research, and no trustee was named, it was held that the court properly gave the money to the American Cancer Society and thereby entitled the relatives to a share although it might have given it to a university, in which case, under the statute, the relatives would not have been so entitled.

[7]In Deeds v. Deeds, 58 Ohio Abs. 129, 94 N.E.2d 332 (1950), the testatrix left the residue to her husband, and the court held that it was immaterial whether her only son did or did not execute a waiver.

In Watson v. Manley, 257 Iowa 92, 130 N.W.2d 693 (1964), a statute invalidated bequests for charity in excess of one fourth of the testator's estate if he left a spouse, child, child of a deceased child, or parent surviving. He left the proceeds of his farm to two churches, but provided that if the bequest should exceed the share that could be bequeathed to them, he decreased the gift so that the churches should receive one quarter of his estate, and gave the amount by which the bequest should be decreased to his two granddaughters. He left a son and the two granddaughters, children of the son. The lower court held that the churches took the whole of the proceeds on the ground that the son could not object because he would not take, and the granddaughters could not object because they were not within the class of relatives specified in the statute. The judgment was reversed. The court said that the testator intended the churches to receive no more than one fourth of his estate, whether or not anyone had a standing to invoke the statute, and that it was therefore unnecessary to decide whether the son could have done so.

In Wolf Estate, 69 D.&C.2d 371 (Pa. 1974), a testator died within 30 days

testator's death, and the testator makes a charitable bequest in a will not executed within the designated period, and thereafter revokes the will and executes a new will making the same charitable disposition and dies within the period, the courts have upheld the bequest.[8] This seems clearly sound, since the testa-

---

of executing a will making gifts to charity, but left a valid remainder. It was held that his heir could not set aside the legacy to charity.

In Woods v. Neissen, 11 Ohio App. 3d 62, 11 Ohio B.R. 96, 463 N.E.2d 92 (1983), the parties agreed that a statute, providing that if the will was executed less than six months before death, charitable bequests are valid up to 25 percent of the net probate estate and any disposition made invalid is to be distributed to the testator's issue, applied to a will that bequeathed the residue to charity and provided that taxes should be paid from the residue. The statute defined net probate estate as that existing prior to payment of estate and inheritance taxes. It was held that the taxes should be paid from the portion of the residue invalidated by the statute before reducing the charities' share to less than 25 percent of the pre-tax estate.

[8] In re Nutting's Estate, 82 F. Supp. 689 (D.D.C. 1949); Estate of Kaufman, 25 Cal. 2d 854, 155 P.2d 831 (1945); Estate of Herbert, 131 Cal. App. 2d 666, 281 P.2d 57 (1955); Linkins v. Protestant Episcopal Cathedral Foundation, 87 App. D.C. 351, 187 F.2d 357 (1950), noted in 39 Geo. L.J. 346, 64 Harv. L. Rev. 686, 37 Va. L. Rev. 461.

But see Ely v. Megie, 219 N.Y. 112, 113 N.E. 800 (1916); Newman v. Newman, 94 Ohio Abs. 321, 199 N.E.2d 904 (1964); Melville's Estate, 245 Pa. 318, 91 A. 679 (1914); Hartman's Estate, 320 Pa. 321, 182 A. 234 (1936) (where the charitable dispositions in the second will were different from those in the original will).

Crosby v. Alton Ochsner Medical Found. 276 So.2d 661, 75 A.L.R.3d 853 (Miss. 1973) (three judges dissenting).

See Note, Revival under doctrine of dependent relative revocation, of charitable bequest in will, expressly revoked in later will containing same charitable bequest, 75 A.L.R.3d 877 (1977).

In Kuntz Estate, 77 D.&C. 337 (Pa. 1950), a testator executed a will more than thirty days before his death, creating a trust with a remainder interest in specified amounts to certain charities. He executed a codicil within thirty days of his death. It was held that the dispositions were valid where he did not increase the amount given to a particular charity, although he restricted the use of it, and where he increased the amount or decreased it, the disposition was valid to the extent of the lesser amount.

By the Pennsylvania Wills Act of 1947 (20 Pa. Stat., §180.7(1)), superseded by 20 Pa. Cons. Stat., §2507(1), which was repealed by Laws 1976, c. 135, after providing that a bequest or devise for charitable purposes included in a will or codicil executed within thirty days of the death of the testator shall be invalid, it was provided that "Unless the testator directs

tor is not in reality making a deathbed charitable disposition. It

---

otherwise, if such a will or codicil shall revoke or supersede a prior will or codicil executed at least thirty days before the testator's death, and not theretofore revoked or superseded and the original of which can be produced in legible condition, and if each instrument shall contain an identical gift for substantially the same religious or charitable purpose, the gift in the later will or codicil shall be valid; or if each instrument shall give for substantially the same religious or charitable purpose a cash legacy or a share of the residuary estate or a share of the same asset, payable immediately or subject to identical prior estates and conditions, the later gift shall be valid to the extent to which it shall not exceed the prior gift." See Witmer Estate, 2 Fiduciary Rep. 113 (Pa. 1952); Baum Estate, 418 Pa. 404, 211 A.2d 521 (1965), noted in 69 Dick. L. Rev. 407.

In McGuigen Estate, 388 Pa. 475, 131 A.2d 124 (1957), it was held that, under the Pennsylvania statute quoted in this note, where a testatrix by her will executed more than thirty days prior to her death left the residue in trust to pay the income to a charitable organization for its general purposes, and by a will executed within five days of her death left the residue, which was less in value than the residue under the earlier will, to the corporation itself for its general purposes, the disposition made by the later will was valid.

For other cases involving the question whether the later charitable bequest was substantially the same as the earlier one, see York Estate, 3 Fiduciary Rep. 1 (Pa. 1952); Benner Estate, 6 Fiduciary Rep. 150 (Pa. 1956); King Estate, 7 Fiduciary Rep. 252 (Pa. 1957); Pearl Estate, 16 D.&C.2d 227 (Pa. 1959); Yeakel Estate, 23 D.&C.2d 17 (Pa. 1960); Hilsberg Estate, 31 D.&C.2d 686 (Pa. 1963); La Touche Estate, 36 D.&C.2d 88 (Pa. 1965).

Grubnau Estate, 39 D.&C.2d 335 (Pa. 1966); Leonard Estate, 17 Fiduciary Rep. 102 (Pa. 1967); Wise Estate, 49 D.&C.2d 82 (Pa. 1970); O'Brien Estate, 63 D.&C.2d 376 (Pa. 1973); Riley Estate, 459 Pa. 428, 329 A.2d 511 (1974), *cert. denied,* 421 U.S. 971 (1975).

In Riddle Estate, 4 Fiduciary Rep. 601 (Pa. 1954), it was held that the earlier disposition would not be upheld under the doctrine of dependent relative revocation.

In Gearhart Estate, 434 Pa. 344, 255 A.2d 557 (1969), noted in 74 Dick. L. Rev. 352, a testator executed a will leaving property to a hospital, and later within 30 days of his death executed a second will revoking the first but making substantially the same disposition, and thereafter executed a third will making the same disposition to the hospital. It was held (two justices dissenting) that the legacy failed because the second will revoked the first will.

In Smith Estate, 435 Pa. 258, 256 A.2d 130 (1969), a woman made a will leaving one half of the residue to certain charities, and within 30 days of her death executed a new will pouring over her property into a revocable trust which she created at that time under which she gave one half to the same charities. It held that the trust failed as to the charities under the statute as to gifts that made no reference to earlier dispositions, and held that there was

would seem that even if in the new will he makes a different

---

a resulting trust for her estate, and that because all the property passed under her will it was valid because of the earlier will.

In Prynn Estate, 455 Pa. 192, 315 A.2d 265 (1974), where a testatrix bequeathed her residuary estate to four charitable beneficiaries and by a new will executed within 30 days of her death, left it to three of the beneficiaries, it was held that her heirs could not object to the validity of the later will.

In Cavill Estate, 459 Pa. 411, 329 A.2d 503 (1974), it was held that the statute (20 Pa. Stat., §2507) was unconstitutional as denying equal protection of the laws, two justices dissenting.

As to whether the decision in Cavill Estate is retroactive, see Heffner Estate, 71 D.&C.2d 413 (Pa. 1975); Heilig Estate, 13 D.&C.3d 1 (Pa. 1979) (not retroactive so as to avoid transfers to bona fide purchasers).

In White v. Conference Claimants Endowment Commn., 81 Idaho 17, 336 P.2d 674 (1959), where a testator executed a will containing a legacy for charitable purposes, and subsequently married, thereby invalidating the will, and thereafter within thirty days of his death he executed a codicil, it was held that, although this operates as a revival of the original will, it was ineffective to validate the charitable bequest.

In In re Estate of Pratt, 88 So. 2d 499 (Fla. 1956), where a testator bequeathed a share of his estate to charitable corporations and within three days of his death executed a new will making the same charitable bequests, it was held that the disposition failed, the court refusing to apply the doctrine of dependent relative revocation. But in Matter of Pratt, 5 A.D.2d 501, 172 N.Y.S.2d 965 (1958), aff'd mem., 8 N.Y.2d 855, 168 N.E.2d 709 (1960), it was held that the Florida statute was not applicable to a trust created in New York under which the settlor by the will exercised a power of appointment.

In In re Blankenship's Estate, 122 So. 2d 466 (Fla. 1960), rev'g 114 So. 2d 519 (1959), noted in 14 U. Fla. L. Rev. 198, 15 U. Miami L. Rev. 309, where a testator executed a will more than six months before he died, bequeathing property for charitable purposes, and within the six-month period he executed two new wills making substantially the same charitable dispositions, it was held that the dispositions failed. The reason was that the statute provided that the bequest should be valid if the testator by will executed immediately next prior to his last will and more than six months before his death made substantially the same charitable disposition. The court held that it was fatal that the will immediately preceding the last will was itself made within the six-month period, although the earlier will was executed more than six months before he died. The court felt that the statute should be applied literally. See s.c. 136 So. 2d 23 (Fla. App. 1961).

But see In re Estate of Rauf, 213 So. 2d 31 (Fla. App. 1968), upholding a somewhat different charitable disposition made in the later will.

By Ohio Rev. Code, §2107.06, as amended by laws 1965, repealed effective August 1, 1985, and held unconstitutional in Shriners' Hosp. for Crippled Children v. Hester, 23 Ohio St. 3d 198, 492 N.E.2d 153 (1986), it was provided

charitable disposition, and the new disposition is therefore invalid, the old disposition should stand if the testator would presumably have intended it to stand should the new disposition be invalid. This is an application of the doctrine of dependent relative revocation.

If a statute invalidates a bequest for charitable purposes of more than a designated proportion of the testator's estate or where the will is executed within a certain time before the testator's death, the question arises whether these restrictions are applicable where the donee of a general power of appointment by will makes an appointment for charitable purposes. In *Farmers' Loan & Trust Co. v. Shaw*[9] a testatrix left the residue of her estate in trust to pay the income to a woman for life and on her death as she should appoint by will with a gift over to the heirs of the testatrix in default of appointment. The beneficiary made an appointment to charity. Her husband survived her. By statute it was provided that no person having a husband or certain other relatives should devise or bequeath for charity more than one half of his estate. It was held that the appointment was valid. The court held that the statute was applicable only when one is disposing of his own property, and not where he is exercising a power of appointment. In *In re Estate of Lowe*[10] a testator left

that "(B) The execution of a codicil to the testator's will within six months of his death shall not affect the validity of any such devises and bequests made by will or codicil executed more than six months prior to his death, except as the same are revoked or modified by the codicil. If a codicil executed within such period increases the aggregate of such devises and bequests to more than twenty-five per cent of the value of the testator's net probate estate, such increase by codicil is invalidated to the extent that such increases, plus the aggregate contained in the will and not revoked by the codicil, exceeds twenty-five per cent of the value of the testator's net probate estate; and the amount of the codicil's increase of each such devise and bequest in the will and each such devise and bequest contained in the codicil which was not contained in the will shall be abated proportionately."

See Fisch, Restrictions on Charitable Giving, 10 N.Y. L.F. 307, 329 (1964); Schwartz, The Ohio Mortmain Statute — As Amended, 17 W. Res. L. Rev. 83 (1965).

[9]127 A.D. 656, 111 N.Y.S. 1118 (1908), *aff'g* 56 Misc. 201, 107 N.Y.S. 337 (1907).

[10]119 Ohio App. 303, 191 N.E.2d 196 (1963), *aff'g* 90 Ohio Abs. 399, 186 N.E. 2d 648 (1962), noted in 34 U. Cin. L. Rev. 169.

As to the validity of an appointment to charity where the settlor reserves a general power of appointment, see §362.6, n. 7.

his estate in trust for his wife for life, giving her a general power of appointment by will. He died within a year after execution of the will, leaving issue. After his death the wife executed a will making an appointment to charity and died within a year, leaving no issue. By statute it was provided that if a testator dies leaving issue, a devise or bequest for charitable purposes shall be invalid unless the will is executed at least one year prior to the death of the testator. It was held that the appointment was valid.

Restrictions on power of corporations to take by devise or bequest. In some states there are, or have been, restrictions on the power of corporations, whether charitable or noncharitable, to take land by devise unless the corporation is specially authorized to do so by its charter or by statute.[11] In some of these states the

[11]*California:* Prob. Code, §27, amended by Laws 1961, c. 2027, and Laws 1970, c. 965, so as to remove the restrictions.

Montana: Rev. Code 1947, §91-104, repealed by Laws 1975, c. 263.

New York: Decedent Estate Law, §12, superseded by Estates, Powers and Trusts Law, §3-1.3(a), which provides that "A testamentary disposition of property may be made to any person having capacity to acquire and hold such property."

North Dakota: Cent. Code, §56-02-05, repealed by the enactment of the Uniform Probate Code.

Oklahoma: Stat. Ann., tit. 84, §45.

South Dakota: Codified Laws 1967, §29-2-15.

Virgin Islands: Code Ann., tit. 15, §4.

In Utah Code Ann., §74-1-4, it is provided that testamentary dispositions may be made to any person or corporation capable of taking by deed or assignment. See 26 Cal. L. Rev. 309 (1938). See Manatakis' Estate v. Walker Bank & Trust Co., 5 Utah 2d 412, 303 P.2d 701 (1956).

By Kansas Stat. Ann., §59-602, it is provided that devises and bequests by residents to any foreign country or city or corporation or in trust to any trustee or agent thereof except devises and bequests to institutions created and existing exclusively for religious, educational, or charitable purposes, are prohibited. In In re Weeks' Estate, 154 Kan. 103, 114 P.2d 857 (1941), the court held invalid a bequest to a town in Switzerland in trust for the purpose of building and equipping a hospital, Allen, J., dissenting on the ground that a charitable trust was created and that even if the town could not act as trustee the trust should not fail.

By the Mississippi Constitution and by statute (Code 1972, §91-5-31) it is provided that if land is devised to a charitable institution it may be held by the devisee for not longer than 10 years, and that if it is not sold within that period it shall revert to the heirs of the testator. It is held that the forfeiture statutes apply to bequests of personalty as well as to devises of land.

Restrictions as to amount that charitable corporations may own. In some states there are, or have been, restrictions on the amount of property that may be held by charitable corporations, particularly by religious corporations.[12] The effect of such stat-

---

cannot be avoided by the creation of a trust for the institution. See Methodist Hosp. v. Slack, 330 So. 2d 882 (Miss. 1976); see Johnson v. Board of Trustees of the Miss. Annual Conference of the Methodist Church, 492 So. 2d 269 (Miss. 1986) (where land was devised to Methodist Conference on trust for "needy colored children," title reverted to heirs of testatrix ten years after her death because of conference's failure to dispose of it, even though it was in the possession of a tenant under a lease given by the testatrix throughout the period).

[12]*Arizona:* Rev. Stat. Ann., §10-454.

Arkansas: Stat. 1947, §50-201.

Kansas: Stat. Ann., §17-5904, enacted by Laws 1981, c. 106, prohibits, under $50,000 penalty, ownership by a charitable trust unless created by will of agricultural land.

Kentucky: Rev. Stat. Ann., §273.090, repealed by Laws 1968, c. 165.

Maine: Rev. Stat. Ann., tit. 13, §§903, 931.

Maryland: Constitution, Declaration of Rights, art. 38; see Corporations and Associations Article, §5-701, as enacted by Laws 1975, c. 311 (removing charter restrictions).

Massachusetts: Ann. Laws, c. 68, §9, repealed by Laws 1965, c. 40; c. 180, §9. Ann. Laws, c. 180, §6, as inserted by Laws 1971, c. 819, provides that "any corporation may hold real and personal estate to an unlimited amount, which estate or its income shall be devoted to the purposes set forth in its charter or articles of association or in any amendment thereof, and it may receive and hold, in trust or otherwise, funds received by gift or bequest to be devoted by it to such purposes; this provision shall be applicable notwithstanding the specification of a limited amount in any special law."

Michigan: By Stat. Ann., §21.165, it is provided that charitable corporations shall have power to take and hold for any of its purposes property without limitation as to amount of value, except such limitations, if any, as the legislature shall hereafter specifically impose.

Missouri: Constitution, art. XI, §5 (real estate not necessary for carrying on legitimate business of the corporation).

Nebraska: Rev. Stat., §§76-1511 to 76-1516, added by Laws 1981, L.B. 9, appears to prohibit, under $50,000 penalty, ownership of agricultural land by charitable trusts unless created by will.

Nevada: Rev. Stat., §86.160.

New Hampshire: Rev. Stat. Ann., §306:10.

utes on devises or bequests to a charitable corporation depends on the construction of the statute. If the purpose of the statute is to prevent the testator from devising or bequeathing property to the corporation so that it would then own an amount in excess of that permitted by the statute, the corporation cannot take the property beyond the permitted amount, but it passes to the heirs or next of kin or residuary devisees or legatees of the testator. The right to the property vests in them immediately upon the death of the testator, and they cannot be deprived of the property even though the legislature may thereafter enlarge the amount that the corporation is entitled to take and hold. On the other hand, if the purpose of the statute is to prevent the corporation from holding an amount of property in excess of that permitted by the statute, but is not to prevent the testator from devising or bequeathing property to the corporation, the corporation may take and hold the property if the legislature even after the death of the testator enlarges the amount that the corporation is entitled to hold.

The leading case for the view that a devise or bequest giving a charitable corporation an amount in excess of the permitted amount fails altogether as to such excess, with the result that the heirs or next of kin of the testator are entitled to it, is the case of *Matter of McGraw,* [13] decided by the Court of Appeals of New York. In that case a testatrix bequeathed the residue of her estate to Cornell University to be applied for the purposes of a library fund that had previously been given by her father. By its charter the university was permitted to hold real and personal

---

North Dakota: Cent. Code, §10-28-19.

Ohio: Rev. Code Ann., §1715.16.

Pennsylvania: Stat. Ann. (Purdon), tit. 10, §§31 to 36, 71 to 73, have been repealed.

Rhode Island: Gen. Laws, 1956, §7-6-8 as amended by Laws 1972, c. 228.

Vermont: Stat. Ann., tit. 11, §132, repealed by Laws 1967, c. 59.

Virginia: Code 1950, §57-12, as amended by Laws 1973, c. 515.

West Virginia: Code, §35-1-8.

See D.C. Code 1961, §29-602 (doing away with former $25,000 limitation); Ill. Rev. Stat., c. 32, §171.

See Estate of Lawlor, 52 T.C. 268 (1969) (a tax case).

[13] 111 N.Y. 66, 19 N.E. 233, 2 L.R.A. 387 (1888), *aff'd sub nom.* Cornell Univ. v. Fiske, 136 U.S. 152, 10 S. Ct. 775, 34 L. Ed. 427 (1890).

property not exceeding three million dollars. The amount of the bequest was such as to enlarge the property of the university beyond three million dollars. After the death of the testatrix the legislature removed the limitation. The court held that the bequest failed as to the excess and that the next of kin of the testatrix were entitled to it. Counsel for the university contended that only the state could take advantage of the violation of the restriction, and that the bequest was not open to attack by the next of kin, and that the legislature by removing the restriction authorized the university to retain the bequest. It was held, however, that the purpose of the restriction was to prevent the corporation from taking and not merely from holding the property. The court said that the effect of the prohibition was different from that contained in the English mortmain laws, under which a corporation could take land and could hold it until the overlord or Crown brought a proceeding to enforce a forfeiture. The court also distinguished cases holding that where land is transferred inter vivos to a corporation that is not entitled to hold it, the grantor is precluded from attacking his own conveyance. The court said that it was the intention of the legislature to prevent the corporation from taking property in excess of the permitted amount, and not merely to permit the state to penalize it by enforcing a forfeiture of the property or a forfeiture of the charter of the corporation. This view has been taken in some other states.[14]

The leading case for the opposite view is *Hubbard v. Worcester Art Museum,*[15] decided by the Supreme Judicial Court of Massachusetts. In that case a testator bequeathed the residue of his estate to a charitable corporation organized to maintain an art

[14]St. Peter's Roman Catholic Congregation v. Germain, 104 Ill. 440 (1882); Wood v. Hammond, 16 R.I. 98, 17 A. 324, 18 A. 198 (1889).

See Simler v. Wilson, 210 F.2d 99 (10th Cir. 1954), *cert. denied sub nom.* Wilson v. Simler, 347 U.S. 954 (1954).

By statute in Rhode Island it is provided that where property shall be given to a charitable corporation in excess of the amount that it is entitled to take and hold, the corporation shall take the property on a condition subsequent that it obtain from the legislature authority to take and hold the property and that the application to the legislature be made within one year. R.I. Gen. Laws 1956, §7-1-17.

[15]194 Mass. 280, 80 N.E. 490, 9 L.R.A. (N.S.) 689, 10 Ann. Cas. 1025 (1907).

museum. The value of the estate was over two million dollars. By statute such corporations were permitted to hold real and personal property to an amount not exceeding one and a half million dollars. After the death of the testator the legislature enlarged the permitted amount to five million dollars. The heirs of the testator brought a proceeding to reach the property. The court dismissed the petition. It held that the bequest was valid except as against the state, and such proceedings as the state might have taken were precluded by the subsequent action of the legislature. The purpose of the restriction was not to limit the power of a testator to dispose of his property for charitable purposes, but merely to prevent charitable corporations from holding too much property. The court said, moreover, that even if the corporation could not take and hold the property, a new trustee might be appointed to administer it for the charitable purposes intended by the testator.[16] The court said that in the mind of the testator the general charitable purpose was predominant and not a desire to give to a particular corporation. In some other states the courts have taken the same view.[17]

It is impossible, of course, to say whether the view of the New York court or that of the Massachusetts court is to be preferred. The answer must depend on considerations of policy. In Massachusetts the policy of the legislature and of the courts has always been to encourage gifts for charitable purposes, to a greater extent perhaps than in any other state. The legislature has imposed few restrictions, and the courts by the adoption of a very liberal attitude on the doctrine of cy pres have gone far to uphold charitable dispositions. In New York, on the other hand, the legislature and the courts have taken a much less

[16]Chase v. Dickey, 212 Mass. 555, 99 N.E. 410 (1912).
See §397.3.
[17]*Federal:* Jones v. Habersham, 107 U.S. 174, 2 S. Ct. 336, 27 L. Ed. 401 (1882); Brigham v. Peter Bent Brigham Hosp., 134 Fed. 513 (1st Cir. 1904).
Connecticut: Eliot's Appeal, 74 Conn. 586, 51 A. 558 (1902).
Maine: Farrington v. Putnam, 90 Me. 405, 37 A. 652, 38 L.R.A. 339 (1897).
Maryland: In re Stickney's Will, 85 Md. 79, 36 A. 654, 60 Am. St. Rep. 308 (1897).
Missouri: McCaleb v. Shantz, 318 S.W.2d 199 (Mo. 1958).
Pennsylvania: Darlington's Estate, 289 Pa. 297, 137 A. 268 (1927).
South Dakota: Jordheim v. Bottum, 77 S.D. 80, 85 N.W.2d 731 (1957).

liberal view with respect to charitable dispositions. The legislature has forbidden devises to corporations unless they are authorized by charter or by statute to take land by devise. It has provided that a testator can leave only a certain part of his property for charitable purposes. Indeed, the New York courts held that charitable trusts, as distinguished from dispositions to charitable corporations, were invalid. It is only since the enactment of the Tilden Act in 1893 that a somewhat more liberal attitude toward charitable dispositions has prevailed in New York. In New York there has always been a feeling that the family of a testator should be protected against his somewhat vicarious deathbed generosity, and a feeling also that there is some danger in the acquisition of great wealth by charitable organizations.[18] In Massachusetts, on the other hand, there has always been a strong tendency to encourage charitable dispositions. Which view is to be preferred depends on the mores of the community.

We shall consider hereafter questions as to the conflict of laws relating to restrictions on charitable dispositions by will.[19]

§362.5.   **Agreement by devisee or legatee or heir or next of kin to hold upon charitable trust.**   We have seen that where a testator bequeaths property to a person in reliance on his agreement to hold the property upon a charitable trust, the legatee can be compelled to apply the property to the charitable purposes for which he agreed to hold it.[1] The disposition in such a case is held not to be so far testamentary in character as to be invalid for failure to comply with the requirements of the Statute of Wills. The result is different, however, where a testamentary disposition in favor of charity is forbidden by statute. Where a legatee promised the testator to apply the legacy to charitable purposes, the disposition is so far testamentary that it falls within the scope of the statute. It has been so held under the Georgian Statute of Mortmain in England, and has been so held under American statutes restricting testamentary devises or bequests for charitable purposes. In such a case the legatee cannot be compelled and will not be permitted to apply the property to

---

[18]See Scott, Charitable Trusts in New York, 26 N.Y.U. L. Rev. 251 (1951).
[19]See §§589, 594, 649.
§362.5.   [1]See §359.

the charitable purposes agreed upon, but holds it upon a resulting trust for the estate of the testator.[2] Obviously it would defeat the purpose of the statute, which is to prevent the disinheriting of the family of the testator by dispositions in favor of charity, even though the disposition does not appear on the face of the will, if the legatee were compelled to apply the property to a charitable purpose. On the other hand, just as obviously the legatee would be unjustly enriched if he were permitted to keep the property. Accordingly, where a testator bequeaths property to a person who promises him to apply the property to charitable purposes, he holds the property upon a resulting trust for the estate of the testator if the will was executed and the agreement made within a year of the death of the testator, and if by statute it is provided that a bequest for charitable purposes made within a year of the death of the testator is invalid. So also where by statute it is provided that a testator can bequeath only a half of his estate for charitable purposes, and he bequeaths the whole of his estate to a person who promised him to hold the property in trust for charitable purposes, the legatee holds a half of the property upon a resulting trust for the estate of the testator. Thus in *Trustees of Amherst College v. Ritch*[3] a testator left the residue of his estate to his three executors. Although the be-

---

[2]*England:* Strickland v. Aldridge, 9 Ves. 516 (1804); Russell v. Jackson, 10 Hare 204 (1852); Tee v. Ferris, 2 Kay & J. 357 (1856); Moss v. Cooper, 1 J.&H. 352 (1861); Sweeting v. Sweeting, 10 Jur. (N.S.) 31 (1864); In re Spencer's Will, 57 L.T. 519 (1888).

Missouri: Kenrick v. Cole, 61 Mo. 572 (1876).

New York: Matter of O'Hara, 95 N.Y. 403, 47 Am. Rep. 53 (1884); Trustees of Amherst College v. Ritch, 151 N.Y. 282, 45 N.E. 876, 37 L.R.A. 305 (1897), *reargument denied,* 152 N.Y. 627, 46 N.E. 1152 (1897); Edson v. Bartow, 154 N.Y. 199, 215, 48 N.E. 541, 61 Am. St. Rep. 609 (1897).

Pennsylvania: Stirk's Estate, 232 Pa. 98, 81 A. 187 (1911).

Ireland: Geddis v. Semple, [1903] 1 I.R. 73.

See §55.6.

Kansas and Nebraska impose a fine of $50,000 on any charitable trust that acquires an interest in agricultural land but exempt testamentary trusts from the penalty. §362.4, n. 12. Would a charitable trust created by absolute devise to a devisee who promised the testator to hold for charity be subject to the penalty or is it a testamentary trust for this purpose? If a trust is treated as testamentary for the purpose of defeating it, should it not be so treated for the purpose of enforcing it?

[3]151 N.Y. 282, 45 N.E. 876, 37 L.R.A. 305 (1897), *reargument denied,* 152 N.Y. 627, 46 N.E. 1152 (1897).

quest was absolute it appeared that it was made upon a secret trust for certain colleges to which the residuary legatees agreed to convey it. By statute it was provided that no person having a husband, wife, child, or parent should devise or bequeath to any charitable corporation more than one half of his estate. The court held that the trust was enforceable to the extent of one half of the testator's estate, and that as to the balance there would be a resulting trust for the widow and next of kin, but that because they had waived their rights the whole trust became enforceable. Vann, J., pointed out that although a secret trust of this sort is not so far a testamentary disposition as to be invalid under the Statute of Wills, yet it is so far testamentary as to fall within the policy of the statute imposing restrictions on devises or bequests for charity.[4]

The result is different, however, where the legatee did not expressly or impliedly agree to hold the property in trust. As we have seen, where a testator makes an absolute bequest, the mere fact that he intended that the legatee should hold the legacy in trust imposes no obligation on him in the absence of an agreement by him with the testator to hold the property in trust.[5] If, for example, the intention of the testator was not communicated to the legatee, but on the death of the testator a letter is found directing the legatee to hold the property in trust, the legatee can hold the legacy free of trust. He is not under any obligation to perform the intended trust, nor does he hold the property upon a resulting trust for the estate of the testator. The result is the same although the intended trust is a charitable trust, and although there are statutory restrictions on testamentary dispositions for charitable purposes.[6] Thus in *Schultz's*

---

[4]In Matter of Watson, 177 Misc. 308, 30 N.Y.S.2d 577 (1941), where the testatrix bequeathed more than half of her property to charity and after the execution of the will her children agreed with her that if any portion of the estate was not effectually disposed of by the will they would give the property to the designated charities, it was held that the children were entitled to the excess over one half and were not bound to give it to the charities. See §362.4, n. 5.

[5]See §359.

[6]*England:* Adlington v. Cann, 3 Atk. 141 (1744); Stickland v. Aldridge, 9 Ves. 516 (1804), *semble;* Wallgrave v. Tebbs, 2 Kay & J. 313 (1855); Moss v. Cooper, 1 J.&H. 352, 365 (1861), *semble;* Jones v. Badley, L.R. 3 Ch. App. 362 (1868); Juniper v. Batchelor, [1868] W.N. 197.

Appeal[7] a testator desired to leave property by will for charitable purposes, and being informed that if he should die within thirty days such a disposition would be ineffectual, but that he might make an absolute bequest to some individual with the expectation that he might carry out the intended charitable purposes, he executed a will bequeathing property to a bishop of the church to which he belonged. The bishop was not informed of the will until some time after the death of the testator. When informed of it he declared his intention to carry out the testator's wishes. It was held that the bequest was valid and that the bishop took the property free and clear of any trust, although

California: Estate of Holt, 61 Cal. App. 464, 215 P. 124 (1923); Estate of Sanderson, 58 Cal. 2d 522, 375 P.2d 37 (1962).

Massachusetts: Boynton v. Gale, 194 Mass. 320, 80 N.E. 448 (1907).

New Jersey: Nash v. Bremner, 84 N.J. Eq. 131, 92 A. 938 (1915).

Pennsylvania: Schultz's Appeal, 80 Pa. 396 (1876); Flood v. Ryan, 220 Pa. 450, 69 A. 908, 22 L.R.A. (N.S.) 1262, 13 Ann. Cas. 1189 (1908); Bickley's Estate, 270 Pa. 101, 113 A. 68 (1921).

Ireland: Geddis v. Semple, [1903] I.R. 73.

But compare Gore v. Clarke, 37 S.C. 537, 16 S.E. 614, 20 L.R.A. 465 (1892) (bequest for uncommunicated purpose of giving testator's mistress and illegitimate children more than one fourth of his estate in violation of a statute).

For cases where the trust was agreed to by one only of several joint tenants or tenants in common, see:

England: Burney v. Macdonald, 15 Sim. 6 (1845); Russell v. Jackson, 10 Hare 204 (1852); Tee v. Ferris, 2 Kay & J. 357 (1856); Moss v. Cooper, 1 J.&H. 352 (1861); In re Stead, [1900] 1 Ch. 237.

Michigan: Hooker v. Axford, 33 Mich. 453 (1876).

New Jersey: Powell v. Yearance, 73 N.J. Eq. 117, 67 A. 892 (1907).

New York: Trustees of Amherst College v. Ritch, 151 N.Y. 282, 45 N.E. 876, 37 L.R.A. 305 (1897), *reargument denied,* 152 N.Y. 627, 641, 46 N.E. 1152 (1897); Edson v. Bartow, 154 N.Y. 199, 48 N.E. 541, 61 Am. St. Rep. 609 (1897).

Ohio: Winder v. Scholey, 83 Ohio St. 204, 93 N.E. 1098, 33 L.R.A. (N.S.) 995, 21 Ann. Cas. 1379 (1910).

For cases in which the testator or intestate communicated to one other than the devisee, legatee, or heir his intention to create a trust, see:

California: Simons v. Bedell, 122 Cal. 341, 55 P. 3, 68 Am. St. Rep. 35 (1898).

Missouri: Mead v. Robertson, 131 Mo. App. 185, 110 S.W. 1095 (1908).

Pennsylvania: Stirk's Estate, 232 Pa. 98, 81 A. 187 (1911).

[7]80 Pa. 396 (1876).

he could devote the property to charity in accordance with the testator's wishes if he should choose to do so.

So also statutory restrictions on bequests for charitable purposes are not applicable where the testator in the will manifests an intention not to impose a duty on the legatee to apply the property to charitable purposes, but merely expresses a wish that he will so apply it.[8]

§362.6. Where settlor of trust created inter vivos reserves power to revoke or modify. We have seen that where a charitable trust is created by a transaction inter vivos, the disposition is not invalid for failure to comply with the formalities required by the Statute of Wills merely because the settlor reserves a beneficial life estate and a power to revoke or modify the trust.[1] The disposition is not so far testamentary as to require that the trust instrument be executed with the formalities of a will. The question arises, however, whether the result is different in jurisdictions in which there are restrictions imposed by statute on testamentary dispositions for charitable purposes. In England under the Georgian Statute of Mortmain[2] it was expressly provided that no land should be given in trust except by deed sealed and delivered in the presence of two or more witnesses at least twelve months before the death of the donor, and

> unless the same be made to take effect in possession for the charitable use intended, immediately from the making thereof, and be without any power of revocation, reservation, trust, condition, limitation, clause, or agreement whatsoever, for the benefit of the donor or grantor, or of any person or persons claiming under him.

[8]Matter of Will of Keleman, 126 N.Y. 73, 26 N.E. 968 (1891).

See Matter of Hayes, 263 N.Y. 219, 188 N.E. 716 (1934), *reargument denied,* 264 N.Y. 459, 191 N.E. 513 (1934), noted in 19 Iowa L. Rev. 574, 9 Notre Dame Law. 473, 8 St. John's L. Rev. 308, 43 Yale L.J. 146.

As to the situation where, although the language of the will is precatory, the legatee agrees with the testator to hold the property for a designated purpose, see §55.1, n. 15.

§362.6. [1]See §361.

[2]Stat. 9 Geo. II, c. 36 (1736).

It is clear that this statute forbade not only devises for charitable purposes but also dispositions inter vivos where the settlor reserved either a beneficial life interest or a power of revocation.

In the United States the statutes in jurisdictions in which restrictions on the creation of charitable trusts are imposed are not so clear. As we have seen, these statutes provide either that no devise or bequest for a charitable purpose shall be good if the will is executed within a certain time before the death of the testator, or that the testator can devise or bequeath for charitable purposes not more than a half or a third of his estate. The question then is whether these statutes are applicable where a trust is created inter vivos for charitable purposes, and the settlor reserves a life estate and a power of revocation or modification. The question is whether such a disposition is so far testamentary as to fall within these restrictive statutes. It is held that it does not.[3] In *City Bank Farmers Trust Co., v. Charity Organization Society*[4] the settlor executed a trust indenture transferring property to a trust company in trust to pay the income to himself for life and on his death to certain charitable organizations. He reserved power to revoke the trust and provided that the trustee should not make investments except with his consent. He died without having revoked the trust. After his death his daughter sought to set aside the trust, contending that it was invalid on the ground that it was a testamentary disposition and the trust instrument was not executed in accordance with the requirements of the Statute of Wills, and that it was in violation of the Decedent Estate Law, §17,[5] which provided that no person leav-

[3] *Federal:* President of Bowdoin College v. Merritt, 75 F. 480 (C.C.N.D. Cal. 1896).

New York: Robb v. Washington & Jefferson College, 185 N.Y. 485, 78 N.E. 359, 384 N.Y.S.2d 429 (1906), cited also in §57.5, n. 25; City Bank Farmers Trust Co. v. Charity Org. Socy., 238 A.D. 720, 265 N.Y.S. 267 (1933), *aff'd mem.*, 264 N.Y. 441, 191 N.E. 504 (1934); but see Worthington v. Redkey, 86 Ohio St. 128, 99 N.E. 211 (1912).

See §§57.5, 58.5.

[4] 238 A.D. 720, 265 N.Y.S. 267 (1933), *aff'd mem.*, 264 N.Y. 441, 191 N.E. 504 (1934).

[5] New York Decedent Estate Law, §17 (cited in the text) was superseded by Estates, Powers and Trusts Law, §5-3.3, as inserted by Laws 1967, c. 683, and by Laws 1973, c. 45. New York Estates, Powers and Trusts Law, §5-3.3 was repealed by New York Laws 1981, c. 461.

ing a husband, wife, child, or parent should devise or bequeath for charitable purposes more than one half of his estate, and that the disposition was made fraudulently for the purpose of evading the statute. The court held that the trust was valid.

The question is at least open to argument. If the settlor can create a living trust under which the property is ultimately to go to charity, but he reserves the same potential control that he would have if the disposition were made by will, it is arguable that the purpose of the statute is defeated. Where a settlor creates a trust inter vivos and reserves a power of revocation, it is possible for him to enjoy the property if he so wishes at any time as long as he lives, and the persons who are to take the beneficial interest on his death are in a precarious position until he dies, because they may be deprived by the exercise of the power of revocation of all interest under the trust. In substance the situation is not very different from that which arises where the owner of property has made a will. Even though a revocable trust created inter vivos has some of the aspects of a testamentary disposition, the courts have wisely refused to hold such trusts invalid merely because they are not executed with the formalities of a will. The purpose of the Statute of Wills is to prevent fraudulent claims, but in the case of a trust created inter vivos there is no more danger of fraud where a power of revocation is reserved than where the trust is irrevocable. Different considerations enter in, however, where a settlor attempts to do by means of a revocable trust created inter vivos what he could not do by will. The policy underlying the restriction on dispositions by will may well be held to be equally applicable to revocable trusts created inter vivos. In states in which there is a policy forbidding a testamentary disposition in favor of charitable purposes of more than a certain proportion of a man's estate, it may be contended that the policy is applicable to dispositions inter vivos where the settlor reserves a power of revocation. A similar problem arises, as we have seen, with respect to the statutory rights of a surviving spouse in the estate of a deceased spouse.[6] The courts, however, have sometimes held that these statutes impose no restrictions on the creation of a trust inter vivos, even though the settlor reserves a life interest and a power of revocation.

[6]See §57.5.

The question may arise whether these statutes restricting charitable dispositions by will are applicable where a settlor creates a trust for himself for life and on his death as he may appoint by will. We have seen that where a power of appointment is given to another person, it has been held that the exercise of the power does not fall within the statutory restriction.[7] It may be different, however, where a power of appointment is reserved by the settlor. In such a case it would seem that the policy of the statute is applicable.[8]

§363. The Trust Property

A charitable trust, like a private trust, cannot be created unless there is trust property of such a nature as to be the proper subject of a trust. This requirement as to private trusts has been treated elsewhere.[1] A charitable trust is not invalid merely because the trustee is authorized to apply as much of the trust property as is necessary to accomplish the charitable purposes specified, or because he is authorized to exercise his discretion as to the amount to be so applied. Thus in *Wright's Estate*,[2] where a testator bequeathed his estate in trust for the education of poor boys and girls and authorized the trustees to pay to his

[7]See §362.4, nn. 9, 10.

[8]In Matter of Pratt, 5 A.D.2d 501, 172 N.Y.S.2d 965 (1958), *aff'd mem.*, 8 N.Y.2d 855, 168 N.E.2d 709 (1960), it was unnecessary to decide the question. In that case a settlor created a trust in New York, reserving a general testamentary power. He executed a will leaving bequests to charity. He died three days after the execution of the will, domiciled in Florida. The Florida court held that the disposition of his property was invalid under a Florida statute invalidating bequests to charity made within six months of the testator's death. In re Pratt's Estate, 88 So.2d 499 (Fla. 1956). The New York court held, however, that the validity of the appointment was governed by the law of New York, where there was no such restrictive statute.

§363. [1]See §§74-88.2.

See National Bank of Commerce Trust & Sav. Assn. v. Crowell Memorial Home, 181 Neb. 341, 148 N.W.2d 304 (1967).

Kansas and Nebraska impose a fine of $50,000 on any charitable trust that acquires an interest in agricultural land but exempt testamentary trusts from the penalty. §362.4, n. 12. Query whether a self-declaration of trust of agricultural land or a conveyance upon trust of such land for charitable purposes creates a trust or is void as illegal.

[2]284 Pa. 334, 131 A. 188 (1925), noted in 39 Harv. L. Rev. 659.

nieces and nephews such sums as in their discretion might be necessary, it was held that the trust was valid. It was a trust partly for charitable purposes and partly for private beneficiaries, but this fact did not invalidate it. So far as it was a private trust it did not violate the rule against perpetuities, because the testator intended to include only such nephews and nieces as were living at the time of his death.

§364. Indefinite Beneficiaries

The most important distinction between a private trust and a charitable trust is with reference to the beneficiaries. As has been stated, a private trust is not valid unless there is a beneficiary who is definitely ascertained at the time of the creation of the trust or definitely ascertainable within the period of the rule against perpetuities.[1] In the case of a private trust no one except a beneficiary or one suing on his behalf can maintain a suit to enforce the trust.[2] In the case of a charitable trust the beneficial interest is not given to individual beneficiaries, but the property is devoted to the accomplishment of purposes that are beneficial or are supposed to be beneficial to the community, and the persons who are to receive benefits from the trust need not be designated. A charitable trust is enforceable at the suit of the Attorney General, and ordinarily is not enforceable at the suit of any individual beneficiary, although in the case of some charitable trusts there may be beneficiaries having such a special interest in the performance of the trust as to entitle them to maintain a suit to enforce it.[3]

The mere fact that the beneficiaries of a charitable trust are indefinite does not invalidate it; on the contrary, a trust is not a charitable trust where all of the beneficiaries are definitely ascertained.[4] Ordinarily, where the method of selecting persons to benefit from the performance of the trust is not stated in the

---

§364. [1] See §112.

[2] See §200.

[3] See §391.

[4] See §§375-375.3; Tinnin v. First United Bank of Miss., 502 So. 2d 659 (Miss. 1987), citing text.

trust instrument, the trustees are authorized to make the selection;[5] but even if the trustees are not to make the selection, the court may determine how the beneficiaries shall be selected.[6]

§365.   Duration of Charitable Trusts

A charitable trust is valid although it is to continue beyond the period of the rule against perpetuities. It is valid even though it is to continue indefinitely.[1] It is not essential to a

[5]See §396.

In Rice v. Morris, 541 S.W.2d 627 (Tex. Civ. App. 1976), *writ dismissed,* a testator left his property in trust to make distributions in the trustee's discretion to churches and hospitals in Texas, and to five named persons. The distributions were to be made within 20 years. It was held that the trust was valid, both as to the charities and as to the named individuals.

[6]Galiger v. Armstrong, 114 Colo. 397, 165 P.2d 1019 (1946) (citing the text). See §§397-399.5.

See Eldridge v. Marshall Natl. Bank, 527 S.W.2d 222 (Tex. Civ. App. 1975), *writ refused, n.r.e.*

§365. [1]The cases so holding are so numerous that it is unnecessary to cite them; indeed, most charitable trusts are of indefinite duration. See:

Arkansas: Bakos v. Kryder, 260 Ark. 621, 543 S.W.2d 216 (1976) (quoting Restatement of Trusts §365).

Colorado: Smith v. United States Natl. Bank, 120 Colo. 167, 207 P.2d 1194 (1949), noted in 49 Mich. L. Rev. 281.

Connecticut: Mitchell v. Reeves, 123 Conn. 549, 196 A. 785, 115 A.L.R. 1114 (1938) (citing Restatement of Trusts §365).

Delaware: Hutton v. St. Paul Bhd. of People's Church, 20 Del. Ch. 413, 178 A. 584 (1935).

Illinois: Smith v. Renne, 382 Ill. 26, 46 N.E.2d 587 (1943).

Iowa: In re Estate of Small, 244 Iowa 1209, 58 N.W.2d 477 (1953).

Kansas: Commercial Natl. Bank of Kan. City v. Martin, 185 Kan. 116, 340 P.2d 899 (1959); In re Estate of Freshour, 185 Kan. 434, 345 P.2d 689, 81 A.L.R.2d 806 (1959) (citing Restatement of Trusts §365).

Kentucky: Epperson v. Clintonville Cemetery Co., 303 Ky. 852, 199 S.W.2d 628 (1947) (endowment of public cemetery); Hatcher v. Southern Baptist Theological Seminary, 632 S.W.2d 251 (Ky. 1982).

New Jersey: National Newark & Essex Banking Co. v. Arthur Sunshine Home, 113 N.J. Eq. 313, 166 A. 635 (1933); Guaranty Trust Co. of N.Y. v. New York Community Trust, 139 N.J. Eq. 144, 50 A.2d 161 (1946), 141 N.J. Eq. 238, 56 A.2d 907 (1948), *aff'd mem.,* 142 N.J. Eq. 726, 61 A.2d 239 (1948); Martin v. Haycock, 140 N.J. Eq. 450, 55 A.2d 60 (1947); Wendell v. Hazel Wood Cemetery, 7 N.J. Super. 117, 72 A.2d 383 (1950), *aff'g* 3 N.J. Super. 457,

charitable trust, however, that it should continue indefinitely. Thus although a charitable trust may be created under which the income is to be expended for charitable purposes for an indefinite period but the principal is to be held intact, a charitable trust may be created for the purpose of applying the principal immediately for charitable purposes, as for example to distribute the principal immediately to aid the poor, or, as in the case of some modern foundations, to expend the principal within a limited period such as twenty years.

---

67 A.2d 219 (1949); Burlington County Trust Co. v. New Jersey Socy., 12 N.J. Super. 369, 79 A.2d 710 (1951) (citing Restatement of Trusts §365).

New York: Matter of Gardini, 5 Misc. 2d 335, 164 N.Y.S.2d 262 (1957); Matter of Reese, 21 Misc. 2d 29, 195 N.Y.S.2d 144 (1960).

North Carolina: Williams v. Williams, 215 N.C. 739, 3 S.E.2d 334 (1939); Z. Smith Reynolds Found. v. Trustees of Wake Forest College, 227 N.C. 500, 42 S.E.2d 910 (1947).

Oregon: Good Samaritan Hosp. and Medical Center v. United States Natl. Bank, 246 Or. 748, 425 P.2d 541 (1967) (citing Restatement of Trusts §365).

South Dakota: In re Geppert's Estate, 75 S.D. 96, 59 N.W. 727 (1953).

Texas: Boyd v. Frost Natl. Bank, 145 Tex. 206, 196 S.W.2d 497, 168 A.L.R. 1326 (1946), noted in 25 Tex. L. Rev. 434; Moore v. Sellers, 201 S.W.2d 248 (Tex. Civ. App. 1947).

Virginia: Maguire v. Loyd, 193 Va. 138, 67 S.E.2d 885 (1952).

Canada: In re Hart, [1951] 2 D.L.R. 30 (N.S.); In re Armstrong, 7 D.L.R.3d 36 (N.S. 1969); Wasilenko v. Saskatchewan Council for Crippled Children & Adults, 41 Sask. R. 77 (Sur. Ct. 1985).

See Restatement of Property §398, which states that "A charitable trust of perpetual duration can be validly created." This is assumed by Restatement (Second) of Property (Donative Transfers) §2.1 (1979).

See Lynn, Perpetuities: The Duration of Charitable Trusts and Foundations, 13 U.C.L.A. Law Rev. 1074 (1966); Chaffin, The Rule Against Perpetuities as Applied to Georgia Wills and Trusts: A Survey and Suggestions for Reform, 16 Ga. L. Rev. 235 (1982) (citing the text).

In several states statutes expressly permit charitable trusts with indefinite duration:

Arizona: Rev. Stat. Ann., §33-261.

Louisiana: Rev. Stat. Ann., §§9:2291, 9:2295.

Michigan: Stat. Ann., §§26.1191, 26.1201.

Minnesota: Stat. Ann., §501.12.

North Carolina: Gen. Stat., §36A-43.

Oklahoma: Stat. Ann., tit. 60, §175.47.

South Carolina: Code Ann., §§21-27-50, 21-29-20.

Tennessee: Code Ann., §35-1-114, enacted by Laws 1986, c. 566.

Wisconsin: Stat., §700.16.

It is not entirely accurate to say that the rule against perpetuities although applicable to private trusts is not applicable to charitable trusts. The rule against perpetuities, according to Professor Gray's classic statement, is that "No interest is good unless it must vest, if at all, not later than twenty-one years after some life in being at the creation of the interest."[2] If an interest vests within the period, it is not invalid merely because it may continue beyond the period. This is true, according to the better view, in the case of private trusts,[3] and is undoubtedly true in the case of charitable trusts. Because of the requirement, however, that all interests under a private trust must vest within the period, it rarely happens that a private trust will continue beyond the period. A charitable trust usually is to continue beyond the period. Because a charitable trust is for the benefit of an indefinite number of persons, the beneficial interest in the trust property does not vest in any person during the continuance of the trust.

The exceptional situation with respect to perpetuities in the case of a charitable trust can best be appreciated by contrasting such a trust with the situation that arises where property is bequeathed for a noncharitable purpose and there is no person to benefit from the accomplishment of the purpose. In that case, as we have seen, if the purpose is specific and is not capricious, the person to whom the property is bequeathed has a power to apply it to the designated purpose although he cannot be compelled to do so.[4] It is so held, for example, where money is bequeathed for the erection of a tomb. But where by the will it is provided that the property shall or may be applied to the purpose for a period longer than the period of the rule against perpetuities, the disposition fails.[5] Thus, for example, a bequest of money to apply the income forever in maintaining a tomb is invalid in the absence of a statute otherwise providing. On the other hand, a bequest of money to apply the income forever to some charitable purpose is valid.

Although a charitable trust may continue for a period lon-

[2]Gray, Rule Against Perpetuities §201 (4th ed. 1942).
[3]See §62.10.
[4]See §124.
[5]See §124.1.

ger than the period of the rule against perpetuities, a contingent disposition in favor of a charity, following a disposition for non-charitable purposes, is invalid under the rule against perpetuities if the contingency may not occur within the period of the rule.[6] To this extent the rule against perpetuities is applicable to charitable dispositions. On the other hand, a gift over from one charity to another is valid although it is to take effect upon the happening of a contingency that may not occur within the period of the rule against perpetuities.[7] Although a charitable trust may continue beyond the period of the rule against perpetuities, and although a provision for the termination of the charitable trust upon the happening of an event that is not within the period is valid, a gift over for noncharitable purposes upon the happening of such an event is invalid.[8]

A charitable trust is not invalid merely because the creation of such a trust results in the creation of inalienable and indestructible interests. In the case of a private trust, as we have seen, it is held in England and in a few American states that a restraint on the alienation by a beneficiary of his interest is invalid.[9] On the other hand, in a majority of the states a restraint on the alienation of a beneficiary's right to income under a trust, and in some states a restraint on the alienation of his right to the principal, is valid. It would seem, however, that such a restraint on alienation may be invalid if it is to continue for a period beyond that of the rule against perpetuities. On the other hand, in the case of a charitable trust the beneficial interest is always inalienable as long as the trust continues because there is no beneficiary who has an interest that he can transfer, but the property is to be devoted to the accomplishment of the desig-

[6]See §401.7.

In Re Green's Will Trusts, [1985] 3 All E.R. 455 (Ch. D.), an estate was devised on trust for a son of the testatrix who had been reported missing in action in World War II, with a proviso that, if the son failed to claim by January 1, 2020, the estate should be held on trust to prevent cruelty to animals. It was held that, as Perpetuities and Accumulations Act 1964, c. 55, §1(1) permits the election of an alternative perpetuity period of 80 years, the charitable disposition was bound to vest or fail within the statutory 80-year period and so was valid.

[7]See §401.5.
[8]See §401.6.
[9]See §152.1.

nated purposes. The fact that the beneficial interest in the subject matter of the trust, or even the subject matter of the trust itself, is inalienable, and the fact that it is inalienable for a period beyond the period of the rule against perpetuities, or even forever, does not invalidate the charitable trust. If it did, indeed, most charitable trusts would fail.

We shall consider hereafter the question of the termination of a charitable trust, particularly where property is held by trustees in trust to pay the income to a charitable corporation.[10] We shall also consider the question of the authority of trustees for charitable purposes to organize a charitable corporation to administer the charity.[11]

§366. Rescission and Reformation

The principles governing the rescission or reformation of a charitable trust are the same as those applicable to private trusts.[1] A charitable trust can be rescinded where the settlor has been induced to create it by fraud, duress, undue influence, or mistake.

§367. Revocation and Modification

As has been stated, where a private trust is created inter vivos the settlor has power to revoke the trust or to modify it only if he has reserved such a power, or if the omission to reserve such a power is due to a mistake.[1] The same principle is applicable to charitable trusts. It is true that in the case of a private trust created inter vivos the settlor can revoke or modify the trust if all of the beneficiaries are ascertained and are under no legal incapacity and consent.[2] In the case of a charitable trust, however, the beneficiaries are indefinite, and it is therefore impossible to obtain the consent of the beneficiaries. It would

[10]See §367A.
[11]See §§367A, 385A.
§366. [1]See §333.
§367. [1]See §§330-331.2.
[2]See §339.

seem, however, that the consent of the Attorney General may be effective. In *Matter of Schlussel*[3] a settlor created a trust, by its terms irrevocable, to pay the income to himself and his wife, and on the death of the survivor to pay the principal to their children, and, if none, to his brother and sister, or if neither were then living to such charitable institution as the survivor might appoint, and in the absence of appointment as the trustee might appoint. No children of the settlor having been born, he sought to revoke the trust. It was held that he could revoke it with the consent of his wife and brother and sister and the Attorney General. The Attorney General had consented in return for an

[3] 195 Misc. 1008, 89 N.Y.S.2d 47 (1949), noted in 50 Colum. L. Rev. 105, 35 Cornell L.Q. 449, 24 N.Y.U. L.Q. Rev. 1231. See §340, n. 12.

In Matter of Martin v. Lefkowitz, 40 Misc. 2d 857, 243 N.Y.S.2d 709 (1963), the court held that the compromise of the rights of charitable beneficiaries consented to by the Attorney General would be set aside if he exercised his discretion without inquiry or investigation and for expediency in violation of the trust imposed on him.

In Sigmund Sternberger Found. v. Tannenbaum, 273 N.C. 658, 161 S.E.2d 116 (1968), it was held that a charitable corporation could make a compromise agreement with the heirs of the testator, even though the Attorney General did not consent. See §340, n. 14; §380, n. 7.

In In re Estate of Horton, 11 Cal. App. 3d 680, 90 Cal. Rptr. 66 (1970), a testator created a trust to pay $40,000 to a person for life, and on his death the remainder was to be paid to four charitable corporations, and no disposition of the income in excess of $40,000 was made. The court approved a compromise agreement between the life beneficiary and the charitable corporations under which the life beneficiary was to receive a larger sum and the balance of the income was to be paid to the corporations, although the Attorney General did not approve of the compromise.

In In re Estate of Reeder, 380 Mich. 655, 158 N.W.2d 451 (1968), it was held that the court could properly approve a compromise settlement of a charitable trust even though the Attorney General objected.

In Estate of Beckley, 63 A.D.2d 855, 405 N.Y.S.2d 861 (1978), *appeal dismissed,* 45 N.Y.2d 837 (1978), it was held that, where the will was ambiguous as to which of two charitable organizations was the legatee, a compromise agreement made by both organizations and the Attorney General for payment to the two organizations jointly should be approved.

By Texas Civ. Stat. Ann., art. 4412a, as inserted by Laws 1959, c. 115, amended by Texas Laws 1981, c. 501, §1, and Laws 1983, c. 657, the Attorney General is authorized to enter into such compromises and settlement agreements as in his judgment may be in the best interest of the public, with or without the approval of the court. If the attorney general is not joined, the judgment is voidable at his option.

agreement to create a trust for certain charitable corporations to arise on the death of the other beneficiaries. The court said that it was unnecessary to determine whether the consent of the Attorney General would have been effective in the absence of any such agreement.[4]

§367.1. **Revocation of charitable trust.** Where the owner of property transfers it inter vivos to trustees for charitable purposes, or where he declares himself trustee, he cannot revoke the trust unless he has reserved a power of revocation.[1] Even though the trustees consent to the revocation of the trust, the revocation is ineffective because they would thereby commit a breach of trust.[2] The settlor may, however, reserve a power of revocation where the trust is a charitable trust as well as where it is a private trust.[3] We have dealt elsewhere with the question

[4]By Michigan Stat. Ann., §27.2681, it is provided that, when the probate of a will containing a gift for charitable purposes without naming any person or corporation as donee is contested, no settlement shall be approved against the objection of the Attorney General.

§367.1. [1]See the following cases:

Federal: Teachers Annuity & Aid Assn. v. Riggs Natl. Bank, 278 F.2d 452, 108 App. D.C. 7 (1960) (citing the text).

Connecticut: Langdon v. Plymouth Congregational Socy., 12 Conn. 113 (1837); Christ Church v. Trustees, 67 Conn. 554, 35 A. 552 (1896).

Kansas: Daughters of the Am. Revolution of Kan., Topeka Chapter v. Washburn College, 160 Kan. 583, 164 P.2d 128 (1945) (citing Restatement of Trusts §367).

Minnesota: City of Fergus Falls v. Whitlock, 247 Minn. 347, 77 N.W.2d 194 (1956).

Missouri: Pilgrim Evangelical Lutheran Church of the Unaltered Augsburg Confession v. Lutheran Church-Missouri Synod Found., 661 S.W.2d 833 (Mo. App. 1983), *transfer to S. Ct. denied* (1984), citing text and Restatement (Second) of Trusts §367.

Virginia: Penn v. Keller, 178 Va. 131, 16 S.E.2d 331 (1941), noted in 22 B.U.L. Rev. 159, 30 Geo. L.J. 216, 28 Va. L. Rev. 307.

[2]*New York:* Application of Dana, 119 Misc. 2d 815, 465 N.Y.S.2d 102 (Sup. 1982) (sale of all assets of charitable trust to settlors, who were also the trustees, did not invalidate or revoke the trust).

Ohio: O'Brien v. Physicians Hosp. Assn., 96 Ohio St. 1, 116 N.E. 975, L.R.A. 1917F 741 (1917).

Oregon: In re Kulka's Estate, 142 Or. 104, 18 P.2d 1036 (1933).

[3]*Federal:* President of Bowdoin College v. Merritt, 75 F. 480 (C.C.N.D. Cal. 1896).

whether the reservation of such a power makes the trust so far testamentary as to cause it to fail if it is not created with the formalities required in the case of a will,[4] or to cause it to fail in states in which there are restrictions on testamentary dispositions for charitable purposes.[5] Indeed, if the charitable trust fails because the purposes cannot be accomplished, and if the doctrine of cy pres is not applicable, a resulting trust arises in favor of the settlor or his estate.[6] But unless the charitable trust fails and the doctrine of cy pres is not applicable, neither the settlor nor his heirs or personal representatives can compel the trustees to reconvey the property to them.

§367.2. Modification of charitable trust.   Where a charitable trust is created inter vivos, the settlor has no power to compel or to permit a deviation from the terms of the trust, unless he has reserved a power of modification.[1] So also where

---

California: American Bible Socy. v. Mortgage Guar. Co., 217 Cal. 9, 17 P.2d 105 (1932).

New York: Robb v. Washington & Jefferson College, 185 N.Y. 485, 78 N.E. 359 (1906); City Bank Farmers Trust Co. v. Charity Org. Socy., 238 A.D. 720, 265 N.Y.S. 267 (1933), *aff'd mem.,* 264 N.Y. 441, 191 N.E. 504 (1934).

See In re Sir Robert Peel's School, L.R. 3 Ch. App. 543 (1868).

[4]See §361.

[5]See §362.6.

[6]See §413.

§367.2. [1]*England:* Attorney-General v. Dulwich College, 4 Beav. 255, 267 (1841).

See In re Hartshill Endowment, 30 Beav. 130 (1861).

Arkansas: Bailey v. Sebastian County Humane Socy., 201 Ark. 354, 144 S.W.2d 716 (1940).

Massachusetts: St. Paul's Church v. Attorney Gen., 164 Mass. 188, 41 N.E. 231 (1895); Thorp v. Lund, 227 Mass. 474, 116 N.E. 946, Ann. Cas. 1918B 1204 (1917); Eustace v. Dickey, 240 Mass. 55, 132 N.E. 852 (1921).

New York: Matter of Reese, 21 Misc. 2d 29, 195 N.Y.S.2d 144 (1960).

Oregon: State ex rel. Crutze v. Toney, 141 Or. 406, 17 P.2d 1105 (1933).

Vermont: Franklin County Grammar School v. Bailey, 62 Vt. 467, 20 A. 820, 10 L.R.A. 405 (1889).

West Virginia: Grand Lodge of Indep. Order of Odd Fellows v. Gunnoe, 154 W. Va. 594, 177 S.E.2d 150 (1970) (citing Restatement of Trusts §367; removal of trustees).

By New York Estates, Powers and Trusts Law, §8-1.3, which was first enacted before charitable trusts were generally permitted, it is provided that a person may by conveyance create a trust for certain charitable purposes, and

a charitable trust has been created by several persons who have subscribed money for the purposes of the trust, the subscribers cannot thereafter modify the purposes to which the property is to be applied.[2] It is clear also that where a charitable trust is created by will, or where it is created inter vivos and the settlor later dies, the heirs or personal representatives of the settlor have no power to compel or to permit a modification of the purposes to which the property is to be applied.[3] Even though the trustees and the settlor or his heirs or personal representatives all consent to the modification of the trust, the modification is ineffective.[4]

---

that he may reserve for himself or his wife certain powers of administration and also power to modify the terms of the trust.

In Elliott v. Teachers College, 177 Misc. 746, 31 N.Y.S.2d 796 (1941), *aff'd*, 264 A.D. 839, 35 N.Y.S.2d 761 (1942), *aff'd mem.*, 290 N.Y. 747, 50 N.E.2d 97 (1943), and in Teachers College v. Goldstein, 70 N.Y.S.2d 778 (1947), *mod.*, 273 A.D. 11, 75 N.Y.S.2d 250 (1947), *aff'd*, 297 N.Y. 969, 80 N.E.2d 357 (1948), the court found it unnecessary to determine the effect of a release by the settlor of restrictions on the gifts.

[2]See Attorney-General v. Kell, 2 Beav. 575 (1840).

In Baldry v. Feintuck, [1972] 2 All E.R. 81, a students' union of Sussex University was created to encourage the corporate life of the union in cultural, social, and athletic fields, to participate in university administration, to foster the academic, social, and personal welfare of members of the university, and to safeguard the interests of the members of the union. At its annual meeting a new constitution was adopted providing that "The aims and objects of the union shall be the promotion of any matter whatsoever of interest to its members." A student member brought an action to enjoin a proposed gift of funds to a charitable institution conducting a war on want, and to promote a political campaign against ending free milk supplies to schoolchildren. The court granted the injunction, because the purposes, whether charitable or not, were beyond those for which the union was created.

See London Hosp. Medical College v. Inland Revenue Commrs., [1976] 2 All E.R. 113, [1976] 1 W.L.R. 613.

[3]Attorney-General v. Margaret & Regius Professors, 1 Vern. 55 (1682); Cary Library v. Bliss, 151 Mass. 364, 25 N.E. 92, 7 L.R.A. 765 (1890).

See Trustees of Dartmouth College v. Woodward, 4 Wheat. 518, 642, 4 L. Ed. 629 (U.S. 1819).

[4]O'Brien v. Physicians Hosp. Assn., 96 Ohio St. 1, 116 N.E. 975, L.R.A. 1917F 741 (1917); In re Kulka's Estate, 142 Or. 104, 18 P.2d 1036 (1933).

In Brown v. National Victoria & Grey Trust Co., 35 Man. R. 2d 300 (Q.B. 1985), the residue of an estate was bequeathed on trust to pay the widow a life annuity, then to divide the trust fund into three shares, one to be paid over to a named charity, the others to be retained in trust forever and the income

If, indeed, it becomes impossible or impracticable or illegal to carry out the particular purpose for which the property was given, the court may direct the application of the property to some other charitable purpose that falls within the general charitable intention of the settlor.[5] This is the doctrine of cy pres. The power to permit such a deviation from the terms of the trust is in the court, however, and not in the settlor. The settlor's control over the property ceases as soon as the trust is created, unless he has reserved a power of control. The court in the exercise of the cy pres power may undoubtedly take into consideration the wishes of the settlor when he is still living, although he cannot insist on the court giving effect to his wishes expressed after the creation of the trust.

In New York in the statutes that permit the court to make an order under the cy pres doctrine, it is provided that no such order shall be made without the consent of the donor of the property, if he be living.[6]

It would seem that in minor matters the consent of the settlor may be effective to remove restrictions on the trustees in the administration of a charitable trust.[7]

By the Uniform Management of Institutional Funds Act §7,[8] approved in 1972, provision is made for the release of

---

paid in the discretion of the trustee to two other named charities. The court varied the trust by terminating it at once, the widow to receive $250,000 and the balance to be divided among the three named charities.

[5]See §§399-399.5.

[6]New York Estates, Powers and Trusts Law, §8-1.1, amended by Laws 1971, c. 1058, and Laws 1985, c. 492.

See also Minnesota Stat. Ann., §501.12; South Dakota Codified Laws, §§55-9-1 to 55-9-5.

[7]See St. Paul's Church v. Attorney Gen., 164 Mass. 188, 199, 41 N.E. 231 (1895); City of Fergus Falls v. Whitlock, 247 Minn. 347, 77 N.W.2d 194 (1956); Scholler Estate, 403 Pa. 97, 169 A.2d 554 (1961), aff'g 20 D.&C.2d 318 (Pa. 1960) (citing Restatement of Trusts, §367, Comment c).

For statutes and decisions as to the reformation of the terms of the trust to meet the requirements of the federal Tax Reform Act of 1969, see §348.4, n. 3.

[8]For other provisions of the Act, see §§379, 389.

This section of the Uniform Act has been substantially enacted in New York, Not-for-Profit Corporation Law, §522, as enacted by Laws 1978, c. 690.

In Williams College v. Attorney Gen., 375 Mass. 220, 375 N.E.2d 1225 (1978), it was held that a probate court in the county where the charitable

restrictions on the use or investment of funds held by charitable institutions. In Section 7 of the Act it is provided

(a) With the written consent of the donor, the governing board may release, in whole or in part, a restriction imposed by the applicable gift instrument on the use or investment of an institutional fund.

(b) If written consent of the donor cannot be obtained by reason of his death, disability, unavailability, or impossibility of identification, the governing board may apply in the name of the institution to the [appropriate] court for release of a restriction imposed by the applicable gift instrument on the use or investment of an institutional fund. The [Attorney General] shall be notified of the application and shall be given an opportunity to be heard. If the court finds that the restriction is obsolete, inappropriate, or impracticable, it may by order release the restriction in whole or in part. A release under this subsection may not change an endowment fund to a fund that is not an endowment fund.

(c) A release under this section may not allow a fund to be used for purposes other than the educational, religious, charitable, or other eleemosynary purposes of the institution affected.

(d) This section does not limit the application of the doctrine of cy pres.

§367.3.   Modification of charitable trusts by the legislature.   Where a charitable trust has been created and it is possible to carry out the purposes for which the property was given, the legislature has no power to alter the purposes to which the property is to be devoted. It has been held that an act of the legislature altering a charitable trust is in violation of the provision in the federal Constitution forbidding the states to impair the obligation of contracts.[1] In the famous *Dartmouth College*

---

corporation was located had jurisdiction to allow removal of restrictions on investments.

§367.3.   [1]Cary Library v. Bliss, 151 Mass. 364, 25 N.E. 92, 7 L.R.A. 765 (1890); Crawford v. Nies, 220 Mass. 61, 107 N.E. 382 (1914), 224 Mass. 474, 113 N.E. 408 (1916).

In City of Hartford v. Larrabee Fund Assn., 161 Conn. 312, 288 A.2d 71 (1971), funds were given to a city in trust to apply the income for needy women, an association of ladies to determine the beneficiaries. It was held that

Case[2] it was held that the state legislature had no power to alter the charter of a charitable corporation without the consent of the corporation.[3] It was said that the charter was a contract and that the amendment of the charter involved an impairment of the contract. In the case of an unincorporated charitable trust there is no charter to be altered. It was said, however, in the Dartmouth College Case that it was an impairment of the obligation of contract to divert property given by donors for one purpose to a different purpose. In *Cary Library v. Bliss*[4] the Supreme Judicial Court of Massachusetts said that the rule in the Dartmouth College Case as to the alteration of the charter of a charitable corporation "is a mere extension of the doctrine which gives a similar effect to the written statement of a scheme that is made the foundation of donations to unincorporated trustees of a public charity." It held, accordingly, that an act of the legislature making changes in a charitable trust for the maintenance of a library was unconstitutional.

---

a special act incorporating the trust was unconstitutional because the courts had exclusive power to determine whether a charitable trust should be incorporated and to determine whether the purposes of the corporation were in accordance with the terms of the trust.

As to the modification of charitable trusts by the legislature, where a town is trustee, see §348.1, n. 11.

As to the exercise of the cy pres power by the legislature, see §399.5.

[2]Trustees of Dartmouth College v. Woodward, 4 Wheat. 518, 4 L. Ed. 629 (U.S. 1819).

See Hite v. Queen's Hosp., 36 Haw. 250 (1942); Board of Regents v. Trustees of Endowment Fund, 206 Md. 559, 112 A.2d 678 (1955), *cert. denied,* 350 U.S. 836 (1955); Goldstein v. Trustees of the Sailors' Snug Harbor, 277 A.D. 269, 98 N.Y.S.2d 544 (1950).

[3]Where, however, the governing body of the corporation consents to the amendment of the charter, it has been held that the statute authorizing the amendment is not unconstitutional. See University of Md. v. Williams, 9 G.&J. 365, 31 Am. Dec. 72 (Md. 1838), *semble;* Visitors, etc. of St. John's College v. Comptroller, 23 Md. 629 (1865); Trustees of Rutgers College v. Richman, 41 N.J. Super. 259, 125 A.2d 10 (1956); In re Probate of Will of Seabrook, 90 N.J. Super. 553, 218 A.2d 648 (1966); Case of St. Mary's Church, 7 S.&R. 517 (Pa. 1822).

But see State ex rel. Pittman v. Adams, 44 Mo. 570 (1869).

See Scott, Education and the Dead Hand, 34 Harv. L. Rev. 1 (1920).

[4]151 Mass. 364, 378, 25 N.E. 92, 7 L.R.A. 765 (1890).

We shall consider hereafter the question of the power of the legislature with respect to the exercise of the cy pres power.[5]

§367A. *Termination of Charitable Trust*

The principle that a trust will not be terminated, even though all of the beneficiaries wish to terminate it, where such termination would be contrary to the intention of the settlor,[1] is applicable to charitable as well as to private trusts.

A charitable trust may be terminated where its continuance would no longer serve the purpose for which it was created. This is sometimes the case where the assets of the trust are small.[2] By a statute in Rhode Island[3] it is provided that a charitable trust with assets of less than $25,000 may be terminated at the discretion of the trustees with the consent of the Attorney General and the beneficiary or beneficiaries; and that where the trustees have discretion in the selection of the beneficiaries, only the consent of the Attorney General shall be required, and the discretion in the selection of the beneficiary or beneficiaries shall be exercised by the trustees; and that the beneficiary or beneficiaries to whom the trust estate shall be delivered shall hold and apply the trust estate for the uses and purposes set forth in the trust instrument. The statute evidently contemplates turning over the assets to one or more charitable institutions.

In New Hampshire[4] it is provided by statute that

[5]See §399.5, n. 18.

As to the power of the legislature to permit a sale of property of a charitable institution, see §381, n. 18.

§367A. [1]See §§337-337.8.

[2]Arner Estate, 65 D.&C.2d 421 (Pa. 1974) (where administration would be difficult to conform to Tax Reform Act of 1969, court authorized transfer to a charitable corporation).

As to the termination of private trusts, see §336.

[3]Rhode Island Gen. Laws 1956, §18-9-16, as inserted by Laws 1973, c. 208.

See California Prob. Code, §§15408, 15409, cited in §336, n. 2.

[4]New Hampshire Rev. Stat. Ann., §498:4-E, as inserted by Laws 1973, c. 234.

If the superior court, upon application of the trustee, or trustees, finds that the continuance of charitable trust is impracticable or unfeasible, and that the charitable purpose of the settlor or testator can be accomplished by a transfer of the trust assets to another charitable trust or corporation, or to the beneficiaries of said trust, the trust is subject to termination by the court upon such terms and conditions as it may impose. This section shall not be construed to limit or restrict the general equitable jurisdiction of the court over trustees, trusts or trust funds.

In Connecticut it is provided by statute[5] that

In any case where the current market value of the assets of a testamentary or inter vivos charitable trust is less than sixty-five thousand dollars, any trustee thereof, any charitable beneficiary specifically designated in the governing instrument or the attorney general may petition the court of probate for the district in which any such trustee resides or has its principal place of business for an order terminating the trust. Upon receipt of such a petition, the court shall order a hearing and cause notice thereof to be given to the attorney general, the trustees, the grantor of the trust, if living, and any charitable beneficiary of the trust specifically designated in the governing instrument. If at such a hearing the court determines that continuation of the trust is uneconomic when the costs of operating the trusts, probable income and other relevant factors are considered or not in the best interest of the beneficiaries, the court may order termination of the trust and distribution of the trust assets to any charitable beneficiary specifically designated in the governing instrument or, in the event no such beneficiary exists, to such other charitable trusts or charitable corporations, including any community trust or foundation, as the court may determine will fulfill the charitable purposes of the trust being so terminated.

Where income is payable indefinitely to a charitable corporation. Where a testator leaves property to trustees upon a trust of unlimited duration to pay the income to a charitable corporation, the court will not compel or permit the termination of the trust by the transfer of the principal of the trust estate to the corporation, even though the corporation is the sole beneficiary

[5]Connecticut Gen. Stat., §45-79b, as amended by Laws 1986, c. 86-234.

of the trust and desires to terminate it.[6] In *Winthrop v. Attorney*

[6]*England:* In re Levy, [1960] Ch. 346.

Kansas: In re Estate of Yetter (Simmons v. Reynolds), 183 Kan. 340, 328 P.2d 738 (1958).

Massachusetts: Winthrop v. Attorney Gen., 128 Mass. 258 (1880).

Pennsylvania: Unruh's Estate, 248 Pa. 185, 93 A. 1000 (1915); Baughman's Estate, 281 Pa. 23, 126 A. 58 (1924); Bowman's Estate, 332 Pa. 197, 2 A.2d 725 (1938); Yeager's Estate, 345 Pa. 463, 47 A.2d 813 (1946); Craig Estate, 356 Pa. 564, 52 A.2d 650 (1947), *semble;* Jordan Estate, 83 D.&C. 1 (Pa. 1952); Updegrove Estate, 12 D.&C.2d 216 (Pa. 1956) (trust held to be active).

Texas: But see City of Austin v. Austin Natl. Bank, 503 S.W.2d 759 (Tex. 1974) (bequest of income to a charitable organization gave it the property outright, no trust being intended). See §128.2.

Vermont: See In re Estate of Copeland, 123 Vt. 32, 179 A.2d 475 (1962) (citing the text).

Virginia: Maguire v. Loyd, 193 Va. 138, 67 S.E.2d 885 (1952).

Wisconsin: Estate of Goodrich, 271 Wis. 59, 72 N.W.2d 698 (1955).

Australia: Congregational Union of N.S.W. v. Thistlethwayte, 87 C.L.R. 375 (Austl., 1952); In re Dehnert, [1973] Vict. Rep. 449.

Canada: But see Brown v. National Victoria & Grey Trust Co., 35 Man. R. 2d 300 (Q.B. 1985), §367.2, n. 4, *supra.*

New Zealand: In re Flannagan, [1962] N.Z.L.R. 480; In re Clark, [1961] N.Z.L.R. 635.

But compare Syfer v. Fidelity Trust Co., 184 Md. 391, 41 A.2d 293 (1945).

In Armstrong Estate, 29 D.&C.2d 220 (Pa. 1963), a testatrix devised land to a trust company in trust to permit the use of it for a certain church and she bequeathed money to it, the income to be used for the maintenance of the church. She provided that if the church failed to use the premises as a church for five years, the land and money should go to two other charities. The church sought to terminate the trust by having the property conveyed to it, the other charities assenting. It was held that the trust should not be terminated because this would defeat the purpose of the testatrix. The court cited the text and Restatement of Trusts §337.

In Ulman Estate, 12 D.&C.2d 619 (Pa. 1957), where $5000 was left to a bank in trust to pay the income to a church for its maintenance and the principal diminished so that it was less than $1000, the court ordered that the principal be paid over to the church.

In Estate of Goodrich, 271 Wis. 59, 72 N.W.2d 698 (1955), it was held that a decree terminating a trust was not res judicata because the Attorney General had not been made a party. See §§391, 399.

In Parker v. Banks, 118 App. D.C. 60, 331 F.2d 806 (1964), a testator named an individual trustee under a trust to pay the income to Howard University. The lower court removed the trustee and appointed successor trustees. The Court of Appeals remanded with instructions to consider whether it would not be advisable under the circumstances to pay over the principal to the University and terminate the trust.

General[7] a donor gave a large sum of money to trustees in trust to invest it and to apply the income to maintain in Harvard University a museum and a professorship. Many years later the trustees and the University desired that the fund be turned over to the University to be managed by it as a part of its general funds, the University paying the income to the trustees to be applied to the purposes designated by the donor. The court refused to permit the trustees to surrender the fund to the University, on the ground that the donor intended to entrust the fund to the care and management of the trustees selected by him and their successors. In *Unruh's Estate*[8] a testatrix left the residue of her estate to trustees in trust to pay an annuity to a woman and to pay any balance of the income to an orphanage and on the death of the annuitant to pay the whole of the income to the orphanage. After the death of the annuitant the orphanage brought suit to terminate the trust by a conveyance of the corpus to the orphanage. The court refused to permit this because it would be contrary to the intention of the testatrix. Similarly, in *Baughman's Estate,*[9] where a testator left the residue of his estate in trust to pay the income to a church, it was held that the church could not compel the surrender of the trust property to it, since the testator intended that the property should be managed by the trustees and not by the church.

The court may permit the termination of the trust where its continuance would not promote the wishes of the testator. Thus in *Portsmouth Hospital v. Attorney General,*[10] where a testator left property in trust to pay the income to his sisters and after their deaths to erect and maintain an annex to an incorporated hospital, and thereafter the sisters died and the annex had been so remodeled as to form a part of the hospital building, and it was found that to continue the trust would be inefficient, the court held that the trustees should transfer the trust property to the hospital to be administered by it.

---

[7]128 Mass. 258 (1880).
[8]248 Pa. 185, 93 A. 1000 (1915).
[9]281 Pa. 23, 126 A. 58 (1924).
See Fox Estate, 16 D.&C.2d 425 (Pa. 1959).
[10]104 N.H. 51, 178 A.2d 516 (1962).

It has been held that where property is left to trustees in trust to divide the income among two or more charitable corporations, the court will not permit the termination of the trust by dividing the principal of the trust estate among the corporations, even though they all desire to terminate the trust.[11] Thus in *National Newark & Essex Banking Co. v. Arthur Sunshine Home*[12] a testatrix left the residue of her estate to her executor in trust to invest the same and divide the yearly income into three parts, one third to be paid to each of three named charitable corporations. The three corporations contended that since the income of the fund was given to them without limitation as to time, this amounted to a gift of the corpus, and that they were therefore entitled to terminate the trust and divide the corpus. The court held that they were entitled only to the income and that the trust should not be terminated.

Accelerating payment of principal to a charitable corporation. In the cases heretofore considered, a perpetual trust was intended, under which the income, and the income only, was to be paid to the charitable corporations; and the court held that it would be contrary to the intention of the creator of the trust to terminate it. There are other cases in which the creator of the trust intended that it should be terminated at a particular time, and the question was presented whether it should be terminated before that time. The answer here, as in the case of a private trust, depends on whether such termination would or would not be contrary to a material purpose of the settlor in creating the trust.[13] The court has permitted the termination of the trust when it finds that such termination would not defeat the settlor's

---

[11]*New Jersey:* National Newark & Essex Banking Co. v. Arthur Sunshine Home, 113 N.J. Eq. 313, 166 A. 635 (1933).

Pennsylvania: Smith's Estate, 56 D.&C. 60 (Pa. 1946) (citing Restatement of Trusts p. 1093).

But in Biehl Estate, 35 D.&C.2d 148 (Pa. 1965), where a testator bequeathed $12,000 to a savings fund society in trust to pay the income to four charitable corporations and the trustee disclaimed, it was held that the fund should be paid over to the four corporations.

[12]113 N.J. Eq. 313, 166 A. 635 (1933).

[13]See §§337-337.8.

purpose.[14] Thus in *Stafford's Estate,* [15] where a testatrix devised her real estate to a trust company in trust to pay the income to her brothers during their lives and then to a sister for life and on the death of the survivor to pay the principal to a charitable corporation, and after the death of one of the brothers the surviving brother and sister conveyed their interests to the charitable corporation, it was held that the corporation was entitled to a conveyance of the principal. The court found that the only purpose of the testatrix in creating the trust was to make provision for the life beneficiaries, and that because their interests had been transferred to the remainderman there was no longer any reason for continuing the trust. The court applied the same rule where the remainderman was, as here, a charitable corporation, as is applied in the case of successive interests under a private trust.[16] In *Estate of Robinson,* [17] a testatrix left her estate to three women friends for the establishment of a professorship in the University of Wisconsin always to be held by a woman, the income to be accumulated until it reached $6000 a year when it was to be paid to the Regents of the University. It was held that the court in order to save expense might properly direct that the funds be paid over to the Regents and permit them to accumulate the income.

On the other hand, the court will not compel or permit the termination of the trust where its termination would be contrary to the purpose of the settlor.[18] Thus in *Baer v. Hospital of St.*

---

[14]Citizens Natl. Bank v. St. Peters Lodge of Masons, 102 N.H. 352, 156 A.2d 768 (1959) (citing the text).

Stafford's Estate, 258 Pa. 595, 102 A. 222 (1917); Pender Estate, 68 D.&C.2d 265 (Pa. 1974) (to a hospital for the purposes designated by the testator).

[15]258 Pa. 595, 102 A. 222 (1917).

[16]See §337.1.

[17]248 Wis. 203, 21 N.W.2d 391 (1946).

[18]*Kentucky:* Plymouth Congregational Church v. Young's Trustee, 299 S.W.2d 807 (Ky. 1957).

Massachusetts: Abbott v. Williams, 268 Mass. 275, 167 N.E. 357 (1929); Springfield Safe Deposit & Trust Co. v. Friele, 304 Mass. 224, 23 N.E.2d 138 (1939); Taylor v. Albree, 309 Mass. 248, 34 N.E.2d 601 (1941) (same will as in Abbott v. Williams).

New Jersey: Baer v. Hospital of St. Barnabas, 133 N.J. Eq. 264, 31 A.2d 823

Barnabas[19] a testator left the residue of his estate to a trust company in trust to pay the income to one brother for life and on his death to pay the income to another brother for life and on the death of the survivor to pay over the corpus to a certain hospital to endow a room. The brothers and the hospital entered into an agreement for the division among them of the estate in three equal parts, and a bill was filed to terminate the trust. It was held that the bill should be dismissed. The court said that the testator intended not only that his brothers should have the protection of the income from his entire estate, but also that on their death the entire corpus should go to the hospital.

Partial termination of a charitable trust. A similar principle is applicable to the partial termination of a trust. As in the case of a private trust,[20] the trust is terminable if, but only if, the termination would not be contrary to a material purpose of the settlor in creating the trust. In some cases, however, the court has permitted the termination of the trust.[21] Thus in *Welch v. Episcopal Theological School,*[22] where a testator bequeathed his estate in trust to pay the income in equal shares to his wife, his son, or his son's wife and to a theological school, with a provision that

---

(1943), *aff'g* Baer v. Fidelity Union Trust Co., 132 N.J. Eq. 333, 28 A.2d 275 (1942).

Pennsylvania: Estate of Tonner, 508 A.2d 1237 (Pa. Super. 1986).

In Franklin Found. v. Attorney Gen., 340 Mass. 197, 163 N.E.2d 662 (1960), where Benjamin Franklin created a trust to make loans to young artificers and, after 200 years, to pay the principal and accumulated income to the Commonwealth of Massachusetts and to the City of Boston, and such loans became impossible and the funds were invested, it was held that the trust should not be terminated by conveying the property to the Franklin Foundation, even though the Commonwealth and City consented. The court said that the testator's purpose was not merely to aid artificers but was to accumulate the fund for the Commonwealth and City. The court cited the text.

[19]133 N.J. Eq. 264, 31 A.2d 823 (1943), *aff'g* Baer v. Fidelity Union Trust Co., 132 N.J. Eq. 333, 28 A.2d 275 (1942).

[20]See §337.8.

[21]Welch v. Episcopal Theological School, 189 Mass. 108, 75 N.E. 139 (1905); State Historical Socy. v. Foster, 172 Wis. 155, 177 N.W. 16 (1920). See Queen's Hosp. v. Hite, 38 Haw. 494 (1950).

[22]189 Mass. 108, 75 N.E. 139 (1905).

on the death of the wife and on the death of the son and his wife their thirds were to be paid to the school, and the principal was payable to the school on the death of the life beneficiaries, it was held that after the death of the wife and son and with the consent of the son's wife the school was entitled to a conveyance of two thirds of the corpus. In *State Historical Society v. Foster*,[23] where a testator left property in trust to pay an annuity to his son and if he should marry to pay an annuity to his wife, with a gift over to a charitable corporation on his death without issue, it was held that on the death of the son without issue leaving a wife, the charitable corporation could compel the trustees to convey the trust estate to it subject to a charge to pay the annuity to the son's widow.

On the other hand, the court will not direct or permit a partial termination of the trust where this would be contrary to the settlor's intention.[24]

The experience in Pennsylvania is interesting. In *Biddle's Appeal*[25] a testator left his property in trust to pay a number of annuities and on the death of the survivor of the annuitants to pay the principal to a charitable corporation. Shortly afterward the corporation brought suit to compel the trustees to pay over the principal sum, after setting aside a sufficient amount for the payment of the annuities. The court held that the termination of the trust would be contrary to the intention of the testator and that no part of the principal should be paid to the corporation. Thereafter, another action was brought and the court again declined to terminate the trust.[26] Thereafter, a statute was passed providing that when in a trust created by deed or by will by a person who before or after the passage of the statute has

[23]172 Wis. 155, 177 N.W. 16 (1920).

[24]First Methodist Episcopal Church v. Hull, 225 Iowa 306, 280 N.W. 531 (1938) (court refused to compel annuitant to accept an annuity purchased from an insurance company); Abbott v. Williams, 268 Mass. 275, 167 N.E. 357 (1929); Weeks v. Pierce, 279 Mass. 108, 181 N.E. 231 (1932); Biddle's Appeal, 99 Pa. 525 (1882); Derbyshire's Estate, 239 Pa. 389, 86 A. 878 (1913).

See Teplitz Trust, 75 D.&C.2d 601 (Pa. 1975), where the testator directed an accumulation of income.

[25]99 Pa. 525 (1882).

[26]Derbyshire's Estate, 239 Pa. 389, 86 A. 878 (1913).

died domiciled in the state the payment of annuities or estates
for lives or for years is directed with a vested remainder to a
charitable corporation, and the annuitants or life beneficiaries
and corporation agree on the termination of the trust or have
assigned their interests to the corporation, the court may direct
the termination of the trust, except where the trust instrument
provides for an accumulation for the benefit of the corporation.[27] Thereafter, a proceeding was brought for the termination of the trust with the consent of the surviving annuitants and
the corporation, and it was held that the trust should be terminated.[28] Even under the statute, however, it has been held
that the court will not terminate the trust where the interests of
the annuitants are not assignable by them or reachable by their
creditors, in other words, where it is a spendthrift trust.[29] It has
also been held that the statute does not apply where by the terms
of the trust the income is to be paid to a charitable corporation
forever.[30] The statute was, however, repealed in 1947 and an
entirely new provision was made with respect to the termination
of trusts, giving the court, within limitations, a broad discretionary power.[31]

Power to form or convey to a charitable corporation. We consider
elsewhere the question whether, where property is given to
trustees in trust for charitable purposes, they can properly dele-

[27]Pa. Stat. Ann. (Purdon), tit. 20, §3251.

[28]Derbyshire's Estate, 306 Pa. 278, 159 A. 439 (1932), *aff'g* 16 D.&C. 200
(Pa. 1931).

[29]Harrison's Estate, 322 Pa. 532, 185 A. 766 (1936), *aff'g* 25 D.&C. 133
(Pa. 1935).

Compare Slater's Estate, 316 Pa. 56, 173 A. 399 (1934).

[30]Yeager's Estate, 345 Pa. 463, 47 A.2d 813 (1946).

[31]20 Pa. Cons. Stat., §6102, as amended by Laws 1976, c. 135, and by Laws
1980, P.L. 565, Laws 1982, P.L. 45. 20 Pa. Cons. Stat., §6110(b) and (c), added
by Laws 1982, Act No. 1982-26, §10, empowers the trustee of a charitable trust
with assets not exceeding $10,000, with the approval of the Attorney General,
to terminate the trust and apply the assets cy pres. It also empowers the court
to direct termination and cy pres application of the property of charitable
trusts that have administrative expenses or other burdens unreasonably out of
proportion to the charitable benefits.

See §337.2, n. 5.

gate the administration of the trust by conveying the property to an existing corporation; we also consider the question whether the trustees can properly form a corporation for the purpose of taking over the administration of the trust.[32]

TOPIC 3.　NATURE OF CHARITABLE PURPOSES

§368.　What Purposes Are Charitable

It is impossible to enumerate all the purposes that have been held by the courts to be charitable purposes or that may hereafter be held to be charitable purposes. Certain purposes are clearly charitable. These include the relief of poverty, the promotion of education, the advancement of religion. So too, it is well settled that the promotion of health is a charitable purpose. So are governmental or municipal purposes, such as the erection of public buildings, the laying out of highways, the erection of bridges, and the like. In addition to these purposes there must be added a more general and indefinite category, a general catchall, to include the vast number of miscellaneous purposes that are properly held to be charitable. Perhaps these can best be included under the heading of other purposes the accomplishment of which is beneficial to the community. This category is, indeed, broad enough to cover all charitable purposes, including those more specifically enumerated above. It is helpful, however, to consider separately those types of purposes that are and have long been definitely classified as charitable purposes, before dealing with the more doubtful cases.[1]

In the leading case of *Commissioners for Special Purposes of Income Tax v. Pemsel*,[2] Lord Macnaghten thus expressed the judicial idea of the scope of charitable purposes:

[32]See §385A.

§368.　[1]See §348.

[2][1891] A.C. 531, 583.

See Arnold v. Commissioner of Corps. & Taxation, 327 Mass. 694, 100 N.E.2d 851 (1951) (citing the text and Restatement of Trusts, §368, Comment *a*).

See Brunyate, The Legal Definition of Charity, 61 L.Q. Rev. 268 (1945).

'Charity' in its legal sense comprises four principal divisions: trusts for the relief of poverty; trusts for the advancement of education; trusts for the advancement of religion; and trusts for other purposes beneficial to the community, not falling under any of the preceding heads. The trusts last referred to are not the less charitable in the eye of the law, because incidentally they benefit the rich as well as the poor, as indeed, every charity that deserves the name must do either directly or indirectly.

A much-quoted definition of charitable trusts is that of Mr. Justice Gray. He says that

A charity, in the legal sense, may be more fully defined as a gift, to be applied consistently with existing laws, for the benefit of an indefinite number of persons, either by bringing their minds or hearts under the influence of education or religion, by relieving their bodies from disease, suffering or constraint, by assisting them to establish themselves in life, or by erecting or maintaining public buildings or works or otherwise lessening the burdens of government.[3]

The only difficulty with this definition is that it is not broad enough; it includes purposes that are undoubtedly charitable, but these are not the only purposes that are held to be charitable.

Another frequently quoted definition is that of Horace Binney in his argument in *Vidal v. Girard's Executors.*[4] He defined a charitable trust as "whatever is given for the love of God, or for the love of your neighbor, in the catholic and universal sense — given from these motives and to these ends — free from the stain or taint of every consideration that is personal, private or selfish." From the legal point of view, perhaps, no definition could be worse than this. It makes the matter depend on the motive of the donor, rather than the purpose to which the property is to be applied. It is well settled that the motive of the

---

[3]Jackson v. Phillips, 14 Allen 539, 556 (Mass. 1867).

[4]2 How. 127, 11 L. Ed. 205 (U.S. 1844). See Girard Will Case, p. 62, published in 1854, containing the arguments of the defendants' counsel. See §348.

donor is immaterial.[5] A trust is none the less charitable although

[5]*England:* Hoare v. Osborne, L.R. 1 Eq. 585 (1866); In re King, [1923] 1 Ch. 243 (memorial window in church).

Federal: Holdeen v. Ratterree, 292 F.2d 338 (2d Cir. 1961) (citing the text, §348).

California: Estate of Loring, 29 Cal. 2d 423, 175 P.2d 524 (1946), *mod'g* 168 P.2d 224 (Cal. App. 1946); Estate of Butin, 81 Cal. App. 2d 76, 183 P.2d 304 (1947), noted in 46 Mich. L. Rev. 705; Estate of Robbins, 57 Cal. 2d 718, 371 P.2d 573 (1962) (citing the text and Restatement of Trusts, §368, Comment *d*), noted in 48 Iowa L. Rev. 1019, 8 Utah L. Rev. 152, 20 Wash. & Lee L. Rev. 1019; In re Mayer's Estate, 237 Cal. App. 2d 549, 47 Cal. Rptr. 44 (1965) (citing Restatement of Trusts, §368, Comment *d*); In re Estate of Zahn, 16 Cal. App. 3d 106, 93 Cal. Rptr. 810 (1970), *cert. denied,* 404 U.S. 938 (1971), *rehearing denied,* 404 U.S. 996 (1971).

Illinois: French v. Calkins, 252 Ill. 243, 96 N.E. 877 (1911); First National Bank of Chicago v. Elliott, 406 Ill. 44, 92 N.E.2d 66 (1950).

Indiana: Scobey v. Beckman, 111 Ind. App. 574, 41 N.E.2d 847 (1942) (memorial to son of testatrix), noted in 41 Mich. L. Rev. 332; Quinn v. Peoples Trust & Sav. Co., 223 Ind. 317, 60 N.E.2d 281, 157 A.L.R. 885 (1945) (citing Restatement of Trusts, §368, Comment *d*).

Kentucky: Goode's Admr. v. Goode, 238 Ky. 620, 38 S.W.2d 691 (1931).

Maine: Bills v. Pease, 116 Me. 98, 100 A. 146, L.R.A. 1917D 1060 (1917).

Massachusetts: Massachusetts Inst. of Technology v. Attorney Gen., 235 Mass. 288, 126 N.E. 521 (1920); Mackey v. Bowen, 332 Mass. 167, 124 N.E.2d 254 (1955) (citing the text).

Missouri: Odom v. Langston, 355 Mo. 109, 195 S.W.2d 466 (1946), noted in 12 Mo. L. Rev. 443.

New Jersey: First Camden Natl. Bank & Trust Co. v. Collins, 110 N.J. Eq. 623, 160 A. 848 (1932), *rev'd on other grounds,* 114 N.J. Eq. 59, 168 A. 275 (1933), noted in 3 Mercer Beasley L. Rev. 117, 31 Mich. L. Rev. 1167, 20 Va. L. Rev. 365; Woodstown Natl. Bank & Trust Co. v. Snelbaker, 136 N.J. Eq. 62, 40 A.2d 222 (1944), *aff'd mem.,* 137 N.J. Eq. 256, 44 A.2d 210 (1945); Martin v. Haycock, 140 N.J. Eq. 450, 55 A.2d 60 (1947); Mirinda v. King, 11 N.J. Super. 165, 78 A.2d 98 (1951) (quoting Restatement of Trusts, §368, Comment *d*).

New York: Matter of Browning, 165 Misc. 819, 1 N.Y.S.2d 825 (1938), *aff'd mem.,* 254 A.D. 843, 6 N.Y.S.2d 339 (1938), *aff'd mem.,* 281 N.Y. 577, 22 N.E.2d 160 (1939); Matter of Everson, 268 A.D. 425, 52 N.Y.S.2d 395 (1944), *aff'd mem.,* 295 N.Y. 622, 64 N.E.2d 653 (1945); Matter of Rupprecht, 271 A.D. 376, 65 N.Y.S.2d 909 (1946), *aff'd mem.,* 297 N.Y. 462, 74 N.E.2d 175 (1947); Matter of Merritt, 273 A.D. 79, 75 N.Y.S.2d 828 (1947), *aff'g* 185 Misc. 979, 61 N.Y.S.2d 537 (1945).

Ohio: Becker v. Fisher, 112 Ohio St. 284, 147 N.E. 744 (1925); Heinlein v. Elyria Sav. & Trust Co., 75 Ohio App. 353, 62 N.E.2d 284 (1945); Murr v. Youse, 52 Ohio Abs. 321, 80 N.E.2d 788 (1946).

Pennsylvania: Fire Ins. Patrol v. Boyd, 120 Pa. 624, 15 A. 553, 1 L.R.A. 417,

the donor was actuated by a desire to glorify himself or by a desire to spite his relatives. On the other hand, the fact that the donor was actuated by the highest motives in creating the trust or the fact that he regarded it as a charitable trust does not make it so, if the purposes to which the property is to be devoted are not such as are recognized by the courts as charitable.[6] St. Paul, it is true, in his tribute to the virtue of charity, was speaking of the motive rather than the purpose; but St. Paul was not attempting to define charitable trusts or to deal with the question of their validity under the Anglo-American system of jurisprudence.[7]

The truth of the matter is that it is impossible to frame a perfect definition of charitable purposes. There is no fixed standard to determine what purposes are charitable. In the Restatement of Trusts it is pointed out that a purpose is charitable if its accomplishment is of such social interest to the community as to justify permitting property to be devoted to the purpose in perpetuity. The interests of the community, however, vary with time and place. Purposes that may be regarded as laudable at one time may at other times be regarded as serving no useful purpose or even as being illegal. So too what in one community is regarded as beneficial to the community may in another be regarded as useless if not detrimental. As to some purposes there is a general agreement as to their value to the community in all civilized places, but as to others there are conflicting opin-

---

6 Am. St. Rep. 745 (1888); Smith's Estate, 181 Pa. 109, 37 A. 114 (1897) (memorial to include bronze statue of testator); Archambault's Estate, 308 Pa. 549, 162 A. 801 (1932); Abel v. Girard Trust Co., 365 Pa. 44, 73 A.2d 682 (1950), noted in 24 Temp. L.Q. 373; McKee Estate, 378 Pa. 607, 108 A.2d 214 (1954).

Texas: Wooten v. Fitz-Gerald, 440 S.W.2d 719 (Tex. Civ. App. 1969), *writ refused, n.r.e.* (citing Restatement of Trusts §368).

New Zealand: Grant v. Commissioner of Stamp Duties, [1943] N.Z.L.R. 113.

See §374.9.

[6]*Federal:* See Paris v. United States, 381 F. Supp. 597 (N.D. Ohio 1974).

New York: See Matter of Frasch, 245 N.Y. 174, 182, 156 N.E. 656 (1927).

Ohio: Barton v. Parrott, 25 Ohio Misc. 2d 8, 495 N.E.2d 973 (Ohio C.P. 1984), citing text (trust to run annual horse race in memory of testatrix's daughter).

[7]1 Corinthians 13.

ions. We shall attempt in the sections that follow to point out the purposes that have generally been recognized in England and in the United States as charitable purposes.[8]

In the so-called Nathan Report,[9] presented to Parliament in 1952, the committee made the following recommendation:

[8]By Georgia Code 1981, §53-12-70, it is provided that the following subjects are proper matters of charity for the jurisdiction of equity: (1) relief of aged, impotent, diseased, or poor people; (2) every educational purpose; (3) religious instruction or worship; (4) construction or repair of public works, or highways, or other public conveniences; (5) promotion of any craft or persons engaging therein; (6) redemption or relief of prisoners or captives; (7) improvement or repair of cemeteries or tombstones; (8) other similar subjects, having for their object the relief of human suffering or the promotion of human civilization.

In Pennsylvania by the Estates Act of 1947 (20 Pa. Cons. Stat., §6101,) it is provided: " 'Charity' or 'charitable purpose' includes but is not limited to the relief of poverty, the advancement of education, the advancement of religion, the promotion of health, governmental or municipal purposes, or other purposes the accomplishment of which is beneficial to the community." This is substantially the language of the Restatement of Trusts §368.

For a broad statutory definition of charity, see Oklahoma Stat. Ann., tit. 60, §601.

See Wisconsin Stat., §701.10 (using the language of the Restatement of Trusts §368).

See the statutes cited in §398.1, n. 20.

Thus in the New York Estates, Powers and Trusts Law, §8-1.1, it is provided that "no disposition of property for religious, charitable, educational or benevolent purposes, otherwise valid under the laws of this state, is invalid by reason of the indefiniteness or uncertainty of the persons designated as beneficiaries." Note that the word "charitable" is used, and not "relief of poverty," and that the word "benevolent" is used as a catchall to cover other charitable purposes.

Although in the statutes the word "charity" is generally interpreted broadly as covering all the purposes that are held to be charitable at common law, the courts occasionally in the cases involving tax exemption interpret it as limited to the popular sense of relief of poverty. See §372 (hospitals); §374.9 (cemeteries); §374.11A (housing for the aged).

See Shenandoah Valley Natl. Bank v. Taylor, 192 Va. 135, 63 S.E.2d 786, 25 A.L.R.2d 1104 (1951) (citing the text and quoting Restatement of Trusts §368), noted in 23 Miss. L.J. 62, 20 U. Cin. L. Rev. 505, 37 Va. L. Rev. 642, 9 Wash. & Lee L. Rev. 310.

See Atiyah, Public Benefit in Charities, 21 Mod. L. Rev. 138 (1958); Sacks, The Role of Philanthropy: An Institutional View, 46 Va. L. Rev. 516 (1960).

[9]Report of the Committee on the Law and Practice Relating to Charitable Trusts (Cmd. 8710) 36.

We consider that a rewording of the 'definition' of charity is needed and we favour a definition which would allow of flexibility in interpretation. We recommend that the existing 'definition' of charity by reference to the Preamble of the Statute of Charitable Uses should be repealed and that in its stead there should be put on the Statute book a 'definition' based on Lord Macnaghten's classification, but preserving the case law as it stands.

For the reasons stated above, it would seem that even the Parliament cannot frame a definition that would successfully include what should be included and exclude what should not be included. Matters of grave policy like this cannot be solved by definition.

Statutory provisions. The statutes dealing with dispositions for charitable purposes are often somewhat rambling in the choice of adjectives. This is so whether the statute deals with the validity of a charitable trust,[10] or with the disposition cy pres on the failure of the purpose,[11] or with the dissolution of a charitable corporation,[12] or with exemptions from taxation.[13]

In New York, where charitable trusts were held to be invalid under the common law of the state, a statute[14] provides that "No disposition of property for religious, charitable, educational, or benevolent purposes is invalid for the indefiniteness of the beneficiaries." Here there are interspersed two specific words, "religious" and "educational," and two general words, "charitable" and "benevolent." It seems clear that the word "charitable" was not intended to be restricted to the relief of poverty, but was intended to include other purposes recognized generally as

---

[10]See §348.3, n. 9.

[11]See §399, n. 2.

[12]See §397.3, n. 15.

[13]See §348.4, n. 1.

[14]New York Estates, Powers and Trusts Law §8-1.1, as amended by Laws 1971, c. 1058, and Laws 1985, c. 492.

The same words are used in subsections dealing with cy pres, accumulations, and the standing of the Attorney General.

In the New York Not-for-Profit Corporation Law §201, dealing with the dissolution of charitable corporations, the words are "charitable, educational, religious, scientific, literary, cultural or for the prevention of cruelty to children or animals."

charitable. There is a question as to the scope of the word "benevolent." The better view is that it is not intended to go beyond "charitable," although when a settlor uses the word, it is unfortunately held in England and in some states not to be limited to charity, and to cause the intended trust to fail.[15]

In several of the statutes the word "eleemosynary" is used. Thus in Maine a statute[16] relating to the dissolution of a charitable corporation uses the words "charitable, religious, eleemosynary, benevolent or educational." A Connecticut statute[17] uses the same words but adds "or similar purposes." The Uniform Management of Institutional Funds Act[18] is applicable to organizations "for educational, religious, charitable, or other eleemosynary purposes, or a governmental organization to the extent that it holds funds exclusively for any of these purposes." The word "eleemosynary" is generally defined in the dictionaries both in a narrow sense as "almsgiving" and in a broad sense as "charitable." It seems clear that in the statutes it is used in the broad sense as synonymous with "charitable."[19]

A case dealing with the interpretation of loose language as to the scope of charity arose in Massachusetts.[20] A statute[21] provided that on the dissolution of a "charitable corporation constituting a public charity," the Supreme Judicial Court should have exclusive jurisdiction to authorize the disposition of its funds "for such similar public charitable purpose" as the court might determine. The plaintiff, a Congregational church, brought suit in the Superior Court, seeking a decree of dissolution and the disposition of its assets. That court awarded the assets to two other churches. On appeal the suit was dismissed for lack of jurisdiction of the Superior Court. It was contended by the plaintiff that the statute did not apply to religious organi-

[15]See §398.1.

[16]Maine Rev. Stat. Ann., tit. 13-B, §407, as amended by Laws 1978, c. 592.

[17]Connecticut Gen. Stat. 1958, §33-490.

[18]See §389, n. 16.

[19]See People v. Cogswell, 113 Cal. 129, 45 P. 270 (1896).

The word is used in both the Greek and Latin versions of the New Testament. In the King James version it is translated as alms-giving. Matthew 6:2-4.

[20]Congregational Church of Chicopee Falls v. Attorney Gen., 376 Mass. 545, 381 N.E.2d 1305 (1978).

[21]Mass. Ann. Laws, c. 180, §11A.

zations because it used only the words "charitable" and "charity," whereas in another section of the statute dealing with the formation of an organization it used the words "any civic, educational, charitable, benevolent or religious purpose."[22] The court held that the word "charitable" was not distinct from but included "religious."[23] It was also contended that the statute used the words "public charity," and that a church served only a part of the community. The court rejected the contention. The word "public" adds nothing. Every charitable trust is a public trust as distinguished from a private trust. It is not limited to trusts for governmental or municipal purposes, such as public schools and hospitals, and parks and public buildings.[24]

In Wisconsin it was formerly provided that "no trust for charitable or public purposes" should be invalid. But in 1971 a statute[25] was enacted, based on the Restatement of Trusts, which provided: "A charitable trust may be created for any of the following charitable purposes: relief of poverty, advancement of education, advancement of religion, promotion of

---

[22]Mass. Ann. Laws, c. 180, §4.

[23]As to this the court said: "This might suggest a line of demarcation between 'charitable' and 'religious'; but to hold that 'charitable' is not thus distinct from 'religious,' and encompasses or engrosses 'religious,' appeals to common sense and conforms to ordinary speech."

[24]See §§370.5, 373, 373.1.

As to the cy pres doctrine, see Mass Ann. Laws, c. 12, §8K, using the words "public charitable purpose."

In the Congregational Church case the court said: "That the church was a 'public charity' might be challenged on the ground of the private or limited rather than general or indefinite range of its beneficiaries. Such a contention, which commanded some support in earlier days (citing cases), is overwhelmed by our more recent authority" (citing cases and the Restatement of Trusts §§368, 371, and the text).

Minnesota Stat. Ann., §501.12, uses the words, "any charitable, benevolent, educational, religious or other public use or trust."

Although the fact that the word "public" is used in a statute or trust instrument adds or subtracts nothing from the word "charitable," so far as the validity of the trust is concerned, in statutes as to exemption from taxation is concerned it may be construed to require a wider scope as to those who are to benefit. See, for example, Brattleboro Child Dev. v. Town of Brattleboro, 138 Vt. 402, 416 A.2d 152 (1980).

See §§348.4, 370.5, 373, 373.1.

[25]Wis. Stats. §701.10.

health, governmental or municipal purposes or any other purpose the accomplishment of which is beneficial to the community."

This is indeed the effect generally given to statutes dealing
with charitable trusts and corporations, even though they are
unclear in their wording. It is in accordance with the results
reached by the courts in the absence of a statute as to the scope
of charity.

There are generally more elaborate statutory provisions
dealing with exemption from taxation, state and federal.[26]

§368.1. The Statute of Charitable Uses. In 1601,
shortly before the death of Queen Elizabeth, Parliament enacted
the famous statute known as the Statute of Charitable Uses.[1]
This statute provided that the chancellor might from time to
time award commissions to the bishop of every diocese and to
other persons, authorizing them to inquire into abuses and
breaches of trust where property is given for charitable purposes, and to make such orders, judgments, and decrees as
should be necessary to carry out the purposes for which the
donors had given the property, and which should be valid until
altered by the chancellor. The statute thus provided machinery
for the enforcement of charitable trusts. The importance of the
statute, however, lies not in the procedure thus authorized, for
it appears after a time to have been little employed, but in the
provisions of the preamble of the statute, which contains an
enumeration of charitable purposes. The preamble states that
property given for charitable purposes has frequently been
misapplied, and enumerates among the purposes for which
property has been given:

> some for relief of aged, impotent and poor people, some for
> maintenance of sick and maimed soldiers and mariners, schools
> of learning, free schools, and scholars in universities, some for
> repair of bridges, ports, havens, causeways, churches, sea-banks
> and highways, some for education and preferment of orphans,

[26]See §348.4, n. 1.
See Ginsberg, The Real Property Tax Exemption of Nonprofit Organizations: A Perspective, 53 Temp. L.Q. 291 (1980).
§368.1. [1]Stat. 43 Eliz. I, c. 4 (1601).

some for or towards relief, stock or maintenance for houses of correction, some for marriages of poor maids, some for supportation, aid and help of young tradesmen, handicraftsmen and persons decayed, and others for relief or redemption of prisoners or captives, and for aid or ease of any poor inhabitants concerning payments of fifteens, setting out of soldiers and other taxes.

This enumeration is not and clearly was not intended to be exhaustive. It merely gives typical instances of purposes that are charitable. The courts, both in England and in the United States, have frequently had recourse to the statute as showing the kind of purpose that is charitable. Any purpose is charitable that falls within one of these types, but it may also be charitable although it does not, if the purpose is more or less analogous to one or more of the purposes specified in the statute. Many of the purposes specified have to do with the relief of poverty in one way or another. Some of them have to do with the advancement of education. One of them has to do with public works. One of them deals with the promotion of health, although it actually refers only to sick and maimed soldiers and mariners. Some of the purposes combine relief of poverty with educational purposes. It is interesting to note that the only mention of religion is the repair of churches, and yet it soon was held by the courts that the promotion of religion, or at least of what was regarded as the proper religion, is charitable. The tendency of the courts through the centuries that have elapsed since the enactment of the statute has been gradually to enlarge the scope of charitable purposes, with the result that the purposes enumerated in the statute include only a few of those that are now regarded as charitable.[2]

[2]Scottish Burial Reform and Cremation Socy. v. Glasgow Corp., [1968] A.C. 138 (Scottish corporation to encourage and provide facilities for cremation held tax exempt, since cremation is for the public benefit within the spirit of the Statute of Charitable Uses); Incorporated Council of Law Reporting v. Attorney-General, [1972] Ch. 73, noted in 88 L. Quar. Rev. 171, *aff'g* [1971] Ch. 626 (nonprofit corporation formed for reporting judicial decisions: held within the spirit of the Statute of Charitable Uses, either as an educational purpose or one for the public benefit and not merely for the profit of lawyers); Incorporated Council of Law Reporting (Queensland) v. Federal Commr. of Taxation, [1972] A.L.R. 127 (Austl.) (nonprofit corporation formed for reporting judicial decisions).

As we have seen, it was once thought by some judges and writers that the law of charitable trusts had its origin in the Statute of Charitable Uses, and that charitable trusts could not be upheld in a state which rejected that statute.[3] It was later learned that charitable trusts were enforced in the Court of Chancery prior to the enactment of the statute, and that charitable trusts never depended for their validity on the provisions of the statute.

§369. Relief of Poverty

Trusts for the relief of poverty have always been held to be charitable. A large proportion of the charitable trusts created prior to the Statute of Charitable Uses and mentioned in the Calendars of Chancery, and in the Reports of the Charity Commissioners, to which reference has heretofore been made, were trusts for the relief of poverty. The preamble to the Statute of Charitable Uses makes reference to this purpose in various forms, mentioning relief of aged, impotent and poor people, education and preferment of orphans, marriages of poor maids, aid of young tradesmen, handicraftsmen and persons decayed, and aid of poor inhabitants concerning taxes. These are, of course, merely instances of trusts for the relief of poverty, and there are numerous cases of other trusts to relieve the poor that have been upheld as charitable.[1]

In Royal Natl. Agric. & Indus. Assn. v. Chester, [1974] 48 A.L.J.R. 304 (Austl.), noted in 91 L.Q. Rev. 167, it was held that a trust to spend the income "in improving the breeding and racing of Homer pigeons," was not within the purposes of the Statute of Charitable Uses and was invalid.

[3] See §348.3.

§369.   [1] *England:* Attorney-General v. Wansey, 15 Ves. 231 (1808) (apprenticing poor boys); Thompson v. Thompson, 1 Coll. 381 (1844) (distribution of bread at testator's mausoleum); Biscoe v. Jackson, 35 Ch. D. 460 (1886) (soup kitchen and cottage hospital); In re Gardom, [1914] 1 Ch. 662, 84 L.J. Ch. 749 (1915) (temporary house of residence for ladies of limited means); In re Monk, [1927] 2 Ch. 197 (coal fund and loan fund for poor), noted in 165 L.T. 186; In re James, [1932] 2 Ch. 25 (to establish a home for rest); In re Tree, [1945] Ch. 325 (to assist persons to emigrate to British Dominions), noted in 19 Aust. L.J. 122, 10 Convey. (N.S.) 53, 61 L.Q. Rev. 339, 199 L.T. 197; In re Sahal's Will Trusts, [1958] 3 All E.R. 428 (for a hostel for young soldiers,

The methods of aiding the poor have varied from time to

sailors, airmen, or merchant seamen or for poor aged and infirm people), noted in 75 L.Q. Rev. 22; In re Paylings Will Trusts, [1969] 3 All E.R. 698 (home for the aged, although fund insufficient to do more than supply rent-free housing).

Arizona: Olivas v. Board of Missions, 1 Ariz. App. 543, 405 P.2d 481 (1965) (homesite for Indians, citing the text).

California: In re Wood, 108 Cal. App. 694, 292 P. 144 (1930) (to purchase useful and pleasing Christmas presents for inmates of orphans' home); Pacific Home v. County of Los Angeles, 41 Cal. 2d 844, 264 P.2d 539 (1953), *aff'g* 256 P.2d 36 (1953) (a home for aged and infirm persons held exempt from taxation); Samarkand of Santa Barbara v. County of Santa Barbara, 216 Cal. App. 2d 341, 31 Cal. Rptr. 151 (1963) (nonprofit corporation to provide food, lodging, and medical care to elderly persons, a tax case); John Tennant Memorial Home v. City of Pacific Grove, 27 Cal. App. 3d 372, 103 Cal. Rptr. 215 (1972) (retirement home; a tax case).

Connecticut: Strong's Appeal from Probate, 68 Conn. 527, 37 A. 395 (1897) (to aid worthy poor by providing food and clothing).

Georgia: Strother v. Kennedy, 218 Ga. 180, 127 S.E.2d 19 (1962) (to establish home for indigent colored people residing in Augusta).

Illinois: First Natl. Bank of Chicago v. Elliott, 406 Ill. 44, 92 N.E.2d 66 (1950) (to establish and maintain orphans' home).

Kansas: Treadwell v. Beebe, 107 Kan. 31, 190 P. 768, 10 A.L.R. 1359 (1920) (to buy food and fuel for needy residents of city).

Massachusetts: City of Boston v. Doyle, 184 Mass. 373, 68 N.E. 851 (1903) (loan fund); Lord v. Miller, 277 Mass. 276, 178 N.E. 649 (1931) (to assist persons in need); City Bank Farmers Trust Co. v. Carpenter, 319 Mass. 78, 64 N.E.2d 636 (1946) (to town to maintain home for poor); Clark v. Mayor of Gloucester, 336 Mass. 631, 147 N.E.2d 191 (1958) (to city to maintain home for indigent females, of sixty years of age or over, natives of city).

Missouri: Missouri Goodwill Indus. v. Gruner, 357 Mo. 647, 210 S.W.2d 38 (1948) (corporation obtaining donations of secondhand articles and reconditioning and selling them in order to give employment to handicapped persons, held exempt from property tax).

Nebraska: In re Estate of Creighton, 91 Neb. 654, 136 N.W. 1001, Ann. Cas. 1913D 128 (1912) (home for poor working girls).

New Hampshire: Towle v. Nesmith, 69 N.H. 212, 42 A. 900 (1897) (to buy meal, flour, and fish for poor widows and children under ten years of age).

New Jersey: Hilliard v. Parker, 76 N.J. Eq. 447, 74 A. 447 (1909) (to purchase fuel for most needy women of a town); McCran v. Kay, 93 N.J. Eq. 352, 115 A. 649 (1921) (lodging-house for destitute women); Guaranty Trust Co. of N.Y. v. New York Community Trust, 139 N.J. Eq. 144, 50 A.2d 161 (1946), 141 N.J. Eq. 238, 56 A.2d 907 (1948), *aff'd mem.,* 142 N.J. Eq. 726, 61 A.2d 239 (1948) (furnishing shoes for needy actors).

New York: Matter of Robinson, 203 N.Y. 380, 96 N.E. 925, 37 L.R.A. (N.S.) 1023 (1911) (to provide shelter and financial aid to persons in need); Matter

time. Good-hearted testators, ignorant of sociological science,

---

of Martyn, 99 N.Y.S.2d 28 (1945) (to such indigent persons as executrices deem proper); Matter of Murray, 198 Misc. 45, 99 N.Y.S.2d 32 (1948) (to assist needy Salvation Army officers); Matter of Hare, 1 Misc. 2d 114, 149 N.Y.S.2d 428 (1955) (vacations for underprivileged children); Belle Harbor Home v. Tishelman, 100 Misc. 2d 911, 420 N.Y.S.2d 343 (1979), *aff'd,* 81 A.D.2d 886, 441 N.Y.S.2d 413 (1981) (home for the aged; a tax case).

North Carolina: Bennett v. Attorney Gen., 245 N.C. 312, 96 S.E.2d 46 (1957) (home for aged and homeless ladies).

Ohio: Danner v. Shanafelt, 159 Ohio St. 5, 110 N.E.2d 772 (1953) (distribution of income each year among the poor of a town); Lewis v. Board of County Commrs., 98 Ohio App. 192, 128 N.E.2d 818 (1954) (to county to support home for old ladies); Edgeter v. Kemper, 73 Ohio Abs. 297, 136 N.E.2d 630 (1955) (fund bequeathed to the United States for benefit of indigent American Indians; citing the text and Restatement of Trusts §369).

Pennsylvania: McIlvaine Estate, 349 Pa. 380, 37 A.2d 580 (1944) (home for aged); Myers Estate, 351 Pa. 472, 41 A.2d 570 (1945) (homes for friendless); Lycoming House v. Board of Revision of Taxes, 64 D.&C. (Pa. 1948) (residence and grounds used as retreat for aged and needy gentlewomen; tax case).

Tennessee: Eledge v. Dixon, 193 Tenn. 654, 249 S.W.2d 886 (1952) (needy children).

Texas: Morse v. First Natl. Bank of Galveston, 194 S.W.2d 578 (Tex. Civ. App. 1946) (to distribute among poor of the Island of Jersey; citing Restatement of Trusts §369); Wooten v. Fitz-Gerald, 440 S.W.2d 719 (Tex. Civ. App. 1969), *writ refused, n.r.e.* (to establish a home for aged men).

Virginia: McClure v. Carter, 202 Va. 191, 116 S.E.2d 260 (1960) (to maintain a home for indigent widows and maiden ladies).

Wisconsin: Stat., §§701.27, 853.40, as amended by Laws 1983, c. 189.

Australia: Armenian Gen. Benevolent Union v. The Union Trustee Co., 87 C.L.R. 597 (Austl., 1952) (orphans whose fathers fought with the Russian Army in the Second World War).

Canada: In re O'Brien, 15 D.L.R.2d 484 (N.S. 1958) (for the relief of the poor, sick, and needy of a town); In re Forgan, 29 D.L.R.2d 585 (Alta. 1961) (to establish a home for the care of children); In re Gun, 38 D.L.R.3d 197 (Ont. 1973) (to Canadian Red Cross Society for the Benefit of Elgin County returned soldiers).

New Zealand: In re Booth, [1954] N.Z.L.R. 1114 (needy New Zealand servicemen in Second World War); In re Elgar, [1957] N.Z.L.R. 556, *appeal dismissed,* [1957] N.Z.L.R. 1221 (for the re-establishment in civil life of New Zealand men discharged from the armed services and for their children).

In Matter of Byrd, 62 Misc. 2d 232, 308 N.Y.S.2d 97 (1970), it was held that a trust for orphan boys was intended to include boys either of whose parents had died; and, if not, the doctrine of cy pres was applicable to permit their inclusion.

In Downing v. Federal Commr. of Taxation, [1971] A.L.R. 139 (Vict. 1970), where a testator created a trust for "the amelioration of the condition

if it can even yet be called a science, have frequently done more harm than good through their generous impulses. One method of assisting the needy that was frequently employed by testators in England in the seventeenth century was the dole, a periodic and promiscuous distribution of money or goods among the poor. The results of these charities were most unfortunate, often causing rather than curing pauperism.[2] Where the distribution was confined to the poor of a particular district, the result was frequently to enable the landlords to raise their rents, because the landlords in other communities where similar doles were not available could not compete with them on equal terms. The indirect result was to enrich the landlords and not to help the poor. Perhaps the nadir of all such trusts was one created by a testator of more imagination than good sense who provided that each year the trustees should throw sixpences upon his grave to be scrambled for by aged women. The evil effects of the doles became so manifest that Parliament finally felt compelled to intervene and in the middle of the nineteenth century authorized the application of the funds to the purposes of education.[3] Fortunately in the United States this particular form of aiding the poor has not often been used by testators.

§369.1. **General trusts for the poor.** In creating a trust for the relief of poverty, the settlor may specify the manner in which the poor are to be assisted. A trust for the relief of poverty, however, is valid as a charitable trust although no method of relief is specified.[1] Thus a trust "for the poor," or "to aid the poor," or to "help the needy," or "for the relief of poverty" is charitable. In such cases if it appears that the trustees were to have discretion as to the manner of assisting the poor, they may

---

of the dependants of any member or ex-member of her Majesty's naval military or air forces or the naval military or air forces of the Commonwealth," it was held that the trust was valid because it could under a statute be limited to needy dependents; but because it was not limited to persons in Australia it was not exempt from tax.

[2]Kenny, Endowed Charities (1880) 40-52. See also Hobhouse, The Dead Hand (1880).

[3]Endowed Schools Act, 1869, 32 & 33 Vict., c. 56, §30.

§369.1. [1]Scudder v. Security Trust Co., 238 Mich. 318, 213 N.W. 131 (1927); Palmer v. Oiler, 102 Ohio St. 271, 131 N.E. 362 (1921).

adopt any reasonable method for effectuating this purpose. If this discretion is not conferred upon the trustees, the court will frame a scheme for the application of the property to the purpose.[2]

§369.2. Words indicating purpose of relieving poverty. A trust may be upheld as a trust for the relief of poverty even though there is no express reference to the poor, no provision in express words that the benefits of the trust shall be confined to the poor, provided that it sufficiently appears from the language of the trust instrument that the benefits are to be so limited.[1] Thus in *In re Lucas*[2] a testator directed that the income

---

[2]Palmer v. Oiler, 102 Ohio St. 271, 131 N.E. 362 (1921).

§369.2. [1]*England:* Powell v. Attorney-General, 3 Mer. 48 (1817) (widows and children of seamen of a particular port); Attorney-General v. Comber, 2 S.&S. 93 (1824) (widows and orphans of a particular place); Thompson v. Corby, 27 Beav. 649 (1860) (aged widows and spinsters of a parish); In re Dudgeon, 74 L.T. 613 (1896) (respectable single women above age of sixty); In re Gosling, 48 W.R. 300 (1900) (old and worn-out clerks of a certain firm); In re Elliott, 102 L.T. 528 (1910) (blind residents of a district); In re Lucas, [1922] 2 Ch. 52 (oldest respectable inhabitants to receive five shillings a week); In re Tree, [1945] Ch. 325 (to assist persons to emigrate to British Dominions), noted in 19 Aust. L.J. 122, 10 Convey. (N.S.) 53, 61 L.Q. Rev. 339, 199 L.T. 197.

See Collinson v. Pater, 2 Russ. & M. 344 (1831) (widows of respectable tradesmen).

New York: Matter of Antoni, 186 Misc. 988, 61 N.Y.S.2d 349 (1946) (widows and orphans of German village; citing the text).

Washington: In re Hunter's Estate, 147 Wash. 216, 265 P. 466 (1928) (to aid children or aged people).

Canada: In re Fallis Estate, [1948] 1 D.L.R. 27 (Sask.) (relief of suffering and distress); In re Forgan, 29 D.L.R.2d 585 (Alta. 1961) (to establish a home for the care of children); Canada Permanent Trust Co. v. MacFarlane, 27 D.L.R.3d 480 (B.C. 1972) (such Protestant homes for the care and welfare of children as the trustee in its uncontrolled discretion shall elect).

New Zealand: In re Bingham, [1951] N.Z.L.R. 491 (to support home to care for aged women).

In Downing v. Federal Commr. of Taxation, [1971] A.L.R. 139 (Vict. 1970), a bequest in trust for "the amelioration of the condition" of the dependents of members or ex-members of the armed forces in the Commonwealth was held to be charitable because it was construed to be limited to necessitous dependents. Compare §374.3, n. 1.

See Carr, The Charitable Status of Trusts for the Working Class, 123 Solic. J. 88 (1979).

[2][1922] 2 Ch. 52.

of the trust should be given to "the oldest respectable inhabitants in Gunville to the amount of five shillings per week each." It was held that the purpose of the testator was to benefit old people in straitened circumstances, and not to include those who were well-to-do, and that a valid charitable trust was created. The court expressed the opinion that the requirement of old age would not of itself be sufficient to constitute a charitable trust, although the Statute of Charitable Uses in its enumeration of charitable purposes includes "relief of aged, impotent and poor people." But in *In re Robinson*[3] the court held that a trust for the benefit of the aged was charitable even though not limited to the poor. In that case a testator left property in trust for "the old people over 65 years" of a certain village to be given as the trustees should think best. The trust was upheld as charitable. The court took the view that even though it was not expressly or impliedly limited to the poor, it was sufficient that it was for the aged, since the provision in the Statute of Elizabeth for the relief of aged, impotent, and poor people was to be treated distributively. But surely it is not in the public interest to uphold a perpetual trust for the distribution of the income among old people, rich or poor.

In *In re Lewis*[4] a testator left £100 each to ten blind girls and ten blind boys, Tottenham residents if possible. It was held that the trust was charitable although the court found that there was no requirement, express or implied, of poverty. The court said that the words in the preamble of the Statute of Elizabeth, "aged, impotent and poor," were to be read disjunctively, and that blind persons, although not aged or poor, were impotent. But surely the result should not depend on a narrow question of construction of the very loose list of instances mentioned in the preamble of that old statute. The ultimate test is undoubt-

[3][1951] Ch. 198, noted in 67 L.Q. Rev. 164.
See also In re Glyn, [1950] 2 All E.R. 1150 (building cottages for old women of working classes of age of sixty years or upwards), noted in 67 L.Q. Rev. 164; In re Bradbury, [1951] 1 T.L.R. 130 (maintenance of an aged person or persons in nursing home), noted in 67 L.Q. Rev. 164; In re Cottam's Will Trusts, [1955] 3 All E.R. 704.
[4][1955] Ch. 104, noted in 71 L.Q. Rev. 16, 18 Mod. L. Rev. 76.
See In re Fraser, 22 Ch. D. 827 (1883) (to invest and apply income for benefit of blind in Invernessshire).
See In re McIntosh, [1976] 1 N.Z.L.R. 308.

edly benefit to the community.[5] Surely, the payment of a sum of money to blind persons, rich or poor, is not a purpose of benefit to the community. But in this case, where an immediate distribution was to be made, there is no question of perpetuity involved, and even if the trust is not charitable, it might be upheld. The only difficulty is that the class of recipients is pretty general, but, as we have seen, some courts at least are willing to permit the distribution to be made even though no one can compel it to be made.[6]

§369.3. Destitution unnecessary. A trust for the relief of poor persons is charitable although it is not limited to those who are destitute.[1] It is sufficient that the persons to benefit

[5] If the trust were to assist in the relieving of the disabilities of the blind, it would be a charitable trust although not confined to the poor because it would be a trust for the promotion of health. See §372.

[6] See §122.

§369.3. [1] *England:* Spiller v. Maude, 32 Ch. D. 158n (1881) (incapacitated actors not having an income of more than £50); In re Lacy, [1899] 2 Ch. 149 (aid for persons in receipt of less than £120); In re Estlin, 89 L.T. 88 (1903) (home for lady teachers who were to contribute ten shillings a week); Trustees of the Mary Clark Home v. Anderson, [1904] 2 K.B. 645 (home for ladies in reduced circumstances having an income of not less than £25 and not more than £50); In re Gardom, [1914] 1 Ch. 662, 84 L.J. Ch. 749 (1915) (maintenance of temporary house of residence for ladies of limited means); In re Cohen, 36 T.L.R. 16 (1919) (to pay dowries to deserving Jewish girls); In re de Carteret, [1933] 1 Ch. 103 (to provide annual allowances of £40 each to widows or spinsters having an income of not less than £80 nor more than £120); In re Clarke, [1923] 2 Ch. 407 (nursing home for persons of moderate means ineligible to benefit under health insurance acts); In re Harvey, [1941] 3 All E.R. 284 (to found home for needy, poor, and aged persons of genteel birth who have not been able to earn a sufficient income adequate to provide for their old age), noted in 6 Convey. (N.S.) 139; In re Central Employment Bureau, [1942] 1 All E.R. 232 (loans to help educated women and girls to become self-supporting), noted in 6 Convey. (N.S.) 282; In re Hillier, [1944] 1 All E.R. 480, noted in 8 Convey. (N.S.) 227, 60 L.Q. Rev. 221; In re Tree, [1945] Ch. 325 (to assist persons to emigrate to British Dominions), noted in 19 Aust. L.J. 122, 10 Convey. (N.S.) 53, 61 L.Q. Rev. 339, 199 L.T. 197; In re Coulthurst, [1951] Ch. 661, *aff'g* [1951] Ch. 193 (to apply income for benefit of widows and orphaned children of deceased officers of bank), noted in 11 Camb. L.J. 97, 282; Guinness Trust (London Fund) v. West Ham Borough Council, [1959] 1 W.L.R. 233, *rev'g* [1958] 2 All E.R. 237 (working persons' hostel; tax case); In re Armitage, [1972] Ch. 438 (nursing homes for elderly women, with preference to those who had lost their savings); In re Niyazi's Will

from the trust are in needy circumstances although they have a

---

Trusts, [1978] 3 All E.R. 785, [1978] 1 W.L.R. 910 (for or towards the construction of a workingmen's hostel in a town in Cyprus); Joseph Rowntree
Memorial Trust Hous. Assn. v. Attorney-General, [1983] 1 Ch. 159, [1983] 2
W.L.R. 284, [1983] 1 All E.R. 288 (scheme for small dwellings to be leased
for long terms to aged persons was charitable even though the lessees were
not necessarily poor).

Federal: Aid to Artisans v. Commissioner, 71 T.C. 202 (1978) (for disad-
vantaged artisans, and promotion and sale of products of handicraft).

Alaska: Matanuska-Susitna Borough v. King's Lake Camp, 439 P.2d 441
(Alaska 1968) (children's camp).

California: Fredericka Home for the Aged v. County of San Diego, 35 Cal.
2d 789, 221 P.2d 68 (1950) (home for aged); Estate of Robbins, 57 Cal. 2d
718, 371 P.2d 573 (1962), noted in 48 Iowa L. Rev. 1019, 8 Utah L. Rev. 152,
20 Wash. & Lee L. Rev. 85; John Tennant Memorial Home v. City of Pacific
Grove, 27 Cal. App. 3d 372, 103 Cal. Rptr. 215 (1972), *semble,* (retirement
home).

Connecticut: Camp Isabella Freedman of Conn. v. Town of Canaan, 147
Conn. 510, 162 A.2d 700 (1960) (camp to provide assistance to underprivileged young people in their problems and social adjustments; tax case).

Georgia: Perkins v. Citizens & S. Natl. Bank, 190 Ga. 29, 8 S.E.2d 28 (1940)
(assistance of aged females and of underprivileged children of a county);
Houston v. Mills Memorial Home, 202 Ga. 540, 43 S.E.2d 680 (1947) (old
folks' home; citing the text).

Illinois: Continental Ill. Natl. Bank & Trust Co. v. Harris, 359 Ill. 86, 194
N.E. 250 (1935) (farmers' home for worthy, honest, respectable, law-abiding,
American citizens).

Indiana: Barr v. Geary, 82 Ind. App. 5, 142 N.E. 622 (1924) (home giving
short period of rest for girls).

Maine: Bills v. Pease, 116 Me. 98, 100 A. 146, L.R.A. 1917D 1060 (1917)
(worthy persons whose means fall just short of a comfortable support).

Maryland: Second Natl. Bank v. Second Natl. Bank, 171 Md. 547, 190 A.
215, 111 A.L.R. 711 (1937) (home for unfortunate girls).

Massachusetts: Thornton v. Franklin Square House, 200 Mass. 465, 86 N.E.
909, 22 L.R.A. (N.S.) 486 (1909) (home for working girls at moderate cost);
Bowditch v. Attorney Gen., 241 Mass. 168, 134 N.E. 796, 28 A.L.R. 713 (1922)
(trust for promotion of best interests of sewing girls in Boston); Staman v.
Board of Assessors of Chatham, 351 Mass. 479, 221 N.E.2d 861 (1966) (citing
Restatement of Trusts, §369, Comments *c, d*).

Missouri: Bader Realty & Inv. Co. v. St. Louis Hous. Auth., 358 Mo. 747,
217 S.W.2d 189 (1949) (providing housing for low-income tenants; tax case);
Delmo Hous. Corp. v. Finnegan, 85 F. Supp. 220 (E.D. Mo. 1949) (to assist
needy persons to purchase homes); Franciscan Tertiary Province v. State Tax
Commn., 566 S.W.2d 213 (Mo. 1978), noted in 44 Mo. L. Rev. 154 (1979)
(apartment building to house the elderly; a tax case).

certain amount of property, but not enough to afford the neces-

---

New Jeresy: Kitchen v. Pitney, 94 N.J. Eq. 485, 493, 119 A. 675 (1923) (home for persons who through misfortune have become wholly or partially unable to support themselves); Woodstown Natl. Bank & Trust Co. v. Snelbaker, 136 N.J. Eq. 62, 40 A.2d 222 (1944), *aff'd mem.*, 137 N.J. Eq. 256, 44 A.2d 210 (1945) (home for worthy white women over fifty years of age born in a certain county); Mirinda v. King, 11 N.J. Super. 165, 78 A.2d 98 (1951) (to found and maintain home for aged and blind).

New York: Matter of MacDowell, 217 N.Y. 454, 112 N.E. 177, L.R.A. 1916E 1246, Ann. Cas. 1917E 853 (1916) (home for gentlewomen whose means are small and whose home is made unhappy by having to live with relatives); Matter of Nevins, 16 Misc. 2d 425, 184 N.Y.S.2d 405 (1959) (home for persons practically incapable of supporting themselves or in need of charitable aid; held, institution may admit persons paying what they can).

But see *contra* People v. Chambers, 276 A.D. 755, 757, 92 N.Y.S.2d 919 (1949), *aff'd mem.*, 301 N.Y. 575, 93 N.E.2d 455 (1950), *rev'g* 196 Misc. 367, 88 N.Y.S.2d 459 (1949) (aiding persons in need of pecuniary assistance by making secured loans; tax case); Matter of Valeria Home, Inc. v. Cook, 22 N.Y.2d 388, 239 N.E.2d 631, 292 N.Y.S.2d 882 (1968) (home for recreation and convalescence for people of education and refinement who cannot afford independent homes or to pay charges exacted at health resorts or sanitaria; a tax case).

Oregon: Pape v. Title & Trust Co., 187 Or. 175, 210 P.2d 490 (1949) (erection of home for homeless self-supporting women), noted in 1 Hastings L.J. 158, 29 Or. L. Rev. 153.

Pennsylvania: Daly's Estate, 208 Pa. 58, 57 A. 180 (1904) (to furnish aid to industrious girls and women); Saulino Estate, 8 D.&C.2d 721 (Pa. 1957) (for needy musicians; citing Restatement of Trusts, §369, Comment *d*); Shepp Estate, 29 D.&C.2d 385 (Pa. 1962) (quoting Restatement of Trusts §369 and the comments thereon); Appeal of Calvary Fellowship Homes, 43 Pa. Commw. 485, 403 A.2d 150 (1979) (a tax case).

Texas: Clevenger v. Rio Farms, 204 S.W.2d 40 (Tex. Civ. App. 1947) (to provide homes for low-income farmers; citing Restatement of Trusts, §369, Comment *g*).

Washington: Kenney Presbyterian Home v. State, 174 Wash. 19, 24 P.2d 403 (1933) (home for poor who are unable wholly to provide for themselves); Spokane Methodist Homes v. Department of Labor, 81 Wash. 2d 283, 501 P.2d 589 (1972) (home for elderly people).

Canada: In re Pearse, [1955] 1 D.L.R. 801 (B.C.) (for young governesses who may be sick or overworked); In re Bethel, 17 D.L.R.3d 652 (Ont. 1971) *aff'd sub nom.* Jones v. The T. Eaton Co., 35 D.L.R.3d 97 (1973) (for needy or deserving Toronto members of a club of elderly employees of a corporation), noted in 52 Can. Bar Rev. 114 (1974); Assessment Commr. v. Mennonite Home Assn., 31 D.L.R.3d 237 (S. Ct. Can., 1972) (nursing home; a tax case); In re Public Trustee, London, Eng., 74 D.L.R.3d 545 (Alta. 1977) (a home for Anglican girls of low earning ability).

sities or the comforts of life. Thus the benefits of the trust may be limited to persons whose means fall short of a comfortable support, or whose means are so limited that they are unable entirely to support themselves. A trust to establish a home for such persons is a valid charitable trust, although the inmates are required to make some contribution to the expense of maintaining the home. The mere fact that the persons to benefit from a trust are required to make contributions does not prevent it from being a charitable trust, provided that the income, if it should exceed the costs of administration, is not to be devoted to a private use.[2]

§369.4. **Incidental benefit to others.** A trust for the benefit of the poor is nonetheless charitable although incidentally it is of benefit to those who are not poor. Thus to the extent to which a trust relieves the poor, the public authorities are relieved of the burden of caring for the poor, and the taxpayers are thereby assisted. As we shall see, however, a trust for the

---

New Zealand: In re Strong, [1956] N.Z.L.R. 275 (girls' hostel).

See §374.11.

As to a possible distinction between destitute and indigent persons, see Destitute of Bennington County v. Henry W. Putnam Memorial Hosp., 125 Vt. 289, 215 A.2d 134 (1965), 126 Vt. 146, 225 A.2d 71 (1966).

In Bakos v. Kryder, 260 Ark. 621, 543 S.W.2d 216 (1976), a testatrix bequeathed a fund to pay $100 to each child departing from a designated children's home. It was held to be a charitable disposition. The children were generally poor children, and the purpose fell, in any event, within the broad class of dispositions for a purpose beneficial to the community. The court quoted the Restatement of Trusts §§365, 374.

In Hilder v. Church of Eng. Deaconess' Inst., [1973] 1 N.S.W.R. 506 (N.S.W.), the court upheld as charitable a devise of land for providing homes for elderly people. It was held to be immaterial that there was no requirement of poverty, although a trust for the aged wealthy or to provide luxuries for the aged would not be charitable.

See Carr, The Charitable Status of Trusts for the Working Class, 123 Solic. J. 88 (1979).

[2]See §376.

A payment to a charitable institution for commensurate benefits in return is not a charitable gift for tax purposes. Sedam v. United States, 518 F.2d 242 (7th Cir. 1975) (a son paid money to a charitable home in return for its undertaking to care for his mother for life).

See Note on this case in 34 A.L.R. Fed. 840 (1977).

purpose of reducing taxes is charitable even though it is uncon-nected with the relief of poverty.[1]

§369.5. Limited classes of beneficiaries. A trust is not a charitable trust if the persons who are to benefit are not of a sufficiently large or indefinite class so that the community is interested in the enforcement of the trust.[1] This is true even though the benefits of the trust are limited to poor persons, although where it is so limited the class can be narrower than in the case where it is not so limited. A trust for the relief of poverty is charitable although the benefits are limited to the inhabitants of a particular place, such as a specified city or town or village or parish. In an early English case it was held that a trust for the benefit of the poor on the testator's estate was charitable.[2] It may well be doubted, however, whether the class was not so narrow as to prevent the purpose from being a charitable purpose. A trust for the relief of poverty is charita-ble although the benefits are confined to the members of a particular church. A trust for the benefit of poor members, or the widows and orphan children of members, of a particular fraternal organization is held to be charitable, although a gift to the organization for its general purposes is not charitable. This is true also of other organizations. A trust for the relief of poverty is valid although the persons to be benefited are lim-ited to those of a particular sex or condition, such as widows or maidens; or of a particular age, such as aged persons or children; or of a particular religious denomination;[3] or persons having certain qualifications, such as pious persons, respect-

§369.4. [1]See §373.1.
§369.5. [1]See §375.

In Matter of Martyn, 99 N.Y.S.2d 28 (1945), where a bequest was made to pay the income to such indigent persons as the executrices might deem advisable and proper, the bequest was held to be charitable, although the testatrix stated a desire to benefit some of the most worthy persons that she had in mind.

In McClure v. Carter, 202 Va. 191, 116 S.E.2d 260 (1960), where a testatrix left her property in trust to maintain a home for indigent women and requested that preference be given to her nieces, it was held that this provision was merely precatory and that the trust was a valid charitable trust.

[2]Bristow v. Bristow, 5 Beav. 289 (1842).

[3]Catholic Bishop of Chicago v. Murr, 3 Ill. App. 3d 107, 120 N.E.2d 4 (1954) (cemetery for Catholics of a town).

able persons, or the like; or persons of a particular trade or calling; or persons of a certain social status, such as gentlewomen. A trust is nonetheless charitable although the settlor has provided for a combination of these various requirements. Thus in a case in Connecticut, a trust was upheld as charitable although limited to "worthy, deserving, poor, white, American, Protestant, Democratic widows and orphans residing in the town of Bridgeport."[4]

On the other hand, a trust for the benefit of named beneficiaries is not charitable although the beneficiaries are poor. So also a trust for such of the next of kin of the testator as are in need is not a charitable trust. In these cases the class of beneficiaries is a definite and narrow class, and the benefit to the community is not sufficient to make the trust a charitable trust. The trust, however, is a private trust, since the beneficiaries are sufficiently definite to enforce it, and will be valid unless the disposition is of such a character that it violates the principle of the rule against perpetuities. The question whether a trust for poor descendants of the testator, or of another person, living or dead at the time of the creation of the trust, is a charitable trust will be dealt with hereafter.[5]

§370. Advancement of Education

Trusts for the advancement of education are charitable. In the Statute of Charitable Uses the enumeration of charitable purposes includes "schools of learning, free schools, and scholars in universities." It also includes "education and preferment of orphans," in which the ideas of education and the relief of poverty are combined. The cases in which trusts for the advancement of education have been upheld as charitable are numerous.[1] The methods of advancing education include the

---

[4]Beardsley v. Selectmen of Bridgeport, 53 Conn. 489, 3 A. 557, 55 Am. Rep. 152 (1885).

As to trusts with racial or religious restrictions, see §§96.4, 370.5, 373, 399.4.

[5]See §375.3.

§370. [1]*England:* University of London v. Yarrow, 23 Beav. 159 (1856), *aff'd,* 1 De G.&J. 72 (1857) (free lectures in connection with establishing institute for investigation and healing of diseases of animals or birds useful to

establishment and maintenance of educational institutions; con-

man); In re Shakespeare Memorial Trust, [1923] 2 Ch. 398 (to provide national theater as memorial to Shakespeare); In re Cranstoun, [1932] 1 Ch. 537 (to maintain certain picturesque Elizabethan cottages); In re Central Employment Bureau, [1942] 1 All E.R. 232 (loans to help educated women and girls to become self-supporting), noted in 6 Convey. (N.S.) 282; Royal Choral Socy. v. Commissioner of Inland Revenue, [1943] 2 All E.R. 101 (society to promote choral singing in London held exempt from income tax), noted in 59 L.Q. Rev. 113, 307, 7 Mod. L. Rev. 158; The Abbey, Malvern v. Minister of Town and Country Planning, [1951] 2 All E.R. 154 (unincorporated school held its property upon charitable trust within the meaning of Town and Country Planning Act, 1947, §85); In re Shaw's Will Trusts, [1952] Ch. 163 (bringing masterpieces of fine art within the reach of the Irish people, and teaching in Ireland of self-control, elocution, oratory, deportment, the arts of personal contact, of social intercourse, and the other arts of public, private, professional, and business life), noted in 11 Camb. L.J. 281, 68 L.Q. Rev. 155; O'Sullivan v. English Folk Dance and Song Socy., [1955] 1 W.L.R. 907, noted in 71 L.Q. Rev. 451; In re Levien, [1955] 3 All E.R. 35 (fund to employ the income in making yearly advances to distinguished persons in professions connected with singing; another fund to use the income to assist musicians or students in music so as to produce better organists and organ music); In re Delius, [1957] Ch. 299 (to advance musical works of testatrix's husband, a famous composer), noted in 74 L.Q. Rev. 15; In re North of Eng. Zoological Socy. v. Chester Rural Dist. Council, [1959] 3 All E.R. 116 (zoological society exempt from tax); George Drexler Ofrex Found. Trustees v. Inland Revenue Commrs., [1965] 3 All E.R. 529, [1966] Ch. 675 (to enable a student to travel abroad so as to acquire experience in commercial methods employed outside the United Kingdom); Re South Place Ethical Socy.; Barralet v. Attorney-General, [1980] 3 All E.R. 918 (Ch. Div.) (society for study and dissemination of ethical principles); Inland Revenue Commrs. v. White, Re Clerkenwell Green Assn. for Craftsmen, [1980] T.R. 155, [1981] C.L. 16 (association that maintained library, open to the public, and workshop, with specialized tools open to all bona fide craftsmen, was charitable); Re Koeppler's Will Trusts; Barclays Bank Trust Co. v. Slack, [1986] 1 Ch. 423, [1985] 2 All E.R. 869 (C.A.).

Federal: President and Fellows of Harvard College v. Jewitt, 11 F.2d 119 (6th Cir. 1925) (to preserve land containing Indian relics); Lewis v. United States, 189 F. Supp. 950 (D. Wyo. 1961) (education of worthy youth of community; tax case); City of Chattanooga v. Louisville & N.R.R., 298 F. Supp. 1 (E.D. Tenn. 1969), *aff'd*, 427 F.2d 1154 (6th Cir. 1970), *cert. denied*, 400 U.S. 903 (1970) (exhibition of historic locomotive, *semble*); Industrial Natl. Bank v. United States, 187 F. Supp. 810 (D.R.I. 1960) (club for art culture; a tax case).

Alabama: Tarver v. Weaver, 221 Ala. 663, 130 So. 209 (1930) (art museum); Stariha v. Hagood, 252 Ala. 158, 40 So. 2d 85 (1949) (to establish a

tributions to existing educational institutions; provisions for

---

school or scholarship for workers).

Arkansas: Bossen v. Woman's Christian Natl. Library Assn., 216 Ark. 334, 225 S.W.2d 336 (1949) (to maintain religious library), noted in 4 S.W.L.J. 352.

California: Estate of Bailey, 19 Cal. App. 2d 135, 65 P.2d 102 (1937) (to school; quoting Restatement of Trusts, §370, Comment *a*); Estate of Yule, 57 Cal. App. 2d 652, 135 P.2d 386 (1943) (student loan fund); Estate of Fleming, 183 P.2d 295 (Cal. App. 1947), *rev'd on other grounds,* 31 Cal. 2d 514, 190 P.2d 611 (1948) (scholarships, the recipients to be chosen from those obtaining best scores in annual golf tournament); Estate of Mealy, 91 Cal. App. 2d 371, 204 P.2d 971 (1949) (to distribute educational material); Davenport v. Davenport Found., 36 Cal. 2d 67, 222 P.2d 11 (1950), *mod'g* 215 Cal. App. 467 (Cal. App. 1950) (to establish in college a department of philosophy and religion); In re Los Angeles County Pioneer Socy., 40 Cal. 2d 852, 257 P.2d 1 (1953) (association to preserve data on history of county and state; citing Restatement of Trusts §374); Estate of Rollins, 163 Cal. App. 2d 225, 328 P.2d 1005 (1958) (research fund); Estate of Peck, 168 Cal. App. 2d 25, 335 P.2d 185 (1959) (to establish a foundation to provide education for newspapermen in international affairs), *cert. and rehearing denied,* 361 U.S. 826, 903 (1959); Estate of Moore, 190 Cal. App. 2d 833, 12 Cal. Rptr. 436 (1961) (to some creditable nonprofit science investigation society of sister's choice); Greek Theatre Assn. v. County of Los Angeles, 76 Cal. App. 3d 768, 142 Cal. Rptr. 919 (1977) (nonprofit organization providing theatrical and musical attractions; a tax case); Younger v. Wisdom Socy., 121 Cal. App. 3d 683, 175 Cal. Rptr. 542 (1981) (charitable corporation); Hardman v. Feinstein, 195 Cal. App. 3d 157, 240 Cal. Rptr. 483 (1987), citing text (art museum).

Colorado: Ireland v. Jacobs, 114 Colo. 168, 163 P.2d 203, 161 A.L.R. 1413 (1945) (scholarship in college); Galiger v. Armstrong, 114 Colo. 397, 165 P.2d 1019 (1946) (to educate needy theological or medical students; citing the text); In re Estate of Gardner, 31 Colo. App. 361, 505 P.2d 50 (1973) (scholarships).

Connecticut: Hoyt v. Bliss, 93 Conn. 344, 105 A. 699 (1919) (scholarship in college); Hoenig v. Lubetkin, 137 Conn. 516, 79 A.2d 278 (1951) (musical foundation).

Delaware: Woodlen v. Brodnax, 30 Del. Ch. 227, 57 A.2d 752 (1948) (scholarship in college, for graduates of a particular high school); Wilmington Trust Co. v. Sloane, 30 Del. Ch. 103, 54 A.2d 544 (1947) (scholarships in a school; citing Restatement of Trusts §§368, 370).

District of Columbia: Board of Directors of City Trust v. Maloney, 78 App. D.C. 371, 141 F.2d 275 (1944), *cert. denied sub nom.,* Maloney v. Board of Directors of City Trusts, 323 U.S. 714 (1944) (medical scholarship); District of Columbia v. Catholic Educ. Press, 91 App. D.C. 126, 199 F.2d 176, 34 A.L.R.2d 1214 (1952), *cert. denied,* 344 U.S. 896 (1953) (publication of educational, literary, scientific, and religious matter; tax case).

Florida: Holsey v. Atlantic Natl. Bank, 115 Fla. 604, 155 So. 821 (1934)

teaching particular subjects in an educational institution, includ-

---

(student loan fund); Pattillo v. Glenn, 150 Fla. 73, 7 So. 2d 328 (1942) (student loan fund; citing the text); Miller v. Flowers, 158 Fla. 51, 27 S.E.2d 667 (1946) (education of deserving young men and women).

Georgia: Duffee v. Jones, 208 Ga. 639, 68 S.E.2d 699 (1952) (to the trustees of a school district).

Illinois: Morgan v. National Trust Bank of Charleston, 331 Ill. 182, 162 N.E. 888 (1928) (student loan fund), noted in 3 Temp. U.L.Q. 226; Summers v. Chicago Title & Trust Co., 335 Ill. 564, 167 N.E. 777 (1929) (student loan fund), noted in 24 Ill. L. Rev. 687, 39 Yale L.J. 437; People ex rel. Hellyer v. Morton, 373 Ill. 72, 25 N.E.2d 504 (1940) (foundation to carry on practical scientific research in horticulture and arboriculture); People ex rel. Scott v. George F. Harding Museum, 58 Ill. App. 3d 408, 16 Ill. Dec. 960, 374 N.E.2d 756, (1978) (perpetuation of knowledge of ancient arts and sciences; quoting the text and citing Restatement of Trusts §370).

Indiana: Quinn v. Peoples Trust & Sav. Co., 223 Ind. 317, 60 N.E.2d 281, 157 A.L.R. 885 (1945) (to educate children of employees of railroad at college or university; citing Restatement of Trusts §370); State ex rel. Emmert v. Union Trust Co., 74 N.E.2d 833 (1947), *rev'd,* 227 Ind. 571, 86 N.E.2d 450, 12 A.L.R.2d 836 (1949) (to publish and distribute diaries of testatrix' grandfather relating to early history of state).

Iowa: Wilson v. First Natl. Bank, 164 Iowa 402, 145 N.W. 948, Ann. Cas. 1916D 481 (1914) (to establish industrial training school for children); Iowa Fed. of Women's Clubs v. Dilley, 234 Iowa 417, 12 N.W.2d 815 (1944) (student loan fund); In re Will of Hagan, 234 Iowa 1001, 14 N.W.2d 638, 152 A.L.R. 1296 (1944) (scholarships; citing Restatement of Trusts §370); Eckles v. Lounsberry, 253 Iowa 172, 111 N.W.2d 638 (1961) (to promote instruction in vocal music and proper development of the lungs of children attending kindergarten and first and second grades in the schools of Iowa; citing Restatement of Trusts §§370, 372).

Kansas: Daughters of the Am. Revolution of Kansas, Topeka Chapter v. Washburn College, 160 Kan. 583, 164 P.2d 128 (1945) (to college for scholarship; quoting Restatement of Trusts, §370, Comment *a*); In re Estate of Porter, 164 Kan. 92, 187 P.2d 520 (1947) (student scholarship or loan fund); Commercial Natl. Bank of Kansas City v. Martin, 185 Kan. 116, 340 P.2d 899 (1959) (to pay income to a schoolmistress).

Kentucky: Owens v. Owens' Exr., 236 Ky. 118, 32 S.W.2d 731 (1930) (student loan fund); Commonwealth v. Isaac W. Bernheim Found., 505 S.W.2d 762 (Ky. 1974) (bird sanctuary, art gallery, museum of natural history; a tax case).

Louisiana: Succession of Maguire, 228 La. 1096, 85 So. 2d 4 (1956) (loan fund to enable young girls to fit themselves to earn a living); In re Succession of Abraham, 136 So. 2d 471 (La. App. 1962) (to a Catholic bishop to be used to build a school or orphanage); Oroszy v. Burkard, 158 So. 2d 405 (La. 1963) (loans to boys and girls who wish to go to college).

ing the endowment of a professorial chair and contributions

Maryland: Rosser v. Prem, 52 Md. App. 367, 449 A.2d 461 (1982) (trust to publish and distribute book written by testatrix about her daughter, who died at the age of eight, is charitable even though the book contained errors in grammar; citing the text and Restatement (Second) of Trusts §370).

Massachusetts: American Academy of Arts and Sciences v. President and Fellows of Harvard College, 12 Gray 582 (Mass. 1832) (prize for research; delivery of lectures); Lowell, Appellant, 22 Pick. 215 (Mass. 1839) (public lectures); Society for Promoting Theological Educ. v. Attorney Gen., 135 Mass. 285 (1883) (scholarships); Cary Library v. Bliss, 151 Mass. 364, 25 N.E. 92, 7 L.R.A. 765 (1890) (public library); Bartlett, Petitioner, 163 Mass. 509, 40 N.E. 899 (1895) (medals for scholars in public schools); Dexter v. President and Fellows of Harvard College, 176 Mass. 192, 57 N.E. 371 (1900) (to pay salary of professor); Richardson v. Essex Inst., 208 Mass. 311, 94 N.E. 262, 21 Ann. Cas. 1158 (1911) (botanical gardens and employment of instructor in botany and free lectures); Briggs v. Merchants Natl. Bank, 323 Mass. 261, 81 N.E.2d 827 (1948) (art museum); Worcester County Trust Co. v. Grand Knight, 325 Mass. 748, 92 N.E.2d 579 (1950) (to provide annual prize for students in Catholic colleges and schools in New England); M.I.T. Student House v. Board of Assessors, 350 Mass. 539, 215 N.E.2d 788 (1966) (to provide living quarters for needy students of a college; a tax case); Fulton v. Trustees of Boston College, 372 Mass. 350, 361 N.E.2d 1297 (1977) (accumulation until year 2000 and then paid to a college for the erection of a building; citing Restatement of Trusts §370); Cummington School of the Arts v. Board of Assessors, 373 Mass. 597, 369 N.E.2d 457 (1977) (art school conducting summer sessions for art educators and advanced art students; a tax case).

Michigan: Wanstead v. Fisher, 278 Mich. 68, 270 N.W. 218 (1936) (student loan fund); De Groot v. Edison Inst., 306 Mich. 339, 10 N.W.2d 907 (1943) (historical museum).

Minnesota: Junior Achievement of Greater Minneapolis v. State, 271 Minn. 385, 135 N.W.2d 881 (1965) (corporation organized to provide place of training for young people in free enterprise system of business); North Star Research Inst. v. Hennepin County, 306 Minn. 1, 236 N.W.2d 754 (1976) (holding nonprofit corporation engaged in research activities for private enterprises exempt from personal property taxes); Mayo Found. v. Commissioner of Revenue, 306 Minn. 25, 236 N.W.2d 767 (1975) (holding that the Mayo Clinic and Mayo Foundation are exempt from sales and use tax, because private practice of medicine was incidental to educational and research activities).

Mississippi: Alden v. Lewis, 254 Miss. 704, 182 So. 2d 600 (1966) (municipal art museum, citing the text); In re Estate of Hall, 193 So. 2d 587 (Miss. 1967) (for the education of poor boys and girls at a church school; citing the text); Estate of Bunch v. Heirs of Bunch, 485 So. 2d 284 (Miss. 1986).

Missouri: Lackland v. Walker, 151 Mo. 210, 52 S.W. 414 (1899) (lectures on botany and allied sciences in connection with botanical garden, museum,

toward the payment of the salary of a teacher; provisions for the

---

and library); Parsons v. Childs, 345 Mo. 689, 136 S.W.2d 327 (1940), *cert. denied,* 310 U.S. 640 (1940), *rehearing denied,* 311 U.S. 724 (1940) (art museum); Bogdanovich v. Bogdanovich, 360 Mo. 753, 230 S.W.2d 695 (1950) (to build school in Yugoslavia); Voelker v. St. Louis Mercantile Library Assn., 359 S.W.2d 689 (Mo. 1962) (library for use of members); First Natl. Bank of Kansas City v. Jacques, 470 S.W.2d 557 (Mo. 1971) (grants or loans to students; citing Restatement of Trusts §370); Flynn v. Danforth, 547 S.W.2d 132 (Mo. App. 1977) (city library; citing the text).

New Hampshire: Hills v. D'Amours, 95 N.H. 130, 59 A.2d 551 (1948) (to establish and endow school).

New Jersey: In re Butler, 137 N.J. Eq. 48, 42 A.2d 857 (1945), *aff'd mem.,* 137 N.J. Eq. 457, 45 A.2d 598 (1946) (scholarships); Cinnaminson Library Assn. v. Fidelity-Philadelphia Trust Co., 141 N.J. Eq. 127, 56 A.2d 417 (1948) (public library); Wilber v. Owens, 2 N.J. 167, 65 A.2d 843 (1949), *aff'g* Wilber v. Asbury Park Natl. Bank & Trust Co., 142 N.J. Eq. 99, 59 A.2d 570 (1948) (scientific and philosophical research; citing the text); Litcher v. Trust Co. of N.J., 11 N.J. 64, 93 A.2d 368 (1952), *aff'g* 18 N.J. Super. 101, 86 A.2d 601 (1952) (to educate a youth for the priesthood and to establish a chair of public speaking); Princeton Township v. Institute for Advanced Study, 59 N.J. Super. 46, 157 A.2d 136 (1960) (premises of Institute for Advanced Study exempt from local property taxation as a college, although its purpose was research and not instruction); Chester Theatre Group v. Borough of Chester, 115 N.J. Super. 360, 279 A.2d 878 (1971) (corporation organized to stimulate, perpetuate, and develop interest in dramatic arts; a tax case).

New York: Butterworth v. Keeler, 219 N.Y. 446, 114 N.E. 803 (1916) (to establish school for girls); Matter of Davidge, 200 A.D. 437, 193 N.Y.S. 245 (1922) (student loan fund); Matter of Frasch, 245 N.Y. 174, 156 N.E. 656 (1927) (research in field of agricultural chemistry); Matter of Everson, 268 A.D. 425, 52 N.Y.S.2d 395 (1944), *aff'd mem.,* 295 N.Y. 622, 64 N.E.2d 653 (1945) (to found and maintain art museum; citing the text and Restatement of Trusts §370); Matter of Futterman, 197 Misc. 558, 95 N.Y.S.2d 876 (1950) (to make musical recordings available to public through public lending libraries); Matter of Lewis, 199 Misc. 463, 99 N.Y.S.2d 986 (1950) (scholarship in university); Matter of Morgan, 200 Misc. 645, 107 N.Y.S.2d 180 (1951) (student loan fund; citing the text and Restatement of Trusts §370); Matter of Howell, 109 N.Y.S.2d 270 (1951) (teachers' loan fund); Matter of Folsom, 155 N.Y.S.2d 140 (1956), *aff'd,* 6 A.D.2d 691, 174 N.Y.S.2d 116 (1958), *aff'd mem.,* 6 N.Y.2d 886, 160 N.E.2d 857 (1959) (to form corporation for vocational training of young men); Bes Corp. v. Tully, 61 A.D.2d 1097, 403 N.Y.S.2d 342 (1978), *rev'd,* 46 N.Y.2d 1038, 389 N.E.2d 1065, 416 N.Y.S.2d 544 (1979), on the ground that the uniforms were sold to parents rather than to the schools (corporation supplying uniforms to students in parochial schools; a tax case).

North Carolina: Board of Trustees of the Univ. of N.C. at Chapel Hill v.

payment of pensions to retired professors or other teachers;

Unknown Heirs of Prince, 311 N.C. 644, 319 S.E.2d 239 (1984) (erection of a theatre to be used by state university dramatic society).

Ohio: Murr v. Youse, 52 Ohio Abs. 321, 80 N.E.2d 788 (1946) (to erect library building, *semble*); Baily v. McElroy, 120 Ohio App. 85, 195 N.E.2d 559 (1963) (to educate worthy young people in veterinary science or general sanitation; citing Restatement of Trusts §370).

Oklahoma: Noble v. Oklahoma Tax Commn., 560 P.2d 185 (Okla. 1977) (loan fund for students; a tax case).

Oregon: Unander v. United States Natl. Bank (In re Jenkins' Estate), 224 Or. 144, 355 P.2d 729 (1960) (student loan fund; but subject to inheritance tax because it might be used outside the state).

Pennsylvania: Hill School Tax Exemption Case, 370 Pa. 21, 87 A.2d 259 (1952) (preparatory school; tax case); Wilstach Estate, 1 D.&C.2d 197 (Pa. 1954) (to found art museum); McClain Estate, 435 Pa. 408, 257 A.2d 245 (1969) (for scholarships; citing Restatement of Trusts §368); Glant Will, 48 D.&C.2d 791 (Pa. 1969) (educational loan fund); Barnwell Estate, 52 D.&C.2d 698 (Pa. 1971) (rewarding the practice of high principles of honor and moral courage by the students and graduates of a public school of which the testator was a graduate).

Rhode Island: Carpenter, For an Opinion, 47 R.I. 461, 134 A. 16, 47 A.L.R. 60 (1926) (retirement fund for public school teachers of Providence); McLyman v. Art Assn., 51 R.I. 273, 154 A. 117 (1931) (art museum); Pennsylvania Co. for Ins. on Lives and Granting Annuities v. Contributors to Pa. Hosp., 63 R.I. 466, 9 A.2d 269 (1939) (establishment of scholarships for foundations in such colleges as trustees may select); Industrial Trust Co. v. Nolan, 74 R.I. 178, 59 A.2d 542 (1948) (public library); Champlin v. Powers, 80 R.I. 30, 90 A.2d 787, 33 A.L.R.2d 1176 (1952) (student loan fund); Smith v. Powers, 83 R.I. 415, 117 A.2d 844 (1955) (to preserve house as example of colonial architecture and furnishings); Alumnae Assn. of Newport Hosp. School of Nursing v. Nugent, 101 R.I. 26, 219 A.2d 763 (1966) (graduate scholarships for nurses); Alumnae Assn. of Newport Hosp. School of Nursing v. De Simone, 106 R.I. 196, 258 A.2d 80 (1969).

South Dakota: In re McNair's Estate, 74 S.D. 369, 53 N.W.2d 210 (1952) (scholarship fund for needy students).

Tennessee: Gibson v. Frye Inst., 137 Tenn. 452, 193 S.W. 1059, L.R.A. 1917D 1062 (1916) (building for free use of working people, with rooms for lectures, library, and dance hall); Ratto v. Nashville Trust Co., 178 Tenn. 457, 159 S.W.2d 88, 141 A.L.R. 341 (1942) (education of any child or children whom trustee deems worthy of assistance).

See also Carson v. Nashville Bank & Trust Co., 204 Tenn. 396, 321 S.W.2d 798 (1959).

Texas: Powers v. First Natl. Bank, 138 Tex. 604, 161 S.W.2d 273 (1942), *aff'g* 137 S.W.2d 839 (Tex. Civ. App. 1940) (loans to ambitious and worthy boys and girls who are financially unable to secure an education), noted in 19

provisions enabling students to attend educational institutions,

---

Tex. L. Rev. 102; Harrold v. First Natl. Bank of Fort Worth, 93 F. Supp. 882 (N.D. Tex. 1950) (scholarships for worthy boys unable to pay their own expenses in designated university); Taysum v. El Paso Natl. Bank, 256 S.W.2d 172 (Tex. Civ. App. 1953) (to set up a research foundation in electricity); Eldridge v. Marshall Natl. Bank, 527 S.W.2d 222 (Tex. Civ. App. 1975), *writ refused, n.r.e.* (scholarship fund; citing Restatement of Trusts §370).

Virginia: Triplett v. Trotter, 169 Va. 440, 193 S.E. 514 (1937) (to found and maintain business college).

West Virginia: Mercantile Banking & Trust Co. v. Showacre, 102 W. Va. 260, 135 S.E. 9, 48 A.L.R. 1138 (1926) (annual course of lectures on art, literature, history, or economics), noted in 31 Law Notes 74, 34 W. Va. L.Q. 386.

Wisconsin: Steenis v. City of Appleton, 230 Wis. 530, 284 N.W. 492 (1939) (conveyance of log cabin to city to be maintained as historical landmark); Estate of Robinson, 248 Wis. 203, 21 N.W.2d 391 (1946) (to establish professorship to be held by a woman).

Australia: Royal North Shore Hosp. of Sydney v. Attorney-General, 60 C.L.R. 396 (Austl., 1938) (biennial awards for essays promoting prevention of death of infants, improvement of Australian food habits, and extension of technical education in state schools in Australia); Perpetual Trustee Co. v. Commissioner of Stamp Duties, [1975] 1 N.S.W.R. 111 (N.S.W.) (a center for the cultivation, education, and performance of musical and dramatic arts); Perpetual Trustee Co. v. Groth, [1985] 2 N.S.W. L. Rep. 278 (Sup. Ct.) (bequest to establish an annual competition for portrait painting is an educational charity).

Canada: In re Macdonald, 18 D.L.R.3d 521 (Ont. 1971) (to collect historical objects for exhibition); In re Societa Unita and Town of Gravenhurst, 79 D.L.R.3d 281 (Ont. 1977) (a children's camp to train children of immigrants in Italian language and history; a tax case).

New Zealand: In re Mason (deceased), [1971] N.Z.L.R. 714 (to Auckland District Law Society for library purposes); Canterbury Orchestra Trust v. Smitham, [1978] 1 N.Z.L.R. 787 (C.A.) (a trust for advancement of musical education is charitable but a society to promote music for the amusement of the members is not).

In In re Dupree's Trusts, [1945] Ch. 16, it was held that a trust to promote annual tournaments in chess among boys of a city under twenty-one was charitable, since the evidence showed that the playing of chess was of considerable educational value. The case is noted in 61 L.Q. Rev. 12, 9 Convey. (N.S.) 84.

In Noble v. Union Township, 140 N.J. Eq. 513, 55 A.2d 222 (1947), where a testator left $25,000 to erect a permanent memorial to himself to be placed in a certain town, the trustees to have absolute discretion as to the nature of the memorial, it was held that they could properly create scholarships in Rutgers and Princeton Universities for students coming from the town.

In Mohonk Trust v. Board of Assessors, 47 N.Y.2d 476, 392 N.E.2d 876,

such as scholarship and loan funds. A trust is a valid charitable trust as one for the advancement of education although it is not connected with an educational institution. Thus trusts to establish or maintain public libraries, art museums, or botanical or zoological or similar institutions are charitable. So also are trusts for the advancement of knowledge by research or otherwise. So too are trusts for the dissemination of knowledge or beliefs through the publication or distribution of books or pamphlets or the delivery of lectures.

In *In re Shaw*[2] George Bernard Shaw made a bequest of money in trust for a period of 21 years to ascertain how much time and expense could be saved by the substitution of a new alphabet for the present English alphabet and to transliterate one of his plays into the proposed alphabet. It was held that the trust was not a charitable trust and failed. The court said that an increase of knowledge is not an educational purpose unless combined with an element of teaching. It is submitted that this is an unnecessarily narrow view, because research is often a necessary foundation for education. It further said that the trust could not be upheld as beneficial to the community. Appeals by the Attorney-General and the trustee were dismissed by consent on terms agreed to by the parties and with the concurrence of the Attorney-General. Under the agreed terms of compromise, a sum of money was to be devoted to the purposes that the

---

418 N.Y.S.2d 763 (1979), a trust was created of a large tract of undeveloped mountain wilderness, to be used for a variety of environmental, conservation, educational, and recreational purposes. It was held to be charitable and free of tax.

See Levi, Financing Education and the Effect of the Tax Laws, 39 Law & Contemp. Probs. 75 (Duke U., 1975); Buckley, Educational Benefit Trusts — A New Breath of Life, 20 Wake Forest L. Rev. 343 (1984).

See 46 A.L.R. 827 (1927); 47 id. 63 (1927); 48 id. 1126, 1142 (1927); 110 id. 1369 (1937).

See Note, Validity, as for a charitable purpose, of trust for dissemination or preservation of material of historical or other educational interest or value, 12 A.L.R.2d 849 (1950).

See Note, Validity, as a charity, of trust to lend money to students, 33 id. 1183 (1954).

See Note, What is a "scientific institution" within property tax exemption provisions, 34 id. 1221 (1954).

[2][1957] 1 All E.R. 745, noted in 73 L.Q. Rev. 305.

testator had expressed in his will in regard to a new alphabet, the trusts to be carried out within 21 years from the testator's death, any sum left over going to the residuary legatees.[3]

In *In re Hopkins' Will Trusts*[4] the court took a broader view as to research as an educational purpose. In that case a testatrix made a legacy to the Francis Bacon Society, Incorporated to be applied toward finding the Bacon-Shakespeare manuscripts. The main purpose of the society was "to encourage the general study of the evidence in favour of Francis Bacon's authorship of the plays commonly ascribed to Shakespeare." The court held that the purpose was charitable, and that the degree of improbability of discovering manuscripts of the plays was not so great as to justify rejecting the trust as wholly impracticable or futile.

A trust for educational purposes may fail because the performance of the trust would be of little or no value to the community. Thus it has been held that a trust to publish the writings of the testator, which were of no value whatever, was not enforceable as a charitable trust.[5] Similarly, a trust to establish an

[3]In re Shaw, [1958] 1 All E.R. 245.

[4][1965] Ch. 669.

[5]Wilber v. Asbury Park Natl. Bank & Trust Co., 142 N.J. Eq. 99, 59 Å.2d 570 (1948), *aff'd sub nom.* Wilber v. Owens, 2 N.J. 167, 65 A.2d 843 (1949), noted in 63 Harv. L. Rev. 348.

In this case the court found that the testator showed a general intent to apply the legacy for scientific and philosophical research and therefore applied the cy pres doctrine. See §399.2, n. 33.

In Fidelity Title & Trust Co. v. Clyde, 143 Conn. 247, 121 A.2d 625 (1956), a trust to publish pamphlets written by the testator, which the court found to be objectionable, was held invalid. The court cited the Restatement of Trusts §§60, 62, 370.

In Hanson Estate, 8 D.&C.2d 620 (Pa. 1956), a testatrix directed that a novel written by her should be sent to a designated publisher and that the royalties were to be given for a certain charitable purpose. The publisher offered to publish it on payment of a certain sum. Since it was clear that there would be no royalties because the novel was worthless, the court ordered that the amount offered be paid to the charity.

In In re Pinion, [1965] Ch. 85, noted in 80 L.Q. Rev. 311, the testator gave his studio and the contents, which included paintings by himself and others, furniture, china, glass, and bric-a-brac to trustees and directed that the residue of his estate should be used to endow the studio as a museum for the display of his collection. It was shown by expert evidence that the contents of the studio were practically worthless. It was held that the intended trust failed. It could not be upheld as a charitable trust for educational purposes.

art museum in which to exhibit objects acquired by the testatrix that were of little or no artistic value was held not to be valid as a charitable trust.[6]

A trust for educational purposes is charitable although the persons to be educated are not limited to the poor.[7] Where a trust is created for the education of poor children it is charitable not merely as a trust to promote education but also as a trust for the relief of poverty.[8] But a trust for the promotion of education has no necessary connection with the relief of poverty.

In In re Elmore, [1968] Vict. Rep. 390, where a testator left money in trust to publish a book by his wife and to publish his own manuscripts in prose and poetry, and the writings had no literary merit or educational value, it was held the trust failed.

In Matter of Manschinger, 74 Misc. 2d 373, 343 N.Y.S.2d 426 (1973), a testatrix left funds in trust to publish musical compositions of her husband that were shown to be of artistic merit. It was held that it was a valid charitable trust.

In In re Estate of Rood, 41 Mich. App. 405, 200 N.W.2d 728, 67 A.L.R.3d 390 (1972), a testator left his estate to three college presidents in trust to use the income to teach political science in the colleges in a manner that should take account of his writings on the subject. It was held that to comply with his directions would abridge academic freedom; but that the trust would not fail and the property should be applied cy pres, by the submission by the colleges of plans for a course dealing with conservative political philosophy without relying on the specific philosophy of the testator. (But query.)

See Note, Application of cy pres doctrine to trust for promulgation of particular political or philosophical doctrines, 67 A.L.R.3d 417 (1975).

As to the creation of trusts for capricious purposes, see §62.14.·

[6]Medical Socy. of S.C. v. South Carolina Natl. Bank, 197 S.C. 96, 14 S.E.2d 577 (1941). See also Charleston Library Socy. v. Citizens & S. Natl. Bank, 200 S.C. 96, 20 S.E.2d 623 (1942), noted in 7 U.S.C. Selden Soc. Year Book 48.

In People ex rel. Redfern v. Hopewell Farms, 9 Ill. App. 3d 16, 291 N.E.2d 288 (1972), where a farm was carried on ostensibly for experimental research, but was in fact a profit-oriented enterprise, it was held subject to tax.

In In re Estate of Hermann, 454 Pa. 292, 312 A.2d 16 (1973), the court said that it was powerless to determine the question of the artistic merit of the objects of art to be exhibited in a museum.

See §374.7.

[7]Hoyt v. Bliss, 93 Conn. 344, 105 A. 699 (1919) (competitive scholarship in college).

[8]In re Estate of Grblny, 147 Neb. 117, 22 N.W.2d 488 (1946) (citing Restatement of Trusts §370).

§370.1.   General trusts to promote education.   A trust
for the promotion of education generally, without specifying
any particular method for achieving the purpose, is a valid charitable trust.[1] Thus in *Whicker v. Hume*[2] a trust for the advancement of education and learning in every part of the world was
upheld. In *President of the United States v. Drummond*[3] a trust for the
increase of knowledge among men was held to be a valid charitable trust. In such a case the trustees may apply the property in
their discretion in any reasonable method of effectuating the
testator's purpose, or if he did not intend to confer such discretion on them they may submit a scheme to the court for the
application of the property.

§370.2.   Physical training.   A trust for educational purposes need not be limited to the training of the mind but may
include the training of the body. A trust to provide athletic
facilities in a school is charitable.[1] Such a trust is nonetheless
charitable although it is not connected with a particular educa-

§370.1.   [1]Westport Bank & Trust Co. v. Fable, 126 Conn. 665, 13 A.2d
862 (1940) (citing Restatement of Trusts §§370, 376); In re Morton, [1941]
4 D.L.R. 763 (B.C.).

[2]7 H.L.C. 124 (1858).

[3]7 H.L.C. 155 (cited) (1838).

§370.2.   [1]*England:* In re Mariette, [1915] 2 Ch. 284; London Hosp. Medical College v. Inland Revenue Commrs., [1976] 1 W.L.R. 613, [1976] 2 All
E.R. 113 (to promote social, cultural, and athletic activities of students of a
medical college; a tax case).; Inland Revenue Commrs. v. McMullen, [1980]
2 W.L.R. 416, [1980] 1 All E.R. 884 (H.L.) (a football association set up a trust
to encourage pupils at schools and universities in the United Kingdom to play
association football or other games or sports and thereby to give physical
education to the students).

Illinois: People v. Catholic Bishop, 311 Ill. 11, 142 N.E. 520 (1924) (lake
used for swimming and boating).

Massachusetts: Wheaton College v. Town of Norton, 232 Mass. 141, 122
N.E. 280 (1919) (wild land used for recreation).

New York: Harvey School v. Town of Bedford, 34 A.D.2d 965, 312
N.Y.S.2d 586 (1970) (skating rink).

Ohio: College Preparatory School for Girls v. Evatt, 144 Ohio St. 408, 59
N.E.2d 142 (1945).

In Board of Trustees, etc. v. County of Santa Clara, 86 Cal. App. 3d 79,
150 Cal. Rptr. 109 (1978), it was held that land used by Stanford University
as a golf course was exempt from taxation as used exclusively for educational
purposes, although it could be used by faculty and alumni as well as students.

tional institution. Thus a bequest to a city to provide suitable playgrounds for children is charitable,[2] as is also a trust to provide an annual field day for schoolchildren.[3] A trust to maintain playgrounds or athletic fields for the public generally is a charitable trust, and it is immaterial that the enjoyment of the facilities thus afforded is not limited to children but extends to adults. Such trusts can be upheld not merely on the ground that they are educational, but also on the broader ground that they are of benefit to the community, particularly for the benefit of the underprivileged in the community. Thus in *In re Hadden*[4] a bequest to "give open-air recreation to as large a number of people as possible" was upheld as charitable. Clauson, J., pointed out that the purpose of the trust was to promote the health and welfare of the working classes, and not to encourage mere sport.

On the other hand, trusts for the promotion of sport have been held not to be charitable. Thus in *In re Nottage*[5] a trust to

---

[2]Greenman v. Phillips, 241 Mich. 464, 217 N.W. 1 (1928); Saint John v. Attorney-General, 51 N.B.R.2d 354, 134 A.P.R. 354 (N.B.Q.B. 1983) (trust to finance city skating rink for children).

[3]In re Melody, 34 T.L.R. 122 (1917); Re Porter: Porter v. Porter, 52 N.B.R.2d 130, 137 A.P.R. 130 (N.B.Q.B. 1983) (bequest to dance society in Scotland to establish scholarship for attending summer school).

In Estate of Fleming, 183 P.2d 295 (Cal. App. 1947), *rev'd on other grounds*, 31 Cal. 2d 514, 190 P.2d 611 (1948), a testator left property in trust to give scholarships to boys and girls, and directed that the recipients should be selected from those making the lowest scores in a golf tournament to be held annually for the purpose. It was held that the trust was exempt from an inheritance tax as a charitable trust.

In Bohemian Gymnastic Assn. Sokol v. Higgins, 144 F.2d 774 (2d Cir. 1945), noted in 45 Colum. L. Rev. 789, it was held that an association to promote various physical and mental undertakings among its members was an association exclusively for educational purposes and not a mere social club, for the purposes of the federal Social Security Act.

In Pomeroy v. Little League Baseball of Collingswood, 142 N.J. Super. 471, 362 A.2d 39 (1976), a little league baseball organization was held to be charitable and exempt from tort liability.

See Hutchinson, Recreational Charities — A Change of Tactics Required?, [1978] Conv. 355.

[4][1932] 1 Ch. 133, noted in 11 Can. B. Rev. 53, 18 Convey. 37, 172 L.T. 338.

See §§374.10, 374.11.

[5][1895] 2 Ch. 649.

See Bryan, Charity Law on the Football Field, 129 New L.J. 86 (1979).

promote yacht racing was held not to be charitable; and in *In re Clifford*[6] a trust to promote angling was held not to be charitable. These cases can also be supported on the ground that the trusts were for the benefit of the members of limited organizations. But a trust to encourage rifle shooting has been upheld, since it tends to train citizens in an art useful for the public defense.[7] On the same ground a trust to promote various sports among the members of a military regiment has been upheld.[8]

The question of trusts to promote sports is considered further hereafter.[9]

§370.3. Training for citizenship. A trust for the purpose of training young people in the duties and responsibilities of citizenship is charitable. Thus it is held that a trust to carry out the purposes of the Boy Scouts of America in training boys in citizenship, character, and leadership is a valid charitable trust for educational purposes.[1] Such a trust is charitable although not limited to children, as for example a trust to instruct immi-

---

[6] 81 L.J. Ch. (N.S.) 220 (1911).

[7] In re Stephens, 8 T.L.R. 792 (1892).

[8] In re Gray, [1925] Ch. 362.

[9] See §374.6A.

§370.3. [1] *England:* In re Webber, [1954] 3 All E.R. 712.

California: Young v. Boy Scouts of Am., 9 Cal. App. 2d 760, 51 P.2d 191 (1935).

Connecticut: See Charter Oak Council, Boy Scouts of Am. v. New Hartford, 121 Conn. 466, 185 A. 575 (1936).

Georgia: Tharpe v. Central Ga. Council of Boy Scouts of Am., 185 Ga. 810, 196 S.E. 762, 116 A.L.R. 373 (1938).

New Jersey: Stoolman v. Camden County Council Boy Scouts, 77 N.J. Super. 129, 185 A.2d 436 (1962).

Ohio: Westlake v. Ohio Northern Univ., 21 Ohio Misc. 202, 50 Ohio Ops. 2d 417, 256 N.E.2d 642 (1969) ("for recreational, educational and character-building activities, primarily for Union County rural people and their organizations").

Pennsylvania: Darlington's Estate, 289 Pa. 297, 137 A. 268 (1927); Wayne County Bd. of Assessment v. Rolling Hills Girl Scout Council, 19 Pa. Commw. 484, 353 A.2d 498 (1975) (girl scouts; a tax case).

Rhode Island: Tillinghast v. Boy Scouts of Am. Council at Narragansett Pier, 47 R.I. 406, 133 A. 662, 46 A.L.R. 823 (1926), noted in 30 Law Notes 213.

See 46 A.L.R. 827 (1927); 116 id. 378 (1938).

grants or others with respect to the duties of citizenship. In a case in Australia a trust to establish a training farm for delinquent boys, and to establish a home for difficult, wayward, or underprivileged boys, was held to be free of tax as a charitable trust.[2]

§370.4. **Dissemination of beliefs and doctrines.** A trust for the dissemination of beliefs or doctrines or information is not a valid charitable trust if they are of such a character that their dissemination is illegal.[1] Even though the beliefs or doctrines to be disseminated are not illegal, the trust is not a valid charitable trust if they are so irrational that it cannot be said that their dissemination can be of any benefit to the community.[2]

The mere fact, however, that the beliefs or doctrines to be disseminated are those of a minority group does not preclude the trust from being a valid charitable trust.[3] The difficult task is imposed on the courts to determine whether a belief or doctrine is of such a character that its dissemination is illegal, or at least that its dissemination cannot be of benefit to the community because of its absurdity, or whether it is merely one that is displeasing to the majority. In *George v. Braddock*[4] a lower court

---

[2]Salvation Army (Vict.) Property Trust v. Fern Tree Guffey Corp., 85 C.L.R. 159 (Austl., 1952).

See San Francisco Boys' Club v. County of Mendocino, 254 Cal. App. 2d 548, 62 Cal. Rptr. 294 (1967) (a tax case; part of expense came from timber sales).

§370.4. [1]See §377.

[2]See Girard Trust Co. v. Commissioner, 122 F.2d 108, 138 A.L.R. 448 (3d Cir. 1941) (citing the text), noted in 46 Dick. L. Rev. 199, 30 Geo. L.J. 316, 14 Rocky Mt. L. Rev. 70, 90 U. Pa. L. Rev. 365, 27 Wash. U.L.Q. 276.

[3]Estate of Mealy, 91 Cal. App. 2d 371, 204 P.2d 971 (1949).

California: In re Estate of Connolly, 48 Cal. App. 3d 129, 121 Ca. Rptr. 325 (1975) (citing the text and Restatement of Trusts §370).

In Leubuscher v. Commissioner, 54 F.2d 998 (2d Cir. 1932), it was held that in determining the estate tax a legacy for teaching and propagating the ideas of Henry George was a charitable trust exclusively for educational purposes.

See Note, Tax exemptions for educational institutions: discretion and discrimination, 128 U. Pa. L. Rev. 849 (1980).

[4]45 N.J. Eq. 757, 18 A. 881, 6 L.R.A. 511, 14 Am. St. Rep. 754 (1889).

In Ross v. Freeman, 21 Del. Ch. 44, 180 A. 527 (1935), where land was conveyed to establish a village in which the only taxes would be derived from

in New Jersey held invalid a trust to publish the works of Henry George, in which the capitalistic system with reference to the holding of land was vigorously attacked and the "single tax" was advocated, but the highest court of the state upheld the trust. In *Peth v. Spear*[5] the Supreme Court of Washington upheld a trust to provide a place where the doctrines of socialism could be taught by example as well as by precept. On the other hand, it has been held in England that a trust to establish a college for the training of spiritualist mediums is not charitable.[6] It is arguable, however, that since there are intelligent persons who believe in spiritualism and the possibility of communication with the dead through the instrumentality of mediums, the purpose is not so irrational as to prevent it from being a charitable purpose.

§370.5. Public and private institutions. A trust for the promotion of public education is charitable. There is no difficulty in upholding trusts for the benefit of public schools or other educational institutions conducted by the state or one of its subdivisions, where all citizens possessing the proper educational qualifications are admitted within their doors.[1] Such

---

land rentals, thus applying the notions of Henry George as to the single tax, it was held that the disposition was charitable. See also Broeker v. Ware, 27 Del. Ch. 8, 29 A.2d 591 (1942).

See Annotation, Validity, as for a charitable purpose, of trust for publication or distribution of particular books or writings, 34 A.L.R.4th 958 (1984).

[5]63 Wash. 291, 115 P. 164 (1911).

Cf. People *ex rel.* Hartigan v. National Anti-Drug Coalition, 124 Ill. App. 3d 269, 79 Ill. Dec. 786, 464 N.E.2d 690 (1984) (society to disseminate propaganda against the use of drugs is charitable); Planned Parenthood League of Mass. v. Attorney Gen., 391 Mass. 709, 464 N.E.2d 55, *cert. denied,* 469 U.S. 858, 105 S. Ct. 189, 83 L. Ed. 2d 122 (1984) (society to disseminate propaganda in favor of planned parenthood is charitable).

[6]In re Hummeltenberg, [1923] 1 Ch. 237.

In Lockwood's Estate, 344 Pa. 293, 25 A.2d 168 (1942), it was held that an outright gift to an incorporated spiritualistic college was valid.

In Stephan's Estate, 129 Pa. Super. 396, 195 A. 653 (1937), a trust for the perpetual upkeep of a spiritualist memorial was held invalid.

§370.5. [1]*Iowa:* Liggett v. Abbott, 192 Iowa 742, 185 N.W. 569 (1921).

Kentucky: Trustees Stewart Common School Fund v. Lewis, 234 Ky. 286, 28 S.W.2d 27 (1930).

Massachusetts: Davis v. Inhabitants of Barnstable, 154 Mass. 224, 28 N.E. 165 (1891); Bartlett, Petitioner, 163 Mass. 509, 40 N.E. 899 (1895).

trusts may be supported not merely on the ground that they promote education, but also on the ground that they assist the government in the performance of one of its governmental functions.[2] A trust in aid of public education is charitable not only where the property is to be used for the establishment or maintenance of a public school, but also where it is to be used to aid in the establishment or maintenance of a pension or retirement fund for the teachers in the public schools.[3] Such a trust is not merely for the benefit of the individuals who ultimately become recipients of the benefits of the fund, but is a trust to promote education by affording financial security to the teachers and, indeed, in the case of public school teachers it assists the government in the performance of its functions. Such a trust is as clearly charitable as a trust for the payment of salaries to the teachers.

An interesting case involving the question whether a bequest was for the benefit of a state institution arose in California.[4] A testator made a bequest to the state university of which

---

New Hampshire: Reed v. Pittsfield School Dist., 91 N.H. 209, 16 A.2d 704 (1940).

Oregon: In re John's Will, 30 Or. 494, 47 P. 341, 50 P. 226, 36 L.R.A. 242 (1896).

See 48 A.L.R. 1126 (1927).

In In re Mackenzie, [1962] 2 All E.R. 890, where a testator bequeathed £5000 to a county council in Scotland to assist pupils at a public primary school to continue their education at a secondary school by a provision for bursaries, it was held that the trust failed because students were entitled to support from the government.

In Board of Regents of Univ. of Neb. v. Exon, 199 Neb. 146, 256 N.W.2d 330 (1977), it was held that under the constitution of Nebraska the Board of Regents of the state university had independent authority, and that a statute providing that gifts to the university of more than $10,000 must be approved by the governor was unconstitutional as infringing on the authority of the Board of Regents.

In In re South Place Ethical Socy., [1980] 1 W.L.R. 1565, it was held that a society to promote ethical principles, whose members were agnostics but not atheists, was charitable not as advancing religion but as educational.

[2]See §373.

[3]Carpenter, For An Opinion, 47 R.I. 461, 134 A. 16, 47 A.L.R. 60 (1926); Powers v. Home for Aged Women, 55 R.I. 187, 192 A. 770, 110 A.L.R. 1361 (1937).

See 47 A.L.R. 63 (1927); 110 id. 1369 (1937).

[4]Estate of Purington, 199 Cal. 661, 250 P. 657 (1926).

In Attorney-General v. Ross, [1986] 1 W.L.R. 252 (Ch.D.), it was held that

the income was to be used in giving free scholarships to deserving students. A statute in California forbids a bequest of more than one third of the testator's property for charitable purposes, but excepts bequests to any state institution for the use of the institution. It was held that the bequest in question came within the exception. It was contended by the next of kin that the bequest was not for the benefit of the institution but only for the benefit of the recipients of the scholarships. In that case it would be a charitable bequest, but it would not come within the exception. The court held that the bequest was for the benefit of the institution and not merely for the benefit of the students.

On the other hand, a trust is nonetheless charitable although it is for the benefit of a private educational institution, provided that it is not a proprietary institution. The fact that the institution is not conducted by the government, and the fact that all of the members of the public are not accepted as students in the institution, does not prevent it from being a charitable institution. A trust to establish or maintain an educational institution not conducted for private profit is charitable, although it is provided that the students shall pay fees.[5] A trust to establish a fund to lend money to students to assist them in acquiring an education is charitable, although the borrowers are required to pay interest on the loans, provided that the interest is to be used for the same purpose or for other charitable purposes.[6]

On the other hand, a trust is not a charitable trust if any

---

public funds paid over to a polytechnic student union to advance the education of the students were held upon charitable trust for education and that the Attorney-General had standing to maintain a suit for an injunction against use of the funds to aid a miners' strike and to relieve famine in Ethiopia.

[5]Younger v. Wisdom Socy., 121 Cal. App. 3d 683, 175 Cal. Rptr. 542 (1981) (charitable corporation).

See §376.

[6]*Illinois:* Morgan v. National Trust Bank of Charleston, 331 Ill. 182, 162 N.E. 888 (1928), noted in 3 Temp. U.L.Q. 226; Summers v. Chicago Title & Trust Co., 335 Ill. 564, 167 N.E. 777 (1929), noted in 24 Ill. L. Rev. 687, 39 Yale L.J. 437.

Kentucky: Owens v. Owens' Exr., 236 Ky. 118, 32 S.W.2d 731 (1930); Goode's Admr. v. Goode, 238 Ky. 620, 38 S.W.2d 691 (1931).

New York: Matter of Davidge, 200 A.D. 437, 193 N.Y.S. 245 (1922).

Pennsylvania: Wright's Estate, 284 Pa. 334, 131 A. 188 (1925), noted in 39 Harv. L. Rev. 659.

profits arising from it are to be devoted to private uses. Thus where an educational institution is conducted for private profit it is not a charitable institution.[7]

A question as to the distinction between a public and a private institution arose in the case of Girard College. In the *Girard Will Case*[8] it was held that, where property was given to a city to establish a school for poor male white orphan children, the school was not a public school and racial segregation was not prohibited by the Fourteenth Amendment to the Constitution of the United States. The judgment was reversed by the Supreme Court of the United States in *Pennsylvania v. Board of Directors of City Trusts.*[9] Thereafter the Orphans' Court in Pennsylvania removed the Board of Directors of City Trusts as trustees and appointed individual trustees. Its action was approved by the Supreme Court of Pennsylvania.[10] The Supreme Court of the United States denied certiorari and dismissed an appeal.[11] Ten years later it denied certiorari to a court of appeals decision that the change of trustees was a state involvement and that Girard College must admit black children.[12]

In *Evans v. Newton*[13] a testator devised land to the City of

[7]Radosevic v. Virginia Intermont College, 633 F. Supp. 1084 (W.D. Va. 1986).

See §376.

[8]386 Pa. 548, 127 A.2d 287 (1956), *aff'g* 4 D.&C.2d 671 (Pa. 1955).

In Bob Jones Univ. v. United States, 461 U.S. 574, 103 S. Ct. 2017, 76 L. Ed. 2d 157 (1983), citing §377, *infra*, a private university with a racially discriminatory policy based on religious reasons was denied federal tax exemption as a charity.

[9]353 U.S. 230, 989, 77 S. Ct. 806, 1281, 1 L. Ed. 2d 792, 1146 (1957).

[10]391 Pa. 434, 138 A.2d 844 (1958).

[11]357 U.S. 570 (1958), noted in 20 Ohio St. L.J. 132.

See Note, Constitutionality of restricted scholarships, 33 N.Y.U.L. Rev. 604 (1958); Note, Restricted Scholarships: Problems in Standing to Challenge, Constitutionality, Cy Pres, and Legislative Policy, 1963 Wis. L. Rev. 254.

See §96.4. Compare §373.

[12]Commonwealth v. Brown, 392 F.2d 120 (3d Cir. 1968), 25 A.L.R.3d 724, *cert. denied,* 391 U.S. 921 (1968).

Cf. Trustees of Univ. of Del. v. Gebelin, 420 A.2d 1191 (Del. Ch. 1980) (trust for scholarship for white females in state university amended cy pres to delete "white" but not "female").

As to the effect of racial and religious restrictions, see §399.4.

[13]220 Ga. 280, 138 S.E.2d 573 (1964).

Macon in trust to maintain a park for white people only. It was held by the Supreme Court of Georgia that the lower court properly accepted the resignation of the city as trustee and appointed individuals as successor trustees. The judgment was reversed by the Supreme Court of the United States.[14] Mr. Justice Douglas, speaking for the majority, said that the service rendered by a park of this character is municipal in nature and that it should be treated as a public institution whether administered by a municipality or by private trustees. Three of the justices dissented on the ground that it was within the power of the state court to substitute new trustees and that its judgment did not involve the question of segregation. Thereafter the Supreme Court of Georgia held that the sole purpose for which the trust was created had become impossible of accomplishment and that it should be terminated, and the court remitted the case to the lower court to determine who was entitled to the property under a resulting trust.[15]

§370.6. Limited classes of beneficiaries. A trust is not a charitable trust if the persons who are to benefit are not of a sufficiently large or indefinite class so that the community is interested in the enforcement of the trust.[1] This is true even though the purpose of the trust is to promote education. Thus a trust to educate a particular person or named persons, though valid, is not charitable.[2] Such a trust is a private trust and is valid

---

[14]Evans v. Newton, 382 U.S. 296, 86 S. Ct. 486, 15 L. Ed. 2d 373 (1966).

[15]Evans v. Newton, 221 Ga. 870, 148 S.E.2d 329 (1966). In Evans v. Abney, 224 Ga. 826, 165 S.E.2d 160 (1968), *aff'd,* 396 U.S. 435, 90 S. Ct. 628, 24 L. Ed. 3d 634 (1970) (Douglas and Brennan, JJ., dissenting), it was held that the doctrine of cy pres was not applicable and that heirs of the testator were entitled to the property.

§370.6. [1]See §375.

In In re Co-operative College of Can., 64 D.L.R.3d 531 (Sask. 1975), a college was created for the purpose of benefiting all phases of co-operative and credit union development and operation. It was held not to be a charitable institution, although it was for educational purposes and not for individual profit, because it was so limited in its purpose as not to be of public benefit. The purpose was similar to political purposes. See §374.6.

[2]See Sherwin v. Smith, 282 Mass. 306, 185 N.E. 17 (1933).

But see In re Regan, 8 D.L.R.2d 541 (N.S. 1957).

See §§369.5, 375.2.

unless it violates the principle of the rule against perpetuities. So also a trust to educate the descendants of the testator, or of another person, is not charitable.[3]

On the other hand, a trust for education is nonetheless charitable although the persons to receive the education are of a limited class if the class is not so small that the purpose is not of benefit to the community. Thus a trust for the education of children living in a certain district is charitable. So is a trust to educate persons of a particular race or sex or religion.[4] So is a trust for the education of children of persons of a particular profession or trade or of a particular social class.[5] Similarly, the beneficiaries of a scholarship may be limited to persons living in a particular place or belonging to a certain class. It would seem also that a scholarship may be limited to persons bearing a certain surname, at least if the name is not too uncommon.

A trust is charitable where the possible beneficiaries do not belong to too limited a class, although the trustees are to select

---

In Bauer v. United States, 449 F. Supp. 755 (W.D. La. 1978), *aff'd,* 594 F.2d 44 (5th Cir. 1979), a settlor created a trust fund to provide each year a scholarship for a student in each of several high schools to be selected by the principal. It was held that the trust was charitable for tax purposes, even though the settlor knew which students had been selected, because he had no power to make the selection.

[3]See §375.3.

[4]*Connecticut:* Lockwood v. Killiam, 172 Conn. 496, 375 A.2d 998 (1977) (citing the text and Restatement of Trusts §370, Comment *j*), *modified,* 179 Conn. 62, 425 A.2d 909 (1979).

New York: Matter of Johnson, 93 A.D.2d 1, 460 N.Y.S.2d 932 (1983), citing the text, *rev'd,* Matter of Estate of Wilson, 59 N.Y.2d 461, 452 N.E.2d 1228, 465 N.Y.S.2d 900 (1983), noted in 53 U. Cin. L. Rev. 297 (1984), and in 12 Hastings Const. L.Q. 127 (1984), citing §370.

See §399.4A, nn. 27, 37. But see §370.5, n. 8, *supra.*

[5]See Hall v. Derby Sanitary Auth., 16 Q.B.D. 163 (1885), which was distinguished in Oppenheim v. Tobacco Sec. Trust Co., [1951] A.C. 297, where the House of Lords held that a trust for the education of children of employees of a particular tobacco company was not charitable.

See §375.2.

Re Porter; Porter v. Porter, 52 N.B.R.2d 130, 137 A.P.R. 130 (N.B.Q.B. 1983) (bequest to university to establish scholarships for deserving students from particular school district): Native Communications Socy. of B.C. v. Minister of National Revenue, 86 D.T.C. 6353, 67 N.R. 146, [1986] 2 C.T.C. 170 (Fed. Ct. App.) (society to communicate to Indians and Eskimos).

from time to time a single beneficiary. Thus in *Ashmore v. New-man*[6] a testator bequeathed $1000 to pay the income as a prize to that boy or girl who should produce in any year the best calf or pig. It was held that the trust was a charitable trust. In the same case it was held that another bequest of $2000 in trust to pay the interest to the highest-ranking student of the graduating class of a named high school was charitable.

§371. Advancement of Religion

A trust for the advancement of religion is a charitable trust. It is true that the Statute of Charitable Uses made no mention of this purpose in its enumeration of charitable purposes, the only reference to religion in any form being "repair of bridges, forts, havens, causeways, *churches,* sea-banks and highways." Indeed, Sir Francis Moore, the draftsman of the act, explained that religious purposes were omitted intentionally

> lest the gifts intended to be employed upon purposes grounded upon charity, might, in change of times (contrary to the minds of the givers) be confiscate into the King's treasury. For religion being variable, according to the pleasure of succeeding princes, that which at one time is held for orthodox, may at another, be accounted superstitious, and then such lands are confiscate.[1]

The struggle between Protestantism and Catholicism under the Tudor sovereigns was present to the mind of the draftsman of the act. Nevertheless, as early as 1639 it was held that a trust to maintain a preaching minister was a valid charitable trust.[2] From then on the courts in England had no doubt that a trust to

[6]350 Ill. 64, 183 N.E. 1 (1932).

Cf. Estate of Bunch v. Heirs of Bunch, 485 So. 2d 284 (Miss. 1986) ("to help one or two young men through medical school").

But see Re Miller Estate, 22 E.T.R. 107 (B.C. Sup. Ct. 1986) (trust to establish award for "beautiful lyric" or for prose that "portrays the beautiful" is not charitable).

§371. [1]Moore, Readings upon the Statute of 43 Elizabeth, contained in Duke, Law of Charitable Uses, 131, 132 (1676).

[2]Pember v. Inhabitants of Knighton, Duke, Law of Charitable Uses, 82 (1639).

promote in any way the established religion is a valid charitable trust. Only gradually, however, did the English courts come to uphold, as charitable, trusts for other religions than that of the establishment. In 1754 in the well-known case of *Da Costa v. De Pas*[3] a Jewish testator left money to be applied toward establishing a Jesuba or assembly for reading the Jewish law and instructing the people in the Jewish religion. The court held that the trust was illegal, but that under the doctrine of cy pres the king might apply the fund to other charitable purposes.

Gradually, the disabilities of religions other than that of the established church were removed. The disabilities of Protestant dissenters were done away with by the Toleration Act, 1688, and other succeeding acts. This toleration was extended in the middle of the nineteenth century to Roman Catholics and to Jews. Accordingly, trusts for the promotion of the Roman Catholic religion[4] and for the promotion of the Jewish religion[5] were upheld. In 1842 the House of Lords upheld a trust for the promotion of Unitarianism.[6] In the United States the courts have had no difficulty in upholding trusts for the promotion of any form of religion.[7]

[3] 1 Amb. 228 (1754).
[4] Bradshaw v. Tasker, 2 Myl. & K. 221 (1834).
[5] Straus v. Goldsmid, 8 Sim. 614 (1837).
[6] Shore v. Wilson, 9 Cl. & Fin. 355 (1842).
See Holmes v. Attorney-General, [1981] 2 C.L. §234a (Ch. Div. 1981) (trust to provide a meeting room for the Plymouth Brethren, "an ultra puritan sect," charitable).

Cf. Re South Place Ethical Socy.; Barralet v. Attorney-General, [1980] 3 All E.R. 918 (Ch. Div.) (society for study and dissemination of ethical principles and that did not believe in God was not a religious charity but was an educational charity).

[7] *Federal:* Girard Trust Co. v. Commissioner, 122 F.2d 108, 138 A.L.R. 448 (3d Cir. 1941) (bequest to Board of Temperance, Prohibition and Public Morals of the Methodist Episcopal Church held deductible under federal estate tax; quoting the text), noted in 46 Dick. L. Rev. 199, 30 Geo. L.J. 316, 14 Rocky Mtn. L. Rev. 70, 90 U. Pa. L. Rev. 365, 27 Wash. U.L.Q. 276.

Arkansas: Garrett v. Mendenhall, 209 Ark. 898, 192 S.W.2d 972 (1946) (bequest to unincorporated church for best interests of church and community).

Iowa: Quinn v. Shields, 62 Iowa 129, 17 N.W. 437, 49 Am. Rep. 141 (1883) (support of charitable institutions of Roman Catholic faith).

Kansas: In re Estate of Freshour, 185 Kan. 434, 345 P.2d 689, 81 A.L.R.2d

§371.1. **Methods of advancing religion.** Trusts for the advancement of religion may assume various forms, such as the erection or maintenance of a church; the erection of a memorial window in a church; the care of a graveyard attached to a church; the payment of or augmentation of the salary of a minister; the payment of the salary of an organist or of a choir; the preaching of sermons; the distribution of religious literature; the promotion of the work of home and foreign missions.[1]

---

806 (1959) (to a Catholic bishop for the benefit of a parish, and to the trustees of a church for the benefit of the members of the church).

Massachusetts: Chase v. Dickey, 212 Mass. 555, 99 N.E. 410 (1912) (Christian Science); Glaser v. Congregation Kehillath Israel, 263 Mass. 435, 161 N.E. 619 (1928) (Jewish religion).

Missouri: Glidewell v. Glidewell, 360 Mo. 713, 230 S.W.2d 752 (1950) (devise to unincorporated church).

New Hampshire: Glover v. Baker, 76 N.H. 393, 83 A. 916 (1912) (Christian Science).

New Jersey: Jones v. Watford, 62 N.J. Eq. 339, 50 A. 180 (1901), *modified,* 64 N.J. Eq. 785, 53 A. 397 (1902) (spiritualism); Vineland Trust Co. v. Westendorf, 86 N.J. Eq. 343, 98 A. 314 (1916), *aff'd,* 87 N.J. Eq. 675, 103 A. 1054 (1917) (metaphysical thought).

Pennsylvania: Arnold's Estate, 56 D.&C. 662 (Pa. 1946) (citing Restatement of Trusts §371).

Tennessee: Kopsombut-Myint Buddhist Center v. State Bd. of Equalization, 728 S.W. 2d 327 (Tenn. App. 1986) (Buddhist temple and ecumenical center for Buddhist studies).

Virginia: Maguire v. Loyd, 193 Va. 138, 67 S.E.2d 885 (1952) (Christian Science church; citing the text and Restatement of Trusts §371).

See Re Orr, 40 Ont. L. Rep. 567 (1917) (Christian Science).

In this treatise we do not consider the problems that arise where there is a conflict of doctrine and a local church withdraws from its parent organization. See Protestant Episcopal Church v. Graves, 161 N.J. Super. 230, 391 A.2d 563 (1978). See §397.3.

See 15 Williston, Contracts (3 ed.) §1746.

In In re South Place Ethical Socy., [1980] 1 W.L.R. 1565, *sub nom.* Barralet v. Attorney-General, [1980] 3 All E.R. 918, noted in [1981] Conv. 150, it was held that a society to promote ethical principles, whose members were agnostics but not atheists, was charitable not as advancing religion but as educational.

See Annot., What constitutes church, religious society, or institution exempt from property tax under state constitutional or statutory provisions, 28 A.L.R.4th 344 (1984).

§371.1 [1]*England:* Pember v. Inhabitants of Knighton, Duke, Law of Charitable Uses 82 (1639) (to maintain preaching minister); Attorney-General

v. City of London, 1 Ves. Jr. 243 (1780) (advancement of Christianity among infidels); Attorney-General v. Stepney, 10 Ves. 22 (1804) (distribution of Bibles and other religious books); Thornton v. Howe, 31 Beav. 14 (1862) (distribution of literature of particular sect); Commissioners for Special Purposes of Income Tax v. Pemsel, [1891] A.C. 531 (maintenance of missionary establishment); In re Forster, [1939] Ch. 22 (to society for the relief of sick and aged priests — not limited to poor priests); In re Royce, [1940] Ch. 514 (church choir), noted in 4 Convey. (N.S.) 424; In re Mylne, [1941] Ch. 204 (benefit of missionaries, active or retired), noted in 5 Convey. (N.S.) 312, 76 Ir. L.T. 111, 57 L.Q. Rev. 171; In re Moon's Will Trusts, [1948] 1 All E.R. 300 (mission work); In re Norton's Will Trusts, [1948] 2 All E.R. 842 (benefit of church and parish); Glasgow Corp. v. Johnstone, [1965] A.C. 609 (house for church officer; tax case); In re Watson, [1973] 1 W.L.R. 1472, [1973] 3 All E.R. 678 (for the continuance of the work of God as it has been maintained by H. and myself); Holmes v. Attorney-General, [1981] 2 C.L. §234a (Ch. Div. 1981) (trust to provide a meeting room for the Plymouth Brethren, "an ultra puritan sect," charitable).

Federal: King v. Richardson, 136 F.2d 849 (4th Cir. 1943), *cert. denied sub nom.* Richardson v. King, 320 U.S. 777 (1943) (benefit of home and foreign missions and benevolent causes of church in such proportion as trustees of church deem best); Elisian Guild v. United States, 412 F.2d 121 (1st Cir. 1969) (to collect, publish, and distribute religious books; a tax case); Parkersburg Natl. Bank v. United States, 228 F. Supp. 375 (N.D. W. Va. 1964) (income to be paid to persons in charge of a choir of a named church; a tax case).

Alaska: Bolshanin v. Zlobin, 76 F. Supp. 281 (D. Alaska, 1948) (to archbishop for benefit of church).

Arizona: In re Estate of Kidd, 106 Ariz. 554, 479 P.2d 697 (1971), *cert. denied,* 404 U.S. 842, 92 S. Ct. 138, 30 L. Ed. 2d 77, *rehearing denied,* 404 U.S. 960, 92 S. Ct. 311, 30 L. Ed. 2d 279 (1971) (the money to go "in a research of some scientific proof of a soul of the human body which leaves at death").

California: Estate of Moore, 219 Cal. App. 2d 737, 33 Cal. Rptr. 427 (1963) (to a church for its missionary work; citing the text).

Connecticut: FitzGerald v. East Lawn Cemetery, 126 Conn. 286, 10 A.2d 683 (1940) (memorial chapel; citing Restatement of Trusts §371).

Delaware: Hutton v. St. Paul Bhd. of People's Church, 20 Del. Ch. 413, 178 A. 584 (1935) (to church to establish foundation for lectures on Christian subjects); Girard Trust Co. v. St. Anne's P.E. Church, 30 Del. Ch. 1, 52 A.2d 591 (1947) (erection of chapel and parish house; citing Restatement of Trusts §368); Delaware Trust Co. v. Graham, 30 Del. Ch. 330, 61 A.2d 110 (1948) (foreign missions; citing the text), noted in 9 Md. L. Rev. 359.

Florida: In re Williams' Estate, 59 So. 2d 13 (Fla. 1952) (broadcasting the Gospel over radio).

Georgia: Roughton v. Jones, 225 Ga. 774, 171 S.E.2d 536 (1969) (for home and foreign missions).

Idaho: In re Coleman's Estate, 66 Idaho 567, 163 P.2d 847 (1945) (to be distributed among churches).

Illinois: People ex rel. Marsters v. Missionaries, 409 Ill. 370, 99 N.E.2d 186 (1951) (seminary for education of students and conduct of retreats).

Indiana: Scobey v. Beckman, 111 Ind. App. 574, 41 N.E.2d 847 (1942) (devise of house as parsonage; quoting Restatement of Trusts §371), noted in 41 Mich. L. Rev. 332; Bible Inst. Colportage Assn. v. St. Joseph Bank & Trust Co., 118 Ind. App. 592, 75 N.E.2d 666 (1947) (publication and dissemination of evangelical Christian literature; citing Restatement of Trusts §371).

Iowa: Gray v. Watters, 243 Iowa 430, 51 N.W.2d 885 (1952) (to be disposed of to religious organizations).

Kansas: Leeper v. Salvation Army, 158 Kan. 396, 147 P.2d 702 (1944) (Salvation Army); In re Estate of Yetter (Simmons v. Reynolds), 183 Kan. 340, 328 P.2d 738 (1958) (toward the salary of the minister of a church; citing Restatement of Trusts §371).

Kentucky: Shrader v. Erickson's Exr., 284 Ky. 449, 145 S.W.2d 63 (1940) (education of young priests).

Massachusetts: Going v. Emery, 16 Pick. 107, 26 Am. Dec. 645 (Mass. 1834) (to cause of Christ, for benefit and promotion of true evangelical piety and religion); Hinckley v. Thatcher, 139 Mass. 477, 1 N.E. 840, 52 Am. Rep. 719 (1885) (missions); Sears v. Attorney Gen., 193 Mass. 551, 79 N.E. 772, 9 Ann. Cas. 1200 (1907) (support of dignity of bishop); Howard v. Howard, 227 Mass. 395, 116 N.E. 937 (1917) (parsonage); Reed v. Fogg, 248 Mass. 336, 143 N.E. 47 (1924) (to keep church edifice in repair and to provide organist); Curtis v. First Church in Charlestown, 285 Mass. 73, 188 N.E. 631 (1933) (church chimes); Mackey v. Bowen, 332 Mass. 167, 124 N.E.2d 254 (1955) (altar in church; citing the text and Restatement of Trusts §371).

Minnesota: In re Estate of Lundquist, 193 Minn. 474, 259 N.W. 9 (1935) (missions).

Missouri: Board of Trustees of Hannibal Presbytery v. Taylor, 359 Mo. 417, 221 S.W.2d 964 (1949) (church building to be used by all denominations of Christians; quoting Restatement of Trusts, §371, Comment *b*), noted in 18 U. Kan. L. Rev. 78; First Natl. Bank of Kansas City v. Stevenson, 293 S.W.2d 362 (Mo. 1956) (to church for specified purposes); McMenomy v. Williford, 526 S.W.2d 880 (Mo. App. 1975) (to a named trustee to be used in his discretion for evangelistic and mission purposes); Pilgrim Evangelical Lutheran Church of the Unaltered Augsburg Confession v. Lutheran Church-Missouri Synod Found., 661 S.W.2d 833 (Mo. App. 1983), *transfer to S. Ct. denied* (1984), citing text and Restatement (Second) of Trusts, §371, Comment *a* (maintenance of local church).

New Jersey: Jones v. Watford, 62 N.J. Eq. 339, 50 A. 180 (1901), *modified,* 64 N.J. Eq. 785, 53 A. 397 (1902) (to purchase and make available books upon philosophy of spiritualism); Parker v. Fidelity Union Trust Co., 2 N.J. Super. 362, 63 A.2d 902 (1944) (floral decorations and memorial window or clock); Wendell v. Hazel Wood Cemetery, 3 N.J. Super. 457, 67 A.2d 219 (1949), *aff'd,* 7 N.J. Super. 117, 72 A.2d 383 (1950) (to erect and maintain chapel in cemetery); Litcher v. Trust Co. of N.J., 11 N.J. 64, 93 A.2d 368 (1952), *aff'g* 18 N.J. Super. 101, 86 A.2d 601 (1952) (to educate a youth for the priesthood and to promote Roman Catholic missions).

New Mexico: Rhodes v. Yater, 27 N.M. 489, 202 P. 698, 22 A.L.R. 692 (1921) (preaching the Gospel).

New York: Matter of Thomson, 135 Misc. 62, 237 N.Y.S. 622 (1929) (salary of minister of particular church); Matter of Merritt, 273 A.D. 79, 75 N.Y.S.2d 828 (1947), *aff'g* 185 Misc. 979, 61 N.Y.S.2d 537 (1945) (to erect chapel in England); Matter of MacFarland, 95 N.Y.S.2d 258 (1950) (to furnish flowers weekly for pulpit of church); Matter of Liebeck, 109 N.Y.S.2d 147 (1951) (to a pastor, who predeceased testatrix, as he may see fit for church purposes); Matter of Kearney, 13 Misc. 2d 106, 177 N.Y.S.2d 855 (1958) (to a pastor or his successors to assist young men financially in their study for the priesthood); Gospel Volunteers v. Village of Speculator, 29 N.Y.2d 622, 273 N.E.2d 139, 324 N.Y.S.2d 412 (1971), *aff'g* 33 A.D.2d 407, 308 N.Y.S.2d 785 (organization maintaining camps for the purpose of promoting the Christian religion through Bible study, religious meetings, and recreation; held exempt from tax on the land); Rudolf Steiner Educ. & Farming Assn. v. Brennan, 65 A.D.2d 868, 410 N.Y.S.2d 404 (1978) (education as to farming methods; a tax case); Mount Trempler Lutheran Camp v. Board of Assessors, 70 A.D.2d 984, 417 N.Y.S.2d 796 (1979) (a Christian camping project).

North Carolina: Whitsett v. Clapp, 200 N.C. 647, 158 S.E. 183 (1931) (to keep up preaching in weak churches and for home missionary work).

Pennsylvania: Archambault's Estate, 308 Pa. 549, 162 A. 801 (1932) (to make a pew free).

Rhode Island: Thomas v. General Bd. of Church of Nazarene, 76 R.I. 197, 68 A.2d 66 (1949) (for the purpose of church worship and religious service of the Almighty God); Gott v. Norberg, 417 A.2d 1352 (R.I. 1980) (Watch Tower Bible and Tract Society of Pennsylvania; a tax case).

South Dakota: In re Geppert's Estate, 75 S.D. 96, 59 N.W.2d 727 (1953) (to Catholic bishop to be used by him and his successors for support of work of church in poorer parishes of state).

Tennessee: Lewis v. Darnell, 580 S.W.2d 572 (Tenn. App. 1979) (for missions).

Texas: San Antonio Indep. School Dist. v. Division of World Missions, 161 Tex. 471, 341 S.W.2d 896 (1961), *aff'g* Division of World Missions v. National Bank of Commerce, 326 S.W.2d 934 (Tex. Civ. App. 1959) (to a missionary society in trust for needy Chinese); Bode v. Loeffler, 540 S.W.2d 465 (Tex. Civ. App. 1976), *writ refused* (fund for retired ministers).

Washington: Gwinn v. Church of the Nazarene, 66 Wash. 2d 838, 405 P.2d 602 (1965) (to a church to be used in foreign missions as directed by a committee of named persons).

Canada: In re Meikle, [1943] 3 D.L.R. 668 (Alta.) (to church to use income as part of minister's salary); In re Anderson, [1943] 4 D.L.R. 268 (Ont.) (to provide religious book for use in grade schools); In re MacKay Estate, [1948] S.C.R. 500 (Can.) (to church as endowment fund).

Ireland: Maguire v. Attorney-General, [1943] I.R. 238 (to found a convent of Perpetual Adoration of the Blessed Sacrament); In re MacCarthy, [1958] I.R. 311 (to apply the income for traveling expenses of two or more invalids each year on an organized religious pilgrimage to Lourdes).

§371.2. General trusts for religion. A trust for the advancement of religion without specifying any method of achieving the purpose is a valid charitable trust. Thus in *Matter of Durbrow* [1] a testatrix left the residue of her estate to her executor to distribute it as he or his successor should consider as "most effective to the advancement of Christ's kingdom on earth." The lower court held that this was too indefinite a purpose and that the intended trust failed, but the Court of Appeals upheld the trust. There are numerous other cases in which a trust to promote religion was upheld in spite of the generality of the purpose.[2] Occasionally, it is true, there is a decision to the effect that

---

New Zealand: In re Macdonald, [1951] N.Z.L.R. 502 (to aid missionary work by scholarships, providing place for clerical workers to stay during transit or on holidays, and to repair vessels used in the missionary work); Centrepoint Community Growth Trust v. Commissioner of Inland Revenue, [1985] 1 N.Z.L.R. 673 (H.C.) (trust to maintain a religious community for persons who transferred all their property to the trust and received from it food, shelter, and health care, is charitable).

See Crowther, Religious Trusts (1954); Newark, Public Benefit and Religious Trusts, 62 L.Q. Rev. 234 (1946); Note, Charitable Trusts for Religious Purposes, 22 St. John's L. Rev. 241 (1948).

In Jewish Natl. Fund v. Royal Trust Co., [1965] S.C.R. 784 (Canada), *aff'g* In re Schechter, 43 D.L.R.2d 417 (B.C. 1964), a testator left his estate to the Jewish National Fund, a New York corporation, to be used to purchase land in Palestine, the United States, or one of the Dominions, for the establishment therein of a Jewish colony or colonies. It was held that the bequest failed because the purpose was not charitable (not for the promotion of religion, to relieve poverty, or for the benefit of the community).

In New York the court has taken a very strict view as to the tax on real estate. See American Bible Soc. v. Lewisohn, 40 N.Y.2d 78, 351 N.E.2d 697, 386 N.Y.S.2d 49 (1976) (a corporation for the distribution of Bibles). See also Swedenborg Found. v. Lewisohn, 40 N.Y.2d 87, 351 N.E.2d 702, 386 N.Y.S.2d 54 (1976) (a foundation for dissemination of the religious and philosophical writings of a famous theologian).

§371.2. [1] 245 N.Y. 469, 157 N.E. 747 (1927), noted in 13 Cornell L.Q. 310, 22 Ill. L. Rev. 454.

[2] *England:* Attorney-General v. Stepney, 10 Ves. 22 (1804) (increase and improvement of Christian knowledge and promoting religion); Attorney-General v. Pearson, 3 Mer. 353, 409 (1817) (worship of God); Townsend v. Carus, 3 Hare 257 (1843) (purposes having regard to the glory of God in the spiritual welfare of his creatures); Wilkinson v. Lindgren, L.R. 5 Ch. App. 570 (1870) (such religious purposes as trustees think proper); In re Lea, 34 Ch. D. 528 (1887) (spread of the gospel); In re Rees, [1920] 2 Ch. 59 (missionary purposes); In re Barker's Will Trust, 64 T.L.R. 273 (1948) (for God's

such a trust fails because the purpose is too general.[3] By the great weight of authority, however, it is held that if the purpose is limited to the advancement of religion the mere fact that the testator has not specified a particular religion and has not specified any method by which religion is to be advanced is not fatal to the validity of the trust. If discretion is conferred on the trustees, they may exercise it in any reasonable manner; and if

---

work, with indications that the fund was to be applied for Baptist religious purposes).

California: Estate of Schloss, 56 Cal. 2d 248, 363 P.2d 875 (1961) (to promote progress of mankind, particularly among people in accord with the teachings of a named church).

Connecticut: Cheshire Bank & Trust Co. v. Doolittle, 113 Conn. 231, 155 A. 82 (1931) (to be used for either home or foreign missions).

Iowa: In re Estate of Small, 244 Iowa 1209, 58 N.W.2d 477 (1953) (to distribute income to such persons and for such purposes as the trustees or their successors may feel is directed by God the Father, Jesus Christ the Son, and as they believe would be acceptable to the testator); In re Will of Faber, 259 Iowa 1, 141 N.W.2d 554 (1966) (to such Christian organizations as trustee may deem worthy in their work of advancing the cause of Christianity).

Massachusetts: Going v. Emery, 16 Pick. 107, 26 Am. Dec. 645 (Mass. 1834) (to the cause of Christ, for benefit and promotion of true evangelical piety and religion).

New Mexico: Rhodes v. Yater, 27 N.M. 489, 202 P. 698, 22 A.L.R. 692 (1921) (preaching the gospel).

Ohio: Miller v. Teachout, 24 Ohio St. 525 (1874) (to be applied in trustee's judgment to advancement of Christian religion).

Canada: In re Morton, [1941] 4 D.L.R. 763 (B.C.) (educational and religious objects in connection with Baptist Denomination in Province of British Columbia); In re Brooks, 4 D.L.R.3d 694 (Sask. 1969) (given to the work of the Lord).

Ireland: Powerscourt v. Powerscourt, 1 Moll. 616 (Ir., 1824) (to be employed "in the service of my Lord and Master").

New Zealand: In re Palmerston North Hall Trust Bd., [1976] 2 N.Z.L.R. 161 (to be used exclusively for meetings of Christians).

See 14 L.R.A. (N.S.) 49 (1908); 22 A.L.R. 697 (1923).

[3]Methodist Episcopal Church of United States v. Walters, 50 F.2d 416 (D. Mo. 1928).

In Kinnear v. Ballagh, 109 N.J. Eq. 27, 156 A. 269 (1931), where a testator expressed the wish that his house should be devoted to some purpose of value to Presbyterian missionaries, it was held that the provision was too indefinite and the gift failed.

See §396, and Fratcher, Powers of Appointment to Unspecified Charities, 32 Mo. L. Rev. 443, 449-456 (1967), for citations to other cases of this type.

the trustees have not such discretion, a scheme will be approved by the court for carrying out the purpose of the testator.

§371.3.   **Words indicating religious purposes.**   Where it is not expressly stated in the trust instrument that the purpose of the trust is the advancement of religion, it is a question of interpretation whether that is the purpose of the trust. Such a purpose may be gathered from the nature of the persons or organization to whom the property is given. Thus in *In re Garrard*[1] where property was left to the vicar of a church and the churchwardens for the time being to be applied by them in such manner as they should in their sole discretion think fit, it was held that the property was intended by the testator to be applied for religious purposes and a valid charitable trust was created. On the other hand, in *In re Davidson,*[2] where property was left in trust for the Roman Catholic Archbishop of Westminster for the time being to be distributed and given by him at his absolute discretion among such charitable, religious, or other societies, institutions, persons, or objects in connection with the Roman Catholic faith in England as he should in his absolute discretion think fit, the court held that the property might be applied to other than charitable purposes, and that the intended trust failed. In view of all the circumstances, however, it is difficult to believe that the testator did not intend to devote the property to religious purposes. So in *In re Flinn,*[3] where a testatrix left the residue of her estate to a Roman Catholic archbishop for the time being "to be used by him for such purposes as he shall in his absolute discretion think fit," it was held that the bequest was not a beneficial gift to the archbishop but was a gift upon a valid trust for ecclesiastical purposes.

There are many cases in which the court held that the fact that the legatee was a religious organization or a person holding a religious office indicated an intention of the settlor that the property should be applied for religious purposes, although his language was general and did not in express words direct that the property should be applied for religious purposes.[4] There

§371.3.   [1][1907] 1 Ch. 382.
[2][1909] 1 Ch. 567.
[3][1948] Ch. 241, noted in 11 Mod. L. Rev. 343. See §351, n. 17.
[4]*England:* Attorney-General v. Gladstone, 13 Sim. 7 (1842); Thornber v. Wilson, 4 Drew. 350 (1858); In re Delany, [1902] 2 Ch. 642; In re Ray's Will

are other cases, however, in which the court held, as in *In re Davidson,* that the testator did not expressly or by implication limit the trustees to charitable purposes and that the intended trust therefore failed.[5]

Trusts, [1936] Ch. 520; In re Simson, [1946] Ch. 299 (more fully reported in [1946] 2 All E.R. 220), noted in 11 Convey. (N.S.) 57, 10 Mod. L. Rev. 214; In re Norman, [1947] Ch. 349, noted in 11 Convey. (N.S.) 283; In re Eastes, [1948] Ch. 257, noted in 11 Mod. L. Rev. 343, 93 Sol. J. 298; In re Rumball, [1956] Ch. 105.

See also In re Ward, [1941] Ch. 308, *rev'g* [1941] 1 All E.R. 315, noted in 5 Convey. (N.S.) 227, 57 L.Q. Rev. 168, 316, 4 Mod. L. Rev. 311, 85 Sol. J. 295.

Kansas: In re Estate of Freshour, 185 Kan. 434, 345 P.2d 689, 81 A.L.R.2d 806 (1959) (citing the text and Restatement of Trusts §371).

Kentucky: Goode's Admr. v. Goode, 238 Ky. 620, 38 S.W.2d 691 (1931).

Maine: Bates v. Schillinger, 128 Me. 14, 145 A. 395 (1929).

North Carolina: Williams v. Williams, 215 N.C. 739, 3 S.E.2d 334 (1939).

Pennsylvania: Gibbons Estate, 40 D.&C.2d 84 (Pa. 1966).

Canada: See In re MacKay Estate, [1948] S.C.R. 500 (Can.), *rev'g* [1947] 1 D.L.R. 477 (B.C.); Blais v. Touchet, [1963] S.C.R. 358 (Can.), *rev'g* Touchet v. Blais, 34 D.L.R.2d 521 (Sask. 1962) (bequest by priest to his bishop "pour ses oeuvres, mais pour les oeuvres qui aideraient la cause des Canadiens Français dans son diocèse").

Ireland: Robb v. Dorian, Ir. R. 9 C.L. 483 (1875), *aff'd,* Ir. R. 11 C.L. 292 (1877); Gibson v. Representative Church Body, 9 L.R. Ir. 1 (1881); In re Howley, [1940] I.R. 109.

In In re Gare, [1952] Ch. 80, where a testator gave a legacy to a certain parish church, it was held that he thereby created a charitable trust for purposes connected with the services of the church and that unless the Attorney-General and the solicitors for the parochial church council, a corporate body appointed by statute, should agree on a method for using the fund, a scheme should be framed for the administration of the fund.

In Public Trustee v. Federal Commr. of Taxation, 112 C.L.R. 326 (Austl. 1964), where a testator left the residue upon trust for the Roman Catholic Archbishop of Adelaide to be expended for the benefit of Catholic charities in his absolute discretion, it was held that, although it was a charitable trust, it was not limited to religion and was not tax exempt under the statute.

See Oaks, Trust Doctrines in Church Controversies (1984).

See Note, Validity, as a charitable trust, of gift to church, church society, or trustees or officers thereof, without declaration or restriction as to its use or purpose, 81 A.L.R.2d 819 (1962).

[5]Doe v. Copestake, 6 East 328 (1805); Aston v. Wood, L.R. 6 Eq. 419 (1868); In re Freeman, [1908] 1 Ch. 720; In re The Friends' Free School, [1909] 2 Ch. 675; Dunne v. Byrne, [1912] A.C. 407; In re Ashton, [1938] 1 Ch. 482, *aff'd sub nom.* Farley v. Westminster Bank, [1939] A.C. 430, noted in 17 Can. B. Rev. 751, 4 Convey. (N.S.) 217, 56 L.Q. Rev. 8; In re Lawton, [1940]

On the other hand, it may appear that the intention of the testator was not to create a trust but to make a beneficial gift to the legatee. Thus in *Matter of Devitt*,[6] where a testatrix bequeathed $5000 to the pastor of a church, requesting that the money should be used by him for whatever purpose he should deem proper, it was held that this was a gift to the pastor for his

---

Ch. 984; In re Moore, [1919] 1 I.R. 316; Trustees of the Londonderry Presbyterian Church House v. Commissioners, [1946] N. Ir. L.R. 178.

In McNamee v. Mansfield, [1945] I.R. 13, it was held that a bequest to the head of a religious order for the purposes of the order was not charitable because most of its purposes were not charitable, but the court held that the trust was valid as a noncharitable trust. See §119.

In In re Simson, [1946] Ch. 299 (more fully reported in [1946] 2 All E.R. 220), where the court upheld a legacy to a clergyman for his work, it held that another legacy to another clergyman "for his benevolent work" in the parish failed because the evidence showed that the work which he carried on in the parish was not limited to purposes of charity. Compare §398.1.

In Oxford Group v. Inland Revenue Commrs., [1949] 2 All E.R. 537, it was held that an association called the Oxford Group, which included in its purposes not merely the advancement of the Christian religion but also the support of the Oxford Group Movement in every way, was not exempt from income tax because the purposes extended beyond religious activities. See §398.2, n. 31.

In Inland Revenue Commrs. v. Baddeley, [1955] A.C. 572, *rev'g* Baddeley v. Inland Revenue Commrs., [1953] Ch. 504, *rev'g* [1953] 1 All E.R. 63, noted in [1956] Camb. L.J. 20, 33 Can. B. Rev. 898, land on which were a mission church, lecture room, and store was conveyed in trust to be used by the leaders of a mission "for the promotion of the religious social and physical well-being" of the residents of a borough, by providing facilities for religious services and instruction and for the social and physical training and recreation of these residents. It was held by the House of Lords (Lord Reid dissenting) that the trust was not exclusively for religious purposes, and was not a charitable trust.

In In re Endacott, [1960] Ch. 232, where a testator left the residue to a Parish Council "for the purpose of providing some useful memorial to myself," it was held that the character of the legatee did not indicate that the purpose was charitable, and the disposition failed. See §123, n. 24.

In Lawrence v. Board of Selectmen, 350 Mass. 354, 214 N.E.2d 893 (1966), a conveyance to a pastor of a church was held to be a conveyance to him beneficially and not upon trust.

In Fides Publishers Assn. v. United States, 263 F. Supp. 924 (N.D. Ind. 1967), it was held that a profit-making publisher of religious books was not exempt from income tax because it was operated for a business purpose. See §398.2, n. 31.

[6] 12 Misc. 2d 168, 172 N.Y.S.2d 848 (1958).

own benefit. In *Gilbert Estate*[7] a house was devised to the minister of a church. It was held that the minister took beneficially and that the devise did not fail because made within thirty days of the death of the testator. In *In re Meehan*[8] a testatrix left the residue of her estate to be distributed among certain named charitable legatees. She provided that if any bequest should fail she bequeathed it to the bishop for the time being of a certain diocese absolutely. The legacies failed because she died within three months of the making of her will. It was held that the bishop at her death was entitled beneficially. In *Lucey v. Catholic Orphanage of Prince Albert*[9] a legacy was held to lapse because given to a priest personally and not upon a charitable trust. In some cases where there is a bequest to a priest for the saying of masses it has been held that the testator intended to make a beneficial gift to the priest conditioned on his saying of the masses.[10]

§371.4.   The legality of the purpose.   In the attitude of the state toward unorthodox religions there are several stages on the road to toleration. At first the state may attempt to compel conformity to the orthodox religion, imposing criminal penalties on those who do not conform. Next, the state may not compel conformity but may impose silence on those who do not conform, imposing criminal penalties on those who advocate unorthodox religions, or who otherwise attack the doctrines of the orthodox religion. Thirdly, the state may impose no criminal penalties on the unorthodox but may hold that the devotion of property to the promotion of an unorthodox religion is illegal with the result that the disposition fails. Fourthly, it may be held that although such a disposition is not illegal it is not a disposition for charitable purposes and is not entitled to the special form of protection that is afforded to dispositions for charitable purposes. Finally, of course, the state may treat all religions alike, giving the same measure of protection to all.

In England the law has proceeded through these various stages. The intolerance of Tudor times has yielded step by step

[7] 5 Fiduciary Rep. 47 (Pa. 1954).
[8] [1960] I.R. 82.
[9] [1951] S.C.R. 690 (Can.).
[10] See §124.4, n. 7; §371.5, n. 7.

to the tolerance of the twentieth century. No longer is it criminal or illegal to encourage "the propagation of a false religion."[1] Criminal penalties have been gradually removed. Dispositions for the promotion of unorthodox religions have been upheld. The last traces of the old intolerance are disappearing. In 1919 it was held by the House of Lords that a bequest for the saying of masses is not illegal, although the courts had held otherwise for centuries.[2] Finally, it was held in 1934 that such a bequest is for a charitable purpose,[3] but it has been said in the House of Lords that this question is still open.[4]

It is immaterial that the particular religious sect or doctrine to be promoted is one that has few adherents or is one that seems to others to be somewhat absurd. In the well-known case of *Thornton v. Howe*[5] a testatrix left property to be applied to the "propagation of the sacred writings of the late Joanna South-cote." This eccentric person had declared that she was with child by the Holy Ghost and that she was to give birth to a second Messiah, but she had died without issue. The court held that the trust was charitable.

In England today and in the United States a trust for the promotion of religion is a valid charitable trust, although the religion has few adherents and although its doctrines may seem foolish to most people. On the other hand, illegal practices will not be protected even though they are permitted by the tenets of a particular religion. It was held by the Supreme Court of the United States that Congress might dissolve a church corporation organized in a territory of the United States if the church advocated the practice of polygamy as one of its fundamental tenets.[6]

Even though there is nothing positively illegal in the tenets of a religious sect, if they appear to be so absurd as to be

§371.4.   [1]Rex v. Lady Portington, 1 Salk. 162 (1692).

[2]Bourne v. Keane, [1919] A.C. 815.

[3]In re Caus, [1934] 1 Ch. 162.

[4]See Gilmour v. Coats, [1949] A.C. 426. See §371.5, n. 4.

[5]31 Beav. 14 (1862).

This case was followed in In re Watson, [1973] 1 W.L.R. 1472, [1973] 3 All E.R. 678.

[6]Mormon Church v. United States, 136 U.S. 1, 10 S. Ct. 792, 34 L. Ed. 478 (1890).

irrational it is arguable that a trust to promote the religion is not a charitable trust. The difficulty is, however, that very frequently the tenets of one religion seem absurd and irrational to the adherents of other religions and to those who have no religious convictions. Where the purpose of the trust is not the promotion of religion but merely the promotion of purposes that are of a character beneficial to the community, it is obvious that a distinction must be drawn between what may rationally be thought to be beneficial to the community and what is clearly absurd.[7] Where the purpose is to promote a particular religion, however, it is almost impossible to draw such a line. In an English case it was held that a trust to establish a college to train suitable persons as spiritualistic mediums was not a charitable trust.[8] It was not contended in that case, however, that the trust was for the promotion of religion, but the contention was that it might be upheld as a trust for the advancement of education or a trust generally beneficial to the community.

§371.5. **Masses.** In England for many centuries a bequest of money to be used for the saying of masses for the soul of the testator or of others was held to be illegal as a superstitious use.[1] In 1919, however, the earlier decisions were overruled by the House of Lords in the case of *Bourne v. Keane.*[2] In that case bequests to a church and to certain Jesuit priests for the saying of masses were upheld. The court did not deal with the question whether the trust was charitable. It is possible to maintain that such a trust, although not illegal, is not charitable

[7]See §374.7.

[8]In re Hummeltenberg, [1923] 1 Ch. 237.

In Lockwood's Estate, 344 Pa. 293, 25 A.2d 168 (1942), it was held that an outright gift to an incorporated spiritualistic college was valid.

In Stephan's Estate, 129 Pa. Super. 396, 195 A. 653 (1937), a trust for the perpetual upkeep of a spiritualist memorial was held invalid.

§371.5. [1]West v. Shuttleworth, 2 Myl. & K. 684, 696 (1835); Heath v. Chapman, 2 Drew. 417 (1854); In re Blundell's Trusts, 30 Beav. 360 (1861).

It was formerly provided by the Constitution of Missouri that every gift to take place after the death of the donor for the support of any minister or religious sect should be void. Under this provision it was held that a bequest for masses was illegal. In the Matter of Schmucker's Estate v. Reel, 61 Mo. 592 (1876).

[2][1919] A.C. 815.

beçause it is for the benefit of specific persons who are dead and not for the benefit of an indefinite number of persons. Under this view a gift for masses is valid if it is not to continue beyond the period of the rule against perpetuities. This was the view once taken by the Irish court and in Ontario and in a few American cases. In a few decisions it was held that even though the trust was not to continue beyond the period of the rule against perpetuities it was invalid because there was no beneficiary to enforce it.[3]

In 1934, however, it was held in England that a trust for masses is charitable. In *In re Caus*[4] a testator bequeathed money for masses, the income to be applied for that purpose for 25 years, and the principal then to be turned over to a named church. He made another bequest for a foundation mass, where the interest only was to be used forever. It was held that these were valid charitable trusts. The court pointed out that the trusts were for the performance of a ritual act that is the central act of the religion of a large proportion of Christian people, and that they assisted in the endowment of priests whose duty it is to perform the act. By the great weight of authority in the United States it is now held that a trust for masses is a charitable trust.[5]

[3]See §124.4.

[4][1934] 1 Ch. 162.

In the House of Lords, however, doubt has been expressed as to the soundness of this decision. In Gilmour v. Coats, [1949] A.C. 426 (see §371.6, n. 3), in speaking of this case and of the Irish cases holding that a gift for the saying of masses is charitable, Lord Simonds said, "I would expressly reserve my opinion on the question whether these decisions should be sustained in this House." See also the speech of Lord du Parcq (p. 454), and that of Lord Reid (p. 460).

See Crowther, Religious Trusts, c. 4 (1954).

[5]*California:* Estate of Hamilton, 181 Cal. 758, 186 P. 587 (1919).

Delaware: Delaware Trust Co. v. FitzMaurice, 27 Del. Ch. 101, 31 A.2d 383 (1943) (citing the text), *aff'd sub nom.* Crumlish v. Delaware Trust Co., 27 Del. Ch. 374, 38 A.2d 463 (1944).

District of Columbia: Sedgwick v. National Sav. & Trust Co., 76 App. D.C. 177, 130 F.2d 440 (1942).

Illinois: Hoeffer v. Clogan, 171 Ill. 462, 49 N.E. 527, 40 L.R.A. 730, 63 Am. St. Rep. 241 (1898); Gilmore v. Lee, 237 Ill. 402, 86 N.E. 568, 127 Am. St. Rep. 330 (1908).

Indiana: Ackerman v. Fichter, 179 Ind. 392, 101 N.E. 493, 46 L.R.A. (N.S.) 221, Ann. Cas. 1915D 1117 (1913) (all poor souls).

These cases seem clearly sound. Although the saying of a mass

---

Iowa: Seda v. Huble, 75 Iowa 429, 39 N.W. 685, 9 Am. St. Rep. 495 (1888).

Kentucky: Obrecht v. Pujos, 206 Ky. 751, 268 S.W. 564 (1925).

Massachusetts: Schouler, Petitioner, 134 Mass. 426 (1883); Mahoney v. Nollman, 309 Mass. 522, 35 N.E.2d 265 (1941) (valid although legatee died before legacy paid).

Missouri: Minturn v. Conception Abbey, 227 Mo. App. 1179, 61 S.W.2d 352 (1933). Kane v. Mercantile Trust Co., 513 S.W.2d 362 (Mo. 1974).

New Hampshire: Webster v. Sughrow, 69 N.H. 380, 45 A. 139, 48 L.R.A. 100 (1898).

New Jersey: Kerrigan v. Tabb, 39 A. 701 (N.J. Ch. 1898).

New York: Matter of Eppig, 63 Misc. 613, 118 N.Y.S. 683 (1909); Matter of Welch, 105 Misc. 27, 172 N.Y.S. 349 (1918); Matter of Morris, 227 N.Y. 141, 124 N.E. 724 (1919); Matter of Korzeniewska, 163 Misc. 323, 297 N.Y.S. 997 (1937); Matter of Breckwoldt, 176 Misc. 549, 27 N.Y.S.2d 938 (1941) (valid although legatee renounced); Matter of Neary, 194 Misc. 200, 86 N.Y.S.2d 312 (1949) (valid although legatee predeceased testatrix); Matter of Lawless, 194 Misc. 844, 87 N.Y.S.2d 386 (1949), *aff'd mem.,* 277 A.D. 1045, 100 N.Y.S.2d 537 (1950); Matter of Liebeck, 109 N.Y.S.2d 147 (1951); Matter of Dobbins, 206 Misc. 64, 132 N.Y.S.2d 236 (1954); Matter of Yadach, 5 A.D.2d 355, 172 N.Y.S.2d 340 (1958) (invalid as to excess over one half of testator's estate); Matter of Jeglich, 14 Misc. 2d 982, 178 N.Y.S.2d 363 (1958) (applied cy pres where legatee renounced); Matter of Klein, 39 Misc. 2d 960, 242 N.Y.S.2d 241 (1963) (bequest to Daughters of Israel for perpetual religious services for decedent and her deceased husband); Matter of McCarthy, 75 Misc. 2d 193, 347 N.Y.S.2d 490 (1973).

Ohio: Lanza v. Di Fronzo, 56 Ohio Abs. 310, 92 N.E.2d 299 (1949) (citing the text), noted in 26 Notre Dame Law. 162 (1950).

Pennsylvania: Rhymer's Appeal, 93 Pa. 142, 39 Am. Rep. 736 (1880), *semble;* Duffy Estate, 2 D.&C.2d 250 (Pa. 1954) (income to be used in perpetuity for masses for testatrix and members of her family; citing the text and Restatement of Trusts §§371, 375); Harrigan Estate, 29 D.&C.2d 119 (Pa. 1963) (citing Restatement of Trusts, §371, Comment *g*); Selewicz Estate, 29 D.&C.2d 742 (Pa. 1962) (quoting the text and Restatement of Trusts, §371, Comment *d*).

Wisconsin: Will of Kavanaugh, 143 Wis. 90, 126 N.W. 672, 28 L.R.A. (N.S.) 470 (1910), overruling McHugh v. McCole, 97 Wis. 166, 72 N.W. 631, 65 Am. St. Rep. 106, 40 L.R.A. 724 (1897).

Canada: In re Samson, 59 D.L.R.2d 132 (N.S. 1966).

Ireland: O'Hanlon v. Logue, [1906] 1 I.R. 247 (to be said in public); In re Howley, [1940] I.R. 109; Kelly v. Walsh, [1948] I.R. 388.

Scotland: Lindsay's Exr. v. Forsyth, [1940] Sess. Cas. 568 (Scot.).

See 14 Ann. Cas. 1025 (1909); Ann. Cas. 1915D 1122; 14 L.R.A. (N.S.) 49, 96 (1908).

See §124.4.

may be for the particular benefit of a specific person who has died, the benefits are not confined to the particular soul but extend to the other members of the church and to all the world, according to the doctrines of the Roman Catholic church.[6]

In Mahoney v. Nollman, 309 Mass. 522, 35 N.E.2d 265 (1951), *supra,* it was said that only the Attorney General could enforce a trust for the saying of masses.

In Moran v. Kelly, 95 N.J. Eq. 380, 124 A. 67 (1924), *aff'd,* 96 N.J. Eq. 699, 126 A. 924 (1924), a trust for masses was upheld, not on the ground that it was a charitable trust, but on the ground that it was a trust for the benefit of the testator. The trust did not involve a perpetuity.

In Chelsea Natl. Bank v. Our Lady Star of the Sea, 105 N.J. Eq. 236, 147 A. 470 (1929), noted in 78 U. Pa. L. Rev. 573, the court upheld a bequest for masses for the soul of the testatrix as a funeral expense, but said that the bequest was not charitable.

In Matter of De Molina, 35 N.Y.S.2d 24 (1942), it was held that a trust for masses for the souls of the testatrix and of her husband who had predeceased her was not entitled to priority as a funeral expense, but was merely a charitable bequest. See also Matter of Nolan, 198 Misc. 979, 99 N.Y.S.2d 622 (1950).

In In re Estate of Reilly, 138 Ohio St. 145, 33 N.E.2d 987 (1941), it was held that a bequest for masses was not exempt from an inheritance tax under a statute that exempted bequests for purposes of public charity. To the same effect, see In re Shanahan, 159 Ohio St. 487, 112 N.E.2d 665 (1953), *rev'g* 64 Ohio Abs. 259, 101 N.E.2d 917 (1951).

In Kelly v. Walsh, [1948] I.R. 388, where a testator made a bequest to a priest for masses for his soul, and the priest was one of the attesting witnesses, it was held that the disposition was valid because it was a charitable bequest.

In Matter of Fleishfarb, 151 Misc. 399, 271 N.Y.S. 736 (1934), a trust for a Jewish Yahrzeit was held charitable.

In Matter of Goldberg, 33 N.Y.S.2d 1021 (1942), a trust for the celebration of Kaddish or Jewish memorial services on the anniversaries of the deaths of the testator's parents, his wife, and himself was held charitable.

In In re Estate of Khoo Cheng Teow, [1932] Straits Settlements L.R. 226, the court held that a gift to hold Sin Chew, a Chinese religious ceremony, was not charitable because, unlike the mass, it does not benefit those other than the decedent.

In Matter of Connolly, 40 Misc. 2d 673, 243 N.Y.S.2d 727 (1963), where a testator gave half the residue to the pastor of a church for masses and the pastor survived the testator but died before the estate could be distributed, it was held that the fund should be given to his successor for masses and not to the legatees under his will, because a charitable trust was created.

See Cafardi, Bequests for Masses: Doctrine, History and Legal Status, 20 Duq. L. Rev. 403 (1982).

[6]For an exposition of the Catholic doctrine, see Attorney-General v. Delaney, 10 Ir. R.C.L. 104, 107 (1875). See also Catholic Encyclopaedia, tit.

In several cases where a bequest was made to a particular priest for the saying of masses, the bequest was upheld not as a charitable trust but as a beneficial gift to the priest conditioned on his saying masses.[7]

§371.6. Where class is too narrow. Where a trust is created for the religious benefit of a particular person or specific persons only, it is not a charitable trust. Thus in *Cocks v. Manners*[1] it was held that a trust to aid in promoting the spiritual welfare of a group of nuns was not a charitable purpose. In *In re Thackrah*,[2] where a bequest was made to the secretary or other proper officer of the Oxford Group, which was not an association with a constitution or membership list but was a name for a group of persons who had "surrendered their lives to God," it was held that the bequest was not for a charitable purpose and was invalid. In *Gilmour v. Coats*[3] money was given to trustees in

---

Mass; Curran, Trusts for Masses, 7 Notre Dame Law. 42 (1931); O'Brien, Seventy Years of Bequests for Masses in New York Courts, 23 Fordham L. Rev. 147 (1954).

See 23 B.U.L. Rev. 260 (1945); 48 Dick. L. Rev. 179 (1944); 13 Fordham L. Rev. 175 (1944); 17 S. Calif. L. Rev. 144 (1944).

See Curran, Charitable Trusts for Masses 1931-1956, 5 De Paul L. Rev. 246 (1956).

[7]*California:* Estate of Holtermann, 206 Cal. App. 2d 460, 23 Cal. Rptr. 685 (1962).

Kansas: Harrison v. Brophy, 59 Kan. 1, 51 P. 883, 40 L.R.A. 721 (1898).

Rhode Island: Sherman v. Baker, 20 R.I. 446, 40 A. 11, 40 L.R.A. 717 (1898); Slattery v. Ward, 45 R.I. 54, 119 A. 755 (1923).

In Matter of Beckley, 63 A.D.2d 855, 405 N.Y.S.2d 861 (1978), *appeal denied,* 45 N.Y.2d 837 (1978), where a testator gave a legacy to a religious organization with the request that masses be said, the provision was held to be merely precatory.

See §124.4, n. 7.

§371.6. [1]L.R. 12 Eq. 574 (1871).

See also In re Joy, 60 L.T. 175 (1888); In re Warre's Will Trusts, [1953] 2 All E.R. 99.

[2][1939] 2 All E.R. 4, noted in 13 Austl. L.J. 241, 1939 Scot. L.T. 166.

See also Oxford Group v. Inland Revenue Commrs., [1949] 2 All E.R. 537, cited in §371.3, n. 5, §398.2, n. 31.

[3][1949] A.C. 426, *aff'g* In re Coats' Trusts, [1948] Ch. 340, *aff'g* [1948] Ch. 1, noted in 21 Austl. L.J. 270, 22 id. 278, 23 id. 259, 10 Camb. L.J. 104, 11 id. 97, 26 Chi.-Kent L. Rev. 333, 12 Convey. (N.S.) 294, 377, 60 Jurid. Rev.

trust for the purposes of a Carmelite priory, a convent belonging to one of the strictly cloistered and clearly contemplative orders of the Roman Catholic church, with a gift over if the purposes were not charitable. It was held that the purposes were not charitable. But in Ireland the courts take a different view. Thus in *In re Howley*[4] the court criticized the decision in *Cocks v. Manners* and said: "The assumption that the Irish public finds no edification in cloistered lives, devoted to purely spiritual ends, postulates a close assimilation of the Irish outlook to the English, not obviously warranted by the traditions and mores of the Irish people."

As we have seen, it has been held in some cases that a trust for the saying of masses for the soul of a particular person is not a charitable trust, because it is for the benefit of a specified individual; but by the great weight of authority, however, as we have seen, it is held that such a trust is charitable because masses are not for the exclusive benefit of the souls of particular persons.[5] In an Irish case[6] it was held that a trust for the Perpetual Adoration of the Blessed Sacrament was valid because it was for a pious use and was not merely for the benefit of the nuns.

A trust for the religious benefit of particular persons may be valid if it does not violate the rule against perpetuities, even though it is not charitable. In *In re Doering*[7] a testator left the residue of his estate in trust to use the income to educate the male descendants of his father so as to imbue them with the father's religious faith. It was provided that the trust should terminate 21 years after the death of the last survivor of those descendants who were living at the testator's death, and that the property should then be given to two charitable institutions. It

---

244, 99 L.J. 267, 63 L.Q. Rev. 424, 65 id. 427, 12 Mod. L. Rev. 378, 4 Res Judicatae 92, 22 St. John's L. Rev. 241, 16 Sol. J. 195.

See Leahy v. Attorney-General for N.S.W., [1959] A.C. 457, noted in 76 L.Q. Rev. 204, *aff'g* Attorney-General v. Donnelly, 98 C.L.R. 538 (Austl. 1958).

[4][1940] I.R. 109, 113.

See Bank of Ir. Trustee Co. v. Attorney-General, [1957] I.R. 257.

But see McNamee v. Mansfield, [1945] I.R. 13.

[5]See §371.5.

[6]Maguire v. Attorney-General, [1943] I.R. 238.

[7][1949] 1 D.L.R. 267 (Ont.).

As to the legality of provisions restraining religious freedom, see §62.7.

was held that the trust as to the income was valid although not charitable.

§372. *Promotion of Health*

A trust for the promotion of health is a charitable trust. The only reference to this purpose in the Statute of Charitable Uses is the inclusion of trusts "for maintenance of sick and maimed soldiers and mariners." The cases in which trusts for the promotion of health have been upheld as charitable trusts are numerous. They include trusts to establish or maintain a hospital or a ward or a bed in a hospital;[1] to furnish nurses to attend the

§372. [1]*England:* In re James, [1932] 2 Ch. 25; In re Chaplin, [1933] Ch. 115; In re White's Will Trusts, [1951] 1 All E.R. 528 (home of rest for nurses of hospital), noted in 65 Harv. L. Rev. 704; Royal College of Surgeons v. National Provincial Bank, [1952] A.C. 631, *rev'g* In re Bland-Sutton's Will Trusts, [1951] Ch. 485, *aff'g* [1951] Ch. 70 (Royal College of Surgeons), noted in 11 Camb. L.J. 435, 94 Sol. J. 795; In re Tacon, [1958] Ch. 477 (convalescent home for nurses or patients or both); In re Adams, [1968] Ch. 80 (endowing beds for paying patients in a hospital); In re Resch's Will Trusts, [1969] 1 A.C. 514 (hospital for women able to pay reasonable fees).

Federal: Wallace v. Graff, 104 F. Supp. 925 (D.D.C. 1952) (hospital for crippled children and needy residents of District of Columbia); Wilkin v. Wilkin Trust, 261 F. Supp. 977 (D.C. Okla. 1966) (care and treatment of needy crippled children of Oklahoma County); National Sav. & Trust Co. v. Sarolea, 269 F. Supp. 4 (D.D.C. 1967) (to organizations caring for sufferers of tubercular consumption in New Orleans designated by governing bodies of certain churches).

Alabama: Hinson v. Smyer, 246 Ala. 644, 21 So. 2d 825 (1945) (to some institution for research as to cause and cure of arthritis).

Connecticut: Connecticut Bank & Trust Co. v. Ajello, 39 Conn. Supp. 80, 468 A.2d 942 (1983), citing text.

Idaho: See In re Coleman's Estate, 66 Idaho 567, 163 P.2d 847 (1945) (relief and treatment of crippled children).

Illinois: Hart v. Taylor, 301 Ill. 344, 133 N.E. 857 (1922); Rubel v. Friend, 344 Ill. App. 450, 101 N.E.2d 445 (1951) (to establish home for convalescents); Raser v. Johnson, 9 Ill. App. 2d 375, 132 N.E.2d 819 (1956) (for hospitalization and medical supplies for worthy persons in need).

Iowa: In re Estate of Anderson, 244 Iowa 325, 56 N.W.2d 913 (1953); National Bank of Burlington v. Huneke, 250 Iowa 1030, 98 N.W.2d 7 (1959) (tax case; citing Restatement of Trusts §372).

Massachusetts: McDonald v. Massachusetts Gen. Hosp., 120 Mass. 432, 21 Am. Rep. 529 (1876); Roosen v. Peter Bent Brigham, 235 Mass. 66, 126 N.E.

392, 14 A.L.R. 563 (1920); Kirwin v. Attorney Gen., 275 Mass. 34, 175 N.E. 164 (1931), noted in 19 Geo. L.J. 507; Anna Jaques Hosp. v. Attorney Gen., 341 Mass. 179, 167 N.E.2d 875 (1960) (citing the text).

Michigan: Floyd v. Smith, 303 Mich. 137, 5 N.W.2d 695 (1942); Love v. Sullivan, 5 Mich. App. 201, 146 N.W.2d 117 (1967) (to help those having harelip or cleft palates, under direction of a third person; quoting Restatement of Trusts §185).

See Gifford v. First Natl. Bank, 285 Mich. 58, 280 N.W. 108 (1938) (furthering of medical arts, care of the sick, child welfare, etc.).

Minnesota: Mayo Found. v. Commr. of Revenue, 306 Minn. 25, 236 N.W.2d 767 (1975) (holding that the Mayo Clinic and Mayo Foundation are exempt from sales and use tax, because private practice of medicine was incidental to educational and research activities).

Missouri: Rice v. Hawley, 239 Mo. App. 901, 203 S.W.2d 158 (1947) (to trustees of fraternal organization to erect hospital); Ramsey v. City of Brookfield, 237 S.W.2d 143 (1951) (citing Restatement of Trusts §374).

New Jersey: Parker v. Fidelity Union Trust Co., 2 N.J. Super. 362, 63 A.2d 902 (1944) (to maintain bed in hospital); Wendell v. Hazel Wood Cemetery, 3 N.J. Super. 457, 67 A.2d 219 (1949), *aff'd,* 7 N.J. Super. 117, 72 A.2d 383 (1950).

New York: Schloendorff v. Society of N.Y. Hosp., 211 N.Y. 125, 105 N.E. 92, 52 L.R.A. (N.S.) 505, Ann. Cas. 1915C 581 (1914); Matter of Lawless, 194 Misc. 844, 87 N.Y.S.2d 386 (1949), *aff'd mem.,* 277 A.D. 1045, 100 N.Y.S.2d 537 (1950) (to provide free home for cancer patients).

See City Bank Farmers Trust Co. v. Bennett, 159 Misc. 779, 287 N.Y.S. 784 (1936) (to pay income to charitable organizations engaged in work for prevention and relief of cancer, and to those engaged in work for care and education of crippled children).

North Carolina: Wachovia Bank & Trust Co. v. McMullan, 229 N.C. 746, 51 S.E.2d 473 (1949).

Ohio: O'Brien v. Physicians Hosp. Assn., 96 Ohio St. 1, 116 N.E. 975, L.R.A. 1917F 741 (1917); Aultman Hosp. Assn. v. Evatt, 140 Ohio St. 114, 42 N.E.2d 646 (1942) (nurses' home connected with hospital); Fitton v. Beeler, 44 Ohio Abs. 615, 67 N.E.2d 95 (1943) (to erect and establish hospital).

South Carolina: Gilbert v. McLeod Infirmary, 219 S.C. 174, 64 S.E.2d 524 (1951) (hospital), noted in 4 S.C.L.Q. 325.

See Porcher v. Cappelmann, 187 S.C. 491, 198 S.E. 8 (1938) (to provide medical and surgical attention to crippled children, not limited to the poor).

Utah: Manatakis' Estate v. Walker Bank & Trust Co., 5 Utah 2d 412, 303 P.2d 701 (1956).

Virginia: Hospital of St. Vincent v. Thompson, 116 Va. 101, 81 S.E. 13, 51 L.R.A. (N.S.) 1025 (1914).

Australia: In re List, [1949] N.Z.L.R. 78; Kytherian Assn. of Queensland v. Sklavos, 101 C.L.R. 56 (Austl. 1958).

In In re Dean's Will Trusts, [1950] 1 All E.R. 882, noted in 94 Sol. J. 622 (1950), it was held that a trust to provide accommodation in a certain hospital for relatives of patients critically ill was valid as a charitable trust.

poor;[2] to increase medical knowledge by research or otherwise;[3] to remove the causes of the spread of disease, as by draining swamps. Frequently, of course, a trust for the promotion of

---

For cases holding that a hospital is exempt from liability for tort on the ground that it is a charitable institution, see §402.

[2]In re Webster, [1912] 1 Ch. 106; Royal College of Nursing v. St. Marylebone Corp., [1959] 3 All E.R. 663, *aff'g* [1958] 1 All E.R. 129 (to promote the advance of nursing as a profession).

In General Nursing Council for Eng. and Wales v. St. Marylebone Borough, [1959] A.C. 540, *aff'g* [1958] Ch. 421, noted in 75 L.Q. Rev. 145, 293, it was held that land occupied by an organization of nurses was subject to tax on the ground that the main purpose of the organization was the enhancement of the status of nurses and nursing and not merely the benefit of the public when sick.

[3]*Arizona:* In re Harber's Estate, 99 Ariz. 323, 409 P.2d 31 (1965) (citing the text and Restatement of Trusts §372).

California: Estate of McKenzie, 227 Cal. App. 2d 167, 38 Cal. Rptr. 496, 7 A.L.R.3d 1275 (1964) (citing the text and Restatement of Trusts §372; for a reward for discovering a cure for arthritis).

Illinois: Estate of Tomlinson, 65 Ill. 2d 382, 3 Ill. Dec. 699, 359 N.E.2d 109 (1976) (citing Restatement of Trusts §372).

Massachusetts: Barrett v. Brooks Hosp., 338 Mass. 754, 157 N.E.2d 638 (1959).

New Jersey: Sheen v. Sheen, 126 N.J. Eq. 132, 8 A.2d 136 (1939) (annual prize to outstanding Doctor of Medical Science in the United States each year; citing Restatement of Trusts §372).

New York: Matter of Judd, 242 A.D. 389, 274 N.Y.S. 902 (1934), *aff'd,* 270 N.Y. 516, 200 N.E. 297 (1936) (trust to pay $1000 each year to person making greatest advancement toward discovery of cure for cancer; and if cure discovered, half of principal to discoverer and half to a hospital for research).

Tennessee: Pierce v. Tharp, 58 Tenn. App. 362, 430 S.W.2d 787 (1968), *cert. denied,* 402 U.S. 929 (1970) (trust to pay income to whoever has contributed most toward solving problem of alcoholism during the year).

New Zealand: McGregor v. Commissioner of Stamp Duties, [1942] N.Z.L.R. 164 (promotion of scientific study of obstetrics and gynecology and promoting maternal welfare in New Zealand); In re Travis, [1947] N.Z.L.R. 382 (scientific investigation of remedies for consumption and cancer).

In In re Estate of Carlson, 187 Kan. 543, 358 P.2d 669 (1961), a testator left his estate to a city in trust for the education of a medical student who should promise to practice in the city. The court upheld the trust as charitable on the ground that it would promote health in the city where physicians were scarce.

See 35 Colum. L. Rev. 305 (1935).

health may be also a trust for the relief of poverty, or a trust for the advancement of education. Thus a trust to afford medical assistance to the poor, or a trust for medical research, is charitable. A trust for the promotion of health, however, is nonetheless charitable although the benefits are not limited to the poor. Thus a trust to establish a hospital for all persons whether rich or poor is charitable.[4] Most hospitals, indeed, are of this character. Moreover, trusts for the increase of medical knowledge by research are unconnected with the relief of poverty.

Indeed, a nonprofit hospital is a charitable institution, even if it requires payment by all of its patients, and does not provide free or reduced-rate services for those who are unable to pay. A trust for the promotion of health is a charitable trust and is valid even though it is not a trust for the relief of poverty. See §372.1, note 2; §376, note 3.

If the question is not one of validity, but of exemption from federal or state taxation, the result depends on the terms of the statutes and on how they are interpreted. But if the statute exempts charitable institutions and trusts without any further restriction, a nonprofit hospital should come within the exemption, quite apart from the question of whether it gives free services to the poor.

As to federal taxes, the question arose in *Eastern Kentucky Welfare Rights Organization v. Simon.*[5] An earlier ruling by the Internal Revenue Service provided that a hospital qualified for exemption only if it provided free or below-cost service to those unable to pay. It changed this position in 1969 by a ruling that a nonprofit hospital was exempt even though it did not provide free or below-cost services to those unable to pay. An action was

---

[4]*England:* Le Cras v. Perpetual Trustee Co., [1967] 3 All E.R. 915 (P.C.).
Alabama: See Stallworth v. Andalusia Hosp., 470 So. 2d 1158 (Ala. 1985).
Illinois: Hart v. Taylor, 301 Ill. 344, 133 N.E. 857 (1922).
Kansas: Lutheran Home v. Board of County Commrs. of Dickinson County, 211 Kan. 270 (1973), 505 P.2d 1118, overruling Topeka Presbyterian Manor v. Board of County Commrs., n. 8, *infra.*

In In re Mills' Will, 57 N.M. 577, 260 P.2d 1111 (1953), a bequest to deformed and crippled children in such manner as the executors might arrange for was upheld as charitable, although its benefits were not limited to the poor. The court cited the text.

[5]506 F.2d 1278 (D.C. Cir. 1974) (citing the text and Restatement of Trusts §368).

brought by several indigents, and organizations representing indigents, against the Secretary of the Treasury and the Commissioner of Internal Revenue, seeking injunctive relief as to the later ruling. The district court granted summary judgment for the plaintiffs.[6] The court of appeals reversed and held that the ruling was proper and should not be set aside. It said that the term "charitable" included the promotion of health independently of aid to the poor. It pointed out that in earlier times hospitals, like almshouses, were generally created to serve the poor; other patients could be taken care of at home. But the situation has drastically changed; the institutions of Medicare and Medicaid, and the growth of medical and hospital insurance, have greatly reduced the number of poor people requiring free or below-cost hospital services. It said, "To continue to base the 'charitable' status of a hospital strictly on the relief it provides for the poor fails to account for these major changes in the area of health care." It said, however, that to be tax exempt it must provide emergency service for the poor.

The case was reversed by the Supreme Court on the ground that the plaintiffs had no standing to bring the action, hence the court made no ruling as to the merits.[7]

In the state courts similar questions as to taxation have arisen relating to hospitals, nursing homes, and homes for the aged. In many cases it is held that these institutions are tax exempt, even though the beneficiaries are all required to pay the charges.[8] In some cases, however, the courts have ruled that

[6]Eastern Ky. Welfare Rights Org. v. Shulz, 370 F. Supp. 325 (D.D.C. 1973), *rev'd,* 506 F.2d 1278 (D.C. Cir. 1974).

[7]Simon v. Eastern Ky. Welfare Rights Org., 426 U.S. 26, 96 S. Ct. 1917, 48 L. Ed. 3d 450 (1976), noted in 90 Harv. L. Rev. 205 (1976).

As to the matter of standing of the plaintiffs in this case, see Tushnet, The New Law of Standing: A Plea for Abandonment, 62 Cornell L. Rev. 663, 680 (1977).

See Sound Health Assn. v. Commissioner, 71 T.C. 158 (1978), holding that an association promoting health was charitable for tax purposes, even though its purpose was not relief of poverty. The court quoted the text.

[8]See, for example, Peachtree on Peachtree Inn v. Camp, 120 Ga. App. 403, 170 S.E.2d 709 (1969), *rehearing denied, cert. denied;* State Bd. of Tax Commrs. v. Methodist Home for Aged, 143 Ind. 119, 241 N.E.2d 84 (1968), *aff'g* 143 Ind. App. 419, 241 N.E.2d 84 (1968) (citing Restatement of Trusts §368); Topeka Presbyterian Manor v. Board of County Commrs., 195 Kan. 90, 402 P.2d 802 (1965); Assembly Homes v. Yellow Medicine County, 273 Minn. 197, 140 N.W.2d 336 (1966); Bozeman Deaconess Found. v. Ford, 151 Mont.

there was no exemption from taxes because there were not sufficient services to the poor.[9]

A trust for the promotion of mental health is charitable. In *In re James*[10] a trust to establish a home of rest for the members of a religious community and for the clergy of a diocese and for such persons as the Mother Superior of the community should nominate was upheld as charitable. In *In re Chaplin*[11] a testator left property "to provide a Home of Rest that shall afford a means of physical and/or mental recuperation to persons in need of rest by reason of the stress and strain caused or partly caused by the conditions in which they ordinarily live and/or work." He expressed a wish that in considering the suitability of a candidate for admission to the home his financial position

---

143, 439 P.2d 915 (1968); Evangelical Lutheran Good Samaritan Soc. v. Board of Commrs., 219 N.W.2d 900 (N.D. 1974); Joseph Rowntree Memorial Trust Housing Assn. v. Attorney-General, [1983] 1 Ch. 159 (small self-contained dwellings for sale to elderly people on long leases in consideration of a capital payment).

[9]Small v. Pangle, 60 Ill. 2d 517, 328 N.E.2d 285 (1975), *rev'g* Small v. Nelson, 17 Ill. App. 3d 1082, 309 N.E.2d 308 (1974), *appeal dismissed,* 423 U.S. 918 (1975); Iowa Methodist Hosp. v. Board of Review, 252 N.W.2d 390 (Iowa 1977); Lutheran Home v. Board of County Commrs. of Dickinson County, 211 Kan. 270 (1973), 505 P.2d 1118, overruling Topeka Presbyterian Manor v. Board of County Commrs., n. 8, *supra;* Michigan Baptist Homes v. City of Ann Arbor, 396 Mich. 660, 242 N.W.2d 749 (1976) (one judge dissenting); Oregon Methodist Homes v. Horn, 226 Or. 298, 360 P.2d 293 (1961).

See Note, Receipt of pay from beneficiaries as affecting tax exemption of charitable institutions, 37 A.L.R.3d 1191 (1971); Note, Homes of the aged as exempt from property taxation, 37 A.L.R.3d 565 (1971); Note, Nursing home as exempt from property taxation, 45 A.L.R.3d 610 (1972); Bronberg, Financing Health Care and the Effect of the Tax Laws, 39 Law & Contemp. Probs. 656 (Duke U., 1975). See §374.12, *infra.*

In Georgia it is provided by Code 1981, §48-7-25, that exemption from the state income tax shall be given to those corporations and organizations that are exempt under the federal statute.

See also the proposed amendment to the constitution of Georgia as to the exemption from ad valorem taxation of nonprofit homes for the aged that are qualified under the federal law. Internal Rev. Code of 1954, §501 (Resolution, 1976, No. 164).

[10][1932] 2 Ch. 25.

[11][1933] Ch. 115.

See In re Pearse, [1955] 1 D.L.R. 801 (B.C.) (for young governesses who may be sick or overworked).

should not be taken into account, and that persons might be required to pay according to their means for board, lodging, and medical treatment. The court upheld the bequest as charitable because it was for the promotion of health, and it was immaterial that the benefits were not limited to the poor. In *In re Clark*[12] the court upheld a trust for such nursing homes or similar institutions as assist persons of moderate means, such as clerks, governesses, and others who might not be eligible to benefit under the health insurance, old age pension, or similar statutes, to have either surgical operations performed or medical treatment given on payment of some moderate contribution. In *In re Osmund*[13] a testatrix bequeathed all her estate to trustees "upon trust in their absolute discretion to apply the same to the medical profession for the furtherance of psychological healing in accordance with the teaching of Jesus Christ." The lower court held that the intended trust failed, on the ground that the purpose was not charitable because the trustees might in their discretion apply funds for the psychological healing of a rich man, but the Court of Appeal reversed the judgment, holding that a valid charitable trust was created.

A trust for the promotion of health is invalid if by the terms of the trust it is provided that a method of treatment shall be used that has been shown by experience to be an improper method, tending rather to impair health.[14]

§372.1. Proprietary institutions. An institution for the promotion of health is not a charitable institution if it is privately owned and is run for the profit of the owners.[1] Thus a hospital or nursing home or sanitarium is not a charitable institution if the profits resulting from its operation inure to the benefit of private owners. Similarly, a proprietary school for medical education is not a charitable institution. The fact that salaries are paid to persons rendering service to the institution does not prevent it from being charitable; but if the payment of salaries is a mere device for securing to the beneficial owners the profits

[12][1923] 2 Ch. 407.
[13][1944] Ch. 206, *rev'g* [1944] Ch. 66, noted in 8 Convey. (N.S.) 227, 60 L.Q. Rev. 221, 197 L.T. 218, 11 Sol. J. 100.
[14]See §377.
§372.1. [1]See §§376, 402.

that may accrue, the institution is not charitable. The mere fact, however, that persons receiving medical or surgical treatment are required to pay fees does not prevent the institution from being a charitable institution, provided that the profits, if any, resulting from its operation are to be applied solely for charitable purposes.[2]

A medical institution owned and operated by the state or one of its subdivisions is clearly charitable. A trust to aid in the establishment or maintenance of such an institution is not merely one to promote health but is also one to assist the government in the performance of its functions.[3] An institution to promote health, however, is charitable although it is a private institution, provided that it is not one the profits of which inure to the benefit of any individual.

§372.2. Limited classes of beneficiaries. A trust is not a charitable trust if the persons who are to benefit are not of a sufficiently large or indefinite class so that the community is interested in the enforcement of the trust. This is true even

[2]*England:* Le Cras v. Perpetual Trustee Co., [1967] 3 All E.R. 915 (P.C.); In re Resch's Will Trusts, [1969] 1 A.C. 514.

Alabama: Moore v. Walker County, 236 Ala. 688, 185 So. 175 (1938).

Florida: Miami Retreat Found. v. Ervin, 62 So. 2d 748 (Fla. 1953).

Massachusetts: Barrett v. Brooks Hosp., 338 Mass. 754, 157 N.E.2d 638 (1959).

Minnesota: But see Share v. Commr. of Revenue, 363 N.W.2d 47 (Minn. 1985) (nonprofit health maintenance organization is not charitable if it receives no donations and charges fees to all persons who receive care).

Nebraska: Evangelical Lutheran Good Samaritan Socy. v. County of Gage, 181 Neb. 831, 151 N.W.2d 446 (1967).

North Carolina: Darsie v. Duke Univ., 48 N.C. App. 20, 268 S.E.2d 554 (1980), *cert. denied.*

Washington: Weiss v. Swedish Hosp., 16 Wash. 2d 446, 133 P.2d 978 (1943).

In Estate of Orphanos, 67 T.C. 780 (1977), a testator domiciled in Kentucky devised land in trust to accumulate the income and erect a hospital in a village in Greece, and then to terminate the trust and sell the land for the purpose of purchasing equipment for the hospital. The court held, reversing the Commissioner, that a deduction under the estate tax was allowable because the hospital did not pass to the testator's heirs, but was to be held by the village or its representative for charitable purposes.

See §376, n. 3. But see §374.11A.

[3]See §373.

though the purpose of the trust is to promote health. Thus a trust to afford medical assistance to named persons is not charitable, although it may be valid as a private trust. On the other hand, a trust for the promotion of health may be charitable although the persons to receive the benefits are of a limited class, if the class is not so small that the purpose is not of benefit to the community. Thus a trust to establish a hospital for the employees of a particular railroad is upheld as charitable.[1]

§373. Governmental or Municipal Purposes

A trust for the erection or construction or maintenance of public works is charitable. In the Statute of Charitable Uses are included trusts "for repair of bridges, ports, havens, causeways, churches, sea-banks and highways." It has been held that a trust for the purpose of supplying the community with these or other facilities, which are usually supplied at the expense of taxpayers, is charitable. Thus the courts have upheld trusts for the erection of a town hall or similar public building; for the construction or repair of highways; for the erection or maintenance of bridges; for the establishment or maintenance of public parks; for the construction of water works; for protection against fire; and the like.[1] A trust may be charitable, not only because it is for a

§372.2. [1]Union P. Ry. v. Artist, 60 F. 365, 23 L.R.A. 581 (8th Cir. 1894) (hospital for employees of railroad); Louisville & N. R.R. v. Foard, 104 Ky. 456, 47 S.W. 342 (1898) (same); Illinois Cent. R.R. v. Buchanan, 126 Ky. 288, 103 S.W. 272 (1907) (same).

Cf. London Hosp. Medical College v. Inland Revenue Commrs., [1976] 2 All E.R. 113, [1976] 1 W.L.R. 613 (to promote social, cultural, and athletic activities of students of a medical college; a tax case).

See §375.

In Hassett v. Assoc. Hosp. Serv. Corp. of Mass., 125 F.2d 611 (1st Cir. 1942), noted in 55 Harv. L. Rev. 1055, *cert. denied sub nom.* Associated Hosp. Serv. Corp. v. Hassett, 316 U.S. 672 (1942), it was held that a nonprofit hospital service corporation providing hospital care for subscribers was not exempt as a charitable corporation under the provisions of the federal Social Security Act.

§373. [1]*England:* Collison's Case, Hob. 136 (1523) (repair of highways); Jones v. Williams, Amb. 651 (1767) (to bring spring water to town); Attorney-General v. Shrewsbury, 6 Beav. 220 (1843) (repair and fortification of bridges, gates, towers, and walls of town); Forbes v. Forbes, 18 Beav. 552 (1854)

governmental or municipal purpose, but also because it is for

(bridge); Wilson v. Barnes, 38 Ch. D. 507 (1886) (repair of sea dike); Attorney-General v. Day, [1900] 1 Ch. 31 (repair of road); In re Jones, [1948] Ch. 67 (erection of village hall); Brisbane City Council v. Attorney-General, [1979] A.C. 411, [1978] 3 W.L.R. 299, 3 All E.R. 30 (P.C.) (land given to a city for park and recreational purposes).

Federal: Stuart v. City of Easton, 74 Fed. 854 (3d Cir. 1896), *aff'd,* 170 U.S. 383, 18 S. Ct. 650, 42 L. Ed. 1078 (1898) (county courthouse).

Alabama: Mastin v. First Natl. Bank, 278 Ala. 251, 177 So. 2d 808 (1965) (citing Restatement of Trusts §368).

California: Estate of Butin, 81 Cal. App. 2d 76, 183 P.2d 304 (1947) (to erect tower to memory of all those who strove to make Madera County what it is), noted in 46 Mich. L. Rev. 705; Estate of Hart, 151 Cal. App. 2d 271, 311 P.2d 605 (1957) (public park; citing the text and Restatement of Trusts §373).

Connecticut: Hamden v. Rice, 24 Conn. 350 (1856) (repair of highways and bridges); Town of Winchester v. Cox, 129 Conn. 106, 26 A.2d 592 (1942) (park; citing Restatement of Trusts §373).

Delaware: Trustees of New Castle Common v. Gordy, 33 Del. 334, 93 A.2d 509, 40 A.L.R.2d 544 (1952) (city common), noted in 101 U. Pa. L. Rev. 1087.

Illinois: In re Estate of Graves, 242 Ill. 23, 89 N.E. 672, 24 L.R.A. (N.S.) 283, 134 Am. St. Rep. 302, 17 Ann. Cas. 137 (1909) (erection of drinking fountain for horses); Scanlan v. Kirby, 230 Ill. App. 505 (1923) (public bath-house); Stowell v. Prentiss, 323 Ill. 309, 154 N.E. 120, 50 A.L.R. 584 (1926) (water supply), noted in 31 Law Notes 133; Carlstrom v. Frackelton, 263 Ill. App. 250 (1931) (memorial bridge).

Iowa: In re Estate of Nugen, 223 Iowa 428, 272 N.W. 638 (1937) (municipal public library); Blackford v. Anderson, 226 Iowa 1138, 286 N.W. 735 (1939) (construction of highway), noted in 24 Minn. L. Rev. 298, 5 Mo. L. Rev. 123; Jensen v. Nelson, 236 Iowa 569, 19 N.W.2d 596 (1945) (county court-house), noted in 31 Iowa L. Rev. 291.

Kansas: In re Trust Estate of Woods, 181 Kan. 271, 311 P.2d 359 (1957) (parks and playgrounds).

Maine: In re Estate of Clark, 131 Me. 105, 159 A. 500 (1932) (town hall); State v. Rand, 366 A.2d 183 (Me. 1976).

Maryland: Mayor and City Council of Baltimore v. Peabody Inst., 175 Md. 186, 200 A. 375 (1938) (public park).

Massachusetts: Burbank v. Burbank, 152 Mass. 254, 25 N.E. 427, 9 L.R.A. 748 (1890) (public park); Bartlett, Petitioner, 163 Mass. 509, 40 N.E. 899 (1895) (public park); Higginson v. Turner, 171 Mass. 586, 51 N.E. 172 (1898) (water supply); City of Boston v. Doyle, 184 Mass. 373, 68 N.E. 851 (1903) (water supply); Richardson v. Mullery, 200 Mass. 247, 86 N.E. 319 (1908) (lifesaving station); Fay v. Locke, 201 Mass. 387, 87 N.E. 753, 131 Am. St. Rep. 402 (1909) (to aid Federal Bureau of Fisheries); Burr v. City of Boston, 208 Mass. 537, 95 N.E. 208, 34 L.R.A. (N.S.) 143 (1911) (public park); Briggs v. Merchants Natl. Bank, 323 Mass. 261, 81 N.E.2d 827 (1948) (municipal park and art museum); Arnold v. Commr. of Corps. and Taxation, 327 Mass. 694,

the relief of poverty, or for the advancement of education, or for

100 N.E.2d 851 (1951) (to create and maintain park); Peakes v. Blakely, 333 Mass. 281, 130 N.E.2d 564 (1955) (to acquire and cultivate forests; citing the text and Restatement of Trusts §373).

Michigan: Hosmer v. City of Detroit, 175 Mich. 267, 141 N.W. 657 (1913) (to erect fountain in public park with life-size statue of testator).

Minnesota: Schaeffer v. Newberry, 235 Minn. 282, 50 N.W.2d 477 (1951) (to village for public park; citing the text and Restatement of Trusts §§373, 374).

Missouri: Stewart v. Coshow, 238 Mo. 662, 142 S.W. 283 (1911) (to establish public cemetery).

Montana: Hames v. City of Polson, 123 Mont. 469, 215 P.2d 950 (1950) (public park and golf course).

New Hampshire: Petition of Simpson, 89 N.H. 550, 3 A.2d 97 (1938) (to town for its best interests); City of Keene v. Martin, 96 N.H. 482, 79 A.2d 13 (1951) (chimes on public building).

New Jersey: Lawrence v. Prosser, 89 N.J. Eq. 248, 104 A. 772 (1918) (to erect and maintain a monument to a public character).

But see *contra* Morristown Trust Co. v. Morristown, 82 N.J. Eq. 521, 91 A. 736 (1913) (base for flagstaff in public park in memory of testator's father).

New York: Coggeshall v. Pelton, 7 Johns. Ch. 292, 11 Am. Dec. 471 (N.Y. 1823) (town hall); Sherman v. Richmond Hose Co., 230 N.Y. 462, 130 N.E. 613 (1921) (fire protection); Matter of Elliston, 110 N.Y.S.2d 139 (1952) (public park).

Ohio: Heinlein v. Elyria Sav. & Trust Co., 75 Ohio App. 353, 62 N.E.2d 284 (1945) (public parks); Anderson v. Malone, 95 Ohio Abs. 211, 205 N.E.2d 131 (1963) (police pension fund).

Oklahoma: Board of County Commrs. v. Warram, 285 P.2d 1034 (Okla. 1955) (to provide water and fire protection and other services).

Pennsylvania: Cresson's Appeal, 30 Pa. 437 (1858) (shade trees); Fire Ins. Patrol v. Boyd, 120 Pa. 624, 15 A. 553, 1 L.R.A. 417, 6 Am. St. Rep. 745 (1888) (fire protection); Franklin v. Philadelphia, 2 Pa. Dist. Rep. 435 (1893) (provision under will of Benjamin Franklin for accumulation of income for a hundred years, a portion of the accumulated fund to be then given to Philadelphia to be laid out in public works, such as fortifications, bridges, aqueducts, baths, and pavements, with a recommendation that part be employed in bringing water into the town); Abel v. Girard Trust Co., 365 Pa. 44, 73 A.2d 682 (1950) (public park; citing Restatement of Trusts §373), noted in 24 Temp. L.Q. 373; Bangor Park Assn. Case, 370 Pa. 442, 88 A.2d 769 (1952) (public park); Deichelmann Estate, 21 D.&C.2d 659 (Pa. 1959) (public park; citing the text and Restatement of Trusts §373); Dayon Estate, 33 D.&C.2d 91 (Pa. 1964) (drinking fountains in public park: bequest failed because will executed within 30 days of death).

Texas: Rissman v. Lanning, 276 S.W.2d 356 (Tex. Civ. App. 1955) (to the Board of Control of the state of Texas for the state orphans' home; citing Restatement of Trusts §368).

the promotion of health. Thus a trust to maintain a public alms-

---

Utah: Staines v. Burton, 17 Utah 331, 53 P. 1015, 70 Am. St. Rep. 788 (1898) (schools, parks, water works, planting forests, acclimatizing foreign plants).

Australia: In re Smith, [1967] Vict. Rep. 341 (land given as a garden park or for the use of the public or for municipal markets or other similar purposes).

Canada: Re Gemmill, [1946] 2 D.L.R. 716 (Ont.), *rev'g* [1946] 1 D.L.R. 480 (Ont.) (public parks, and public abattoir for humane slaughter of animals).

New Zealand: Kaikoura County v. Boyd, [1949] N.Z.L.R. 233 (conveyance of land to county in trust for improvement and protection of named river); In re Lushington, [1964] N.Z.L.R. 161 (devise of land to public authority for park purposes).

Northern Ireland: Commissioner of Valuation v. Lurgan Borough Council, [1968] N. Ireland L.R. 104 (public swimming pool).

In In re Hayward's Estate, 65 Ariz. 228, 178 P.2d 547 (1947), property was bequeathed to two trustees "for any purpose deemed by them beneficial to the town of Paonia, Colorado, or the Paonia schools." It was held that the trust failed because under the language used the trustees would be authorized to erect a race track or department store or engage in a commercial adventure in the town. Such an interpretation of the language of the testatrix cannot be well justified.

In Assessors of Quincy v. Cunningham Found., 305 Mass. 411, 26 N.E.2d 335 (1940), a charitable corporation was formed to beautify the town of Milton. It purchased land partly in the town of Quincy as a public park for the citizens of Milton. It was held that the land was exempt from the real estate tax in Quincy as well as in Milton.

In Butler v. Shelton, 408 S.W.2d 530 (Tex. Civ. App. 1966), *writ refused, n.r.e.,* a trust for a park for the benefit of landowners in a particular tract was held to be not a charitable trust. See §375.2.

In Monterey Pub. Parking Corp. v. United States, 481 F.2d 175 (9th Cir. 1973), a nonprofit public parking corporation was held not liable for federal income tax because it served the public interest and relieved the city of a burden.

See Ann. Cas. 1914A 1215; 50 A.L.R. 593 (1927); Note, Legacy or devise to or for benefit of municipality as subject to payment of inheritance, succession, or estate taxes, 120 A.L.R. 1388 (1939).

By Arkansas Stat. 1947, §§58-401 to 58-408, provision is made for the creation of trusts for the furtherance of public and governmental purposes and functions.

By Georgia Code 1981, §53-12-71, it is provided that all gifts to the United States or to any state or to any subdivision thereof for any public purpose shall be charitable.

In several states, provision is made for the creation and administration of trusts in which the beneficiary is the state or a subdivision or an instrumentality of the state. Louisiana Laws 1970, c. 135; Montana Code Ann. 1983, §17-3-1001; Oklahoma Stat. Ann., tit. 60, §§176 to 180, as inserted by Laws 1976, c. 222.

house, or a public school, or a municipal hospital, is clearly charitable.[2]

On the other hand, it has been held in England[3] that where a house was devised to the National Trust in trust

> for the use of the High Commissioner or other person representing the Government of the Commonwealth of Australia in England for the time being to be used by him as a country residence in a way similar to that in which Chequers is used by the Prime Minister of England,

the purpose was not charitable.

The question has arisen as to the validity of a trust to establish and maintain a park with a racial discrimination. Undoubtedly, if the municipality is trustee, the racial discrimination is unconstitutional.[4] But suppose that private trustees are originally named or are later substituted for the municipality. This question came before the Supreme Court of the United States in 1966. In *Evans v. Newton*[5] a testator devised land to the city of Macon in trust to maintain a park for white people only. It was held by the state court that the lower court properly accepted

---

See State ex rel. Brennan v. Bowman, 88 Nev. 582, 503 P.2d 454 (1972).

As to municipal corporations as trustees, see §§96.4, 348.1, n. 11.

See Note, Taxpayer's conveyance or dedication of land to or for use of governmental entity as charitable contributions qualifying for tax deduction under 26 U.S.C. §170, 30 A.L.R. Fed. 796 (1976).

[2]In Construction Indus. Training Bd. v. Attorney-General, [1972] 2 All E.R. 1339, noted in 87 Law Q. Rev. 468, it was held that a board created by the Minister of Labour for training persons in the construction industry and for research was entitled to be registered as a charity. It was not disqualified merely because it was under the control of the Ministry, because the courts had jurisdiction to prevent diversion of its funds.

[3]In re Spensley's Will Trusts, [1954] Ch. 233, *rev'g* [1952] Ch. 886, noted in 70 Law Q. Rev. 149.

In MacDonald v. Manning, 103 R.I. 538, 239 A.2d 640 (1968), it was held that a bequest to the state of Rhode Island for the benefit of the fire wardens and fish and game wardens for a residence or meeting place was not charitable.

[4]Pennsylvania v. Board of Directors of City Trusts, 353 U.S. 230, 989, 77 S. Ct. 806, 1181, 1 L. Ed. 2d 792, 1146 (1957).

In Commonwealth v. Brown, 392 F.2d 120 (3d Cir. 1968), 25 A.L.R.3d 724, *cert. denied,* 391 U.S. 921 (1968), it was held that the change of trustees was a state involvement, and that Girard College must admit black children.

See §96.4.

[5]220 Ga. 280, 138 S.E.2d 573 (1964).

the resignation of the city as trustee and appointed individuals as successor trustees. The judgment was reversed by the Supreme Court of the United States.[6] Mr. Justice Douglas, speaking for the majority, said that the service rendered by a park of this character is municipal in nature and that it should be treated as a public institution whether administered by a municipality or by private trustees. Justices Black, Harlan, and Stewart dissented on the ground that it was within the power of the state court to substitute new trustees, and that its judgment did not involve the question of segregation. Mr. Justice White, concurring with the majority, expressed the view that a trust for community purposes like this was not charitable if it discriminated against a part of the community.[7] A statute of the state that permitted dedication of parks limited to the white race involved an unconstitutional discrimination.

§373.1.   General trusts for public purposes.   A trust for the benefit of the nation or a state or municipality is charitable, although the particular method of applying the property is not provided for. Thus trusts for the following purposes have been upheld: for the benefit of a town; for purposes conducing to the good of a certain county and parish; for public works of a city; for the benefit of the nation; for general town expenses; for the benefit and ornament of a town; for the improvement of a city.[1]

---

[6]Evans v. Newton, 382 U.S. 296, 86 S. Ct. 486, 15 L. Ed. 2d 373 (1966).

See Evans v. Newton, 221 Ga. 870, 148 S.E.2d 329 (1966), holding that the trust failed.

In Evans v. Abney, 224 Ga. 826, 165 S.E.2d 160 (1968), aff'd. 396 U.S. 435, 90 S. Ct. 628, 24 L. Ed. 3d 634 (1970) (Douglas and Brennan, JJ., dissenting), it was held that the doctrine of cy pres was not applicable and that the heirs of the testator were entitled to the property.

As to the effect of racial and religious restrictions, see §399.4.

[7]Citing Restatement of Trusts §§368, 374, 375; and the text §§368, 375.2.

§373.1.   [1]*England:* Howse v. Chapman, 4 Ves. 542 (1799); Attorney-General v. Heelis, 2 S.&S. 67 (1824); Attorney-General v. Lonsdale, 1 Sim. 105 (1827); Mitford v. Reynolds, 1 Phil. 185 (1841), 16 Sim. 105 (1848); Faversham v. Ryder, 18 Beav. 318 (1854), aff'd, 5 De G.M.&G. 350 (1854); Mayor v. Tamplin, 21 W.R. 768 (1873).

Federal: Estate of Lucy Latham Boyles, 4 T.C. 1092 (1945) ("civic purposes"; tax case; citing Restatement of Trusts, §373, Comment *c*); Holdeen v. Ratterree, 292 F.2d 338 (2d Cir. 1961) (citing the text).

In an English case it was held that a bequest toward the payment of the national debt of England was a valid charitable bequest.[2] In another case a bequest for the benefit of Great Britain was upheld.[3] In a more recent case[4] a testator bequeathed all his property "unto my country England" for its own use and benefit absolutely. On a summons taken out by the Public Trustee as executor for a determination of the validity of the bequest, the Attorney-General contended that it was a valid charitable bequest and should be administered by the Crown under the sign manual for charitable purposes because no trustee was named to administer it. The Solicitor-General contended that it was a charitable bequest but that it was a direct

---

Delaware: New Castle Common v. Megginson, 1 Boyce 361, 77 A. 565 (Del. 1910).

Illinois: City of Aurora v. Young Men's Christian Assn., 9 Ill. 2d 286, 137 N.E.2d 347 (1956) (citing the text).

Massachusetts: Collector of Taxes of Norton v. Oldfield, 219 Mass. 374, 106 N.E. 1014 (1914); Pierce v. Attorney Gen., 234 Mass. 389, 125 N.E. 609 (1920).

Pennsylvania: Garrison Estate, 391 Pa. 234, 137 A.2d 321 (1958) (citing the text and Restatement of Trusts §373).

Australia: Schellenberger v. Trustees Exrs. & Agency Co., 86 C.L.R. 454 (Austl. 1952) (for beautification and advancement of township).

In In re Endacott, [1960] Ch. 232, where a testator left the residue to a Parish Council "for the purpose of providing some useful memorial to myself," it was held that the character of the legatee did not indicate that the purpose was charitable, and the disposition failed. See §123, n. 24.

In Continental Ill. Natl. Bank & Trust Co. v. United States, 403 F.2d 721 (Ct. Cl. 1968), *cert. denied,* 394 U.S. 973 (1969), it was held that a bequest to the Mayor and Magistratsraete of a German city for the benefit of the city was not deductible as a gift to charity.

But see National Sav. & Trust Co. v. United States, 436 F.2d 458 (Ct. Cl. 1971) (to a foreign town to build a home for the aged).

[2]Newland v. Attorney-General, 3 Mer. 684 (1809).

See also Girard Trust Co. v. Russell, 179 F.446 (3d Cir. 1910).

In Matter of Bertram, 89 Misc. 2d 55, 389 N.Y.S.2d 999 (1976), *aff'd,* 63 A.D.2d 650, 404 N.Y.S.2d 987 (1978), the court upheld a bequest to the Chancellor of the Exchequer of Great Britain for the payment of its national debt to the United States.

[3]Nightingale v. Goulburn, 5 Hare 484, 2 Phil. 594 (1847).

[4]In re Smith, [1932] 1 Ch. 153, *rev'g* [1931] 2 Ch. 364, noted in 11 Can. B. Rev. 52, 72 Law J. 281, 48 Law Q. Rev. 142.

This case is criticized in Albery, Trusts for the Benefit of the Inhabitants of a Locality, 56 Law Q. Rev. 49 (1940).

gift to the king, not as a personal gift, but in right of his crown. The next of kin contended that the bequest was not charitable and was void for uncertainty. The court upheld the contention of the Attorney-General.

§373.2.   Relieving burdens of government.   In many of the cases cited in the two preceding sections there was a gift directly to the nation, or to a state, or to a municipality. In others a trust was created, the performance of which would relieve the government of a burden that it would or might otherwise have had to bear out of its own resources, and thus was a relief to the taxpayers. This is the case where provision is made for the establishment or maintenance of parks, water supply, fire protection, public or community buildings, roads and bridges, or for various other purposes that are normally taken care of by the government. Trusts for such purposes are charitable, although they benefit the rich as well as the poor.

In *Burr v. City of Boston,* [1] where a bequest was made to a city to use the income for the maintenance of its parks, it was held that it was a valid charitable trust. The court said, "It supplies funds for a purpose which otherwise must be provided for by taxation, and so far tends to lighten the public burdens. This is strictly a public use."

In *Dulles v. Johnson*[2] it was held that certain bar associations were charitable organizations, and bequests to them were deductible as to the federal estate tax. In dealing with their purpose in regulating unauthorized practice of law, Waterman, C.J., said: "If these activities were not undertaken by the Associations, the cost of the necessary regulation would descend upon the public. Hence we conclude that as to regulation of the unauthorized practice of the law the Associations must be deemed 'charitable.' "

In *Incorporated Council of Law Reporting v. Attorney-General*[3] the court upheld as charitable a nonprofit corporation formed for reporting judicial decisions. Russell, L.J., said, "It cannot I think

---

§373.2.   [1]208 Mass. 537, 95 N.E. 208 (1911).

See also Monterey Pub. Parking Corp. v. United States, 481 F.2d 175 (9th Cir. 1973) (nonprofit public parking corporation; a tax case).

[2]273 F.362 (2d Cir. 1958), *cert. denied,* 364 U.S. 934 (1960).

[3][1972] Ch. 73, noted in 88 Law Q. Rev. 171.

be doubted that if there were not a competent and reliable set of reports of judicial decisions, it would be a proper function and responsibility of government to secure their provision for the administration of the law."

There are other situations in which the courts have upheld as charitable trusts for purposes that would relieve the government of burdens.[4]

§374. Promotion of Other Purposes Beneficial to the Community

In classifying the purposes that are held to be charitable, it is possible to enumerate some of them, as has been done in the preceding sections. But no matter how many types of purposes are thus enumerated, there will always be another class to include the miscellaneous purposes that cannot be classified under a single heading. The common element is that the purposes are of a character sufficiently beneficial to the community to justify permitting property to be devoted for an indefinite time to their accomplishment. These purposes include the relief of poverty, the advancement of education and of religion, the promotion of health, and governmental or municipal purposes, which have been discussed in the preceding sections. There are in addition many other purposes that have been held to be of such benefit to the community as to be charitable. What purposes can properly be included in this broad category depends a good deal on time and place; it depends on the views of social policy prevailing at the time of the creation of the trust in the state whose law governs the validity of the trust. At any rate, trusts to promote various "causes," such as those considered in the following sections, have been generally upheld as charitable.

§374.1. Promotion of temperance. In numerous cases it has been held that a trust for the promotion of temperance in the use of intoxicating liquors is charitable.[1] There can be no

---

[4] As to trusts for nonprofit cemeteries, see §374.9.

§374.1. [1] *England:* See In re Hood, [1931] 1 Ch. 240, noted in 4 Austl. L.J. 18, 11 Can. B. Rev. 53, 169 Law T. 158, 281, 170 id. 73, 171 id. 222, 74 Sol. J. 143 (1930).

doubt, as the Greeks recognized, that moderation in all things is desirable. There is no doubt that the excessive use of intoxicating liquors is detrimental not merely to the individual guilty of the excess but also to the community. Drunkenness is accountable for many crimes and for much damage to life and property, particularly today in connection with the use of motor vehicles. The courts have had no difficulty in holding that the promotion of temperance in the use of intoxicating liquors is of such benefit to the community as to make a trust to accomplish the purpose a charitable trust.

The only questions that have raised any difficulty are those relating to the means for achieving the purpose. If the trust is one to promote temperance by educational methods, as by the use of pamphlets or lectures or by a study of the causes and cures of intemperance, the trust is undoubtedly charitable.[2] For the most part the courts have had no difficulty in upholding trusts for the promotion of temperance by attempting to bring about legislation prohibiting the manufacture and sale of intoxicating liquors.[3] Whether this method of achieving temperance

---

Federal: Girard Trust Co. v. Commissioner, 122 F.2d 108, 138 A.L.R. 448 (3d Cir. 1941) (citing the text), noted in 46 Dick. L. Rev. 199, 30 Geo. L.J. 316, 14 Rocky Mtn. L. Rev. 70, 90 U. Pa. L. Rev. 365, 27 Wash. U.L.Q. 276.

California: People v. Dashaway Assn., 84 Cal. 114, 24 P. 277, 12 L.R.A. 117 (1890).

Indiana: Haines v. Allen, 78 Ind. 100, 41 Am. Rep. 555 (1881).

Massachusetts: Saltonstall v. Sanders, 11 Allen 446 (Mass. 1865); Sherman v. Congregational Home Missionary Socy., 176 Mass. 349, 57 N.E. 702 (1900); Bowditch v. Attorney Gen., 241 Mass. 168, 134 N.E. 796, 28 A.L.R. 713 (1922).

New York: Buell v. Gardner, 83 Misc. 513, 144 N.Y.S. 945, 149 N.Y.S. 803 (1914).

Ohio: Dirlam v. Morrow, 102 Ohio St. 279, 131 N.E. 365 (1921).

Wisconsin: Harrington v. Pier, 105 Wis. 485, 82 N.W. 345, 50 L.R.A. 307, 76 Am. St. Rep. 924 (1900).

Canada: Farewell v. Farewell, 22 Ont. Rep. 573 (1892); In re McDougall, [1939] 1 D.L.R. 783 (Ont.).

See 21 A.L.R. 951, 952 (1922); 73 id. 1361 (1931).

[2]Haines v. Allen, 78 Ind. 100, 41 Am. Rep. 555 (1881).

[3]*England:* In re Hood, [1931] 1 Ch. 240, noted in 4 Austl. L.J. 18, 11 Can. B. Rev. 53, 169 Law T. 158, 281, 170 id. 73, 171 id. 222, 74 Sol. J. 143.

Federal: See Girard Trust Co. v. Commissioner, 122 F.2d 108, 138 A.L.R. 448 (3d Cir. 1941) (bequest to Board of Temperance, Prohibition and Public

is effective is a question on which reasonable persons differ. Some persons believe that it is effective if limited to the several states but is ineffective when applied to the whole country. Some believe that it is effective if limited to those subdivisions of the state where the preponderant sentiment is in favor of prohibition, and that local option is the most desirable method of achieving the purpose. Some believe that temperance cannot be brought about by the compulsion of law. The courts are not concerned with the question of what method of promoting temperance is best adapted to the purpose. A trust for the promotion of temperance is a valid charitable trust if any method is to be employed that reasonable persons may believe is adapted to that end. Moreover, a trust providing generally for the promotion of temperance, without specifying the method to be employed, is charitable.[4]

The mere fact that the method provided by the terms of the trust involves a change in the law does not prevent it from being charitable.[5] The fact that such changes in the law might conceivably be brought about through illegal methods, as by bribery or duress, does not invalidate the trust. The court will properly assume that the settlor intended that only proper methods should be employed. Thus it has been held that where a testator bequeathed money in trust to use the income for temperance and the overthrow of the liquor traffic in a particular county and

---

Morals of the Methodist Episcopal Church held deductible under federal estate tax; quoting the text), noted in 46 Dick. L. Rev. 199, 30 Geo. L.J. 316, 14 Rocky Mtn. L. Rev. 70, 90 U. Pa. L. Rev. 365, 27 Wash. U.L.Q. 276.

District of Columbia: See International Reform Fed. v. District Unemployment Compensation Bd., 76 U.S. App. D.C. 282, 131 F.2d 337 (1942), *cert. denied sub nom.* District Unemployment Compensation Bd. v. International Reform Fed., 317 U.S. 693 (1942) (corporation to promote prohibition of liquor traffic and kindred evils held exempt from unemployment tax of District of Columbia), noted in 11 Geo. Wash. L. Rev. 125.

Massachusetts: Sherman v. Congregational Home Missionary Socy., 176 Mass. 349, 57 N.E. 702 (1900).

Canada: Farewell v. Farewell, 22 Ont. Rep. 573 (1892).

[4]Saltonstall v. Sanders, 11 Allen 446 (Mass. 1865); Harrington v. Pier, 105 Wis. 485, 82 N.W. 345, 76 Am. St. Rep. 924, 50 L.R.A. 307 (1900).

[5]See §374.4.

In Inland Revenue Commrs. v. Temperance Council, 42 Tax L. Rev. 618 (1926), it was held that a temperance society was not exempt from the payment of an income tax because its purpose was to change the existing liquor laws.

to defray the expenses of the No-License League, the Anti-Saloon League, the Prohibition Party, or any kindred organization in the county, the trust was valid; and the court said that it would not construe the will as authorizing any illegal method of accomplishing the purpose such as defraying the expenses of a political party in violation of a statute.[6]

During the period after the passage of the Eighteenth Amendment to the Constitution of the United States prohibiting the manufacture and sale of intoxicating liquor throughout the United States and prior to its repeal, the question arose whether charitable trusts to secure the prohibition by law of the liquor traffic failed because the purpose had been accomplished. In one case it was held that the trust failed for this reason.[7] Unless it clearly appeared, however, that the purpose of the settlor was solely to secure prohibitory laws and did not include the combatting of efforts to repeal the laws or to assist in securing the enforcement of the law, it could not be said that the whole purpose of the trust had been fully accomplished.[8]

§374.2. Relief of animals. A trust to prevent or alleviate the suffering of animals is charitable. The courts have sometimes emphasized the benefit to the human beings in the community who would either suffer in seeing animals suffer or would be degraded if they did not suffer in seeing animals suffer. It is quite sufficient, however, that the animals are protected from suffering or that their sufferings are diminished. The purpose was not one of those mentioned in the Statute of Charitable Uses, and perhaps in the time of Elizabeth there was no general sentiment against causing animals to suffer. Today, at any rate, the purpose is recognized as one in which the community has an interest. Thus it has been held that the prevention of cruelty to animals is a charitable purpose.[1] So is the establishment or

[6]Buell v. Gardner, 83 Misc. 513, 144 N.Y.S. 945 (1914).

[7]Women's Christian Temperance Union v. Cooley, 25 S.W.2d 171 (Tex. Civ. App. 1930).

[8]Bowditch v. Attorney Gen., 241 Mass. 168, 134 N.E. 796, 28 A.L.R. 713 (1922); Dirlam v. Morrow, 102 Ohio St. 279, 131 N.E. 365 (1921).

See Lee Trust, 5 D.&C.3d 159 (Pa. 1974), stated in §187, n. 3.

§374.2. [1]*England:* In re Marchant, 54 Sol. J. 425 (1910); Simmonds v. Heffer [1983] 6 C.L. 418 (Ch. Div.); Re Green's Will Trusts, [1985] 3 All E.R. 455 (Ch.D.).

maintenance of a home for domestic animals such as cats and dogs and horses.[2] A trust to found an institution for studying and curing maladies of animals useful to man is charitable.[3] Trusts to promote vegetarianism have been upheld, partly because they are intended to promote the welfare of the animals that would otherwise be used for food, and partly on the theory that they are intended to promote the health of mankind.[4] In other cases as well, trusts for the benefit of animals have been upheld.[5]

Colorado: In re Forrester's Estate, 86 Colo. 221, 279 P. 721 (1929), noted in 2 Rocky Mt. L. Rev. 125.

Massachusetts: Minns v. Billings, 183 Mass. 126, 66 N.E. 593, 5 L.R.A. (N.S.) 686, 97 Am. St. Rep. 420 (1903).

New Jersey: Burlington County Trust Co. v. New Jersey Socy., 12 N.J. Super. 369, 79 A.2d 710 (1951).

New York: Matter of Manville, 57 N.Y.S.2d 439 (1945) (citing the text).

North Carolina: Woodcock v. Wachovia Bank & Trust Co., 214 N.C. 224, 199 S.E. 20 (1938) (*semble,* but held void for uncertainty), noted in 37 Mich. L. Rev. 1132, 6 U. Chi. L. Rev. 332.

Oregon: In re Kulka's Estate, 142 Or. 104, 18 P.2d 1036 (1933).

Pennsylvania: Siemens Estate, 346 Pa. 610, 31 A.2d 280, 153 A.L.R. 483 (1943) (court taking judicial notice as to the meaning of "S.P.C.A."); Towne Estate, 75 D.&C. 215 (Pa. 1951) (quoting the text).

Wisconsin: Estate of Goodrich, 271 Wis. 59, 72 N.W.2d 698 (1955) (citing the text).

Canada: In re Smith, [1953] 3 D.L.R. 510 (B.C.).

[2]*England:* In re Douglas, 35 Ch. D. 472 (1887); In re Murawski's Will Trusts, [1971] 2 All E.R. 328.

Connecticut: Shannon v. Eno, 120 Conn. 77, 179 A. 479 (1935).

New Jersey: Bankers Trust Co. v. New York Women's League for Animals, 17 N.J. Super. 398, 86 A.2d 138 (1952) (citing Restatement of Trusts, §374, Comment *c*), *rev'd on other grounds,* 23 N.J. Super, 170, 92 A.2d 820 (1952).

New York: Matter of Hamilton, 185 Misc. 660, 57 N.Y.S.2d 359 (1945), *aff'd,* 270 A.D. 634, 63 N.Y.S.2d 265 (1946), *aff'd mem.,* 296 N.Y. 578, 68 N.E.2d 872 (1946) (citing the text and quoting Restatement of Trusts, §374, Comment *c*), noted in 32 Cornell L.Q. 458, 21 St. John's L. Rev. 87.

Texas: Georg v. Animal Defense League, 231 S.W.2d 807 (Tex. Civ. App. 1950).

Australia: Attorney-General (S.A.) v. Bray, 111 C.L.R. 402 (Austl. 1964).

Ireland: Swifte v. Attorney-General, [1912] 1 I.R. 133.

[3]University of London v. Yarrow, 1 De G.&J. 72 (1857).

[4]In re Cranston, [1898] 1 I.R. 431; Lackland v. Walker, 151 Mo. 210, 52 S.W. 414 (1899).

[5]*England:* In re Wedgwood, [1915] 1 Ch. 113; In re Moss, [1949] 1 All E.R. 495 (to a woman to aid her in her work for welfare of cats and kittens).

The question has arisen whether a trust for the suppression of vivisection is a valid charitable trust. Such a trust was upheld in *In re Foveaux.* [6] The question was raised again 50 years later. In *National Anti-Vivisection Society v. Inland Revenue Commissioners* [7] the House of Lords took the view that in the light of the evidence

---

California: Estate of Coleman, 167 Cal. 212, 138 P. 992, Ann. Cas. 1915C 682 (1914) (drinking fountain for thirsty animals and birds).

Illinois: In re Estate of Graves, 242 Ill. 23, 89 N.E. 672, 24 L.R.A. (N.S.) 283, 134 Am. St. Rep. 302, 17 Ann. Cas. 137 (1909) (drinking fountain for horses).

Massachusetts: Peakes v. Blakely, 333 Mass. 281, 130 N.E.2d 564 (1955) (reserve for birds; citing Restatement of Trusts §374).

New Jersey: More Game Birds in America, Inc. v. Boettger, 125 N.J.L. 97, 14 A.2d 778 (1940) (corporation to conserve game birds in America, to establish hatcheries and refuges, and to teach vermin control; citing Restatement of Trusts §374), noted in 29 Geo. L.J. 245, 5 U. Newark L. Rev. 407.

Canada: Re Gemmill, [1946] 2 D.L.R. 716 (Ont.), *rev'g* [1946] 1 D.L.R. 480 (public abattoirs for humane slaughtering of animals).

See 66 A.L.R. 465 (1930).

In Towne Estate, 75 D.&C. 215 (Pa. 1951), a testator left money in trust to maintain a drinking fountain for horses and dogs, and to pay any surplus to a society for the prevention of cruelty to animals. It appeared that no horses used the highways and that dogs were prohibited from wandering at large. It was held that the trust should not be terminated, but the income should be paid to the society except such part as might be needed to pay for the removal of the fountain.

[6][1895] 2 Ch. 501.

See also Old Colony Trust Co. v. Welch, 25 F. Supp. 45 (D. Mass. 1938); Armstrong v. Reeves, 25 L.R. Ir. 325 (1890); Glasgow Socy. for Prevention of Cruelty to Animals v. National Anti-Vivisection Socy., [1915] Sess. Cas. 757 (Scot.).

[7][1948] A.C. 31, noted in 63 Law Q. Rev. 403, *aff'g* Commissioners of Inland Revenue v. National Anti-Vivisection Socy., [1946] K.B. 185, noted in 10 Camb. L.J. 104, 62 Law Q. Rev. 111, 23 Sol. J. 435.

Their Lordships also took the view that because the purpose of the society involved the repeal of a statute permitting vivisection, thus changing the existing law, the purpose was political and therefore not charitable. As to this, see §374.4.

For later cases, see In re Wightwick's Will Trusts, [1950] Ch. 260, noted in 15 Convey. (N.S.) 180, 94 Sol. J. 513; Animal Defence and Anti-Vivisection Socy. v. Inland Revenue Commrs., 94 Sol. J. 725, [1950] T.L.R. (66 Pt. 1) 1112, noted in 60 Law Q. Rev. 438, 67 id. 36.

In Commonwealth v. American Anti-Vivisection Socy., 32 Pa. Commn. 70, 377 A.2d 1378 (1977), it was held that an anti-vivisection society was not exempt from a state sales tax, because it was not a "purely public charity."

offered it appeared that the purpose could no longer be held to be charitable and that a society for the suppression of vivisection was not exempt from income tax, and it expressly overruled *In re Foveaux.* It was held that the purpose was such as to impede medical research, and that it therefore could not be beneficial to the community.

Where a disposition is made by a testator for the care of specific animals that he owned, and not for the benefit of an indefinite number of animals, the trust is not a charitable trust. But in such a case the disposition does not fail if the legatee is willing to carry it out and there is no violation of the principle of the rule against perpetuities.[8] Where a testator left the residue of his estate to a state board in perpetuity to afford relief to neglected animals and provided that his pet dog should be given a good home, the court held that the trust was charitable and that the provision for the particular dog did not invalidate the bequest, the court treating the provision for the dog as merely precatory.[9]

Where in the opinion of the court a trust for the benefit of animals is of a quixotic character, the court has refused to uphold it. In an English case the court said that a trust to feed sparrows would not be charitable.[10] In a more recent English case[11] a testatrix left money to establish and maintain an institu-

[8]See §124.3.

[9]Johnston v. Colorado State Bureau, 86 Colo. 221, 279 P. 721 (1929).

[10]Attorney-General v. Whorwood, 1 Ves. Sr. 534 (1750).

[11]In re Grove-Grady, [1929] 1 Ch. 57, 66 A.L.R. 448, noted in 4 Camb. L.J. 82, 45 Law Q. Rev. 426.

In Royal Socy. for the Prevention of Cruelty to Animals, N.S.W. v. Benevolent Socy. of N.S.W., 102 C.L.R. 629 (Austl. 1960), it was held that a trust to maintain a sanctuary for birds was, because of certain circumstances, not a charitable trust.

In Holbrook Island Sanctuary v. Inhabitants of Town of Brooksville, 161 Me. 476, 214 A.2d 660 (1965), it was held that real estate held by a corporation as a wildlife sanctuary was not exempt from tax as a charitable institution. The court said that there was no benefit to the community.

In In re Green, [1970] Vict. Rep. 442, it was held that a bequest to buy land and maintain on it native fauna and flora was not a charitable disposition. But query.

In In re Kitchener-Waterloo Humane Socy., 31 D.L.R.3d 438 (1981), it was held that a humane society directed to the welfare of animals was not conducted on "philanthropic" principles and was subject to tax.

tion as a refuge to preserve from molestation or destruction by man "animals, birds or other creatures not human," with a further provision that the institution should be controlled by anti-vivisectionists and opponents of sport involving the pursuit or death of animals. A majority of the Court of Appeal was of the opinion that the institution would not afford any advantage to animals that are useful to mankind or any protection to other animals from cruelty, and held that the trust failed. Certainly the fact that the animals to be protected are not animals useful to man should not prevent a trust from being a charitable trust.

§374.3. Patriotic purposes. Trusts for the promotion of the security of the nation have been upheld as charitable, whether the method to be employed is through increasing preparations for war or stimulating the desire for peace or inculcating patriotic emotions. Thus trusts have been upheld for the benefit of military organizations, not only by increasing the professional competence of the soldier but also by improving his health and morale through facilities for sports, or through supplying better food for his stomach or literature for his mind.[1] It

---

In Matter of North Manursing Wildlife Sanctuary v. City of Rye, 75 A.D.2d 855, 427 N.Y.S.2d 843 (1980), it was held that a corporation formed to preserve wildlife was charitable and not subject to tax.

In Commonwealth v. Isaac W. Bernheim Found., 505 S.W.2d 762 (Ky. 1974), it was held that a trust to establish a bird sanctuary was charitable and not subject to tax.

In Greiss v. United States, 146 F. Supp. 505 (N.D. Ill. 1956), it was held that a sportsman's club was not exempt from federal tax although its purposes included, but were not limited to, conservation of wildlife. It was held to be immaterial that the state court had held it charitable and exempt from a state tax.

In Silverman v. Town of Alton, 451 A.2d 103 (Me. 1982), it was held that land conveyed to trustees for maintenance as a wildlife refuge for the benefit of the University of Maine was not exempt from taxation.

See §374.10, on community purposes.

§374.3. [1]In re Lord Stratheden and Campbell, [1894] 3 Ch. 265 (benefit of volunteer military corps); In re Good, [1905] 2 Ch. 60 (books and plates for officers' mess of certain regiment); In re Donald, [1909] 2 Ch. 410 (benefit of mess of regiment); In re Gray, [1925] Ch. 362 (promotion of shooting, fishing, cricket, and polo in regiment); In re Driffill, [1950] Ch. 92 (to protect the United Kingdom from attack by hostile aircraft), noted in 14 Convey. (N.S.) 65; Scott v. Sterrett, 234 S.W.2d 917 (Tex. Civ. App. 1950) (erection of armory for militia organization).

has been held that a trust to promote rifle shooting among the people is charitable because it tends to make them more efficient if called on to serve in the army.[2] On the other hand, a trust to promote yacht racing has been held to be not charitable,[3] although it might be suggested that the encouragement of the sport might tend to make the people more efficient sailors if called on to serve in the navy. In England a trust to provide an Eton fives court in a school was held to be a charitable trust;[4] it might be regarded as a trust to promote the public defense if, as has been suggested, the battle of Waterloo was won on the playing fields of Eton; but at any rate it can be supported as a trust for the advancement of education.

Trusts to stimulate patriotism have been upheld as charitable, such as a trust in England to ring a peal of bells on the anniversary of the restoration of the monarchy;[5] or a trust for

---

A trust to assist disabled war veterans is of course charitable. In re Schikowsky's Estate, 155 Kan. 815, 130 P.2d 598 (1942).

In In re Meyers, [1951] 1 All E.R. 538, the court held invalid a trust for charitable or benevolent institutions or funds having as their object the assistance of members of the Royal Navy whether past, present, or future or their wives or children. The difficulty was that it included former members of the Navy.

But see Re Perry and Kovacs, 12 D.L.R. 4th 751 (B.C. Sup. Ct. 1984) (trust to provide rest for navy personnel is not charitable because "rest" might mean "comfort"; trust fails because court will not apply the cy pres doctrine).

In In re Thomas's Will Trust, [1969] 3 All E.R. 1492, the court held invalid a bequest to the colonel of a regiment in trust to use the income for the benefit of the officers and men who belong or have belonged to the regiment.

In In re Chitty's Will Trusts, [1970] Ch. 254, a bequest to the colonel for the time being of a regiment in trust to use the income for the benefit of the officers and men who belong or have belonged to the regiment was assumed not to be a charitable trust.

[2]In re Stephens, 8 T.L.R. 792 (1892).

In In re Corbyn, [1941] Ch. 400, noted in 5 Convey. (N.S.) 311, 57 L.Q. Rev. 455, the court upheld as charitable a trust to train boys for commissions in the Royal Navy or as officers in the mercantile marine on the ground that such a trust was beneficial to the community.

[3]In re Nottage, [1895] 2 Ch. 649.

As to trusts for the promotion of sports, see §374.6A.

[4]In re Mariette, [1915] 2 Ch. 284.

[5]In re Pardoe, [1906] 2 Ch. 184.

the purchase and display of the flag;[6] or a trust for the celebration of Memorial Day;[7] or a trust for the inculcation of patriotism.[8]

Love of country finds expression not merely in the desire to assist in the winning of wars but also in the desire to prevent war. Accordingly, it has been held that a trust for the promotion of peace is charitable.[9]

Although trusts for these various patriotic purposes have been upheld as charitable, it has been held in England that a trust for "patriotic purposes" is not charitable, because the expression is so broad that it would include purposes not recognized as charitable, even though the motive of the testator might be patriotic.[10]

§374.4. Changes in existing law. It has sometimes been said that a trust is not charitable if the accomplishment of the purposes of the trust involves a change in existing law. Thus in the famous case of *Jackson v. Phillips*[1] a testator made a bequest in trust to promote the cause of "women's rights." The court interpreted this to mean not the advancement of the social or economic condition of women but the extension to women of

[6]Sargent v. Cornish, 54 N.H. 18 (1873).

[7]Matter of De Long, 140 Misc. 92, 250 N.Y.S. 504 (1931).

[8]Thorp v. Lund, 227 Mass. 474, 116 N.E. 946, Ann. Cas. 1918B 1204 (1917).

[9]*California:* Estate of Peck, 168 Cal. App. 2d 25, 335 P.2d 185 (1959) (to promote peace and world understanding), *cert. and rehearing denied,* 361 U.S. 826, 903 (1959).

Maine: Tappan v. Deblois, 45 Me. 122 (1858).

Massachusetts: Parkhurst v. Treasurer & Receiver Gen.. 228 Mass. 196, 17 N.E. 39 (1917).

New York: Matter of Harmon, 80 N.Y.S.2d 903 (1948) (citing the text).

[10]Attorney-General v. National Provincial & Union Bank, [1924] A.C. 262.

But in Valley Forge Historical Socy. v. Washington Memorial Chapel, 479 A.2d 1011 (Pa. Super. 1984), deeds of land upon trust "for patriotic purposes" were held to create a valid charitable trust although the particular patriotic purposes were not specified, citing Restatement (Second) of Trusts §374.

§374.4. [1]14 Allen 539, 571 (1867).

But see Planned Parenthood League of Mass. v. Attorney Gen., 391 Mass. 709, 464 N.E.2d 55, *cert. denied,* 105 S. Ct. 189, 83 L. Ed. 2d 122 (1984) (society engaged in lobbying for legislation favorable to planned parenthood is charitable).

the right to vote and to hold office. It was held that this was not a charitable purpose. Mr. Justice Gray said:

> This bequest differs from the others in aiming directly and exclusively to change the laws; and its object cannot be accomplished without changing the Constitution also. Whether such an alteration of the existing laws and frame of government would be wise and desirable is a question upon which we cannot, sitting in a judicial capacity, properly express any opinion. Our duty is limited to expounding the laws as they stand. And those laws do not recognize the purpose of overthrowing or changing them, in whole or in part, as a charitable use.

Further on he said that

> trusts whose expressed purpose is to bring about changes in the laws or the political institutions of the country are not charitable in such a sense as to be entitled to peculiar favor, protection and perpetuation from the ministers of those laws which they are designed to modify or subvert.

It is interesting to observe that Mr. Justice Gray in speaking of a change in the law each time throws in another verb that has an offensive connotation, showing hostility to the particular change — "overthrowing or changing," "to modify or subvert." One cannot escape the feeling that the learned justice felt that the extension of the suffrage to women would be unfortunate. At any rate, curiously enough, in the same case the court upheld a bequest in trust to create a public sentiment that would put an end to black slavery in the United States; and yet this purpose involved a change in the Constitution of the United States, a change that was in fact effected after the death of the testator and before the decision in the case. In a later case in Massachusetts the court again refused to uphold a trust to promote "women's rights,"[2] but the opposite view was taken in a case in Illinois.[3]

In England it seems to be held that a court cannot take the

[2]Bowditch v. Attorney Gen., 241 Mass. 168, 134 N.E. 796, 28 A.L.R. 713 (1922).
[3]Garrison v. Little, 75 Ill. App. 402 (1898).

position that a change in the law is for the public benefit, and it is held that a trust to bring about a change in the law is not charitable. In *National Anti-Vivisection Society v. Inland Revenue Commissioners*[4] it was held by the House of Lords that an anti-vivisection society was not a charitable organization and was not exempt from taxes. This result was reached on two grounds. In the first place it was held that the evidence showed that animal experimentation was necessary for medical research and that because the suppression of vivisection would impede medical progress the purpose was against public policy.[5] Their Lordships gave as a further ground for the decision the fact that a purpose of the society was to repeal a statute that permitted vivisection, and that where the purpose is to bring about a change in the law it is not charitable. Lord Wright quoted with approval a statement in Tyssen on Charitable Bequests that "The law could not stultify itself by holding that it was for the public benefit that the law itself should be changed," and that "each court . . . must decide on the principle that the law is right as it stands." It seems difficult indeed to justify such a view as to the perfection of the law.

In the United States the notion that a trust for a purpose otherwise charitable is not charitable if the accomplishment of its purposes involves a change in existing laws has been pretty thoroughly rejected. Many reforms can be accomplished only by

[4][1948] A.C. 31, noted in 10 Camb. L.J. 104, 63 Law Q. Rev. 403.

For other English cases in which the court has said that a purpose is not charitable if it involves a change in existing law, see Bowman v. Secular Socy., [1917] A.C. 406, 442 (per Lord Parker); Inland Revenue Commrs. v. Temperance Council, 42 Tax L.R. 618, 136 Law T. 27 (1926); In re Trusts of the Arthur McDougall Fund, [1956] 3 All E.R. 867, *semble;* McGovern v. Attorney-General, [1981] 3 All E.R. 493 (Ch.D.) (Amnesty International; purposes were (1) relief of needy prisoners of conscience and their families; (2) release of prisoners of conscience; (3) abolition of torture; (4) research into human rights; (5) dissemination of results of such research; (6) other actions to further the preceding. Held: (2) and (3) were not charitable objects because they involved change in foreign law).

In In re Jenkins' Will Trusts, [1966] Ch. 249, noted in 82 Law Q. Rev. 159, where a share of the residue was left to an anti-vivisection society to procure an Act of Parliament forbidding vivisection, it was held that the legacy failed and that it could not be upheld under the cy pres doctrine, although the other shares were given to valid charitable purposes for the relief of animal suffering.

[5]See §374.2, n. 7.

a change in the law, and there seems to be no good reason why the mere fact that they can be accomplished only through legislation should prevent them from being valid charitable purposes. The courts have upheld trusts for the improvement of the structure and methods of government,[6] trusts for the prohibition of the manufacture and sale of liquor,[7] and trusts for various other objects,[8] although in each case the accomplishment of the purposes of the trust involved a change in existing law. If, indeed, the purposes to be achieved are not charitable purposes, the intended trust fails. As we shall see, if the purposes are purely political in character, they are not charitable purposes.[9]

A decision to the effect that the donor or donee is not entitled to an exemption from the payment of a tax does not necessarily mean that the gift is not for other purposes a charitable gift. Thus it has been held that where a gift was made to the American Birth Control League the donor was not entitled to a deduction from the payment of an income tax that was allowed in the case of gifts made to any corporation organized and operated exclusively for charitable or educational purposes.[10]

[6]See §384.5.

[7]See §374.1.

Cf. People *ex rel.* Hartigan v. National Anti-Drug Coalition, 124 Ill. App. 3d 269, 79 Ill. Dec. 786, 464 N.E.2d 690 (1984) (society actively campaigning against public officials who favor decriminalization of drugs is charitable).

[8]Register of Wills for Baltimore City v. Cook, 241 Md. 264, 216 A.2d 542 (1966) (to eliminate discrimination against women, citing the text and Restatement of Trusts, §374, Comment *j*).

See 21 A.L.R. 951 (1922); 16 Cal. L. Rev. 478 (1928).

See Leubuscher v. Commissioner, 54 F.2d 998 (2d Cir. 1932) (trust for teaching and propagating the ideas of Henry George).

See Note, Validity of charitable trust to promote change in laws or systems or methods of government, 22 A.L.R.3d 886 (1968).

[9]See §374.6.

[10]Slee v. Commissioner, 42 F.2d 184, 72 A.L.R. 400 (2d Cir. 1930).

By Internal Revenue Code of 1954, §170, a deduction is permitted in the case of gifts to a charitable organization "no substantial part of the activities of which is carrying on propaganda, or otherwise attempting to influence legislation."

There are many cases where federal tax exemptions or deductions are not allowed because of the attempt to influence legislation, often involving a close question whether the attempt is substantial. See, for example, League of Women Voters v. United States, 180 F. Supp. 379 (Ct. Cl. 1960) (two judges dissenting), *cert. denied,* 364 U.S. 822, 81 S. Ct. 57, 5 L. Ed. 2d 51 (1960);

The purposes of the league were to collect and disseminate lawful information regarding the consequences of uncontrolled procreation, to maintain a medical clinic for the giving of advice to married women as to birth control if in the judgment of the physicians such advice was necessary for the protection of their health, and also to enlist support of legislators and others to effect the lawful repeal and amendment of statutes dealing with the prevention of conception. Learned Hand, J., said that the league was not operated exclusively for charitable purposes within the meaning of the revenue statute because one of the purposes was to agitate for a change in the law. He expressed no doubt, however, on the question whether the purposes of promoting health and education are charitable, as they undoubtedly are; and undoubtedly a trust to promote these purposes, even though they might involve a change in the law, would be a valid charitable trust. In *Faulkner v. Commissioner of Internal Revenue*[11] it was held that a gift to the Birth Control League of Massachusetts was deductible from the federal income tax, the league having decided to abandon political and legislative objects prior to the time of the gift. In another case[12] it was held that the International Reform Federation was a charitable corporation and exempt from the unemployment tax of the District of Columbia. Its purposes were to promote prohibition of the liquor traffic, of the white slave traffic, and of drugs, and the suppression of gambling and of political corruption. One judge dissented on the ground that the purposes were not exclusively charitable.

Haswell v. United States, 500 F.2d 1133 (Ct. Cl. 1974), *cert denied,* 419 U.S. 1107, 95 S. Ct. 779, 42 L. Ed. 2d 803 (1975); Regan v. Taxation with Representation of Washington, 461 U.S. 540, 103 S. Ct. 1997, 76 L. Ed. 2d 129 (1983).

See Fratcher, Bequests for Purposes, 56 Iowa L. Rev. 773, 777-778 (1971).

[11]112 F.2d 987 (1st Cir. 1940), noted in 41 Colum. L. Rev. 335.

In Planned Parenthood Assn. v. Tax Commr., 5 Ohio St. 2d 117, 214 N.E.2d 222 (1966), it was held that the Planned Parenthood Association was a charitable corporation and was exempt from succession tax. The purpose was to give information to married or about-to-be married women as to contraception.

[12]International Reform Fedn. v. District Unemployment Compensation Bd., 76 App. D.C. 282, 131 P.2d 337 (1942), *cert. denied sub nom.* District Unemployment Compensation Bd. v. International Reform Fedn. (1942), noted in 11 Geo. Wash. L. Rev. 125.

§374.5. Improvement of government. Trusts for the improvement of the structure and methods of government have been held to be charitable. It is immaterial that the court and a majority of the citizens may not believe that the accomplishment of the particular purpose would be an improvement, if rational persons can reasonably hold the opposite view. In *Taylor v. Hoag*[1] the court in Pennsylvania upheld as charitable a trust to promote improvements in the structure and methods of government with special reference to the initiative, referendum and recall, ballot reform, and similar purposes, with a view to promote efficiency and popular control of government. In *Collier v. Lindley*[2] the California court upheld a trust to promote improvements in the structure and methods of government, national, state, and local, by furthering in all legitimate ways public ownership and operation of public utilities, the initiative, referendum and recall, and popular nomination and election of public officials. In *Peth v. Spear*[3] the Washington court upheld a trust to provide a place where the doctrines of socialism could be taught by example as well as by precept. In *George v. Braddock*[4] a trust to distribute the works of Henry George, who advocated the single tax, was upheld.

§374.6. Political objects. A line must be drawn, though it is not always easy to draw it, between objects that are merely political and objects that are of general social significance. It is clear that a trust to promote the success of a particular political party is not a charitable trust. It is against public policy to permit the perpetual endowment of a political party.[1] It is immaterial

§374.5. [1]273 Pa. 194, 116 A. 826, 21 A.L.R. 946 (1922).
See In re Trusts of the Arthur McDougall Fund, [1956] 3 All E.R. 867 (to promote study in connection with the art or science of government or other branches of political or economic science).
[2]203 Cal. 641, 266 P. 526 (1928).
[3]63 Wash. 291, 115 P. 164 (1911).
[4]45 N.J. Eq. 757, 18 A. 881, 6 L.R.A. 511, 14 Am. St. Rep. 754 (1889).
In Leubuscher v. Commissioner, 54 F.2d 998 (2d Cir. 1932), it was held that in determining the estate tax a legacy for teaching and propagating the ideas of Henry George was a charitable trust exclusively for educational purposes.
§374.6. [1]Boorse Trust, 64 D.&C. 447 (Pa. 1948) (quoting the text).
See Note, Charitable Trusts for Political Purposes, 37 Va. L. Rev. 988 (1951).

whether the endowment is for the purpose of electing to office the candidates of the party or for the purpose of otherwise promoting the success of the party. Thus in an English case it was held that a trust for the furtherance of the principles of a particular political party was not a charitable trust and was subject to the income tax.[2] In that case a bequest was made to an association organized for the promotion of the principles of the Conservative party. The governing body was composed of eminent members of the Conservative party and one of the purposes was to give instruction in political history and such other subjects as the governing body might determine. On the other hand, in an earlier English case the court upheld as charitable a gift for the furtherance of Conservative principles, but the testator had required that this be combined with religious and mental improvement.[3] It would seem, however, that this should hardly be enough to sweeten the pill. In another English case[4] a testator bequeathed a share of his estate to a prominent member of the Liberal party to be distributed by him among such political bodies having as their object or one of their objects the promotion of Liberal principles in politics as he should in his absolute discretion select. The court held that the bequest was valid and that it was immaterial whether or not it was a charitable trust because the beneficiaries of the trust were ascertainable organizations among whom the distribution was to be immediately made. In a more recent English case[5] a testator left prop-

[2]Bonar Law Memorial Trust v. Inland Revenue Commrs., 49 Tax L.R. 220 (1933).

[3]In re Scowcroft, [1898] 2 Ch. 638.

[4]In re Ogden, [1933] Ch. 678, noted in 49 Law Q. Rev. 469.

[5]In re Hopkinson, [1949] 1 All E.R. 346.

In In re Bushnell (deceased), [1975] 1 All E.R. 721, [1975] 1 W.L.R. 1596, noted in 38 Mod. L. Rev. 471, a trust "for the advancement and propagation of the teaching of Socialised Medicine" with detailed provisions as to what was to be taught, was held to be not for a charitable purpose, and failed. The court said that the purpose was political rather than educational.

See In re Grant's Will Trusts, [1980] 1 W.L.R. 360, [1979] 3 All E.R. 359 (a Labour Party unincorporated association).

In Simmonds v. Heffer, [1983] 6 C.L. 418 (Ch. Div.), it was held that £50,000 donated by the League Against Cruel Sports to the Labour Party's general election fund in 1979 was not within the League's objects, but £30,000 given to the party to be spent on publicizing animal welfare was.

erty to four prominent members of the Labour party in trust to apply both capital and income for the advancement of adult education, with particular reference to a certain memorandum relating to the purpose of the party. The purpose stated in the memorandum was to advance the cause of the party by improving methods of propaganda and increasing its electoral efficiency. The court held that the object of the trust was political and therefore not charitable.

In a case in Canada[6] a testator left his property to his executor "for the purpose of promoting and propagating the doctrines and teachings of Socialism." It was held that the purpose, although not illegal, was not charitable and therefore failed for lack of definite beneficiaries.

There have been similar decisions in the United States. Thus it has been held that a legacy to the Socialist-Labor Party, an unincorporated political association, could not be upheld as a gift for charitable purposes.[7] In another case[8] it was held that a corporation organized for the purpose of promoting the interests of the Socialist party and of workers' organizations by education of the young and by lectures was not exempt from the payment of a tax on its real estate. In *Liapis Estate*[9] the court upheld a bequest to the Socialist-Labor Party of the United States, an unincorporated association, although the will was executed within thirty days of the testator's death, on the ground that the legacy was not for a charitable purpose and therefore was not invalid under a statute invalidating bequests for charitable purposes in a will executed within thirty days of

[6]In re Loney, [1953] 4 D.L.R. 539 (Man.).

[7]Matter of Andrejevich, 57 N.Y.S.2d 86 (1945); Matter of Grossman, 190 Misc. 521, 75 N.Y.S.2d 335 (1947) (citing Restatement of Trusts §374).

In Estate of Carlson, 9 Cal. App. 3d 479, 88 Cal. Rptr. 229, 41 A.L.R.3d 825 (1970), it was held that a bequest to the Socialist Labor Party of California was invalid under a statute permitting bequests to unincorporated charitable associations and to fraternal associations.

See Note, Validity and construction of testamentary gift to political party, 41 A.L.R.3d 833 (1972); Note, Charity and Politics, 38 Mod. L. Rev. 471 (1975).

[8]Workmen's Circle Educ. Center v. Assessors of Springfield, 314 Mass. 616, 51 N.E.2d 313 (1943) (citing the text and Restatement of Trusts §374).

[9]88 D.&C. 303 (Pa. 1954) (citing the text and Restatement of Trusts, §374, Comment *k*).

the testator's death. In *Deichelmann Estate*[10] it was held that a bequest to an institution organized to create a center of education and a bureau of information for the Republican women of Pennsylvania was for political and not for charitable purposes and was not invalid on the ground that the will was executed within thirty days of the death of the testatrix.

On the other hand, in another case[11] a testator provided that his executors should distribute the remainder of his estate "among any socialist, labor, educational, cultural or charitable societies." It was held that the provision was valid, and that the executors properly made a payment to an incorporated association devoted to the propagation of the principles of socialism and trade unionism, and to the promotion of social intercourse among the members and to the dissemination of economic, social, and political knowledge. The court said that the association although not strictly charitable was an educational institution and not a partisan political organization.

Where the trust is one to promote not the general purposes of a political party but a particular cause, a more difficult question arises. The mere fact that one political party favors and another opposes the particular cause does not necessarily prevent a trust to promote that cause from being charitable, if it is one that apart from politics would be recognized as a charitable purpose. Thus the fact that there is a Prohibition party has not prevented the court from holding that a trust to promote the prohibition of the manufacture and sale of intoxicating liquor is charitable. Undoubtedly the question of the abolition of slavery prior to the Civil War long dominated the political scene, but in Massachusetts, at least, the court had no difficulty in upholding a trust created by a testator, a famous abolitionist, who died in 1861, for the preparation and circulation of books and the delivery of lectures to create a public sentiment that would put an end to slavery in the United States.[12]

On the other hand, there are some questions that, although they may have social significance, have become recognized as primarily political questions. What questions are to be consid-

[10]21 D.&C.2d 659 (Pa. 1959) (citing the text and Restatement of Trusts §§373, 374).

[11]In re Cahan's Estate, 122 N.Y.S.2d 716 (1953).

[12]Jackson v. Phillips, 14 Allen 539 (Mass. 1867).

ered as primarily political depends a good deal on the time and place. In a case decided by the House of Lords, Lord Parker of Waddington said: "The abolition of religious tests, the disestablishment of the Church, the secularization of education, the alteration of the law touching religion or marriage, or the observation of the Sabbath, are purely political objects. Equity has always refused to recognize such objects as charitable."[13] This was but a dictum, however, because the bequest in question was to a corporation organized to promote these objects, and the court held that the bequest, though not for a charitable purpose, was valid. In another case, Russell, J., said: "Subsidizing a newspaper for the promotion of particular political or fiscal opinions would be a patriotic purpose in the eyes of those who considered that the triumph of those opinions would be beneficial to the community. It would not be an application of funds for a charitable purpose."[14] In an Australian case,[15] where a testator left a part of his estate to a Catholic archbishop and three bishops to establish a Catholic daily newspaper, it was held that the bequest was not for a charitable purpose and that it failed. On the other hand, in *Tribune Press v. Punjab Income Tax Commissioner*,[16] where an inhabitant of the Punjab bequeathed his newspaper to trustees to maintain the newspaper, keeping up its liberal quality and devoting the surplus income to improving it and placing it on a footing of permanence, it was held that the purpose was charitable and that the undertaking was not subject to income tax. The court said that the purpose was not educational but was one of general public utility in supplying an organ of educated public opinion. In a case in New York[17] a testator left property in trust "for the foundation of a Universal Journal or of any other enter-

[13]Bowman v. Secular Socy., [1917] A.C. 406, 442.

In Baldry v. Feintuck, [1972] 2 All E.R. 81, the court said that a contribution to a political campaign of protest against the government's policy of ending free milk supplies to school children was not charitable. See §367.2, n. 2.

[14]In re Tetley, [1923] 1 Ch. 258, 262, *aff'd sub nom.* Attorney-General v. National Provincial & Union Bank, [1924] A.C. 262.

[15]In re Lawlor, [1934] Vict. L.R. 22, *aff'd by an equally divided court sub nom.* Roman Catholic Archbishop of Melbourne v. Lawlor, 51 C.L.R. 1 (Austl. 1934).

[16][1939] 3 All E.R. 469, noted in 14 Austl. L.J. 9.

[17]Matter of Tackian, 109 Misc. 519, 179 N.Y.S. 188 (1919).

prise which shall have for its purpose the betterment and improvement of the conditions of suffering mankind in general or in particular." The court held that the foundation of such a journal was not a charitable purpose and that the trust failed.

In other cases it has been held that the trust failed because it was for political purposes. Thus in a Scottish case[18] it was held that an association to assist the government or the public in resisting any strike, lockout, or civil commotion interfering with essential public services was not exempt from taxation because its purposes were predominantly political. In a case in New Zealand[19] it was held that a trust for the League of Nations of New Zealand was a trust for a political purpose and was therefore invalid under the rule against perpetuities. On the other hand, in an Australian case[20] it was held that a trust to prevent the death of infants, to improve Australian food habits, and to extend technical education was not for political purposes and was valid.

On the question of the validity of a trust to promote women's suffrage there has been a conflict of opinion. In Illinois such a trust was upheld,[21] but in Massachusetts the court reached the opposite result.[22] Although in Massachusetts the court gave as a reason that the accomplishment of the purposes of the trust involved a change in existing law, we have seen that by the great weight of authority that is immaterial. The only justification for the decisions in Massachusetts is that the question was purely political. It would seem, however, that it was more than a political question; it involved indirectly social and

[18]Trustees for the Roll of Voluntary Workers v. Commissioners of Inland Revenue, [1942] Sess. Cas. 47 (Scot.), noted in 58 Law Q. Rev. 167.

[19]In re Wilkinson, [1941] N.Z.L.R. 1065.

[20]Royal North Shore Hosp. of Sydney v. Attorney-General, 60 C.L.R. 396 (Austl. 1938).

[21]Garrison v. Little, 75 Ill. App. 402 (1898).

See Register of Wills for Baltimore City v. Cook, 241 Md. 264, 216 A.2d 542 (1966), holding that the National Woman's Party, whose purpose was to eliminate discrimination against women, was not a political party and a legacy to it was not taxable.

See Note, Validity of charitable trust to promote change in laws or systems or methods of government, 22 A.L.R.3d 886 (1968).

[22]Jackson v. Phillips, 14 Allen 539 (Mass. 1867); Bowditch v. Attorney Gen., 241 Mass. 168, 134 N.E. 796, 28 A.L.R. 713 (1922).

economic considerations that transcended party lines. At any rate the question is now an academic one since the enactment of the Nineteenth Amendment to the Constitution of the United States.

There are other matters in which there is little room for doubt, because the trust is for a social rather than a political purpose and is charitable. Thus in one case a trust to employ all legal and moral means to prevent discrimination against blacks in America was upheld.[23] In another case a trust to promote justice for the American Indians by assisting and procuring legislation or otherwise was held to be a valid charitable trust.[24] In another case, however, the intended trust failed.[25] In that case a testator left his estate to trustees to be applied for any purpose that would in their opinion be designed to strengthen the bonds of unity between the Union of South Africa and England, and which incidentally would conduce to the appeasement of racial feelings between the Dutch and English-speaking sections of the South African community. It was held that the intended trust failed, because it was possible to imagine modes of application within the declared purpose that would not be charitable.

As we have seen, trusts for the improvement of government have been upheld, although the methods advocated included those frequently advocated or opposed by one or another of the political parties.[26]

§374.6A. Promotion of sports. A trust for the mere promotion of sports is not charitable.[1] This is clearly so where

[23]Lewis's Estate, 152 Pa. 477, 25 A. 878 (1893).

[24]Collier v. Lindley, 203 Cal. 641, 266 P. 526 (1928).

[25]In re Strakosch, [1949] Ch. 529, [1948] Ch. 37, noted in 13 Convey. (N.S.) 378.

In Re Koeppler's Will Trusts; Barclays Bank Trust Co. v. Slack, [1984] 1 Ch. 243, [1984] 2 All E.R. 111 (Ch. D.), it was held that a bequest on trust to finance conferences of leaders of opinion in western countries with a view to the formation of an informed international public opinion and the promotion of greater cooperation in Europe and the West was not charitable because it contemplated education to promote political views; *reversed* by the Court of Appeal, [1986] 1 Ch. 423 (C.A.), [1985] 2 All E.R. 869.

[26]See §374.5.

§374.6A. [1]*England:* In re Nottage, [1895] 2 Ch. 649 (yacht racing); In re Clifford, 81 Law J. Ch. 220 (1911) (angling); In re Lipinski's Will Trusts, [1976] 3 W.L.R. 522, [1977] 1 All E.R. 33 (cricket and other sports).

a limited group of persons are to take part in or benefit from the sport.[2] A trust to promote rifle shooting, however, has been upheld on the ground that it tends to promote the national defense.[3] So also it has been held that a trust to promote sports among children may be upheld on the ground that it is a part of the education of children to improve their bodies as well as their minds.[4] A stricter view, however, was taken by an English court in *In re Patten*.[5] In that case it was held that a bequest of £300 to a cricket club in trust to pay the income to a fund to train boys of the working or lower middle classes to become professional cricketers was not a charitable trust. The court said that it could not be supported as a trust for the "supportation, aid and help of young tradesmen, handicraftsmen and persons decayed" within the meaning of the Statute of Elizabeth, but

---

Arkansas: Weaver v. First Natl. Bank, 216 Ark. 199, 224 S.W.2d 813 (1949) (outing club).

Illinois: Halbert v. Springfield Motor Boat Club, 342 Ill. App. 685, 97 N.E.2d 592 (1951) (boat club).

Massachusetts: In re Troy, 364 Mass. 15, 306 N.E.2d 203 (1973). But see Attorney Gen. v. International Marathons, 392 Mass. 370, 467 N.E.2d 51 (1984); Boston Athletic Assn. v. International Marathons, 392 Mass. 356, 467 N.E.2d 58 (1984).

Pennsylvania: Maxwell Memorial Football Club v. Commonwealth, 336 A.2d 460 (Pa. Commw. 1975) (a tax case).

West Virginia: Contra, In re Teubert's Estate, 298 S.E.2d 456 (W. Va. 1982) (perpetual foundation to provide, inter alia, annual prizes in golf tournament and to pay for little league baseball equipment was valid).

Canada: But see Re Laidlaw Found., 48 O.R.2d 549 (Ont. Div. Ct. 1984).

New Zealand: Laing v. Commissioner of Stamp Duties, [1948] N.Z.L.R. 154 (amateur athletic association).

See Evans, Sport and Charitable Status 1 Trust L.&P. 16 (1986).

As to sports in schools and universities, see §370.2.

[2]Barton v. Parrott, 25 Ohio Misc. 2d 8, 495 N.E.2d 973 (Ohio C.P. 1984) (trust to run annual horse race in memory of testatrix's daughter).

See §375.2.

[3]In re Stephens, 8 T.L.R. 792 (1892).

As to trusts for patriotic purposes, see §374.3.

[4]In re Mariette, [1915] 2 Ch. 284 (fives court for school); Inland Revenue Commrs. v. McMullen, [1980] 1 All E.R. 884 (House of Lords) (trust for association football and other sports for pupils at school and universities is an educational charity); College Preparatory School for Girls v. Evatt, 144 Ohio St. 408, 59 N.E.2d 142 (1945).

See §370.2.

[5][1929] 2 Ch. 276, 289.

that it was "reasonably clear that the object of the fund is the encouragement of the game of cricket and nothing else."

§374.7. **Unpopular causes.** The charitable trust has played a notable part in promoting the interests of minority groups in the community. As we have seen, various religious sects in England have been enabled to establish themselves and to break down the monopoly of the established church. Similarly, the charitable trust has played a great part in the field of education. It has been possible through privately endowed institutions to try many experiments to which it would be improper to devote the public funds, or that the public would be unwilling to support until convinced by proof of their success. And so it has been in other fields. The mere fact that the members of the court and the great majority of the people believe that a particular purpose is unwise does not prevent a trust to accomplish that purpose from being charitable, if the general purposes for which the trust is created may reasonably be thought to promote the interests of the community. In an Irish case[1] in which the court upheld a trust to promote vegetarianism, Lord Justice Fitz Gibbon said:

> What is the tribunal which is to decide whether the object is a beneficent one? It cannot be the individual mind of a Judge, for he may disagree, *toto coelo*, from the testator as to what is or is not beneficial. On the other hand, it cannot be the *vox populi*, for charities have been upheld for the benefit of insignificant sects, and of peculiar people. It occurs to me that the answer must be — that the benefit must be one which *the founder* believes to be of public advantage, and his belief must be at least rational, and not contrary either to the general law of the land, or to the principles of morality. A gift of such a character, dictated by benevolence, believed to be beneficent, devoted to an appreciably important object, and neither *contra bonos mores* nor *contra legem*, will, in my opinion, be charitable in the eye of the law, as settled by decisions which bind us. It is not for us to say that these have gone too far.

In a case in New Jersey the lower court held invalid a trust to disseminate the writings of Henry George advocating the

§374.7. [1]In re Cranston, [1898] 1 I.R. 431, 446-447.

single tax, but the upper court held that it was a valid charitable trust.[2] In Massachusetts in an early case the court upheld a trust to establish and maintain a school to be taught by females in which no books of instruction were to be used except spelling books and the Bible.[3] If in the course of time experiments like this prove to be a failure, relief can be given through a liberal exercise of the cy pres power.[4]

On the other hand, if the purpose for which a trust is created is wholly irrational it is not a charitable trust. But it is not always easy to draw the line between purposes believed to be irrational and those believed to be merely unwise. The test is not what the court believes, and not what the majority believe, but what rational persons may believe. In England a trust to maintain an institution to educate and train spiritualistic mediums was held invalid.[5] It is difficult, however, to say that the purpose was irrational, because undoubtedly a belief in spiritualism has been entertained by a not inconsiderable number of quite rational and not undistinguished persons. At any rate, it was held in Pennsylvania that an outright gift to an incorporated spiritualistic college was valid.[6]

In a case in New York,[7] a trust created by the will of a Theosophist to pay the income to such highly evolved individuals with much occult knowledge who are ceaselessly working for the advancement of the race and the alleviation of the sufferings of humanity as the trustee might deem worthy was held not to be charitable and it failed. In another case,[8] where a testator left his property to the trustees of the Theosophical Society in India

---

[2]George v. Braddock, 45 N.J. Eq. 757, 18 A. 881, 6 L.R.A. 511, 14 Am. St. Rep. 754 (1889).

In Leubuscher v. Commissioner, 54 F.2d 998 (2d Cir. 1932), it was held that in determining the estate tax a legacy for teaching and propagating the ideas of Henry George was a charitable trust exclusively for educational purposes.

[3]Tainter v. Clark, 5 Allen 66 (Mass. 1862).

[4]See §399.3.

[5]In re Hummeltenberg, [1923] 1 Ch. 237.

Compare Stephan's Estate, 129 Pa. Super. 396, 195 A. 653 (1937) (trust for perpetual upkeep of spiritualist memorial held invalid).

[6]Lockwood's Estate, 344 Pa. 293, 25 A.2d 168 (1942).

[7]Matter of Carpenter, 163 Misc. 474, 297 N.Y.S. 649 (1937).

[8]Korsstron v. Barnes, 167 F. 216 (C.C.W.D. Wash. 1909).

to be used in obtaining translations into English of the Ancient Hieratic Scriptures, the bequest was held to be void for uncertainty. A trust for the promotion of religion, however, is not invalid merely because the religious views to be promoted are those of a small minority.[9]

As we have seen, a trust for educational purposes may fail because the testator's project was of little or no value, as where he directs that his worthless writings be published or that a museum be established to exhibit works of art of slight value.[10] We have seen also that a trust for the suppression of vivisection has been held in England to be invalid on the ground that such a purpose is an impediment to medical progress.[11]

§374.8. Charity outside the state. A trust is charitable where its purposes are or may reasonably be supposed to be beneficial to the community. A trust is nonetheless charitable although the community to be benefited is not that of the state in which the trust is created. Thus it is held in England that a trust is charitable although it is for the benefit of persons in another part of the United Kingdom or in a foreign country, as, for example, where it is for the benefit of the poor of another country or to establish a school in a foreign country.[1] Similarly, in the United States the courts have had no difficulty in upholding trusts as charitable although they are for the benefit of members of a community outside the state in which the trust is

[9]See §371.4.

[10]See §370.

[11]See §374.2.

§374.8. [1]In re Marr's Will Trusts, [1936] Ch. 671; In re Robinson, [1931] 2 Ch. 122 (German soldiers disabled in the late war); In re Niyazi's Will Trusts, [1978] 1 W.L.R. 910 (for or towards the construction of a "working men's hostel" in a town in Cyprus).

See: In re Stone, 91 W.N. (N.S.W.) 704 (1970) (bequest to a fund the object of which was to acquire land in Israel for the purpose of settling Jews thereon).

See Williams v. Attorney-General, [1946] N.Z.L.R. 118.

See Carr, The Charitable Status of Trusts for the Working Class, 123 Sol. J. 88 (1979).

As to the conflict of laws relating to charities outside the state of the testator's domicile, see §594.

created or outside the United States.[2] Whether the trust prop-

[2]*California:* Estate of Moeller, 199 Cal. 705, 251 P. 311 (1926); Estate of McDole, 215 Cal. 328, 10 P.2d 75 (1932) (home for aged in another state).

Iowa: Beidler v. Dehner, 178 Iowa 1338, 161 N.W. 32 (1917) (poor curates in foreign country); Martinson v. Jacobson, 200 Iowa 1054, 205 N.W. 849 (1925) (Swedish society), noted in 12 Iowa L. Rev. 66, 85.

Massachusetts: Teele v. Bishop of Derry, 168 Mass. 341, 47 N.E. 422, 38 L.R.A. 629, 60 Am. St. Rep. 401 (1897) (to build chapel in Ireland); Thorp v. Lund, 227 Mass. 474, 116 N.E. 946, Ann. Cas. 1918B 1204 (1917) (to such national or philanthropic purpose in Norway as daughter of testatrix should direct); Staman v. Board of Assessors of Chatham, 351 Mass. 479, 221 N.E.2d 861 (1966) (citing the text and Restatement of Trusts, §374, Comment *i*).

Missouri: Bogdanovich v. Bogdanovich, 360 Mo. 753, 230 S.W.2d 695 (1950) (to build school in Yugoslavia).

New Jersey: Lawrence v. Prosser, 89 N.J. Eq. 248, 104 A. 772 (1918) (to erect monument in Maine); Bloomer v. Bloomer, 98 N.J. Eq. 576, 131 A. 388 (1925), *aff'd,* 100 N.J. Eq. 361, 134 A. 915 (1926) (to assist poor of Ireland); Rowe v. Rowe, 113 N.J. Eq. 344, 167 A. 16 (1933); Haas v. Canton of Bern, 140 N.J. Eq. 240, 54 A.2d 213 (1947); Martin v. Haycock, 140 N.J. Eq. 450, 55 A.2d 60 (1947) (for library in Irish town).

New Mexico: Farmers & Merchants Bank v. Woolf, 86 N.M. 320, 523 P.2d 1346 (1974).

New York: Matter of Dreyfuss, 154 Misc. 47, 276 N.Y.S. 438 (1934) (to city officials of German city for charitable purposes); Matter of Antoni, 186 Misc. 988, 61 N.Y.S.2d 349 (1946) (widows and orphans of German village); Matter of Byrne, 71 N.Y.S.2d 359 (1947) (to parish priest in Ireland to equip parochial schools in Ireland to train children in trades and handicrafts); Matter of Merritt, 273 A.D. 79, 75 N.Y.S.2d 828 (1947), *aff'g* 185 Misc. 979, 61 N.Y.S.2d 537 (1945) (to erect chapel in England); Matter of Hinckey, 86 N.Y.S.2d 579 (1949) (to church organization in Ireland to supply clothes for poor children).

North Dakota: Hagen v. Sacrison, 19 N.D. 160, 123 N.W. 518, 26 L.R.A. (N.S.) 724 (1909) (to establish children's home in Sweden).

Pennsylvania: Crawford's Estate, 294 Pa. 201, 143 A. 912 (1928) (fatherless children of France).

Texas: Morse v. First Natl. Bank of Galveston, 194 S.W.2d 578 (Tex. Civ. App. 1946).

Canada: See In re Oldfield, [1949] 2 D.L.R. 175 (Man.) (upkeep of municipal cemetery in France); In re Burnham, 17 D.L.R.2d 298 (B.C. 1958) (the income to be devoted to voluntary organizations for the poor, sick, and afflicted of Montenegro, Macedonia, and Armenia); In re Masoud, 28 D.L.R.2d 646 (Ont. 1961) (to establish and maintain a school in Syria).

A trust for charitable purposes is not invalid merely because its benefits may extend to persons throughout the world. Ratto v. Nashville Trust Co., 178 Tenn. 457, 159 S.W.2d 88, 141 A.L.R. 341 (1942).

In Matter of Muckl, 174 Misc. 35, 19 N.Y.S.2d 1009 (1940), where a legacy was left to a religious order to educate missionaries in Germany, and it ap-

erty will be administered by trustees within the state, or whether it will be turned over to trustees or organizations in the other state or country, depends on the intention of the testator.[3]

We shall consider hereafter the questions of the conflict of laws that arise where the law as to the validity of the trust in the state in which the trust is to be administered is different from the law of the state in which the testator was domiciled.[4]

Whether a gift for charitable purposes to be administered

---

peared that if the legacy were sent to Germany it would not be so applied, it was held it should be given to a branch of the order in Nebraska.

In Brownell v. Fidelity Union Trust Co., 119 F. Supp. 755 (D.N.J. 1954), where property was left in trust before World War II for the benefit of a German charity, the trust did not fail and there was no resulting trust to the settlor or need for the application of the doctrine of cy pres.

In San Antonio Indep. School Dist. v. Division of World Missions, 161 Tex. 471, 341 S.W.2d 896 (1961), *aff'g* Division of World Missions v. National Bank of Commerce, 326 S.W.2d 934 (Tex. Civ. App. 1959), where a testator left money to a missionary society to be used for needy Chinese people in China, with a gift over if it should refuse to accept or qualify, it was held that since, owing to the Communist domination, the money could not be used to help Chinese on the mainland of China, it might be used to aid Chinese in Formosa and Hong Kong.

In Freedman v. Scheer, 223 Ga. 705, 157 S.E.2d 875 (1967), it was held that a bequest of personalty, but not a devise of land, to the state of Israel was valid, but that the land should be sold and the proceeds paid to Israel.

See Note, Charitable trust as affected by lack of territorial limitation as regards beneficiaries, 141 A.L.R. 346 (1942).

As to the question of exemption from inheritance taxes of institutions of other states, see 27 Iowa L. Rev. 155 (1941).

[3]*Illinois:* People v. First Natl. Bank, 364 Ill. 262, 4 N.E.2d 378, 108 A.L.R. 277 (1936).

Iowa: Beidler v. Dehner, 178 Iowa 1338, 161 N.W. 32 (1917).

Australia: Kytherian Assn. of Queensland v. Sklavos, 101 C.L.R. 56 (Austl. 1958).

See Note, Foreign location of charity as determining proper situs for administration of trust settled upon it by local donor, 58 A.L.R.2d 1135 (1958).

See Alford, Voluntary Foreign Aid and American Foreign Policy: The Elements of State Control, 46 Va. L. Rev. 477 (1960).

[4]See §§592-594.

In Arkansas v. Texas, 346 U.S. 368, 74 S. Ct. 109, 98 L. Ed. 80 (1953), it was held that the question whether a Texas charitable corporation had authority to contribute funds to the University of Arkansas is a question of the law of Texas.

in another state is entitled to tax advantages under state income or inheritance or estate tax laws depends on the terms of the statute.[5] By the terms of the Internal Revenue Code[6] a taxpayer can to a limited extent deduct from gross income for the purposes of the income tax gifts for charitable purposes to a corporation, trust, or community chest, fund, or foundation, "created or organized in the United States or in any possession thereof, or under the law of the United States, any State, the District of Columbia, or any possession of the United States."

§374.9. **Monuments and tombs.** A bequest for the erection or maintenance of a tomb or monument does not ordinarily create a charitable trust. The bequest does not fail, however, if there is no violation of the principle of the rule against perpetuities and if the legatee is ready and willing to carry out the intended purpose.[1] There are cases, however, in which trusts for the erection or maintenance of tombs or monuments are held to be charitable trusts. Thus a trust to erect and maintain a monument to a person of note is a charitable trust because it is considered of benefit to the community that such tributes be

[5]Unander v. United States Natl. Bank (In re Jenkins' Estate), 224 Or. 144, 355 P.2d 729 (1960).

See Note, Succession and estate tax construction of statute or regulation exempting gifts to foreign charitable, educational or religious body on reciprocal basis, 12 A.L.R.3d 918 (1967). See §348.4, n. 1.

[6]26 U.S.C. §170(c). See §348.4.

In England, the exemption from income tax is limited to charitable trusts established in the United Kingdom. Camille & Henry Dreyfus Found. v. Inland Revenue Comms., [1956] A.C. 39.

§374.9. [1]See §124.2.

In Proprietors of the Cemetery of Mt. Auburn v. Unemployment Compensation Commn., 305 Mass. 288, 25 N.E.2d 759 (1940), noted in 25 Marq. L. Rev. 95, it was held that a cemetery was not a charitable organization so as to be exempt from unemployment compensation tax, even though no one profited from its operation.

In Metairie Cemetery Assn. v. United States, 282 F.2d 225 (5th Cir. 1960), where purchasers of cemetery lots made agreements with the cemetery corporation to deposit money in trust for the perpetual care of their lots, the corporation agreeing to keep the lots in repair, it was held that the corporation was subject to an income tax with respect to the trust income that it paid to itself in return for its services, even though the trust funds were invested in tax-exempt securities.

paid to its dead leaders.[2] The question how prominent the decedent must have been and how great his services to his country or state or local community is one of degree. There seems to be no difficulty in the case of military leaders or officeholders; but in an English case the court refused to uphold as charitable a trust for a monument of the philosopher John Locke.[3] On the other hand, in New Jersey the court had no difficulty in upholding a trust to erect a monument to a brother of the testator, although his fame was confined to his immediate community;[4] and a similar result was reached in a Scottish case.[5] So also have bequests been upheld as charitable where they are for the upkeep of a public cemetery or one attached to a church,[6] or for the erection or maintenance of a memorial window in a church.[7] Similarly a trust to erect headstones for the poor is charitable.[8] So also a trust for the erection or maintenance of a monument not to individuals but to a class of persons who have rendered service to the nation or to the community, such as a soldiers' or sailors' monument, is charitable.[9]

Where a trust is created for educational, religious, or other

[2]*Alabama:* Gilmer's Legatees v. Gilmer's Exrs., 42 Ala. 9 (1868) (General Stonewall Jackson and Colonels Cobb and Bartow).

Kentucky: Owens v. Owens' Exr., 236 Ky. 118, 32 S.W.2d 731 (1930) (Washington, Lincoln, Jefferson, and Andrew Jackson).

Massachusetts: Eliot v. Trinity Church, 232 Mass. 517, 122 N.E. 648 (1919) (Bishop Phillips Brooks).

Wyoming: Town of Cody v. Buffalo Bill Memorial Assn., 64 Wyo. 468, 196 P.2d 369 (1948) (William F. Cody; quoting the text).

In Gilmer's Legatees v. Gilmer's Exrs., 42 Ala. 9, 23 (1868), it was held that a bequest for assisting to raise monuments to the memory of all officers and soldiers from Alabama who distinguished themselves or were killed in the War Between the States was void on account of impossibility of performance.

[3]In re Jones, 79 Law T. 154 (1898).

[4]Lawrence v. Prosser, 89 N.J. Eq. 248, 104 A. 772 (1918).

[5]M'Caig's Trustees v. Kirk-Session of United Free Church of Lismore, [1915] Sess. Cas. 426 (Scot.).

[6]See §124.2, n. 10.

[7]See §124.2, n. 11.

[8]In re Pardoe, [1906] 2 Ch. 184; Estate of Coleman, 167 Cal. 212, 138 P. 992, Ann. Cas. 1915C 682 (1914).

[9]*Kentucky:* Owens v. Owens' Exr., 236 Ky. 118, 32 S.W.2d 731 (1930).

New York: Matter of Barnard, 170 Misc. 875, 11 N.Y.S.2d 115 (1939) (monument dedicated to Gold Star Mothers of America).

Rhode Island: Ogden, Petitioner, 25 R.I. 373, 55 A. 933 (1903).

charitable purposes, the mere fact that it is to serve as a memorial to the testator or another does not prevent it from being a charitable trust.[10] It has been held that where a bequest was made for the erection of a drinking fountain, with a provision that there should be a life-size statue of the testator[11] or a statue of his horse,[12] the provision did not prevent the trust from being a charitable trust.

Statutes.　　In a number of states it is provided by statute that trusts for the perpetual care of individual graves shall be valid.[13]

[10]*District of Columbia:* Noel v. Olds, 78 App. D.C. 155, 138 F.2d 581 (1943), *cert. denied,* 321 U.S. 773 (1945) (quoting the text), s.c. 80 App. D.C. 63, 149 F.2d 13 (1945), s.c. *sub nom.* Olds v. Rollins College, 84 App. D.C. 299, 173 F.2d 639 (1949), noted in 43 Mich. L. Rev. 211, 32 Geo. L.J. 425, 27 N.C.L. Rev. 591, 35 Va. L. Rev. 649.

Massachusetts: Massachusetts Inst. of Technology v. Attorney Gen., 235 Mass. 288, 126 N.E. 521 (1920); Old Colony Trust Co. v. O. M. Fisher Home, 301 Mass. 1, 16 N.E.2d 10 (1938).

Ohio: Murr v. Youse, 52 Ohio Abs. 321, 80 N.E.2d 788 (1946), *semble.* See §368, n. 5.

[11]Hosmer v. City of Detroit, 175 Mich. 267, 141 N.W. 657 (1913).

[12]In re Estate of Graves, 242 Ill. 23, 89 N.E. 672, 24 L.R.A. (N.S.) 283, 134 Am. St. Rep. 302, 17 Ann. Cas. 137 (1909).

[13]*Alabama:* Code 1975, §§11-17-13 to 11-17-16.

Arizona: Rev. Stat. Ann., §33-261.

Arkansas: Code, §82-427.

Colorado: Rev. Stat. 1973, §38-30-110.

Connecticut: Gen. Stat. 1958, §47-2. See §19-151a, providing for payment to the cemetery association of funds left in trust with a county treasurer for perpetual care.

See Fairlawns Cemetery Assn. v. Zoning Commn., 138 Conn. 434, 86 A.2d 74 (1952).

Florida: Stat. Ann., §689.13.

Georgia: Code 1981, §53-12-70.

Illinois: Rev. Stat., c. 21, §68; c. 32, §288a, as amended by Laws 1967, c. 1674; c. 30, §153, as amended by Laws 1969, c. 76-1427 (providing that restrictions on accumulation shall not be applicable to trusts created for the care of burial places).

Kansas: Stat. Ann., §12-1419a.

Louisiana: Rev. Stat. Ann., §§8:1 to 8:903, enacted by Laws 1974, c. 417.

Maryland: Ann. Code, Estates and Trusts Article, §11-102.

Michigan: Stat. Ann., §26.1191.

Minnesota: Stat. Ann., §§307.05 to 307.07.

Mississippi: Code 1972, §41-43-3.

In some states the statute provides for gifts for perpetual care when made to a cemetery corporation or association.[14] Where

---

Missouri: Rev. Stat., §§214.140, 214.270 to 214.410.

See Powers v. Johnson, 306 S.W.2d 616 (Mo. 1957).

New Jersey: Rev. Stat., §8:2-30.

New Mexico: Stat. Ann. 1978, §§58-17-1 to 58-17-17.

New York: Estates, Powers and Trusts Law, §§8-1.5 and 8-1.6.

North Carolina: Gen. Stat., §36A-43.

Oregon: Rev. Stat., §97.730. See §97.010.

Pennsylvania: 9 Pa. Stat., §§303 to 308; 20 Pa. Cons. Stat., §6104.

See Note, Cemetery Trusts in Pennsylvania, 60 Dick. L. Rev. 264 (1956).

Rhode Island: Gen. Laws 1956, §45-5-11, as amended by Laws 1976, c. 13.

South Carolina: Code Ann., 1976, §§21-29-20; §27-5-70.

Texas: Civ. Stat. Ann., arts. 912 to 915.

Utah: Code Ann., §8-2-1.

Vermont: Stat. Ann., tit. 18, §§5306 to 5309, 5382. Section 5309 as amended by Laws 1980, c. 144.

West Virginia: Code §§35-5-6, 35-5A-1 to 35-5A-8.

Wisconsin: Stat. §§157.11(9)(g), 157.125, as amended by Laws 1979, c. 175.

For cases applying these statutes, see §124.2, n. 15.

New Hampshire Rev. Stat. Ann., §289:14, provides that cemetery corporations holding funds in trust may establish and maintain common trust funds. See §227.9, n. 26.

In Perry v. Twentieth Street Bank, 137 W. Va. 963, 206 S.E.2d 421 (1974), it was held that under a statute permitting perpetual care of a grave, a bequest in trust to establish a flower fund and to expend the income in buying flowers to be placed on the graves of the testatrix and of her father and mother was valid.

In Indiana Dept. of State Revenue v. Estate of Wallace, 408 N.E.2d 150 (Ind. App. 1980), a legacy in trust to place flowers on certain cemetery lots was held not exempt from inheritance tax as a charity.

[14]*Arkansas:* Stat. 1947, §82-423 (cited in this note) as amended by Laws 1971, c. 463.

California: Health and Safety Code, §8733.5.

Connecticut: Gen. Stat. 1958, §§19-150 to 19-156.

Delaware: Code Ann., tit. 12, §3552.

District of Columbia: Code Ann. 1981, §27-113.

Georgia: Code 1981, §36-7-5.

Idaho: Code, §28-404, as amended by Laws 1967, c. 233.

Illinois: Rev. Stat. c. 21, §§64 to 64.24, as amended by Laws 1973, c. 78-592; §185, as amended by Laws 1973, c. 78-866.

Indiana: Code 1971, §§23-14-1-1, 23-14-1-12, 23-14-16-1, 23-14-29-1.

Iowa: Code Ann., §566.1.

Kansas: Stat. Ann., §17-1338.

a statute permits a trust for the perpetual upkeep of a grave or

---

Kentucky: Rev. Stat. Ann., §§307.190 to 307.991 (Kentucky Cemetery Law), as enacted by Laws 1976, c. 294.

Louisiana: Rev. Stat. Ann., §§8:1 to 8:903.

See Metairie Cemetery Assn. v. United States, 282 F.2d 225 (5th Cir. 1960).

Maine: Rev. Stat. 1964, tit. 13, §§1222, 1261, 1301.

Massachusetts: Ann. Laws, c. 114, §§5, 28; c. 206, §15.

Michigan: Stat. Ann., §§5.3131, 5.3165, 21.855.

Minnesota: Stat. Ann., §§306.30 to 306.57.

Missouri: Rev. Stat., §214.130.

Montana: Code Ann. 1983, §§35-20-212, 35-20-215, 35-20-301 to 35-20-315, 35-21-206, and 35-21-601 to 35-21-625.

Nebraska: Rev. Stat. 1943, §§12-509 to 12-512; Laws 1953, c. 20.

Nevada: Rev. Stat., §452.160, as amended by Laws 1983, p. 139.

New Hampshire: Rev. Stat. Ann., §§289:13, 654:10-a (city or town)

New Jersey: Rev. Stat., §8:2-34.

New York: Not-for-Profit Corporation Law, §1401, as amended by Laws 1971, c. 458, and by Laws 1977, c. 871.

See Town Law 291. See also Application of Town of Penfield, 97 Misc. 2d 233, 410 N.Y.S.2d 795 (1978).

As to public cemetery corporations, see N.Y. Not-for-Profit Corporation Law, §§1501 to 1507.

Ohio: Rev. Code Ann., §§9:20, 1721.12, 2113.37.

Oklahoma: Stat. Ann., tit. 8, §§51 to 53; tit. 60, §175.47.

Pennsylvania: 9 Pa. Stat., §§303 to 308.

Rhode Island: Gen. Laws 1956, §45-5-11, as amended by Laws 1976, c. 13.

South Dakota: Codified Laws 1967, §47-29-22.

Tennessee: Code Ann., §46-1-103.

Texas: Civ. Stat. Ann., arts. 912 to 915, as amended by Laws 1975, c. 40.

In Foshee v. Republic Natl. Bank, 600 S.W.2d 358 (Tex. Civ. App. 1980), it was held that the statute is not unconstitutional under a provision that "Perpetuities and monopolies are contrary to the genius of a free government, and shall never be allowed." On appeal it was held, however, that the statute did not, and constitutionally could not, authorize perpetual trusts for the care of individual burial sites unless the trustee was authorized to expend principal. Foshee v. Republic Natl. Bank, 617 S.W.2d 675 (Tex. 1981) (citing Restatement (Second) of Trusts, §374, Comment *h*).

Washington: Rev. Code, §§68.44.010, 68.44.170.

West Virginia: Code, §35-5-3. See Code, §§35-5A-1 to 35-5A-8.

Wisconsin: Stat., §701.11. Stat., §157.12 as amended by Laws 1977, c. 449, Laws 1979, c. 221, and Laws 1981, c. 1483.

By Wisconsin Stat., §66.04(2), as amended by Laws 1961, c. 97, Laws 1979, c. 293, Laws 1981, c. 187, and Laws 1983, cc. 189, 368, municipal cemetery perpetual care funds may be invested in accordance with the prudent man rule.

tomb, the trust is undoubtedly valid, but the question remains whether it is to be treated for all purposes or for any purpose as a charitable trust. Under some of these statutes the legislature clearly treats the trust as a charitable trust.[15] In Pennsylvania it has been held that a trust for the upkeep of a cemetery lot, although valid, is not a charitable trust and that the doctrine of cy pres is inapplicable.[16] In another case in Pennsylva-

---

Wyoming: Stat. 1945, §38-102 (providing for cemetery companies using part of proceeds of sale as perpetual fund for maintenance of cemetery).

For cases citing the statutes cited in this and the preceding notes, see §124.2, n. 15.

In In re Lathrop's Estate, 100 N.H. 393, 128 A.2d 199 (1956), a testatrix bequeathed $100,000 to a town for the perpetual care of a certain cemetery lot, and left a share of the residue to the town. It was held that the residuary gift to the town was intended to be used for cemetery purposes.

See Indiana Dept. of State Revenue v. Estate of Wallace, 408 N.E.2d 150 (Ind. App. 1980), holding that a bequest to a trustee (not to the cemetery owner) for perpetual care of a grave was not exempt from inheritance tax as a charity.

[15]See the following cases:

Iowa: In re Estate of Scott, 240 Iowa 35, 34 N.W.2d 177 (1948).

Nebraska: Root v. Morning View Cemetery Assn., 174 Neb. 438, 805, 118 N.W.2d 633, 119 N.W.2d 696 (1963).

New Hampshire: Opinion of the Justices, 101 N.H. 531, 133 A.2d 792 (1957).

New Jersey: Woodstown Natl. Bank & Trust Co. v. Snelbaker, 136 N.J. Eq. 62, 40 A.2d 222 (1944), *aff'd mem.* 137 N.J. Eq. 256, 44 A.2d 210 (1945); Parker v. Fidelity Union Trust Co., 2 N.J. Super. 362, 63 A.2d 902 (1944).

New York: Matter of Myers, 81 N.Y.S.2d 505 (1948); Matter of Meyers, 93 N.Y.S.2d 859 (1949).

In Hartsdale Canine Cemetery v. Lefkowitz, 37 A.D.2d 548, 322 N.Y.S.2d 330 (1971), *aff'd mem.*, 29 N.Y.2d 702, 275 N.E.2d 26 (1971), it was held that the Attorney General had standing to investigate a large perpetual care fund in an animal cemetery.

Canada: Attorney-General v. Smallwood, [1946] 2 D.L.R. 58 (P.E.I.).

In Matter of Bryant, 8 Misc. 2d 738, 168 N.Y.S.2d 21 (1957), where a testator left $500 in trust for the care of a cemetery lot and the income was insufficient and the town took over the care of the lot, it was held that it was a charitable trust and under the doctrine of cy pres the money should be paid to the town.

In Anderson v. Mount Zion Cemetery Assn., 40 Del. Ch. 442, 184 A.2d 86 (1962), it was held that a nonprofit cemetery association not connected with a church did not hold its property upon a charitable trust.

[16]Devereux's Estate, 48 D.&C. 491 (Pa. 1943), noted in 93 U. Pa. L. Rev. 226; Essig Estate, 167 Pa. Super. 66, 74 A.2d 787 (1950).

nia[17] it was held that a direction to accumulate income to erect a mausoleum was invalid because, although a statute permitted accumulations for charitable purposes, and although a statute provided that a disposition for the care of a place of burial or a monument should not be invalid as a perpetuity but should be held to be made for a charitable use, the purpose was not charitable within the statute as to accumulations.

Administration.   Various questions have arisen as to the administration of cemetery trusts. It has been held that where a bequest is made to a cemetery association for perpetual care of a lot, the money so bequeathed need not be kept separate from the general fund for perpetual care maintained by the corporation.[18] But the income from such a trust cannot properly be used

---

In Chester Monthly Meeting Petition, 23 D.&C.2d 728 (Pa. 1961), where a cemetery company connected with a church petitioned for authority to sell the cemetery, it was held that it was not a charitable organization and the Attorney General had no standing to intervene in order to see that it was sold for the highest price obtainable.

In Clark v. Portland Burying Ground Assn., 151 Conn. 527, 200 A.2d 468 (1964), where a testatrix bequeathed the residue of her estate amounting to $15,000 to a cemetery corporation for the perpetual care of a cemetery lot, it was held that $3000 should be held for the purpose and that the balance should be paid to the next of kin. Although the bequest of a reasonable amount for perpetual care was valid under a statute, the disposition was not charitable and the balance should not be applied cy pres to the care of the cemetery. The court cited the text.

Wierman Trust, 68 D.&C.2d 525 (Pa. 1975) (citing Restatement of Trusts §374).

See Earney v. Clay, 516 S.W.2d 59 (Mo. App. 1974).

[17]Nixon v. Nixon, 67 D.&C. 173 (Pa. 1948).

In Duffy Estate, 2 D.&C.2d 250 (Pa. 1954), it was held that a trust for the perpetual care of a family cemetery lot is valid and not subject to an inheritance tax.

[18]Trust Co. of N.J. v. Greenwood Cemetery, 21 N.J. Misc. 169, 32 A.2d 519 (1943).

By California Health and Safety Code, §8748, as inserted by Laws 1953, c. 1161, provision is made for the merger of endowment funds for the care of mausoleums.

By Maine Rev. Stat. 1964, tit. 13, §1223, it is provided that cemetery trust funds may be combined with other similar trust funds in making investments, unless otherwise provided by the terms of the trust.

By the New York City Admin. Code, §93f-2.0, as inserted by Laws 1954,

for the general purposes of the cemetery.[19] Where, as is usually the case, the income alone is directed to be used for the upkeep of the lot, the principal cannot be used.[20] It has been held that where the testator directed that a trust company should hold a fund in trust for the perpetual upkeep of his family lot, and a statute permitted a city or cemetery association to hold funds for such perpetual care, it was held that the court would not permit the trust to fail for want of a trustee, and that the funds should be paid to the city that operated the cemetery.[21]

Questions have arisen as to the amount of money that may be left in trust for the perpetual care of a cemetery lot. In *Matter of Baeuchle*[22] a testatrix left the whole of her estate, valued at over $170,000, in trust to purchase a burial lot and to erect a mausoleum for herself and her husband, and to apply the income for the perpetual care of the lot and mausoleum. The court took the

---

c. 568, the New York City Comptroller is empowered to maintain common trust funds for money held by him for the perpetual care of burial lots.

In Baer Trust, 6 D.&C.2d 215 (Pa. 1956), the trustees of a small cemetery fund were permitted to transfer the fund to the cemetery trustees; but in Baumgardner Trust, 6 D.&C.2d 219 (Pa. 1956), where the cemetery fund was larger, the court refused to permit such transfer. See Sixty Cemetery Trusts, 5 Fiduciary Rep. 505 (Pa. 1952).

By Pennsylvania Stat. (9 Pa. Stat., §§303 to 308), it is provided that funds received by a corporation for perpetual care may be combined for purposes of investment.

By the California Health and Safety Code, §8734, as enacted by Laws 1976, c. 524, provision is made as to the duties of trustees of endowment cemetery care funds.

By New Hampshire Rev. Stat. Ann., §31:22a, as enacted by Laws 1977, c. 128, provision is made for the cy pres application of accumulated excess income from burial lot trusts.

[19]Town of Boscawen v. Attorney Gen., 93 N.H. 444, 43 A.2d 780 (1945).

[20]Epperson v. Clintonville Cemetery Co., 303 Ky. 852, 199 S.W.2d 628 (1947).

See Evans Trust, 7 D.&C.2d 121 (Pa. 1956).

In Hetrick Estate, 13 D.&C.2d 77 (Pa. 1957), the court directed an accumulation of income to meet future repairs.

See Kansas Stat. Ann., §17-1319, as enacted by Laws 1973, c. 88, and amended by Laws 1977, c. 54.

[21]Heinlein v. Elyria Sav. & Trust Co., 75 Ohio App. 353, 62 N.E.2d 284 (1945).

[22]82 N.Y.S.2d 371 (1948), *aff'd*, 276 A.D. 925, 94 N.Y.S.2d 582 (1950), *aff'd mem.*, 301 N.Y. 582, 93 N.E.2d 491 (1950), noted in 1 Baylor L. Rev. 382.

view that a provision in the Personal Property Law, §13-a, as to the court's power to fix a reasonable sum for such purposes is inapplicable where the testatrix directs that the whole of the residue shall be applied to such purposes. The result thus reached seems to be against sound public policy.[23] In *Dreisbach Estate,*[24] where a testator left his estate in trust for the perpetual care of a cemetery plot, and the estate was very large, it was held that the trust should include only an amount that at 3 percent interest would be reasonable for the purpose, and that the next of kin were entitled to the balance of the principal. In *In re Byrne's Estate*[25] a testatrix left almost her entire estate to her uncle, whom she named executor and trustee, to be expended for the erection of a tomb on her family lot. Her uncle predeceased her. The estate was worth more than $19,000. The officials of the cemetery refused to permit the erection of a tomb on the lot. The administrator asked for instructions. It was held that the purpose was not charitable, and that no trust was created, and that the administrator should use a reasonable amount in the erection of a monument as he would be justified in doing if there were no provision in the will.

We have been considering trusts for the erection or maintenance of a particular tomb or monument or grave or cemetery. There is a further question whether a cemetery association or a trust for the establishment or maintenance of a cemetery is charitable. When the cemetery is that of a church it is undoubtedly charitable; most of the early cases involve a churchyard or

---

[23]See §§124.2, 124.7.

[24]384 Pa. 535, 121 A.2d 74 (1956), noted in 18 U. Pitt. L. Rev. 341.

In Wood Estate, 12 D.&C.2d 577 (Pa. 1957), where a testatrix left $2000 in trust for the perpetual care of a cemetery lot, and after forty years the fund amounted to over $15,000, it was held that $2000 should be paid to the cemetery company for the perpetual care of the lot and the balance should be paid to the residuary legatees.

In Clark v. Portland Burying Ground Assn., 151 Conn. 527, 200 A.2d 468 (1964), where a testatrix bequeathed the residue of her estate amounting to $15,000 to a cemetery corporation for the perpetual care of a cemetery lot, it was held that the bequest was valid as to $3000 and that the balance should be distributed to the next of kin. The court cited the text. See §124.2, n. 6.

[25]98 N.H. 300, 100 A.2d 157 (1953) (citing Restatement of Trusts, §374, Comment *h;* §418).

cemetery attached to a church.[26] It is clear also that a cemetery maintained by a municipality is charitable.[27] So also is a cemetery for the burial of paupers, a potter's field.[28] But the modern cases go beyond this. A nonprofit cemetery in which lots are owned or may be purchased by persons seeking burial for themselves or others is a charitable institution.[29] This is so even though there is no provision for free lots for the poor.[30] The burial of the dead is a matter of public concern; it is indeed ultimately a responsibility of the government, and the establishment or maintenance of such a cemetery relieves the government of a burden.[31]

In *Scottish Burial Reform and Cremation Society, Ltd.,*[32] the

[26]In re Vaughan, 33 Ch. D. 187 (1886); In re Manser, [1905] 1 Ch. 681 (for use of Quakers); In re Eighmie, [1935] Ch. 524.

[27]Chapman v. Newell, 146 Iowa 415, 125 N.W. 324 (1910); Johnson v. South Blue Hill Cemetery Assn., 221 A.2d 280 (Me. 1966) (citing the text §124.2 and Restatement of Trusts §374); McElwain v. Attorney Gen., 241 Mass. 112, 134 N.E. 620 (1922).

[28]See In re Pardoe, [1906] 2 Ch. 184 (headstones for the poor).

[29]*Illinois:* Catholic Bishop of Chicago v. Murr, 3 Ill. App. 2d 107, 120 N.E.2d 4 (1951).

Missouri: Newton v. Newton Burial Park, 326 Mo. 901, 34 S.W.2d 118 (1931); Crawford v. Bashor, 564 S.W.2d 323 (Mo. App. 1978).

Nebraska: Root v. Morning View Cemetery Assn., 174 Neb. 438, 118 N.W.2d 633, 119 N.W.2d 696 (1952).

New Jersey: Woodstown Natl. Bank & Trust Co. v. Snelbaker, 136 N.J. Eq. 62, 40 A.2d 222 (1944), aff'd mem. 137 N.J. Eq. 256, 44 A.2d 210 (1945); Wendell v. Hazel Wood Cemetery, 3 N.J. Super. 457, 67 A.2d 219 (1948).

Ohio: Baily v. McElroy, 120 Ohio App. 85, 28 Ohio Ops. 2d 286, 195 N.E.2d 559 (1963) (statutory).

Oklahoma: Estate of Anderson, 571 P.2d 880 (Okla. App. 1977).

Tennessee: Pope v. Alexander, 194 Tenn. 146, 250 S.W.2d 51 (1952).

Canada: In re Robinson, 75 D.L.R.3d 532 (Ont. 1976).

See §124.2, n. 10.

But see Anderson v. Mount Zion Cemetery Assn., 40 Del. Ch. 442, 184 A.2d 86 (1962).

In Armack's Estate v. State, 561 S.W.2d 109 (Mo. 1978), it was held that a bequest to a cemetery for the care of graves of certain members of the testator's family was not charitable and was subject to the state inheritance tax, although the cemetery itself was a charitable institution.

See Comment, Exempt Cemetery Companies, 28 Emory L.J. 1081 (1979).

[30]See §376, n. 3.

[31]See §373.2.

[32][1968] A.C. 138.

House of Lords held as charitable and exempt from taxation a nonprofit society organized to promote reform in burial and to promote cremation. It charged fees to those to whom it rendered burial services. Lord Upjohn said, "The disposal of the dead is, and always has been, not merely a purpose beneficial to the community but a matter of public necessity." Lord Wilberforce, after stating that a disposition is charitable when a cemetery is connected with a church, or owned by a local authority, said, "Now what we have to consider is whether to take the further step of holding charitable the purpose of providing burial, or facilities for the disposal of mortal remains, without any connection with a church, by an independent body. I have no doubt that we should."

In *Catholic Bishop of Chicago v. Murr*,[33] where land was conveyed in trust to be used as a cemetery for the Catholic population of a town, it was held that a condition against alienation was valid because it was a charitable trust. Schaefer, C.J., said, "There is a recognized difference between establishing a trust for the upkeep of a private grave and donating land for use as a cemetery.[34] The public character of the latter is precisely the factor which distinguishes a charitable from a private trust." He held that the restriction of benefit to Catholics of the town does not make the trust too limited in its benefits.

The question arises whether for tax purposes a nonprofit cemetery is a charitable institution; whether it is exempt from taxation, or a gift to it is deductible by the giver from his income tax, or a bequest to it is deductible under the estate tax.

Under an express provision of the Internal Revenue Code, the cemetery is exempt from federal income tax.[35] So also the Code expressly allows a deduction for the income tax of a contribution to the cemetery.[36] In these cases, therefore, it is im-

---

[33] 3 Ill. 2d 107, 120 N.E.2d 4 (1951) (citing the Restatement of Trusts, §374, Comment *h*).

[34] At 120 N.E.2d 7, citing cases and the Restatement of Trusts, §374, Comment *h*.

[35] 26 U.S.C., §501(C)(13).

There are similar statutes in some of the states. See New York Real Property Tax Law, §421; John D. Rockefeller Family Cemetery Corp., 63 T.C. 355 (1964).

[36] 26 U.S.C., §170(C)(5).

material whether the cemetery is a charitable institution. But in the case of the estate tax there is no provision as to cemeteries, and the question, therefore, is whether a bequest to a cemetery comes within the general provision allowing a deduction for bequests for charitable purposes.[37]

In *Child v. United States*[38] it was held that bequests to certain nonprofit cemetery associations were not deductible for the estate tax because they were not for charitable purposes (not for religious purposes and not providing for the burial of indigents). One judge dissented on the ground that the burial of the dead by the associations relieved a burden on the government, and that the statute was intended to follow the common law as to the scope of charitable purposes. He said, as to such cemeteries, "They render a great public benefit at no cost to the public treasury and clearly come within the general concept of a charitable use, even from the point of view of the tax law."

§374.10. Community purposes. The promotion of the happiness and enjoyment of the members of a community is a charitable purpose. It is not material that the benefits are not limited to the poor. In the well-known case of *Goodman v. Mayor of Saltash*[1] the House of Lords upheld a prescriptive right in the

[37] 26 U.S.C., §2055(a)(2).
[38] 540 F.2d 579 (2d Cir. 1976).
    See Gund's Estate v. Commissioner, 113 F.2d 61 (5th Cir. 1940), *cert. denied,* 311 U.S. 696; Estate of Amick, 67 T.C. 924 (1977), disallowing deduction on the ground that the bequests were not for a charitable or public purpose.
    To the same effect, see First Natl. Bank of Omaha v. United States, 532 F. Supp. 251 (D. Neb. 1981), *aff'd,* 681 F.2d 534 (8th Cir. 1982), *cert. denied,* 459 U.S. 1104, 103 S. Ct. 726, 74 L. Ed. 2d 952 (1982); Mellon Bank, N.A. v. United States, 762 F.2d 283 (3d Cir. 1985).
    In Davie v. Rochester Cemetery Assn., 91 N.H. 494, 23 A.2d 377 (1941), it was held that a nonprofit cemetery was not subject to a tax under the State Unemployment Compensation Act exempting charitable institutions. The court said that "a cemetery, though maintained by a private corporation, may fairly be deemed a public burial ground if it is 'open, under reasonable regulations to the use of the public for the burial of the dead.' "
    In Rosehill Cemetery Co. v. United States, 285 F. Supp. 21 (N.D. Ill. 1968), it was held that a trust to pay the income to a profit-making cemetery for perpetual care of the graves was not exempt from income tax.
    §374.10. [1] 7 App. Cas. 633 (1882).

free inhabitants of a borough to dredge for oysters during a certain season of the year. The court said that if there had been a grant in trust to permit the inhabitants or a particular class of the inhabitants to dig oysters it would be a charitable trust that would not be invalid as a perpetuity.

The erection or maintenance of a community building in a village to be used for the benefit of the inhabitants is a charitable purpose.[2] So also the gift of a theater in trust for the use of the people of a small city has been held to be charitable.[3] In an English case[4] it was held that property owned by a voluntary fire brigade, received from subscriptions and donations, was held upon a charitable trust for the benefit of the community, and on its dissolution should be applied cy pres. In an Australian case[5] it was held that a bequest for the erection of a public hall for the holding of concerts, dramatic entertainments, and meetings of a cultural or educational value is charitable.

[2]*England:* In re Spence, [1938] 1 Ch. 96, noted in 82 Sol. J. 167.

See In re Morgan, [1955] 2 All E.R. 632 (trust for public recreation ground for amateur activities).

Connecticut: Klein v. City of Bridgeport, 125 Conn. 129, 3 A.2d 675 (1939).

Idaho: In re Eggan's Estate, 86 Idaho 328, 386 P.2d 563 (1963).

Kansas: In re Estate of Denton, 166 Kan. 411, 201 P.2d 625 (1949), *semble.*

Maine: Perry v. Town of Friendship, 237 A.2d 405 (Me. 1968); Miller v. Inhabitants of Town of Friendship, 265 A.2d 608 (Me. 1970).

Massachusetts: Holmes v. Welch, 314 Mass. 106, 49 N.E.2d 461, 157 A.L.R. 896 (1943).

New Jersey: New Jersey Title Guar. & Trust Co. v. Smith, 90 N.J. Eq. 386, 108 A. 16 (1919).

North Carolina: Shannonhouse v. Wolfe, 191 N.C. 769, 133 S.E. 93 (1926).

Northern Ireland: Springhill Hous. Action Comm. v. Commissioner of Valuation, [1983] 5 N.I.J.B. (C.A.) (community center on a housing estate).

In In re Wright, [1951] 2 D.L.R. 429 (N.S.) it was held that a legacy given for the erection of a building to bring people together to uplift and train them to higher ideals and to provide clean amusement in order to check the lure of the streets was charitable.

In In re Stone, 91 W.N. (N.S.W.) 704 (1970), the court upheld as charitable a bequest to a fund the purpose of which was to acquire land in Israel for the purpose of settling Jews thereon.

[3]Nixon v. Brown, 46 Nev. 439, 214 P. 524 (1923).

[4]In re Wokingham Fire Brigade Trusts, [1951] Ch. 373.

See Sherman v. Richmond Hose Co., 230 N.Y. 462, 130 N.E. 613 (1921), cited in §348.1, n. 3.

[5]Monds v. Stackhouse, 77 C.L.R. 232 (Austl. 1948).

There are other cases in which a trust for the benefit of the community has been upheld as charitable. A trust for the encouraging of choruses by the residents of a certain town is charitable.[6] A bequest for the peaceful recreation of the inhabitants of a town was held to be charitable, and a scheme was framed for carrying out the purpose.[7] So also where a testator left property in trust for "the Common Good Fund" of a town council, it was held that a valid charitable trust was created.[8] In another case[9] a trust of money to be applied by a church council for the benefit of a particular church or parish was held to be charitable. So also it has been held that a trust to hold the Crystal Palace in London as a place of public resort and for other purposes including education and "the promotion of industry, commerce and art," was created solely for charitable purposes.[10] In a Scottish case,[11] where the owners of property executed an obligation to apply the property as certain officials should direct for any purpose tending "to promote the moral intellectual physical or social improvement bodily health and recreation of the inhabitants" of a town, it was held that the obligation was valid and binding.

So also in the United States courts have upheld trusts for community purposes. Thus in *People ex rel. Untermeyer v. McGregor,*[12] where an estate was devised to the state to maintain it as a public park and garden, and the state disclaimed, and a charitable corporation was formed to carry out the purpose, it was held that the corporation was exempt from tax as a charitable corporation. In *Attinson v. Consumer-Farmer Milk Cooperative*[13] it was

[6]Shillington v. Portadown Urban Dist. Council, [1911] 1 I.R. 247.

See also Royal Choral Socy. v. Commissioners of Inland Revenue, [1943] 2 All E.R. 101 (tax case), noted in 59 Law Q. Rev. 113, 307, 7 Mod. L. Rev. 158.

[7]In re Gorham's Charity Gift, [1939] Ch. 600, noted in 3 Convey. (N.S.) 336, 187 L.T. 242.

[8]In re Baynes, [1944] 2 All E.R. 597, noted in 95 L.J. 197.

[9]In re Norton's Will Trusts, [1948] 2 All E.R. 852.

[10]In re Town and Country Planning Act, 1947 (Crystal Palace Trustees v. Minister of Town and Country Planning), [1951] Ch. 132.

[11]Denny's Trustee v. Dumbarton Magistrates, [1945] Sess. Cas. 147 (Scot.).

[12]295 N.Y. 237, 66 N.E.2d 292 (1946). See §373.

[13]197 Misc. 336, 94 N.Y.S.2d 891 (1950).

held that a cooperative corporation organized to benefit farmers and consumers through the distribution of milk and other products and otherwise to serve the economic and cultural welfare of its members and of the public was a charitable corporation, and that on its dissolution its property should be applied cy pres and not divided among the members. A trust is charitable where the purpose is to contribute to the aesthetic enjoyment of the community.[14] Thus the courts have upheld a trust for the development of the Palisades along the Hudson River;[15] a trust for promoting the permanent preservation of lands of beauty or historic interest;[16] a trust to beautify a city by the planting and maintaining of shade trees;[17] a trust to preserve a forest and wild lands intact as a park to which visitors shall be allowed access.[18]

On the other hand, there are cases in which it was held that the trust was not charitable. Thus it was held that a trust for the perpetual maintenance of the house of the testator at Stratford-upon-Avon as a place for the entertainment of distinguished

[14]See General Municipal Law, §§301 to 323 (New York State Cultural Resources Act); Re Cotton Trust for Rural Beautification, [1980] 118 D.L.R. 3d 542 (P.E.I.S.C.).

[15]Noice v. Schnell, 101 N.J. Eq. 252, 137 A. 582, 52 A.L.R. 965 (1927), *cert. denied,* 276 U.S. 625 (1928), noted in 32 Law Notes 33.

See City of Englewood v. Allison Land Co., 25 N.J. Super. 466, 96 A.2d 702 (1953), involving the question whether the trustees could properly sell Palisades land to a development company. See also City of Englewood v. Allison Land Co., 45 N.J. Super. 538, 133 A.2d 680 (1957), *aff'g* 40 N.J. Super. 495, 123 A.2d 591 (1956).

[16]In re Verrall, [1916] 1 Ch. 100, 114.

[17]Bartlett, Petitioner, 163 Mass. 509, 40 N.E. 899 (1895); Cresson's Appeal, 30 Pa. 437 (1858).

See Nickols v. Commissioners of Middlesex County, 341 Mass. 13, 166 N.E.2d 911 (1960) (involving a conveyance of Walden Pond reservation to the Commonwealth; citing the text and Restatement of Trusts §374).

In Commonwealth Commn. on Charitable Orgs. v. Acorn, 463 A.2d 406 (Pa. 1983), it was held that a society organized to enhance the quality of neighborhoods by promoting better housing conditions, more police protection, vacant lot clean-ups, more recreation facilities, improved traffic safety, public transportation, increased city support for public health, day care facilities, and the paving of streets, mainly by bringing pressure to bear on public officials, was required to register as a charity before soliciting funds.

[18]Middlebury College v. Central Power Corp., 101 Vt. 325, 143 A. 384 (1928); Middlebury College v. Town of Hancock, 115 Vt. 157, 55 A.2d 194 (1947).

visitors from far countries was not charitable and failed.[19] In another case,[20] where a testatrix directed her executor to erect and maintain a hotel in a town as a memorial to her, it was held that the bequest failed on the ground that it was not charitable and involved a perpetuity. Two of the judges dissented, holding that the purpose was charitable. In a case in New Zealand[21] a trust to provide the facilities of a club and educational societies for farmers was held to be noncharitable and invalid. On the other hand, it has been held that a trust to promote the general welfare of the farming population of the United States and the improvement of the conditions of rural life is charitable.[22]

We have seen that a trust for the promotion of sport has been held not to be charitable, except insofar as it can be regarded as educational in character, or as it can be regarded as tending to promote the national defense.[23]

As we shall see, not infrequently a disposition is held not to be a charitable disposition because the class to be benefited thereby is too limited.[24]

§374.11. Trusts for persons of limited opportunities.
As we have seen, a trust to aid poor persons is charitable even

[19]In re Corelli, [1943] Ch. 332, noted in 8 Convey. (N.S.) 112, 11 Sol. J. 36.

See Town of Norwood v. Norwood Civic Assn., 340 Mass. 327, 165 N.E.2d 124 (1960), where it was not shown that the corporation was operated predominantly for civic purposes.

[20]In re Swayze's Estate, 120 Mont. 546, 191 P.2d 322 (1948) (citing the text and Restatement of Trusts §§124, 374, 398), noted in 23 Ind. L.J. 502.

[21]In re Cumming, [1951] N.Z.L.R. 498.

Cf. Attorney Gen. v. Weymouth Agric. & Indus. Socy., 400 Mass. 475, 509 N.E.2d 1193 (1987) (corporation organized to encourage agriculture and conduct agricultural exhibits that operated a county fair at which livestock and farm products were displayed, prizes were awarded, and horse and dog racing were conducted is not a charity for purposes of a statute requiring charities to make annual reports).

As to social clubs, see §375.2.

[22]People v. First Natl. Bank, 364 Ill. 262, 4 N.E.2d 378, 108 A.L.R. 277 (1936).

See Note, Farmland Preservation in Vermont and the Creative Use of Land Trusts, 11 Vt. L. Rev. 603 (1986).

[23]See §§370.2, 374.3, 374.6A.

[24]See §375.2.

though the persons to be aided are not actually destitute.[1] The community has an interest in the promotion of the happiness and well-being of the underprivileged. Thus a trust to maintain a home for working girls at moderate cost is charitable.[2] A trust to erect a building to include a library and dance hall for the free use of working men and women of a city and their families is charitable.[3] A bequest "for the promotion of the best interests of sewing girls in Boston" was upheld as a charitable trust.[4] The court said that it was nonetheless charitable although not limited to the relief of poverty; it was charitable because it was for the purpose of assisting an indefinite number of working girls by adding to their welfare and assisting them in their establishment in life.

The question has been raised in a number of cases whether the Young Men's Christian Association and the Young Women's Christian Association are charitable organizations. The answer depends on the scope of the purposes for which they are created and maintained. In numerous cases it has been held that they are charitable organizations, it appearing that their purposes are to provide rooming and boarding facilities and facilities for health and recreation mainly for working young men and women, and for their intellectual and moral improvement.[5] Where

§374.11. [1]See §369.3.

[2]Thornton v. Franklin Square House, 200 Mass. 465, 86 N.E. 909, 22 L.R.A. (N.S.) 486 (1909).

[3]Gibson v. Frye Inst., 137 Tenn. 452, 193 S.W. 1059, L.R.A. 1917D 1062 (1916).

[4]Bowditch v. Attorney Gen., 241 Mass. 168, 134 N.E. 796, 28 A.L.R. 713 (1922).

[5]*Illinois:* People v. Young Men's Christian Assn. of Chicago, 365 Ill. 118, 6 N.E.2d 166 (1937) (exempt from taxation); Myers v. Young Men's Christian Assn., 316 Ill. App. 177, 44 N.E.2d 755 (1942) (not liable in tort), noted in 21 Chi.-Kent L. Rev. 256, 10 U. Chi. L. Rev. 211; Saffron v. Young Men's Christian Assn., 317 Ill. App. 149, 45 N.E.2d 555 (1942) (not liable in tort), noted in 27 Marq. L. Rev. 164.

Iowa: Andrews v. Young Men's Christian Assn., 226 Iowa 374, 284 N.W. 186 (1939) (*semble,* but held liable in tort to nonmember), noted in 24 Iowa L. Rev. 769, 87 U. Pa. L. Rev. 1015; Servison v. Young Men's Christian Assn., 230 Iowa 86, 296 N.W. 769 (1941) (not liable in tort to member).

Massachusetts: Springfield Young Men's Christian Assn. v. Board of Assessors, 284 Mass. 1, 187 N.E. 104 (1933) (exempt from personal property tax); Carpenter v. Young Men's Christian Assn., 324 Mass. 365, 86 N.E.2d 634

it did not appear that these were the purposes of the organi-

---

(1949) (not liable in tort; citing the text and Restatement of Trusts, §374, Comment *g*); Staman v. Board of Assessors of Chatham, 351 Mass. 479, 221 N.E.2d 861 (1966) (citing the text).

Missouri: Eads v. Young Women's Christian Assn., 325 Mo. 577, 29 S.W.2d 701 (1930) (not liable in tort), noted in 30 Colum. L. Rev. 1073; Salvation Army v. Hoehn, 354 Mo. 107, 188 S.W.2d 826 (1945) (building used by Salvation Army to provide board and lodging for girls, held tax-exempt).

New Hampshire: Young Women's Christian Assn. v. Portsmouth, 89 N.H. 40, 192 A.2d 617 (1937) (exempt from taxation).

New Jersey: Leeds v. Harrison, 7 N.J. Super. 558, 72 A.2d 371 (1950), *rev'd on other grounds,* 9 N.J. 202, 87 A.2d 713 (1952), noted in 40 Geo. L.J. 122, 100 U. Pa. L. Rev. 457; Terracciona v. Magee, 53 N.J. Super. 557, 148 A.2d 68 (1959); Hauser v. Young Men's Christian Assn., 91 N.J. Super. 172, 219 A.2d 532 (1966).

As to the incorporation of Young Men's Christian Associations and similar organizations, see New Jersey Rev. Stat., §§16:19-1 to 16:19-9.

By New Jersey Rev. Stat., §54:4-3.24, property used for the purposes of the Young Men's Christian Association, Young Women's Christian Association, Young Men's Hebrew Association and Young Women's Hebrew Association are exempt from taxation.

New York: Matter of Moses, 138 A.D. 525, 123 N.Y.S. 443 (1910) (exempt from transfer tax); Matter of Rowland, 225 A.D. 118, 232 N.Y.S. 127 (1928) (bequest of more than half of testator's estate invalid); Young Men's Christian Assn. v. City of N.Y., 159 Misc. 539, 287 N.Y.S. 287 (1935), *aff'd mem.,* 251 A.D. 821, 298 N.Y.S. 191 (1937), *aff'd mem.,* 276 N.Y. 619, 12 N.E.2d 605 (1938) (not liable for local sales tax); Young Women's Christian Assn. v. Wagner, 96 Misc. 2d 361, 409 N.Y.S.2d 167 (1978) (a tax case).

By New York Not-for-Profit Corporation Law, §1404, provision is made for the incorporation of young men's and young women's Christian associations.

North Carolina: Young Women's Christian Assn. v. Morgan, 281 N.C. 485, 189 S.E.2d 169 (1972).

Ohio: Waddell v. Young Women's Christian Assn., 133 Ohio St. 601, 15 N.E.2d 140 (1938) (not liable in tort), noted in 24 Iowa L. Rev. 164; Emrick v. Pennsylvania R.R. Young Men's Christian Assn. of Crestline, 69 Ohio App. 353, 43 N.E.2d 733 (1942) (not liable in tort); Goldman v. Friar's Club, 158 Ohio St. 205, 107 N.E.2d 518 (1952) (club connected with a church furnishing dormitory and dining facilities held tax-exempt).

Pennsylvania: Young Men's Christian Assn. v. City of Philadelphia, 139 Pa. Super. 332, 11 A.2d 529 (1940), *rev'g* 33 D.&C. 539 (1938) (not liable for local sales tax).

South Carolina: Caughman v. Columbia Young Men's Christian Assn., 212 S.C. 337, 47 S.E.2d 788 (1948) (Y.M.C.A. not subject to Workmen's Compensation Act), noted in 33 Minn. L. Rev. 440; by Code 1962, §65-1522, as

zation, it was held that it was not a charitable organization.[6]

In an English case[7] the court took a narrower view of the scope of charities. In that case a director of a company bequeathed shares of the company in trust for the purpose of

---

amended by Laws 1975, c. 162, premises of the Young Men's Christian Association are exempt from taxation, when used for its purposes.

Texas: Moore v. Sellers, 201 S.W.2d 248 (Tex. Civ. App. 1947) (trust for work of Y.M.C.A. or Y.W.C.A. or other charitable purposes held valid).

Washington: Susmann v. Young Men's Christian Assn., 101 Wash. 487, 172 P. 554 (1918) (not liable for tort if shown to be not a profit-making institution).

Wisconsin: Estate of Briggs, 189 Wis. 524, 208 N.W. 247 (1926) (bequest to a Young Women's Christian Association that was not yet in existence held bequest for charitable purposes and therefore valid); Waldman v. Young Men's Christian Assn., 227 Wis. 43, 277 N.W. 632 (1938) (not liable in tort).

By Wisconsin Stat., §70.11(10), provision is made for the exemption from taxation, at least in part, of the buildings of the Y.M.C.A. and Y.W.C.A.

Canada: In re Young Women's Christian Assn. & Minister of Mun. Affairs, 4 D.L.R.3d 713 (N.B. 1969).

Ireland: In In re Macnamara, [1943] I.R. 372, it was held that although a devise to the Young Men's Christian Association of Cork was charitable because it was for a religious purpose, a provision that the property should be used as a rest and holiday home for Protestant men invalidated the devise.

Northern Ireland: See Belfast Young Men's Christian Assn. v. Commissioner of Valuation, [1969] N. Ir. L.R. 3 (charitable except as it permitted the use of its premises by schools and other clubs).

[6]*Massachusetts:* Chapin v. Holyoke Young Men's Christian Assn., 165 Mass. 280, 42 N.E. 1130 (1896) (liable for tort).

Pennsylvania: Young Men's Christian Assn. v. City of Philadelphia, 323 Pa. 401, 187 A. 204 (1936) (not exempt from real estate tax on building used as dormitory, in which rooms were rented commercially).

In Goldman v. The L.B. Harrison, 158 Ohio St. 181, 107 N.E.2d 530 (1952), it was held that an organization maintaining a building to promote the welfare of young working men by providing them with living, recreational, and auxiliary facilities was not exempt from taxation because it rented rooms and operated a cafeteria in the building.

[7]In re Drummond, [1914] 2 Ch. 90.

See also Wernher's Charitable Trust v. Internal Revenue Commrs., [1937] 2 All E.R. 488, stated in §375.2, n. 34.

In In re Sanders' Will Trusts, [1954] Ch. 205, it was held that a trust to provide or assist in providing dwellings for the working classes and their families in a designated area with preference to dockworkers was not charitable, because it was not limited to relief of the poor.

In In re Hart, [1951] 2 D.L.R. 30 (N.S.), a bequest to a trust company to apply the income to enable poor children and their parents in a named city to have outings during the summer months was upheld as charitable.

contribution to the holiday expenses of the work people employed in one of the departments of the company. In that department were employed over 400 persons, chiefly girls, whose average weekly wages were 15 shillings. There had been for some time a holiday fund to which the workers could contribute. It was held that the bequest failed. The court said that the beneficiaries could not be regarded as being poor people within the Statute of Elizabeth, and that the class of persons to be benefited was not large enough to make the trust one for general public purposes.[8]

The English court was more liberal, however, in another case[9] in which the trustees were to select a deserving Jewish girl once in every three years and to pay her on her marriage the income from the trust fund as a dowry. It was admitted that the recipients were not limited to poor girls. The court said that the trust was for the benefit of the Jewish religion, but this ground for the decision seems difficult to justify. But if the gift is to be interpreted as intended to assist underprivileged girls, even though not poverty-stricken, the trust may well be held to be for a charitable purpose. The assisting of poor maids by enabling them to be married was one of the purposes mentioned in the Statute of Charitable Uses. It is quite in accordance with modern authority to hold that the recipients need not be destitute.

In the Statute of Charitable Uses one of the purposes mentioned as charitable is "supportation, aid and help of young

[8] For cases where the class to be benefited is limited, see §375.2.

By the Recreational Charities Act, 1958, 6 & 7 Eliz. II, c. 17, noted in 21 Mod. L. Rev. 534, it is provided that it shall be and be deemed always to have been charitable to provide facilities for recreation or other leisure-time occupation, if the facilities are provided in the interests of "social welfare," provided that this should not be taken to derogate from the principle that a trust or institution to be charitable must be for the public benefit. It is further provided that the requirement as to social welfare shall not be treated as satisfied unless the facilities are provided with the object of improving the conditions of life for the persons for whom the facilities are primarily intended; and that those persons have need of such facilities by reason of their youth, age, infirmity or disablement, poverty, or social and economic circumstances; or that the facilities are to be available to the members or female members of the public at large.

Warburton, Football and the Recreational Charities Act 1958, [1980] Conv. 173-81.

[9] In re Cohen, 36 Tax L.R. 16 (1919), noted in 33 Harv. L. Rev. 472.

tradesmen, handicraftsmen and persons decayed." It has been held that trusts to assist young men and women to establish themselves are charitable although the recipients are not paupers. Thus a trust to assist young artisans or apprentices or other workers to establish themselves in life by making loans to them is charitable.[10]

On the other hand, it is not enough that the purpose of the trust is to afford pleasure to an indefinite number of persons. In one English case it was held that a trust to provide a pennyworth of sweets for every boy and girl under the age of 14 within a certain parish was not charitable.[11] In another English case it was held that a trust to apply the income in annually providing knickers for boys between ten and fifteen years of age in a particular district, not being limited to poor boys, was not charitable.[12] In a case in Virginia[13] a trust to divide the income annually just before Easter and Christmas among all the pupils in the first, second, and third grades of a designated public school, in order to further their education, was held not charitable, and it was held that the intended trust failed as a perpetuity. On the other hand, a court in New York upheld a bequest to a church organization in Ireland to clothe the children of a parish for Holy Communion and Confirmation when the parents possessed less than one acre of land.[14]

---

[10]Higginson v. Turner, 171 Mass. 586, 51 N.E. 172 (1898); City of Boston v. Doyle, 184 Mass. 373, 68 N.E. 851 (1903); Neech's Executors, [1947] Sess. Cas. 119 (Scot.).

See Franklin Found. v. Attorney Gen., 340 Mass. 197, 163 N.E.2d 662 (1960), and the numerous earlier cases dealing with the will of Benjamin Franklin.

[11]In re Pleasants, 39 Tax L.R. 675 (1923).

[12]In re Gwyon, [1930] 1 Ch. 255.

In New Zealand Socy. of Accountants v. Commissioner of Inland Revenue, [1986] 1 N.Z.L.R. 147, a society of accountants maintained a fidelity fund to indemnify persons whose funds were stolen by accountants or solicitors. It was held that the income from this fund was not exempt from income tax as a charity when the benefits of the fund were not confined to the poor.

See Note, Trust for school children as charitable, or merely benevolent, 25 A.L.R.2d 1114 (1952).

[13]Shenandoah Valley Natl. Bank v. Taylor, 192 Va. 135, 63 S.E.2d 786 (1951) (quoting Restatement of Trusts, §374, Comment *f*), noted in 23 Miss. L.J. 62, 20 U. Cin. L. Rev. 505, 37 Va. L. Rev. 642, 9 Wash. & Lee L. Rev. 310.

[14]Matter of Hinckey, 86 N.Y.S.2d 579 (1949).

In *In re Cole*[15] a testator left property in trust to apply the income "for the general benefit and general welfare of the children for the time being in Southdown House," a home conducted by a city for juvenile delinquents and refractory children from five to fifteen years of age. It was held by the Court of Appeal, Lord Evershed, M.R., dissenting, that the trust failed because it was not limited to charitable purposes. The court held that under the terms of the gift the income might be used to amuse and interest the children by providing such amenities as television or record players and that the disposition did not fall within the spirit and intendment of the Statute of Elizabeth. But surely the supplying of amenities would play a proper and perhaps a necessary part in the rehabilitation of such children.

§374.11A. Housing and services for elderly and handicapped persons. During the current century the average life expectancy has risen dramatically.[1] In consequence, the proportion of elderly persons in the population has increased substantially. It has become more difficult for the elderly to make satisfactory living arrangements, even if their financial means are adequate. At the beginning of the century most families lived on farms or in small villages, commonly in spacious homes; now most live in urban areas. The size of modern dwelling units and the tendency of both members of a married couple to be employed frequently makes it difficult or impossible for children to

[15][1958] Ch. 877, noted in 74 Law Q. Rev. 481.

See In re Sahal's Will Trusts, [1958] 3 All E.R. 428, noted in 75 Law Q. Rev. 22.

In In re Mitchell, [1963] N.Z.L.R. 934, a testator left a legacy in trust to apply the income for the inmates of a certain home for "either creature comforts additional to those already enjoyed or the means of obtaining such creature comforts or actual necessities." It was held that the trust failed because it included supplying amenities.

But see In re McIntosh, [1976] 1 N.Z.L.R. 308, where the income was to be used not for luxuries but for the care, recreation, and recovery of patients.

In In re Banfield, [1968] 2 All E.R. 276, the court upheld a bequest to an unincorporated religious association whose purpose was to help members of the public who should need help because of addiction to drugs or drink, or having been in prison, or suffering from loneliness.

§374.11A. [1]See Langbein, The Twentieth-Century Revolution in Family Wealth Transmission, 86 Mich. L. Rev. 722, 740-741 (1988).

take elderly parents into their homes. Domestic servants are unavailable to all but the very wealthy. The corner grocery and the streetcar line at the end of the block have disappeared. With suburban living and shopping centers, it is often necessary to drive miles to buy groceries, medicine, and clothing. Elderly persons sometimes cannot drive automobiles, climb stairs, or walk long distances; some are confined to wheelchairs. They need apartments or rooms in establishments that provide at least some meals, transportation to church and the grocery store, and help in securing medical care. There has been a great growth in the number of such establishments. Some are operated for profit and so are clearly not charitable. Some, which serve the indigent elderly without charge, are clearly charitable. Most elderly persons have some income from Social Security or another public source, though it may be small. The problem case is the nonprofit establishment that charges elderly residents what they can afford to pay and makes up the difference between what the less affluent can afford and the cost of their housing by (1) charging the well-to-do residents more than cost, (2) securing contributions from a church or charitable foundation or society, or (3) both of these means. Many of these establishments are operated by nonprofit corporations organized by churches.

The question of the charitable status of such establishments is ordinarily raised in litigation involving an ad valorem property tax on the real property of the establishment. This type of tax is the main source of funds of many municipalities that supply police and fire protection, street cleaning, and other necessary services to their residents. If large and valuable housing blocks are exempt from taxation as charities, such a municipality may have difficulty in financing its operations. This may be an acute problem in an area that, for climatic or other reasons, attracts numerous establishments for the well-to-do elderly. If the residents of an establishment for the elderly have average incomes that are higher than those of most of the younger residents of the municipality, their exemption from payment of any part of the cost of municipal services that they enjoy may seem unfair to many. If the trust or nonprofit corporation that operates the establishment was formed by wealthy elderly persons for their own benefit and the amenities of the establishment are luxurious as compared to those of most local residents, tax exemption may seem unfair to most people. Denial of charitable status for property tax purposes is not necessarily conclusive on the question of the validity and charitable nature of a trust for housing the elderly, but in England, and in the United States, a decision that a purpose is not charitable for tax purposes tends to influence decisions on such questions as validity under the rule against perpetuities and the application of the cy pres doctrine.[2]

The Preamble to the Statute of Charitable Uses of 1601, often used by the courts as a guide in formulating a list of permissible charitable purposes, lists first as a charitable purpose, "Relief of aged, impotent and poor people."[3] Several English cases hold that the words "aged, impotent and poor" are to be read disjunctively, that is, that a trust for the elderly is charitable even though not confined to those who are sick or poor or both.[4] A nonprofit home for elderly people of modest means has been held to be charitable in England,[5] and decisions in the United States made before 1965 were usually to the same

[2]In re Shaw, [1957] 1 All E.R. 745 (Ch. D.), *appeal dismissed,* [1958] 1 All E.R. 245 (C.A.); Scottish Burial Reform and Cremation Socy. v. Glasgow Corp., [1968] A.C. 138; M. Fremont-Smith, Foundations and Government 71 (1965); Cross, Some Recent Developments in the Law of Charity, 72 Law Q. Rev. 187, 203-204 (1956).

[3]43 Eliz. I, c. 4 (1601), §368.1. M. Fremont-Smith, Foundations and Government 1-111 (1965); L. Kutner, Legal Aspects of Charitable Trusts and Foundations 16-120 (1970).

[4]In re Glyn's Will Trusts, [1950] 2 All E.R. 1150 n. (free cottages for old women of the working classes); In re Bradbury, [1950] 2 All E.R. 1150 n. (nursing home for the aged); Re Robinson; Davis v. Robinson, [1951] Ch. 198; In re Lewis, [1955] Ch. 104; 4 Halsbury's Laws of England 213-214 (Simonds 3d ed., 1953).

[5]In re Estlin; Prichard v. Thomas, 89 L.T.R. 88, 89 (1903) (home for lady teachers who were to pay for room and board); Trustees of the Mary Clark Home v. Anderson, [1904] 2 K.B. 645, 657 (home for ladies of the professional and mercantile classes who have limited independent means); In re Gardom, [1914] 1 Ch. 662, *rev'd on other grounds,* 84 L.J. Ch. 749, 751 (House of Lords 1915) (home for ladies of limited means); In re Harvey, [1941] 3 All E.R. 284 (home for aged persons of genteel birth with limited income); cases cited in preceding note.

effect.[6] Elderly people who cannot climb stairs, walk long dis-

[6]*Arizona:* Memorial Hosp. v. Sparks, 9 Ariz. App. 478, 453 P.2d 989 (1969).

California: Fredericka Home for the Aged v. County of San Diego, 35 Cal. 2d 789, 796, 221 P.2d 68, 72 (1950); Pacific Home v. Los Angeles County, 41 Cal. 2d 844, 264 P.2d 539 (1953); Fifield Manor Wilshire v. County of Los Angeles, 188 Cal. App. 2d 1, 12, 10 Cal. Rptr. 242, 249 (1961).

Delaware: Electra Arms Apartment v. Wilmington, 254 A.2d 244 (Del. Super. 1969).

Florida: Jasper v. Mease Manor, 208 So. 2d 821 (Fla. 1968).

Georgia: Houston v. Mills Memorial Home, 202 Ga. 540, 549, 43 S.E.2d 680, 686 (1947); General Bd. of Care of Jewish Aged v. Henson, 120 Ga. App. 627, 171 S.E.2d 747 (1969).

Illinois: Continental Ill. Natl. Bank & Trust Co. v. Harris, 359 Ill. 86, 92-94, 194 N.E. 250, 253-254 (1935).

Indiana: State Bd. of Tax Commrs. v. Methodist Home for the Aged, 241 N.E.2d 84, 90 (Ind. App. 1968).

Iowa: South Iowa Methodist Homes v. Board of Review, 173 N.W.2d 526 (Iowa 1970).

Kansas: Topeka Presbyterian Manor v. Board of County Commrs., 195 Kan. 90, 99, 402 P.2d 802, 809 (1965).

Minnesota: Assembly Homes v. Yellow Medicine County, 273 Minn. 197, 204, 140 N.W.2d 336, 341 (1966).

Missouri: Missouri United Methodist Retirement Homes v. State Tax Commn., 522 S.W.2d 745 (Mo. 1975) (cost above what residents were able to pay was met by church); Franciscan Tertiary Province of Mo. v. State Tax Commn., 566 S.W.2d 213 (Mo. 1978), noted in 44 Mo. L. Rev. 154 (1979) (costs above what residents were able to pay were met by a charitable organization and the federal government, the court saying that the test for homes for the elderly is the same as that for hospitals: (1) Is the institution nonprofit? and (2) Is there direct or indirect benefit to the public as well as to the residents, poor or otherwise?).

Montana: Bozeman Deaconess Found. v. Ford, 151 Mont. 143, 439 P.2d 915, 918 (1968).

Nebraska: Evangelical Lutheran Good Samaritan Socy. v. County of Gage, 181 Neb. 831, 151 N.W.2d 446 (1967).

New Jersey: Kitchen v. Pitney, 94 N.J. Eq. 485, 489-490, 119 A. 675, 678 (1923); Woodstown Natl. Bank & Trust Co. v. Snelbaker, 136 N.J. Eq. 62, 66, 40 A.2d 222, 225 (1944), *aff'd,* 137 N.J. Eq. 256, 44 A.2d 210 (1945).

New York: In re MacDowell, 217 N.Y. 454, 464, 112 N.E. 177, 180 (1916).

Ohio: Carmelite Sisters, St. Rita's Home v. Board of Review, 18 Ohio St. 2d 41, 45, 247 N.E.2d 477, 479 (1969).

Pennsylvania: In re Tax Appeals of United Presbyterian Homes, 428 Pa. 145, 154, 236 A.2d 776, 780-781 (1968).

Texas: Texas Retired Teachers Residence Corp. v. Waco, 453 S.W.2d 236 (Tex. 1970).

tances, or drive automobiles are in obvious need of special housing if they are to live without servants and attendants. Furthermore, one does not need to be destitute in order to be "poor" for purposes of the law of charity.[7] Housing of this type is for the "relief of aged, impotent and poor people," and it promotes the public health and welfare. For all purposes except taxation, there should be no doubt that nonprofit homes for the elderly are charitable. But there are a number of recent decisions that they are not charities for the purpose of exemption from the ad valorem property tax on their real property.[8]

Wisconsin: Fairbanks v. City of Appleton 249 Wis. 476, 484-485, 24 N.W.2d 893, 897 (1946).

[7]Bowditch v. Attorney Gen., 241 Mass. 168, 134 N.E. 796 (1922); Restatement (Second) of Trusts, §369, Comment *d*, §374, Comment *g*, §376, Comment *c*; §§369.3, 374.11, *supra,* 376, *infra;* 4 Halsbury's Laws of England 214 (Simonds 3d ed., 1953).

[8]*Colorado:* United Presbyterian Assn. v. Board of County Commrs., 448 P.2d 967 (Colo. 1969).

Connecticut: Huntington v. Swedish Baptist Home, 90 Conn. 504, 97 A. 860 (1916).

Florida: Haines v. St. Petersburg Methodist Home, 173 So. 2d 176 (Fla. App. 1965); Presbyterian Homes of Synod v. Bradenton, 190 So. 2d 771 (1966).

Illinois: Methodist Old Peoples Home v. Korzen, 39 Ill. 2d 149, 233 N.E.2d 537 (1968); People ex rel. Nordlund v. Association of Winnebago Home for Aged, 40 Ill. 2d 91, 237 N.E.2d 533 (1968); Willows v. Munson, 43 Ill. 2d 203, 251 N.E.2d 249 (1969).

Minnesota: Madonna Towers v. Commissioner of Taxation, 283 Minn. 111, 167 N.W.2d 712 (1969).

Missouri: Defenders' Townhouse v. Kansas City, 441 S.W.2d 365 (Mo. 1969); Paraclete Manor v. State Tax Commn., 447 S.W.2d 311 (Mo. 1969); Westminster Gerontology Found. v. State Tax Commn., 522 S.W.2d 754 (Mo. 1975); John Calvin Manor v. State Tax Commn., 522 S.W.2d 754 (Mo. 1975) (well-to-do residents paid the cost to the extent that other residents could not afford to do so).

Nebraska: County of Douglas v. OEA Senior Citizens, 172 Neb. 696, 111 N.W.2d 719 (1961).

New Mexico: Mountain View Homes v. State Tax Commn., 77 N.M. 649, 427 P.2d 13 (1967).

Ohio: Beerman Found. v. Board of Tax Appeals, 152 Ohio St. 179, 39 Ohio Ops. 462, 87 N.E.2d 474 (1949); Philada Home Fund v. Board of Tax Appeals, 5 Ohio St. 2d 135, 214 N.E.2d 431 (1966); In re Exemption of Real Property From Taxation by Lutheran Senior City, 9 Ohio St. 2d 151, 224 N.E.2d 352 (1967); Crestview of Ohio v. Donahue, 14 Ohio St. 2d 121, 236

§374.12. **Humanitarian purposes.** One of the charitable purposes enumerated in the preamble to the Statute of Charitable Uses is "relief or redemption of prisoners or captives." In an English case that was decided in 1833 it was held that a trust for the redemption of British captives in Turkey or Barbary is a charitable purpose.[1] The trust was created by a testator in 1723. When the case was decided, however, there were no more British slaves in Turkey or Barbary, and the court held that a scheme should be framed for the application cy pres of the income under the trust. So also in Massachusetts in 1867 the court upheld a trust, created by a testator who died in 1861, for the benefit of fugitive slaves and another trust to create a public sentiment that would put an end to slavery in the United States.[2] The court pointed out that although purposes may be charitable that are not enumerated in the preamble to the Statute of Charitable Uses, yet one of the purposes there stated was the relief or redemption of prisoners and captives, and although the captives principally contemplated were doubtless Englishmen held as slaves in Turkey and Barbary, there is no reason for confining the words of the statute to such captives. A trust to put an end to slavery is for a charitable purpose. Since slavery was abolished in the United States by the enactment of the Thirteenth Amendment to the Constitution of the United States,

---

N.E.2d 668 (1968). But see Carmelite Sisters, St. Rita's Home v. Board of Review, 18 Ohio St. 41, 247 N.E.2d 477 (1969), overruling the *Donahue* and *Lutheran Senior City* cases.

Oregon: Friendsview Manor v. State Tax Commn., 247 Or. 94, 420 P.2d 77 (1966); Oregon Methodist Homes v. Horn, 226 Or. 298, 360 P.2d 293 (1960).

Texas: Hilltop Village v. Kerrville Indep. School Dist., 426 S.W.2d 943 (Tex. 1968).

See Fratcher, Bequests for Purposes, 56 Iowa L. Rev. 773, 778-779 (1971); Annot., Homes for the aged as exempt from property taxation, 37 A.L.R.3d 565 (1971); Annot., Receipt of pay from beneficiaries as affecting tax exemption of charitable institutions, 37 A.L.R.3d 1191 (1971).

§374.12. [1]Attorney-General v. The Ironmongers' Co., 2 Myl. &K. 576 (1833).

[2]Jackson v. Phillips, 14 Allen 539 (Mass. 1867). See Abrams v. Richmond County S.P.C., 125 Misc. 2d 530, 479 N.Y.S.2d 624 (Sup. Ct. 1984) (Society for the Prevention of Cruelty to Children).

which was ratified in 1865, the court directed that a scheme should be framed for the application cy pres of the property held upon these trusts.

Similarly, it is clear that a trust to assist prisoners who have served their sentences to rehabilitate themselves is for a charitable purpose.

An intended trust for humanitarian purposes may be couched in such broad language that it is not limited to charitable purposes and therefore fails.[3] In *Matter of Hayes*[4] a testatrix left a legacy to a man "to use at his discretion in promoting the ends of justice." The lower court held that the legacy was given upon a trust that was not charitable and that failed. The judgment was reversed on the ground that there was a beneficial gift to the legatee.

§375. Definite Beneficiaries

A trust will not be upheld as charitable unless the accomplishment of the purposes of the trust is of benefit or supposed benefit to the community. A trust may fail because the class of persons who are to benefit is so narrow that the community has no interest in the performance of the trust. It is a question of degree whether the class is large enough to make the performance of the trust of sufficient benefit to the community so that it will be upheld as a charitable trust. If the purpose of the trust is to relieve poverty, promote education, advance religion, or protect health, the class need not be as broad as it must be where the benefits to be conferred have no relation to any of these purposes. On the other hand, the class of persons to be benefited may be so limited that the trust is not charitable even though the purpose of the trust is to relieve their poverty, to educate them, to save their souls, or to promote their health.[1]

[3] See §398.1.

[4] 263 N.Y. 219, 18 N.E. 716, 264 N.Y. 459, 191 N.E. 513 (1934). See §25.2, n. 8.

§375. [1] See the following federal tax cases: United States v. Bank of Am. Natl. Trust & Sav. Assn., 326 F.2d 51 (9th Cir. 1964) (free bed in hospital for designated beneficiaries); Tripp v. Commissioner, 337 F.2d 432 (7th Cir. 1964) (to educate a specified person); Sedam v. United States, 518 F.2d 242,

Although the trust is not a charitable trust, however, it may be a valid private trust if the beneficiaries are sufficiently definite and if the trust does not involve a violation of the principle of the rule against perpetuities.

The question whether a trust is charitable or not may be of importance for several reasons. If it is a charitable trust it is valid although the trust is to continue for an indefinite period,[2] whereas if it is not a charitable trust it may fail because of the rule against perpetuities. If it is a charitable trust it is valid although there is no definite beneficiary to enforce it because it is enforceable at the suit of the Attorney General,[3] whereas if it is not a charitable trust it cannot be enforced unless there are beneficiaries to enforce it. On the other hand, if it is a charitable trust created by will, it may fail because of statutory provisions limiting the power of a testator to devise or bequeath property for charitable purposes.[4] So also if it is a charitable trust it may be exempt from taxation.[5] Whether it is exempt depends on the terms of the statute imposing the tax, and it is to be borne in mind that although a trust may be held to be valid as a charitable trust, it may nevertheless not be exempt from taxation. So also a charitable institution may be exempt from liability in tort, where a noncharitable institution would not be exempt.[6]

§375.1. Where the number of recipients is limited. Where the class of persons from whom the recipients of benefits are to be selected is sufficiently large, the fact that the number of persons who are to receive the benefits is small does not prevent the trust from being charitable. This is clear enough where the income of the trust fund is to be applied for the benefit of one person or a limited number of persons for an indefinite period. In such a case the number of persons who are to receive benefits under the trust at any one time is limited, but the total number is unlimited. The number of recipients of

---

34 A.L.R. Fed. 833 (7th Cir. 1975) (donor's mother to live in retirement home).

  [2]See §365.
  [3]See §364.
  [4]See §362.
  [5]See §348.4.
  [6]See §402.

benefits is narrow horizontally but vertically is indefinitely long. Thus a bequest of a sum of money in trust to pay the income annually as a prize to the highest ranking student of the graduating class of a particular school, or to pay the income to the boy or girl who shall produce the best calf or pig, is charitable.[1] The purpose of such a trust is to promote education, and the class from whom the recipients of benefits are to be selected is sufficiently wide, and the fact that there is to be but a single recipient in any year does not prevent the trust from being a charitable trust. Similarly, a trust of money to apply the income for the education through high school of white girl inmates of a home, the girls to be selected by the trustees, is charitable.[2] A trust to pay the income to one person or several persons to assist him or them to prepare for their lifework is charitable.[3]

So also a bequest in trust to pay $1000 each year from the income to the person who in the judgment of the trustees shall have made the greatest advancement toward discovery of a cure for cancer is charitable.[4] The purpose of such a trust is to pro-

§375.1. [1]Ashmore v. Newman, 350 Ill. 64, 183 N.E. 1 (1932).

See Worcester County Trust Co. v. Grand Knight, 325 Mass. 748, 92 N.E.2d 579 (1950) (citing the text).

See also Matter of Lewis, 199 Misc. 463, 99 N.Y.S.2d 986 (1950) (scholarship fund).

[2]Humphrey v. Board of Trustees, 203 N.C. 201, 165 S.E. 547 (1932), noted in 11 N.C.L. Rev. 179.

See also In re Welton, [1950] 2 D.L.R. 280 (N.S.).

[3]Matter of Davidge, 200 A.D. 437, 193 N.Y.S. 245 (1922).

In In re Estate of Carlson, 187 Kan. 543, 358 P.2d 669 (1961), a testator left his estate to a city in trust for the education of a medical student who should promise to practice in the city. The court upheld the trust as charitable on the ground that it would promote health in the city, where physicians were scarce.

See Chapman Estate, 39 D.&C.2d 701 (Pa. 1966) (to a clergyman "to pay for the education of a fine boy of his selection, preferably one who is handicapped").

[4]Matter of Judd, 242 A.D. 389, 274 N.Y.S. 902 (1934), aff'd, 270 N.Y. 516, 200 N.E. 297 (1936).

See Estate of McKenzie, 227 Cal. App. 2d 167, 38 Cal. Rptr. 496, 7 A.L.R.3d 1275 (1964) (for a reward for discovering a cure for arthritis); Sheen v. Sheen, 126 N.J. Eq. 132, 8 A.2d 136 (1939) (annual prize to outstanding Doctor of Medical Science in the United States each year).

See Note, Validity, as charitable trust, of gift for prize or award to person or persons accomplishing specified result, 7 A.L.R.3d 1281 (1966).

mote the public health, and the class of persons from whom the recipients of the prize are to be drawn is of indefinite extent, and the fact that each year only one person is to receive the prize does not prevent the trust from being charitable. In another case[5] the court upheld as charitable a trust to give annual prizes for the best results achieved in the accomplishment of various purposes, such as the prevention of cruelty, the promotion of peace, the spreading of the gospel, the uplifting of moral conditions, the production of serviceable inventions or works of art, discoveries in medicine and surgery, and agricultural improvements.

A trust may be a valid charitable trust for the advancement of religion although the persons who are directly to benefit are limited in number. Thus a perpetual trust to pay or to contribute to the payment of the salary of a minister of a particular church is charitable.[6] Although the direct beneficiary for the time being is a single person, the incumbent of the office, the effect of the trust is to promote religion. Similarly, a trust to use the income for the support of the widows and children of former ministers of a particular church is charitable.[7] Thus in *Sears v. Attorney General*[8] a fund was raised by subscriptions from persons con-

---

[5]Matter of Browning, 165 Misc. 819, 1 N.Y.S.2d 825 (1938), *aff'd mem.*, 254 A.D. 843, 6 N.Y.S.2d 339 (1938), *aff'd mem.*, 281 N.Y. 577, 22 N.E.2d 160 (1939).

[6]Curtis v. First Church in Charlestown, 285 Mass. 73, 188 N.E. 631 (1933); Matter of Bell, 141 Misc. 720, 253 N.Y.S. 118 (1931); In re Clark, [1961] N.Z.L.R. 635.

So also a trust to supply the minister with a parsonage is charitable. Bartlett, Petitioner, 163 Mass. 509, 40 N.E. 899 (1895).

In Heckler Estate, 5 Fiduciary Rep. 110 (Pa. 1955), the court upheld as charitable a trust to pay the income forever in equal shares to the preachers and deacons of a designated Mennonite church.

[7]Sears v. Attorney Gen., 193 Mass. 551, 79 N.E. 772, 9 Ann. Cas. 1200 (1907); Matter of Edge, 159 Misc. 505, 288 N.Y.S. 437 (1936) (citing Restatement of Trusts §375).

See Morey v. Riddell, 205 F. Supp. 918 (S.D. Cal. 1962), holding that gifts to a church for its support were for a charitable purpose, although they included payment of a reasonable salary for the minister.

[8]193 Mass. 551, 79 N.E. 772, 9 Ann. Cas. 1200 (1907).

In In re Clark, [1961] N.Z.L.R. 635, however, where a testatrix created a trust to pay £50 a year to the wife (if any) of the minister from time to time of a designated church, to be used by her for her own private use, it was held that the trust was not charitable and failed.

nected with Trinity Church in Boston "for the benefit of the widows and orphan children that may be left by the future ministers of this church." Payments were to be made only to such widows and orphans as were in need. It was held that the trust was charitable both because it was for the relief of poverty and because it tended to promote religion. As a trust for the relief of poverty it was charitable although the class to be relieved was at any one time a small one, because it included an indefinite number of persons in future generations. Moreover, the trust tended to benefit religion by increasing the remuneration of ministers of the church by providing for their families. But if the trust had not been limited to needy widows and orphans and if the persons to be benefited had not been connected with a religious vocation, it would seem that the trust would not have been charitable because the class to be benefited would have been too narrow. Thus it would seem that a trust for the benefit of the families of the presidents of a fraternal organization without regard to poverty would not be charitable.

Where the purpose of the trust is charitable and the class of persons who are to receive benefits under the trust is sufficiently large, the trust is charitable even though the number of recipients of benefits is limited both horizontally and vertically. A trust to make immediate distribution of the principal among a specified number of poor persons is a valid charitable trust.[9] Thus a bequest of $1000 to the testator's executor to be applied by him in shares of $100 each for the benefit of ten poor boys to be selected by him is a valid charitable trust, and if the executor dies without making the selection the court will appoint a new trustee to perform the trust.[10] Similarly, in an early English case it was held that a gift of £600 to be distributed among 60

---

[9]Brett v. Attorney-General, [1945] I.R. 526 (to be distributed among such poor persons in an Irish county as executor should select).

In In re Wedge, 67 D.L.R.2d 433 (B.C. 1968), the court upheld a trust where the property was to be given to some needy displaced family of European origin who wished to make a new start in life in Canada and engage in farming.

[10]Sherman v. Shaw, 243 Mass. 257, 137 N.E. 374 (1922).

In Brady v. Ceaty, 349 Mass. 180, 207 N.E.2d 49 (1965), the court upheld a trust for the education of one or more deserving boys or girls to be chosen by the trustee; citing the text and Restatement of Trusts §375.

pious ejected ministers was a valid charitable trust.[11] On the other hand, in a later English case a bequest of money to each of ten poor clergymen to be selected by the testator's executor was held not to be a charitable trust within the meaning of the mortmain statutes.[12] In a California case it was held that a bequest to be used to help defray the expense of educating some boy or girl in music or art to be selected by a designated person was invalid because the will provided for a single recipient of the benefit of the trust.[13] This would seem to be immaterial, however, because the purpose of the trust was to promote education and the class of persons from whom the selection was to be made was indefinite in extent.[14]

§375.2. Where the class to be benefited is limited.
A trust is upheld as a charitable trust because it is of benefit to the community. It is not essential, however, that every member of the community should be a beneficiary or potential beneficiary of the trust. Even though the purposes of the trust are charitable in character, the trust is not a valid charitable trust if the benefits are limited to too small a class of persons. The difficulty is, of course, in determining just where to draw the line. It must be remembered that if the beneficiaries are sufficiently definite, the trust may be valid as a private trust if there is no violation of the rule against perpetuities. On the other hand, the class of beneficiaries may be sufficiently indefinite so that the trust cannot be enforced as a private trust, and yet may not be broad enough to make the trust valid as a charitable trust.

The cases are numerous in which property is given to or in trust for unincorporated associations. The trust does not fail merely because the association is not a legal entity. But if the association is not a charitable organization and if the property is so tied up that it cannot be expended for the benefit of the

[11]Attorney-General v. Hughes, 2 Vern. 105 (1689), *rev'g* Attorney-General v. Baxter, 1 Vern. 248 (1684).

[12]Thomas v. Howell, L.R. 18 Eq. 198 (1874).

[13]Estate of Huebner, 127 Cal. App. 244, 15 P.2d 758 (1932).

[14]In Young v. Redmon's Trustee, 300 Ky. 418, 189 S.W.2d 401 (1945), a trust to educate some poor Christian worthy girl was held to be a valid charitable trust.

Cf. Estate of Bunch v. Heirs of Bunch, 485 So. 2d 284 (Miss. 1986) ("to help one or two young men through medical school").

association within the period of the rule against perpetuities, the gift or trust fails.[1] If the association is a charitable organization, however, a gift in trust for it or a gift directly to it is valid.[2] The disposition is valid even though it is to continue for an indefinite time, as, for example, where the principal is to be held intact and the income expended in perpetuity for the promotion of the purposes of the association. Where property is bequeathed in trust for an unincorporated association and it is provided that the trust shall continue beyond the period of the rule against perpetuities, the validity of the trust depends on whether the association is a charitable organization or one existing merely for the benefit of the members.

Fraternal organizations and social clubs. A trust for the benefit of the members of a Masonic lodge or other fraternal organization is not a charitable trust if the purposes of the organization are not limited to charitable purposes.[3] But where a trust is

§375.2. [1]See §119.
[2]See §397.2.
[3]*England:* National Deposit Friendly Socy. Trustees v. Skegness Urban Dist. Council, [1959] A.C. 293, *aff'g* [1957] 2 Q.B. 573 (tax case); Independent Order of Odd Fellows Manchester Unity Friendly Socy. v. Manchester Corp., [1958] 3 All E.R. 378 (tax case); United Grand Lodge of Ancient Free and Accepted Masons of England v. Holborn Borough Council, [1957] 1 W.L.R. 1080 (tax case); Waterson v. Hendon Borough Council, [1959] 2 All E.R. 760; Working Men's Club & Inst. Union v. Swansea Corp., [1959] 3 All E.R. 769, *rev'g* [1958] 3 All E.R. 414 (tax case).
Federal: Levey v. Smith, 103 F.2d 643 (7th Cir. 1939), *cert. denied,* 308 U.S. 578 (1939) (no deduction under federal estate tax).
California: Kauffman v. Foster, 3 Cal. App. 741, 86 P. 1108 (1906) (Masons); Estate of Wirt, 207 Cal. 106, 277 P. 118 (1929) (case sent back to determine whether purposes of Masonic Lodge charitable or not); In re Estate of Allen, 17 Cal. App. 3d 401, 94 Cal. Rptr. 648 (1971) (Scottish Rite Bodies); In re Kober Trust Fund, 26 Cal. App. 3d 265, 103 Cal. Rptr. 1 (1972).
Illinois: Klopp v. Benevolent Protective Order of Elks, 309 Ill. App. 145, 33 N.E.2d 161 (1941) (liable in tort), noted in 26 Marq. L. Rev. 163.
Indiana: Indianapolis Elks Bldg. Corp. v. State Bd. of Tax Commrs., 145 Ind. App. 2d 522, 251 N.E.2d 673 (1969) (land tax).
Maine: Bangor v. Masonic Lodge, 73 Me. 428, 40 Am. Rep. 369 (1882) (Masons); MacDonald v. Stubbs, 142 Me. 235, 49 A.2d 765 (1946) (Masons; not exempt from Maine inheritance tax); Thirkell v. Johnson, 150 Me. 131, 107 A.2d 489 (1954) (Masons; though bylaw provided that unrestricted gifts should constitute a permanent charity fund).

created for the relief of poverty or the advancement of educa-

---

Massachusetts: Peakes v. Blakely, 333 Mass. 281, 130 N.E.2d 564 (1955).

Minnesota: High v. Supreme Lodge of the World, Loyal Order of Moose, 214 Minn. 164, 7 N.W.2d 675, 144 A.L.R. 810 (1943) (Loyal Order of Moose).

New York: Matter of Shaul, 58 Misc. 2d 967, 297 N.Y.S.2d 209 (1969).

Oregon: State v. Sunbeam Rebekah Lodge No. 180, 169 Or. 253, 127 P.2d 726 (1942) (Odd Fellows).

Pennsylvania: Swift's Exrs. v. Easton Beneficial Socy., 73 Pa. 362 (1873).

Rhode Island: Mason v. Perry, 21 R.I. 475, 48 A. 671 (1901) (Masons).

Texas: Most Worshipful Prince Hall Grand Lodge v. City of Fort Worth, 435 S.W.2d 274 (Tex. Civ. App. 1968) (a tax case).

In the following cases, however, it was held that the purposes of the organization were charitable:

Alabama: Moseley v. Smiley, 171 Ala. 593, 55 So. 143 (1911) (Tabernacle Alliance).

Georgia: Mayor, etc. of Savannah v. Solomon's Lodge, 53 Ga. 93 (1874) (Masons; statutory).

Illinois: Grand Lodge v. Board of Review, 281 Ill. 480, 117 N.E. 1016 (1917) (Masons).

Indiana: Cruse v. Axtell, 50 Ind. 49 (1875) (Masons).

Massachusetts: King v. Parker, 9 Cush. 71 (Mass. 1851).

Missouri: In re Estate of Burroughs, 357 Mo. 10, 206 S.W.2d 340, 174 A.L.R. 524 (1947) (Masons; exempt from Missouri succession tax).

New Mexico: Santa Fe Lodge No. 460, B.P.O.E. v. Employment Sec. Commn., 49 N.M. 149, 159 P.2d 312 (1945) (Elks lodge, exempt from New Mexico Unemployment Compensation Law).

New York: Matter of Manville, 57 N.Y.S.2d 439 (1945) (any fraternal societies operating under lodge system).

Oregon: Brown v. Webb, 60 Or. 526, 120 P. 387, Ann. Cas. 1914A 148 (1912) (Independent Order of Good Templars).

Virginia: Manassas Lodge v. County of Prince William, 218 Va. 220, 237 S.E.2d 102 (1977) (Loyal Order of Moose held exempt from state tax).

In Wilbur v. Portland Trust Co., 121 Conn. 535, 186 A. 499 (1936), a trust for an unincorporated Masonic lodge was held valid, although not a charitable trust, where the income and principal were payable to the lodge at any time in the discretion of the trustee. See §119.

In Spotz's Estate, 51 D.&C. 427 (Pa. 1944), where a bequest was made to a chapter of the Order of Eastern Star, an unincorporated association affiliated with the Masons, it was held that the association was not a charitable organization, and that the bequest was valid, although a bequest for charitable purposes would have been invalid because the will was made within thirty days of the death of the testatrix. See §§119, 362.4.

See Note, Exemption from succession, estate, or inheritance tax of devise or bequest of property to fraternal society, 174 A.L.R. 531 (1948).

As to the exemption from federal taxes of fraternal societies, see 26 U.S.C., §501(c)(8); as to the deduction from income tax of a gift to such

tion or the promotion of health, the trust is charitable although the beneficiaries are limited to the members or relatives of members of such an organization.[4] Thus a trust for the benefit of

---

societies, see 26 U.S.C., §170(c)(4); as to the estate tax, see 26 U.S.C., §2055(a)(3).

[4]*England:* Spiller v. Maude, 32 Ch. D. 158n (1881) (Royal General Theatrical Fund Association, to provide for indigent members); Pease v. Pattinson, 32 Ch. D. 154 (1886) (Miners' Permanent Relief Fund Friendly Society); In re Buck, [1896] 2 Ch. 727 (Commercial Travellers' Society for the relief of sick and distressed members, their widows and orphans); In re Lacy, [1899] 2 Ch. 149 (Royal General Theatrical Fund Association); In re Young's Will Trusts, [1955] 3 All E.R. 689 (for pensions or grants to members of a social club who might fall on evil days).

California: Estate of Willey, 128 Cal. 1, 60 P. 471 (1900) (bequest to certain Masonic Lodges for the use of their widows' and orphans' funds); Estate of Henderson, 17 Cal. 2d 853, 112 P.2d 605 (1941) (citing the text and Restatement of Trusts §375), noted in 30 Calif. L. Rev. 218; Estate of Clippinger, 75 Cal. App. 2d 426, 171 P.2d 567 (1946) (Eastern Star Home); Estate of Brown, 140 Cal. App. 2d 677, 295 P.2d 566 (1956) (Shriners Hospitals for Crippled Children).

District of Columbia: Van Horn v. Lewis, 79 F. Supp. 541 (D.D.C. 1948) (welfare and retirement fund of United Mine Workers; held majority of trustees can act).

Illinois: Guilfoil v. Arthur, 158 Ill. 600, 41 N.E. 1009 (1895) (bequest on trust for widows and orphans of deceased members of brotherhood of Locomotive Engineers); Slenker v. Grand Lodge, 344 Ill. App. 1, 100 N.E.2d 354 (1951), *cert. denied,* 344 U.S. 830, 888 (1952) (Grand Lodge of the Independent Order of Odd Fellows, maintaining fund for aged members).

Indiana: Quinn v. Peoples Trust & Sav. Co., 223 Ind. 317, 60 N.E.2d 281, 157 A.L.R. 885 (1945) (to afford college education to children of employees of the Pennsylvania Railroad Company living in certain city).

Kansas: In re Estate of Bauer, 192 Kan. 538, 390 P.2d 16 (1964) (devise to Masonic lodge, held valid but to be applied to charitable purposes only).

Kentucky: Widows' & Orphans' Home of O. F. v. Commonwealth, 126 Ky. 386, 103 S.W. 354, 16 L.R.A. (N.S.) 829 (1907) (Widows' and Orphans' Home of the Odd Fellows of Kentucky); Green's Admrs. v. Fidelity Trust Co. of Louisville, 134 Ky. 311, 120 S.W. 283, 20 Ann. Cas. 861 (1909) (bequest to erect and maintain institution for support and education of poor orphans of Free Masons of Indiana).

Massachusetts: Masonic Educ. & Charity Trust v. Boston, 201 Mass. 320, 87 N.E. 602 (1909) (bequest to establish and maintain home for needy Masons in Boston and vicinity).

By Mass. Ann. Laws, c. 176, §14, as inserted by Laws 1958, c. 540, it is provided that a fraternal benefit society may maintain charitable institutions for the benefit of its members and their families and dependents.

needy members or the needy widows and orphans of members of a fraternal organization, or a trust to provide medical or surgical assistance for the members or their families, is a charitable trust. There are cases, indeed, in which it has been held that a trust for such purposes is not exempt from taxation, but these cases can be supported on the ground that it was not the intention of the legislature to exempt all charitable trusts but it was

Missouri: Rice v. Hawley, 239 Mo. App. 901, 203 S.W.2d 158 (1947) (to erect a hospital).

New Hampshire: Roberts v. Corson, 79 N.H. 215, 107 A. 625, 5 A.L.R. 1172 (1919) (to Masonic Lodge for needy members).

New York: Matter of Brown, 93 N.Y.S.2d 881 (1949) (one half for employees of particular trust company and their dependents, one half for Masonic asylum fund); Matter of Reese, 21 Misc. 2d 29, 195 N.Y.S.2d 144 (1960) (trust to pay income to a Christmas fund for employees of what was apparently a social club upheld as charitable); Matter of Shaul, 58 Misc. 2d 967, 297 N.Y.S.2d 209 (1969) (Masonic Home).

Oregon: State ex rel. Crutze v. Toney, 141 Or. 406, 17 P.2d 1105 (1933) (educational fund of Masonic Grand Lodge).

Pennsylvania: Channon's Estate, 266 Pa. 417, 109 A. 756 (1920) (Masonic home); Lowe's Estate, 326 Pa. 375, 192 A. 405, 111 A.L.R. 518 (1937) (Odd Fellows Home for the Aged and Infirm of Pennsylvania; bequest held invalid because will executed within thirty days of death); Hatzfeld's Estate, 54 D.&C. 60 (Pa. 1945) (Odd Fellows Home for the Aged of a town; bequest held invalid because will executed within thirty days of death); James Estate, 414 Pa. 80, 199 A.2d 275 (1964) (for the use of a Masonic home; citing Restatement of Trusts §368).

Tennessee: Heiskell v. Chickasaw Lodge, 87 Tenn. 668, 11 S.W. 825, 4 L.R.A. 699 (1889) (for widows and orphans of deceased members of lodge of Odd Fellows).

Virginia: City of Petersburg v. Petersburg Benevolent Mechanics Assn., 78 Va. 431 (1884) (Benevolent Mechanics Association).

Washington: In re Quick's Estate, 33 Wash. 2d 568, 206 P.2d 489 (1949) (needy Masons).

Wisconsin: In re Thronson's Estate, 243 Wis. 73, 9 N.W.2d 641 (1943) (Masonic Home).

In Samuels v. Attorney Gen., 373 Mass. 844, 370 N.E.2d 698 (1977), it was held that funds given to a fraternal organization for the relief of distress among its members could not be used for the general purposes of the organization. The court cited the text and the Restatement of Trusts, §375, Comment *e.*

But see *contra* Troutman v. De Boissiere Odd Fellows' Orphans' Home & Indus. School Assn., 66 Kan. 1, 71 P. 286 (1903) (trust to provide home for orphan children of deceased Odd Fellows of Kansas); In re Hartung, 40 Nev. 262, 160 P. 782, 161 P. 715 (1916), *semble.*

intended only to exempt those in which the general public has a more direct interest.[5]

There are other cases in which the question has arisen whether a trust for the benefit of an organization of limited membership is a charitable trust. The answer depends on the purposes of the organization. Where the purpose of the organization is merely to afford pleasure to the members or to promote their social interests, it is not a charitable organization.[6] It has been held that college fraternities are not charitable organizations.[7] Neither are the English friendly societies, which are

[5]La Societe Française de Bienfaisance Mutuelle v. California Employment Commn., 56 Cal. App. 2d 534, 133 P.2d 47 (1943), *cert. denied,* 320 U.S. 736 (1943); In re La Societe Française de Bienfaisance Mutuelle, 75 Cal. App. 2d 770, 171 P.2d 544 (1946); In re Estate of Salisbury, 90 Ohio App. 17, 101 N.E.2d 304 (1951), *appeal dismissed,* 155 Ohio St. 615, 99 N.E.2d 671 (1952); Philadelphia v. Masonic Home, 160 Pa. 572, 28 A. 954, 23 L.R.A. 545, 40 Am. St. Rep. 736 (1894).

See Channon's Estate, 266 Pa. 417, 109 A. 756 (1920).

But see Louise H. Haessler Memorial Fund's Appeal, 41 D.&C. 202 (Pa. 1941) (corporation for relief of needy teachers of Philadelphia public schools).

In Rotary Intl. v. Paschen, 14 Ill. 2d 480, 153 N.E.2d 4 (1958), it was held that the Rotary International was not exempt from the Illinois property tax.

In Miller v. Davis, 136 Tex. 299, 150 S.W.2d 973 (1941), it was held that a special act of the legislature incorporating a charitable foundation created by a testator was unconstitutional because such a corporation is not a public but a private corporation within the meaning of a constitutional provision forbidding the incorporation of private corporations by special act.

[6]See §374.6A.

In In re Women's Club of Harrisburg, 23 D.&C.2d 356 (Pa. 1960), it was held that a woman's club established to promote good fellowship and to develop the social, educational, and recreational opportunities for its members was not charitable and that on its dissolution its property was distributable among its members. See §430.4.

In Lynch v. Spilman, 67 Cal. 2d 406, 431 P.2d 636, 62 Cal. Rptr. 12 (1967), it was held that on the dissolution of a lodge organized for the benefit of its members and for service for boys, the Attorney General was not entitled to a summary judgment forbidding the members to divide its property on its dissolution, because it did not appear that its purpose was wholly charitable.

[7]*Federal:* Phinney v. Dougherty, 307 F.2d 357 (5th Cir. 1962) (a tax case).

Illinois: Knox College v. Board of Review, 308 Ill. 160, 139 N.E. 56, 35 A.L.R. 1041 (1923); People v. Phi Kappa Sigma, 326 Ill. 573, 158 N.E. 213, 54 A.L.R. 1376 (1927).

Kansas: Sigma Alpha Epsilon Fraternal Assn. v. Board of County Commrs., 207 Kan. 514, 485 P.2d 1297 (1971).

created to promote the social and financial interests of the members.[8]

In some cases the courts have found greater difficulty in determining whether a club or society was a charitable or merely social organization. In *In re Topham*[9] a testator left his estate to trustees for the benefit of the Christ Church Club, half of the legacy to be used in the purchase of premises for the club and the other half to be invested to form a permanent yearly income for the maintenance of the club. The club was connected with a church. Its object was the religious, moral, intellectual, physical, and social improvement of its members. Under the rules of the club its property might be used for the benefit of the members in any way in which the members saw fit. The court held that the club was not a charitable organization. It was a club "of an ordinary social type, with a particular tendency towards religious, moral, intellectual and physical improvement." It was held accordingly that the trust failed as involving a perpetuity for noncharitable purposes. In *Williams' Trustees v. Inland Revenue Commissioners*[10] it was held that a trust to establish an institute for the moral, spiritual, and educational welfare of Welsh people was for social as well as charitable purposes and was subject to the income tax. In *In re Barnett*[11] a bequest to a trade guild in

---

Massachusetts: See Bancroft v. Cook, 264 Mass. 343, 162 N.E. 691 (1928).

Nebraska: Iota Benefit Assn. v. County of Douglas, 165 Neb. 330, 85 N.W.2d 726, 66 A.L.R.2d 898 (1957).

Pennsylvania: Langfitt v. United States, 321 F. Supp. 360 (W.D. Pa. 1970) (bequest in trust to use income to pay dues of students joining the Phi Delta Theta fraternity who cannot afford the cost; a tax case).

In University of Rochester v. Wagner, 63 A.D.2d 341, 408 N.Y.S.2d 157 (1978), *aff'd mem.* 47 N.Y.2d 833, 392 N.E.2d 569, 418 N.Y.S.2d 583 (1979), where the fraternities had been turned over to the university, it was held that they were tax exempt as held for educational purposes.

See Note, Exemption from taxation of college fraternity or sorority house, 66 A.L.R.2d 904 (1959).

[8]In re Clark's Trust, 1 Ch. D. 497 (1875); Cunnack v. Edwards, [1896] 2 Ch. 679; Braithwaite v. Attorney-General, [1909] 1 Ch. 510.

See Moran v. Plymouth Rubber Co. Mut. Benefit Assn., 307 Mass. 444, 30 N.E.2d 238 (1940) (mutual benefit association of employees of company selling food to members held liable in tort for personal injury).

[9][1938] 1 All E.R. 181, 185, noted in 11 Austl. L.J. 554.

[10][1947] A.C. 447, *aff'g* [1945] 2 All E.R. 236, noted in 63 Law Q. Rev. 18, 64 id. 5.

[11]24 T.L.R. 788 (1908).

trust to give a dinner on each anniversary of the testator's birthday was held invalid. In an Irish case[12] a bequest was made to a branch of the Catholic Young Men's Society of Ireland. It was shown that the society had a charitable object, namely the promotion of Catholic action, but also had as other objects the spiritual, intellectual, social, and physical welfare of its members. It was held that the latter objects were not charitable, and the legacy failed. The court said that it was not a valid gift to the individual members of the society, and was therefore void as infringing the rule against perpetuities. In *Tennant Plays, Ltd. v. Inland Revenue Commissioners*[13] it was held that a company that included in its purposes not merely the advancement of education and of educational plays and arts such as the drama, dance, singing, and music, but also the conducting of entertainments that were not educational, was not exempt from the income tax. In *Inland Revenue Commissioners v. City of Glasgow Police Association*[14] the purposes of a police association were to promote athletic sports among the members, and also, as shown by parol evidence, to encourage recruiting and improve the police force. It was held by the House of Lords that the association was not exempt from tax, because the noncharitable purpose of providing recreation for its members was not merely incidental to the charitable purposes. There are other cases in which clubs or associations have been held to be noncharitable.[15]

[12]Munster & Leinster Bank v. Attorney-General, [1940] I.R. 19. But compare In re Howley, [1940] I.R. 106. See §371.6, n. 1.

[13][1948] 1 All E.R. 506.

[14][1953] 1 All E.R. 747, noted in 69 Law Q. Rev. 313, 69 id. 517.

[15]*Connecticut:* Bentley v. Hamden Post 88, 27 Conn. 56, 229 A.2d 32 (1967) (social club not exempt from tort liability).

Illinois: Oak Park Club v. Lindheimer, 369 Ill. 462, 17 N.E.2d 32 (1938) (social club engaged also in charitable undertakings held not exempt from real estate tax).

Massachusetts: In re Troy, 364 Mass. 15, 306 N.E.2d 203 (1973) (association for benefit of members, not of public; held not a charitable organization).

New York: Matter of Kennedy, 240 A.D. 20, 269 N.Y.S. 136 (1934), *aff'd mem.,* 264 N.Y. 691, 191 N.E. 629 (1934) (to promote fellowship and to secure clubhouse for the members of association of graduate nurses of hospital; tax case).

Northern Ireland: In re the Lord Mayor of Belfast's Air Raid Distress Fund, [1962] N. Ir. L.R. 161 (to erect a war memorial building for ex-servicemen as a social and recreational center).

In Dissolution of Labor Lyceum, 40 D.&C.2d 580 (Pa. 1965), it was held

On the other hand, somewhat similar trusts have been upheld as charitable. In *Tollinger Estate*[16] a bequest in trust to pay the income to an unincorporated men's club connected with a church, to be expended for food for banquets at its meetings, was held to be valid as a charitable trust. In *Worcester County Trust Co. v. Grand Knight*[17] the court upheld a trust to pay income to the treasurers of certain Catholic colleges for the purpose of providing annual dinners for the priests and sisters of those institutions. In *In re Charlesworth*[18] a small bequest in trust to use the income to pay for dinners at meetings of a clerical society was held to be a valid charity, because it would tend to promote

---

that a nonprofit corporation for the education of its members was not charitable and that on its dissolution the assets should be divided among the members. See §430.4.

In Ladies Literary Club v. City of Grand Rapids, 409 Mich. 948, 298 N.W.2d 422 (1980), *rev'g* 92 Mich. App. 567, 285 N.W.2d 212 (1979), a ladies literary club was held not exempt from the property tax, three justices dissenting.

In Society of Cincinnati v. Exeter, 92 N.H. 348, 31 A.2d 52 (1943), it was held that the incorporated New Hampshire branch of the Society of the Cincinnati was not exempt from real estate taxes as a charitable organization because its purpose was to promote patriotism and friendship among the members, and the benefits did not extend to the public generally.

In Matter of Emil Hubsch Post No. 596, Veterans of Foreign Wars of the United States of America, 303 N.Y. 682, 102 N.E.2d 836 (1951), *aff'g* 278 A.D. 460, 106 N.Y.S.2d 727 (1951), it was held that a post of the Veterans of Foreign Wars was not exempt from unemployment insurance contributions because the evidence showed that it was organized not merely for charitable purposes but also for fraternal and social activities.

See also In re Application of the American Legion, 20 Ohio St. 2d 121, 49 Ohio Ops. 2d 442, 254 N.E.2d 21 (1969).

In Goldman v. Robert E. Bentley Post No. 50, American Legion, 158 Ohio St. 205, 107 N.E.2d 528 (1952), it was held that an American Legion post did not hold its property exclusively for charitable purposes, and that it was not exempt from a state property tax.

Under 26 U.S.C., §170(c)(3), an individual may for the purposes of the income tax deduct gifts to posts or organizations of war veterans where no part of their earnings inures to the benefit of any private shareholder or individual.

For cases holding that certain organizations with religious purposes were not charitable because they had other purposes also, or the class to benefit was too narrow, see §§371.3, 371.6.

[16]349 Pa. 393, 37 A.2d 500 (1944).
[17]325 Mass. 748, 92 N.E.2d 579 (1950).
[18]101 L.T.R. 908 (1910).

the charitable purposes for which the meetings were held. In *In re Coxen*[19] a testator left £200,000 in trust to apply annually a sum not exceeding £100 to provide a dinner for the six trustees, and to pay each of them a guinea at each meeting, and to apply the balance for the benefit of charitable hospitals. It was held that the whole trust was valid because a provision for the dinners and the fees for the trustees tended to promote efficient administration of the charity. The court was further of the opinion that even if these provisions were invalid, the trust would not fail and that the whole of the property should be devoted to the charitable purposes.[20]

In *Newton Centre Woman's Club, Inc. v. Newton*[21] it was held that a women's club was a charitable organization and was exempt from taxation. The club had 700 members and owned a clubhouse. The membership was limited to residents of a town, the members being elected by the directors of the club. The purposes were to promote ethical, social, and intellectual culture in the community and to promote the mutual improvement of the members in literary and educational interests, to aid charity and to promote social intercourse. The court held that the club was a charitable organization and that the social pleasure and mutual improvement of the members were only incidental to its broader charitable purposes. In *Lawson's Estate*[22] a bequest to an unincorporated society having for its objects relief from distress of its own members and all other needy persons of British nativity and descent in Philadelphia and the promotion of social intercourse among its members was held to be charitable, and therefore to fail because the testator died within thirty days after making his will, and a statute invalidated charitable bequests when made within that period. In *In re Los Angeles*

[19][1948] Ch. 747, noted in 22 Austl. L.J. 413, 13 Convey. (N.S.) 131, 133, 138, 99 Law J. 102.

See also Queen's Univ. v. Attorney-General for N. Ir., [1966] N. Ir. L.R. 115.

[20]See §398.2, n. 12.

[21]258 Mass. 326, 154 N.E. 846 (1927).

See Neville Estates v. Madden, [1961] 3 All E.R. 769, where it was held that a trust for the members of a synagogue was charitable as a religious trust, although social activities were also carried on by the members.

[22]264 Pa. 77, 107 A. 376 (1919).

County Pioneer Society[23] a corporation organized to preserve data on the history of the county and state was held to be charitable, and its assets not distributable on dissolution among its members, although one of its purposes was to cultivate social intercourse among the members. In *Bohemian Gymnastic Association Sokol v. Higgins*[24] it was held that an association to promote various physical and mental undertakings among its members was an association exclusively for educational purposes and not a mere social club, for the purposes of the federal Social Security Act.

Whether or not a Young Men's Christian Association is a charitable organization or merely a social organization for the benefit of its members depends on the purposes of the particular association. As we have seen, it has generally been held that these associations are charitable associations, because their purposes are to provide rooming and boarding facilities and facilities for health and recreation mainly for working young people, and for their intellectual and moral improvement.[25]

It is to be constantly borne in mind that a decision that a trust or organization is not exempt from inheritance or estate taxes or income taxes or property taxes is not necessarily a decision that it is not charitable. A bequest in trust for a particular purpose may be valid as creating a charitable trust, although it may be held that there is no exemption from taxation.[26] This is clear enough where the statute giving the exemption is applicable only to certain classes of charities, as for example in Pennsylvania where the Constitution provides for exemption of institutions of purely public charity.[27] Even though there is no express limitation in the statute, it may be construed as not embracing all charities. The distinction is important where the trust is to benefit primarily a limited class or portion of the community. Thus it has been held in Massachusetts that the Boston Symphony Orchestra was subject to a property tax on its hall because it charged admission and permitted certain renew-

[23]40 Cal. 2d 852, 257 P.2d 1 (1953).
[24]147 F.2d 774 (2d Cir. 1945), noted in 45 Colum. L. Rev. 789.
[25]See §374.11.
[26]See §§348.4, 374.8.
[27]In re Hill School Tax Exemption Case, 370 Pa. 21, 87 A.2d 259 (1952) (preparatory school held exempt from tax).

able season ticket privileges.[28] Whether the decision is sound depends on questions of the interpretation of the statute permitting exemptions and on state policy. It seems perfectly clear, however, that a trust to endow a symphony orchestra in a city is not invalid as a trust in perpetuity for a noncharitable purpose. There is no doubt that the establishment of such an orchestra, which affords enjoyment and which contributes to the appreciation of fine music in the community, is a charitable purpose. If, indeed, only a limited class of persons were permitted to attend the concerts given by the orchestra, the purpose would not be charitable. The mere fact, however, that fees for admission are charged does not prevent a trust from being charitable, so long as any profits that may accrue do not inure to the benefit of private individuals.

Employees. A trust to relieve the necessities of persons who are or have been employed in a particular trade or profession is charitable.[29] Such a trust is charitable where the persons to be assisted are of small means although not in actual need. Thus a trust for the benefit of young seamstresses of a city has been upheld as charitable,[30] and a trust has been upheld to supply medical or surgical care to any member of the Customs Service in the Port of New York.[31]

[28]Boston Symphony Orchestra v. Board of Assessors, 294 Mass. 248, 1 N.E.2d 6 (1936), noted in 50 Harv. L. Rev. 489.

In Boxer v. Boston Symphony Orchestra, 339 Mass. 369, 159 N.E.2d 336 (1959) (citing the text), 342 Mass. 537, 174 N.E.2d 363 (1961) (citing the text), it was held that the Boston Symphony Orchestra is a charitable organization and not subject to tort liability. The court said that it had amended its charter so as to limit the charges for use by others of its hall to the actual expenses incurred.

[29]Thompson v. Thompson, 1 Coll. 381 (1844) (unsuccessful literary men); Hayes v. Pratt, 147 U.S. 557, 13 S. Ct. 503, 37 L. Ed. 279 (1892) (home for disabled or aged and infirm and deserving American mechanics); Minns v. Billings, 183 Mass. 126, 66 N.E. 593, 5 L.R.A. (N.S.) 686, 97 Am. St. Rep. 420 (1903) (disabled members of an association of printers or teachers or bank officers).

[30]Bowditch v. Attorney Gen., 241 Mass. 168, 134 N.E. 796, 28 A.L.R. 713 (1922).

[31]Matter of Skuse, 165 Misc. 554, 1 N.Y.S.2d 202 (1937).

In Hall v. Derby Sanitary Auth., 16 Q.B.D. 163 (1885), it was held that an institution for the support and education of children of railway employees is exempt from tax as a public charity.

Where a trust is created for the relief of poverty or the promotion of health, the fact that the benefits are confined to the employees of a particular railroad or industrial organization does not prevent the trust from being a valid charitable trust.[32]

[32]*England:* In re Gosling, 48 W.R. 300 (1900) (pensions for old and worn-out clerks of particular firm); In re Rayner, 122 L.T.R. 577 (1920) (to relieve incapacitated employees of company, and to educate children of employees) (which was disapproved in part in In re Compton, [1945] Ch. 123, 134, and in Oppenheim v. Tobacco Sec. Trust Co., [1951] A.C. 297); Gibson v. South American Stores, [1950] Ch. 177, noted in 13 Convey. (N.S.) 377, 14 id. 66, 66 Law Q. Rev. 161, 93 Sol. J. 818, *aff'g* [1949] Ch. 572; In re Coulthurst, [1951] Ch. 661, *aff'g* [1951] Ch. 193 (to apply income for benefit of widows and orphaned children of deceased officers of bank), noted in 11 Camb. L.J. 97.

Federal: Union P. R. v. Artist, 60 F. 365, 23 L.R.A. 581 (8th Cir. 1894) (hospital for employees of railroad); Eagan v. Commissioner, 43 F.2d 881, 71 A.L.R. 863 (5th Cir. 1930) (to provide living wage and protection against unemployment and sickness and to pay pensions); Harrison v. Barker Annuity Fund, 90 F.2d 286 (7th Cir. 1937) (for payment of pensions to aged members of association of employees of manufacturing company; held, association not subject to income and capital stock taxes).

California: Estate of Tarrant, 38 Cal. 2d 42, 237 P.2d 505 (1951), *rev'g* 232 P.2d 43 (1951) (bequest to the pension fund of a Canadian railway, of a domestic railway, and to the pension fund of the Railroad Retirement Board; citing the text).

Georgia: Burgess v. James, 73 Ga. App. 857, 38 S.E.2d 637 (1946) (trust for benefit of employees of manufacturing company, by relieving sick and needy, by making loans, and by affording recreation; tort case).

Kentucky: Illinois Cent. R.R. v. Buchanan, 126 Ky. 288, 103 S.W. 272 (1907) (hospital for employees of railroad).

But see Coe v. Washington Mills, 149 Mass. 543, 21 N.E. 966 (1889).

In several states it is provided by statute that a trust created as a part of an employees' pension or bonus or disability or death benefit plan is not subject to the rule against perpetuities or accumulations. See §§62.10, 62.11, 112.

In Smith v. Reynolds, 43 F. Supp. 510 (D. Minn. 1942), it was held that a beneficial association of employees of a railroad, the purpose of which was to supply medical care for its members, was not a charitable corporation for the purposes of the federal Social Security Act.

In Wachovia Bank & Trust Co. v. Steele's Mills, 225 N.C. 302, 34 S.E.2d 425 (1945), where a trust was created by a corporation for such employees as might be in need, and it was limited in duration to twenty years, it was held that a valid private trust was created.

In In re Miners' & Laborers' Beneficial Fund, 445 Pa. 65, 282 A.2d 689 (1971), where a coal company and its employees alone contributed to a fund

Even though the benefits under the trust are to be extended to employees who are not actually poverty-stricken, if they are among the underprivileged the trust may be charitable.[33]

In the English cases, however, the courts have tended to take a stricter view. Thus it has been held that a bequest for the purpose of contributing to the holiday expenses of the employees of a certain company was not charitable, it being shown that the employees were all paid as much as fifteen shillings a week and could not therefore, so said the court, be classified as poor.[34] In another

---

to provide for injuries suffered by employees, it was held that a charitable trust was not created and the cy pres doctrine was not applicable, but that it was a beneficial association whose purposes could be extended by vote of its members.

See Note, Gift to or for employees' pension fund as valid charitable gift or trust, 28 A.L.R.2d 428 (1953).

[33]Eagan v. Commissioner, 43 F.2d 881, 71 A.L.R. 863 (5th Cir. 1930); Estate of Carlson v. Commissioner, 21 T.C. 291 (1953) (to be used as retirement or welfare fund, to be distributed to employees of corporation as its directors may promulgate after counseling with committee of employees; tax case); Matter of Fanelli, 207 Misc. 719, 140 N.Y.S.2d 334 (1955) (for children of employees of a subsidiary of American Telephone & Telegraph Co.); Matter of Barbieri, 8 Misc. 2d 753, 167 N.Y.S.2d 962 (1957) (to maintain pension fund for employees of corporation).

In Matter of Reese, 21 Misc. 2d 29, 195 N.Y.S.2d 144 (1960), a trust to pay the income to a Christmas fund for employees of what was apparently a social club was upheld as charitable.

In Watson v. United States, 355 F.2d 269 (3d Cir. 1969), it was held that a bequest creating a pension trust for the employees of a corporation, without any restriction as to need, was not exempt from the federal estate tax, although a state court had held that the trust was a charitable trust and did not violate the rule against perpetuities. Two judges dissented.

In Armantrout v. Commissioner, 570 F.2d 210 (7th Cir. 1978), a corporation created a trust for the payment of educational expenses of the children of certain key employees. It was held that the employees were subject to income tax on the money so applied.

[34]In re Drummond, [1914] 2 Ch. 90.

In In re Patten, [1929] 2 Ch. 276, 289, it was held that a bequest of £100 to pay the income to the staff Christmas funds of two social clubs was not a charitable bequest. Romer, J., said that even if a trust for the encouragement of good servants is charitable, "I cannot think that the public are in any way interested in the question whether the members of the two Clubs are well or ill served."

In Wernher's Charitable Trust v. Internal Revenue Commrs., [1937] 2 All

E.R. 488, land was conveyed in trust for the benefit of the employees of a large manufacturing company as a recreation field. It was held that it was not exempt from taxation. The court held that the trust was not charitable because, although it was for the promotion of health, it was for the benefit of too limited a class of beneficiaries. No question as to the validity of the trust was involved in the decision.

In In re Koettgen's Will Trusts, [1954] Ch. 252, a testatrix bequeathed her estate in trust for the furtherance of commercial education of British-born subjects, giving preference to employees of a named company or members of their families. It was held that it was valid as a charitable trust.

In Vernon v. Inland Revenue Commrs., [1956] 3 All E.R. 14, a testator left property in trust to use the income for some organization or charity for the benefit of the employees of the testator's firm. The testator died in 1919, and on a summons brought by the trustees, the Attorney-General being a party, a compromise was effected and approved by the court, permitting the use of the funds to maintain a clubhouse for the employees and others in the village whom the trustees might select. Over thirty years later it was claimed that the trustees were liable for an income tax. It was held that they were liable. Although the disposition made was valid because it was approved by the court, the purpose was not a charitable purpose and the trustees were not exempt from the income tax.

In In re Wykes' Will Trusts, [1961] Ch. 229, noted in 24 Mod. L. Rev. 387, where a testator left property in trust for welfare purposes for the benefit of employees of a company, the court said that the trust would fail, because it was not limited to relief of poverty of the employees, but should be upheld under the Charitable Trusts (Validation) Act, 1954, because it might be applied for the relief of poverty of the employees. See §398.2, n. 31.

In Inland Revenue Commrs. v. Educational Grants Assn., [1967] Ch. 993, *aff'g* [1967] Ch. 123, where a commercial corporation created an association for the advancement of education, it was held that although the association was charitable, to the extent that it made grants for the education of children of those connected with the corporation it was subject to a tax. The court criticized In re Koettgen, [1954] Ch. 252, cited in this note.

In In re Denley's Trust Deed, [1969] 1 Ch. 373, noted in 32 Mod. L. Rev. 96, a conveyance of land was made in trust, during the lives of named persons, to use it for recreation or sports primarily for the benefit of the employees of a company, and secondarily for others whom the trustees might allow. It was held that the trust was not invalid for uncertainty as to the beneficiaries, although it was not a charitable trust.

In In re Bethel, 14 D.L.R.3d 129 (Ont. 1970), a testator made a bequest to the officers of a business corporation "to be used by them as a trust fund for any needy or deserving Toronto members of the Eaton Quarter Century Club as the said [officers] in their absolute discretion may decide." The Club was an unincorporated club of elderly employees of the corporation. It was held that the bequest failed for uncertainty and as violating the rule against perpetuities. The trust was held not to be charitable because it was for "deserving" as well as "needy" members. But the decision was reversed by the Court

case,[35] where employees of a company through weekly contributions created a benevolent fund to assist them when sick or suffering from air raids, it was held that the trust was not a charitable trust and that the doctrine of cy pres could not be applied.

At length the question of the validity of trusts for employees of a corporation came before the House of Lords. In *Oppenheim v. Tobacco Securities Trust Co.*[36] a settlor conveyed property to a trustee in trust to apply the income to the education of children of employees of a large tobacco company and its allied companies, which had 110,000 employees. It was held by the House of Lords that the trust was not charitable because the beneficiaries constituted too limited a class even though the trust was for their education, and that the trust failed. Lord Simonds hinted that the House of Lords might repudiate the cases upholding trusts for the relief of poverty of members of a limited class of persons, such as relatives.[37]

In *Dingle v. Turner*[38] the House of Lords upheld as charita-

---

of Appeal, which held that it was a charitable trust, although the beneficiaries included persons of moderate means and not merely the destitute. In re Bethel, 17 D.L.R.3d 652 (Ont. 1971). The judgment of the Court of Appeal was affirmed by the Supreme Court of Canada *sub nom.* Jones v. The T. Eaton Co., 35 D.L.R.3d 97 (1973), noted in 52 Can. B. Rev. 114 (1974).

See Stevens, Certainty and Charity, Recent Developments in the Law of Trusts, 52 Can. B. Rev. 372 (1974).

In Oesterlin v. Sands, 120 C.L.R. 346 (Austl. 1969), where a testator left shares in a company to build up a fund to be held in trust for the employees of the company, but without guidelines to the trustee, it was held that the trust failed as violating the rule against perpetuities.

[35]In re Hobourn Aero Components, Limited's Air Raid Distress Fund, [1946] Ch. 194, *aff'g* [1946] Ch. 86.

[36][1951] A.C. 297.

In George Drexler Ofrex Found. Trustees v. Inland Revenue Commrs., [1965] 3 All E.R. 529, where a trust was created for the advancement of education among employees or former employees of a large corporation or its associated companies, or the families of such persons, it was held that the trust was not for a charitable purpose and was subject to tax.

[37]See §375.3.

See Fridman, Charities and Public Benefits, 31 Can. B. Rev. 537 (1953).

[38][1972] A.C. 601, noted in 88 Law Q. Rev. 316; 36 Mod. L. Rev. 532; [1974] Camb. L.J. 63.

See Gravells, Public Purpose Trusts, 40 Mod. L. Rev. 397 (1977); Watkin, Charity: The Purport of "Purpose," [1978] Conv. 297.

ble a trust to apply the income in paying pensions to poor employees of a company largely owned by the testator. The company had over 700 employees. Their lordships examined the earlier cases on "poor relatives" and distinguished the Oppenheim case. They questioned the soundness of holding that if a trust is upheld as charitable it is necessarily exempt from taxation.

A similar question was presented to the Supreme Court of Canada in *In re Cox.* [39] In that case a testator, domiciled in Ontario, left his estate in trust to pay the income in perpetuity for charitable purposes only, adding that the persons to benefit directly were to be only employees of a certain insurance company, and that the board of directors of the company should have absolute discretion, subject to these restrictions, as to the application of the income, including the amounts to be expended and the persons to benefit therefrom. It was held that the class to be benefited, although it numbered more than 30,000, was too narrow, that the trust was therefore not charitable and failed. Two of the judges dissented on the ground that, although the direct benefits were limited to too narrow a class, there was a general charitable intention. The judgment was affirmed by the Judicial Committee of the Privy Council.

Other limited classes. Where a trust is created for the relief of poverty, it is a charitable trust although the beneficiaries are limited to the inhabitants of a particular town or parish or even

---

See also In re Denison, 42 D.L.R.3d 652 (Ont. 1974) (income for relief of impoverished members of the Law Society of Upper Canada and their wives and children).

[39] [1953] 1 S.C.R. 94 (Can.), *aff'g* [1951] 2 D.L.R. 326 (Ont.), *rev'g* [1950] 2 D.L.R. 449, noted in 31 Can. B. Rev. 1166.

The decision was affirmed in In re Cox (Baker v. National Trust Co.), [1955] A.C. 627, 51 A.L.R.2d 1285, noted in 33 Can. B. Rev. 898, 19 Mod. L. Rev. 92.

In In re Massey Trust, 21 D.L.R.2d 477 (Ont. 1959), noted in 38 Can. B. Rev. 405, a trust for the relief of poverty among employees of a business corporation was held to be valid as a charitable trust.

See Note, Gift, other than one to pension fund, for employees or former employees of a particular business or company, or their families, as valid charitable gift or trust, 51 A.L.R.2d 1290 (1957).

to the members of a particular church.[40] There are other cases in which trusts have been upheld as charitable although the recipients of benefits are to be drawn from a more or less narrow class of persons. A trust is undoubtedly charitable where it is to relieve needy veterans of a war.[41] In one case a trust was upheld in which the testator limited the class of beneficiaries to "worthy, deserving, poor, white, American, Protestant, Democratic widows and orphans" residing in a certain town, although there might not be many persons to whom all these adjectives could be applied.[42]

A trust is charitable where it is for the relief of persons suffering from a particular disaster such as a fire[43] or

[40]*Kansas:* In re Estate of Freshour, 185 Kan. 434, 345 P.2d 689, 81 A.L.R.2d 806 (1959) (for a parish and for the members of a particular church; citing the text).

New Jersey: Wilkinson's Exrs. v. Trustees, 38 N.J. Eq. 514 (1884), *aff'g* 36 N.J. Eq. 141 (1882).

North Carolina: Keith v. Scales, 124 N.C. 497, 32 S.E. 809 (1899) (particular school).

Pennsylvania: Witman v. Lex, 17 S.&R. 88, 17 Am. Dec. 644 (Pa. 1827); Reeser Estate, 1 D.&C.2d 731 (Pa. 1954) (to provide for medical education of boy belonging to particular church; citing Restatement of Trusts §375).

Wisconsin: Richtman v. Watson, 150 Wis. 385, 136 N.W. 797 (1912).

See Dawson, "Old Presbyterian Persons" — a Sufficient Section of the Public? [1987] Conv. 114.

[41]*Massachusetts:* Holmes v. Coates, 159 Mass. 226, 34 N.E. 190 (1893) (disabled soldiers and sailors who served in Union Army in the Civil War).

New Hampshire: Carter v. Whitcomb, 74 N.H. 482, 69 A. 779, 17 L.R.A. (N.S.) 733 (1908) (needy members of Grand Army of the Republic in vicinity of certain town).

New Zealand: In re Booth, [1954] N.Z.L.R. 1114 (needy New Zealand servicemen in Second World War).

[42]Beardsley v. Selectmen of Bridgeport, 53 Conn. 489, 3 A. 557, 55 Am. Rep. 152 (1885).

[43]Doyle v. Whalen, 87 Me. 414, 32 A. 1022, 31 L.R.A. 118 (1895); Hill v. Moors, 224 Mass. 163, 112 N.E. 641 (1916).

See Kirwin v. Attorney Gen., 275 Mass. 34, 175 N.E. 164 (1931), noted in 19 Geo. L.J. 507.

In Boenhardt v. Loch, 129 A.D. 355, 113 N.Y.S. 747 (1908), where funds were contributed for the relief of sufferers from the destruction by fire of a ship, it was held that one who suffered from the disaster had no standing to compel the payment of a part of the fund to him. See §391, n. 37.

flood.[44] A trust has been upheld as charitable where it is for the benefit of persons suffering from a widespread strike.[45]

In England the court went perhaps too far in upholding as charitable a trust for the benefit of the poor on a particular estate.[46] So also it was held that a statutory trust under which a portion of a common was to be allotted to the occupiers for the time being of certain cottages was a charitable trust.[47] On the other hand, in an Irish case it was held that a trust for the benefit of the tenantry of the settlor was not a charitable trust.[48]

In *Davies v. Perpetual Trustee Co.*[49] a resident of New Zealand left his estate after the termination of life interests

---

[44]Kerner v. Thompson, 293 Ill. App. 454, 13 N.E.2d 110 (1938), *cert. denied sub nom.* Thompson v. Kerner, 308 U.S. 635 (1938), noted in 26 Ill. B.J. 385.

[45]Attorney Gen. v. Bedard, 218 Mass. 378, 105 N.E. 993 (1914).

[46]Bristow v. Bristow, 5 Beav. 289 (1842).

[47]In re Christchurch Inclosure Act, 38 Ch. D. 520 (1888), *aff'd sub nom.* Attorney-General v. Meyrick, [1895] A.C. 1.

[48]Browne v. King, 17 L.R. Ir. 448 (1885).

[49][1959] A.C. 439.

In England the law as to the exemption from tax on land was liberalized by an Act of Parliament in 1955. Rating and Valuation (Miscellaneous Provisions) Act, 1955, 4 & 5 Eliz. II, c. 9, §8. The Act exempted any hereditaments occupied for the purposes of an organization not established or conducted for profit and whose main objects were charitable or were otherwise concerned with the advancement of religion, education, "or social welfare." In Skegness Urban Dist. Council v. Derbyshire Miners' Welfare Comm., [1959] A.C. 807, *aff'g* [1958] 1 Q.B. 298, noted in 75 Law Q. Rev. 293, it was held·that a trust of premises used for recreation for coal mine workers in Derbyshire was one for social welfare and was exempt from the tax. Although the trust was not a charitable trust because it afforded benefits for only a limited class in the community, it fell within the broader concept of social welfare. Lord Simonds said, "There is no justification for supposing that the legislature intended to import the highly artificial considerations, which distinguish or disfigure the law of charity, into the latter part of the subsection. Neither the words themselves nor the context demand it and I think that all the court has to do is to forget all the refinements of charity law and ask itself the simple question that I have already posed."

On the other hand, it was held by the House of Lords in National Deposit Friendly Socy. Trustees v. Skegness Urban Dist. Council, [1959] A.C. 293, *aff'g* [1957] 2 Q.B. 573, that the Act did not exempt a friendly society from liability with respect to a convalescent home conducted for the benefit of the members who numbered more than 700,000.

to the Presbyterians the descendants of those settled in the Colony hailing from or born in the North of Ireland to be held in trust for the purpose of establishing a college for the education and tuition of their youth in the standards of the Westminster Divines as taught in the Holy Scriptures.

The disposition was upheld as charitable by the Supreme Court of New South Wales, but its judgment was reversed by the Judicial Committee of the Privy Council, which held that although the trust was concerned with education and religion, it was not charitable because the beneficiaries constituted a fluctuating body of private individuals and the element of public benefit was therefore lacking.

As we have seen, a trust to promote the happiness or well-being of members of the community is charitable, although it is not a trust to relieve poverty, advance education, promote religion, or protect health.[50] In such a case, however, the trust must be for the benefit of the members of the community generally and not merely for the benefit of a class of persons. It is true that it need not directly benefit all the members of the community. Thus a trust to employ all legal and moral means to destroy and prevent discrimination against blacks in the United States has been held to be charitable.[51] A trust is nonetheless charitable although the persons to be benefited are limited to the inhabitants of a particular town, even though the trust is one for the general benefit of the inhabitants and is not limited to the relief of poverty or the advancement of education or religion or health. Thus in the well-known English case of *Goodman v. Mayor of Saltash*,[52] decided by the House of Lords, it was said that a grant of a fishery subject to a provi-

---

Section 8 of the 1955 Act was superseded by the Rating and Valuation Act 1961, §11, which is superseded by the General Rate Act 1967, §§39, 40. This gives full land tax exemption only to places of religious worship. Hereditaments held on trust and used for charity or almshouses get a 50 percent reduction in taxes.

In In re Mason (deceased), [1971] N.Z.L.R. 714, the court held a gift to a noncharitable society for library purposes was valid only as to purposes that would benefit the community at large.

[50]See §§374-374.12.

[51]Lewis's Estate, 152 Pa. 477, 25 A. 878 (1893).

[52]7 App. Cas. 633 (1882).

sion that the free inhabitants of a borough should be entitled to fish during a certain season created a charitable trust that was not invalid as a perpetuity.

But a trust unconnected with the relief of poverty or the advancement of education or religion or health in order to be charitable must be for the benefit of a larger class than need be benefited if the trust is connected with such purposes. Thus although, as we have seen, a trust for the relief of poverty is charitable even if confined to persons following a particular calling or persons in a particular employment, a trust for the general benefit of such persons is not charitable. In an English case it was held that a trust "for the benefit of individuals who have been engaged in the Oporto Red or Port St. Mary's White Sherry Wine Trade" was not charitable.[53] In an Irish case it was held that a bequest made by one O'Laverty to contribute toward the support and education in Ireland of any Roman Catholic boys of the surname of O'Laverty or Laverty or O'Lafferty or Lafferty, between the ages of 11 and 23, was not charitable.[54] The purpose of the trust was not limited to the relief of poor boys of the designated names nor was it limited to education. According to the terms of the trust the money might be used to support wealthy boys of the designated surnames. The court said of this trust: "Its purposes can hardly be regarded as one of those general purposes beneficial to the community, or to some class of the community, which have been held charitable without any element of the relief of poverty, or advancement of religion or education." In *Bullock v. Commissioner of Corporations and Taxation*[55] it was held that a gift to a private cemetery corporation was not free of tax, because the burial services were limited to the owners of lots in the cemetery, although there was no restriction on the attendance by others at services in the chapel.[56]

[53]In re Gassiot, 70 L.J. Ch. 242 (1901).
[54]Laverty v. Laverty, [1907] 1 I.R. 9, 13.
[55]260 Mass. 129, 156 N.E. 743 (1927).
[56]In Illinois Hosp. & Health Serv., v. Aurand, 58 Ill. App. 3d 79, 15 Ill. Dec. 549, 373 N.E.2d 1021 (1978), *cert. denied,* 440 U.S. 916 (1978), a health organization gave services only to members who paid dues. It was held that it was not a charitable organization even though there was a gift over on dissolution for charitable purposes.

Business purposes. A purpose may be held to be noncharitable because it is for the financial or commercial benefit of a group of persons. In most of the cases in which it has been so held the question was whether an organization was exempt from taxation as a charitable institution. It is to be borne in mind that a holding that the purposes are not charitable within a statute granting exemption from taxation does not necessarily mean that the purposes may not be held to be charitable when the question is not one of such exemption. In *Better Business Bureau v. United States*[57] it was held that a corporation formed "for the mutual welfare protection and improvement of business methods . . . and for the educational and scientific advancements of business methods" in the District of Columbia was not exempt as a charity from taxation under the Social Security Act. In *Boston Chamber of Commerce v. Assessors of Boston*[58] it was held that the Boston Chamber of Commerce, the dominant purpose of which was to foster and promote good business and commerce in Boston and New England, was not exempt from tax as a charitable organization. In *Assessors of Boston v. Boston Pilots' Relief Society*[59] a corporation organized to furnish aid and relief to the pilots of Boston and their families was held not to be exempt from taxation as a benevolent or charitable corporation, because the members paid substantial admission and annual dues, and on retirement were entitled to substantial monthly payments irrespective of need, and in case of death the widow and children of a member were entitled to such payments regardless of need. In an English case[60] a corporation formed "to watch over and protect the interests and rights of holders of public securities wherever issued but especially of foreign and colonial securities issued in the United Kingdom" was held not exempt

[57] 326 U.S. 279, 66 S. Ct. 112, 90 L. Ed. 67 (1945).

[58] 315 Mass. 712, 54 N.E.2d 199, 152 A.L.R. 174 (1944).

To the same effect, see Memphis Chamber of Commerce v. City of Memphis, 144 Tenn. 291, 232 S.E. 73 (1921).

But compare Corporation of Chamber of Commerce v. Bennett, 143 Misc. 513, 257 N.Y.S. 2 (1932).

[59] 311 Mass. 232, 40 N.E.2d 889 (1942).

[60] Corporation of Foreign Bondholders v. Commissioners of Inland Revenue, [1944] K.B. 63, *aff'd,* [1944] K.B. 403, noted in 60 Law Q. Rev. 120, 224, 7 Mod. L. Rev. 234.

from tax as a charity. The court pointed out that the primary object was to see that creditors were paid and only indirectly was the public benefited. In a case in Northern Ireland[61] it was held that a corporation created by the Ministry of Agriculture to market pigs for the purpose of assisting the depressed business of pig marketing was not exempt from income tax as a charitable corporation. In a Canadian case[62] it was held that the Saskatchewan Farmers' Union, the chief purpose of which was to influence legislation and trade in farm products, was an organization with political and commercial objects and was not charitable. In a case decided by the Judicial Committee of the Privy Council[63] a testator left his estate in trust to establish a bank, the object being primarily to assist the planters and agriculturists in a district, by making loans at as low a rate of interest as is compatible with the proper operation of the bank. It was held that the disposition was not for a charitable purpose and that it failed.

On the other hand, there are cases upholding trusts where the purpose is to promote the economic benefit of a community. In *Powell Estate*[64] a trust of $100,000 to apply the income in making a quadrennial award to the citizen of Philadelphia who should by his application to its manufacturing and commercial interests produce the best results for the prosperity of the city was upheld as charitable. In *Attinson v. Consumer-Farmer Milk Corporation*[65] it was held that a cooperative corporation organized to benefit farmers and consumers through the distribution of milk and other products and otherwise to serve the economic and cultural welfare of its members and of the public was a charitable corporation, and that on its dissolution its property should be applied cy pres and not divided among the members.

A trust may fail to be a charitable trust because it is primarily of benefit to a particular business corporation.[66] In *In re*

[61]Pig Mktg. Bd. (N. Ir.) v. Commissioners of Inland Revenue, [1945] N. Ir. L.R. 155.

[62]In re Patriotic Acre Fund, [1951] 2 D.L.R. 624 (Sask.).

[63]Hadaway v. Hadaway, [1955] 1 W.L.R. 16.

[64]71 D.&C. 51 (Pa. 1950).

[65]197 Misc. 336, 94 N.Y.S.2d 891 (1950).

[66]In Martin v. North Hill Christian Church, 64 Ohio App. 2d 192, 18 Ohio Ops. 3d 147, 412 N.E.2d 413 (1979), it was held that a student loan fund to aid students in a school was not charitable, because it was of benefit to the shareholders of the school.

Leverhulme[67] Lord Leverhulme, the head of Lever Bros., Ltd., a manufacturing corporation, bequeathed property in trust for a Staff Training College, an unincorporated organization for the technical and general education of the employees of the corporation. It was held that the purpose was not charitable and that the trust failed. Morton, J., said:

> I think there is no doubt that one of the excellent objects which the late Lord Leverhulme had in view when he formulated this scheme was to make the employees of Lever Bros., Ltd., better fitted to discharge their duties, although no doubt he may have had in mind their general education from other aspects as well.

He held that there was not a beneficial gift to the corporation itself.

In *Northeast Osteopathic Hospital v. Keitel*[68] it was held that an osteopathic hospital was not operated exclusively for charitable purposes within the meaning of the Missouri Unemployment Compensation Act, because one of its purposes was to foster facilities for the practice of osteopathy by the physicians.

So also an organization of employees formed for their financial benefit is not a charitable organization. Thus a trust for a trade union is not a charitable trust.[69] But it has been held that

[67][1943] 2 All E.R. 143, noted in 60 Law Q. Rev. 27.

[68]355 Mo. 740, 197 S.W.2d 970 (1946).

See Harding Hosp. v. United States, 505 F.2d 1069 (6th Cir. 1974) (hospital not exempt from federal income tax).

[69]In re Amos, [1891] 2 Ch. 159; County Assessor v. United Bhd. of Carpenters, 202 Okla. 162, 211 P.2d 790 (1949).

In Langham v. Peterson, 87 L.T. (N.S.) 744 (1903), legacies to two trade guilds "for the benefit of hospitality" were upheld as absolute gifts.

In Commonwealth, by Packel of Pa. v. Frantz Advertising, 23 Pa. Commw. 526, 353 A.2d 492 (1976), it was held that a police fraternal organization was not a charitable organization because it was essentially a labor organization existing solely for the benefit of its members.

In International Found. of Employee Benefit Plans v. City of Brookfield, 95 Wis. 2d 444, 290 N.W.2d 720 (1980), *aff'd.* 100 Wis. 2d 66, 301 N.W.2d 175 (1981), it was held that an organization formed to provide educational help to trustees of employee benefit plans was not exempt from a property tax.

In In re Mead's Trust Deed, [1961] 2 All E.R. 836, where a trust was created to establish a home for the aged members of a trade union, it was held that the trust was not charitable, because it was limited to members of the

a trust for the benefit of members of a particular local of a trade union to be used for the benefit of members in periods of unemployment and members over the age of 65 is charitable.[70]

Professional associations.   The question has arisen whether bar associations are charitable organizations for tax purposes.[71] In *Dulles v. Johnson*[72] it was held that bequests to certain bar associations were deductible in computing the net taxable estate under the Internal Revenue Code of 1939, §812(b). The court below took the view that the associations "exist primarily to benefit members of the legal profession, and to provide a method whereby their views and recommendations as a body on legislation of various kinds is made known to the legislators," and that their purposes were not solely charitable. The Court of Appeals reversed, holding that the purposes of the associations were charitable. In *Rhode Island Hospital Trust Co. v. United States*[73] it was held that a bequest to the Rhode Island Bar Association to be used for the advancement of standards of the legal profession was a gift in trust for a charitable purpose and was deductible in computing the estate tax. In *Pennsylvania Bar Association Endowment v. Robins,*[74] however, it was held that a building owned by the Pennsylvania Bar Association was subject to a property tax.

---

union and was not exclusively for the relief of poverty. The court held, however, that the provision was an "imperfect trust provision" within the Charitable Trusts (Validation) Act, 1954 (see §398.2, n. 31).

[70]Matter of Pattberg, 282 A.D. 770, 123 N.Y.S.2d 564 (1953), *aff'd mem.,* 306 N.Y. 835, 118 N.E.2d 903 (1954), noted in 23 Fordham L. Rev. 220.

[71]See Note, Bequests to bar associations as deductible or exempt from estate and succession taxes, 80 A.L.R.2d 1350 (1961).

[72]273 F.2d 362, 80 A.L.R.2d 1338 (2d Cir. 1959), *cert. denied,* 364 U.S. 834 (1960), *rev'g* 155 F. Supp. 275 (S.D.N.Y. 1957).

In St. Louis Union Trust Co. v. United States, 374 F.2d 427 (8th Cir. 1967), it was held that a bequest to the Bar Association of St. Louis was tax deductible as charitable.

In Association of Bar of City of N.Y. v. Lewisohn, 34 N.Y.2d 143, 313 N.E.2d 30, 356 N.Y.S.2d 555 (1974), reversing the courts below, it was held that the Association of the Bar of the City of New York was not a charitable institution and that its premises were subject to the city property tax.

[73]159 F. Supp. 204 (D.R.I. 1958).

[74]10 D.&C.2d 637 (Pa. 1955).

Apart from questions of taxation, the question may arise whether the bar association is a charitable organization. In *Thomas v. Harrison*[75] it was held that a bequest to the Cleveland Bar Association was charitable and therefore failed because of violation of a statute forbidding charitable bequests by a will executed within one year of the testator's death.

In *Massachusetts Medical Society v. Assessors of Boston*[76] it was held that the Massachusetts Medical Society was not exempt as a charity from a property tax, because it was organized and operated for the benefit of its members as well as to aid needy medical students and doctors.[77]

§375.3. **Trusts for relatives.** As we have seen, a valid trust may be created in favor of such relatives of the testator as the trustee may select.[1] In such a case, unless it is otherwise provided by the terms of the trust, the trustee may select relatives who are not among the next of kin of the testator; but if he makes no selection, the next of kin are entitled to the property in equal shares. Such a trust is not, of course, a charitable trust. A testator may make a bequest for the benefit of his poor relations. Whether the benefits of the trust are to be confined to such poor relations as are included among his next of kin or extend to persons more remotely related to him is a question of

[75]92 Ohio Abs. 175, 191 N.E.2d 862 (1962).

In Smith v. Brooklyn Bar Assn., 266 A.D. 1038, 44 N.Y.S.2d 620 (1943), *aff'd sub nom.* Claim of Smith, 292 N.Y. 593, 55 N.E.2d 368 (1944), it was held that in view of the activities of the Brooklyn Bar Association in the furtherance of the economic advancement of its members, it was not a charitable organization for the purposes of the Unemployment Insurance Law.

[76]340 Mass. 327, 164 N.E.2d 325 (1960).

See Appeal of Lanchester Medical Center Assn., 23 Pa. Commw. 596, 353 A.2d 75 (1976) (a tax case).

In Hammerstein v. Kelley, 349 F.2d 928 (8th Cir. 1965), it was held that a bequest to the St. Louis Medical Society was not tax deductible as a charity. The same result was reached in Krohn v. United States, 246 F. Supp. 341 (D. Colo. 1965).

[77]See American Inst. of Indus. Engrs. v. Chilivis, 236 Ga. 793, 225 S.E.2d 308 (1976) (organization of dues-paying members to promote advancement of industrial engineering held to be for the benefit of the members and not exempt from taxation).

§375.3. [1]See §121.

construction of the will.[2] In any event it would seem that the trust is not a charitable trust, because the class of persons to be benefited is too narrow, but it is valid as a private trust.[3] In some cases the courts have called the trust a charitable trust even though the benefits were confined to such poor relations as were included among the testator's next of kin; but these dicta can hardly be supported.

A more interesting question arises where a trust in favor of the relatives of the testator is not a trust for immediate distribution but one that is to continue indefinitely. Where a testator bequeaths money in trust to apply the income for the benefit of

---

[2]Carr v. Bedford, 2 Rep. Ch. 77 (1679); Griffith v. Jones, 2 Rep. Ch. 179 (1687); Edge v. Salisbury, Amb. 70 (1749); Gower v. Mainwaring, 2 Ves. Sr. 87, 110 (1750); Isaac v. DeFriez, Amb. 595, 17 Ves. 373n (1754); Brunsden v. Woolredge, Amb. 507 (1765); Widmore v. Woodroffe, Amb. 636 (1766); Bronson v. Strouse, 57 Conn. 147, 17 A. 699 (1889).

See Webster v. Morris, 66 Wis. 366, 28 N.W. 353, 57 Am. Rep. 278 (1886).

For the early cases on trusts for relatives, see Jones, History of the Law of Charity, 1532-1827 (1969).

[3]In re Scarisbrick, [1950] Ch. 226, *rev'd,* [1951] 1 Ch. 622, noted in 11 Camb. L.J. 97, 282, 14 Convey, (N.S.) 66, 66 Law Q. Rev. 161, 68 id. 9, 209 Law T. 137.

In Matter of Baumwald, 192 Misc. 846, 81 N.Y.S.2d 779 (1948), a testator left property in trust to expend the income and principal in bringing the testator's relatives to the United States and to provide for their support. It was held that the trust was not charitable, and because it was to last beyond two lives it failed.

In In re Doering, [1949] 1 D.L.R. 267 (Ont.), a testator left the residue of his estate in trust to use the income to educate the male descendants of his father so as to imbue them with the father's religious faith. It was provided that the trust should terminate 21 years after the death of the last survivor of such descendants who were living at the testator's death, and the property was then given to two charitable institutions. It was held that the trust as to the income was valid although not charitable. See §371.6, n. 7.

In Salveson's Trustees v. Wye, [1954] Sess. Cas. 440 (Scot.), a testator directed that a share of the residue should be disposed of by his trustees among "any poor relations, friends or acquaintances of mine" or former employees of his firm, or their wives, or to certain charitable purposes. It was held that the disposition failed altogether and that the property passed by intestacy. The court held that the trust was not charitable, although limited to poor persons, since the class was too indefinite. See §122, n. 7.

In Will of Scales, [1972] 2 N.S.W.R. 108 (N.S.W.), the court said that a trust for needy relatives was charitable, but that it did not violate the rule against perpetuities and would be valid even if not charitable.

his descendants, and the purposes of the trust are not limited to the relief of poverty or the promotion of education, the trust is not a charitable trust, and if it is to continue beyond the period of the rule against perpetuities it fails.[4] Where the trust is for the benefit of needy descendants of the testator, however, or where it is a trust to educate his descendants, there is a conflict of opinion on the question whether a valid charitable trust is created. In England the courts have upheld such trusts.[5] But in more recent decisions the English courts have tended to hold that such trusts are not charitable trusts and will therefore fail. In *In re Compton*[6] a testatrix left money in trust to use the income

[4]St. Paul's Church v. Attorney Gen., 164 Mass. 188, 41 N.E. 231 (1895); Amory v. Trustees of Amherst College, 229 Mass. 374, 118 N.E. 933 (1918).

In In re Zeagman, 37 Ont. L. Rep. 536 (1916), a bequest for the saying of masses for the souls of the descendants of the testator forever was held invalid, the court holding that the purpose was not charitable.

Some schools of Islamic jurisprudence treat as charitable and valid trusts for the benefit of descendants of the settlor in perpetuity, at least if the ultimate remainder upon the descendants becoming extinct is to public charity. See Fratcher, The Islamic Wakf, 36 Mo. L. Rev. 153, 161 (1971).

[5]Flood's Case, Hob. 136 (1571) (to college to find a scholar of testator's poor relations); White v. White, 7 Ves. 422 (1802) (perpetual fund to apprentice testator's poor relations); Attorney-General v. Price, 17 Ves. 371 (1810) (annual distribution among testator's poor kinsmen); Attorney-General v. Sidney Sussex College, 34 Beav. 654 (1865), L.R. 4 Ch. 722 (1869) (to college for education of descendants of testator's brothers and sisters); Gillam v. Taylor, L.R. 16 Eq. 581 (1873) (permanent fund for needy descendants of testator's uncle); Attorney-General v. Duke of Northumberland, 7 Ch. D. 745 (1877) (perpetual fund for poor kindred of testator); In re Scarisbrick, [1951] Ch. 622, *rev'g* [1950] Ch. 226 (for needy relatives of children of testatrix); In re Lavelle, [1914] 1 I.R. 194 (perpetual fund to educate testator's relatives).

In In re Cohn, [1952] 3 D.L.R. 833 (N.S.), the court upheld as charitable a trust to apply the income for the support of poor and needy relatives of the testatrix for a period of twenty years.

In In re Cohen, [1973] 1 All E.R. 889, a testatrix made a bequest in trust to apply the whole or any parts for the benefit of any of her relatives whom the trustees shall consider to be in special need. The trustees were given absolute and uncontrolled discretion without accountability. It was held that this did not confer a special power of appointment but created a valid charitable trust for her needy relatives, whether born or not at the time of her death.

See Zweibel, Looking the Gift Horse in the Mouth: an Examination of Charitable Gifts which Benefit the Donor, 31 McGill L.J. 417 (1986).

[6][1945] Ch. 123, *rev'g* [1944] Ch. 378, noted in 18 Austl. L.J. 292, 19 id. 21, 20 id. 432, 9 Convey. (N.S.) 86, 152, 179, 79 Ir. L.T. 91, 94 Law J. 413, 61 Law Q. Rev. 20, 62 id. 234, 199 Law T. 61, 201 id. 41, 7 Mod. L. Rev. 231.

to educate the descendants of three named persons, including her grandfathers. It was held that the trust failed. The Court of Appeal took the view that the cases involving the relief of poverty of descendants of the testator or of other named persons should not be extended to permit a trust for the education of such descendants when not in need. In *Oppenheim v. Tobacco Securities Trust Co.,* [7] where the House of Lords held invalid a trust for the education of children of employees of a large tobacco company, Lord Simonds suggested that the House of Lords might not follow the lower courts in upholding trusts for the relief of poverty of members of a limited class such as relatives of the settlor or of others.

In several cases in the United States it has been held that the class of beneficiaries is too narrow and that the intended trust fails.[8] It is believed that the American cases are based on

---

To the same effect, see In re McEnery, [1941] I.R. 323.

In Caffoor v. Income Tax Commr., [1961] A.C. 584, a person domiciled in Ceylon created there a trust under which the income was to be applied for the education of deserving youths of the Islamic faith. It was further provided that the beneficiaries should be selected from the descendants of the grantor or of his brothers or sisters, failing whom other youths of the Islamic faith might be selected. It was held that this was a family trust and was not exempt from income tax in Ceylon as a charitable trust. The members of the family were given absolute priority and not merely a preference.

Some schools of Islamic jurisprudence would treat such a trust as charitable and valid. Fratcher, The Islamic Wakf, 36 Mo. L. Rev. 153, 161 (1971).

[7][1951] A.C. 297. See §375.2, n. 36.

In George Drexler Ofrex Found. Trustees v. Inland Revenue Commrs., [1966] Ch. 675, the principal shareholder of a commercial corporation created a trust for education and the relief of poverty. It was provided that if the directors so directed, 60 percent of surplus income should be applied for needy former employees of the corporation or their families or for their education. It was held that the trust for this purpose was not charitable, but that the trust was otherwise valid and entitled to tax exemption. See the text, §375.2, n. 36.

[8]*Federal:* Brennan v. United States, 129 F. Supp. 155 (D. Conn. 1954) (for medical care of descendants of donor's parents; tax case).

Georgia: Hardage v. Hardage, 211 Ga. 80, 84 S.E.2d 54 (1954) (for medical care of testator's needy relatives and for educational loans to their dependents; quoting the text and Restatement of Trusts §375).

Kentucky: Johnson v. De Pauw Univ., 116 Ky. 671, 76 S.W. 851 (1903) (for educating descendants of two named persons).

Massachusetts: Kent v. Dunham, 142 Mass. 216, 7 N.E. 730, 56 Am. Rep.

sound policy. There is no good reason why a man who has acquired property should be permitted to make provision for the perpetual care or education of his descendants.

The same principles are applicable where a trust is created for the descendants of a person other than the testator himself. Thus in *Matter of Beekman*[9] it was held that the Beekman Family Association was not a charitable organization. This was a corporation whose objects were to educate such members of the Beekman family as might be designated by the directors, to aid poor members of the family, to preserve heirlooms, to publish the history of the family, and to care for burial lots of members of the family. All descendants of William Beekman who came to America in 1647 were eligible as members of the family. The court held that a bequest to the corporation was subject to a transfer tax, because it was not a charitable organization.

On the other hand, in the United States as well as in England it is held that a trust for the relief of poverty or the promotion of education is charitable, although by the terms of the trust it is provided that in selecting beneficiaries preference

---

667 (1886) (for aid and support of destitute descendants of testator); Talbot v. Riggs, 287 Mass. 144, 191 N.E. 360, 93 A.L.R. 964 (1934) (perpetual trust for support, education, or comfort of needy descendants of testator's parents), noted in 15 B.U.L. Rev. 404, 19 Minn. L. Rev. 127, 2 U. Chi. L. Rev. 156.

New Jersey: In re Butler, 137 N.J. Eq. 48, 42 A.2d 857 (1945) (*semble;* citing the text), *aff'd mem.,* 137 N.J. Eq. 457, 45 A.2d 598 (1946).

New York: Matter of MacDowell, 217 N.Y. 454, 112 N.E. 177, L.R.A. 1916E 1246, Ann. Cas. 1917E 853 (1916) (home for benefit of poor relatives and descendants of designated persons; *semble*).

Ohio: Jones v. Webster, 133 Ohio St. 492, 14 N.E.2d 928 (1938) (perpetual trust for scholarships for descendants of testator).

Pennsylvania: Ramsey Estate, 7 D.&C.2d 763 (Pa. 1955) (trust for benefit of indigent orphan descendants of testator's father for 200 years and then for charity; quoting the text and Restatement of Trusts, §375, Comment *c*).

[9] 232 N.Y. 365, 134 N.E. 183 (1922).

See In re Tree, [1945] Ch. 325, noted in 19 Austl. L.J. 122 (1945), 10 Convey. (N.S.) 53 (1945), 61 Law Q. Rev. 339 (1945), 199 Law T. 197 (1945), upholding a trust to assist in the emigration to the British Dominions of persons who had resided in a certain borough prior to 1880 and their descendants.

See also Matter of Gottlieb, 193 Misc. 940, 85 N.Y.S.2d 701 (1948), holding that a gift to a corporation organized for the benefit of needy relatives of the testator was not exempt from transfer tax as a charitable corporation.

should be given to relatives or descendants of the testator or of other designated persons.[10]

[10]*England:* Spencer v. All Souls College, Wilm. Notes 163 (1762) (for establishing fellowship in college, preference to be given to testator's poor relations); Braund v. Earl of Devon, L.R. 3 Ch. App. 800 (1868) (for founding free school, preference to be given to lineal descendants of testator's grandfather).

Federal: Perin v. Carey, 24 How. 465, 16 L. Ed. 701 (U.S. 1860) (for founding college, preference to be given in applications for admission to relatives and descendants of the testator and of other designated persons); Canal Natl. Bank v. United States, 258 F. Supp. 626 (D. Me. 1966) (precatory provision; a tax case; citing the text and Restatement of Trusts, §375, Comment *d*).

See Schoellkopf v. United States, 124 F.2d 982 (2d Cir. 1942) (citing Restatement of Trusts, §375, Comment *c*), *aff'g* 36 F. Supp. 617 (W.D.N.Y. 1941) (provision that descendants of donor's father may be beneficiaries if needy, held not taxable).

Alabama: Tarver v. Weaver, 221 Ala. 663, 130 So. 209 (1930) (trust for university scholarships with preference to descendants of named relative of testator).

Georgia: Trammell v. Elliott, 230 Ga. 841, 199 S.E.2d 194 (1973) (scholarship fund with preference to descendants of testatrix's parents).

Illinois: Continental Ill. Natl. Bank & Trust Co. v. Harris, 359 Ill. 86, 194 N.E. 250 (1935) (farmers' home).

Massachusetts: Darcy v. Kelley, 153 Mass. 433, 26 N.E. 1110 (1891) (perpetual fund for poor, preference to be given to testator's poor relatives); Dexter v. President and Fellows of Harvard College, 176 Mass. 192, 57 N.E. 371 (1900) (to college for the education of descendants of testator's grandparents, any excess to be expended for the general purposes of the college).

New Jersey: In re Butler, 137 N.J. Eq. 48, 42 A.2d 857 (1945), *aff'd mem.,* 137 N.J. Eq. 457, 45 A.2d 598 (1946) (scholarships, preference to be given to descendants of testator's brothers and sisters if in need of assistance; citing the text and Restatement of Trusts, §375, Comment *c*).

New York: Matter of MacDowell, 217 N.Y. 454, 112 N.E. 177, L.R.A. 1916E 1246, Ann. Cas. 1917E 853 (1916) (home for poor gentlewomen, preference to be given to descendants of testatrix and of other designated persons).

Pennsylvania: Commonwealth Trust Co. of Pittsburgh v. Granger, 57 F. Supp. 502 (W.D. Pa. 1944) (scholarships, with preference to needy relatives having the testator's surname; quoting the text and Restatement of Trusts, §375, Comment *c*); Stewart's Estate, 48 D.&C. 526 (Pa. 1943) (scholarship fund, with preference to kinsfolk of testatrix; quoting Restatement of Trusts, §375, Comment *c*); Glant Will, 48 D.&C.2d 791 (Pa. 1969) (to establish educational loan funds, with the expression of a desire that applications from the descendants of certain relatives "be regarded kindly," and a statement that this is "precatory and not mandatory," held charitable).

See also Eberhardt Estate, 2 D.&C.3d 154 (Pa. 1976) (citing the text and

In *Stanton v. Stanton*[11] a testator left his estate to trustees and directed that his residence should be maintained as a memorial to his parents and for the benefit of their descendants as long as there should be any living. It was held that the testator intended to provide only for such of the descendants as were living at the time of his death, and that the trust was valid, although it was not a charitable trust, because there was no violation of the rule against perpetuities.

§376. *Private Profit*

If an undertaking is conducted for private profit, it is not charitable. This is true although the purposes are such that, if it were not conducted for private profit, it would be charitable. Thus an educational institution or a hospital or a home that is privately owned and conducted for the financial benefit of the owner is not a charitable institution.[1] Such an institution is, of

---

Restatement of Trusts, §370, Comment *k,* and §375, Comment *d;* a tax case); Blackwood Estate, 2 D.&C.3d 80 (Pa. 1977).

West Virginia: Gallaher v. Gallaher, 106 W. Va. 588, 146 S.E. 623 (1929) (scholarships in college, with preference to descendants of certain relatives of testator).

Canada: Herbert v. Cyr & Lynch, [1944] 2 D.L.R. 374 (N.B.) (for education of poor boys, with preference to relatives of testatrix).

See Note, Provision for relief or education of member of family or relatives as creating charitable trust, 131 A.L.R. 1277 (1941).

In Griffin v. United States, 267 F. Supp. 142 (E.D. Ky. 1967), where a testator created a trust to educate his grandchildren, not exceeding $750 a year for each grandchild, the trust to terminate in 21 years, and subject thereto for financial assistance for needy students, it was held that because the amount available for charitable purposes could not be ascertained, the federal estate tax was not subject to a charitable deduction.

[11]140 Conn. 504, 101 A.2d 789 (1953) (citing the text and Restatement of Trusts §375).

§376. [1]*Federal:* Founding Church of Scientology v. United States, 412 F.2d 1197 (Ct. Cl. 1969), *cert. denied,* 397 U.S. 1009, 95 S. Ct. 1237, 25 L. Ed. 2d 422 (for a church, but with many benefits for the founder and his family; a tax case); Christian Manner Intl. v. Commissioner, 71 T.C. 661 (1979) (sale by religious association of books written by founder, giving him a profit; a tax case); EST of Hawaii v. Commissioner, 71 T.C. 1067 (1979) (a tax case).

California: Alcoser v. County of San Diego, 111 Cal. App. 3d 907, 169 Cal. Rptr. 90 (1980) (vocational school for the benefit of employers; a tax case).

course, not exempt from taxation nor is a devise or bequest to

---

Connecticut: Hawthorne v. Blythewood, 118 Conn. 617, 174 A. 81 (1934).

Delaware: Sussex Trust Co. v. Beebe Hospital, 25 Del. Ch. 172, 15 A.2d 246 (1940) (citing the text and Restatement of Trusts §376).

Illinois: People ex rel. Redfern v. Hopewell Farms, 9 Ill. App. 3d 16, 291 N.E.2d 288 (1972) (farm carried on ostensibly for experimental research, but in fact a profit-oriented enterprise; a tax case); People ex rel. County Collector v. Hopedale Medical Found., 46 Ill. 2d 450, 264 N.E.2d 4 (1970) (a tax case); Hopedale Medical Found. v. Tazewell County Collector, 59 Ill. App. 3d 816, 17 Ill. Dec. 92, 375 N.E.2d 1376 (1978), *cert. denied,* 440 U.S. 916 (a tax case).

In Oasis, Midwest Center for Human Potential v. Rosewell, 55 Ill. App. 2d 851, 13 Ill. Dec. 97, 370 N.E.2d 1124 (1977), a nonprofit organization conducting programs for members in humanistic psychology was held on the evidence not to be a charitable institution inasmuch as it did not benefit the public, and was held to be subject to a real estate tax.

Indiana: Fowler v. Norways Sanatorium, 112 Ind. App. 347, 42 N.E.2d 415 (1942) (sanatorium).

Kentucky: Lexington Hosp. v. White, 245 S.W.2d 927 (Ky. 1952) (hospital).

Massachusetts: Stratton v. Physio-Medical College, 149 Mass. 505, 21 N.E. 874, 5 L.R.A. 33, 14 Am. St. Rep. 442 (1889) (medical school); Hall v. College of Physicians & Surgeons, 254 Mass. 95, 149 N.E. 675 (1925) (medical school).

Michigan: Scarney v. Clarke, 282 Mich. 56, 275 N.W. 765 (1937) (medical clinic), noted in 18 Mich. S.B.J. 44.

Nebraska: Malcolm v. Evangelical Lutheran Hosp. Assn., 107 Neb. 101, 185 N.W. 330 (1921) (hospital).

New Jersey: Carteret Academy v. State Bd., 102 N.J.L. 525, 133 A. 886 (1926), *aff'd,* 104 N.J.L. 165, 138 A. 919 (1927) (school), noted in 25 Mich. L. Rev. 204; Montclair v. The Kimberly School, 25 N.J. Misc. 165, 51 A.2d 228 (1947), *aff'd sub nom.* Kimberly School v. Montclair, 137 N.J.L. 402, 60 A.2d 312 (1948), *rev'd,* 2 N.J. 28, 65 A.2d 500 (1949) (school; tax case).

New York: Hendrickson v. Hodkin, 276 N.Y. 252, 11 N.E.2d 899 (1937) (hospital); Claim of Carroll, 288 N.Y. 447, 43 N.E.2d 484 (1942) (school; subject to state unemployment tax).

Ohio: Cleveland Osteopathic Hosp. v. Zangerle, 153 Ohio St. 222, 91 N.E.2d 261 (1950) (hospital; tax case); Shaker Medical Center Hosp. v. Blue Cross of N.E. Ohio, 115 Ohio App. 497, 183 N.E.2d 628 (1962) (proprietary hospital not entitled to Blue Cross services); Martin v. North Hill Christian Church, 64 Ohio App. 2d 192, 18 Ohio Op. 3d 147, 412 N.E.2d 413 (1979) (business college operated for profit).

Oregon: Benton County v. Allen, 170 Or. 481, 133 P.2d 991 (1943) (hospital).

Texas: Malone-Hogan Hosp. Clinic Found. v. City of Big Spring, 288 S.W.2d 550 (Tex. Civ. App. 1956) (quoting Restatement of Trusts, §376, Comment *b*).

Virginia: Stuart Circle Hosp. Corp. v. Curry, 173 Va. 136, 3 S.E.2d 153,

it tax exempt. Even in jurisdictions in which charitable organizations are exempt from liability for torts, such an institution is not exempt from such liability.[2]

A trust to establish or maintain an institution may be charitable, however, although it is provided that some or all of the persons to receive benefits from the institution are to pay fees or otherwise contribute to the expense of maintaining the insti-

---

124 A.L.R. 176 (1939) (hospital); Danville Community Hosp. v. Thompson, 186 Va. 746, 43 S.E.2d 882, 173 A.L.R. 525 (1947) (hospital).

Washington: Mueller v. Winston Bros. Co., 165 Wash. 130, 4 P.2d 854 (1931) (hospital); Miller v. Mohr, 198 Wash. 619, 89 P.2d 807 (1939).

Wisconsin: Prairie du Chien Sanitarium Co. v. City of Prairie du Chien, 242 Wis. 262, 7 N.W.2d 832, 144 A.L.R. 1480 (1943) (hospital); Riverview Hosp. v. City of Tomahawk, 243 Wis. 581, 11 N.W.2d 188 (1943) (hospital; tax case).

See In re Knox, [1937] Ch. 109, noted in 1 Convey. (N.S.) 274.

See Note, Liability of private, noncharitable hospital or sanitarium for improper care or treatment of patients, 22 A.L.R. 341 (1923), 39 id. 1431 (1925), 124 id. 186 (1940).

See Note, Hospital as within tax exemption provision not specifically naming hospital, 144 A.L.R. 1483 (1943).

See 48 Yale L.J. 81 (1938).

In John Robinson Hosp. v. Cross, 279 Mich. 407, 272 N.W. 724 (1937), a testatrix left money to a trustee in trust to use the income in maintaining a room and bed in a named hospital. At her death it was a charitable institution, but later became noncharitable. It was held that the hospital was still entitled to the income. Two of the judges dissented on the ground that the trust failed when the hospital was taken over for private profit, citing Restatement of Trusts §§124, 376.

In In re Farmers' Union Hosp. Assn. of Elk City, 190 Okla. 661, 126 P.2d 244 (1942), it was held that a hospital association was subject to property taxes because it was conducted for the benefit of the members, the profits being used to reduce the cost of hospital care to the members.

In Coyne Elec. School v. Paschen, 12 Ill. 2d 387, 146 N.E.2d 73 (1957), an institution for instruction in electricity was held not exempt from taxation. It had been a proprietary institution but was changed into a nonprofit institution but the former proprietor received a benefit from the operation of the school, because he held bonds issued by it. Moreover, the standards of instruction were very low.

In Milward v. Paschen, 16 Ill. 2d 302, 157 N.E.2d 1 (1959), the court held subject to tax a foundation to promote education for persons engaged in the mortuary profession, because the instruction was superficial, and was more a symposium on how to conduct a funeral than a course of instruction in funeral science.

[2] See §402.1.

tution.[3] It has been so held in numerous cases of educational

[3]*England:* In re Estlin, 89 L.T. 88 (1903) (home of rest); In re Webster, [1912] 1 Ch. 106 (for nurses to attend the poor); Guinness Trust (London Fund) v. West Ham Borough Council, [1959] 1 W.L.R. 233, *rev'g* [1958] 2 All E.R. 237 (hostel for workingmen at moderate rentals; tax case); Campbell College, Belfast v. Northern Ireland Valuation Commr., [1964] 1 W.L.R. 912 (fee-paying school); In re Resch's Will Trusts, [1969] 1 A.C. 514 (hospital primarily for paying patients, but any surplus was not for private profit).

Federal: Ettlinger v. Trustees of Randolph-Macon College, 31 F.2d 869 (4th Cir. 1929) (college); Commissioner v. Battle Creek, 126 F.2d 405 (5th Cir. 1942) (sanitarium); Berry v. Odom, 222 F. Supp. 467 (N.C. 1963) (North Carolina law; university).

Alabama: Moore v. Walker County, 236 Ala. 688, 185 So. 175 (1938) (county hospital).

Alaska: Matanuska-Susitna Borough v. King's Lake Camp, 439 P.2d 441 (Alaska 1968) (children's camp).

California: Estate of Bailey, 19 Cal. App. 2d 135, 65 P.2d 102 (1937) (school; quoting Restatement of Trusts, §370, Comment *c*); Scripps Memorial Hosp. v. California Employment Commn., 24 Cal. 2d 669, 151 P.2d 109, 155 A.L.R. 360 (1944); Fredericka Home for the Aged v. County of San Diego, 35 Cal. 2d 789, 221 P.2d 68 (1950) (home for aged).

Connecticut: Waterbury Trust Co. v. Porter, 131 Conn. 206, 38 A.2d 598 (1944) (*semble;* school).

Florida: Miami Retreat Found. v. Ervin, 62 So. 2d 748 (Fla. 1953) (retreat for alcoholics).

Georgia: Peachtree on Peachtree Inn v. Camp, 120 Ga. App. 403, 170 S.E.2d 709 (1969), *rehearing denied, cert. denied* (home for aged, charging rentals to those able to pay; a tax case).

Illinois: Parks v. Northwestern Univ., 218 Ill. 381, 75 N.E. 991, 2 L.R.A. (N.S.) 556, 4 Ann. Cas. 103 (1905) (university); Hart v. Taylor, 301 Ill. 344, 133 N.E. 857 (1922) (hospital); School of Domestic Arts v. Carr, 322 Ill. 562, 153 N.E. 669 (1926) (school of domestic science); Summers v. Chicago Title & Trust Co., 335 Ill. 564, 167 N.E. 777 (1929) (university), noted in 24 Ill. L. Rev. 687, 39 Yale L.J. 437; Myers v. Young Men's Christian Assn., 316 Ill. App. 177, 44 N.E.2d 755 (1942) (Y.M.C.A.), noted in 21 Chi.-Kent L. Rev. 256, 10 U. Chi. L. Rev. 211; People v. Southern Ill. Hosp. Corp., 404 Ill. 66, 88 N.E.2d 20 (1949) (hospital); American College of Surgeons v. Korzen, 36 Ill. 2d 340, 224 N.E.2d 7 (1967) (College of Surgeons), *overruled on other grounds,* Christian Action Ministry v. Department of Local Govt. Affairs, 74 Ill. 2d 51, 23 Ill. Dec. 87, 383 N.E.2d 958 (1978).

Iowa: National Bank of Burlington v. Huneke, 250 Iowa 1030, 98 N.W.2d 7 (1959) (tax case; citing Restatement of Trusts §376).

Maryland: Fletcher v. Safe Deposit & Trust Co., 193 Md. 400, 67 A.2d 386 (1949) (home of rest).

Massachusetts: McDonald v. Massachusetts Gen. Hosp., 120 Mass. 432, 21 Am. Rep. 529 (1876) (hospital); Thornton v. Franklin Square House, 200

institutions and hospitals and homes. The question is not

Mass. 465, 86 N.E. 909, 22 L.R.A. (N.S.) 486 (1909) (home for working girls); Little v. City of Newburyport, 210 Mass. 414, 96 N.E. 1032, Ann. Cas. 1912D 425 (1912) (Y.M.C.A.); Roosen v. Peter Bent Brigham Hosp., 235 Mass. 66, 126 N.E. 392, 14 A.L.R. 563 (1920); Beverly Hosp. v. Early, 292 Mass. 201, 197 N.E. 641, 100 A.L.R. 1332 (1935) (hospital); Assessor of Lancaster v. Perkins School, 323 Mass. 418, 82 N.E.2d 883 (1948) (school for retarded children), noted in 24 Notre Dame Law, 403; Carpenter v. Young Men's Christian Assn., 324 Mass. 365, 86 N.E.2d 634 (1949) (Y.M.C.A.); Barrett v. Brooks Hosp., 338 Mass. 754, 157 N.E.2d 638 (1959).

Michigan: De Groot v. Edison Inst., 306 Mich. 339, 10 N.W.2d 907 (1943) (historical museum); Retirement Homes of Detroit v. Sylvan Township, 92 Mich. App. 560, 285 N.W.2d 375 (1979) (retirement home; a tax case).

Missouri: Voelker v. St. Louis Mercantile Library Assn., 359 S.W.2d 689 (Mo. 1962) (citing the text); Jewish Community Centers Assn. v. State Tax Commn., 520 S.W.2d 23 (Mo. 1975) (summer camp; a tax case).

Montana: Bozeman Deaconess Found. v. Gallatin Co., 151 Mont. 143, 439 P.2d 915 (1969) (home for the aged).

New Jersey: Alfred Univ. v. Hancock, 69 N.J. Eq. 470, 46 A. 178 (1900) (university); Mayor & Common Council of Princeton v. State Bd., 96 N.J.L. 334, 115 A. 342 (1921) (girls' school).

New York: Schloendorff v. Society of N.Y. Hosp., 211 N.Y. 125, 105 N.E. 92, 52 L.R.A. (N.S.) 505, Ann. Cas. 1915C 581 (1914) (hospital); Matter of MacDowell, 217 N.Y. 454, 112 N.E. 177, L.R.A. 1916E 1246, Ann. Cas. 1917E 853 (1916) (home for gentlewomen); Butterworth v. Keeler, 219 N.Y. 446, 114 N.E. 803 (1916) (school).

North Dakota: Evangelical Lutheran Socy. v. Board of City Commrs., 219 N.W.2d 900 (N.D. 1974) (home for the aged; a tax case).

Ohio: Taylor v. Protestant Hosp. Assn., 85 Ohio St. 90, 96 N.E. 1089, 39 L.R.A. (N.S.) 427 (1911) (hospital); O'Brien v. Physicians Hosp. Assn., 96 Ohio St. 1, 116 N.E. 975, L.R.A. 1917F 741 (1917) (hospital); Graham v. Bergin, 18 Ohio App. 35 (1923) (home for aged women); College Preparatory School for Girls v. Evatt, 144 Ohio St. 408, 59 N.E.2d 142 (1945) (preparatory school); Vick v. Cleveland Memorial Medical Assn., 2 Ohio St. 2d 30, 206 N.E.2d 2 (1965), *semble.*

Pennsylvania: Daly's Estate, 208 Pa. 58, 57 A. 180 (1904) (home for industrious girls); Channon's Estate, 266 Pa. 417, 109 A. 756 (1920) (home); Four Freedoms House v. City of Philadelphia, 443 Pa. 215, 279 A.2d 155 (1971) (apartment home operated by nonprofit corporation to provide low-cost housing for aged people; a tax case); City of Harrisburg v. Presbyterian Apartments, 337 A.2d 297 (Pa. Commw. 1975) (same; a tax case); Wayne County Bd. of Assessment v. Rolling Hills Girl Scout Council, 19 Pa. Commw. 484, 353 A.2d 498 (1975) (camping ground for girl scouts; a tax case).

In Vaughn Estate, 69 D.&C.2d 32 (Pa. 1974), where a testator creating a home for aged women provided that no one should be admitted unless she conveyed all her assets to the home, it was held that the trust was charitable.

whether the institution may receive a profit, but what disposition

---

Rhode Island: Webster v. Wiggin, 19 R.I. 73, 31 A. 824, 28 L.R.A. 510 (1895) (tenements for laboring classes).

Texas: Goelz v. J. K. & Susie L. Wadley Research Inst. & Blood Bank, 350 S.W.2d 573 (Tex. Civ. App. 1961) (blood bank); City of McAllen v. Evangelical Lutheran Good Samaritan Soc., 530 S.W.2d 806 (Tex. 1975) (three justices dissenting), *aff'g* 518 S.W.2d 557 (Tex. Civ. App. 1975) (nonprofit nursing home; a tax case).

Virginia: Hospital of St. Vincent v. Thompson, 116 Va. 101, 81 S.E. 13, 51 L.R.A. (N.S.) 1025 (1914) (hospital).

Washington: Weiss v. Swedish Hosp., 16 Wash. 2d 446, 133 P.2d 978 (1943) (hospital); Spokane Methodist Homes *v.* Department of Labor, 81 Wash. 2d 283, 501 P.2d 589 (1972) (home for elderly people).

Wisconsin: Maxcy v. City of Oshkosh, 144 Wis. 238, 128 N.W. 899, 1136, 31 L.R.A. (N.S.) 787 (1910) (manual training school); Fairbanks v. City of Appleton, 249 Wis. 476, 24 N.W.2d 893 (1946) (old people's home; citing Restatement of Trusts, §376, Comment *c*), noted in Wis. L. Rev. 467.

Ireland: Barrington's Hosp. v. Commissioner of Valuation, [1957] I.R. 299 (hospital).

The opposite result was reached in Trust Co. of Georgia v. Williams, 184 Ga. 706, 192 S.E. 913 (1937). In that case a testator left his estate to a trust company in trust to accumulate the income for 25 years and then to erect a memorial hospital. He made a "special request that all charges at said hospital be reasonable." It was held that the trust failed on the ground that there was no provision for free service to any patient, that it was not for charity, and that it violated the rule against perpetuities. The court said that while the hospital would be a charitable institution even though some patients were to pay compensation, the terms of the gift must themselves require that the hospital be operated at least in substantial part for the gratuitous relief of its inmates. Such a result seems wholly unsound. The hospital was not to be conducted for profit. The case is criticized in 16 Tex. L. Rev. 289.

Some of the cases involving property taxes on homes for the elderly cited in §374.11A, n. 8, *supra,* also appear to be contrary to those cited above in this note.

In Hassett v. Associated Hosp. Serv. Corp. of Massachusetts, 125 F.2d 611 (1st Cir. 1942), noted in 55 Harv. L. Rev. 1055, *cert. denied sub nom.* Associated Hosp. Serv. Corp. v. Hassett, 316 U.S. 672 (1942), it was held that a nonprofit hospital service corporation providing hospital care for subscribers was not exempt as a charitable corporation under the federal Social Security Act.

In Matter of Futerman, 197 Misc. 558, 95 N.Y.S.2d 876 (1950), it was held that where money was given in trust to make musical recordings available to the public through public lending libraries, it was not improper for the libraries to charge a modest rental fee.

In Degn Estate (No. 2), 14 D.&C.2d 343 (Pa. 1956), where a testatrix left her home as a museum, it was held that the devise was exempt from an inheritance tax, although the trustees were authorized to charge admission.

is to be made of the profit, if any, that may be received. If the profits are to inure to the benefit of individuals, the institution is not charitable. But if the profits, if any, are to be applied wholly to charitable purposes, the institution is charitable.[4] Thus it has been held that where an educational institution conducts a restaurant but any profits made from the operation of the restaurant are to be applied to educational purposes, the trust is charitable.[5] Similarly, where an institution to assist the poor is authorized to receive by gift or purchase secondhand articles and to conduct a store for the sale of such articles, the profits to be applied to the assistance of the poor, the institution is charitable.[6]

A trust to maintain a loan fund for students is charitable although interest is charged on the loans, the income thus received being applicable to the making of further loans and not to inure to the profit of any individual.[7]

In Bowers v. Akron City Hosp., 16 Ohio St. 2d 94, 243 N.E.2d 95, 33 A.L.R.3d 934 (1968), it was held that a parking lot owned and used by a hospital was exempt from taxation, although fees were charged but were used solely for parking facilities for the hospital.

See Note, Garage and parking lot as within tax exemption extended to property of educational, charitable, or hospital organizations, 33 A.L.R.3d 938 (1970); Note, Receipt of pay from beneficiaries as affecting tax exemption of charitable institutions, 37 A.L.R.3d 1191 (1971); Note, Nursing homes as exempt from property taxation, 45 A.L.R.3d 610 (1972); Chaffin, The Rule Against Perpetuities as Applied to Georgia Wills and Trusts: A Survey and Suggestions for Reform, 16 Ga. L. Rev. 235 (1982) (citing the text).

On the question whether a hospital or nursing home or home for the aged is subject to taxation if it does not provide for the poor, see §372.

On the question whether a nonprofit cemetery association is subject to taxation, see §374.9.

[4]Gingrich v. Blue Ridge Memorial Gardens & Marlon Corp., 444 Pa. 420, 282 A.2d 315 (1971) (quoting the text).

[5]School·of Domestic Arts v. Carr, 322 Ill. 562, 153 N.E. 669 (1926).

[6]See McKay v. Morgan Memorial Coop. Indus. & Stores, 272 Mass. 121, 172 N.E. 68 (1930) (held not exempt from liability in tort).

See also Holder v. Massachusetts Horticultural Socy., 211 Mass. 370, 97 N.E. 630 (1912); Conklin v. John Howard Indus. Home, 224 Mass. 222, 112 N.E. 606 (1916).

See §402.1.

[7]*California:* Estate of Yule, 57 Cal. App. 2d 652, 135 P.2d 386 (1943).

Illinois: Morgan v. National Trust Bank of Charleston, 331 Ill. 182, 162

An institution for the promotion of charitable purposes is charitable although salaries are paid to its managers, officers, and employees. Thus in *Hart v. Taylor*[8] it was held that a bequest to establish a memorial hospital was a valid charitable bequest, although it was provided that the trustees should receive compensation for their services. But if the fixing of a salary is merely a device for taking the profits of the institution and not to afford compensation for services rendered, the institution is not a charitable institution.[9]

N.E. 888 (1928), noted in 3 Temp. U.L.Q. 226; Summers v. Chicago Title & Trust Co., 335 Ill. 564, 167 N.E. 777 (1929), noted in 24 Ill. L. Rev. 687.

Iowa: In re Estate of Pierce, 245 Iowa 22, 60 N.W.2d 894 (1953).

Kentucky: Goode's Admr. v. Goode, 238 Ky. 620, 38 S.W.2d 691 (1931).

Louisiana: Oroszy v. Burkard, 158 So. 2d 405 (La. 1963).

New York: Matter of Morgan, 200 Misc. 645, 107 N.Y.S.2d 180 (1951); Matter of Howell, 109 N.Y.S.2d 270 (1951) (teachers' loan fund).

See §370, n. 1.

[8]301 Ill. 344, 133 N.E. 857 (1922).

See City Bank Farmers Trust Co. v. Bennett, 159 Misc. 779, 287 N.Y.S. 784 (1936).

[9]Scholarship Endowment Fund Found. v. Nicholas, 25 F. Supp. 511 (D. Colo. 1938) (tax case; citing Restatement of Trusts, §376, Comment *b*), *aff'd,* 106 F.2d 552 (10th Cir. 1939), *cert. denied,* 308 U.S. 623 (1940), noted in 25 Cornell L.Q. 634; Hall v. College of Physicians & Surgeons, 254 Mass. 95, 149 N.E. 675 (1925).

In Virginia Mason Hosp. Assn., v. Larson, 9 Wash. 2d 284, 114 P.2d 976 (1941), it was held that although the hospital was mortgaged, this was not a device by which net earnings should inure to the benefit of any individual and that the hospital was charitable within the provisions of the federal Unemployment Compensation Act.

In Benton County v. Allen, 170 Or. 481, 133 P.2d 991 (1943), it was held that where the stockholders of a corporation maintaining a proprietary hospital that was incurring losses transferred it to a new corporation organized as a charitable corporation in consideration of second-mortgage bonds in the amount of the capital stock of the old corporation, the new corporation was not exempt from taxation as a charitable corporation.

In Mayberry v. Foster, 194 Okla. 205, 148 P.2d 983 (1944), where the defendant, a physician who owned a private hospital, sold it to a charitable association and thereafter the plaintiff was injured by falling down an elevator shaft, it was held that the plaintiff had not proved that the sale was a subterfuge to escape taxation.

In Gordon v. Commissioner of Stamp Duties, [1946] N.Z.L.R. 625, it was held that a trust to establish a maternity hospital to be conducted as the trustees should determine, with a provision that any profit should be used in

Not infrequently it happens that a testator leaves money in trust to be applied to such educational institutions as the trustees may select. Occasionally it has been held that such a trust is not a charitable trust because the trustees might select educational institutions organized for private profit.[10] Thus in *Matter of Shattuck*[11] a testator left money in trust to pay the income to religious or educational or eleemosynary institutions. The court held that the trustees might under the terms of the will select an educational institution organized for private profit and that the trust was not therefore limited to charitable purposes and failed. Although it is true that the language of the will was literally broad enough to include proprietary institutions, it would seem that it would have been more reasonable to hold that the testator intended to afford aid only to such institutions as were nonproprietary in character and therefore charitable. This is the view taken in later decisions.[12]

---

improving the hospital, was not charitable and failed, the court being of the opinion that the trustees might receive only selected patients and might carry on the hospital on a purely commercial basis.

[10]Estate of Sutro, 155 Cal. 727, 102 P. 920 (1909); Estate of Vance, 118 Cal. App. 163, 4 P.2d 977 (1931); Estate of Kline, 138 Cal. App. 514, 32 P.2d 677 (1934); Matter of Shattuck, 193 N.Y. 446, 86 N.E. 455 (1908).

In In re Peabody's Estate, 21 Cal. App. 2d 690, 70 P.2d 249 (1937), noted in 51 Harv. L. Rev. 561, a testatrix left her property "to go to an institution for old people in memory of" her mother and father, and designated a person to make the choice of the institution. It was held that the choice was not limited to charitable institutions and that the trust failed. It seems clear, however, that the testatrix did not intend to include any proprietary institutions for old people. The case is criticized in 51 Harv. L. Rev. 561.

In Estate of Rollins, 163 Cal. App. 2d 225, 328 P.2d 1005 (1958), it was held that a bequest of the residue to "some charitable institution, or research fund, or for a suitable memorial to my mother and father (no statue or monument)" was valid. The court criticized the cases cited above. See Estate of Peck, 168 Cal. App. 2d 25, 335 P.2d 185 (1959), *cert. and rehearing denied,* 361 U.S. 826, 903 (1959).

[11]193 N.Y. 446, 86 N.E. 455 (1908).

[12]*New York:* Matter of Frasch, 245 N.Y. 174, 156 N.E. 656 (1927); Matter of Durbrow, 245 N.Y. 469, 157 N.E. 747 (1927), noted in 22 Ill. L. Rev. 454, 13 Cornell L.Q. 310; Matter of Everson, 268 A.D. 425, 52 N.Y.S.2d 395 (1944), *aff'd mem.,* 295 N.Y. 622, 64 N.E.2d 653 (1945); Matter of Cohen, 58 N.Y.S.2d 924 (1945).

Rhode Island: Rhode Island Hosp. Trust Co. v. Metcalf, 48 R.I. 411, 137 A. 875 (1927).

Where a trust inures to the benefit of private individuals, although the benefits are not pecuniary, the trust is not charitable.[13] Where the home of a famous person is privately owned, a trust to maintain it is not a charitable trust, although if it were not privately owned it would be upheld as a charitable trust for educational purposes. Thus in *Thomson v. Shakespear*[14] it was held that a trust to restore Shakespeare's house and maintain a museum in it was not charitable, because the house was privately owned by the subscribers to the fund. Similarly in *Thorp v. Lund*[15] a testatrix, who was the widow of the famous violinist Ole Bull, by her will authorized her daughter to apply a part of the estate for some national or philanthropic purpose in Norway associated with the name of Ole Bull. It was held that the daughter was not authorized to appoint a part of the estate for the

---

Canada: Canada Permanent Trust Co. v. MacFarlane, 27 D.L.R.3d 480 (B.C. 1972).

See Estate of Blanch B. Gilbert, 4 T.C. 1006 (1945) (bequest for purchase of iron lungs to be given to hospitals that need them); Westport Bank & Trust Co. v. Fable, 126 Conn. 665, 13 A.2d 862 (1940) (citing Restatement of Trusts, §376, Comment *a*); Matter of Hamilton, 185 Misc. 660, 57 N.Y.S.2d 359 (1945), *aff'd*, 270 A.D. 634, 63 N.Y.S.2d 265 (1946), *aff'd mem.*, 296 N.Y. 578, 68 N.E.2d 872 (1946), noted in 32 Cornell L.Q. 458, 21 St. John's L. Rev. 87.

In In re Smith's Will Trusts, [1962] 2 All E.R. 563, *rev'g* [1961] 3 All E.R. 824, noted in 79 Law Q. Rev. 3, where a testator left a fund to a bank in trust for such hospitals and/or charitable institutions as the chairman of the bank should in his absolute and uncontrolled discretion think fit, it was held that the testator intended to include only charitable hospitals and that the trust was valid.

In Estate of Moore, 190 Cal. App. 2d 833, 12 Cal. Rptr. 436 (1961), where a testatrix left her property to be given to some creditable nonprofit science investigation society of her sister's choice, it was held that the disposition was charitable.

Where trustees are authorized to distribute the testator's estate among charitable institutions to be selected by them, it is to be inferred that they are to select only such charitable institutions as are exempt from taxes. Matter of Heit, 26 Misc. 2d 774, 206 N.Y.S.2d 59 (1960). See §396, n. 3.

[13]A gift to a charitable organization may be held for tax purposes not to be a gift to charity, if it is subject to a provision conferring benefits on the donor or others designated by him.

See Note. Taxation: Liberal Standard Proposed for Deducting Charitable Contributions to Religious Schools, 61 Minn. L. Rev. 887 (1977).

[14]1 De G.F.&J. 399 (1860).

[15]227 Mass. 474, 116 N.E. 946, Ann. Cas. 1918B 1204 (1917).

purpose of maintaining his home as a memorial to his memory, because the home was privately owned by her. There are other cases in which a trust was held not to be charitable, although the purposes were such that it otherwise would be charitable, because the resulting benefits were primarily for specific individuals rather than for the community. In *Matter of DeForest*[16] a testator bequeathed $100,000 to the Adirondack Mountain Reserve, stating that his purpose was to preserve the forests, lakes, and mountains in their natural condition and that the fund should be used for this purpose. The Adirondack Mountain Reserve was a business corporation empowered to buy and sell land, to cut timber, to manufacture and sell lumber, and the like. The shareholders and others had conducted a club of restricted membership to enjoy the land. The court held that because the corporation was operated for private profit and enjoyment, a charitable trust was not created.

A trust for the benefit of a library privately owned by an individual or group of individuals and conducted for the benefit of the owners is not a charitable trust.[17] The trust is charitable, however, if, although privately owned, the public is entitled to share in its use. In *Minns v. Billings*[18] a testator left his estate to his executors in trust to apply it to such charitable purposes as they might determine. It was held that they might properly apply a part of the estate to the Boston Athenaeum. This was a corporation the shareholders of which contributed to the cost of its maintenance and were permitted to use its library. It appeared, however, that any citizen was permitted as a matter of right to inspect some of its publications and that the library was to a large extent accessible to inquirers and students as well as to its members. The court held that it was a charitable corporation and not merely a private institution conducted for the benefit of its members.

We have already dealt with the question how far various

[16]147 Misc. 82, 263 N.Y.S. 135 (1933).

[17]Carne v. Long, 2 De G.F.&J. 75 (1860); In re Dutton, 4 Ex. D. 54 (1878). See In re Prevost, [1930] 2 Ch. 383, noted in 170 Law T. 489.

[18]183 Mass. 126, 66 N.E. 593, 5 L.R.A. (N.S.) 686, 97 Am. St. Rep. 420 (1903).

See Voelker v. St. Louis Mercantile Library Assn., 359 S.W.2d 689 (Mo. 1962) (library for members).

types of associations are charitable organizations and how far they are noncharitable on the ground that they are organized and conducted merely for the benefit of the members.[19]

§377. Illegal Purposes

A trust cannot be created for a purpose that is illegal. The purpose is illegal if the trust property is to be used for an object that is in violation of the criminal law, or if the trust tends to induce the commission of crime, or if the accomplishment of the purpose is otherwise against public policy. Questions of public policy are not fixed and unchanging, but vary from time to time and from place to place. A trust fails for illegality if the accomplishment of the purposes of the trust is regarded as against public policy in the community in which the trust is created and at the time when it is created.[1] Where a policy is articulated in a statute making certain conduct a criminal offense, then, of course, a trust is illegal if its performance involves such criminal conduct, or if it tends to encourage such conduct. Thus in an early English case a bequest to trustees "to make seats for poor people to beg in by the highways" was held invalid since such begging was a criminal offense.[2]

A trust is illegal, even if it does not involve the performance of an illegal act by the trustees, if the natural result of the enforcement of the trust would be to induce the commission of crime. Thus a bequest to purchase the release of persons committed to prison for nonpayment of fines under the game laws was held illegal.[3]

On the other hand, the mere fact that the trust may indirectly induce the commission of a crime does not make the

[19]See §375.2.

§377. [1]By Michigan Stat. Ann., §27.3178(71a), as added by Laws 1951, no. 157, it is provided that a devise or bequest to or for any association or corporation for subversion as defined in the constitution shall be invalid.

See the Final Report of the Select Committee to Investigate Foundations and Other Organizations (1953) (pursuant to H. R. Res. 561, 82d Cong.).

See §§60-65.3 (effect of illegality); §401.2 (illegal condition subsequent); §401.10 (illegal condition precedent); §§422-422.6, 444 (resulting trusts).

[2]Anonymous, Duke, Law of Charitable Uses, 133.

[3]Thrupp v. Collett, 26 Beav. 125 (1858).

trust invalid. In *Estate of Robbins*[4] a testator left property in trust to support minor black children whose father or mother has been convicted of a crime of a political nature such as violation of the Smith Act, refusal to answer questions as to beliefs or affiliations and the like. It was held, three judges dissenting, that the trust was a valid charitable trust. Traynor, J., said, "Any risk that a parent might be induced to commit a crime he otherwise would not commit because of the possibility that his child might become a beneficiary of this trust is far outweighed by the interests of the innocent children involved and society's interest in them." He said further

> We may assume that the testator intended to benefit the children of those convicted of even valid laws of which he disapproved and that his motive in part at least was to encourage challenges to such laws by violations of them. It is the purpose for which the property is to be used, however, not the motives of the testator, that determines whether a trust is a valid charitable trust.

A trust is illegal where the performance of the trust involves a violation of the law of another country. Thus an English trust the purpose of which involved a violation of the law of Scotland was held invalid.[5] In an English case decided in 1851, a trust to restore the Jews to Jerusalem, then under Turkish rule, was held invalid as tending to promote a revolution in a friendly country.[6] But a similar trust was upheld in 1924, Palestine being no longer under Turkish rule.[7] In a case in New York in 1925, a gift to "further the development of the Irish Republic" was held to be for a political rather than a charitable purpose, and it might be against public policy as having a tendency to embroil the United States with a friendly power.[8]

A trust to promote religion may be illegal as against public policy. In England, as we have seen, it was once held that a trust to promote any religion but that of the established church was illegal. Long after this view was abandoned, the courts con-

---

[4]457 Cal. 2d 718, 371 P.2d 573 (1962), noted in 48 Iowa L. Rev. 1019, 8 Utah L. Rev. 152, 20 Wash. & Lee L. Rev. 1019.

[5]Attorney-General v. Guise, 2 Vern. 266 (1692).

[6]Habershon v. Vardon, 4 De G. & Sm. 467 (1851).

[7]In re Rosenblum, 131 L.T. 21 (1924).

[8]Matter of Killen, 124 Misc. 720, 209 N.Y.S. 206 (1925).

tinued to hold that trusts for certain religious purposes were illegal. A trust for the saying of masses was held illegal as a superstitious use until the House of Lords in 1919 overthrew the earlier decisions.[9] Such trusts were never held illegal in the United States, although in some of the earlier cases it was held that such trusts are not charitable.[10] In England it was also held that a trust to publish a treatise advocating the doctrine of papal supremacy was invalid.[11] In the United States a trust to promote any religious doctrine or sect is a valid charitable trust unless it involves conduct that is illegal. In *Mormon Church v. United States*[12] it was held that the Congress might constitutionally dissolve a church corporation that advocated the practice of polygamy as one of its tenets.

Is the promotion of atheism an illegal purpose? Until recent times the courts, both in England and in the United States, had no difficulty in answering this question in the affirmative. In England it was once held that the promulgation of atheistic doctrines was a criminal offense. To deny the existence of God was an offense not only against God but against the state. Lord Hale said: "To say religion is a cheat is to dissolve all those obligations whereby the civil societies are preserved, and that Christianity is parcel of the laws of England; and therefore to reproach the Christian religion is to speak in subversion of the law."[13] In a number of cases, both English and American, it has been held that an attack on the fundamental doctrines of the Christian religion is a criminal offense, regardless of the method of the attack.[14] Today, however, the speaking or writing of

[9]Bourne v. Keane, [1919] A.C. 815.

[10]See §371.5.

[11]De Themmines v. De Bonneval, 5 Russ. 288 (1828).

[12]136 U.S. 1, 10 S. Ct. 792, 34 L. Ed. 478 (1890).

[13]Taylor's Case, 1 Vent. 293, 3 Keb. 607, 621 (1675). The actual decision was undoubtedly right, because the defendant's words were indecent.

[14]Rex v. Woolston, 2 Str. 820, Fitzg. 64, 1 Barnard, 162, 266 (1779) (denial of miracles of Christ); Rex v. Williams, 26 How. St. Tr. 653 (1797) (publishing Paine's "Age of Reason"); Regina v. Moxon, 4 St. Tr. (N.S.) 694 (1841) (publishing Shelley's "Queen Mab"); Regina v. Petcherini, 7 Cox C.C. 79 (1855) (burning an authorized version of the Bible); Commonwealth v. Kneeland, 20 Pick. 206 (Mass. 1838) (promulgation of pantheistic ideas); Updegraph v. Commonwealth, 11 S.&R. 394 (Pa. 1824) (denial of infallibility of the Bible).

words denying the fundamentals of the Christian religion is not an offense unless the circumstances are such as to make the attack improper either as a nuisance or as tending to a breach of the peace.[15] A decorous discussion of the fundamentals of religion is no longer a criminal offense.[16]

Even if the promotion of atheism is not a criminal offense, the question remains whether it is illegal in any sense. In 1822 Lord Eldon refused to enjoin a pirated edition of a medical book because it seemed to throw doubt on the doctrine of the immortality of the soul.[17] In the same year Lord Eldon refused to restrain the publication of a pirated edition of Lord Byron's "Cain."[18] In 1850 the English court held illegal a legacy for the best original essay on natural theology, treating it as a science, and demonstrating its adequacy and sufficiency when so treated and taught to constitute a true, perfect, and philosophical system of universal religion.[19] In 1867 the English court held illegal a contract to let rooms for the purpose of delivery of lectures on such subjects as "The Character and Teachings of Christ: the former defective, the latter misleading."[20] There are similar decisions in Canada.[21] In a well-known Pennsylvania case in 1870, Sharswood, J., was of the opinion that a legacy to the "Infidel Society of Philadelphia hereafter to be incorporated, and to be held and disposed of by them, for the purpose of

[15]A judge in Delaware has pointed out that the atheist would be roughly handled not by true Christians but by the near Christians. "The professing and devout Christian would indeed look on the scene more in sorrow than anger, but his relatives and friends, who are not strictly professors of Christianity or members of any church or sect, and the great mass who have been educated in the Christian's belief, though not professing to act up to it, would probably do as outraged and insulted men have in all ages been accustomed to do." State v. Chandler, 2 Har. 553, 570 (Del. 1873).

[16]Regina v. Bradlaugh, 15 Cox C.C. 217 (1883); Regina v. Ramsay, 15 Cox C.C. 231 (1883); Rex v. Boulther, 72 J.P. 188 (1908). See Shore v. Wilson, 9 Cl. & Fin. 355, 524, 539 (1842).

See Note, Blasphemy, 70 Colum. L. Rev. 694 (1970).

[17]Lawrence v. Smith, Jac. 471 (1822).

[18]Murray v. Benbow, 4 St. Tr. (N.S.) 1410 (1822).

[19]Briggs v. Hartley, 19 L.J. Ch. 416 (1850).

[20]Cowan v. Milbourn, L.R. 2 Ex. 230 (1867).

[21]Pringle v. Napanee, 43 U.C.Q.B. 285 (1878); Kinsey v. Kinsey, 26 Ont. Rep. 99 (1894).

building a hall for the free discussion of religion, politics, etc.," was illegal.[22]

This was the state of the authorities when in 1917 the case of *Bowman v. Secular Society, Ltd.* [23] was decided by the House of Lords. In that case a testator made a bequest in trust for the Secular Society, Ltd., a registered company, the objects of which were inter alia to promote "the principle that human conduct should be based upon natural knowledge, and not upon supernatural belief, and that human welfare in this world is the proper end of all thought and action." It was held that the trust was not illegal. In this case it was unnecessary to decide whether the trust was charitable or not because the bequest was made to a registered company. The only question for decision was whether the purpose was illegal, not whether it was a charitable purpose. Lord Parker in a dictum expressed the opinion that the trust was not charitable. A decision to that effect was rendered in an Australian case, where a bequest was made to the "Incorporated Body of Freethinkers of South Australia," which advocated the doctrine "that science provides for life, and that materialism can be relied upon in all phases of society."[24] At the time of the death of the testator the corporation had ceased to exist, and the question was whether the legacy could be applied cy pres. The court held that the purposes of the society were not charitable and that it could not be so applied. It may well be contended, however, that a trust to promote atheism, although not a trust for the advancement of religion, can nevertheless be upheld as a trust for the advancement of education.[25] A trust for

[22]Zeisweiss v. James, 63 Pa. 465, 3 Am. Rep. 558 (1870).

See also Manners v. Philadelphia Library Co., 93 Pa. 165, 39 Am. Rep. 741 (1880).

[23][1917] A.C. 406.

[24]In re Jones, [1907] S. Austl. L.R. 190.

[25]In Knight's Estate, 159 Pa. 500, 28 A. 303 (1894), the court was of the opinion that a legacy to promote atheism was charitable so as to be invalid under a statute invalidating bequests made less then one month before the testator's death.

In the famous case of Vidal v. Girard's Exrs., 2 How. 127, 198, 11 L. Ed. 205 (U.S. 1844), the Supreme Court of the United States had no difficulty in holding that a provision in a bequest for the founding of a school that ecclesiastics of all denominations should not be allowed to teach or even to enter on the premises did not invalidate the bequest or prevent the trust from being charitable. See §348.

educational purposes is nonetheless charitable although it does not involve unbiased inquiry and research to ascertain the truth but involves the promulgation of particular doctrines or beliefs, provided that those doctrines or beliefs are such as rational persons may and do entertain. It is not for the courts to decide among conflicting views which is true or wise.[26]

Where a trust is created for the promotion of health, the trust or a provision in the terms of the trust is illegal if it appears that the effect would be injurious to health. Thus in a case decided by the Supreme Court of Washington[27] a testator left money to apply the income for instruction at some homeopathic school of medicine and directed that in the lectures the physicians should use certain treatises as textbooks. It was shown in evidence that these textbooks were no longer the basis for instruction in homeopathic schools of medicine and that it would be dangerous to health to apply the theories advocated in these textbooks. The court held that the provision for such teaching was illegal as detrimental to the public health. In a case in New York[28] it was held that where a bequest was made to a hospital

---

In Old Colony Trust Co. v. Welch, 25 F. Supp. 45 (D. Mass. 1938), it was held that a bequest to "Freethinkers of America, Incorporated," a nonprofit corporation engaged primarily in conducting litigation to prevent expenditure of public money in promotion of religion, was not exclusively charitable and could not be deducted under the federal estate tax.

In In re Estate of Connolly, 48 Cal. App. 3d 129, 121 Cal. Rptr. 325 (1975), a bequest to "World's Agnostics Groups, a non-profit California corporation" was held to be a valid gift for educational purposes, and the court held that the cy pres doctrine was applicable.

[26]In Faulkner v. Commissioner, 112 F.2d 987, 992 (1st Cir. 1940), noted in 41 Colum. L. Rev. 335, it was held that a gift to the Birth Control League of Massachusetts was deductible under the federal Revenue Act of 1934, although subsequent to the making of the gift persons in charge of an office operated by the League were convicted of violating the Massachusetts law against the distribution of contraceptives. See §374.4, n. 11.

[27]In re Hill's Estate, 119 Wash. 62, 204 P. 1055, 207 P. 689 (1922).

Compare Hoffstot v. Fifth Ave. Hosp. 140 Misc. 206, 249 N.Y.S. 399 (1931), aff'd, 236 A.D. 667, 257 N.Y.S. 1034 (1932), aff'd mem., 262 N.Y. 479, 188 N.E. 28 (1933).

As to the situation that arises where a trust was created for a homeopathic hospital and homeopathic treatment ceased to be practiced as a separate medical system, see The Sydney Homeopathic Hosp. v. Turner, 102 C.L.R. 188 (Austl. 1959).

[28]Matter of Sterne, 147 Misc. 59, 263 N.Y.S. 304 (1933).

on condition that all physicians practicing in the hospital should be required to pay a percentage of their fees to the hospital, the condition was illegal as tending to promote fee-splitting, which was against public policy.[29]

In *Wilson v. Smith*[30] a testator died domiciled in Texas leaving his property, which was situated in Texas, to three residents of Texas in trust for charitable purposes. One of the purposes was to establish and maintain a clinic-hospital in California in which various methods of non-medicinal healing in the field of chiropractic were to be employed. In an action brought by the trustees in Texas for a declaratory judgment, it was held that the provision was invalid because such practice was in violation of the civil and criminal laws of Texas, even though it would not be illegal in California. The court said that this was governed by the law of Texas because it was in all respects a Texas trust, except that the trustees were to establish and maintain the hospital in California. The court said that it would not permit Texas property administered in Texas by trustees under Texas law to send the revenue to another state for a purpose that is criminal under Texas law, although it is not illegal in the other state.

TOPIC 4. THE ADMINISTRATION OF CHARITABLE TRUSTS

§378. Who May Be Trustee

A natural person who has capacity to be trustee of a private trust may be trustee of a charitable trust. The question of capacity to be trustee has been heretofore considered.[1]

The United States, as a juristic person, has capacity to take and hold the title to property, and can hold it upon a charitable

---

[29]In Rice v. Sayers, 98 F. Supp. 634 (D. Kan. 1951), *rev'd on other grounds,* 198 F.2d 724 (10th Cir. 1952), *cert. denied,* 344 U.S. 877 (1952), the court upheld a trust to pay the income to two universities to establish chairs in their medical schools in which the incumbents were to teach the utter uselessness of narcotic drugs when taken internally, with a gift over if this should not be taught.

[30]373 S.W.2d 514 (Tex. Civ. App. 1963), *cert. denied,* 379 U.S. 973.

§378. [1]See §§89-94.

trust. It can administer charitable trusts, however, only for such purposes as are within the powers conferred on it by the Constitution of the United States, expressly or otherwise. The trust is not enforceable against the United States in the courts, except to the extent to which by statute it has consented to be sued.[2]

A state can take and hold property upon a charitable trust and can administer a trust for any charitable purpose unless restrained by the provisions of the Constitution of the United States or by the laws of the United States or of the state itself. The trust cannot be enforced against the state, however, except to the extent to which it has consented to be sued.[3]

A town or city or county or other subdivision of the state may accept and administer trusts for charitable purposes.[4]

Whether a private corporation has capacity to take and hold property upon a charitable trust and to administer the trust depends on the extent of its corporate powers.[5] Trust companies and banks authorized to administer trusts have capacity to take and hold property upon a charitable trust and to administer the trust.[6]

Ordinarily, an unincorporated association has no power to act as trustee of a private trust or of a charitable trust.[7] An intended trust, however, does not fail for lack of capacity of the trustee.[8]

§379. The Duties of the Trustee

The duties of the trustee of a charitable trust are similar to those of trustees of a private trust. The chief difference is that the duties of the trustees of a charitable trust are not ordinarily owed to specific beneficiaries, but are enforced at the suit of the

---

[2]See §95.

[3]See §95.

[4]See §96.4.

As to the enforceability of trusts of property held by municipal corporations, see §348.1, n. 11.

[5]See §96.3.

[6]See §96.5.

[7]See §97.

[8]See §397.

Attorney General.[1] The liabilities of a trustee of a charitable trust for violations of his duty are dealt with hereafter.[2]

The trustees are under a duty to exercise due diligence in the administration of the trust, and are under a duty not to delegate the administration to others.[3] It is improper, for example, to permit another person to invest the funds of the charity.[4]

There is a question, however, whether the strict rules as to delegation applicable to individual trustees[5] are applicable to the board of trustees or directors of a charitable institution. There is, in the first place, a question whether the board may entrust the power to make investments to an executive committee or other committee of the board or to an officer. There is no doubt that in practice this is often done.[6] The board, which has to pass on many matters as to the proper carrying out of the

§379. [1]See Donaldson v. Madison Borough, 88 N.J. Super. 574, 213 A.2d 33 (1965) (citing Restatement of Trusts §379); State v. Taylor, 58 Wash. 2d 252, 362 P.2d 247, 86 A.L.R.2d 1365 (1961) (citing the text and Restatement of Trusts §379).

See §391.

[2]See §386.

[3]See Chapin v. Benwood Found., 402 A.2d 1295 (Del. Ch. 1979), as to choice of successors.

[4]City of Boston v. Curley, 276 Mass. 549, 177 N.E. 557 (1931).

Where a city is named as trustee it can entrust the management of the trust to a board subject to its control. City of Bangor v. Beal, 85 Me. 129, 26 A. 1112 (1892).

In Ray v. Homewood Hosp., 223 Minn. 440, 27 N.W.2d 409 (1947), it was held that an agreement by some of the trustees of a charitable corporation not to participate in the management of the corporation is illegal.

As to the power of charitable trustees to convey the property of the trust to a charitable corporation, see §385A.

In Wallace v. Graff, 104 F. Supp. 925 (D.D.C. 1952), where a fund was left in trust to establish and maintain a hospital, and under the authority of the will the trustees formed a corporation to administer the fund, it was held that the corporation was under a duty to account to the court.

In Denckla v. Independence Found., 41 Del. Ch. 247, 193 A.2d 538 (1963), aff'g 40 Del. Ch. 268, 181 A.2d 78 (1962), it was held that where a charitable corporation was authorized to establish and maintain charitable agencies and institutions and to contribute to and aid institutions established for such purposes, it had power to give 55 percent of its assets to another separately administered charitable corporation with the same purposes.

[5]See §§171 to 171.4.

[6]Note, Delegation of Investment Responsibility by Trustees of Charitable Trusts and Corporations, 9 Real Prop., Prob. & Tr. J. 583 (1974).

purposes of the institution, can rarely give full consideration to the making of investments. It would seem to be not improper to delegate the power of investment to a committee or officer, as long as the board itself prudently exercises a general supervision over the matter.[7]

There is a further question whether the board of trustees or directors of a charitable institution can properly delegate the power to make or retain investments to an outsider, such as an investment counselor or a bank. This is harder to justify, but it seems reasonable to permit it. At any rate, it may be permitted by statute.[8]

By the Uniform Management of Institutional Funds Act,

[7]The question as to delegation by trustees or directors of charitable institutions is dealt with fully by Gesell, D.J., in Stern v. Lucy Webb Hayes Natl. Training School, 381 F. Supp. 1003 (D.D.C. 1974). He applied the broader rules applicable to corporate directors rather than the stricter rules applicable to trustees.

See also Midlantic Natl. Bank v. Frank G. Thompson Found., 170 N.J. Super. 728, 405 A.2d 866 (1979) (citing the text and Restatement of Trusts, §379, Comment *b*).

See Mace, Standards of Care for Trustees, Harv. Bus. Rev., Jan.-Feb. 1976, p. 14, commenting on the Stern case.

See also Massachusetts Charitable Mechanic Assn. v. Beede, 320 Mass. 601, 70 N.E.2d 825 (1947).

See Cary and Bright, The Law and the Lore of Endowment Funds (Report to the Ford Foundation, 1969); Cary and Bright, The "Income" from Endowment Funds, 69 Colum. L. Rev. 396 (1969).

[8]The California Corporation Code, §10204, provides that in the case of charitable corporations: "the articles of incorporation may prescribe that the matter of controlling, managing, investing, and disposing of the property of the corporation for the purpose of earning an income therefrom, as distinguished from the matter of applying property and funds to charitable and eleemosynary purposes, shall be exclusively in a finance committee consisting of not less than three members of the board, designated or appointed in some particular manner. The matter of controlling, managing, investing, and disposing of the property of the corporation for the purpose of earning an income therefrom may be delegated either in whole or in part to one or more trust companies or banks duly authorized to conduct a trust or banking business in this State."

By Pennsylvania Corporation Not-for-Profit Code, 15 Pa. Stat., §7551, it is provided that a nonprofit corporation may transfer assets to a bank or trust company as trustee for investment purposes.

Compare the provisions of the Employee Retirement Income Security Act as to the employment of investment managers. See §185.

§5,[9] approved in 1972, delegation of investment management of funds held by charitable institutions is permitted. In Section 5 of the Act it is provided:

> Except as otherwise provided by the applicable gift instrument or by applicable law relating to governmental institutions or funds, the governing board may (1) delegate to its committees, officers or employees of the institution or the fund, or agents, including investment counsel, the authority to act in place of the board in investment and reinvestment of institutional funds, (2) contract with independent investment advisors, investment counsel or managers, banks, or trust companies, so to act, and (3) authorize the payment of compensation for investment advisory or management services.

The trustees of a charitable trust, like those of a private trust, are under a duty of loyalty; they must administer the trust solely with a view to the accomplishment of the purposes of the trust and not with a view to promoting their own interests. Self-dealing is clearly improper. The trustees of a charitable trust, like those of a private trust, commit a breach of trust when they sell trust property to themselves individually, or when they sell their individual property to themselves as trustees.[10] They

---

[9]For other provisions of the Act, see §§367.2, 389.

This section of the Uniform Act has been substantially enacted in New York, Not-for-Profit Corporation Law, §514, as enacted by Laws 1978, c. 690.

[10]*Federal:* People of State of Cal. v. Larkin, 413 F. Supp. 978 (N.D. Cal. 1976) (California law).

California: Gbur v. Cohen, 93 Cal. App. 3d 296, 155 Cal. Rptr. 507 (1979), *vacating* 91 Cal. App. 3d 117, 153 Cal. Rptr. 794 (1979) (citing the text).

Illinois: Eurich v. Korean Found., 31 Ill. App. 2d 474, 176 N.E.2d 692 (1961).

South Carolina: Gilbert v. McLeod Infirmary, 219 S.C. 174, 64 S.E.2d 524 (1951).

Wisconsin: In re Taylor Orphan Asylum, 36 Wis. 534 (1875).

In Kenney Presbyterian Home v. State, 174 Wash. 19, 24 P.2d 403 (1933), it was held that where one of several trustees of a charitable corporation who was engaged in the business of mortgage loans and insurance sold mortgages to the corporation and received premiums for placing insurance on its property, he was not subject to liability for the profit that he made thereby.

In Matter of Schiff, 203 Misc. 805, 118 N.Y.S.2d 828 (1952), where the beneficiaries of a charitable trust were to be selected by the presidents for the time being of three charitable institutions, it was held that they could properly include these institutions in making such selection.

are not permitted to profit in other ways through the administration of the trust. Thus it has been held that where one of the trustees of a charitable trust purchases at a discount a claim against the trust estate, he will not be permitted to profit by enforcing the claim for more than the amount that he paid for it.[11] It is, of course, the duty of the trustees of a charitable trust, like those of a private trust, to keep the trust funds separate from their individual funds.[12]

Where property is given to a charitable corporation for a particular purpose, the property must be devoted to that purpose.[13] If it complies with the terms of the gift, however, it can properly take into consideration the promotion of the general purposes for which the gift was made. Thus in *Attorney General v. President and Fellows of Harvard College*[14] land was conveyed to a university for the purpose of establishing an arboretum, and gifts were made to maintain the arboretum. It was held that the university could properly remove books and dried specimens for deposit in its library and herbarium because this was in the interests of botany as a whole and involved no departure from the terms of the gifts. Whittemore, J., said:

> There is a dominant public interest that public charitable trusts in private educational hands be so managed under the particular trust provisions as to be of maximum usefulness, thus serving to the greatest possible extent the public as the ultimate beneficiary. In the light of this, in a gift to a university of trust funds to create a specific subdivision of scientific or cultural activity of the university (that is, broadly, a department), there is, we think, an implied intention that the managers of the university shall determine in their best judgment what policies, in respect of that

---

In George Pepperdine Found. v. Pepperdine, 126 Cal. App. 2d 154, 271 P.2d 600 (1954), where the defendant, a philanthropist, created a charitable corporation of which he was president, and he so invested the funds as to incur large losses, it was held that neither he nor the directors were liable, although the investments may have been improper investments. This decision was partially disapproved in Holt v. College of Osteopathic Physicians & Surgeons, 61 Cal. 2d 750, 394 P.2d 932, 40 Cal. Rptr. 244 (1964).

In general, as to the trustees' duty of loyalty, see §§170 to 170.25.

[11]Attorney Gen. v. Armstrong, 231 Mass. 196, 120 N.E. 678 (1918).

[12]Attorney Gen. v. Bedard, 218 Mass. 378, 105 N.E. 993 (1914).

[13]See §348.1.

[14]350 Mass. 125, 213 N.E.2d 840 (1966) (citing the text).

department, within the express trust purposes, will give that department and the trust assets used therein their greatest usefulness. Certainly it is implied that to such end the managers may decide to correlate the activities of the department with the overall policies of related departments, provided all applicable restrictions are regarded, and the trust assets are used advantageously for the specific purposes of the trust.

He said that the university was not required to act solely in the interests of the arboretum.

§380. Extent of Trustee's Powers

The trustees of a charitable trust, like the trustees of a private trust, have such powers as are conferred on them in specific words by the terms of the trust or are necessary or appropriate to carry out the purposes of the trust and are not forbidden by the terms of the trust. The powers of trustees of a private trust have been considered elsewhere.[1] The fact that a charitable trust may continue for an indefinite period may have the effect of giving the trustees more extensive powers than they have in the case of a private trust, which is of limited duration. Thus long leases of property held for charitable purposes may be proper, where such leases would not be proper if made by the trustees of a private trust because they would continue beyond the period of the trust.[2]

§380. [1]See §§186-193.4.

[2]*England:* Attorney-General v. South Sea Co., 4 Beav. 453 (1841); In re Cross's Charity, 27 Beav. 592 (1859).

Kentucky: Trustees of Madison Academy v. Board of Educ., 16 Ky. L. Rep. 51, 26 S.W. 187 (1894).

Pennsylvania: Pennsylvania Horticultural Socy. v. Craig, 240 Pa. 137, 87 A. 678 (1913).

South Carolina: Black v. Ligon, Harper's Eq. (5 S.C. Eq.) 205 (1824).

A lease made by the trustees of a charity is invalid if improvidently made. Attorney-General v. Owen, 10 Ves. 555 (1805); Attorney-General v. Foord, 6 Beav. 288 (1843).

Leases made by trustees of a charity, if for a reasonable time, are valid and binding on successor trustees. Jeanes v. Burke, 226 S.W.2d 908 (Tex. Civ. App. 1950).

California Probate Code, §§1032, 1035, added by Laws 1982, c. 41, as

By the terms of the trust the trustees may have a power, express or implied, to sell land.[3] Even though no power of sale is conferred by the terms of the trust, or even though a sale is expressly forbidden, the court may direct or permit the trustees to sell the property where such a sale is necessary to accomplish the purposes of the trust.[4] In the case of a charitable trust as in the case of a private trust, the trustees cannot properly mortgage the trust property unless a power to mortgage is conferred, expressly or impliedly, by the terms of the trust.[5] The trustees of a charitable trust can properly incur expenses that are necessary or appropriate to carry out the purposes of the trust, and are entitled to indemnity out of the trust estate for such expenses.[6] The trustees of a charitable trust, like the trustees of a

---

amended by Laws 1986, c. 820, provide that if a will manifests an intention to create a marital deduction trust or charitable remainder trust the powers of the trustee are limited and the distributive provisions modified to the extent necessary to make the trust qualify under federal law in the intended category.

In Sayre College v. General Assembly of Presbyterian Church, 308 Ky. 404, 214 S.W.2d 601 (1948), where there was a provision in a deed of land to a college that the land should not be alienated or encumbered, it was held that the college could properly make ordinary leases, but not a lease for 99 years.

[3]Harvard College v. Weld, 159 Mass. 114, 34 N.E. 175 (1893).

Where no power of sale is conferred expressly or by implication, the trustees cannot sell land held upon a charitable trust without the authorization of the court. Congregational Church Union of Boston v. Attorney Gen., 290 Mass. 1, 194 N.E. 820 (1935).

In Wilstach Estate, 1 D.&C.2d 197 (Pa. 1954), it was held that where a testatrix left her works of art to found an art museum, the trustees had power to sell some of the objects without applying to the court.

By Virginia Code 1950, §13.1-246.1, as enacted by Laws 1973, c. 476, it is provided that an incorporated educational institution may in certain circumstances by vote of its trustees or directors sell land in excess of 1000 acres, notwithstanding any provision in its charter or in the deed or will under which it holds the land.

See Thurston, Disposals of Land by Charities [1987] 1 Trust L. & P. 138.

[4]See §§381, 399-399.5.

[5]Emmerglick v. Vogel, 131 N.J. Eq. 257, 24 A.2d 861 (1942) (citing Restatement of Trusts §380); Shannonhouse v. Wolfe, 191 N.C. 769, 133 S.E. 93 (1926).

Cf. Rosemary Simmons Memorial Hous. Assn. v. United Dominions Trust, [1987] 1 All E.R. 281, [1986] 1 W.L.R. 1440 (Ch.D.), §191, n. 1.

[6]Estate of Bishop, 36 Haw. 403 (1943) (quoting the text), noted in 32 Calif. L. Rev. 208; Bradbury v. Birchmore, 117 Mass. 569 (1875); Nelson v. Georgetown, 190 Mass. 225, 76 N.E. 606 (1906).

private trust, can properly compromise or submit to arbitration claims by or against third persons.[7]

By the terms of the trust the legal title to the trust property may be vested in a designated trustee or in several trustees and the control of the administration of the trust may be conferred on others.[8] In such a case the trustees have no active duties. So also by the terms of the trust the financial administration of the trust may be committed to the trustee and the power to determine the purposes to which the trust property shall be applied may be vested in others. This method of administering the trust is that which is employed in the so-called community trusts. The title to the trust property and the power to invest and reinvest is conferred upon a bank or trust company, but the charitable purposes to which the property shall be applied from time to

---

In Parkinson v. Murdock, 183 Kan. 706, 332 P.2d 273 (1958), it was held that where property was left in trust to maintain a municipal art museum, the trustee could properly employ a person to inspect the objects of art and to see that they are properly housed and cared for, and make expenditures to prepare a catalogue of the objects; and the court authorized payment to the trustee for her services in preparing the catalogue. The court quoted the text.

By Hawaii Rev. Stat., §607-20, it is provided that the trustees of a charitable trust shall be entitled "to just and reasonable allowances for bookkeeping, clerical and special services and expenses incidental thereto."

[7]*Massachusetts:* Morville v. American Tract Socy., 123 Mass. 129, 25 Am. Rep. 40 (1877) (charitable corporation);

North Carolina: Sigmund Sternberger Found. v. Tannenbaum, 273 N.C. 658, 161 S.E.2d 116 (1968) (charitable corporation; quoting the text).

Texas: Robbins v. Simmons Estate, 252 S.W.2d 970 (Tex. Civ. App. 1952) (citing Restatement of Trusts §391).

See §192.

By New Hampshire Rev. Stat. Ann., §556:27, it is provided that the Attorney General or the Director of the Register of Charitable Trusts shall be a necessary party to any agreement between an executor and creditors or legatees or heirs-at-law whenever such agreement may directly or indirectly affect a charitable interest, residuary or otherwise, created in any estate.

See §337.8, n. 5; §340, n. 15; §367, n. 3.

[8]*Massachusetts:* Cary Library v. Bliss, 151 Mass. 364, 25 N.E. 92, 7 L.R.A. 765 (1890); City of Boston v. Doyle, 184 Mass. 373, 68 N.E. 851 (1903); Worcester City Missionary Socy. v. Memorial Church, 186 Mass. 531, 72 N.E. 71 (1904); City of Boston v. Curley, 276 Mass. 549, 177 N.E. 557 (1931).

Pennsylvania: Garrison Estate, 391 Pa. 234, 137 A.2d 321 (1958) (quoting the text).

time are determined by a group of persons selected in accordance with the terms of the trust instrument.[9]

§381. Deviation from Terms of the Trust

The power of a court of equity to permit or direct a deviation from the terms of the trust is at least as extensive in the case of charitable trusts as it is in the case of private trusts.[1] The courts will direct or permit a deviation from the terms of the trust where compliance is impossible or illegal, or where owing to circumstances not known to the settlor and not anticipated by him compliance would defeat or substantially impair the accomplishment of the purposes of the trust. It has been held in numerous cases that the court may authorize the sale of property held upon a charitable trust although such sale is not authorized or is forbidden by the terms of the trust.[2] Thus where a settlor

[9]In Taylor v. Baldwin, 362 Mo. 1224, 247 S.W.2d 741 (1952), it was held that the trustees of a hospital corporation properly exercised their discretion in authorizing an affiliation with a university medical center. The court cited the Restatement of Trusts §380.

§381. [1]See §§165-167.2.

England: Re J. W. Laing Trust; Stewards' Co. v. Attorney-General, [1984] 1 All E.R. 50 (Ch.D.) (where trust property had increased substantially more than settlor contemplated, court will permit charitable trustee to deviate from direction to distribute all of the property within ten years).

Illinois: Matter of Estate of Offerman, 153 Ill. App. 3d 299, 106 Ill. Dec. 107, 585 N.E.2d 413 (1987), citing Restatement (Second) of Trusts §381.

Canada: Saint John v. Attorney-General, 51 N.B.R.2d 354, 134 A.P.R. 354 (N.B.Q.B. 1983).

[2]*Federal:* Stanley v. Colt, 5 Wall. 119, 18 L. Ed. 502 (U.S. 1866).

Alabama: Heustess v. Huntingdon College, 242 Ala. 272, 5 So. 2d 777 (1942) (citing Restatement of Trusts, §381, Comment *d*); Thurlow v. Berry, 249 Ala. 597, 32 So. 2d 526 (1947) (citing the text and Restatement of Trusts §381).

See Dallas Art League v. Weaver, 240 Ala. 432, 199 So. 831 (1941).

But see Lovelace v. Marion Inst., 215 Ala. 271, 110 So. 381 (1926), noted in 2 Ala. L.J. 254, 36 Yale L.J. 582.

Arizona: State v. Coerver, 100 Ariz. 135, 412 P.2d 259 (1966) (citing the text).

Arkansas: Bossen v. Woman's Christian Natl. Library Assn., 216 Ark. 334, 225 S.W.2d 336 (1949) (citing Restatement of Trusts §§380, 381, 399), noted

conveyed to trustees her residence, to be used as an old ladies'

in 4 Sw. L.J. 352; Anderson v. Ryland, 232 Ark. 335, 336 S.W.2d 52 (1960) (citing Restatement of Trusts §§167, 381).

California: O'Hara v. Grand Lodge I.O.G.T., 213 Cal. 131, 2 P.2d 21 (1931).

Connecticut: Bristol Baptist Church v. Connecticut Baptist Convention, 98 Conn. 677, 120 A. 497 (1923); Williams Memorial Inst. v. Beers, 18 Conn. Supp. 512 (1954); Goetz v. Dietz, 20 Conn. Supp. 360, 135 A.2d 369 (1957); See Charlotte Hungerford Hosp. v. Mulvey, 26 Conn. 394, 225 A.2d 495 (1966); Harris v. Attorney Gen., 31 Conn. 93, 324 A.2d 279 (1974) (sale of a house connected with a museum).

Delaware: Trustees of New Castle Common v. Gordy, 33 Del. Ch. 334, 93 A.2d 509, 40 A.L.R.2d 544 (1952) (*semble;* citing the text), noted in 101 U. Pa. L. Rev. 1087.

Illinois: Catholic Bishop of Chicago v. Murr, 3 Ill. 2d 107, 120 N.E.2d 4 (1954); City of Aurora v. Young Men's Christian Assn., 9 Ill. 2d 286, 137 N.E.2d 347 (1956); Catholic Bishop of Chicago v. Castle (Catholic Bishop of Chicago v. Elliott), 14 Ill. App. 2d 495, 144 N.E.2d 874 (1957).

Indiana: Foust v. William E. English Found., 118 Ind. App. 484, 80 N.E.2d 303 (1948) (quoting the text and Restatement of Trusts, §381, Comment *e*), noted in 24 Ind. L.J. 464.

Kentucky: Sawyer v. Lamar, 230 Ky. 168, 18 S.W.2d 971 (1929), noted in 8 Tenn. L. Rev. 52; Board of Trustees of Madison Academy v. Board of Educ., 282 Ky. 671, 139 S.W.2d 766 (1940); Kelly v. Second Presbyterian Church, 288 Ky. 592, 157 S.W.2d 123 (1941); Pennebaker v. Pennebaker Home for Girls, 297 Ky. 670, 181 S.W.2d 49 (1944) (quoting Restatement of Trusts, §381, Comment *e*).

Louisiana: Ada C. Pollack-Blundon Assn. v. Heirs of Evans, 273 So. 2d 552 (La. App. 1973).

Massachusetts: Weeks v. Hobson, 150 Mass. 377, 23 N.E. 215, 6 L.R.A. 147 (1890); Amory v. Attorney Gen., 179 Mass. 89, 60 N.E. 391 (1901); Ford v. Rockland Trust Co., 331 Mass. 25, 116 N.E.2d 669 (1954) (citing the text).

Mississippi: City of Jackson v. Trustees of Young Women's Christian Assn., 224 Miss. 298, 80 So. 2d 50 (1955); Hengen v. Perpetual Care Cemeteries, 230 So. 2d 795 (Miss. 1970) (citing the text, §190.4).

Missouri: Lackland v. Walker, 151 Mo. 210, 52 S.W. 414 (1899).

Nebraska: Matteson v. Creighton University, 105 Neb. 219, 179 N.W. 1009 (1920).

New Hampshire: Methodist Episcopal Socy. v. Harriman, 54 N.H. 444 (1874); Rolfe and Rumford Asylum v. Lefebre, 69 N.H. 238, 45 A. 1087 (1897); Smart v. Durham, 77 N.H. 56, 86 A. 821 (1913); Trustees of Pittsfield Academy v. Attorney Gen., 95 N.H. 51, 57 A.2d 161 (1948) (citing the text); Souther v. Schofield, 95 N.H. 379, 63 A.2d 796 (1949) (quoting the text); Trustees of Protestant Episcopal Church v. Danais, 108 N.H. 344, 235 A.2d 516 (1967), 108 N.H. 347, 235 A.2d 518 (1967).

New Jersey: Trustees of the First Presbyterian Church v. Wheeler, 106 N.J.

home, and securities, the income of which was to be used to

Eq. 8, 149 A. 589 (1930), *semble,* noted in 40 Yale L.J. 143; Trinity Cathedral
in the Diocese of N.J. v. Etz, 137 N.J. Eq. 261, 44 A.2d 394 (1945) *(semble;* citing
Restatement of Trusts, §381, Comment *e*); Mirinda v. King, 11 N.J. Super.
165, 78 A.2d 98 (1951); Paterson v. Paterson Gen. Hosp., 97 N.J. Super. 514,
235 A.2d 487 (1967) (hospital removed to suburb).

New York: Trustees of Sailors' Snug Harbor v. Carmody, 211 N.Y. 286,
105 N.E. 543 (1914); Application of Arms, 189 Misc. 576, 64 N.Y.S.2d 693
(1946); Matter of Krantz, 13 Misc. 2d 800, 178 N.Y.S.2d 537 (1958); Application of Bd. of Educ. of Utica City School Dist., 18 Misc. 2d 192, 184 N.Y.S.2d
735 (1959); Matter of Randall, 68 Misc. 2d 119, 326 N.Y.S.2d 603 (1971), *aff'd.*
38 A.D.2d 1012, 330 N.Y.S.2d 998 (1972); Matter of Randall, 71 Misc. 2d
1063, 338 N.Y.S.2d 269 (1972).

North Carolina: Grace Church v. Ange, 161 N.C. 314, 77 S.E. 239 (1913);
Holton v. Elliott, 193 N.C. 708, 138 S.E. 3 (1927); Johnson v. Wagner, 219
N.C. 235, 13 S.E.2d 419 (1941) (citing the text); Brooks v. Duckworth, 234
N.C. 549, 67 S.E.2d 752 (1951) (citing the text); Wachovia Bank & Trust Co.
v. John Thomasson Constr. Co., 3 N.C. App. 157, 164 S.E.2d 519 (1968), *aff'd,*
275 N.C. 399, 168 S.E.2d 358 (1969).

Ohio: First Presbyterian Church of Salem v. Tarr, 63 Ohio App. 286, 26
N.E.2d 597 (1939); Board of Educ., v. Unknown Heirs of Aughinbaugh, 99
Ohio App. 463, 134 N.E.2d 872 (1955) (citing Restatement of Trusts §§165,
167); Baily v. McElroy, 120 Ohio App. 85, 195 N.E.2d 559 (1963).

Pennsylvania: Myers v. Crick, 271 Pa. 399, 114 A. 255 (1921); Daniels v.
Ralpho Township School Dist. 13 Northumberland Leg. J. 209 (Pa. 1937)
(quoting Restatement of Trusts §§381, 399); Lehigh Univ. v. Hower, 159 Pa.
Super. 84, 46 A.2d 516 (1946) *(semble;* citing Restatement of Trusts §167);
Girard Estate, 73 D.&C. 42 (Pa. 1950); Hill Trust, 23 D.&C.2d 791 (Pa. 1961)
(citing Restatement of Trusts §§167, 381, and 399).

Rhode Island: Brown v. Meeting St. Baptist Socy., 9 R.I. 177 (1869); Town
of South Kingstown v. Wakefield Trust Co., 48 R.I. 27, 134 A. 815, 48 A.L.R.
1122 (1926); Buchanan v. McLyman, 51 R.I. 177, 153 A. 304 (1931).

South Carolina: Furman Univ. v. McLeod, 238 S.C. 475, 120 S.E.2d 865
(1961) (citing the text and Restatement of Trusts, §381, Comment *d*).

Tennessee: Henshaw v. Flenniken, 183 Tenn. 232, 191 S.W.2d 541, 168
A.L.R. 1010 (1946) (quoting the text), noted in 19 Tenn. L. Rev. 483; Goodman v. State, 49 Tenn. App. 96, 351 S.W.2d 399 (1961).

Wyoming: Bentley v. Whitney Benefits, 41 Wyo. 11, 281 P. 188 (1929).

New Zealand: In re Martin (Decd.), [1968] N.Z.L.R. 289.

See Note, Power of court to authorize sale of property contrary to provisions of trust, 168 A.L.R. 1018 (1947).

In Glatfelder Trust Deed Case (Appeal of School Dist. of Borough of
Columbia), 372 Pa. 502, 94 A.2d 723 (1953), where land was conveyed to a
school district as a playground, the court refused to permit a sale of a part of
it, and held that if it should prove impracticable to maintain it, a cy pres
application could be made.

maintain the home, and later the income became insufficient, the court permitted the use of principal to make up the deficiency.[3] The court, however, will not permit the sale of trust property in spite of the change in conditions, if there is a provision in the trust instrument for reverter if the property should no longer be used for the designated charitable purpose.[4]

In some states there are statutes providing that the court may authorize or direct the sale of land held for charitable purposes:

Kentucky: Rev. Stat. Ann., §273.140.

Michigan: Stat. Ann., §26.1211.

New Jersey: Rev. Stat., §§15:14-7, 16:1-22.

New York: Estates, Powers and Trusts Law, §8-1.1, amended by Laws 1971, c. 1058, and Laws 1985, c. 492. Matter of Reiger, 60 A.D.2d 299, 400 N.Y.S.2d 881 (1977).

In Application of Guaranty Trust Co. (Matter of Petroleum Research Fund), 15 Misc. 2d 23, 507, 184 N.Y.S.2d 413 (1959), s.c. 22 Misc. 2d 83, 200 N.Y.S.2d 118 (1960), where several oil companies created a charitable trust for purposes of research, substantially the whole of the corpus being shares of a company, and it was provided that these shares should not be sold unless authorized by the court, the court authorized a sale where it appeared that such sale because of change of circumstances was necessary to effectuate the purposes of the trust.

In Succession of Rogers, 138 So. 2d 251 (La. 1962), it was held that where land was devised for the construction of a college chapel, a restriction on the sale of the land was invalid under Louisiana Civil Code, §1519.

[3]Merchants Bank & Trust Co. v. Garrett, 203 Miss. 182, 33 So. 2d 603 (1948) (quoting the Restatement of Trusts §167).

See Knickerbocker Hosp. v. Goldstein, 181 Misc. 540, 41 N.Y.S.2d 32 (1943).

But compare Application of Brooklyn Children's Aid Socy., 269 A.D. 789, 55 N.Y.S.2d 323 (1945); Lutheran Hosp. of Manhattan v. Goldstein, 182 Misc. 913, 46 N.Y.S.2d 705 (1944).

In Givens v. Third Natl. Bank, 516 S.W.2d 356 (Tenn. 1974), where the income became more than enough to pay the annuitants, the court held that the income should not be paid immediately to the charitable institution, which was given the remainder, but should be accumulated, even though this made the income taxable. The court found that the settlor intended such accumulation and was probably aware of the tax consequences. Hence the court refused to permit a deviation from the terms of the trust.

By Vermont Stat. Ann., tit. 16, §§3681 to 3684, it is provided that if an educational corporation holds a fund of which, whether by statute or by usage, only the income may be expended, and it is unable to pay its expenses from its current receipts, the court may on petition permit use of the principal.

[4]Roberds v. Markham, 81 F. Supp. 38 (D.D.C. 1948), noted in 2 Okla. L. Rev. 384, 18 U. Cin. L. Rev. 228. See §401.2.

Where by the terms of the trust the trustees are forbidden to sell the trust property, it is improper for them to sell the property without application to the court even though a sale becomes necessary to carry out the purposes of the trust.[5] But if the circumstances are such that the court would have authorized the sale, the court may subsequently approve it.[6] The court will not authorize a sale if it does not appear that such sale would be for the benefit of the trust.[7] Where the trustees apply to the court for permission to sell, the Attorney General should be joined as a party to the proceeding.[8]

So also the court will not permit the sale if there is a provision in the trust instrument for a gift over to another charity in the event that the property should no longer be used for the designated charitable purpose. Mississippi Children's Home Socy. v. City of Jackson, 230 Miss. 546, 93 So. 2d 483 (1957). See §§399.2, 401.5.

See Matter of Reiger, 60 A.D.2d 299, 400 N.Y.S.2d 881 (1977), where it was held that no condition or limitation was imposed.

[5]Trustees of the First Presbyterian Church v. Wheeler, 106 N.J. Eq. 8, 149 A. 589 (1930), noted in 40 Yale L.J. 143; Seif v. Krebs, 239 Pa. 423, 86 A. 872 (1913); Woodring v. Lesher, 147 Pa. Super. 340, 24 A.2d 42 (1942).

See Congregational Church Union of Boston v. Attorney Gen., 290 Mass. 1, 194 N.E. 820 (1935).

See Milner v. Staffordshire Congregational Union, [1956] Ch. 275, where the trustees made a contract to sell without having obtained the approval of the Charity Commissioners.

In Petition of Acchione, 425 Pa. 23, 227 A.2d 816 (1967), it was held that where a township bought and dedicated land to park purposes it could not sell the land without order of the court.

In Sullivan v. Roman Catholic Archbishop of Boston, 368 Mass. 253, 331 N.E.2d 57 (1975), where a testator devised his farm to be devoted to such charitable purposes as the trustee might select, it was held that the trustee had power to sell the land.

[6]O'Hara v. Grand Lodge I.O.G.T., 213 Cal. 131, 2 P.2d 21 (1931).

[7]City of St. Louis v. McAllister, 281 Mo. 26, 218 S.W. 312 (1920); City of Englewood v. Allison Land Co., 25 N.J. Super. 466, 96 A.2d 702 (1953); City of Englewood v. Allison Land Co., 40 N.J. Super. 495, 123 A.2d 591 (1956), aff'd 45 N.J. Super. 538, 133 A.2d 680 (1957).

In In re Trust of McDonough, 252 Iowa 870, 109 N.W.2d 29 (1961), where land was devised in trust to pay the rents and profits to a charitable corporation, the court refused to permit a sale of the land and the investment of the proceeds in securities, because the land was producing a fair income and there was no exigency. The court quoted Restatement of Trusts, §381, Comment *d.*

[8]*Massachusetts:* Congregational Church Union of Boston v. Attorney Gen., 290 Mass. 1, 194 N.E. 820 (1935);

The court may authorize the trustees of a charitable trust to mortgage trust property where such mortgage is necessary to carry out the purposes of the trust, although by the terms of the trust the trustee is not authorized to mortgage the property.[9]

There are other situations in which the court may authorize a deviation from the terms of the trust.[10] Thus it has been held

---

New Jersey: Bernardsville Methodist Episcopal Church v. Seney, 85 N.J. Eq. 271, 96 A. 388 (1915);

New York: Trustees of Sailors' Snug Harbor v. Carmody, 211 N.Y. 286, 105 N.E. 543 (1914).

Rhode Island: Donnelly v. Israel, 113 R.I. 29, 317 A.2d 443 (1974).

[9]Long v. Simmons Female College, 218 Mass. 135, 105 N.E. 553 (1914); Bond v. Town of Tarboro, 217 N.C. 289, 7 S.E.2d 617, 127 A.L.R. 695 (1940).

See Note, Power of trustees of charitable trust to mortgage trust property, 127 A.L.R. 705 (1940).

By New York Estates, Powers and Trusts Law, §8-1.1 as amended by Laws 1971, c. 1058, and by Laws 1985, c. 492, it is provided that the supreme court may authorize the sale or mortgage of real estate held for charitable purposes that has or is likely to become unproductive or has depreciated or is likely to depreciate in value, or where it is advisable to raise money to improve or erect buildings on the property, or where it is expedient for any other reason that such property be sold or mortgaged.

[10]*Connecticut:* Britton v. Killian, 27 Conn. Supp. 483, 245 A.2d 289 (1968) (where the testator directed that not more than 20 percent of the principal should be used to construct a home for the aged, the court refused to permit the expenditure of a greater sum; the court cited Restatement of Trusts §381).

New Jersey: Rev. Stat., §3B:14-24, enacted by Laws 1968, c. 270, repealed and reenacted by Laws 1981, c. 405, provides, "The court having jurisdiction of the estate or trust may authorize the fiduciary to exercise any other power which in the judgment of the court is necessary for the proper administration of the estate or trust."

New York: Application of Trustees of Diocesan Convention, 126 Misc. 2d 860, 484 N.Y.S.2d 407 (Sur. 1984).

Pennsylvania: Coleman Estate, 456 Pa. 163, 317 A.2d 361 (1974) (a provision in the terms of a charitable foundation that no one could serve as trustee unless his or her spouse was a Protestant was whimsical and should be disregarded).

Texas: Gregory v. Mbank Corpus Christi, N.A., 716 S.W.2d 662 (Tex. App. 1986).

As to the authorization by the court to widen the powers of trustees of charitable trusts, as well as those of private trusts, in making investments, see §167, nn. 15 to 24.

As to the scope of investments of funds held in trust for charitable purposes, see §389.

that where a legacy was given in trust to invest in certain government bonds and to use the income in giving a prize for discoveries in the realm of physics, the court might authorize the investment in other securities, because it appeared that the investment in the designated securities had become almost impossible owing to the diminution in the amount of those securities.[11]

The court may permit a deviation from or modification of the terms of the trust in order to avoid unfavorable tax consequences.[12]

There is greater occasion for the exercise of the power of the court to permit or direct a deviation from the terms of the trust in the case of charitable trusts than in the case of private trusts, because charitable trusts may continue for an indefinite period and changes in conditions not foreseen by the settlor are therefore more likely to occur.[13] Moreover, in the case of chari-

---

As to the scope of the Uniform Management of Institutional Funds Act, see §§367.2, 379, 389.

[11]American Academy of Arts & Sciences v. President and Fellows of Harvard College, 12 Gray 582 (Mass. 1832).

See John A. Creighton Home for Girls' Trust v. Waltman, 140 Neb. 3, 299 N.W. 261 (1941); Long Asylum Trustees' Petition, 63 D.&C. 284 (Pa. 1948) (quoting Restatement of Trusts §381); In re Kirby Memorial Health Center, 36 Luz. Legal Reg. 70 (Pa. 1941) (citing Restatement of Trusts §381). See §227.11.

In In re Harvey, [1941] 3 All E.R. 284, noted in 6 Convey. (N.S.) 139, where two sisters made identical residuary bequests to found a home for needy persons, it was held that although the trustee had no power to blend the estates the court could under Trustee Act, 1925, §57(1), confer such power on him. See §179.2, n. 4.

In In re Shipwrecked Fishermen & Mariners' Royal Benevolent Socy., [1959] Ch. 220, noted in 75 Law Q. Rev. 21, it was held that under Trustee Act, 1925, §57(1), the court had jurisdiction to widen the powers of investment of a charitable corporation beyond those specified in the statute creating the corporation.

In Bank of Del. v. Allmond, 40 Del. Ch. 372, 183 A.2d 188 (1962), it was held that the trustees were not permitted to invade the principal of a charitable fund contrary to the terms of the trust unless the court should permit it.

[12]See §167, n. 20; §348.4, n. 2.

[13]See Estate of Loring, 29 Cal. 2d 423, 175 P.2d 524 (1946), mod'g 168 P.2d 224 (Cal. App. 1946) (citing the text and Restatement of Trusts §§157, 381); City of Springfield v. Patterson, 26 Ohio Misc. 242, 55 Ohio Ops. 2d 323, 270 N.E.2d 683 (1970) (citing the text and Restatement of Trusts §381).

table trusts the court has power not merely, as in the case of private trusts, to permit deviations as to matters relating to the

---

In Reed v. Eagleton, 384 S.W.2d 578 (Mo. 1964), where a testator left the residue in trust for a city and directed the trustees to use the trust estate for the purchase of land to be used for public parks, the court authorized the use of the estate in the making of improvements on parks already owned by the city. The court said that it was immaterial whether this be treated as a deviation from administration terms or an application of the cy pres doctrine, quoting Restatement of Trusts §381.

In Gordon v. City of Baltimore, 258 Md. 682, 267 A.2d 98 (1970), it was held that the Peabody Institute of the City of Baltimore could transfer its library to the Enoch Pratt Free Library. The court gave a liberal interpretation to the words of the founder of the Peabody Institute, quoting the text and citing Restatement of Trusts §381.

In Matter of Barkey, 65 Misc. 2d 738, 318 N.Y.S.2d 843 (1971), where the trustees were authorized to make payments to charities exempt by law from New York state and federal income taxes, the court allowed an amendment to take account of the federal Tax Reform Act of 1969. The court quoted the text. For statutes and decisions as to the reformation of the terms of the trust to meet the requirements of the federal Tax Reform Act of 1969, see §348.4, n. 3.

In In re Estate of Hermann, 454 Pa. 292, 312 A.2d 16 (1973), where land and objects of art were conveyed to trustees to maintain a museum, and the settlor by will gave money to a bank in trust to pay for the maintenance of the museum with a provision that if the museum should cease to exist the money was to go to other charities, it was held that the sale of the land and the placing of the objects of art in a public library did not cause the museum to cease to exist.

In Mills v. Ball, 380 So. 2d 1134 (Fla. App. 1980), the court permitted an increase in the number of trustees of a charitable trust, citing Restatement of Trusts §381.

See Note, Cy Pres and Deviation: Current Trends in Application, 8 Real Prop., Prob. & Tr. J. 391 (1973).

The modern tendency is to extend the doctrine of deviation, where this seems desirable, whether or not the settlor had foreseen the circumstances.

In Klein Estate, 66 D.&C.2d 627 (Pa. 1974), where the testator included detailed provisions as to a trust for the benefit of a church, the court said that "it certainly does no violence to the expressed intent of a testator to carry out his wishes in more modern or efficient ways than were known to him."

By Wisconsin Stat., §701.10(2)(b), it is provided that "If any administrative provision of a charitable trust or part of a plan set forth by the settlor to achieve his charitable purpose is or becomes impractical, unlawful, inconvenient or undesirable, and a modification of such provision or plan will enable the trustee to achieve more effectively the basic charitable purpose, the court may by appropriate order modify the provision or plan."

administration of the trust, but also as to the purposes of the trust. This power of the court, under the so-called doctrine of cy pres, goes quite beyond anything that is permitted in the case of private trusts. Where the court permits a sale of property held upon a charitable trust, however, it is not necessary to resort to the doctrine of cy pres, although such sale is not permitted or is forbidden by the terms of the trust. The court can permit the sale in the exercise of its ordinary power over the administration of trusts. This is true even where by the terms of the trust the trustees are directed to conduct the charitable enterprise on the particular land given to them. Thus in a Rhode Island case, where land was given in trust to maintain thereon a schoolhouse and for no other purpose whatever, and subsequently the land became unsuitable as a site for a schoolhouse, the court authorized a sale of the land.[14] Sweetland, C.J., said: "The circum-

---

[14]Town of S. Kingstown v. Wakefield Trust Co., 48 R.I. 27, 32, 134 A. 815, 48 A.L.R. 1122 (1926).

See also Craft v. Shroyer, 81 Ohio App. 253, 74 N.E.2d 589 (1947) (citing the text and Restatement of Trusts §381), noted in 9 Ohio St. L.J. 181.

In Furman Univ. v. McLeod, 238 S.C. 475, 120 S.E.2d 865 (1961), it was held that a university might substitute a new women's campus. The court said that the doctrine of deviation was applicable even though the cy pres doctrine was not accepted in South Carolina.

Re J. W. Laing Trust; Stewards' Co. v. Attorney-General, [1984] 1 Ch. 143; [1984] 1 All E.R. 50 (Ch. Div.) involved an inter vivos trust for charity providing that all principal and income must be distributed during the settlor's lifetime or within ten years after his death. The value of the trust property increased unexpectedly to £24,000,000 and the trustees requested permission to defer distribution. It was held that such permission could be granted within the inherent jurisdiction of the court to permit deviation from administrative provisions of trusts and that it did not involve change in the purposes of the trust under the cy pres doctrine or §13 of the Charities Act 1960, 8 & 9 Eliz. II, c. 58.

In Northern Ill. Medical Center v. Home State Bank of Crystal Lake, 136 Ill. App. 3d 129, 90 Ill. Dec. 802, 482 N.E.2d 1085 (1985), it was said that, although the cy pres doctrine will not be applied if the settlor directed another disposition of his bounty should it be impossible to carry out a particular charitable purpose, deviation from administrative provisions may be permitted.

In First Natl. Bank & Trust Co. v. Brimmer, 504 P.2d 1367 (Wyo. 1973), where a testatrix left funds for scholarships in the Casper Community College, it was held that the funds could not be used for scholarships in the Laramie Community College, because neither the doctrine of cy pres nor that of devia-

stances of the case do not call for the application of the cy pres doctrine, but merely for the exercise of the ordinary jurisdiction of the Superior Court, sitting in equity, over the administration of trusts." In some of the cases, however, in which the court has permitted the sale of land given as a site for a charitable institution, it has treated the matter as one involving the exercise of the cy pres power.[15] In a case in Alabama[16] the court held that a deviation from the terms of a charitable trust was permissible even if the doctrine of cy pres were rejected. We shall consider hereafter the situations in which the court exercises the cy pres power.[17]

There is some authority to the effect that the legislature, as well as the court, may authorize a sale of property held upon a charitable trust, where a power of sale is not conferred on the trustees by the terms of the trust or where such sale is expressly forbidden by the terms of the trust.[18] The legislature, however,

---

tion was applicable. The court cited the text and Restatement of Trusts §381.

See South Carolina Natl. Bank v. Bonds, 260 S.C. 327, 195 S.E.2d 835, 68 A.L.R.3d 983 (1973), in which there was a trust to aid students of the high schools of a city, and owing to changes unforeseen by the testator the court permitted aid to students of high schools in the county.

See Note, Effect on charitable trust or bequest for particular school or school district, or students or graduates thereof, of change in school or district structure or organization, 68 A.L.R.3d 997 (1975).

[15]Weeks v. Hobson, 150 Mass. 377, 23 N.E. 215, 6 L.R.A. 147 (1890). See §399.

[16]Thurlow v. Berry, 249 Ala. 597, 32 So. 2d 526 (1947) (citing the text and Restatement of Trusts §381).

[17]See §§399-399.4.

[18]*Federal:* Stanley v. Colt, 5 Wall. 119, 18 L. Ed. 502 (U.S. 1866).

Delaware: Trustees for the Baptist Church v. Laird, 10 Del. Ch. 118 (1913) (where sale not expressly forbidden); Trustees of New Castle Common v. Gordy, 33 Del. 334, 93 A.2d 509 (1952) (citing the text), noted in 101 U. Pa. L. Rev. 1087.

Massachusetts: Sohier v. Trinity Church, 109 Mass. 1 (1871); Crawford v. Nies, 220 Mass. 61, 107 N.E. 382 (1914), 224 Mass. 474, 113 N.E. 408 (1916).

Rhode Island: Van Horne, Petitioner, 18 R.I. 389, 28 A. 341 (1893).

But in Bridgeport Pub. Library & Reading Room v. Burroughs Home, 85 Conn. 309, 82 A. 582 (1912), it was held that the power to authorize a sale of the property of a specific charitable trust is a judicial power and cannot be exercised by the legislature.

See Second Ecclesiastical Socy. v. Attorney Gen., 133 Conn. 89, 48 A.2d

has no power to authorize the use of property held upon a charitable trust for other purposes than those designated by the settlor.[19]

§382. Control of Discretionary Powers

Where discretion is conferred on the trustees of a charitable trust, the court will not interfere with the exercise of their discretion except to prevent an abuse of discretion. The principles are the same as those that are applicable to private trusts.[1] If the trustees act within the bounds of a reasonable judgment in the exercise of the discretion conferred on them, the court will not interfere.[2] The result is different, however, where the trustees

---

266 (1946); Tharp v. Fleming, 1 Houst. 580 (Del. 1858) (sale expressly forbidden by the trust instrument).

In Matter of Randall, 68 Misc. 2d 119, 326 N.Y.S.2d 603 (1971), *aff'd,* 38 A.D.2d 1012, 330 N.Y.S.2d 998 (1972), it was held that the Surrogates Court had jurisdiction to permit "The Trustees of the Sailors' Snug Harbor in the City of New York," a charitable corporation created by special act of the New York legislature, to sell its land and buildings on Staten Island and to transfer the institution to North Carolina. It was unnecessary to apply to the legislature.

See Matter of Randall, 71 Misc. 2d 1063, 338 N.Y.S.2d 269 (1972).

See Note, Power of Legislature to Authorize Deviations in Terms of a Trust, 101 U. Pa. L. Rev. 1087 (1953).

See Note, Constitutionality, construction, and effect of legislation authorizing sale of charitable trust property, 40 A.L.R.2d 556 (1955).

See an opinion of the Attorney General of Kansas to the effect that the legislature had no power to sell land given to the state for charitable purposes, quoted in 3 U. Kan. L. Rev. 295 (1955).

[19]See §§367.3, 399.5.

§382. [1]See §187.

[2]*Connecticut:* Harris v. Attorney Gen., 31 Conn. Supp. 93, 324 A.2d 279 (1974) (quoting the text).

Hawaii: Takabuki v. Ching, 695 P.2d 319 (Haw. 1985), citing text.

Massachusetts: Hawes Place Congregational Socy. v. Trustees of Hawes Fund, 5 Cush. 454 (Mass. 1850); Attorney Gen. v. Butler, 123 Mass. 304 (1877); Bradway v. Shattuck, 325 Mass. 168, 89 N.E.2d 753 (1950) (citing the text); Boston Seaman's Friend Socy. v. Attorney Gen., 379 Mass. 414, 398 N.E.2d 721 (1980) (citing the text).

Missouri: Taylor v. Baldwin, 362 Mo. 1224, 247 S.W.2d 741 (1952) (citing Restatement of Trusts §382); Ranken-Jordan Home v. Drury College, 449 S.W.2d 161 (Mo. 1970) (citing Restatement of Trusts §381).

act beyond the bounds of a reasonable judgment. Thus it has been held that where a testator left his estate to a town in trust to apply the income to the support of public schools in the town, in such way as the town shall judge best, the court would not permit the town to devote the income to purchasing books and presenting them to the scholars.[3]

§383. Several Trustees

As has been stated, where there are several trustees of a private trust, the powers conferred on them cannot be exercised without the concurrence of all the trustees, unless it is otherwise provided by the terms of the trust or by statute.[1] In the case of charitable trusts, the rule is different; powers conferred on the trustees can be exercised by the concurrence of a majority of them, unless it is otherwise provided by the terms of the trust.[2]

New Jersey: Larkin v. Wikoff, 75 N.J. Eq. 462, 72 A. 98 (1909), *aff'd,* 77 N.J. Eq. 589, 78 A. 1134 (1910).

Ohio: Carrel v. State, 11 Ohio App. 281 (1919).

Pennsylvania: See Williams's Appeal, 73 Pa. 249 (1873).

[3]Davis v. Inhabitants of Barnstable, 154 Mass. 224, 28 N.E. 165 (1891).

In Matter of James, 119 N.Y.S.2d 259 (1953), a testator left property to a charitable foundation and directed that the income be paid to specified charitable corporations, but provided that this should not limit the authority of the trustees of the foundation to discontinue distributions to any of the corporations in the event that they in their discretion should determine that changes in the charitable work should justify discontinuance of distribution. It was held that the discretion thus conferred on the trustees was not absolute.

In City of Englewood v. Allison Land Co., 45 N.J. Super. 538, 133 A.2d 680 (1957) (citing the text), *aff'g* 40 N.J. Super. 495, 123 A.2d 591 (1956), where a trust was created to preserve the beauties of the Palisades along the Hudson, and the trustees were authorized to sell land if found essential to carry out the terms of the trust, it was held that they were not authorized to sell for residential purposes in order to develop recreational or picnic parks.

§383. [1]See §194.

[2]*Federal:* Van Horn v. Lewis, 79 F. Supp. 541 (D.D.C. 1948).

Hawaii: Richards v. Midkiff, 48 Haw. 32, 396 P.2d 49 (1964) (citing the text and Restatement of Trusts §383); Takabuki v. Ching, 695 P.2d 319 (Haw. 1985), citing text.

Illinois: Gorin v. McFarland, 108 Ill. App. 2d 348, 247 N.E.2d 620 (1969) (citing Restatement of Trusts §383).

Massachusetts: City of Boston v. Doyle, 184 Mass. 373, 68 N.E. 851 (1903).

By the terms of the trust it may be provided, either expressly or by implication, that the powers or some of them shall be exercised only by the concurrent action of all of the trustees.[3]

§384. Surviving Trustees

If one of several trustees of a charitable trust dies or otherwise ceases to be trustee, the powers conferred on the trustees can be exercised by the surviving trustees, unless it is otherwise provided by the terms of the trust. The rule is the same as that which is applicable to private trusts.[1] In the case of a charitable trust of indefinite duration it would be rare indeed to find that the settlor intended the powers to cease merely because one of the trustees died or otherwise ceased to act. Whether it is necessary to fill the vacancy before the powers conferred on the trustees can be exercised depends on the language of the trust instrument and all the circumstances. Even though the broadest discretion is conferred on the trustees to determine to what charitable purposes the estate shall be devoted, it is to be in-

---

Missouri: Columbia Union Natl. Bank & Trust Co. v. Bundschu, 641 S.W.2d 864 (Mo. App. 1982).

New Jersey: Donaldson v. Madison Borough, 88 N.J. Super. 574, 213 A.2d 33 (1965) (citing the text and Restatement of Trusts §383).

Pennsylvania: Stewart's Estate, 48 D.&C. 526 (Pa. 1943) (citing the text and quoting Restatement of Trusts §383).

By Kentucky Rev. Stat. Ann., §273.110, it is provided that a majority of the trustees of a religious society may sue or be sued in their own names on behalf of the society in any action concerning the property of the society.

[3]Morville v. Fowle, 144 Mass. 109, 10 N.E. 766 (1887).

In Attorney Gen. v. Olson, 346 Mass. 190, 191 N.E.2d 132 (1963), where the trustees of a charitable trust were authorized to establish by-laws and rules for the governance of their conduct, it was held not improper to adopt a rule requiring unanimous action. The court cited the text and Restatement of Trusts, §383, Comment *b.*

As to the situation that arises where the trustees cannot agree, see Stuart v. Continental Illinois Natl. Bank & Trust Co., 68 Ill. 2d 502, 12 Ill. Dec. 248, 369 N.E.2d 1262, (1977), *cert. denied,* 444 U.S. 844, 100 S. Ct. 86, 62 L. Ed. 2d 56 (1979) (citing Restatement of Trusts §383), *aff'g* Northern Trust Co. v. Continental Illinois Natl. Bank & Trust Co., 43 Ill. App. 3d 169, 11 Ill. Dec. 767, 356 N.E.2d 1049 (1976), stated in §194, n. 15.

§384. [1]See §195.

ferred that the testator intended that the power to make the selection might be exercised by the surviving trustees.[2]

In rare cases it has been held that powers conferred on the original trustees cannot be exercised by the surviving trustees. Thus in *Hadley v. Hadley*[3] a testator left his estate to three persons in trust to devote it if thought practicable to the erection and maintenance of an institution for the education of poor children, and provided that if the erection of such an institution was not in the judgment of the said trustees deemed practicable the property should be divided among his heirs. One of the trustees predeceased the testator. The court held that the testator intended that the power to apply the property to the stated charitable purpose should be exercised only by the three trustees named by him, that the power was personal to them and could not be exercised by the survivors. Accordingly it was held that the charitable trust failed.

§385. Successor Trustees

Ordinarily, the powers conferred on the trustees of a charitable trust can be exercised by successor trustees.[1] The rule as to this is the same as in the case of trustees of a private trust.[2] If the settlor manifested an intention that the powers should be exercised only by the trustees originally named, they cannot be exercised by successor trustees.[3] But in the case of charitable trusts, which are to last for an indefinite period, such an intention is rarely found. Even where property is left to a person in trust for such charitable purposes as he may select, the trust will not ordinarily fail merely because the person named is unable or unwilling to act as trustee.[4]

[2]Coffin v. Attorney Gen., 231 Mass. 579, 121 N.E. 397 (1919).
[3]147 Ind. 423, 46 N.E. 823 (1897).
See §397.
§385. [1]Woodroof v. Hundley, 147 Ala. 287, 39 So. 907 (1905); Hartford Natl. Bank & Trust Co. v. Oak Bluffs Baptist Church, 116 Conn. 347, 164 A. 910 (1933); In re Estate of Grblny, 147 Neb. 117, 22 N.W.2d 488 (1946) (citing Restatement of Trusts §385); Taysum v. El Paso Natl. Bank, 256 S.W.2d 172 (Tex. Civ. App. 1953).
[2]See §196.
[3]Binney v. Attorney Gen., 259 Mass. 539, 156 N.E. 724 (1927), *semble*.
[4]See §397.

§385A. Power of Trustees to Convey to or to Form a Charitable Corporation

We have seen that trustees of a private trust cannot properly delegate to others the administration of the trust,[1] and that the same principle is applicable to trustees of a charitable trust.[2] Where property is given to trustees for charitable purposes, they cannot delegate the administration of the trust to an existing charitable corporation unless authorized to do so by the terms of the trust or by order of the court.[3]

The question arises, however, whether the trustees may form a corporation to administer the trust. It has been held that they can properly do so, if this does not involve a departure from the purpose of the donor.[4] But if it would be contrary to his

§385A. [1]See §171.1.

[2]See §379.

[3]*Iowa:* In re Estate of Owens, 244 Iowa 533, 57 N.W.2d 193 (1953).

Massachusetts: Harvard College v. Society for Promoting Theological Educ., 3 Gray 280 (Mass. 1855); Winthrop v. Attorney Gen., 128 Mass. 258 (1880); Morville v. Fowle, 144 Mass. 109, 10 N.E. 766 (1887); Massachusetts Charitable Mechanic Assn. v. Beede, 320 Mass. 601, 70 N.E.2d 825 (1947).

Canada: In re Partanen, [1944] 2 D.L.R. 473 (Ont.).

In Continental Ill. Natl. Bank & Trust Co. v. Sever, 324 Ill. App. 613, 59 N.E.2d 197 (1945), where a testator left his property for the purpose of establishing an educational institution of a certain character, it was held that the trustee could properly select an existing institution to receive the property.

In Pierce v. How, 153 Me. 180, 136 A.2d 510 (1957), where a testator created a trust to use the income for indigent seamen, it was held that the trustee might do this directly or by turning over the income to worthy associations organized for that purpose.

By Georgia Code 1981, §53-12-78, it is provided that the trustees of any charitable trust having as its object the relief of aged, impotent, diseased, and poor people by providing hospitals and hospital services are authorized to contract with any hospital for the care of such people and with the written consent of the donors may contribute trust funds for the construction and equipment of such hospitals where the beneficiaries of such trusts may receive treatment.

In Louisa T. York Orphan Asylum v. Erwin, 281 A.2d 453 (Me. 1971), where money was bequeathed to an orphan asylum to aid orphan children, it was held that it could properly make grants to similar organizations.

[4]*Federal:* Wallace v. Graff, 104 F. Supp. 925 (D.D.C. 1952) (express authorization).

Hawaii: Midkiff v. Kobayashi, 54 Haw. 299, 507 P.2d 724 (1973).

Massachusetts: Sanderson v. White, 18 Pick. 328, 29 Am. Dec. 591 (Mass.

purpose to administer the trust in this way, the trustees are not permitted to form a corporation to administer it.[5] Where the trustees can properly form a charitable corporation to administer a trust created by a testator's will, the provisions of the charter or certificate of incorporation must be such as are in accordance with the will.[6] In Louisiana it is provided by

---

1836); Nelson v. Cushing, 2 Cush. 519 (Mass. 1848); City of Boston v. Curley, 276 Mass. 549, 177 N.E. 557 (1931); Curtis v. First Church in Charlestown, 285 Mass. 73, 188 N.E. 631 (1933); Briggs v. Merchants Natl. Bank, 323 Mass. 261, 81 N.E.2d 827 (1948); Attorney Gen. v. Olson, 346 Mass. 190, 191 N.E.2d 132 (1963); Davenport v. Attorney Gen., 361 Mass. 372, 280 N.E.2d 193 (1972) (incorporation authorized by terms of the will).

New York: Matter of Folsom, 155 N.Y.S.2d 140 (1956), *aff'd,* 6 A.D.2d 691, 174 N.Y.S.2d 116 (1958), *aff'd mem.,* 6 N.Y.2d 886, 160 N.E.2d 857 (1959) (express authorization to form corporation).

Ohio: Westlake v. Ohio N. Univ., 21 Ohio Misc. 202, 50 Ohio Ops. 2d 417, 256 N.E.2d 642 (1969) (will directed trustee to form a corporation).

Oklahoma: Goss and Hamlyn Home v. State, 285 P.2d 428 (Okla. 1955).

Pennsylvania: Jacobs Estate, 62 D.&C.2d 167 (Pa. 1973) (incorporation permitted by will; held executor should pay fund directly to the corporation).

Washington: Reagh v. Hamilton, 194 Wash. 449, 78 P.2d 555 (1938); State of Washington v. Salvation Army, 47 Wash. 2d 113, 286 P.2d 709 (1955).

See also Ferguson v. Rippel, 23 N.J. Super. 132, 92 A.2d 647 (1952) (express authorization to form corporation); People ex rel. Untermyer v. McGregor, 295 N.Y. 237, 66 N.E.2d 292 (1946); Matter of Futterman, 197 Misc. 558, 95 N.Y.S.2d 876 (1950) (express authorization to form corporation); Stevens's Estate, 200 Pa. 318, 49 A. 985 (1901).

In Riddle Estate, 8 D.&C.2d 716 (Pa. 1956), a testator left his estate in trust to establish and maintain a hospital and directed the trustees to form a nonprofit corporation. They had not formed such a corporation within four years after the death of the testator, and the Attorney General brought suit asking for the appointment of a new trustee. The court denied the petition but without prejudice to the right to make a similar future request if it should become expedient to do so.

See Note, The Charitable Corporation, 64 Harv. L. Rev. 1168 (1951).

As to the power of the trustees to form a corporation to administer a private trust, see §171.1.

[5]*Connecticut:* Cochran v. McLaughlin, 128 Conn. 638, 24 A.2d 836 (1942).

Florida: Jordan v. Landis, 128 Fla. 604, 175 So. 241 (1937).

Massachusetts: Shattuck v. Wood Memorial Home, 319 Mass. 444, 66 N.E.2d 568 (1946) (citing the text).

[6]Appeal of Vaux, 109 Pa. 497 (1885); Curran Found. Charter, 297 Pa. 272, 146 A. 908 (1929).

See Davenport v. Attorney Gen., 361 Mass. 372, 280 N.E.2d 193 (1972)

statute[7] that where gifts are made to individual trustees for charitable purposes, they can form a corporation to administer the trust.

Where property is given to trustees to hold for an unincorporated charitable association that is incapable of taking the legal title to property, and thereafter the association is incorporated, the court may direct the conveyance of the trust property to the corporation, where this is not contrary to the intention of the settlor.[8] So also if property is bequeathed directly to an unincorporated charitable association, the disposition does not fail merely because the association is incapable of taking the legal title to the property,[9] and the court may appoint trustees to administer the trust; and if the association is thereafter incorporated the court may direct a conveyance of the trust property to the corporation. By the terms of the trust it may be provided that property shall be transferred to a charitable corporation to be organized and, if the corporation is to be organized within the period of the rule against perpetuities, the bequest is valid; and even if there is no requirement that it must be organized within that period, the bequest is valid if the organization of the corporation is not a condition precedent to the gift.[10]

We have considered elsewhere the question whether, where trustees hold property in trust to pay the income to a charitable corporation, either for an indefinite period or until the happening of some event, the corporation can compel the trustees to convey the trust property to it.[11]

(citing the text); In re Petition of Downer Home, 67 Wis. 2d 55, 226 N.W.2d 444 (1975) (quoting the text).

In City of Hartford v. Larrabee Fund Assn., 161 Conn. 312, 288 A.2d 71 (1971), where funds were given to a city in trust to apply the income for needy women, an association of ladies to determine the beneficiaries, it was held that a special act incorporating the trust was unconstitutional, because the courts had exclusive power to determine whether a charitable trust should be incorporated and to determine whether the purposes of the corporation were in accordance with the terms of the trust.

[7]La. Rev. Stat. Ann., §9:2275.
[8]See Street v. Pitts, 238 Ala. 531, 192 So. 258 (1939).
[9]See §397.2.
[10]See §401.8.
[11]See §367A.

§386. The Liabilities of the Trustee

Where a trustee of a charitable trust commits a breach of trust, he incurs a liability to the same extent to which a trustee of a private trust incurs a liability.[1] Thus if the trustee of a charitable trust makes an improper investment, he is liable for any loss that results.[2] Similarly, if the trustee misappropriates or otherwise expends trust funds in breach of trust, he is under a liability to restore the money to the trust.[3] So also the trustee is liable for a loss resulting from the improper failure to convert property into proper trust investments, but not where his retention of the property is not a breach of trust.[4] Similarly, the

§386. [1]See §§201-213.2.

[2]Schroeder v. American Natl. Red Cross, 215 Wis. 54, 254 N.W. 371 (1934).

In Stuart v. Continental Ill. Natl. Bank & Trust Co., 68 Ill. 2d 502, 12 Ill. Dec. 248, 369 N.E.2d 1262 (1977), *cert. denied,* 444 U.S. 844, 100 S. Ct. 86, 62 L. Ed. 2d 56 (1979), *modifying* Northern Trust Co. v. Continental Ill. Natl. Bank & Trust Co., 43 Ill. App. 3d 169, 11 Ill. Dec. 767, 356 N.E.2d 1049 (1976), a corporate co-trustee was held liable for making an improper distribution of funds of a charitable trust.

But see George Pepperdine Found. v. Pepperdine, 126 Cal. App. 2d 154, 271 P.2d 600 (1954), cited in §379, n. 10, partially disapproved in Holt v. College of Osteopathic Physicians & Surgeons, 61 Cal. 2d 750, 394 P.2d 932, 40 Cal. Rptr. 244 (1964).

As to the standard of care required of trustees for charitable purposes in making investments, see John A. Creighton Home for Girls' Trust v. Waltman, 140 Neb. 3, 299 N.W. 261 (1941).

See Mulreeny, Foundation Trustees — Selection, Duties, and Responsibilities, 13 U.C.L.A. Law Rev. 1060 (1966); Rogerson, Fiduciary Responsibilities of Charitable Foundation Trustees, 7 Real Prop., Prob. & Trust J., 770 (1972).

[3]Stuart v. Continental Ill. Natl. Bank & Trust Co., 68 Ill. 2d 502, 12 Ill Dec. 248, 369 N.E.2d 1262 (1977), *cert. denied,* 444 U.S. 844, 100 S. Ct. 86, 62 L. Ed. 2d 56 (1979) (citing the text), *aff'g* Northern Trust Co. v. Continental Ill. Natl. Bank & Trust Co., 43 Ill. App. 3d 169, 11 Ill. Dec. 767, 356 N.E.2d 1049 (1976); White v. Ditson, 140 Mass. 351, 4 N.E. 606, 54 Am. Rep. 473 (1885); Attorney Gen. v. Bedard, 218 Mass. 378, 105 N.E. 993 (1914); Attorney Gen. v. City of Lowell, 246 Mass. 312, 141 N.E. 45 (1923).

See City of Bangor v. Beal, 85 Me. 129, 26 A. 1112 (1892).

[4]First Natl. Bank of Boston v. Truesdale Hosp., 288 Mass. 35, 192 N.E. 150 (1934), noted in 48 Harv. L. Rev. 347, 21 Va. L. Rev. 334.

trustees of a charitable trust are liable for an improper failure to invest the funds held upon a charitable trust.[5]

A trustee of a charitable trust who commits a breach of trust may be guilty of a criminal offense. If he misappropriates trust property he may be guilty of embezzlement or larceny.[6] He may be guilty of a lesser offense.[7]

If the trustees of a charitable trust have deliberately and inexcusably misapplied the whole or a part of the income, they will be held accountable for such misapplication, and will not have a defense of laches or of the statute of limitations. But, where they acted in good faith and over a considerable period of time, the court may refuse to hold them liable.[8]

§387. Removal of Trustee

A trustee of a charitable trust may be removed as trustee for the same reasons for which a trustee of a private trust may be removed.[1] Thus he may be removed for serious breaches of

---

[5]Attorney-General v. Alford, 4 De G.M.&G. 843 (1855); Lynch v. John M. Redfield Found., 9 Cal. App. 3d 293, 88 Cal. Rptr. 86, 51 A.L.R.3d 1311 (1970).

See Note, Charitable trusts: Liability of trustee for permitting trust income to accumulate in noninterest-bearing account, 51 A.L.R.3d 1293 (1972).

[6]See §12.7.

[7]By N.J. Rev. Stat., §2A:111-30, it is made a misdemeanor for any officer, agent, or member of a charitable, fraternal, benevolent, or philanthropic organization, whether or not incorporated, to use or expend or authorize the use or expenditure of funds contributed to the organization for a particular charitable, benevolent, or philanthropic purpose, for any other purpose, or for its general purposes.

[8]Attorney Gen. v. Old South Socy., 13 Allen 474 (Mass. 1866).

As to the effect on the enforcement of a trust of a long-continued deviation from the terms of the trust, see §392.

§387. [1]*Federal:* Sunday School Union of African M.E. Church v. Walden, 121 F.2d 719 (6th Cir. 1941) (friction).

Alabama: Birmingham Trust Natl. Bank v. Henley, 371 So. 2d 883 (Ala. 1979), *cert. denied,* 445 U.S. 915 (1979) (quoting the text).

California: In re Los Angeles County Pioneer Socy., 40 Cal. 2d 852, 257 P.2d 1 (1953) (substitution of one charitable corporation for another; citing the text and Restatement of Trusts §387); Brown v. Memorial Natl. Home Found., 162 Cal. App. 2d 513, 329 P.2d 118, 75 A.L.R.2d 427 (1955), *cert.*

trust, for unfitness, for long-continued absence and the like. He can also be removed where his views are hostile to the purposes of the trust, as in the case of a religious trust where he ceases to hold religious views that it is the purpose of the trust to promote.[2] Although ordinarily the court alone has the power of removal, by the terms of the trust third persons may be empowered to remove trustees.[3] Where such power is by the terms of the trust to be exercised only for good cause, it cannot be exer-

---

denied, 358 U.S. 943 (1959) (charitable corporation; quoting the text and citing Restatement of Trusts §387).

Georgia: Simmons v. City of Cave Spring, 211 Ga. 284, 85 S.E.2d 419 (1955).

Illinois: Carlstrom v. Frackelton, 263 Ill. App. 250 (1931) (negligence); Stuart v. Continental Ill. Natl. Bank & Trust Co., 68 Ill. 2d 502, 12 Ill. Dec. 248, 369 N.E.2d 1262 (1977), *cert. denied,* 444 U.S. 844, 100 S. Ct. 86, 62 L. Ed. 2d 56 (1979), *aff'g* Northern Trust Co. v. Continental Ill. Natl. Bank & Trust Co., 43 Ill. App. 3d 169, 11 Ill. Dec. 767, 356 N.E.2d 1049 (1976) (corporate trustee not removed for improper distribution of trust funds).

Massachusetts: Attorney Gen. v. Garrison, 101 Mass. 223 (1869) (refusal to obey decree); Attorney Gen. v. Armstrong, 231 Mass. 196, 120 N.E. 678 (1918) (improper self-dealing); Attorney Gen. v. Olson, 346 Mass. 190, 191 N.E.2d 132 (1963) (failure to file annual account not sufficient ground for removal).

Nebraska: In re Estate of Grblny, 147 Neb. 117, 22 N.W.2d 488 (1946) (breaches of trust and refusal to give bond).

New York: Petition of Grace, 25 A.D.2d 277, 268 N.Y.S.2d 901 (1966) (removal of trustee of charitable corporation; citing the text and Restatement of Trusts §107).

Oregon: Leahey v. Commission for Blind, 253 Or. 527, 456 P.2d 77 (1969) (public trustees; citing the text and Restatement of Trusts §§379, 387).

In Smith v. Board of Pensions of the Methodist Church, 54 F. Supp. 224 (E.D. Mo. 1944), the court refused to remove the trustees, because the losses to the trust were not due to misconduct.

As to the removal of trustees of a private trust, see §107.

See Note, Grounds for removal of trustee of charitable trust, 75 A.L.R.2d 449 (1961).

[2] Attorney-General v. Pearson, 7 Sim. 290 (1835); Ross v. Crockett, 14 La. Ann. 811 (1859).

See Baker v. Lee, 8 H.L.C. 495 (1860).

But compare Attorney-General v. St. John's Hosp., 2 Ch. D. 554 (1876).

By Mississippi Code 1972, §§91-9-301 to 91-9-305, provision is made for the removal of trustees of a charity at the suit of a majority of the contributors on the ground of irreconcilable hostility or tension between them and the trustees. See also Louisiana Rev. Stat. Ann., §9:2282.

[3] Éustace v. Dickey, 240 Mass. 55, 132 N.E. 852 (1921); Dittemore v. Dickey, 249 Mass. 95, 144 N.E. 57 (1924).

cised arbitrarily but only when sufficient cause for removal appears.[4]

§388.   *Appointment of New Trustees*

As in the case of private trusts,[1] where a charitable trust is created and the settlor fails to designate a trustee or the trustee designated by him is unwilling or unable to act or he subsequently ceases to be trustee by death, resignation, or for some other reason, a new trustee may be appointed by the court.[2] Thus where a testator leaves property in trust for a charitable purpose and fails to designate a trustee to administer the trust, the court will appoint a trustee to administer it.[3] Where property is bequeathed to an unincorporated charitable association that has no capacity to take title to the property, the court will appoint a trustee.[4] Where property is bequeathed to a charitable corporation upon a charitable trust and the corporation declines to accept the legacy, the court may appoint another charitable corporation as trustee.[5] So also if the designated corporation has ceased to exist, the court may appoint another as trustee.[6]

[4]Kenney Presbyterian Home v. State, 174 Wash. 19, 24 P.2d 403 (1933).
§388. [1]See §108.
[2]Bethel Farm Bureau v. Anderson, 217 Ga. 529, 123 S.E.2d 754 (1962); Davenport v. Attorney Gen., 361 Mass. 372, 280 N.E.2d 193 (1972) (citing the text and Restatement of Trusts §388).

In Macy v. Cunningham, 140 Conn. 124, 98 A.2d 800 (1953), it was held that the appointment of a successor trustee is a judicial function and that the legislature has no power to direct the court as to whom to appoint.

By Tennessee Code Ann. §35-121, it is provided that in the case of a charitable trust the court may on its own motion appoint trustees.
[3]See §397.
[4]Craven v. Wilmington Teachers Assn., 29 Del. Ch. 180, 47 A.2d 580 (1946) (citing the text); Tillinghast v. Boy Scouts of Am. Council at Narragansett Pier, 47 R.I. 406, 133 A. 662, 46 A.L.R. 823 (1926), noted in 30 Law Notes 213; Taylor v. Salvation Army, 49 R.I. 316, 142 A. 335 (1928) (court-appointed trust company).

See §397.2.
[5]Mears's Estate, 299 Pa. 217, 149 A. 157 (1930), noted in 39 Yale L.J. 1219.

See §397.3.
[6]Read v. Willard Hosp., 215 Mass. 132, 102 N.E. 95, 45 L.R.A. (N.S.) 574 (1913).

Where a corporation holds property upon a charitable trust and wishes to resign and have the trust administered by another corporation, the court may authorize the transfer of the trust property to the second corporation to be administered by it for the same charitable purposes as those on which the first corporation held it.[7] Where property is conveyed to several trustees in trust for charitable purposes and a vacancy occurs among the trustees, the court will fill the vacancy by the appointment of successor trustees, unless by the terms of the trust another method for the appointment of new trustees is provided.[8]

It is to be remembered, however, that although ordinarily a trust will not fail for want of a trustee, the settlor may manifest an intention that the trust should arise only if the particular trustee named by him should act as trustee and that the trust should continue only as long as the named trustee is able and willing to act. In such a case the court cannot save the trust by appointing a new trustee.[9]

By the terms of the trust it may be provided that vacancies in the office of trustee may be filled by some method other than by appointment by the court. In such a case new trustees may be appointed by the method designated. Thus it may be provided that where a vacancy occurs it may be filled by the remaining trustees.[10] It may be provided that trustees shall be appointed by the action of a church board or other organization.[11]

[7]Bible Readers' Aid Socy. v. Katzenbach, 97 N.J. Eq. 416, 128 A. 628 (1925).

[8]Glader v. Schwinge, 336 Ill. 551, 168 N.E. 658, 66 A.L.R. 172 (1929).

Where the trustees named by the settlor are able and willing to act, the court cannot substitute other trustees. Hartman v. Orr, 35 Ohio Abs. 528, 41 N.E.2d 406 (1941).

See Kekoa v. Supreme Court of Haw., 55 Haw. 104, 516 P.2d 1239 (1973), *cert. denied,* 417 U.S. 930 (1973), where the power to appoint trustees of a charitable trust was conferred upon the justices of the Supreme Court of Hawaii as individuals.

[9]See §397.

[10]Selleck v. Thompson, 28 R.I. 350, 67 A. 425 (1907).

As to the power of a court to appoint additional trustees of a charitable trust, see §108.2, n. 12.

[11]Methodist Episcopal Church v. Roach, 51 S.W.2d 1100 (Tex. Civ. App. 1932).

§389. Investments

The principles governing the investments that trustees may properly make are the same whether the trust is a private trust or a charitable trust. Unless it is otherwise provided by the terms of the trust or by statute, the trustees are under a duty to make such investments as a prudent man would make of his own property having primarily in view the preservation of the trust estate and the amount and regularity of the income to be derived.[1] Indeed, the leading case in which this principle was laid down, the case of *Harvard College v. Amory*,[2] was a case of a charitable trust. The courts have in other cases applied the same principles to the making and the retention of investments of property held upon a charitable trust as are applied in the case of private trusts.[3]

§389. [1]See §§227-227.16.

[2]9 Pick. 446 (Mass. 1830).

[3]*Massachusetts:* American Academy of Arts & Sciences v. President & Fellows of Harvard College, 12 Gray 582 (Mass. 1832) (court may permit deviation from directions as to investment if circumstances change); Worcester City Missionary Socy. v. Memorial Church, 186 Mass. 531, 72 N.E. 71 (1904) (duty to follow testator's directions); First Natl. Bank of Boston v. Truesdale Hosp., 288 Mass. 35, 192 N.E. 150 (1934) (retention of original investments), noted in 48 Harv. L. Rev. 347, 21 Va. L. Rev. 334.

New York: Matter of Hoagland, 74 N.Y.S.2d 156 (1947), *aff'd mem.,* 272 A.D. 1040, 74 N.Y.S.2d 911 (1947), *aff'd mem.,* 297 N.Y. 920, 79 N.E.2d 746 (1948) (authorization to invest in non-legal securities authorized investment in a common trust fund).

Rhode Island: Bowen for an Opinion, 68 R.I. 200, 27 A.2d 181 (1942) (deviation from testator's directions not permitted).

Vermont: Bellows Free Academy v. Sowles, 76 Vt. 412, 57 A. 996 (1904).

See Graham Bros. Co. v. Galloway Woman's College, 190 Ark. 692, 81 S.W.2d 837 (1935).

In Rand v. McKittrick, 346 Mo. 466, 142 S.W.2d 29 (1940), noted in 39 Mich. L. Rev. 1051, 9 U. Kan. City L. Rev. 44, 26 Wash. U.L.Q. 580, it was held that trustees of a charitable trust could properly invest in common stocks. The court drew no distinction between charitable trusts and private trusts and laid down as governing in both cases the rule stated in Restatement of Trusts §227, as applied in Massachusetts.

In Application of United States Trust Co. of N.Y., 66 N.Y.S.2d 72 (1946), where a settlor transferred $31,000 par value of bonds of a certain railroad in trust for a charitable purpose with a provision that on maturity the proceeds should be invested in railroad bonds or municipals, the court refused the

Where it is provided by statute that trustees shall be permitted to invest only in certain types of securities, it is a question of interpretation of the statute whether the restrictions are applicable to the trustees of charitable trusts. Ordinarily, it would seem that the restrictions are applicable in the case of charitable as well as of private trusts. Thus in *Schroeder v. American National Red Cross*[4] it was held that the trustees of a trust for the benefit of soldiers who served in the First World War were liable for investing in securities other than those provided for by statute as proper trust investments.

Charitable corporations. There is a question whether the rules governing investment by trustees are applicable to charitable corporations. We have seen that courts sometimes say that a charitable corporation is a trustee of property given to it, at least where there are restrictions on the use of the property, but sometimes say that it is not a trustee.[5] At any rate, many, but not all, of the principles applicable to charitable trusts are applicable to charitable corporations. How is it as to investments?

In states like Massachusetts, where trustees can properly make such investments as a prudent man would make of his own property with a view to the preservation of the property and the amount and regularity of the income to be derived, it seems clear enough that the same principle is applicable to charitable corporations. Under this rule a charitable corporation, like a private trustee, can properly invest in shares of stock, common or preferred, provided that proper prudence is exercised in their selection.[6] Where trustees are limited, by statute or other-

---

trustee permission to sell any of the bonds and to invest the proceeds in legal trust investments, because no special reasons were shown for deviating from the terms of the trust.

As to investments by an unincorporated charitable association, see In re Tobacco Trade Benevolent Assn., [1958] 3 All E.R. 353.

By New Hampshire Rev. Stat. Ann., §387:17-A, as amended by Laws 1971, c. 286, the investment of funds of a nonprofit trust in participating mortgages is permitted.

See Note, Charitable trusts: liability of trustee for permitting trust income to accumulate in noninterest-bearing account, 51 A.L.R.3d 1293 (1972).

[4]215 Wis. 54, 254 N.W. 371 (1934).

[5]See §348.1.

[6]See §§227-227.16.

wise, to certain types of investment, it is a question of interpretation whether the statute is applicable to charitable corporations. Unless the statute is interpreted as applicable to charitable corporations, it would seem that in making investments they are bound only to comply with the general rule of prudent management. It would seem that this is so not only with respect to investments of unrestricted funds but also where funds are given to be used as an endowment, that is, where the principal is to be invested and only the income is to be used, and also where funds are given to be used only for a specified purpose, such as to maintain a bed in a hospital or to endow a professorship.[7] In a case in Ohio[8] it was held that a cemetery association, in making investments of funds given to it for the care of a cemetery or a burial lot therein, was bound only to act with proper prudence and was not limited by the statute as to investments by trustees.

In several states there are statutes governing investments by charitable corporations or by trustees holding funds for charitable purposes.[9]

[7]In Soldiers', Sailors' & Airmen's Families Assn. v. Attorney-General, [1968] 1 W.L.R. 313, it was held that a charitable corporation could invest only in the securities prescribed by statute for trustees, unless it was otherwise provided in its charter.

See Taylor, A New Chapter in the New York Law of Charitable Corporations, 25 Cornell L.Q. 382, 391 (1940); Lincoln, Gifts to Charitable Corporations, 25 Va. L. Rev. 764 (1939); Blackwell, The Charitable Corporation and the Charitable Trust, 24 Wash. U.L.Q. 1 (1938); Daines, Theory and Procedure for Pooled Investments in Colleges and Universities, 69 J. Accountancy 114 (1940); Christie, Legal Aspects of Changing University Investment Strategies, 58 N.C.L. Rev. 189 (1980).

[8]Freeman v. Norwalk Cemetery Assn., 88 Ohio App. 446, 100 N.E.2d 267 (1950).

By Illinois Rev. Stat., c. 21, §64.3, trustees of funds for the care of cemeteries or burial lots are permitted to follow the prudent-man rule as to trust investments.

[9]*California:* Corporations Code, §§10206, 10250.

Kansas: Stat. Ann., §17-5002, as amended by Laws 1974, c. 99.

Michigan: Stat. Ann., §§21.149, 21.154.

Missouri: Laws 1976, c. 58. Rev. Stat., §402.025.

New Jersey: Rev. Stat., §3B:14-24, enacted by Laws 1968, c. 270, repealed and reenacted by Laws 1981, c. 405, provides, "The court having jurisdiction of the estate or trust may authorize the fiduciary to exercise any other power which in the judgment of the court is necessary for the proper administration of the estate or trust."

There is a further question whether a charitable corpora-

New York: Not-for-Profit Corporation Law, §512, as amended by Laws 1978, c. 690. See also §§102, 513. Religious Corporations Law, §§5-a, 5-b.

Pennsylvania: 15 Pa. Cons. Stat., §7550.

Tennessee: Code Ann., §48-1108.

West Virginia: Code, §44-6-2a.

In New York by Not-for-Profit Corporation Law, §512, as amended by Laws 1978, c. 690, it is provided that "Subject to the limitations and conditions contained in any gift, devise or bequest, a membership corporation, created by or under a general or special law, may invest its funds in such mortgages, bonds, debentures, shares of preferred and common stock and other securities as the directors shall deem advisable." See Application of Arms, 193 Misc. 427, 81 N.Y.S.2d 246 (1948).

In New York by Religious Corporations Law, §§5-a and 5-b, as inserted by Laws 1950, c. 225, it is provided that religious corporations may invest their funds as they shall deem advisable without being restricted to those classes of securities that are lawful for the investment of trust funds; and that any investment theretofore made should not be deemed to have been restricted to such securities.

In Pennsylvania (15 Pa. Cons. Stat., §7550), it is provided that unless it is otherwise provided by the trust instrument, the directors of a charitable corporation shall have power to invest in such investments as in the honest exercise of their judgment they may, after investigation, determine to be safe and proper investments. They are required to keep accurate accounts of all trust funds, separate and apart from the other funds of the corporation. They are authorized to transfer funds to a corporate trustee to invest them and to keep investments in the name of the corporation or of a nominee of the corporation.

In West Virginia, by Code, §44-6-2a, as enacted by Laws 1951, c. 2, the prudent-man rule for investments is made applicable to charitable institutions.

By Michigan Stat. Ann., §21.165, it is provided that charitable foundations shall have power to invest and reinvest the principal and income in accordance with the laws of the state governing authorized investments for trustees.

In Nebraska Rev. Stat. 1943, §24-601, which prescribes the investments that are legal for trustees, it is provided that the statute shall not be construed to apply to any incorporated religious, charitable, or eleemosynary institution, the board of trustees of any college or university, or any endowment fund of any college or university, except to the extent that any such board or corporation may be named as specific trustee under a will or other trust instrument.

As to permissible investments of trust funds of the University of Wisconsin, see Wis. Stat., §36.065(1), and as to other state colleges, see Stat., §37.-115(1). As to permissible investments of state colleges or universities in Ohio, see Ohio Rev. Code Ann., §3345.16.

In the Report of the Committee on the Law and Practice Relating to Charitable Trusts (1952) (Cmd. 8710), p. 69, the Committee recommended

tion is bound to keep separate from its other funds those funds that are given to it for restricted purposes, or whether it may mingle all the funds in one common pool. Private trustees are ordinarily not permitted to mingle funds of different trusts.[10] It is believed that in the absence of restrictions in the terms of the gift as to this matter, such mingling by a charitable corporation is not improper.[11]

---

that the range of investments for trustees of charitable trusts should be extended to comprise debentures and stock and shares of financial, industrial, and commercial companies quoted on the London Stock Exchange, and that they should be permitted to invest up to 50 percent of their funds in securities within the extended range.

In In re Shipwrecked Fishermen & Mariners' Royal Benevolent Socy., [1959] Ch. 220, noted in 75 Law Q. Rev. 21, it was held that under Trustee Act, 1925, §57(1), the court had jurisdiction to widen the powers of investment of a charitable corporation beyond those specified in the statute creating the corporation. See §381, n. 11.

In Sendak v. Trustees of Indiana Univ., 254 Ind. 390, 260 N.E.2d 601 (1970), it was held that the Board of Trustees of Indiana University could properly invest gifts in stock of corporations, although the constitution of the state provided that the state should not be a stockholder in any corporation.

See the A.B.A. Model Non-Profit Corporations Act, §5, which has been adopted in several states, which confers a general power to invest in shares and obligations of domestic or foreign organizations.

By the Uniform Management of Institutional Funds Act, large investment powers are conferred on the governing boards of charitable institutions. See *infra*, n. 16. As to the delegation by the governing boards of the power to invest, see §379.

[10]See Latham, Trustee Investments and American Practice, 7 Current Legal Probs. 139 (1954).

See §179.2.

[11]By California Corporations Code, §10250, as amended by Laws 1968, c. 88, and by Laws 1972, c. 1057, charitable corporations are authorized to establish common trust funds.

See also California Corporations Code, §10251, as inserted by Laws 1972, c. 417, as amended by Laws 1986, c. 820.

By Maine Rev. Stat. 1964, tit. 22, §1819, it is provided that hospitals may treat any two or more trust funds as a single fund for the purpose of investment, if not prohibited by the terms of the trust.

By Massachusetts Ann. Laws, c. 68, §32, as inserted by Laws 1971, c. 595, charitable organizations may invest in common trust funds established by The Common Fund for Nonprofit Organizations, a New York corporation.

By New Hampshire Rev. Stat. Ann., §§292:18 to 292:21, it is provided that any charitable corporation may establish common trust funds for the collective

Income and principal. Where funds are given to a charitable institution as an endowment, questions may arise as to the allo-

---

investment of property belonging to trusts in its care, unless the trust instrument prohibits collective investments.

By New Hampshire Rev. Stat. Ann., §§564:2-a to 564:2-c, the judge of probate is empowered to appoint a public trustee to administer such small charitable trusts as the court may assign to him, where it is found that the difficulties or expense involved in each trust would tend to defeat its purpose, provided the trustee consents; and the public trustee is authorized to establish common trust funds in which he may combine funds belonging to the various trusts in his care.

By Pennsylvania Corporation Not-for-Profit Code, 15 Pa. Cons. Stat., §§7581 to 7585, as enacted by Laws 1972, c. 271, nonprofit corporations are authorized to establish common trust funds.

The Attorney General of Pennsylvania has rendered an opinion that municipalities may combine several accounts for investment purposes, and that two or more municipalities may join together for this purpose. Investment of Municipal Funds, 68 D.&C.2d 744 (Pa. 1974).

By Vermont Stat. Ann., tit. 16, §3641, it is provided that an educational institution may associate together for common investment the funds of individual trusts or individual funds held by it whether created by order of court or otherwise, if the terms of the trust or gift do not require a separate investment.

By West Virginia Code, §44-6-2a, as inserted by Laws 1961, c. 158, it is provided that the board of trustees or a fiduciary of a charitable association may make collective investments, and if they are held by a corporate fiduciary they may be invested in its common trust fund.

By the Uniform Management of Institutional Funds Act, §4(3), it is provided that charitable institutions may include all or any part of an institutional fund in any pooled or common fund maintained by the institution.

This provision of the Uniform Act is enacted in New York, Not-for-Profit Corporation Law, §512, as enacted by Laws 1978, c. 690.

See also the New Jersey Educational Endowment Management Act, N.J. Stat. Ann., §§15:18-1 to 15:18-14, providing for an endowment pool for educational institutions.

In In re Royal Society's Charitable Trusts, [1956] Ch. 87, noted in 19 Mod. L. Rev. 93, the court permitted a charitable corporation to mingle its trust funds in making investments and to allocate the income to the various trusts, and permitted investment partly in non-legals. See also In re Royal Naval & Royal Marine Children's Homes v. Attorney-General, [1959] 2 All E.R. 716; In re University of London Charitable Trusts, [1963] 3 All E.R. 859.

By Charities Act, 1960, 8 & 9 Eliz. II, c. 58, §22, provision is made for the establishment of common investment funds for charities.

See Richardson, A Common Trust Fund for Charitable Trusts, 113 Tr. & Est. 296 (1974).

cation to income or principal. It would seem that the mere fact that the trustees have allocated income to principal does not preclude them from later allocating it to income. But where a donor has given discretion to the trustees to allocate income to principal, and they have done so, it has been held that they cannot thereafter allocate it to income if this would be contrary to the donor's intent.[12]

Although profits realized on the sale of property held in trust are usually allocable to principal,[13] the question arises whether this is true in the case of the property of a charitable corporation. It is to be noted that here there is no conflict between income beneficiary and principal beneficiary but simply a question as to how and when the property is to be used. Hence even if a donor specifies that his gift shall be used as an endowment or that the income shall be used but the principal preserved, the question arises as to just what is principal for this purpose.[14]

By the Pennsylvania Corporation Not-for-Profit Code,[15] it is provided that so much of the net realized capital gains as of the end of any fiscal year of the corporation as the directors or other body shall, within four months after the end of such year, in their sole discretion, allocate to income for such fiscal year shall be deemed income. The amount so allocated is not to exceed 9 percent of the market value at the end of the year of the remaining principal.

By the Uniform Management of Institutional Funds Act, §2, the governing board in the case of an endowment fund is per-

---

[12]Davison v. Duke Univ., 282 N.C. 676, 194 S.E.2d 761, 57 A.L.R.3d 1008 (1973).

[13]See §233.1, n. 2.

[14]See Cary and Bright, The Law and the Lore of Endowment Funds (Report to the Ford Foundation) (1969); Cary and Bright, The "Income" from Endowment Funds, 69 Colum. L. Rev. 396 (1969); Cary and Bright, The Developing Law of Endowment Funds, "The Law and the Lore" Revisited (Report to the Ford Foundation) (1974); Wilde, Corporate Management of Endowment Funds, 31 Bus. Law. 399 (1975).

By Idaho Laws 1969, c. 244, it is provided that in the case of state endowment funds income shall not include capital gains derived from the sale of investments or securities.

[15]15 Pa. Cons. Stat., §7550(c), as enacted by Laws 1972, c. 271. See Maryland Estates and Trusts Article, §§15-401 to 15-408.

mitted to expend so much of the net appreciation, realized and
unrealized, in the fair value of the assets of the fund over the
historic dollar value of the fund as is prudent, unless the gift
instrument indicates the donor's intention that net appreciation
shall not be expended.[16]

[16]The Act contains the following provisions:

Section I. [*Definitions.*] In this Act:

(1) "institution" means an incorporated or unincorporated organization
organized and operated exclusively for educational, religious, charitable, or
other eleemosynary purposes, or a governmental organization to the extent
that it holds funds exclusively for any of these purposes;

(2) "institutional fund" means a fund held by an institution for its exclusive use, benefit, or purposes, but does not include (i) a fund held for an
institution by a trustee that is not an institution or (ii) a fund in which a
beneficiary that is not an institution has an interest, other than possible rights
that could arise upon violation or failure of the purposes of the fund;

(3) "endowment fund" means an institutional fund, or any part thereof,
not wholly expendable by the institution on a current basis under the terms
of the applicable gift instrument;

(4) "governing board" means the body responsible for the management
of an institution or of an institutional fund;

(5) "historic dollar value" means the aggregate fair value in dollars of (i)
an endowment fund at the time it became an endowment fund, (ii) each
subsequent donation to the fund at the time it is made, and (iii) each accumulation made pursuant to a direction in the applicable gift instrument at the time
the accumulation is added to the fund. The determination of historic dollar
value made in good faith by the institution is conclusive.

Section 2. [*Appropriation of Appreciation.*] The governing board may appropriate for expenditure for the uses and purposes for which an endowment fund
is established so much of the net appreciation, realized and unrealized, in the
fair value of the assets of an endowment fund over the historic dollar value of
the fund as is prudent under the standard established by Section 6. This
Section does not limit the authority of the governing board to expend funds
as permitted under other law, the terms of the applicable gift instrument, or
the charter of the institution.

Section 3. [*Rule of Construction.*] Section 2 does not apply if the applicable
gift instrument indicates the donor's intention that net appreciation shall not
be expended. A restriction upon the expenditure of net appreciation may not
be implied from a designation of a gift as an endowment, or from a direction
or authorization in the applicable gift instrument to use only "income," "interest," "dividends," or "rents, issues or profits," or "to preserve the principal
intact," or a direction which contains other words of similar import. This rule
of construction applies to gift instruments executed or in effect before or after
the effective date of this Act.

Section 4. [*Investment Authority.*] In addition to an investment otherwise authorized by law or by the applicable gift instrument, and without restriction to investments a fiduciary may make, the governing board, subject to any specific limitations set forth in the applicable gift instrument or in the applicable law other than law relating to investments by a fiduciary, may:

(1) invest and reinvest an institutional fund in any real or personal property deemed advisable by the governing board, whether or not it produces a current return, including mortgages, stocks, bonds, debentures, and other securities of profit or non-profit corporations, shares in or obligations of associations, partnerships, or individuals, and obligations of any government or subdivision or instrumentality thereof;

(2) retain property contributed by a donor to an institutional fund for as long as the governing board deems advisable;

(3) include all or any part of an institutional fund in any pooled or common fund maintained by the institution; and

(4) invest all or any part of an institutional fund in any other pooled or common fund available for investment, including shares or interests in regulated investment companies, mutual funds, common trust funds, investment partnerships, real estate investment trusts, or similar organizations in which funds are commingled and investment determinations are made by persons other than the governing board. [See §389, n. 11.]

Section 5. [*Delegation of Investment Management.*] Except as otherwise provided by the applicable gift instrument or by applicable law relating to governmental institutions or funds, the governing board may (1) delegate to its committees, officers or employees of the institution or the fund, or agents, including investment counsel, the authority to act in place of the board in investment and reinvestment of institutional funds, (2) contract with independent investment advisors, investment counsel or managers, banks, or trust companies, so to act, and (3) authorize the payment of compensation for investment advisory or management services. [See §379.]

Section 6. [*Standard of Conduct.*] In the administration of the powers to appropriate appreciation, to make and retain investments, and to delegate investment management of institutional funds, members of a governing board shall exercise ordinary business care and prudence under the facts and circumstances prevailing at the time of the action or decision. In so doing they shall consider long and short term needs of the institution in carrying out its educational, religious, charitable, or other eleemosynary purposes, its present and anticipated financial requirements, expected total return on its investments, price level trends, and general economic conditions.

Section 7. [*Release of Restrictions on Use or Investment.*]

(a) With the written consent of the donor, the governing board may release, in whole or in part, a restriction imposed by the applicable gift instrument on the use or investment of an institutional fund.

(b) If written consent of the donor cannot be obtained by reason of his death, disability, unavailability, or impossibility of identification, the governing board may apply in the name of the institution to the [appropriate] court for release of a restriction imposed by the applicable gift instrument on the use or investment of an institutional fund. The [Attorney General] shall be notified of the application and shall be given an opportunity to be heard. If the court finds that the restriction is obsolete, inappropriate, or impracticable, it may by order release the restriction in whole or in part. A release under this subsection may not change an endowment fund to a fund that is not an endowment fund.

(c) A release under this section may not allow a fund to be used for purposes other than the educational, religious, charitable, or other eleemosynary purposes of the institution affected.

(d) This section does not limit the application of the doctrine of cy pres. [See §367.2.]

The Act has been adopted in a number of states.

California: Education Code, §§94600 to 94610, enacted by Laws 1986, c. 820.

Colorado: Rev. Stat. 1973, §§15-1-1101 to 15-1-1109.

Connecticut: Gen. Stat. 1958, §45-100.

Delaware: Code Ann., tit. 12, §§4701 to 4708.

District of Columbia: Code 1981, §§32-401 to 32-409.

Georgia: Code Ann., §§44-15-1 to 44-15-8.

Illinois: Rev. Stat. c. 32, §§1101 to 1110.

Kansas: Stat. Ann., §§58-3601 to 58-3610.

Kentucky: Rev. Stat. Ann., §§273.510 to 273.590.

Louisiana: Rev. Stat. Ann., §§9:2337.1 to 9:2337.8.

Maine: Rev. Stat. 1964, tit. 13, c. 95 (applicable only to educational institutions; see Laws 1973, c. 286).

Maryland: Ann. Code, Estates and Trusts, §§15-401 to 15-409.

Massachusetts: Ann. Laws, c. 180A, §§1-11.

Michigan: Comp. Laws Ann., §§451.1201 to 451.1210.

Minnesota: Stat. Ann., §309.62 to 309.71.

Montana: Code Ann. 1983, §§72-30-101 to 72-30-207.

New Hampshire: Rev. Stat. Ann., §§292-B:1 to 292-B:9.

New Jersey: Rev. Stat., §§15:18-15 to 15:18-24.

New York: Not-for-Profit Corporation Law, §§102, 512, 522, as enacted by Laws 1978, c. 690 (substantial adoption).

North Carolina: Gen. Stat., §§36B-1 to 36B-10, enacted by Laws 1985, c. 98.

North Dakota: Cent. Code, §§15-67-01 to 15-67-09; Laws 1975, c. 182.

Ohio: Rev. Code Ann., §§1715.51 to 1715.59.

Oregon: Rev. Stat., §§128.310 to 128.355.

Rhode Island: Gen. Laws, §§18-12-1 to 18-12-9, as amended by Laws 1976, c. 154.

Tennessee: Code Ann., §§35-10-101 to 35-10-109.

Vermont: Stat. Ann., tit. 14, §§3401 to 3407.

Virginia: Code 1950, §§55-268.1 to 55-268.10.

Washington: Rev. Code, §§24.44.010 to 24.44.090.

West Virginia: Code, §§44-6A-1 to 44-6A-8.

Wisconsin: Stat., §112.10.

Section 2 of the Act has in substance been enacted in New York.[17]

§390. Trustee's Compensation

The trustees of a charitable trust may be entitled to compensation to the same extent as private trustees.[1] In the case of

See Note, The Uniform Management of Institutional Funds Act — A Commentary, 8 Real Prop. Prob. & Tr. J. 405 (1973).

[17]N.Y. Not-for-Profit Corporation Law, §513, as enacted by Laws 1978, c. 690. See also §102.

§390. [1]Donaldson v. Madison Borough, 88 N.J. Super. 574, 213 A.2d 33 (1965) (citing the text and Restatement of Trusts §390).

Dolfinger Estate, 45 D.&C.2d 404 (Pa. 1968); Keasbey Trust, 1 D.&C.3d 701 (Pa. 1977).

In Pender Estate, 68 D.&C.2d 265 (Pa. 1974), the court held that in the case of a perpetual charitable trust the trustees were entitled to compensation out of income and to a terminal commission payable out of income, but not to interim commissions on principal. The court cited the text and Restatement of Trusts §390.

In Matter of Cornell, 63 Misc. 2d 234, 311 N.Y.S.2d 49 (1970), a provision in the terms of a charitable trust was interpreted as providing that the original and successor individual trustees were not to receive compensation, but only the corporate trustees.

Where a fund is left to a corporate trustee or to individual trustees to invest it and to pay the income to a charitable organization, the trustee is ordinarily entitled to the same commissions as would be payable to the trustees of a private trust. Matter of Belknap, 184 Misc. 272, 50 N.Y.S.2d 228 (1944).

In Matter of Finck, 17 Misc. 2d 300, 184 N.Y.S.2d 827 (1959), it was held that under New York Surrogate's Court Act, §285-a(5), although commissions on principal are not allowable to trustees of a charitable trust, or where the same trustee holds upon a private trust for life and then upon a charitable trust, where one trustee holds upon a private trust for life he is entitled to such commission where another trustee is then to hold upon a charitable trust.

See also Matter of Griffith, 66 Misc. 2d 349, 320 N.Y.S.2d 767 (1971).

In In re The French Protestant Hosp., [1951] Ch. 567, it was held that the governor and directors of an unincorporated hospital could not properly amend the by-laws to permit persons employed by the corporation to serve as directors.

By Illinois Rev. Stat., c. 148, §31, it is provided that the county court may fix the compensation of trustees of charitable trusts created by will if compensation is not expressly forbidden by the will; but that trustees of charitable

charitable trusts, however, it is more common to provide expressly or impliedly in the terms of the trust that the trustees are to serve without compensation. In the case of the so-called community trusts, where contributions are made by various testators and other contributors to a fund to be administered by a trust company or other trust institution and the income or principal is to be applied to such charitable purposes as may be determined from time to time by a committee or board, the trustee is entitled to compensation for administering the trust, but the members of the committee or board serve without compensation, unless it is otherwise provided by the terms of the trust. In the case of charitable corporations the members of the board of trustees ordinarily serve without compensation.[2]

§391. Who Can Enforce a Charitable Trust

We have seen that in the case of a private trust no one except a beneficiary or one suing on his behalf can maintain a

---

institutions shall not be entitled to compensation. See Gorin v. McFarland, 80 Ill. App. 2d 398, 224 N.E.2d 615 (1967); Ill. Rev. Stat. c. 148, §31 is repealed by Laws 1973, c. 78-625.

By Hawaii Rev. Stat., §607-20, provision is made for trustee's fees and expenses in the case of charitable trusts. As to decisions prior to the enactment of the statute, see Estate of Bishop, 36 Haw. 403 (1943), noted in 32 Calif. L. Rev. 208; Estate of Bishop, 37 Haw. 111 (1945).

By New Hampshire Rev. Stat. Ann., §564:21, it is provided that "in the case of trusts held exclusively for charitable purposes the compensation should be payable out of income only, unless otherwise provided in the trust instrument or where the judge determines that certain unusual and non-recurring services and expenses such as the distribution of principal are involved that should be charged to the corpus."

As to the compensation of trustees of a charitable trust in New York, see New York Surrogate's Court Procedure Act, §2309(5), as amended by Laws 1984, c. 936. See Matter of Durland, 64 Misc. 2d 810, 315 N.Y.S.2d 1011 (1970), aff'd mem., 38 A.D.2d 722, 329 N.Y.S.2d 999 (1972).

In Matter of Gabeline, 288 N.W.2d 341 (Iowa 1980), a testator bequeathed property to the Board of Supervisors of a county in trust to provide additional services and facilities for residents of a county home. It was held that the members of the Board were entitled to compensation as trustees, because their duties as trustees went beyond their duties as public officers to manage the home.

[2]Midlantic Natl. Bank v. Frank G. Thompson Found., 170 N.J. Super. 728, 405 A.2d 866 (1979).

suit to enforce the trust.[1] In the case of a charitable trust the beneficial interest is not given to individual beneficiaries, but the property is devoted to purposes beneficial to the community.[2] How then is a charitable trust enforced?

The Attorney General. In England the records show that even before the enactment of the Statute of Charitable Uses in 1601 suits were brought by the Attorney-General to enforce charitable trusts. The community has an interest in the enforcement of such trusts and the Attorney General represents the community in seeing that the trusts are properly performed.[3] In

§391. [1]See §§200, 204.

[2]See §364.

[3]*England:* Attorney-General v. Ross, [1986] 1 W.L.R. 252 (Ch.D.).

California: Brown v. Memorial Natl. Home Found., 162 Cal. App. 2d 513, 329 P.2d 118, 75 A.L.R.2d 427 (1955) (quoting the text), *cert. denied,* 358 U.S. 943 (1959); Estate of Ventura, 217 Cal. App. 2d 50, 31 Cal. Rptr. 490 (1963).

Connecticut: Lieberman v. Rogers, 40 Conn. Supp. 116, 481 A.2d 1295 (1984), citing text (Attorney General has standing to sue to set aside inter vivos transfers induced by fraud that reduced amounts available for distribution under will to charities).

Florida: Delaware v. Florida First Natl. Bank, 381 So. 2d 1075 (Fla. App. 1979) (Attorney General of Delaware had standing to sue to enforce a Florida testamentary charitable trust created for the benefit of inhabitants of Delaware); Delaware v. Belin, 453 So. 2d 1177 (Fla. App. 1984) (Attorney General of Delaware not entitled to reimbursement for the cost of employing Florida counsel to conduct the preceding case because the Attorney General is paid a salary to do this kind of work).

Massachusetts: Budin v. Levy, 343 Mass. 644, 180 N.E.2d 74 (1962); Davenport v. Attorney Gen., 361 Mass. 372, 280 N.E.2d 193 (1972) (citing the text).

Minnesota: In re Estate of Quinlan, 233 Minn. 35, 45 N.W.2d 807 (1951) (citing Restatement of Trusts §391).

New Hampshire: Attorney Gen. v. Rochester Trust Co., 115 N.H. 74, 333 A.2d 718 (1975).

New York: Matter of Stanley, 59 Misc. 2d 232, 299 N.Y.S.2d 47 (1969) (accounting by executor); Matter of Lown, 59 Misc. 2d 987, 301 N.Y.S.2d 746 (1969).

Pennsylvania: Pruner Estate, 390 Pa. 529, 136 A.2d 107 (1957) (citing the text and Restatement of Trusts §391); Musical Fund Socy. of Philadelphia, 73 D.&C.2d 115 (Pa. 1975) (member of charitable corporation sues for misuse of funds; held Attorney General should be added as a party).

South Dakota: In re Geppert's Estate, 75 S.D. 96, 59 N.W.2d 727 (1953) (citing Restatement of Trusts §391).

Washington: State v. Taylor, 58 Wash. 2d 252, 362 P.2d 247, 86 A.L.R.2d 1365 (1961) (citing the text).

some states such a suit may be maintained by the local district

---

Wisconsin: Estate of Goodrich, 271 Wis. 59, 72 N.W.2d 698 (1955) (citing Restatement of Trusts §391).

In In re Katz' Estate, 40 N.J. Super. 103, 122 A.2d 185 (1956), it was held that the Attorney General or the state is not entitled to counsel fees out of the estate.

As to which Attorney General should be a party where more than one state is involved, see National City Bank of N.Y. v. Beebe, 131 N.Y.S.2d 67 (1954), *aff'd mem.,* 285 A.D. 874, 139 N.Y.S.2d 238 (1955), *appeal dismissed,* 308 N.Y. 960, 127 N.E.2d 100 (1956), in which a trust was created by a testator who died domiciled in Rhode Island. By the exercise of a power to appoint successor trustees, a New York bank was named as the successor trustee, and thereafter the trust was administered in New York. In an accounting action brought by the trustee in New York, it was held that the Attorney General of New York was the proper party to represent the dispositions for charitable purposes under the trust. See also Israel v. Natl. Bd. of Young Men's Christian Assn., 117 R.I. 614, 369 A.2d 646 (1977), stated in §594.

In Commonwealth v. Barnes Found., 398 Pa. 458, 159 A.2d 500 (1960), noted in 22 U. Pitt. L. Rev. 280, it was held that the Attorney General could compel the trustees of a charitable art museum to admit the public under reasonable regulation.

In Grace v. Carroll, 219 F. Supp. 270 (S.D.N.Y. 1963), where the settlor brought an action in a federal court based on diversity of citizenship to recover property held in trust partly for charitable purposes, it was held that the Attorney General was a necessary party.

In Brown v. Concerned Citizens, 56 Ohio St. 2d 85, 382 N.E.2d 1155 (1978), it was held that the Attorney General had power to maintain a suit to impose a constructive trust on funds collected for charitable purposes that had been subsequently diverted to other purposes.

As to the duty to notify the Attorney General where a will leaves property to charity, see California Prob. Code, §328, as amended by Laws 1970, c. 1014.

But the court and not the Attorney General has power to permit deviation from the terms of the trust, or to determine whether and how to apply the cy pres doctrine. See §399, n. 15.

In Glenmede Trust Co. v. Dow Chemical Co., 384 F. Supp. 423 (E.D. Pa. 1974), where the trustee of a charitable trust brought a proceeding in a Pennsylvania court to approve a sale of stock, the court denied removal to the federal court, on the ground that under Pennsylvania law the Attorney General was a party defendant and was a resident of Pennsylvania as was the plaintiff also, and that he did not consent to the removal.

In Matter of Estate of Birch, 50 A.D.2d 475, 378 N.Y.S.2d 792 (1976), the court held that the Attorney General and the trustee had standing to raise an objection to a compromise agreement by the individual and charitable beneficiaries of a trust.

It is held that even though the proceeding by the Attorney General is of

attorney or county attorney.[4] In most states, as in England, the suit is brought in the name of the Attorney General, although in some states it is brought in the name of the people of the state but is prosecuted by the Attorney General.[5] The suit may be brought by the Attorney General on his own initiative, or it may be brought by him on the relation of a third person.[6] The relator need not have any direct interest in the enforcement of the trust. He is liable for the costs that would otherwise have to be paid by the state. Even though the suit is brought on the relation of

---

benefit to the charity, he and counsel employed by him are not entitled to payment for their services out of the trust property. Bush v. Arrowood, 293 Minn. 243, 198 N.W.2d 263 (1972); Matter of Dow, 90 Misc. 2d 950, 396 N.Y.S.2d 979 (1977); Wemme v. First Church of Christ, Scientist, 110 Or. 179, 219 P. 618, 223 P. 250 (1924).

But see Matter of Rothko, 95 Misc. 2d 492, 407 N.Y.S.2d 954 (1978).

[4]*Connecticut:* Dailey v. City of New Haven, 60 Conn. 314, 22 A. 945, 14 L.R.A. 69 (1891).

Illinois: People ex rel. Smith v. Braucher, 258 Ill. 604, 101 N.E. 944 (1913); People ex rel. Courtney v. Wilson, 327 Ill. App. 231, 63 N.E.2d 794 (1945) (citing the text).

Massachusetts: Parker v. May, 5 Cush. 336 (Mass. 1850) (under early statute).

Michigan: In re Powers Estate, 362 Mich. 222, 106 N.W.2d 833 (1961) (holding that under the statute the prosecuting attorney of the county was the proper party to represent the public and that the court should not appoint a special guardian for this purpose; quoting the text and citing Restatement of Trusts §391).

Canada: Re Baker, 47 O.R.2d 415, 17 E.T.R. 168 (Ont. H.C. 1984) (public trustee now has standing like Attorney General to participate in cy pres proceedings).

[5]*Federal:* Mount Vernon Mortgage Corp. v. United States, 98 App. D.C. 429, 236 F.2d 724 (1956), *aff'g* United States v. Mount Vernon Mortgage Corp., 128 F. Supp. 629 (D.D.C. 1954) (suit by United States as parens patriae by its Attorney General), *cert. denied,* 352 U.S. 988 (1957).

California: People v. Cogswell, 113 Cal. 129, 45 P. 270, 35 L.R.A. 269 (1896).

Illinois: People ex rel. Courtney v. Wilson, 327 Ill. App. 231, 63 N.E.2d 794 (1945).

Bell & Bell, Supervision of Charitable Trusts in California, 32 Hastings L.J. 433 (1980).

[6]*California:* Brown v. Memorial Natl. Home Found., 162 Cal. App. 2d 513, 329 P.2d 118, 75 A.L.R.2d 427 (1955), *cert. denied,* 358 U.S. 943 (1959).

Massachusetts: Attorney Gen. v. Butler, 123 Mass. 304 (1877); Attorney Gen. v. Parker, 126 Mass. 216 (1879).

a third person, the Attorney General and not the relator has charge of the conduct of the suit. In a number of states there are statutes expressly providing that the Attorney General may enforce charitable trusts.[7]

Not only may the Attorney General bring a proceeding to enforce a charitable trust or to enforce the obligations of a charitable corporation,[8] but also he is ordinarily a necessary party and is entitled to be heard when a proceeding is brought

[7]*California:* Corporations Code, §§9505, 10207.

Florida: Stat. Ann., §737.251, as inserted by Laws 1957, c. 57-149.

Georgia: Code 1981, §53-12-79.

Idaho: Code 1947, §67-1401, as amended by Laws 1963, c. 161; §15-1132A, as inserted by Laws 1963, c. 164.

Maine: Rev. Stat. 1964, tit. 5, §194.

Maryland: Ann. Code, Estates and Trusts Article, §§14-301, 14-302.

Massachusetts: Ann. Laws, c. 12, §§8, 8c, as amended by Laws 1979, c. 716.

Michigan: Comp. Laws Ann., §554.351 (Attorney General not local prosecuting attorney). See Oleksy v. Sisters of Mercy, 74 Mich. App. 374, 253 N.W.2d 772 (1977).

Minnesota: Stat. Ann., §501.12.

New York: Estates, Powers and Trusts Law, §8-1.1, as amended by Laws 1971, c. 1058, §43, and by Laws 1985, c. 492.

North Carolina: Gen. Stat., §§36A-41, 36A-42, 36A-46.

Ohio: Rev. Code Ann., §§109.23 to 109.33 are amended by Laws 1975, c. 93 and by Laws 1976, H.B. No. 347.

See Monroe v. Brown, 56 Ohio App. 2d 153, 8 Ohio Ops. 3d 467, 381 N.E.2d 1151 (1978) (gambling facility operated for the benefit of a charitable organization).

South Carolina: Code 1976, §1-7-130.

Tennessee: Code Ann., §§29-35-102 to 29-35-109.

In Tennessee it is held that the Attorney General has no power to enforce charitable trusts except to the extent to which a statute has conferred such power on him. State v. Hollinsworth, 193 Tenn. 491, 246 S.W.2d 345 (1952).

Texas: Rev. Civ. Stat., art. 4412a, as amended by Laws 1981, c. 501, §1, and by Laws 1983, c. 657.

As to the extent of the duty of the Attorney General, see Attorney Gen. v. Flynn, 331 Mass. 413, 120 N.E.2d 296 (1954).

In Commonwealth v. Gardner, 327 S.W.2d 947, 74 A.L.R.2d 1059 (Ky. 1959), noted in 14 Vand. L. Rev. 428, it was held that where a will gave a legacy for charitable purposes, the Attorney General had no power to intervene in an action contesting the will.

See Note, Right of attorney general to intervene in will contest case involving charitable trust, 74 A.L.R.2d 1066 (1960).

[8]See §348.1, n. 2.

for permission to deviate from the terms of the trust,[9] or to apply the doctrine of cy pres.[10] So too he is entitled to be heard in a proceeding to terminate a charitable trust,[11] or in a proceeding to approve a compromise.[12] However, in all these matters his consent or non-consent, though important, is not binding on the court.[13] So also if a charitable corporation has a claim against a third person, the action should be brought by the corporation and not by the Attorney General, unless the corporation improperly failed to act.[14]

A person having no special interest in the performance of a charitable trust cannot maintain a proceeding, by mandamus or otherwise, to compel the Attorney General to bring an action to enforce a charitable trust.[15]

Both in England and in the United States the Attorney General is charged with many duties that have nothing to do with the enforcement of charitable trusts. The result has been that, in the absence of statutory changes in the law, the enforcement of charitable trusts is bound to be more or less sporadic. This is the reason why in 1601 the Statute of Charitable Uses was enacted. The preamble of that statute recited that property given to charitable uses had frequently been misapplied by reason of fraud, breaches of trust, and negligence. The statute then

[9]See §381, n. 8.

[10]See §399, nn. 15, 16.

[11]See §337.8, n. 5.

[12]See §340, n. 15, 16; §367, n. 3.

[13]See §§108.2, n. 12; 337.8, n. 5; §340, nn. 15, 16; §367, n. 3; §367.2, n. 8.

In In re Wilson, 372 Mass. 525, 361 N.E.2d 1281 (1977), it was held that the court might appoint as successor trustee of a charitable trust a person recommended by the other trustees, although the Attorney General recommended a different person.

[14]Matter of Gebbie's Will, 33 A.D.2d 1093, 307 N.Y.S.2d 1002 (1970). See §393, n. 3.

In In re Estate of Sharp, 63 Wis. 2d 254, 217 N.W.2d 258 (1974), it was held that under the Wisconsin statutes the Attorney General had no right to intervene in probate proceedings involving a charitable trust.

In Berge v. Gorton, 88 Wash. 2d 756, 567 P.2d 187 (1977), it was held that the Attorney General had discretion whether to sue to recover funds allegedly improperly disbursed, and that an action by taxpayers to compel such suit should be dismissed.

[15]Ames v. Attorney Gen., 332 Mass. 246, 124 N.E.2d 511 (1955).

provided as a remedy that the chancellor should appoint commissioners to inquire into the administration of charitable trusts. It was found, however, that this method of appointing commissioners ad hoc did not work very well, and gradually it ceased to be employed. It so happened that early in the nineteenth century Lord Brougham became interested in the problem of enforcing charitable trusts. Under his leadership a commission was appointed by Parliament to investigate the administration of charitable trusts throughout England, and the reports of this commission, contained in some sixty volumes, disclosed a state of affairs that showed the need of some regular form of public supervision. Accordingly, in 1853 Parliament provided for a permanent Board of Charity Commissioners, with authority to examine into all charities in England or Wales, both as to the objects and management and the value of the property, and to require all trustees to furnish accounts and statements, except in the case of the universities and colleges and churches and certain other charities.[16] The board exercises general supervision over charitable trusts, and has not only administrative powers but also certain judicial powers, subject to appeal to the court from orders of the board. In 1899 the jurisdiction of the board over endowments solely for educational purposes was transferred to the Board of Education[17] and was in 1944 transferred to the Minister of Education, a corporation.[18] Further changes in the control over the administration and enforcement of charitable trusts were advocated in a parliamentary report in 1952.[19]

[16]Charitable Trusts Act, 1853, 16 & 17 Vict., c. 137.

See also Charitable Trusts (Amendment) Act, 1855, 18 & 19 Vict., c. 124; Charitable Trusts Act, 1860, 23 & 24 Vict., c. 136.

[17]Board of Education Act, 1899, 62 & 63 Vict., c. 33.

[18]Education Act, 1944, 7 & 8 Geo. VI, c. 31. This official was redesignated as the Secretary of State for Education and Science by an order issued in 1964, S.I. 1964 No. 490.

[19]Report of the Committee on the Law and Practice of the Law Relating to Charitable Trusts (1952) (Cmd. 8710), the so-called Nathan Report.

By Charities Act, 1960, 8 & 9 Eliz. II, c. 58, further provisions are made as to the functions of the Charity Commissioners and the Minister of Education and for the registration of charities.

In §28 of the Act it is provided that charity proceedings may be taken either by the charity, or by any of the charity trustees, or by any person

In the United States we have lagged far behind England in the matter of the supervision of the administration of charitable trusts. As in England in the middle of the nineteenth century, the enforcement of charitable trusts is left to the more or less sporadic action of the Attorney General. In most of the states there is no officer who is charged with the duty of exercising any general supervision over the administration of charitable trusts, and no one knows how much property is held upon such trusts or to what extent they are being properly administered. In a few states there are statutes providing that trustees for charitable purposes must account annually to the court.[20] More recently statutes have been enacted in several states, led by New Hampshire, reorganizing the office of the Attorney General so as to enable him to deal more effectively with the supervision and enforcement of charitable trusts.[21]

---

interested in the charity, or by any two or more inhabitants of the area of the charity, if it is a local charity, but not by any other person; but that no such proceeding shall be entertained in any court unless the taking of the proceeding is authorized by order of the Commissioners. It is provided that these restrictions shall not apply to the taking of proceedings by the Attorney-General, with or without a relator.

See Nathan on the Charities Act, 1960 (1962).

[20]*Indiana:* Code 1971, §30-2-2-1.

North Carolina: Gen. Stat., §36A-41.

Oregon: Rev. Stat., §128.670, as amended by Laws 1973, c. 506, and by Laws 1975, c. 388.

Vermont: Stat. Ann., tit. 14, §2501.

Wisconsin: Stat., §317.06.

[21]*California:* Government Code, §§12580 to 12598, enacted by Laws 1987, c. 892 (Uniform Supervision of Trustees for Charitable Purposes Act).

Georgia: Code 1981, §§53-12-90 to 53-12-102, providing for supervision by the State Revenue Commissioner instead of the Attorney General.

Idaho: Code 1947, §30-601, as amended by Laws 1971, c. 18.

Illinois: Rev. Stat., c. 14, §§51 to 64, as amended by Laws 1976, c. 79-1361 (Uniform Supervision of Trustees for Charitable Purposes Act).

Iowa: Code Ann., §§682.48 to 682-59.

Massachusetts: Ann. Laws, c. 12, §§8A to 8J, as amended by Laws 1979, c. 716.

Michigan: Stat. Ann., §26.1200(3), as amended by Laws 1967, c. 295 (Uniform Supervision of Trustees for Charitable Purposes Act).

Minnesota: Stat. Ann., §§501.71 to 501.81, as enacted by Laws 1975, c. 243; Stat. Ann., §§501.75, 501.76, 501.77 and 501.78, were amended by Laws 1981, c. 39.

Trustees. It is frequently said in the cases that the Attorney General alone has power to maintain suits for the enforcement of charitable trusts. This, however, is not strictly true. It is clear, for example, that where there are several trustees, one of them may maintain an action against the others to enforce the trust

---

New Hampshire: Rev. Stat. Ann., §§17:19, 17:21, 17:28, 17:31, as amended by Laws 1971, c. 439; Rev. Stat. Ann., §7:32-a, as inserted by Laws 1967, c. 203. See Souhegan Natl. Bank v. Kenison, 92 N.H. 117, 26 A.2d 26 (1942); Portsmouth Hosp. v. Attorney Gen., 104 N.H. 51, 178 A.2d 516 (1962).

New York: Estates, Powers and Trusts Law, §8-1.4, as amended by Laws 1969, c. 504, Laws 1983, c. 309, and Laws 1987, c. 573, exempts charitable trusts with assets worth less than $25,000 from reporting requirements.

Ohio: Rev. Code Ann., §§109.25 and 109.26, as amended by Laws 1975, c. 93, and by Laws 1976, H.B. No. 347.

Oregon: Rev. Stat., §§128.610 to 128.990, as amended by Laws 1971, c. 589, and by Laws 1981, c. 593, and Laws 1985, c. 730 (Uniform Supervision of Trustees for Charitable Purposes Act).

Rhode Island: Gen. Laws 1956, §§18-9-1 to 18-9-15.

South Carolina: Code 1976, §§21-31-10 to 21-31-50.

Washington: Rev. Code, §§11.110.010 to 11.110.090, as recodified by Laws 1984, c. 149.

A Uniform Supervision of Trustees for Charitable Purposes Act was adopted in 1954. It was enacted in some of the states enumerated above.

See Taylor, Public Accountability of Foundations and Charitable Trusts (1953), published by the Russell Sage Foundation; Note, Supervision of Charitable Trusts, 21 U. Chi. L. Rev. 118 (1953); Bogert, Proposed Legislation Regarding State Supervision of Charities, 52 Mich. L. Rev. 633 (1954); Bogert, The Nathan Report and the Supervision and Enforcement of Charitable Trusts, 29 N.Y.U.L. Rev. 1069 (1954); Forer, Forgotten Funds: Suggesting Disclosure Laws for Charitable Funds, 105 U. Pa. L. Rev. 1044 (1957); Vestal, Critical Evaluation of the Charitable Trust as a Giving Device, Wash. U.L.Q. 195 (1957); Ball, Accountability of Charitable Trustees, 98 Tr. & Est. 970 (1959); D'Amours, The Benefits to Fiduciaries from the Supervision of Charities, 2 N.H. Bar J. 161 (1960); Karst, The Efficiency of the Charitable Dollar: An Unfulfilled State Responsibility, 73 Harv. L. Rev. 433 (1960); Report of the Committee on Charitable Trusts and Foundations, 100 Tr. & Est. 895 (1961); Fremont-Smith, Regulating Charitable Trusts, 103 Tr. & Est. 845 (1964); Fremont-Smith, Duties and Powers of Charitable Fiduciaries: The Law of Trusts and the Correction of Abuses, 13 U.C.L.A. Law Rev. 1041 (1966); Howland, The History of the Supervision of Charitable Trusts and Corporations in California, 13 U.C.L.A. Law Rev. 1029 (1966).

See Note, 18 Syracuse L. Rev. 618 (1967); Note, Charitable Trust Enforcement in Virginia, 56 Va. L. Rev. 716 (1970); Bell & Bell, Supervision of Charitable Trusts in California, 32 Hastings L.J. 433 (1980); Hamilton, The Regulation of Charities: The Ideal, 5 Philanthropist No. 3, 30 (1985).

or to compel the redress of a breach of trust.[22] So also where the trustees bring a bill for instructions the court may make a decree as to the enforcement of the trust.[23] Where a suit is brought by the trustees of a charitable trust for the construction of the instrument creating it, or to determine its validity, or where a suit is brought by others to invalidate a charitable trust, the Attorney General is a necessary party.[24] In litigation involv-

[22]*California:* Holt v. College of Osteopathic Physicians & Surgeons, 61 Cal. 2d 750, 394 P.2d 932 (1964) (citing the text and Restatement of Trusts §391).

Florida: Ball v. Mills, 376 So. 2d 1174 (Fla. App. 1979).

Hawaii: Richards v. Midkiff, 48 Haw. 32, 396 P.2d 49 (1964) (citing the text and Restatement of Trusts §391).

Massachusetts: Morville v. Fowle, 144 Mass. 109, 10 N.E. 766 (1887); Eastman v. Allard, 149 Mass. 154, 21 N.E. 235 (1889); Crawford v. Nies, 220 Mass. 61, 107 N.E. 382 (1914), 224 Mass. 474, 113 N.E. 408 (1916).

Compare, as to private trusts, §200.2.

[23]Drury v. Inhabitants of Natick, 10 Allen 169 (Mass. 1865).

[24]*England:* Brooks v. Richardson, [1986] 1 W.L.R. 385 (Ch. D.).

Alabama: Thurlow v. Berry, 247 Ala. 631, 25 So. 2d 726 (1946).

California: In re Los Angeles County Pioneer Socy., 40 Cal. 2d 852, 257 P.2d 1 (1953) (citing Restatement of Trusts §391).

Delaware: Trustees of New Castle Common v. Gordy, 33 Del. Ch. 196, 91 A.2d 135 (1952); Carlisle v. Delaware Trust Co., 34 Del. Ch. 133, 99 A.2d 764, 775 (1953).

Indiana: State ex rel. Emmert v. Union Trust Co., 74 N.E.2d 833 (1947), *rev'd on other grounds,* 227 Ind. 571, 86 N.E.2d 450, 12 A.L.R.2d 836 (1949).

Massachusetts: Loring v. Marshall, 396 Mass. 166, 484 N.E.2d 1315 (1985), §411.5 (but a decree instructing the trustee is not void if the Attorney General is not joined).

Nebraska: In re Estate of Grblny, 147 Neb. 117, 22 N.W.2d 488 (1946) (citing Restatement of Trusts §391).

New Hampshire: Burtman v. Butman, 94 N.H. 412, 54 A.2d 367 (1947), *semble.*

New Jersey: But see Matter of Estate of Yablick, 218 N.J. Super. 91, 526 A.2d 1134 (1987) (settlement of litigation between trustees of charitable trust was binding despite failure to join Attorney General as a party where he was notified and failed to intervene).

Pennsylvania: Voegtly Estate, 396 Pa. 90, 151 A.2d 593 (1959).

Rhode Island: Leo v. Armington, 74 R.I. 124, 297, 59 A.2d 371, 60 A.2d 475 (1948).

Texas: Akin Found. v. Trustees for the Preston Rd. Church, 367 S.W.2d 351 (Tex. Civ. App. 1962). See Tex. Rev. Civ. Stat., art. 4412a, as inserted by Laws 1959, c. 115, as amended by Laws 1981, c. 501, §1, and by Laws 1983, c. 657.

But see In re Estate of Roberts, 190 Kan. 248, 373 P.2d 165 (1962),

ing a charitable trust the Attorney General is attorney for the public and not for the trustee. Hence it has been held that in a suit brought to contest a will under which a charitable trust was created, the trustees properly employed an attorney and could properly pay him a reasonable fee out of the trust estate.[25]

Persons having special interests. A person who has a special interest in the performance of a charitable trust can maintain a suit for its enforcement.[26] He must show that he is entitled to receive a benefit under the trust that is not merely the benefit to which members of the public in general are entitled. Although it is true that a trust for the benefit of definite persons is not a charitable trust, nevertheless definite persons may be entitled to receive certain benefits under the trust. Thus where a trust is created to pay or contribute toward the payment of the salary of the minister of a particular church, the minister for the time being can maintain a suit to compel the trustees to pay him the amount specified by the terms of the trust.[27] The trust is a charitable trust because it is for the promotion of religion, which is of benefit to the community generally, but the minister for the time being has a special interest in the performance of the trust. The same thing is true where a trust is created for the endowment of a professorial chair in an educational institution; the incumbent of the chair for the time being has a special interest in the performance of the trust and can maintain a suit to enforce his interest. Similarly, where by the terms of the trust it is provided that in awarding the benefits under the trust a prefer-

---

holding that in an action involving the validity of a charitable trust created by will the Attorney General was not a necessary party.

[25]Murphey v. Dalton, 314 S.W.2d 726, 67 A.L.R.2d 1278 (Mo. 1958) (citing the text and Restatement of Trusts §391).

[26]German Evangelical St. Marcus Congregation v. Archambault, 404 S.W.2d 705 (Mo. 1966) (owners of cemetery lots in public cemetery).

See Newman v. Forward Lands, 430 F. Supp. 1320 (E.D. Pa. 1977) (citing Restatement of Trusts §391).

[27]See First Congregational Socy. in Raynham v. Trustees, 23 Pick. 148 (Mass. 1839).

In Howe v. School Dist. No. 3, 43 Vt. 282 (1870), it was held that where a trust was created to maintain a church, persons having pew rights in the church could bring a bill in equity to enjoin the use of the land for school purposes.

ence shall be given to certain persons, these persons can maintain a suit against the trustee to enforce the provision.[28] Where property is given in trust for a charitable corporation, the corporation can maintain a suit against the trustees for the enforcement of the trust.[29] In a case in Delaware it was held that where land was conveyed in trust to establish a colony for the purpose of applying in a practical way the single-tax theory, the trustees being authorized to make leases and to permit the lessees the use of common land and generally to conduct the colony on the land in the manner authorized, a lessee had such an interest under the trust as to permit him to maintain a suit to enjoin the trustees from creating a rent charge on the property.[30]

[28]See Darcy v. Kelley, 153 Mass. 433, 26 N.E. 1110 (1891); Alco Gravure v. Knapp Found., 64 N.Y.2d 458, 479 N.E.2d 752, 490 N.Y.S.2d 116 (1985), citing text and Restatement (Second) of Trusts §391.

In Braund v. Earl of Devon, L.R. 3 Ch. App. 800 (1868), it was held that where a testator left his estate in trust to establish a school for the gratuitous education of boys, with preference to the lineal descendants of his grandfather, a suit to enforce the trust could not be maintained by such descendants without obtaining the permission of the Charity Commissioners.

See §375.3, n. 10.

[29]*Massachusetts:* Harvard College v. Amory, 9 Pick. 446 (Mass. 1830); Bradbury v. Birchmore, 117 Mass. 569 (1875).

Michigan: St. John's-St. Luke Evangelical Church v. National Bank, 92 Mich. App. 1, 283 N.W.2d 852 (1979) (citing Restatement of Trusts §391).

Oklahoma: Matter of Estate of Doan, 727 P.2d 574 (Okla. 1986) (where property was bequeathed to foundation upon trust to pay a third of the income to the YMCA, YMCA had standing to commence proceeding to determine whether this legacy was charged with part of the federal estate tax).

But in Estate of Vanderbilt, 109 Misc. 2d 914, 441 N.Y.S.2d 153 (Sur. 1981), it was held that a charitable corporation could sue the Attorney General for allowance of its accounts.

[30]Cannon v. Stephens, 18 Del. Ch. 276, 159 A. 234 (1932).

In Matter of Jones, 191 Misc. 617, 78 N.Y.S.2d 34 (1948), a testatrix made a bequest to a hospital to endow two beds to be used by persons who might from time to time be designated by a named church. It was held that the church could maintain a proceeding for a construction of the will, but that a person designated by the church to occupy one of the beds could not.

In San Diego County Council v. City of Escondido, 14 Cal. App. 3d 189, 92 Cal. Rptr. 186 (1971), land was conveyed to a bank in trust for the Boy Scouts and Girl Scouts of certain districts. The district associations were not incorporated, but there was a parent incorporated association, the County Council. It was held that the Council could maintain an action to enforce the trust, joining the Attorney General as a party defendant. A representative sent

In the situations just discussed it is clear enough that the persons suing have such special interests under the trust as to enable them to maintain a suit against the trustees for the protection of their interests. There are other situations where the matter is more doubtful. It would seem, however, that where a charitable trust is created for the benefit of a small class of persons, any member of the class can maintain a suit on behalf of himself and the other members of the class for the enforcement of the trust. A study of the Calendars in Chancery, listing numerous cases brought prior to the enactment of the Statute of Charitable Uses in 1601, shows that although in many of these cases the suit was brought by the Attorney-General, in many others it was brought by third persons. In many of the cases the trust was for the benefit of the poor of a particular church or parish or town, and the suit was brought either by the church-wardens or other officials or was brought by church members or inhabitants suing on behalf of themselves and the other church members or inhabitants. There are modern cases to the same effect.[31]

---

by individual scouts was dropped, because they were represented by the Council.

[31]*Federal:* Schell v. Leander Clark College, 10 F.2d 542 (D. Iowa, 1926) (temporary injunction against diversion but not suit for approval of a scheme).

Connecticut: Dailey v. City of New Haven, 60 Conn. 314, 22 A. 945, 14 L.R.A. 69 (1891).

District of Columbia: Young Men's Christian Assn. of the City of Washington v. Covington, 484 A.2d 589 (D.C. Ct. App. 1984) (members of a Y.M.C.A. branch housed in the building held on trust).

Missouri: Harger v. Barrett, 319 Mo. 633, 5 S.W.2d 1100 (1928).

New Jersey: Larkin v. Wikoff, 75 N.J. Eq. 462, 72 A. 98 (1909), *aff'd,* 77 N.J. Eq. 589, 78 A. 1134 (1910); Leeds v. Harrison, 15 N.J. Super. 82, 83 A.2d 45 (1951) (citing the text), *rev'd on other grounds,* 9 N.J. 202, 87 A.2d 713 (1952), noted in 40 Geo. L.J. 122, 100 U. Pa. L. Rev. 457; Township of Cinnaminson v. First Camden Natl. Bank & Trust Co., 99 N.J. Super. 115, 238 A.2d 701 (1968) (citing the text).

Texas: Lokey v. Texas Methodist Found., 479 S.W.2d 260 (Tex. 1972), *rev'g* 468 S.W.2d 945; Gray v. St. Matthews Cathedral Endowment Fund, 544 S.W.2d 488, 94 A.L.R.3d 1197 (Tex. Civ. App. 1976) (citing the text and Restatement of Trusts, §391, Comments *c* and *d*).

But see Krauthoff v. Attorney Gen., 240 Mass. 88, 132 N.E. 865 (1921), where a suit had already been brought by the Attorney General.

Where a person having a special interest in the performance of a charitable trust brings suit for the enforcement of the trust, the Attorney General is ordinarily a necessary party to the suit, since his presence is necessary for the protection of the interests of the community in the performance of the trust.[32] Where the

In Town of Leesburg v. First Natl. Bank, 209 Va. 795, 167 S.E.2d 109 (1969), where a lot was dedicated for the burial of paupers, it was held that the town in which the lot was situated had a standing to enforce the trust.

See Note, Standing of minister or member of religious society to seek enforcement, termination, or proper administration of charitable trust, 94 A.L.R.3d 1204 (1979).

[32] *England:* Strickland v. Weldon, 28 Ch. D. 426 (1885); Brooks v. Richardson, [1986] 1 W.L.R. 385 (Ch.D.).

California: Estate of Schloss, 56 Cal. 2d 248, 363 P.2d 875 (1961) (citing the text); San Diego County Council v. City of Escondido, 14 Cal. App. 3d 189, 92 Cal. Rptr. 186 (1971).

Connecticut: Copp v. Barnum, 160 Conn. 557, 276 A.2d 893 (1970) (suit for declaratory judgment).

New Jersey: Larkin v. Wikoff, 75 N.J. Eq. 462, 72 A. 98 (1909), *aff'd,* 77 N.J. Eq. 589, 78 A. 1134 (1910).

In Elliott v. Teachers College, N.Y. L.J. June 12, 1941, p. 2643, col. 1, a suit was brought to enjoin a charitable corporation from merging an endowed school owned by it with another school which it also owned, and asking for a declaration of rights. The suit was brought by three pupils of the endowed school, suing by their guardians, and the parents of other pupils and a contributor to the funds of the schools all suing on behalf of themselves and all others similarly situated, and by the president of its Parent-Teachers Association suing on behalf of the association. The Attorney General was made a party defendant and in his answer prayed for a declaration of rights. The court denied a motion to dismiss the action on the ground that the plaintiffs lacked legal capacity to maintain the suit. The court said that it was unnecessary to determine whether the plaintiffs had a special interest entitling them to maintain the suit but held that because the Attorney General was a party and asked for a declaration of rights, the action could be maintained. Subsequently, judgment was given against the plaintiffs on the ground that the merger was not a violation of the terms of the grants made to the endowed school. Elliott v. Teachers College, 177 Misc. 746, 31 N.Y.S.2d 796 (1941), *aff'd,* 264 A.D. 839, 35 N.Y.S.2d 761 (1942), *aff'd,* 290 N.Y. 747, 50 N.E.2d 97 (1943).

In Frank v. Clover Leaf Park Cemetery Assn., 29 N.J. 193, 148 A.2d 488 (1959), an action was brought by a manufacturer of grave markers against a charitable cemetery corporation that sold markers manufactured by others to be used in the cemetery. The Attorney General was not made a party but intervened. It was held that the action lay. See Terwilliger v. Graceland Memorial Park Assn., 59 N.J. Super. 205, 157 A.2d 567 (1960).

interests of the community are unaffected by the result of the suit, however, the Attorney General is not a necessary party.[33] Indeed, in *Attorney General v. Clark,*[34] it was held that an information filed by the Attorney General at the relation of the trustees of a church to compel the defendants to deliver to the trustees property wrongfully taken from them should be dismissed, because the church was a definite body for whose use the property was intended and that was capable of enforcing its rights.

Persons having no special interest.   On the other hand, a person who has no interest in the performance of the trust, no interest other than as a member of the community, cannot main-

---

In Matter of Langeloth, 200 Misc. 551, 102 N.Y.S.2d 978 (1951), where the Attorney General was already a party, the court gave leave to other interested persons to intervene.

In Kolin v. Leitch, 343 Ill. App. 622, 99 N.E.2d 685 (1951), a suit was brought by a pupil in a school and his mother on behalf of themselves and all others similarly situated and on behalf of the Parents Committee of the school to enjoin the closing of the school. The Attorney General was made a party. It was held that he was entitled to control the litigation and that his motion to dismiss the suit should be granted.

By California Probate Code, §328, as amended by Laws 1963, c. 984, it is provided that "Whenever the instrument offered for probate involves or may involve a testamentary trust of property for charitable purposes other than a charitable trust with a designated trustee, resident in this State, notice of the hearing on the petition for probate accompanied by a copy of the petition and the will, must be personally served upon the Attorney General or mailed, postage prepaid, from a post office within this State addressed to him at the office of the Attorney General at Sacramento, California." See also Probate Code, §1080, as amended by Laws 1963, c. 1326, and by Laws 1969, c. 124.

[33]Amundson v. Kletzing-McLaughlin Memorial Found. College, 247 Iowa 91, 73 N.W.2d 114 (1955) (citing Restatement of Trusts §391); Eustace v. Dickey, 240 Mass. 55, 132 N.E. 852 (1921).

See Miller v. Davis, 136 Tex. 299, 150 S.W.2d 973 (1941).

In Rohlff v. German Old People's Home, 143 Neb. 636, 10 N.W.2d 686 (1943), property was bequeathed to a charitable corporation for a particular purpose that failed. It was held that the Attorney General was not a necessary party in an action brought by the heirs, who claimed that the doctrine of cy pres was not applicable and that the property reverted to them. It would seem, however, that in the absence of the Attorney General there was no party adequately representing the interest of the public.

[34]167 Mass. 201, 45 N.E. 183 (1896).

tain a suit for the enforcement of the trust.[35] He may, if he can,

[35]*England:* Feoffees of Heriot's Hosp. v. Ross, 12 Cl. & Fin. 507 (1846); In re Belling, [1967] 1 All E.R. 105; Hauxwell v. Barton-upon-Humber Urban Dist. Council, [1973] 2 All E.R. 1022, [1973] 3 W.L.R. 41.

Federal: Kemmerer v. John D. & Catherine T. MacArthur Found., 594 F. Supp. 121 (N.D. Ill. 1984).

Alabama: Moseley v. Smiley, 171 Ala. 593, 55 So. 143 (1911).

California: Hart v. County of Los Angeles, 260 Cal. App. 2d 512, 67 Cal. Rptr. 242 (1968); Hardman v. Feinstein, 195 Cal. App. 3d 157, 240 Cal. Rptr. 483 (1987).

Connecticut: Averill v. Lewis, 106 Conn. 582, 138 A. 815 (1927), noted in 12 Minn. L. Rev. 653, 76 U. Pa. L. Rev. 332.

District of Columbia: Mount Vernon Mortgage Corp. v. United States, 98 App. D.C. 429, 236 F.2d 724 (1956), *aff'g* United States v. Mount Vernon Mortgage Corp., 128 F. Supp. 629 (D.D.C. 1954) (*semble;* quoting Restatement of Trusts, §391, Comment *d*), *cert. denied,* 352 U.S. 988 (1957).

Illinois: Barker v. Hauberg, 325 Ill. 538, 156 N.E. 806 (1927); Greene v. Art Inst. of Chicago, 16 Ill. App. 2d 84, 147 N.E.2d 415 (1958) (citing the text); Stoner Mfg. Corp. v. Young Men's Christian Assn., 13 Ill. 2d 162, 148 N.E.2d 441 (1958).

Indiana: Boice v. Mallers, 121 Ind. App. 210, 96 N.E.2d 342 (1950), *petition for transfer to Supreme Court denied,* 229 Ind. 325, 98 N.E.2d 368 (1951) (unsuccessful bidder; citing Restatement of Trusts §391).

Kentucky: See Greenway v. Irvine's Trustee, 279 Ky. 632, 131 S.W.2d 705, 124 A.L.R. 1229 (1939) (quoting Restatement of Trusts §391).

Massachusetts: See Elias v. Steffo, 310 Mass. 280, 37 N.E.2d 991 (1941).

Michigan: Oleksy v. Sisters of Mercy, 74 Mich. App. 374, 253 N.W.2d 772 (1977); s.c. 92 Mich. App. 770, 285 N.W.2d 455 (1979).

Minnesota: See Longcor v. City of Red Wing, 206 Minn. 627, 289 N.W. 570 (1940) (citing Restatement of Trusts §391), noted in 24 Minn. L. Rev. 568; Schaeffer v. Newberry, 227 Minn. 259, 35 N.W.2d 287 (1948) (citing Restatement of Trusts §391); John Wright & Assocs., v. City of Red Wing, 259 Minn. 111, 106 N.W.2d 205 (1960); In re Trust in Estate of Everett, 263 Minn. 398, 116 N.W.2d 601 (1962) (citing Restatement of Trusts §391).

Missouri: Dickey v. Volker, 321 Mo. 235, 11 S.W.2d 278, 62 A.L.R. 858 (1928), *cert. denied,* 279 U.S. 839 (1929); Voelker v. St. Louis Mercantile Library Assn., 359 S.W.2d 689 (Mo. 1962) (citing the text).

New Jersey: Di Cristofaro v. Laurel Grove Memorial Park, 43 N.J. Super. 244, 128 A.2d 281 (1957) (*semble;* citing the text).

New York: Female Assn. of N.Y. v. Beekman, 21 Barb. 565 (N.Y. 1854); Caputo v. Officers & Trustees of N.Y. Dispensary, 92 N.Y.S.2d 547 (1949); Balluffi v. Montross, 199 Misc. 220, 102 N.Y.S.2d 543 (1950) (citing the text); Revici v. Conference of Jewish Material Claims, 11 Misc. 2d 354, 174 N.Y.S.2d 825 (1958).

See Application of Herman, 177 Misc. 276, 30 N.Y.S.2d 448 (1941);

induce the Attorney General to bring a suit, and the Attorney

---

Matter of James, 123 N.Y.S.2d 520 (1953) (citing the text and Restatement of Trusts §391).

North Carolina: Kania v. Chatham, 297 N.C. 290, 254 S.E.2d 528 (1979) (candidate for scholarship seeking to remove trustees; citing the text and Restatement of Trusts §391).

Oklahoma: Sarkeys v. Independent School Dist., 592 P.2d 529 (Okla. 1979); McFarland v. Atkins, 594 P.2d 758 (Okla. 1979).

Oregon: Associated Students of Univ. of Or. v. Oregon Inv. Council, 82 Or. App. 145, 728 P.2d 30 (1986), *review denied,* 303 Or. 74, 734 P.2d 354 (1987).

Pennsylvania: Wiegand v. Barnes Found., 374 Pa. 149, 97 A.2d 81 (1953) (quoting Restatement of Trusts §391).

Texas: See Clevenger v. Rio Farms, 204 S.W.2d 40 (Tex. Civ. App. 1947) (citing Restatement of Trusts §391); Gray v. St. Matthews Cathedral Endowment Fund, 544 S.W.2d 488, 94 A.L.R.3d 1197 (Tex. Civ. App. 1976), *semble* (citing the text and Restatement of Trusts §391); Gregory v. Mbank Corpus Christi, N.A., 716 S.W.2d 662 (Tex. App. 1986).

In Wiegand v. Barnes Found., 374 Pa. 149, 97 A.2d 81 (1953) (quoting Restatement of Trusts §391), it was held that an action against a charitable corporation to enforce its charitable obligations could not be maintained by a private person even though the Attorney General consented to the bringing of the suit.

In People ex rel. Courtney v. Wilson, 327 Ill. App. 231, 63 N.E.2d 794 (1945), a testatrix left money in trust to erect such a memorial as the trustees might determine, but provided that if the erection of a memorial should be commenced by her in her lifetime, they should complete it. She had engaged an architect to draw plans and she had accepted the plans, but the erection had not been begun in her lifetime. It was held that the architect had no standing to maintain an action to enforce the trust. The court cited the text.

In Voelker v. St. Louis Mercantile Library Assn., 359 S.W.2d 689 (Mo. 1962), where a charitable corporation was created by the legislature to maintain a library for the benefit of elected members, it was held that the members had no such special interest as to entitle them to maintain a suit to enjoin an alleged breach of trust. The court cited the text.

In Application of Herman, 177 Misc. 276, 30 N.Y.S.2d 448 (1941), *supra,* it was held that although suit was begun for the enforcement of a charitable trust by a person having no special interest, nevertheless the suit would not be dismissed because the court can on its own initiative enforce such a trust under New York Personal Property Law, §12(2), and Real Property Law, §113 (now superseded by Estates, Powers and Trusts Law, §8-1.1, amended by Laws 1971, c. 1058, and Laws 1985, c. 492), providing that "the supreme court shall have control over gifts, grants and bequests" for educational purposes.

In Longcor v. City of Red Wing, 206 Minn. 627, 289 N.W. 570 (1940), *supra,* the court suggested that if the Attorney General had, upon adequate showing, refused to act, an action might have been maintainable by a private person.

General may, if he chooses, bring the suit only if the complaining person is willing to act as relator and assume responsibility for the payment of costs. But a third person who has no special interest cannot himself maintain the suit. If a third person were permitted to sue as a matter of right it would be possible to subject the charity to harassing litigation. Thus where a testator left his estate in trust to establish and maintain an art museum in a city, a resident and taxpayer of the city cannot maintain a suit to enforce the trust.[36] The mere fact that a person may in the discretion of the trustee become a recipient of the benefit under the trust does not entitle him to maintain a suit for the enforcement of the trust. Thus in a case in Connecticut where an estate was left in trust to maintain a home for needy female teachers in a certain county, it was held that a suit to enforce the trust could not be maintained by a group of needy teachers.[37]

In Day v. City of Hartford, 16 Conn. 228 (1949), it was held that a citizen-taxpayer of a city could maintain a suit to enjoin the city from destroying two bridges given to it.

A person having no special interest in the performance of a charitable trust cannot maintain a proceeding, by mandamus or otherwise, to compel the Attorney General to bring an action to enforce a charitable trust. See n. 15, *supra.*

In People v. American Socy. for Prevention of Cruelty to Animals, 20 A.D.2d 762, 247 N.Y.S.2d 487 (1964), *aff'd mem.,* 15 N.Y.2d 511, 202 N.E.2d 561 (1964), it was held that members of the public could not maintain an action to rescind the charter of a charitable corporation, the Attorney General having refused to bring such an action.

As to the right to intervene, see §399, n. 16.

In Fitzgerald v. Baxter State Park Auth., 385 A.2d 189 (Me. 1978), land was conveyed to the state of Maine as a state park. The state by legislation designed the defendant Park Authority to carry out the terms of the trust. The plaintiffs, as Maine citizens, domiciliaries, voters, and property holders, brought a class suit against the Park Authority to enjoin a deviation from the terms of the trust. The Attorney General was a member of the Park Authority and was therefore precluded from suing, and was named co-defendant. The court held that the plaintiffs had standing to sue. It said that it expressed no opinion whether the plaintiffs would have standing as having a special interest if the Attorney General were not precluded. The court cited the text, §391.

[36]Dickey v. Volker, 321 Mo. 235, 11 S.W.2d 278, 62 A.L.R. 858 (1928), *cert. denied,* 279 U.S. 839 (1929).

[37]Averill v. Lewis, 106 Conn. 582, 138 A. 815 (1927), noted in 12 Minn. L. Rev. 653, 76 U. Pa. L. Rev. 332.

In Boenhardt v. Loch, 129 A.D. 355, 113 N.Y.S. 747 (1908), where funds

Chief Justice Wheeler, however, dissented on the ground that the class of beneficiaries was small enough so that its members had a sufficient interest to permit them to maintain a suit for the enforcement of the trust. Where a trust is created to maintain a charitable institution, the managers and other agents or employees engaged in the conducting of the institution have not such an interest in the performance of the trust as to permit them to maintain a suit for its enforcement.[38]

Standing; class actions. In recent times the question has often arisen whether plaintiffs have a standing to maintain an action. It has arisen in the case of charitable trusts. Thus in *Simon v. Eastern Kentucky Welfare Rights Association*[39] the Supreme Court held that indigents and various organizations representing indigents had no standing to maintain an action against the Secretary of the Treasury and the Internal Revenue Commissioner to set aside a ruling by the Internal Revenue Service that a nonprofit hospital was a charitable institution and as such was exempt from a federal tax, even though it did not provide free or below-cost services to the poor. In some other cases standing has also been denied.[40] But in other cases it was held that the plaintiffs had standing.[41]

---

were contributed for the relief of sufferers from the destruction by fire of a ship, it was held that one who suffered from the disaster had no standing to compel the payment of a part of the fund to him. See §375.2, n. 43.

[38]Barker v. Hauberg, 325 Ill. 538, 156 N.E. 806 (1927).

[39]426 U.S. 26, 96 S. Ct. 1917, 48 L. Ed. 2d 450 (1976). See §372, n. 7.

[40]In Askew v. Hold the Bulkhead — Save Our Bays, 269 So. 2d 696 (Fla. App. 1972), where land was devised to the state, and the will provided that any resident taxpayer of the state should have the right to enforce the trust, it was held that a taxpayer having no special interest had no standing to sue.

In Miller v. Alderhold, 228 Ga. 65, 184 S.E.2d 172 (1971), *appeal dismissed,* 405 U.S. 908 (1971), it was held that students in a college had no standing to maintain a class suit against its trustees, claiming that the trustees had been guilty of breaches of trust in its administration.

In Fuchs v. Bidwell, 65 Ill. 2d 503, 359 N.E.2d 158 (1977), it was held that plaintiffs representing citizens of the state had no standing to sue to impose a constructive trust of bribes received by public officers (three justices dissenting).

[41]In Jones v. Grant, 344 So. 2d 1210 (Ala. 1977), it was held that members of the faculty, staff, and students had standing to bring a class action against the president and directors of a college for the misuse of funds.

The settlor or his heirs or personal representatives. The question remains whether the settlor or his heirs or personal representatives can maintain a suit for the enforcement of a charitable trust. As we have seen, the settlor cannot revoke or modify a charitable trust created by him unless he has reserved a power to do so.[42] After the trust is once created, he has no beneficial interest in the trust property. Accordingly, it has been held in a number of cases that the settlor has no standing to maintain a suit for the enforcement of a charitable trust.[43] There are,

---

In Parsons v. Walker, 28 Ill. App. 3d 517, 328 N.E.2d 920 (1975), where a gift of land was made to a state university for a park, it was held that citizens had standing to maintain a suit to enjoin deviation.

In Gordon v. City of Baltimore, 258 Md. 682, 267 A.2d 98 (1970), it was held that a taxpayer had standing to sue to prevent a transfer by a charitable corporation of its library to another charitable corporation under an agreement by the City of Baltimore to support the library. The court cited the text.

See Connecticut Gen. Stat., §§47-42a to 47-42c, as to the enforcement of conservation and preservation restrictions.

As to class actions in case of mortgage escrow agreements, see §12.2, n. 32.

As to class actions against a municipality as trustee, see §348.1, n. 11.

See Tushnet, The New Law of Standing: A Plea for Abandonment, 62 Cornell L. Rev. 663, 680 (1977); Parker & Stone, Standing and Public Law Remedies, 78 Colum. L. Rev. 771 (1978).

[42]See §367.

[43]*California:* O'Hara v. Grand Lodge I.O.G.T., 213 Cal. 131, 2 P.2d 21 (1931), *semble;* Marin Hosp. Dist. v. State Dept. of Health, 92 Cal. App. 3d 442, 154 Cal. Rptr. 838 (1979) (citing Restatement of Trusts, §391, Comment *e*).

Illinois: Smith v. Thompson, 266 Ill. App. 165 (1932); Holden Hosp. Corp. v. Southern Ill. Hosp. Corp., 22 Ill. 2d 150, 174 N.E.2d 793 (1961) (citing Restatement of Trusts §391); Skokie Valley Professional Bldg. v. Skokie Valley Community Hosp., 74 Ill. App. 3d 569, 30 Ill. Dec. 474, 393 N.E.2d 510 (1979).

Kentucky: Greenway v. Irvine's Trustee, 279 Ky. 632, 131 S.W.2d 705, 124 A.L.R. 1229 (1939) (*semble;* quoting Restatement of Trusts §391); Eitel v. John N. Norton Memorial Infirmary, 441 S.W.2d 438 (Ky. 1969), *semble,* (citing Restatement of Trusts §391).

Massachusetts: Trustees of Andover Theological Seminary v. Visitors, 253 Mass. 256, 301, 148 N.E. 900 (1925), *semble,* noted in 35 Yale L.J. 643; Dillaway v. Burton, 256 Mass. 568, 153 N.E. 13 (1926), *semble.*

Mississippi: Freedman's Aid & S. Educ. Socy. v. Scott, 125 Miss. 299, 87 So. 659 (1921).

Missouri: Tyree v. Bingham, 100 Mo. 451, 13 S.W. 952 (1890).

New Jersey: Ludlam v. Higbee, 11 N.J. Eq. 342 (1857), *semble;* Leeds v.

however, cases in which the opposite result has been reached.[44] But where the settlor has a special interest in the performance of the trust he can maintain a suit to enforce it. Thus in a case in New York it was held that where an association of the alumni of an educational institution gave a fund to the institution for the establishment of a professorship, reserving power to nominate the professor, the association could maintain a suit to enforce the trust.[45]

Where a charitable trust is created by will, or where it is created inter vivos and the settlor has subsequently died, the heirs or personal representatives of the settlor cannot maintain

---

Harrison, 7 N.J. Super. 558, 72 A.2d 371 (1950) (citing Restatement of Trusts §391).

New York: Balluffi v. Montross, 199 Misc. 220, 102 N.Y.S.2d 543 (1950); Application of Italian Benevolent Inst., 157 N.Y.S.2d 485 (1956).

Ohio: Kemper v. Trustees of Lane Seminary, 17 Ohio 293 (1848).

Oklahoma: Sarkeys v. Independent School Dist., 592 P.2d 529 (Okla. 1979); McFarland v. Atkins, 594 P.2d 758 (Okla. 1979) (a contributor).

Virginia: Clark v. Oliver, 91 Va. 421, 22 S. E. 175 (1895).

Wisconsin: Strong v. Doty, 32 Wis. 381 (1873); Steenis v. City of Appleton, 230 Wis. 530, 284 N.W. 492 (1939) (*semble;* citing Restatement of Trusts, §391, Comment *e*); Fairbanks v. City of Appleton, 249 Wis. 476, 24 N.W.2d 893 (1946) (*semble;* citing Restatement of Trusts, §391, Comment *e*).

In Wisconsin it is provided by statute Stat., §701.10, that a proceeding to enforce a charitable trust may be brought by any settlor or group of settlors who contributed half or more of the principal.

See 62 A.L.R. 881, 897 (1929); 124 id. 1237 (1940); 37 Yale L.J. 533 (1928).

As to the right of the settlor of a private trust and his successors in interest to maintain a suit to enforce it, see §200.1.

[44]*Iowa:* Citizens for Washington Square v. City of Davenport, 277 N.W.2d 882 (Iowa 1979) (suit by settlor's descendant against city as to land given to it for park purposes).

Kentucky: Chambers v. Baptist Educ. Socy., 1 B. Mon. 215 (Ky. 1841), *semble;* Baptist Church at Lancaster v. Presbyterian Church, 18 B. Mon. 635 (Ky. 1857), *semble;* Tate v. Woodyard, 145 Ky. 613, 140 S.W. 1044 (1911).

New Jersey: Mills v. Davison, 54 N.J. Eq. 659, 35 A. 1072, 35 L.R.A. 113, 55 Am. St. Rep. 594 (1896), *semble.*

New York: Hascall v. Madison Univ., 8 Barb. 174 (N.Y. 1850).

Oregon: Chapman v. Wilbur, 4 Or. 362 (1873), *semble.*

[45]Associate Alumni v. Theological Seminary, 163 N.Y. 417, 57 N.E. 626 (1900).

Compare Hopkins v. Women's Medical College, 331 Pa. 42, 200 A. 32 (1938), noted in 5 U. Pitt. L. Rev. 114.

a suit for the enforcement of the trust.[46] In a few cases, however, the opposite result has been reached.[47]

Where on the termination or failure of a charitable trust the settlor or his heirs or personal representatives are entitled to receive the property, they can of course maintain a suit to recover the property.[48] In such a case they are enforcing rights

[46]*Federal:* Gredig v. Sterling, 47 F.2d 832 (5th Cir. 1931), *semble, cert. denied,* 284 U.S. 629 (1931).

Delaware: Wier v. Howard Hughes Medical Inst., 407 A.2d 1051 (Del. Ch. 1979) (holding that personal representative of the settlor who was trustee of a charitable corporation has no standing).

Massachusetts: Sanderson v. White, 18 Pick. 328, 29 Am. Dec. 591 (Mass. 1836); Holmes v. Welch, 314 Mass. 106, 49 N.E.2d 461, 157 A.L.R. 896 (1943), *semble.*

New Hampshire: Petition of Burnham, 74 N.H. 492, 69 A. 720 (1908).

New Jersey: MacKenzie v. Trustees of Presbytery, 67 N.J. Eq. 652, 61 A. 1027, 3 L.R.A. (N.S.) 227 (1905); In re St. Michael's Church, 76 N.J. Eq. 524, 74 A. 491 (1909) (residuary legatee; *semble*).

Oregon: Wemme v. Noyes, 134 Or. 590, 294 P. 602, 295 P. 465 (1930).

Pennsylvania: In re Conveyance of Land Belonging to City of Du Bois, 461 Pa. 161, 335 A.2d 352 (1975).

Tennessee: Nolfe v. Byrne, 142 Tenn. 309, 219 S.W. 1 (1919), *semble.*

In First Camden Natl. Bank & Trust Co. v. Hiram Lodge No. 81, 134 N.J. Eq. 303, 35 A.2d 490 (1944), *aff'd,* 135 N.J. Eq. 505, 39 A.2d 371 (1944), it was held that where a legacy is given to a charitable corporation and it makes a compromise with the next of kin, the executor has no standing to object to the compromise. The court quoted Restatement of Trusts §391.

[47]Garrison v. Little, 75 Ill. App. 402, 417 (1898), *semble;* McGee v. Vandeventer, 326 Ill. 425, 158 N.E. 127 (1927), *semble,* noted in 37 Yale L.J. 533; Mott v. Morris, 249 Mo. 137, 149, 155 S.W. 434 (1913), *semble.*

[48]*Illinois:* Miller v. Riddle, 227 Ill. 53, 81 N.E. 48, 118 Am. St. Rep. 261 (1907); Green v. Old People's Home, 269 Ill. 134, 109 N.E. 701 (1915).

Kentucky: Eitel v. John N. Norton Memorial Infirmary, 441 S.W.2d 438 (Ky. 1969) (citing Restatement of Trusts §391).

Maryland: Carter v. Mayor & City Council of Baltimore, 197 Md. 70, 78 A.2d 212 (1951).

Massachusetts: Chase v. Dickey, 212 Mass. 555, 99 N.E. 410 (1912).

Michigan: In re Estate of Rood, 41 Mich. App. 405, 200 N.W.2d 728, 67 A.L.R.3d 390 (1972).

Missouri: Thatcher v. City of St. Louis, 343 Mo. 597, 122 S.W.2d 915 (1938) (citing Restatement of Trusts §381 [391?]).

Nebraska: Rohlff v. German Old People's Home, 143 Neb. 636, 10 N.W.2d 686 (1943).

In an action brought by the heirs of the settlor to recover the property on the ground that the charitable trust had failed, the Attorney General is a

adverse to the trust and are not attempting to enforce it. Similarly, where by the terms of the trust there is a gift over on the failure of the charity to a charitable institution, that institution can maintain an action.[49]

The visitorial power.   Under the law of England, where property is given to a charitable corporation founded by the donor, he may reserve or may confer on others a power of visitation. An English writer[50] says: "The power of electing and removing the members of a corporation and of its officers, of regulating the management of the property, or deciding the construction of the statute of foundation, and judging claims and complaints by members concerning the internal affairs of the corporation is vested in visitors." Where property is given to trustees for charitable purposes rather than to a charitable corporation, there is no such visitorial power. In the United States it has not been usual for the founder of a charitable corporation to provide for supervision by visitors. There are, however, occasional cases involving the exercise of this power.[51]

---

necessary party. Pruner Estate, 390 Pa. 529, 136 A.2d 107 (1957) (citing the text and Restatement of Trusts, §391, Comment *f*).

[49]In Trustees of Dartmouth College v. City of Quincy, 331 Mass. 219, 118 N.E.2d 89 (1954), where property was devised to a town to establish a school with a gift over to a college if the town should cease to maintain the school, it was held that the college could maintain a suit to prevent the town from using the principal for the upkeep of the school. The court cited the Restatement of Trusts §391.

[50]Tudor, Law of Charitable Trusts 194 (5th ed. 1929).

For a recent case on the scope of the visitorial power, see Patel v. University of Bradford, [1979] 1 W.L.R. 1066, [1978] 3 All E.R. 841.

[51]See Trustees of Andover Theological Seminary v. Visitors, 253 Mass. 256, 148 N.E. 900 (1925); Trustees of Putnam Free School v. Attorney Gen., 321 Mass. 94, 67 N.E.2d 658 (1946).

See Wier v. Howard Hughes Medical Inst., 407 A.2d 1051 (Del. Ch. 1979), holding that the old common law as to visitors is not to be followed either in the case of a charitable trust or a charitable corporation.

See Sarkeys v. Independent School Dist., 592 P.2d 529 (Okla. 1979).

In State v. Taylor, 58 Wash. 2d 252, 362 P.2d 247, 86 A.L.R.2d 1365 (1961), it was held that the Attorney General could maintain a suit to enforce a charitable trust, although the settlor had reserved a visitorial power for himself. The court cited the text.

See Note, Duty of trustees of charitable trust to furnish information and

Intervening parties and parties aggrieved. Where a proceeding involving a charitable trust is properly brought by the Attorney General or by the trustees or by persons having a special interest, a third person may seek to intervene in the proceeding. It is within the discretion of the court whether to permit such intervention.[52] A further question may arise whether the intervening party can appeal from a decision of the court as a party aggrieved. The question most frequently arises where the third person is a charitable organization asking the court to award the property to it under the doctrine of cy pres. We shall consider this matter hereafter.[53]

§392. Nature of Remedies

The remedies for the enforcement of charitable trusts or for the redress of breaches of trust are equitable rather than legal.[1]

---

records to attorney general relating to trust administration, 86 A.L.R.2d 1375 (1962).

[52]Gibault Home for Boys v. Terre Haute First Natl. Bank, 227 Ind. 410, 85 N.E.2d 824 (1949); Stackpole v. Brewster Free Academy, 355 Mass. 774, 247 N.E.2d 599 (1969).

[53]See §399.

In In re Trust in Estate of Everett, 263 Minn. 398, 116 N.W.2d 601 (1962), where land was devised to a university for the use of its Forestry Department with a provision that if the university should not accept within six months, the land was to be conveyed to the Boy Scouts of America, the university brought an action to determine whether it would be bound to use the land for such purpose. Before a decision was rendered, the university accepted the gift without qualification. Thereafter the court held that the university was not bound to use it for its Forestry Department. From this judgment the Boy Scouts of America appealed. It was held that it was not a party aggrieved, because its interest was extinguished by the acceptance by the university. The court cited the Restatement of Trusts §391.

In Levings v. Danforth, 512 S.W.2d 207 (Mo. App. 1974) (citing the text and Restatement of Trusts §399), it was held that in a suit for the application cy pres of trust funds, the court should not allow legal fees to intervening parties.

See Nevil Estate, 414 Pa. 122, 199 A.2d 419 (1964), holding that in a cy pres proceeding, notice to a charitable institution having similar purposes was not required.

§392. [1]First Congregational Socy. in Raynham v. Trustees, 23 Pick. 148 (Mass. 1839); Fairbanks v. City of Appleton, 249 Wis. 476, 24 N.W.2d 893

The rule is the same as in the case of private trusts, except that in certain cases the beneficiaries of a private trust can maintain an action at law against the trustees where the trustees are under a duty to make an immediate payment of money or an immediate conveyance of a chattel to the beneficiaries.[2] In the case of charitable trusts there is no such exception because there are no beneficiaries who are entitled to demand an immediate payment or conveyance. The remedies in the case of a charitable trust are exclusively equitable, whether the suit is brought, as is usually the case, by the Attorney General, or by a third person who has a special interest in the performance of the trust, or by the settlor or his heirs or personal representatives where they are entitled to bring suit for the enforcement of the trust.[3]

The mere fact that the trustees of a charitable trust have for a long time applied the trust property to purposes other than those designated by the settlor does not preclude the court from directing that the trust should be administered according to its terms.[4]

The failure on the part of the Attorney General or of an interested party to enforce the trust does not bar its enforcement on the ground of laches or the statute of limitations.[5] But where the intention of the settlor is not clearly manifested, length of time and acquiescence in a particular mode of adminis-

---

(1946) (citing Restatement of Trusts §392), noted in 1947 Wis. L. Rev. 467.

[2]See §§197-198.3.

[3]See §391.

[4]*England:* In re Ingleton Charity, [1956] Ch. 585; Attorney-General v. Ross, [1986] 1 W.L.R. 252 (Ch.D.).

Massachusetts: Trustees of Andover Theological Seminary v. Visitors, 253 Mass. 256, 298, 148 N.E. 900 (1925); Davenport v. Attorney Gen., 361 Mass. 372, 280 N.E.2d 193 (1972) (citing the text).

See Franklin Found. v. City of Boston, 336 Mass. 39, 142 N.E.2d 367 (1957) (citing the text), noted in 37 B.U.L. Rev. 504.

Wisconsin: Estate of Mead, 227 Wis. 311, 277 N.W. 694, 279 N.W. 18 (1838).

[5]Brown v. Memorial Natl. Home Found., 162 Cal. App. 2d 513, 329 P.2d 118, 75 A.L.R.2d 427 (1955), *cert. denied,* 358 U.S. 943 (1959); Mosk v. Summerland Spiritualist Assn., 225 Cal. App. 2d 376, 37 Cal. Rptr. 366 (1964); Mount Vernon Mortgage Corp. v. United States, 98 App. D.C. 429, 236 F.2d 724 (1956), *aff'g* United States v. Mount Vernon Mortgage Corp., 128 F. Supp. 629 (D.D.C. 1954), *cert. denied,* 352 U.S. 988 (1957).

tration may be taken as good evidence of the settlor's purpose and of the manner in which the trust ought to be administered.[6]

§393. Actions Against Third Persons

In the case of charitable trusts, as in the case of private trusts,[1] the trustees can maintain such actions at law or suits in equity against a third person acting adversely to the trust as they could maintain if they held the property free of trust. Thus the trustees can maintain an action at law against a third person who commits a tort with reference to the trust property, either to recover the property or to recover damages for the tort. Similarly, they can maintain actions at law for breach of contract or suits in equity for the specific performance of contracts, as, for example, where they have made a proper contract for the sale of property of the trust and the purchaser refuses to perform the contract. So also where a testator makes a bequest upon a charitable trust, the trustees can maintain a suit against his personal representatives to recover the property bequeathed to them.

Where an action at law or suit in equity is brought by the trustees of a charitable trust against a third person acting adversely to the trust, the Attorney General is not a necessary party, because the question of the application of the property to the charitable purposes is not involved.[2] The situation is different from that which arises where a suit is brought for the en-

---

[6]*Federal:* Church of Christ v. Reorganized Church, 71 F. 250 (8th Cir. 1895).

Massachusetts: Attorney Gen. v. Proprietors of the Meeting House in Federal St., 3 Gray 1 (Mass. 1854); Trustees of Andover Theological Seminary v. Visitors, 253 Mass. 256, 298, 148 N.E. 900 (1925), *semble.*

South Carolina: Presbyterian Church of James Island v. Pendarvis, 227 S.C. 50, 86 S.E.2d 740 (1955) (citing Restatement of Trusts §219).

§393. [1]See §280.

[2]Halladay v. Verschoor, 381 F.2d 100 (8th Cir. 1967) (Minnesota law; quoting the text and Restatement of Trusts §393); Black United Fund of N.J. v. Kean, 593 F. Supp. 1567 (D.N.J. 1984); Pease v. Parsons, 259 Mass. 86, 156 N.E. 4 (1927) (charitable corporation allowed to maintain suit against governor of state for injunction against his barring all charities except the United Way from soliciting in state offices), *rev'd on other grounds,* 763 F.2d 156 (3d Cir. 1985).

forcement of a charitable trust. In the latter case the Attorney General is ordinarily a necessary party, because it is his duty to see that the charitable trust is properly administered. But where the trustees are seeking merely to protect the trust property from outsiders, they sufficiently represent the public interest in the trust.[3]

§394. Application to Court for Instructions

The trustees of a charitable trust, like the trustees of a private trust,[1] can maintain a suit for instructions. The trustees are entitled to instructions as to the proper construction of the trust instrument, as to the validity of the trust, and as to the extent of their powers and duties.[2] The purpose of the giving of

---

[3]In Matter of Gebbie's Will, 33 A.D.2d 1093, 307 N.Y.S.2d 1002 (1970), *leave to appeal denied*, 27 N.Y.2d 482, 261 N.E.2d 270, 313 N.Y.S.2d 1025 (1970), it was held that a claim of a charitable corporation was enforceable by it, and not by the Attorney General, unless the trustees of the corporation improperly failed to act. The court cited the text.

In Matter of Notkin, 45 A.D.2d 849, 358 N.Y.S.2d 491 (1974), where a bequest was made to a charitable institution and it agreed to pay part of the legacy to another legatee, it was held that the objection of the Attorney General to the payment should be sustained. The court said that to the extent that Matter of Gebbie expresses a different view, the court disagreed.

In Lefkowitz v. Lebensfeld, 51 N.Y.2d 442, 415 N.E.2d 919, 434 N.Y.S.2d 929 (1980), it was held that the Attorney General was not empowered to enforce a liability of a third person to a charitable corporation.

In Carswell v. Creswell, 217 N.C. 40, 7 S.E.2d 58 (1940), where trustees of land held for a charitable purpose sold the property, it was held that the purchasers acquired a good title by adverse possession.

§394.　[1]See §259.

[2]*England:* In re Lucas, [1922] 2 Ch. 52.

Delaware: Delaware Trust Co. v. Graham, 30 Del. Ch. 330, 61 A.2d 110 (1948) (citing the text), noted in 9 Md. L. Rev. 359.

Hawaii: Takabuki v. Ching, 695 P.2d 319 (Haw. 1985), citing text (but one of five trustees may not sue a second for instructions without joining the others).

Massachusetts: Jackson v. Phillips, 14 Allen 539 (Mass. 1867); Minot v. Baker, 147 Mass. 348, 17 N.E. 839, 9 Am. St. Rep. 713 (1888); City of Quincy v. Attorney Gen., 160 Mass. 431, 35 N.E. 1066 (1894); St. Paul's Church v. Attorney Gen., 164 Mass. 188, 41 N.E. 231 (1895); Bowden v. Brown, 200 Mass. 269, 86 N.E. 351, 128 Am. St. Rep. 419 (1908); Bowditch v. Attorney

instructions by the court is to enable the trustees to properly discharge their duties under the trust and to protect them in the discharge of these duties. As was said in a Massachusetts case:

> Unless a petitioner for instructions has real and serious doubts as to his duty, and the advice of the court is required for his protection and the discharge of his trust, the court is without jurisdiction to entertain such a petition. The right to instructions does not extend to the determination of questions which do not require any action by the trustee, or which should properly be submitted to some other tribunal, or where events which must control the rights of the parties and the duties of the trustee have not transpired.[3]

Accordingly, the court will not give instructions where there is no room for reasonable doubt as to the duties and powers of the trustees, and will not give instructions as to questions that may never arise or that will arise only at some time in the future.[4] So also the court will not give instructions on a question relating to the past administration of the trust.[5] Where the trustees have discretion, the court will not instruct them as to the manner in which they should exercise their discretion.[6]

Where a bill is filed by the trustees of a charitable trust for instructions as to the validity of the trust or as to the scope of

---

Gen., 241 Mass. 168, 134 N.E. 796, 28 A.L.R. 713 (1922); Kirwin v. Attorney Gen., 275 Mass. 34, 175 N.E. 164 (1931), noted in 19 Geo. L.J. 507 (1931).

New Jersey: Trustees of Princeton Univ. v. Wilson, 78 N.J. Eq. 1, 78 A. 393 (1910).

New York: Butterworth v. Keeler, 219 N.Y. 446, 114 N.E. 803 (1916).

Rhode Island: Selleck v. Thompson, 28 R.I. 350, 67 A. 425 (1907); Rhode Island Hosp. Trust Co. v. Rhode Island Homeopathic Hosp., 87 A. 177 (R.I. 1913).

[3]Hill v. Moors, 224 Mass. 163, 165, 112 N.E. 641 (1916).

[4]Bullard v. Chandler, 149 Mass. 532, 21 N.E. 951, 5 L.R.A. 104 (1889); Bullard v. Attorney Gen., 153 Mass. 249, 26 N.E. 691 (1891); Oldfield v. Attorney Gen., 219 Mass. 378, 106 N.E. 1015 (1914).

[5]Sohier v. Burr, 127 Mass. 221 (1879); Hill v. Moors, 224 Mass. 163, 112 N.E. 641 (1916).

[6]*Hawaii:* Takabuki v. Ching, 695 P.2d 319 (Haw. 1985), citing text.

Massachusetts: Sohier v. Burr, 127 Mass. 221 (1879).

New York: Matter of Jacobs, 127 Misc. 2d 1020, 487 N.Y.S.2d 992 (Sur. 1985), §194, n. 15, *supra.*

their duties or powers, the Attorney General is a proper party and ordinarily a necessary party.[7]

TOPIC 5. FAILURE OF CHARITABLE TRUSTS — THE DOCTRINE OF CY PRES

§395. *Where Settlor Fails to State Charitable Purposes*

Where a testator leaves property in trust for charitable purposes, the trust does not fail merely because the testator does not state any particular charitable purpose to which the property is to be applied. Thus where he leaves property in trust for such charitable purposes as the trustee may select, the trust does not fail if the trustee is able and willing to make the selection;[1] and even if the trustee is unable or unwilling to make the selection, the trust does not fail unless the testator manifested an intention that the selection by the particular trustee should be an essential part of his scheme.[2]

The situation is different, however, where the testator manifested an intention that the property should be applied only to a particular charitable purpose but he does not properly manifest his intention as to what the particular purpose is. In such a case the testator has not manifested a general intention to devote the property to charitable purposes, but only an intention to devote it to some particular charitable purpose. If it cannot be ascertained what that purpose is, the intended charitable trust fails.

In England, however, it has been held in a number of cases that the trust does not fail but the property will be applied to

---

[7]*Delaware:* Delaware Trust Co. v. Graham, 30 Del. Ch. 330, 61 A.2d 110 (1948) (*semble;* citing the text), noted in 9 Md. L. Rev. 359.

Hawaii: Takabuki v. Ching, 695 P.2d 319 (Haw. 1985), citing text (one of five trustees may not sue a second for instructions without joining the other trustees as well as the Attorney General).

New Jersey: Trustees of Princeton Univ. v. Wilson, 78 N.J. Eq. 1, 78 A. 393 (1910).

Texas: Rev. Civ. Stat., art. 4412a, as amended by Laws 1981, c. 501, §1.

§395. [1]See §396.

[2]See §397.

charitable purposes under a scheme approved by the court.[3] Thus in 1702 it was held that where a testator bequeathed money to such charitable uses as he should direct by a codicil to be annexed to his will or by a note in writing, and he died without having executed such codicil or note, the Court of Chancery had power to dispose of the property to such charitable uses as it should think fit.[4] In another case it was held that where a will provided that a sum of money was to be applied to such charitable uses as the testator had directed, and no such direction could be found, the trust did not fail.[5] In another case it was held that where a bequest was made "to the following religious societies, viz.," and the names of the societies were not inserted in the will, which left a blank space where they were to have been inserted, the intended charitable trust did not fail.[6] Similarly, it was held that where property was bequeathed for charitable purposes to be set forth in a codicil and no codicil was executed the trust did not fail.[7] It is difficult to justify the results reached in these cases. It would seem that the testator intended to devote his property to a particular charitable purpose and had no intention to devote it to other charitable purposes; and because the particular purpose cannot be ascertained, it would seem that the trust should fail. The Judicial Committee of the Privy Council, indeed, has indicated its view that the decision in some of these cases cannot be justified.[8] Moreover, the English courts have not upheld such trusts where it did not appear in the will that the property was to be devoted exclusively to charitable purposes. Thus in one case it was held that where a testator in a codicil to his will made a bequest for the same purpose as he had named in a previous codicil, and no such codicil was found, the bequest failed for uncertainty because it was not limited to

[3]Attorney-General v. Syderfen, 1 Vern. 224, 7 Ves. 43n (1683); Anonymous, Freem. C.C. 261 (1702); Mills v. Farmer, 1 Mer. 55, 19 Ves. 482 (1815); In re White, [1893] 2 Ch. 41; In re Pyne, [1903] 1 Ch. 83.

See Gillan v. Gillan, 1 L.R. Ir. 114 (1878); In re Gott, [1944] Ch. 193 (referring to Restatement of Trusts §395), noted in 8 Convey. (N.S.) 228, 60 Law Q. Rev. 221, 11 Sol. 100.

[4]Anonymous, Freem. C.C. 261 (1702).

[5]Attorney-General v. Syderfen, 1 Vern. 224, 7 Ves. 43n (1683).

[6]In re White, [1893] 2 Ch. 41.

[7]In re Pyne, [1903] 1 Ch. 83.

[8]Dunne v. Byrne, [1912] A.C. 407, 411.

charity.[9] In another case where a testator made a bequest of a sum of money to his trustees, the money to be appropriated according to a statement appended, and after his death a statement was found appropriating the money to certain charitable purposes, it was held that the trust failed because the will did not show that it was to be used solely for charitable purposes and the statement could not be admitted to probate because it was not properly attested.[10] In another case it was held that where a testator made a bequest "for some one or more purposes charitable, philosophic or _____," the bequest failed because it did not appear that the purposes were limited to charitable purposes.[11]

In the United States it seems clear that the intended charitable trust fails if it appears that the testator intended that the property should be devoted to a particular charitable purpose and it cannot be ascertained what that purpose was. Thus it has been held that where a testator made a bequest for such charitable purposes as he might designate in a letter to be found with his will, the intended trust failed even though the letter was found, because it was not admissible to probate.[12] In another case it was held that where a testator provided for the establishment of a school on plans to be thereafter described by him, or in case of his death before perfecting such plans then on plans that he had from time to time described to most of the trustees, and he never formulated such plans, the intended trust failed.[13]

[9]Mayor of Gloucester v. Osborn, 1 H.L.C. 272 (1846).

[10]Aston v. Wood, L.R. 6 Eq. 419 (1868).

[11]In re Macduff, [1896] 2 Ch. 451; In re Gott, [1944] Ch. 193, noted in 8 Convey. (N.S.) 228, 60 Law Q. Rev. 221, 11 Sol. 100.

[12]*Illinois:* Phelps v. La Moille, Ill., Lodge No. 270, 52 Ill. App. 2d 159, 201 N.E.2d 634 (1964).

Massachusetts: Thayer v. Wellington, 9 Allen 283, 85 Am. Dec. 753 (Mass. 1864).

See §358.

See In re Jones, [1942] Ch. 328, noted in 7 Convey. (N.S.) 45, 59 Law Q. Rev. 23, cited in §54.3, n. 19; Delaware Trust Co. v. Young, 33 Del. Ch. 357, 93 A.2d 496 (1952) (citing Restatement of Trusts, §395, Comment *c*; §413, Comment *e*).

See Note, Charitable gifts; definiteness, 163 A.L.R. 784, 804 (1946).

[13]Smith v. Smith, 54 N.J. Eq. 1, 32 A. 1069 (1895), *aff'd mem.*, 55 N.J. Eq. 821, 41 A. 1116 (1896).

On the other hand, where it appears that the particular purposes were not an essential part of the testator's scheme, the charitable trust does not fail even though the particular purposes cannot be ascertained. Thus where a testator left the residue of his estate in trust to develop the Palisades along the Hudson River and stated that he would formulate plans for the purpose, but he died without formulating any such plans, the court held that the trust did not fail because the testator's general charitable purpose sufficiently appeared in the will and the particular plans that he intended to formulate were not an essential part of his purpose.[14] The same result was reached in another case where a testator devised land as a home for working girls or as an old ladies' home, "the plan to be hereafter devised or left in care of said executor," and no such plan was formulated by the testator.[15] In *Ervin Estate*[16] a testatrix left her property to a charitable institution for crippled children that she would name in the will, but she failed to name any such institution. It was held that the trust did not fail and that the property should be given to an existing home for crippled children. In *Souhegan National Bank v. Kenison*[17] a testator left the residue of

[14]Noice v. Schnell, 101 N.J. Eq. 252, 137 A. 582, 52 A.L.R. 965 (1927), *cert. denied,* 276 U.S. 625 (1928), noted in 32 Law Notes 33.

See City of Englewood v. Allison Land Co., 25 N.J. Super. 466, 96 A.2d 702 (1953), involving the question whether the trustees could properly sell Palisades land to a development company. See also City of Englewood v. Allison Land Co., 45 N.J. Super. 538, 133 A.2d 680 (1957), *aff'g* 40 N.J. Super. 495, 123 A.2d 591 (1956).

[15]Sherman v. Congregational Home Missionary Socy., 176 Mass. 349, 57 N.E. 702 (1900).

[16]367 Pa. 58, 79 A.2d 264 (1951), noted in 23 Temp. L.Q. 159.

[17]92 N.H. 117, 26 A.2d 26 (1942).

See Taylor v. Republic Natl. Bank, 452 S.W.2d 560 (Tex. Civ. App. 1970), where a testator left his property for a hospital, described in an attached document. It was held that the document was not incorporated by reference but was not intended to have a legal effect, and that the trust was valid.

In Barnwell Estate, 52 D.&C.2d 698 (Pa. 1971), a testator created a trust to reward the practice of high principles of honor and moral courage by the students and graduates of a high school, and provided that, although he intended to make codicils to carry out the purpose, if he did not the trustees should use their own judgment. It was held the trust was valid.

In Application of Price (Matter of Carper), 67 A.D.2d 333, 415 N.Y.S.2d 550 (1979), *aff'd mem.,* 50 N.Y.2d 974, 409 N.E.2d 941, 431 N.Y.S.2d 468

his estate in trust for charitable purposes, "in accordance with a suggestive memorandum which I have prepared and hereby make a part of this will." No memorandum was prepared by him then or later. It was held that the trust was valid, because the word "suggestive" showed that the memorandum was not intended to be mandatory.

Where a testator devises or bequeaths property to a person in trust for such charitable purposes as he has communicated to the devisee or legatee, and the latter has agreed to hold the property for these purposes, there is, as has been stated, a difference of opinion on the question whether the devisee or legatee can be compelled to hold the property upon a constructive trust for such purposes, or whether there is a resulting trust to the estate of the testator.[18] In states in which a constructive trust will not be imposed, the intended charitable trust fails altogether, because although it appears in the will that a charitable trust is intended it also appears that the testator intended the property to be applied to particular charitable purposes and these purposes cannot be ascertained from the will. Thus in *Olliffe v. Wells*[19] a woman bequeathed the residue of her estate to a clergyman "to distribute the same in such manner as in his discretion shall appear best calculated to carry out wishes which I have expressed to him or may express to him." On a bill brought by the heirs and next of kin of the testatrix, it was held that the intended trust failed. Although the legatee alleged that the testatrix had communicated to him the charitable purposes to which she desired the property to be applied, the court held that because these purposes were not declared in the will and because the trust declared in the will was too indefinite to be

---

(1980), a testatrix left the residue to her sister and the sister's husband "to be used by them in their sole discretion for the purpose of establishing in a charitable institution or institutions" memorials of her parents and husband "in such manner and to such extent as I shall make known to them." The testatrix did not make known to them any purpose except for a gift of $26,000 to one institution. It was held that she had a general charitable intent and that the trust did not fail.

[18]See §359.

[19]130 Mass. 221 (1881).

See also Wilcox v. Attorney Gen., 207 Mass. 198, 93 N.E. 599, Ann. Cas. 1912A 833 (1911).

carried out, a resulting trust arose in favor of the heirs and next of kin.

§396. Where the Selection of Charitable Objects Is Left to the Trustee and He Makes the Selection

A testator may devise or bequeath property in trust for charitable purposes without designating the particular purposes to which he wishes the property to be applied. He may leave the property to trustees for such charitable purposes as they may select. Such a disposition is valid according to the great weight of authority. If the trustee is ready and willing to make the selection, there is no reason why he should not be permitted to do so.[1] This is true where the testator designates the general

§396. [1]*Federal:* District of Columbia v. Castiello, 97 App. D.C. 289, 230 F.2d 839 (1956) (to trustees to distribute to such worthy charity or charities in the District of Columbia as they might select in their discretion).

Massachusetts: Gill v. Attorney Gen., 197 Mass. 232, 83 N.E. 676 (1908) (to executors to distribute among such charitable institutions, persons, or objects as they decide to be most worthy); Sullivan v. Roman Catholic Archbishop of Boston, 368 Mass. 253, 331 N.E.2d 57 (1975) (to the Archbishop of Boston to be devoted to such charitable uses as he may select).

New Jersey: Mills v. Montclair Trust Co., 139 N.J. Eq. 56, 49 A.2d 889 (1946) (for such charitable purposes as a charitable foundation should determine).

New York: Matter of Estate of Bush, 124 Misc. 2d 40, 475 N.Y.S.2d 311 (Sur. Ct. 1984).

Pennsylvania: Trexler Estate, 39 D.&C.2d 101 (Pa. 1965) (charitable organizations and objects as in discretion of the trustees, but limited to a particular county and to certain types of institutions).

Virginia: McClure v. Carter, 202 Va. 191, 116 S.E.2d 260 (1960) (gift over on failure of charitable trust to a charitable organization to be selected by the trustee).

Canada: Canada Permanent Trust Co. v. MacFarlane, 27 D.L.R.3d 480 (B.C. 1972) (such Protestant homes for the care and welfare of children as the trustee in its uncontrolled discretion shall elect). Re McIntosh; McIntosh v. McIntosh, [1982] 40 N.B.R.2d 101, 105 A.P.R. 101 (N.B.Q.B.) (trust to educate named relatives; surplus "may be used . . . for other educational purposes, or the same may be paid over directly to a recognized university or universities," which created valid charitable trust despite uncertainty of objects).

Even though the trustee is unable or unwilling to make the selection, the trust will not fail unless the settlor intended that the selection should be made only by the original trustee. See §397.

nature of the charitable purposes to which he desires the property to be applied.[2] It is true also where the trustee is left free

---

See Fratcher, Powers of Appointment to Unspecified Charities, 32 Mo. L. Rev. 443 (1967).

[2]*England:* In re Eastes, [1948] Ch. 257 (to vicar and churchwardens of a church to be used for any purposes in connection with the church that they may select), noted in 11 Mod. L. Rev. 343, 93 Sol. J. 298.

Alabama: Tarver v. Weaver, 221 Ala. 663, 130 So. 209 (1930) (to relieve the poor and maintain beds in hospitals and for scholarships).

California: Estate of Moore, 190 Cal. App. 2d 833, 12 Cal. Rptr. 436 (1961) (to some creditable nonprofit science investigation society of sister's choice).

Connecticut: Cheshire Bank & Trust Co. v. Doolittle, 113 Conn. 231, 155 A. 82 (1931) (to be used by T for either home or foreign missions).

Iowa: Gray v. Watters, 243 Iowa 430, 51 N.W.2d 885 (1952) (for religious organization); In re Estate of Small, 244 Iowa 1209, 58 N.W.2d 477 (1953) (to distribute income to such persons and for such purposes as trustees or their successors may feel is directed by God the Father, Jesus Christ the Son, and Holy Spirit, and as they believe would be acceptable to me).

Kentucky: Kentucky Christian Missionary Socy. v. Moren, 267 Ky. 358, 102 S.W.2d 335 (1937) (to a religious society to use income for benefit of Christian churches of certain counties in such ways as might seem wisest).

Louisiana: Succession of Baker, 432 So. 2d 817 (La. 1983).

Maryland: Rabinowitz v. Wollman, 174 Md. 6, 197 A. 566 (1938) (such religious, charitable, scientific, literary, or educational Hebrew corporations or associations as might be selected by executors; citing Restatement of Trusts §396).

Massachusetts: Rotch v. Emerson, 105 Mass. 431 (1870) (for promotion of agricultural or horticultural improvements, or other philosophical or philanthropic purposes at T's discretion); Peirce v. Attorney Gen., 234 Mass. 389, 125 N.E. 609 (1920) (for benefit of town as T may determine).

Missouri: Altman v. McCutchen, 210 S.W.2d 63 (Mo. 1948) (to charitable institutions devoted to alleviation of human suffering and want; citing Restatement of Trusts §396); Epperly v. Mercantile Trust & Sav. Bank, 415 S.W.2d 819 (Mo. 1967), *mod.,* 457 S.W.2d 1 (Mo. 1970) (to distribute at discretion of trustee to Protestant churches and religious organizations to be used to save souls and not for buildings; quoting Restatement of Trusts §396). McMenomy v. Williford, 526 S.W.2d 880 (Mo. App. 1975) (to a named trustee to be used at his discretion for evangelistic and mission purposes; citing the text and Restatement of Trusts §§395 to 397).

New York: Matter of Robinson, 203 N.Y. 380, 96 N.E. 925, 37 L.R.A. (N.S.) 1023 (1911) (to provide necessaries, education, and such other financial aid as may seem to T proper, to such persons as T shall select as being in need of the same), noted in 12 Colum. L. Rev. 356; Matter of Kaufman, 30 Misc. 2d 860, 219 N.Y.S.2d 627 (1961) (to a home for the aged in Israel within the discretion of the trustees).

to devote the property to any charitable purpose he may select.[3]

Ohio: Miller v. Teachout, 24 Ohio St. 525 (1874) (to Christian religion in T's judgment).

Pennsylvania: Barnwell Estate, 52 D.&C.2d 698 (Pa. 1971) (to reward the practice of high principles of honor and moral courage by the students and graduates of a high school of which the testator was a graduate).

Texas: Zweig v. Zweig, 275 S.W.2d 201 (Tex. Civ. App. 1955) (trustees to select deserving Jewish charities); Rice v. Morris, 541 S.W.2d 627 (Tex. Civ. App. 1976), *appeal for writ dismissed* (churches and hospitals in Texas; citing Restatement of Trusts §364).

Virginia: Roller v. Shaver, 178 Va. 467, 17 S.E.2d 419 (1941) (to be given by executor to trustees of some Methodist institution or institutions for the poor or what in his judgment is worthy of the same); Allaun v. First & Merchants Natl. Bank, 190 Va. 104, 56 S.E.2d 83 (1949) (to the white poor of county).

Canada: Cox v. Hogan, 35 Brit. Col. R. 286 (1925) (for some good public purpose such as a hospital, woman's home, or park); In re Fallis Estate, [1948] 1 D.L.R. 27 (Sask.) (for relief of suffering and distress as committee might direct).

Ireland: In re Salter, [1911] 1 I.R. 289 (to such other charitable or religious purposes for benefit of members of Church of Ireland within county of C).

Scotland: Wordie's Trustees v. Wordie, [1915] Sess. Cas. 310 (Scot.) (charitable institutions for benefit of women and children); Denny's Trustee v. Dumbarton Magistrates, [1945] Sess. Cas. 147 (Scot.) (to promote moral, intellectual, physical or social improvement, bodily health and recreation of inhabitants of a certain town in such manner as certain officials should determine).

[3] *England:* In re Best, [1904] 2 Ch. 354 (such charitable and benevolent institutions as T shall determine); In re Pardoe, [1906] 2 Ch. 184 (to such public charities and institutions or for such charitable purposes as T shall consider fitting); In re Garrard, [1907] 1 Ch. 382 (to vicar and churchwardens for the time being of K, to be applied by them in such manner as they shall in their sole discretion think fit); In re Flinn, [1948] Ch. 241 (to a Roman Catholic archbishop for the time being, to be used for such purposes as he should think fit), noted in 11 Mod. L. Rev. 343; In re Beesty's Will Trusts, [1966] Ch. 223 ("to my brother and sister for their lives and at their deaths to go to charities which they may have selected during their lives;" held, the survivor may select the charities).

But see In re Warre's Will Trusts, [1953] 2 All E.R. 99.

Federal: Chicago Bank of Commerce v. McPherson, 2 F. Supp. 110 (W.D. Mich. 1931), *aff'd,* 62 F.2d 393 (6th Cir. 1932), *cert. denied,* 289 U.S. 736 (1933) (such charitable, benevolent, educational, and public welfare uses as T might select); Michigan Trust Co. v. United States, 21 F. Supp. 482 (W.D. Mich. 1937) (such corporate charity or corporate benevolence or public purpose as testator's widow may by will appoint); Beggs v. United States, 27 F. Supp. 599 (Ct. Cl. 1939) (to such charities and worthy objects as executor and testator's

There are indeed a few cases in which it was held that the

sister should determine); Commissioner v. Upjohn's Estate, 124 F.2d 73 (6th Cir. 1941) (such civic, charitable, educational, or religious purposes and for such purposes of general and public welfare as T may select).

Alabama: Biles v. Martin, 288 Ala. 231, 259 So. 2d 258 (1972) (to such charitable organizations as the executors might select; citing the text).

Arkansas: Curry v. Guaranty Loan & Trust Co., 212 Ark. 988, 208 S.W.2d 465 (1948) (to some organization selected by trustees to discover a cure for rheumatism and, if the trustees cannot agree, to any charitable institution on which they may agree).

California: Estate of Bunn, 33 Cal. 2d 897, 206 P.2d 635 (1949), *rev'g* 200 P.2d 810 (Cal. App. 1948) (to worthy charity selected by executors), noted in 23 So. Cal. L. Rev. 632; Estate of Hurwitz, 109 Cal. App. 2d 302, 240 P.2d 990 (1952) (to such charity as T might designate).

Connecticut: Mitchell v. Reeves, 123 Conn. 549, 196 A. 785, 115 A.L.R. 1114 (1938) (to corporations, institutions, and trusts devoted exclusively to religious, charitable, scientific, literary, historical, or educational purposes); Westport Bank & Trust Co. v. Fable, 126 Conn. 665, 13 A.2d 862 (1940) (to such charitable and educational purposes as corporate trustee might deem wise and prudent); Nash v. Danbury Natl. Bank, 138 Conn. 676, 88 A.2d 397 (1952) (to charitable organizations and agencies to be selected by an "allocator").

Florida: In re Estate of Stewart, 242 So. 2d 781 (Fla. App. 1971) (to such of my relatives and among such charitable corporations as A may designate; quoting the text), *rev'd on other grounds,* 271 So. 2d 754 (Fla. 1973).

Georgia: Pace v. Dukes, 205 Ga. 835, 55 S.E.2d 367 (1949) (to be devoted to religious, charitable, educational, and humanitarian purposes); Marshall v. Trust Co. of Ga., 231 Ga. 415, 202 S.E.2d 94 (1973) (to pay the income to charitable, educational, or religious institutions to be selected by the trustee).

Illinois: Welch v. Caldwell, 266 Ill. 488, 80 N.E. 1014 (1907) (charitable and religious purposes in the discretion of T); Northern Ill. Medical Center v. Home State Bank of Crystal Lake, 136 Ill. App. 3d 129, 90 Ill. Dec. 802, 482 N.E.2d 1085 (1985).

Indiana: Hulet v. Crawfordville Trust Co., 117 Ind. App. 125, 69 N.E.2d 823 (1946) (charitable and benevolent purposes as corporate trustee should determine; citing Restatement of Trusts §396).

Iowa: In re Estate of Ditz, 254 Iowa 444, 117 N.W.2d 825 (1962) (organizations operated exclusively for religious, charitable, and educational purposes; citing the text and Restatement of Trusts §396).

Louisiana: Pires v. Youree, 170 La. 986, 129 So. 552 (1930) (to use income in charitable work as T may deem wise).

Maine: Fox v. Gibbs, 86 Me. 87, 29 A. 940 (1893) (benevolent and charitable purposes at T's discretion).

Massachusetts: Wells v. Doane, 3 Gray 201 (Mass. 1855) (to such charities as shall be deemed by T most useful); Saltonstall v. Sanders, 11 Allen 446 (Mass. 1865) (purposes of benevolence or charity at T's discretion); Suter v.

trust failed for uncertainty even though the trustee was given

Hilliard, 132 Mass. 412, 42 Am. Rep. 444 (1882) (to assist poor persons and to assist or cooperate with such charitable, benevolent, religious, literary, and scientific associations as T shall think most deserving); Weber v. Bryant, 161 Mass. 400, 37 N.E. 203 (1894) (such objects of benevolence and charity, public or private, including educational or charitable institutions and the relief of individual need as T deems worthy).

Missouri: Standley v. Allen, 349 Mo. 1115, 163 S.W.2d 1012 (1942) (to some worthy charitable organization to be selected by trustee; quoting Restatement of Trusts §396); Yeager v. Johns, 484 S.W.2d 211 (Mo. 1972) (to a minister "to be used by him at his discretion for religious and educational purposes").

Nebraska: St. James Orphan Asylum v. Shelby, 60 Neb. 796, 84 N.W. 273, 83 Am. St. Rep. 553 (1900) (to some charity according to T's judgment).

New Hampshire: Souhegan Natl. Bank v. Kenison, 92 N.H. 117, 26 A.2d 26 (1942) ("for religious, charitable and relief purposes in any part of the world"; citing the text).

New Jersey: De Camp v. Dobbins, 29 N.J. Eq. 36 (1878), *aff'd,* 31 N.J. Eq. 671 (1879) (to religious society for missionary, educational, and benevolent purposes).

New York: Matter of Cunningham, 206 N.Y. 601, 100 N.E. 437 (1912) (to such charitable and benevolent associations and institutions of learning as T may select); Matter of Olmstead, 131 Misc. 238, 226 N.Y.S. 637 (1928) (for such worthy, charitable and benevolent works as T may select); Matter of Macaulay, 173 Misc. 887, 19 N.Y.S.2d 418 (1940) (for charitable or religious uses as trustee might select); Matter of Manville, 57 N.Y.S.2d 439 (1945) (to such political subdivision of New York for public purposes, or for the use of such corporations organized and operated exclusively for religious, charitable, scientific, literary, or educational purposes, or for such fraternal societies, as trustees should select); Matter of Manville, 117 N.Y.S.2d 220 (1952) (such charitable purposes or corporations as the trustees, in their absolute and uncontrolled discretion, might select); Matter of Schiff, 203 Misc. 805, 118 N.Y.S.2d 828 (1952); National City Bank of N.Y. v. Beebe, 155 N.Y.S.2d 347 (1956) (to distribute income and principal among charitable corporations; Rhode Island law); Matter of Michaels, 7 Misc. 2d 439, 165 N.Y.S.2d 234 (1957) (to distribute among educational institutions and charities as the trustee in his uncontrolled discretion shall deem to be in conformity with testator's ideals and principles; citing the text and Restatement of Trusts §396); Matter of Manville, 8 Misc. 2d 201, 163 N.Y.S.2d 695 (1957) (such charitable purposes or corporations as the trustees, in their absolute and uncontrolled discretion, might select; held selection may be made during the lifetime of life beneficiaries); Matter of Sullivan, 38 Misc. 2d 971, 235 N.Y.S.2d 278 (1962) (to sister and on her death to any charitable institution selected by her; court held that she may by deed direct that the money be divided between two named charitable institutions); Matter of Linson, 38 Misc. 2d 971, 239 N.Y.S.2d 459 (1963) (to be distributed by executor bank in its sole discretion

authority to select the charitable purposes to which it should be

for such purposes and to such institutions as it deems best); Matter of Clark, 54 Misc. 2d 1015, 284 N.Y.S.2d 244 (1967) (to such religious and charitable corporations as the corporate trustee may select); Application of Price (Matter of Carper), 67 A.D.2d 333, 415 N.Y.S.2d 550 (1979) aff'd mem., 50 N.Y.2d 974, 409 N.E.2d 941, 431 N.Y.S.2d 648 (1980) (to establish a memorial for the parents or husband of the testatrix).

Ohio: Moskowitz v. Federman, 72 Ohio App. 149, 51 N.E.2d 48 (1943) (power to distribute among charitable organizations and testator's next of kin at T's uncontrolled discretion), noted in 7 U. Det. L.J. 50; In re Estate of Luce, 116 Ohio App. 420, 185 N.E.2d 559 (1962) (to be expended by trustee for any charities that she may select as a memorial to the testator).

Pennsylvania: Murphy's Estate, 184 Pa. 310, 39 A. 70, 63 Am. St. Rep. 802 (1898) (to be divided among such benevolent, charitable, and religious institutions and associations as shall be selected by T); Dulles's Estate, 218 Pa. 162, 67 A. 49, 12 L.R.A. (N.S.) 1177 (1907) (among such religious, charitable, and benevolent purposes and objects or institutions as at T's discretion shall be best and proper); Kimberly's Estate (No. 1), 249 Pa. 469, 95 A. 82 (1915) (such charitable uses, objects and purposes as T may select); Little Estate, 403 Pa. 247, 168 A.2d 738 (1961) (to be used as a suitable memorial for the testator's brother and parents, seeking advice from a friend of the testator as to the nature of the memorial).

Rhode Island: Pell v. Mercer, 14 R.I. 412 (1884) (such works of religion and benevolence as T shall select); Selleck v. Thompson, 28 R.I. 350, 67 A. 425 (1907) (such charitable purposes as T shall judge will do the most real good).

Tennessee: Eledge v. Dixon, 193 Tenn. 654, 249 S.W.2d 886 (1952) (for needy children in vicinity of town).

Texas: Powers v. First Natl. Bank, 138 Tex. 604, 161 S.W.2d 273 (1942), aff'g 137 S.W.2d 839 (Tex. Civ. App. 1940) (for worthy objects of charity, including support of Christian religion), noted in 19 Tex. L. Rev. 102; Boyd v. Frost Natl. Bank, 145 Tex. 206, 196 S.W.2d 497, 168 A.L.R. 1326 (1946), aff'g Frost Natl. Bank v. Boyd, 188 S.W.2d 199 (Tex. Civ. App. 1945) (to pay income in perpetuity to such charitable association as trustee should in its absolute discretion select; quoting the text and Restatement of Trusts §396), noted in 25 Tex. L. Rev. 434.

Washington: In re Stewart's Estate, 26 Wash. 32, 66 P. 148, 67 P. 723 (1901) (such charitable purposes and uses as T may deem fit); In re Planck's Estate, 150 Wash. 301, 272 P. 972 (1928) (executrix authorized to dispose to worthy charities).

Wisconsin: Kronshage v. Varrell, 120 Wis. 161, 97 N.W. 928 (1904) (to relieve distress from storms, floods, fires, and other accidental and natural causes); Will of Monaghan, 199 Wis. 273, 226 N.W. 306 (1929) (to trust company to distribute income in its discretion among charities in county and at end of a hundred years to divide principal among worthy charities in its discretion).

Australia: Smith v. West Australian Trustee Exr. & Agency Co., 81 C.L.R.

applied and was ready and willing to exercise this authority.[4] In

320 (Austl. 1950) (such charitable institutions, bodies, and organizations as the trustee might select).

Canada: Toronto Gen. Trusts Corp. v. Shaw, [1942] 1 D.L.R. 802 (Sask.) (such Protestant charitable institutions and agencies in Saskatchewan as T may select); In re Cohn, [1952] 3 D.L.R. 833 (N.S.) (for such charitable purposes as the executors should think proper).

In In re Finkle, 82 D.L.R.3d 445 (Man. 1977), a testator left the residue to his executors to be distributed among "such religious, educational and charitable institutions" as he might direct in writing, and on his failure to give directions to distribute as they in their sole discretion might deem fit. He gave no directions. It was held that they should distribute among such religious or educational or charitable institutions as they might select.

Ireland: Rickerby v. Nicholson, [1912] I.R. 343 (such religious or charitable purposes as T shall think fit).

New Zealand: Williams v. Attorney-General, [1946] N.Z.L.R. 118 (for such charitable and religious purposes as the trustees might think fit); Williams v. Commr. of Stamp Duties, [1948] N.Z.L.R. 662 (such charitable and religious purposes as my said trustees may in their absolute discretion think fit; tax case).

Scotland: Paterson's Trustees v. Paterson, [1909] Sess. Cas. 485 (Scot.) (such charities or benevolent or beneficent institutions as T shall think proper); M'Phee's Trustees v. M'Phee, [1912] Sess. Cas. 75 (Scot.) (such religious and charitable institutions in Glasgow as T may select); Cameron's Trustees v. Mackenzie, [1915] Sess. Cas. 313 (Scot.) (such charitable institutions, persons, or objects as T may think desirable); Bannerman's Trustees v. Bannerman, [1915] Sess. Cas. 398 (Scot.) (religious or charitable institutions conducted according to Protestant principles).

See the cases cited in §398.1, n. 21.

See Note, Charitable gifts; definiteness, 163 A.L.R. 784, 816, 824 (1946).

See Note, Validity of charitable gift or trust contemplating that property shall go to such charitable bodies or be devoted to such charitable purposes as trustee or other person may select, 168 A.L.R. 1350 (1947).

Where trustees are authorized to distribute the testator's estate among charitable institutions to be selected by them, it is to be inferred that they are to select only such charitable institutions as are exempt from taxes. Matter of Heit, 26 Misc. 2d 774, 206 N.Y.S.2d 59 (1960).

In In re Estate of Luce, 116 Ohio App. 420, 185 N.E.2d 559 (1962), where the trustee was authorized to expend for any charities that she might select, it was held that the disposition was subject to the state inheritance tax, because it might be expended in other states.

See §376, n. 12.

[4]*Alabama:* Woodroof v. Hundley, 147 Ala. 287, 39 So. 907 (1905) (to such objects of charity and benevolence as presbytery of certain church may indicate); Crim v. Williamson, 180 Ala. 179, 60 So. 293 (1912) (aiding worthy objects of charity at T's discretion).

these cases the clear intention of the testator is defeated, and no

---

But see Alabama Code 1975, §35-4-251.

Connecticut: Bristol v. Bristol, 53 Conn. 242, 5 A. 687 (1885) (to trustees for such charitable purposes as testator's widow might deem proper).

In Connecticut it was later provided by statute (Conn. Gen. Stat. 1958, §45-80, as amended by Laws 1980, c. 80-476, §224) that the particular charitable purpose need not be designated in the trust instrument, provided that the trustee or any other person is given the power to select the charitable purpose. See Nash v. Danbury Natl. Bank, 138 Conn. 676, 88 A.2d 397 (1952).

Idaho: Hedin v. Westdala Lutheran Church, 59 Idaho 241, 81 P.2d 741 (1938) (for such charitable or religious purposes as trustee may select); Yribar v. Fitzpatrick, 91 Idaho 105, 416 P.2d 164 (1966) (to some worthy charitable or public institution as executors and testator's attorney might select).

But see In re Eggan's Estate, 86 Idaho 328, 386 P.2d 563 (1963) (to a city to build or furnish a Youth Center building for the recreation of the youth of the area); Dolan v. Johnson, 95 Idaho 385, 509 P.2d 1306 (1973) (upholding a foundation for various charitable purposes as the managers may direct).

Kentucky: Spalding v. St. Joseph's Indus. School, 107 Ky. 382, 54 S.W. 200 (1899) (for charitable objects in diocese of Louisville according to T's discretion); Coleman v. O'Leary's Ex., 114 Ky. 388, 70 S.W. 1068 (1902) (to any charitable uses so as to do most good); Gooding v. Watson's Trustee, 235 Ky. 562, 31 S.W.2d 919 (1930) (to distribute to such charitable organization as T should deem proper); Stoeer v. Meyer, 285 Ky. 387, 147 S.W.2d 1041 (1941) (such charitable and educational institutions in town in Germany as might be designated by highest official of town); Hoenig v. Newmark, 306 S.W.2d 838 (Ky. 1957) (to such educational or charitable institutions or to such individual or individuals as the trustees should determine to be worthy); Bank of Maysville v. Calvert, 481 S.W.2d 24 (Ky. 1972) (to be divided among such charitable and religious organizations as the executor might deem deserving; citing but not following the text).

Louisiana: Succession of Burke, 51 La. Ann. 538, 25 So. 387 (1899) (to use for any charitable institution T may select); Succession of McCloskey, 52 La. Ann. 1122, 27 So. 705 (1900) (for such charitable uses and purposes in Ireland as T thinks proper); Succession of Villa, 132 La. 714, 61 So. 765 (1913) (to be used for any good work T may see fit to use it for).

Missouri: Wentura v. Kinnerk, 319 Mo. 1068, 5 S.W.2d 66 (1928) (such charitable uses as executor might determine).

Other Missouri cases are collected in Fratcher, Powers of Appointment to Unspecified Charities, 32 Mo. L. Rev. 443 (1967).

North Carolina: See Woodcock v. Wachovia Bank & Trust Co., 214 N.C. 224, 199 S.E. 20 (1938), criticized in 37 Mich. L. Rev. 1132, 6 U. Chi. L. Rev. 332.

But see *infra* n. 6.

Tennessee: Johnson v. Johnson, 92 Tenn. 559, 23 S.E. 114, 22 L.R.A. 179, 36 Am. St. Rep. 104 (1893) (for some charitable purpose, preferably something of an educational nature, although permissible to appropriate income as

good reason can be given for defeating it. As long as the purposes to which the property is to be applied are limited to charitable purposes, there is no reason why the trust should not be carried out in accordance with the intention of the testator.

So also a charitable trust will not fail where a third person is authorized to select the particular purposes to which the property shall be applied. Thus in *Reilly v. McGowan*[5] a testator left property to his wife for life and on her death for their children and on their deaths to such charitable uses and purposes as one of the children should appoint. It was held that the trust did not fail.

By statute in a number of states it is provided that a charitable trust shall not fail because of the failure of the settlor to designate the particular purpose.[6]

T may elect); Davis v. Bullington, 164 Tenn. 272, 47 S.W.2d 555 (1931) (to erect memorial to testator's mother), noted in 18 Va. L. Rev. 891.

See Caffrey, Charitable Bequests: Delegation; Discretion to Choose the Objects of the Testator's Beneficence, 40 Tenn. L. Rev. 307 (1977).

Wisconsin: Webster v. Morris, 66 Wis. 366, 28 N.W. 353, 57 Am. Rep. 278 (1886) (to be expended by T for charitable purposes).

But see Wisconsin Stat., §701.10.

In Lutheran Church v. Farmers' Co-operative, [1970] A.L.R. 545 (Austl.), a testatrix left the residue to trustees, giving them discretionary power to convey the property to a designated charitable corporation to build a home for the aged. The lower court held that the disposition failed because the power was discretionary. The High Court was equally divided. The result seems shocking.

For criticisms of the view that the trust fails for uncertainty when the selection of the charitable object is left to the trustee, see Fratcher, Powers of Appointment to Unspecified Charities, 32 Mo. L. Rev. 443 (1967); Caffrey, Charitable Bequests: Delegating Discretion to Choose the Objects of the Testator's Benevolence, 44 Tenn. L. Rev. 307 (1977).

[5]267 Mass. 268, 166 N.E. 766 (1929).

In Estate of Stewart, 271 So. 2d 754 (Fla. 1973), where on the death of the income beneficiary the trustees were directed to distribute the principal among the surviving relatives of the testatrix or among charitable corporations in such proportions as a third person should determine, it was held that the power of the third person could not be exercised until after the death of the income beneficiary.

[6]*California:* Corporations Code, §10206 (gift to charitable corporation).
Connecticut: Gen. Stat. 1958, §15-81.
Georgia: Code 1981, §53-12-73.
Minnesota: Stat. Ann., §501.12.

§397. Failure of Trustee

In the case of a charitable trust, as in the case of a private trust,[1] equity will not ordinarily allow a trust to fail for want of a trustee. A trust will not fail because no trustee is named, or because the trustee named dies, is under an incapacity, is removed, resigns, or renounces. This is true whether the failure of the trustee occurs at the time of the creation of the trust or subsequently. A charitable trust, like a private trust, will fail for want of a trustee only if the settlor showed an intention that the trust should not arise or should not continue unless the person named by him as trustee should accept the trust and continue to act as trustee. In a number of states it is provided by statute that a charitable trust shall not fail for want of a trustee.[2]

Where a particular charitable purpose is designated. Where the property is to be applied to a particular charitable purpose, it has been held in numerous cases that the trust will not fail merely because no trustee was named by the testator or because the trustee named by him was unable or unwilling to perform the trust.[3] The result reached in these cases is clearly sound,

---

North Carolina: Gen. Stat., §§36A-43, 36A-46.

See Banner v. North Carolina Natl. Bank, 266 N.C. 337, 146 S.E.2d 89 (1966) (to some charitable organization selected by executor).

South Carolina: Code 1976, §21-27-60.

Virginia: Code 1950, §55-31.

West Virginia: Code, §35-1-4.

Wisconsin: Stat., §701.10.

§397. [1]See §§33, 101.

[2]*Kentucky:* Rev. Stat. Ann., §381.270.

Michigan: Stat. Ann., §26.1191.

Nebraska: Rev. Stat. 1943, §30-239.

New York: Estates, Powers and Trusts Law, §8-1.1, amended by Laws 1971, c. 1058, and Laws 1985, c. 492.

North Carolina: Gen. Stat., §36A-43.

South Carolina: Code 1976, §§21-29-20, 21-27-60.

Tennessee: Code Ann., §35-1-114, enacted by Laws 1986, c. 566.

West Virginia: Code, §35-2-2.

[3]*England:* Mayor of Reading v. Lane, Duke 81 (1601) (to poor people maintained in hospital of A forever); Attorney-General v. Hickman, W. Kel. 34, 2 Eq. Cas. Abr. 193 (1732) (for encouraging nonconforming ministers and dissenting ministers); Attorney-General v. Clarke, Amb. 422 (1762) (to poor

even though the method of accomplishing the charitable pur-

---

inhabitants of A); Attorney-General v. Downing, Amb. 549, 571, Wilm. 1, 21 (1766) (for erecting college); White v. White, 1 Bro. C.C. 12 (1778) (to such lying-in hospital as T appoints); Attorney-General v. Gladstone, 13 Sim. 7 (1842) (to be applied by T for use of Roman Catholic priests in and near London).

Federal: John v. Smith, 102 F. 218 (9th Cir. 1900), *aff'g* 91 F. 827 (C.C.D. Or. 1899) (for free public schools in A).

Arizona: In re Estate of Kidd, 106 Ariz. 554, 479 P.2d 697 (1971) (citing Restatement of Trusts §397) (the money to go "in a research of some scientific proof of a soul of the human body which leaves at death").

California: Fay v. Howe, 136 Cal. 599, 69 P. 423 (1902) (for aid of deserving aged native poor of A); Estate of De Mars, 20 Cal. App. 2d 514, 67 P.2d 374 (1937) (to poor soldiers in named hospital; quoting Restatement of Trusts, §397, Comment *f*); Estate of Hart, 151 Cal. App. 2d 271, 311 P.2d 605 (1957) (devise to a county to maintain a public park); Estate of McKenzie, 227 Cal. App. 2d 167, 38 Cal. Rptr. 496, 7 A.L.R.3d 1275 (1964) (for a reward for discovering a cure for arthritis); In re Estate of Thomason, 245 Cal. App. 2d 793, 54 Cal. Rptr. 229 (1966) (to be turned over to cancer research); In re Estate of Gatlin, 16 Cal. App. 3d 644, 94 Cal. Rptr. 295 (1971) (to be equally divided between a home for the blind and a home for crippled children in San Francisco; quoting Restatement of Trusts §399).

Colorado: Jeffreys v. Intl. Trust Co., 97 Colo. 188, 48 P.2d 1019 (1935) (to Denver Foundation, a community trust, for benefit of needy Denver people), noted in 14 Tenn. L. Rev. 118.

Connecticut: Eliot's Appeal, 74 Conn. 586, 51 A. 558 (1902) (for aiding destitute seamen frequenting port of A); Shannon v. Eno, 120 Conn. 77, 179 A. 479 (1935) (to found and support home for cats).

Florida: In re Serrill's Estate, 159 So. 2d 246 (Fla. App. 1964) (to a home for children to be selected by the executors; one executor had died and the other was ineligible; held, the administrator may select the home).

Georgia: Thompson v. Hale, 123 Ga. 305, 51 S.E. 383 (1905) (school); Simpson v. Anderson, 220 Ga. 155, 137 S.E.2d 638 (1964) (to attorney of testatrix to be distributed by him among child welfare organizations). Roughton v. Jones, 225 Ga. 774, 171 S.E.2d 536 (1969) (to two churches for home and foreign missions; the churches disclaimed).

Illinois: Heuser v. Harris, 42 Ill. 425, 436 (1867) (to poor of A county); Hunt v. Fowler, 121 Ill. 269, 12 N.E. 331, 17 N.E. 491 (1887) (to distribute among worthy poor of A as Court of Chancery may direct); Grand Prairie Seminary v. Morgan, 171 Ill. 444, 49 N.E. 516 (1898) (for education of poor young boys of Illinois); Hitchcock v. Board of Home Missions, 259 Ill. 288, 102 N.E. 741, Ann. Cas. 1915B 1 (1913) (for Presbyterian home and foreign missions and for educating poor children).

Indiana: Dykeman v. Jenkines, 179 Ind. 549, 101 N.E. 1013, Ann. Cas. 1915D 1011 (1913) (hospital).

Iowa: Grant v. Saunders, 121 Iowa 80, 95 N.W. 411, 100 Am. St. Rep. 310

poses of the testator is not specified by him. The testator either

---

(1903) (for benefit of poor; *semble*); Klumpert v. Vrieland, 142 Iowa 434, 121 N.W. 34 (1909) (to poor of A).

Kentucky: Young v. Redmon's Trustee, 300 Ky. 418, 189 S.W.2d 401 (1945) (to educate some worthy girl).

Maine: Howard v. American Peace Socy., 49 Me. 288 (1860) (to suffering poor of A); Webber Hospital Assn. v. McKenzie, 104 Me. 320, 71 A. 1032 (1908) (hospital); Dunn v. Morse, 109 Me. 254, 83 A. 795 (1912) (to be given to institutions for relief of suffering humanity); Petition of Pierce, 109 Me. 509, 84 A. 1090 (1912) (for founding home for indigent seamen), s.c. Petition of Pierce, 153 Me. 180, 136 A.2d 510 (1957).

Maryland: Fletcher v. Safe Deposit & Trust Co., 193 Md. 400, 67 A.2d 386 (1949) (citing the text).

Massachusetts: Darcy v. Kelley, 153 Mass. 433, 26 N.E. 1110 (1891) (to nonexistent association as fund for poor); Sears v. Chapman, 158 Mass. 400, 33 N.E. 604, 35 Am. St. Rep. 502 (1893) (for benefit of inhabitants of A for educational purposes); Attorney Gen. v. Goodell, 180 Mass. 538, 62 N.E. 962 (1902) (to be divided among poor colored people of A); Chase v. Dickey, 212 Mass. 555, 99 N.E. 410 (1912) (for promotion of Christian Science); Sherman v. Shaw, 243 Mass. 257, 137 N.E. 374 (1922) (to pay certain sum to ten poor boys to be selected by T); Binney v. Attorney Gen., 259 Mass. 539, 156 N.E. 724 (1927) (for relief of poor and unfortunate as judgment of sisters of testator may dictate); Town of Milton v. Attorney Gen., 314 Mass. 234, 49 N.E.2d 909 (1943) (to town for erection and maintenance of hospital; cy pres applied by giving bequest to existing hospital; citing the text); Davenport v. Attorney Gen., 361 Mass. 372, 280 N.E.2d 193 (1972) (citing the text and Restatement of Trusts §397).

Michigan: Gifford v. First Natl. Bank, 285 Mich. 58, 280 N.W. 108 (1938) (for furthering medical arts, care of the sick, child welfare, etc.).

Mississippi: Estate of Bunch v. Heirs of Bunch, 485 So. 2d 284 (Miss. 1986), citing text.

New Hampshire: French v. Lawrence, 76 N.H. 234, 81 A. 705 (1911) (to feeble Congregational churches of N.H.).

New Jersey: Bruere v. Cook, 63 N.J. Eq. 624, 52 A. 1001 (1902), *aff'd mem.*, 67 N.J. Eq. 724, 63 A. 1118 (1903) (for home and foreign missions of Baptist Church); Case v. Hasse, 83 N.J. Eq. 170, 93 A. 728 (1914) (to poor children of A for summer home).

New York: Bowman v. Domestic & Foreign Missionary Socy., 182 N.Y. 494, 75 N.E. 535 (1905) (for Indian and domestic missions); Matter of Liebeck, 109 N.Y.S.2d 147 (1951) (to pastor as he might see fit for church purposes); Matter of Jones, 27 Misc. 2d 569, 213 N.Y.S.2d 92 (1961) (to divide among Protestant and nonsectarian incorporated charitable institutions in Brooklyn whose general objects are ministering to the poor); Matter of Thomas, 38 Misc. 2d 48, 235 N.Y.S.2d 601 (1962) (to society for assistance of war refugees to be selected by executor).

See Matter of Van Vechten, 169 Misc. 328, 7 N.Y.S.2d 502 (1938).

may have left wholly undetermined the method to be pursued
or he may have left the method to the discretion of a trustee who

---

North Carolina: State v. Gerard, 2 Ired. Eq. 210 (N.C. 1842) (to poor of A);
Lassiter v. Jones, 215 N.C. 298, 1 S.E.2d 845 (1939).

North Dakota: Hagen v. Sacrison, 19 N.D. 160, 123 N.W. 518, 26 L.R.A.
(N.S.) 724 (1909) (for poor children of A).

Ohio: Urmey's Exrs. v. Wooden, 1 Ohio St. 160, 59 Am. Dec. 615 (1853)
(to poor and needy of A).

Pennsylvania: Crawford's Estate, 294 Pa. 201, 143 A. 912 (1928) (for benefit of fatherless children of France); Millero Estate, 20 D.&C.2d 532 (Pa. 1959)
(citing Restatement of Trusts §397).

Tennessee: Carson v. Nashville Bank & Trust Co., 204 Tenn. 396, 321
S.W.2d 798 (1959) (to a named individual to be used by him for the education
of children whom he deems worthy of assistance; quoting the text); Lewis v.
Darnell, 580 S.W.2d 572 (Tenn. App. 1979).

Texas: Morse v. First Natl. Bank of Galveston, 194 S.W.2d 578 (Tex. Civ.
App. 1946) (to be distributed in discretion of trustee among poor of Island of
Jersey); Taysum v. El Paso Natl. Bank, 256 S.W.2d 172 (Tex. Civ. App. 1953)
(to set up research foundation in electricity); Taylor v. Republic Natl. Bank,
452 S.W.2d 560 (Tex. Civ. App. 1970) (to an unincorporated church conference for a hospital); Eldridge v. Marshall Natl. Bank, 527 S.W.2d 222 (Tex.
Civ. App. 1975), *writ refused, n.r.e.* (to form a scholarship fund; no trustee
named).

Washington: In re Preston's Estate, 141 Wash. 619, 252 P. 139 (1927) (to
poor people of Spokane).

Wisconsin: Sawtelle v. Witham, 94 Wis. 412, 69 N.W. 72 (1896) (for support and education of indigent orphan children of A); Hood v. Dorer, 107 Wis.
149, 82 N.W. 546 (1900) (for support and maintenance of superannuated
preachers of a church).

Australia: Kytherian Assn. of Queensl. v. Sklavos, 101 C.L.R. 56 (Austl.
1958) (to an unincorporated association to erect a hospital).

Canada: In re O'Brien, 15 D.L.R.2d 484 (N.S. 1958) (to be put into a trust
fund for the poor to be looked after by an unincorporated branch of the
Salvation Army).

See 5 A.L.R. 315 (1920); 78 U. Pa. L. Rev. 573 (1930).

In Matter of Saalberg, 190 Misc. 966, 75 N.Y.S.2d 707 (1947), where a
testator bequeathed money to an alien enemy in trust for the upkeep of the
graves of the testator's parents in Germany, it was held that a charitable trust
was created that would not fail because the trustee was an alien enemy, and
that the Alien Property Custodian was not entitled to the legacy.

In Matter of Hill (In re Hill's Will), 45 Misc. 2d 36, 255 N.Y.S.2d 898
(1965), where a testatrix made a bequest to a corporation to be formed for the
relief of animals and directed that it should be formed with the guidance and
help of a veterinarian, and he predeceased her, it was held that the trust did
not fail.

is unable or unwilling to exercise this discretion. For this reason it has been held in a few cases that the intended charitable trust fails for uncertainty if the testator names no trustee or if the trustee named by him is unable or unwilling to administer the trust.[4] This is, however, too narrow a view of the matter. The uncertainty may be removed by an appointment by the court of a trustee to administer the trust or by the framing of a scheme by the court. There is no principle of public policy that would require the trust to fail, and such failure would be contrary to the intention of the testator. It is true, as we shall see, that where the testator intended that the method of applying the property to the intended charitable purposes should lie wholly and solely within the discretion of the person whom he names as trustee, the trust may fail. But ordinarily the method to be pursued is a merely secondary consideration, the primary purpose of the testator being that the property should be applied to the designated charitable purposes.

Where property is devised or bequeathed for a particular charitable purpose, it may appear that the testator intended that the administration of the trust by the particular trustee named by him should be an essential part of his scheme. In such a case the trust fails if the trustee named is unwilling or unable to accept and administer the trust.[5] Thus in *Bullard v. Inhabitants of*

[4]*New Jersey:* Brown v. Condit, 70 N.J. Eq. 440, 61 A. 1055 (1905); Bankers Trust Co. v. New York Women's League for Animals, 23 N.J. Super. 170, 92 A.2d 820 (1952), *rev'g* 17 N.J. Super. 398, 86 A.2d 138 (1952) (bequest to charitable corporation to acquire farm for care of animals).

[5]*Arkansas:* Cammack v. Chalmers, 284 Ark. 161, 680 S.W.2d 689 (1984) (land conveyed to state university in consideration of its contract to use it as a campus will revert to heirs of grantrix if university fails for fifty years to use it for a campus).

Indiana: Hadley v. Hadley, 147 Ind. 423, 46 N.E. 823 (1897) (for erection and maintenance of institution for education of poor children if thought practicable).

Massachusetts: Bullard v. Inhabitants of Shirley, 153 Mass. 559, 27 N.E. 766, 12 L.R.A. 110 (1891).

New York: Beekman v. Bonsor, 23 N.Y. 298, 80 Am. Dec. 269 (1861) (to apply property or as much as executors should think proper to one or more societies for support of indigent persons).

Ohio: Reichert v. Mikesell, 73 Ohio App. 504, 57 N.E.2d 160 (1943) (to humane society for dog pound and animal shelter).

Pennsylvania: See Farrell's Estate, 38 D.&C. 238 (Pa. 1940).

Shirley[6] a woman left a sum of money to a town "strictly on this condition, namely, that said town shall support fairly and permanently a Unitarian clergyman, in which case all interest accruing on above sum shall be used to aid in payment of his salary, failing which it shall revert to my heirs at law." It was admitted that the town could not lawfully support the clergyman,[7] and the question was whether the gift failed. The court said that "support by the town, and not merely in the town, is of the essence of the condition. . . . We cannot doubt that what she required from the town went to the root of her gift." The court held that the bequest therefore failed, and that the next of kin of the testatrix were entitled to the money. Whether the testatrix intended to create a charitable trust or to impose a condition, the decision can be supported if the intention of the testatrix was that the administration of her bounty by the town was of the essence of her gift. Perhaps in view of the language used by her it was so; but ordinarily the settlor is primarily concerned with the disposition of the beneficial interest and only secondarily concerned with its administration, and in most cases where the purpose of the trust is clearly declared the trust will not fail because the trustee named is not competent or not willing to administer it.

Where no particular charitable purpose is designated. In the cases that we have been considering, the testator has designated the kind of charitable purpose that he has in mind, although he has left it to the trustees to determine the method of applying the property for the accomplishment of his purpose. It frequently happens, however, that the testator has merely indicated his intention that the property should be devoted to charitable purposes. Even though the trustee is authorized to apply trust property to any charitable purpose he may select, and the trustee named by the testator is unable or unwilling to make the selection, the trust does not fail unless the testator

---

Washington: Chellew v. White, 127 Wash. 382, 221 P. 3 (1923) (to executor in trust to expend as he saw fit for benefit of widows and orphans of World War in two parishes in England), noted in 10 Va. L. Rev. 486.

[6]153 Mass. 559, 27 N.E. 766, 12 L.R.A. 110 (1891).

[7]See §96.4.

manifested a different intention.[8] It is ordinarily to be inferred that the testator's primary purpose was that the property should

[8]*England:* Moggridge v. Thackwell, 7 Ves. Jun. 36, 32 Eng. Rep. 15 (1803), discussed in Fratcher, Powers of Appointment to Unspecified Charities, 32 Mo. L. Rev. 443, 448 (1967); In re Cammell, [1925] W.N. 36.

Florida: In re Estate of Gold, 189 So. 2d 905 (Fla. App. 1966) (gift over to two universities).

Massachusetts: Schouler, Petitioner, 134 Mass. 426 (1883); Minot v. Baker, 147 Mass. 348, 17 N.E. 839, 9 Am. St. Rep. 713 (1888); Kirwin v. Attorney Gen., 275 Mass. 34, 175 N.E. 164 (1931), noted in 19 Geo. L.J. 507.

Missouri: Epperly v. Mercantile Trust & Sav. Bank, 415 S.W.2d 819 (Mo. 1967), *modified,* 457 S.W.2d 1 (Mo. 1970) (to distribute in discretion of trustee to Protestant churches and religious organizations to be used to save souls and not for buildings; quoting Restatement of Trusts §396).

New Hampshire: Petition of Madden, 86 N.H. 583, 172 A. 435 (1934).

New Jersey: Levin v. Attorney Gen., 136 N.J. Eq. 568, 42 A.2d 870 (1945) (citing Restatement of Trusts §397).

New York: Stewart v. Franchetti, 167 A.D. 541, 153 N.Y.S. 453 (1915); Matter of Groot, 173 A.D. 436, 159 N.Y.S. 1003 (1916), *aff'd,* 226 N.Y. 576, 123 N.E. 867 (1919); Matter of McLoghlin, 139 Misc. 202, 248 N.Y.S. 253 (1931), *aff'd,* 233 A.D. 886, 251 N.Y.S. 876 (1931); Matter of Michaels, 7 Misc. 2d 439, 165 N.Y.S.2d 234 (1957) (citing the text and Restatement of Trusts §397); Matter of Harrigan, 23 A.D.2d 667, 257 N.Y.S.2d 299 (1965) (citing the text and Restatement of Trusts §397), *aff'd mem.,* 18 N.Y.2d 881, 223 N.E.2d 33 (1966); Matter of O'Connor, 45 Misc. 2d 1033, 258 N.Y.S.2d 688 (1965) (for such residue to executor for distribution among Catholic charities as he deemed wise; he died and court awarded it to the pastor of the testator's church for its purposes); Matter of Rose, 58 Misc. 2d 576, 296 N.Y.S.2d 656 (1967), *aff'd,* 29 A.D.2d 635, 286 N.Y.S.2d 458 (1968), *aff'd mem.,* 23 N.Y.2d 870, 245 N.E.2d 808, 298 N.Y.S.2d 77 (1969); Application of Price (Matter of Carper), 67 A.D.2d 333, 415 N.Y.S.2d 550 (1979), *aff'd mem.,* 50 N.Y.2d 974, 409 N.E.2d 941, 431 N.Y.S.2d 468 (1980).

Pennsylvania: Thompson's Estate, 282 Pa. 30, 127 A. 446 (1925), noted in 73 U. Pa. L. Rev. 322; Funk Estate, 353 Pa. 321, 45 A.2d 67, 163 A.L.R. 780 (1946), *aff'g* 46 D.&C. 667 (Pa. 1942), noted in 44 Mich. L. Rev. 846; Ayres Estate, 11 D.&C.2d 383 (Pa. 1957).

Wisconsin: In re Raulf's Estate, 28 Wis. 2d 514, 137 N.W.2d 416 (1965) (citing Restatement of Trusts §397).

Canada: In re Gilliland, 10 D.L.R.2d 769 (N.S. 1956).

So also the trust does not fail merely because the trustees cannot agree, but the court may direct a disposition of the property. See Stuart v. Continental Ill. Natl. Bank & Trust Co., 68 Ill. 2d 502, 12 Ill. Dec. 248, 369 N.E.2d 1262 (1977), *cert. denied,* 444 U.S. 844, 100 S. Ct. 86, 62 L. Ed. 2d 56 (1979) (quoting Restatement of Trusts §397, Comment *c*), *aff'g* Northern Trust Co. v. Continental Ill. Natl. Bank & Trust Co., 43 Ill. App. 3d 169, 11 Ill. Dec. 767, 356 N.E.2d 1049 (1976), stated in §194, n. 15.

be devoted to charitable uses, and the selection of those uses by the trustee whom he names is a secondary matter. The leading case is *Minot v. Baker*. [9] In that case a testator left the residue of his estate to one Healy, whom he also appointed executor, "to be disposed of by him for such charitable purposes as he shall think proper." Although Healy survived the testator, he died before he had disposed of more than a small portion of the estate for charitable purposes. A bill for instructions was brought by the administrator de bonis non to determine whether the remainder of the estate should be paid to the next of kin of the testator or should be applied to charitable purposes. The court held that it should be applied to charitable purposes according to a scheme to be framed under the direction of the court. Holmes, J., said that it was a matter of construction "whether the limitation to charities was conditional upon Healy's making an appointment, or whether it should be construed as a gift to charitable uses out and out, with a superadded power to Healy to specify them if he saw fit." He held that it was an unconditional gift to charitable purposes, that "The nature of the gift shows that an application of the funds to charity is the dominant object, and that the selection by the trustee is subordinate, or means to an end." He said that it was no objection that there was nothing more specific to guide the court than a general direction to apply the funds to charitable purposes.

The same result has been reached where property is given to trustees in trust for such charitable purposes as a third person may designate, and the third person fails to make the designation. In such a case the disposition does not fail unless the testator showed an intention that the selection by the third person was an essential part of his scheme.[10] Thus in an English case[11] where a testatrix left her estate in trust for her sister for life and on the death of her sister to such charitable institution

[9]147 Mass. 348, 349, 17 N.E. 839, 9 Am. St. Rep. 713 (1888).

[10]*England:* In re Willis, [1921] 1 Ch. 44.

Massachusetts: Binney v. Attorney Gen., 259 Mass. 539, 156 N.E. 724 (1927).

Pennsylvania: Dutton Estate, 54 D.&C.2d 698 (Pa. 1972) (person to select charity predeceased testatrix without making any selection).

[11]In re Willis, [1921] 1 Ch. 44.

or society in England, Russia, or elsewhere as might be selected by a designated friend of the testatrix, and the sister and the friend predeceased her, it was held that the intended charitable trust did not fail.

On the other hand, the testator may show an intention to make the selection of the charitable purposes by the trustee named by him a primary and essential part of his scheme. In such a case the trust fails if the trustee named by him is unable or unwilling to make the selection.[12] In the cases cited the court found that the power of selection was to be exercised only by the trustees named in the will, and that the selection by them was an essential part of his scheme. Ordinarily, however, the selection of the charitable purposes by the original trustee is presumed to be a secondary consideration and only incidental to the primary purpose that the property should be devoted to charitable uses.

Direct gift to charity.   Where a testator leaves property directly to purposes of charity, without using language indicating that the property is to be held in trust, the disposition does not fail, but the court will appoint a trustee to hold and dispose of the property for the intended objects. Thus where a testator leaves a sum of money "to the poor," the bequest will be treated as a gift in trust to assist the poor, although in form the gift was made directly to the poor; and the court will appoint a trustee to administer the trust, or will frame a scheme for the application of the legacy to the intended purpose.

Similarly, a direct bequest "to charity" is valid.[13] So also the

---

[12]*Federal:* Fontain v. Ravenel, 17 How. 369, 15 L. Ed. 80 (U.S. 1854) (for use of charitable institutions in Pennsylvania and South Carolina as T may deem most beneficial to mankind).

Florida: Estate of Stewart, 271 So. 2d 754 (Fla. 1973) (power to appoint among relatives or charitable corporations).

Missouri: Hadley v. Forsee, 203 Mo. 418, 101 S.W. 59, 14 L.R.A. (N.S.) 49 (1907) (to testator's wife to advance cause of religion and promote cause of charity in such manner as she may think would be most conducive to carrying out his wishes).

Ohio: Rogers v. Rea, 98 Ohio St. 315, 120 N.E. 828 (1918) (for such charitable purposes as T may deem proper).

[13]*California:* Estate of Quinn, 156 Cal. App. 2d 684, 320 P.2d 219 (1958) (citing Restatement of Trusts, §397, Comment *f*); Estate of Gutierrez, 189 Cal.

disposition is valid where a testator leaves property directly to something that has no legal existence as an entity, as where he makes a bequest to a designated home or other institution. In such a case the court will treat the disposition as though it were made to the trustees of the institution in trust for the purposes for which the institution is conducted.[14] Occasionally, however,

---

App. 2d 165, 11 Cal. Rptr. 51 (1961) ("the rest to different charities"); In re Estate of Cafferty, 246 Cal. App. 2d 711, 55 Cal. Rptr. 173 (1967) (help for the blind).

See Estate of Quinn, 273 P.2d 47 (Cal. App. 1954) (citing Restatement of Trusts §397), *rev'd on statutory procedural ground,* 43 Cal. 2d 785, 278 P.2d 692 (1955).

Mississippi: Estate of Bunch v. Heirs of Bunch, 485 So. 2d 284 (Miss. 1986) ("to help one or two young men through medical school").

New York: Matter of Finkelstein, 189 Misc. 180, 70 N.Y.S.2d 596 (1947).

Pennsylvania: Jordan's Estate, 329 Pa. 427, 197 A. 150 (1938) (citing Restatement of Trusts §397).

In Streeper Estate, 71 D.&C.2d 326 (Pa. 1975), a testatrix bequeathed $10,000 "for a memorial in memory of my sister." The court upheld the disposition as a charitable bequest and awarded it to two churches, one of which had been attended by her, and the other by her sister.

Texas: Wilson v. Franz, 359 S.W.2d 630 (Tex. Civ. App. 1962) (devise of home to be sold for the blind and crippled, and mortgages and land left to needed charity; quoting the text and Restatement of Trusts, §397, Comments *d* and *e*).

But see Brezinski v. Breves, 109 N.J. Eq. 206, 156 A. 429 (1931); Levin v. Attorney Gen., 136 N.J. Eq. 568, 42 A.2d 870 (1945); Angus's Exr. v. Batchan's Trustees, [1949] Sess. Cas. 335 (Scot.).

In Estate of Rollins, 163 Cal. App. 2d 225, 328 P.2d 1005 (1958), it was held that a bequest of the residue to "some charitable institution, or research fund, or for a suitable memorial to my mother and father (no statue or monument)" was valid. The court cited Restatement of Trusts, §397, Comment *f.*

In In re Mills' Will, 57 N.M. 577, 260 P.2d 1111 (1953), the court upheld a bequest to "deformed and crippled children in such manner as my executors may arrange for."

See Note, Charitable gifts; definiteness, 163 A.L.R. 784, 834 (1946).

[14]*England:* In re Faraker, [1912] 2 Ch. 488 (bequest to pre-existing charity).

California: Estate of Moeller, 199 Cal. 705, 251 P. 311 (1926) (bequest to workhouse); Estate of McDole, 215 Cal. 328, 10 P.2d 75 (1932) (bequest to home).

Iowa: Meeker v. Lawrence, 203 Iowa 409, 212 N.W. 688 (1927) (bequest to cemetery).

New Jersey: First Natl. Bank & Trust Co. of Summit v. Board of Freeholders, 123 N.J. Eq. 415, 198 A. 292 (1938) (bequest to sanitarium).

the courts have taken a more technical view, and have held that the disposition failed because it was not labeled in the will as a gift in trust. Thus in a case in Missouri it was held that a bequest to the "capital" of a public school fund failed because a gift could not be made to an inanimate thing, although it appeared that there was such a fund in existence held and administered by trustees.[15] Obviously, the intention of the testator was to make a gift to the trustees of the fund to be applied for the purposes for which the fund was administered, which were clearly charitable purposes. This case has now been overruled

---

New York: Matter of Feehan, 135 Misc. 903, 241 N.Y.S. 669 (1929) (bequest to fund); Matter of Tiffany, 157 Misc. 873, 285 N.Y.S. 971 (1935) (bequest to charitable foundation); Petition of the Roman Catholic Diocese of Brooklyn, 138 N.Y.S.2d 174 (1954) (bequest to seminary held payable to ecclesiastical association conducting seminary).

Texas: Bode v. Loeffler, 540 S.W.2d 465 (Tex. Civ. App. 1976), *writ refused* (legacy to "Retired Ministers' Fund" of a church conference. There was no such fund, but the court appointed the Board of Pensions of the conference to administer the trust. The court cited the text.).

In Matter of Calkins, 182 Misc. 44, 43 N.Y.S.2d 15 (1943), a bequest to the "Manse Fund" of a church was upheld as a gift to the trustees of the church for the purposes of the fund.

In Matter of Hernberg, 180 Misc. 764, 41 N.Y.S.2d 72 (1943), a bequest to the "Rector's Fund" of a church was upheld as a gift to the church corporation for the purposes of the fund.

In Carr v. Hart, 220 La. 833, 57 So. 2d 739 (1952), where a testatrix left a legacy to "the cemetery fund," it was held that the legacy failed because there was no fund and no person or body to hold any funds for the upkeep of the cemetery that she intended to benefit.

In In re Gare, [1952] Ch. 80, where a testator gave a legacy to a certain parish church, it was held that he thereby created a charitable trust for purposes connected with the services of the church and that unless the Attorney-General and the solicitors for the parochial church council, a corporate body appointed by statute, should agree on a method for using the fund, a scheme should be framed for the administration of the fund.

[15]Robinson v. Crutcher, 277 Mo. 1, 209 S.W. 104 (1918).

In American Cancer Socy., Mo. Div. v. Damon Runyon Memorial Fund for Cancer Research, 409 S.W.2d 222 (Mo. App. 1966), criticized in 32 Mo. L. Rev. 583 (1967), there was a bequest to the Damon Runyon Memorial Fund for Cancer Research, St. Joseph, Missouri, Division. Testatrix was an active member of the St. Joseph Chapter of the American Cancer Society. The Damon Runyon Fund had no St. Joseph chapter or division. It was held that the bequest failed because the legatee did not exist.

in another case[16] where the court upheld a bequest to "the Macon County Mo, school fund." In *White v. Corinthian Lodge, F. & A.M.,*[17] the court upheld a legacy to "the proposed Central School of Epsom, N.H." There was no such school, but the testator was familiar with plans for the construction of such a school, and the court awarded the legacy to the school district.

Where a bequest is made directly to an unincorporated charitable association, the courts have generally upheld the disposition, even though the association is incapable of holding the legal title to the property bequeathed.[18]

§397.1. Procedure on failure of trustee. As we have seen, the court will not ordinarily permit a charitable trust to fail for want of a trustee. The question remains, however, as to the proper procedure for the administration of the trust. Where the particular charitable purposes and the methods for the administration of the trust are designated in the trust instrument, the

[16]Burrier v. Jones, 338 Mo. 679, 92 S.W.2d 885 (1936).

In Carlock v. Ladies Cemetery Assn., 317 S.W.2d 432 (Mo. 1958), a testator devised land to an Illinois cemetery. The cemetery was owned by a city that had conferred control of it to the defendant, a nonprofit corporation. It was held that a valid charitable trust was created and that the court would name a trustee in Missouri to sell the land and pay the proceeds to the corporation. The court cited the text.

In Succession of Quillou, 221 So. 2d 651 (La. App. 1969), where a testator left his estate to the New Orleans Library, the bequest was upheld as one to the city for the purposes of its public library.

[17]100 N.H. 138, 121 A.2d 795 (1956).

But see *contra,* In re Estate of Loomis, 202 Kan. 668, 451 P.2d 195 (1968) (bequest to a proposed home for the aged).

In Eckles v. Lounsberry, 253 Iowa 172, 111 N.W.2d 638 (1961), where a bequest was made to the Iowa State Public School Fund, and there was no such entity, the court held that the trust did not fail but that it was a bequest to the state and that, if it should not accept, the court would appoint a trustee. The court cited the text and Restatement of Trusts §397.

In Matter of Kashiwabara, 11 Misc. 2d 426, 171 N.Y.S.2d 1001 (1958), where a legacy was given to the United States Navy Hospital, without naming any specific hospital, it was held that the legacy should be given to the General Gift Fund of the Department of the Navy.

In In re Barwick, 11 D.L.R.2d 341 (Ont. 1957), where a legacy was given directly to the sick nurses' benefit fund of a hospital, the legacy was upheld as a charitable gift to the corporation that administered the fund.

[18]See §397.2.

court will appoint a new trustee to administer the trust.[1] This is
true whether the failure of the trustee occurs at or before the
time of the creation of the trust or at some subsequent time. The
successor trustee can properly exercise the powers conferred by
the terms of the trust even though they involve the exercise of
discretion, unless the testator manifested an intention that the
powers should be exercised only by the trustee originally named
by him.

Where property is left in trust for such charitable purposes
as the trustee may select, and the trustee named by the testator
is unable or unwilling to make the selection, and the selection
by the particular trustee is not an essential part of the scheme
of the testator, the court will either appoint a new trustee to
make the selection or will approve a scheme for the administration of the trust. No definite rules have been laid down by the
courts as to which method shall be adopted. In a number of
cases the court has appointed a new trustee and clothed him
with authority to exercise the discretion that was reposed in the
original trustee.[2] This would seem to be in accordance with the

§397.1.   [1]Estate of Briggs, 189 Wis. 524, 208 N.W. 247 (1926).

In re Poulsen Found., 173 Cal. App. 3d 1212, 219 Cal. Rptr. 375 (1985),
involved an irrevocable charitable trust of land created inter vivos. After nine
years of operation, a mudslide from the land damaged improved land down-
hill. The county attorney having informed the trustee that he would be personally liable for damage caused by any other mudslides, the trustee resigned and
the court could find no one willing to act as trustee. A decree requiring the
settlors to act as trustees without their consent was reversed and the trial court
was directed to appoint a receiver to administer the trust without individual
liability for acts of God.

[2]*Massachusetts:* Schouler, Petitioner, 134 Mass. 426 (1883); Davenport v.
Attorney Gen., 361 Mass. 372, 280 N.E.2d 193 (1972) (citing the text and
Restatement of Trusts §397).

Michigan: Gifford v. First Natl. Bank, 285 Mich. 58, 280 N.W. 108 (1938).

New Jersey: Levin v. Attorney Gen., 136 N.J. Eq. 568, 42 A.2d 870 (1945).

New York: Matter of Jacobs, 127 Misc. 2d 1020, 487 N.Y.S.2d 992 (Sur.
1985), §194, n. 15, *supra.*

Rhode Island: Selleck v. Thompson, 28 R.I. 350, 67 A. 425 (1907).

Canada: In re Gilliland, 10 D.L.R.2d 769 (N.S. 1956).

In Litcher v. Trust Co. of N.J., 11 N.J. 64, 93 A.2d 368 (1952), *aff'g* 18
N.J. Super. 101, 86 A.2d 601 (1952), a testator authorized the trustees to
appoint a committee to divide the residue of his estate among certain charitable purposes. It was held that the power to appoint the committee could be
exercised by successor trustees.

probable intention of the testator where the trust is a continuing trust and the discretion is to be exercised throughout the duration of the trust.

On the other hand, in a number of cases where property was left in trust for such charitable purposes as the trustee might select and he was unable or unwilling to make the selection, it was held that there should be a reference to a master to frame a scheme for the administration of the trust.[3] This, as we shall see, is the method employed where it becomes impossible to carry out the particular charitable purpose for which property is given and it becomes necessary to apply the property cy pres.[4]

In some cases the courts seem to have employed a method slightly different from either appointing a new trustee and clothing him with discretionary power to select the particular charitable purposes, or referring the matter to a master to frame a scheme for submission to the court for its approval. Thus in a case in Pennsylvania, where a testator left his estate to his executors in trust with full and unlimited power to distribute the property among such religious and charitable purposes, objects, and institutions as might commend themselves to the executors

---

In Mackay & Another, Petitioners, [1955] Sess. Cas. 361 (Scot.), where the trusteeship was vacant and the charitable purposes could not be accomplished, the court refused to frame a scheme but appointed new trustees to decide as to the necessity for a cy pres scheme.

By Wisconsin Stat., §701.10, it is provided that "If a particular charitable purpose is not indicated and no trustee is named in the creating instrument, the court may appoint a trustee with such an implied power to select or may direct that the property be transferred outright to one or more established charitable entities."

[3]*England:* Attorney-General v. Gladstone, 13 Sim. 7 (1842); In re Willis, [1921] 1 Ch. 44.

Massachusetts: Minot v. Baker, 147 Mass. 348, 17 N.E. 839, 9 Am. St. Rep. 713 (1888).

New York: Matter of Grueby, 133 Misc. 248, 232 N.Y.S. 424 (1928).

Pennsylvania: Jordan's Estate, 329 Pa. 427, 197 A. 150 (1938).

Canada: Herbert v. Cyr & Lynch, [1944] 2 D.L.R. 374 (N.B.); In re Bobier, [1949] 4 D.L.R. 288 (Ont.) (municipal corporation incompetent to take title to land as trustee).

It will not be necessary to appoint a master if the court can itself determine a proper disposition of the property. Matter of Thomas, 38 Misc. 2d 48, 235 N.Y.S.2d 601 (1962).

[4]See §§399-399.5.

in their discretion and as in their judgment were in accordance with his wishes and preferences, and one of the executors renounced and the other died without having selected the charities, the court chose a member of the bar to make the disposition.[5] Apparently he was not appointed trustee by the court, nor did the court refer the matter to a master to frame a scheme.

In *Kirwin v. Attorney General*[6] a testator left the residue of his estate to his executors in trust for such public charitable purposes as should meet their approval under the conditions in which they might be called to act. After the administration of the estate had been completed but before the residue had been distributed the survivor of the executors died. An administrator de bonis non of the testator's estate was appointed, and he filed a petition alleging that the surviving executor had designated his purpose to distribute the residue to certain charities in certain amounts and asked that it be so distributed. It appeared that he had prepared a list of the intended charities and had consulted the Attorney General and secured his approval. The court found the scheme just and adopted it as the scheme of the court and decreed that the property be applied to the purposes designated by the executor before his death. One of the heirs appealed on the ground that the trust had failed. The court held that the decree of the lower court should be affirmed.

In *Binney v. Attorney General*[7] a testatrix left her estate to a trustee and directed that her sisters should apply the income to the relief of the poor and unfortunate whom they had aided in past years and also to others as their judgment might dictate. After the death of the sisters many years later the trustee brought a bill for instructions. The court directed that the trustee should continue to apply the income as the sisters had applied it, and if he was unwilling to do so the court said that it would appoint others to act as almoners.

§397.2. Gift to an unincorporated charitable association. If a devise or bequest is made in trust for a particular

---

[5]Thompson's Estate, 282 Pa. 30, 127 A. 446 (1925), noted in 73 U. Pa. L. Rev. 322.
[6]275 Mass. 34, 175 N.E. 164 (1931), noted in 19 Geo. L.J. 507.
[7]259 Mass. 539, 156 N.E. 724 (1927).

charitable purpose and the testator names as trustee an unincorporated charitable association which has no capacity to take title to the property, the trust does not fail, but the court will appoint a trustee to administer the trust. By the great weight of authority the result is the same where a devise or bequest is made to the association directly without mention of the purposes for which the property is given to it.[1] A bequest to such an association is

§397.2. [1]*England:* In re Schoales, [1930] 2 Ch. 75, noted in 4 Austl. L.J. 123, 169 Law T. 323, 29 Mich. L. Rev. 651; In re Meyers, [1951] 1 All E.R. 538 (to unincorporated hospital to be added to its invested funds); In re Gare, [1952] Ch. 80 (to unincorporated parish church); In re Banfield, [1968] 2 All E.R. 276 (to an unincorporated community house); In re Finger's Will Trusts, [1972] 1 Ch. 286; In re Lipinski's Will Trusts, [1976] 3 W.L.R. 522, [1977] 1 All E.R. 33 (to be used in constructing buildings for the association); Re Koeppler's Will Trusts; Barclays Bank Trust Co. v. Slack, [1986] 1 Ch. 423; [1985] 2 All E.R. 869 (C.A.).

Alabama: Tarver v. Weaver, 221 Ala. 663, 130 So. 209 (1930); Stariha v. Hagood, 252 Ala. 158, 40 So. 2d 85 (1949) (to unincorporated foundation for education of workers); McLean v. Church of God, 254 Ala. 134, 47 So. 2d 257 (1950) (*semble* as to personalty, but devise of land held invalid); Murphy v. Traylor, 292 Ala. 78, 289 So. 2d 584 (1973) (to an unincorporated church; quoting Restatement of Trusts, §397, Comment *f*).

See Arnold v. Methodist Episcopal Church, 281 Ala. 297, 202 So. 2d 83 (1967).

Arkansas: Garrett v. Mendenhall, 209 Ark. 898, 192 S.W.2d 972 (1946) (bequest to unincorporated church for best interests of church and community).

California: McDole's Estate, 215 Cal. 328, 10 P.2d 75 (1932); Estate of Clippinger, 75 Cal. App. 2d 426, 171 P.2d 567 (1946) (to trustees of Eastern Star Home at Rockford, Illinois; citing Restatement of Trusts, §397, Comments *f, g*).

Colorado: In re McLaughlin's Will, 128 Colo. 581, 265 P.2d 691 (1954) (devise to School of Medicine of the University of Texas).

Connecticut: Brinsmade v. Beach, 98 Conn. 322, 119 A. 233 (1922); New York E. Annual Conference of Methodist Church v. Seymour, 151 Conn. 517, 199 A.2d 701 (1964).

Delaware: Craven v. Wilmington Teachers Assn., 29 Del. Ch. 180, 47 A.2d 580 (1946).

District of Columbia: Sedgwick v. National Sav. & Trust Co., 76 App. D.C. 177, 130 F.2d 440 (1942) (citing the text).

Florida: Jordan v. Landis, 128 Fla. 604, 175 So. 241 (1937), *semble.*

Illinois: Burke v. Burke, 259 Ill. 262, 102 N.E. 293 (1913); Estate of Tomlinson, 65 Ill. 2d 382, 3 Ill. Dec. 699, 359 N.E.2d 109 (1976), *rev'g* 30 Ill. App. 3d 502, 333 N.E.2d 663 (1975) (Cancer Research Fund).

Iowa: In re Estate of Durham, 203 Iowa 497, 211 N.W. 358 (1927).

a bequest to be applied to the purposes for which the association

---

Kansas: Barnhart v. Bowers, 143 Kan. 866, 57 P.2d 60 (1936) (citing Restatement of Trusts §397), noted in 35 Mich. L. Rev. 656.

Maine: Bates v. Schillinger, 128 Me. 14, 145 A. 395 (1929); Johnson v. South Blue Hill Cemetery Assn., 221 A.2d 280 (Me. 1966).

Massachusetts: Bartlett v. Nye, 4 Met. 378 (Mass. 1842); Washburn v. Sewall, 9 Met. 280 (Mass. 1845); Winslow v. Cummings, 3 Cush. 358 (Mass. 1849); Peakes v. Blakely, 333 Mass. 281, 130 N.E.2d 564 (1955) (citing the text and Restatement of Trusts §397).

Missouri: Schneider v. Kloepple, 270 Mo. 389, 193 S.W. 834 (1917); Harger v. Barrett, 319 Mo. 633, 5 S.W.2d 1100 (1928); Glidewell v. Glidewell, 360 Mo. 713, 230 S.W.2d 752 (1950).

New Jersey: Hadden v. Dandy, 51 N.J. Eq. 154, 26 A. 464, 32 L.R.A. 625 (1893), *aff'd mem. sub nom.* Dandy v. Methodist Socy. of Ir., 51 N.J. Eq. 330, 30 A. 429 (1893); American Bible Socy. v. American Tract Socy., 62 N.J. Eq. 219, 50 A. 67 (1901); New Jersey Title Guar. & Trust Co. v. American Natl. Red Cross, 111 N.J. Eq. 12, 160 A. 842 (1932).

New Mexico: Farmers & Merchants Bank v. Woolf, 86 N.M. 320, 523 P.2d 1346 (1974) (bequest to Alcoholics Anonymous, an unincorporated association in Texas).

New York: Matter of Idem, 256 A.D. 124, 8 N.Y.S.2d 970 (1939), *aff'd,* 280 N.Y. 756, 21 N.E.2d 522 (1939) (Ohio law); Matter of Lamborn, 171 Misc. 734, 13 N.Y.S.2d 732 (1939) (Pennsylvania law); Matter of Macaulay, 173 Misc. 887, 19 N.Y.S.2d 418 (1940) (Connecticut law); Matter of Rathbone, 170 Misc. 1030, 11 N.Y.S.2d 506 (1939), *aff'd mem.,* 262 A.D. 706, 27 N.Y.S.2d 993 (1941), *aff'd mem.,* 287 N.Y. 708, 39 N.E.2d 930 (1942) (Pennsylvania law); Matter of Merritt, 273 A.D. 79, 75 N.Y.S.2d 828 (1947),˙*aff'g* 185 Misc. 979, 61 N.Y.S.2d 537 (1945) (English law); Matter of Schmadeke, 80 N.Y.S.2d 372 (1948) (Connecticut law); Matter of Jackson, 192 Misc. 618, 81 N.Y.S.2d 48 (1948) (Missouri law); Matter of MacKenzie, 197 Misc. 979, 96 N.Y.S.2d 241 (1950) (New Jersey law); Application of Goldberg, 99 N.Y.S.2d 101 (1950). See §594.

Ohio: American Diabetes Assn. v. Diabetes Socy. of Clinton County, 31 Ohio App. 3d 136, 31 O.B.R. 224, 509 N.E.2d 84 (1986).

Oklahoma: Estate of Anderson, 571 P.2d 880 (Okla. App. 1977) (cemetery association; quoting Restatement of Trusts, §397, Comment *f*).

Oregon: State v. Sunbeam Rebekah Lodge No. 180, 169 Or. 253, 127 P.2d 726 (1942) (*semble;* citing Restatement of Trusts, §397, Comment *g*); Good Samaritan Hosp. & Medical Center v. United States Natl. Bank. 246 Or. 478, 425 P.2d 541 (1967) (citing Restatement of Trusts §119).

Pennsylvania: Frazier v. Rector of St. Luke's Church, 147 Pa. 256, 23 A. 442 (1892); Shand's Estate, 275 Pa. 77, 118 A. 623 (1922).

Rhode Island: St. Peter's Church v. Brown, 21 R.I. 367, 43 A. 642 (1899); Guild v. Allen, 28 R.I. 430, 67 A. 855 (1907); Tillinghast v. Boy Scouts of Am., Council at Narragansett Pier, 47 R.I. 406, 133 A. 662, 46 A.L.R. 823 (1926), noted in 30 Law Notes 213; Taylor v. Salvation Army, 49 R.I. 316, 142 A. 335

is created and is in substance if not in form a bequest in trust

(1928); Bliven v. Borden, 56 R.I. 283, 185 A. 239, 249 (1936); Industrial Trust Co. v. City of Central Falls, 60 R.I. 218, 197 A. 467 (1938); Industrial Natl. Bank of Providence v. Nugent, 97 R.I. 236, 197 A.2d 278 (1964); Rhode Island Association for the Blind v. Nugent, 99 R.I. 187, 206 A.2d 527 (1965).

Tennessee: Nashville Trust Co. v. Johnson, 34 Tenn. App. 197, 236 S.W.2d 100 (1951).

See Sales v. Southern Trust Co., 182 Tenn. 270, 185 S.W.2d 623 (1945).

Virginia: Fitzgerald v. Doggett's Exr., 115 Va. 112, 155 S.E. 129 (1930); Owens v. Bank of Glade Spring, 195 Va. 1138, 81 S.E.2d 565 (1954).

Wisconsin: In re Thronson's Estate, 243 Wis. 73, 9 N.W.2d 641 (1943); Estate of Rowell, 248 Wis. 520, 22 N.W.2d 604 (1946).

Canada: See In re Oldfield, [1949] 2 D.L.R. 175 (Man.).

In Reisig v. Associated Jewish Charities of Baltimore, 182 Md. 432, 34 A.2d 842 (1943), the court upheld a devise to the Hebrew University Association, an association that under the laws of Palestine was a legal entity.

In St. Alfred's Temple of Pittsburgh v. Colburn (Colburn v. St. Alfred's Temple), 416 Pa. 214, 205 A.2d 857 (1965), where the money of an unincorporated church was used in the purchase of land in the name of individuals, they held upon a resulting trust for the church. See §440.

As to the validity of a bequest made in trust for or directly to unincorporated noncharitable associations, see §119.

See Note, Charitable gifts; definiteness, 163 A.L.R. 784, 801 (1946).

By California Prob. Code, §27, it is provided that testamentary dispositions may be made to unincorporated religious, benevolent, or fraternal associations or branches of such associations. See also Colorado Rev. Stat. 1973, §7-50-107.

But in In re Estate of Carlson, 9 Cal. App. 3d 479, 88 Cal. Rptr. 229 (1970), it was held that a bequest to an unincorporated noncharitable association failed.

California Prob. Code, §27 (cited in this note) is amended by Laws 1970, c. 965, so as to permit testamentary dispositions to any unincorporated associations or lodges. See also California Corporations Code, §§21200 and 21201, as amended by Laws 1970, c. 965.

By Virginia Code 1950, §§57-18 to 57-21, it is provided that where any gift or devise of land for charitable purposes to an unincorporated body or society is made, whether made directly to it or to it in trust for charitable uses, trustees may be appointed to hold the property.

See Note, Gifts to Unincorporated Associations: Where There's a Will There's a Way, 40 Mod. L. Rev. 231 (1977).

As to trusts for unincorporated noncharitable associations, see §119.

In Estate of King, 39 Or. App. 239, 592 P.2d 231 (1979), a testator made a bequest to an unincorporated church "for general charitable purposes." It was held that the trust did not fail and that after the church became incorporated it could administer the trust.

for the purposes of the association. It is immaterial that the bequest is in the form of a direct gift to the association and that the association has no capacity to take title to the property given to it.

In New York, however, it has been held that a devise or bequest directly to an unincorporated charitable association fails because the association cannot take title to the gift and the testator has failed to state that he is making the gift in trust for one or any of the purposes of the association.[2] The result is that a disposition for charitable purposes fails because of the form in which the disposition is made. It seems absurd to defeat the lawful intention of the testator on a ground which is purely technical. Certainly, in New York a charitable trust may be created although the gift is not expressly stated to be in trust.[3] It is well established in New York that a bequest to an unincorporated branch or subdivision of a charitable corporation does not fail but that the corporation will hold the property for the purposes of the branch or subdivision.[4] The more recent cases

---

In Louisiana a gift to an unincorporated charitable organization is valid. Lord v. District VIII Baptist Convention, 391 So. 2d 942 (La. App. 1981).

[2]Mount v. Tuttle, 183 N.Y. 358, 367, 76 N.E. 873, 2 L.R.A. (N.S.) 428 (1906); Ely v. Megie, 219 N.Y. 112, 143, 113 N.E. 800 (1916); Matter of Idem, 256 A.D. 124, 8 N.Y.S.2d 970 (1939), aff'd, 280 N.Y. 756, 21 N.E.2d 522 (1939) (realty); Fisher v. Lister, 130 Misc. 1, 223 N.Y.S. 321 (1927), mod. in other respects, 222 A.D. 841, 226 N.Y.S. 484 (1928), noted in 37 Yale L.J. 258; Matter of Grossman, 190 Misc. 521, 75 N.Y.S.2d 335 (1947); Matter of Hackett, 37 Misc. 2d 1029, 236 N.Y.S.2d 837 (1962).

See Matter of Merritt, 280 N.Y. 391, 21 N.E.2d 365 (1939); Ratto v. Nashville Trust Co., 178 Tenn. 457, 159 S.W.2d 88, 141 A.L.R. 341 (1942).

[3]Manley v. Fiske, 139 A.D. 665, 124 N.Y.S. 149 (1910), aff'd mem., 201 N.Y. 546, 95 N.E. 1133 (1911); Matter of Durbrow, 245 N.Y. 469, 157 N.E. 747 (1927), noted in 13 Cornell L.Q. 310, 22 Ill. L. Rev. 454; Matter of Idem, 256 A.D. 124, 8 N.Y.S.2d 970 (1939), aff'd, 280 N.Y. 756, 21 N.E.2d 522 (1939) (bequest to unincorporated association for masses); Matter of Merritt, 273 A.D. 79, 75 N.Y.S.2d 828 (1947), aff'g 185 Misc. 979, 61 N.Y.S.2d 537 (1945) (bequest to unincorporated church in England for erection of chapel); Matter of Howell, 109 N.Y.S.2d 270 (1951) (bequest to teachers' loan fund).

[4]Prudential Ins. Co. v. New York Guild for Jewish Blind, 252 A.D. 493, 299 N.Y.S.2d 917 (1937); Matter of Clendenin, 9 N.Y.S.2d 875 (1939); Matter of Farrell, 175 Misc. 430, 24 N.Y.S.2d 49 (1940); Matter of Walters, 172 Misc. 207, 15 N.Y.S.2d 8 (1939), aff'd, 259 A.D. 1078, 21 N.Y.S.2d 37 (1940), mod.

in the lower courts in New York have held that a direct gift to an unincorporated charitable association may be upheld as a charitable trust, the court appointing a competent trustee to administer the trust.[5]

The difficulties that troubled the New York courts have been removed by statutory provisions. By Decedent Estate Law,

---

on other grounds, 285 N.Y. 158, 33 N.E.2d 72 (1941), noted in 20 Chi.-Kent L. Rev. 109, 41 Colum. L. Rev. 1130, 26 Cornell L.Q. 739, 27 Iowa L. Rev. 163, 18 N.Y.U.L.Q. Rev. 603, 50 Yale L.J. 701; New York City Mission Socy. v. Board of Pensions, 261 A.D. 823, 24 N.Y.S.2d 395 (1941), *leave to appeal denied,* 285 N.Y. 862, 33 N.E.2d 568 (1941); Matter of Winslow, 53 N.Y.S.2d 220 (1945); Matter of Lemcke, 53 N.Y.S.2d 253 (1945); Matter of Eaton, 62 N.Y.S.2d 348 (1946); Matter of Stymus, 64 N.Y.S.2d 304 (1946); First Methodist Church of Penn Yan v. Putnam, 189 Misc. 519, 72 N.Y.S.2d 70 (1947); Matter of Sands, 73 N.Y.S.2d 791 (1947); Matter of Jackson, 192 Misc. 618, 81 N.Y.S.2d 48 (1948); Matter of Jones, 90 N.Y.S.2d 598 (1949); Matter of Cromwell, 197 Misc. 734, 95 N.Y.S.2d 746 (1950); Matter of MacKenzie, 197 Misc. 979, 96 N.Y.S.2d 241 (1950); Matter of Martin, 96 N.Y.S.2d 842 (1950); Matter of Levine, 98 N.Y.S.2d 680 (1950); Matter of Lawless, 194 Misc. 844, 87 N.Y.S.2d 386 (1949), *aff'd mem.,* 277 A.D. 1045, 100 N.Y.S.2d 537 (1950); Matter of Lane, 201 Misc. 1003, 106 N.Y.S.2d 987 (1951); Matter of Smith, 129 N.Y.S.2d 130 (1954); Matter of Cornwall, 208 Misc. 1054, 145 N.Y.S.2d 427 (1955); In re Welton's Will, 156 N.Y.S.2d 628 (1956); Matter of Bradford, 17 Misc. 2d 954, 188 N.Y.S.2d 617 (1959); Matter of Bergen, 22 Misc. 2d 762, 193 N.Y.S.2d 817 (1959); In re Estate of Devlin, 46 Misc. 2d 399, 259 N.Y.S.2d 531 (1964).

See Matter of Kunze, 282 A.D. 300, 122 N.Y.S.2d 884 (1953) (noncharitable association).

To the same effect, see Estate of Mealy, 91 Cal. App. 2d 371, 204 P.2d 971 (1949); Hutton v. St. Paul Bhd. of People's Church, 20 Del. Ch. 413, 178 A. 584 (1935); Society for Propagation of Faith v. Joswick, 40 Del. Ch. 260, 180 A.2d 617 (1962); Christian Herald Assn. v. First Natl. Bank, 40 So. 2d 563 (Fla. 1949); In re Pfizer's Estate, 33 N.J. Super. 242, 110 A.2d 40 (1954), *aff'd mem.,* 17 N.J. 40, 110 A.2d 54 (1954) (under New Jersey and New York law); Wachovia Bank & Trust Co. v. Board of Natl. Missions, 226 N.C. 546, 39 S.E.2d 621 (1946).

[5]Matter of Winburn, 139 Misc. 5, 247 N.Y.S. 584 (1931); Matter of Patterson, 139 Misc. 872, 249 N.Y.S. 441 (1931); Matter of Smith, 70 N.Y.S.2d 797 (1947); Matter of Pattberg, 282 A.D. 770, 123 N.Y.S.2d 564 (1953), *aff'd mem.,* 306 N.Y. 835, 118 N.E.2d 903 (1954), noted in 23 Fordham L. Rev. 220; Matter of Bishop, 3 N.Y.2d 294, 144 N.E.2d 63 (1957), *aff'g* 1 A.D.2d 612, 152 N.Y.S.2d 310 (1956) (bequest to an unincorporated hospital in Scotland, authorized by Scottish law to take).

See §97.

§47-e,[6] it was provided that if a devise or bequest is made to an unincorporated association that is authorized to become incorporated by the law of New York or of the jurisdiction in which it has its principal office, the devise or bequest shall not be invalid because of the lack of capacity of the association if it becomes incorporated within one year, or within any period during which the vesting of the devise or bequest is otherwise lawfully postponed by the will, whichever period is greater. It is provided that this shall not limit other methods available for the enforcement of such devise or bequest. In the next year Personal Property Law, §12,[7] was amended by the insertion of the following provision:

> The supreme court and the surrogate's court shall have control over gifts, grants and legacies made for a religious, charitable, educational or benevolent purpose to a corporation or an unincorporated association, and the jurisdiction of the court to prevent failure of such a gift, grant or legacy and give effect to the general purpose thereof is not defeated by the fact that the donee, grantee or legatee does not exist or lacks capacity to take at the time the gift, grant or legacy would otherwise become effective, whether or not the gift, grant or legacy creates an express trust for such purpose.
>
> Where a bequest is made to an unincorporated association that never existed or had ceased to exist at the death of the testator or subsequently ceased to exist, the charitable trust does not fail where the existence of the particular organization is not

---

[6]As inserted by New York Laws 1952, c. 832, as recommended by the Law Revision Commission. Decedent Estate Law, §47-e is superseded by Estates, Powers and Trusts Law, §3-1.3.

See Note, Devise or Bequest to Unincorporated Association, 19 Brooklyn L. Rev. 113 (1952).

In Matter of Staheli, 158 N.Y.S.2d 317 (1956), where a testatrix made a bequest to a certain convalescent home that was an unincorporated activity of a religious corporation, and at her death in 1954 the home had ceased to exist, it was held that under the doctrine of cy pres the bequest should be paid to the corporation to be used in a similar charitable activity.

[7]New York Personal Property Law, §12(2-a), as inserted by Laws 1953, c. 715. There is a similar provision as to real estate in N.Y. Real Property Law, §113(2-a). Personal Property Law, §12, and Real Property Law, §113, are superseded by Estates, Powers and Trusts Law, §8-1.1, amended by Laws 1971, c. 1058, and Laws 1985, c. 492.

of the essence of the gift and where the primary purpose of the testator was that the property should be applied to the charitable purposes of the association.[8] But where the identity of the association is of the essence of the gift, the disposition fails.[9]

§397.3. **Gift to a charitable corporation.** Where property is devised or bequeathed to a charitable corporation, and the gift fails because the corporation is unable or unwilling to take the property, the question arises whether the disposition fails altogether. The question arises where the corporation renounces the gift, or where it is incapable of taking title to the property or of administering it for the intended purposes, or where the corporation never existed or has ceased to exist. The answer depends on whether the testator manifested an intention merely to make a gift to the corporation or whether he manifested a more general intention to devote the property to certain charitable purposes.

Where a testator devises or bequeaths property to a charitable corporation to be applied to a particular charitable purpose, it is to be inferred that the application of the property to the designated purpose is the testator's primary intention, and that the choice of the organization to make the application is second-

---

[8]*Rhode Island:* Industrial Natl. Bank of Providence v. Nugent, 97 R.I. 187, 197 A.2d 278 (1964).

Australia: In re Goodson, [1971] Vict. Rep. 801.

Canada: In re Scott, 11 D.L.R.2d 223 (Ont. 1957); In re Abbott, 45 D.L.R.3d 478 (Sask. 1974).

New Zealand: In re Cohen, [1954] N.Z.L.R. 1097.

[9]Morristown Trust Co. v. Morristown, 82 N.J. Eq. 521, 91 A. 736 (1913); Matter of Hackett, 37 Misc. 2d 1029, 236 N.Y.S.2d 837 (1962).

In In re Thackrah, [1939] 2 All E.R. 4, noted in 13 Austl. L.J. 241, 1939 Scots Law Times 166, where a bequest was made to the secretary or other proper officer of the Oxford Group, which was not an association with a constitution or membership list but was a name for a group of persons who had "surrendered their lives to God," it was held that the bequest was not for a charitable purpose and was invalid.

In Matter of Jones, 201 Misc. 881, 108 N.Y.S.2d 812 (1951), where a testatrix gave a legacy to an unincorporated church that was a subsidiary of an incorporated church, but the unincorporated church was dissolved prior to her death, and the testatrix intended to benefit only the unincorporated church, the court held that the cy pres doctrine was inapplicable and the legacy failed.

ary. In such a case the fact that the corporation named is unwilling or unable to accept the gift and to apply the property to the designated purpose does not cause the disposition to fail. Even though the gift is to a corporation for its general purposes, the disposition does not fail if the primary intention of the testator was that the property should be applied to those purposes, and the choice of the particular donee was merely incidental and not of the essence.

Disclaimer. The question of the failure of the disposition arises where it is made to a corporation that refuses to accept the gift. If the identity of the donee is not of the essence of the gift, the disposition will not fail.[1] Thus where a testator left the

§397.3. [1]*England:* In re Packe, [1918] 1 Ch. 437; In re Woodhams (Decd.); Lloyds Bank v. London College of Music, [1981] 1 W.L.R. 493 (Ch. Div.) (bequest to two musical colleges to establish scholarships for "absolute orphans"; colleges would not accept restriction to orphans because the government paid the expenses of orphans; restriction deleted).

California: Estate of Faulkner, 128 Cal. App. 2d 575, 275 P.2d 818 (1954) (citing Restatement of Trusts §§397, 399).

Connecticut: Dailey v. City of New Haven, 60 Conn. 314, 22 A. 945, 14 L.R.A. 69 (1891).

District of Columbia: Noel v. Olds, 78 App. D.C. 155, 138 F.2d 581 (1943), *cert. denied,* 321 U.S. 773 (1945) (quoting the text), s.c. 80 App. D.C. 63, 149 F.2d 13 (1945), s.c. *sub nom.* Olds v. Rollins College, 84 App. D.C. 299, 173 F.2d 639 (1949), noted in 32 Geo. L.J. 425, 43 Mich. L. Rev. 211, 27 N.C.L. Rev. 591, 35 Va. L. Rev. 649.

Illinois: But see Matter of Estate of Offerman, 153 Ill. App. 3d 299, 186 Ill. Dec. 107, 505 N.E.2d 413 (1987).

Maine: Manufacturers Natl. Bank v. Woodward, 138 Me. 70, 21 A.2d 705 (1941), 140 Me. 117, 34 A.2d 471 (1943), 141 Me. 28, 38 A.2d 657 (1944).

New Jersey: Rowe v. Davis, 138 N.J. Eq. 122, 47 A.2d 36 (1946); Mirinda v. King, 11 N.J. Super. 165, 78 A.2d 98 (1951).

New York: City Bank Farmers Trust Co. v. Arnold, 268 N.Y. 297, 197 N.E. 288 (1935); City Bank Farmers Trust Co. v. Arnold, 283 N.Y. 184, 27 N.E.2d 984 (1940); Matter of Duke, 181 Misc. 529, 41 N.Y.S.2d 745 (1943).

Ohio: Danner v. Shanafelt, 159 Ohio St. 5, 110 N.E.2d 772 (1953).

Pennsylvania: Mear's Estate, 299 Pa. 217, 149 A. 157 (1930).

New Zealand: In re Strong, [1956] N.Z.L.R. 275.

In Howard Sav. Inst. v. Peep, 34 N.J. 494, 170 A.2d 39 (1961) (citing the text and Restatement of Trusts §399), noted in 40 N.C.L. Rev. 308, *aff'g* Howard Sav. Inst. v. Trustees of Amherst College, 61 N.J. Super. 119, 160 A.2d 177 (1960), noted in 61 Colum. L. Rev. 111, 40 N.C.L. Rev. 308, 36 Notre Dame Law, 74, 16 Rutgers L. Rev. 366, 36 Tul. L. Rev. 176, where a testator

residue of his estate to Harvard University to found a course of lectures in eugenics in accordance with the principles contained in a book written by the testator, and the corporation of Harvard refused to accept the legacy, it was held that the gift did not fail and that another college might be appointed by the court to receive the legacy and to apply it to the giving of such a course.[2] The primary purpose of the testator was that the lectures should be given and not that they should be given at the institution that he named. On the other hand, where the identity of the donee is of the essence of the gift, and the donee renounces, the disposition fails.[3]

---

made a bequest to Amherst College for scholarships for "deserving American born, Protestant, Gentile boys of good moral repute, not given to gambling, smoking, drinking or similar acts" and the college refused to accept the bequest because of the religious restrictions, it was held that under the cy pres doctrine the bequest should be given to the college free of the religious restrictions.

In In re Lysaght, [1966] Ch. 191, noted in 82 Law Q. Rev. 9, where a testatrix left money to apply the income for scholarships in a medical college, excluding students of the Jewish or Roman Catholic faith, the college refused to accept the legacy subject to the restrictions. The court held that under the cy pres power it would permit the college to receive the legacy free of the restrictions.

In Weaver Trust, 43 D.&C.2d 245 (1967), where a settlor by deed of trust gave property to a trust company and provided that it should report annually to a college the amount of income available, and that the college officers should distribute it as scholarships among deserving, white, male Protestant students, and after some years the college notified the trustee that such a discrimination among students was against its policy, and that it would not certify students for the scholarships, the court refused to remove the restriction, and held that the trustee may adopt a plan for the selection of students.

As to the effect of racial and religious restrictions, see §399.4.

[2]Mears's Estate, 299 Pa. 217, 149 A. 157 (1930), noted in 39 Yale L.J. 1219.

See Jordan v. Warnke, 205 Cal. App. 2d 621, 23 Cal. Rptr. 300 (1962).

[3]*Colorado:* See Estate of Nicholson, 104 Colo. 561, 93 P.2d 880 (1939) (citing Restatement of Trusts §397), noted in 12 Rocky Mtn. L. Rev. 40.

Illinois: Chicago Daily News Fresh Air Fund v. Kerner, 305 Ill. App. 237, 27 N.E.2d 310 (1940).

Indiana: See In re Lowe's Estate, 117 Ind. App. 554, 70 N.E.2d 187 (1946).

Iowa: Simmons v. Parsons College, 256 N.W.2d 225 (Iowa 1977) (gift over to testator's heirs if trustee should fail to perform).

Kentucky: Hampton v. O'Rear, 309 Ky. 1, 215 S.W.2d 539 (1948).

Incapacity.   The question of the failure of the disposition arises where it is made to a corporation for certain charitable purposes and the corporation, although it has capacity to take title to the property, has no capacity to administer a trust for the particular purposes. Thus it has been held that where land was conveyed to a school district for the purpose of supplying water to the community, and the school district was not empowered to hold land for such a purpose because it was not germane to its corporate purposes, the trust did not fail but the court would appoint a trustee to administer it.[4]

Massachusetts: Bowden v. Brown, 200 Mass. 269, 86 N.E. 351, 128 Am. St. Rep. 419 (1908).

New Jersey: Bankers Trust Co. v. New York Women's League for Animals, 23 N.J. Super. 170, 92 A.2d 820 (1952), *rev'g* 17 N.J. Super. 398, 86 A.2d 138 (1952).

New York: Matter of Herr, N.Y.L.J., Nov. 25, 1942, p. 1612, col. 6; Matter of Colgan, 204 Misc. 109, 120 N.Y.S.2d 683 (1953); Matter of Zumstine, 13 A.D.2d 780, 215 N.Y.S.2d 11 (1961), *aff'g* 23 Misc. 2d 305, 200 N.Y.S.2d 861 (1960), *aff'd mem.*, 10 N.Y.2d 957, 180 N.E.2d 60 (1961).

Rhode Island: Edwards v. De Simone, 105 R.I. 335, 787, 252 A.2d 327 (1969).

Canada: In re Metcalfe, 29 D.L.R.3d 60 (Ont. 1972).

In White's Estate, 340 Pa. 92, 16 A.2d 394, 131 A.L.R. 1273 (1940), where a mother bequeathed property to a charitable home as compensation for taking care of her defective daughter after her death, and the home refused to receive the daughter and renounced the legacy and the daughter died shortly thereafter, it was held that the bequest should not be applied cy pres.

[4]Stowell v. Prentiss, 323 Ill. 309, 154 N.E. 120, 50 A.L.R. 584 (1926), noted in 31 Law Notes 133.

In Barclay Estate, 18 D.&C.2d 489 (Pa. 1959), a testatrix left a legacy to a college or university in Germany to be designated by her or her niece, the income to be used for specified purposes. No such designation was made by her or her niece. Under German law, colleges and universities have no power to act as trustees for specific purposes but legacies to them become a part of their general assets. The court held that the money bequeathed should be given to two trustees in Pennsylvania to disburse the income in Germany for the designated purposes.

In In re Armitage, [1972] Ch. 438, where the trustee was directed to make annual payments to a town council for nursing homes for elderly women, and the council lacked power to act, it was held that the trust did not fail.

In Matter of Gerber, 652 P.2d 937 (Utah 1982), property was bequeathed to a church for a children's hospital run by it. The church transferred the hospital to a nonprofit corporation before the death of the testatrix. It was held that the bequest should be applied cy pres to the corporation for the benefit of the hospital.

The question of the failure of the disposition arises also where it is made to a corporation that does not have capacity to accept the gift. If the purpose of the gift and not the identity of the donee was the primary consideration of the testator, the disposition does not fail but the court will appoint a trustee to apply the property to the intended purposes.[5] In *Chase v. Dickey,* [6] Mary Baker G. Eddy, the founder of Christian Science, left the residue of her estate to the First Church of Christ, Scientist, in Boston, Massachusetts, in trust to keep in repair the church building and other buildings belonging to the church and to use the balance of the income for the promotion and extension of the religion of Christian Science. The heirs at law of the testatrix claimed the property on the ground that by statute the income of gifts made to or for the use of any one church should not exceed $2000 a year. The Attorney General contended that the church should not be permitted to take the property because it already had property giving an income of the amount specified in the statute. The court held that because the Commonwealth had raised the objection of the statute, the church should not be permitted to take the property. Because the gift was not made to the church for its own special needs, however, but for the broader purpose of promoting and extending the Christian Science religion, it was not an absolute gift to the church but a gift to it in trust for these broader purposes. Although the statute precludes the acceptance of the gift by the church, whether the gift is an absolute gift to it or a gift in trust for broader charitable purposes, the court held that the trust would not be permitted

---

[5]*California:* Estate of Barter, 30 Cal. 2d 549, 184 P.2d 305 (1947), *aff'g* 177 P.2d 574 (1947) (bequest to the British government for benefit of British refugee children).

Connecticut: Dailey v. City of New Haven, 60 Conn. 314, 22 A. 945, 14 L.R.A. 69 (1891).

Massachusetts: Chase v. Dickey, 212 Mass. 555, 99 N.E. 410 (1912).

See Hubbard v. Worcester Art Museum, 194 Mass. 280, 80 N.E. 490, 9 L.R.A. (N.S.) 689, 10 Ann. Cas. 1025 (1907).

Nebraska: Stork v. Evangelical Lutheran Synod, 129 Neb. 311, 261 N.W. 552 (1935).

In In re Hill's Will, 261 Wis. 290, 52 N.W.2d 867 (1952), where property was left to a charitable foundation to be used for a particular charitable purpose and the purpose was not included in its articles, the corporation was entitled to the property if it should amend its articles.

[6]212 Mass. 555, 567, 99 N.E. 410 (1912).

to fail because of the incapacity of the trustee to take the property and administer the trust. Chief Justice Rugg said:

> The facts disclosed on the record and appearing in the will do not lead to the conclusion that the intent of the testatrix was fixed on the donee named so profoundly that if the donee fails the gift fails. The purpose of the gift and the trustee are not so inextricably combined that they must stand or fall together. The support of a branch of the Christian religion being the declared purpose of the trust and this being a public charity, the gift will stand unless it appears that the discretion of the particular trustee named is of the essence. There is disclosed no exceptional reliance upon the particular corporation named beyond that which appears commonly. The establishment of the trust does not seem to depend upon the particular instrument for execution nominated in the will. It is the not unusual case of a plain charitable intent, where the legatee is incapable of taking, and the trust is not permitted to fail for lack of a trustee.

On the other hand, where the identity of the donee is of the essence of the gift, and the donee has no capacity to take the gift, the disposition fails.

Nonexistence. The question of the failure of the disposition also arises where it is made to a corporation that never existed or had ceased to exist at the time when the disposition was made or subsequently ceased to exist. Where the existence of the particular organization is not of the essence of the gift, where the primary purpose of the testator was that the property should be applied to certain charitable purposes, the disposition does not fail.[7] On the other hand, where the identity of the donee is

[7]*England:* In re Davis, [1902] 1 Ch. 876; In re Magrath, [1913] 2 Ch. 331; In re Wedgwood, [1914] 2 Ch. 245; In re Harwood, [1936] 1 Ch. 285; In re Knox, [1937] Ch. 109, noted in 1 Convey. (N.S.) 274; In re Tharp, [1943] 1 All E.R. 257, *rev'g* [1942] 2 All E.R. 358, noted in 7 Convey. (N.S.) 104, 8 id. 42, 59 Law Q. Rev. 22, 117; In re Lucas, [1948] Ch. 424, *rev'g* [1948] Ch. 175; In re Gartside, [1949] 2 All E.R. 546, noted in 208 Law T. 231; In re Kellner's Will Trusts, [1950] Ch. 46; In re Hutchinson's Will Trusts, [1953] Ch. 387; In re Little, [1953] 2 All E.R. 852; In re Bagshaw, [1954] 1 All E.R. 227; In re Roberts, [1963] 1 All E.R. 674; In re Satterthwaite's Will Trusts, [1966] 1 All E.R. 919; In re Finger's Will Trusts, [1972] 1 Ch. 286; In re Vernon's Will

Trusts, [1972] 1 Ch. 300; Re Koeppler's Will Trusts; Barclays Bank Trust Co. v. Slack, [1986] 1 Ch. 423; [1985] 2 All E.R. 869 (C.A.).

Alabama: Frye v. Community Chest, 241 Ala. 591, 4 So. 2d 140 (1941).

California: In re Estate of Lamb, 19 Cal. App. 3d 859, 97 Cal. Rptr. 46 (1971) (citing the text and Restatement of Trusts §399); In re Estate of Connolly, 48 Cal. App. 3d 129, 121 Cal. Rptr. 325 (1975) (citing the text and Restatement of Trusts §397).

Connecticut: Ministers & Missionaries Benefit Bd. v. Meriden Trust & Safe Deposit Co., 139 Conn. 435, 94 A.2d 917 (1953).

Delaware: Marvel v. Sadtler, 25 Del. Ch. 288, 18 A.2d 231 (1941).

Florida: Christian Herald Assn. v. First Natl. Bank, 40 So. 2d 563 (Fla. 1949); In re Williams' Estate, 59 So. 2d 13 (Fla. 1952).

Georgia: Goree v. Georgia Indus. Home, 187 Ga. 368, 200 S.E. 684 (1938); Houston v. Mills Memorial Home, 202 Ga. 540, 43 S.E.2d 680 (1947); Creech v. Scottish Rite Hosp. for Crippled Children, 211 Ga. 195, 84 S.E.2d 563 (1954); Hines v. Village of St. Joseph, 227 Ga. 431, 181 S.E.2d 54 (1971).

Iowa: Starr v. Morningside College, 186 Iowa 790, 173 N.W. 231 (1919); Lupton v. Leander Clark College, 194 Iowa 1008, 187 N.W. 496 (1922).

Kansas: Daughters of the Am. Revolution of Kan., Topeka Chapter v. Washburn College, 160 Kan. 583, 164 P.2d 128 (1945); Estate of Coleman, 2 Kan. App. 2d 567, 584 P.2d 1255 (1978) (divided between other charitable legatees).

Kentucky: Kentucky Children's Home v. Woods, 289 Ky. 20, 157 S.W.2d 473 (1941); Orphan Socy. of Lexington v. Board of Educ., 437 S.W.2d 194 (Ky. 1969).

Maine: Lynch v. South Congregational Parish, 109 Me. 32, 82 A. 432 (1912).

See Snow v. President & Trustees of Bowdoin College, 133 Me. 195, 175 A. 268 (1934), noted in 34 Mich. L. Rev. 142.

Maryland: Loats Female Orphan Asylum v. Essom, 220 Md. 11, 150 A.2d 742 (1959); Miller v. Mercantile-Safe Deposit & Trust Co., 224 Md. 380, 168 A.2d 184 (1961) (citing the text and Restatement (Second) of Trusts, §399, Comment *o*), noted in 22 Md. L. Rev. 340; Wesley Home v. Mercantile-Safe Deposit & Trust Co., 265 Md. 185, 289 A.2d 337 (1972).

Massachusetts: Old Colony Trust Co. v. Winchester Home for Aged Women, 324 Mass. 258, 85 N.E.2d 622 (1949); Sleeper v. Camp Menotomy, 352 Mass. 47, 223 N.E.2d 696 (1967) (citing the text).

See Old Colony Trust Co. v. Board of Governors, 355 Mass. 776, 247 N.E.2d 583 (1969).

Missouri: Board of Trustees of Hannibal Presbytery v. Taylor, 359 Mo. 417, 221 S.W.2d 964 (1949), noted in 18 U. Kan. City L. Rev. 78; First Natl. Bank of Kansas City v. Jacques, 470 S.W.2d 557 (Mo. 1971) (citing the text and Restatement of Trusts §399). But see American Cancer Socy., Mo. Div. v. Damon Runyon Memorial Fund for Cancer Research, 409 S.W.2d 222 (Mo. App. 1966), noted in 32 Mo. L. Rev. 583 (1967), §397, n. 15, *supra.*

New Jersey: Reed v. Institute of Musical Art, 141 N.J. Eq. 111, 56 A.2d 124

(1947); Burlington County Trust Co. v. New Jersey Socy., 12 N.J. Super. 369, 79 A.2d 710 (1951) (citing Restatement of Trusts, §399, Comment *j*).

New York: Sherman v. Richmond Hose Co., 230 N.Y. 462, 130 N.E. 613 (1921); Matter of Walter, 150 Misc. 512, 269 N.Y.S. 400 (1934); New York City Mission Socy. v. Board of Pensions, 261 A.D. 823, 24 N.Y.S.2d 395 (1941), *leave to appeal denied,* 285 N.Y. 862, 33 N.E.2d 568 (1941); Matter of Hoagland, 74 N.Y.S.2d 156 (1947), *aff'd mem.,* 272 A.D. 1040, 74 N.Y.S.2d 911 (1947), *aff'd mem.,* 297 N.Y. 920, 79 N.E.2d 746 (1948); Matter of Dillenback, 189 Misc. 538, 74 N.Y.S.2d 473 (1947), *aff'd mem.,* 273 A.D. 1051, 81 N.Y.S.2d 169 (1948); Matter of Martin, 96 N.Y.S.2d 842 (1950) (citing the text and Restatement of Trusts, §397, Comment *h*); Matter of Potter, 307 N.Y. 504, 121 N.E.2d 522 (1954), *rev'g* 281 A.D. 981, 120 N.Y.S.2d 636 (1953); Matter of Dobbins, 206 Misc. 64, 132 N.Y.S.2d 236 (1954) (to nonexistent organization for masses); In re Olmsted's Will, 133 N.Y.S.2d 197 (1954); Matter of Clark, 1 Misc. 2d 869, 150 N.Y.S.2d 65 (1956); Matter of Kittinger, 6 Misc. 2d 125, 160 N.Y.S.2d 214 (1957); Matter of Sanders, 7 Misc. 2d 800, 161 N.Y.S.2d 982 (1957); Matter of Wolf, 7 Misc. 2d 799, 162 N.Y.S.2d 645 (1957); Matter of Bank, 10 Misc. 2d 492, 169 N.Y.S.2d 528 (1957); Matter of Bowne, 11 Misc. 2d 597, 173 N.Y.S.2d 723 (1958); Matter of Goodrich, 17 Misc. 2d 503, 186 N.Y.S.2d 879 (1959); Matter of Phoenix, 18 Misc. 2d 1025, 189 N.Y.S.2d 963 (1959); Matter of McCarthy, 49 A.D.2d 204, 374 N.Y.S.2d 203 (1975); Matter of Estate of Brown, 109 A.D.2d 955, 486 N.Y.S.2d 446 (1985).

Ohio: Fenn College v. Nance, 4 Ohio Misc. 183, 210 N.E.2d 418 (1965) (citing the text); American Diabetes Assn. v. Diabetes Socy. of Clinton County, 31 Ohio App. 3d 136, 31 O.B.R. 224, 509 N.E.2d 84 (1986).

Oklahoma: In re Nuckols' Estate, 199 Okla. 175, 184 P.2d 778 (1947); Estate of Shaw, 620 P.2d 483 (Okla. App. 1980).

Oregon: Quick v. Hayter (In re Stouffer's Trust), 188 Or. 218, 215 P.2d 374 (1950) (citing Restatement of Trusts §399).

Pennsylvania: Craig Estate, 356 Pa. 564, 52 A.2d 650 (1947); In re Kensington Hosp. for Women Case, 358 Pa. 458, 58 A.2d 154, 3 A.L.R.2d 73 (1948), noted in 10 U. Pitt. L. Rev. 101; Abel v. Girard Trust Co., 365 Pa. 44, 73 A.2d 682 (1950) (citing the text), noted in 24 Temp. L.Q. 373; Bangor Park Assn. Case, 370 Pa. 442, 88 A.2d 769 (1952); Dobbins Estate, 4 D.&C.2d 763 (Pa. 1955); Dwier Estate, 5 D.&C.2d 371 (Pa. 1955); Brooks Estate, 2 Fiduciary Rep. 57 (Pa. 1952); Women's Homeopathic Hosp. of Philadelphia Case, 393 Pa. 313, 142 A.2d 292 (1958); Turner Estate, 28 D.&C.2d 251 (Pa. 1962) (citing Restatement of Trusts §399); Schimpf Estate, 57 D.&C.2d 35 (Pa. 1972) (citing Restatement of Trusts §399); Pennsylvania Home Teaching Socy., 69 D.&C.2d 1 (Pa. 1975).

In Kay Estate, 456 Pa. 43, 317 A.2d 193, 67 A.L.R.3d 427 (1974), where there was a legacy to a nonexistent home for the blind, the court held that under cy pres the legacy should be divided between two institutions for the blind.

Rhode Island: Rhode Island Hosp. Trust Co. v. Williams, 50 R.I. 385, 148 A. 189, 74 A.L.R. 664 (1929); Wood v. Hartigan, 59 R.I. 333, 195 A. 507 (1937); Rhode Island Hosp. Trust Natl. Bank v. Israel, 119 R.I. 298, 377 A.2d 341 (1977) (citing Restatement of Trusts §399).

Tennessee: First Am. Natl. Bank v. DeWitt, 511 S.W.2d 698 (Tenn. App. 1974).

Texas: Stahl v. Shriner's Hosp., 581 S.W.2d 227 (Tex. Civ. App. 1979), *rev'd on other grounds,* 610 S.W.2d 147 (Texas 1981).

West Virginia: Stephenson v. Kuntz, 131 W. Va. 599, 49 S.E.2d 235 (1948).

Wisconsin: Will of Lott, 193 Wis. 409, 214 N.W. 391 (1927); Estate of Bletsch, 25 Wis. 2d 40, 130 N.W.2d 275 (1964); In In re Estate of Ganser, 79 Wis. 2d 180, 255 N.W.2d 483 (1977), a testatrix made a devise in trust for "Marquette University for its medical school." The medical school later severed its ties with the university but continued to be associated with it. It was held that the devise did not fail.

Australia: In re Mulcahy, [1969] Vict. Rep. 545; In re Daniels, [1970] Vict. Rep. 72; In re Constable, [1971] Vict. Rep. 742; In re Tyrie, [1972] Vict. Rep. 168; In re Flynn, [1975] Vict. Rep. 633; In re Bryning, [1976] Vict. Rep. 100.

Canada: In re Hogle, [1939] 4 D.L.R. 817 (Ont.); In re Brown, [1950] 1 D.L.R. 777 (N.S.); In re Smith, [1953] 3 D.L.R. 510 (B.C.); In re Armour, 38 D.L.R.2d 204 (Sask. 1963); In re Johnston, 66 D.L.R.2d 688 (Ont. 1968); In re Boyd, 6 D.L.R.3d 110 (Ont. 1969); In re Barnes, 72 D.L.R.3d 651 (Alta. 1976); In re Jacobsen, 80 D.L.R.3d 122 (B.C. 1977); In Re Roberts, [1981] 120 D.L.R.3d 74 (P.E.I.S.C.); Montreal Trust Co. v. Richards, [1983] 1 W.W.R. 437, 40 B.C.L.R. 114 (B.C. S. Ct.); Re Ellis, 43 Sask. R. 38 (Sur. 1985).

In Guilford Trust Co. v. La Fleur, 148 Me. 162, 91 A.2d 17 (1952), where a testator left his estate to a high school of a town that before his death was enlarged to include other towns, it was held that the legacy did not fail because the school still existed, and that it was unnecessary to resort to the doctrine of cy pres.

See Note, Cy pres doctrine as affected by sectarian or doctrinal differences or factors, 3 A.L.R.2d 78 (1949).

By New York Estates, Powers and Trusts Law, §8-1.1, amended by Laws 1971, c. 1058, and Laws 1985, c. 492, it is provided: "The supreme court and the surrogate's court shall have control over gifts, grants and legacies made for a religious, charitable, educational or benevolent purpose to a corporation or an unincorporated association, and the jurisdiction of the court to prevent failure of such a gift, grant or legacy and give effect to the general purpose thereof is not defeated by the fact that the donee, grantee or legatee does not exist or lacks capacity to take at the time the gift, grant or legacy would otherwise become effective, whether or not the gift, grant or legacy creates an express trust for such purpose." See §397.2, n. 7.

By the Pennsylvania Corporation Not-for-Profit Code, 15 Pa. Cons. Stat., §7552, enacted by Laws 1972, c. 271, it is provided that "a devise, bequest or gift to be effective in the future, in trust or otherwise, to or for a nonprofit corporation which has (1) changed its purposes; (2) sold, leased away or exchanged all or substantially all its property and assets; (3) been converted into a business corporation; (4) become a party to a consolidation or a division; (5) become a party to a merger which it did not survive; or (6) been dissolved; after the execution of the document containing such devise, bequest or gift shall be effective only as a court having jurisdiction over the assets may order under the Estates Act of 1947 or other applicable provision of law."

By the National Health Service Act, 1946, 9 & 10 Geo. VI, c. 81, it is provided that on July 5, 1948, the property of voluntary hospitals and hospitals vested in a local authority vests in the Minister of Health, free of any trust then existing, and the Minister may use such property for the purpose of any of his functions under the act, but shall so far as practicable secure that the objects for which any such property was then used are not prejudiced. As to the effect of this legislation on testamentary gifts to hospitals made before or after the appointed day, see In re Gartside, [1949] 2 All E.R. 546; In re Kellner's Will Trusts, [1950] Ch. 46; Minister of Health v. Fox, [1950] Ch. 369; In re Morgan's Will Trusts, [1950] Ch. 637, noted in 209 Law T. 342, 94 Sol. J. 622; In re Glass' Will Trusts, [1950] 2 All E.R. 953; In re Meyers, [1951] 1 All E.R. 538; In re Frere, [1951] Ch. 27; Royal College of Surgeons v. National Provincial Bank, [1952] A.C. 631, rev'g In re Bland-Sutton's Will Trusts, [1951] Ch. 485, aff'g [1951] Ch. 70, noted in 11 Camb. L.J. 435, 94 Sol. J. 795; In re Hunter, [1951] Ch. 190; In re Ginger, [1951] 1 All E.R. 422; In re Marjoribanks, [1952] Ch. 181; In re Couchman, [1952] Ch. 391; In re Lowry's Will Trusts, [1967] Ch. 638; In re Vernon's Will Trusts, [1972] 1 Ch. 300.

See also In re Pearson, [1951] N. Ir. L. Rep. 152; Montrose Maternity Hosp. Govan, [1948] Sess. Cas. 491 (Scot.); Board of Management for Dundee Gen. Hosp. v. Bell's Trustees, [1950] Sess. Cas. 406 (Scot.).

See Speller, Law Relating to Hospitals (2d ed. 1949); 206 Law T. 124 (1948).

In First Natl. Bank of Chicago v. King Edward's Hosp. Fund, 1 Ill. App. 2d 338, 117 N.E.2d 656 (1954), a testator who died in 1936 left his estate in trust for certain beneficiaries for life and on their deaths to a London hospital. It was held that the gift over did not fail because of the nationalization of the hospital in 1946.

In Pennsylvania Co. for Banking & Trusts v. Board of Governors of London Hosp., 79 R.I. 74, 83 A.2d 881 (1951), noted in 65 Harv. L. Rev. 704, a testator left property in trust for several beneficiaries for life and, on the death of the survivor, for such charitable purposes as his executrix might select. The testator died in 1882, and the executrix selected various charitable institutions including a London hospital, and the selection was approved by the court. After the death of the last survivor of the beneficiaries the trustees brought suit for instructions. It was held that the trust failed because the hospital was taken over by the Ministry of Health under the National Health Service Act, 1946. But the same court held that a similar trust did not fail where the nationalization took place after the testator's death, although before the death of a life beneficiary. Rhode Island Hosp. Trust Co. v. Johnston, 81 R.I. 115, 99 A.2d 12 (1953).

In New York the Court of Appeals has upheld bequests to English and Scottish hospitals that were nationalized after the testator's death. Matter of Ablett, 3 N.Y.2d 261, 144 N.E.2d 46 (1957), aff'g 2 A.D.2d 205, 153 N.Y.S.2d 816 (1956), aff'g 206 Misc. 157, 132 N.Y.S.2d 488 (1954); Matter of Perkins, 3 N.Y.2d 281, 144 N.E.2d 56 (1957), aff'g 2 A.D.2d 655, 152 N.Y.S.2d 315 (1956), aff'g 1 Misc. 2d 589, 145 N.Y.S.2d 775 (1954); Matter of Bishop, 3 N.Y.2d 294, 144 N.E.2d 63 (1957), aff'g 1 A.D.2d 612, 152 N.Y.S.2d 310

of the essence of the gift, and the donee is a corporation that has never existed or has ceased to exist, the disposition fails.[8] Where

---

(1956), *aff'g* 206 Misc. 7, 129 N.Y.S.2d 387 (1954), noted in 40 Cornell L.Q. 163.

See Note, Division of charitable gift among several claimants where named donee is nonexistent, 67 A.L.R.3d 442 (1975).

[8] *England:* Clark v. Taylor, 1 Drew, 642 (1853); In re Ovey, 29 Ch. D. 560 (1885); In re Rymer, [1895] 1 Ch. 19; In re Harwood, [1936] Ch. 285; In re Goldney, 115 L.J. Ch. 337 (1946); In re Slatter's Will Trusts, [1964] Ch. 512; In re Stemson's Will Trusts, [1970] Ch. 16; In re Spence, Dec'd, [1978] 3 W.L.R. 483, [1978] 3 All E.R. 92, [1979] 1 Ch. 483.

California: Estate of Klinkner, 85 Cal. App. 3d 942, 151 Cal. Rptr. 20 (1978) (citing Restatement of Trusts, §397, Comment *f*).

Connecticut: Duncan v. Higgins, 129 Conn. 136, 26 A.2d 849 (1942) (citing the text); Mears v. Conway, 17 Conn. 319 (1951).

Illinois: Miller v. Riddle, 227 Ill. 53, 81 N.E. 48, 118 Am. St. Rep. 261 (1907); Quimby v. Quimby, 175 Ill. App. 367 (1912).

Iowa: In re Estate of Staab, 173 N.W.2d 866 (Iowa 1970).

Kansas: Estate of Coleman, 2 Kan. App. 2d 567, 584 P.2d 1255 (1978).

In In re Estate of Loomis, 202 Kan. 668, 451 P.2d 195 (1968), the court held invalid a bequest to a proposed home for the aged. But query.

Kentucky: State Bank & Trust Co. of Harrodsburg v. Vandyke, 311 Ky. 202, 223 S.W.2d 750 (1949); Dunn v. Ellis, 245 S.W.2d 945 (Ky. 1952).

Maine: Brooks v. Belfast, 90 Me. 318, 38 A. 222 (1897); Bancroft v. Maine State Sanatorium Assn., 119 Me. 56, 109 A. 585 (1920); First Universalist Socy. of Bath v. Swett, 148 Me. 142, 90 A.2d 812 (1952), noted in 5 Baylor L. Rev. 205.

Mississippi: National Bank of Greece v. Savarika, 167 Miss. 571, 148 So. 649 (1933).

Missouri: American Cancer Socy. v. Damon Runyon Memorial Fund, 409 S.W.2d 222 (Mo. App. 1967).

New York: Wright v. Wright, 225 N.Y. 329, 122 N.E. 213 (1919); Matter of Rappolt, 140 Misc. 239, 250 N.Y.S. 377 (1931); Barnum v. D'Hendecourt, 28 N.Y.S.2d 143 (1941); Matter of Brunzel, 51 N.Y.S.2d 483 (1944); Matter of Walker, 185 Misc. 1046, 53 N.Y.S.2d 106 (1944); Matter of Joseph, 62 N.Y.S.2d 197 (1946); Matter of Westheimer, 124 N.Y.S.2d 784 (1953); Matter of Alsop, 127 N.Y.S.2d 551 (1953); Matter of Koons, 206 Misc. 856, 135 N.Y.S.2d 733 (1954); Matter of Aker, 21 A.D.2d 935, 251 N.Y.S.2d 144 (1964).

Ohio: Ward v. Worthington, 28 Ohio App. 325, 162 N.E. 714 (1928), noted in 29 Colum. L. Rev. 90; Cheney v. State Council of Ohio Junior Order of U.A.M., 81 Ohio Abs. 395, 162 N.E.2d 242 (1959).

Pennsylvania: See In re Leffmann's Trust, 378 Pa. 128, 105 A.2d 115 (1954) (terms of trust required separate corporate existence).

Rhode Island: Gladding v. St. Matthew's Church, 25 R.I. 628, 57 A. 860, 65 L.R.A. 225, 105 Am. St. Rep. 904, 1 Ann. Cas. 537 (1904); Industrial Natl.

a bequest is made to a corporation that was in existence at the time of the testator's death but that ceased to exist before the legacy was paid to it, it has been held that the bequest does not fail even though it would have failed if the corporation had ceased to exist at the testator's death.[9]

Bank v. Glocester Manton Free Pub. Library, 107 R.I. 161, 265 A.2d 724 (1970).

Washington: Horton v. Board of Educ., 32 Wash. 2d 99, 201 P.2d 163 (1948) (citing the text), noted in 48 Mich. L. Rev. 127, 25 Wash. L. Rev. 199.

Canada: In re Hart, [1951] 2 D.L.R. 30 (N.S.); In re Ogilvy, [1953] 1 D.L.R. 44 (Ont.); In re Allendorf, 38 D.L.R.2d 459 (Ont. 1963); In re Hunter, 34 D.L.R.3d 602 (B.C. 1973).

In In re Montreal Trust Co. & Boy Scouts of Can. 88 D.L.R.3d 99 (B.C. 1978), it was held that the fact that a charitable corporation had been struck off the register of charities for failure to make reports did not cause it to cease to exist, and that a legacy to it was effective.

In In re Goldschmidt, [1957] 1 All E.R. 513, noted in 73 Law Q. Rev. 166, a testatrix left a legacy to "the Fund for the Relief of Distressed German Jews in England," and left the residue to a hospital. There was no such organization or fund, and the court was asked to give the legacy to certain organizations having a similar purpose. The court held that the testatrix had a particular organization in mind, and that the organization did not exist, and that the legacy fell into the residue. The court said that because the residue was to a charity, there was no reason for finding a general charitable intent as to the legacy that failed.

In First Portland Natl. Bank v. Kaler-Vaill Memorial Home, 155 Me. 50, 151 A.2d 708 (1959), a testator bequeathed a share of the residue to the "Kaler-Vaill Memorial Home located at Scarborough for the general purposes of said Home." His name was Vaill and his wife's name was Kaler. No such home existed at his death. It was held that the disposition failed.

[9]*England:* In re Slevin, [1891] 2 Ch. 236; In re Moon's Will Trusts, [1948] 1 All E.R. 300, noted in 12 Convey. (N.S.) 222.

Indiana: Indiana Masonic Home v. Association of Franciscans, 142 Ind. App. 443, 235 N.E.2d 708 (1968).

Maine: Freme v. Maher, 480 A.2d 783 (Me. 1984) (bequest of residue to incorporated college on trust for its general purposes did not fail when college had been operating at death of testatrix, then ceased to operate before distribution but retained its corporate existence; dictum that cy pres doctrine could be applied if the college could not take).

New Jersey: Fidelity Union Trust Co. v. Ackerman, 18 N.J. Super. 314, 87 A.2d 47 (1952) (quoting the text); Montclair Natl. Bank & Trust Co. v. Seton Hall College of Medicine & Dentistry, 96 N.J. Super. 428, 233 A.2d 195 (1967), rev'g 90 N.J. Super. 419, 217 A.2d 897 (1966).

New York: In re Tapper's Will, 139 N.Y.S.2d 110 (1954); Matter of Leventhal, 27 Misc. 2d 594, 212 N.Y.S.2d 475 (1961).

Misnomer. The cases are numerous in which there is a devise or bequest to a named corporation, but there is in fact no

---

Canada: In re Enderton, [1954] 4 D.L.R. 710 (Man.); In re Gordon, 52 D.L.R.2d 197 (Ont. 1965); Richards v. Central Trust Co., 16 E.T.R. 1 (N.B.Q.B. 1983) (remainder bequeathed to organization that was operating an orphanage when testator died but not when the remainder became possessory).

See Scott-Lees Collegiate Inst. v. Charles, 283 Ky. 234, 140 S.W.2d 1060 (1940); Drake v. Chappel, 288 Ky. 610, 157 S.W.2d 117 (1941); Saunders v. President & Fellows of Harvard College, 318 Mass. 447, 61 N.E.2d 839 (1945); Matter of Mohr, 175 Misc. 706, 24 N.Y.S.2d 977 (1941).

But see Morristown Trust Co. v. Morristown, 82 N.J. Eq. 521, 91 A. 736 (1913); Matter of Hough, 11 Misc. 2d 183, 172 N.Y.S.2d 669 (1958) (corporation ceased to exist prior to enactment of New York Personal Property Law, §12(2-a), now Estates, Powers and Trusts Law, §8-1.1, cited *supra* n. 7).

In Baker Estate, 9 D.&C.2d 125 (Pa. 1957), where there was a bequest to trustees to pay the income to a sanatorium for its general purposes and it subsequently ceased to receive patients but continued its research, it was held that it could apply the income to research. The court said that it was unnecessary to resort to the doctrine of cy pres.

In Montclair Natl. Bank & Trust Co. v. Seton Hall College of Medicine & Dentistry, 90 N.J. Super. 419, 217 A.2d 897 (1966), a bequest was made to a college of medicine that was carrying on its activities at the testator's death but before the legacy was payable it was in process of dissolution. It was held that the legacy should not be paid to the college to be used for the payment of its debts but should be applied cy pres by giving it to a similar institution.

In In re Estate of Daley, 6 Ariz. App. 443, 433 P.2d 296 (1967), it was held that the charitable corporation, though inactive, had not ceased to exist.

In In re Estate of Hermann, 454 Pa. 292, 312 A.2d 16 (1973), where land and objects of art were conveyed to trustees to maintain a museum, and the settlor by will gave money to a bank in trust to pay for the maintenance of the museum with a provision that if the museum should cease to exist the money was to go to other charities, it was held that the sale of the land and the placing of the objects of art in a public library did not cause the museum to cease to exist.

In Town of Lee v. Town of Lincoln, 351 A.2d 554 (Me. 1976), where a school was combined with another school, it was held that the school had not ceased to exist under the terms of the donor's will.

In Matter of Beckley, 63 A.D.2d 855, 405 N.Y.S.2d 861 (1978), where there was doubt which of two charitable institutions was entitled to a legacy, and they agreed to share it, it was held that the surrogate's refusal to allow the compromise was erroneous.

See Note, Charity — Cy-Pres — Supervening Impossibility, 52 Can. B. Rev. 598 (1974).

See §399.3, n. 13.

corporation having that name. In such a case evidence is admissible as to the intention of the testator. It may appear that there are two or more corporations with somewhat similar names, none having the name stated in the will. The misnomer will not ordinarily result in the failure of the devise or bequest, and the property will be given to the corporation that on the evidence appears to have been the one probably intended by the testator.[10]

[10]*England:* In re Spence, Dec'd, [1979] 1 Ch. 483, [1978] 3 W.L.R. 483, [1978] 3 All E.R. 92.

Delaware: Equitable Sec. Trust Co. v. Home for Aged Women, 35 Del. Ch. 553, 123 A.2d 117 (1956).

Illinois: Strong v. Strong, 326 Ill. App. 513, 62 N.E.2d 135 (1945); Hays v. Illinois Indus. Home for the Blind, 12 Ill. 2d 625, 147 N.E.2d 287 (1958); First Natl. Bank of Chicago v. Canton Council of Campfire Girls, 85 Ill.2d 507, 55 Ill. Dec. 824, 426 N.E.2d 1198, (1981).

Iowa: Hollenbeck v. Gray, 185 N.W.2d 767 (Iowa 1971).

Kentucky: Davis v. Cary, 429 S.W.2d 411 (Ky. 1968).

Massachusetts: Pope v. Hinckley, 209 Mass. 323, 95 N.E. 798 (1911); Kingman v. New Bedford Home for Aged, 237 Mass. 323, 129 N.E. 449 (1921); Bosworth v. Massachusetts W.C.T. Union, 299 Mass. 93, 11 N.E.2d 916 (1937); Phipps v. Barbera, 23 Mass. App. 1, 498 N.E.2d 411 (1986), quoting this paragraph.

New Hampshire: In re Morrison's Estate, 106 N.H. 388, 211 A.2d 904 (1965).

New York: Matter of Chapman, 32 N.Y.S.2d 290 (1941); Matter of Comfort, 116 N.Y.S.2d 851 (1952), s.c. 201 Misc. 1119, 113 N.Y.S.2d 876 (1952); In re Yungel's Will, 153 N.Y.S.2d 418 (1956); In re Welton's Will, 156 N.Y.S.2d 628 (1956); In re Little's Will, 157 N.Y.S.2d 340 (1956); Matter of Locke, 7 Misc. 2d 474, 162 N.Y.S.2d 799 (1957); Matter of Momand, 13 Misc. 2d 990, 177 N.Y.S.2d 115 (1958), *rev'd on other grounds,* 7 A.D.2d 280, 182 N.Y.S.2d 565 (1959); Matter of Bergen, 22 Misc. 2d 762, 193 N.Y.S.2d 817 (1959); Matter of Hodges, 26 Misc. 2d 771, 208 N.Y.S.2d 357 (1960).

North Carolina: Redd v. Taylor, 270 N.C. 14, 153 S.E.2d 761 (1967).

Ohio: American Diabetes Assn., v. Diabetes Socy. of Clinton County, 31 Ohio App. 3d 136, 31 O.B.R. 224, 509 N.E.2d 84 (1986).

Pennsylvania: Black Estate, 398 Pa. 390, 158 A.2d 133 (1960); Burch Estate, 64 D.&C.2d 310 (Pa. 1973) (although the name used was that of a corporation not known to the testator).

Canada: In re Johnston, 66 D.L.R.2d 688 (Ont. 1968).

See Berks County Tuberculosis Socy. Appeal (In re Girard Trust Corn Exch. Bank), 418 Pa. 112, 208 A.2d 857 (1965), as to the admissibility of extrinsic evidence.

In In re Raven, [1915] 1 Ch. 673, where a legacy was given to a charitable association and it was provided in the will that if any doubt should arise as to

Merger and consolidation. Where a devise or bequest is made to a charitable corporation that either before or after the death of the testator has been consolidated with another corporation, or has been merged in another corporation, the consolidated corporation or that into which the other has been merged will be entitled to receive the property, unless the settlor manifested a different intention.[11] There are statutes in

---

the identity of the institution intended, the question should be decided by the trustees, and that their decision should be binding, it was held that the provision was invalid as ousting the courts of jurisdiction. It would seem, however, that there is no public policy that should prevent a testator from thus avoiding litigation.

In Estate of Black, 211 Cal. App. 2d 75, 27 Cal. Rptr. 418 (1962), a testatrix left her estate "To The University of Southern California known as The U.C.L.A." The lower court held that extrinsic evidence as to her intention was not admissible and awarded the legacy to the University of California at Los Angeles. The judgment was reversed and the case remanded to admit extrinsic evidence.

In In re Songest, [1956] 2 All E.R. 765, *order varied,* [1956] 3 All E.R. 489, a testatrix left her estate upon trust for the Disabled Soldiers, Sailors and Airmen's Association. There never was such an association. Two societies organized for the care of disabled ex-servicemen each claimed the property. There were no other similar organizations. It was held by the Court of Appeal that, subject to the approval of the Attorney-General, the residue should be equally divided between the two institutions, in order to carry out the general purpose of the testatrix.

In In re Conroy, 35 D.L.R.3d 752 (B.C. 1973), a testator left the residue to "The Cancer fund of British Columbia." There was no such organization. There were two organizations dealing with cancer in British Columbia. The court held that the residue should be divided equally between them.

In Vadman v. American Cancer Socy., 26 Wash. App. 697, 615 P.2d 500 (1980), where the bequest was to a correctly named existing charitable corporation, it was held that evidence was not admissible to show that the testator intended to make the gift to a corporation with a somewhat similar name.

[11]*England:* See In re Dawson's Will Trusts, [1957] 1 All E.R. 177 (merger of unincorporated association).

California: In re Kober Trust Fund, 26 Cal. App. 3d 265, 103 Cal. Rptr. 1 (1972).

Illinois: In re Estate of Fuller, 10 Ill. App. 3d 460, 294 N.E.2d 313 (1973); Strand v. United (Methodist) Church of Sheldon, 16 Ill. App. 3d 744, 307 N.E.2d 621 (1974); In re Estate of Trimmer, 29 Ill. App. 3d 209, 330 N.E.2d 241 (1975) (as to all except land devised with a provision for a gift over on dissolution or change of affiliation to some other church denomination).

Indiana: Stockton v. Northwestern Branch of Women's Foreign Missionary Socy., 127 Ind. App. 193, 133 N.E.2d 875 (1955).

Kentucky: Eitel v. John N. Norton Memorial Infirmary, 441 S.W.2d 438 (Ky. 1969).

Massachusetts: Anna Jaques Hosp. v. Attorney Gen., 341 Mass. 179, 167 N.E.2d 875 (1960) (citing the text); First Bank & Trust Co. v. Attorney Gen., 371 Mass. 796, 359 N.E.2d 938 (1977).

Missouri: First Natl. Bank of Kansas City v. Jacques, 470 S.W.2d 557 (Mo. 1971) (citing the text and Restatement of Trusts §399); Flynn v. Danforth, 547 S.W.2d 132 (Mo. App. 1977) (city library merged into county library; citing the text).

New York: Matter of Chiprout, 8 Misc. 2d 648, 166 N.Y.S.2d 570 (1957); Matter of Clarke, 24 Misc. 2d 177, 200 N.Y.S.2d 284 (1960); Matter of Morris, 36 Misc. 2d 1094, 234 N.Y.S.2d 122 (1962); Matter of Drenning, 48 Misc. 2d 1082, 266 N.Y.S.2d 625 (1966); People v. Branham, 53 Misc. 2d 346, 278 N.Y.S.2d 494 (1967); Matter of Dorning, 37 A.D.2d 943, 326 N.Y.S.2d 495 (1971).

See Matter of Hoagland, 74 N.Y.S.2d 156 (1947), *aff'd mem.,* 272 A.D. 1040, 74 N.Y.S.2d 911 (1947), *aff'd mem.,* 297 N.Y. 920, 79 N.E.2d 746 (1948); Congregation Bnai Jacob-Tifereth Israel v. Stolitzky, 3 Misc. 2d 54, 151 N.Y.S.2d 143 (1956).

North Dakota: Mercy Hosp. of Williston v. Stillwell, 358 N.W.2d 506 (N.D. 1984).

Ohio: In re Will of Barker, 162 Ohio St. 531, 124 N.E.2d 421 (1955); Fenn College v. Nance, 4 Ohio Misc. 183, 210 N.E.2d 418 (1965) (citing the text).

Pennsylvania: Davis Trust, 47 D.&C.2d 184 (Pa. 1969) (citing the text and Restatement of Trusts, §399, Comment *o*); Rothschild Estate, 60 D.&C.2d 337 (Pa. 1973) (citing the text and Restatement of Trusts, §399, Comment *o*); Dellinger Trust, 75 D.&C.2d 649 (Pa. 1975) (nonprofit tennis club).

Canada: In re Kappele, [1955] 1 D.L.R. 29 (Ont.).

In Matter of Syracuse Univ. (Matter of Hendricks), 1 Misc. 2d 904, 148 N.Y.S.2d 245 (1955), *aff'd mem.,* 3 A.D.2d 890, 161 N.Y.S.2d 855 (1957), *aff'd mem.,* 4 N.Y.2d 744, 148 N.E.2d 911 (1958), a bequest was made to Syracuse University as an endowment fund for its medical college, and it was permitted to use its funds and property for a medical center at the state university. But see Matter of Syracuse Univ. (Matter of Heffron), 3 N.Y.2d 665, 148 N.E.2d 671 (1958), *rev'g* 2 A.D.2d 466, 156 N.Y.S.2d 779 (1956), *rev'g* 2 Misc. 2d 446, 150 N.Y.S.2d 251 (1956).

In Matter of Dunbar, 41 Misc. 2d 1044, 247 N.Y.S.2d 512 (1964), where a testator bequeathed money to the University of Buffalo as an endowment and before his death the university was merged into the State University of New York, it was held that the latter university was entitled to the legacy to be used as an endowment fund for the benefit of the branch at Buffalo.

In Matter of Boasberg, 51 Misc. 2d 684, 273 N.Y.S.2d 717 (1966), *aff'd mem.,* 30 A.D.2d 638, 291 N.Y.S.2d 780 (1968), a bequest to the University of Buffalo for certain purposes passed to the State University of New York with which it was merged after the death of the testator.

In Bodine Trust, 429 Pa. 260, 239 A.2d 315, 34 A.L.R.3d 743 (1968), it was held that in the case of a merger it was not necessary to resort to the cy

many states dealing with the effect of such merger or consolidation.[12]

---

pres doctrine, and that a gift over to another charitable corporation, if an event should occur that would necessitate the application of the cy pres doctrine, did not take effect. The court cited the text and Restatement of Trusts, §399, Comment *o*.

In Curators of Univ. of Mo. v. University of Kansas City, 442 S.W.2d 66 (Mo. 1969), where an endowment fund was given to the University of Kansas City, a private institution, with a provision that if it should cease to exist the fund was to go to Park College, and the University became a part of the state University of Missouri, it was held (two justices dissenting) that the gift over to Park College took effect.

See Note, Merger or consolidation of corporation as a testamentary charitable trust of which corporation is beneficiary, 34 A.L.R.3d 749 (1970).

[12]*Arizona:* Rev. Stat. Ann., §§10-1038 to 10-1043, as enacted by Laws 1979, c. 65.

California: Corporations Code, §§6010 to 6018 and §§8010 to 8018.

Colorado: Rev. Stat. 1973, §§7-40-108 to 7-40-113, as amended by Laws 1977, c. 72. See also Rev. Stat. 1973, §§7-25-101 to 7-25-121.

District of Columbia: Code 1981, §§29-539 to 29-546.

Illinois: Rev. Stat., c. 32, §163a41.

Indiana: Code 1971, §23-7-1-1 (Not-For-Profit Corporation Act).

Iowa: Code, §504A, as inserted by Laws 1979, c. 122.

Kansas: Stat. Ann., §17-1738, enacted by Laws 1972, c. 56.

Kentucky: Rev. Stat. Ann., §273.291.

Louisiana: Nonprofit Corporation Law, §246 (as enacted by Laws 1968).

Maryland: Ann. Code, Corporations and Associations Article, §5-207, as enacted by Laws 1975, c. 311.

Missouri: Ann. Stat., §§352.160, 355.215.

New Jersey: Rev. Stat., §15:2-8.

New York: Not-for-Profit Corporation Law, §§901 to 909.

See Note, New York's Not-for-Profit Corporation Law, 47 N.Y.U.L. Rev. 761 (1972).

North Dakota: Cent. Code, §10-25-01 to 10-25-07.

North Carolina: Gen. Stat., §55A-42.1, as enacted by Laws 1973, c. 314.

Ohio: Rev. Code, §1702.41.

Oregon: Rev. Stat., §§61.455 to 61.481.

Pennsylvania: 15 Pa. Cons. Stat., §§7549, 7552, 7929.

See also 7 Pa. Stat., §§7101 et seq.

Rhode Island: Gen. Laws 1956, §7-6-18, as added by Laws 1968, c. 66.

Utah: Non-Profit Corporation Act, §§37 to 43.

Vermont: Nonprofit Corporation Act, Stat. Ann., tit. 11 §§2301 et seq., as enacted by Laws 1971, c. 237.

Washington: Washington Nonprofit Corporation Act, Rev. Code, §24.06.-005 et seq., enacted by Laws 1967, c. 235.

Dissolution. On the dissolution of a charitable corporation the question arises as to the disposition of property that had been given to it. If the property was given to it for a particular charitable purpose the doctrine of cy pres is applicable, and the disposition does not fail unless the existence of the particular corporation was of the essence of the gift. Where the gift to the charitable corporation was unrestricted, a more difficult question arises. It has been held in some cases that the property reverts to the donor either on the ground that a determinable fee was created with a possibility of reverter or on the ground of a resulting trust.[13] It would seem, however, that the doctrine of cy pres should be applied, and that the property should not revert to the donor unless he had manifested an intention that it should revert on the dissolution of the corporation.[14] In many

---

In Connecticut Children's Aid Socy. v. Connecticut Bank & Trust Co., 147 Conn. 554, 163 A.2d 317 (1960), where a legacy was given to a charitable corporation with a gift over to another charity if it should cease to exist, it was held that the gift over did not take effect on the merger of the corporation with a similar corporation under a special act of the legislature.

[13]*California:* See Victoria Hosp. Assn. v. All Persons, 169 Cal. 455, 147 P. 124 (1915).

Illinois: Mott v. Danville Seminary, 129 Ill. 403, 21 N.E. 927 (1889); Danville Seminary v. Mott, 136 Ill. 289, 28 N.E. 54 (1891).

Minnesota: Cone v. Wold, 85 Minn. 302, 88 N.W. 977 (1902).

Mississippi: Daniel v. Jacoway, Freem. Ch. 59 (Miss. 1844).

Rhode Island: Nugent v. St. Dunstans College, 133 R.I. 666, 324 A.2d 654 (1974).

Washington: Jenkins v. Jenkins Univ. 17 Wash. 160, 49 P. 247, 50 P. 785 (1897).

In Industrial Natl. Bank v. Drysdale, 83 R.I. 172, 114 A.2d 191 (1955), 84 R.I. 385, 125 A.2d 87 (1956) (citing the text), where a testator left money to a trust company on a perpetual trust to pay the income to a religious corporation, and the corporation was dissolved some years after his death, it was held that the testator had no general charitable intent and that the trustee held upon a resulting trust for the next of kin. See §399.3, nn. 14 to 18.

See Gray, Rule Against Perpetuities §§44-51.1 (4th ed. 1942); Kales, Estates §§300-302 (2d ed. 1920); 18 Mich. L. Rev. 144 (1919).

As to the effect of an express condition or limitation, see §401.2, 401.3.

[14]*England:* Liverpool & Dist. Hosp. for Diseases of the Heart v. Attorney-General, [1981] 2 W.L.R. 379 (Ch. Div.).

Federal: Stevens Bros. Found. v. Commissioner, 324 F.2d 633 (8th Cir. 1963) (Delaware law, citing the text), *cert. denied,* 376 U.S. 969.

California: In re Los Angeles County Pioneer Socy., 40 Cal. 2d 852, 257

states there are statutes dealing with the dissolution of nonprofit

---

P.2d 1 (1953), noted in 1 U.C.L.A. L. Rev. 117; Veterans' Indus. v. Lynch, 8
Cal. App. 3d 902, 88 Cal. Rptr. 303 (1970); In re Estate of MacPherson, 14
Cal. App. 3d 450, 92 Cal. Rptr. 574 (1971); Metropolitan Baptist Church v.
Younger, 48 Cal. App. 3d 850, 121 Cal. Rptr. 899 (1975) (assets given to other
churches).

Illinois: Rosewell v. Chicago Park Dist., 126 Ill. App. 3d 30, 81 Ill. Dec.
428, 466 N.E.2d 1230 (1984).

Mississippi: Allgood v. Bradford, 473 So. 2d 402 (Miss. 1985).

New York: Matter of Scott, 1 Misc. 2d 206, 145 N.Y.S.2d 346 (1955), s.c.
Matter of Scott, 5 Misc. 2d 690, 160 N.Y.S.2d 210 (1956); Matter of Richmond
County Socy. for the Prevention of Cruelty to Children, 11 A.D.2d 236, 204
N.Y.S.2d 707 (1960), *aff'd mem.,* 9 N.Y.2d 913, 176 N.E.2d 97 (1961).

Virginia: Wellford v. Powell, 197 Va. 685, 90 S.E.2d 791 (1956); Hanshaw
v. Day, 202 Va. 818, 120 S.E.2d 460 (1961).

In In re Enderton, [1954] 4 D.L.R. 710 (Man.), where the charitable
corporation was in existence at the testator's death, but before distribution its
charter was revoked, it was held that the property did not revert to the testator's estate but passed to the Crown as bona vacantia. The court pointed out
that in such a case it is the practice of the Crown in England to dispose of the
property for analogous charitable purposes. See In re Slevin, [1891] 2 Ch. 236.

In Lynch v. Spilman, 64 Cal. 2d 406, 431 P.2d 636, 62 Cal. Rptr. 12
(1967), it was held that on the dissolution of a lodge organized for the benefit
of its members and for service for boys, the Attorney General was not entitled
to a summary judgment forbidding the members to divide its property on its
dissolution, because it did not appear that its purpose was wholly charitable.

In In re Farren, 27 Ohio App. 2d 31, 272 N.E.2d 162 (1971), where a
testatrix left her property in trust to pay the income to a privately owned
hospital for the care of indigents, and the hospital ceased to exist, it was held
that the hospital was given the property on a charitable trust and the trust did
not fail, but the income should be paid to other hospitals for the care of
indigent patients. The court cited the text.

In In re MacAulay, 18 D.L.R.3d 726 (P.E.I. 1971), a testatrix left a legacy
to a Roman Catholic college, to use the income for scholarships for needy boys
from a certain area of Prince Edward Island attending the college. Some years
after her death the college, although continuing as an entity, no longer continued its educational functions. It was held that the college should disburse
the income for scholarships in other colleges.

In McDaniel v. Frisco Employees' Hosp. Assn., 510 S.W.2d 752 (Mo. App.
1974), it was held that the trustees of a nonprofit corporation, an employees'
hospital association, had no power to dissolve it without a vote of the members
of the association.

In St. Dunstan's Univ. v. Canada Permanent Trust Co., 67 D.L.R.3d 480
(P.E.I. 1976), there was a bequest to a university that ceased teaching and
became a foundation to distribute funds for educational purposes. It was held
that the university should not take the legacy but that, under the cy pres

corporations, whether charitable or otherwise.[15] A few of them

---

doctrine, the legacy should be given to a university that had been created to take over the educational purpose of the legatee.

In Greil Memorial Hosp. v. First Ala. Bank, 387 So. 2d 778 (Ala. 1980), a testatrix made a bequest to a sanitorium that before she died was reincorporated for different purposes. It was held that the legacy lapsed and passed to the charities named as residuary legatees.

[15]*Arizona:* Rev. Stat. Ann., §10-1046, as enacted by Laws 1979, c. 65.

Arkansas: Stat., 1947, §64-1924 (for exempt charitable organization as the board of trustees shall determine, otherwise as the court may determine).

California: Corporations Code, §§6713, 6716, 7412, 8713, 8716, and 8717.

Colorado: Rev. Stat. 1973, §7-26-103.

Connecticut: Gen. Stat. 1958, §33-490.

District of Columbia: Code 1981, §§29-548 to 29-550.

Georgia: Code 1981, §14-3-210.

Illinois: Rev. Stat., c. 32, §§163a44, 163a54.

Indiana: Code 1971, §23-7-1-1 (Not-For-Profit Corporation Act).

Iowa: Nonprofit Corporation Act, §§48, 57.

Kentucky: Rev. Stat. Ann., §273.303, as amended by Laws 1974, c. 156. See also §386.365, as inserted by Laws 1974, c. 155.

Louisiana: Nonprofit Corporation Law, §249, as enacted by Laws 1968.

Maine: Rev. Stat. 1964, tit. 13, §938, as inserted by Laws 1971, c. 373. See tit. 13-B, §407, as enacted by Laws 1977, c. 525, and amended by Laws 1978, c. 592.

Maryland: Corporations and Associations Article, §5-208, as enacted by Laws 1975, c. 311.

Massachusetts: Ann. Laws, c. 180, §§11A and 11B, inserted by Laws 1962, c. 472, amended by Laws 1971, c. 819. See also c. 214, §3(12) as to the disposition of property of inactive religious societies. See First Christian Church v. Brownell, 332 Mass. 143, 123 N.E.2d 603 (1954).

In Congregational Church of Chicopee v. Attorney Gen., 376 Mass. 545, 381 N.E.2d 1305 (1978), it was held that under the statute the Supreme Judicial Court alone had jurisdiction to determine the disposition of its property on the dissolution of a church.

Michigan: Stat. Ann., §§21.290(1) to 21.290(3).

Missouri: Stat. Ann., §§352.210, 355.230.

New Jersey: Rev. Stat., 15:1-20.

New Mexico: Stat. Ann. 1978, §53-8-48.

New York: Not-for-Profit Corporation Law, §§1005, 1008(15), 1115, as amended by Laws 1970, c. 847.

North Carolina: Gen. Stat., §55A-45(3).

North Dakota: Cent. Code, §10-26-02.

Ohio: Rev. Code Ann., §1702.49.

Oklahoma: Stat. Ann., tit. 18, §864, as inserted by Laws 1975, c. 114.

Oregon: Rev. Stat., §61.525(3).

deal specifically with charitable corporations in general, or with specific types of charitable corporations. Thus in Illinois it is provided that on the voluntary or involuntary dissolution of a charitable corporation, in the absence of a condition its assets shall be conveyed to organizations engaged in activities substantially similar to those of the dissolving corporation.[16] In New York it is provided that on the dissolution of such a corporation the Supreme Court is authorized to order a transfer of its assets to another corporation or association to be administered in such manner as in the judgment of the court will best accomplish the general purposes for which the corporation so dissolved was organized, and that bequests or gifts to the corporation made before or after the dissolution shall inure to the corporation or association acquiring the assets of the dissolved corporation.[17]

Pennsylvania: 15 Pa. Cons. Stat., §§7549, 7552, 7968.

Utah: Code Ann., §16-6-12.1, as amended by Laws 1980, c. 17.

Vermont: Nonprofit Corporation Act, Stat. Ann. tit 11, §§2301 et seq., as enacted by Laws 1971, c. 237.

Virginia: Code 1950, §31.1-258(c).

Washington: Nonprofit Corporation Act, Laws 1967, c. 235.

In Bertram v. Berger, 1 Ill. App. 3d 743, 274 N.E.2d 667 (1971), it was held that a charitable corporation could properly convey property given to it to a similar charitable corporation, even though the former corporation was not dissolved.

By the Model Non-Profit Corporation Act, prepared by the Committee on Corporate Laws of the Section of Corporation, Banking and Business Law of the American Bar Association (1952) §46, it is provided that assets held by a nonprofit corporation for charitable purposes, and not held upon a condition requiring their return, shall on the dissolution of the corporation be transferred to one or more domestic or foreign corporations or organizations engaged in activities substantially similar to those of the dissolving corporation.

See Boyer, Nonprofit Corporation Statutes 77, 179 (1957).

[16]Illinois Rev. Stat., c. 32, §§163a44, 163a54.

The statute is applicable even though the settlor did not have a general charitable intent. See McDonough County Orphanage v. Burnhart, 5 Ill. 2d 230, 125 N.E.2d 625 (1955); Holden Hosp. Corp. v. Southern Ill. Hosp. Corp., 22 Ill. 2d 150, 174 N.E.2d 793 (1961).

[17]New York Not-for-Profit Corporation Law, §§1005, 1115; Alco Gravure v. Knapp Found., 64 N.Y.2d 458, 479 N.E.2d 752, 490 N.Y.S.2d 116 (1985), *motion denied,* 67 N.Y.2d 717, 490 N.E.2d 861, 499 N.Y.S.2d 942 (1986).

In Matter of Goehringer, 69 Misc. 2d 145, 329 N.Y.S.2d 516 (1972), a testator bequeathed $20,000 to a named Jesuit preparatory school in per-

Colleges and universities. In order to more effectively promote education it is frequently desirable that a college or university should merge into another college or university. The latter institution may be another private institution. Where the trustees of both institutions have consented, the courts have approved such merger.[18] So also the courts have approved the transfer of the assets of a private college or university to a state institution or the change of the private institution into a state institution.[19] In such a case the assets of the old institution may be transferred to the new institution,[20] except such assets as

---

petuity to provide funds for the education of boys of the school. The school was dissolved a year after his death. It was held that the money should go to similar Jesuit schools, in accordance with the terms of the Not-for-Profit Corporation Law.

In Matter of Multiple Sclerosis Serv. Org. of N.Y., 107 A.D.2d 644, 487 N.Y.S.2d 805 (1985), it was held that on dissolution of a corporation furnishing recreational services to sufferers from multiple sclerosis, all of its assets must be distributed to organizations aiding sufferers from this particular disease and none could go to organizations aiding sufferers from other diseases. This decree was reversed and a new hearing ordered, 68 N.Y.2d 32, 496 N.E.2d 861, 505 N.Y.S.2d 841 (1986), the court saying that the standard for distribution of the assets of a charitable corporation is less restrictive than that under the common law cy pres doctrine that applies to charitable trusts, citing the text and Restatement (Second) of Trusts §399 for the latter.

See Application of Italian Benevolent Inst., 157 N.Y.S.2d 485 (1956).

[18]*California:* People v. President & Trustees of College of Cal., 38 Cal. 166 (1869).

Illinois: Rush Medical College v. Chicago Univ., 312 Ill. 109, 143 N.E. 434 (1924).

Iowa: Starr v. Morningside College, 186 Iowa 790, 173 N.W. 231 (1919); Lupton v. Leander Clark College, 194 Iowa 1008, 187 N.W. 496 (1922).

As to the power to amend the charter of a charitable institution, see §399.5.

In Bell v. Carthage College, 103 Ill. App. 2d 289, 243 N.E.2d 23 (1968), it was held that a legacy to "Carthage College, Carthage, Illinois," was not defeated by the removal of the college to Wisconsin.

[19]*Missouri:* First Natl. Bank of Kansas City v. Jacques, 470 S.W.2d 557 (Mo. 1971) (citing the text and Restatement of Trusts §399).

New Jersey: Trustees of Rutgers College v. Richman, 41 N.J. Super. 259, 125 A.2d 10 (1956).

Ohio: Fenn College v. Nance, 4 Ohio Misc. 183, 210 N.E.2d 418 (1965).

As to the effect of the English nationalization of hospitals, see n. 7, *supra.*

[20]Matter of Syracuse Univ. (Matter of Hendricks), 1 Misc. 2d 904, 148 N.Y.S.2d 245 (1955), *aff'd mem.,* 3 A.D.2d 890, 161 N.Y.S.2d 855 (1957), *aff'd*

were so restricted by the terms of the trust that it would defeat the intention of the donor to transfer them.[21]

Withdrawals by a local organization from its parent. Where a state or national organization has a local branch or chapter that withdraws from it, the question arises whether the property of the local organization may be retained by it or vests in the parent organization. The answer depends on the nature of the relation between them and requires an examination of the extent to which the local organization is dependent on or independent of the parent, not whether it is an integral part of the parent.[22]

The most difficult questions arise where a local church withdraws from the parent organization. Here enters in the principle that the civil courts will not, and constitutionally cannot, inquire into and determine matters of faith and doctrine. In general, where the church has a hierarchical organization, as in the Catholic and Protestant Episcopal churches, the property will go to the parent. So also in the case of the Presbyterian church, which

---

mem., 4 N.Y.2d 744, 148 N.E.2d 911 (1958); Matter of Dunbar, 41 Misc. 2d 1044, 247 N.Y.S.2d 512 (1964) (University of Buffalo).

[21]Matter of Syracuse Univ. (Matter of Heffron), 3 N.Y.2d 665, 148 N.E.2d 671 (1958). See n. 11, *supra.*

[22]See New Jersey Assn. for Children with Learning Disabilities v. Burlington County Assn., 163 N.J. Super. 199, 394 A.2d 406 (1978), *modified,* 174 N.J. Super. 149, 415 A.2d 1196 (1980); Woman's Christian Temperance Assn. v. Bearhalter, 6 D.&C.3d 207 (Pa. 1977); Polish Veterans' Corps v. Army, etc. Veterans, 87 D.L.R.3d 449 (Ont. 1978).

In Collins v. Beinecke, 67 N.Y.2d 479, 495 N.E.2d 335, 504 N.Y.S.2d 72 (1986), a business corporation established a nonprofit corporation as a charitable foundation and transferred over $6 million in assets to it. All of the stock of the business corporation was purchased by a holding company. The directors of the charitable foundation refused to allow the holding company to be represented on the board or in the membership of the foundation. It was held that the directors could not be compelled to resign or to permit representation of the holding company although all members and directors of the foundation had been representatives of the business corporation prior to the takeover.

The question may arise as to labor unions. See Note. The Legal Consequences of Labor Union Schisms, 63 Harv. L. Rev. 1413 (1950); Note, Rights to Local Union Property after Secession, 58 Yale L.J. 1171 (1948).

It may arise as to fraternal organizations.

Similar questions may arise where a local chapter of a college fraternity withdraws from the national fraternity. See Bancroft v. Cook, 264 Mass. 343, 162 N.E. 691 (1928).

has a central government, it will not go to the local church. In the churches having a congregational government, as in the case of Baptist and Congregational and Unitarian churches, the local church can keep the property. But the problems are complicated and there is an enormous amount of litigation that we shall not consider in this treatise.[23]

[23]For recent cases, see Trinity Presbyterian Church v. Tankersley, 374 So. 2d 861 (Ala. 1979), *cert. denied,* 445 U.S. 904 (1980); Presbytery of Riverside v. Community Church of Palm Springs, 89 Cal. App. 3d 910, 152 Cal. Rptr. 854 (1979), *cert. denied,* 444 U.S. 974, 100 S. Ct. 469, 62 L. Ed. 2d 389 (1979); Protestant Episcopal Church v. Barker, 115 Cal. App. 3d 599, 171 Cal. Rptr. 541 (1981), *cert. denied,* 454 U.S. 864, 102 S. Ct. 323, 70 L. Ed. 2d 163 (1981); Bishop and Diocese of Colorado v. Mote, 716 P.2d 85 (Colo.), *cert. denied,* 107 S. Ct. 102, 93 L. Ed. 2d 52 (1986) (corporate articles of local church constituted a declaration of trust in favor of the diocese and the national church); Crumbley v. Solomon, 243 Ga. 343, 254 S.E.2d 330 (1979); Emberry Community Church v. Bloomington Dist. Missionary & Church Extension Socy., 482 N.E.2d 288 (Ind. App. 1985) (as United Methodist Church is hierarchical, property passes to parent organization by way of implied trust when local congregation ceases to be affiliated to denomination); Wheeler v. Roman Catholic Archdiocese, 79 Mass. 1230, 389 N.E.2d 966 (1979), *cert. denied,* 444 U.S. 899, 100 S. Ct. 208, 162 L. Ed. 2d 135 (1979); Protestant Episcopal Church v. Graves, 161 N.J. Super. 230, 391 A.2d 563 (1978), *aff'd,* 167 N.J. Super. 563, 401 A.2d 548 (1979), aff'd, 83 N.J. 572, 417 A.2d 19 (1980), *cert. denied;* Tea v. Protestant Episcopal Church, 96 Nev. 399, 610 P.2d 182 (1980); Presbytery of Beaver-Butler v. Middlesex Presbyterian Church, 507 Pa. 255, 489 A.2d 1317 (1985), *cert. denied,* 474 U.S. 887, 106 S. Ct. 198, 88 L.Ed.2d 167 (1985) (in absence of declaration of trust or provision in national constitution, local church does not hold its property upon trust for superior ecclesiastical body); Presbytery of Elijah Paris Lovejoy v. Jaeggi, 682 S.W.2d 465 (Mo. 1984), *cert. denied,* 471 U.S. 1117, 105 S. Ct. 2361, 86 L. Ed. 2d 262 (1985); Misa v. Congregational Christian Church of Samoa Trust Bd., [1984] 2 N.Z.L.R. 461 (C.A.).

Many cases in the state courts, and one in the United States Supreme Court, were decided before the First Amendment as to religion became applicable to the states. Many of the state cases involved Congregational churches that became Unitarian. For an early case in the federal courts, see Watson v. Jones, 13 Wall. (80 U.S.) 679, 20 L. Ed. 666 (1872).

On the constitutional questions, see Presbyterian Church v. Mary Elizabeth Blue Hill Memorial Presbyterian Church, 393 U.S. 440, 89 S. Ct. 601, 21 L. Ed. 2d 658 (1969); Maryland and Virginia Eldership v. Church of God, 396 U.S. 367, 90 S. Ct. 499, 24 L. Ed. 2d 582 (1970); Serbian Eastern Orthodox Diocese v. Milivojevich, 426 U.S. 696, 96 S. Ct. 2372, 49 L. Ed. 2d 151 (1976); Jones v. Wolf, 443 U.S. 595, 61 L. Ed. 2d 775, 99 S. Ct. 3020 (1979) (see Jones v. Wolf, 244 Ga. 388, 260 S.E.2d 84 (1979)); United Methodist Church v. St. Louis Crossing, 150 Ind. App. 574, 276 N.E.2d 916, 52 A.L.R.3d 311 (1972).

§397.4. **Power to distribute among specified charities.**
In the case of a private trust, where the trustee is authorized to
select among several persons who shall take and in what proportions and the trustee fails to make the selection, the trust does
not fail, but the trust fund will be divided among the beneficiaries in equal shares.[1] Similarly, where the trustee is authorized to
distribute the trust fund among two or more specified charities
and he fails to make the distribution, the fund may be divided
equally among the charities.

Where an equal division among the several charities would
not be in accordance with the probable intention of the testator,
however, such division will not be made. Thus if the maximum
amount required for the accomplishment of one of the charitable purposes can be ascertained, no more than that amount will
be applied to that purpose, and the balance will be divided
among the other charitable purposes. Where the power to make
the division among the several charitable purposes is conferred
not only on the original trustee but on successor trustees,
whether or not it is expressly so provided in the trust instrument, the court will not divide the property in equal shares
among several charities but will appoint a new trustee who will
be empowered to make the division.

Where the power to make the division among the several
charities is confined to the original trustee, and where an equal
division among the several charities would not be in accordance
with the probable intention of the testator, the court may frame
a scheme for the division of the property. Such a method of
saving the trust goes beyond anything that is permitted in the
case of private trusts and is an application of the general doctrine of cy pres.

See Note, Judicial Intervention in Disputes over the Use of Church Property, 75 Harv. L. Rev. 1142 (1962); Note, Judicial Intervention in Church
Property Disputes — Some Constitutional Considerations, 74 Yale L.J. 1113
(1965); Note, Determination of property rights between local church and
parent church body: modern view, 52 A.L.R.3d 324 (1973); Note, Judicial
Resolution of Church Property Disputes, 31 Ala. L. Rev. 307 (1980); Adams
and Hanlon, Jones v. Wolf: Church Autonomy and the Religion Clauses of the
First Amendment, 128 U. Pa. L. Rev. 1291 (1980); Oaks, Trust Doctrines in
Church Controversies, 1981 B.Y.U. L. Rev. 805.

§397.4. [1]See §§27, 120, 414.

§397.5. Power to distribute among charitable and other valid objects. Where property is given in trust for two or more objects, some of which are charitable and others are not, the trustee being clothed with discretion as to the amount to be applied to each of the objects, and the trustee fails to apply the property among the objects, the question arises whether the disposition fails and, if not, how the property is to be distributed. Where the noncharitable objects are objects for which a trust can properly be created, the trust does not fail unless the distribution by the trustee named by the testator was an essential part of his scheme, which would rarely be the case. If the testator manifested an intention that the division among the several objects might be made not only by the trustee named by him but also by any successor trustee, the court may appoint a successor trustee to make the division; but this would rarely be his intention.

Ordinarily, where the trustee named by the testator fails to make the division among the several objects, the court will decree that the property be equally divided among the several objects. It is true that the trustee might have made a different division, but if he dies without exercising his discretion, the court will not attempt to exercise the discretion but will make an equal division among the several objects. The principle here applied is similar to that which is applied in the case of a private trust where the trustee is given discretion to determine which members of a class of beneficiaries shall take and in what proportions; if the trustee fails to exercise this discretion, the property will be divided among the members of the class in equal shares.[1]

In *Attorney General v. Doyley*[2] a testator left all his property to two trustees in trust to pay the income to his niece for life, and if she should die without issue the trustees were to dispose of the estate to such of his relations on his mother's side who should be most deserving, and in such manner and proportion as they should think fit to such charitable use as they should think proper. On the death of the life tenant without issue the next of kin on the mother's side brought a bill to reach the

§397.5. [1] See §120.
[2] 7 Ves. 58n, 4 Vin. Abr. 485 (1735).

estate, and a cross bill by the Attorney General was filed asking that the property be applied to charitable uses. The court held that the estate should be divided into halves and that one half be distributed in equal shares among all the relations of the testator on his mother's side who were within the degree of third cousins and that a scheme should be framed for distributing the other half in charity.

In *Salusbury v. Denton*[3] a testator left money

> to be at the disposal, by her will, of my dear wife therewith to apply a part to the foundation of a charity school, or such other charitable endowment for the benefit of the poor of Offley as she may prefer, and under such regulations as she may prescribe herself; and the remainder of said [fund] to be at her disposal among my relatives, in such proportions as she may be pleased to direct.

The widow died without having made any disposition of the fund. The court held that the trust did not fail, and that because the widow had not divided the property, it should be divided in equal shares, one half for the charitable purpose and the other half for the testator's only child.

There are, it is true, a few cases in which it was held that where the trustee has power to divide the property among charitable objects and other objects, the disposition fails even though a trust for these other objects would have been a valid private trust and even though the trustee was ready and willing to make the division. Thus in a case in Rhode Island[4] a testator provided that the residue of his estate should be given to such charities as his executor should determine or in the discretion of the executor to the testator's surviving brothers and sisters in equal shares. It was held that the whole disposition failed on the ground that it was too indefinite. It seems impossible to support the decision. Each purpose was in itself valid, and the fact that the executor was given discretion to divide the property between the two objects should not invalidate the disposition. Even if the executor had died without making the division between the two objects, an equal division would have been made

[3] 3 K.&J. 529 (1857).
[4] Slattery v. Ward, 45 R.I. 54, 119 A. 755 (1923).

under the decisions cited above. In a case in Illinois[5] a testator left his estate in trust to give such portion of it as the trustees might think best to any one or more of his brothers or sisters who might stand in need, the remainder to be devoted to certain charitable purposes. One trustee died and the other resigned and the plaintiffs were named as successor trustees by the court. It was held that the disposition of the residue was void. The court said that if the trustees were given power to choose between charities or if a definite part was for charity and a definite part for the private trust, the disposition would be valid. But clearly there is no reason why the trustees should not have been permitted to make the decision in the exercise of the discretion conferred on them by the testator.

On the other hand, in a case in Ohio it was held that the mere fact that a trust had two objects, one of which was charitable, did not cause the disposition to fail if each object separately was valid.[6] In that case, a testator left his property in trust for the establishment and maintenance of a home for aged women and provided that certain relatives should receive life annuities out of the income and that certain friends and relatives should be entitled to support in the home even though they were not in need. The court held that this mixing of private purposes with charitable purposes was not fatal to the trust so long as the private purposes did not involve a perpetuity and were not otherwise invalid.

§398. Charitable and Invalid Purposes

Where property is left to a trustee to be applied among charitable purposes and other purposes, and the other purposes are such that an intended trust for their accomplishment would

---

[5]Wilce v. Van Anden, 248 Ill. 358, 94 N.E. 42, 140 Am. St. Rep. 212, 21 Ann. Cas. 153 (1911).

[6]Graham v. Bergin, 18 Ohio App. 35 (1923).

See Estate of Moore, 219 Cal. App. 2d 737, 33 Cal. Rptr. 427 (1963) Woodstown Natl. Bank & Trust Co. v. Snelbaker, 136 N.J. Eq. 62, 40 A.2d 222 (1944), aff'd mem., 137 N.J. Eq. 256, 44 A.2d 210 (1945).

By Wisconsin Stat., c. 615, it is provided that charitable corporations may receive gifts conditioned on or in return for an agreement to pay an annuity to the donor or his nominee.

fail, the whole disposition fails unless it is possible to carry out in part the intention of the testator by making a division of the property among the purposes, in which case the trust is valid as to the part that is apportioned to the charitable purposes and fails as to the balance; or unless it was the primary purpose of the testator to devote the property to charitable purposes.

We shall consider first the situation that arises where the donor states no specific purposes but directs that the property shall be applied to purposes that may include charity but are broader than charity, as, for example, where he directs that the property be applied to benevolent purposes.[1] We shall then consider the situation where the donor specifies the purposes, but they are not all charitable purposes.[2]

§398.1. **Indefinite purposes not limited to charity.** When the first and second editions of this treatise were published (1939 and 1956), there were thought to be two corollary rules restricting the ability of a settlor to confer on the trustee power to select the beneficiaries or purposes of a trust. Rule One was that, if a trust was created for such members of a class of *persons* as the trustee might select, the class must be so defined that every member of the class could be ascertained. Rule Two was that, if a trust was created for such *purposes* as the trustee might select, (1) all purposes eligible for selection must be listed or (2) the selection must be confined to charitable purposes. These rules were thought to ensure that, if the trustee failed to select, the court could enforce the trust by giving equal shares to each noncharitable member of the class. Rule One was rejected in 1959 by the Restatement of Trusts[1] and in 1971 by the House of Lords.[2] In jurisdictions that have rejected Rule One, it is possible to create a trust for such persons as the trustee may select, even though all members of the class from which he is to select cannot be ascertained. Rule Two was also rejected in 1959 by the Restatement of Trusts,[3] but it has not yet been rejected

§**398.** [1]See §398.1.
[2]See §398.2.
§**398.1.** [1]Restatement (Second) of Trusts, §122. See §122, n. 37.
[2]McPhail v. Doulton; In re Baden's Deed Trusts, [1971] A.C. 424, noted in Camb. L. J. 210, 37 Mod. L. Rev. 643, 87 Law Q. Rev. 31, §122, n. 30, *supra.*
[3]Restatement (Second) of Trusts, §123. See §123, p. 238.

by the House of Lords or by most courts in the United States and the Commonwealth. This being so, it is necessary to examine the principles of construction used to determine whether a trust for purposes to be selected by the trustee is restricted to charitable purposes and so is valid under Rule Two.

Where a testator leaves property for general or indefinite purposes, and does not specifically limit them to charitable purposes, the question in each case is whether he has indicated an intention to confine the disposition of the property to charitable purposes. Thus in the leading case of *Morice v. Bishop of Durham* [4] a testatrix left the residue of her estate to the Bishop of Durham upon trust "to dispose of the ultimate residue to such objects of benevolence and liberality as the Bishop of Durham in his own discretion shall most approve of." A bill was filed by the next of kin to have the bequest declared void, and the Attorney-General and the bishop were made defendants. The court held that the words "benevolence" and "liberality" indicated pur-

---

[4] 10 Ves. Jun. 521, 32 Eng. Rep. 947 (1805), affirming the decree of Sir William Grant, Master of the Rolls, 9 Ves. Jun. 399, 32 Eng. Rep. 656 (1804). This was the third case in two years in which a testamentary trust was attacked by Sir Samuel Romilly, as counsel for the next of kin, and defended by Spencer Perceval, then the Attorney-General (Prime Minister 1809; murdered 1812). In the first, Moggridge v. Thackwell, 7 Ves. Jun. 36, 32 Eng. Rep. 15 (1803), Perceval won a decree that a trust for such charities as the trustee might select was valid although the trustee predeceased the testatrix and so could not select. In the second, Attorney-General v. Stepney, 10 Ves. Jun. 22, 32 Eng. Rep. 751 (1804), Perceval won a decree that a trust "to purchase bibles and other religious books, pamphlets, and tracts" as the trustees should think fit was a valid charitable trust. Perceval's argument in the *Morice* case was that "objects of benevolence and liberality" were confined to charity and so validated by the *Moggridge* decision. Sir Samuel exploded this argument by the sly suggestion that the bishop's entertaining his hunting companions with liquor would be an object of liberality. Sir Samuel's suggestion really endangered his clients' case. If the trust was to enable the bishop to entertain his hunting companions with liquor it might be destroyed by merger because the bishop was the sole beneficiary (§99, n. 1) but then the bishop would be entitled to the legacy beneficially; he would not hold it upon resulting trust for the next of kin of the testatrix. Neither counsel adequately addressed the problem of whether purpose trusts are valid even if they are not charitable. The *Morice* case is discussed in Fratcher, Powers of Appointment to Unspecified Charities, 32 Mo. L. Rev. 443 at 443-448 (1967). The problem not addressed by counsel in the *Morice* case is discussed in Fratcher, Bequests for Purposes, 56 Iowa L. Rev. 773 at 780-783 (1971). See §124.

poses broader than those that are recognized as charitable; and because there was not a beneficial gift to the bishop, he held upon a resulting trust for the next of kin. Although the bishop expressed his willingness to carry out the purposes of the testatrix, the court held that he would not be permitted to do so, but must surrender the property to the next of kin.

In the century and a half that followed the decision in this case, the principle there laid down has been applied in numerous English cases, culminating in the decision of the House of Lords in *Chichester Diocesan Fund v. Simpson.*[5] In that case a testator who died without near relatives left the residue of his estate to his executors in trust to apply it "for such charitable institution or institutions or other charitable or benevolent object or objects in England as my acting executors or executor may in their or his absolute discretion select." It was held by Farwell, J., sitting in the Chancery Division of the High Court of Justice, that the purposes were limited to charity and that the bequest was valid. The decision was reversed by the Court of Appeal, and on appeal to the House of Lords the decision of the Court of Appeal was sustained and the appeal dismissed. The law lords held, Lord Wright dissenting, that because the executors were authorized to apply the property for "charitable or benevolent" purposes it was not a charitable trust. All five of the law lords agreed that if the purposes were not limited to charitable purposes the disposition was invalid.

The question whether a testator intends that the trustees should apply the property only to charitable purposes, or whether he intends to give them a broader discretion, is a question of construction on which there is usually room for a difference of opinion. In a long line of cases extending back to the preamble of the Statute of Charitable Uses[6] and before, the courts have decided that certain purposes are charitable purposes and certain others are not. Although there still are and always will be situations where it is doubtful on which side of the line a particular disposition will fall, the term "charitable" has

[5][1944] A.C. 341, *aff'g* In re Diplock, [1941] Ch. 253, which *rev'd* [1940] Ch. 988, noted in 19 Can. B. Rev. 213, 5 Convey. (N.S.) 65, 266, 9 id. 85, 56 Law Q. Rev. 451, 57 id. 166, 60 id. 311, 198 Law T. 14, 88 id. 427, 4 Mod. L. Rev. 311, 2 Res Judicatae 229, 85 Sol. J. 395.

[6]Stat. 43 Eliz. I. c. 4 (1601).

acquired a fairly definite meaning. When a testator directs that the property shall be applied to charitable purposes, the inference is strong that he uses the term in its legal sense, that he means to authorize the trustees to apply the property to such purposes and only such purposes as are held by the courts to be charitable. It is, of course, possible that a testator may use the word in a narrower sense, so as to include only the relief of poverty and exclude other purposes such as the promotion of education or religion. On the other hand, it is possible that he uses the word in a broader sense so as to include purposes that the courts have not recognized as charitable, in which case the trust may fail. However, it will ordinarily be inferred that he uses the word "charitable" in the same sense in which the courts use it when they determine whether a disposition shall be upheld as a valid charitable trust.[7]

Difficulty arises when a testator uses as a substitute, or uses in addition, some word like "benevolent," which has not acquired a technical meaning. The English courts, and to a lesser extent the American courts, have been prone to construe the word "benevolent" and similar words as not limiting the purposes to charitable purposes, even though the effect is to invalidate the bequest. The notion is that to determine what is benevolent one should apply a subjective test as to whether the disposition proceeds from a well-wishing mind. On the other hand, a purpose is charitable, regardless of the donor's state of mind, if it falls within the scope of those purposes that the courts consider sufficiently in the public interest to be upheld and enforced at the suit of the Attorney General. Thus a purpose that is benevolent may not be charitable, and a purpose that is charitable may not be benevolent, although ordinarily a purpose that is charitable is also benevolent.

Some ingenuity has been expended in imagining purposes that are benevolent but not charitable. It has been suggested that a trust to provide music on the village green is for a benevo-

---

[7]Where the question is one of exemption from taxation, the word "charitable" in a tax statute may be used in a narrower sense. In the leading English case of Commissioners for Special Purposes of the Income Tax v. Pemsel, [1891] A. C. 531, two out of the five law lords took the view that the exemption of trusts for "charitable purposes" in an income tax act included only trusts for the relief of poverty.

lent but not a charitable purpose.[8] But it has now been held that such a purpose is charitable.[9] It has been suggested that a trust to provide oysters for the Benchers of the Inns of Court is benevolent but not charitable. But Lord Wright has said that he would not be disposed to regard the fund for oysters as either benevolent or charitable. It has been held in England that a trust to provide a pennyworth of sweets for all boys and girls under the age of fourteen within a certain parish was not charitable;[10] and in another case it was held that a trust was not charitable where the purpose was to apply the income annually in providing knickers for boys between the ages of ten and fifteen in a particular district, the bounty not being limited to poor boys.[11] These are perhaps illustrations of a purpose that might be called benevolent although not charitable.

Certainly it is possible for a testator to use these words with these distinctions in mind. But the distinctions are difficult to grasp and are certainly not understood by anyone except such lawyers as have an expert knowledge of the law of charitable trusts. In many of the cases where the disposition was held invalid the will was drawn by a lawyer who, of course, never suspected that the disposition would fail. As Sir Wilfred Greene, M.R. (later Lord Greene), said: "The phrase 'charitable or benevolent' as applied by testators to gifts in favour of institutions or purposes is all too familiar. It is a trap into which the unskilled draftsman not infrequently falls, with the result that the gift fails for uncertainty."[12]

In the *Chichester* case, Goddard, L.J., who concurred with

---

[8]This suggestion was made by Lord Bramwell in Commissioners for Special Purposes of Income Tax v. Pemsel, [1891] A.C. 531, 565. See Lord Wright's comments in the Chichester case, [1944] A.C. 341, 358.

[9]In Shillington v. Portadown Urban Dist. Council, [1911] 1 Ir. R. 247, a trust for the encouraging of choruses by the residents of a town was held to be charitable. See also Royal Choral Socy. v. Inland Revenue Commrs., [1943] 2 All E.R. 101 (tax case).

[10]In re Pleasants, 39 T.L.R. 675 (1923).

[11]In re Gwyon, [1930] 1 Ch. 255.

[12]In re Horrocks, [1939] P. 198, 209.

In King v. Richardson, 136 F.2d 849 (4th Cir. 1943), *cert. denied sub nom.* Richardson v. King, 320 U.S. 777 (1943), it was held that the erection of a church, which is clearly a charitable purpose, was not a benevolent cause within the meaning of the terms of a trust.

the other judges in the Court of Appeal because he felt that the precedents obliged him to hold that the bequest was void, said that if it had been pointed out to the testator that the result of the insertion of the words "or benevolent" would be that the money would not go to charity but to his first cousins once removed of whose existence the testator probably did not even know, there is not the least doubt in the world that he would, provided he was of sound mind and memory and understanding, have said, "Cut out the word 'benevolent.' "

Where the word "benevolent" or some similar word is used, and the word "charitable" is not also used, as where property is bequeathed in trust for such benevolent purposes as the trustee may select, it has been held in a number of cases that the word denotes purposes not limited to charity, that the word is not synonymous with the word "charitable," and that the trust fails.[13] It is quite possible, however, to construe the will differ-

[13]*England:* Morice v. Bishop of Durham, 9 Ves. 399 (1804), 10 Ves. 522 (1805), n. 4, *supra,* (to such objects of benevolence and liberality as trustee should most approve of); James v. Allen, 3 Mer. 17 (1817) (for such benevolent purposes as trustees may unanimously agree on); In re Barnett, 24 T.L.R. 788 (1908) (to trade guild to apply toward its general benevolent objects or purposes); In re Rowe, 30 T.L.R. 528 (1914) (to city company to be employed and bestowed according to their discretion); In re Atkinson's Will Trusts, [1978] 1 All E.R. 1275, [1978] 1 W.L.R. 586 (to divide the residue between such "worthy causes as have been communicated to me by my trustees;" no communication; held word "worthy" was not limited to charity and trust failed).

Compare Harris v. Du Pasquier, 26 L.T. (N.S.) 689 (1872) (to trustees for such objects as they consider deserving).

In In re Endacott, [1960] Ch. 232, noted in 76 Law Q. Rev. 20, where a testator left the residue to a parish council "for the purpose of providing some useful memorial to myself," it was held that the character of the legatee did not indicate that the purpose was charitable, and the disposition failed. See §123, n. 24.

Alabama: Read v. McLean, 240 Ala. 501, 200 So. 109 (1941) (for benevolent purposes in trustee's discretion).

Arizona: In re Hayward's Estate, 65 Ariz. 228, 178 P.2d 547 (1947) (for any purpose deemed beneficial to certain town; citing Restatement of Trusts §§123, 398), noted in 15 U. Chi. L. Rev. 432.

Connecticut: Adye v. Smith, 44 Conn. 60 (1876) (for any benevolent purposes that trustee thinks fit).

Compare Bristol v. Bristol, 53 Conn. 242, 5 A. 687 (1885) (to such worthy persons and objects as executrix might deem proper).

Florida: In re Estate of Jones, 318 So. 2d 231 (Fla. App. 1975).

ently, and there are decisions in the United States holding a trust for benevolent purposes to be a charitable trust.[14] Thus in *Goodale v. Mooney*[15] a testator left the residue of his estate to his executors to be distributed by them "among my relatives, and for benevolent objects, in such sums as in their judgment shall be for the best." The court said that the construction should be such as would preserve rather than destroy the gift; that the construing of a will according to technical rules results as often in defeating as in promoting the testator's intent; that it was quite probable that the testator did not know that there is any legal difference between the words "charitable" and "benevolent," and that most persons probably use the words indifferently as meaning the same thing. The court held, therefore, that the testator had created a valid trust for charitable purposes.

Massachusetts: Chamberlain v. Stearns, 111 Mass. 267 (1873) (solely for benevolent purposes in discretion of trustees).

Compare Nichols v. Allen, 130 Mass. 211 (1881) (to be distributed to such persons, societies, or institutions as trustee may consider most deserving).

Oregon: In re Johnson's Estate, 100 Or. 142, 196 P. 385, 1115 (1921) (for benevolent purposes).

Wisconsin: In re Estate of Kradwell, 44 Wis. 2d 40, 170 N.W.2d 773 (1969) (to distribute among testator's heirs, legatees, and such other persons as the executrix should deem deserving and for benevolent objects).

Canada: Lawrence v. Lawrence, 13 D.L.R. 737 (N.B. 1913) (for benevolent purposes as the trustees may see fit); In re Street, 29 Ont. W. Notes 428 (1926) (to be donated to benevolent institution to be selected by officers of trust company); In re Albery, 42 D.L.R.2d 201 (Ont. 1963) (any worthy object or purpose); In re Aydt, 54 D.L.R.2d 771 (Sask. 1965) (for such worthy objects as legatee considers fit).

Compare Planta v. Greenshields, [1931] 2 D.L.R. 189 (B.C.) (to aid any worthy cause as executor shall think fit).

Scotland: Baird's Trustees v. Lord Advocate, 15 Sess. Cas. (4th series) 682 (Scot. 1888) (holding that in Scotland religious purposes are not charitable).

[14]*Federal:* St. Louis Union Trust Co. v. Burnet, 59 F.2d 922 (8th Cir. 1932) (to such benevolent purposes as in opinion of trustee may constitute a fitting memorial; tax case).

New Hampshire: Goodale v. Mooney, 60 N.H. 528 (1881) (for benevolent objects).

New Jersey: Smith v. Pond, 92 N.J. Eq. 211, 111 A. 154 (1920), *rev'g* 90 N.J. Eq. 445, 107 A. 800 (1919) (for support of church or such benevolent purposes as trustees of church shall direct).

[15]60 N.H. 528 (1881).

The reasoning of the court and the result it reached seem eminently sensible.

In most cases where the word "benevolent" or some similar word is used, it is used in connection with the word "charitable" or in connection with other words clearly denoting charitable purposes. Thus a bequest may be made for such "charitable or benevolent objects" as the trustee may select. In such a case it is possible to construe "benevolent" as synonymous with "charitable." It is true that if the words are synonymous it is unnecessary to use both of them. But, as Lord Wright pointed out in the *Chichester* case, such tautology is common. Laymen as well as lawyers like to use two or three words where one would do, since the balanced structure is thought to be artistic. The Bible and the works of Shakespeare, as well as deeds and wills, are full of tautological expressions. It is possible in such cases to apply the principle of ejusdem generis. However, in the great majority of cases that have arisen in England the court has held that the words are not synonymous and that the trust fails.[16] In a few

[16]Vezey v. Jamson, 1 Sim. & St. 69 (1822) (to apply to any charitable or public purposes or to any person or persons as executors should think would have been agreeable to testator); Ommanney v. Butcher, 1 Turn. & R. 260 (1823) (to be given in private charity); Williams v. Kershaw, 5 Cl. & Fin. 111n. 5 L.J. Ch. (N.S.) 84 (1835) (such benevolent, charitable, and religious purposes as trustees think most beneficial); Kendall v. Granger, 5 Beav. 300 (1842) (assisting indigent individuals or encouraging undertakings of general utility in discretion of trustees); In re Jarman's Estate, 8 Ch. D. 584 (1878) (to any charitable or benevolent purpose trustees might agree on); In re Riland's Estate, [1881] W.N. (pt. 1) 173 (such charitable institutions or such charitable or benevolent objects and purposes as trustees think proper); In re Hewitt's Estate, 53 L.J. Ch. (N.S.) 132 (1883) (to mayor of city to be expended by him in acts of hospitality or charity); In re Woodgate, 2 T.L.R. 674 (1886) (for sick poor, or any other utilitarian purposes trustee may select); In re Macduff, [1896] 2 Ch. 451 (charitable or philanthropic purposes); Langham v. Peterson, 87 L.T. (N.S.) 744 (1903) (to be expended in charity or works of public utility); In re Sidney, [1908] 1 Ch. 126, 488 (such charitable uses or such emigration uses as trustees should think fit); In re Freeman, [1908] 1 Ch. 720 (to Charitable Organization Society to pay income to such societies as are most in need of help); In re Da Costa, [1912] 1 Ch. 337 (for sole benefit of such person or persons and for such public purposes as Governor-in-Chief for the time being of South Australia should in writing direct); Attorney-General for N.Z. v. Brown, [1917] A.C. 393 (such charitable, benevolent, religious, and educational institutions and objects as trustees should select); In re Eades, [1920] 2 Ch. 353 (such religious, charitable, and philanthropic objects as executors

English cases the words have been construed in the light of the context as synonymous and the trust upheld as a charitable trust.[17] In the Scottish cases the court has been more inclined

---

should jointly appoint); In re Davis, [1923] 1 Ch. 225 (charitable or public institutions in Wales as trustees deem advisable); In re Clarke, [1923] 2 Ch. 407 (such other funds, charities, and institutions as executors in their absolute discretion should think fit); Attorney-General v. National Provincial & Union Bank, [1924] A.C. 262 (such patriotic purposes and charitable objects in British Empire as trustees should select); In re Horrocks, [1939] P. 198 (such charitable institutions or other charitable or benevolent objects); In re Bawden's Settlement, [1953] 2 All E.R. 1235 (to such objects of charity or benevolence or amelioration of human suffering or advancement of knowledge as trustees might select); Berry v. St. Marylebone Borough Council, [1958] Ch. 406, *aff'g* [1957] 1 All E.R. 681 (to a Theosophical Society having as one of its objects the forming of a nucleus of the Universal Brotherhood of Humanity without distinction of race, creed, sex, caste, or color; tax case); In re Gillingham Bus Disaster Fund, [1958] Ch. 300, *aff'd,* [1959] Ch. 62 (for Royal Marine Cadets killed and injured in a road accident, then to such worthy causes in their memory as the trustees might determine), noted in 74 Law Q. Rev. 190, 489, [1959] Camb. L.J. 41; Attorney-General of the Bahamas v. Royal Trust Co., [1986] 1 W.L.R. 1001 (P.C.) (education and welfare of Bahamian children); In re Jacques, 63 D.L.R.2d 673 (B.C. 1967) (to finance such community project in accordance with such wishes as I may have expressed to my surviving trustee).

See also In re White, [1933] S. Austl. St. R. 129 (for such charitable, religious, philanthropic, educational, or scientific institutions as trustee should select); In re Greaves, [1917] 1 W.W.R. 997 (B.C.) (such charitable or benevolent institutions in N as trustees should consider deserving of support); In re Poole, 40 Ont. W. N. 558 (1931) (for some religious or philanthropic cause); In re Metcalfe, [1947] 1 D.L.R. 567 (Ont.) (to such religious, charitable, and benevolent purposes as executors should determine); In re Eacrett, [1949] 1 D.L.R. 305 (Ont.) (for such charitable purposes or civic betterment or for relief of poverty as trustee should see fit); Brewer v. McCauley (Matter of Loggie), [1954] S.C.R. 645 (Can.) (for such charitable, religious, educational, or philanthropic purposes as the trustees should appoint), noted in 33 Can. B. Rev. 334; Trustees of the Londonderry Presbyterian Church House v. Commissioners, [1946] N. I. L.R. 178 (helping in religious, moral, social, and recreative life of those connected with Presbyterian churches in city); In re White, [1963] N.Z. L.R. 788 (to dispose of as the trustee in his absolute discretion should think fit).

[17]Dolan v. Macdermot, L.R. 5 Eq. 60 (1867), *aff'd,* L.R. 3 Ch. App. 676 (1868) (for such charitable and other public purposes as lawfully might be in certain parish); In re Douglas, 35 Ch. D. 472 (1887) (such charities, societies, and institutions as third person should nominate or, if he neglects, as trustee should nominate); In re Allen, [1905] 2 Ch. 400 (for such charitable, educa-

to construe the words as synonymous,[18] although occasionally the opposite result has been reached.[19] In the United States

---

tional, or other institutions in certain town as trustees should think fit); In re Pardoe, [1906] 2 Ch. 184 (to such public charities and institutions or for such charitable purposes as trustees should consider worthy); In re Bennett, [1920] 1 Ch. 305 (for benefit of schools and charitable institutions and poor, and other objects of charity or any other public objects in certain parish); In re Baron Ludlow, [1923] W.N. (pt. 1) 126, 314, 93 L.J. 30 (for hospitals or other charitable or benevolent institutions).

See Wilson v. Toronto Gen. Trusts Corp., [1954] 3 D.L.R. 136 (Sask.) (to pay the income to board of governors of university for scholarships or for such other purposes as board might determine).

In several cases it has been held that a bequest for religious or charitable purposes is not invalid on the ground that the testator intended to include some religious purposes that are not charitable. In re Tomkinson, 74 Sol. J. 77 (1930); In re Sinclair's Trust, 13 L.R. Ir. 150 (1884); In re Salter, [1911] 1 Ir. R. 289; Rickerby v. Nicholson, [1912] 1 Ir. R. 343.

In Muir v. The Open Brethren, 96 C.L.R. 166 (Austl. 1956), a testator bequeathed his residuary estate to a religious body to be employed in relieving cases of need and distress and in assisting persons in indigent circumstances and in particular "in assisting and relieving persons who have been or shall be adversely affected by the effects of" the Second World War. It was held that the trust was charitable, because the context showed that the testator intended to assist only persons in indigent circumstances.

[18]Miller v. Rowan, 5 Cl. & Fin. 99 (1873) (such benevolent and charitable purposes as trustee should think proper); Paterson's Trustees v. Paterson, [1909] Sess. Cas. 485 (Scot.) (such charities or benevolent or beneficent institutions as trustees should think proper); Mackinnon's Trustees v. Mackinnon, [1909] Sess. Cas. 1041 (Scot.) (such charitable or philanthropic institutions in the west of Scotland as trustees might select as in their opinion the most deserving); Wink's Exrs. v. Tallent, [1947] Sess. Cas. 470 (Scot.) (such societies or institutions of a benevolent or charitable nature as executors might select); Milne's Trustees v. Davidson, [1956] Sess. Cas. 81 (Scot.) (among various charities, nursing associations, infirmaries, etc., to be selected by them).

[19]Blair v. Duncan, [1902] A.C. 37 (such charitable or public purposes as trustee thinks proper); Grimond v. Grimond, [1905] A.C. 124 (such charitable or religious institutions and societies as trustees might select); Houston v. Burns, [1918] A.C. 337, aff'g Turnbull's Trustees v. Lord Advocate, [1917] Sess. Cas. 591 (Scot.) (such public, benevolent, or charitable purposes in parish of L as trustees should think proper); Symmers's Trustees v. Symmers, [1918] Sess. Cas. 337 (Scot.) such charitable institutions or deserving agencies in a place as trustees might select); Reid's Trustees v. Cattanach's Trustees, [1929] Sess. Cas. 727 (Scot.) (such charitable, educational, or benevolent societies or public institutions in Scotland as trustees should select).

there are cases holding that the intended trust fails.[20] But in a large and increasing number of cases it has been held that the disposition was for charitable purposes and the trust has been upheld.[21]

[20]*Illinois:* Taylor v. Keep, 2 Ill. App. 368 (1878) (such charitable or other institution as in opinion of trustees is most needed).

Kentucky: Hoenig v. Newmark, 306 S.W.2d 838 (Ky. 1957) (to such educational or charitable institutions or to such individual or individuals as the trustees should determine to be worthy).

Massachusetts: Minot v. Attorney Gen., 189 Mass. 176, 75 N.E. 149 (1905) (to be distributed by executors to charitable or worthy objects and particularly for relatives whom testator may have overlooked).

New Jersey: Norris v. Thomson's Exrs., 19 N.J. Eq. 307 (1868), *aff'd sub nom.* Thomson's Exrs. v. Norris, 20 N.J. Eq. 489 (1869) (to benevolent, religious, or charitable institutions as widow should appoint); Livesey v. Jones, 55 N.J. Eq. 204, 35 A. 1064 (1896), *aff'd mem. sub nom.* Chadwick v. Livesey, 56 N.J. Eq. 453, 41 A. 1115 (1897) (for promotion of religious, moral, and social welfare of the people as legatee should think most needful); Hyde's Exrs. v. Hyde, 64 N.J. Eq. 6, 53 A. 593 (1902) (such religious, charitable, or educational or other purposes as trustees might deem advisable); Hegeman's Exrs. v. Roome, 70 N.J. Eq. 562, 62 A. 392 (1905) (such religious, benevolent, or charitable objects as trustee might select).

New York: Matter of Sheifer, 178 Misc. 340, 34 N.Y.S.2d 302 (1942) (to any charitable institution or institutions or to any person, persons, individual, or individuals that my executors and trustees see proper).

Texas: Allred v. Beggs, 125 Tex. 584, 84 S.W.2d 233 (1935) (such charities and worthy objects as executor and a third person should determine), noted in 21 Cornell L.Q. 667, 34 Mich. L. Rev. 582, 14 Tex. L. Rev. 124, 45 Yale L.J. 1515.

West Virginia: Goetz v. Old Natl. Bank, 140 W. Va. 422, 84 S.E.2d 759 (1954) (to two banks to distribute to such religious, charitable, scientific, literary, educational, or fraternal corporations and associations as they may select), noted in 43 Geo. L.J. 699.

But see Sands v. Security Trust Co., 143 W. Va. 522, 102 S.E.2d 733 (1958) (to some educational, scientific, religious, charitable, or other public benevolent use).

[21]*Federal:* Gossett v. Swinney, 53 F.2d 772 (8th Cir. 1931), *cert. denied,* 286 U.S. 545 (1932) (for such charitable, benevolent, hospital, infirmary, public, educational, scientific, literary, library, or research purposes in city as trustees should determine); Chicago Bank of Commerce v. McPherson, 2 F. Supp. 110 (W.D. Mich. 1931), *aff'd,* 62 F.2d 393 (6th Cir. 1932), *cert. denied,* 289 U.S. 736 (1933) (such charitable, benevolent, educational, and public welfare uses as trustees should select); Commissioner v. Upjohn's Estate, 124 F.2d 73 (6th Cir. 1941) (such civic, charitable, educational, or religious purposes and for such purposes of general and public welfare as trustees might select; tax case);

In many states there are statutes relating to charitable

Beggs v. United States, 27 F. Supp. 599 (Ct. Cl. 1939) (to such charities and worthy objects as executor and testator's sister should determine; tax case); Hight v. United States, 256 F.2d 795 (2d Cir. 1958), *rev'g* 151 F. Supp. 202 (D. Conn. 1957) (for such charitable, benevolent, religious, or educational institutions as the executors should determine; tax case; citing Restatement of Trusts, §398, Comment *b*); Rosamond Gifford Charitable Corp. v. United States, 170 F. Supp. 239 (N.D.N.Y. 1958) (to a charitable corporation to be created and operated exclusively for religious, educational, scientific, charitable, or benevolent uses; tax case).

California: Estate of Hinckley, 58 Cal. 457, 507 (1881) (to establish fund to be devoted perpetually to human beneficence and charity).

Colorado: Smith v. United States Natl. Bank, 120 Colo. 167, 207 P.2d 1194 (1949) (public or educational, charitable, or benevolent purposes), noted in 49 Mich. L. Rev. 281.

Georgia: Pace v. Dukes, 205 Ga. 835, 55 S.E.2d 367 (1949) (to be devoted to religious, charitable, educational, and humanitarian purposes).

Kansas: Robinson v. Hammel, 154 Kan. 654, 121 P.2d 200 (1942) (charitable or benevolent organization).

Kentucky: Druker v. Levy, 262 S.W.2d 681 (Ky. 1953) (to make selection of Jewish charities and organizations or institutions; citing the text).

Maine: Fox v. Gibbs, 86 Me. 87, 29 A. 940 (1893) (benevolent and charitable purposes at Trustee's discretion); Prime v. Harmon, 120 Me. 299, 113 A. 738 (1921) (to certain charitable societies and to other moral and useful associations).

Massachusetts: Saltonstall v. Sanders, 11 Allen 446 (Mass. 1865) (to furtherance of cause of piety and good morals, or in aid of purposes of benevolence or charity, public or private, or temperance or for education of deserving youths at trustees' discretion); Rotch v. Emerson, 105 Mass. 431 (1870) (for promotion of agricultural or horticultural improvements, or other philosophical or philanthropic purposes, at discretion of trustees); Suter v. Hilliard, 132 Mass. 412 (1882) (to assist poor persons and to assist and cooperate with such charitable, benevolent, religious, literary, and scientific associations as trustee should think most deserving); Weber v. Bryant, 161 Mass. 400, 37 N.E. 203 (1894) (such objects of benevolence or charity, public or private, including educational or charitable institutions and relief of individual needs as trustees should deem worthy); Amory v. Attorney Gen., 179 Mass. 89, 60 N.E. 391 (1901); Thorp v. Lund, 227 Mass. 474, 116 N.E. 946, Ann. Cas. 1918B 1204 (1917) (national or philanthropic purposes in Norway).

Michigan: Michigan Trust Co. v. United States, 21 F. Supp. 482 (W.D. Mich. 1937) (such corporate charity or corporate benevolence or public purpose as testator's widow may by will appoint); Cleveland v. Second Bank & Trust Co., 354 Mich. 202, 92 N.W.2d 449 (1958) (to charitable and social welfare institutions or movements in a designated city).

Minnesota: In re Estate of Quinlan, 233 Minn. 35, 45 N.W.2d 807 (1951)

trusts. In many of these statutes the word "benevolent" is

(worthy religious, educational, scientific, medical, surgical, social, or charitable organizations in Minnesota).

New Hampshire: Clark v. Cummings, 83 N.H. 27, 137 A. 660 (1927) (charitable, fraternal, benevolent, and educational uses).

New Jersey: De Camp v. Dobbins, 29 N.J. Eq. 36 (1878), *aff'd*, 31 N.J. Eq. 671 (1879) (to a religious society to promote its religious interests, and to aid the missionary, educational, and benevolent enterprises to which it is in the habit of contributing); in Wilson v. Flowers, 58 N.J. 250, 277 A.2d 199 (1971), a testator bequeathed a share of his estate "to such philanthropic causes as my Trustees may select." The court held that, in light of the evidence as to the testator's intent, the disposition was for charitable purposes and was valid. The court cited the text.

New York: Matter of Cunningham, 206 N.Y. 601, 100 N.E. 437 (1912) (to such charitable and benevolent associations and institutions of learning as executors might select); Buell v. Gardner, 83 Misc. 513, 144 N.Y.S. 945 (1914) (for benefit of such institutions and persons who may be worthy, needy, and deserving of the same, and to use income for educational and benevolent purposes); Baptist Home of Monroe County v. Gardner, 145 N.Y.S. 275 (1914) (for benefit of worthy institutions and worthy persons); Matter of Olmstead, 131 Misc. 238, 226 N.Y.S. 637 (1928) (for such worthy, charitable, and benevolent works as trustees might select).

Ohio: Becker v. Fisher, 112 Ohio St. 284, 147 N.E. 744 (1925) (to perpetuate my interest in a certain church and to assist needy and worthy causes and persons as Trustee understands my wishes and practices).

Pennsylvania: Murphy's Estate, 184 Pa. 310, 39 A. 70 (1898) (to be divided among such benevolent, charitable, and religious institutions and associations as shall be selected by executors); Dulles's Estate, 218 Pa. 162, 67 A. 49, 12 L.R.A. (N.S.) 1177 (1907) (among such religious, charitable, and benevolent purposes and objects or institutions as in Trustee's discretion shall be best and proper); Anderson's Estate, 269 Pa. 535, 112 A. 766 (1921) (to distribute residue among such institutions or to do such acts of charity therewith as in judgment of executors might seem best); Funk Estate, 353 Pa. 321, 45 A.2d 67, 163 A.L.R. 780 (1946), *aff'g* 46 D.&C. 667 (1942) (to be given to some worthy cause or institution; quoting Restatement of Trusts §123 and §398, Comment *b*), noted in 41 Mich. L. Rev. 846; Voegtly Estate, 396 Pa. 90, 151 A.2d 593 (1959) (to distribute within five years to charities or causes that the trustee might select); Little Estate, 403 Pa. 247, 168 A.2d 738 (1961) (to be used as a suitable memorial for the testator's brother and parents, seeking advice from a friend of the testator as to the nature of the memorial).

Rhode Island: Pell v. Mercer, 14 R.I. 412, 422 (1884) (for works of religion or benevolence as executors should select).

Texas: Moore v. Sellers, 201 S.W.2d 247 (Tex. Civ. App. 1947) (benevolent, charitable, religious, or educational undertakings).

West Virginia: Sands v. Security Trust Company, 143 W. Va. 522, 102

used.[22] In most of the cases involving these statutes it seems to be assumed that the legislature did not intend to include purposes other than charitable purposes and that the word "benevolent" was used as though it were synonymous with "charitable."[23] Surely if a testator uses the very words that are used in the statute, the disposition should not be held invalid.

Even if the word "benevolent" is given a wider connotation than that of the word "charitable," it may be possible to find that the testator intended that any disposition which the trustee should make should be for an object that has both characteristics, that is, one which is both charitable and benevolent. In a

---

S.E.2d 733 (1958) (to some educational, scientific, religious, charitable, or other public benevolent use).

Canada: In re Armstrong, 7 D.L.R.3d 36 (N.S. 1969) (for the benefit of a particular church and ancillary projects as the trustee directs).

See Scott, Trusts for Charitable and Benevolent Purposes, 58 Harv. L. Rev. 548 (1945); Benas, Quasi-Charities, 9 Convey. (N.S.) 67, 104 (1945); 115 A.L.R. 1123 (1938).

For somewhat similar cases in which it was held that the language of the trust instrument was to be construed as limiting the application of the property to charitable purposes, see §396.

Where the purposes are so broad as to indicate a beneficial gift to the legatee, the gift is valid and no resulting trust arises. But where the purposes are not quite broad enough to make the bequest a beneficial gift to the legatee, the gift is invalid and a resulting trust arises. See §125.

[22]*Colorado:* Rev. Stat. 1963, §153-16-1.

Idaho: Code 1947, §14-326.

Indiana: Code 1971, §30-2-2-1.

Kentucky: Rev. Stat. Ann., §381.260, as amended by Laws 1980, c. 123.

Louisiana: Rev. Stat. Ann., §9:2291.

Maine: Rev. Stat. 1964, tit. 13, §3062.

Michigan: Stat. Ann., §26.1191.

Minnesota: Stat. Ann., §501.12.

Missouri: Stat. Ann., §§252.010 to 252.220.

Nebraska: Rev. Stat. 1943, §30-239.

New Jersey: Rev. Stat., §15:14-6.

New York: Estates, Powers and Trusts Law, §8-1.1, amended by Laws 1971, c. 1058, and Laws 1985, c. 492.

North Carolina: Gen. Stat., §§36A-43, 36A-46.

South Carolina: Code 1976, §§21-29-20, 21-27-60.

South Dakota: Codified Laws, §§55-9-1 to 55-9-5.

West Virginia: Code, §35-2-1.

Wyoming: Stat. Ann., §§34-93 to 34-96.

See Kentucky Rev. Stat. Ann., §381.260 (humane purposes).

[23]See §123.

number of cases the courts have so held, laying stress on the fact that the testator had stated the matter conjunctively, as where he has provided that the property shall be applied to such "charitable and benevolent objects" as the trustees may select.[24] In one English case,[25] where it was provided that the residue should be held in trust for "charitable or benevolent objects," the unfortunate solicitor who drafted the will unsuccessfully attempted to convince the court that the word "or" was the result of the typist's mistake and that the will should be reformed by striking it out. In the *Chichester* case, Goddard, L.J., remarked, "Indeed, when I find a rule which says that if property is left to trustees to give to charitable and benevolent purposes, that is good, but if it is for charitable or benevolent purposes, it is not, I regard it with some distaste."[26]

There are cases, indeed, in which the testator used the word

[24]*England:* Attorney-General v. Herrick, 2 Amb. 712 (1772) (charitable and pious uses); In re Sutton, 28 Ch. D. 464 (1885) (charitable and deserving objects); In re Lloyd Greame v. Attorney-General, 10 T.L.R. 66 (1893) (religious and benevolent societies or objects); In re Best, [1904] 2 Ch. 354 (charitable and benevolent institutions).

Maine: Fox v. Gibbs, 86 Me. 87, 29 A. 940 (1893) (benevolent and charitable purposes).

Michigan: Cleveland v. Second Bank & Trust Co., 354 Mich. 202, 92 N.W.2d 449 (1958) (to charitable and social welfare institutions or movements in a designated city).

Canada: In re Huyck, 10 Ont. L.R. 480 (1905) (to religious society to be applied in charitable and philanthropic purposes); In re McPherson, 17 Ont. W.N. 22 (1919) (religious, benevolent, and charitable purposes and uses); In re Massey Trust, 21 D.L.R.2d 477 (Ont. 1959) (charitable and relief work), noted in 38 Can. B. Rev. 405; In re Shortt, 42 D.L.R.3d 673 (Ont. 1974) (for charitable and benevolent purposes).

Scotland: Caldwell's Trustees v. Caldwell, [1921] Sess. Cas. 82 (Scot.) (charitable and benevolent institutions in Glasgow), noted in 65 Sol. J. 765.

See also In re Scowcroft, [1898] 2 Ch. 638; In re Hood, [1931] 1 Ch. 240, noted in 4 Austl. L.J. 18, 11 Can. B. Rev. 53, 169 Law T. 158, 281, 170 id. 73, 171 id. 222, 94 Sol. J. 143; In re Morton, [1941] 4 D.L.R. 763 (B.C.) (educational and religious objects).

[25]In re Horrocks, [1939] P. 198.

The language used in the will in this case, as in so many of the English cases, is based on a form given in Key and Elphinstone, Precedents in Conveyancing. In the tenth edition, that of 1914, the form is, "to or for such charitable institution or institutions or other charitable [& benevolent] object or objects. . . ." 2 id. at 859. The words that were there inserted in brackets are omitted in later editions. See 2 id. at 861 (14th ed. 1940).

[26]In re Diplock, [1941] Ch. 253, 266.

"or," but the court interpreted it as meaning "and," with the result that the trust was upheld as a charitable trust.[27] On the other hand, to complete the circle there are cases in which the court has interpreted "and" as "or," with the result that where one of the objects was not charitable the trust failed.[28]

In construing the will, is it legitimate to consider that under one construction the disposition will fail but under another it will be valid and effective? The earlier view perhaps was that the question of meaning must be entirely divorced from the question of the legal effect. But this view has long since yielded to the more rational one that in case of ambiguity a construction may be preferred that will make the disposition effective.[29] Even in the case of the rule against perpetuities, it is permissible if there is an ambiguity to prefer the construction that will save the disposition.[30] In the *Chichester* case Lord Simonds admitted that "If there is an ambiguity, it may be that I am at liberty to choose that construction which will give legal effect to the instrument rather than that which will invalidate it." However, the fact that Lord Wright, and Farwell, J., in the lower court, thought that the testator meant by his language to devote his estate to charitable

[27]In re Bennett, [1920] 1 Ch. 305 (for benefit of schools and charitable institutions and poor, and other objects of charity or any other public objects in certain parish); Robinson v. Hammel, 154 Kan. 654, 121 P.2d 200 (1942) (some charitable or benevolent organization); Thorp v. Lund, 227 Mass. 474, 116 N.E. 946 (1917) (national or philanthropic purpose in Norway).

[28]Williams v. Kershaw, 5 Cl. & Fin. 111n (1835) (such benevolent, charitable, and religious purposes as trustees think most beneficial); Attorney-General for N.Z. v. Brown, [1917] A.C. 393 (such charitable, benevolent, religious, and educational institutions and objects as trustees should select); In re Eades, [1920] 2 Ch. 353 (such religious, charitable, and philanthropic objects as executors should jointly appoint); Attorney-General v. National Provincial & Union Bank, [1924] A.C. 262 (such patriotic purposes and charitable objects in the British Empire as trustees should select); In re Metcalfe, [1947] 1 D.L.R. 567 (Ont.) (to such religious, charitable, and benevolent purposes as executors should determine); Trustees of the Londonderry Presbyterian Church House v. Commissioners, [1946] N. I. L.R. 178 (helping in religious, moral, social, and recreative life of those connected with Presbyterian churches in city).

[29]See Restatement of Property §243.

[30]See Pearks v. Moseley, 5 App. Cas. 714, 719 (1880); Shepard v. Union & New Haven Trust Co., 106 Conn. 627, 138 A. 809, 813 (1927); Gray, Rule Against Perpetuities §633 (4th ed. 1942).

purposes only did not induce Lord Simonds to think that there was even an ambiguity.

We have been considering in this section the question of construction, the question whether the testator manifested an intention to devote the property to charity only, or whether he intended that it should be devoted to purposes that are broader than charity although they may include charity. If the property is to be devoted only to charity, the disposition is valid even though no specific charitable purposes are designated by the testator.[31] On the other hand, where the disposition is not limited to charity, it is generally held that it fails,[32] although it has sometimes been held that even though the trustees cannot be compelled to carry out the testator's purposes, they may be permitted to do so. We have discussed this matter at length elsewhere.[33]

§398.2. **Specified objects.** Where a testator leaves property in trust to be applied by the trustee in his discretion among several specified objects, and some of these objects are charitable but others are objects for which a trust cannot validly be created, several possible dispositions of the property may be made. The following results have been reached:

(1) the property has been divided equally among the purposes, and the trust has been upheld as to the shares allotted to the charitable purposes and has failed as to the balance;

(2) all of the property has been applied to the charitable purposes;

(3) the property has been applied to the charitable purposes, except the amount that would be required for the invalid purposes, the trust failing as to that amount;

(4) the trust has failed altogether.

[31]See §§396-397.5.

[32]Baarslag v. Hawkins, 12 Wash. App. 756, 531 P.2d 1283 (1975) (citing Restatement of Trusts §398).

In Paris v. United States, 381 F. Supp. 597 (N.D. Ohio 1974), where a testator bequeathed $25,000 as a "memorial" to be erected in Israel for his parents and other relatives, it was held that the purpose was not limited to charity and was subject to tax. But query.

[33]See §123.

The character of the disposition will determine which of these results will be reached.

(1) Equal division among the purposes, failure pro tanto. It has been held in a number of cases that where property is bequeathed in trust for charitable purposes and other purposes that fail, the property should be divided into as many shares as there are named purposes, and the trust upheld as to the shares allocated to the charitable purposes but failed as to the shares allocated to the other purposes.[1] It is to be remembered that the method of making an equal division among the several objects is applied where the trustee has discretion to distribute the property among the members of a class and dies without making the distribution.[2] The same method has been applied where the trustee has discretion to distribute the property among charitable objects and valid noncharitable objects and dies without making the distribution.[3] The same method is applicable where the trustee in his discretion may distribute among several charitable objects and dies without making the disposition.[4]

In *In re Clarke*[5] a testator left the residue of his property

> to *(a)* such institution society or nursing home or nursing homes or similar institutions as assist or provide for persons of moderate means . . . to have either surgical operations performed together with medical treatment or medical treatment alone on payment of some moderate contribution *(b)* the Royal National Lifeboat Institution *(c)* the Lister Institute of Preventive Medicine *(d)* and such other funds, charities and institutions as my executors in their absolute discretion shall think fit. And I direct that such residue shall be divided amongst the legatees named in the paragraphs *(a) (b) (c)* and *(d)* lastly hereinbefore contained in such shares and proportions as my trustees shall determine.

The executors brought a summons to determine the validity of the disposition. The court held that the first three objects were

§398.2. [1]Hoare v. Osborne, L.R. 1 Eq. 585 (1866); In re Rigley's Trusts, 36 L.J. Ch. 147 (1866); In re Clarke, [1923] 2 Ch. 407; In re Gavacan, [1913] 1 I.R. 276.
[2]See §§120, 121.
[3]See §397.5.
[4]See §397.4.
[5][1923] 2 Ch. 407.

charitable, but that the fourth was not exclusively charitable. It was contended by the next of kin that because the trustees might have applied the whole fund for the fourth object and might therefore have applied it all for noncharitable purposes, the whole bequest failed, under the rule laid down in *Morice v. Bishop of Durham*. [6] The court held, however, that although the gift for the object stated in clause *(d)* was invalid, this did not cause the whole disposition to fail. It is true that by the terms of the power conferred on the trustees they might have appointed the whole fund to the set of objects stated in clause *(d)*;[7] but the court held that the power was invalid, because it was a power to appoint to indefinite noncharitable objects. There was therefore a gift to the four objects with a superadded power of appointment that was invalid. The court held that the property should therefore be divided into four equal shares, one for each of the first three objects, and the other for the testator's next of kin.

The same method of upholding the trust as to a pro rata share of the property has been applied where a trust is created for several charitable objects, but as to one or more of the objects the trust is invalid under a mortmain act. Thus in an English case[8] it was held that where a testator left the residue of his estate in trust for opening new schools, subscribing to schools already open, and for purchasing land to let to the poor at a low rent, the rent to be applied to benevolent purposes, the provision for the purchase of land was invalid under the mortmain acts, which forbade a devise of land or a bequest of money to be laid out in land for charitable purposes. The court held, however, that the trust did not fail altogether. The only question was whether it failed as to one half or as to one third. The court said that the provision for opening new schools and for subscribing to schools already open constituted in the mind of the testator a single educational purpose, and because the trust failed as to the other purpose it was valid as to one half of the estate.

A similar method of saving the trust in part has been applied where the trust is created for two charitable objects and one of them fails because it is impracticable to perform it. Thus

[6] 9 Ves. 399 (1804), 10 Ves. 522 (1805).
[7] Lord Selborne's Act, 37 & 38 Vict., c. 37 (1874).
[8] Crafton v. Frith, 4 De G. & Sm. 237 (1851).

in a case in New South Wales[9] a testator bequeathed the residue of his estate toward the cost of the erection of a new cathedral and for the erection of a church window. The intended trust for the cathedral failed because there was no prospect of the erection of a new cathedral by the chapter. It was held, however, that the trust for the erection of the window was valid because it might be erected in the old cathedral. The court held that the residue should be divided into two equal parts, that one of the parts should be applied to the erection of a window, and that there was a resulting trust of the other part.

(2) All given to charity. It has been held in a number of cases that where property is bequeathed in trust for charitable purposes and other purposes that fail, the whole of the property should be applied to the charitable purposes. Where the primary purpose of the settlor is to give all the property to a charitable purpose, but there is superadded a power to apply a part of the property to invalid objects, there is a valid charitable trust of the whole of the property. The situation is somewhat analogous to that which arises where property is given subject to an equitable charge that fails, or where property is given upon trust for one purpose and subject thereto for another purpose. In these cases the intention of the testator is that all the property shall be applied to the charitable purpose, except so much as is actually used for the other purpose. Thus in a case in Michigan[10] a testator bequeathed his property in trust to apply the income for a charitable purpose and provided that a part of the income should be used to purchase flowers to be placed on his grave and that of his wife each year. It was held that this provision was invalid as a perpetuity and that the whole of the income should be applied for the designated charitable purpose. In an Irish case[11] a testator devised land in trust to apply the income to erect a chapel and thereafter to pay one half to the parish priest for masses and to divide the other half among the poor annually. It was held that the trust to erect the chapel failed because the bishop refused to consent to the erection of the chapel. The

[9]Muir v. Archdall, 19 N.S.W. St. R. 10 (1918).
[10]Kostarides v. Central Trust Co., 370 Mich. 690, 122 N.W.2d 729 (1963).
[11]Kelly v. Attorney-General, [1917] 1 I.R. 183.

heirs claimed that the whole trust failed. The priest claimed that there should be an application cy pres toward improving the existing church. The court held that the gift for masses and for the poor was a gift of the whole trust property subject to a gift that failed and that therefore the whole was applicable to these purposes.

In *In re Coxen*[12] a testator left £200,000 in trust to apply annually a sum not exceeding £100 to provide a dinner for the six trustees, and to pay each of them a guinea at each meeting, and to apply the balance for the benefit of charitable hospitals. It was held that the whole trust was valid because the provision for the dinners and the fees for the trustees tended to promote efficient administration of the charitable purpose.[13] The court was further of the opinion that if this provision were invalid the whole of the property should be devoted to the charitable purpose, because the testator clearly intended to devote the whole income to the charitable purpose, although subjecting a part of it to trusts designed to promote that purpose by a particular means to which effect might not perhaps legally be given. The court further said that even if the whole trust could not be upheld it would be invalid only as to the maximum amount that would be needed to pay for the dinners and the fees.

The English courts have held in a number of cases that where a testator bequeaths property in trust for the maintenance of a tomb, the balance to be applied to charitable purposes, and the provision with respect to the tomb is invalid as a perpetuity, the whole of the property should be applied to the charitable purposes.[14] The ground for these decisions would seem to be that the primary purpose of the testator was to apply the prop-

---

[12][1948] Ch. 747, noted in 22 Austl. L.J. 413, 13 Convey. (N.S.) 131, 133, 138, 99 Law J. 102.

See Scholler Estate, 403 Pa. 97, 169 A.2d 554 (1961), *aff'g* 20 D.&C.2d 318 (Pa. 1960) (quoting Restatement of Trusts §398).

[13]See §375.2, n. 19.

[14]Fisk v. Attorney-General, L.R. 4 Eq. 521 (1867); Hunter v. Bullock, L.R. 14 Eq. 45 (1872); Dawson v. Small, L.R. 18 Eq. 114 (1874); In re Williams, 5 Ch. D. 735 (1877); In re Birkett, 9 Ch. D. 576 (1878); In re Vaughan, 33 Ch. D. 187 (1886); In re Rogerson, [1901] 1 Ch. 715; In re Norton's Will Trusts, [1948] 2 All E.R. 842.

See Stubblefield v. Peoples Bank, 406 Ill. 374, 94 N.E.2d 127 (1950); In re Oldfield, [1949] 2 D.L.R. 175 (Man.).

erty to charitable purposes, and that he intended that all of the property should be so applied except so much as should be actually applied to the maintenance of the tomb. In *In re Birkett*, [15] Jessel, M.R., questioned the soundness of these decisions. In that case a testator bequeathed money in trust for the maintenance of a tomb and directed that the balance be applied to charitable purposes. The Master of the Rolls, although holding that under the authorities the whole of the fund was applicable to the charitable purposes, said that on principle the charitable trust should be valid only as to the residue over the amount that might readily be ascertained as necessary for the maintenance of the tomb, and that the amount that would be necessary for its maintenance should go to the next of kin of the testator. The result reached by the English courts may, perhaps, be justified on the ground that the testator would have preferred to have the whole of the property applied to the charitable purposes rather than to have the disposition fail in part.

A result similar to that reached by the English courts in these tombstone cases was reached in *Heinlein v. Elyria Savings & Trust Co.* [16] A testator left a large estate in trust, and directed the trustee to expend not less than $600 annually in the upkeep of his burial lot and to apply the balance to the establishment and maintenance of public parks. The court held that it would be unreasonable to expend more than $125 annually on the upkeep of the lot, and that the trustee should therefore pay $5000 to the city that maintained the cemetery, a sum which at 2½ percent would yield $125. The court said that to comply with the testator's direction to expend $600 annually, the sum of $24,000 would be required if the interest rate were 2½ percent. The question therefore arose whether $19,000 should go

[15] 9 Ch. D. 576 (1878).

[16] 75 Ohio App. 353, 62 N.E.2d 284 (1945).

In Ohio a trust of a reasonable sum for perpetual care of a cemetery lot is valid. See §374.9.

In Walker Estate, 21 D.&C.2d 512 (Pa. 1959), where a beneficiary of an employees' trust designated two persons to take his interest on his death and instructed them to dispose of the property for charitable purposes and also for the benefit of any member of his family who might require assistance, it was held that the whole of the fund should be disposed of for charitable purposes. The court quoted Restatement of Trusts §398(2).

as intestate property or should be applied to the charitable purpose of maintaining the parks. It was held that it should be applied for this charitable purpose.

In *In re Dalziel,* [17] however, a provision as to the perpetual maintenance of a tomb was held to invalidate the whole disposition. In that case a testatrix bequeathed a large sum of money to a hospital corporation, and directed that the income should be used as far as necessary for the upkeep and rebuilding of a mausoleum, and she provided that if the corporation should fail to carry out this purpose the legacy should go to another charity, to be selected by the trustees, which would be willing to accept the legacy subject to the same condition. It was held that the legacy failed altogether.

In *Brennan v. United States* [18] a woman conveyed property in trust to maintain a hospital room in memory of her brother and provided that the hospital should care for her during her lifetime and after her death should care for the descendants of her parents, the remainder of the income to be used for the benefit of the hospital. It was held that on her death the amount of the gift could not be deducted in ascertaining the estate tax. The court held that the provision for her descendants was void under the rule against perpetuities and that the whole trust failed because the donor's primary purpose was not to benefit the hospital.

(3) All given to charity except amount required for invalid purposes. It has been held in a number of cases that where property is bequeathed in trust for charitable purposes and other purposes that fail, and it is possible to ascertain the maximum amount that could properly be applied for the other purposes if they were valid purposes, the trust fails as to that amount, but the balance of the property is applicable to the charitable purposes. Thus in an English case where a testator directed that a part of his estate should be used for the erection of a monument and that the remainder should go to the government of Bengal to be applied to charitable purposes, it was held that the direction as to the

[17][1943] Ch. 277, noted in 8 Convey. (N.S.) 166, 60 Law Q. Rev. 26, 196 Law T. 74, 80, 11 Sol. 36.

See §124.2, n. 16; §401.5, n. 6.

[18]129 F. Supp. 155 (D. Conn. 1954).

monument was invalid, but that after ascertaining the amount that it would have cost for the monument the balance of the estate should go as directed to the government of Bengal, the amount applicable to the monument passing to the next of kin of the testator.[19] In a Rhode Island case[20] a testator bequeathed to a certain church $3000 in trust to use the income for the care of his grave, adding that if the income should be more than sufficient for this purpose the balance should be used at the discretion of the vestry. It was held that the trust for the care of the grave was invalid; that under a statute executors were authorized to pay to a cemetery corporation or town a reasonable sum for the perpetual care of the testator's grave; that $500 was amply sufficient for the purpose; and that the trust of the balance of $2500 being given for religious purposes was valid. In a California case[21] property was left in trust for charitable purposes, subject to the payment of an annuity that was invalid as a perpetuity. It was held that a resulting trust arose as to the amount required for the annuity, and that the balance should be applied for the designated charitable purposes.

(4) Whole disposition fails.   On the other hand, it has been held in many cases that where property is bequeathed in trust for charitable purposes and other purposes for which a trust cannot be validly created, the trust fails altogether. In these cases the court has found it to be impossible or impracticable or contrary to the intention of the testator to uphold the trust, either in whole or in part, as a charitable trust.

As we have seen in the preceding section, it has been held in England and quite generally in the United States that where property is left in trust for purposes that are not limited to charity, although they may be broad enough to include charity, the intended trust fails altogether. In a few of these cases it has been argued that a pro rata division should be made between charitable and noncharitable objects, and that the trust should

[19]Mitford v. Reynolds, 1 Phil. 185 (1841), 16 Sim. 105 (1848).

See In re Coxen, [1948] Ch. 747, noted in 22 Austl. L.J. 413, 13 Convey. (N.S.) 131, 133, 138, 99 Law J. 102.

[20]Todd v. St. Mary's Church, 45 R.I. 282, 120 A. 577 (1923).

[21]Davenport v. Davenport Found., 36 Cal. 2d 67, 222 P.2d 11 (1950), *mod'g* 215 P.2d 467 (Cal. App. 1950).

be upheld in part. The courts have held, however, that the method of making a pro rata division of the property among the valid and invalid objects is not applicable where the testator has not enumerated several objects but has merely grouped together in general language objects that are charitable and objects that are not charitable. Where the testator has used several adjectives or nouns, of which some connote charity and others do not, the court will not direct a division of the property into as many shares as there are adjectives or nouns. The question of such an apportionment was raised in *Morice v. Bishop of Durham*.[22] In that case the testatrix left the residue of her estate to such objects of "benevolence and liberality" as the legatee should most approve of. The Attorney-General contended that although the word "liberality" did not connote charity, the word "benevolence" did, and that the court should divide the fund into two equal parts and uphold the trust as to one half of the estate. Lord Eldon held, however, that even assuming that the word "benevolence" connoted charity, no apportionment should be made. In a later English case[23] a testator bequeathed one-fifth of his residuary estate in trust "for such patriotic purposes or objects and such charitable institution or institutions or charitable object or objects in the British Empire as my trustees may in their absolute discretion select in such shares and proportions as they shall think proper." The court held that the trust failed, because "patriotic" purposes are not necessarily charitable. Lord Sterndale, M.R., said:

> Then the third and last resort was that, at any rate, assuming patriotic purposes and objects to be outside the definition of charity, and therefore bad in law, the fund can be divided between patriotic objects which are not charitable, and patriotic objects which are charitable. I do not see how that can be done. There is no distribution at all between the different objects. The trustees are to apply the fund either to one or to the other, or to one and the other in quite undefined proportions, and it is therefore open to them, on the wording of the will, to apply the whole of the fund to purposes which are not charitable, and have noth-

[22]9 Ves. 399 (1804), 10 Ves. 522 (1805).
[23]In re Tetley, [1923] 1 Ch. 258, 269, *aff'd sub nom.* Attorney-General v. National Provincial & Union Bank, [1924] A.C. 262.

ing left for charity, and, in those circumstances, it seems to me an apportionment such as is suggested, whether in equal or in other proportions, is impossible.

Even where the testator has specified several objects, of which some are valid charitable objects and the others are invalid noncharitable objects, it has been held that the whole trust fails where an equal division of the property among the several objects would not be in accordance with the probable intention of the testator, and where the maximum amount applicable to the invalid objects could not be ascertained, and where the charitable purposes were not the primary purposes.[24] Thus in *In re Porter*[25] a testator bequeathed £10,000 to the trustees of a Masonic temple to apply the income to the maintenance of the temple in their sole discretion, the balance if any to be applied annually in favor of any Masonic charity that the trustees might select. It was held that the trust for the maintenance of the temple was not charitable and was invalid as a perpetuity, and that because the trustees might have applied all of the income to the maintenance of the temple the whole trust failed. The court distinguished the cases in which it is held in England that where the income of a fund is to be applied to the maintenance

[24]*England:* Fowler v. Fowler, 33 Beav. 616 (1864); Hunter v. Attorney-General, [1899] A.C. 309; In re Porter, [1925] Ch. 746.

Connecticut: Coit v. Comstock, 51 Conn. 352, 50 Am. Rep. 29 (1884).

Georgia: Green v. Austin, 222 Ga. 409, 150 S.E.2d 346 (1966).

Illinois: Hampton v. Dill, 354 Ill. 415, 188 N.E. 419 (1933).

New Jersey: Van Syckel v. Johnson, 80 N.J. Eq. 117, 70 A. 657 (1908).

Rhode Island: Kelly v. Nichols, 17 R.I. 306, 21 A. 906 (1891), 19 L.R.A. 413, 18 R.I. 62, 25 A. 840 (1892).

Texas: Carr v. Jones, 403 S.W.2d 181 (Tex. Civ. App. 1966).

Canada: Klassen Estate v. Klassen, [1986] 5 W.W.R. 746 (Sask. Q.B.).

In The Equity Trustees Exrs. & Agency Co. v. Epstein, [1984] Vict. R. 577, land was devised to trustees to pay 20 percent of the income to grandchildren and their descendants forever, 20 percent to a college forever, and to accumulate the other 60 percent of income forever. It was held that although the college was a charity and Victoria Property Law Act §158 applies to trusts for charities and individuals, the entire trust failed.

See Note, Gift to charity as affected by conjoined noncharitable gift invalid under rule or statute against perpetuities or rule against accumulations, 170 A.L.R. 760 (1947).

[25][1925] Ch. 746.

of a tomb and the balance is to be applied for charitable purposes, the trust as to the tomb fails but the whole of the trust fund can be applied to the charitable purposes, on the ground that these cases are sui generis. In a Connecticut case[26] a testator made a bequest to an ecclesiastical society to apply the income or as much as should be necessary in keeping certain burial lots in good order, the remainder of the income if any to be applied to the maintenance of religious services. The court held the bequest wholly invalid. In a case in New Jersey[27] a testator bequeathed $6000 to his executors in trust to pay the income in keeping in repair a part of a graveyard where his family was buried, and secondly in keeping the rest of the graveyard in repair, and thirdly to apply the balance for certain charitable purposes. The court held that the whole trust failed; that a bequest for the perpetual maintenance of a graveyard is void as a perpetuity; that when an unascertainable part of a fund is given upon a void trust and the residue upon a valid trust, the whole fails. In a Rhode Island case[28] a testator bequeathed his estate in trust to keep a grave in repair, to keep a clock in repair, to keep his house open for the reception of ministers and others of his faith when traveling in the service of truth, and if the means permitted to publish religious books. The court held that the trust for the first three purposes was invalid, and that although the fourth purpose was charitable the whole trust failed, because the amount applicable to the first three purposes could not be ascertained. The same result was reached in another case in the same state.[29] In that case a testator left $1000 to a cemetery corporation and directed that the interest therefrom should be used for flowers on Decoration Day and for keeping his monument in condition. It was held that although under a statute a trust to keep a monument in condition was charitable, a trust to place flowers each year for an indefinite period on a grave was not charitable and failed as a perpetuity. The question

---

[26]Coit v. Comstock, 51 Conn. 352, 50 Am. Rep. 29 (1884).

[27]Van Syckel v. Johnson, 80 N.J. Eq. 117, 70 A. 657 (1908).

[28]Kelley v. Nichols, 17 R.I. 306, 21 A. 906, 19 L.R.A. 413 (1891), 18 R.I. 62, 25 A. 840 (1892).

[29]Rhode Island Hosp. Trust Co. v. Proprietors of Swan Point Cemetery, 62 R.I. 83, 141, 3 A.2d 236 (1938), 63 R.I. 79, 7 A.2d 205 (1939).

See MacDonald v. Manning, 103 R.I. 538, 239 A.2d 640 (1968).

then arose whether the disposition failed altogether. The court held that it was impossible to say that either purpose was a primary purpose, and held that the intended trust failed altogether.

Similarly, in a number of English cases it has been held that where property was bequeathed in trust for two or more charitable purposes and one of the purposes involved the purchase of real estate and was therefore invalid under the mortmain statutes, the whole trust failed.[30] In these cases it was impossible to ascertain the maximum amount applicable to the purposes that failed, and the other charitable purposes did not appear to have been the testator's primary purposes, and it was felt that an equal division of the property among the several purposes would not be in accordance with the probable intention of the testator.

Where the purposes of a corporation or association include purposes that are charitable and others that are not charitable, it has been held that it is not a charitable organization.[31]

---

[30]Chapman v. Brown, 6 Ves. 404 (1801) (to build or purchase a chapel and to apply the surplus if any to the support of a minister and for other charitable purposes); Attorney-General v. Hinxman, 2 Jac. & W. 270 (1820) (devise of land for school and bequest of money to keep schoolhouse in repair and to apply residue for poor); Kirkmann v. Lewis, 38 L.J. Ch. 570 (1869) (for construction of public well, the surplus if any for benefit of school); In re Taylor, 58 L.T. 538 (1888) (to build hospital and keep it in repair and to apply balance if any for poor).

[31]In re Corelli, [1943] Ch. 332, noted in 8 Convey. (N.S.) 112, 11 Sol. 36; Tennant Plays v. Inland Revenue Commrs., [1948] 1 All E.R. 506; Inland Revenue Commrs. v. Baddeley, [1955] A.C. 572, *rev'g* Baddeley v. Inland Revenue Commrs., [1953] Ch. 504, *rev'g* [1953] 1 All E.R. 63, noted in Camb. L.J. 20, 33 Can. B. Rev. 898; McNamee v. Mansfield, [1945] 1 I.R. 13; Oxford Group v. Inland Revenue Commrs., [1949] 2 All E.R. 537; Associated Artists v. Inland Revenue Commrs., [1956] 2 All E.R. 583.

See also Dulles v. Johnson, 155 F. Supp. 275 (S.D.N.Y. 1957), *rev'd,* 275 F.2d 362, 80 A.L.R.2d 1338 (2d Cir. 1959) on the ground that the purposes were wholly charitable, *cert. denied,* 364 U.S. 834 (1960). See §371.3, n. 5.

But see North of Eng. Zoological Socy. v. Chester Rural Dist. Council, [1959] 3 All E.R. 116 (zoological society whose main purposes were educational); Congregational Union of N.S.W. v. Thistlethwayte, 87 C.L.R. 375 (Austl. 1952).

In the Report of the Committee on the Law and Practice Relating to Charitable Trusts (1952) (Cmd. 8710) c. 12, the Oxford Group case was discussed and it was recommended that where a trust had a primary charitable

As we have seen, where property is bequeathed in trust for

---

object it should not fail so long as the property was devoted to the charitable object. Parliament thereupon enacted a statute retroactively validating trusts containing such "imperfect trust provisions" created before December 15, 1952. Charitable Trusts (Validation) Act, 1954, 2 & 3 Eliz. II, c. 58. See 18 Mod. L. Rev. 152 (1955).

In In re Wykes' Will Trusts, [1961] Ch. 229, noted in 24 Mod. L. Rev. 387, a testator left a share of his estate to the board of directors of a company "to be used at their discretion as a benevolent or welfare fund or for welfare purposes for the sole benefit of the past, present and future employees of the company." It was held that the trust was validated by the Charitable Trusts (Validation) Act, 1954, and the property should be applied for the relief of poverty of the employees of the company.

In In re Mead's Trust Deed, [1961] 2 All E.R. 836, where a trust was created to establish a home for the aged members of a trade union, it was held that the trust was not charitable, because it was limited to members of the union and was not exclusively for the relief of poverty. See §375.2, n. 69. The court held, however, that the provision was an "imperfect trust provision" within the Charitable Trusts (Validation) Act, 1954, and that the trustees could admit to the home only members of the union who could not support themselves.

But see the following cases holding that the Act was not applicable: In re Gillingham Bus Disaster Fund, [1958] Ch. 300, aff'd, [1959] Ch. 62, noted in 74 Law Q. Rev. 190, 489, Camb. Law J. 41; In re Harpur's Will Trusts, [1962] Ch. 78, aff'g [1961] Ch. 38; In re The Lord Mayor of Belfast's Air Raid Distress Fund, [1962] N. Ir. L.R. 161.

In In re Harpur's Will Trusts, [1962] Ch. 78, aff'g [1961] Ch. 38, where a testatrix left her estate to be divided at the uncontrolled discretion of the trustee between institutions having for their *main* object the assistance of wounded or incapacitated members of the armed forces, it was held that the trust was not charitable and failed.

In In re McCullough, [1966] N. Ir. L.R. 73, a testator left the residue of his estate to a Masonic lodge, "the interest annually to be used at the sole discretion of the said Provincial Grand Master for such purposes within the province as he shall from time to time direct." It was held that because the purposes were not limited to charity the trust failed. The court said that it might have been upheld under the Charities Act (Northern Ireland) 1964, §24, validating such imperfect trust provisions, but the Act was not retroactive.

In Belfast Assn. v. Commissioner of Valuation, [1968] N. Ir. L.R. 21, it was held that a shop in which articles made by the blind were sold was not used exclusively for charitable purposes if other goods were also sold. MacDermott, L.C.J., dissented on the ground that the sale of other articles was merely incidental.

See note, Warburton, Football and the Recreational Charities Act 1958, [1980] Conv. 173-181.

purposes that are not limited to charity, although they are broad enough to include charity, it is arguable that the legatee should be permitted, although he cannot be compelled, to apply the property to the designated purposes, and that the trust should fail only if he fails to do so. This argument, however, has been rejected in England and in most of the American decisions. It is arguable that the legatee should be permitted, or even compelled, to apply the property to the designated charitable purposes, on the ground that the testator would have preferred this disposition to be made of the property rather than to have the trust fail. This argument has been rejected by the courts, although it has induced the legislatures in Australia and in New Zealand to provide by statute for such a disposition of the property.[32]

§399. Failure of Particular Purpose Where Settlor Had General Charitable Intention; the Doctrine of Cy Pres

Where property is given in trust for a particular charitable purpose, the trust will not ordinarily fail even though it is impossible to carry out the particular purpose. In such a case the court will ordinarily direct that the property be applied to a similar charitable purpose. The theory is that the testator would have desired that the property be so applied if he had realized that it would be impossible to carry out the particular purpose. The courts usually put it this way, that although the testator intended that the property should be applied to the particular charitable purpose named by him, yet he had a more general intention to devote the property to charitable purposes. The testator would presumably have desired that the property should be applied to purposes as nearly as may be like the purposes stated by him rather than that the trust should fail altogether.

The principle under which the courts thus attempt to save a charitable trust from failure by carrying out the more general

---

As to the provisions of the Recreational Charities Act, 1958, 6 & 7 Eliz. II, c. 17, see §374.11, n. 8.

[32]See §123.

purpose of the testator and carrying out approximately though not exactly his more specific intent is called the doctrine of cy pres. The phrase is in the Anglo-French and is equivalent to the modern French *si près,* meaning so near or as near.[1] The intention of the testator is carried out as nearly as may be.

In a number of states there are statutes embodying the doctrine of cy pres.[2] The Model Act Concerning the Administra-

§399. [1]See Oxford English Dictionary, "cy pres."

See Delaware Trust Co. v. Graham, 30 Del. Ch. 330, 61 A.2d 110 (1948) (citing the text), noted in 9 Md. L. Rev. 359.

Chester, Cy Pres: A Promise Unfulfilled, 54 Ind. L.J. 407 (1979) (charity).

[2]*Alabama:* Code 1975, §35-4-251.

Delaware: Code Ann., tit. 12, §3541, as enacted by Laws 1979, c. 131.

Georgia: Code 1981, §§53-2-99, 53-12-77.

Illinois: Ann. Stat. c. 30 ¶601, added by Laws 1983, P.A. 83-478.

Indiana: Code 1971, §§30-4-3-27, 36-1-4-10.

Louisiana: Rev. Stat. Ann., §§9:2331 to 9:2337, as amended by Laws 1970, c. 43.

Maryland: Code Ann., art. 16, §196.

Minnesota: Stat. Ann., §501.12.

New Hampshire: Rev. Stat. Ann., §§498:4a to 498:4c, as inserted by Laws 1971, c. 516.

New York: Estates, Powers and Trusts Law, §8-1.1, amended by Laws 1971, c. 1058, and Laws 1985, c. 492.

North Carolina: Gen. Stat., §36A-47. See Wachovia Bank & Trust Co. v. Morgan, 279 N.C. 265, 182 S.E.2d 356 (1971) (citing the text); Edmisten v. Sands, 307 N.C. 670, 300 S.E.2d 387 (1983).

Oklahoma: Stat. Ann., tit. 60, §201.

Pennsylvania: 20 Pa. Cons. Stat., §6110.

Rhode Island: Gen. Laws 1956, §18-4-1.

South Dakota: Codified Laws 1967, §§55-9-1 to 55-9-5.

Vermont: Stat. Ann., tit. 14, §2328, as amended by Laws 1985, c. 144.

Virginia: Code, §55-31.1, as amended by Laws 1980, c. 361.

West Virginia: Code, §35-2-2.

Wisconsin: Stat., §701.10 (stating its purpose to broaden the power of the courts to make charitable gifts more effective).

By Massachusetts Ann. Laws, c. 12, §8K, as inserted by Laws 1974, c. 562, it is provided that "A gift made for a public charitable purpose shall be deemed to have been made with a general intention to devote the property to public charitable purposes, unless otherwise provided in a written instrument of gift." This is made applicable to gifts made thereafter.

By Massachusetts Ann. Laws, c. 214, §10B, as inserted by Laws 1974, c. 562, it is provided that "Upon a petition commenced after the death of the donor for the application cy pres to similar public charitable purposes of a gift for a public charitable purpose which has become impossible or impracticable of fulfillment, the court may exercise jurisdiction without requiring that the

tion of Charitable Trusts, Devises and Bequests, recommended by the National Conference of Commissioners on Uniform State Laws in 1944, provides that:

> If a trust for charity is or becomes illegal, or impossible or impracticable of fulfillment or if a devise or bequest for charity, at the time it was intended to become effective is illegal, or impossible or impracticable of fulfillment, and if the settlor, or testator, manifested a general intention to devote the property to charity, [a court of equity] may, on application of any trustee, or any interested party or the attorney general of the state, order an administration of the trust, devise or bequest as nearly as possible to fulfill the general charitable intention of the settlor or testator.[3]

It is not true that a charitable trust never fails where it is impossible to carry out the particular purpose of the testator. In some cases, as we shall see, it appears that the accomplishment of the particular purpose and only that purpose was desired by the testator and that he had no more general charitable intent and that he would presumably have preferred to have the whole trust fail if the particular purpose is impossible of accomplishment. In such a case the cy pres doctrine is not applicable.

The doctrine of cy pres is also invoked where a testator makes a bequest "for charity," without making any provision with respect to the person who is to determine to what charitable

---

heirs or next of kin of the donor or others who would be entitled to take upon failure of any charitable gift be joined as parties." Notice to such persons is not required except in certain cases. This is a very liberal extension of the cy pres doctrine.

See Clark v. Mayor of Gloucester, 336 Mass. 631, 147 N.E.2d 191 (1958).

In some of these statutes, as in Minnesota, New York, and South Dakota, it is provided that the court shall not make an order applying the property cy pres without the consent of the donor of the property if he be living.

In Minnesota the statute requires the consent of the trustees.

In a few states there are statutes providing for the application cy pres in particular situations:

Indiana: Code Ann. §30-4-3-27, added by Acts 1971, P.L. 416.

Maine: Rev. Stat. 1964, tit. 13, §§3061, 3062 (pious purposes, where no proper custodian).

See the Uniform Management of Institutional Funds Act, §389, n. 16.

[3]This statute has been enacted in Maryland, Oklahoma, and Vermont. See n. 2, *supra.*

purposes the property should be devoted. In such a case, as in the case where property is left in trust for a particular charitable purpose the accomplishment of which is impossible, the court will direct the framing of a scheme for the disposition of the property.[4] On the other hand, where a testator leaves property for such charitable purposes as a trustee named by him shall select, and the trustee is willing and able to make the selection, it is unnecessary to frame a scheme for the disposition of the property, but the trustee may dispose of the property for any charitable purposes he may select. In such a case, however, if the trustee named by the testator is unable or unwilling to make the selection, and the selection by the named trustee is not an essential part of the scheme of the testator so that the trust does not fail, the court will direct the framing of a scheme, unless it would be more in accordance with the intention of the testator to name a successor trustee to make the selection.[5]

The cy pres doctrine is applicable only to dispositions for charitable purposes, including gifts to individual trustees and gifts to charitable corporations.[6] It is true, however, even in the case of private trusts that the court may to a limited extent permit a modification of the trust in order to prevent its failure. Thus, as we have seen, the court may permit or direct a deviation from the terms of the trust if, owing to circumstances not known to the settlor and not anticipated by him, compliance with the terms of the trust would defeat or substantially impair the accomplishment of the purposes of the trust.[7] In permitting a deviation the court is merely exercising its general power over the administration of trusts. It not infrequently exercises the same power to permit a deviation from the terms of the trust in the case of a charitable trust.[8] Thus, both in the case of a private trust and in the case of a charitable trust, the court may permit a sale of land although the sale is not permitted or is expressly

---

[4]See §397.

[5]See §397.1.

[6]See §348.1.

Martin v. North Hill Christian Church, 64 Ohio App. 2d 192, 18 Ohio Op. 3d 147, 412 N.E.2d 413 (1979) (business college operated for profit).

See Edwards v. De Simone, 105 R.I. 335, 787, 252 A.2d 327 (1969) (citing Restatement of Trusts §399).

[7]See §167.

[8]See §381.

forbidden by the terms of the trust. In the exercise of this power in the case of a private trust, however, the court will not substitute different beneficiaries from those designated by the terms of the trust nor will it enlarge the interest of one beneficiary at the expense of another. Similarly, in the exercise of this power in the case of a charitable trust the court will not substitute one charitable purpose for another. In the exercise of the cy pres power, however, the court may permit the trust property to be applied to a charitable purpose other than that designated by the terms of the trust, where it has become impossible to accomplish the designated purpose. In other words, the cy pres doctrine involves the exercise of a power much more extensive than the ordinary power of the court to permit deviations from the terms of the trust.

Where property is given in trust for a particular charitable purpose that fails, but the trust does not fail because the cy pres doctrine is applicable, the proper procedure is to apply to the court for its determination as to the purposes to which the property should be applied.[9] Frequently, the court will refer the matter to a master with directions to report a scheme of application of the property to the court. The court may accept the scheme so proposed or may reject or modify it.[10] If the situation is one in which there is no difficulty in the framing of a scheme the court may frame a scheme itself or adopt one proposed by the trustees.[11] It is improper, however, for the trustees themselves, without applying to the court for its instructions, to proceed to make an application of the property cy pres.[12] But if the court would have directed the trustees to make

[9]As to the way in which the court proceeds to frame a scheme, see Jackson v. Phillips, 14 Allen 539, 596 (Mass. 1867); Town of Milton v. Attorney Gen., 314 Mass. 234, 49 N.E.2d 909 (1943); Matter of Lawless, 194 Misc. 844, 87 N.Y.S.2d 386, 403 (1949), *aff'd mem.*, 277 A.D. 1045, 100 N.Y.S.2d 537 (1950).

As to the English practice, see Tudor, Law of Charitable Trusts 186-193 (5th ed. 1929); Husband, *Cy-pres* and Charities, 146 Law Q. Rev. 1115 (1982).

[10]Jackson v. Phillips, 14 Allen 539 (Mass. 1867); Du Pont Estate, 37 D.&C.2d 456 (Pa. 1965).

[11]In re Robinson, [1923] 2 Ch. 332; Osgood v. Rogers, 186 Mass. 238, 71 N.E. 306 (1904).

[12]*Illinois:* City of Aurora v. Young Men's Christian Assn., 9 Ill. 2d 286, 137 N.E.2d 347 (1956) (citing Restatement of Trusts §399); Bertram v. Berger, 1 Ill. App. 3d 743, 274 N.E.2d 667 (1971), *semble.*

the application of the property that they made, it may approve the application so made.[13]

In a proceeding for the application of the cy pres doctrine, the Attorney General is a necessary party.[14] The determination of the proper scheme, however, is for the court, and the Attorney General has no power to control the disposition.[15]

Massachusetts: Trustees of Andover Theological Seminary v. Visitors, 253 Mass. 256, 297, 148 N.E. 900 (1925), *semble,* noted in 35 Yale L.J. 643; First Christian Church v. Brownell, 332 Mass. 143, 123 N.E.2d 603 (1954).

Missouri: Lewis v. Brubaker, 322 Mo. 52, 14 S.W.2d 982 (1929).

New Jersey: Mackenzie v. Trustees of Presbytery, 67 N.J. Eq. 652, 671, 61 A. 1027, 3 L.R.A. (N.S.) 227 (1905); Trustees of First Presbyterian Church v. Wheeler, 106 N.J. Eq. 8, 149 A. 589 (1930), noted in 40 Yale L.J. 143; Miranda v. King, 11 N.J. Super. 165, 78 A.2d 98 (1951).

Pennsylvania: Johnson Estate, 15 D.&C.2d 407 (Pa. 1958).

Wyoming: Town of Cody v. Buffalo Bill Memorial Assn., 64 Wyo. 468, 196 P.2d 369 (1948) (conveyance by a charitable corporation to a town; citing Restatement of Trusts §399).

[13]O'Hara v. Grand Lodge I.O.G.T., 213 Cal. 131, 2 P.2d 21 (1931); Lakatong Lodge v. Franklin Bd. of Educ., 84 N.J. Eq. 112, 92 A. 870 (1915).

See American Natl. Red Cross v. Felzner Post, 86 Ind. App. 709, 159 N.E. 771 (1928), noted in 2 U. Cin. L. Rev. 417; Gordon v. City of Baltimore, 258 Md. 682, 267 A.2d 98 (1970) (citing the text).

In Stuart v. Continental Ill. Natl. Bank & Trust Co., 68 Ill. 2d 502, 12 Ill. Dec. 248, 369 N.E.2d 1262 (1977), *cert. denied,* 444 U.S. 844, 100 S. Ct. 86, 62 L. Ed. 2d 56 (1979), (citing Restatement of Trusts §399), *aff'g* Northern Trust Co. v. Continental Ill. Natl. Bank & Trust Co., 43 Ill. App. 3d 169, 11 Ill. Dec. 767, 356 N.E.2d 1049 (1976), the court refused to condone an unauthorized distribution by one of the trustees of a charitable trust.

[14]In re Estate of Owens, 244 Iowa 533, 57 N.W.2d 193 (1953); Matter of McIntyre, 257 A.D. 972, 13 N.Y.S.2d 35 (1939), *appeal dismissed,* 281 N.Y. 817, 24 N.E.2d 486 (1939); Alco Gravure v. Knapp Found., 64 N.Y.2d 458, 479 N.E.2d 752, 490 N.Y.S.2d 116 (1985).

The Attorney General is a necessary party in an action brought by the heirs of the settlor to recover property on the ground that the charitable trust had failed. Pruner Estate, 390 Pa. 529, 136 A.2d 107 (1957). See §391, n. 48.

By Texas Civ. Stat. Ann., art. 4412a, as inserted by Laws 1959, c. 115, as amended by Laws 1981, c. 501, §1, it is provided that the Attorney General is a necessary party in proceedings for the application of the doctrine of cy pres.

[15]Town of Brookline v. Barnes, 327 Mass. 201, 97 N.E.2d 651 (1951). In this case Spalding, J., in a very clear opinion set forth the principles and methods governing the framing of schemes under the cy pres doctrine.

See Application of Guaranty Trust Co. (Matter of Petroleum Research

Intervening parties and parties aggrieved. If a proceeding involving a charitable trust is properly brought by the Attorney General or by the trustees or by persons having a special interest, a third person may seek to intervene in the proceeding. It is within the discretion of the court whether to permit such intervention. The question frequently arises where the doctrine of cy pres is applicable and a charitable institution seeks to have the trust fund awarded to it.[16]

If the court refuses to award the trust fund to the intervening party, a question arises whether it can maintain an appeal. It is held that the party is not a party aggrieved and has no standing to appeal.[17] In *Coffee v. William Marsh Rice Univer-*

Fund), 15 Misc. 2d 23, 507, 184 N.Y.S.2d 413 (1959), s.c. 22 Misc. 2d 83, 200 N.Y.S.2d 118 (1960); Veterans' Indus. v. Lynch, 8 Cal. App. 3d 902, 88 Cal. Rptr. 303 (1970) (citing the text); In re Estate of Horton, 11 Cal. App. 3d 680, 90 Cal. Rptr. 66 (1970); Midkiff v. Kobayashi, 54 Haw. 229, 507 P.2d 724 (1973) (as to deviations from the terms of the trust); Estate of Thompson, 414 A.2d 881 (Me. 1980).

[16]*California:* Veterans' Indus. v. Lynch, 8 Cal. App. 3d 902, 88 Cal. Rptr. 303 (1970).

Illinois: Art Inst. of Chicago v. Castle, 9 Ill. App. 2d 473, 133 N.E.2d 748 (1956).

Maine: Estate of Thompson, 414 A.2d 881 (Me. 1980).

Minnesota: In re Application of Sister Elizabeth Kenny Found. (Sister Elizabeth Kenny Found. v. National Found.), 267 Minn. 352, 126 N.W.2d 640 (1964).

New Hampshire: In Concord Natl. Bank v. Haverhill, 101 N.H. 416, 145 A.2d 61 (1958), noted in 39 B.U.L. Rev. 262, where a trust was created to assist needy students at Dartmouth College from two towns and in a proceeding brought by the trustees for an application cy pres of surplus income the towns were named as defendants, it was held that their counsel were entitled to reasonable compensation out of the trust funds.

[17]*Massachusetts:* Bolster v. Attorney Gen., 306 Mass. 387, 28 N.E.2d 475 (1940); Stackpole v. Brewster Free Academy, 355 Mass. 774, 247 N.E.2d 599 (1969).

New Jersey: See In re Rogers, 15 N.J. Super. 189, 83 A.2d 268 (1951), noted in 32 B.U.L. Rev. 126.

New York: Matter of Richmond County Socy. for the Prevention of Cruelty to Children, 11 A.D.2d 236, 204 N.Y.S.2d 707 (1960), *aff'd mem.,* 9 N.Y.2d 913, 176 N.E.2d 97 (1961).

Pennsylvania: Atlee Estate, 406 Pa. 528, 178 A.2d 722 (1962).

In Hinckley v. Beardsley, 28 Ill. App. 2d 379, 171 N.E.2d 401, 88 A.L.R.2d 686 (1961), a testatrix left property in trust to establish a home for worthy women. It was impracticable to establish such a home and proceedings were

sity[18] the founder of a university provided for the admission of white students only and provided that no tuition should be charged. The university brought suit to determine whether it might admit students without regard to color and to charge tuition to those able to pay. The Attorney General was named as defendant. Two of the alumni were permitted to intervene as representing alumni and contributors. The trial court held that because the purpose of the founder was to establish a first-class institution, it should be permitted to admit students without regard to color and to charge tuition. The intervenors, but not the Attorney General, appealed. The lower court held that the intervenors had no standing to appeal, but its decision was reversed, three justices dissenting.

A further question arises as to the standing of the trustee of a charitable trust to appeal from a judgment of the court involving the disposition of the trust property. The question arises where the court renders a judgment for the application cy pres of the trust property, and the Attorney General does not appeal. Because the judgment authorizes a deviation from the terms of the trust, it has been held that the trustee has a standing to appeal. In *Howard Savings Institution v. Peep*[19] where a testator made a bequest to Amherst College for scholarships for Protestant gentile boys and the college refused to accept the bequest because of the religious restriction and the court held that under

---

brought for an application cy pres of the property. A charitable corporation intervened asking that the property be given to it, but the court gave it to another institution. It was held that the intervening claimant was not entitled to attorneys' fees out of the property.

In Veterans' Indus. v. Lynch, 8 Cal. App. 3d 902, 88 Cal. Rptr. 303 (1970) (citing the text), it was suggested that in case the lower court abused its discretion in refusing to permit intervention, mandamus would be the remedy.

[18]387 S.W.2d 132 (Tex. Civ. App. 1965), *rev'd,* 403 S.W.2d 340 (1966).

Thereafter the appellate court affirmed the decision of the trial court. 408 S.W.2d 269 (Tex. Civ. App. 1966) (citing the text). See §399.4A, n. 24.

In Howard Hughes Medical Inst. v. Neff, 640 S.W.2d 942 (Tex. App. 1982), *writ refused n.r.e.,* a medical institute established by Howard Hughes in 1953 petitioned for probate of an alleged lost 1925 will of Hughes providing for the establishment of a medical institute. It was held that the possibility that petitioner would be designated as beneficiary cy pres was not enough to give petitioner standing to seek probate.

[19]34 N.J. 494, 170 A.2d 39 (1961).

the cy pres doctrine the bequest should be given to the college free of the religious restriction, it was held that the executor had standing to appeal. So also where the judgment results in the extinguishment of the charitable trust, the trustee or executor has a standing to appeal.[20]

§399.1.   Judicial and prerogative cy pres.   In the preceding section we discussed the judicial doctrine of cy pres. Under this doctrine the courts attempt in part at least and as nearly as practicable to carry out the testator's intention. At common law in England, however, there was a prerogative doctrine of cy pres as well as a judicial doctrine. Under the prerogative doctrine the Crown, as parens patriae, was permitted in certain cases to apply the property for any charitable purpose it might select. The king in the exercise of this prerogative power was under no duty, save perhaps a moral duty, to consider what would probably have been the wishes of the testator. He would indicate in writing over his sign manual (signature) the disposition that he wished to be made of the property, and the chancellor would thereupon order that disposition to be made.

It is not entirely clear exactly where the line was to be drawn between the situations in which the disposition would be made by the Crown under the prerogative power and the situations where the disposition would be made under a scheme approved by the chancellor under the judicial power. Indeed, the line seems to have shifted, with a tendency to enlarge the judicial power at the expense of the prerogative power. It would seem that the disposition under the prerogative power was made in

---

[20]Waterbury Trust Co. v. Porter, 130 Conn. 494, 35 A.2d 837 (1944) (citing Restatement of Trusts §178).

In Thompson Will, 416 Pa. 249, 206 A.2d 21 (1965), where the residue was bequeathed to the executor to be disposed of for such local charities as he should select, and the lower court held that the will was revoked, it was held that he could appeal as a party aggrieved, because as trustee it was his duty to uphold the trust.

But see Trusts of Holdeen, 486 Pa. 1, 403 A.2d 978 (1979), holding that the trustee had no standing to appeal.

See Note, Right of executor or administrator to appeal from order granting or denying distribution, 16 A.L.R.3d 1274 (1967).

As to the standing of a trustee to appeal as a party aggrieved by a judgment involving conflicting interests of the beneficiaries of a private trust, see §183, n. 9.

two classes of cases: first, where property was given for a purpose that was illegal but that except for such illegality would be charitable; and secondly, where property was given directly to charity, without indicating further the character of the purpose and without indicating that a trustee was to administer the charity.[1] It was once thought that where property was bequeathed in trust for charitable purposes to be thereafter stated in a codicil, and such purposes were never stated, the property should be disposed of by the Crown in the exercise of its prerogative power; but the court later held that the disposition in such a case should be made by the court under a scheme in the exercise of the judicial power.[2] In the United States, however, in such a case the trust fails, and the cy pres doctrine is not applicable.[3] On the other hand, where property is given to charity generally and no one is named as trustee to select the charity it would seem that today this will be treated as a situation calling for the exercise of the judicial cy pres power and not that of the prerogative, and the court will approve a scheme for the distribution of the property.[4]

§399.1.   [1]Moggridge v. Thackwell, 7 Ves. 36, 76 (1802); Cary v. Abbot, 7 Ves. 490 (1802); Mills v. Farmer, 1 Mer. 55, 19 Ves. 482 (1815); West v. Shuttleworth, 2 Myl. & K. 684 (1835); In re White, [1893] 2 Ch. 41.

See Jackson v. Phillips, 14 Allen 539 (Mass. 1867); Puget Sound Natl. Bank v. Easterday, 56 Wash. 2d 937, 350 P.2d 444 (1960) (quoting the text), noted in 36 Wash. L. Rev. 205.

In In re Bennett, [1960] Ch. 18, where a testatrix left a share of the residue to a nonexisting hospital for incurables, it was held that the court should not frame a scheme but that the prerogative cy pres doctrine was applicable, because it was a direct gift and not a trust.

In In re Conroy, 35 D.L.R.3d 752 (B.C. 1973), where a testator left the residue to a nonexisting organization, the court said that although in such a case the disposition was subject to the prerogative power of the Crown, it could itself, with the consent of the Attorney General, make a cy pres disposition, and gave the property to two organizations in equal shares.

As to the prerogative cy pres in the earlier English law, see Jones, History of the Law of Charity, 1532-1827 (1969).

See 8 Cornell L.Q. 179 (1923); 13 id. 310 (1928).

[2]In re Pyne, [1903] 1 Ch. 83; In re Leslie, [1940] 3 D.L.R. 790 (Ont.).

[3]See §395.

[4]See Estate of Quinn, 156 Cal. App. 2d 684, 320 P.2d 219 (1958); In re Estate of Cafferty, 246 Cal. App. 2d 711, 55 Cal. Rptr. 173 (1967) (help for the blind); First Congregational Socy. of Bridgeport v. City of Bridgeport, 99 Conn. 22, 121 A. 77 (1923); Klumpert v. Vrieland, 142 Iowa 434, 121 N.W.

The exercise of the prerogative power by a biased or cynical or whimsical king sometimes resulted in devoting the property of the testator to purposes of which he never would have approved, purposes that might run entirely counter to his wishes. A famous instance of this is to be found in the case of *Da Costa v. De Pas.*[5] In that case a Jewish testator left a sum of money in trust to apply the income toward establishing a jesuba, or assembly for reading the Jewish law and instructing people in the Jewish religion. The case was decided in 1754, when such a gift was illegal as promoting a religion contrary to the established religion. Lord Chancellor Hardwicke held, however, that because the trust was for religious purposes, it was a charitable trust and did not fail and the next of kin of the testator were not entitled to the fund. He held that the matter of the disposition of the money should be referred to the king for his direction. The king thereupon by his sign manual directed that the fund should be applied to the support of a preacher in the Foundling Hospital and to instruct the children in that institution in the Christian religion. Surely this is the last thing that the testator would have desired. In a case decided a few years later Chief Justice Wilmot expressed the opinion that in a case like this, had he not been bound by authority, he would have been inclined to hold that the trust should fail and that the next of kin should be entitled to the money.[6] He thought that the testator should not be made to disinherit his heir or next of kin for a charity he never thought of, perhaps for a charity repugnant to his intention and that directly opposed the charity he meant to establish. He then said:

> But this doctrine is now so fully settled that it cannot be departed from; and the reason upon which it is founded, seems to be this: The donation was considered as proceeding from a general principle of piety in the testator. Charity was an expiation of sin and to be rewarded in another state; and therefore, if political reasons

---

34 (1909); Matter of Finkelstein, 189 Misc. 180, 70 N.Y.S.2d 596 (1947); Jordan's Estate, 329 Pa. 427, 197 A. 150 (1938).

See §397.

[5] 1 Amb. 228, 2 Swanst. 487 (1754).

See also Neech's Exrs., [1947] Sess. Cas. 119 (Scot.).

[6] Attorney-General v. Downing, Wilm. 1, 32, Amb. 549 (1767).

negatived the particular charity given, this Court thought the merits of the charity ought not to be lost to the testator, nor to the public, and that they were carrying on his general pious intention; and they proceeded upon a presumption, that the principle, which produced one charity, would have been equally active in producing another, in case the testator had been told the particular charity he meditated could not take place. The Court thought one kind of charity would embalm his memory as well as another, and being equally meritorious, would entitle him to the same reward.

To the modern mind this reason appears naive if not cynical. A Jew leaves money in trust to promote the Jewish religion, but the promotion of that religion is illegal. His motive was to secure approval in this world and a reward hereafter. How much greater will be his fame in this world and how much greater his reward hereafter if the fund is used for the promotion of the Christian religion! Therefore let the money not be returned to his next of kin, but let it be applied to promote the Christian religion. How could a Jewish testator object to anything so reasonable?

This particular difficulty no longer arises, because a trust to promote religions other than the Christian religion is no longer illegal in England and, of course, is not illegal in the United States.[7] The fundamental difficulty with the prerogative power of cy pres still remains, however. In the exercise of this power the king can disregard entirely the probable desires of the testator. The power is an arbitrary one, and the king is not accountable for the manner in which he exercises it. The situation is quite different from that which arises in the exercise by the court of the judicial power of cy pres. Such a power is exercised only for the purpose of carrying out what would probably have been in accordance with the intention of the testator.[8] For this reason

[7]See §371.

[8]*Federal:* Noel v. Olds, 78 App. D.C. 155, 138 F.2d 581 (1943), *cert. denied,* 321 U.S. 773 (1945), s.c. 80 App. D.C. 63, 149 F.2d 13 (1945), s.c. *sub nom.* Olds v. Rollins College, 84 App. D.C. 299, 173 F.2d 639 (1949), noted in 32 Geo. L.J. 425, 43 Mich. L. Rev. 211, 27 N.C.L. Rev. 591, 35 Va. L. Rev. 649.

Delaware: Delaware Trust Co. v. Graham, 30 Del. Ch. 330, 61 A.2d 110 (1948) (citing the text and Restatement of Trusts §399), noted in 9 Md. L. Rev. 359.

the prerogative power has no place in American jurisprudence. Certainly no one can exercise the power in the United States unless it may be the legislature. There are some statements in the cases to the effect that the legislature has succeeded to the prerogative power of the Crown.[9] It is believed, however, that this is not so. If the intended charitable trust does not fail although it is impossible or illegal to carry out the particular purpose of the testator, the property should nevertheless be applied only to purposes approximating those of the testator. No one, whether king or legislature, should have an arbitrary power to apply it to any charitable purposes that to him or it may seem fitting.[10]

In *Opinion of the Justices*[11] the Supreme Court of New Hampshire was called on to give an opinion as to the constitutionality of a proposed amendment to a statute. The statute[12] authorized towns to hold gifts, legacies, and devises made to them for the care of cemeteries and burial lots and authorized towns to receive funds from cemetery associations or individuals for the care of cemeteries or lots and provided that the income should be expended by the town in accordance with the terms of the trust. The proposed amendment added a provision that the income accumulation of a burial lot trust fund might be used for the general care of the cemetery where the lot is located, if the terms of the trust do not otherwise provide, and if it can be reasonably anticipated that an accumulation of income would

---

Nebraska: Rohlff v. German Old People's Home, 143 Neb. 636, 10 N.W.2d 686 (1943).

Wisconsin: Estate of Bletsch, 25 Wis. 2d 40, 130 N.W.2d 275 (1964) (citing Restatement of Trusts §399).

[9] Mormon Church v. United States, 136 U.S. 1, 10 S. Ct. 792, 34 L. Ed. 478 (1890); Williams' Estate, 52 D.&C. 107 (Pa. 1944); Will of Lott, 193 Wis. 409, 214 N.W. 391 (1927).

[10] In some cases it has been held that the legislature, as well as the court, has power to authorize a sale of property held upon a charitable trust, although such sale is not authorized or is forbidden by the terms of the trust. See §381.

Certainly the legislature has no power to divert the property to other charitable purposes if it is possible to carry out the original purpose. See §399.5.

[11] 101 N.H. 531, 133 A.2d 792 (1957) (citing the text, §§367.3, 399.1, 399.5, and Restatement of Trusts, §399, Comment *e*).

[12] New Hampshire Rev. Stat. Ann., §§31:20, 31:21.

not be required for the care of the particular lot, and it was provided that if thereafter the income of a fund should become insufficient for the care of the lot, the town should appropriate the funds necessary to maintain it. The justices were of the opinion that the proposed amendment was unconstitutional as an invasion of established equitable powers of the courts and in violation of Part 1, Article 37 of the New Hampshire Constitution, which provided for the separation of the legislative, executive, and judicial powers.

It is to be noted that the proposed amendment was not concerned with a particular charity, but with all dispositions of this kind, namely those made to towns for maintaining burial lots, which in New Hampshire are held to be charitable trusts.[13] It related apparently to dispositions theretofore as well as thereafter made. It is to be noted also that in a previous decision[14] the same court had refused under the exercise of the power of cy pres to authorize the expenditure for the general care of the cemetery of a fund held in trust for the care of a particular lot. The court said,

> In effect the bill would be an exercise of what amounts to a legislative power of cy pres with respect to all cemetery trusts having surplus income, without regard to established principles of law relating to the use of such funds, or the terms of the trusts so long as they did not expressly forbid the use.

The justices were of the opinion that the cy pres power must be exercised through the courts by the application of established principles of law to the circumstances of each particular trust.[15]

§399.2. **The exercise of the cy pres power.** Where property is given in trust for a particular charitable purpose, and it is impossible or impracticable to carry out that purpose, the trust does not fail if the testator has a more general intention to

---

[13]See §374.9, n. 15.

[14]Town of Boscawen v. Attorney Gen., 93 N.H. 444, 43 A.2d 780 (1945).

[15]By Connecticut Gen. Stat., §4716, it is provided that towns, ecclesiastical societies, and cemetery associations holding donations for the care of cemeteries and burial lots may expend any surplus wholly or in part for the general care or improvement of the cemeteries in the town.

devote the property to charitable purposes. In such a case the property will be applied under the direction of the court to some charitable purpose falling within the general intention of the testator. This principle is easy to state but is not always easy to apply. It is seldom that the testator's intention can be definitely analyzed and divided into a particular and a general intention. It is ordinarily impossible to determine what disposition the testator intended should be made of the property if his particular purpose could not be carried out. Indeed, it is ordinarily true that the testator does not contemplate the possible failure of his particular purpose, and all that the court can do is to make a guess not as to what he intended but as to what he would have intended if he had thought about the matter.[1]

In the great majority of states the cy pres doctrine has been accepted.[2] In a few states the courts have said that the doctrine has not been accepted as a part of the law of the state.[3] The

---

§399.2.   [1]Rice v. Stanley, 42 Ohio St. 2d 209, 327 N.E.2d 774, 71 Ohio Op. 2d 205 (1975) (quoting the text), noted in 37 Ohio St. L.J. 685.

[2]See the cases cited in the notes to this section.

See Fisch, The Cy Pres Doctrine in the United States (1950); Fisch, The Cy Pres Doctrine and Changing Philosophies, 51 Mich. L. Rev. 375 (1953); Fisch, Judicial Attitude Towards the Application of the Cy Pres Doctrine, 25 Temp. L.Q. 177 (1951); Note, A Revaluation of *Cy Pres,* 49 Yale L.J. 303 (1939); Note, Recent Trends in the *Cy Pres* Doctrine in New York, 39 Colum. L. Rev. 1358 (1939); Note, Cy Pres Reaffirmed in the District of Columbia, 32 Geo. L.J. 425 (1944); Note, The *Cy Pres* Doctrine in Kentucky, 35 Ky. L.J. 95 (1946); Note, *Cy Pres* in Pennsylvania, 54 Dick. L. Rev. 77 (1949); Gray, The History and Development in England of the Cy-Pres Principle in Charities, 33 B.U.L. Rev. 30 (1953); Sheridan, The Cy-pres Doctrine, 32 Can. B. Rev. 599 (1954); Robinson, Cy Pres in Maine Today, Portland U.L. Rev. (1954); Sheridan, The Cy Pres Doctrine (1959); Fisch, Changing Concepts and Cy Pres, 44 Cornell L.Q. 382 (1959); Note, The Cy Pres Doctrine in West Virginia, 58 W. Va. L. Rev. 168 (1956); Note, Cy Pres in Alabama, 16 Ala. L. Rev. 428 (1964); Report of Committee on Charitable Trusts, 104 Tr. & Est. 990 (1965); Peters, A Decade of Cy Pres: 1955-1965, 39 Temp. L.J. 256 (1966); Di Clerico, Cy Pres: A Proposal for Change, 47 B.U.L. Rev. 153 (1967); Hatton, The Lapse of Charitable Bequests, 32 Mod. L. Rev. 283 (1969); Note, Cy Pres and Deviation: Current Trends in Application, 8 Real Prop. Prob. & Tr. J. 391 (1973).

As to statutes adopting the cy pres doctrine, see §399, n. 2.

[3]*Arizona:* In re Hayward's Estate, 65 Ariz. 228, 178 P.2d 547 (1947), *semble.*

But see Olivas v. Board of Natl. Missions, 1 Ariz. App. 543, 405 P.2d 481 (1965).

courts of some states have gone much further than others in applying the doctrine.

Mississippi: National Bank of Greece v. Savarika, 167 Miss. 571, 148 So. 649 (1938).

See Note, The Doctrine of Cy Pres in Charitable Trusts — Its Need in Mississippi, 30 Miss. L.J. 301 (1959).

North Carolina: Woodcock v. Wachovia Bank & Trust Co., 214 N.C. 224, 199 S.E. 20 (1938), noted in 37 Mich. L. Rev. 1132, 6 U. Chi. L. Rev. 332; Edmisten v. Sands, 307 N.C. 670, 300 S.E.2d 387 (1983) (cy pres applied under statutory authorization).

South Carolina: City of Columbia v. Monteith, 139 S.C. 262, 137 S.E. 727 (1926); Furman Univ. v. McLeod, 238 S.C. 475, 120 S.E.2d 865 (1961), *semble;* Estate of Woodworth, 47 T.C. 193 (1966) (a tax case; holding bequest to establish a Catholic hospital in Spartansburg County, South Carolina, failed).

The court in South Carolina has been increasingly liberal in allowing deviations and in reaching results that are ordinarily reached under the cy pres doctrine. South Carolina Natl. Bank v. Bonds, 260 S.C. 327, 195 S.E.2d 835, 68 A.L.R.3d 983 (1973).

In Colin McK. Grant Home v. Medlock, 349 S.E.2d 655 (S.C. App. Ct. 1986), the court, after stating that South Carolina does not accept the cy pres doctrine, authorized a charitable corporation, to which property had been devised for the purpose of maintaining a home on particular land for elderly white Presbyterians, to sell the land and use the proceeds to subsidize housing for elderly Presbyterians of all races.

Tennessee: Henshaw v. Flenniken, 183 Tenn. 232, 191 S.W.2d 541 (1946).

In Bell v. Shannon, 212 Tenn. 28, 367 S.W.2d 761 (1963), where a testator left his estate in trust to erect a charity hospital after the death of his wife, and before her death a county hospital had been erected and the funds were insufficient to erect a new hospital, it was held that they might be applied to the construction of a wing to the existing hospital. The court said that this did not involve an application of the cy pres doctrine, which had been rejected in Tennessee, but was at most a permissible deviation from the terms of the trust. The court cited the text, §381.

See Hardin v. Independent Order of Odd Fellows, 51 Tenn. App. 586, 370 S.W.2d 844 (1963), noted in 17 Vanderbilt L. Rev. 633, holding that a bequest to a home for orphans did not fail merely because the home was closed.

The cy pres doctrine was rejected also in Alabama, Maryland, Virginia, and West Virginia, but is now authorized by statute. See §399, n. 2. See Fisch, Cy Pres Doctrine in the United States (1950).

In some states in which the court has said that it rejects the doctrine of cy pres, much the same results are reached under a doctrine of approximation. Thus in Smith v. Moore, 343 F.2d 594 (4th Cir. 1965), *mod'g* 225 F. Supp. 434 (D.C. Va. 1963), where a testator directed his trustees to erect a hospital and the funds were insufficient for the purpose, the court authorized the erection

The terms of the trust. If the testator makes an express provision as to the disposition of the property in case the particular purpose fails, that provision is controlling.[4] Thus if he

---

of a wing to an existing building. The court said that there was some doubt how far the Virginia statute accepted the doctrine of cy pres, but that the variations could be upheld on the ground of equitable approximation, citing Restatement of Trusts §167, and the text, §381.

It has come to be generally recognized that the rejection of the cy pres doctrine means only the rejection of the prerogative cy pres and not the judicial cy pres. Estate of Bletsch, 25 Wis. 2d 40, 130 N.W.2d 275 (1964) (citing Restatement of Trusts §399).

See Note, Effect on charitable trust or bequest for particular school or school district, or students or graduates thereof, of change in school or district structure or organization, 68 A.L.R.3d 997 (1975).

[4]*Federal:* Roberds v. Markham, 81 F. Supp. 38 (D.D.C. 1948) (quoting Restatement of Trusts, §399, Comment *l*), noted in 2 Okla. L. Rev. 384, 18 U. Cin. L. Rev. 228.

Arkansas: Greene v. Thompson, 227 Ark. 1089, 305 S.W.2d 136 (1957); Little Rock Univ. v. George W. Donaghey Found., 252 Ark. 1148, 483 S.W.2d 230 (1972).

California: Hart v. County of Los Angeles, 260 Cal. App. 2d 512, 67 Cal. Rptr. 242 (1968).

Connecticut: Connecticut Bank & Trust Co. v. Johnson Memorial Hosp., 30 Conn. Supp. 1, 294 A.2d 586 (1972) (citing the text and Restatement of Trusts §399); Harris v. Attorney Gen., 31 Conn. 93, 324 A.2d 279 (1974), *semble.*

Florida: Jewish Guild for the Blind v. First Natl. Bank, 226 So. 2d 414 (Fla. App. 1969).

Georgia: Smyth v. Anderson, 238 Ga. 343, 232 S.E.2d 835 (1977) (citing the text and Restatement of Trusts, §399, Comment *c*).

Illinois: First Natl. Bank of Chicago v. American Bd. of Commrs. for Foreign Missions, 328 Ill. App. 481, 66 N.E.2d 446 (1946); First Natl. Bank of Chicago v. Canton Council of Campfire Girls, 85 Ill. 2d 507, 55 Ill. Dec. 824, 426 N.E.2d 1198 (1981); Northern Ill. Medical Center v. Home State Bank of Crystal Lake, 136 Ill. App. 3d 129, 111 Ill. Dec. 802, 482 N.E.2d 1085 (1985).

Kentucky: Hail v. Cook, 294 S.W.2d 87 (Ky. 1956); Defenders of Fur Bearers v. First Natl. Bank & Trust Co., 306 S.W.2d 100 (Ky. 1957).

Maine: City of Belfast v. Goodwill Farm, 150 Me. 17, 103 A.2d 517 (1954) (citing the text and Restatement of Trusts §§401, 413).

Massachusetts: Bowditch v. Attorney Gen. 241 Mass. 168, 134 N.E. 796, 28 A.L.R. 713 (1922); Harrison v. Marcus, 396 Mass. 424, 486 N.E.2d 710 (1985).

Missouri: Curators of Univ. of Mo. v. University of Kansas City, 442 S.W.2d 66 (Mo. 1969) (citing the text); Pilgrim Evangelical Lutheran Church of the Unaltered Augsburg Confession v. Lutheran Church-Missouri Synod Found., 661 S.W.2d 833 (Mo. App. 1983), *transfer to S. Ct. denied* (1984), citing text.

Nebraska: In re Estate of Harrington, 151 Neb. 81, 36 N.W.2d 577 (1949);

provides that if the particular purpose should fail the property

Board of Trustees of York College v. Cheney, 158 Neb. 292, 63 N.W.2d 177 (1954) (citing the text).

New Hampshire: Trustees of Pittsfield Academy v. Attorney Gen., 95 N.H. 51, 57 A.2d 161 (1948) (citing the text).

New York: Matter of Price, 264 A.D. 29, 35 N.Y.S.2d 111 (1942), *aff'd mem.,* 289 N.Y. 751, 46 N.E.2d 354 (1942) (citing Restatement of Trusts §§399, 413), *aff'd mem.,* 289 N.Y. 751, 46 N.E.2d 354 (1942), noted in 17 St. John's L. Rev. 42; Matter of Shapiro, 201 Misc. 968, 112 N.Y.S.2d 46 (1952); Matter of Loomis, 17 Misc. 2d 693, 186 N.Y.S.2d 811 (1959); Matter of Zumstine, 23 Misc. 2d 305, 200 N.Y.S.2d 861 (1960), *aff'd,* 13 A.D.2d 780, 215 N.Y.S.2d 11 (1961), *aff'd mem.,* 10 N.Y.2d 957, 180 N.E.2d 60 (1961); Matter of Dunton, 28 Misc. 2d 939, 214 N.Y.S.2d 157 (1961); Matter of Eckert, 43 A.D.2d 365, 352 N.Y.S.2d 48 (1974).

Ohio: Harrah v. Meigs County Memorial Hosp., 77 Ohio Abs. 68, 145 N.E.2d 566 (1957).

Oregon: Good Samaritan Hosp. & Medical Center v. United States Natl. Bank, 246 Or. 478, 425 P.2d 541 (1967) (citing the text).

Pennsylvania: Johnson Trust, 435 Pa. 303, 255 A.2d 571 (1969).

Rhode Island: Pennsylvania Co. for Banking & Trusts v. Board of Governors of London Hosp., 79 R.I. 74, 83 A.2d 881 (1951), noted in 65 Harv. L. Rev. 704, 51 Mich. L. Rev. 128; Champlin v. Powers, 80 R.I. 30, 90 A.2d 787, 33 A.L.R.2d 1176 (1952); Edwards v. De Simone, 105 R.I. 335, 252 A.2d 327 (1969) (citing Restatement of Trusts §399).

Texas: San Antonio Indep. School Dist. v. Division of World Missions, 161 Tex. 471, 341 S.W.2d 896 (1961) (majority held that the trust did not fail; dissenting opinion quoted Restatement of Trusts, §399, Comment *a*).

Wisconsin: In re Berry's Estate, 29 Wis. 2d 506, 139 N.W.2d 72 (1966) (citing the text).

In Wanamaker's Estate, 312 Pa. 362, 167 A. 592 (1933), where a testator bequeathed money to Princeton University to establish scholarships for students studying the mercantile business, in the event that the university should establish a permanent course in that subject, and it did not establish such a course, it was held that the bequest failed and that the doctrine of cy pres would not be applied because it was subject to an express condition precedent.

In Dobbins Estate, 74 D.&C. 106 (Pa. 1951), where the testatrix made gifts in trust for a number of charitable institutions and provided that if any trust should fail the other institutions should share in that part of the property pro rata, it was held that the subsequent dissolution of a hospital that was a beneficiary was not such failure as was contemplated by the testatrix and that the property should be given to another hospital under the cy pres doctrine.

The doctrine of cy pres will be applicable, of course, if the trust instrument expressly so provides. Puget Sound Natl. Bank v. Easterday, 56 Wash. 2d 937, 350 P.2d 444 (1960), noted in 36 Wash. L. Rev. 205.

In Matter of Kittinger, 36 Misc. 2d 385, 232 N.Y.S.2d 922 (1962), where a testator bequeathed property in trust for the needy employees of a desig-

should be devoted to certain other charitable purposes, it will be so applied.[5] It is immaterial that the gift over to the other

---

nated company and provided that in the event of the dissolution or other termination of the company the trust property should be applied to charitable or benevolent purposes as nearly as may be like the purpose expressed, and the company was merged into another company, it was held that the property should be applied for the benefit of the needy employees of the latter company.

In Geo. W. Donaghey Found. v. Little Rock Univ., 231 Ark. 748, 332 S.W.2d 497 (1960), where property was conveyed to trustees for the benefit of Little Rock University and it was provided that if it should at any time cease to be operated by the public school authorities the trustees should have discretion to select some other public school, it was held that the income should be paid to the university, although it had ceased for the time being to be operated by the public school authorities.

In Orphan Socy. of Lexington v. Board of Educ., 437 S.W.2d 194 (Ky. 1969), a gift was made to a civic league for certain educational purposes in connection with a model school to be erected by the Board of Education of the city of Lexington, and it was provided that if the school should not be erected or should cease to exist the fund should go to a certain orphan society, and the school was erected but was later discontinued. It was held that the gift over did not take effect but the fund should be used for the designated educational purposes.

In Matter of Goehringer, 69 Misc. 2d 145, 329 N.Y.S.2d 516 (1972), a testator bequeathed $20,000 to a named Jesuit preparatory school in perpetuity to provide funds for the education of boys of the school. The school was dissolved a year after his death. It was held that the money should go to similar Jesuit schools, in accordance with the terms of the Not-for-Profit Corporation Law.

In In re Estate of Hermann, 454 Pa. 292, 312 A.2d 16 (1973), land and objects of art were conveyed to trustees to maintain a museum, and the settlor by will gave money to a bank in trust to pay for the maintenance of the museum with a provision that if the museum should cease to exist the money was to go to other charities. It was held that the sale of the land and the placing of the objects of art in a public library did not cause the museum to cease to exist.

In Psychic Research & Dev. Inst. v. Gutbrodt, 46 Md. 21, 415 A.2d 611 (1980), a testatrix gave a legacy to a designated charitable corporation "if in existence at the time of" her death. Before her death its charter was forfeited, but after her death it was revived. It was held that the legacy failed.

In Rourk v. Brunswick County, 46 N.C. App. 795, 266 S.E.2d 401 (1980), the court refused to reform the trust instrument by inserting a provision for reverter if the particular purpose should fail.

[5]*California:* Estate of Klinkner, 85 Cal. App. 3d 942, 151 Cal. Rptr. 20 (1978) (citing Restatement of Trusts, §399, Comment *c*); Estate of Zabriskie, 96 Cal. App. 3d 571, 158 Cal. Rptr. 154 (1979).

charity may happen beyond the period of the rule against perpetuities, because that rule is not applicable to a gift over from
one charity to another. See §401.5. So also the doctrine of cy
pres is inapplicable where there is a valid gift over to an individ-

---

Illinois: Matter of Estate of Offerman, 153 Ill. App. 3d 299, 186 Ill. Dec.
107, 505 N.E. 2d 413 (1987).

Maine: Town of Lee v. Town of Lincoln, 351 A.2d 554 (Me. 1976).

Massachusetts: Rogers v. Attorney Gen., 347 Mass. 126, 196 N.E.2d 855
(1964).

Mississippi: Mississippi Children's Home Socy. v. City of Jackson, 230 Miss.
546, 93 So. 2d 483 (1957) (citing the text).

New Jersey: Fidelity Union Trust Co. v. Laise, 127 N.J. Eq. 287, 12 A.2d
882 (1940); Camden Trust Co. v. Christ's Home of Warminster, 28 N.J. Super.
466, 101 A.2d 84 (1953); Estate of Thornton, 169 N.J. Super. 360, 404 A.2d
1222 (1979).

New York: Matter of Manila, 16 Misc. 2d 937, 182 N.Y.S.2d 769 (1959);
Matter of Martin, 32 A.D.2d 849, 300 N.Y.S.2d 751 (1969), *aff'g* 58 Misc. 2d
851, 296 N.Y.S.2d 425 (1969).

Washington: In re Lemon's Estate, 47 Wash. 2d 23, 286 P.2d 691 (1955).

In Saulino Estate, 8 D.&C.2d 721 (Pa. 1957), a testator directed that a
portion of the income be paid to the Philadelphia Musical Association, a
nonprofit corporation, for the benefit of needy musicians, and that if the
Association refused the gift or if it disbanded, the corpus should be turned
over to the Judges of the Orphans' Court of Philadelphia for division by them
among nonsectarian charitable institutions of the City of Philadelphia. The
Association had been disbanded. It was held that the corpus should be paid
to the Board of City Trusts for the benefit of needy musicians who had been
members of the Association, and subject thereto for nonsectarian charitable
institutions.

If the alternative gift also fails and the doctrine of cy pres is not applicable,
there is a resulting trust for the testator's estate. In re Adams, [1966] 3 All E.R.
825, *rev'd on other grounds.* [1968] Ch. 80.

In Ranken-Jordan Home v. Drury College, 449 S.W.2d 161 (Mo. 1970),
the gift over did not take effect, because the use of the property was within the
discretionary power of the trustees.

In Matter of Estate of Charouleau, 25 Ariz. App. 507, 544 P.2d 1108
(1976), a testator provided for the establishment of a home for the aged and
needy residents of a certain county. He further provided that if the funds are
insufficient, the funds should be used for the charity most likely to carry out
his purpose, and if there should be no such charity then to a charitable organization on its agreement to use the funds for the benefit of persons residing
in the county, and suggesting a particular home for children. The trustee gave
it to this home. It was held that this was improper, because there were in the
county existing institutions for the aged and needy residents of the county.

ual if the gift for charity should fail.[6] So, on the other hand, where the testator provides that if the purpose should fail the trust should terminate, the property will not be applied cy pres but will be held upon a resulting trust for his heirs or next of kin or residuary devisees or legatees.[7] See §401.2. The fact that a testator provides in the will that his heirs or next of kin shall not take any part of his estate does not preclude them from taking under a resulting trust if the doctrine of cy pres is not applicable, because the mere expression of an intention to exclude them is ineffective unless there is a gift to someone else.[8] Such a provision, however, may be some indication that the testator intended that the property should be applied for charitable purposes even if the particular purpose should fail.[9]

In *In re Hanbey's Will Trusts*[10] a testator who died in 1786 left money for the benefit of poor persons in a certain parish, with

---

[6]Phipps v. Barbera, 23 Mass. App. 1, 498 N.E.2d 411 (1986); Matter of Fletcher, 259 A.D. 335, 19 N.Y.S.2d 214 (1940); Matter of Merritt, 280 N.Y. 391, 21 N.E.2d 365 (1939).

In Matter of Will of Kraetzer, 119 Misc. 2d 436, 462 N.Y.S.2d 1009 (Sur. 1983), *A*'s will bequeathed property upon trust for *B* for life, remainder to be distributed "by valid and absolute disposition by will of" *B*, and in default of such exercise of the power, to *B*'s next of kin. *B* died, leaving a will by which he appointed the property upon trust for his wife, *C*, for life, remainder to *D* hospital "or its successor or successors, to its sole use, benefit and behoof, absolutely and forever." After the death of *C* but before the trustee designated by *B*'s will had distributed the remainder, the hospital became bankrupt and ceased operations. It was held that the remainder vested in *D* hospital on the death of *B* and that, therefore, *A*'s gift in default to the next of kin of *B* did not operate. It was also held that the remainder should be applied cy pres, the court rejecting a proposal that it be deemed assets available to *D*'s creditors in bankruptcy.

But see Society of Cal. Pioneers v. McElroy, 63 Cal. App. 2d 332, 146 P.2d 962 (1944), holding that a gift over to the trustees absolutely did not preclude application of the cy pres doctrine.

[7]See Nelson v. Kring, 225 Kan. 499, 592 P.2d 438 (1979) (citing the text and Restatement of Trusts, §399, Comment *c*).

[8]Matter of Merritt, 280 N.Y. 391, 21 N.E.2d 365 (1939).

[9]Howard Sav. Inst. v. Peep, 34 N.J. 494, 170 A.2d 39 (1961), noted in 40 N.C.L. Rev. 308.

[10][1956] Ch. 264, criticized in 10 Mod. L. Rev. 405.

See Trustees of Dartmouth College v. City of Quincy, 357 Mass. 521, 258 N.E.2d 745 (1970), citing the text and Restatement of Trusts §§399, 401, stated in §401.4.

detailed directions as to how it should be applied. The will provided that if the trustee should at any time fail to distribute the income in accordance with the testator's directions, the property should be given to Christ's Hospital, a charitable institution. It became impossible to comply with these directions and the trustee applied the property for other purposes. Subsequently, the trustee asked the court to decide whether the gift over had taken effect or whether a scheme should be settled under the cy pres doctrine. The court held that in the exercise of its discretion it would under the circumstances decline to frame a scheme and that the gift over took effect. The court said, however, that it had power to direct a scheme and thus to prevent the gift over from taking effect. It is to be noted that, although it was provided that the gift over should take effect if the trustee should fail to distribute the income in accordance with the testator's directions, the provision did not specifically deal with the situation where it became impossible to do so. In effect the court was suggesting that relief might be given against forfeiture on the ground of impossibility. See §401.4.

In *Burr v. Brooks*[11] a testator directed the payment of the residue to a city in trust to erect and maintain a hospital for needy persons. He provided that if the city should decline to accept the trust, the trustees under the will should procure the incorporation of an industrial school for girls to receive the property. The creation of a hospital became impracticable. The court held that the gift to the city for the hospital did not fail, and that the property should be applied by it for the health care of the poor and needy. The gift over for a home for girls did not take effect, especially since it was also impractical, and the property could only have been applied cy pres.

Where property is given to a charitable corporation or association for a particular charitable purpose, and the purpose fails, the court has in some cases permitted the corporation or association to use the trust property or part of it for its general purposes.[12]

---

[11]75 Ill. App. 3d 80, 30 Ill. Dec. 744, 393 N.E.2d 1091 (1979), *aff'd*, 83 Ill. 2d 488, 48 Ill. Dec. 200, 416 N.E.2d 231 (1981). The result seems sound under the cy pres doctrine rather than on the doctrine of deviation (see §381).

[12]In Grace Episcopal Church v. Nichols, 341 Mass. 736, 171 N.E.2d 285 (1961), where a testatrix devised a house to a church and bequeathed $7000

On the other hand, where the testator has not manifested an intention that the charitable corporation or association should receive any benefit, it will not be entitled to use the property for its own purposes on the failure of the trust.[13]

The fact that the property is given "upon condition" that it be applied to a particular charitable purpose does not ordinarily create a condition, and such a provision is usually construed

---

as a permanent fund for the payment of taxes and repairs on the house, and the house became useless, it was held that the money could be used for the general purposes of the church.

In Matter of Fairchild, 15 Misc. 2d 272, 178 N.Y.S.2d 886 (1958), where money was bequeathed to a charitable corporation to be used for the benefit of a home maintained by it, and the home ceased to exist, it was held that the corporation might use the money for its general charitable purposes.

In Matter of Scott, 8 N.Y.2d 419, 171 N.E.2d 326 (1960), *rev'g* 10 A.D.2d 556, 196 N.Y.S.2d 597 (1960), which *aff'd,* 19 Misc. 2d 18, 189 N.Y.S.2d 87 (1959), a testator gave the remainder of his estate, after the death of the life beneficiaries, to a designated church for the purpose of erecting and maintaining a building for the care of persons suffering from tuberculosis, to be called the Scott Memorial Home. The value of the estate was $1,600,000. It appeared that outdoor treatment for relief had become the proper treatment. The lower courts held that the fund should be applied cy pres for such outdoor relief. The Court of Appeals reversed, holding that one of the purposes of the testator was to benefit the church, and therefore the lower courts erred in directing that the whole fund should be used for outdoor relief, and that a part of the fund could be used for the purposes of the church.

In Brooke Estate, 45 D.&C.2d 670 (Pa. 1968), where a testator made a bequest to a medical college to establish a chair of orthopedic surgery and the fund was insufficient, it was held that the college could use it with other funds to construct a new hospital building devoted to orthopedic medicine.

In Hess v. Sommers, 4 Ohio App. 3d 281, 4 Ohio B.R. 500, 448 N.E.2d 494 (1982), the residue was bequeathed to a church "for the building fund." The church had had a building fund at the date of the will but had none at the date of the testatrix's death. It was held that the church could take the residuary bequest.

[13]Mary J. Drexel Home Petition, 13 D.&C.2d 371 (Pa. 1957).

In In re Eastman, 10 D.L.R.3d 516 (Ont. 1970), where a testator made a bequest to The Children's Aid Society for the use of their work among boys and girls at Lynwood Hall, and Lynwood Hall was a separate institution not operated by the Aid Society, it was held that the Aid Society was not entitled to use the bequest for its own purposes but was to hold it in trust for Lynwood Hall.

See Wilson v. First Presbyterian Church, 284 N.C. 284, 200 S.E.2d 769 (1973).

merely as a direction that the property should be applied to the particular purpose.[14] Accordingly, if it is impossible or impracticable to apply the property to the designated purpose, there is room for the operation of the cy pres doctrine. Similarly, where property is given in trust for a particular purpose "and no other purpose," these words do not necessarily preclude the court from applying the property to other purposes if the particular purpose fails.[15] The words may be construed as merely indicating by way of emphasis the intention of the testator that the property should be applied to the particular purpose so long as it is possible and practicable to so apply it. The words do not necessarily indicate that the testator would prefer that the trust should fail altogether if the particular purpose should fail. So also a direction that the property should be applied "forever" to a particular purpose does not prevent the application of the cy pres doctrine if that purpose fails.[16]

The application of the cy pres doctrine. Where there is no provision in the terms of the trust with respect to the possible failure of the charitable purpose to which the property is to be devoted, and the purpose fails, the question arises whether the trust should fail altogether or whether the doctrine of cy pres should be applied. The intended purpose may fail for various reasons, such as that the funds available are insufficient, the purpose has already been accomplished through other means, the purpose has become impossible of accomplishment, the property is given to a corporation or association that never existed or has ceased to exist, the property is unsuitable for the purpose for which it was given, or for other reasons. We shall consider these situations.

Insufficient funds. The particular purpose of the testator may fail for a variety of reasons. Thus the amount bequeathed

[14]See §§351, 401.2.

[15]Fairbanks v. City of Appleton, 249 Wis. 476, 24 N.W.2d 893 (1946) (citing Restatement of Trusts, §399, Comment *b*), noted in 1947 Wis. L. Rev. 467.

See §401.2.

But see In re Estate of Yetter (Simmons v. Reynolds), 183 Kan. 340, 328 P.2d 738 (1958).

[16]City of Newport v. Sisson, 51 R.I. 481, 155 A. 576 (1931).

by him may be insufficient to accomplish the particular purpose for which it is given. Whether the trust fails altogether or whether the money will be applied cy pres depends on whether the particular purpose was not an essential part of the scheme of the testator. If the particular purpose was not an essential part of his scheme, the court will approve a scheme for the application of the property to some other purpose falling within the general charitable intention of the testator.[17] Thus where a tes-

[17]*England:* Biscoe v. Jackson, 35 Ch. D. 460 (1886); Attorney-General v. Belgrave Hosp., [1910] 1 Ch. 73; In re Whittaker, [1951] 2 T.L.R. 955; In re Bradwell's Will Trusts, [1952] Ch. 575; In re Whitworth Art Gallery Trusts, [1958] Ch. 461.

Federal: Smith v. Moore, 343 F.2d 594 (4th Cir. 1965), *mod'g* 225 F. Supp. 434 (D.C. Va. 1963) (Virginia law; citing the text and Restatement of Trusts §399).

Arkansas: Bossen v. Woman's Christian Natl. Library Assn., 216 Ark. 334, 225 S.W.2d 336 (1949) (citing Restatement of Trusts §§380, 381, 399), noted in 4 Sw. L.J. 352.

California: See Estate of Loring, 29 Cal. 2d 423, 175 P.2d 524 (1946), *mod'g* 168 P.2d 224 (Cal. App. 1946) (citing the text and Restatement of Trusts §399).

Connecticut: Shannon v. Eno, 120 Conn. 77, 179 A. 479 (1935); Citizens & Mfrs. Natl. Bank v. Guilbert, 121 Conn. 520, 180 A. 564 (1936); Howood House v. Trustees of Donations & Bequests, 27 Conn. Supp. 176, 233 A.2d 5 (1967); Harris v. Attorney Gen., 31 Conn. Supp. 93, 324 A.2d 279 (1974) (citing Restatement of Trusts §399).

District of Columbia: Fay v. Hunster, 86 App. D.C. 224, 181 F.2d 289 (1950), *rev'g* 80 F. Supp. 729 (1948).

Illinois: Bruce v. Maxwell, 311 Ill. 479, 143 N.E. 82 (1924); Village of Hinsdale v. Chicago City Missionary Socy., 375 Ill. 220, 30 N.E.2d 657 (1940); First Natl. Bank of Chicago v. Elliott, 406 Ill. 44, 92 N.E.2d 66 (1950) (quoting Restatement of Trusts §399); Hardy v. Davis, 16 Ill. App. 2d 516, 148 N.E.2d 805 (1958) (citing the text); Hinckley v. Caldwell, 35 Ill. App. 2d 121, 182 N.E.2d 230 (1962) (quoting the text).

Indiana: Burke v. Crawfordsville Trust Co., 103 Ind. App. 1, 2 N.E.2d 817 (1936).

Iowa: Eckles v. Lounsberry, 253 Iowa 172, 111 N.W.2d 638 (1961).

Kentucky: Citizens Fidelity Bank & Trust Co. v. Isaac W. Bernheim Found., 305 Ky. 802, 205 S.W.2d 1003 (1947).

Maine: Stevens v. Smith, 134 Me. 175, 183 A. 344 (1936); Town of Lee v. Town of Lincoln, 351 A.2d 554 (Me. 1976); Estate of Thompson, 414 A.2d 881 (Me. 1980) (citing the text and Restatement of Trusts §399).

Massachusetts: Ely v. Attorney Gen., 202 Mass. 545, 89 N.E. 166 (1909); Norris v. Loomis, 215 Mass. 344, 102 N.E. 419 (1913); Town of Milton v. Attorney Gen., 314 Mass. 234, 49 N.E.2d 909 (1943) (citing the text); Trustees

tatrix left $2000 to found a home for cats and the sum was

---

of Putnam Free School v. Attorney Gen., 320 Mass. 94, 67 N.E.2d 658 (1946); Rogers v. Attorney Gen., 347 Mass. 126, 196 N.E.2d 855 (1964); Fulton v. Trustees of Boston College, 372 Mass. 350, 361 N.E.2d 1297 (1977) (accumulation until year 2000 and then paid to a college for the erection of a building; citing Restatement of Trusts, §399, Comment *i*).

Michigan: Gifford v. First Natl. Bank, 285 Mich. 58, 280 N.W. 108 (1938); Knights of Equity Memorial Scholarships Commn. v. University of Detroit, 359 Mich. 235, 102 N.W.2d 463 (1960).

Missouri: Ramsey v. City of Brookfield, 237 S.W.2d 143 (Mo. 1951) (citing the text and Restatement of Trusts §399); Levings v. Danforth, 512 S.W.2d 207 (Mo. App. 1974) (intensive care unit instead of building a hospital; citing the text and Restatement of Trusts §399).

Nebraska: First Trust Co. of Lincoln v. Thompson, 147 Neb. 366, 23 N.W.2d 339 (1946), 147 Neb. 817, 25 N.W.2d 394 (1946).

New Hampshire: Adams v. Page, 76 N.H. 96, 79 A. 837 (1911).

New Jersey: Patton v. Pierce, 114 N.J. Eq. 548, 169 A. 284 (1933); Cinnaminson Library Assn. v. Fidelity-Philadelphia Trust Co., 141 N.J. Eq. 127, 56 A.2d 417 (1948) (bequest to be used toward construction of library building, held income payable to existing libraries, quoting Restatement of Trusts §399); Mirinda v. King, 11 N.J. Super. 165, 78 A.2d 98 (1951) (citing the text).

New York: Matter of Swan, 237 A.D. 454, 261 N.Y.S. 428 (1933), *aff'd sub nom.* In the Matter of St. John's Church of Mt. Morris, 263 N.Y. 638, 189 N.E. 734 (1934); Matter of Neher, 279 N.Y. 370, 18 N.E.2d 625 (1939) (citing Restatment of Trusts §399); Matter of Lawless, 194 Misc. 844, 87 N.Y.S.2d 386 (1949), *aff'd mem.,* 277 A.D. 1045, 100 N.Y.S.2d 537 (1950); Matter of Grossbard, 101 N.Y.S.2d 527 (1950); Matter of Lewis, 308 N.Y. 795, 125 N.E.2d 598 (1955) (s.c. 208 Misc. 968, 145 N.Y.S.2d 829 (1953)) (funds insufficient to establish home for old ladies); Matter of Folsom, 23 Misc. 2d 817, 199 N.Y.S.2d 571 (1960) (consolidation of two trusts); Matter of Angel, 33 Misc. 2d 122, 225 N.Y.S.2d 419 (1962).

Ohio: Gearhart v. Richardson, 109 Ohio St. 418, 142 N.E. 890 (1924); Craft v. Shroyer, 81 Ohio App. 253, 74 N.E.2d 589 (1947) (citing the text and Restatement of Trusts §399), noted in 9 Ohio St. L.J. 181; First Natl. Bank v. Unknown Heirs of Donnelly, 96 Ohio App. 509, 122 N.E.2d 672 (1954); Kingdom v. Saxbe, 82 Ohio Abs. 6, 161 N.E.2d 461 (1958) (citing the text).

Pennsylvania: Keeler's Estate, 41 D.&C. 182 (Pa. 1941); Williams Estate, 353 Pa. 638, 46 A.2d 237 (1946) (citing Restatement of Trusts, §399, Comment *g*); Cameron v. Kranich (Cameron v. Shahedy), 359 Pa. 472, 59 A.2d 88 (1948); Ashbridge's Estate, 61 D.&C. 279 (Pa. 1948); Wanamaker Estate, 364 Pa. 248, 72 A.2d 106 (1950) (citing Restatement of Trusts §399), *aff'g* 67 D.&C. 517 (Pa. 1949); McKee Estate, 378 Pa. 607, 108 A.2d 214 (1954); Miller Estate, 380 Pa. 172, 110 A.2d 200 (1955) (citing Restatement of Trusts §399); Spoerl Estate, 5 D.&C.2d 130 (Pa. 1955); Melson Estate, 27 D.&C.2d 66 (Pa. 1962); Brooke Estate, 45 D.&C.2d 670 (Pa. 1968); Vaughn Estate, 69 D.&C.2d

insufficient for the purpose the court held that the money should

---

32 (Pa. 1974) (to establish a home; given to a charitable corporation maintaining such a home).

Wisconsin: Fairbanks v. City of Appleton, 249 Wis. 476, 24 N.W.2d 893 (1946) (citing Restatement of Trusts, §399, Comment *g*), noted in 1947 Wis. L. Rev. 467.

Australia: In re Tyrie, [1970] V.R. 264; Phillips v. Roberts, [1975] 2 N.S.W.R. 207 (N.S.W.).

Canada: In re Wright, [1951] 2 D.L.R. 429 (N.S.) (to erect building to bring people together to uplift and train them to higher ideals); In re Pearse, [1955] 1 D.L.R. 801 (B.C.); Re McSweeney, (1982) 41 N.B.2d 419.

Ireland: In re McGwire, [1941] I.R. 33, noted in 20 Can. B. Rev. 165; In re ffrench, [1941] I.R. 49 (note).

Scotland: Hay's Judicial Factor v. Hay's Trustees, [1950] Sess. Cas. 576 (Scot.).

In Teachers College v. Goldstein, 70 N.Y.S.2d 778 (1947), *mod.,* 273 A.D. 11, 75 N.Y.S.2d 250 (1947), *aff'd,* 297 N.Y. 969, 80 N.E.2d 357 (1948), a charitable foundation conveyed land and a building to a college for the purpose of maintaining an experimental school. It also gave the college several million dollars as an endowment fund. It was held that under the terms of the grant of money the college was at liberty to apply the fund for purposes other than to maintain the school, but that the land was given only for the purpose of maintaining the school. It was held, however, that since it was impracticable to carry on the school without the use of the money, the doctrine of cy pres was applicable, and the college might discontinue the school and sell the land and building and apply the proceeds to experimental education in the public schools.

In Pennsylvania (20 Pa. Stat., §6110), it is provided that the court may permit a combination of two or more trusts created for substantially the same charitable purposes if it finds that they can be more effectively administered if they are combined. This supersedes a prior statute (10 Pa. Stat., §116), which applied only where the income was insufficient to carry them on separately. See Williams' Estate, 52 D.&C. 107 (Pa. 1944); Grace Lutheran Church Petition, 2 Fiduciary Rep. 64 (Pa. 1951).

In In re Sundry Cemetery Trusts (No. 1), 57 D.&C.2d 677 (Pa. 1972), the court permitted consolidation of 26 cemetery trusts, although they were not charitable trusts.

By Charities Act, 1960, 8 & 9 Eliz. II, c. 58, §13, it is provided that the doctrine of cy pres can be applied "where the property available by virtue of the gift and other property applicable for similar purposes can be more effectively used in conjunction, and to that end can suitably, regard being had to the spirit of the gift, be made applicable to common purposes."

In Thomas v. Bryant, 185 Va. 845, 40 S.E.2d 487, 169 A.L.R. 257 (1946), where a testator left the residue of his estate to establish a home for aged

be given to the Connecticut Humane Society, which cared for homeless animals.[18] In the same case it was held that where the testatrix devised real estate to be used for an old ladies' home for poor women living in or near a certain town and bequeathed $5000 to the home when established, but the property given was insufficient to establish such a home, the property should go to a hospital for the care of poor women. On the other hand, where money is bequeathed for a particular purpose and is insufficient to accomplish the purpose, the trust fails altogether if the testator manifested an intention that it should be applied to that purpose only.[19] Ordinarily, where the amount bequeathed is

---

people, and the estate was sufficient for the establishment of such a home although on a smaller scale than that contemplated by the testator, it was held that the trust was valid without resorting to the doctrine of cy pres, the court expressing doubt whether the doctrine of cy pres is accepted in Virginia.

In Graham Hosp. Assn. v. Talley, 29 Ill. App. 3d 190, 329 N.E.2d 918 (1975), a man conveyed property in trust to build a hospital within 15 years. After 12 years, a hospital brought suit asking that under the cy pres doctrine the property be turned over to it. The court held that it would not apply the cy pres doctrine, because although at present it was impossible to erect a hospital it might become possible before the end of the 15-year period.

In James Emmet Tower Memorial Fund v. Rutland Hosp., 133 Vt. 381, 340 A.2d 54 (1975), where a testator made a bequest for founding and supporting an old people's home, and this was impracticable, it was held that under the cy pres doctrine the fund should not be given to a hospital because this would not be a home, but should be given to other charitable institutions that did provide homes for the elderly.

See Note, Charitable trust as affected by insufficiency of assets, 169 A.L.R. 266 (1947).

[18]Shannon v. Eno, 120 Conn. 77, 179 A. 479 (1935).

[19]*England:* Cherry v. Mott, 1 Myl. & Cr. 123 (1835); In re White's Trusts, 33 Ch. D. 449 (1886); In re Good's Will Trusts, [1950] 2 All E.R. 653; In re Ulverston & Dist. New Hosp. Bldg. Trusts, [1956] Ch. 622, noted in 34 Can. B. Rev. 1066, 20 Mod. L. Rev. 61.

Colorado: Fisher v. Minshall, 102 Colo. 154, 78 P.2d 363 (1938).

Connecticut: Waterbury Trust Co. v. Porter, 131 Conn. 206, 38 A.2d 598 (1944).

Maine: Gilman v. Burnett, 116 Me. 382, 102 A. 108, L.R.A. 1918A 794 (1917).

Massachusetts: Teele v. Bishop of Derry, 168 Mass. 341, 47 N.E. 422, 38 L.R.A. 629, 60 Am. St. Rep. 401 (1897); Dodge v. Anna Jacques Hosp., 301 Mass. 431, 17 N.E.2d 308 (1938) (gift inter vivos, citing Restatement of Trusts §399); City Bank Farmers Trust Co. v. Carpenter, 319 Mass. 78, 64 N.E.2d 636 (1946), *semble.*

insufficient for the purpose, the court will not direct that the money should be invested and the income accumulated until a sum sufficient for the purpose is realized.[20] But where the amount does not fall far short of the required sum, so that it would be possible within a reasonably short time to accumulate the difference, the court may direct such accumulation.[21] In

---

Nebraska: Rohlff v. German Old People's Home, 143 Neb. 636, 10 N.W.2d 686 (1943) (citing Restatement of Trusts §399).

New Hampshire: Green v. Parker, 92 N.H. 419, 32 A.2d 316 (1943) (citing Restatement of Trusts, §399, Comment *g*), noted in 42 Mich. L. Rev. 323.

New Jersey: McCran v. Kay, 93 N.J. Eq. 352, 115 A. 649 (1921); Fidelity Union Trust Co. v. Laise, 142 N.J. Eq. 366, 60 A.2d 250 (1948) (citing the text); In re Stevens, 18 N.J. Super. 176, 86 A.2d 812 (1952).

New York: Matter of Fletcher, 280 N.Y. 86, 19 N.E.2d 794, 21 N.E.2d 623 (1939); Matter of Merritt, 280 N.Y. 391, 21 N.E.2d 365 (1939); Matter of Fletcher, 259 A.D. 335, 19 N.Y.S.2d 214 (1940).

North Carolina: Wilson v. First Presbyterian Church, 284 N.C. 284, 200 S.E.2d 769 (1973).

Ohio: Allen v. City of Bellefontaine, 47 Ohio App. 359, 191 N.E. 896 (1934), noted in 9 U. Cin. L. Rev. 91.

Pennsylvania: Hildebrand's Estate, 47 D.&C. 537 (Pa. 1942).

Australia: In re Tyrie, [1970] V.R. 264.

Scotland: Cuthbert's Trustees v. Cuthbert, [1958] Sess. Cas. 629 (Scot.).

[20]Ely v. Attorney Gen., 202 Mass. 545, 89 N.E. 166 (1909); Norris v. Loomis, 215 Mass. 344, 102 N.E. 419 (1913); Town of Milton v. Attorney Gen., 314 Mass. 234, 49 N.E.2d 909 (1943); Trustees of Putnam Free School v. Attorney Gen., 320 Mass. 94, 67 N.E.2d 658 (1946).

See Tainter v. Clark, 5 Allen 66 (Mass. 1862).

In In re Burton's Charity, [1938] 3 All E.R. 90, where stock was left in trust to employ three curates for not more than an aggregate sum of £400 a year, and it became impossible to secure curates at that price, it was held that two curates should be employed, and the court declined to direct an accumulation of income until there was enough to hire three curates.

In Nevil Estate, 414 Pa. 122, 199 A.2d 419 (1964), where the fund was to establish an asylum for the deaf, dumb, or blind, with a direction to accumulate until the fund was sufficient, and it appeared after 30 years that there was no prospect of acquiring a sufficient amount, the court directed payment to existing institutions.

As to the effect of a direction to accumulate, see §401.9.

[21]*Federal:* Graff v. Wallace, 59 App. D.C. 64, 32 F.2d 960 (1929), *cert. denied,* 280 U.S. 579 (1929) (see s.c. Wallace v. Graff, 104 F. Supp. 925 (D.D.C. 1952)).

Alabama: Noble v. First Natl. Bank, 236 Ala. 499, 183 So. 393 (1938), 241 Ala. 85, 1 So. 2d 289 (1941).

Missouri: Levings v. Danforth, 512 S.W.2d 207 (Mo. App. 1974) (citing the text and Restatement of Trusts §399).

Estate of Robinson[22] a testatrix bequeathed her estate to the University of Wisconsin to establish a professorship, to be held by a woman who was to be paid a salary of at least $6000 a year. The estate amounted to less than $50,000. The court ordered that the funds be paid over by the trustee to the university, to be invested and the income accumulated until the fund was sufficient for the designated purpose.

Purpose already accomplished. So also it may be impracticable to apply the property to the particular purpose stated by the testator because the purpose has been already accomplished. In such a case the court may direct the application of the property to a similar purpose falling within the general charitable intention of the testator.[23] Thus in the famous case of *Jackson v. Phillips*[24] the testator, a well-known abolitionist who died in 1861, bequeathed $10,000 in trust for the preparation and circulation of books and newspapers and for the delivery of

[22]248 Wis. 203, 21 N.W.2d 391 (1946).

[23]*England:* In re Morgan, [1955] 2 All E.R. 632 (recreation ground for amateur activities applied cy pres for parish hall or gymnasium).

California: Society of Cal. Pioneers v. McElroy, 63 Cal. App. 2d 332, 146 P.2d 962 (1944) (bequest to erect a monument for California pioneers; monument already erected).

Illinois: Burr v. Brooks, 75 Ill. App. 3d 80, 30 Ill. Dec. 744, 393 N.E.2d 1091 (1979), aff'd, 83 Ill. 2d 488, 48 Ill. Dec. 200, 416 N.E.2d 231 (1981).

Massachusetts: Jackson v. Phillips, 14 Allen 539 (Mass. 1867); Bowditch v. Attorney Gen., 241 Mass. 168, 134 N.E. 796, 28 A.L.R. 713 (1922).

Nebraska: School Dist. No. 70, Red Willow County v. Wood, 144 Neb. 241, 13 N.W.2d 153 (1944).

New Hampshire: Adams v. Page, 76 N.H. 96, 79 A. 837 (1911).

North Carolina: Board of Trustees of the Univ. of N.C. at Chapel Hill v. Unknown Heirs of Prince, 311 N.C. 644, 319 S.E.2d 239 (1984) (bequest of $135,000 to state university to accumulate income until, with other funds, it could be used to build theatre for university dramatic society; after some of the trust funds had been used to pay for the planning of the theatre, the state legislature appropriated the whole cost of construction; trust varied, cy pres, to permit use of funds for related dramatic purposes).

Rhode Island: City of Newport v. Sisson, 51 R.I. 481, 155 A. 576 (1931).

Tennessee: Bell v. Shannon, 212 Tenn. 28, 367 S.W.2d 761 (1963).

Australia: Kytherian Assn. of Queensl. v. Sklavos, 101 C.L.R. 56 (Austl. 1958).

[24]14 Allen 539 (Mass. 1867).

See Briggs v. Merchants Natl. Bank, 323 Mass. 261, 81 N.E.2d 827 (1948) (citing the text).

speeches and lectures and such other means as in the judgment of the trustees would create a public sentiment that would put an end to slavery in the United States, and bequeathed $2000 in trust for the benefit of fugitive slaves. The case came up for argument in March 1863 and finally was decided in 1867. In the meantime the Thirteenth Amendment to the Constitution of the United States abolishing slavery was ratified in December 1865. The court held that a valid charitable trust was created at the death of the testator and that it did not fail because the particular purposes had been accomplished by the adoption of the amendment. A scheme was framed under which the legacies were applied to purposes beneficial to blacks. But if the testator manifested an intention that the property should be applied only to the particular purpose, the trust will fail.[25]

Purpose impossible of accomplishment, refusal of trustee or third person to cooperate.   So also the intended trust may be impossible of accomplishment because of the refusal of the trustee to accept the trust, or because of the refusal of a third person to cooperate where his cooperation is necessary to carry out the particular purpose. In such a case the trust does not fail but the property will be applied cy pres if the particular purpose was not an essential part of the testator's scheme.[26] Thus where a testa-

---

[25]Murr v. Youse, 52 Ohio Abs. 321, 80 N.E.2d 788 (1946) (citing the text and Restatement of Trusts §339); Women's Christian Temperance Union v. Cooley, 25 S.W.2d 171 (Tex. Civ. App. 1930).

In In re Mackenzie, [1962] 2 All E.R. 890, where a testator bequeathed £5000 to a county council in Scotland to assist pupils at a public primary school to continue their education at a secondary school by a provision for bursaries, it was held that the trust failed because students were entitled to support from the government. The court refused to apply the funds cy pres on the ground that the testator had no general charitable intention.

[26]*England:* In re Lysaght, [1966] Ch. 191, noted in 82 Law Q. Rev. 9 (bequest to a medical college for scholarships for students who were not of the Jewish or Roman Catholic faith, the college rejecting the restrictions as against its policy); In re Woodhams (Decd.); Lloyds Bank v. London College of Music, [1981] 1 W.L.R. 493 (Ch. Div.) (bequest to two musical colleges to establish scholarships for "absolute orphans"; colleges would not accept restriction to orphans because the government paid the expenses of orphans; restriction deleted).

Connecticut: Williams Memorial Inst. v. Beers, 18 Conn. Supp. 512 (1954).

Illinois: First Natl. Bank of Chicago v. Elliott, 406 Ill. 44, 92 N.E.2d 66 (1950) (quoting Restatement of Trusts §399).

trix bequeathed the residue of her estate to be given to the

Louisiana: Succession of Mizell, 468 So. 2d 1371 (La. App. 1985), 475 So. 2d 765 (La. 1985), *rehearing denied.* 477 So. 2d 94 (La. 1985) (devise of lot and bequest of money for erection of a church on the lot; this could not be done because widow would not release her community property interest in the lot).

Massachusetts: Town of Brookline v. Barnes, 324 Mass. 632, 87 N.E.2d 843 (1949); Town of Brookline v. Barnes, 327 Mass. 201, 97 N.E.2d 651 (1951) (bequest to town to establish and maintain public general hospital applied to establishment and maintenance of health center); Wesley United Methodist Church v. Harvard College, 366 Mass. 247, 316 N.E.2d 620 (1974) (for scholarships at Harvard for worthy male members of a church, and no members qualified or were likely to qualify, held restriction to church members removed; citing the text and Restatement of Trusts §399).

New Jersey: Howard Sav. Inst. v. Peep, 34 N.J. 494, 170 A.2d 39 (1961), *aff'g* Howard Sav. Inst. v. Trustees of Amherst College, 61 N.J. Super. 119, 160 A.2d 177 (1960) (bequest to a college for scholarships for Protestant Gentile students, where the charter of the college forbade religious discrimination; citing the text and Restatement of Trusts §399), noted in 61 Colum. L. Rev. 111, 40 N.C.L. Rev. 308, 36 Notre Dame Law. 74, 16 Rutgers L. Rev. 366, 36 Tulane L. Rev. 176.

New York: Matter of Johnson, 93 A.D.2d 1, 460 N.Y.S.2d 932 (1983), citing the text (where school district named as trustee could not under federal law administer trust for scholarships for males, restriction to males would be deleted under the cy pres doctrine). This decision was reversed in Matter of Estate of Wilson, 59 N.Y.2d 461, 452 N.E.2d 1228, 465 N.Y.S.2d 900 (1983), noted in 53 U. Cin. L. Rev. 297 (1984) and in 12 Hast. C.L.Q. 127 (1984), and a private trustee was appointed to administer the trust for males only. In the same opinion the Court of Appeals affirmed a decree modifying a provision of a trust for scholarships for males that the candidates be certified as qualified by a superintendent of schools who could not, under federal law, make such certifications, by eliminating the requirement of certification.

Pennsylvania: Atlee Estate, 406 Pa. 528, 178 A.2d 722 (1962) (bequest to a Presbyterian church that rejected the legacy but the Presbytery, the superior judicatory of the church, intervened).

Australia: Royal North Shore Hosp. of Sydney v. Attorney-General, 60 C.L.R. 396 (Austl. 1938).

New Zealand: In re List, [1949] N.Z.L.R. 78.

Northern Ireland: Re Dunwoodie (Decd.); Northern Bank Exr. & Trustee Co. v. Moss, [1977] N.Ir. 141, involved a bequest upon trust for an Irish church indicating that the money should be used to purchase bells. The church decided not to install bells. The bequest was applied cy pres to the religious purposes of the same church.

In In re Metcalfe, 29 D.L.R.3d 60 (Ont. 1972), a testator created a trust fund for a scholarship in the medical faculty of McGill University for a Protestant of good moral character, and the university disclaimed because of the religious restriction. It was held that the trust failed and the fund went to the testator's next of kin.

lifesaving station to be built and established in Marblehead or Nahant, and the United States declined to accept the legacy, which amounted to $6000, it was held that the trust did not fail.[27] The court said that the purpose of the testatrix was not limited to the maintenance of a lifesaving station but that she had a more general purpose to assist persons exposed to the perils of the sea in the neighborhood, and the court directed that a scheme should be devised to carry out the general purpose. On the other hand, if the testator manifested an intention that the property should be applied only to the particular purpose, the trust will fail.[28] Thus it has been held that where a testator bequeathed money in trust to purchase land and build a chapel in a village in Ireland, the title to be vested in the bishop of the diocese, and the village was so small and the population so poor that it would be impossible to support the chapel and the bishop declined to accept the chapel or to undertake its support, the trust failed.[29] The court held that the erection of the chapel in the village was of the essence of the testator's plan and that he had no general charitable intent to aid religion in any other way. Similarly, where a testatrix left the residue of her estate to a town "toward the erection of a building that should be for the sick and poor" and the town declined to accept the legacy, it was held that the trust failed.[30] The amount of the estate was quite insufficient to erect a building without the assistance of the town. The court said that there was nothing to indicate that the testatrix intended to make provision generally for the sick and poor of the town and that the property could not therefore be applied cy pres.

Nonexisting corporation or association.   The particular purpose of the testator may fail because the property was bequeathed to

[27]Richardson v. Mullery, 200 Mass. 247, 86 N.E. 319 (1908).

[28]Bankers Trust Co. v. New York Women's League for Animals, 23 N.J. Super. 170, 92 A.2d 820 (1952), *rev'g* 17 N.J. Super. 398, 86 A.2d 138 (1952) (citing the text and quoting Restatement of Trusts, §399, Comment *g*).

[29]Hampton v. O'Rear, 309 Ky. 1, 215 S.W.2d 539 (1948); Teele v. Bishop of Derry, 168 Mass. 341, 47 N.E. 422, 38 L.R.A. 629, 60 Am. St. Rep. 401 (1897).

See also Morristown Trust Co. v. Morristown, 82 N.J. Eq. 521, 91 A. 736 (1913).

[30]Bowden v. Brown, 200 Mass. 269, 86 N.E. 351, 128 Am. St. Rep. 419 (1908).

a corporation or association that did not exist at the time of the creation of the trust or subsequently ceased to exist, or that was unwilling or unable to receive the property and administer the trust. In such a case, as we have seen, the disposition does not fail unless the identity of the donee was of the essence of the gift.[31]

Unsuitability of premises. Where land is devised as a site for a particular charitable institution, it may happen that the land is or becomes unsuitable for the purpose. As we have seen, the court may authorize or direct the sale of land held upon a charitable trust even though by the terms of the trust the trustees are not authorized to sell the land or even though they are expressly forbidden to sell it.[32] This power is exercised where otherwise the purposes of the trust would be defeated or substantially impaired. Even though by the terms of the trust it is provided that the land shall be used as the site of the charity, the court may permit a removal to another site if the original site has become unsuitable for the purpose.[33] Where it is provided by

[31]See §§397.2, 397.3.
[32]See §381.
[33]*Arkansas:* Bossen v. Woman's Christian Natl. Library Assn., 216 Ark. 334, 225 S.W.2d 336 (1949) (citing Restatement of Trusts §§380, 381, 399), noted in 4 Sw. L.J. 352.

California: O'Hara v. Grand Lodge I.O.G.T., 213 Cal. 131, 2 P.2d 21 (1931).

Connecticut: Hinman v. Windham Natl. Bank, 14 Conn. Supp. 14 (1946); Goetz v. Dietz, 20 Conn. Supp. 360, 135 A.2d 369 (1957).

Delaware: Delaware Land & Dev. Co. v. First & Cent. Church, 16 Del. Ch. 410, 147 A. 165 (1929).

District of Columbia: Shoemaker v. American Sec. & Trust Co., 82 App. D.C. 270, 163 F.2d 585 (1947) (citing the text and Restatement of Trusts §399); Stead v. American Sec. & Trust Co., 84 App. D.C. 358, 173 F.2d 650 (1949).

Illinois: Bruce v. Maxwell, 311 Ill. 479, 143 N.E. 82 (1924); Board of Educ. v. City of Rockford, 372 Ill. 442, 24 N.E.2d 366 (1939) (citing Restatement of Trusts §399), noted in 28 Geo. L.J. 853; Village of Hinsdale v. Chicago City Missionary Socy., 375 Ill. 220, 30 N.E.2d 657 (1940).

Kentucky: Sawyer v. Lamar, 230 Ky. 168, 18 S.W.2d 971 (1929), noted in 8 Tenn. L. Rev. 52.

Louisiana: Ada C. Pollock-Blundon Assn. v. Heirs of Evans, 273 So. 2d 552 (La. App. 1973).

Massachusetts: Weeks v. Hobson, 150 Mass. 377, 23 N.E. 215, 6 L.R.A. 147 (1890); Ely v. Attorney Gen., 202 Mass. 545, 89 N.E. 166 (1909); Norris v.

the terms of the trust, however, that the trust should continue

Loomis, 215 Mass. 344, 102 N.E. 419 (1913); Rogers v. Attorney Gen., 347 Mass. 126, 196 N.E.2d 855 (1964).

Mississippi: Kilpatrick v. Graves, 51 Miss. 432 (1875).

Missouri: Academy of the Visitation v. Clemens, 50 Mo. 167 (1872) (site of convent of contemplative order became unsuitable when city put street through the tract); Missouri Historical Socy. v. Academy of Science of St. Louis, 94 Mo. 459 (1888) (site too small for intended use); Catron v. Scarritt Collegiate Inst., 264 Mo. 713, 175 S.W. 571 (1915) (college merged with another in a town some miles away).

New Jersey: St. James Church v. Wilson, 82 N.J. Eq. 546, 89 A. 519 (1913), *aff'd on this point sub nom.* West v. St. James' Episcopal Church, 83 N.J. Eq. 324, 91 A. 101 (1914); In re Young Women's Christian Assn., 96 N.J. Eq. 568, 126 A. 610 (1924); Trustees of the First Presbyterian Church v. Wheeler, 106 N.J. Eq. 8, 149 A. 589 (1930), *semble,* noted in 40 Yale L.J. 143.

New York: Matter of Barnard, 170 Misc. 875, 11 N.Y.S.2d 115 (1939); Matter of Lawless, 194 Misc. 844, 87 N.Y.S.2d 386 (1949), *aff'd mem.,* 277 A.D. 1045, 100 N.Y.S.2d 537 (1950); Matter of Wornock, 124 N.Y.S.2d 8 (1953).

North Carolina: Holton v. Elliott, 193 N.C. 708, 138 S.E. 3 (1927).

See Trustees of Rex Hosp. v. Board of Commrs., 239 N.C. 312, 79 S.E.2d 892 (1954).

Pennsylvania: Wilkey's Estate, 337 Pa. 129, 10 A.2d 425 (1940) (quoting Restatement of Trusts §399); Emlen's Estate, 57 D.&C. 404 (Pa. 1946); Salvation Army Petition, 72 D.&C. 157 (Pa. 1950); Hill Trust, 23 D.&C.2d 791 (Pa. 1961) (citing Restatement of Trusts §§167, 381, and 399).

Rhode Island: Town of S. Kingstown v. Wakefield Trust Co., 48 R.I. 27, 134 A. 815, 48 A.L.R. 1122 (1926); Buchanan v. McLyman, 51 R.I. 177, 153 A. 304 (1931); City of Newport v. Sisson, 51 R.I. 481, 155 A. 576 (1931).

Tennessee: Goodman v. State, 49 Tenn. App. 96, 351 S.W.2d 399 (1961).

Australia: Attorney-General v. Perpetual Trustee Co., 63 C.L.R. 209 (Austl. 1940).

Canada: Re MacGregor Estate, 22 E.T.R. 192 (Ont. H.C. 1986).

Scotland: Robertson's Trustees, [1948] Sess. Cas. 1 (Scot.).

See 63 A.L.R. 880 (1929).

As to the power of the legislature to authorize a sale, see §381.

In Matter of Krantz, 13 Misc. 2d 800, 178 N.Y.S.2d 537 (1958), where land was devised to two persons for life and then to be used as a home for young women, and the premises could not be used for that purpose without financially prohibitive alterations, it was held that the land might be sold with the consent of the life beneficiaries, and the proceeds of the remainder interest applied cy pres.

In Union Congregational Socy. v. South Shore Natl. Bank, 342 Mass. 41, 172 N.E.2d 92 (1961), where a testator left money in trust to pay the income to a church to keep the edifice in repair, and subsequently it merged with another church and the original edifice was no longer used, it was held that the income could be used for the repair of the new church building. The court

only so long as the land shall be used as a site for the charity, or that the trust shall terminate if the land ceases to be used for this purpose, the court cannot authorize the removal to a different site. In such a case there is an express limitation or condition subsequent.[34] Even though it is provided in the trust instrument that the premises shall be forfeited if they are not used for the purposes of the charity, or if the trustees should sell or attempt to sell them, it has been held that the forfeiture will not be enforced where the property is taken on eminent domain.[35] In rare cases it has been held that the conducting of the charity on the particular site is an essential part of the testator's scheme even though no express limitation or condition is created by the terms of the trust; and in such a case the court cannot authorize the removal to a different site.[36] In another case[37] a testator devised a ranch to a county to use the income for the relief of crippled and blind residents of the county. In the will it was stated that the gift was in memory of his wife. The will provided that if the county should sell or mortgage the ranch, it should revert to the testator's heirs. The ranch was taken on

---

said it was unnecessary to resort to the doctrine of cy pres, or even to the doctrine of deviation, because the new use fell within the implied intent of the testator. The court quoted Restatement (Second) of Trusts, §399, Comment *p*.

In Samuel Estate, 47 D.&C.2d 116 (Pa. 1969), where a testator gave the residue to a college as an endowment fund to be used for the upkeep of a farm, and the college sold the land that was not suited for farming or instructional purposes, it was held that the endowment fund could be used to promote the agricultural program of the college.

In Jacobs Estate, 62 D.&C.2d 167 (Pa. 1973), where a testator left a fund in trust to erect a library, and expressed a wish that it should not be erected on a community center, it was held that the trustees could erect it there, because the reason for the testator's wish had ceased to operate.

[34]See §§401.2, 401.3.

[35]State v. Federal Square Corp., 89 N.H. 538, 3 A.2d 109 (1938). See §401.4.

[36]Edwards v. Packard, 129 Me. 74, 149 A. 623 (1930).

The court has refused to permit a sale of the site and the removal to another site in states in which the doctrine of cy pres has been rejected. King v. Banks, 220 Ala. 274, 124 So. 871 (1929).

[37]Pedrotti v. Marin County, 152 F.2d 829 (9th Cir. 1946), *cert. denied sub nom.* County of Marin v. Pedrotti, 328 U.S. 853 (1946), *rev'g* United States v. 263.5 Acres of Land, 54 F. Supp. 692 (N.D. Cal. 1944).

eminent domain. It was held that because the object of making the ranch a memorial to his wife had failed, it reverted to his heirs.

Other reasons for failure of purpose. There are numerous other situations in which the doctrine of cy pres has been applied where the particular purpose of the testator failed, but it was held that the particular purpose was not an essential part of his plan and that he would probably have preferred to have the property applied to similar purposes rather than that the trust should fail altogether.[38] On the other hand, the trust has been

---

[38]*England:* Attorney-General v. The Ironmongers' Co., 2 Myl. & K. 576 (1833) (trust to redeem British captives in Turkey or Barbary); In re Hillier, [1954] 2 All E.R. 59, *rev'g* [1953] 2 All E.R. 1547 (contributions for erection of voluntary hospital), noted in 70 Law Q. Rev. 454, 6 Stan. L. Rev. 729; In re Woodhams (Decd.); Lloyds Bank v. London College of Music, [1981] 1 W.L.R. 493 (Ch. Div.) (bequest to two musical colleges to establish scholarships for "absolute orphans"; colleges would not accept restriction to orphans because the government paid the expenses of orphans; restriction deleted).

But compare In re Ulverston & Dist. New Hosp. Bldg. Trusts, [1956] Ch. 622 (contributions for erection of voluntary hospital), noted in 34 Can. B. Rev. 1066, 20 Mod. L. Rev. 61.

Federal: Tincher v. Arnold, 147 F. 665, 7 L.R.A. (N.S.) 471, 8 Ann. Cas. 917 (7th Cir. 1906) (income to pay teachers applied partly for maintenance of school); Laswell v. Hungate, 256 F. 635 (7th Cir. 1918), *cert. denied,* 249 U.S. 612 (1919) (educational purposes).

Connecticut: Trustees of the Watkinson Library v. Attorney Gen., 16 Conn. Supp. 448 (1950) (library given to be maintained in connection with Connecticut Historical Society; permission given to transfer it to Trinity College); Goetz v. Dietz, 20 Conn. Supp. 360, 135 A.2d 369 (1957) (home devised for men's club of a church; church permitted to sell and erect parish house with quarters for men's club).

Delaware: Delaware Trust Co. v. Graham, 30 Del. Ch. 330, 61 A.2d 110 (1948) (trust for a missionary society that was taken over by a new board; citing the text), noted in 9 Md. L. Rev. 359; Union Methodist Episcopal Church v. Equitable Trust Co., 32 Del. Ch. 197, 83 A.2d 111 (1951) (to assist worthy aged members of two designated churches to enter designated homes; citing the text and quoting Restatement of Trusts §399).

In Union Methodist Episcopal Church v. Equitable Security Trust Co., 40 Del. Ch. 154, 177 A.2d 217 (1962), the court refused to permit the use of surplus funds involved in Union Methodist Episcopal Church v. Equitable Trust Co., 32 Del. Ch. 197, cited in this note, for the construction of a new home for the aged.

District of Columbia: Noel v. Olds, 78 App. D.C. 155, 138 F.2d 581 (1943), *cert. denied,* 321 U.S. 773, (1945), s.c. 80 App. D.C. 63, 149 F.2d 13 (1945), s.c. *sub nom.* Olds v. Rollins College, 84 App. D.C. 299, 173 F.2d 639 (1949) (bequest to university to establish art museum, disclaimed by university), noted in 32 Geo. L.J. 425, 43 Mich. L. Rev. 211, 27 N.C.L. Rev. 591, 35 Va. L. Rev. 649.

Florida: Fenske v. Coddington, 57 So. 2d 452 (Fla. 1952) (transfer to public body of property given for black school).

Illinois: Mason v. Bloomington Library Assn., 237 Ill. 442, 86 N.E. 1044 (1909) (to establish art studio or gallery in connection with a library that conveyed all its property to another library association and ceased to exist); Community Unit School Dist. No. 4 v. Booth, 1 Ill. 2d 545, 116 N.E.2d 161 (1953) (enlargement of school district); Kelly v. Guild, 42 Ill. App. 2d 143, 191 N.E.2d 377 (1963) (bequest to a home that had transferred its assets to another corporation).

Kentucky: Pennebaker v. Pennebaker Home for Girls, 297 Ky. 670, 181 S.W.2d 49 (1944) (where school failed, scheme allowed for selling land, investing proceeds, and educating in some other way as through scholarships). ·

Louisiana: In re Succession of Milne, 230 La. 729, 89 So. 2d 281 (1956) (home for destitute orphans); In re Succession of Abraham, 136 So. 2d 471 (La. App. 1962) (to Catholic bishop to be used to build school or orphanage).

Maine: Manufacturers Natl. Bank v. Woodward, 141 Me. 28, 38 A.2d 657 (1944) (income given for repair of library building and purchase of books, held applicable to payment of running expenses if trust would otherwise fail); Grigson v. Harding, 154 Me. 146, 144 A.2d 870 (1958); State v. Rand, 366 A.2d 183 (Me. 1976) (lot transferred to city for a memorial public park, taken by eminent domain; held that the proceeds should be used to acquire another lot as a park).

Maryland: Gray v. Harriet Lane Home for Invalid Children, 192 Md. 251, 64 A.2d 102 (1949) (income to be applied to wards in hospital for treatment of diseases that ceased to be prevalent); Fletcher v. Safe Deposit & Trust Co., 193 Md. 400, 67 A.2d 386 (1949) (trust to found home; funds insufficient; citing the text); Loats Female Orphan Asylum v. Essom, 220 Md. 11, 150 A.2d 742 (1959) (devise to orphans' home that was closed and property applied to pay for foster home).

Massachusetts: McElwain v. Attorney Gen., 241 Mass. 112, 134 N.E. 620 (1922) (legacy for adornment of cemetery later abandoned applied to another cemetery to which testator's body removed); Worcester County Trust Co. v. Grand Knight, 325 Mass. 748, 92 N.E.2d 579 (1950) (method of awarding prizes in Catholic colleges and schools modified); Ford v. Rockland Trust Co., 331 Mass. 25, 116 N.E.2d 669 (1954) (old ladies' home no longer needed because of old-age assistance); Stackpole v. Brewster Free Academy, 355 Mass. 774, 247 N.E.2d 599 (1969) (for free schools in two New Hampshire towns that had ceased to exist; held should be used for scholarships); New England Hosp. v. Attorney Gen., 362 Mass. 401, 286 N.E.2d 474 (1972) (to a hospital to enable students to study abroad; citing Restatement of Trusts §399).

Nebraska: Garwood v. Drake Univ., 188 Neb. 605, 198 N.W.2d 336 (1972) (bequest to Divinity School of Drake University; the school was phased out before death of testatrix and a department of religion created for undergraduates); In re Last Will & Testament of Teeters, 205 Neb. 576, 288 N.W.2d 735 (1980) (for the benefit of nurses residing at a hospital's nursing home, which was later discontinued; citing Restatement of Trusts §399).

New Hampshire: Petition of Rochester Trust Co., 94 N.H. 207, 49 A.2d 922 (1946) (where fund given to a strictly Protestant charitable institution in one city and there was no such institution, held it should be given to such an institution elsewhere in state; citing Restatement of Trusts §399); Exeter v. Robinson Heirs, 94 N.H. 463, 55 A.2d 622 (1947) (where income to maintain a girls' school became insufficient, held it may be used to contribute to support of coeducational school; citing the text and Restatement of Trusts §399).

New Jersey: Rowe v. Davis, 138 N.J. Eq. 122, 47 A.2d 36 (1946) (bequest to home and nursery school for blind that had closed); Morristown Trust Co. v. Protestant Episcopal Church, 1 N.J. Super. 418, 61 A.2d 762 (1948) (trust to support particular Protestant Episcopal church whose communicants moved away held applicable for support of another church sixty miles distant); Wilber v. Owens, 2 N.J. 167, 65 A.2d 843 (1949) (citing Restatement of Trusts, §399, Comment *m*), *aff'g* Wilber v. Asbury Park Natl. Bank & Trust Co., 142 N.J. Eq. 99, 59 A.2d 570 (1948) (trust to publish worthless writings of testator, and for scientific and philosophical research), noted in 63 Harv. L. Rev. 348.

New York: Matter of Brundrett, 87 N.Y.S.2d 851 (1940) (bequest to charitable corporation that ceased to exist after death of testatrix and before death of life beneficiary); Matter of Shelton, 87 N.Y.S.2d 853 (1942) (like preceding case); Matter of Borden, 180 Misc. 988, 42 N.Y.S.2d 560 (1943) (trust to establish Masonic home on testator's farm; income insufficient to maintain home; court authorized sale of farm and use of proceeds to support similar home); People ex rel. Untermyer v. McGregor, 295 N.Y. 237, 66 N.E.2d 292 (1946) (devise of park and garden to state, which renounced); Matter of Rupprecht, 271 A.D. 376, 65 N.Y.S.2d 909 (1946), *aff'd mem.*, 297 N.Y. 462, 74 N.E.2d 175 (1947) (property devised and bequeathed to corporation to be formed to maintain orphanage; funds insufficient and orphanage unnecessary and corporation could not be formed because of refusal of consent by Board of Social Welfare; held, trust to be administered by church); Conway v. Bowe, 116 N.Y.S.2d 182 (1952) (scholarships in colleges that make certain courses of study compulsory); Matter of Swope, 204 Misc. 510, 121 N.Y.S.2d 181 (1953) (to support theological seminary in China that later passed under communist control); Matter of Stern, 159 N.Y.S.2d 308 (1953); Matter of Aramian, 9 Misc. 2d 148, 166 N.Y.S.2d 1006 (1957) (for study in Armenia, which came under communist control); Stephens v. Domestic & Foreign Missionary Socy., 20 Misc. 2d 1061, 197 N.Y.S.2d 369 (1959) (for establishment of missionary school in China that came under communist control); Matter of Hastings, 28 Misc. 2d 1089, 217 N.Y.S.2d 810 (1961) (court authorized sale of tuberculosis sanatorium and entering into contract with university for research).

North Carolina: Edmisten v. Sands, 307 N.C. 670, 300 S.E.2d 387 (1983) (where will manifested intent to create charitable remainder unitrust but omitted provisions required by federal Internal Revenue Service to qualify as such a trust, court will insert the required provisions by construction).

Oregon: Quick v. Hayter (In re Stouffer's Trust), 188 Or. 218, 215 P.2d 374 (1950) (to endowment fund of college that later ceased to exist; citing Restatement of Trusts §399).

Pennsylvania: Curran's Estate, 310 Pa. 434, 165 A. 842 (1933) (legacy for female education in college in or adjacent to Philadelphia; held, if no suitable college near Philadelphia, legacy can be used to support suitable college situated 156 miles away); Hoff's Estate, 315 Pa. 286, 172 A. 645 (1934) (bequest for maintenance of hospital wing where wing destroyed by fire and building sold); Sheridan Estate, 16 Fiduciary Rep. 439 (Pa. 1966) (trust company appointed to administer trust for crippled boys; quoting Restatement of Trusts §399).

Rhode Island: Industrial Natl. Bank v. Guiteras, 107 R.I. 379, 267 A.2d 706 (1970) (to support a library in Cuba, which was later taken over for political purposes under the Castro government, citing the text).

Tennessee: Vanderbilt Univ. v. Mitchell, 162 Tenn. 217, 36 S.W.2d 83 (1931) (college loan fund; gifts to poor students permitted).

Texas: Scott v. Sterrett, 234 S.W.2d 917 (Tex. Civ. App. 1950) (for erection of armory for militia organization).

Virginia: Campbell v. Board of Trustees, 220 Va. 516, 260 S.E.2d 204 (1979) (substitution of a treatment center for a school).

Canada: In re Scott, 11 D.L.R.2d 223 (Ont. 1957) (bequest to unincorporated charitable association that discontinued its work before testator's death); In re Stewart, 13 D.L.R.2d 654 (B.C. 1958) (trust for a church fund that had ceased to exist); In re Denison, 42 D.L.R.3d 652 (Ont. 1974) (for impoverished members of the Law Society of Upper Canada; held may include students-at-law of the Society); In re Abbott, 45 D.L.R.3d 478 (Sask. 1974) (to a hospital that later became a ward); Re Tufford, 2 O.A.C. 45 (Ont. C.A. 1983) (bequest of residue to trustees of church operating cemetery; there were no such trustees and the township was operating the cemetery).

Ireland: In re McGwire, [1941] I.R. 33 (to religious society for sanitarium in Ireland and if the society should renounce then to government of Switzerland for needy poor there; held, both renouncing, applicable for benefit of sick poor in Ireland), noted in 20 Can. B. Rev. 165.

Northern Ireland: Re Stewart's Will Trusts, [1983] 11 N.I.J.B. (trust to support Presbyterian ministers who "use the hymn book the hymns of which are unaltered and unabridged in any way"; there was no such hymn book; the requirement of its use was removed cy pres).

In Township of Cinnaminson v. First Camden Natl. Bank & Trust Co., 99 N.J. Super. 115, 238 A.2d 701 (1968), where the specific purpose failed and the court directed a cy pres application, and many years later it became possible to carry out the specific purpose, it was held that the court would not disturb the disposition that it had directed.

In In re Estate of Rood, 41 Mich. App. 405, 200 N.W.2d 728, 67 A.L.R.3d 390 (1972), a testator left his estate to three college presidents in trust to use the income to teach political science in the colleges in a manner that should

held to fail where the particular purpose was held to be an essential part of the testator's plan.[39] In some states it has been

---

take account of his writings on the subject. It was held that to comply with his directions would abridge academic freedom; but that the trust would not fail and the property should be applied cy pres, by the submission by the colleges of plans for a course dealing with conservative political philosophy without relying on the specific philosophy of the testator. (But query.) The court cited the text and Restatement of Trusts §399.

In Garbrick Estate, 68 D.&C.2d 599 (Pa. 1974), a testator left his estate in trust to use the income for Christian education in a designated Presbyterian church under the supervision of its officers or for aiding boys and girls to study for the ministry, provided that they declare their belief in certain dogmas. The officers refused to require such declarations. Later the church was dissolved. It was held that under the cy pres doctrine the bequest should be given to the Princeton Theological Seminary, for scholarships for students whose theological position is conservative.

See Note, Application of cy pres doctrine to trust for promulgation of particular political or philosophical doctrine, 67 A.L.R.3d 417 (1975). See 74 A.L.R. 671 (1931).

[39] *England:* In re University of London Medical Sciences Inst. Fund, [1909] 2 Ch. 1 (bequest to fund to establish medical institution scheme that proved impracticable); In re Wilson, [1913] 1 Ch. 314 (bequest to support schoolmaster in school to be erected by voluntary contributions; no such school erected); In re White's Will Trusts, [1955] Ch. 188 (devise of cottages for missionary homes).

See Hall, Recent Developments in the Cy-Prés Doctrine, [1957] Camb. L.J. 87.

Federal: President & Fellows of Harvard College v. Jewett, 11 F.2d 119 (6th Cir. 1925) (lot to be kept for preservation of Indian relics).

Alabama: General Assembly of Colored Cumberland Presbyterian Church v. Patterson, 256 Ala. 50, 53 So. 2d 621 (1951) (trust to support school that ceased to exist).

Arkansas: Sloan v. Robert Jack Post No. 1322, V.F.W., 218 Ark. 917, 239 S.W.2d 591 (1951) (to build hut for Veterans of Foreign Wars but available for all veterans).

California: Estate of Zabriskie, 96 Cal. App. 3d 571, 158 Cal. Rptr. 154 (1979) (failure to incorporate religious organization, as required by will).

Connecticut: City Bank Farmers Trust Co. v. Frauen Verein Von Riegel, 18 Conn. Supp. 346 (1953) (bequest to establish home for aged in German town, project becoming impracticable).

Delaware: Equitable Trust Co. v. Delaware Trust Co., 30 Del. Ch. 348, 61 A.2d 529 (1948) (bequest of antique furniture and money to maintain an exhibition at homestead, title to the whole of which could not be acquired).

New Jersey: Grebenstein v. St. John's Evangelical Lutheran Church, 3 N.J. Super. 422, 66 A.2d 461 (1949) (bequest to church to be applied toward

held that where the particular purpose fails the trust fails even though the particular purpose was not an essential part of the testator's scheme, the reason being that the doctrine of cy pres is rejected.[40]

§399.3. **Subsequent failure of particular purpose.** The doctrine of cy pres may be applied where the particular purpose of the testator fails at the outset. Where this purpose is at the time of the testator's death impossible of accomplishment or where it is impracticable to carry out his purpose, the trust does not fail if the testator would presumably have desired that it should be applied to other purposes if he had known that it would be impossible or impracticable to carry out his particular purpose. Not infrequently, however, the trust fails because the particular purpose is held to be of the essence of the intended trust.

---

payment of mortgage, which was discharged before testator's death); Estate of Thornton, 169 N.J. Super. 360, 404 A.2d 1222 (1979) (to a village for a clubhouse for teenagers; village took no steps to carry out the purpose).

New York: Saltsman v. Greene, 136 Misc. 497, 243 N.Y.S. 576 (1930), *aff'd,* 231 A.D. 781, 246 N.Y.S. 913 (1930), *aff'd,* 256 N.Y. 636, 691, 177 N.E. 172 (1931) (to repair and beautify particular church that had ceased to function).

Ohio: Barton v. Parrott, 25 Ohio Misc. 2d 8, 495 N.E.2d 973 (Ohio C.P. 1984) (trust to run annual horse race in memory of testatrix's daughter; no charitable intent).

Pennsylvania: Randall's Estate, 341 Pa. 501, 19 A.2d 272 (1941) (to establish home for the poor, which proved impracticable); Pruner Estate, 400 Pa. 629, 162 A.2d 626 (1960) (to provide a home for friendless children; suitable children were not available), noted in 22 U. Pitt. L. Rev. 277.

Rhode Island: Nugent v. St. Dunstans College, 133 R.I. 666, 324 A.2d 654 (1974) (bequest to a college of music that ceased to exist).

Wisconsin: Nelson v. Madison Lutheran Hosp. & Sanatorium, 237 Wis. 518, 297 N.W. 424 (1941), 243 Wis. 97, 9 N.W.2d 599 (1943) (subscriptions to erect hospitals where purpose could not be carried out), noted in 1942 Wis. L. Rev. 89.

Australia: In re Barry, [1971] V.R. 395; In re Goodson, [1971] V.R. 801 (devised for a home for elderly ladies, but unfit for the purpose).

Northern Ireland: McCormick v. Queen's Univ., [1958] N. Ir. L.R. 1 (trust to maintain a house for educational purposes, but house never conveyed).

On the question whether the doctrine of cy pres will be applied where the settlor fails to state the particular charitable purpose that he had in mind, see §395.

[40]See n. 3, *supra.*

On the other hand, where at the time of the creation of the trust it is possible and practicable to carry out the specific directions of the testator, but in course of time conditions change so that it becomes impossible or impracticable to carry out these directions, the cy pres doctrine is almost invariably applied, and it is rare indeed that the trust is held to fail altogether.[1] If the trust fails, a resulting trust arises in favor of the persons who have succeeded to the estate of the testator; and if many years and perhaps centuries have elapsed since the creation of the trust, it is frequently impossible and always expensive to ascertain the persons who would be entitled to the property. There is stronger reason, therefore, to apply the cy pres doctrine where the particular purpose of the testator fails at a subsequent time than there is where the purpose fails at the outset.

If, indeed, the testator has expressly provided that the charitable trust shall terminate if the specific purpose can no longer be accomplished, it will so terminate.[2] In the absence of such a provision, however, it is rarely held that the trust fails altogether because of the impossibility of carrying out the specific directions of the testator, where the trust was a permanent trust and the impossibility was due to circumstances happening after the trust had been created. In England it has been said that there is no case of a resulting trust arising upon the failure of a charitable trust that has once taken effect.[3] If the testator, however,

---

§399.3. [1]In re Petition of Downer Home, 67 Wis. 2d 55, 226 N.W.2d 444 (1975) (quoting the text and Restatement of Trusts, §399, Comment *i*).

See Simmons v. Parsons College, 256 N.W.2d 225 (Iowa 1977) (citing Restatement of Trusts, §399, Comment *i*).

[2]See 401.2.

[3]In re Slevin, [1891] 2 Ch. 236.

See Attorney-General v. The Ironmongers' Co., 2 Myl. & K. 576 (1833); Campbell v. Mayor of Liverpool, L.R. 9 Eq. 579 (1870); In re Peel's Release, [1921] 2 Ch. 218.

See the language of Jenkins, L.J., in In re Ulverston & Dist. New Hosp. Bldg. Trusts, [1956] Ch. 622, 635–637, noted in 34 Can. B. Rev. 1066, 20 Mod. L. Rev. 61, on the distinction between failure at the outset and subsequent failure.

See In re Hardy, [1933] N. Ir. L.R. 150; In re the Lord Mayor of Belfast's Air Raid Distress Fund, [1962] N. Ir. L.R. 161; Davidson's Trustees v. Arnott, [1951] Sess. Cas. 42 (Scot.).

In In re Wokingham Fire Brigade Trusts, [1951] Ch. 373, it was held that property owned by a voluntary fire brigade received by subscriptions and

appears to have contemplated that the particular charitable purpose would be accomplished sooner or later, it has been held that the property reverts to the testator's estate upon the accomplishment of that purpose. Thus in *In re Stanford*[4] it was held that where money was bequeathed in trust for the publication of a dictionary, and the dictionary was completed without exhaust-

---

donations was held upon a charitable trust for the benefit of the community, and on the dissolution of the brigade should be applied cy pres.

In In re Hart, [1951] 2 D.L.R. 30 (N.S.), where a testator made a bequest to a charitable corporation, showing an intention to benefit only that corporation, and the legacy was payable on the death of his widow, and the corporation ceased to exist before the death of the widow, it was held that the bequest failed.

In In re Cooper's Conveyance Trusts, [1956] 3 All E.R. 28, noted in 34 Can. B. Rev. 1066, land was conveyed in 1864 to establish an orphanage with a gift over on failure of the orphanage. The gift over was invalid because it was noncharitable and violated the rule against perpetuities. It was held that on the failure of the orphanage the doctrine of cy pres was not applicable and a resulting trust arose. It is submitted that the result thus reached is unfortunate.

In Cuthbert's Trustees v. Cuthbert, [1958] Sess. Cas. 629 (Scot.), where a testator left his house as a holiday home for nurses and provided that the income of the residue of his estate should be applied for its maintenance, and the trustees attempted to run the home for several years but the funds were insufficient, it was held that the trust failed. The court said that the experiment proved that the funds were never sufficient for the purpose.

In Edinburgh Corp. v. Cranston's Trustees, [1960] Sess. Cas. 244 (Scot.), where a testator directed his trustees to pay a fund to a corporation to pay annuities to 12 poor tailors who complied with certain conditions and for several years only two such tailors could be found, it was held that the trust had not failed at the outset and that on the subsequent failure of the trust the property should be applied cy pres and not revert to the testator's estate.

In In re Royal Kilmainham Hosp., [1966] I.R. 451, the court said (p. 469) that "where property is given absolutely and perpetually to charity for a particular purpose and has vested in the charity the fund can be applied *cy-près* irrespective of the donor's particular intention."

In In re Rowhook Mission Hall, Horsham; Chaning-Pearce v. Morris, [1985] Ch. 62 (Ch. D.), land was conveyed to trustees so long as they operated a school on it. They ceased to operate the school in 1904. It was held that the possibility of reverter of the grantors became a possessory estate in 1904 and so was barred by the statute of limitations. The trustees having acquired a fee simple absolute by adverse possession held for such charitable purpose as the court should direct cy pres.

See Luxton, Cy-Pres and the Ghost of Things That Might Have Been, [1983] Conv. 107.

[4][1924] 1 Ch. 73.

ing the money, the trustees held the surplus upon a resulting trust for the estate of the testator. In *In re British Red Cross Balkan Fund*[5] it was held that where funds were received by popular subscription for assisting the sick and wounded in the Balkan War and the funds were not wholly expended when the war ended, the subscribers were entitled to receive back the surplus in proportion to their subscriptions. No suggestion was made in the case that the surplus should be applied to relieve the suffering caused by the war; but in a later case the court said that if such a suggestion had been made, the court would have made such an application of the property under the cy pres doctrine.[6]

On the other hand, where there is an absolute perpetual gift for charitable purposes, even though the trusts declared are only for the accomplishment of particular charitable purposes, it would seem that in England the trust will never fail if it is valid at the outset, even though the particular purpose becomes impossible of accomplishment unless the testator otherwise provided.[7]

In the United States it has been held that the doctrine of cy

[5][1914] 2 Ch. 419.

[6]In re Welsh Hosp. Fund, [1921] 1 Ch. 655.

Compare American Natl. Red Cross v. Felzner Post, 86 Ind. App. 709, 159 N.E. 771 (1928), where it was held that a fund subscribed as a "war chest" to assist men and women in the military service of the United States could be applied after the end of the war for the benefit of ex-servicemen and their families. The case is noted in 2 U. Cin. L. Rev. 417.

[7]In re Prison Charities, L.R. 16 Eq. 129 (1873); Biscoe v. Jackson, 35 Ch. D. 460 (1886); In re Buck, [1896] 2 Ch. 727; In re Cunningham, [1914] 1 Ch. 427; In re British School of Egyptian Archaeology, [1954] 1 All·E.R. 887; In re Whitworth Art Gallery Trusts, [1958] Ch. 461; Avalon Consol. School Bd. v. United Church of Can., 42 Nfld. & P.E.I.R. 8, 122 A.P.R. 8 (Nfld. T.D.), *aff'd*, 47 Nfld. & P.E.I.R. 261, 139 A.P.R. 261 (Nfld. Ct. App. 1984).

See Hall, Recent Developments in the Cy-prés Doctrine, [1957] Camb. L.J. 87.

Even if the testator made express provision for reverter, it should be recalled that, under English law, unlike the rules in the United States, rights of entry on breach of condition subsequent, possibilities of reverter, and resulting trusts are subject to the rule against perpetuities. Law of Property Act 1925, 15 & 16 Geo. V, c. 20, §43(3); Perpetuities and Accumulations Act 1964, c. 55, §12; Simes & Smith, The Law of Future Interests §§1220, 1238, 1239 (2d ed. 1956 and 1987 Pocket Part by Fratcher); §62.10, pp. 340–341. See Fratcher, Differences Between the English and American Rules Against Perpetuities, 28 Conv. 244, 245 (1964).

pres is not always applicable where the purpose for which a charitable trust is created subsequently fails. Mr. Justice Holmes once said that "there is no absolute rule of law that prevents the charity terminating when the donee ceases to exist, although, no doubt, in such cases courts have gone still further in straining the meaning of wills, in order to uphold the supposed general intent."[8] Where it clearly appears that the testator intended that the property should be applied only to the particular purpose that failed, or for the benefit of a particular association or corporation that was dissolved, it has been held that the doctrine of cy pres is not applicable and that the property reverts to the settlor or his estate.[9] The cases, however, are far more numer-

[8]Stratton v. Physio-Medical College, 149 Mass. 505, 508, 21 N.E. 874, 5 L.R.A. 33, 14 Am. St. Rep. 442 (1889).

[9]*Federal:* President & Fellows of Harvard College v. Jewett, 11 F.2d 119 (6th Cir. 1925).

Connecticut: Mears v. Conway, 17 Conn. Supp. 319 (1951); Connecticut Bank & Trust Co. v. Coles, 150 Conn. 569, 192 A.2d 202 (1963).

Kansas: Shannep v. Strong, 160 Kan. 206, 160 P.2d 683 (1945).

Maine: Bancroft v. Maine State Sanatorium Assn., 119 Me. 56, 109 A. 585 (1920); First Universalist Socy. of Bath v. Swett, 148 Me. 142, 90 A.2d 812 (1952), noted in 5 Baylor L. Rev. 205.

Massachusetts: Dodge v. Anna Jaques Hosp., 301 Mass. 431, 17 N.E.2d 308 (1938) (citing Restatement of Trusts §399); Board of Selectmen of Provincetown v. Attorney Gen., 15 Mass. App. Ct. 639, 447 N.E.2d 677 (1983), citing text.

Missouri: Comfort v. Higgins, 576 S.W.2d 331 (Mo. 1979) (trust for old peoples' home; no attempt to create such a home for many years).

New Jersey: McCran v. Kay, 93 N.J. Eq. 352, 115 A. 649 (1921).

New York: Matter of Merritt, 258 A.D. 188, 16 N.Y.S.2d 1 (1939); Matter of Syracuse Univ. (Matter of Heffron), 3 N.Y.2d 665, 148 N.E.2d 671 (1958) (citing the text and Restatement of Trusts, §399, Comment *k*); De Pew v. Union Free School Dist., 41 A.D.2d 308, 342 N.Y.S.2d 560 (1973) (holding it error to dismiss claim by the settlor's heirs, because the question of settlor's intent should be determined by a trial; citing the text).

Pennsylvania: Pruner Estate, 400 Pa. 629, 162 A.2d 626 (1960), noted in 22 U. Pitt. L. Rev. 277.

Washington: Townsend v. Charles Schalkenbach Home for Boys, 33 Wash. 2d 255, 205 P.2d 345 (1949); McLaren v. Charles Schalkenbach Home for Boys, 41 Wash. 2d 123, 247 P.2d 691 (1952), noted in 28 Wash. L. Rev. 76.

See 38 A.L.R. 44 (1925); 14 Mass. L.Q., No. 6, p. 50 (1929).

In 1859 one Bryan Mullanphy made a bequest to the city of St. Louis in trust to furnish relief to all poor emigrants and travelers coming to St. Louis, on their way bona fide to settle in the West. Several attempts were made by

ous in which it has been held that the doctrine of cy pres should be applied.[10] In a New Jersey case it was said that where a

---

the heirs of the testator to reach the fund on the ground that the trust had failed and that it should revert to them. The court held, however, that the purposes of the trust had not become impossible of accomplishment. City of St. Louis v. McAllister, 281 Mo. 26, 218 S.W. 312 (1920), 302 Mo. 152, 257 S.W. 425 (1924); Thatcher v. City of St. Louis, 335 Mo. 1130, 76 S.W.2d 677 (1934).

In Industrial Natl. Bank v. Drysdale, 83 R.I. 172, 114 A.2d 191 (1955), 84 R.I. 385, 125 A.2d 87 (1956) (citing the text), where a testator left money to a trust company on a perpetual trust to pay the income to a religious corporation, and the corporation was dissolved some years after his death, it was held that the testator had no general charitable intent and that the trustee held upon a resulting trust for the next of kin.

In Payne v. City of Providence, 182 F.2d 888 (1st Cir. 1950), it was held that in case of diversity of citizenship the heirs of the testator could maintain suit in a federal court to enforce a resulting trust on the failure of a charitable trust. The court cited Restatement of Trusts §413.

In Matter of Syracuse Univ. (Matter of Heffron), 3 N.Y.2d 665, 148 N.E.2d 671 (1958), rev'g 2 A.D.2d 466, 156 N.Y.S.2d 779 (1956), rev'g 2 Misc. 2d 446, 150 N.Y.S.2d 251 (1956), where a legacy was given to Syracuse University as an endowment for the support of its College of Medicine, and because of financial difficulties the College of Medicine closed, it was held that the fund should not be transferred under the cy pres doctrine to the Medical Center of the State University of New York, on the ground that the testator intended to benefit only the Medical College of Syracuse University. The court quoted the text and Restatement of Trusts, §399, Comment k.

As to the disposition of its property on the dissolution of a charitable corporation, see §397.3.

[10]England: Liverpool & Dist. Hosp. for Diseases of the Heart v. Attorney-General, [1981] 1 All E.R. 994 (Ch. Div.) (National Health Service had taken over the functions of the charitable corporation and its own memorandum of association provided for judicial application cy pres if the corporation could not function).

Arkansas: State Natl. Bank of Texarkana v. Bann, 202 Ark. 850, 153 S.W.2d 158 (1941); Trevathan v. Ringgold Noland Found., 241 Ark. 758, 410 S.W.2d 132 (1967).

Connecticut: Williams Memorial Inst. v. Beers, 18 Conn. Supp. 512 (1954); New York E. Annual Conference of Methodist Church v. Seymour, 151 Conn. 517, 199 A.2d 701 (1964) (dissolution of unincorporated church); Connecticut Bank & Trust Co. v. Ajello, 39 Conn. Supp. 80, 468 A.2d 942 (1983).

Georgia: Alexander v. Georgia Baptist Found., 245 Ga. 545, 266 S.E.2d 165 (1980).

Illinois: Hardy v. Davis, 16 Ill. App. 2d 516, 148 N.E.2d 805 (1958) (bequest to maintain a home for orphan children, who ceased to attend, was

charitable trust has taken effect initially with no limitation of

---

applied for scholarships for orphan children; citing the text); Rosewell v. Chicago Park Dist., 126 Ill. App. 3d 30, 81 Ill. Dec. 428, 466 N.E.2d 1230 (1984).

Kentucky: Harwood v. Dick, 286 Ky. 423, 150 S.W.2d 704 (1941); Pennebaker v. Pennebaker Home for Girls, 297 Ky. 670, 181 S.W.2d 49 (1944); Zevely v. City of Paris, 298 S.W.2d 12 (Ky. 1957) (for memorial room in hospital that was closed on erection of another hospital).

Louisiana: In re Succession of Milne, 230 La. 729, 89 So. 2d 281 (1956); In re Succession of Abraham, 136 So. 2d 471 (La. App. 1962); Ada C. Pollock-Blundon Assn. v. Heirs of Evans, 273 So. 2d 552 (La. App. 1973).

See Bonner v. Board of Trustees, 181 So. 2d 255 (La. 1966).

Maine: Pierce v. How, 153 Me. 180, 136 A.2d 510 (1957) (quoting the text and Restatement of Trusts, §399, Comment *f;* interpretation of terms of trust as well as application cy pres); State v. Rand, 366 A.2d 183 (Me. 1976) (citing the text).

Maryland: Wesley Home v. Mercantile-Safe Deposit & Trust Co., 265 Md. 185, 289 A.2d 337 (1972).

Massachusetts: Jackson v. Phillips, 14 Allen 539 (Mass. 1867); Trustees of Putnam Free School v. Attorney Gen., 320 Mass. 94, 67 N.E.2d 658 (1946); Clark v. Mayor of Gloucester, 336 Mass. 631, 147 N.E.2d 191 (1958); Anna Jaques Hosp. v. Attorney Gen., 341 Mass. 179, 167 N.E.2d 875 (1960) (citing the text); Rogers v. Attorney Gen., 347 Mass. 126, 196 N.E.2d 855 (1964); Trustees of Dartmouth College v. City of Quincy, 357 Mass. 521, 258 N.E.2d 745 (1970); Boston Seaman's Friend Socy. v. Attorney Gen., 379 Mass. 414, 398 N.E.2d 721 (1980) (citing the text and Restatement of Trusts §399).

Michigan: Knights of Equity Memorial Scholarships Commn. v. University of Detroit, 359 Mich. 235, 102 N.W.2d 463 (1960).

Missouri: Lewis v. Brubaker, 322 Mo. 52, 14 S.W.2d 982 (1929).

New Hampshire: Exeter v. Robinson Heirs, 94 N.H. 463, 55 A.2d 622 (1947) (citing the text and Restatement of Trusts §399); Trustees of Pittsfield Academy v. Attorney Gen., 95 N.H. 51, 57 A.2d 161 (1948) (citing the text).

New Jersey: MacKenzie v. Trustees of Presbytery, 67 N.J. Eq. 652, 61 A. 1027, 3 L.R.A. (N.S.) 227 (1905); Cuthbert v. McNeill, 103 N.J. Eq. 184, 142 A. 667 (1928), *aff'd,* 104 N.J. Eq. 495, 146 A. 881 (1929).

New York: Sherman v. Richmond Hose Co., 230 N.Y. 462, 130 N.E. 613 (1921); Matter of Swope, 204 Misc. 510, 121 N.Y.S.2d 181 (1953) (citing the text); Heckscher's Trust, 131 N.Y.S.2d 191 (1954); Matter of Scott, 1 Misc. 2d 206, 145 N.Y.S.2d 346 (1955) (citing Restatement of Trusts §399), s.c. Matter of Scott, 5 Misc. 2d 690, 160 N.Y.S.2d 210 (1956); Matter of Syracuse Univ. (Matter of Hendricks), 1 Misc. 2d 904, 148 N.Y.S.2d 245 (1955), *aff'd mem.,* 3 A.D.2d 890, 161 N.Y.S.2d 855 (1957), *aff'd mem.,* 4 N.Y.2d 744, 148 N.E.2d 911 (1958); Matter of Clark, 1 Misc. 2d 869, 150 N.Y.S.2d 65 (1956); Matter of Lee, 3 Misc. 2d 1072, 156 N.Y.S.2d 813 (1956); Matter of Kittinger, 6 Misc. 2d 125, 160 N.Y.S.2d 214 (1957); Matter of Bowne, 11 Misc. 2d 597, 173 N.Y.S.2d 723 (1958); Matter of Hampton, 15 Misc. 2d 846, 182 N.Y.S.2d 439

time for its accomplishment and no provision for reverter, the

---

(1958); Application of Bd. of Educ. of Utica City School Dist., 18 Misc. 2d 192, 184 N.Y.S.2d 735 (1959); Matter of Hawley, 32 Misc. 2d 624, 223 N.Y.S.2d 803 (1961); Matter of Will of Kraetzer, 119 Misc. 2d 436, 462 N.Y.S.2d 1009 (Sur. 1983), §399.2, n. 6, *supra.*

North Carolina: Trustees of Watts Hosp. v. Commissioners of Durham, 231 N.C. 604, 58 S.E.2d 696 (1950); Board of Trustees of the Univ. of N.C. v. Unknown & Unascertained Heirs of Prince, 311 N.C. 644, 319 S.E.2d 239 (1984).

Pennsylvania: Pentz's Estate, 42 D.&C. 296 (Pa. 1941) (citing the text and Restatement of Trusts §399); Dobbins Estate, 74 D.&C. 106 (Pa. 1951); Towne Estate, 75 D.&C. 215 (Pa. 1951) (quoting the text); Magee Estate, 1 D.&C.2d 447 (Pa. 1954).

Rhode Island: Powers v. Home for Aged Women, 55 R.I. 187, 192 A. 770, 110 A.L.R. 1361 (1937) (citing Restatement of Trusts §399); City of Providence v. Powers, 83 R.I. 512, 120 A.2d 811 (1956); New England Yearly Meeting of Friends v. Anthony, 95 R.I. 251, 186 A.2d 340 (1962); Industrial Natl. Bank v. Guiteras, 107 R.I. 379, 267 A.2d 706 (1970) (citing the text).

South Carolina: Colin McK. Grant Home v. Medlock, 349 S.E.2d 655 (S.C. App. Ct. 1986) (although South Carolina does not accept the cy pres doctrine, a charitable corporation to which property was devised to maintain a home on particular land for elderly white Presbyterian will be allowed, on a showing that racial attitudes have changed and the site has become unsuitable, to sell the home and use the proceeds to subsidize housing for elderly Presbyterians of all races).

Virginia: Penn v. Keller, 178 Va. 131, 16 S.E.2d 331 (1941), noted in 22 B.U.L. Rev. 159, 30 Geo. L.J. 216, 28 Va. L. Rev. 307; Wellford v. Powell, 197 Va. 685, 90 S.E.2d 791 (1956).

Washington: Puget Sound Natl. Bank v. Easterday, 56 Wash. 2d 937, 350 P.2d 444 (1960), noted in 36 Wash. L. Rev. 205.

Wisconsin: First Wis. Trust Co. v. Board of Trustees of Racine College, 225 Wis. 34, 272 N.W. 464 (1937).

Canada: Re Fitzpatrick, 6 D.L.R. 4th 644 (Man. Q.B. 1984).

Northern Ireland: Re Currie, McClelland v. Gamble. [1985] 7 N.I.J.B. 69.

In Robert W. Traip Academy v. Staples, 317 A.2d 816 (Me. 1974), where a testator created an academy in a town, and after 100 years it was impractical to continue it, it was held that the building should be sold and the proceeds and endowment used by the town not for its regular educational work in its schools but rather to supplement its budgetary capabilities.

In In re Los Angeles County Pioneer Socy., 40 Cal. 2d 852, 257 P.2d 1 (1953), a corporation was organized to preserve data on the history of a county and state, and an incidental purpose was to cultivate social intercourse among the members. It was held that it was a charitable corporation, and that on its dissolution its assets should not be divided among its members or returned to the donor but should be given to another charitable corporation to administer.

trust will never fail, and the property will never revert to the heirs of the testator.[11]

It sometimes happens that the particular purpose for which property is bequeathed is practicable at the time of the death of the testator but becomes impracticable before it is to come into

---

In Attinson v. Consumer-Farmer Milk Coop., 197 Misc. 336, 94 N.Y.S.2d 891 (1950), it was held that a cooperative corporation organized to benefit farmers and consumers through the distribution of milk and other products and otherwise to serve the economic and cultural welfare of its members and of the public was a charitable corporation, and that on its dissolution its property should be applied cy pres and not divided among the members. See §374.10, n. 13.

In Morristown School v. Parsons, 23 N.J. Super. 146, 92 A.2d 646 (1952), a school gymnasium was destroyed, and the school did not have sufficient funds to replace it, and its replacement was necessary for the continuance of the school. It was held that the school might use the principal of its endowment fund to complete the construction, taking a second mortgage on the gymnasium to secure the repayment to the fund.

In Trustees of Alexander Linn Hosp. Assn. v. Richman, 46 N.J. Super. 594, 135 A.2d 221 (1957), a testatrix left her estate to a hospital to use the income for its purposes. It was held that the hospital might use the principal to pay for the completion of a building, giving a second mortgage to secure the repayment, since otherwise it might be compelled to close its doors. The court cited Restatement of Trusts §167.

In Reeser Estate, 1 D.&C.2d 731 (Pa. 1954), where property was left in trust for the medical education of a boy belonging to a particular church, it was held that a girl might be chosen as a beneficiary.

In Brown Trust, 10 D.&C.2d 93 (Pa. 1957), where a testator left $1000 to a trust company in trust as an endowment fund for a named hospital, one half of the income to be accumulated and the other half to be used as the hospital managers should think best, and the hospital was dissolved, it was held unnecessary to appoint a master and to attempt to apply cy pres, and the court ordered that the sum be paid over to another hospital without restrictions.

In a number of cases the question has arisen as to the disposition of funds raised during the First World War for the benefit of soldiers. See Fennel v. McGuire, 5 Conn. Supp. 367 (1937) (quoting Restatement of Trusts §399); Niles Post No. 2074 of Veterans of Foreign Wars of U.S. v. Niles Memorial Hosp. Assn., 65 Ohio App. 238, 29 N.E.2d 631 (1936); In re Distribution of Funds of Y.M.C.A. War Fund, 63 Ohio App. 213, 25 N.E.2d 956 (1939); Connors v. Ahearn, 342 Pa. 5, 19 A.2d 388 (1941).

In many of the cases cited in the preceding section where the property was applied cy pres, the particular purpose failed after the death of the testator.

[11]Cuthbert v. McNeill, 103 N.J. Eq. 184, 142 A. 667 (1928), aff'd, 104 N.J. Eq. 495, 146 A. 881 (1929).

operation, as in the case where the testator creates a trust for a beneficiary for life and directs that the property be applied to the charitable purpose on the beneficiary's death. This is not quite like the case where the charitable trust fails after it has gone into operation, where the failure might take place at some indefinite time; nor is it quite like the case where it fails on the death of the testator. In England it would seem that it is treated as a case of subsequent, not original, failure, and the cy pres doctrine will almost automatically be applied.[12] In the United States, where the distinction between original and subsequent failure is not so marked, the courts are a little more ready, but not much more ready, to apply the cy pres doctrine than in the case where the purpose fails at the death of the testator.[13]

A further question may arise as to the disposition of the trust property on the failure of a charitable trust. If the doctrine of cy pres is not applicable, the question is whether there is a resulting trust for the heirs or next of kin of the testator or whether there is a resulting trust for the residuary devisee or legatee. The question arises, of course, only where there is a specific devise or bequest or general legacy for charitable purposes, followed by a disposition of the residue. If the charitable trust fails at the outset, there is a resulting trust for the residuary devisee or legatee, because all the property not effectively disposed of falls into the residue. A more difficult question arises where the failure of a charity occurs at some time subsequent to the death of the testator. In such a case a provision that, if the charitable trust should terminate, the property should be paid

---

[12]In re Slevin, [1891] 2 Ch. 236; In re Moon's Will Trusts, [1948] 1 All E.R. 300, noted in 12 Convey. (N.S.) 222; In re Wright, [1954] Ch. 347; In re White's Will Trusts, [1955] Ch. 188; In re Tacon, [1958] Ch. 447.

See In re Whittaker, [1951] 2 T.L.R. 955; In re Gordon, 52 D.L.R.2d 197 (Ont. 1965); Attorney-General v. Perpetual Trustee Co., 115 C.L.R. 581 (Austl. 1966).

[13]Horton v. Board of Educ., 32 Wash. 2d 99, 201 P.2d 163 (1948).

See In re Estate of McPherson, 14 Cal. App. 3d 450, 92 Cal. Rptr. 574 (1971).

In McKee Estate, 378 Pa. 607, 108 A.2d 214 (1954), the doctrine of cy pres was applied after the death of the life beneficiaries although at the time of the testator's death the statutory law of cy pres was unsettled.

As to the effect of the dissolution of a charitable corporation after the testator's death but before the death of a life beneficiary, see §397.3.

to a designated person is invalid where the termination might take place at a time beyond the period of the rule against perpetuities.[14] The question remains, however, whether on the failure of the charitable trust the testator intends to and can effectively give the property to a third person by giving the residue of his estate to the third person.

In *Industrial National Bank v. Drysdale*[15] a testator bequeathed $10,000 to a trust company in trust to pay the income forever to a designated charitable corporation and left the residue to designated individuals. Eighteen years after his death the corporation was dissolved. The court had held that the doctrine of cy pres should not be applied.[16] The court granted a rehearing on the question whether the next of kin of the testator or the residuary legatees were entitled to the property. It was held that, because the trust did not fail at the outset, there should be a resulting trust for the next of kin and not for the residuary legatees. In *President and Fellows of Harvard College v. Jewett*[17] a testatrix devised to a museum land containing an ancient Indian cemetery, for the preservation of the remains and relics therein. All of the relics, which consisted of skeletons, were subsequently

---

[14]See §399.3, n. 7, and §401.6.

[15]84 R.I. 385, 125 A.2d 87, 62 A.L.R.2d 756 (1956).

In Rhode Island Hosp. Trust Co. v. Votolato, 102 R.I. 467, 231 A.2d 491, 30 A.L.R.3d 1299 (1967), it was held that on the failure at the outset of a private trust, the residuary legatees and not the next of kin were entitled to the legacy. The court distinguished Industrial National Bank v. Drysdale, cited *supra*. The court quoted Restatement of Trusts §411, and cited the text, §430.1. See also MacDonald v. Manning, 103 R.I. 538, 239 A.2d 640 (1968); Industrial Natl. Bank v. Glocester Manton Free Pub. Library, 107 R.I. 161, 265 A.2d 724 (1970).

See Martin v. North Hill Christian Church, 64 Ohio App. 2d 192, 18 Ohio Ops. 3d 147, 412 N.E.2d 413 (1979), and In re Goodson, [1971] V.R. 801, where an intended charitable trust failed at the outset and it was held that the devised property fell into the residue.

See Note, Disposition of property of inter vivos trust falling in after death of settlor, who left will making no express disposition of the trust property, 30 A.L.R.3d 1318 (1970).

As to the respective rights of the next of kin and of a residuary legatee in case of the failure of a private trust, see §422A.

[16]Industrial Natl. Bank v. Drysdale, 83 R.I. 172, 114 A.2d 191 (1955). See n. 9, *supra.*

[17]11 F.2d 119 (6th Cir. 1925).

removed and placed in the museum. It was held that the purpose for which the land was given having ceased, and the doctrine of cy pres not applying, the land reverted to the heirs of the testatrix and did not fall into the residue.

A different result was reached in *Brown v. Independent Baptist Church.* [18] In that case a testator devised land to a church and provided that if it should ever be dissolved the property should go to certain persons whom he also named as residuary legatees. Many years later the church was dissolved. It was held that the residuary legatees and not the heirs of the testator were entitled to the property. The court held that the church took a determinable fee and that the possibility of reverter fell into the residue.

It would seem that, in the absence of language indicating a contrary intention, the testator intends to include in the residue

[18]325 Mass. 645, 91 N.E.2d 922 (1950). See §401.6, n. 7.

To the same effect see Shannep v. Strong, 160 Kan. 206, 160 P.2d 683 (1945); Matter of Syracuse Univ. (Matter of Heffron), 2 Misc. 2d 446, 150 N.Y.S.2d 251 (1956), *rev'd,* 2 A.D.2d 466, 156 N.Y.S.2d 779 (1956), *rev'd,* 3 N.Y.2d 665, 148 N.E.2d 671 (1958); Ewing Estate, 22 D.&C.2d 445 (Pa. 1960).

In Nelson v. Kring, 225 Kan. 499, 592 P.2d 438 (1979), a testator who died in 1931 made a bequest in trust to pay the income to a hospital. He provided that if it should fail to be operated for a year the fund should be paid to a George Green, or if he should be dead, to his heirs. He also provided that if any bequest should be adjudged void, it should go to Green. In 1972 the hospital ceased to operate. It was held that the gift over to Green was invalid under the rule against perpetuities, that the trust property should not be applied cy pres by giving it to another hospital, and that there was a resulting trust to the heirs of Green as residuary legatees and not to the testator's next of kin. The court cited the text.

In Board of Selectmen of Provincetown v. Attorney Gen., 15 Mass. App. Ct. 639, 447 N.E.2d 677 (1983), the testatrix devised her home to the town to be used for or as a site for a public library and directed her executors to sell the land and pay the proceeds to Harvard University if at the time of her death the town already owned a public library building or site or if the town refused to accept within a year. The town accepted at once but later built its public library elsewhere and sued more than thirty years after the death of the testatrix for a determination that it owned her home in fee simple absolute. It was held that the town held the home in fee simple absolute upon trust for use as a library, that the charitable purpose had failed, that the testatrix had no general charitable intent, that the cy pres doctrine was inapplicable, and that the town held the home on resulting trust for Harvard University.

See Note, Devolution of property to testator's heirs or next of kin, or to his residuary devisees or legatees, where testamentary charitable trust which became operative later fails, 62 A.L.R.2d 763 (1958).

not only property not effectively disposed of at his death, but also all the property that might ultimately come back to his estate, by way of resulting trust or possibility of reverter or right of entry for condition broken. His intention is to exclude his heirs and next of kin in favor of the residuary devisee or legatee. If that is his intention, the only question is whether he can exclude his heirs or next of kin and give the property to his residuary devisee or legatee, where the termination of the disposition may occur beyond the period of the rule against perpetuities. Does the public policy that prevents his making a gift over for noncharitable purposes preclude him from including the property in the residue of his estate? These questions would never arise if it were held that the doctrine of cy pres should always be applied where the trust fails at some time subsequent to his death, or if it were held that the rule against perpetuities is applicable to rights of reverter and to rights of entry for condition broken.[19] It would seem that, if the property is allowed to revert to the estate of the testator, it should revert to the residuary devisee or legatee rather than to the heirs or next of kin.

§399.4. **Where the accomplishment of the particular purpose is not impossible or illegal.** Where property is given in trust for a particular charitable purpose and it is legal and possible and practicable to carry out that purpose, the courts will not ordinarily permit the property to be applied to other purposes, although the other purposes appear to the court to be more useful and desirable than the purpose designated by the testator. On the other hand, it is not fatal to the application of the cy pres doctrine that the designated purpose is possible of accomplishment if it appears that under the circumstances the application of the property to the designated purpose would fail to accomplish the general charitable intention of the testator. In other words, the cy pres doctrine is applicable where it is impracticable to carry out the specific directions of the testator even though it is possible to do so. As was said by the court in one case, "The necessity that will authorize and warrant an order from the court deviating from the exact plan as indicated

---

[19]See §399.3, n. 7, *supra.*

by the will of the donor, need however be only a reasonable necessity and not an absolute physical impossibility."[1] It is difficult, of course, to draw any exact line between the situations where it would be impracticable to carry out the specific directions of the testator and situations where it would merely be undesirable to do so. The distinction is one of degree rather than one of kind.[2]

In the earlier English cases the chancellors showed a reluctance to permit departures from the express directions of the donor where it was possible to carry out those directions, even though as a result of a change of circumstances a departure from those directions had become necessary to make the gift serve a useful purpose. In the sixteenth century it was quite common in England for testators to establish grammar schools, that is, as the term was then used, schools for instruction in Latin and Greek. At the beginning of the nineteenth century some of the more ambitious of the governors and masters of these schools wished to extend the curriculum so as to include writing and arithmetic and modern languages and even physical science. But Lord Eldon, a very great judge, but as conservative a man as ever sat upon the woolsack, held that this could not be done, that the founders had shown their devotion to the classics and that the will of the founders must be respected.[3] Such a doctrine, how-

§399.4.   [1]Women's Christian Assn. v. Kansas City, 147 Mo. 103, 127, 48 S.W. 960 (1898).

New York Estates, Powers and Trusts Law, §7-1.9(c), added by Laws 1985, c. 492, empowers the court, if the settlor is dead or consents, to terminate a charitable trust when the assets are reduced to $100,000 or less and administration is uneconomic and to order the assets applied cy pres to accomplish charitable purposes.

[2]"I have heard it suggested that the difference is one of degree. I am the last man in the world to quarrel with a distinction simply because it is one of degree. Most distinctions, in my opinion, are of that sort, and are none the worse for it." Holmes, J., in Haddock v. Haddock, 201 U.S. 562, 631, 26 S. Ct. 525, 50 L. Ed. 867 (1906).

[3]"The question is, not what are the qualifications most suitable to the rising generation of the place where the charitable foundation subsists, but what are the qualifications intended." Attorney-General v. Whiteley, 11 Ves. 241, 247 (1805). See also Attorney-General v. Earl of Mansfield, 2 Russ. 501 (1826). Lord Eldon was probably historically in error in thinking that the founders of grammar schools intended to exclude everything but the classics. 1 Report of Commission on Popular Education (1861) 458. See also 1 Report of Schools Inquiry Commission, 1867-1868, p. 452.

ever, rendered many of the schools practically useless — some of them worse than useless.[4] It could not stand. Lord Eldon's successors had already shown signs of taking a more liberal view, holding that the school curriculums might be revised and other changes made,[5] when Parliament took a hand. Several statutes were enacted providing a simple method whereby the changes necessary to enable the schools to play their proper part in modern education could be systematically made under the supervision of the courts or of public officials, who should have regard to, but who should not be absolutely bound by, the intentions of the founders and benefactors.[6] Similarly, Parliament empowered the universities of Oxford and Cambridge to make such changes as should be necessary to enable them to awake from the dreams of the Middle Ages and adjust themselves to the needs of modern society.[7]

[4]See Report of Commission on Popular Education (1861); Reports of Schools Inquiry Commission (1867-1868); the reports of Lord Brougham's commissions; and the annual reports of the Charity Commissioners.

As to the evils resulting in course of time from other charitable trusts, see Hobhouse, The Dead Hand (1880). As to the disastrous consequences of that once popular form of charity known as doles, i.e., the promiscuous distribution of money or goods among the poor, see Kenny, Endowed Charities 40-52 (1880). In the case of doles and certain allied forms of charity, Parliament has authorized the application of the funds to education by the Charity Commissioners with the consent of the governing body. Endowed Schools Act, 1869, 32 & 33 Vict. c. 56, §30.

[5]See Attorney-General v. Gascoigne, 2 Myl. & K. 647 (1832); Attorney-General v. Caius College, 2 Keen 150 (1837).

[6]See the Grammar Schools Act, 1840; the Endowed Schools Acts, 1860, 1869, 1873, 1874; the Elementary Education Act, 1870; the Board of Education Act, 1899; the Education Act, 1902; Education Act, 1944. Under these acts authority to authorize new schemes was vested in, first, the Endowed Schools Commissioners, later the Charity Commissioners, and now the Ministry of Education. These acts authorized among other things changes of curriculum and changes as to religious qualifications of governors and masters and pupils. Under the Education Act, 9 & 10 Geo. V, c. 41 (1919), if the governing body of an educational institution applies for a Parliamentary grant, provisions in any instrument regulating the trusts or management of the institution that are inconsistent with the conditions prescribed by the Board of Education for the receipt of Parliamentary grants may be modified.

These statutes have been repealed in whole or in part, as obsolete or as superseded, by Charities Act, 1960, 8 & 9 Eliz. II, c. 58.

[7]See Oxford University Acts, 1854-1869; Cambridge University Act, 1856; University Tests Abolition Act, 1871; Universities of Oxford and Cambridge Act, 1877. Under the last-named act changes may be authorized by

In the more recent English cases the courts have shown a greater readiness to permit a departure from the directions of the donor, even though it is possible to comply with those directions, if the result of such compliance would because of changed conditions impair the usefulness of the gift. Thus in *In re Robinson*[8] a testatrix who died in 1889 bequeathed money toward the endowment of a proposed evangelical church. She made it an "abiding" condition that a black gown should be worn in the pulpit, unless there should be an alteration in the law rendering it illegal. At the time of her death the wearing of a black gown was not unusual among clergymen of the evangelistic school of the Church of England, but later the wearing of such a gown became so unusual that it would be looked upon as eccentric and would disturb the feelings of the congregation. The court held that the requirement should be dispensed with because, although it was not impossible to comply with it, it had become impracticable. To enforce the specific provision would tend to defeat the general object of the testatrix.[9]

As we have seen, the reluctance of the courts in England in the early part of the nineteenth century to permit departures from the directions of the donor led to legislation by Parliament authorizing such departures. In the United States, however, there arise constitutional obstacles to such action by the legislature. It is possible of course to provide by legislation that as to charitable gifts thereafter made such departures may be permitted. As to trusts already created it has been held that the legislature cannot by special acts constitutionally direct that property devoted to one charitable purpose shall be applied to another charitable purpose, nor can it interfere with the control or administration of a charitable trust.[10] If in the course of time changes take place that make desirable a departure from the terms of the trust, the remedy is in the application by the courts

---

commissioners who "shall have regard to the main design of the founder, except where the same has ceased to be observed before the passing of this Act, or where the trusts, conditions, or directions affecting the emolument have been altered in substance by or under any other Act."

[8][1923] 2 Ch. 332.

[9]As to the removal of racial or religious restrictions, see the concluding paragraphs of this section.

[10]See §399.5.

of the cy pres doctrine. If the courts are too reluctant to apply that doctrine, the danger is that charitable trusts may become useless or worse than useless.

In a number of cases it has been held that the doctrine of cy pres was inapplicable because it was practicable even if undesirable to carry out the particular purpose designated by the testator.[11]

[11]*England:* In re Weir Hosp., [1910] 2 Ch. 124.

Federal: Connecticut College v. United States, 276 F.2d 491, 107 App. D.C. 245 (1960) (attempt to change location and to erect an addition instead of a building).

Arkansas: Hicks Memorial Christian Assn. v. Locke, 178 Ark. 892, 12 S.W.2d 866 (1939) (attempt to change location of recreation building where designated site was still as suitable as when will was written).

California: Queen of Angels Hosp. v. Younger, 66 Cal. App. 3d 359, 136 Cal. Rptr. 36 (1977) (hospital not permitted to lease its premises and conduct clinics).

Colorado: Moore v. City & County of Denver, 133 Colo. 190, 292 P.2d 986 (1956) (attempt to enlarge class of beneficiaries of trust to establish and maintain school for poor, white, male orphans, funds greatly increased); City & County of Denver v. Currigan, 147 Colo. 125, 362 P.2d 1060 (1961) (municipal improvements).

Connecticut: Newton v. Healy, 100 Conn. 5, 122 A. 654 (1923) (where income to be used to support higher education, principal cannot be used to furnish established school); Healy v. Loomis Inst., 102 Conn. 410, 128 A. 774 (1925) (attempt to exclude girls from coeducational school); Ludorf v. Hadden, 16 Conn. Supp. 312 (1949) (income given for one type of memorial cannot properly be used for another).

Connecticut: Connecticut Bank & Trust Co. v. Hartford Hosp., 29 Conn. Sup. 158, 276 A.2d 792 (1971) (fund for free bed in named hospital; held fund cannot be used for other purposes of the hospital, although there was no present demand for beds).

See Seymour v. Attorney Gen., 124 Conn. 490, 200 A. 815 (1938).

Illinois: State Bank & Trust Co. v. Park Ridge School for Girls, 34 Ill. App. 2d 396, 181 N.E.2d 204 (1962) (for school so long as it is operated as a Protestant institution, with a gift over if the membership on the board of directors, or teaching staff, or housing administration should be a person of the Roman Catholic faith; held, not applicable to employment of Roman Catholics as janitor, maid, or house mother).

Louisiana: Succession of Correjolles, 206 La. 581, 19 So. 2d 259 (1944) (where large legacy given to erect hospital building, permission to erect pavilion to serve as waiting room denied).

Maine: Manufacturers Natl. Bank v. Woodward, 140 Me. 117, 34 A.2d 471 (1943), s.c. 141 Me. 28, 38 A.2d 657 (1944) (income given for repair of library

It is believed that the courts have not infrequently been too

---

building and purchase of books cannot be used for expenses of operation of library).

Massachusetts: Harvard College v. Society for Promoting Theological Educ., 3 Gray 280 (Mass. 1855) (attempt to separate divinity school from Harvard College); Winthrop v. Attorney Gen., 128 Mass. 258 (1880) (attempt to allow Harvard College to administer funds given to individual trustees to maintain a museum in connection with Harvard College); President & Fellows of Harvard College v. Attorney Gen., 228 Mass. 396, 117 N.E. 903 (1917) (attempt to allow Massachusetts Institute of Technology to cooperate in use of funds given to Harvard College for engineering school); Eliot v. Trinity Church, 232 Mass. 517, 122 N.E. 648 (1919) (attempt to remove memorial statue and substitute a different statue); City of Salem v. Attorney Gen., 344 Mass. 626, 183 N.E.2d 859 (1962) (city to which land was devised for park purposes wished to erect schoolhouse on the land); City of Worcester v. Directors of Worcester Free Pub. Library, 349 Mass. 601, 211 N.E.2d 356 (1965) (provisions as to management of library fund given to town; citing Restatement of Trusts, §399, Comment *a*).

New Hampshire: Town of Boscawen v. Attorney Gen., 93 N.H. 444, 43 A.2d 780 (1945) (cemetery trust).

New York: Matter of Niven, 180 Misc. 767, 42 N.Y.S.2d 739 (1943) (where income directed to be used to maintain church in France and church suspended its activities because of war conditions but such suspension was presumably temporary, use of income to pay rector's salary not permitted); Matter of Thorne, 200 Misc. 30, 102 N.Y.S.2d 386 (1951) (land to be used as park for walking and driving but not for picnics, and fund to be used only as endowment).

Ohio: Findley v. City of Conneaut, 145 Ohio St. 480, 62 N.E.2d 318 (1945), *mod'g* 76 Ohio App. 153, 63 N.E.2d 449 (1945) (citing Restatement of Trusts §381), noted in 32 Va. L. Rev. 666.

See Kingdom v. Saxbe, 82 Ohio Abs. 6, 161 N.E.2d 461 (1958) (quoting the text).

Wisconsin: In re Berry's Estate, 29 Wis. 2d 506, 139 N.W.2d 72 (1966) (student scholarships not substituted for student loans, citing Restatement of Trusts §399); In re Oshkosh Found., 61 Wis. 2d 432, 213 N.W.2d 54, 68 A.L.R.3d 1041 (1973) (charitable foundation for inhabitants of a city; court refused to permit inclusion of inhabitants of neighboring area; citing the text).

In In re Petition of Downer Home, 67 Wis. 2d 55, 226 N.W.2d 444 (1975), a testatrix who died in 1888 devised land and her residuary estate to the elders of a Presbyterian church, to be used as a home for aged clergymen and their wives, to be called the Downer Home. She provided that it first receive Presbyterians and then those of other Protestant denominations. The Home was incorporated and carried on until 1965, when it petitioned to be allowed to sell the building because it had become dilapidated and there was not much demand for admittance, and to use the proceeds to pay the living expenses of aged clergymen; and this was permitted by the court. In 1973, the home

reluctant to permit a deviation from the directions of the testator. The result of a too strict adherence to the words of the testator often means the defeat rather than the accomplishment of his ultimate purpose. He intends to make the property useful to mankind, and to render it useless is to defeat his intention.[12] Said John Stuart Mill.

> Under the guise of fulfilling a bequest, this is making a dead man's intentions for a single day a rule for subsequent centuries, when we know not whether he himself would have made it a rule even for the morrow. . . . No reasonable man, who gave his money, when living, for the benefit of the community, would have desired that his mode of benefiting the community should be adhered to when a better could be found.[13]

Some vain and obstinate donors indeed might prefer to have their own way forever, whether that way should ultimately

---

brought this proceeding asking permission to use part of the funds for a series of seminars at Carleton College for the continuing education of Presbyterian and other Protestant pastors. The court below granted the petition, but the Supreme Court of Wisconsin reversed the order. It was not impractical to continue the practice permitted in 1965, and the beneficiaries should not be enlarged to include clergymen who were not aged or in need.

Canada: Rector, Wardens & Vestry of Parish of Christ Church v. Canadian Permanent Trust Co., 18 E.T.R. 150, 66 N.S.R. 2d 132, 152 A.P.R. 132 (N.S.T.D. 1985) (trust to erect new church building will not be varied cy pres to permit restoration of old building because original purpose not impossible or impracticable).

New Zealand: See In re Goldwater, [1967] N.Z.L.R. 754.

Scotland: Galloway v. Elgin Magistrates, [1946] Sess. Cas. 353 (Scot.); Scotstown Moor Children's Camp, [1948] Sess. Cas. 630 (Scot.).

In Ogontz School Trust, 67 D.&C.2d 402 (Pa. 1974), a settlor created a trust to use the income for scholarships in a named school. As there was no great demand for scholarships, the income had accumulated. The school asked for permission to use the income for the library. The Attorney General objected. The court refused permission on the ground that the request for scholarships might increase and the income should be, for the time at least, accumulated.

See Note, Extension of charitable trust benefits to persons residing outside geographic area prescribed by trust instrument, under doctrines of cy pres or equitable deviation, 68 A.L.R.3d 1049 (1975).

[12]Dunbar v. Board of Trustees of George W. Clayton College, 170 Colo. 327, 461 P.2d 28 (1969) (quoting the text).

[13]1 Mill, Dissertations 32, 36.

prove beneficial or not. But why should effect be given to such an unreasonable desire? A man is not allowed to control the disposition of property for private purposes beyond the period of perpetuities. He is permitted to devote his property in perpetuity to charitable purposes only because the public interest is supposed to be promoted by the creation of charities. The public interest is not promoted by the creation of a charity that by the lapse of time ceases to be useful. The founder of a charity should understand therefore that he cannot create a charity that shall be forever exempt from modification. This idea is expressed by the Commissioners on Popular Education in England, who said:

> It seems, indeed, desirable in the interest of charities in general, and of educational charities in particular, that it should be clearly laid down as a principle, that the power to create permanent institutions is granted, and can be granted, only on the condition implied, if not declared, that they be subject to such modifications as every succeeding generation shall find requisite.[14]

It might be suggested that unless donors can rely on the strict observance of all their directions they will be dissuaded from making gifts for charitable purposes. But experience in England shows the fact to be otherwise. Charitable gifts were never more common in England than in the early days of the Reformation, when the fact that Henry VIII had defeated the intentions of many a founder of religious institutions was fresh in the mind of every Englishman. Bequests to the English universities increased after Parliament had authorized them to depart from the directions of their founders and benefactors.[15] It would seem rather that the charitable-minded would be discouraged by the sight of charitable institutions gradually ceasing

[14] 1 Report of Commission on Popular Education (1861) 477.

See Trustees of Dartmouth College v. City of Quincy, 357 Mass. 521, 258 N.E.2d 745 (1970) (citing the text).

[15] 4 Report of Commission on Popular Education (1861) 308.

See Endowed Schools Act (1869) 32 & 33 Vict., and subsequent acts relating to education.

Connecticut: Pub. Act, §82-155 (1982), amends Conn. Gen. Stat., §45-79b, to permit termination of charitable trusts with assets less than $15,000. Assets go to charitable beneficiaries or are applied cy pres.

to accomplish the high purposes for which they were created.

There is, it is believed, a tendency in the more recent cases to permit a cy pres application even though it is difficult to say that it is impracticable to carry out the specific purpose, but where it would be so unwise to do so that the testator would presumably not have desired to insist on it.[16] Thus in *Matter of*

[16]*Maryland:* Loats Female Orphan Asylum v. Essom, 220 Md. 11, 150 A.2d 742 (1959) (foster home for orphans substituted for institutional care).

New Jersey: Matter of Crichfield Trust, 177 N.J. Super. 258, 426 A.2d 88 (1980) (state agency acting as trustee of trust to provide $400 annual college scholarship to male graduates of named high school granted variation cy pres to allow a larger amount and permit award to female graduates).

New York: Matter of Swan, 237 A.D. 454, 261 N.Y.S. 428 (1933), *aff'd sub nom.* Matter of St. John's Church of Mount Morris, 263 N.Y. 638, 189 N.E. 734 (1934) (funds insufficient to properly establish and maintain an old ladies' home in testator's residence); Application of Arms, 189 Misc. 576, 64 N.Y.S.2d 693 (1946) (funds insufficient to maintain art institute).

North Carolina: West v. Lee, 224 N.C. 79, 29 S.E.2d 31 (1944) (trust to maintain a common school for poor children that became unnecessary because the state thereafter provided an adequate system of public education); Wachovia Bank & Trust Co. v. Morgan, 9 N.C. App. 460, 176 S.E.2d 860 (1970) (holding that a trust to pay the income of nearly a million dollars to four hospitals for the benefit of charity patients had not become impracticable in spite of the care provided by Medicare and Medicaid).

Pennsylvania: Lippincott Estate, 17 D.&C.2d 80 (Pa. 1959) (trust company trustee of fund of $5000 to aid the blind; held they may pay the income to an institution for the blind).

See Johnson Estate, 15 D.&C.2d 407 (Pa. 1958) (removal of works of art from testator's home); Johnson Estate, 51 D.&C.3d 147 (Pa. 1970) (further arrangements made as to the display of works of art of John G. Johnson).

Australia: Forrest v. Attorney-General, [1986] Vict. L.R. 187 (Sup. Ct.) (testamentary trust to apply income to charities exempt from estate duty at date of testator's death varied to permit application to charities created after testator's death under a 1978 statute that permits variation cy pres even though it is not impossible or impracticable to carry out the precise directions of the settlor).

In Cleveland Museum of Art v. O'Neill, 72 Ohio Abs. 11, 129 N.E.2d 669 (1955) (citing Restatement of Trusts §381), where trusts were created to acquire objects of art for a museum, the court permitted the use of income to acquire better quarters to house its objects of art.

In Matter of Angel, 33 Misc. 2d 122, 225 N.Y.S.2d 419 (1962), where a testator left his property in trust to set up a fund for a particular home for the blind and to provide seeing-eye dogs, and it was found to be impracticable to purchase dogs because of the expense, it was held that the fund might be used by the home for the maintenance of kennels for seeing-eye dogs.

Stuart[17] a testatrix left her books and works of art to a public library, and provided that these things were to be placed in a separate room and separately catalogued. Thereafter owing to lack of space it was found burdensome to carry out these provisions. The court held that the articles might be transferred to a historical society for exhibition. In *Matter of MacFarland*[18] a testatrix left a large legacy to a church to use the income to furnish fresh flowers every Sunday for the pulpit of the church. It was held that to apply the whole of the income to this purpose would discourage others from supplying flowers, that the doctrine of cy pres should be applied, and that the income should be used for church purposes in the discretion of the trustees, subject to a duty to supply an inscribed vase and to use as much of the income as should be necessary to secure a supply of fresh flowers.

A relaxation of the cy pres doctrine is advocated in a report presented to Parliament in 1952.[19] The committee states that its aim is to strike a balance between regard for the spirit of the intention of the founder and the claims of the present. It advocates the relaxing of the cy pres doctrine "so as to admit of trust instruments being altered by scheme in circumstances falling short of the original objects of the trust having become impracticable." It recommends that "Alterations of trusts under the widened powers should not be made within thirty-five years from the foundation of the trust without the consent of the trustees and of the founder of the trust, if living." The scope of the cy pres power was enlarged by Charities Act 1960.[20] This

[17]183 Misc. 20, 46 N.Y.S.2d 911 (1944).

See Schrag, Cy Pres Inexpediency and the Buck Trust, 20 U.S.F. L. Rev. 577 (1986).

[18]95 N.Y.S.2d 258 (1950).

[19]Report of the Committee on the Law and Practice Relating to Charitable Trusts (1952) (Cmd. 8710), c. 9.

[20]The scope of the cy pres doctrine is enlarged by Charities Act, 1960, 8 & 9 Eliz. II, c. 58, §13. This provides:

"13. (1) Subject to subsection (2) below, the circumstances in which the original purposes of a charitable gift can be altered to allow the property given or part of it to be applied cy-près shall be as follows:

provides that the property may be applied cy pres if the trust has ceased "to provide a suitable and effective method of using the property available by virtue of the gift, regard being had to the spirit of the gift."

In most of the states in which there are statutes adopting the cy pres doctrine, it is provided that the doctrine shall apply where it is "impossible or impracticable" to carry out the chari-

---

   (a)   where the original purposes, in whole or in part, (i) have been as far as may be fulfilled; or (ii) cannot be carried out, or not according to the directions given and to the spirit of the gift; or

   (b)   where the original purposes provide a use for part only of the property available by virtue of the gift; or

   (c)   where the property available by virtue of the gift and other property applicable for similar purposes can be more effectively used in conjunction, and to that end can suitably, regard being had to the spirit of the gift, be made applicable to common purposes; or

   (d)   where the original purposes were laid down by reference to an area which then was but has since ceased to be a unit for some other purpose, or by reference to a class of persons or to an area which has for any reason since ceased to be suitable, regard being had to the spirit of the gift, or to be practical in administering the gift; or

   (e)   where the original purposes, in whole or in part, have, since they were laid down, (i) been adequately provided for by other means; or (ii) ceased, as being useless or harmful to the community or for other reasons, to be in law charitable; or (iii) ceased in any other way to provide a suitable and effective method of using the property available by virtue of the gift, regard being had to the spirit of the gift.

"(2) Subsection (1) above shall not affect the conditions which must be satisfied in order that property given for charitable purposes may be applied cy-près, except in so far as those conditions require a failure of the original purposes. . . .

"(5) It is hereby declared that a trust for charitable purposes places a trustee under a duty, where the case permits and requires the property or some part of it to be applied cy-près, to secure its effective use for charity by taking steps to enable it to be so applied."

See Nathan on the Charities Act, 1960 (1962).

The English Charities Act, 1985, c. 20, §§2, 3, 4, authorizes the trustees of an unincorporated charity over 50 years old, by unanimous action, to change the objects of the charity after finding that the original objects are obsolete, lacking in usefulness, or impossible of achievement. Alternatively, they may transfer the assets to another charity. Trustees of very small charitable endowments may expend the entire principal.

See Sladen, Charities Act 1985, [1986] Conv. 78.

table trust in accordance with the directions of the donor. In Minnesota and in South Dakota, however, the word "inexpedient" is inserted.[21]

§399.4A. Racial, sexual, and religious restrictions. Three questions may arise where the creator of a trust for charitable purposes has imposed restrictions, racial, sexual, or religious, as to who should be included in the objects of his bounty. The first is whether the restriction is illegal. The second is whether if it is illegal the trust should fail or should be continued without the restriction. The third is whether the court will permit the removal of the restriction even though it is not illegal.

Where the trust is administered by a municipality, it has been held by the Supreme Court of the United States that a racial restriction is illegal. In *Girard Will Case*[1] a testator died in 1831 leaving a large estate to the City of Philadelphia in trust to establish a school for "poor male white orphan children." Shortly thereafter suit was brought in a federal court by the testator's heirs to set aside the bequest, but it was upheld by the Supreme Court of the United States.[2] In 1954, certain black children applied for admission to the school and were denied admission, and they brought a proceeding in a state court to compel their admission. Their petition was denied. The court held that the doctrine of cy pres was not applicable, because it was not impossible or impracticable to carry on the school for white children only. The court held that segregation was permissible because the school was not a public school. Its decision on this point was reversed by the Supreme Court of the United States.[3] Thereafter the Orphans' Court removed the Board of Directors of City Trusts, the instrumentality through which the city administered its charitable trusts, and appointed individual trustees. Its action was approved by the Supreme Court of Penn-

---

[21]For a list of the statutes, see §399, n. 2.

[1]386 Pa. 548, 127 A.2d 287 (1956), *aff'g* 4 D.&C.2d 671 (Pa. 1955).

[2]Vidal v. Girard's Exrs., 2 How. 127, 11 L. Ed. 205 (U.S. 1844). See §§348, 348.3.

[3]Commonwealth of Pa. v. Board of Directors of City Trusts, 353 U.S. 230, 989, 77 S. Ct. 806, 1281, 1 L. Ed. 2d 792, 1146 (1957).

sylvania.[4] The Supreme Court of the United States denied certiorari and dismissed an appeal.

Because it was impossible legally to carry out the whole of the testator's intention, namely, that the city should administer the trust and that white children alone should be admitted, there were two alternatives available to the state court, either to permit black children to attend the school or to remove the trustee. It would seem that, quite apart from the question of public policy, the state court might properly have applied the cy pres doctrine and held that it would conform more nearly to his intention to remove the restriction rather than to remove the trustee.

It was finally held by the federal courts that the change of trustees by the Pennsylvania courts was a state involvement in racial discrimination, that the exclusion of blacks was illegal, and that the college must admit black children.[5]

[4]In re Girard College Trusteeship, 391 Pa. 434, 138 A.2d 844 (1958), *cert. denied and appeal dismissed,* 357 U.S. 570 (1958).

See Note, 20 Ohio St. L.J. 132 (1959); 18 U. Pitt. L. Rev. 630 (1957); 1963 Wis. L. Rev. 254.

In Fox Estate, 16 D.&C.2d 425 (Pa. 1959), the trustee was by the terms of the trust directed to pay the income to a certain school for blacks, and it was provided that, if the school should be placed under public supervision, the income should be paid to the proper officer, with a gift over to another charity if the school should cease to provide instruction only for blacks. The school was placed under public supervision. It was held that the gift over took effect, because it would be unconstitutional to maintain a public school for blacks only.

[5]Commonwealth v. Brown, 392 F.2d 120, 25 A.L.R.3d 724 (3d Cir. 1968), *cert. denied,* 391 U.S. 921 (1968). Compare Trustees of Univ. of Del. v. Gebelin, 420 A.2d 1191 (Del. Ch. 1980) (trust for scholarship for white females in state university amended cy pres to delete "white" but not "female").

In Matter of Johnson, 93 A.D.2d 1, 460 N.Y.S.2d 932 (1983), a testator without known heirs bequeathed funds to a public school district upon trust to provide scholarships in college for deserving young men who graduated from its high school. It was conceded that the school district could not, for constitutional reasons, administer a trust that discriminated on the basis of sex. The surrogate appointed a private person to act as trustee, instructing him to get advice from the school district. The Appellate Division reversed the decree of the surrogate, left the school district as trustee, and used the cy pres doctrine to change the word "men" to "persons." The Court of Appeals reversed and reinstated the decree of the surrogate. Matter of Estate of Wil-

A similar question has arisen with respect to a racial restriction on the use of a park. In *Evans v. Newton*[6] a testator devised land to the City of Macon in trust to maintain a park for white people only. It was held by the state court that the lower court properly accepted the resignation of the city as trustee and appointed individuals as successor trustees. The judgment was reversed by the Supreme Court of the United States. Mr. Justice Douglas, speaking for the majority, said that the service rendered by a park of this character is municipal in nature and that it should be treated as a public institution whether administered by a municipality or by private trustees. Three of the Justices dissented on the ground that it was within the power of the state to substitute new trustees and that its judgment did not involve the question of segregation. Thereafter the Supreme Court of Georgia held that the sole purpose for which the trust was created had become impossible of accomplishment and that the trust failed, and the court remitted the case to the lower court

---

son, 59 N.Y.2d 461, 452 N.E.2d 1228, 465 N.Y.S.2d 900 (1983), noted in 53 U. Cin. L. Rev. 297 (1984) and in 12 Hast. C.L.Q. 127 (1984), citing this section.

See Parker, Evans v. Newton and the Racially Restricted Charitable Trust, 13 How. L.J. 223 (1967); Note, Mandatory Cy Pres and the Racially Restrictive Charitable Trust, 69 Colum. L. Rev. 1478 (1969); Note, 11 W. & M. L. Rev. 776 (1970); Note, 84 Harv. L. Rev. 54-60 (1970); Note, Validity and effect of gift for charitable purposes which excludes otherwise qualified beneficiaries because of their race or religion, 25 A.L.R.3d 736 (1969); Knowles, The Girard Trust — Past, Present, and Future, 20 Ala. L. Rev. 308 (1968); Glassman, In re Estate of Wilson: Judicial Reformation of Discriminatory Charitable Trusts, 5 Pace L. Rev. 433 (1985).

As to racial discrimination in England, see the Race Relations Act, 1968, 16-17 Eliz. II, c. 71.

See Charter v. Race Relations Bd., [1973] 1 All E.R. 512, as to the applicability of the Act to a club.

See Leacock, Racial Preferences in Educational Trusts: An Overview of the United States Experience, 28 How. L.J. 715 (1985).

[6]382 U.S. 296, 86 S. Ct. 486, 15 L. Ed. 2d 373 (1966), *rev'g* Evans v. Newton, 220 Ga. 280, 138 S.E.2d 573 (1964). See §373.

In La Fond v. City of Detroit, 357 Mich. 362, 98 N.W.2d 530 (1959), a testatrix left her estate to the City of Detroit for a playfield for white children. The Supreme Court of Michigan was equally divided on the question whether the trust failed for illegality or whether the bequest should be applied cy pres for a playground for all children.

to determine who was entitled to the property under a resulting trust.[7]

Thereafter the Georgia court held that there was a resulting trust for the heirs of the testator. It held that the testator would have preferred to let the trust fail rather than to have it continue free of the racial restriction; and that the doctrine of cy pres was therefore not applicable.[8] The judgment was affirmed by the Supreme Court of the United States, Douglas and Brennan, JJ., dissenting.[9]

So also it has been held that if it is expressly provided by the terms of the trust that if the restriction is illegal the property should go to a different charity, the doctrine of cy pres is not applicable and the gift over takes effect. In *Connecticut Bank & Trust Co. v. Johnson*[10] a testatrix left money in trust to be used in a particular hospital for the care of patients of the caucasian race. She provided that if the terms of the trust should be illegal or ineffective, the money should go to other designated charities. It was held that the racial restriction was illegal, and that because there was a gift over, the doctrine of cy pres was not applicable.

On the other hand, it has been held in several cases that where the restriction was illegal, the doctrine of cy pres was applicable, and that the trust should be carried on free of the restriction.

[7]Evans v. Newton, 221 Ga. 870, 148 S.E.2d 329 (1966).

[8]Evans v. Abney, 224 Ga. 826, 165 S.E.2d 160 (1968).

So also in Smyth v. Anderson, 238 Ga. 343, 232 S.E.2d 835 (1977), where a testator left his property to a charitable institution for the benefit of white children and provided that if it were not accepted or were used for any other purpose it should revert to his next of kin, it was held that the cy pres doctrine was inapplicable and that the property reverted to his next of kin. See §399.2, n. 4.

[9]Evans v. Abney, 396 U.S. 435, 90 S. Ct. 628, 24 L. Ed. 3d 634 (1970). Mr. Justice Black, speaking for the court, quoted the text as to the scope of the cy pres doctrine.

See Palmer v. Thompson, 403 U.S. 217, 91 S. Ct. 1940, 29 L. Ed. 3d 438 (1971), where the Supreme Court upheld the closing of public pools because they could not be economically operated when desegregated.

See Swanson, Discriminatory Charitable Trusts: Time for a Legislative Solution, 48 U. Pitts. L. Rev. 153 (1986).

[10]30 Conn. Supp. 1, 294 A.2d 586 (1972) (citing the text and Restatement of Trusts §399).

In *Trammell v. Elliott*[11] a testatrix left the residue of her estate to the Georgia Institute of Technology, a public institution, and Emory University and Agnes Scott College, private institutions, as endowment funds in memory of her parents, "for the benefit of deserving and qualified poor white boys and girls." It was held that in the fund given to the Institute the racial restriction was invalid, but that the testatrix had a general charitable intent, and that the fund should be applied cy pres free of the restriction.

In a case in California[12] a testator left his estate "to some Protestant school that is all white of engineering training, I care not which." The lower court held the bequest invalid. The appellate court reversed and remanded to allow extrinsic evidence to determine whether the testator would prefer to give the property to a school that did not exclude blacks, in which case the doctrine of cy pres would be applied. The court said that otherwise the bequest would fail as an illegal discrimination.

In a case in Delaware[13] a testator bequeathed property in trust for scholarships and provided that applications may be made by white youths residing in Wilmington. He directed his trustees to appoint a committee to make the selections, consisting of the Chief Justice of Delaware, the principal of the Wilmington High School, and the president of a bank. It was held that the selection should not be limited to white students. The court said that the race restriction was illegal and that under the changed conditions the doctrine of cy pres or of deviation was applicable.

In another Delaware case[14] a testator who died in 1843

[11]230 Ga. 841, 199 S.E.2d 194 (1973) (citing the text and Restatement of Trusts §399). See Treen Estate, 13 D.&C.3d 115 (Pa. 1979), as well as the cases stated below.

[12]In re Estate of Vanderhoofven, 18 Cal. App. 3d 940, 96 Cal. Rptr. 260 (1971).

[13]Bank of Del. v. Buckson, 255 A.2d 710 (Del. 1969) (citing the text and Restatement of Trusts §381), noted in 48 Texas L. Rev. 827.

[14]In re Will of Potter, 275 A.2d 574 (Del. Ch. 1971).

See also Milford Trust Co. v. Stabler, 301 A.2d 534 (Del. Ch. 1973), where the trustee in selecting scholars had been accustomed to take the recommendation of public school teachers, although not required to do so by the terms of the trust. The court held that this involved state action, and that the trustee should accept applications without regard to race.

domiciled in Delaware bequeathed the residue of his estate to trustees to distribute the income for the support of "poor white citizens of Kent County." The distribution was to be made by an agent appointed by the court. The agent brought a proceeding for instructions. It was held that the state was so involved that the racial restriction was illegal. It was further held that the doctrine of cy pres was applicable and that the income should be used for any poor citizens of the county.

In a case in Texas[15] a testatrix devised property to an individual trustee to be used for a home for aged white men. The court held that under the cy pres doctrine the word "white" should be eliminated and that the trust was valid. This would more nearly carry out the intention of the testatrix than to have the trust fail for racial discrimination.

In a case in Connecticut[16] a group of donors in 1864 created a permanent fund for orphans of New Haven. The trustees were directed to pay the income to the managers of the New Haven Orphan Asylum "provided they shall all be of the protestant faith." In 1967 as a result of a governor's executive order the religious requirement of the Asylum was removed and some managers were appointed who were not Protestants. It was held that the trustees should continue to pay the income to the asylum.

In a case in the District of Columbia[17] a testator left prop-

---

[15]Wooten v. Fitz-Gerald, 440 S.W.2d 719 (Tex. Civ. App. 1969), *writ refused, n.r.e.*

See also Vaughn Estate, 69 D.&C.2d 32 (Pa. 1974), where a testator provided for a home for white women and the fund was insufficient, and the court said that the restriction was invalid, and awarded the fund to a charitable corporation operated by the Catholic Church. See Long Estate, 5 D.&C.3d 602 (Pa. 1978) (asylum for white women).

[16]Daggett v. Children's Center, 28 Conn. Supp. 468, 266 A.2d 72 (1970) (citing the text and Restatement of Trusts, §39, Comment *q*).

[17]Wachovia Bank & Trust Co. v. Buchanan, 346 F. Supp. 665 (D.D.C. 1972) (citing Restatement of Trusts §§381, 399).

In Tinnin v. First United Bank of Miss., 502 So. 2d 659 (Miss. 1987), the 1962 holographic will of a testator who died in 1968 appointed a lawyer and a church trustees of a trust to provide loans to caucasian students in a state college or university. The named trustees having declined to act, a bank was appointed trustee and it proceeded to administer the trust as if the word "caucasian" were not in the will. The children of an aunt by the half blood,

erty to a bank in trust to provide scholarships for white boys and girls attending the University of North Carolina. In a suit by the trustee for instructions, it was held that the racial discrimination was illegal but that the trust did not fail, and that the fund should be applied for scholarships without racial discrimination.

In *Sweet Briar Institute v. Button*[18] a private college brought suit in a federal court to enjoin the Attorney General of Virginia from enforcing compliance with a provision of the will of the founder of the college restricting enrollment to white girls. The court granted the injunction, on the ground that the enforcement would be state action barred by the Fourteenth Amendment to the Constitution.

Although the restriction is not illegal, it may be impossible to carry out the whole of the testator's intention because of the refusal of the legatee to accept the gift subject to the restriction. In such a case the court may permit the acceptance of the gift free of the restriction. Thus in *Howard Savings Institution v. Peep*[19]

---

who was the sole next of kin, sued the bank, all parties conceding that the trust could not be administered with the word "caucasian" in its terms. The trial court deleted the word. The Supreme Court found the will ambiguous and directed the trial court to receive extrinsic evidence to determine whether the testator would prefer to have the trust administered with the word "caucasian" deleted or have the property go to his half blood cousins.

See also United States v. Hughes Memorial Home, 396 F. Supp. 544 (W.D. Va. 1975) (orphanage for white children of Virginia and North Carolina; held under cy pres race restriction removed).

[18]280 F. Supp. 312 (W.D. Va. 1967).

[19]34 N.J. 494, 170 A.2d 39 (1961), *aff'g* Howard Sav. Inst. v. Trustees of Amherst College, 61 N.J. Super. 119, 160 A.2d 177 (1960) (citing the text), noted in 61 Colum. L. Rev. 111, 40 N.C.L. Rev. 308, 36 Notre Dame Law. 74, 16 Rutgers L. Rev. 366, 36 Tulane L. Rev. 176.

To the same effect see In re Lysaght, [1966] Ch. 91, noted in 82 L.Q. Rev. 9. See §397.3, n. 1.

England: In re Woodhams (Decd.); Lloyds Bank v. London College of Music, [1981] 1 W.L.R. 493 (Ch. Div.) (bequest to two musical colleges to establish scholarships for "absolute orphans"; colleges would not accept restriction to orphans because the government paid the expenses of orphans; restriction deleted).

See also Schaaf Trust, 67 D.&C.2d 163 (Pa. 1974) (bequest to Lafayette College, for scholarships for American-born citizens of the Protestant faith who are children of Masons).

In In re Metcalfe, 29 D.L.R.3d 60 (Ont. 1972), a testator created a trust

a testator made a bequest to Amherst College for scholarships for "deserving American born, Protestant, Gentile boys of good moral repute, not given to gambling, smoking, drinking or similar acts." The college refused to accept the bequest because of the religious restrictions, which were contrary to its charter, but desired to accept it if it could be received free of those restrictions. It was held that the doctrine of cy pres was applicable, and that it came nearer to the intention of the testator to give the money to Amherst College free of the religious restrictions than to appoint a trustee to hold it for Amherst College subject to the restrictions, or to give it to another college, or to the next of kin.

There are other situations in which it had become impossible or at least impracticable to continue to administer the trust subject to the religious or racial restrictions imposed by the testator. In these cases under the doctrine of cy pres the court permitted administration of the trust free of the restrictions.

In *In re Queen's School, Chester,* [20] a donor conveyed land in trust for the maintenance of a school to offer a religious, liberal, and useful education to girls. It was provided in the trust deed that it should be a permanent bylaw of the institution that the headmistress should be a member of the Church of England. About 30 years later it was found that the school could not be carried on unless it received grants-in-aid from the government, but such grants could not be made unless the requirement that the headmistress should be of a particular religious faith were abolished. The court held that a scheme should be framed doing away with the requirement. The primary purpose of the donor to maintain a school for the religious, liberal, and useful education of girls could not be accomplished unless a departure from the requirement as to the religious faith of the headmistress were permitted.

---

fund for a scholarship in the medical faculty of McGill University for a Protestant of good moral character, and the university disclaimed because of the religious restriction. It was held that the trust failed and the fund went to the testator's next of kin.

See Luria, Prying Loose the Dead Hand of the Past: How Courts Apply Cy Pres to Race, Gender and Religiously Restrictive Trusts, 21 U.S.F. L. Rev. 41 (1986).

[20][1910] 1 Ch. 796.

In *In re Dominion Students' Hall Trust*[21] many persons subscribed to establish in London a hostel for male students of European origin from overseas dominions. The trustee petitioned for permission to admit students who were not of European origin, thus removing the color bar. The petition was granted. Evershed, J. (as he then was) said that the purpose of the trust was to promote community of citizenship, culture, and tradition, and when it was established it was thought that the purpose was best promoted by restricting the students to those of European origin. He said,

> But times have changed, particularly as the result of the war; and it is said that to retain the condition, so far from furthering the charity's main object, might defeat it and would be liable to antagonize those students, both white and coloured, whose support and good will it is the purpose of the charity to sustain.

In *Matter of Hawley*[22] a testator bequeathed his estate in trust to award prizes each year to the pupils of highest standing in a school. He provided that no pupil should be entitled to a prize unless he was a communicant in the Protestant Episcopal Church and was the son of native-born American citizens. Over a period of 20 years the number of communicants diminished drastically and it was found impossible to award more than a quarter of the prizes. A proceeding was brought by the trustees asking the court for permission to dispense with the restrictions as to religion and citizenship. The court held that the restrictions should be removed. The doctrine of cy pres was applicable, because it had become impracticable to carry out the testator's specific purpose and because he had a more general charitable intention.

In *Coffee v. William Marsh Rice University*[23] the founder of a

[21][1947] Ch. 183.

See Watkin, Discrimination and Charity, [1981] Conv. 131.

[22]32 Misc. 2d 624, 223 N.Y.S.2d 803 (1961).

[23]387 S.W.2d 132 (Tex. Civ. App. 1965), *rev'd,* 403 S.W.2d 340 (Tex. 1966).

In Colin McK. Grant Home v. Medlock, 349 S.E.2d 655 (S.C. App. Ct. 1986), it was held that although South Carolina does not accept the cy pres doctrine, a charitable corporation to which property had been devised to

university provided for the admission of white students only and provided that no tuition should be charged. The university brought suit to determine whether it might admit students without regard to color and to charge tuition to those able to pay. The Attorney General was named as defendant. Two of the alumni were permitted to intervene as representing the alumni and contributors. The trial court held that because the purpose of the founder was to establish a first-class institution, it should be permitted to admit students without regard to color and to charge tuition. The intervenors, but not the Attorney General, appealed. The appellate court held that the intervenors had no standing to appeal, but its decision was reversed, three Justices dissenting. Thereafter the appellate court affirmed the decision of the trial court.[24]

In some cases, however, the court has refused to permit such a deviation. Thus in *Moore v. City and County of Denver*[25] where a testator left a large sum of money to establish and maintain a school for poor, white, male orphans, and the funds greatly increased, it was held that it was not permissible to enlarge the class of beneficiaries. But in *Dunbar v. Board of Trustees of George W. Clayton College*[26] the court held that it was impracticable to restrict the school to white children and that the doctrine of cy pres was applicable.

In *Lockwood v. Killiam*[27] a testator created a charitable trust, the income to be used for scholarships for needy boys with high records in the schools of a certain county, who are of the cauca-

---

maintain a home at a specified location for elderly white Presbyterians would be authorized to sell the home and use the proceeds to subsidize housing for Presbyterians of all races. It was shown that the neighborhood had so deteriorated that elderly Presbyterians were unwilling to live in it and that racial attitudes had changed.

See Note, 10 S. Tex. L.J. 52 (1968).

[24]408 S.W.2d 269 (Tex. Civ. App. 1966) (citing the text). See §399, n. 18.

[25]133 Colo. 190, 292 P.2d 986 (1956).

[26]170 Colo. 1327, 461 P.2d 28 (1969) (citing the text and Restatement of Trusts, §399, Comment *q*).

[27]172 Conn. 496, 375 A.2d 998 (1977) (citing the text and Restatement of Trusts, §370, Comment *j*, §399), *modified*, 179 Conn. 62, 425 A.2d 909 (1979).

See Note, Connecticut *Cy Pres* and the Restrictive Charitable Trust, 12 Conn. L. Rev. 377 (1980).

sian race and who have professed themselves to be of the Protestant Congregational faith. The trustees were unable to find enough candidates to exhaust the income and applied to the court for instructions. The court held that the religious restriction was neither illegal nor impracticable and should be retained (one judge dissenting); and that the restrictions as to sex and as to race were not illegal, but that they should be dispensed with under the cy pres doctrine if it were shown that this would produce enough candidates for the use of the surplus.

In a case in Pennsylvania[28] where a settlor by deed of trust gave property to a trust company and provided that it should report annually to a college the amount of income available, and that the college officers should distribute it as scholarships among deserving, white, male Protestant students, and after some years the college notified the trustee that such a discrimination among students was against its policy and that it would not certify students for the scholarships, the court refused to remove the restriction and held that the trustee may adopt a plan for the selection of students.

In a case in California[29] a testatrix left land and money to the Salvation Army to establish a rest home for Christian women and girls. It was held that the trust was not invalid, and that the trustee might give preference to Christians, but if it finds this too restrictive it should apply to the court for instructions.

In *First National Bank (of Kansas City) v. Danforth*[30] a testator left a large estate to trustees to use the income for the support of "Protestant Christian Hospitals" in a county, "and/or for the support and care of sick and infirm patients in the said hospitals born of white parents." It was held that these provisions were valid and not a violation of the Constitution.

There is a further question whether under the Internal Revenue Code tax exemptions and deductions are applicable to racially discriminatory private schools. It has been held that such schools are not charitable institutions at least within the meaning of the Code.[31] The court did not have to decide whether this

[28]Weaver Trust, 43 D.&C.2d 245 (Pa. 1967).
[29]In re Estate of Zahn, 16 Cal. App. 3d 106, 93 Cal. Rptr. 810 (1970).
[30]523 S.W.2d 808 (Mo. 1975).
[31]Green v. Connally, 330 F. Supp. 1150 (D.C. 1971), *aff'd mem. sub nom.* Coit v. Connally, 404 U.S. 997, 92 S. Ct. 564, 30 L. Ed. 3d 550 (1972).

ruling is required by the Constitution. It did not have to decide whether such institutions are not charitable institutions for purposes other than for federal tax purposes.

In *McGlotten v. Connally*[32] a three-judge court, in a suit brought by a black American, enjoined the Secretary of the Treasury from granting tax benefits to a fraternal organization that excluded non-whites from membership. It held that a tax exemption was a sufficient governmental involvement as to invoke the Fifth Amendment to the Constitution, and also that it would be a violation of the Civil Rights Act of 1964. It dismissed the suit insofar as an injunction was sought as to nonprofit social clubs.

Finally, the Supreme Court has held that under the Civil Rights Act of 1964 private, commercially operated, nonsectarian schools cannot deny admission to prospective students because they are blacks, and that the act as so applied is constitutional.[33]

See Bittker and Rahdert, The Exemption of Nonprofit Organizations from Federal Income Taxation, 85 Yale L.J. 299 (1976); Note, The Judicial Role in Attacking Racial Discrimination in Tax-Exempt Private Schools, 93 Harv. L. Rev. 378 (1976); Wilson, An Overview as to IRS's Revised Proposed Revenue Procedure on Private Schools as Tax-Exempt Organizations, 57 Taxes 515 (1979).

[32]338 F. Supp. 448 (D.D.C. 1972).

See Pitts v. Wisconsin Dept. of Revenue, 333 F. Supp. 662 (E.D. Wis. 1971), holding unconstitutional a state statute granting tax exemption to organizations with racial discrimination as to membership.

See Bittner and Kaufman, Taxes and Civil Rights, 82 Yale L.J. 51 (1972); Note, The Internal Revenue Code and Racial Discrimination, 72 Colum. L. Rev. 1217 (1972); Lusky, National Policy and the Dead Hand — The Race-Conscious Trust, 112 Tr. & Est. 554 (1973); Note, The IRS, Discrimination, and Religious Schools: Does the Revised Proposed Revenue Procedure Exact Too High a Price?, 56 Notre Dame Law. 141 (1980).

[33]Runyon v. McCrary, 427 U.S. 160, 96 S. Ct. 2586, 49 L. Ed 3d 415 (1976).

See Notes: 124 U. Pa. L. Rev. 714 (1976); 84 Yale L.J. 1441 (1975); 52 Wash. L. Rev. 955 (1977); Bloom, Racial Discrimination in Private Schools, 48 U. Colo. L. Rev. 419 (1977); Neuberger and Crumplar, Tax Exempt Religious Schools under Attack, 48 Fordham L. Rev. 229 (1979); Bagni, Discrimination in the Name of the Lord: A Critical Evaluation of Discrimination by Religious Organizations, 79 Colum. L. Rev. 1514 (1979).

As to charitable foundations that discriminate against blacks in making

In many cases, charitable trusts have been created for the benefit of men only or of women only, of boys or of girls, and no question was raised as to discrimination. Thus it is common to provide for a home for aged women, or a home for aged men.[34] The question arises, however, whether in any case it would be proper to hold such discrimination illegal, and, if so, whether the trust should be upheld free from the sex restriction.

In a case in Pennsylvania[35] property was left in trust for the medical education of a boy belonging to a particular church. It was held that the testator did not intend to exclude girls but merely expressed a preference for boys.

In a more recent case in Massachusetts[36] a testator bequeathed his estate to a bank in trust to assist worthy and ambitious young men to acquire a legal education. The court held that other language in the will indicated that he did not intend to exclude young women. One justice dissented, interpreting the will as showing an intention to include only young men, and said that he did not view the issue as clouded by any constitutional question.

There are, of course, many cases of trusts for scholarships for young men only, or for young women only, that have been upheld without question. Thus in *Lockwood v. Killiam*[37] a trust

---

gifts, see Jackson v. Statler Found., 496 F.2d 623 (2d Cir. 1974), *cert. denied,* 420 U.S. 927.

See Brown v. Dade Christian Schools, 556 F.2d 310 (5th Cir. 1977), involving a sectarian school, but the court by a majority found that racial exclusion was not adopted in the exercise of religion but was of a political or social nature. See Note, Racial Exclusion by Religious Schools, 91 Harv. L. Rev. 879 (1978).

[34]See Long Estate, 5 D.&C.3d 602 (Pa. 1978), where in a trust providing for white women the racial restriction was removed, but not the sex restriction.

[35]Reeser Estate, 1 D.&C.2d 731 (Pa. 1954).

[36]Ebitz v. Pioneer Natl. Bank, 372 Mass. 207, 361 N.E.2d 225 (1977).

[37]172 Conn. 496, 375 A.2d 998 (1977) (citing the text and Restatement of Trusts, §370, Comment *j,* §399), *modified,* 179 Conn. 62, 425 A.2d 909 (1979). See also Matter of Crichfield Trust, 177 N.J. Super. 258, 426 A.2d 88 (1980) (state agency acting as trustee of trust to provide $400 annual college scholarship to male graduates of named high school granted variation cy pres to allow a larger amount and permit award to female graduates). See n. 27, *supra.*

See Attorney-General v. Wansey, 15 Ves. 22 (1808).

was created in which the income was to be used for scholarships for boys who had high records in the schools of a certain county. The trustees could not find enough candidates to exhaust the income, and asked the court for instructions. It was held that although the restriction as to sex was not illegal, under the cy pres doctrine scholarships might be given to girls.

In *Shapiro v. Columbia Union National Bank*[38] a testator created a trust for scholarships for the benefit of "deserving Kansas City, Missouri boys," to attend the University of Kansas City, which was a private university. After his death the university became a part of the University of Missouri, a state institution. The plaintiff, a female law student, applied for and was denied a scholarship and brought suit. It was held that her application was properly denied. The court said that there was no such state involvement as to invalidate the restriction to males.[39] One judge dissented, holding that state action was involved, that the restriction was illegal, and that a deviation from the terms of the trust should be permitted, removing the restriction.

In *Will of Cram*[40] a testator left property in trust to assist boys belonging to two charitable organizations by giving them stipends of $100. A girl who was a member applied for a stipend. It was held that the sex discrimination made by the testator was not illegal. The court said that although the organizations received state aid, the awarding of stipends to the members did not involve state action.

§399.5. The power of the legislature. Although the legislature can properly lay down rules governing charitable trusts, the power of the legislature by special acts to control the administration of charitable trusts already created is limited by provisions of the federal and state constitutions. As we have seen, it has been held in a number of cases that the legislature may by special act authorize the sale of property held upon a charitable trust, where such sale is necessary for the accomplishment of the

[38]576 S.W.2d 310 (Mo. 1979), *cert. denied*, 444 U.S. 831 (1979).

[39]See Cole, Sex-Discriminatory Scholarship Trusts, 44 Mo. L. Rev. 575 (1979); Note, Sex Restricted Scholarships and the Charitable Trust, 59 Iowa L. Rev. 1000 (1974); Ginsburg, Sex Equality and the Constitution, 52 Tul. L. Rev. 451 (1978); Note, Restricted Scholarships, State Universities and the Fourteenth Amendment, 56 Va. L. Rev. 1454, 1471 (1970).

[40]186 Mont. 37, 606 P.2d 145 (1980).

purposes of the trust, although the sale is not authorized or is expressly forbidden by the terms of the trust.[1] There is also some indication in the cases that the legislature has succeeded to the prerogative power of the Crown to apply the property to other charitable purposes where the particular purposes for which the property was given fail on account of illegality or impossibility.[2] In both of these cases it would seem to be more in accordance with the general principles of our law to hold that the legislature has no such power, but that the power to control the administration of charitable trusts as well as of private trusts rests with the courts.

It is clear, at any rate, that where it is possible to carry out the purposes of a charitable trust, the legislature cannot direct that the trust property be applied to other charitable purposes, nor can it control the administration of the trust. The question first arose in the case of a charitable corporation. In the *Dartmouth College Case*[3] the legislature of New Hampshire passed a statute in 1816 "to amend the charter and encourage and improve the corporation of Dartmouth College," changing the name of the corporation to Dartmouth University, increasing the number of trustees to 21, giving the Governor of the state the power to appoint the additional trustees, and creating a board of governors to be appointed for the most part by the Governor; in brief, transferring the control of the institution to the state. This was done over the strenuous objections of the existing board of trustees. The state court upheld the act, and the case was then brought before the Supreme Court of the United States on writ of error. It was held that the statute was unconstitutional as in violation of the provision of Article I, Section 10, of the federal Constitution, which provides that no state shall pass any law impairing the obligation of contracts. Mr.

§399.5. [1]See §381, n. 18.

[2]See §399.1.

[3]Trustees of Dartmouth College v. Woodward, 4 Wheat. 518, 4 L. Ed. 629 (U.S. 1819).

See Hite v. Queen's Hosp., 36 Haw. 250 (1942); Stevens Bros. Found. v. Commissioner, 324 F.2d 633 (8th Cir. 1963), *cert. denied,* 376 U.S. 969.

In Goldstein v. Trustees of the Sailors' Snug Harbor, 277 A.D. 269, 98 N.Y.S.2d 544 (1950), it was held that a statute giving the governor power to appoint additional trustees of a charitable corporation was unconstitutional.

Justice Story said that there was an implied contract on the part of the Crown, which granted the charter, with every benefactor who should give money to the corporation, and that it was a violation of this contract to alter the charter without the consent of the corporation. He said that there was also an implied contract between the corporation and every benefactor that it would administer the property given to it according to the terms stipulated in the charter.

On the other hand, it has been held that such an amendment of the charter of a charitable corporation with the consent of its governing body is not necessarily unconstitutional, and the court in the exercise of its cy pres power may approve the amendment.[4]

After the decision in the *Dartmouth College Case* it was provided in many states by constitution or by statute that the legislature should have power to alter or repeal corporate charters thereafter granted by it. This, however, does not give the legislature an arbitrary power to deal as it likes with the corporation or its property. In *Board of Regents v. Trustees of Endowment Fund*[5] a charter was granted to a charitable corporation. The legislature had reserved a power to amend corporate charters. It was held that a later special act passed without the consent of the governing body of the corporation reconstituting the governing body was unconstitutional. On the other hand, a statute amending the charter of a charitable corporation was upheld in *Matter of Mt. Sinai Hospital.*[6] In that case a statute was enacted amend-

---

[4]*Maryland:* University of Md. v. Williams, 9 G.&J. 365, 31 Am. Dec. 72 (Md. 1838), *semble;* Visitors, etc. of St. John's College v. Comptroller, 23 Md. 629 (1865).

New Jersey: Trustees of Rutgers College v. Richman, 41 N.J. Super. 259, 125 A.2d 10 (1956); Paterson v. Paterson Gen. Hosp., 97 N.J. Super. 514, 235 A.2d 487 (1967).

Pennsylvania: Case of St. Mary's Church, 7 S.&R. 517 (Pa. 1822).

But see State ex rel. Pittman v. Adams, 44 Mo. 570 (1869).

On the power of the legislature to authorize amendments to the charters of charitable corporations, see Scott, Education and the Dead Hand, 34 Harv. L. Rev. 1 (1920).

See §376.3.

[5]206 Md. 559, 112 A.2d 678 (1955), *cert. denied,* 350 U.S. 836 (1955).

[6]250 N.Y. 103, 164 N.E. 871, 62 A.L.R. 564 (1929).

See Pennsylvania College Cases, 13 Wall. 190, 20 L. Ed. 550 (U.S. 1871).

ing the charter of a hospital by transferring the power to elect trustees from the members of the corporation to the trustees themselves. The trustees assented to the amendment. It was held that this was a valid exercise of the power reserved to the legislature by the constitution and statutes of the state, to alter or repeal charters thereafter granted.

The principle laid down in the *Dartmouth College Case* has not been confined to corporations. It has been held that the principle is applicable where property is held by a trustee or an unincorporated group of trustees in trust for charitable purposes. It has been held that the legislature cannot constitutionally interfere with charitable trusts, either by providing that the property shall be devoted to purposes other than those designated by the creators of the trusts, or by changing the method of control or of the administration of the trusts.[7]

See Note, Power of state to amend charter of a private incorporated charity, 62 A.L.R. 573 (1929).

[7] Cary Library v. Bliss, 151 Mass. 364, 25 N.E. 92, 7 L.R.A. 765 (1890); Crawford v. Nies, 220 Mass. 61, 107 N.E. 382 (1914), 224 Mass. 474, 113 N.E. 408 (1916); Opinion of the Justices, 237 Mass. 613, 131 N.E. 31 (1921); Adams v. Plunkett, 274 Mass. 453, 175 N.E. 60 (1931); City of Boston v. Curley, 276 Mass. 549, 177 N.E. 557 (1931); Massachusetts Charitable Mechanic Assn. v. Beede, 320 Mass. 601, 70 N.E.2d 825 (1947) (*semble;* citing the text); City of Salem v. Attorney Gen., 344 Mass. 626, 183 N.E.2d 859 (1962) (legislature authorized city to use for erection of a school part of land devised for park purposes); Mahoney v. Attorney Gen., 346 Mass. 709, 195 N.E.2d 540 (1964) (town cannot interfere with control by trustee provided for in will establishing a public hospital); City of Worcester v. Directors of Worcester Free Pub. Library, 349 Mass. 601, 211 N.E.2d 356 (1965) (provisions as to management of library fund given to town).

In City of Aurora v. Young Men's Christian Assn., 9 Ill. 2d 286, 137 N.E.2d 347 (1956), land was conveyed to a city "to hold and use and permit the use for public purposes" as it might determine. A statute provided that a city acquiring or holding property for any purpose might convey it when it was no longer appropriate for use in the best interests of the city. The city sold the land. It was held that the statute applies only where the city has acquired property free of trust, and did not here apply because it was a gift in trust. The court said that it was unnecessary to determine whether the statute would be unconstitutional if it applied to gifts in trust. The case was remitted to the trial court to determine whether the property should be sold under the cy pres doctrine. The court cited Restatement of Trusts §399. See s.c. Stoner Mfg. Corp. v. Young Men's Christian Assn., 13 Ill. 2d 162, 148 N.E.2d 441 (1958).

As to the modification of charitable trusts by the legislature, see §367.3.

In *Opinion of the Justices to the House of Representatives*[8] the question of the constitutionality of a proposed statute was presented to the court. Benjamin Franklin left £1000 to the town of Boston in trust. He designated as managers of the fund the selectmen and the ministers of certain churches. He provided that after 100 years a part of the fund and its accumulations were to be laid out in public works chosen by the managers. The remainder of the fund was to accumulate for another 100 years, that is, until 1991, at which time one-fourth of the fund was to be left to the disposition of the town of Boston, and three-fourths to the disposition of the state. There were no restrictions as to the distributees. In 1905 a gift was received from Andrew Carnegie matching that of Franklin. The managers then founded an institution called the Franklin Union, later known as the Franklin Technical Institute. In 1908 the legislature incorporated the managers.

In 1977 the House of Representatives asked the opinion of the justices on the constitutionality of a proposed statute authorizing the present transfer by the city of Boston and the Commonwealth of Massachusetts to Boston University of the assets that by the terms of the gifts were to be distributed in 1991. The court in its opinion said that the statute would be unconstitutional. The constitution provided for the separation of legislative and judicial powers. The cy pres power was vested in the courts and not in the legislature. By the terms of the gifts the distribution was to be made by the city and the state in 1991, and they were to make such distributions as they should then determine.[9]

As to the power of the legislature to permit a sale of property of a charitable institution, see §381, n. 18.

On the question whether the legislature has succeeded to the prerogative cy pres power, see §399.1.

The legislature has power, of course, by general acts to liberalize the doctrine of cy pres, applicable to all trusts, whether created before or after the enactment.

As to the modification of a charitable trust by the legislature, where a town is trustee, see §348.1, n. 11.

[8]374 Mass. 843, 371 N.E.2d 1349 (1978) (citing Restatement of Trusts §381, as to deviation, and §399, as to the cy pres doctrine).

[9]The court said that the legislature does possess some authority to alter charitable trusts, but this authority is narrowly limited and does not permit

§400. Application of Surplus

We have been dealing with the situation that arises where it is impossible or impracticable to carry out the particular charitable purpose specified by the testator. A somewhat similar problem arises where the trust property is more than sufficient to carry out completely the particular charitable purpose. In such a case the question arises as to the disposition of the surplus. In this situation several methods of disposing of the surplus are possible. The surplus might be applied cy pres for similar charitable purposes; or the trustee might be permitted to keep the surplus; or there might be a resulting trust of the surplus for the estate of the testator.

Ordinarily, the purpose of the testator is not confined to the particular charitable purpose specified by him, and it is possible to find a more general intention to devote the property to charity. In such a case a resulting trust for the estate of the testator will not arise, but the surplus will be applied cy pres.[1] This is

---

legislative action impairing the title, use, and management of the trust property.

§400. [1]*England:* Merchant Taylors' Co. v. Attorney-General, L.R. 6 Ch. App. 512 (1871); In re Royce, [1940] Ch. 514 (trust for benefit of choir of church), noted in 4 Convey. (N.S.) 424, 5 id. 198;

Indiana: Quinn v. Peoples Trust & Sav. Co., 223 Ind. 317, 60 N.E.2d 281, 157 A.L.R. 885 (1945).

Missouri: Thatcher v. City of St. Louis, 335 Mo. 1130, 76 S.W.2d 677 (1934).

Oregon: Phillips v. Board of Hosp. Trustees, 41 Or. App. 401, 599 P.2d 1134 (1979).

In Vogan Estate, 75 D.&C. 531 (Pa. 1951), where $2000 was left by a testator who died in 1863, in trust to use the income in buying fuel for indigent families in a village, and to add any surplus income to the principal, the court denied permission to use the surplus for other purposes because the surplus was not large.

In Hartford Natl. Bank & Trust Co. v. Billings P. Learned Mission, 22 Conn. Supp. 409, 174 A.2d 49 (1961) (quoting the text), where a testator directed that designated sums be paid annually to a number of charitable corporations and the income became more than enough to pay the amounts, it was held that the surplus income should be divided pro rata among the charitable corporations.

In In re Lepton's Will Trusts, [1972] 1 Ch. 276, a testator died in 1716 leaving land in trust to pay out of the rents and profits £3 yearly to the minister

particularly true where the surplus arises at some time subsequent to the creation of the trust; and the longer the period intervening between the creation of the trust and the arising of the surplus, the less likely the court is to impose a resulting trust. In disposing of the surplus the court will ordinarily approve the framing of a scheme, as it does where the particular purpose of the testator is or becomes impossible of accomplishment.

In framing a scheme as to the disposition of the surplus the court will attempt to carry out the general purpose of the testator. Where the testator has provided that certain sums shall be paid to a certain number of persons, and the income is or becomes more than sufficient for the purpose, the court has sometimes directed that larger sums shall be paid to the same number of persons, and has sometimes directed that the same amounts shall be paid to a larger number of persons. Where the cost of living has increased since the time of the creation of the trust, and the purchasing power of money has thereby diminished, the general purpose of the testator is accomplished by increasing the amounts to be given to the recipients.[2] Thus in the *Case of Thetford School*[3] a testator devised land in 1567 for the

---

of a church and the surplus to the poor of a village. In 1716 the yearly income was £5. It increased to £792. The court held that under the cy pres doctrine of the statute of 1960 the minister should be paid £100 a year and the balance used for the poor.

In Bok Trust, 52 D.&C.2d 111 (Pa. 1971), a trust was created to make an annual award of $10,000 to a resident of Philadelphia in recognition of services to the city. The income greatly increased. It was held that the amount might be increased to not more than $20,000, and that the balance might be applied to scholarships in certain institutions.

In Crippled Children's Found. v. Cunningham, 346 So. 2d 409, 96 A.L.R.3d 945 (Ala. 1977), a trustee was directed by the will to pay $100 each year to two named charitable institutions, with no residuary provision. It was held that the testator intended that any surplus in his estate should be divided between the two institutions. The court cited the text.

See De Jarlais, The Consumer Trust Fund: A Cy Pres Solution to Undistributed Funds in Consumer Class Actions, 38 Hastings L. J. 729 (1987); Note, Disposition of surplus trust income after payment of specific sum to charity, 96 A.L.R.3d 954 (1979).

[2]Case of Thetford School, 8 Rep. 130b (1609); Attorney-General v. Minshull, 4 Ves. 11 (1798); Society for Promoting Theological Educ. v. Attorney Gen., 135 Mass. 285 (1883).

[3]8 Rep. 130b (1609).

purpose of paying out of the income annually a stated sum to a preacher and other sums to a schoolmaster and usher and to a certain number of poor people. The sums amounted altogether to £35, which was the amount of the income of the land at the time of the testator's death. Subsequently the land yielded £100 a year. A private bill was introduced in the House of Lords to make provision for the disposition of the surplus income. The lords referred the question to the judges, who advised that the sums payable to the various beneficiaries should be increased, since owing to the fall in the purchasing power of money such a disposition would conform most nearly to the intention of the testator. So also in *Society for Promoting Theological Education v. Attorney General*, [4] where a testator directed that all of the income should be applied to aid indigent students of theology at Cambridge and that no beneficiary should receive more than $150 annually, and there were not enough students to exhaust the income, the court held that the amount to be paid to each student might be increased.

On the other hand, where the income of the trust has increased so that it is more than sufficient to pay the designated sums to the designated number of persons, the court may increase the number of recipients. This is the method employed where the amounts to be paid are not designated but the trustees are directed to apply as much as is necessary for the support of a designated number of persons. In an English case where a testator left property in trust to use the income to apprentice two poor boys of the congregation of a certain church and the income was more than sufficient for the purpose and moreover there were not always two poor boys in the congregation, the court directed that the surplus income should be applied to apprentice other boys and even girls in the parish or in other parishes.[5] In another case where a testator left his estate in trust to establish a scholarship at Sheffield Scientific School, and the income was more than sufficient to pay the tuition of a student, it was held that the trustee could properly pay the living expenses of the student although he should not use the income to

[4]135 Mass. 285 (1883).
[5]Attorney-General v. Wansey, 15 Ves. 231 (1808).
See §399.4A, nn. 27, 37.

support the student in extravagance or to pay him more than enough to cover his tuition and living expenses.[6] The court said that if the income was more than sufficient to support one student, the surplus should be used to support an additional student. In a case in Tennessee a testator left his estate, one half to the University of Georgia to use the income to assist poor students in obtaining an education there, and the other half to Vanderbilt University to assist poor students from Georgia by making loans to them to enable them to attend Vanderbilt University. It appeared that few students from Georgia cared to go to Vanderbilt and that there were few requests for a loan. The court held that the trustees might support Georgia students coming to Vanderbilt, making gifts instead of loans.[7] In a Massachusetts case[8] a testator left a sum of money in trust and provided that on the death of the life beneficiaries the sum was to be paid to certain charitable organizations, in certain amounts, the total of the amounts equaling the sum bequeathed. The sum was invested and when the time for distribution arrived had increased in value. The court held that the surplus should be divided among the charitable organizations in proportion to the amounts given to them under the will.

In other cases where a surplus remains after the performance of the particular purpose designated by the testator the courts have applied the surplus to other charitable purposes of the same general character.[9] Thus in an English case where in

[6]Hoyt v. Bliss, 93 Conn. 344, 105 A. 699 (1919).

[7]Vanderbilt Univ. v. Mitchell, 162 Tenn. 217, 36 S.W.2d 83 (1931).

In Sendak v. Trustees of Purdue Univ., 151 Ind. App. 372, 279 N.E.2d 840, 50 A.L.R.3d 1109 (1972), where a testator established a loan fund for students, and because of certain restrictions that he imposed no loans could be made, it was held that the restrictions should be removed. The court cited the Restatement of Trusts §381 and §399.

See Note, Charitable trusts: elimination or modification, by court, of restrictions on amount of donation or expenditure which trustee may make for purposes of trust, 50 A.L.R.3d 1116 (1973).

[8]McElwain v. Attorney General, 241 Mass. 112, 134 N.E. 620 (1922).

[9]*England:* Attorney-General v. The Ironmongers' Co., 2 Myl. & K. 576 (1833); In re Avenon's Charity, [1913] 2 Ch. 261; In re King, [1923] 1 Ch. 243; In re N. Devon & W. Somerset Relief Fund Trusts, [1953] 2 All E.R. 1032; In re Raine, [1956] Ch. 417.

Delaware: Union Methodist Episcopal Church v. Equitable Trust Co., 32

1580 land was given in trust to apply the rents for the preaching of a sermon once each year in a certain parish church, and the income greatly increased, it was held that the surplus might be applied to other religious purposes, such as the employment of curates in the church and in other churches in the parish and for the religious instruction of the inhabitants.[10] The court said that

Del. Ch. 197, 83 A.2d 111 (1951) (citing the text and Restatement of Trusts §400); Union Methodist Episcopal Church v. Equitable Security Trust Co., 40 Del. Ch. 154, 177 A.2d 217 (1962).

Maine: Pierce v. How, 153 Me. 180, 136 A.2d 510 (1957) (citing Restatement of Trusts §400; interpretation of terms of trust as well as application cy pres).

Massachusetts: American Academy of Arts & Sciences v. President & Fellows of Harvard College, 12 Gray 582 (Mass. 1832); Eliot v. Trinity Church, 232 Mass. 517, 122 N.E. 648 (1919).

Missouri: Thatcher v. City of St. Louis, 335 Mo. 1130, 76 S.W.2d 677 (1934).

New Hampshire: Concord Natl. Bank v. Haverhill, 101 N.H. 416, 145 A.2d 61 (1958), noted in 39 B.U.L. Rev. 262

New York: Matter of Earl & Mable Nellis Athletic Fund, 42 Misc. 2d 121, 247 N.Y.S.2d 752 (1964) (enlargement of athletic facilities).

Ohio: City of Springfield v. Patterson, 26 Ohio Misc. 242, 55 Ohio Ops. 2d 323, 270 N.E.2d 683 (1971) (citing the text, §399).

Texas: Cushing v. Fort Worth Natl. Bank, 284 S.W.2d 791 (Tex. Civ. App. 1955) (citing the text and Restatement of Trusts §400).

In Kerner v. Thompson, 293 Ill. App. 454, 13 N.E.2d 110 (1938), *cert. denied sub nom.* Thompson v. Kerner, 305 U.S. 635 (1938), noted in 26 Ill. B.J. 385, where money was collected by public subscription for relief of flood sufferers in the Mississippi Valley and a large surplus remained after those who suffered from the flood were taken care of, it was held that the surplus should be applied cy pres by turning it over to the American National Red Cross to relieve future sufferers from similar floods.

In First Natl. Bank & Trust Co. v. First Natl. Bank & Trust Co., 35 Del. Ch. 449, 121 A.2d 296 (1956), where a testator left one sum in trust for the needy poor of a town and another in trust to establish a free public library, and the fund for the library was insufficient, the court refused to permit the use of a possible surplus in the other fund for the purposes of the library. The court cited the text and the Restatement of Trusts §399.

In Hinkley Home Corp. v. Bracken, 21 Conn. Supp. 222, 152 A.2d 325 (1959), where a testator left property in trust to establish and maintain a home for aged residents of a city, the court refused to allow the admission of aged persons of neighboring cities, although the eligible residents of the city did not exhaust more than half of the facilities of the home. See also Bacon Memorial Home v. Bracken, 21 Conn. Supp. 217, 152 A.2d 518 (1959).

[10]In re Avenon's Charity, [1913] 2 Ch. 261.

it would be improper, however, to apply the surplus to nonreligious purposes such as the giving of lectures or for the assistance of a public library.

In *Thatcher v. City of St. Louis* [11] the 1849 will of Judge Mullanphy bequeathed a third of his estate to the City of St. Louis on trust "to furnish relief to all poor immigrants and travelers coming to St. Louis on their way, bona fide, to settle in the west." Due, in part, to the prudent investment and good administration of the trust and, in part, to a decline in the number of poor persons in St. Louis on their way to settle in the west, the income was much more than could be used for the stated purpose. The trial court made a careful investigation of the interests of Judge Mullanphy and the circumstances surrounding the execution of the will and found that there were poor travelers and immigrants going in other directions, or going west without intent to settle, who were stranded in St. Louis without funds. Finding that Judge Mullanphy had a general charitable intent, that is, an intent that the trust should not fail if the particular charitable purpose failed or did not exhaust the fund, the Missouri court affirmed provisions of a decree authorizing the city to aid travelers stranded in St. Louis who were not on their way bona fide to settle in the west.

Where property is given to a charitable corporation or association for a particular charitable purpose, and the purpose is fully accomplished without exhausting the property, the court has in some cases permitted the corporation or association to use the surplus for its general purposes.[12] In these cases the court found an intention on the part of the testator to give to the corporation for its general purposes whatever was not needed for the accomplishment of the particular purpose.

[11]335 Mo. 1130, 76 S.W.2d 677 (1934).

[12]*England:* Mayor etc. of Southmolton v. Attorney-General, 5 H.L.C. 1 (1854); Attorney-General v. Trinity College, 24 Beav. 383 (1856); Attorney-General v. Dean & Canons of Windsor, 8 H.L.C. 369 (1860).

Massachusetts: Attorney General v. Rector & Churchwardens of Trinity Church, 9 Allen 422 (Mass. 1864).

Australia: Armenian Gen. Benevolent Union v. The Union Trustee Co., 87 C.L.R. 597 (Austl. 1952).

As to the situation that arises where property is given to a charitable corporation for a purpose that fails, see §399.2.

Where the testator has manifested no such intention, however, the charitable corporation or association will not be permitted to use the property for its general purposes.[13] Where property is given to private individuals upon a charitable trust, the trustees will not be permitted to keep the surplus beneficially, unless it is clearly so provided by the terms of the trust.

In a few cases it has been held that a resulting trust of the surplus arose in favor of the estate of the testator.[14] In these cases the courts found that the particular purpose stated by the testator was his only purpose, that he had no more general charitable intention, and that presumably he would have preferred to have the surplus returned to his estate rather than to have it applied to other charitable purposes. Thus in *In re Stanford,* [15] where money was left to Cambridge University in trust to apply it for the completion and publication of a certain dictionary, and there was a surplus after the purpose had been carried out, it was held that the surplus should not be applied for other charitable purposes under the cy pres doctrine because the testator had no general charitable intention, but rather a resulting trust arose in favor of the estate of the testator.[16]

---

[13]Merchant Taylors' Co. v. Attorney-General, L.R. 6 Ch. App. 512 (1871); Attorney-General v. Wax Chandlers' Co., L.R. 6 H.L. 1 (1873).

In In re Estate of Yetter (Simmons v. Reynolds), 183 Kan. 340, 328 P.2d 738 (1958), a testatrix bequeathed land to a trustee to pay the income toward the salary of the minister of a certain church and for no other purpose. Later oil was discovered and after the full salary of the minister was paid a surplus of $46,000 remained. The court held that the surplus could not be used for the general purposes of the church. It held, however, that the surplus did not revert to the estate of the testatrix but should be held by the trustee because it might be needed at some time in the future to pay the minister's salary.

[14]Attorney-General v. Mayor of Bristol, 2 Jac. & W. 294, 308 (1820); In re Stanford, [1924] 1 Ch. 73; Holmes v. Welch, 314 Mass. 106, 49 N.E.2d 461, 157 A.L.R. 896 (1943), *semble;* In re Anderson, [1943] 4 D.L.R. 268 (Ont.); In re Waite, [1964] N.Z.L.R. 1034.

See Note, Rights and remedies in respect of claimed surplus over the amount necessary to carry out the expressed purpose of a charitable trust, 157 A.L.R. 903 (1945).

[15][1924] 1 Ch. 73. But see §399.3, n. 7.

[16]In In re Raine, [1956] Ch. 417, where a testatrix left the residue of her estate "for the continuation of the seating" of a parish church, and the estate was more than sufficient to accomplish the purpose, it was held that the balance should be applied cy pres. The court said that even though the testa-

§401. Conditions and Limitations

A charitable trust may be created by the terms of which it is provided that on the happening of a certain event the trust shall terminate. The provision may be in the form of a condition subsequent, as where the property is given for charitable purposes but it is provided that if a certain event should happen the trust should terminate. On the other hand, the property may be given for charitable purposes until the happening of a certain event, or so long as a certain state of affairs continues. In either case the event on which the charitable trust is to terminate may be one that must happen if at all within the period of the rule against perpetuities, or it may be one that may not happen within that period. In either case it may be provided that on the happening of the event the property shall revert to the settlor or his estate, or there may be a gift over. The gift over may be for other charitable purposes or it may be for noncharitable purposes. A gift for charitable purposes may be subject to a condition precedent, that is, the gift to charity may be contingent on the happening of an event, which may or may not be one that must happen within the period of the rule against perpetuities. In the sections that follow we shall consider the validity of such provisions as these.[1]

§401.1. No reverter for breach of trust. The mere fact that the trustees of a charitable trust commit a breach of trust does not cause the trust to fail and entitle the settlor or his successors to enforce a resulting trust. This is true not only

---

trix did not manifest a general charitable intention, she did intend all her property should be used for a charitable purpose and to exclude her next of kin.

In Moore v. City & County of Denver, 133 Colo. 190, 292 P.2d 986 (1956), where a testator left a large sum of money to establish and maintain a school for poor, white, male orphans, and the funds greatly increased, it was held that it was not permissible to enlarge the class of beneficiaries. But in Dunbar v. Board of Trustees of George W. Clayton College, 170 Colo. 327, 461 P.2d 28 (1969), the court held that it was impracticable to restrict the school to white children and that the doctrine of cy pres was applicable.

§401. [1]See Najarian, Charitable Giving and the Rule against Perpetuities, 70 Dick. L. Rev. 455 (1966).

where the trustees merely neglect to apply the property to the designated charitable purposes, but also where they divert it to other purposes. In such a case, if it is not impossible or impracticable to carry out the designated purposes, the remedy is by a suit brought by the Attorney General to compel the trustees to perform the trust, and not by a suit brought by the settlor or his successors to enforce a resulting trust.[1] It is only where the

§401.1. [1]*Federal:* Stuart v. City of Easton, 170 U.S. 383, 18 S. Ct. 650, 42 L. Ed. 1078 (1898); Barnard v. Adams, 58 F. 313 (C.C.N.D. Iowa 1893); Gredig v. Sterling, 47 F.2d 832 (5th Cir. 1931), *cert. denied,* 284 U.S. 629 (1931) (sale of hospital site); Kibbe v. City of Rochester, 57 F.2d 542 (W.D.N.Y. 1932); United States v. Certain Land, etc., 79 F. Supp. 558 (E.D. Mo. 1948) (land taken by the United States), noted in 2 Okla. L. Rev. 247; Polster's Estate v. Commissioner, 274 F.2d 358 (4th Cir. 1960) (Maryland law).

Arkansas: Graham Bros. Co. v. Galloway Woman's College, 190 Ark. 692, 81 S.W.2d 837 (1935).

California: Spence v. Widney, 5 Cal. (unrep.) 516 (1896); Hart v. County of Los Angeles, 260 Cal. App. 2d 512, 67 Cal. Rptr. 242 (1968); In re Poulsen Found., 173 Cal. App. 3d 1212, 219 Cal. Rptr. 375 (1985).

Connecticut: Bridgeport Pub. Library & Reading Room v. Burroughs Home, 85 Conn. 309, 82 A. 582 (1912); Bristol Baptist Church v. Connecticut Baptist Convention, 98 Conn. 677, 120 A. 497 (1923); but see Levine v. The Bess & Paul Sigel Hebrew Academy of Greater Hartford, 39 Conn. Supp. 129, 471 A.2d 679 (1983) (bill of complaint by settlor to terminate interest of beneficiary because it changed its name stated cause of action).

Delaware: Delaware Land & Dev. Co. v. First & Central Church, 16 Del. Ch. 410, 147 A. 165 (1929) (sale of site for meetinghouse).

Florida: Montgomery v. Carlton, 99 Fla. 152, 126 So. 135 (1930) (sale of church site).

Georgia: Huger v. Protestant Episcopal Church, 137 Ga. 205, 73 S.E. 385 (1911).

Illinois: McGee v. Vandeventer, 326 Ill. 425, 158 N.E. 127 (1927), noted in 37 Yale L.J. 533; Village of Hinsdale v. Chicago City Missionary Socy., 375 Ill. 220, 30 N.E.2d 657 (1940); Rubel v. Friend, 344 Ill. App. 450, 101 N.E.2d 445 (1951) (failure to construct convalescent home within ten years as directed); City of Wood River v. Hart, 23 Ill.2d 119, 177 N.E.2d 173 (1961) (delay in converting land into a park).

Indiana: Ebenezer's Old People's Home v. South Bend Old People's Home, 113 Ind. App. 382, 48 N.E.2d 851 (1943) (devise to charitable corporation).

Iowa: Amundson v. Kletzing-McLaughlin Memorial Found. College, 247 Iowa 91, 73 N.W.2d 114 (1955) (citing Restatement of Trusts, §401, Comment *a*).

Kentucky: Carroll County Academy v. Gallatin Academy Co., 104 Ky. 621, 47 S.W. 617 (1898); Pennebaker v. Pennebaker Home for Girls, 291 Ky. 12,

settlor has made the continuance of the trust conditional on the

---

163 S.W.2d 53, 143 A.L.R. 389 (1942) (quoting the text and Restatement of Trusts, §401, Comment *a*); Light v. Third-Woodland Presbyterian Church, 311 S.W.2d 386 (Ky. 1958).

Louisiana: Braquet v. Administrators of Tulane Educ. Fund, 304 So. 2d 720 (La. App. 1974).

Maine: Louisa T. York Orphan Asylum v. Erwin, 281 A.2d 453 (Me. 1971) (quoting the text and Restatement of Trusts, §401, Comment *a*).

Maryland: Fletcher v. Safe Deposit & Trust Co., 193 Md. 400, 67 A.2d 386 (1949).

Massachusetts: Tainter v. Clark, 5 Allen 66 (Mass. 1862); Judkins v. Hyannis Pub. Library Assn., 302 Mass. 425, 19 N.E.2d 727 (1939); Bradway v. Shattuck, 325 Mass. 168, 89 N.E.2d 753 (1949); Davenport v. Attorney Gen., 361 Mass. 372, 280 N.E.2d 193 (1972) (citing the text and Restatement of Trusts §401).

Michigan: Clark v. City of Grand Rapids, 334 Mich. 646, 55 N.W.2d 137 (1952).

Missouri: Goode v. McPherson, 51 Mo. 126 (1872); Mott v. Morris, 249 Mo. 137, 155 S.W. 434 (1913); Lewis v. Brubaker, 322 Mo. 52, 14 S.W.2d 982 (1929); Parsons v. Childs, 345 Mo. 689, 136 S.W.2d 327 (1940), *cert. denied,* 310 U.S. 640 (1940), *rehearing denied,* 311 U.S. 724 (1940).

New Hampshire: Borchers v. Taylor, 83 N.H. 564, 145 A. 666, 63 A.L.R. 874 (1929).

New Jersey: Green v. Blackwell, 35 A. 375 (N.J. Ch. 1896); Mills v. Davison, 54 N.J. Eq. 659, 35 A. 1072, 35 L.R.A. 113, 55 Am. St. Rep. 594 (1896); MacKenzie v. Trustees of Presbytery, 67 N.J. Eq. 652, 61 A. 1027, 3 L.R.A. (N.S.) 227 (1905); Cuthbert v. McNeill, 103 N.J. Eq. 184, 142 A. 667 (1928), *aff'd,* 104 N.J. Eq. 495, 146 A. 881 (1929); Mills v. Montclair Trust Co., 139 N.J. Eq. 56, 49 A.2d 889 (1946).

New York: Associate Alumni v. Theological Seminary, 163 N.Y. 417, 57 N.E. 626 (1900); Van De Bogert v. Reformed Dutch Church, 219 A.D. 220, 220 N.Y.S. 58 (1927) (failure to use site as church cemetery); Montague v. Cooney, 147 Misc. 125, 263 N.Y.S. 346 (1932); Matter of Chaim, 168 Misc. 923, 6 N.Y.S.2d 713 (1938); Ferrari v. Italian Benevolent Inst. & Hosp., 37 N.Y.S.2d 314 (1942); Matter of Stuart, 183 Misc. 20, 46 N.Y.S.2d 911 (1944); De Kay v. Board of Educ. of Central School Dist., 20 Misc. 2d 881, 189 N.Y.S.2d 105 (1959); Application of Dana, 119 Misc. 2d 815, 465 N.Y.S.2d 102 (Sup. Ct. 1982).

North Carolina: Humphrey v. Board of Trustees, 203 N.C. 201, 165 S.E. 547 (1932) (failure to use income as directed), noted in 11 N.C.L. Rev. 179.

Ohio: Taylor v. Dickerson, 113 Ohio App. 344, 178 N.E.2d 46 (1961) (delay in establishing experimental farm).

Oregon: Chapman v. Wilbur, 4 Or. 362 (1873); Wemme v. First Church of Christ, Scientist, 110 Or. 179, 219 P. 618, 223 P. 250 (1924).

Pennsylvania: Barr v. Weld, 24 Pa. 84 (1854); Petition of Sellers Church, 139 Pa. 61, 21 A. 145, 11 L.R.A. 282 (1891); Thornton v. Koch, 317 Pa. 400,

performance of the trust that the failure to perform results in the termination of the trust and the reverter of the trust property to the settlor or his estate.[2]

§401.2. Conditions subsequent. Where land is conveyed or devised upon a charitable trust and it is provided that if the property is not used in the manner directed it shall revert to the settlor or his heirs, the trust is subject to a condition subsequent. In England conditions subsequent were subject to the common law rule against perpetuities.[1] Therefore, if the reverter might occur beyond the perpetuity period, the condition was void *ab initio*. Under the Perpetuities and Accumula-

---

176 A. 3 (1935); Danner Estate, 349 Pa. 82, 36 A.2d 328 (1944); Bangor Park Assn. Case, 370 Pa. 442, 88 A.2d 769 (1952); cf. First Fed. Sav. & Loan Assn. of Erie v. Great Northern Dev. Corp. 422 A.2d 445 (Pa. Super. 1980).

Rhode Island: City of Providence v. Payne, 47 R.I. 444, 134 A. 276 (1926) (sale of site); Buchanan v. McLyman, 51 R.I. 177, 153 A. 304 (1931) (failure to maintain public worship on site); City of Newport v. Sisson, 51 R.I. 481, 155 A. 576 (1931) (failure to use site as school).

Vermont: Middlebury College v. Central Power Corp., 101 Vt. 325, 143 A. 384 (1928), *semble;* Wilbur v. University of Vt., 129 Vt. 33, 270 A.2d 889 (1970) (citing the text, and Restatement of Trusts, §401, Comment *g*).

Washington: Townsend v. Charles Schalkenbach Home for Boys, 33 Wash. 2d 255, 205 P.2d 345 (1949), s.c. *sub nom.* McLaren v. Charles Schalkenbach Home for Boys, 41 Wash. 2d 123, 247 P.2d 691 (1952), noted in 28 Wash. L. Rev. 76.

Wisconsin: Strong v. Doty, 32 Wis. 381 (1873); Estate of Mead, 227 Wis. 311, 277 N.W. 694, 279 N.W. 18, 116 A.L.R. 1127 (1938) (citing Restatement of Trusts, §401, Comment *a*); Steenis v. City of Appleton, 230 Wis. 530, 284 N.W. 492 (1939); Fairbanks v. City of Appleton, 249 Wis. 476, 24 N.W.2d 893 (1946) (citing Restatement of Trusts §401), noted in Wis. L. Rev. 467.

See Note, Failure of trustee to carry out purposes of charitable trust, or diversion of trust property to other purposes, as ground of suit by trustor or his heirs for adjudication of title to him or them, 143 A.L.R. 395 (1943).

[2]Yeshiva v. Rampo Trust, 100 Misc. 2d 1096, 420 N.Y.S.2d 457 (1979) (where it was provided that the charity should refund all contributions if any of the terms of the gift were not complied with).

§401.2. [1]Re Trustees of Hollis Hosp. & Hague's Contract, [1899] 2 Ch. 540, confirming dicta in Re Macleay, L.R. 20 Eq. 186 (1875); Dunn v. Flood, 25 Ch. D. 629 (1883); Law of Property Act 1925, 15 & 16 Geo. V, c. 20, §4(3). See Simes & Smith, The Law of Future Interests §1238 (2d ed. 1956); Maudsley, The Modern Law of Perpetuities 71 (1979); §62.10, p. 341.

tions Act 1964[2] a condition subsequent is enforceable if the breach occurs within the perpetuity period, but not if it occurs after the period has expired. In this country, although the courts do not favor conditions subsequent, they are usually treated as exempt from the rule against perpetuities.[3] If the condition subsequent is exempt from the rule against perpetuities or does not violate the rule, when the condition is breached, the settlor or his heirs are entitled to the property. The character of the interest of the settlor depends on the nature of the disposition. The interest may be legal or equitable. Where the interest transferred is a legal estate in fee subject to a condition subsequent, the settlor has a legal right of entry for condition broken. Where the interest transferred to the trustees is a legal estate in fee simple absolute, but the equitable interest is subject to a condition subsequent, the settlor or his successors upon breach of the condition can enforce a resulting trust.

It is in any case a question of interpretation whether a provision in the trust instrument amounts to a condition or whether it merely imposes duties on the trustees. It is one thing to say that the trustees shall do certain things; it is a different thing to say that if they do not do them the trust shall end. Because a breach of condition results in a forfeiture, the courts are very slow to interpret a provision as imposing a condition. In the absence of language clearly indicating an intention to impose a condition, the courts do not interpret the trust instrument as imposing a condition. In *Bristol Baptist Church v. Connecticut Baptist Convention*[4] land was conveyed in trust to maintain a

---

[2]c. 55, §§3, 12. Simes & Smith, The Law of Future Interests §1220 (1987 Pocket Part by Fratcher); Maudsley, The Modern Law of Perpetuities 190 (1979).

[3]Simes & Smith, The Law of Future Interests §1238 (2d ed. 1956).

[4]98 Conn. 677, 120 A. 497 (1923).

In Application of Mareck, 257 Minn. 222, 100 N.W.2d 758 (1960), *A* transferred land to *B* upon the express condition and covenant that no building, except one used for public park purposes, should be erected on the land and in the event of a breach the land was to revert to *A* and his heirs. *B* conveyed the land to a village in trust to maintain it as a public park with a provision that if it should not do so the land should revert to *B* and his heirs. Thereafter the heirs of *A* and of *B* for consideration executed quitclaim deeds to the village. It was held, over the objection of the Attorney General, that a trust was not created but that the land was held upon a condition that the heirs

meetinghouse thereon, with a provision that if the trustees should permit certain doctrines to be taught in the church the property should revert to the donor. The site becoming unsuitable for a church, the trustees asked permission of the court to sell the land. It was held that the court might authorize a sale. By the terms of the gift it was provided that the church should be maintained on the land, but there was no provision for forfeiture if it should not be so maintained. There was a condition attached to the gift, but the condition related only to the teaching of forbidden doctrines. The property would revert only if the forbidden doctrines were taught.

The mere fact that it is provided in the instrument that the property shall be applied "forever" to certain charitable pur-

---

of the grantors had released, and that therefore the village had a clear title to the land and could pass title to a purchaser.

In Polster's Estate v. Commissioner, 274 F.2d 358 (4th Cir. 1960), where a testator bequeathed his estate to a church for the purchase or erection of buildings and it was provided that only 25 percent of the cost should be paid from the fund, it was held that under the law of Maryland it was an unconditional legacy for charitable purposes and was deductible for the purposes of the estate tax.

In Cummings v. United States, 409 F. Supp. 1064 (M.D.N.C. 1976), a public school unit was anxious to purchase a tract of land for school purposes, and the plaintiff purchased the land and executed a deed of trust as security for the purchase price. The deed provided that it was on the express condition that the plaintiff would not sell except to the school unit, for school purposes, and that if it should cease to be used for such purposes it would revert to the plaintiff. The court held that under North Carolina law there was not a trust or condition but an illegal restraint on alienation. But was it not a trust?

In Matter of Reiger, 60 A.D.2d 299, 400 N.Y.S.2d 881 (1977), a testator devised a house to be retained and used by the Girl and Boy Scouts for the purposes of their organizations. It was held that no condition or limitation was imposed, and that because the premises were unsuitable the house could be sold. See §381, n. 2.

In County of Suffolk v. Greater N.Y. Councils, Boy Scouts of Am., 51 N.Y.2d 830, 413 N.E.2d 363, 433 N.Y.S.2d 42 (1980), a Boy Scout organization paid over the proceeds of a camp owned by it to the defendant, another Boy Scout organization, on condition that the funds be invested in the purchase of a certain tract as a camp. It was so used, but 16 years later the defendant sold the camp. It was held that the conveyance to the defendant did not create a trust, but was on a condition that was performed by the purchase of the land. The condition did not specify that the tract was to be forever used as a camp. The defendant was entitled to retain the proceeds.

poses, or for such purposes "and no other purposes," does not manifest an intention on the part of the testator to create a condition.[5] Even though it is provided in the instrument that the

[5]*England:* Attorney-General v. The Ironmongers' Co., 2 Myl. & K. 576 (1833); In re Ingleton Charity, [1956] Ch. 585.

Federal: Carmack v. United States, 177 F.2d 463 (8th Cir. 1949); United States v. Certain Lands, etc., 79 F. Supp. 558 (E.D. Mo. 1948), noted in 2 Okla. L. Rev. 247.

But see Hopkins v. Grimshaw, 165 U.S. 342, 17 S. Ct. 401, 41 L. Ed. 739 (1897).

Delaware: Delaware Land & Dev. Co. v. First & Central Church, 16 Del. Ch. 410, 147 A. 165 (1929); Executive Council of Protestant Episcopal Church v. Moss, 43 Del. Ch. 379, 231 A.2d 463 (1967) (quoting the text).

Illinois: Downen v. Rayburn, 214 Ill. 342, 73 N.E. 364 (1905); Newton v. Village of Glen Ellyn, 374 Ill. 50, 27 N.E.2d 821 (1940); City of Aurora v. Young Men's Christian Assn., 9 Ill. 2d 286, 137 N.E.2d 347 (1956).

Kentucky: Williams v. Johnson, 284 Ky. 23, 143 S.W.2d 738, 135 A.L.R. 1131 (1940).

Massachusetts: Hillman v. Roman Catholic Bishop of Fall River, 24 Mass. App. 241, 508 N.E.2d 118 (1987).

New Jersey: Hagaman v. Board of Educ., 117 N.J. Super. 446, 285 A.2d 63 (1971), *aff'g* 112 N.J. Super. 221, 270 A.2d 736 (1970).

New York: Camp v. Presbyterian Socy. of Sackett's Harbor, 105 Misc. 139, 173 N.Y.S. 581 (1918); Van De Bogert v. Reformed Dutch Church, 219 A.D. 220, 220 N.Y.S. 58 (1927); Graff v. Harrington, 137 Misc. 712, 244 N.Y.S. 807 (1930); Smith v. Incorporated Village of Patchogue, 285 A.D. 1190, 141 N.Y.S.2d 244 (1955), *aff'g* 129 N.Y.S.2d 422 (quoting the text); De Kay v. Board of Educ. of Cent. School Dist., 20 Misc. 2d 881, 189 N.Y.S.2d 105 (1959).

Ohio: Miller v. Brookville, 152 Ohio St. 217, 89 N.E.2d 85, 15 A.L.R.2d 967 (1949); First Presbyterian Church of Salem v. Tarr, 63 Ohio App. 286, 26 N.E.2d 597 (1939); Taylor v. Dickerson, 113 Ohio App. 344, 178 N.E.2d 46 (1961).

Pennsylvania: Abel v. Girard Trust Co., 365 Pa. 44, 73 A.2d 682 (1950), noted in 24 Temp. L.Q. 373; Bangor Park Assn. Case, 370 Pa. 442, 88 A.2d 769 (1952).

Rhode Island: City of Providence v. Payne, 47 R.I. 444, 134 A. 276 (1926); City of Newport v. Sisson, 51 R.I. 481, 155 A. 576 (1931).

Texas: Toole v. Christ Church, Houston, 141 S.W.2d 720 (Tex. Civ. App. 1940).

See First Natl. Bank of Galveston v. Trinity Protestant Episcopal Church, 219 S.W.2d 828 (Tex. Civ. App. 1949).

Vermont: Wilbur v. University of Vt., 129 Vt. 33, 270 A.2d 889 (1970) (citing the text).

property is given "upon condition" that it be applied to certain purposes, this does not necessarily manifest an intention to create a condition.[6] Unless there is a provision for the reverter of the property, the instrument will rarely be construed as imposing a condition. The word "condition" is frequently used by testators who have no thought of imposing a real condition but who intend merely to impose a duty to apply the property to a particular purpose. But if, on reading the whole instrument and interpreting it in the light of all the circumstances, it appears that the settlor intended to impose a condition, intended that

---

Wisconsin: Fairbanks v. City of Appleton, 249 Wis. 476, 24 N.W.2d 893 (1946), noted in 1947 Wis. L. Rev. 467.

See Note, Character as condition, limitation, covenant, or trust of provision in deed as to purpose for which property is to be used, as affected by introduction with word "provided" or its derivatives, 135 A.L.R. 1135 (1941).

See Note, Nature of estate conveyed by deed for park or playground purposes, 15 A.L.R.2d 975 (1951).

See §§11, 351.

As to the distinction between a condition and a restriction, easement, charge, trust, or specifically enforceable covenant, see 1 American Law of Property §2.8 (1952).

[6]*England:* Merchant Taylors' Co. v. Attorney-General, L.R. 6 Ch. App. 512 (1871); Attorney-General v. Wax Chandlers' Co., L.R. 6 H.L. 1 (1873); Goodman v. Mayor of Saltash, 7 App. Cas. 633 (1882).

Federal: Jones v. Habersham, 107 U.S. 174, 2 S. Ct. 336, 27 L. Ed. 401 (1882).

Kentucky: Hail v. Cook, 294 S.W.2d 87 (Ky. 1956).

Massachusetts: Sohier v. Trinity Church, 109 Mass. 1 (1871); Episcopal City Mission v. Appleton, 117 Mass. 326 (1875).

New Hampshire: Ashuelot Natl. Bank v. Keene, 74 N.H. 148, 65 A. 826, 9 L.R.A. (N.S.) 758 (1907).

New Jersey: Mills v. Davison, 54 N.J. Eq. 659, 35 A. 1072, 55 Am. St. Rep. 594, 35 L.R.A. 113 (1896); MacKenzie v. Trustees of Presbytery, 67 N.J. Eq. 652, 61 A. 1027, 3 L.R.A. (N.S.) 227 (1905).

New York: Matter of Saulpaugh, 15 Misc. 2d 856, 180 N.Y.S.2d 623 (1958) (*semble;* quoting the text).

Rhode Island: Greene v. O'Connor, 18 R.I. 56, 25 A. 692, 19 L.R.A. 262 (1892); City of Providence v. Payne, 47 R.I. 444, 134 A. 276 (1926).

Vermont: Middlebury College v. Central Power Corp., 101 Vt. 325, 143 A. 384 (1928).

Wisconsin: Estate of Mead, 227 Wis. 311, 277 N.W. 694, 279 N.W. 18, 116 A.L.R. 1127 (1938) (*semble;* citing Restatement of Trusts, §401, Comment *b*).

See §399.2.

As to private trusts, see §11.

the property should revert to him or his heirs if the condition should be broken, a condition is created even though there is no express provision for reverter.[7]

Where the trust is subject to a condition subsequent, and the condition is not invalid, a right of entry or resulting trust arises in favor of the settlor or his successors on breach of the condition.[8] It is immaterial that the event upon which the chari-

[7]Roberds v. Markham, 81 F. Supp. 38 (D.D.C. 1948), noted in 2 Okla. L. Rev. 384, 18 U. Cin. L. Rev. 228; Dunne v. Minsor, 312 Ill. 333, 143 N.E. 842 (1924). See §11.

In Hoffman v. Tieton View Community M.E. Church, 33 Wash. 2d 716, 207 P.2d 699 (1949), where a lease of land was made to a church for church purposes and it abandoned the land, it was held that the land reverted to the lessor.

By New Jersey Rev. Stat., §16:1-23, it is provided that an incorporated religious society owning land in trust or on condition that it shall be used for church purposes may by vote of the managing board convey free of the trust, if the donor or his heirs or devisees consent.

In Matter of Goehringer, 69 Misc. 2d 145, 329 N.Y.S.2d 516 (1972), a testator bequeathed money to a named preparatory school to provide funds for the education of boys of the school. He provided that if for any reason the bequest fails, the fund should fall into the residue. The school was in existence at his death but was dissolved a year later before the money was paid over. It was held that the fund should go to similar schools. The court said that the gift over was intended to be effective only if the bequest failed before it vested, and it vested on his death.

In Rourk v. Brunswick County, 46 N.C. App. 795, 266 S.E.2d 401 (1980), the court refused to reform the trust instrument by inserting a provision for reverter if the particular purpose should fail.

See Simes & Smith, The Law of Future Interests, §§247, 248 (2d ed. 1956).

[8]*California:* Mountain Brow Lodge v. Toscano, 257 Cal. App. 2d 22, 64 Cal. Rptr. 816 (1968).

Connecticut: Merchants Bank & Trust Co. v. New Canaan Historical Socy., 133 Conn. 706, 54 A.2d 696 (1947).

Minnesota: Consolidated School Dist. v. Walter, 243 Minn. 159, 66 N.W.2d 881, 53 A.L.R.2d 218 (1954).

New Jersey: Guyer v. Trustees of Young Men's Christian Assn., 142 N.J. Eq. 400, 60 A.2d 276 (1948).

New York: Board of Educ. v. Miles, 15 N.Y.2d 364, 207 N.E.2d 188 (1965), noted in 41 N.Y.U.L. Rev. 657.

Pennsylvania: Randall's Estate, 341 Pa. 501, 19 A.2d 272 (1941) (quoting the text); Ewing Estate, 22 D.&C.2d 445 (Pa. 1960).

Rhode Island: Town of Bristol v. Nolan, 72 R.I. 460, 53 A.2d 466 (1947), noted in 46 Mich. L. Rev. 1120.

table trust is to terminate may happen beyond the period of the rule against perpetuities where there is no gift over on breach of condition. A legal right of entry for condition broken or a possibility of reverter is held not to be within the rule against perpetuities, nor is a resulting trust on termination of a charitable trust,[9] although in England the rule is other-

---

Wisconsin: Saletri v. Clark, 13 Wis. 2d 325, 108 N.W.2d 548 (1961).

In Pedrotti v. Marin County, 152 F.2d 829 (9th Cir. 1946), *cert. denied sub nom.* County of Marin v. Pedrotti, 328 U.S. 853 (1946), *rev'g* United States v. 263.5 Acres of Land, 54 F. Supp. 692 (N.D. Cal. 1944), a testator devised a ranch to a county to use the income for the relief of crippled and blind residents of the county, and provided that if it should sell or mortgage the ranch the property should revert to the testator's heirs, and provided that the gift was in memory of his wife. The ranch was taken on eminent domain. It was held that because the object of making the ranch a memorial to his wife had failed, it reverted to the heirs.

In Foote Memorial Hosp. v. Kelley, 390 Mich. 193, 211 N.W.2d 649 (1973), a woman conveyed land in 1916 to a city with a provision that it should be used for no other purpose than that of a city hospital, and in case of violation of this command it should revert to her, her heirs and assigns. It was proposed, under authority of a statute, to use the land for other purposes. The Attorney General objected on the ground that the city held the land in trust for hospital purposes. It was held that a condition and not a trust was created, and that only the heirs of the settlor had any remedy.

In Lake View Memorial Hosp. v. County of Vermilion, 23 Ill. App. 3d 413, 318 N.E.2d 752 (1974), it was held that there was not a condition but a covenant to reconvey that was specifically enforceable.

[9]*Illinois:* Dunne v. Minsor, 312 Ill. 333, 143 N.E. 842 (1924).

Kansas: Commercial Natl. Bank of Kansas City v. Martin, 185 Kan. 116, 340 P.2d 899 (1959).

Maryland: Mayor & City Council of Ocean City v. Taber, 279 Md. App. 115, 367 A.2d 1233 (1977).

Massachusetts: Hayden v. Inhabitants of Stoughton, 5 Pick. 528 (Mass. 1827) (residuary devisee); Bullard v. Inhabitants of Shirley, 153 Mass. 559, 27 N.E. 766, 12 L.R.A. 110 (1891); Fay v. Locke, 201 Mass. 387, 87 N.E. 753, 131 Am. St. Rep. 402 (1909).

New Jersey: Fidelity Union Trust Co. v. Egenolf Day Nursery Assn., 64 N.J. Super. 445, 166 A.2d 402 (1960) (citing the text).

South Carolina: Purvis v. McElveen, 234 S.C. 94, 106 S.E.2d 913 (1959).

See Gray, Rule Against Perpetuities §§30-42, 299-313, 327.1, 603.8 (4th ed. 1942); Restatement of Property §372; 6 American Law of Property §§24.-17, 24.62 (1952).

As to the validity of a gift over for other charitable purposes, see §401.5.

As to the validity of a gift over for noncharitable purposes, see §401.6.

wise.[10] It might, indeed, have been wiser as an original question to hold that such a terminable charitable trust could not be created.[11]

It has been held that a condition is valid even though the event upon which the charitable trust is to terminate is not connected with the charitable purpose for which the trust was created. Thus in *Dunne v. Minsor*[12] a testator devised land to a bishop for the use of a church as a residence for the priests "upon the condition" that they should at all times see that his grave and the graves of his sister and brother were cared for. It was held that the provision for use of the land as a residence for the priests did not impose a condition, and that when it became no longer useful for this purpose the court might order a sale of the land and the erection with the proceeds of a new residence for the priests; but it was held that the provision with respect to the caring for the graves imposed a condition, and that if the condition were broken the heirs of the testator might enter.

The condition may, however, be invalid as against public policy. In such a case the charitable trust will not terminate even

---

A condition may be construed to be applicable only for a reasonable time. Thus in Independent Congregational Socy. v. Davenport, 381 A.2d 1137 (Me. 1978), land was conveyed to a church organization with a provision that if the land should cease to be used as a place of public religious meetings it should revert to the settlor or his heirs. It was held, a century and a half later, that the condition was applicable only for a reasonable time and was no longer applicable, and the church had a fee simple free of the condition.

To the same effect, see City of Casper v. J. M. Carey & Bros., 601 P.2d 1010 (Wyo. 1979).

See 1 American Law of Property, §2.8.

See Restatement (Second) of Property (Donative Transfers), §1.4, Comment c (1979).

[10]Nn. 1, 2, *supra.*

In In re Smith, [1967] V.R. 341, land was transferred to a municipality "upon condition that it be used as a site for a park," and it was provided that if it was not so used for a certain period the land was to revert to the transferor or his successors who should have a right to re-enter. It was held that the condition was invalid as a perpetuity, but that there was a valid trust.

[11]See §413.

[12]312 Ill. 333, 143 N.E. 842 (1924).

See also Matter of Borden, 180 Misc. 988, 42 N.Y.S.2d 560 (1943); Giblin v. Giblin, 173 Wis. 632, 182 N.W. 357 (1921).

on the happening of the condition. Thus where a testator leaves money in trust to pay the income to a hospital but provides that the trust shall terminate and the property revert to his estate if the hospital should not adopt and enforce a rule compelling physicians practicing in the hospital to share their fees with the hospital, the condition is invalid and the property will not revert for breach of the condition. The condition is invalid because it compels fee-splitting, which is contrary to medical ethics and is against public policy.[13]

The rule that a right of entry for condition broken or a possibility of reverter is not subject to the rule against perpetuities has led to the tying up of property in a way that is most unfortunate, particularly in the case of land. Accordingly, statutes have been passed in several states restricting the power of the owner of property to thus tie it up for an indefinite period or forever.[14]

---

[13]Matter of Sterne, 147 Misc. 59, 263 N.Y.S. 304 (1933). See §65.2.

[14]*California:* Civil Code, §§885.020, 885.050.

Colorado: Rev. Stat. 1963, §§18-1-57 to 18-1-65.

Connecticut: Gen. Stat. 1958, §45-97.

Florida: Stat. Ann., §689.18.

Illinois: Rev. Stat., c. 30, §§37e to 37f.2.

Iowa: Code Ann., §614.24.

Kentucky: Rev. Stat. Ann., §381.220.

Maine: Rev. Stat. 1964, tit. 33, §§101 to 106.

Maryland: Ann. Code, Real Property §§6-101 to 6-105, as enacted by Laws 1972, c. 349.

Massachusetts: Ann. Laws, c. 184, §§23 to 30, as amended by Laws 1969, c. 666.

Michigan: Stat. Ann., §§26.49(11) to 26.49(15).

Minnesota: Stat. Ann., §500.20(2).

Nebraska: Rev. Stat. 1943 (1959 Supp.), §§76-299, 76-2100 to 76-2105.

New York: Real Property Actions and Proceedings Law, §§612, 1951 to 1955.

Oregon: Rev. Stat., §105.770.

Rhode Island: Gen. Laws 1956, §§34-4-19 to 34-4-21.

Virginia: Code 1950, §8-5.1, as enacted by Laws 1975, c. 136 (ten-year limitation as to actions).

In Town of Brookline v. Carey, 355 Mass. 424, 245 N.E.2d 446 (1969), the court upheld the retroactive application of Mass. Ann. Laws, c. 260, §31A,

§401.3. **Limitations.** If property is given to be applied to charitable purposes until a designated event shall occur or so long as a certain state of affairs continues, the settlor has attempted to reserve to himself a legal or equitable possibility of reverter that would, if valid, entitle him or his heirs to the property when the event occurs or the state of affairs ceases. In England such a possibility of reverter is enforceable only if the event occurs or the state of affairs ceases within the perpetuity period.[1] In this country possibilities of reverter are usually

---

imposing a time limitation on the enforcement of a right of entry for condition broken or a possibility of reverter. See also Presbytery of Southeast Iowa v. Harris, 226 N.W.2d 232 (Iowa 1975); Cline v. Johnson County Bd. of Educ., 548 S.W.2d 507, 87 A.L.R.3d 1007 (Ky. 1977); Hiddleston v. Nebraska Jewish Educ. Socy., 186 Neb. 786, 186 N.W.2d 904 (1971).

In Dunphy v. Commonwealth, 368 Mass. 376, 331 N.E.2d 883 (1975), it was held that the statute had no application to a charitable trust. Land was conveyed to a town to be a public park in perpetuity. The court set aside a conveyance of the land to the Commonwealth as a skating rink, although the legislature had enacted a statute permitting it.

As to the validity of the statute insofar as it is retroactive, see Biltmore Village v. Royal, 71 So. 2d 727 (Fla. 1954); Trustees of Schools of Township No. 1 v. Batdorf, 6 Ill. 2d 486, 130 N.E.2d 111 (1955); Board of Educ. v. Miles, 15 N.Y.2d 364, 201 N.E.2d 181 (1965), rev'g 18 A.D.2d 87, 238 N.Y.S.2d 766 (1963).

See also Note, Retroactive Termination of Burdens on Land Use, 65 Colum. L. Rev. 1272 (1965); Note, Validity of statute canceling, destroying, nullifying, or limiting enforcement of possibilities of reverter or rights of re-entry for condition broken, 87 A.L.R.3d 1011 (1978); see Restatement (Second) of Property (Donative Transfers), §1.4, statutory note; Simes & Smith, The Law of Future Interests, §§1239, 1994 (2d ed. 1956, and 1987 Pocket Part by Fratcher).

§401.3. [1]See §401.2, nn. 1, 2.

By Perpetuities and Accumulations Act 1964, c. 55, it is provided that "in the case of (a) a possibility of reverter on the determination of a determinable fee simple, or (b) a possibility of a resulting trust on the determination of any other determinable interest in property, the rule against perpetuities shall apply in relation to the provision causing the interest to be determinable as it would apply if that provision were expressed in the form of a condition subsequent, giving rise, on breach thereof, to a right of re-entry or an equivalent right in the case of property other than land, and where the provision falls to be treated as void for remoteness the determinable interest shall become an absolute interest."

This statute subjects both legal and equitable possibilities of reverter to

treated as being exempt from the rule against perpetuities[2] but,

---

the rule against perpetuities, but modified by the "wait and see" doctrine, so that they are valid if they actually become possessory within the perpetuity period.

Hopper v. Corporation of Liverpool, 88 Sol. J. 213 (1944), noted in 1945 Conv. Y.B. 213 and in 62 Law Q. Rev. 222 (1946), was decided by the Chancery Court of the County Palatine of Lancaster. It involved a conveyance of land to named persons and their heirs so long as the land was used for specified library and other purposes. The Vice-Chancellor, Sir John Bennett, rejected the argument of Professor John Chipman Gray that possibilities of reverter were abolished by the Statute *Quia Emptores Terrarum*, Westminster III, 18 Edw. I, c. 1 (1290) (see Gray, The Rule Against Perpetuities, §§31-37 (3d ed. 1915)), but held that they were subject to the common law rule against perpetuities and so void *ab initio* if there was a possibility that they could become possessory at a time beyond the perpetuity period. Other English cases decided before the enactment of the 1964 statute assumed that possibilities of reverter were valid and exempt from the rule against perpetuities. See Attorney-General v. Pyle, 1 Atk. 435, 26 Eng. Rep. 278 (Ch. 1738), in which land was devised to a charity school, the rents and profits to be applied for the benefit of the school "so long as it shall be endowed with charity." The Lord Chancellor, Lord Hardwicke, said that when the charity ceased the land would revert to the heir of the testator. See also Re Chardon, [1928] Ch. 464; In re Randell, 38 Ch. D. 213 (1888) (to minister of church so long as sittings are free); In re Blunt's Trusts, [1904] 2 Ch. 767 (for school so long as it is conducted in certain manner); Bankes v. Salisbury Diocesan Council of Educ., [1960] Ch. 631 (to trustees to establish a school, the conveyance to be void if it should become impracticable to carry on the school).

See Maudsley, The Modern Law of Perpetuities 70 (1979); Simes & Smith, The Law of Future Interests, §1239 (2d ed. 1956, and 1987 Pocket Part by Fratcher).

[2]*Massachusetts:* Inhabitants of Princeton v. Adams, 10 Cush. 129 (Mass. 1852); Easterbrooks v. Tillinghast, 5 Gray 17 (Mass. 1855); First Universalists Socy. of N. Adams v. Boland, 155 Mass. 171, 29 N.E. 524, 15 L.R.A. 231 (1892) (so long as property used by church for support of certain doctrines); Brown v. Independent Baptist Church, 325 Mass. 645, 91 N.E.2d 922 (1950) (to church so long as it should maintain its present belief and should continue a church), noted in 64 Harv. L. Rev. 864.

See Institution for Sav. in Roxbury v. Roxbury Home for Aged Women, 244 Mass. 583, 139 N.E. 301 (1923).

Mississippi: Kelly v. Wilson, 204 Miss. 56, 36 So. 2d 817 (1948) (to trustees of school so long as land should be used for school purposes); Jones v. Burns, 221 Miss. 833, 74 So. 2d 866 (1954) (to trustees of school so long as land used for school purposes).

Missouri: Donehue v. Nilges, 364 Mo. 705, 266 S.W.2d 553, 45 A.L.R.2d 1150 (1954) (so long as premises used for a school site).

as in the case of rights of entry on breach of condition subsequent, several states have statutes that make possibilities of reverter expire after a stipulated period, commonly 30 or 50 years.[3] Where, before the enactment of legislation causing possibilities of reverter to expire after a period, a bequest was made in this country to a church society, the income to be paid to the pastors so long as they "preach and maintain the same essential doctrines and principles of faith and practice as are now preached and taught" by their present pastor, and the church changed from Unitarianism to Trinitarianism, it was held that

---

New Hampshire: Wood v. County of Cheshire, 32 N.H. 421 (1855) (so long as building is occupied as courthouse).

New York: First Reformed Dutch Church v. Croswell, 210 A.D. 294, 206 N.Y.S. 132 (1924) (to church so long as it occupied the premises as a church).

Oregon: City of Klamath Falls v. Bell, 7 Or. App. 330, 490 P.2d 515 (1971).

Pennsylvania: Reichard Appeal, 188 Pa. Super. 130, 146 A.2d 71 (1958) (for a school reserving a reversionary interest if premises abandoned for school purposes).

Tennessee: Yarbrough v. Yarbrough, 151 Tenn. 221, 269 S.W. 36 (1924) (so long as land used for site of church); Commerce Union Bank v. Warren County, 707 S.W.2d 854 (Tenn. 1986).

Texas: Gibson v. Berry Cemetery Assn., 250 S.W.2d 600 (Tex. Civ. App. 1952) (to trustees of church and of school so long as school and church remain there).

West Virginia: Woman's Club of St. Albans v. James, 158 W. Va. 698, 213 S.E.2d 469 (1975).

Canada: In re Tilbury West Public School Bd. & Hastie, 55 D.L.R.2d 407 (Ont. 1966) (so long as the land shall be used and needed for school purposes and no longer); In re Robinson, 75 D.L.R.3d 532 (Ont. 1976) (provision that graves never be removed held to be a limitation, not a condition, and resulting trust for residuary legatees arose when cemetery abandoned).

In Bonebrake v. McNeill, 491 P.2d 269 (Okla. 1971), land was deeded to a religious corporation for religious and educational purposes, and it was provided that if it should cease to be used for such purposes for a year it should revert to the grantors or their heirs. It was held that a determinable fee simple was granted, and that the possibility of reverter was alienable.

See §62.10.

As to the validity of a gift over for other charitable purposes, see §401.5.

As to the validity of a gift over for noncharitable purposes, see §401.6.

On the question whether the property goes to the heir or next of kin or whether it falls into the residue, see §399.3.

In Moore v. Wells, 212 Ga. 446, 93 S.E.2d 731 (1956), it was held that a limitation and not a trust was created.

[3]§401.2, n. 14.

the trust terminated.[4] Similarly, where a testator devised land in trust to apply the income to the maintenance of a pastor of a church so long as the members of the church should maintain the visibility of a church in a certain faith and practice, and the church was later dissolved, it was held that the land was held by the trustees upon a resulting trust for the heirs of the testator.[5]

§401.4. **Relief against forfeiture.** A provision that a charitable trust shall terminate and that the property shall revert to the donor or his heirs is strictly construed. The court will not permit the donor or his heirs to recover the property unless it is clear that there has been a breach of the condition.[1] Thus in

[4]Inhabitants of Princeton v. Adams, 10 Cush. 129 (Mass. 1852).

[5]Easterbrooks v. Tillinghast, 5 Gray 17 (Mass. 1855).

But if there is a gift over to another charity if the church should cease to exist, there is no reversionary interest in the grantor or his heirs. Trustees of Protestant Episcopal Church v. Danais, 108 N.H. 344, 235 A.2d 516 (1967), 108 N.H. 347, 235 A.2d 518 (1967).

§401.4. [1]*England:* In re Jones, [1948] Ch. 67.

Delaware: Milford Trust Co. v. Milford Memorial Hosp., 24 Del. Ch. 43, 4 A.2d 674 (1939).

Kansas: In re Estate of Roberts, 190 Kan. 248, 373 P.2d 165 (1962) (citing Restatement of Trusts §401).

Kentucky: State Bank & Trust Co. of Richmond v. Madison County, 275 Ky. 501, 122 S.W.2d 99 (1938); Zevely v. City of Paris, 298 S.W.2d 12 (Ky. 1957).

Maine: Bancroft v. Maine State Sanatorium Assn., 119 Me. 56, 109 A. 585 (1920).

Massachusetts: Giles v. Boston Fatherless & Widows' Socy., 10 Allen 355 (Mass. 1865); City of Quincy v. Attorney Gen., 160 Mass. 431, 35 N.E. 1066 (1894); Capen v. Skinner, 177 Mass. 84, 58 N.E. 473 (1900); Woman's Seaman's Friend Socy. v. Boston Y.W.C.A., 240 Mass. 521, 134 N.E. 601 (1922); Attorney Gen. v. Lowell, 246 Mass. 312, 141 N.E. 45 (1923); Miller v. Parish of the Epiphany, 302 Mass. 323, 19 N.E.2d 46 (1939).

Nebraska: Erskine v. Board of Regents of Univ. of Neb., 170 Neb. 660, 104 N.W.2d 285 (1960).

Pennsylvania: Jordan's Estate, 310 Pa. 401, 165 A. 652 (1933); Patterson's Estate, 333 Pa. 92, 3 A.2d 320, 120 A.L.R. 967 (1939); Arnold's Estate, 56 D.&C. 662 (Pa. 1946); Bostwick Trust, 18 D.&C.2d 653 (Pa. 1959) (quoting the text).

In In re Selinger's Will Trusts, [1959] 1 All E.R. 407, where a legacy was left to trustees for such charitable institution as they might select, and it was provided that if no selection was made within one year the legacy should fall into the residue, and the trustees made a selection after two years, it was held that the property should go to the selected charity because it appeared that

Jordan's Estate[2] a testator bequeathed property in trust to pay the income to a certain incorporated academy, and provided that in case the corporation should be dissolved or the academy go out of existence as an academy or the trustees of the academy should fail for five years to maintain a school in which certain subjects should be taught, the income should be paid to a certain church.

---

the property could not have been distributed earlier because of pending litigation.

In Danner v. Shanafelt, 159 Ohio St. 5, 110 N.E.2d 772 (1953), a testator directed that the money bequeathed by him for charitable purposes should be invested only in government bonds, and that the interest should be distributed yearly among the poor of a town. It was provided that if the money were not so invested and the interest so distributed, the bequest should fall into the residue of his estate. It was held that the failure of the named trustee to accept the legacy was not a breach of the conditions.

In Conway v. Emeny, 139 Conn. 612, 96 A.2d 221 (1953), a testatrix provided that if the trustees of a museum established by her should by a two-thirds vote in their absolute discretion determine that there was not sufficient public interest to warrant continuing the museum, the trust should terminate. It was held that it was an abuse of discretion to terminate the trust for financial reasons only.

In Churches Homes for Business Girls v. Manget Found., 110 Ga. App. 539, 139 S.E.2d 138 (1964), where a foundation conveyed land to a home for elderly people and provided that if it should not maintain such a home it would pay $50,000 to the foundation, it was held that the foundation was entitled to recover the money because the home was not operated exclusively for elderly people.

In Harris v. Georgia Military Academy, 221 Ga. 721, 146 S.E.2d 913 (1966), one Colonel Woodward conveyed land to the Georgia Military Academy and provided that if the land should cease to be used for the purposes set forth in its charter, it should revert to the donor or his heirs. On a petition for a declaratory judgment it was held that no forfeiture would result from amendments in the charter abolishing military training, admitting girls, and changing the corporate name to Woodward Academy. Three justices dissented.

In Whetsell v. Jernigan, 291 N.C. 128, 229 S.E.2d 183 (1976), *aff'g* 29 N.C. App. 136, 223 S.E.2d 397, there was a conveyance to a church in fee, but with a provision that the land should revert to the grantor if the church should change its name or should fail to occupy it for three years. It was held (one judge dissenting) that the provision was ineffective.

See Note, Validity, interpretation, and application of provisions of will making devise or bequest to or in trust for religious or educational body dependent upon adherence to particular body of principles or dogmas, or ecclesiastical connection, 120 A.L.R. 971 (1939).

[2] 310 Pa. 401, 165 A. 652 (1933).

The attendance at the academy fell off and an arrangement was made with another institution under which instruction was given in that institution under a reciprocal teaching agreement. The academy was to elect a principal and employ two teachers to teach the required subjects, and all students were to be enrolled as students in both institutions. The trustees of the academy continued to function. It was held that there was no breach of the condition and the church was not entitled to the income. The corporation had not been dissolved and the academy had not gone out of existence as an academy and the required subjects were still taught. The provisions of the will did not require that the academy should continue as an independent self-governing institution.

Even if there has been a breach of the condition, the court may refuse to decree a termination of the charitable trust and a forfeiture of the property if under all the circumstances it would be inequitable to do so. It has long been a function of a court of equity to give equitable relief against a forfeiture where the circumstances are such that there would be an undue hardship in enforcing a forfeiture. This is true where there has been a merely technical breach of a condition or where the persons entitled to the property on breach of the condition have caused the breach, or where they have acquiesced in the breach. Thus it has been held that where land was devised to a church society on condition that the society establish an orphanage on the premises within three years, and it was not established within the period because the heirs of the testator contested the will causing protracted litigation, the heirs were not entitled to the property in spite of the breach of the condition.[3] Similarly, where a testatrix left money to build a memorial bridge and provided that the bequest was on the express condition that within five years from her death the proper authorities should agree to construct suitable approaches to the bridge and lay out a public highway, and, if they should refuse, the money should at the end of five years become a part of her residuary estate, the court would not enforce a forfeiture although no action was taken by

---

[3]Peek v. Woman's Home Missionary Socy., 293 Ill. 337, 127 N.E. 760 (1920), 304 Ill. 427, 136 N.E. 772, 26 A.L.R. 917 (1922).
See In re Harding, [1960] N.Z.L.R. 379.

the public authorities or the trustees within the five-year period because the delay, in part at least, was due to the conduct of the residuary legatees.[4] So also where the persons entitled to the property on breach of the condition have acquiesced in the breach or have delayed in attempting to enforce the forfeiture, they may be barred from enforcing the forfeiture.[5] In *In re Jones*[6] a testatrix directed her trustees to purchase a site for a village hall, and to convey the land to a new set of trustees for the purpose of erecting a hall on the land. She provided that if the latter trustees failed to complete the hall within five years from her death, the site should be sold and the proceeds fall into the residue of her estate. The trustees under the will failed to buy the land, so that the other trustees were unable to erect the hall within the specified period. It was held that the trust did not fail. The court said that a provision for forfeiture should be strictly construed, and that the omission of the trustees to follow the directions of the will should not prejudice one beneficiary in favor of another.

Where the performance of a condition has become impossible, the court may refuse to enforce a forfeiture.[7]

[4]Carlstrom v. Frackelton, 263 Ill. App. 250 (1931).

See Bauer v. Dallas Theater Center, 330 S.W.2d 214 (Tex. Civ. App. 1959).

[5]Faust v. Little Rock School Dist., 224 Ark. 761, 276 S.W.2d 59 (1955); Sanitary Dist. of Chicago v. Chicago Title & Trust Co., 278 Ill. 529, 116 N.E. 161 (1917).

But see Pedrotti v. Marin County, 152 F.2d 829 (9th Cir. 1946), *cert. denied sub nom.* County of Marin v. Pedrotti, 328 U.S. 853 (1946), *rev'g* United States v. 263.5 Acres of Land, 54 F. Supp. 692 (N.D. Cal. 1944).

As to equitable relief against forfeiture for breach of condition in a private trust, see §11.

[6][1948] Ch. 67.

[7]Scobey v. Beckman, 111 Ind. App. 574, 41 N.E.2d 847 (1942), noted in 41 Mich. L. Rev. 332; Keyser v. Calvary Brethren Church, 192 Md. 520, 64 A.2d 748 (1949).

As to private trusts, see §65A.

Where the land is taken on eminent domain, there is no forfeiture. State v. Federal Square Corp., 89 N.H. 538, 3 A.2d 109 (1938), noted in 7 Duke B.A.J. 137; Moses H. Cone Memorial Hosp. v. Cone, 231 N.C. 292, 56 S.E.2d 709 (1949); Banner Baptist Church v. Watson, 193 Tenn. 290, 246 S.W.2d 17 (1952).

In United Baptist Convention v. East Weare Baptist Church, 103 N.H.

Where owing to a change of circumstances the performance of the condition would defeat or substantially impair the purpose of the settlor in creating the trust, it has been held that the court may in the exercise of the cy pres power dispense with the condition. Thus in *In re Robinson*[8] a testatrix who died in 1889 bequeathed money toward the endowment of an evangelical church, and made it an "abiding" condition that a black gown should be worn in the pulpit. Thirty years later the incumbent applied to the court for permission to dispense with the requirement as to the wearing of such a gown and showed that the custom had so changed that the wearing of the gown appeared eccentric and tended to disturb the feelings of the congregation. It was held that the requirement should be dispensed with. The court said that although the performance of the condition was not impossible it had become impracticable. It is to be noted, however, that although the testatrix and the court spoke of the requirement as being a condition of the gift, there was no provision for forfeiture on breach of the condition, and the provision might well have been treated as a mere direction rather than as a true condition. There is no difficulty in the application of the cy pres power to permit a deviation from a particular direction

---

521, 176 A.2d 325 (1961), land was conveyed to a church with a provision that it should revert if the church should fail to use the property for church purposes continuously for one year. The property was taken on eminent domain, and the price was paid to the church, which was using the money to acquire a new church building. It was held that the grantor was not entitled to any part of the proceeds at present (citing the text and Restatement of Property §53). It was held, however, that the plaintiff would be entitled to the property if it should ever cease to be used for church purposes.

In Fairfax County Park Auth. v. Brundage, 208 Va. 622, 159 S.E.2d 831 (1968), there was a devise of land to a charitable corporation as an arboretum and it was provided that if it should not be used for such purpose or if any part should be taken by public authority for any other purpose, the land was to go to a charitable research association, and part of the land was taken on eminent domain as a street. It was held that the gift over took effect.

In In re Macdonald, 18 D.L.R.3d 521 (Ont. 1971), a testatrix left the residue to a public library to be used in collecting historical objects for showing and preservation in a certain house. She provided that the gift was subject to the condition that the city give necessary assurances that the house would never be moved. It was held that the city could not give such assurance, and that the condition was invalid, and that the city took free of condition.

    [8][1923] 2 Ch. 332.

in the terms of the trust where it would defeat the general purpose of the settlor to enforce it.[9]

In *Trustees of Dartmouth College v. City of Quincy* [10] a testator left property to the town of Quincy to establish a school for girls. He provided that the school should be for the education of females who are born in the town "and none other than these, to be allowed to attend this Institute." He further provided that if the town "fails to comply with the words and intent of this will, as determined by good judges . . . or use it for any other purpose than contemplated in this will" the property should go to the Trustees of Dartmouth College. About 75 years later there were about 70 girls in the school, although it had capacity for 100 girls, and the school was in financial difficulties. The governing board approved a proposal to admit non-Quincy-born girls who would pay the full cost of their education. Dartmouth College brought a petition to enjoin the admission of any non-Quincy-born girls. It was held that the petition should be denied. The court said that there is strong reason to avoid any forfeiture of the primary charitable trust. It said that "There is strong ground for disregarding such subordinate details if changed circumstances render them obstructive of, or inappropriate to, the accomplishment of the principal charitable purpose."

In New York the legislature, following a recommendation by the Law Revision Commission, has taken a long step forward in permitting the modification or extinguishment of restrictions on the use of land held for charitable purposes, where the restriction substantially impedes the furthering of the purposes. The Supreme Court is given a discretionary power to extinguish or modify restrictions, even though they are imposed by a special limitation or condition subsequent.[11]

---

[9]See §399.4.

[10]357 Mass. 521, 258 N.E.2d 745 (1970) (citing the text and Restatement of Trusts §§381, 399, 401).

[11]Real Property Actions and Proceedings Law, §1955, as enacted by Laws 1962, c. 142, superseding Real Property Law, §349, inserted by Laws 1958, c. 863. See also Real Property Actions and Proceedings Law, §§1951 to 1954. See Matter of Bayles v. Anderson, 41 Misc. 2d 909, 246 N.Y.S.2d 776 (1964).

§401.5. Gift over from charity to charity. A gift over from one charitable purpose to another upon the happening of an event is valid, even though the event may happen beyond the period of the rule against perpetuities.[1] It is immaterial whether

---

See also Real Property Actions and Proceedings Law, §612, enacting a short statute of limitations in actions to recover real property founded on a claim of reverter for breach of a condition subsequent.

See also Real Property Law, §345.

As to the validity of this legislation insofar as it is retroactive, see Board of Educ. v. Miles, 15 N.Y.2d 364, 201 N.E.2d 181 (1965), *rev'g* 18 A.D.2d 87, 238 N.Y.S.2d 766 (1963), noted in 65 Colum. L. Rev. 1272, 41 N.Y.U.L. Rev. 657.

See §401.2, n. 14.

§401.5. [1]*England:* Christ's Hosp. v. Grainger, 16 Sim. 83 (1848), *aff'd,* 1 Mac. & G. 460 (1849); Royal College of Surgeons v. National Provincial Bank, [1952] A.C. 631, *rev'g* In re Bland-Sutton's Will Trusts, [1951] Ch. 485, *aff'g* [1951] Ch. 70, noted in 11 Camb. L.J. 435, 94 Sol. J. 795.

Federal: Jones v. Habersham, 107 U.S. 174, 185, 2 S. Ct. 336, 27 L. Ed. 401 (1882); Holdeen v. Ratterree, 292 F.2d 338 (2d Cir. 1961) (*semble;* citing Restatement of Trusts, §401, Comment *f*).

Arkansas: Little Rock Junior College v. George W. Donaghey Found., 224 Ark. 895, 277 S.W.2d 79, 51 A.L.R.2d 806 (1955), *semble;* s.c. Geo. W. Donaghey Found. v. Little Rock Univ., 231 Ark. 748, 332 S.W.2d 497 (1960); Little Rock Univ. v. George W. Donaghey Found., 252 Ark. 1148, 483 S.W.2d 230 (1972).

Connecticut: Colonial Trust Co. v. Waldron, 112 Conn. 216, 152 A. 69 (1930).

Illinois: Village of Hinsdale v. Chicago City Missionary Socy., 375 Ill. 220, 30 N.E.2d 657 (1940); Smith v. Renne, 382 Ill. 26, 46 N.E.2d 587 (1943), *semble;* State Bank & Trust Co. v. Park Ridge School for Girls, 34 Ill. App. 2d 396, 181 N.E.2d 204 (1962).

Massachusetts: Odell v. Odell, 10 Allen 1, 8 (Mass. 1865), *semble.*

Compare American Colonization Socy. v. Trustees of Smith Charities, 2 Allen 302 (Mass. 1861).

Mississippi: Mississippi Children's Home Socy. v. City of Jackson, 230 Miss. 546, 93 So. 2d 483 (1957) (citing the text).

Missouri: Pilgrim Evangelical Lutheran Church of the Unaltered Augsburg Confession v. Lutheran Church-Missouri Synod Found., 661 S.W.2d 833 (Mo. App. 1983), *transfer to S. Ct. denied* (1984).

Nebraska: Board of Trustees of York College v. Cheney, 160 Neb. 631, 71 N.W.2d 195 (1955).

New Hampshire: Trustees of Pittsfield Academy v. Attorney Gen., 95 N.H. 51, 57 A.2d 161 (1948).

New Jersey: MacKenzie v. Trustees of Presbytery, 67 N.J. Eq. 652, 61 A. 1027, 3 L.R.A. (N.S.) 227 (1905).

upon the happening of the event the same trustees are to hold the property for other charitable purposes or whether new trustees are to hold the property for the same or other charitable purposes. Similarly, there may be a gift over from one charitable corporation to another charitable corporation. The event upon which the gift over is to take effect may be the failure of the original charitable trust. In such a case the property will not

---

New York: Matter of Dettmer, 178 Misc. 401, 34 N.Y.S.2d 913 (1942), *aff'd mem.*, 266 A.D. 877, 42 N.Y.S.2d 846 (1943), *aff'd mem.*, 292 N.Y. 688, 56 N.E.2d 107 (1944); Matter of Manilla, 16 Misc. 2d 937, 182 N.Y.S.2d 769 (1959) (citing the text).

North Carolina: Williams v. Williams, 215 N.C. 739, 3 S.E.2d 334 (1939).

Pennsylvania: Levan's Estate, 314 Pa. 274, 171 A. 617 (1934); McCann's Estate, 39 D.&C. 215 (Pa. 1940); Lehigh Univ. v. Hower, 159 Pa. Super. 84, 46 A.2d 516 (1946) (quoting Restatement of Trusts, §401, Comments *d, f*).

Rhode Island: Pennsylvania Co. for Banking & Trusts v. Board of Governors of London Hosp., 79 R.I. 74, 83 A.2d 881 (1951) (citing Restatement of Trusts, §401, Comment *f*), noted in 65 Harv. L. Rev. 704, 51 Mich. L. Rev. 128.

Vermont: Wilbur v. University of Vt., 129 Vt. 33, 270 A.2d 889 (1970), *semble* (citing the text and Restatement of Trusts, §401, Comment *f*).

Virginia: McClure v. Carter, 202 Va. 191, 116 S.E.2d 260 (1960) (citing the text).

Washington: In re Lemon's Estate, 47 Wash. 2d 23, 286 P.2d 691 (1955).

In Buchanan v. Willis, 195 Tenn. 18, 255 S.W.2d 8 (1953), it was held that a gift over from one church to another if the first should depart from the teachings of the New Testament was not invalid for uncertainty or as a perpetuity. See §65B.

In In re Campbell's Estate, 20 Cal. App. 3d 474, 97 Cal. Rptr. 726 (1971), a bequest to a church to provide an endowment fund on condition that the church agree to provide perpetual care for a cemetery lot was upheld, because the money given to the church was not to be used for the care of the lot.

See Restatement of Property §397.

Restatement (Second) of Property (Donative Transfers), §1.6, provides: "If under a donative transfer an interest in property transferred to a charity does not vest within the period of the rule against perpetuities, it fails unless it would divest a valid interest in another charity, in which case it does not fail on the ground of the rule against perpetuities, even though the divestiture does not occur within the period of the rule."

See Gray, Rule Against Perpetuities §§597-603.8 (4th ed. 1942); 6 American Law of Property §24.40 (1952); Simes & Smith, The Law of Future Interests §1280 (2d ed. 1956); Chaffin, The Rule Against Perpetuities as Applied to Georgia Wills and Trusts: A Survey and Suggestions for Reform, 16 Ga. L. Rev. 235 (1982) (citing the text and criticizing the rule).

revert to the settlor or his heirs, nor will the doctrine of cy pres be applicable, but the property will be held upon the alternative trust designated by the settlor.[2] It may be provided by the terms of the trust that the gift over shall take effect on the failure to comply with the directions as to the administration of the trust. The leading case is *Christ's Hospital v. Grainger,* [3] where a bequest was made to the corporation of Reading in trust for the poor with a provision that if the corporation should for one year neglect to observe the directions of the will the property should be transferred to the corporation of London in trust for a school.

It has been held that a gift over from charity to charity is valid even though the event upon which the gift over is to take effect is not connected with any of the charitable purposes and may not occur within the period of the rule against perpetuities. Thus it has been held that a gift over from one charity to another may be conditioned on the failure of the trustees of the first charity to keep in repair the tomb or grave of the testator or a third person. As we have seen, a bequest in trust for the perpetual maintenance of a tomb or grave is not a charitable trust and is invalid unless it is otherwise provided by statute.[4] In *In re Tyler,* [5] however, a testator bequeathed money to the trustees of a missionary society and provided that if they should fail to keep his family vault in repair the money should go to a designated educational institution. On a bill for instructions brought by the trustees, it was held that the gift over was valid. The court said

---

[2]In First Church in Somerville v. Attorney Gen., 375 Mass. 332, 376 N.E.2d 1226 (1978), a testator who died in 1881 left the residue to a Unitarian church for certain purposes, and provided that if it should change its religious tenets and cease to inculcate a liberal religion, the legacy should go to two designated charitable organizations. The church ceased to exist. It was held that the property should go to the remaindermen.

But see Matter of Booker, 37 Wash. App. 708, 682 P.2d 320, *review denied,* 102 Wash. 2d 1010 (1984), §401.9, n. 10.

[3]16 Sim. 83, 1 Mac. & G. 460 (1849).

[4]See §124.2.

[5][1891]3 Ch. 252.

In Royal Socy. for the Prevention of Cruelty to Animals, N.S.W. v. Benevolent Socy. for N.S.W., 102 C.L.R. 629 (Austl. 1960) where the first trust was held to be noncharitable and invalid, it was held that the gift over to the other charity was invalid and that there was a resulting trust for the settlor's estate.

that a provision that a part of the money bequeathed should be applied to the repair of the vault would have been invalid, but that a gift over of the money from one charity to another was valid even though conditioned on the failure to keep the vault in repair. If any part of the property bequeathed is to be applied to the maintenance of the vault, the trust as to that part is invalid, and a gift over to a charity on the failure to maintain the vault is invalid, because it is a gift over from a noncharitable purpose to a charity that may not vest within the period of the rule against perpetuities.[6] Similarly, where property is bequeathed in trust for a charitable purpose and it is provided that if the trustees should fail to maintain the vault there should be a gift over to a noncharitable purpose, the gift over is invalid.[7] On the other hand, although a gift over for a noncharitable purpose is invalid, a provision that the property shall revert to the settlor or his heirs on the failure to maintain the vault is valid. In *In re Chardon*[8] the court upheld a bequest to trustees to pay the income to a cemetery corporation so long as a grave

---

[6]In re Barker, 25 T.L.R. 753 (1909).

In In re Dalziel, [1943] Ch. 277, noted in 8 Convey. (N.S.) 166, 60 Law Q. Rev. 26, 196 Law T. 74, 11 Sol. 36, a testatrix bequeathed a large sum of money to a hospital corporation, and provided that the income should be used so far as necessary for the upkeep and rebuilding of a mausoleum, and that if the corporation should fail to carry out this purpose the legacy should go to another charity, to be selected by the trustees, that should be willing to accept the legacy subject to the same conditions. It was held that the legacy failed altogether.

In In re Martin, [1952] W.N. 339, a testatrix left half of the residue in trust to pay to a hospital upon trust to keep certain graves in repair, with a provision that if at any time the graves should fall into disrepair the property should be paid over to another charity. It was held that although the trust to keep the graves in repair was invalid, the gift over was valid. See §398.2.

See §401.7. Adoption of the "wait and see" doctrine may validate a shift from non-charity to charity that occurs within the perpetuity period. See §62.-10.

[7]In re Davies, [1915] 1 Ch. 543. See §401.6. Adoption of the "wait and see" doctrine may validate a shift from charity to non-charity that occurs within the perpetuity period. See §62.10.

[8][1928] Ch. 464, noted in 3 Camb. L.J. 463, 44 Law Q. Rev. 419, 166 Law T. 21, 72 Sol. J. 462.

See §62.10.

should be kept in repair. In *Dunne v. Minsor*[9] a testator bequeathed property to a bishop to hold in trust as a residence for a priest on condition that the priest should at all times see that the graves of the testator and his sister and brother were cared for. The court held that the charitable trust was subject to a valid condition subsequent. So also in order to accomplish his purpose the testator may employ the device of a condition precedent. Thus in *Roche v. M'Dermott*[10] a testator bequeathed money to a charitable society on condition that it should undertake in writing to the executors to keep in repair certain vaults. It was held that this was a valid condition precedent. This particular method of securing the perpetual care of a vault, however, is probably not very effective, because the property would pass to the trustees on the execution of the agreement by them, and it would seem that there is no one who could perpetually enforce the agreement. If, indeed, the court should read into the provisions of the will a condition subsequent, as well as a condition precedent, the testator's purpose would be more likely of fulfillment, because the legacy would be forfeited to his next of kin if the trustees should at any time fail to keep the vault in repair.

These decisions are open to serious objection. Although a gift over from one charitable purpose to another on a remote contingency is valid, it may well be questioned whether such a gift over should be valid where the contingency is wholly unrelated to the charitable purposes. The same objection arises where it is provided that the property held upon a charitable trust shall revert to the settlor or his heirs upon the happening of a contingency unrelated to the charitable purposes. The set-

[9]312 Ill. 333, 143 N.E. 842 (1924).

See also Giblin v. Giblin, 173 Wis. 632, 182 N.W. 357 (1921).

In Giles v. Boston Fatherless & Widows' Socy., 10 Allen 355 (Mass. 1865), Gray, J., doubted whether a provision that a charitable trust should terminate on the failure to maintain a private tomb or burial place was not invalid as tending to create a perpetuity.

See §401.2.

[10][1901] 1 I.R. 394.

In In re Oldfield, [1949] 2 D.L.R. 175 (Man.), where a testator bequeathed money to an association on condition that it would undertake to keep a certain grave in perpetual repair, it was held that if this condition precedent were accepted by the giving of the undertaking, it was immaterial that the undertaking was unenforceable.

tlor is enabled through such provisions to do indirectly what he cannot do directly. If it is against public policy to permit the settlor to create a trust for the perpetual maintenance of a vault or tomb, it would seem to be against public policy to permit him through the creation of a charitable trust indirectly to secure this result. Professor Gray suggested that it might be possible in this way to provide for the perpetual endowment of the settlor's family by a gift of land or money to one college on condition that if it did not pay a certain amount each year to the persons who should then be the heirs of the donor, the land or money should go to another college.[11] The only cases in which indirect provision has been made for the accomplishment in perpetuity of a noncharitable purpose through a charitable trust terminable on the failure to carry out the purpose are the cases cited above involving the perpetual maintenance of a vault or tomb. It is to be hoped that if these cases are not overruled, at least they will not be extended to include other noncharitable purposes.

A condition on which a gift over from charity to charity is to take effect may be invalid as against public policy. In such a case the original charitable trust will not terminate and the gift over will not take effect. Thus in *Matter of Sterne*[12] a testator left money in trust to pay the income to a hospital on condition that it should make a binding rule to the effect that all physicians practicing in the hospital should be required to pay toward its support 10 percent of the fees that they should receive for services performed by them in the hospital, and in the event that it should refuse to make such a rule or should abrogate it or neglect to enforce it, the trust should cease and the money should be paid to the Salvation Army. The court held that the condition was in violation of public policy as compelling fee-splitting, which is prohibited by the canons of ethics of the medical profession, and which would tend to result in the loss of the services of physicians who would refuse to subscribe to the practice and in overcharges by other physicians. Accord-

---

[11]Gray, Rule Against Perpetuities §603.4 (4th ed. 1942).

Chaffin, The Rule Against Perpetuities as Applied to Georgia Wills and Trusts: A Survey and Suggestions for Reform, 16 Ga. L. Rev. 235 (1982) (citing the text).

[12]147 Misc. 59, 263 N.Y.S. 304 (1933).

ingly, the court held that the income should be paid to the hospital free from any condition.

§401.6. Gift over from charity to non-charity. Where property is given in trust for charitable purposes, and it is provided that upon the happening of a designated event the property shall be conveyed to individual beneficiaries, the gift over is valid if the event must happen within the period of the rule against perpetuities.[1] Even if the event may not happen within the period of the rule against perpetuities, the gift over is valid if it is a vested gift at the time of the creation of the trust, or if it must vest, if at all, within the period. Thus in *Holsey v. Atlantic National Bank,*[2] where a testator left money in trust to use the income for scholarships or as a student loan fund for 30 years and then to divide the money among named individuals, it was held that the provision for the distribution of the money among the beneficiaries was valid because their interests became vested at the time of the death of the testator.

On the other hand, the gift over is invalid if it is not for charitable purposes and may not vest within the period of the rule against perpetuities.[3] Thus if property is given in trust for

---

§401.6. [1]Will of Jaeger, 218 Wis. 1, 259 N.W. 842, 99 A.L.R. 738 (1935). [2]115 Fla. 604, 155 So. 821 (1934).

[3]*England:* In re Randell, 38 Ch. D. 213 (1888), *semble;* In re Bowen, [1893] 2 Ch. 491; In re Blunt's Trusts, [1904] 2 Ch. 767, *semble;* In re DaCosta, [1912] 1 Ch. 337; In re Peel's Release, [1921] 2 Ch. 218; In re Talbot, [1933] 1 Ch. 895, *semble,* noted in 50 Law Q. Rev. 21, 1 Sol. 5; In re Engels, [1943] 1 All E.R. 506, noted in 17 Austl. L.J. 219, 8 Convey. (N.S.) 35, 93 Law J. 171, 286, 333, 59 Law Q. Rev. 201, 6 Mod. L. Rev. 242; In re Cooper's Conveyance Trusts, [1956] 3 All E.R. 28, noted in 34 Can. B. Rev. 1066.

Illinois: Green v. Old People's Home, 269 Ill. 134, 109 N.E. 701 (1915).

Kansas: Nelson v. Kring, 255 Kan. 499, 592 P.2d 438 (1979) (citing the text).

Maryland: Starr v. Starr Methodist Protestant Church, 112 Md. 171, 76 A. 595 (1910); McMahon v. Consistory of St. Paul's Reformed Church, 196 Md. 125, 75 A.2d 122 (1950).

Massachusetts: Proprietors of the Church in Brattle Square v. Grant, 3 Gray 142, 63 Am. Dec. 725 (Mass. 1855); Wells v. Heath, 10 Gray 17 (Mass. 1857); Odell v. Odell, 10 Allen 1, 7 (Mass. 1865), *semble;* Society for Promoting Theological Educ. v. Attorney Gen., 135 Mass. 285 (1883); First Universalist Socy. of N. Adams v. Boland, 155 Mass. 171, 29 N.E. 524, 15 L.R.A. 231 (1892); Davenport v. Attorney Gen., 361 Mass. 372, 280 N.E.2d 193 (1972) (citing the text and Restatement of Trusts §401).

charitable purposes and it is provided that if the trustees should at any time fail to apply the property as directed it should be conveyed to a third person and his heirs, the gift over is invalid. So also if property is given in trust for charitable purposes until a certain event should happen, and it is provided that on the happening of the event the property should be conveyed to a third person and his heirs, the gift over is invalid.

Where the gift over is invalid, the question arises whether the charitable trust continues or whether there is a resulting trust for the settlor or his heirs. As we have seen, a provision that the property shall revert to the settlor or his heirs on the termi-

---

Missouri: Donehue v. Nilges, 364 Mo. 705, 266 S.W.2d 553, 45 A.L.R.2d 1150 (1954).

New Hampshire: Rolfe & Rumford Asylum v. LeFebre, 69 N.H. 238, 45 A. 1087 (1897).

Ohio: Church of Christ, E. Seventh Ave. v. Ezzell, 95 Ohio Abs. 89, 202 N.E.2d 212 (1964).

Oregon: City of Klamath Falls v. Bell, 7 Or. App. 330, 490 P.2d 515 (1971).

Pennsylvania: Pruner Estate, 400 Pa. 629, 162 A.2d 626 (1960), noted in 22 U. Pitt. L. Rev. 277.

Rhode Island: Palmer v. Union Bank, 17 R.I. 627, 24 A. 109 (1892).

West Virginia: Woman's Club of St. Albans v. James, 158 W. Va. 698, 213 S.E.2d 469 (1975).

In In re Bawden's Settlement, [1953] 2 All E.R. 1235, by a settlement in 1905 the trustees were directed to distribute the income among several charitable institutions, and it was provided that if any of them should become amalgamated with any other charity, the trustees might pay the share to the amalgamated institution or might pay the income to such other objects of "charity or benevolence or amelioration of human suffering or advancement of knowledge" as the trustees should consider to be most in accordance with the settlor's intention. It was held that the gift over was not limited to charitable objects and was invalid under the rule against perpetuities. See §123.

See Note, Application of rule against perpetuities to limitation over on discontinuance of use for which premises are given or granted, or the commencement of a prohibited use, 45 A.L.R.2d 1154 (1956).

In Harrison v. Marcus, 396 Mass. 424, 486 N.E.2d 710 (1985), land was conveyed to trustees for a Boy Scout troop with a proviso that if the troop ceased to exist, the trustees should convey to the settlor or his heirs. It was held that the gift over was subject to the rule against perpetuities but that it did not fail because, by application of the wait and see doctrine, it appeared that the interest of the heirs actually vested at a time that was not too remote.

See Restatement of Property §396. But adoption of the "wait and see" doctrine may validate a shift from charity to non-charity that occurs within the perpetuity period. See Restatement (Second) of Property (Donative Transfers), §1.6, Illustration 4 (1979).

nation of a charitable trust is valid.[4] The difficulty is that where there is a gift over the settlor has provided that the property shall go to a third person and shall not revert to himself or his heirs. Where the gift over is valid the interest in the property will pass to the person designated and will not revert. If the settlor has expressed an intention as to what should be done with the property if the gift over should be invalid, his intention is controlling on the question whether the trust shall not terminate or whether the property shall revert to him or his heirs. The difficulty arises where he has expressed no such intention.

Where property is conveyed to trustees to hold it upon a charitable trust so long as a certain state of affairs continues and it is provided that if the state of affairs should cease the property should pass to a third person or be used for noncharitable purposes, the charitable trust terminates when the state of affairs ceases, although the gift over is invalid; and the donor or his heirs are entitled to the property.[5] In *Yarbrough v. Yarbrough*[6] the owner of land conveyed it to trustees for so long as it should be used for the site of a Baptist church, and then to the person who might own the adjoining land. It was held that the gift over was invalid for remoteness, but that the grantor was entitled to the land when it ceased to be used as a site for the church. In *Brown v. Independent Baptist Church*[7] a testator devised land to a church for so long as it should retain its present religious beliefs and

---

[4]See §401.2.

[5]*Massachusetts:* First Universalist Socy. of N. Adams v. Boland, 155 Mass. 171, 29 N.E. 524, 15 L.R.A. 231 (1892); Institution for Sav. in Roxbury v. Roxbury Home for Aged Women, 244 Mass. 583, 139 N.E. 301 (1923).

Mississippi: Jones v. Burns, 221 Miss. 833, 74 So. 2d 866 (1954).

Missouri: Donehue v. Nilges, 364 Mo. 705, 266 S.W.2d 553, 45 A.L.R.2d 1150 (1954).

Oregon: City of Klamath Falls v. Bell, 7 Or. App. 330, 490 P.2d 515 (1971).

Tennessee: Yarbrough v. Yarbrough, 151 Tenn. 221, 269 S.W. 36 (1924).

West Virginia: Woman's Club of St. Albans v. James, 213 S.E.2d 469 (W. Va. 1975).

The result is the same where there is an express gift to the settlor's estate. In re Randell, 38 Ch. D. 213 (1888); In re Blunt's Trusts, [1904] 2 Ch. 767.

[6]151 Tenn. 221, 269 S.W. 36 (1924).

[7]325 Mass. 645, 91 N.E.2d 922 (1950), noted in 64 Harv. L. Rev. 864.

On the question whether the property goes to the heir or next of kin or whether it falls into the residue, see §399.3.

continue as a church, with a gift over to named devisees. It was held that the gift over was invalid, but that on the termination of the interest of the church the property passed to the residuary devisees. In cases like this it is said that a limited interest is given to the charity, and the interest given will not be enlarged merely because of the failure of the gift over.

On the other hand, where property is given upon a charitable trust for an indefinite period but subject to a condition subsequent, it is not so clear whether on breach of the condition the charitable trust terminates if there is an invalid gift over. It is generally held, however, that the charitable trust will not terminate.[8]

---

[8]*England:* In re Bowen, [1893] 2 Ch. 491; In re Da Costa, [1912] 1 Ch. 337; In re Peel's Release, [1921] 2 Ch. 218; In re Talbot, [1933] Ch. 895, noted in 50 Law Q. Rev. 21, 1 Sol. 5.

Maryland: Starr v. Starr Methodist Protestant Church, 112 Md. 171, 76 A. 595 (1910); McMahon v. Consistory of St. Paul's Reformed Church, 196 Md. 125, 75 A.2d 122 (1950).

Massachusetts: Proprietors of the Church in Brattle Square v. Grant, 3 Gray 142, 63 Am. Dec. 725 (Mass. 1855); Wells v. Heath, 10 Gray 17 (Mass. 1857); Society for Promoting Theological Educ. v. Attorney Gen., 135 Mass. 285 (1883); Davenport v. Attorney Gen., 361 Mass. 372, 280 N.E.2d 193 (1972) (citing the text and Restatement of Trusts §401).

New Hampshire: Rolfe & Rumford Asylum v. LeFebre, 69 N.H. 238, 45 A. 1087 (1897).

New York: Edward John Noble Hosp. v. Board of Foreign Missions, 13 Misc. 2d 918, 176 N.Y.S.2d 157 (1958); United Methodist Church v. Dobbins, 48 A.D.2d 485, 369 N.Y.S.2d 817 (1975).

Rhode Island: Palmer v. Union Bank, 17 R.I. 627, 24 A. 109 (1892).

But see *contra* Green v. Old People's Home, 269 Ill. 134, 109 N.E. 701 (1915).

In Moses H. Cone Memorial Hosp. v. Cone, 231 N.C. 292, 56 S.E.2d 709 (1949), the court found it unnecessary to decide as to the validity and effect of a provision for forfeiture to the heirs of the settlor's deceased husband.

In In re Cooper's Conveyance Trusts, [1956] 3 All E.R. 28, noted in 34 Can. B. Rev. 1066, where land was conveyed in 1864 to establish an orphanage with a gift over on failure of the orphanage, and the gift over was invalid because it was noncharitable and violated the rule against perpetuities, it was held that on the failure of the orphanage the doctrine of cy pres was not applicable and a resulting trust arose.

In Pruner Estate, 400 Pa. 629, 162 A.2d 626 (1960), noted in 109 U. Pa. L. Rev. 433, 22 U. Pitt. L. Rev. 277, where a devise was made to provide a home for friendless children, with a gift over to the testator's niece if the purpose should fail, and the trust failed, the court held that the doctrine of cy pres was

§401.7. Gift over from non-charity to charity.

Where property is given in trust for noncharitable purposes with a gift over for charitable purposes, the gift over is valid if it is from the outset a vested gift.[1] Thus where a testator left his estate in trust to pay the income to his daughter for life and to her children for their lives and on their death to a charitable corporation, the gift to the corporation is valid, because it is a vested and not a

---

not applicable and that the gift over to the niece was invalid as violating the rule against perpetuities and that a resulting trust arose for the testator's heirs.

In Nelson v. Kring, 225 Kan. 499, 592 P.2d 438 (1979), a testator who died in 1931 made a bequest in trust to pay the income to a hospital. He provided that if it should fail to be operated for a year the fund should be paid to a George Green, or if he should be dead, to his heirs. He also provided that if any bequest should be adjudged void, it should go to Green. In 1972 the hospital ceased to operate. It was held that the gift over to Green was invalid under the rule against perpetuities, that the trust property should not be applied cy pres by giving it to another hospital, and that there was a resulting trust to the heirs of Green as residuary legatees and not to the testator's next of kin. The court cited the text.

§401.7. [1]*Massachusetts:* Seaver v. Fitzgerald, 141 Mass. 401, 6 N.E. 73 (1886).

New York: Matter of Myles, 5 Misc. 2d 163, 159 N.Y.S.2d 434 (1956), *semble.*

Pennsylvania: Gageby's Estate, 293 Pa. 109, 141 A. 842 (1928); Lockhart Estate, 26 D.&C.2d 701 (Pa. 1962).

Texas: Frost Natl. Bank v. Boyd, 188 S.W.2d 199 (Tex. Civ. App. 1945) (citing Restatement of Trusts §401), *aff'd sub nom.* Boyd v. Frost Natl. Bank, 145 Tex. 206, 196 S.W.2d 497 (1946), noted in 25 Tex. L. Rev. 434.

Canada: Richards v. Central Trust Co., 16 E.T.R. 1 (N.B.Q.B. 1983).

In Fidelity Union Trust Co. v. Egenolf Day Nursery Assn., 64 N.J. Super. 445, 166 A.2d 402 (1960), a testatrix left her estate in trust to pay the income to her sister for life and on her death to pay the income to a charitable corporation. She provided that, if the corporation should cease to function during the lifetime of her next of kin or their children, she gave the principal to them, and that, if it should continue to function until after the death of her next of kin and their children, the principal should be paid to the corporation. It was held that the gift of the principal to the corporation was not invalid under the rule against perpetuities, because its continuing to function was not a condition precedent. The gift was subject to a condition subsequent under which the property would revert if the corporation should cease to function during the lives of the next of kin and their children. The court cited the text, §401.2.

See §62.10, n. 30.

contingent gift, although the enjoyment by the charitable corporation is postponed until the death of the children of the testator's daughter who might not be born at the time of his death.

Even though the gift over for charitable purposes is contingent, it is valid if it must vest, if at all, within the period of the rule against perpetuities.[2] Thus if a testator leaves property in trust for his son for life and on the death of the son for his children but if the son dies without children living at his death, then for charitable purposes the gift over to charity is valid. The gift must vest, if at all, on the death of the son. So also where a testator bequeathed property in trust for his children for life and on the death of the survivor to convey the property to a state for certain charitable purposes, provided that the state should first enact legislation making provision for the application of the property to these purposes, it was held that the bequest was valid because the required legislation was to be enacted, if at all, within a reasonable time after the death of the life beneficiaries, and the vesting of the interest for the charitable purposes was not too remote.[3]

On the other hand, if property is given for noncharitable purposes with a contingent gift over to charity upon an event that may not occur within the period of the rule against per-

---

[2]Walliser v. Northern Trust Co., 338 Ill. App. 263, 87 N.E.2d 129 (1949).

See Breault v. Feigenholtz, 250 F. Supp. 551 (N.D. Ill. 1965), *aff'd,* 358 F.2d 39 (7th Cir. 1966).

In In re Regan, 8 D.L.R.2d 541 (N.S. 1957), a testatrix left the residue in trust to educate two named boys for the priesthood, and if they should decide not to study for the priesthood then for some worthy boy designated by the parish priest. It was held that even if the gift to the boys was not charitable the gift over was valid because it must occur before the expiration of lives in being. The court was of the opinion that the provision for the boys was charitable.

See Restatement (Second) of Property (Donative Transfers), §1.6, stated in §401.5, n. 1.

See Note, Remoteness of Vesting and the Charitable Trust, 31 Fordham L. Rev. 782 (1963).

[3]Bell v. Nesmith, 217 Mass. 254, 104 N.E. 721 (1914).

See Smith v. Townsend, 32 Pa. 434 (1859); Stephan's Estate, 129 Pa. Super. 396, 195 A. 653 (1937); In re Metcalfe, [1947] 1 D.L.R. 567 (Ont.).

See Restatement of Property §396.

petuities, the gift over is invalid.[4] Thus it has been held that where land was conveyed to a bank to use so long as it should exist and when the bank should cease to exist it was to be conveyed to a charitable institution, the gift over was invalid.[5] In *Talbot v. Riggs*[6] a testator bequeathed property in trust to pay the income to his needy descendants so long as there should be any, but "failing all such descendants" to a charity. The court held that the trust for needy descendants was not charitable and therefore failed, and that the contingent gift over to charity on an event that might not happen within the period of the rule against perpetuities was also invalid.

Where the gift over to charity is invalid for remoteness, the question arises whether the prior noncharitable gift is absolute or whether the settlor or his heirs can get back the property. The

---

[4]*England:* Attorney-General v. Gill, 2 P. Wms. 369 (1726); In re Johnson's Trusts, L.R. 2 Eq. 716 (1866); In re Wightwick's Will Trusts, [1950] Ch. 260, noted in 14 Convey. (N.S.) 180, 94 Sol. J. 513.

Kentucky: Smith v. Fowler, 301 Ky. 96, 190 S.W.2d 1015 (1945); Letcher's Trustee v. Letcher, 302 Ky. 448, 194 S.W.2d 984 (1946).

Maine: Merritt v. Bucknam, 77 Me. 253 (1885).

Massachusetts: Odell v. Odell, 10 Allen 1, 7 (Mass. 1865); Institution for Sav. in Roxbury v. Roxbury Home for Aged Women, 244 Mass. 583, 139 N.E. 301 (1923); Talbot v. Riggs, 287 Mass. 144, 191 N.E. 360, 93 A.L.R. 964 (1934), noted in 15 B.U.L. Rev. 404, 19 Minn. L. Rev. 127, 2 U. Chi. L. Rev. 156.

New Hampshire: Merrill v. American Baptist Missionary Union, 73 N.H. 414, 62 A. 647, 3 L.R.A. (N.S.) 1143, 111 Am. St. Rep. 632 (1905).

New Jersey: American Natl. Bank of Camden v. Morgenweck, 114 N.J. Eq. 286, 168 A. 598 (1933), *aff'd,* 118 N.J. Eq. 269, 178 A. 727 (1935).

New York: Leonard v. Burr, 18 N.Y. 96, 107 (1858).

Texas: Atkinson v. Kettler, 372 S.W.2d 704 (Tex. Civ. App. 1963) (citing the text), *aff'd. sub nom.* Kettler v. Atkinson, 383 S.W.2d 557 (Tex. 1964).

Ireland: Commissioners of Charitable Donations v. De Clifford, 1 Dr. & War. 245 (1841); In re Macnamara, [1943] I.R. 372.

The adoption of the "wait and see" doctrine may validate such a contingent gift over if it actually vests within the perpetuity period. See Restatement (Second) of Property (Donative Transfers), §1.6, Illustration 2 (1979); Simes & Smith, The Law of Future Interests §§1281-1283 (2d ed. 1956 and 1987 Pocket Part by Fratcher); §62.10.

[5]Institution for Sav. in Roxbury v. Roxbury Home for Aged Women, 244 Mass. 583, 139 N.E. 301 (1923).

[6]287 Mass. 144, 191 N.E. 360, 93 A.L.R. 964 (1934), noted in 15 B.U.L. Rev. 404, 19 Minn. L. Rev. 127, 2 U. Chi. L. Rev. 156.

question is similar to that which arises where there is a gift over from charity to non-charity.[7] Where the property was given to an individual until the happening of a certain event and then over to charity, it was held that, although the gift to charity was invalid for remoteness, the prior gift terminated and the settlor or his heirs were entitled to the property.[8] Similarly, where property was given to a noncharitable corporation so long as it should exist and when it should cease to exist to a charitable organization, it was held that the gift over was invalid but that when the noncharitable corporation ceased to exist the property reverted to the settlor's heirs.[9]

On the other hand, where property is devised to an individual and it is provided that if he should make a certain use of the property it should go over to charity, the gift over is void for remoteness and the original devisee takes the property absolutely.[10]

§401.8. **Gift to charity without intermediate disposition.** Property may be given to be applied to charitable purposes in the future, the donor making no provision for the disposition of the property in the meantime. In such a case the charitable trust is invalid if it is contingent upon an event that may not happen within the period of the rule against perpetuities.[1] Thus in *In re Lord Stratheden and*

[7]See §401.6.

[8]Leonard v. Burr, 18 N.Y. 96 (1858).

[9]Institution for Sav. in Roxbury v. Roxbury Home for Aged Women, 244 Mass. 583, 139 N.E. 301 (1923).

[10]Smith v. Townsend, 32 Pa. 434 (1859).

§401.8. [1]*England:* In re Lord Stratheden & Campbell, [1894] 3 Ch. 265; In re Mander, [1950] Ch. 547.

See Worthing Corp. v. Heather, [1906] 2 Ch. 532 (option to purchase).

Georgia: Murphy v. Johnston, 190 Ga. 23, 8 S.E.2d 23 (1940).

New York: Matter of Roe, 281 N.Y. 541, 24 N.E.2d 322, 131 A.L.R. 707 (1939) (quoting Restatement of Trusts, §401, Comment *j*), noted in 17 N.Y.U.L.Q. Rev. 474, 49 Yale L.J. 1112; In re Miller's Estate, 139 N.Y.S.2d 5 (1954).

Canada: Jewish Home for the Aged v. Toronto Gen. Trusts Corp., [1961] S.C.R. 465 (Can.), *semble.*

Ireland: Kingham v. Kingham, [1897] 1 I.R. 170.

But adoption of the "wait and see" doctrine may validate such a contin-

Campbell[2] a testator left property in trust to pay an annuity to a military organization on the appointment of the next lieutenant colonel. It was held that the disposition was invalid because it was on a contingency that might not happen within the period of the rule against perpetuities. In the Irish case of *Kingham v. Kingham,*[3] where a testator devised land to trustees for a charitable purpose if the trustees of another charity should sell certain premises and pay the proceeds to his trustees, it was held that the devise was invalid because it was upon a condition precedent that might not be performed within the period of the rule against perpetuities.

The same principle has been applied in New York, where it is to be remembered that prior to 1958 the absolute ownership of personal property could not be suspended for longer than the duration of two lives.[4] In *Matter of Roe*[5] a testator left his property in trust for his nephew if he should be found within two

---

gent gift to charity if the event actually occurs within the perpetuity period. See Restatement (Second) of Property (Donative Transfers), §1.6 (1979); Simes & Smith, The Law of Future Interests §1281 (2d ed. 1956 and 1987 Pocket Part by Fratcher); §62.10.

In In re Kagan, [1966] V.R. 538, a testator gave the income to named charitable institutions for 21 years, and directed that at the end of 21 years the properties were to be sold and the proceeds paid to the institutions for the purpose of erecting buildings, which should be named "Cohen Memorial." He provided that the naming of the buildings was a condition precedent to the payment of the proceeds to the institutions. It was held (one judge dissenting) that the gift of the proceeds failed, because the naming of the buildings might take place more than 21 years after the death of the testator. This seems to be an extremely technical decision.

[2][1894] 3 Ch. 265.

[3][1897] 1 I.R. 170.

[4]New York Personal Property Law, §11 was amended by Laws 1958, c. 152, and by Laws 1959, c. 456, by substituting for two lives, any number of lives unless so designated or so numerous as to make proof of their end unreasonably difficult; and by Laws 1960, c. 448, by permitting also a term of not more than 21 years.

Personal Property Law, §11 is superseded by Estates, Powers and Trusts Law, §9-1.1. See §62.10.

[5]281 N.Y. 541, 24 N.E.2d 322, 131 A.L.R. 707 (1939) (quoting Restatement of Trusts, §401, Comment *j*), noted in 17 N.Y.U.L.Q. Rev. 474, 49 Yale L.J. 1112.

years, otherwise for certain charitable purposes. The nephew was not found in spite of diligent search. It was held that the gift to charity was invalid, because the failure to find the nephew was a condition precedent and there was not an immediate gift to charity.

If there is an immediate vested gift to charity, however, the gift is valid although it is provided that the property shall not be applied to the charitable purposes until the happening of an event that may not occur within the period of the rule against perpetuities.[6] The question in each case is whether the gift to charity is subject to a condition precedent or whether there is an immediate unconditional gift to charity. Although the particular method of applying the property to charitable purposes may be subject to a condition precedent that may not happen within the period of the rule against perpetuities, the charitable trust does not fail if the testator had a general unconditional intention to devote the property to charitable purposes.

A common situation is that which arises where a testator leaves property to or in trust for a corporation to be organized after his death for certain charitable purposes. The bequest is of course valid if the corporation must be organized within the period of the rule against perpetuities.[7] Even if the corporation may not be organized within that period, the bequest is nevertheless valid if the testator had a general intention to devote the

---

[6]*Illinois:* Community Unit School Dist. No. 4 v. Booth, 1 Ill. 2d 545, 116 N.E.2d 161 (1953).

Massachusetts: Peakes v. Blakely, 333 Mass. 281, 130 N.E.2d 564 (1955) (citing Restatement of Trusts, §401, Comment *k*).

New Jersey: Wendell v. Hazel Wood Cemetery, 7 N.J. Super. 117, 72 A.2d 383 (1950) (quoting the text and citing Restatement of Trusts, §401, Comment *k*), *aff'g* 3 N.J. Super. 457, 67 A.2d 219 (1949).

New York: National City Bank of N.Y. v. Beebe, 155 N.Y.S.2d 347 (1956) (Rhode Island law).

See Matter of Myles, 5 Misc. 2d 163, 159 N.Y.S.2d 434 (1956).

[7]*Maryland:* Gray v. Orphans' Home, 128 Md. 592, 98 A. 202 (1916).

Minnesota: Watkins v. Bigelow, 93 Minn. 210, 100 N.W. 1104 (1904).

New York: Burrill v. Boardman, 43 N.Y. 254, 3 Am. Rep. 694 (1871); St. John v. Andrews Inst., 191 N.Y. 254, 83 N.E. 981 (1908), *writ of error dismissed sub nom.* Smithsonian Inst. v. St. John, 214 U.S. 19, 29 S. Ct. 601, 53 L. Ed. 892 (1909).

property to the specified charitable purposes.[8] In such a case

[8]*Federal:* Inglis v. Sailor's Snug Harbour, 3 Pet. 99, 7 L. Ed. 617 (1830); Ould v. Washington Hosp., 95 U.S. 303, 24 L. Ed. 450 (1877).

Alabama: Baxley v. Birmingham Trust Natl. Bank, 334 So. 2d 848 (Ala. 1976).

Arizona: In re Harber's Estate, 99 Ariz. 323, 409 P.2d 31 (1965) (citing the text and Restatement of Trusts, §401, Comment *j*).

California: In re Estate of Lamb, 19 Cal. App. 3d 859, 97 Cal. Rptr. 46 (1971) (the testatrix believed the charitable corporation was already in existence but it was created four months after her death; the court held that cy pres was applicable, citing the text).

Connecticut: Coit v. Comstock, 51 Conn. 352 (1884); Hoenig v. Lubetkin, 137 Conn. 516, 79 A.2d 278 (1951).

Georgia: Taylor v. Trustees of Jesse Parker Williams Hosp., 190 Ga. 349, 9 S.E.2d 165 (1940).

Illinois: Franklin v. Hastings, 253 Ill. 46, 97 N.E. 265 (1912); Jansen v. Godair, 292 Ill. 364, 127 N.E. 97 (1920).

Iowa: Wilson v. First Natl. Bank, 164 Iowa 402, 145 N.W. 948 (1914); Palmer v. Evans, 255 Iowa 1176, 124 N.W.2d 856 (1963) (quoting the text).

Kansas: In re Estate of Loomis, 202 Kan. 668, 451 P.2d 195 (1968), *semble.*

Louisiana: H. C. Drew Manual Training School v. Calcasieu Natl. Bank, 194 La. 790, 189 So. 137 (1939).

Maryland: Second Natl. Bank v. Second Natl. Bank, 171 Md. 547, 190 A. 215, 111 A.L.R. 711 (1937).

Massachusetts: Codman v. Brigham, 187 Mass. 309, 72 N.E. 1008 (1905).

New Jersey: Ferguson v. Rippel, 19 N.J. Super. 424, 88 A.2d 647 (1952).

But see First Camden Natl. Bank & Trust Co. v. Collins, 114 N.J. Eq. 59, 168 A. 275 (1933) (trust to accumulate income for lives of young children and 21 years and then to form a charitable corporation).

New York: Matter of Potts, 205 A.D. 147, 199 N.Y.S. 880 (1923), *aff'd mem.,* 236 N.Y. 658, 142 N.E. 323 (1923); Maynard v. Farmers' Loan & Trust Co., 208 A.D. 112, 203 N.Y.S. 83 (1924), *aff'd mem.,* 238 N.Y. 592, 144 N.E. 905 (1924); In re Duprea, 6 N.Y.S.2d 555 (1938) (citing Restatement of Trusts, §401, Comment *k*); Matter of Freund, 33 Misc. 2d 6, 226 N.Y.S.2d 620 (1962).

But see Cruikshank v. Chase, 113 N.Y. 337, 21 N.E. 64 (1889).

North Dakota: In re Myra Found., 112 N.W.2d 552 (N.D. 1961).

Ohio: Rice v. Stanley, 42 Ohio St. 2d 209, 327 N.E.2d 774 (1975) (quoting the text and Restatement of Trusts, §401, Comment *j*), noted in 37 Ohio St. L.J. 685.

Texas: Taysom v. El Paso Natl. Bank, 256 S.W.2d 172 (Tex. Civ. App. 1952).

Virginia: Thomas v. Bryant, 185 Va. 845, 40 S.E.2d 487 (1946).

In Baxley v. Birmingham Trust Natl. Bank, 334 So. 2d 848 (Ala. 1976) (quoting the text), a testatrix, who had a general power of appointment, appointed to "The Allan-Bryant Educational Foundation," and directed that if this corporation was not in existence on her death, her executor should create it in accordance with the terms that she had given to a certain law firm.

there is an immediate gift to charity subject to no condition precedent; and although the particular mode of application is subject to such a condition, that does not invalidate the gift. The general charitable intention of the testator will be effectuated even though the particular method of application specified by him should fail. Where the gift is valid the court will exercise its discretion as to the mode of administering it. If the corporation is formed within a reasonable time, the court will direct that the corporation receive the property. If it appears that the corporation will not be formed within a reasonable time, the court will not wait until it is formed but will direct the application of the property in some other manner to the designated charitable purposes.

There are other situations in which a charitable disposition has been upheld on the ground that there was an immediate and unconditional gift to charity, although the particular method of applying the property might not be possible within the period of the rule against perpetuities.[9] Thus where a testator directs that his land should be sold when business conditions should

---

It was not created prior to her death. The court held (one judge dissenting) that the disposition failed because it could not be supported either on the ground of incorporation by reference or of resorting to facts of independent significance. But query.

See Gray, Rule Against Perpetuities §§607-628 (4th ed. 1942).

By Maryland Ann. Code, Estates and Trusts Article, §4-409, it is provided that no devise or bequest for any charitable uses shall be void if the will directs the formation of a corporation to take the same, and within 12 months from the grant of probate, if the devise or bequest is immediate or within 12 months after the expiration of preceding life estates, a corporation shall be formed capable and willing to receive and administer the devise or bequest.

[9]*New Jersey:* Litcher v. Trust Co. of New Jersey, 11 N.J. 64, 93 A.2d 368 (1952), *aff'g* 18 N.J. Super. 101, 86 A.2d 601 (1952).

South Dakota: In re McNair's Estate, 74 S.D. 369, 53 N.W.2d 210 (1952).

Canada: In re Doering, [1949] 1 D.L.R. 267 (Ont.); In re Pearse, [1955] 1 D.L.R. 801 (B.C.).

In Matter of Cohen, 198 Misc. 466, 96 N.Y.S.2d 398 (1950), a testator gave a legacy to his executors in trust to be paid to a certain charitable institution if it should operate a building as a home for the aged or for orphans within five years of his death, with a gift over, if it should fail to do so within the prescribed time, to the legatees then living. At his death it did not operate such a home. It was held that the gift was valid, the court taking the view that there was an immediate vesting subject to postponement of beneficial enjoyment.

improve, and the proceeds paid to a charity, the bequest does not fail because there is an unconditional gift to charity at the outset.[10] So also a provision postponing the payment of a legacy to a charity for a number of years does not invalidate the legacy because the bequest is not conditional, but the legacy will be payable at the expiration of the period of administration.[11] In a case in Alabama,[12] where a testator directed that money was to be applied at the end of 20 years to building and equipping public schools in a certain county, it was held that there was a gift for charitable purposes that vested within the period of the rule against perpetuities, and that it was immaterial that the doctrine of cy pres was not accepted in Alabama at the time of the death of the testator. In a case in Australia,[13] where a testator left his estate to a city "as a nucleus of a fund to provide" a public building, it was held that the gift was not conditional and was not invalid as violating the rule against perpetuities. So also where a testator authorized his executor to turn over the residue of his estate to the officers of a church when the church building should be completed, it was held that the gift was valid.[14] In another case[15] a testator gave a legacy to a church, to be held by his executors in trust until a parochial school in connection with the church should be erected, upon which event they should pay the legacy to the church as an endowment. It was held that there was an immediate vested gift for charitable purposes and that the legacy was valid.

In some cases it is more doubtful whether there is an unconditional gift to charity with payment postponed or whether the gift is subject to a condition precedent that may not be performed within the period of the rule against perpetuities and is

---

[10]Ashmore v. Newman, 350 Ill. 64, 183 N.E. 1 (1932).

[11]Matter of Stulman, 146 Misc. 861, 263 N.Y.S. 197 (1933).

[12]Henderson v. Troy Bank & Trust Co., 250 Ala. 456, 34 So. 2d 835 (1948). The court reached the same result on a subsequent appeal. Tumlin v. Troy Bank & Trust Co., 258 Ala. 238, 61 So. 2d 817 (1952) (citing the text), noted in 39 Va. L. Rev. 528.

See Mastin v. First Natl. Bank, 278 Ala. 251, 177 So. 2d 808 (1965).

[13]Monds v. Stackhouse, 77 C.L.R. 232 (Austl. 1948).

[14]Reithmiller v. Carr, 137 Neb. 284, 289 N.W. 338 (1939) (citing Restatement of Trusts, §401, Comment *k*).

[15]Matter of Dean, 167 Misc. 238, 3 N.Y.S.2d 711 (1938).

therefore invalid. This question arises where money is left in trust to assist a church or hospital or school or other institution if such institution should at any time be established. If the gift is contingent on the establishment of the institution, it fails because the contingency is too remote.[16] But if the testator had a more general charitable intention, if the establishment of the institution was not an essential part of his scheme, there is an immediate and unconditional gift to charity, and the gift will not fail but the court will apply the money cy pres.[17] Similarly, where property is given in trust to establish a charitable institution when third persons shall give a site for the institution or shall contribute funds for its support, the gift is valid if it is not contingent on the giving of such a site or the making of such contributions.[18] In such a case, if the site is not given or the contributions made, the court can apply the doctrine of cy pres.

If an immediate gift is made for charitable purposes, the gift is not invalid merely because it is subject to a condition subsequent. Thus in *Bancroft v. Maine State Sanatorium Association*[19] a donor paid a large sum of money to trustees in trust to pay the income to a charitable corporation for 40 years and then to pay it the principal. It was provided that if at any time before the principal was paid to it, it should incur a certain amount of indebtedness, the principal should be paid to a third person or his heirs. The court held that a valid trust was created. It was

---

[16]In re De Bancourt's Estate, 279 Mich. 518, 272 N.W. 891, 110 A.L.R. 1346 (1937); Muir v. Archdall, 19 N.S.W. St. R. 10 (1918) (cathedral).

[17]*England:* Sinnett v. Herbert, 12 Eq. 201 (1871), L.R. 7 Ch. App. 232 (1872) (church); Wallis v. Solicitor-General for N.Z., [1903] A.C. 173 (college).

See Attorney-General v. Bishop of Chester, 1 Bro. C.C. 444 (1785) (for establishing bishop in America).

Federal: Ould v. Washington Hosp., 95 U.S. 303, 24 L. Ed. 450 (1877) (home for foundlings).

Illinois: Franklin v. Hastings, 253 Ill. 46, 97 N.E. 265, Ann. Cas. 1913A 135 (1912) (library).

Washington: In re Galland's Estate, 103 Wash. 106, 173 P. 740 (1918) (orphanage).

[18]Chamberlayne v. Brockett, L.R. 8 Ch. App. 206 (1872); Woodruff v. Marsh, 63 Conn. 125, 26 A. 846, 38 Am. St. Rep. 346 (1893).

See In re Galland's Estate, 103 Wash. 106, 173 P. 740 (1918).

[19]119 Me. 56, 109 A. 585 (1920).

immaterial that the charitable corporation was not to receive the principal until the expiration of a period longer than that of the rule against perpetuities or that its right to receive the income and principal was subject to a condition subsequent. In *Matter of Dettmer*,[20] where a testator left property to a county for a hospital, and provided that if the voters of the county should not accept the gift within two years the property should go to other charities, it was held that the acceptance was not a condition precedent and that the bequest was valid.

§401.9. Provisions for accumulation. Where property is given in trust for charitable purposes, the mere fact that the settlor directs that the income shall be accumulated for a period longer than that of the rule against perpetuities does not necessarily invalidate the trust. In such a case there may be an immediate and unconditional gift to charity, and the gift may be valid even though the provision for accumulation is invalid. Where property is given in trust for charitable purposes with a direction that the income shall be accumulated for a certain period, two questions therefore arise. The first question is as to the validity of the provision for accumulation; the second is as to the validity of the trust.

Validity of the provision. Where there is an immediate and unconditional gift for charitable purposes, there is a difference of opinion as to the validity of a provision for accumulation of the income. Because the gift to charity is not contingent, no question of the remoteness of vesting of the interest is involved, and the rule against perpetuities has no application to the situation. Clearly, however, it would be against public policy to permit accumulation for too long a period, during which period no useful disposition would be made of the property or its income. The question then is what limits should be imposed. The courts might conceivably have taken as the standard the same period

---

[20]178 Misc. 401, 34 N.Y.S.2d 913 (1942), *aff'd mem.*, 266 A.D. 877, 42 N.Y.S.2d 846 (1943), *aff'd mem.*, 292 N.Y. 688, 56 N.E.2d 107 (1944). This case was decided at a time when the New York statute prohibiting suspension of the absolute power of alienation for more than two lives in being was deemed to prohibit suspension for any period in gross whatever, even a single day. Fratcher, Perpetuities and Other Restraints 608-610 (1954).

that is applied under the rule against perpetuities to the vesting of future interests, the period of lives in being and 21 years. This, however, they have not done.

In England, it is held that the direction to accumulate for any period is not binding, and that the court may direct the immediate application of the property to the designated charitable purposes.[1] It is to be remembered that in England in the case of a private trust the beneficiaries, if they are all sui juris and all consent, can terminate the trust at any time in spite of a direction in the terms of the trust that the trust shall not be terminated.[2] Thus in England, where property is bequeathed in trust to accumulate the income until the sole beneficiary reaches

§401.9. [1]Wharton v. Masterman, [1895] A.C. 186.

See also In re Beresford, 57 D.L.R.2d 380 (B.C. 1966).

In In re Levy, [1960] Ch. 346, where a testator left property to trustees to pay the income forever to certain charitable corporations, it was held that the corporations were not entitled to have the principal paid to them. The court distinguished Wharton v. Masterman. See §367A.

In Berry v. Geen, [1938] A.C. 575, a testator left all his property in trust to pay certain annuities out of the income and directed that the rest of the income should be accumulated and that on the death of the last annuitant the principal and accumulated income should be paid to a designated charitable institution. By statute accumulations for more than 21 years were forbidden. The question arose as to the disposition of the income after the expiration of 21 years and prior to the death of the last annuitant. It was held that this income passed as intestate property to the next of kin of the testator.

In In re Burns, 25 D.L.R.2d 427 (Alta. 1960), noted in Camb. L.J. 41, where a testator directed that a part of the income should be accumulated and on the termination of the trust a part should be paid to certain beneficiaries and a part to certain charities, and the provision for accumulation was valid only for 21 years, it was held that the first part of the income was payable to the next of kin and the other part under the doctrine of cy pres was to be given to the charities.

In In re Lushington, [1964] N.Z.L.R. 161, a testatrix created a trust to pay £300 a year to her nieces and to accumulate the surplus income and on their death to convey land as a public park and pay the accumulated income to some local authority to be later selected. It was held that the provision for accumulation was invalid under a statute and that the fund fell into the residue.

But see In re Chambers (Decd.), [1971] N.Z.L.R. 703, where the annuitants had no interest in the accumulations, and it was held that the charitable remainderman was entitled.

See §412.1.

[2]See §337.

the age of 30, and then to pay the principal to him or his estate, the beneficiary, if he is of full age, can require the trustee to convey the trust property to him. Somewhat analogously, the Attorney-General can compel the trustees of a charitable trust to make immediate application of the trust property given for charitable purposes in spite of a provision by the testator postponing such application and providing for the accumulation of the income in the meantime.

In the United States, however, the courts are more inclined to give effect to the directions of the testator unless these directions are against public policy. Thus where the testator provides that the principal of a fund held upon a private trust shall not be paid to the sole beneficiary of the trust until he reaches a designated age, the beneficiary cannot compel the trustees to pay him the fund before he reaches the designated age.[3] Where property is given upon an unconditional trust for charitable purposes but it is provided that the income shall be accumulated for a certain time, the American courts have generally held that the provision for accumulation is binding unless under all the circumstances the period of accumulation is unreasonably long.[4] The fact that the period is longer than lives in being

---

[3]See §337.3.

[4]*Federal:* Brigham v. Peter Bent Brigham Hosp., 134 F. 513 (1st Cir. 1904); Girard Trust Co. v. Russell, 179 F. 446 (3d. Cir. 1910), *semble.*

California: Estate of McKenzie, 227 Cal. App. 2d 167, 38 Cal. Rptr. 496, 7 A.L.R.3d 1275 (1964) (citing the text).

Connecticut: Woodruff v. Marsh, 63 Conn. 125, 26 A. 846, 38 Am. St. Rep. 346 (1893); Colonial Trust Co. v. Waldron, 112 Conn. 216, 152 A. 69 (1930).

Delaware: Girard Trust Co. v. St. Anne's P. E. Church, 30 Del. Ch. 1, 52 A.2d 591 (1947) (citing the text and Restatement of Trusts §401); Asche v. Asche, 41 Del. Ch. 481, 199 A.2d 314 (1964); Asche v. Asche, 42 Del. Ch. 307, 210 A.2d 306 (1965) (citing the text), 42 Del. Ch. 545, 216 A.2d 272 (1966).

Massachusetts: Odell v. Odell, 10 Allen 1 (Mass. 1865); St. Paul's Church v. Attorney Gen., 164 Mass. 188, 41 N.E. 231 (1895); Ripley v. Brown, 218 Mass. 33, 105 N.E. 637 (1914); Collector of Taxes of Norton v. Oldfield, 219 Mass. 374, 106 N.E. 1014 (1914); Oldfield v. Attorney Gen., 219 Mass. 378, 106 N.E. 1015 (1914); Frazier v. Merchants Natl. Bank of Salem, 296 Mass. 298, 5 N.E.2d 550 (1936) (citing Restatement of Trusts, §401, Comment *l*).

In Franklin Found. v. Attorney Gen., 340 Mass. 197, 163 N.E.2d 662 (1960), where Benjamin Franklin created a trust to make loans to young artificers and, after 200 years, to pay the principal and accumulated income to the Commonwealth of Massachusetts and to the City of Boston, and such loans

and 21 years does not necessarily invalidate the provision.

---

became impossible and the funds were invested, it was held that the trust should not be terminated by conveying the property to the Franklin Foundation, even though the Commonwealth and City consented. The court said that the testator's purpose was not merely to aid artificers but was to accumulate the fund for the Commonwealth and City.

Missouri: See St. Louis Union Trust Co. v. Bethesda Gen. Hosp., 446 S.W.2d 823 (Mo. 1969) (citing Restatement of Trusts, §401, Comment *k*).

In Mercantile Trust Co. Natl. Assn. v. Shriners Hosp., 551 S.W.2d 864 (Mo. App. 1977), where the testator directed the accumulation of 25 percent of the income, it was held that the trustees were bound thereby, but that if it were later shown that the accumulation was not in the public interest, they might apply to the court for permission to cease to accumulate.

New Hampshire: Attorney Gen. v. Rochester Trust Co., 115 N.H. 74, 333 A.2d 718 (1975) (holding that, although there was a direction to accumulate excess income, the court might order immediate payment to the charitable remainderman; citing the text and Restatement of Trusts, §401, Comment *i*).

New Jersey: Wendell v. Hazel Wood Cemetery, 7 N.J. Super. 117, 72 A.2d 383 (1950) (citing the text and Restatement of Trusts, §401, Comment *l*), *aff'g* 3 N.J. Super. 457, 67 A.2d 219 (1949).

New York: Matter of Whittlesey, 180 Misc. 602, 41 N.Y.S.2d 815 (1943).

North Carolina: Penick v. Bank, 218 N.C. 686, 12 S.E.2d 253 (1940).

Pennsylvania: List Trust, 6 Fiduciary Rep. 119 (Pa. 1955); Balch Estate, 21 D.&C.2d 97 (Pa. 1960), *semble;* James Estate, 414 Pa. 80, 199 A.2d 275 (1964) (citing the text).

Virginia: Collins v. Lyon, 181 Va. 230, 24 S.E.2d 572 (1943).

Washington: Matter of Booker, 37 Wash. App. 708, 682 P.2d 320 (1984), citing text and Restatement (Second) of Trusts §401.

In Restatement of Property §442, it is stated that "An otherwise effective limitation which provides for an accumulation in favor of a charity is subject to judicial supervision as to its duration." See 6 American Law of Property §24.42 (1952); 39 A.L.R. 40, 55 (1925).

A provision for accumulation for charitable purposes for an unreasonably long time may be held to be invalid. Thus in James Estate, 414 Pa. 80, 199 A.2d 275 (1964), *supra,* where a testator bequeathed about $40,000 in trust for a Masonic Home with directions that a portion of the income should be accumulated for 400 years, it was held that the provision for accumulation was invalid and that the whole of the income should be paid currently to the Home. On the other hand, in Morris Estate, 36 D.&C.2d 277 (Pa. 1965), a provision that a part of the income should be added to the endowment fund of the charity was upheld. It is to be noted that the income of the endowment fund was to be used currently. The fund would increase by an arithmetical, not a geometrical, progression.

In Whelan Estate, 54 D.&C.2d 673 (Pa. 1972), where a small sum in a bank was to be accumulated until it reached $100,000 and then paid to a certain

Validity of the trust. If there is an unconditional gift for

---

charitable institution, which would take 30 or 40 years, it was held that the sum should be immediately paid to the institution.

In Finley Trust, 60 D.&C.2d 38 (Pa. 1972), a testator who died in 1919 provided that one-fourth of his estate should be accumulated until it amounted to $3,000,000 and then be used for certain charitable purposes. In 1972 suit was brought to reform the trust by eliminating the direction to accumulate, so that it would not be taxable under the Tax Reform Act of 1969. (See §348.4, n. 3.) The court held that it would not reform the trust because the direction for accumulation was valid, it appearing that it would be accomplished in 1995, and to do away with the accumulation would substantially impair the purposes of the trust.

See also Chauveau Estate, 1 D.&C.3d 471 (Pa. 1976) (accumulation until income amounts to $10,000).

In Teplitz Trust, 75 D.&C.2d 601 (Pa. 1975), a testator left his estate in trust to accumulate the income and to pay from the accumulation certain sums to two charitable institutions. The institutions requested an immediate payment out of principal. The court refused to allow the payment. There was no reason to apply the cy pres doctrine.

In some of the states in which there are statutes against accumulations, exceptions are expressly made with respect to dispositions for charitable purposes.

New York Estates, Powers and Trusts Law, §§8-1.1, 8-1.7, amended by Laws 1971, c. 1058, and Laws 1985, c. 492, provide that where property has been given for any religious, educational, charitable, or benevolent purposes and no valid remainder except for the same or like purposes has been created, a direction for accumulation is valid without regard to the time at which the accumulation is directed to commence or to terminate, but the accumulation is subject nevertheless to the supervision and control of the court. They permit the trustees to accumulate income in their discretion, in the absence of a provision in the terms of the trust, with certain limitations. See the recommendation of the Law Revision Commission, Laws 1961 (McKinney), p. 1853.

In some states it is provided in general terms that income from real and personal property may be accumulated for the benefit of any person or persons for such periods as may be directed by will or other written instrument sufficient to pass such property. 20 Pa. Cons. Stat., §6106.

By Wisconsin Stat., §701.21, it is provided that "A trust containing a direction or authorization to accumulate income from property devoted to a charitable purpose shall be subject to the general equitable supervision of the court with respect to any such accumulation of income, including its reasonableness, amount and duration."

In the Restatement (Second) of Property (Donative Transfers), §2.2(2) (1979), it is provided: "An accumulation of trust income under a charitable trust created in a donative transfer is valid to the extent the accumulation is

charitable purposes, the gift does not fail although it is provided by the terms of the trust that the income shall be accumulated for a period longer than that of the rule against perpetuities.[5]

---

reasonable in the light of the purposes, facts and circumstances of the particular trust."

See Annot., Validity, construction and effect of provisions of charitable trust providing for accumulation of income, 6 A.L.R.4th 903 (1981).

[5]*England:* Martin v. Margham, 14 Sim. 230 (1844); In re Swain, [1905] 1 Ch. 669; In re Bradwell's Will Trusts, [1952] Ch. 575.

Federal: Duggan v. Slocum, 92 F. 806 (2d Cir. 1889); Handley v. Palmer, 103 F. 39 (3d Cir. 1900); Brigham v. Peter Bent Brigham Hosp., 134 F. 513 (1st Cir. 1904).

Alabama: Thurlow v. Berry, 247 Ala. 631, 25 So. 2d 726 (1946), *semble.*

California: Davenport v. Davenport Found., 215 P.2d 467 (Cal. App. 1950), *mod.,* 36 Cal. 2d 67, 222 P.2d 11 (1950) (citing Restatement of Trusts §401).

Connecticut: Colonial Trust Co. v. Waldron, 112 Conn. 216, 152 A. 69 (1930).

Delaware: Girard Trust Co. v. St. Anne's P.E. Church, 30 Del. Ch. 1, 52 A.2d 591 (1947) (citing the text and Restatement of Trusts §401); Asche v. Asche, 41 Del. Ch. 481, 199 A.2d 314 (1964); Asche v. Asche 42 Del. Ch. 307, 210 A.2d 306 (1965) (citing the text), 42 Del. Ch. 545, 216 A.2d 272 (1966).

Georgia: Perkins v. Citizens & S. Natl. Bank, 190 Ga. 29, 8 S.E.2d 28 (1940) (quoting the text).

Illinois: Ingraham v. Ingraham, 169 Ill. 432, 48 N.E. 561, 49 N.E. 320 (1897); Webb v. Webb, 340 Ill. 407, 172 N.E. 730, 71 A.L.R. 404 (1930).

Indiana: Reasoner v. Herman, 191 Ind. 642, 134 N.E. 276 (1922).

See Quinn v. Peoples Trust & Sav. Co., 223 Ind. 317, 60 N.E.2d 281, 157 A.L.R. 885 (1945).

Massachusetts: Odell v. Odell, 10 Allen 1 (Mass. 1865); Codman v. Brigham, 187 Mass. 309, 72 N.E. 1008, 105 Am. St. Rep. 394 (1905).

See American Colonization Socy. v. Trustees of Smith Charities, 2 Allen 302 (Mass. 1861); Dexter v. President & Fellows of Harvard College, 176 Mass. 192, 57 N.E. 371 (1900).

Missouri: Mercantile Trust Co. Natl. Assn. v. Shriners Hosp., 551 S.W.2d 864 (Mo. App. 1977).

New Jersey: Conway v. Third Natl. Bank & Trust Co., 118 N.J. Eq. 61, 177 A. 113 (1935), *aff'd,* 119 N.J. Eq. 575, 182 A. 916 (1936); Wendell v. Hazel Wood Cemetery, 7 N.J. Super. 117, 72 A.2d 383 (1950), *aff'g* 3 N.J. Super. 457, 67 A.2d 219 (1949) (quoting the text and Restatement of Trusts, §401, Comment *l*).

New York: Matter of Potts, 205 A.D. 147, 199 N.Y.S. 880 (1923), *aff'd mem.,* 236 N.Y. 658, 142 N.E. 323 (1923); Matter of Kirkbride, 261 A.D. 853, 24 N.Y.S.2d 375 (1941), *leave to appeal denied,* 285 N.Y. 859, 32 N.E.2d 835 (1941); Matter of Lewis, 199 Misc. 463, 99 N.Y.S.2d 986 (1950); Matter of Grant, 200

If the direction for accumulation is valid, it will be enforced. If
the provision for accumulation is invalid, it will be disregarded
and the court will direct the immediate application of the property to the designated charitable purposes. This is in accordance
with the general principle underlying the cy pres doctrine,
under which a charitable trust does not fail although it is impossible or illegal to carry out the particular purpose of the testator
if that particular purpose is not an essential part of his plan. It
is immaterial whether the testator directs that the funds shall be
accumulated for a designated period that is longer than the lives
of designated persons and 21 years, or whether he directs that
it shall be accumulated until a certain sum is realized although
the sum may not be realized within the period of lives in being
and 21 years. In *Odell v. Odell*[6] a testator bequeathed to a bank
$100 annually for 50 years, to be paid to it by the executors, and
to be safely invested by it and the income accumulated for 50
years. At the end of this period the fund was to be applied to
certain charitable purposes. On a bill for instructions brought
by the executors it was held that the bequest was valid and that
the heirs of the testator were not entitled to the legacy. The

---

Misc. 35, 101 N.Y.S.2d 423 (1950) (law of New South Wales; citing the text);
National City Bank of N.Y. v. Beebe, 155 N.Y.S.2d 347 (1956) (Rhode Island
law).

   Ohio: Third Natl. Bank & Trust Co. v. Eaton, 33 Ohio App. 2d 264, 62
Ohio Ops. 2d 379, 294 N.E.2d 247 (1972).

·   *Pennsylvania:* Balch Estate, 21 D.&C.2d 97 (Pa. 1960); James Estate, 414
Pa. 80, 199 A.2d 275 (1964) (citing the text).

   Virginia: Allaun v. First & Merchants Natl. Bank, 190 Va. 104, 56 S.E.2d
83 (1949) (direction to accumulate one-half of income for 125 years).

   Washington: In re Galland's Estate, 103 Wash. 106, 173 P. 740 (1918).

   Canada: Jewish Home for the Aged v. Toronto Gen. Trusts Corp., [1961]
S.C.R. 465, *rev'g* In re Brier, 23 D.L.R.2d 229 (B.C. 1960); In re Brier, 39
D.L.R.2d 717 (B.C. 1963).

   Australia: Compare Royal North Shore Hosp. of Sydney v. Attorney-General, 60 C.L.R. 396 (Austl. 1938); Attorney-General (S.A.) v. Bray, 111 C.L.R.
402 (Austl. 1964).

   In James Estate, 414 Pa. 80, 199 A.2d 275 (1964), where a testator bequeathed about $40,000 in trust for a Masonic Home, with directions that a
portion of the income should be accumulated for 400 years, it was held that
the provision for accumulation was invalid and that the whole of the income
should be paid currently to the Home. The court cited the text.

   [6] 10 Allen 1 (Mass. 1865).

court said that it was unnecessary to decide whether the direction for accumulation was valid or not. There was an unconditional gift for charitable purposes, and if the provision for accumulation is invalid a court of equity may modify the testator's particular directions so as to carry out his general charitable intent. In *In re Galland's Estate*[7] a testator left his estate to a trust company in trust for the establishment of an orphanage for Jewish children in Seattle, and provided that when the estate should by its own accumulations or by other contributions amount to $50,000 the trust company should deliver the trust funds to five trustees who should establish and control the orphanage. It was held that a valid charitable trust was created. There was an immediate and unconditional bequest for the designated charitable purposes.[8]

Where it appears, however, that the provision for accumulation is an essential part of the testator's plan, a different situation arises. If the provision for accumulation is valid, the trust does not fail.[9] But if the provision for accumulation is invalid, the intended charitable trust fails altogether. In such a case there is not an immediate gift for charitable purposes and the provision for accumulation cannot under the cy pres doctrine be rejected. Thus if property is given in trust to accumulate the income for a period that may exceed the period of the rule against perpetuities, and the accumulation is an essential part of

---

[7]103 Wash. 106, 173 P. 740 (1918).

[8]In Trusts of Holdeen, 486 Pa. 1, 403 A.2d 978 (1979), inter vivos trusts were created in which the income was to be accumulated until the year 2444, when principal and interest were to be paid to the Commonwealth of Pennsylvania "for educational endowment or other public purposes." It was provided that income that is not lawfully subject to accumulation was to be paid to a certain charitable institution for specified charitable uses. It was held that the provision for accumulation was invalid, and that the income accruing from the time of the creation of the trusts, and not merely income accruing from the time of the decision or from the time of the settlor's death, should be paid to the charitable institution. The court cited the text and Restatement of Trusts, §401, Comment *k*.

[9]Summers v. Chicago Title & Trust Co., 335 Ill. 564, 167 N.E. 777 (1929), noted in 24 Ill. L. Rev. 687, 39 Yale L.J. 437; Miller v. Parish of the Epiphany, 302 Mass. 323, 19 N.E.2d 46 (1939); Archambault's Estate, 308 Pa. 549, 162 A. 801 (1932).

the testator's scheme so that the gift to charity is contingent on the accumulation of the income, the trust fails.[10]

The distinction between an immediate absolute gift to charity and a gift subject to a condition precedent is clearly brought out in the case of *Girard Trust Co. v. Russell*.[11] In that case a settlor in 1848 deposited with a trust company a few hundred dollars in trust to be accumulated for the benefit of the state of Pennsylvania in the manner stated in the trust instrument. In that instrument it was provided that the money was to be invested in bonds of the state and the income accumulated until the amount

---

[10]Ewen v. Bannerman, 2 Dow. & Cl. 74, 100 (1830) (criticized in Magistrates of Dundee v. Morris, 3 Macq. 134, 154, 174 (1858)); Girard Trust Co. v. Russell, 179 F. 446 (3d Cir. 1910); First Camden Natl. Bank & Trust Co. v. Collins, 114 N.J. Eq. 59, 168 A. 275 (1933), noted in 3 Mercer Beasley L. Rev. 117, 31 Mich. L. Rev. 1167, 20 Va. L. Rev. 365; Murphy v. Johnston, 190 Ga. 23, 8 S.E.2d 23 (1940); Waterbury Trust Co. v. Porter, 131 Conn. 206, 38 A.2d 598 (1944).

See Porter v. Baynard, 158 Fla. 294, 28 So. 2d 890, 170 A.L.R. 747 (1946), *cert. denied sub nom.* Union Trust Co. v. Genau, 330 U.S. 844 (1947), noted in 45 Mich. L. Rev. 920, 14 U. Chi. L. Rev. 686, 33 Va. L. Rev. 529. The case was criticized in Allaun v. First & Merchants Natl. Bank, 190 Va. 104, 56 S.E.2d 83 (1949).

See Note, Gift to charity as affected by conjoined noncharitable gift invalid under rule or statute against perpetuities or rule against accumulations, 170 A.L.R. 760 (1947).

In Holdeen v. Ratterree, 190 F. Supp. 752 (N.D.N.Y. 1960), where the settlor transferred securities in trust to accumulate the income for 500 years and then to pay the principal and accumulated income to the state of Pennsylvania, for the purpose of concentrating the wealth of the world in a single governmental unit, it was held that the trust failed and that the settlor could not deduct the gift from his income tax liability; but the decision was reversed (292 F.2d 338 (2d Cir. 1961)) on the ground that the provision for accumulation was to be effective only so far as public policy permitted.

In Matter of Booker, 37 Wash. App. 708, 682 P.2d 320, *review denied,* 102 Wash. 2d 1010 (1984), $700,000 was transferred to a trustee with instructions to accumulate income until the fund was sufficient to erect a 40-bed rest home in Town *A* and if that purpose could not be accomplished, to pay over the fund to a hospital in Town *B.* After 12 years the Internal Revenue Service informed the trustee that further accumulation would make the trust taxable. It was held that the court could permit deviation by permitting the erection of a 30-bed rest home in Town *A,* as the provision for 40 beds was not an essential part of the testator's scheme, citing text and Restatement (Second) of Trusts §401.

[11]179 F. 446 (3d Cir. 1910).

should equal the total indebtedness of the state, when the funds were to be transferred to the state in discharge of its indebtedness, and for no other purpose whatsoever. It was further provided that each state bond purchased should be so endorsed as not to be transferable and to release the state from paying the bond except to the trustee, but it was provided that if at any time the state should pay the interest on any such bond by issuing a new obligation the trust should cease and the fund should be paid to the oldest living male heir of the settlor. The settlor died in 1889 and suit was brought by his administrator to enforce a resulting trust on the ground that the trust was invalid. The court held that it was invalid. There was not an absolute immediate gift for charity, but a gift conditional on the accumulation of the amount of the indebtedness of the state. The method of accumulation was an essential part of the testator's scheme. The testator did not manifest a general charitable purpose to benefit the state. The vesting of the fund in charity was subject to a condition precedent that might not be performed within the period of the rule against perpetuities. Accordingly, it was held that the trustee held the fund and its accumulations upon a resulting trust for the estate of the settlor. In view of the language of the trust instrument the result reached seems clearly sound. The settlor intended to benefit the state only in the manner stated by him. The money could not properly be applied, therefore, in any other way for the benefit of the state.

The decision in *First Camden National Bank & Trust Co. v. Collins*[12] is more open to doubt. In that case a testator left the residue of his estate to a trust company in trust to accumulate the income during the life of the survivor of certain designated children and for 21 years thereafter, when the trust company should proceed to form a corporation for certain educational purposes and the fund should be turned over to it. It was held that the bequest was invalid. The property was not to vest in the charity until the corporation should be formed, and because this would necessitate an act of the legislature it might not be formed until after the period of the rule against perpetuities. Now to hold that the provision for accumulation was invalid may be

---

[12]114 N.J. Eq. 59, 168 A. 275 (1933), noted in 3 Mercer Beasley L. Rev. 117, 31 Mich. L. Rev. 1167, 20 Va. L. Rev. 365.

sound. As we have seen, it is held in England that any provision for accumulation of the funds of property devoted to charity is invalid. In the United States it is generally held that such a provision is valid if under all the circumstances the period of accumulation is not unreasonably long. In determining the reasonableness of the period the courts do not necessarily take as a standard the period of the rule against perpetuities. A period longer than that may under some circumstances be proper. On the other hand, a shorter period may under the circumstances be unreasonably long. In the principal case even if there had been no provision for incorporation and the accumulation was limited to lives in being and 21 years, because the testator selected young children as the persons whose lives would determine the period of accumulation, the period might be over 100 years. To enforce such a provision might well be held, as the court held it to be, against public policy. The court, however, did not consider the question whether the provision for accumulation was an essential part of the testator's scheme, whether the bequest was conditional on the carrying out of the provision for accumulation, or, on the other hand, whether there was an immediate absolute gift to charity. The court was troubled by the fact that the corporation might not be formed within the period of perpetuities, but, as we have seen, this does not invalidate the disposition if there is an immediate and unconditional gift to charity. In a later case in New Jersey the court held that where there was an unconditional gift to charity the trust would not fail.[13]

Where there is no provision for accumulation.   Where a testator leaves property in trust for a particular charitable purpose and the amount bequeathed is insufficient to accomplish the purpose, and there is no provision for accumulation, the courts will not ordinarily direct an accumulation, although they have done so in cases where the amount does not fall far short of the required sum so that an accumulation for a short time would be sufficient to raise the necessary sum. Where the particular purpose is not an essential part of the plan of the testator, the court

[13]Conway v. Third Natl. Bank & Trust Co., 118 N.J. Eq. 61, 177 A. 113 (1935), *aff'd,* 119 N.J. Eq. 575, 182 A. 916 (1936).

will order an application cy pres; but if the particular purpose is an essential part of the testator's plan, the trust may fail for insufficiency of funds.[14]

§401.10. Illegal condition precedent. Property may be given upon a charitable trust subject to a condition precedent that is illegal, not because of the rule against perpetuities but because it would be against public policy to enforce the condition. The problem is the same as in the case of a private trust that is subject to an illegal condition precedent.[1] In such a case the validity of the charitable trust will not depend on whether or not the condition is performed. Although this is what the donor intended, it is against public policy to give effect to this intention. Therefore, two possibilities remain. Either the trust will fail even though the condition is performed, or the trust will be upheld even though the condition is not performed. The result should depend on what the donor would probably have preferred if he had realized that the condition was invalid. In the absence of any language or circumstances to indicate a different intent, the inference ordinarily is that the donor would prefer that the trust should not fail. This is the view that was taken in a case decided by one of the lower courts in New York.[2] In that case a testator left money in trust to pay the income to a hospital on condition that it should make a rule that physicians should split their fees with the hospital, and it was provided that if the hospital should refuse to make such a rule or should abrogate it or neglect to enforce it the money should be paid to the Salvation Army. The court held that the condition was illegal because it was against public policy that physicians should split their fees with the hospital. It held that the hospital was entitled to the income without performing the condition.

In *Attorney General v. Lowell*[3] a testator in 1870 bequeathed money to a city for certain charitable purposes on the condition that before the money was paid the proper authorities of the city should legally vote to accept the money and should promise ever thereafter to pay 6 percent interest on it to trustees who

---

[14]See §399.2.
§401.10. [1]See §65.3.
[2]Matter of Sterne, 147 Misc. 59, 263 N.Y.S. 304 (1933).
[3]246 Mass. 312, 141 N.E. 45 (1923).

should apply the fund to the designated charitable purposes. Immediately after the testator's death the city council accepted the bequest and paid 6 percent interest to the trustees until 1918. In 1922 the Attorney General brought suit against the city to compel it to pay the interest to the trustees or to pay the principal to them. The court directed the city to pay the principal to the trustees. It held that the city had no power to bind itself to pay interest. If the provision of the will requiring an agreement to pay such interest was to be regarded as a condition, it was a condition that could not legally be performed. The court held that the charity would not fail, however, because the condition was repugnant to the paramount purpose of the testator.

As we have seen,[4] the law in England as to illegal conditions precedent draws a distinction between realty and personalty, and a distinction between mala prohibita and mala in se, distinctions that seem to be arbitrary and technical, and unrelated to the donor's intention.[5] It is, indeed, the policy of the law that makes the condition illegal, and the donor's intention cannot save it. He can, however, provide what disposition should be made of the property if the condition is illegal, and if he does so his intention should govern. He may provide that in such an event the gift shall be absolute, or he may provide that the gift shall fail. Where he makes no express provision, the question for the court should be what, under all the circumstances, it appears that the donor intended or, had he thought about the matter, would have intended, as to the disposition of the property in the event of the invalidity of the condition.

TOPIC 6.   LIABILITIES TO THIRD PERSONS

§402.   Liability for Tort

The cases that involve the question of the right of tort creditors to reach property held for charitable purposes are very

---

[4]See §65.3.
[5]See Pound, Legacies on Impossible or Illegal Conditions Precedent, 3 Ill. L. Rev. 1 (1908).

numerous. Almost all of them involve property held by a charitable corporation. Such liabilities ordinarily arise out of the operation of a charitable institution, particularly a hospital, although occasionally an educational institution, or church, or home for the poor. Ordinarily, where property is left to individual trustees or to a trust company in trust for charitable purposes, the duty of the trustee is merely to invest the trust funds and apply the income for charitable purposes; and in such a case the question of liability in tort seldom arises. The cases in which a charitable trust rather than a charitable corporation is involved, and that raise questions different from those involved in a proceeding against a charitable corporation, are considered hereafter.[1]

There is a great conflict of authority on the question whether and to what extent a charitable corporation is liable in tort. Three possible bases have been suggested for the exemption of charitable corporations from tort liability; and the circumstances under which there is an exemption depend on which basis is accepted by the courts of the state as the ground for exemption. These bases are: (1) that the trust assets should not be diverted from the charitable purposes for which they were given; (2) that persons benefiting from the charity by the acceptance of such benefits waive any claim for damages; (3) that the doctrine of respondeat superior is inapplicable to charities.

(1) Nondiversion of trust assets. The first suggested basis is that where property is devoted to charitable objects it should not be diverted from those objects, and that to compel the corporation to use its property in paying claims of persons who have been injured is such a diversion. This is sometimes called the "trust fund theory." Thus, in a case in Massachusetts,[2] the court stated as a reason for exempting a hospital from tort liability that "being a charitable institution rendering services to the public without pecuniary profit, if the property of the charity was depleted by the payment of damages its usefulness might be either impaired or wholly destroyed, the object of the founder or donors defeated, and charitable gifts discouraged."

Under this theory the exemption of the institution is very

§402. [1]See §402.2.
[2]Farrigan v. Pevear, 193 Mass. 147, 149, 78 N.E. 855 (1906).

broad. Under it a hospital, for example, is not subject to liability, whether the negligence is that of the directors or trustees or officers or that of its nurses or other employees; it is not subject to liability whether the person injured is a patient, either a paying patient or a charity patient, or is a visitor or an employee or a stranger, as for example a person who is injured on the sidewalk in front of the hospital or a person who is struck by an ambulance. Such a sweeping exemption from liability of charitable institutions seems to be clearly against public policy. The institution should be just before it is generous.

(2) Waiver by beneficiaries.   Another suggested basis is that of waiver or implied agreement. The theory is that a person who receives the benefit of services of a charitable institution impliedly agrees to waive the right to hold it liable for any injuries he may receive. In the Massachusetts decision just cited the court stated as a ground for exemption that "if an individual accepts the benefit of a public charity he thereby enters into a relation which exempts his benefactor from liability for the negligence of servants who are employed in its administration, provided due care has been used in their selection."

Such a waiver, it seems clear, is purely fictitious. It certainly is inapplicable to injured persons other than recipients of benefits, such as patients at a hospital. It does not apply to strangers, such as pedestrians, who are injured by the negligent driving of an ambulance; it does not apply to injured employees of the institution; it does not apply to visitors who are injured on its premises, as, for example, those who fall on an improperly lighted stairway or on a slippery floor. It applies to charity patients at a hospital. It is generally held to apply also to paying patients, although there seems to be little basis for the notion that a patient who pays for the service rendered by the hospital agrees to waive any claim against the hospital. The courts, however, have generally felt that it would be an invidious distinction if they were to hold that damages could be recovered by a paying patient, but none could be recovered by a charity patient. Moreover, even the paying patient seldom pays the full cost of the service rendered.

(3) Nonapplicability of respondeat superior.   A third suggested basis of exemption is that the doctrine under which an employer

is liable for the negligence of his employee, the so-called doctrine of respondeat superior, is not applicable to charitable institutions. The suggestion is that this doctrine should be limited to undertakings carried on for the profit of the employer, to business and not to charitable undertakings. Under this theory there can be no recovery against a hospital by anyone, whether patient or visitor or employee or stranger, where the injury results from the negligence of an employee of the hospital, whether janitor, ambulance driver, orderly, nurse, or physician or surgeon. Thus in a case in Connecticut,[3] where an action was brought against a hospital for injury caused by the negligence of an employee of the hospital, the court said:

> The law which makes one responsible for an act not his own, because the actual wrongdoer is his servant, is based on a rule of public policy. The liability of a charitable corporation for the defaults of its servants must depend upon the reasons of that rule of policy, and their application to such a corporation. . . . This defendant does not come within the main reason for the rule of public policy which supports the doctrine of *respondeat superior;* it derives no benefit from what its servant does, in the sense of that personal and private gain which was the real reason for the rule.

On the other hand, under this theory a charitable institution is not exempt from liability for the negligence of its governing board or of its administrative officers. Thus a hospital is liable where the injuries result from the negligent selection or retention of incompetent employees, from the failure to make proper rules for the conduct of the institution, or from negligence in permitting the premises to be in a dangerous condition. A distinction is drawn under this theory between the negligence of those higher up and the negligence of a mere employee.

The questions of policy. None of the suggested reasons for exemption is altogether satisfactory and in most of the states no one theory is consistently applied. The rules in the various states as to the exemption of charitable institutions from tort liability vary greatly. At one extreme are states like Massachusetts that go the full length in giving exemption, no matter who is injured

[3]Hearns v. Waterbury Hosp., 66 Conn. 98, 123, 125, 33 A. 595, 603, 604 (1895).

and no matter who among the officers or employees of the institution by his negligence caused the injury. At the other extreme are jurisdictions like the District of Columbia, where the Court of Appeals has held that an institution is entitled to no exemption from liability in tort merely because it is a charitable institution. In some other states the courts have taken some intermediate view, some of them holding that a hospital is exempt from liability to its patients but is not exempt from liability to other persons, such as employees, visitors, or strangers, others holding that a hospital is not liable for the negligence of mere employees but is liable for the negligence of its governing board or officers. A review of the more recent decisions shows a strong trend toward the limiting or the abolition of the exemption of hospitals and other charitable institutions.

The rule in the District of Columbia was laid down for the first time in a case in which a hospital was held liable to the plaintiff, a special nurse, who was injured when a student nurse violently pushed a swinging door that struck the plaintiff.[4] Judge Rutledge, after a careful examination of the decisions in the various states with their "welter of conflict," and after examining and rejecting the various bases on which exemption has been granted, held that the fact that the defendant is a charity gives it no immunity. He said,

> The rule of immunity is out of step with the general trend of legislative and judicial policy in distributing losses incurred by individuals through the operation of an enterprise among all who benefit by it rather than in leaving them wholly to be borne by those who sustain them. The rule of immunity itself has given way gradually but steadily through widening, though not too well or consistently reasoned, modifications. It is disintegrating. Each modification has the justification that it is a step in result, if not in reason, from the original error toward eventual correction. As more and more steps are taken, correction becomes more complete. The process is nearing the end.

---

[4]President & Directors of Georgetown College v. Hughes, 76 App. D.C. 123, 130 F.2d 810 (1942), aff'g Hughes v. President & Directors of Georgetown College, 33 F. Supp. 867 (D.D.C. 1940).

He said that insurance should be carried to guard against liabilities and concluded:

> To offset the expense [of insurance] will be the gains of eliminating another area of what has been called "protected negligence" and the anomaly that the institutional doer of good asks exemption from responsibility for its wrong, though all others must pay. The incorporated charity should respond as do private individuals, business corporations and others, when it does good in the wrong way.

Perhaps a real reason for denying recovery is the belief that many such claims are in fact unfounded, and yet there is enough evidence to go to a jury and the jury is likely to be sympathetic to the plaintiff. It is inevitable that many patients in a hospital are not cured in spite of the best efforts of the medical profession, and it is easy to claim that the failure is due to negligence in the treatment the plaintiff has received, and in the present state of the art or science it is difficult to establish definitely whether there has been negligence or not, and in spite of instructions by the court as to the burden of proof juries are inclined to find for the plaintiff and not infrequently to assess heavy damages. The fact that claims may be unfounded may not be a sufficient reason for denying a plaintiff the opportunity to present his case, but undoubtedly this reason has played a part in inducing the courts in so many states to exempt hospitals and other charitable institutions from liability at least to patients at the hospital or the beneficiaries of other charitable institutions.[5]

[5]By the Idaho Hospital Liability Trust Act, Idaho Code, §§41-3701 to 41-3729, provision is made for hospitals to combine to create a trust to protect them against liability.

Maine: Thompson v. Mercy Hosp., 483 A.2d 706 (Me. 1984) (charitable immunity will not be extended to nonprofit hospital that does not obtain any substantial part of its income from charitable donations).

We have not dealt with the question of sovereign immunity where the hospital is a state or municipal organization. The tendency is to do away with sovereign immunity. See, for example, Mayle v. Pennsylvania Dept. of Highways, 479 Pa. 384, 388 A.2d 709 (1978); Poklemba v. Shamokin State Gen. Hosp., 479 Pa. 414, 388 A.2d 722 (1978).

The authorities. The cases on the question of the tort liability of charitable institutions are legion. In many cases it has been held that the institution is not liable for tort, at least under the particular circumstances.[6] In many cases the institution has

---

[6]*Federal:* Matute v. Carson Long Inst., 160 F. Supp. 827 (M.D. Pa. 1958) (Pennsylvania law); Tomlinson v. Trustees of Univ. of Pa., 164 F. Supp. 353 (E.D. Pa. 1958) (university not liable for death of person installing equipment although negligence that of the corporation; Pennsylvania law), *appeal dismissed,* 266 F.2d 569 (3d Cir. 1959); Miller v. Concordia Teachers College, 296 F.2d 100 (8th Cir. 1961) (Nebraska law; college not liable to student for not preventing fellow student from shooting him in dormitory); Webb v. Blount Memorial Hosp., 196 F. Supp. 114 (E.D. Tenn. 1961), *aff'd,* 303 F.2d 437 (6th Cir. 1962) (Tennessee law; county hospital not liable to patient for negligence of employee); Weeks v. Children's Hosp. of Philadelphia, 200 F. Supp. 77 (E.D. Pa. 1961) (Pennsylvania law; hospital not liable to patient for negligence of employee; immunity of charitable institutions not violative of constitutional guaranty of due process and equal protection); Selkow v. City of Philadelphia, 201 F. Supp. 221 (E.D. Pa. 1962) (university and city not liable for defect in sidewalk); Fortugno v. Trachtenberg, 202 F. Supp. 177 (E.D. Pa. 1962) (hospital not liable to patient for negligence of operating surgeon); Berry v. Odom, 222 F. Supp. 467 (D.C.N.C. 1963) (North Carolina law; university not liable for negligent treatment of patient); Egerton v. R.E. Lee Memorial Church, 395 F.2d 381 (4th Cir. 1968) (Virginia law; church not liable to visitor viewing sanctuary because she was a beneficiary); Heirs of Fruge v. Blood Servs., 365 F. Supp. 1344 (W.D. La. 1973), *rev'd* 506 F.2d 841 (5th Cir. 1975) (Louisiana law; charitable corporation furnishing blood services not liable for defective blood); Terry v. Boy Scouts of Am., 471 F. Supp. 28 (D.S.C. 1978), *aff'd mem.* 598 F.2d 616 (4th Cir. 1979) (holding under South Carolina law Boy Scouts not liable for injury to a member in a tent fire); Perloff v. Symmes Hosp., 487 F. Supp. 426 (D. Mass. 1980) (Massachusetts law prior to 1971); Mason v. Southern New England Conference Assn. of Seventh-Day Adventists, 696 F.2d 135 (1st Cir. 1982) (liability limited to $20,000 by Mass. Gen. Laws Ann., c. 231, §85K (1982 Supp.); Hill v. March of Dimes Birth Defects Found., 641 F. Supp. 110 (S.D. Miss. 1986); Seiderman v. American Inst. for Mental Studies, 667 F. Supp. 154 (D.N.J. 1987) (patient in mental hospital operated by Pennsylvania corporation in New Jersey).

Alabama: Thompson v. Druid City Hosp. Bd., 279 Ala. 314, 184 So. 2d 825 (1966) (city hospital).

Arkansas: Michael v. St. Paul Mercury Indem. Co., 92 F. Supp. 140 (W.D. Ark. 1950) (Arkansas law; hospital not liable for negligence of employee), noted in 6 Ark. L. Rev. 209; Cabbiness v. City of N. Little Rock, 228 Ark. 356, 307 S.W.2d 529 (1957) (boys' club not liable for injuries sustained in swimming pool); Helton v. Sisters of Mercy of St. Joseph's Hosp., 234 Ark. 76, 351 S.W.2d 129 (1961) (hospital not liable for negligence of employee), noted in 16 Ark. L. Rev. 289; Williams v. Jefferson Hosp. Assn., 246 Ark. 1200, 442

S.W.2d 243 (1969); Le May v. Trinity Lutheran Church, 248 Ark. 119, 450 S.W.2d 297 (1970) (church not liable for damage to plaintiff's house resulting from fall of tree).

California: Young v. Boy Scouts of Am., 9 Cal. App. 2d 760, 51 P.2d 191 (1935) (Boy Scouts corporation not liable to Boy Scouts where no negligence in selection of Scoutmaster); Calkins v. Newton, 36 Cal. App. 2d 262, 97 P.2d 523 (1940) (county maintaining hospital not liable to patient for negligence of doctors and nurses).

In Tunkl v. Regents of Univ. of Cal., 60 Cal. 2d 92, 383 P.2d 441 (1963), a patient was admitted to a hospital conducted by a university and before his admission he signed an agreement releasing it from liability for the negligence of its employees if it used due care in selecting them. He suffered injuries as a result of the negligence of doctors employed by the hospital. A statute, Cal. Civ. Code, §1668, provided that contracts exempting anyone from responsibility for fraud or wilful injury to person or property or violation of law, whether wilful or negligent, are against the policy of the law. It was held that the defendant was liable. The release was invalid as against the public interest.

Colorado: Hemenway v. Presbyterian Hosp. Assn., 161 Colo. 42, 419 P.2d 312 (1966) (refusing to impose liability, two justices dissenting).

Connecticut: Cashman v. Meriden Hosp., 117 Conn. 585, 169 A. 915 (1933) (hospital not liable to patient for negligence of nurse selected with care); Boardman v. Burlingame, 123 Conn. 646, 197 A. 761 (1938) (institution for insane not liable for inducing patient to submit to confinement); Edwards v. Grace Hosp. Socy., 130 Conn. 568, 36 A.2d 273 (1944) (hospital not liable to patient for negligence of employees if no corporate negligence); Tocchetti v. Cyril & Julia C. Johnson Memorial Hosp., 130 Conn. 623, 36 A.2d 381 (1944) (hospital not liable to patient for negligence of nurse if no corporate negligence); Evans v. Lawrence & Memorial Assocd. Hosps., 133 Conn. 311, 50 A.2d 443 (1946) (hospital not liable to patient for negligence of employee selected with care); Cristini v. Griffin Hosp., 134 Conn. 282, 57 A.2d 262 (1948) (hospital not liable for negligently causing death of premature baby by burning); Coolbaugh v. St. Peter's Roman Catholic Church, 142 Conn. 536, 115 A.2d 662 (1955) (church not liable to regular attendant injured walking across lawn where sexton negligently left a wire); McDermott v. St. Mary's Hosp. Corp., 144 Conn. 417, 133 A.2d 608 (1957) (hospital not liable to patient for negligence of nurse selected with care); Parowski v. Bridgeport Hosp., 144 Conn. 531, 134 A.2d 834 (1957) (hospital not liable for death of patient due to negligence of nurse selected with care); Martino v. Grace-New Haven Community Hosp., 146 Conn. 735, 148 A.2d 259 (1959) (hospital not liable to patient for negligence of employees if no corporate negligence); Fillipone v. Corporation of the Church of the Immaculate Conception, 151 Conn. 717, 202 A.2d 152 (1964) (church not liable to communicant injured by fall on steps after attending mass).

By Connecticut Gen. Stat. 1958, §52-577d, it is provided that "The common law defense of charitable immunity is abolished and shall not constitute a valid defense to any cause of action arising subsequent to the effective date of this act."

District of Columbia: White v. Providence Hosp., 80 F. Supp. 76 (D.D.C. 1943) (hospital not liable for death of patient if no negligence in selecting nurses).

Georgia: Morehouse College v. Russell, 219 Ga. 717, 135 S.E.2d 432 (1964), s.c. 109 Ga. App. 30, 136 S.E.2d 179 (1964) (college not liable for death of student owing to negligence of employee, except as to amount insured); Ponder v. Fulton-DeKalb Hosp. Auth., 256 Ga. 833, 353 S.E.2d 515 (1987), *cert. denied,* 108 S. Ct. 181 (1987).

See Keys v. Enrichment Servs. Program, 183 Ga. App. 8, 357 S.E.2d 852 (1987).

Illinois: Hogan v. Chicago Lying-In Hosp. & Dispensary, 335 Ill. 42, 166 N.E. 461 (1929) (hospital not liable to paying patient injured through negligence of nurse); Mater v. Silver Cross Hosp., 285 Ill. App. 437, 2 N.E.2d 138 (1936) (hospital not liable for negligent injury to patient); Maretick v. South Chicago Community Hosp., 297 Ill. App. 488, 17 N.E.2d 1012 (1938) (hospital held not liable to patient for injuries from defective wiring); Myers v. Young Men's Christian Assn., 316 Ill. App. 177, 44 N.E.2d 755 (1942) (Y.M.C.A.), noted in 21 Chi.-Kent L. Rev. 256, 10 U. Chi. L. Rev. 211; Saffron v. Young Men's Christian Assn., 317 Ill. App. 149, 45 N.E.2d 555 (1942) (Y.M.C.A.), noted in 27 Marq. L. Rev. 164; Piper v. Epstein, 326 Ill. App. 400, 62 N.E.2d 139 (1945) (hospital not liable for negligence in causing death), noted in 24 Chi.-Kent L. Rev. 170, 34 Ill. B.J. 173; Moore v. Moyle, 335 Ill. App. 342, 82 N.E.2d 61 (1948), *rev'd on other grounds,* 405 Ill. 555, 92 N.E.2d 81 (1950) (educational institution not liable to student for negligence of instructor in supplying defective trapeze), noted in 3 Baylor L. Rev. 83, 28 Chi.-Kent L. Rev. 268, 29 id. 107, 38 Ill. B.J. 187, 533, 39 id. 538, 40 id. 138, 45 Ill. L. Rev. 776, 1 Intra. L. Rev. (St. Louis U.) 168, 26 Notre Dame Law. 115, 23 Rocky Mtn. L. Rev. 352, 53 W. Va. L. Rev. 76; Slenker v. Grand Lodge, 344 Ill. App. 1, 100 N.E.2d 354 (1951), *cert. denied,* 344 U.S. 830 (1952) (charitable fraternal organization not liable for negligence of agent in operating automobile damaging plaintiff).

But see Darling v. Charleston Community Memorial Hosp., 33 Ill. 2d 326, 211 N.E.2d 253 (1965), n. 7 *infra.*

Indiana: Richardson v. St. Mary's Hosp., 191 N.E.2d 337 (Ind. App. 1963) (hospital not liable to paying patient for negligence of employee selected with proper care).

Iowa: Servison v. Young Men's Christian Assn., 230 Iowa 86, 296 N.W. 769 (1941) (Y.M.C.A. not liable to member who fell in a shower bath; but this case was expressly overruled in Haynes v. Presbyterian Hosp. Assn., 241 Iowa 1269, 45 N.W.2d 151 (1950), noted in 13 Ga. B.J. 474, 31 Or. L. Rev. 78, 20 U. Cin. L. Rev. 412).

Kansas: Leeper v. Salvation Army, 158 Kan. 396, 147 P.2d 702 (1944) (Salvation Army not liable for negligence of servant in damaging leased premises by fire; overruled by Noel v. Menninger Found., 175 Kan. 751, 267 P.2d 934 (1954), noted in 3 Kan. L. Rev. 62, 23 U. Kan. City L. Rev. 294.

Kentucky: Forrest v. Red Cross Hosp., 265 S.W.2d 80 (Ky. 1954) (hospital not liable to paying patient for food containing foreign substance; citing Restatement of Trusts §402); St. Walburg Monastery v. Feltner's Admr., 275 S.W.2d 784 (Ky. 1955) (hospital not liable for patient's death caused by negligence of nurse). But see Mullikin v. Jewish Hosp. Assn., 348 S.W.2d 930 (Ky. 1961), noted in 50 Ky. L.J. 627.

Louisiana: Jurjevich v. Hotel Dieu, 11 So. 2d 632 (La. App. 1943) (hospital not liable to paying patient for negligence of superintendent), noted in 17 Tulane L. Rev. 621; D'Antoni v. Sara Mayo Hosp., 144 So. 2d 643 (La. App. 1962) (hospital not liable to patient for negligence of employee); Hill v. Eye, Ear, Nose & Throat Hosp., 200 So. 2d 34 (La. 1967) (not liable to paying patient); Tyler v. Touro Infirmary, 223 So. 2d 148 (La. 1969) (three justices dissenting), *aff'g* Grant v. Touro Infirmary, 207 So. 2d 235 (La. App. 1968) (hospital not liable to patient for negligence of employee); Barrios v. Sara Mayo Hosp., 224 So. 2d 846 (La. App. 1969) (patient injured by negligence of physicians).

Maine: Rhoda v. Aroostook Gen. Hosp., 226 A.2d 530 (Me. 1967) (hospital not liable to paying patient for negligence of employees not properly selected by the governing board).

But in Isaacson v. Husson College, 297 A.2d 98 (Me. 1972), it was held that the defense of charitable immunity must be pleaded, and that the plaintiff, a student of the defendant college, who slipped on an icy pavement, was to be treated as a business visitor or invitee.

Maryland: Howard v. South Baltimore Gen. Hosp., 191 Md. 617, 62 A.2d 574 (1948) (hospital not liable to paying patient for negligence of servant); Thomas v. Board of County Commrs., 200 Md. 554, 92 A.2d 452 (1952) (county maintaining hospital not liable to paying patient for negligence of anaesthetist), noted in 7 Miami L.Q. 444; Cornelius v. Sinai Hosp. of Baltimore, 219 Md. 116, 148 A.2d 567 (1959) (hospital not liable to patient for negligence of physician); Howard v. Bishop Byrne Council Home, 249 Md. 233, 238 A.2d 863 (1968) (charitable home not liable to workman injured by negligence of its servant).

See Sanner v. Trustees of Sheppard & Enoch Pratt Hosp., 278 F. Supp. 138 (D. Md. 1968), *aff'd mem.,* 398 F.2d 226 (4th Cir. 1968); James v. Prince George's County, 288 Md. 315, 418 A.2d 1173 (1980) (volunteer fire department company).

Massachusetts: Bearse v. New England Deaconess Hosp., 321 Mass. 750, 72 N.E.2d 743 (1947) (hospital not liable for negligent injury to patient); Carpenter v. Young Men's Christian Assn., 324 Mass. 365, 86 N.E.2d 634 (1949) (Y.M.C.A. conducting playground and charging small fee; citing the text and Restatement of Trusts §402); Mastrangelo v. Maverick Dispensary, 330 Mass. 708, 115 N.E.2d 455 (1953) (hospital not liable to patient for negligence in maintenance of premises); Simpson v. Truesdale Hosp., 338 Mass. 787, 154 N.E.2d 357 (1958) (hospital not liable for negligently causing death of patient); Barrett v. Brooks Hosp., 338 Mass. 754, 157 N.E.2d 638 (1959) (hospital not liable to patient for negligence, although charity patients were not received in the hospital); Boxer v. Boston Symphony Orchestra, 339 Mass. 369, 159 N.E.2d 336 (1959), 342 Mass. 537, 174 N.E.2d 363 (1961) (Boston Symphony Orchestra not liable to musical director for injuries resulting from falling into the orchestra pit); Harrigan v. Cape Cod Hosp., 349 Mass. 765, 208 N.E.2d 232 (1965) (hospital not liable for negligence of employee).

In Colby v. Carney Hosp., 356 Mass. 527, 254 N.E.2d 407 (1969), the court held that the doctrine of charitable immunity is not unconstitutional. The court gave warning "that the next time we are squarely confronted by a legal question respecting the charitable immunity doctrine it is our intention to abolish it." In Trala v. Shea, 335 F. Supp. 81 (D. Mass. 1971), the federal court held that the contemplated change in the law was not intended to be retroactive.

See Ricker v. Northeastern Univ., 361 Mass. 169, 279 N.E.2d 671 (1972), holding a charitable corporation immune from liability for injury suffered prior to the decision in Colby v. Carney Hospital.

Massachusetts Ann. Laws, c. 231, §85K, as inserted by Laws 1971, c. 785, provides for tort liability of charities not exceeding $20,000. The limitation does not apply to torts committed in the course of activities primarily commercial in character. See §402.1, n. 5.

Mullins v. Pine Manor College, 389 Mass. 47, 449 N.E.2d 331 (1983) (applying 1971 statute).

As to the matter of sovereign immunity, see Hannigan v. New Gamma-Delta Chapter, 367 Mass. 658, 327 N.E.2d 882 (1975).

In Johnson v. Wesson Women's Hosp., 367 Mass. 717, 328 N.E.2d 490 (1975), it was held that a charitable hospital was immune from liability for an act prior to the enactment of the statute although subsequent to its announcement of a contemplated denial of immunity.

Michigan: Daszkiewicz v. Detroit Bd. of Educ., 301 Mich. 212, 3 N.W.2d 71 (1942) (municipal university not liable to student who fell down elevator); DeGroot v. Edison Inst., 306 Mich. 339, 10 N.W.2d 907 (1943) (historical museum not liable to paying guest for negligence of employee selected with care); Erwin v. St. Joseph's Hosp., 323 Mich. 114, 34 N.W.2d 480 (1948) (hospital not liable for negligence of physician and nurses); Browning v. Paddock, 364 Mich. 293, 111 N.W.2d 45 (1961) (injury suffered prior to ruling in Parker v. Port Huron Hosp., 361 Mich. 1, 105 N.W.2d 1 (1960)); Cibor v. Oakwood Hosp., 14 Mich. App. 1, 165 N.W.2d 326 (1969) (hospital not liable to patient for negligence of employee; injury suffered prior to ruling in Parker v. Port Huron Hosp.); Ross v. Consumers Power Co., 420 Mich. 567, 363 N.W.2d 641 (1984).

Mississippi: International Order v. Barnes, 204 Miss. 333, 37 So. 2d 487 (1948) (hospital not liable to patient for negligence of nurse if no negligence in selecting nurse).

Missouri: Todd v. Curators of Univ. of Mo., 347 Mo. 460, 147 S.W.2d 1063 (1941) (state university not liable for failure to provide safe place for employee to work), noted in 10 U. Kan. City L. Rev. 65; Stedem v. Jewish Memorial Hosp. Assn., 239 Mo. App. 38, 187 S.W.2d 469 (1945) (hospital not liable to paying patient for negligence in placing boiling water on defective tray); Dille v. St. Luke's Hosp., 355 Mo. 436, 196 S.W.2d 615 (1946) (hospital not liable to patient for negligence of servant); Hinman v. Berkman, 85 F. Supp. 2 (W.D. Mo. 1949) (United Jewish Appeal not liable to stranger injured in automobile collision); Schroeder v. City of St. Louis, 360 Mo. 293, 228 S.W.2d 677 (1950) (city hospital not liable for death of infant paying patient); Krueger v. Schmiechen, 364 Mo. 568, 264 S.W.2d 311 (1954) (governing body of church not liable for injuries resulting from fall on premises); Schulte v. Missionaries of La Salette Corp. of Mo., 352 S.W.2d 636 (Mo. 1962) (religious school not liable for injury to student caused by failure to see that swimming pool was filled), noted in 30 U. Kan. City L. Rev. 255; Koprivica v. Bethesda Gen. Hosp., 410 S.W.2d 84 (Mo. 1966) (patient injured by negligence of employees); Burns v. Owens, 459 S.W.2d 303 (Mo. 1970); Bodard v. Culver-Stockton College, 471 S.W.2d 253 (Mo. 1971) (injury occurred prior to November 10, 1969).

But see n. 7 *infra.*

In Swinford v. Bliley, 513 S.W.2d 381 (Mo. 1974), it was held that the abolition of immunity in the Abernathy case did not apply in the case of injuries incurred prior to the decision, even though the defendant was insured.

Nebraska: Parks v. Holy Angels Church, 160 Neb. 299, 70 N.W.2d 97 (1955) (church corporation not liable to person attending Mass); Muller v. Nebraska Methodist Hosp., 160 Neb. 279, 70 N.W.2d 86 (1955) (hospital not liable to paying patient); Cheatham v. Bishop Clarkson Memorial Hosp., 160 Neb. 297, 70 N.W.2d 96 (1955) (hospital not liable to patient).

But see Myers v. Drozda, 180 Neb. 183, 141 N.W.2d 852 (1966), overruling prior decisions.

Nevada: Springer v. Federated Church of Reno, 71 Nev. 177, 283 P.2d 1071 (1955) (church not liable to member falling on church steps).

New Hampshire: Sandwell v. Elliott Hosp., 92 N.H. 41, 24 A.2d 273 (1942) (hospital not liable to patient's visitor who fell on ice in the grounds because no violation of duty of care).

New Jersey: Boeckel v. Orange Memorial Hosp., 108 N.J.L. 453, 158 A. 832 (1932), *aff'd mem.,* 110 N.J.L. 509, 166 A. 146 (1933) (hospital not liable to mother of paying patient for negligence of supervising nurse); Bianchi v. South Park Presbyterian Church, 123 N.J.L. 325, 8 A.2d 567, 124 A.L.R. 808 (1939) (church not liable to Girl Scouts holding meeting in church and injured by negligence of servant not negligently selected), noted in 6 U. Pitt. L. Rev. 122; Fair v. Atlantic City Hosp., 25 N.J. Misc. 65, 50 A.2d 376 (1946) (hospital not liable to patient for negligence of administrators); Woods v. Overlook Hosp. Assn., 6 N.J. Super. 47, 69 A.2d 742 (1949) (hospital not liable to patient for negligence of nurse), noted in 1 Syracuse L. Rev. 503; Jones v. St. Mary's Roman Catholic Church, 7 N.J. 533, 82 A.2d 187 (1951), *cert. denied,* 342 U.S. 886 (1951) (church not liable to pupil injured by fellow pupil in school conducted by church); Casper v. Cooper Hosp., 26 N.J. Super. 535, 98 A.2d 605 (1953) (hospital not liable to student nurse); Stoolman v. Camden County Council Boy Scouts, 77 N.J. Super. 129, 185 A.2d 436 (1962) (statutory); Schultz v. Roman Catholic Archdiocese of Newark, 95 N.J. 530, 472 A.2d 531 (1984), noted in 15 Seton Hall L. Rev. 907 (1985), 16 Rutgers L.J. 393 (1985) (under N.J. Stat. Ann., §§2A:53A-7 to 2A:53A-11, charity was not liable for intentional tort committed by Scoutmaster against boy in Scout camp even if it was negligent in employing Scoutmaster); Heffelfinger v. Town of Morristown, 209 N.J. Super. 380, 507 A.2d 761 (1985) (persons who fell in town square); Gray v. St. Cecilia's School, 217 N.J. Super. 492, 526 A.2d 264 (1987) (parent of parochial school student).

New York: Robey v. Jewish Hosp. of Brooklyn, 280 N.Y. 533, 807, 20 N.E.2d 6, 21 N.E.2d 694 (1939), *rev'g* 254 A.D. 874, 5 N.Y.S.2d 14 (1938) (hospital not liable for admitting expectant mother where malady affecting infants was prevalent); Steinert v. Brunswick Home, 259 A.D. 1018, 20 N.Y.S.2d 459 (1940), *motion for leave to appeal denied,* 260 A.D. 10, 22 N.Y.S.2d 822 (1940), *appeal denied,* 284 N.Y. 822, 31 N.E.2d 517 (1940) (hospital not liable for negligence of doctor or nurse who is not its servant); Fisher v. Sydenham Hosp., 176 Misc. 7, 26 N.Y.S.2d 389 (1941) (hospital not liable for negligence of special nurse who is not its servant); Kaps v. Lenox Hill Hosp., 51 N.Y.S.2d 791 (1944), *aff'd mem.,* 269 A.D. 830, 930, 56 N.Y.S.2d 415, 57 N.Y.S.2d 843 (1945) (hospital not liable for negligence of nurse who is not its servant); Sutherland v. New York Polyclinic Medical School & Hosp., 273 A.D. 29, 75 N.Y.S.2d 135 (1947), *aff'd mem.,* 298 N.Y. 682, 794, 82 N.E.2d 583, 83 N.E.2d 477 (1948) (hospital not liable for negligence of physician and nurse in burning patient with hot water bottle), noted in 14 Brooklyn L. Rev. 293; Morse v. Syracuse Memorial Hosp., 83 N.Y.S.2d 830 (1948) (hospital not liable for negligence of undergraduate nurse); Bakal v. University Heights Sanitarium, 277 A.D. 572, 101 N.Y.S.2d 385 (1950), *aff'd mem.,* 302 N.Y. 870, 100 N.E.2d 51 (1951) (proprietary hospital not liable for negligence of nurse who is not its servant), noted in 1 Catholic U.L. Rev. 165, 2 Syracuse L. Rev. 396; Bryant v. Presbyterian Hosp., 304 N.Y. 538, 110 N.E.2d 391 (1953) (hospital not liable for negligence of nurse who is not its servant); Schultz v. Boy Scouts of Am., 65 N.Y.2d 189, 480 N.E.2d 679, 491 N.Y.S.2d 90 (1985) (Ohio and Texas charitable corporations whose employee committed an intentional tort in New York not liable for negligent selection of employee because New Jersey law of charitable immunity applied, the employee and his victims being domiciled in New Jersey).

North Carolina: Herndon v. Massey, 217 N.C. 610, 8 S.E.2d 914 (1940) (trustees of Y.W.C.A. not liable to member who slipped on floor in locker room), noted in 19 N.C.L. Rev. 245; Williams v. Union County Hosp. Assn., 234 N.C. 536, 67 S.E.2d 662 (1951) (hospital not liable for negligence of employee if selected with proper care); Williams v. Randolph Hosp., 237 N.C. 387, 75 S.E.2d 303 (1953) (hospital not liable to paying patient for negligence of employee selected with due care); Habuda v. Trustees of Rex Hosp., 3 N.C. App. 11, 164 S.E.2d 17 (1968) (hospital not liable for negligence of nurse selected with due care for injury occurring before decision of Rabon case cited in n. 7 *infra*); Darsie v. Duke Univ., 48 N.C. App. 20, 268 S.E.2d 554 (1980), *appeal denied.*

Ohio: Rudy v. Lakeside Hosp., 115 Ohio St. 539, 155 N.E. 126 (1926) (not liable for negligent loss of jewels entrusted to hospital by patient); Walsh v. Sisters of Charity of St. Vincent's Hosp., 47 Ohio App. 228, 191 N.E. 791 (1933) (hospital not liable to patient injured by explosion of fluoroscope); City Hosp. of Akron v. Lewis, 47 Ohio App. 465, 192 N.E. 140 (1934) (city hospital not liable to patient for negligence of nurse selected with care); Lakeside

Hosp. v. Kovar, 131 Ohio St. 333, 2 N.E.2d 857 (1936) (hospital not liable for negligence of nurse if selected with care); Burgie v. Muench, 65 Ohio App. 176, 29 N.E.2d 439 (1940) (church not liable to member of ladies' aid society who fell downstairs in dark into boiler room); Cullen v. Schmit, 139 Ohio St. 194, 39 N.E.2d 146 (1942) (church authorities not liable to person injured in basement of church where religious articles were sold); Emrick v. Pennsylvania R.R. Y.M.C.A. of Crestline, 69 Ohio App. 353, 43 N.E.2d 733 (1942) (Y.M.C.A. not liable to member for negligence of servants); Lovich v. Salvation Army, 81 Ohio App. 317, 75 N.E.2d 459 (1947) (inmate of home cannot recover for typhoid fever resulting from employment of typhoid carrier in kitchen unless governing authorities were negligent), noted in 9 Ohio S.L.J. 713; Esposito v. Henry H. Stambaugh Auditorium Assn., 49 Ohio Abs. 507, 77 N.E.2d 111 (1948) (auditorium association not liable to patron for injury resulting from negligent failure to furnish employees to assist patrons descending stairway), noted in 23 Notre Dame Law, 606; Tomasello v. Hoban, 60 Ohio Op. 2d 508, 155 N.E.2d 82 (1958) (church not liable for injury to guest from defect in the premises); Gibbon v. Young Women's Christian Assn., 170 Ohio St. 280, 164 N.E.2d 563 (1960), noted in 21 Ohio St. L.J. 247 (Y.W.C.A. not liable for death of child in swimming pool owing to negligence of lifeguard; court refused to overrule prior decisions), noted in 74 Harv. L. Rev. 614; Matthews v. Wittenberg College, 113 Ohio App. 387, 178 N.E.2d 526 (1960) (college not liable to student for negligence of employee selected with due care); Sturdevant v. Youngstown Dist. Girl Scout Council, 118 Ohio App. 489, 195 N.E.2d 914 (1962) (charitable organization not liable to beneficiary for negligence of employee if selected with care); Williams v. First United Church of Christ, 37 Ohio St. 2d 150, 66 Ohio Ops. 2d 311, 309 N.E.2d 924 (1974) (person injured at a church bazaar could recover if he was a non-beneficiary, or if the bazaar was operated for profit unrelated to church purposes).

But see n. 7 *infra*.

Oregon: Gregory v. Salem Gen. Hosp., 175 Or. 464, 153 P.2d 837 (1944) (hospital not liable to paying patients for negligence of nurse); Landgraver v. Emanuel Lutheran Charity Bd., 203 Or. 489, 280 P.2d 301 (1955) (hospital not liable to patient for negligence of employee: citing the text and Restatement of Trusts §402), overruled by Hungerford v. Portland Sanitarium & Benevolent Assn., 235 Or. 412, 384 P.2d 1009 (1963).

Pennsylvania: Siidekum v. Animal Rescue League, 353 Pa. 408, 45 A.2d 59 (1946) (charitable corporation not liable for death caused by its truck); Bond v. Pittsburgh, 368 Pa. 404, 84 A.2d 328 (1951), noted in 25 Temp. L.Q. 488 (religious corporation as abutting owner not liable over to city against whom recovery was had by a person injured because of negligent condition of sidewalk); Michael v. Lancaster School Dist., 11 D.&C.2d 150 (Pa. 1957), *aff'd per curiam*, 391 Pa. 209, 137 A.2d 456 (1958) (school district held not liable to injured child); Knecht v. St. Mary's Hosp., 392 Pa. 75, 140 A.2d 30 (1958) (hospital not liable for injury to patient, two justices dissenting); Polakovic v. Pulcini, 14 D.&C.2d 703 (Pa. 1958) (nonprofit medical service corporation; statute making it exempt from taxation as charitable); Michael v. Hahnemann

Medical College & Hosp., 404 Pa. 424, 172 A.2d 769 (1961) (hospital not liable to patient for negligence of doctors employed by it, three justices dissenting).

But see Flagiello v. Pennsylvania Hosp., 417 Pa. 486, 208 A.2d 193 (1965), overruling prior cases.

Rhode Island: Fournier v. Miriam Hosp., 93 R.I. 299, 175 A.2d 298 (1961), 93 R.I. 1299, 179 A.2d 578 (1962) (hospital not liable to patient for negligence of employees; statute so providing held constitutional); Carroccio v. Roger Williams Hosp., 104 R.I. 617, 247 A.2d 903 (1968).

By Rhode Island Gen. Laws 1956, §7-1-22, it was provided that no charitable hospital should be liable for the negligence of its officers, agents, or employees in the care of patients. Gen. Laws 1956, §7-1-22 was repealed by Laws 1968, c. 43. See n. 7 *infra.*

South Carolina: Caughman v. Columbia Young Men's Christian Assn., 212 S.C. 337, 47 S.E.2d 788 (1948) (Y.M.C.A. not subject to Workmen's Compensation Act), noted in 33 Minn. L. Rev. 440; Decker v. Bishop of Charleston, 247 S.C. 317, 147 S.E.2d 264 (1966) (suit against bishop as corporation sole).

But see S.C. Code Ann. 1962, §10-145.1, as enacted by Laws 1977, c. 182. See n. 7 *infra.*

Texas: Southern Methodist Univ. v. Clayton, 142 Tex. 179, 176 S.W.2d 749 (1944) (university not liable to person injured by collapse of bleachers), noted in 22 Tex. L. Rev. 500; Scott v. Wm. M. Rice Inst., 178 S.W.2d 156 (Tex. Civ. App. 1944) (college not liable to person injured in stadium through negligence of servants employed with due care), noted in 22 Tex. L. Rev. 500; Baptist Memorial Hosp. v. Marrable, 244 S.W.2d 567 (Tex. Civ. App. 1951) (hospital not liable for negligence of employee in failing to supply sideboards to bed), noted in 5 Baylor L. Rev. 199; Felan v. Lucey, 259 S.W.2d 302 (Tex. Civ. App. 1953) (archbishop as trustee of cemetery not liable when monument fell on visitor); Jones v. Baylor Hosp., 284 S.W.2d 929 (Tex. Civ. App. 1955) (hospital not liable for negligence of nurse if no negligence in hiring nurse); Baptist Memorial Hosp. v. McTighe, 303 S.W.2d 446 (Tex. Civ. App. 1957) (hospital not liable to paying patient for injury resulting from hidden step); Penaloza v. Baptist Memorial Hosp., 304 S.W.2d 203 (Tex. Civ. App. 1957) (hospital not liable for negligence of nurse if no negligence in selecting her); Davidson v. Methodist Hosp. of Dallas, 348 S.W.2d 400 (Tex. Civ. App. 1961) (hospital not liable to patient if no negligence in selecting or retaining employee); Goelz v. J.K. & Susie L. Wadley Research Inst. & Blood Bank, 350 S.W.2d 573 (Tex. Civ. App. 1961) (blood bank not liable for wrongful death resulting from negligence of employee); Killen v. Brazosport Memorial Hosp., 364 S.W.2d 411 (Tex. Civ. App. 1963) (hospital not liable where no negligence of the governing board); Watkins v. Southcrest Baptist Church, 399 S.W.2d 530 (Tex. 1966) (hospital not liable to invitee where the governing board was not at fault; two justices dissented and three concurred but were of the opinion that the doctrine of charitable immunity should not be recognized in cases thereafter arising); Mayfield v. Gleichert, 437 S.W.2d 638 (Tex. Civ. App. 1969), *semble* (slander); Sprague v. Memorial Baptist Hosp. Sys., 580 S.W.2d 1 (Tex. Civ. App. 1979) (action arose prior to 1966).

Vermont: Ellsworth v. Brattleboro Retreat, 68 F. Supp. 706 (D. Vt. 1946) (asylum not liable for negligently allowing insane patient to commit suicide).

Virginia: Memorial Hosp. v. Oakes, 200 Va. 878, 108 S.E.2d 388 (1959) (hospital not liable for negligence of employee if no negligence in selection or retention); Hill v. Leigh Memorial Hosp. 204 Va. 501, 132 S.E.2d 411 (1963) (hospital not liable to patient for negligence of employee if no negligence in selection or retention).

Washington: Miller v. Mohr, 198 Wash. 619, 89 P.2d 807 (1939) (hospital not liable for negligence of student nurse if no negligence in selection or retention of nurse); Weiss v. Swedish Hosp., 16 Wash. 2d 446, 133 P.2d 978 (1943) (hospital not liable to paying patient for negligence of nurse or intern if no negligence in their selection or retention).

These cases are overruled in Pierce v. Yakima Valley Memorial Hosp. Assn., 43 Wash. 2d 162, 260 P.2d 765 (1953), noted in 59 Dick. L. Rev. 277.

In Lyon v. Tumwater Evangelical Free Church, 47 Wash. 2d 202, 287 P.2d 128 (1955), it was held that a church was not liable to a child transported without charge on a bus to Sunday School who was injured through negligence of the bus driver.

In Pedersen v. Immanuel Lutheran Church, 57 Wash. 2d 576, 358 P.2d 549 (1961), it was held that a church was not liable for injury to a Ladies Aid member attending a luncheon for which she paid fifty cents and contributed a cake.

In Friend v. Cove Methodist Church, 65 Wash. 2d 174, 396 P.2d 546 (1964), these cases were overruled, and a church was held liable to a visitor injured through the negligence of servants.

See note, 17 Wash. L. Rev. 242 (1962).

West Virginia: Fisher v. Ohio Valley Gen. Hosp. Assn., 137 W. Va. 723, 73 S.E.2d 667 (1952) (hospital not liable to paying patient for negligence of nurse's aide); Meade v. St. Francis Hosp. of Charleston, 137 W. Va. 834, 74 S.E.2d 405 (1953) (hospital not liable to a paying patient for negligence of its servant).

But see Adkins v. St. Francis Hosp., 149 W. Va. 705, 143 S.E.2d 154 (1965).

Wisconsin: Schumacher v. Evangelical Deaconess Socy. of Wis., 218 Wis. 169, 260 N.W. 476 (1935) (hospital not liable to patient for negligence of management in selecting incompetent employee); Waldman v. Young Men's Christian Assn., 227 Wis. 43, 277 N.W. 632 (1938) (Y.M.C.A. not liable to boy in swimming class injured through negligence of employee); Schau v. Morgan, 241 Wis. 334, 6 N.W.2d 212 (1942) (hospital not liable for negligence of employee to paying patient); Baldwin v. St. Peter's Congregation, 264 Wis. 626, 60 N.W.2d 349 (1953) (parochial school not liable to person injured by snow on sidewalk); Grabinski v. St. Francis Hosp., 266 Wis. 339, 63 N.W.2d 693 (1954) (hospital not liable to one slipping on wet floor at entrance); Hooten v. Civil Air Patrol, 161 F. Supp. 478 (E.D. Wis. 1958) (Wisconsin law; charitable corporation incorporated by Congress not liable for injuries to child resulting from attractive nuisance); Duncan v. Steeper, 17 Wis. 2d 226, 116 N.W.2d 154 (1962) (hospital not liable to paying patient for injury occurring

been held liable.[7]   As is shown in the footnotes, the modern

---

before 1961; see n. 7 *infra*); Koenig v. Milwaukee Blood Center, 23 Wis. 2d
324, 127 N.W.2d 50 (1964) (hospital not liable for impure blood transfusion
for injury occurring before 1961); Christy v. Schwartz, 49 Wis. 2d 760, 183
N.W.2d 81 (1971) (holding hospital immune as to cause of action arising
before 1961).

See Esbeck, Tort Claims Against Churches and Ecclesiastical Officers: the
First Amendment Considerations, 89 W. Va. L. Rev. 1 (1986); Note, Liability
of Municipally Run General Hospitals, 32 Wayne L. Rev. 1475 (1986).

[7]*England:* Collins v. Hertfordshire County Council, [1947] K.B. 598
(hospital liable for maintaining a negligent system as to administration of
drugs and for negligence of resident house surgeon), noted in 21 Austl. L.J.
183, 302, 10 Camb. L.J. 124, 25 Can. B. Rev. 646, 63 Law Q. Rev. 410, 64
id. 26, 203 Law T. 303, 10 Mod. L. Rev. 425, 3 Res Judicatae 221; Cassidy
v. Ministry of Health, [1951] 1 All E.R. 574 (Ministry of Health liable for
negligence of surgeon employed by hospital), noted in 30 Can. B. Rev. 423,
95 Sol. J. 213.

Federal: Tuengel v. City of Sitka, Alaska, 118 F. Supp. 399 (D. Alaska 1954)
(city hospital liable to business visitor); Byrd v. Blue Ridge Rural Elec. Coop.,
215 F.2d 542 (4th Cir. 1954), *rev'g* 118 F. Supp. 838 (W.D.S.C. 1954) (non-
profit rural electric cooperative liable for negligence of servant); Fulmer v.
United States, 133 F. Supp. 775 (D. Neb. 1955) (United States liable under
Federal Tort Claims Act for negligence of ambulance driver employed by
Veterans' Administration); Howard v. Sisters of Charity of Leavenworth, 193
F. Supp. 191 (D. Mont. 1961) (hospital liable to paying patient for negligence
of employee, although no state precedent; citing the text and Restatement
(Second) of Trusts §402); White v. United States, 317 F.2d 13 (4th Cir. 1963),
rev'g 205 F. Supp. 662 (E.D. Va. 1962) (United States liable under Federal Tort
Claims Act for negligence of employees); Heirs of Fruge v. Blood Servs., 506
F.2d 841 (5th Cir. 1975) (applying Louisiana law); Bliss v. Allentown Pub.
Library, 534 F. Supp. 356 (E.D. Pa. 1982) (school district operating a public
library as trustee liable for injury to library user even though the school district
enjoyed sovereign immunity); Quinn v. Kent Gen. Hosp. 617 F. Supp. 1226
(D. Del. 1985); Radosevic v. Virginia Intermont College, 633 F. Supp. 1084
(W.D. Va. 1986).

Arizona: Ray v. Tucson Medical Center, 72 Ariz. 22, 230 P.2d 220 (1951)
(hospital liable to patient for negligence of nurse's aide; citing the text), noted
in 13 Ohio St. L.J. 291, 20 U. Cin. L. Rev. 505, 5 U. Fla. L. Rev. 213; Roman
Catholic Church, Diocese of Tucson v. Keenan, 74 Ariz. 20, 243 P.2d 455
(1952) (church maintaining school in which student injured through negligence of employee liable).

California: Silva v. Providence Hosp. of Oakland, 14 Cal. 2d 762, 97 P.2d
798 (1939) (hospital liable to paying patient for negligence of hospital nurse),
noted in 28 Calif. L. Rev. 530, 26 Va. L. Rev. 951; England v. Hospital of the
Good Samaritan, 14 Cal. 2d 791, 97 P.2d 813 (1939) (like preceding case);

Humphreys v. San Francisco Area Council, Boy Scouts of Am., 129 P.2d 118 (Cal. App. 1942), *aff'd,* 22 Cal. 2d 436, 139 P.2d 941 (1943) (Boy Scout corporation liable to employee for negligence of another employee); Welsh v. Mercy Hosp., 65 Cal. App. 2d 473, 151 P.2d 17 (1944) (hospital liable to paying patient for failure to provide reasonably safe bed); Edwards v. Hollywood Canteen, 27 Cal. 2d 802, 167 P.2d 729 (1946) (servicemen's recreation center liable for injury to hostess for failure to protect her against boisterous serviceman); Malloy v. Fong, 37 Cal. 2d 356, 232 P.2d 241 (1951) (religious corporation liable to student of Bible school for negligence of agent causing automobile accident); Sokolow v. City of Hope, 41 Cal. 2d 668, 262 P.2d 841 (1953) (charitable corporation liable to volunteer waitress); Tunkl v. Regents of Univ. of Cal., 60 Cal. 2d 92, 383 P.2d 441 (1963) (hospital liable for negligence of doctors employed by it causing injury to patient).

Colorado: St. Luke's Hosp. Assn. v. Long, 125 Colo. 25, 240 P.2d 917 (1952) (hospital liable for death of infant paying patient resulting from negligence in failing to protect bed by proper sideboards); Michard v. Myron Stratton Home, 144 Colo. 251, 355 P.2d 1078 (1960) (action lies against charitable corporation for injury to leased premises, although execution could not be levied on charity assets).

Connecticut: Cohen v. General Hosp. Socy., 113 Conn. 188, 154 A. 435 (1931) (hospital liable for injury to invitee resulting from condition of premises); Haliburton v. General Hosp. Socy., 133 Conn. 61, 48 A.2d 261 (1946) (*semble,* hospital liable to patient for negligence in employing improper person), noted in 95 U. Pa. L. Rev. 237; Formica v. Hartford Roman Catholic Diocesan Corp., 14 Conn. Supp. 390 (1946) (church liable to visitor though not to worshipper); Kipry v. Grace New Haven Community Hosp., 15 Conn. Supp. 255 (1947) (liable for corporate negligence but not for negligence of employee); Bachino v. Church of the Sacred Heart of Jesus, 16 Conn. Supp. 215 (1949) (church liable for negligence of controlling officers); Daines v. Groton Post, Patrolmen's Benevolent Assn., 17 Conn. Supp. 283 (1951) (charitable association liable to employee); Dickson v. Yale Univ., 141 Conn. 250, 105 A.2d 463 (1954) (university liable to business invitee); Berube v. Salvation Army, 21 Conn. Supp. 487, 157 A.2d 493 (1960) (liable for negligence of employee to customer in store operated by Salvation Army); Bader v. United Orthodox Synagogue, 148 Conn. 449, 172 A.2d 192 (1961) (church liable to member injured by defective premises due to negligence of governing board); By Conn. Gen. Stat. 1958, §52-557d, it is provided that "The common law defense of charitable immunity is abolished and shall not constitute a valid defense to any cause of action arising subsequent to the effective date of this act."

Delaware: Durney v. St. Francis Hosp., 83 A.2d 753 (Del. Super. 1951) (hospital liable to infant patient for negligence of nurse).

District of Columbia: President & Directors of Georgetown College v. Hughes, 76 App. D.C. 123, 130 F.2d 810 (1942), *aff'g* Hughes v. President & Directors of Georgetown College, 33 F. Supp. 867 (D.D.C. 1940) (hospital liable to special nurse employed by patient), noted in 23 B.U.L. Rev. 108, 12 Fordham L. Rev. 89, 6 U. Detroit L.J. 142, 11 U. Kansas City L. Rev. 228, 91 U. Pa. L. Rev. 571; Heimbuch v. President & Directors of Georgetown College,

251 F. Supp. 614 (D.D.C. 1966) (university liable to student for hazing accident).

But see Calomeris v. District of Columbia, 125 F. Supp. 266 (D.D.C. 1954) (hospital operated by District of Columbia).

Florida: Nicholson v. Good Samaritan Hosp., 145 Fla. 360, 199 So. 344, 133 A.L.R. 809 (1940) (hospital liable to paying patient for negligence of hospital nurse though there was no negligence in employing nurse), noted in 15 Fla. L.J. 232; Florida Stat. Ann., §768.28, as amended by Laws 1983, c. 83-257, partially waives sovereign immunity as to some state institutions.

Georgia: Hospital Auth. of City of Marietta v. Misfeldt, 99 Ga. App. 702, 109 S.E.2d 816 (1959) (hospital liable to patient for negligence of employee though selected with proper care); Hipp v. Hospital Auth. of City of Marietta, 104 Ga. App. 174, 121 S.E.2d 273 (1961) (hospital liable to patient for improper conduct of employee not selected with proper care); Medical Center Hosp. Auth. v. Andrews, 250 Ga. 424, 297 S.E.2d 28 (1982) (hospital liable to patient for malpractice to the extent of noncharitable assets); Allgood Rd. United Methodist Church v. Smith, 173 Ga. App. 28, 325 S.E.2d 392 (1984), *cert. denied,* 1985 (by failing to raise it before judgment, church waived defense that plaintiff failed to allege and prove existence of noncharitable assets from which judgment could be collected).

Hawaii: Kamau v. Hawaii County, Cushnie v. Hawaii County, 41 Haw. 527 (1957).

Idaho: Wheat v. Idaho Falls Latter Day Saints Hosp., 78 Idaho 60, 297 P.2d 1041 (1956) (liable to paying patient for negligence of employee); Bell v. Presbytery of Boise, 91 Idaho 374, 421 P.2d 745 (1966) (plaintiff injured by fall on supervised church group outing).

Illinois: Darling v. Charleston Community Memorial Hosp., 33 Ill. 2d 326, 211 N.E.2d 253 (1965) (overruling prior decisions, but not retroactively); Gubbe v. Catholic Diocese of Rockford, 122 Ill. App. 2d 71, 257 N.E.2d 239 (1970) *(semble).*

In Haymes v. Catholic Bishop of Chicago, 41 Ill. 2d 336, 243 N.E.2d 203, 38 A.L.R.3d 473 (1969), it was held that a statute limiting tort liability of private schools to $10,000 that did not apply to public schools and other institutions was unconstitutional as discriminatory.

Indiana: Old Folks' & Orphan Children's Home v. Roberts, 91 Ind. App. 533, 171 N.E. 10 (1930) (charitable home liable to inmate for negligence of servant where negligence in selection or retention of servant); Ball Memorial Hosp. v. Freeman, 196 N.E.2d 274 (Ind. 1964) (hospital liable to patient for failing to employ proper method in preparation, bottling, and dispensing of drugs); Harris v. Young Women's Christian Assn., 250 Ind. 491, 237 N.E.2d 242 (1968) (overruling prior decisions that granted immunity).

Iowa: Andrews v. Young Men's Christian Assn., 226 Iowa 374, 284 N.W. 186 (1939) (Y.M.C.A. liable to carpenter employed by WPA to repair building), noted in 24 Iowa L. Rev. 769, 87 U. Pa. L. Rev. 1015; Haynes v. Presbyterian Hosp. Assn., 241 Iowa 1269, 45 N.W.2d 151 (1950) (hospital liable to patient for negligence of employees), noted in 5 Miami L.Q. 631; Sullivan v. First Presbyterian Church, 260 Iowa 1373, 152 N.W.2d 628 (1967).

Kansas: Noel v. Menninger Found., 175 Kan. 751, 267 P.2d 934 (1954) (denying immunity altogether and overruling prior cases), noted in 3 Kan. L. Rev. 62, 23 U. Kan. City L. Rev. 294: Carroll v. Kittle, 203 Kan. 841, 457 P.2d 21 (1969) (overruling prior cases as to governmental immunity).

Kentucky: Roland v. Catholic Archdiocese of Louisville, 301 S.W.2d 574 (1957) (religious corporation liable to tenant of income-producing property for injury by fire due to failure to comply with safety ordinance); Mullikin v. Jewish Hosp. Assn., 348 S.W.2d 930 (Ky. 1961) (hospital liable for injuries to patients resulting from negligence of employees; overruling prior cases), noted in 50 Ky. L.J. 627; Gillum v. Good Samaritan Hosp., 348 S.W.2d 924 (Ky. 1961) (hospital liable to visitor injured through negligence of employee); Hillard v. Good Samaritan Hosp., 348 S.W.2d 939 (Ky. 1961) (hospital liable for death of patient caused by negligence of employees).

Louisiana: Lusk v. United States Fidelity & Guaranty Co., 199 So. 666 (La. 1941) (*semble,* hospital liable to visitor who slipped on floor); Viosca v. Touro Infirmary, 170 So. 2d 222 (La. App. 1965) (hospital liable to visitor for negligence of employees); White v. Charity Hosp. of La. in New Orleans, 239 So. 2d 385 (La. App. 1970) (charitable immunity not applicable to a government hospital); Garlington v. Kingsley, 289 So. 2d 88 (La. 1973) (overruling prior cases); Jackson v. Doe, 296 So. 2d 323 (La. 1974); Connor v. Methodist Hosp., 297 So. 2d 660 (La. 1974) (holding the decisions refusing immunity are retroactive). See Bourgeois v. Jones, 481 So. 2d 145 (La. App. 1986), *writ denied,* 484 So. 2d 136 (La. 1986).

Maryland: By Ann. Code 1957, art. 43, §556A, as enacted by Laws 1966, c. 673, it is provided that no hospital or related institution shall be immune from liability for tort on the ground that it is a charitable institution, but that if it is insured from such liability in an amount not less than $100,000, it shall not be liable for damages in excess of that amount.

Michigan: Winslow v. Veterans of Foreign Wars Natl. Home, 328 Mich. 488, 44 N.W.2d 19 (1950) (veterans' home liable for death caused by operation of automobile by its employees); Parker v. Port Huron Hosp., 361 Mich. 1, 105 N.W.2d 1 (1960) (hospital liable for death of patient resulting from negligence of employees; overruling prior cases), noted in 36 Notre Dame Law. 93, 16 Sw. L.J. 689.

Minnesota: Swigerd v. City of Ortonville, 246 Minn. 339, 75 N.W.2d 217 (1956) (city liable for death of patient in city hospital resulting from negligence of nurse); Miller v. Macalester College, 262 Minn. 418, 115 N.W.2d 666 (1962) (college liable for injury to student caused by failure of instructor to use reasonable care as to scaffold used in dramatic production).

Mississippi: International Order v. Barnes, 204 Miss. 333, 37 So. 2d 487 (1948) (hospital liable to patient for negligence in selecting nurses); Mississippi Baptist Hosp. v. Holmes, 214 Miss. 906, 55 So. 2d 142, 25 A.L.R.2d 12 (1951), 56 So. 2d 709 (1952) (hospital liable to patient for negligence of technician in causing death of patient; overruling prior cases; citing the text), noted in 51 Mich. L. Rev. 309, 23 Miss. L.J. 152.

Missouri: Abernathy v. Sisters of St. Mary's, 446 S.W.2d 599 (Mo. 1969) (overruling prior cases, applicable to causes of action arising after the decision); Garnier v. St. Andrew Presbyterian Church, 446 S.W.2d 607 (Mo. 1969); Hill v. Boles, 583 S.W.2d 141 (Mo. 1979).

In Swinford v. Bliley, 513 S.W.2d 381 (Mo. 1974), it was held that the abolition of immunity in the Abernathy case did not apply in the case of injuries incurred prior to the decision, even though the defendant was insured.

Nebraska: Wright v. Salvation Army, 125 Neb. 216, 249 N.W. 549 (1933) (*semble,* charitable corporation maintaining a store liable to business visitor injured through defective condition of premises); Myers v. Drozda, 180 Neb. 183, 141 N.W.2d 852 (1966) (liability to patient; overruling prior decisions, applicable to causes of action arising before the decision only if insured).

New Hampshire: Welch v. Frisbie Memorial Hosp., 90 N.H. 337, 9 A.2d 761 (1939) (hospital liable to patient for negligence of X-ray technician, though not for negligence of physician); Nickerson v. Laconia Hosp. Assn., 96 N.H. 482, 79 A.2d 5 (1951) (hospital liable to visitor for knowingly maintaining unsafe railing); Kardulas v. Dover, 99 N.H. 359, 111 A.2d 327 (1955) (city conducting hospital liable to paying patient for negligence of employee); Wheeler v. Monadnock Community Hosp., 103 N.H. 306, 171 A.2d 23 (1961) (hospital liable to child visitor); Dowd v. Portsmouth Hosp., 105 N.H. 53, 193 A.2d 788 (1963) (hospital liable to mother and child visiting a clinic, because there was failure to use care owing to invitees).

New Jersey: Daniels v. Rahway Hosp., 10 N.J. Misc. 585, 160 A. 644 (1932) (hospital liable to stranger injured by negligence of ambulance driver); Simmons v. Wiley Methodist Episcopal Church, 112 N.J.L. 129, 170 A. 237 (1934) (church liable to stranger injured by truck operated by its servant); Kolb v. Monmouth Memorial Hosp., 116 N.J.L. 118, 182 A. 822 (1936) (hospital liable to person other than recipient of benefits); Fields v. Mountainside Hosp., 22 N.J. Misc. 72, 35 A.2d 701 (1944) (hospital liable to paying patient for negligence in selection of employees or for failure to furnish proper equipment); Rose v. Raleigh Fitkin-Paul Morgan Memorial Hosp., 136 N.J.L. 553, 57 A.2d 29 (1948), *aff'g* 25 N.J. Misc. 311, 53 A.2d 178 (1947) (hospital liable to private nurse for injury from fall due to negligence of employee); Lindroth v. Christ Hosp., 21 N.J. 588, 123 A.2d 10 (1956) (hospital liable to surgeon injured in elevator); Dalton v. St. Luke's Catholic Church, 27 N.J. 22, 141 A.2d 273 (1958) (church liable to plaintiff who fell in vestibule while on way to mass); Collopy v. Newark Eye & Ear Infirmary, 27 N.J. 29, 141 A.2d 276 (1958) (hospital liable to patient for negligence, overruling prior cases; citing the text); Benton v. Young Men's Christian Assn., 27 N.J. 67, 141 A.2d 298 (1958), *rev'g* 47 N.J. Super. 372, 136 A.2d 27 (1957) (Y.M.C.A. liable to member injured in fall on slippery stairs).

By N.J. Stat., §§2A:53A-7 to 2A:53A-11, as inserted by Laws 1959, c. 90, it is provided that no charitable association shall be liable for the negligence of any agent or servant to a beneficiary of the works of the association, but that such immunity shall not extend to other persons suffering damage, and that such association organized for hospital purposes shall be liable to a beneficiary for damages resulting from negligence to an amount not exceeding $10,000.

In Turer v. Ahavas Achem Anshe, 53 N.J. Super. 175, 147 A.2d 94 (1958), it was held that a similar 1958 statute was not retroactive so as to preclude recovery against a religious corporation. See also Terracciona v. Magee, 53 N.J. Super. 557, 148 A.2d 68 (1959) (action against Y.M.C.A.). In Anasiewicz v. Sacred Heart Church, 74 N.J. Super. 532, 181 A.2d 787 (1962), it was held that under this statute a church was not liable for injuries sustained by an invited guest at a wedding ceremony in a fall on icy steps of the church, because the plaintiff was a beneficiary.

In La Parre v. Young Men's Christian Assn., 30 N.J. 225, 152 A.2d 340 (1959), it was held that this statute was not retroactive so as to preclude recovery against a Y.M.C.A.

In Mayer v. Fairlawn Jewish Center, 71 N.J. Super. 313, 177 A.2d 40 (1961), aff'd, 38 N.J. 549, 186 A.2d 274 (1962), it was held that a religious social center was not immune from liability to a person making repairs on the buildings.

In Makar v. St. Nicholas etc. Church, 78 N.J. Super. 1, 187 A.2d 353 (1963), it was held that the statute was not unconstitutional as an establishment of religion.

In Gould v. Theresa Grotta Center, 83 N.J. Super. 169, 199 A.2d 74 (1964), it was held that under the statute a nursing home was not a hospital and was immune from liability to a patient.

In Wiklund v. Presbyterian Church of Clifton, 90 N.J. Super. 335, 217 A.2d 463 (1966), a church was held immune from liability to a Sunday school teacher because she was a beneficiary.

In Hauser v. Young Men's Christian Assn., 91 N.J. Super. 172, 219 A.2d 532 (1966), the Y.M.C.A. was held immune from liability to a paying guest because he was a beneficiary.

In Peacock v. Burlington County Historical Socy., 95 N.J. Super. 205, 230 A.2d 513 (1967), it was held that a woman who accompanied her husband in his research in a library was, as beneficiary, precluded under the statute from holding it liable for personal injuries; in Schultz v. Roman Catholic Archdiocese of Newark, 95 N.J. 530, 472 A.2d 531 (1984), noted in 15 Seton Hall L. Rev. 907 (1985) and in 16 Rutgers L.J. 393 (1985), it was held that, under N.J. Stat. Ann., §§2A:53A-7 to 2A:53A-11, a charity was not liable for an intentional tort resulting in death committed against a boy in a scout camp by a scoutmaster employed by it, even if the charity was negligent in employing the scoutmaster; in Jerolamon v. Fairleigh Dickinson Univ., 199 N.J. Super. 179, 488 A.2d 1064 (1985) it was held that a nonprofit university could be liable to an assistant registrar and her husband for malicious libel and assault and battery; in Harrington v. Clara Maass Hosp., 208 N.J. Super. 26, 365, 506 A.2d 26 (1986), it was held that a girlfriend who went with brother of patient to hospital was not a beneficiary.

In Jacobson v. Atlantic City Hosp., 392 F.2d 149 (3d Cir. 1968), it was held that the statutory limit of $10,000 was applicable to actions for wrongful death against a hospital.

In Book v. Aguth Achim Anchai, 101 N.J. Super. 559, 245 A.2d 51 (1968), it was held that a patron of bingo games operated by a religious society was not a beneficiary and could recover for personal injuries.

In Lawlor v. Cloverleaf Memorial Park, 56 N.J. 326, 266 A.2d 569 (1970) (citing the text), it was held that under the statute a privately promoted non-religious cemetery association does not enjoy charitable immunity.

In Muntz v. Newark City Hosp., 115 N.J. Super. 273, 279 A.2d 135 (1971), it was held that the statute is applicable to a city-owned hospital.

In Vitolo v. St. Peter's Church, 118 N.J. Super. 35, 285 A.2d 570 (1972), it was held that under the New Jersey statute a parishioner who had sustained injuries on leaving the church could not recover damages, although the church carried liability insurance.

In Brody v. Overlook Hosp., 121 N.J. Super. 299, 296 A.2d 668 (1972), it was held that the statute gave no immunity where the tort was not based on negligence but on strict liability.

In Sommers v. Union Beach First Aid Squad, 139 N.J. Super. 425, 354 A.2d 347 (1976), where a statute gave charitable immunity to the claim of a beneficiary of the charity, it was held that a woman who fell on ice in entering the premises to make a contribution to the charity because it had rendered a service to her mother was not a beneficiary, and a summary judgment for the defendant was erroneous.

In Pomeroy v. Little League Baseball of Collingswood, 142 N.J. Super. 471, 362 A.2d 39 (1976), it was held that a little league baseball organization was a charity and exempt from liability to an injured spectator and, as such, a beneficiary.

In Jacobs v. North Jersey Blood Center, 172 N.J. Super. 159, 411 A.2d 210 (1979), it was held that a nonprofit organization that extracted blood and sold it was not a charitable organization and was not immune from tort liability.

In Kasten v. Young Men's Christian Assn., 173 N.J. Super. 1, 412 A.2d 1346 (1980), it was held that a nonmember of a Y.M.C.A. injured in a ski area conducted by it for profit, though the profit was devoted to charitable purposes, was not precluded from suing.

New York: Sheehan v. North County Community Hosp., 273 N.Y. 163, 7 N.E.2d 28, 109 A.L.R. 1197 (1937) (hospital liable to paying patient injured through negligence of driver of ambulance); Dillon v. Rockaway Beach Hosp. & Dispensary, 284 N.Y. 176, 30 N.E.2d 373 (1940) (hospital liable to paying patient for negligence of hospital attendant), noted in 15 St. John's L. Rev. 321; Volk v. City of N.Y., 284 N.Y. 279, 30 N.E.2d 596 (1940) (city hospital liable to nurse for negligence of supervisor in administrative function of maintaining proper medicines), noted in 10 Brooklyn L. Rev. 304; Howe v. Medical Arts Center Hosp., 261 A.D. 1088, 26 N.Y.S.2d 957 (1941), *aff'd mem.*, 287 N.Y. 698, 39 N.E.2d 303 (1942) (hospital liable to patient for negligence in employing incompetent undergraduate nurse); Stearns v. Schenectady Day Nursery, 262 A.D. 638, 31 N.Y.S.2d 277 (1941), *aff'd mem.*, 288 N.Y. 574, 42 N.E.2d 24 (1942) (officer injured through negligence of superintendent); Abbott v. New York Pub. Library, 263 A.D. 314, 32 N.Y.S.2d 963 (1942) (public library liable to visitor for negligence in permitting attack on him by insane person); Goldman v. Winkelstein, 263 A.D. 958, 32 N.Y.S.2d 949 (1942) (hospital liable to patient for negligence of employee); Weltman v. New York Univ., 264 A.D. 907, 35 N.Y.S.2d 892 (1942) (university liable to student injured through negligence of professor); Lainen v. Tonsil Hosp., 36 N.Y.S.2d

55 (1942) (hospital liable to patient prematurely discharged by administrative official); Heinemann v. Jewish Agric. Soc., 178 Misc. 897, 37 N.Y.S.2d 354 (1942), *aff'd mem.*, 266 A.D. 907, 43 N.Y.S.2d 746 (1943), *leave to appeal granted,* 291 N.Y. 828, 51 N.E.2d 698 (1944) (New York charitable corporation held not exempt from liability for negligent automobile accident in New Jersey); Martucci v. Brooklyn Children's Aid Socy., 133 F.2d 252 (2d Cir. 1943), 140 F.2d 732 (1944) (nursing home liable for failure to provide safe quarters for patient; New York law); Ranelli v. Society of N.Y. Hosp., 49 N.Y.S.2d 898 (1944), *mod. mem.*, 269 A.D. 906, 56 N.Y.S.2d 481 (1945), *aff'd mem.*, 295 N.Y. 850, 67 N.E.2d 257 (1946) (hospital liable to patient for negligence of non-professional employees); Iacono v. New York Polyclinic Medical School & Hosp., 269 A.D. 955, 58 N.Y.S.2d 244 (1945), *aff'd mem.*, 296 N.Y. 502, 68 N.E.2d 450 (1946) (hospital liable to patient for negligence of nurse); Taylor v. Beekman Hosp., 270 A.D. 1020, 62 N.Y.S.2d 637 (1946) (hospital liable for negligence of X-ray operator); Necolayff v. Genesee Hosp., 270 A.D. 648, 61 N.Y.S.2d 832 (1946), *aff'd mem.*, 296 N.Y. 936, 73 N.E.2d 117 (1947) (hospital liable to paying patient for negligence of intern in giving transfusion intended for another patient), noted in 16 Fordham L. Rev. 263, 4 Wash. & Lee L. Rev. 241; Gordon v. Harbor Hosp., 275 A.D. 1047, 92 N.Y.S.2d 101 (1949) (hospital liable for failure to put up sideboards on patient's bed); White v. Prospect Heights Hosp., 278 A.D. 789, 103 N.Y.S.2d 859 (1951) (hospital liable to patient for negligence of orderly); Pivar v. Manhattan Gen., 279 A.D. 522, 110 N.Y.S.2d 786 (1952) (liable for negligence of staff in failing to erect sideboards on bed); Fox v. Mission of Immaculate Virgin, 202 Misc. 478, 119 N.Y.S.2d 14 (1952), *aff'd mem.*, 280 A.D. 993, 117 N.Y.S.2d 477 (1952) (children's home liable for injury to child who fell through unscreened window); Favale v. Roosevelt Pub. School Dist., 193 N.Y.S.2d 202 (1959) (institution for care of cerebral palsy sufferers liable for negligent injury); Kuncio v. Millard Fillmore Hosp., 91 A.D.2d 1179, 459 N.Y.S.2d 152 (1983).

In Bing v. Thunig, 2 N.Y.2d 656, 143 N.E.2d 3 (1957), *rev'g* 1 A.D.2d 887, 147 N.Y.S.2d 358 (1956), noted in 9 Syracuse L. Rev. 123, the court held a hospital liable to a patient for injuries sustained through the negligence of an employee of the hospital, acting within the scope of his employment, whether the act of the employee was administrative or medical, overruling prior cases, and rejecting the doctrine of hospital immunity. The court cited the text. See Berg v. New York Socy. for the Relief of the Ruptured and Crippled, 1 N.Y.2d 499, 136 N.E.2d 523 (1956), noted in 42 Cornell L.Q. 411.

North Carolina: Turnage v. New Bern Consistory No. 3, 215 N.C. 798, 3 S.E.2d 8 (1939) (Masonic Lodge liable for slander in moving picture show, although proceeds given to crippled children's hospitals); Rabon v. Rowan Memorial Hosp., 269 N.C. 1, 152 S.E.2d 485 (1967) (liable to patient for negligence of employee; overruling prior cases; three justices dissenting); Quick v. High Point Memorial Hosp., 269 N.C. 450, 152 S.E.2d 527 (1967) (hospital immune only from liability to beneficiaries); Helms v. Williams, 4 N.C. App. 391, 166 S.E.2d 852 (1969) (hospital liable for negligence in selection and retention of head nurse).

By N.C. Gen. Stat., §1-539.9, the common-law defense of charitable immunity was abolished as to causes of action arising after September 1, 1967.

See Hill v. James Walker Memorial Hosp., 407 F.2d 1036 (4th Cir. 1969), holding that although the decision in the Rabon case did not apply to liability of a hospital for negligence occurring prior to that decision, it did apply where the hospital was insured.

North Dakota: Rickbeil v. Grafton Deaconess Hosp., 74 N.D. 525, 23 N.W.2d 247, 166 A.L.R. 99 (1946) (hospital liable for libel by secretary of board of trustees), noted in 2 Ark. L. Rev. 240, 9 Ga. B.J. 231, 12 Mo. L. Rev. 77; Granger v. Deaconess Hosp., 138 N.W.2d 443 (N.D. 1965) (hospital liable to patient for injuries resulting from negligence of employees).

Ohio: Duvelius v. Sisters of Charity of Cincinnati, 37 Ohio App. 171, 174 N.E. 256 (1930), *aff'd sub nom.* Sisters of Charity of Cincinnati v. Duvelius, 123 Ohio St. 52, 173 N.E. 737 (1930) (hospital liable to nurse for negligence of operator of elevator); Howard v. Children's Hosp., of the Protestant Episcopal Church, 37 Ohio App. 144, 174 N.E. 166 (1930) (hospital liable under statute for refusal to deliver corpse); Newman v. Cleveland Museum of Natural History, 143 Ohio St. 369, 55 N.E.2d 575 (1944) (museum liable for negligence in selection of servant in charge of elephant on which rides sold to public); Andrews v. Youngstown Osteopathic Hosp. Assn., 77 Ohio Abs. 35, 147 N.E.2d 645 (1956), *appeal dismissed,* 166 Ohio St. 228, 140 N.E.2d 900 (1957) (hospital liable to patient for negligence of intern); Avellone v. St. John's Hosp., 165 Ohio St. 467, 135 N.E.2d 410 (1956) (hospital liable to patient for negligence of employee, overruling earlier cases); Klema v. St. Elizabeth's Hosp., 170 Ohio St. 519, 166 N.E.2d 765 (1960) (holding hospital liable for death of patient due to negligence of hospital staff anesthetist); Bell v. Salvation Army, 172 Ohio St. 326, 175 N.E.2d 738 (1961) (Salvation Army liable to paying guest in hotel operated by it, for injuries caused by its servants); Jones v. Hawkes Hosp., 175 Ohio St. 503, 196 N.E.2d 592 (1964) (hospital liable for negligence of nurses in allowing patient to fall out of bed); Williams v. First United Church of Christ, 37 Ohio St. 2d 150, 66 Ohio Ops. 2d 311, 309 N.E.2d 924 (1974) (person injured at a church bazaar could recover if he was a nonbeneficiary, or if the bazaar was operated for profit unrelated to church purpose); Sears v. City of Cincinnati, 31 Ohio St. 2d 157, 60 Ohio Ops. 2d 113, 285 N.E.2d 732 (1972) (city maintaining a hospital was not immune from liability in tort); Albritton v. Neighborhood Centers Assn. for Child Dev., 12 Ohio St. 3d 210, 12 Ohio B.R. 295, 466 N.E.2d 867 (1984) (Head Start day care program; all vestiges of the doctrine of charitable immunity expressly abolished), noted in 16 U. Toledo L. Rev. 981 (1985), and in 11 U. of Dayton L. Rev. 103 (1985).

Oklahoma: Gable v. Salvation Army, 186 Okla. 687, 100 P.2d 244 (1940) (Salvation Army liable for injury to person employed to repair building resulting from failure to give him safe scaffolding), noted in 39 Mich. L. Rev. 147; Roberts v. South Oklahoma City Hosp. Trust, 742 P.2d 1077 (Okla. 1986).

Oregon: Hungerford v. Portland Sanitarium & Benevolent Assn., 235 Or. 412, 384 P.2d 1009 (1963) (hospital liable to patient for negligence of nurse's aide, overruling prior decisions).

Pennsylvania: Flagiello v. Pennsylvania Hosp., 417 Pa. 486, 208 A.2d 193

(1965) (citing Restatement of Trusts, §402, Comment *d,* and overruling earlier cases).

Puerto Rico: Porto Rico Gas & Coke Co. v. Frank Rullan & Assoc., 189 F.2d 397 (1st Cir. 1951) (Puerto Rican law).

Rhode Island: Brown v. Church of the Holy Name, 105 R.I. 322, 252 A.2d 176 (1969).

By R.I. Gen. Laws 1956, §9-1-26, as added by Laws 1968, c. 43, it is provided that hospitals shall be liable for the neglect, carelessness, or want of skill of their officers, agents, or employees.

South Carolina: Bush v. Aiken Elec. Coop., 226 S.C. 442, 85 S.E.2d 716 (1955) (rural electric cooperative liable for injury to child); Brown v. Anderson County Hosp. Assn., 268 S.C. 479, 234 S.E.2d 873 (1977) (overruling prior cases as to hospitals and denying immunity for causes of action arising after the filing of the opinion, May 10, 1977); Phillips v. Oconee Memorial Hosp., 348 S.E.2d 836 (S.C. 1986).

As to charitable institutions other than hospitals, see Crowley v. Bob Jones Univ., 268 S.C. 492, 234 S.E.2d 879 (1977).

See Code 1962, §10-145.1, as enacted by Laws 1977, c. 182 (not over $100,000).

See Terry v. Boy Scouts of Am., 471 F. Supp. 28 (D.S.C. 1978), *aff'd mem.* 598 F.2d 616 (4th Cir. 1979) (applying South Carolina law).

In Douglass v. Florence Gen. Hosp., 273 S.C. 716, 259 S.E.2d 117 (1979), it was held that a hospital was immune from liability for injuries occurring before the enactment of the statute, even though it was insured; but that it was not immune from liability for an intentional tort.

Tennessee: O'Quin v. Baptist Memorial Hosp., 184 Tenn. 570, 201 S.W.2d 694 (1947) (*semble;* hospital's exemption from liability limited to property used directly for charitable purposes); Spivey v. St. Thomas Hosp., 31 Tenn. App. 12, 211 S.W.2d 450 (1948) (hospital liable for negligently permitting patient to kill himself by jumping from window).

Texas: Medical & Surgical Memorial Hosp. v. Cauthorn, 229 S.W.2d 932 (Tex. Civ. App. 1950) (hospital liable to patient for negligence in providing improper heating cradle); Milner v. Huntsville Memorial Hosp., 398 S.W.2d 647 (Tex. Civ. App. 1966) (hospital liable if governing board at fault); Howle v. Camp Amon Carter, 470 S.W.2d 629 (Tex. 1971) (holding charitable immunity abolished as to causes of action arising after March 9, 1966); Herby v. Abilene Christian College, 470 S.W.2d 311 (Tex. Civ. App. 1971); but in Overton Memorial Hosp. v. McGuire, 518 S.W.2d 528 (Tex. 1975), it was held that a city hospital had no immunity.

In Ritch v. Tarrant County Hosp. Dist., 476 S.W.2d 950 (Tex. Civ. App. 1972), it was held that the abolition of charitable immunity did not render a governmental hospital liable for the death of a paying patient.

Utah: Brigham Young Univ. v. Lillywhite, 118 F.2d 836, 137 A.L.R. 598 (10th Cir. 1941), *cert. denied,* 314 U.S. 638 (1941) (action by student against university for explosion caused by negligence of instructor; Utah law), noted in 20 Tex. L. Rev. 505.

Vermont: Foster v. Roman Catholic Diocese of Vt., 116 Vt. 124, 70 A.2d

230 (1950) (church liable to one who fell on an icy sidewalk in front of its premises), noted in 30 B.U.L. Rev. 419, 38 Geo. L.J. 510, 34 Marq. L. Rev. 29, 49 Mich. L. Rev. 148, 25 Notre Dame Law. 576, 11 Ohio St. L.J. 407, 13 U. Detroit L.J. 234, 5 Wyo. L.J. 143.

Virginia: Walker v. Memorial Hosp., 187 Va. 5, 45 S.E.2d 898 (1948) (*semble;* hospital liable to visitor if negligent); Roanoke Hosp. Assn. v. Hayes, 204 Va. 703, 133 S.E.2d 559, 1 A.L.R.3d 1026 (1963) (hospital liable to practical nurse employed by patient, as an invitee).

By Va. Code 1950, §8-629.2, as enacted by Laws 1974, c. 552, and amended by Laws 1976, c. 765, there is a partial abolition of charitable immunity in the case of hospitals.

Virgin Islands: Soto v. Bradshaw, 351 F. Supp. 602 (D.C.V.I. 1972).

Washington: Miller v. Sisters of St. Francis, 5 Wash. 2d 204, 105 P.2d 32 (1940) (hospital liable for negligent failure to furnish proper equipment, giving bed instead of bassinet to newborn baby), noted in 20 B.U.L. Rev. 709, 4 U. Detroit L.J. 48; Heckman v. Sisters of Charity of the House of Providence, 5 Wash. 2d 699, 106 P.2d 593 (1940) (hospital liable to visitor for negligence in failing to light driveway); Kalinowski v. Young Women's Christian Assn., 17 Wash. 2d 380, 135 P.2d 852 (1943) (Y.W.C.A. liable to invitee injured at a dance); Clampett v. Sisters of Charity of House of Providence in Territory of Wash., 17 Wash. 2d 652, 136 P.2d 729 (1943) (hospital liable to patient for negligent furnishing of defective electric heating pad); Pierce v. Yakima Valley Memorial Hosp. Assn., 43 Wash. 2d 162, 260 P.2d 765 (1953) (denying immunity altogether and overruling prior cases; citing the text), noted in 59 Dick. L. Rev. 277; Friend v. Cove Methodist Church, 65 Wash. 2d 174, 396 P.2d 546 (1964) (holding church liable to invited member of the public injured through negligence of servants, overruling prior cases).

West Virginia: Koehler v. Ohio Valley Gen. Hosp. Assn., 137 W. Va. 764, 73 S.E.2d 673 (1952) (hospital liable to visitor of tenants for negligence in maintaining ramp); Adkins v. St. Francis Hosp., 149 W. Va. 705, 143 S.E.2d 154 (1965) (hospital liable to patient for negligence of orderly; overruling prior cases).

Wisconsin: Treptau v. Behrene Spa, 247 Wis. 438, 20 N.W.2d 108 (1945) (hospital liable to patient for negligence of physician whose services were furnished by hospital); Smith v. Congregation of St. Rose, 265 Wis. 393, 61 N.W.2d 896 (1954) (religious corporation liable to pedestrian slipping on sidewalk on ice resulting from defective spout), noted in 102 U. Pa. L. Rev. 1083; Kojis v. Doctors Hosp., 12 Wis. 2d 367, 107 N.W.2d 131 (1961) (hospital liable to paying patient for negligence of employee; overruling prior cases).

See also Duncan v. Steeper, 17 Wis. 2d 226, 116 N.W.2d 154 (1962), holding hospital immune from liability for injury to paying patient in 1958, and stating that hospitals would have no immunity for injuries arising in the future to charity patients as well as to paying patients. See Kojis v. Doctors Hosp., 12 Wis. 2d 367, 107 N.W.2d 292 (1961) (limiting the rule abolishing immunity to cases arising in the future, though making it applicable to the instant case).

trend is to deny immunity. In a number of states, including
Illinois, Kansas, Michigan, Ohio, Oregon, Pennsylvania, Washington, West Virginia, and Wisconsin, where immunity was formerly permitted, the courts have overruled the earlier cases on
the ground that it is against public policy to permit such immunity,[8] and in a few states statutes have been enacted denying or

---

In Rivera v. Misericordia Hosp., 15 Wis. 2d 351, 112 N.W.2d 918
(1962), it was held that the defendant hospital, if charitable, was immune
from liability where the cause of action arose before the decision in the Kojis
case. See also McCluskey v. Thranow, 31 Wis. 2d 256, 142 N.W.2d 787
(1966).

Wyoming: Lutheran Hosps. & Homes Socy. v. Yepsen, 469 P.2d 409 (Wyo.
1970) (no immunity, at least if most of the charges were paid by the patients
or the government).

Canada: Sisters of St. Joseph v. Fleming, [1938] 2 D.L.R. 417 (Can. S.C.)
(hospital liable to patient for negligence of nurse employed by it), noted in 16
Can. B. Rev. 566, 55 Law Q. Rev. 14; Cox v. Saskatoon, [1942] 2 D.L.R. 412
(Sask.) (city conducting hospital held liable); Sinclair v. Victoria Hosp., [1943]
1 D.L.R. 302 (Man.), *dismissing appeal* from [1942] 4 D.L.R. 652 (infant patient
scalded as a result of negligence of nurse), noted in 17 Austl. L.J. 17; Bugden
v. Harbour View Hosp., [1947] 2 D.L.R. 338 (N.S.) (liable for negligence of
nurses in preparing drugs), noted in 25 Can. B. Rev. 646.

In Tennessee it is held that a charitable corporation is subject to liability
in tort, and that although execution cannot be levied on such of its property
as is used exclusively for charitable purposes, other property that it may
acquire is subject to execution. Anderson v. Armstrong, 180 Tenn. 56, 171
S.W.2d 401 (1943).

In Grigalauskas v. United States, 103 F. Supp. 543 (D. Mass. 1951), *aff'd
sub nom.* United States v. Grigalauskas, 195 F.2d 494 (1st Cir. 1952), it was held
that a United States Army hospital was not a charitable institution because the
United States ran it for its own benefit, and hence such a hospital was liable
under the Federal Tort Claims Act for injury to an enlisted man and his
dependent child for negligently causing injury to the child, although by the law
of Kansas, where the hospital was situated, a charitable institution was immune
from liability except for the negligence of the management.

[8]Hupman v. Erskine College, 281 S.C. 43, 314 S.E.2d 314 (1984) (1981
abrogation of charitable immunity not retroactive).

It will be noted that in many states the courts in overruling cases permitting immunity held that liability should be imposed only as to injuries occurring after the date of the overruling decision.

See Nicol, Prospective Overruling; a New Device for English Courts?, 39
Mod. L. Rev. 542 (1976).

See Note, Prospective or retrospective operation of overruling decision,
10 A.L.R.3d 1371, 1423 (1966).

limiting immunity. The question of the tort liability of charitable institutions has been extensively dealt with in the law reviews and elsewhere.[9]

[9]For an extensive collection of authorities, see Scott, Tort Liability of Hospitals, 17 Tenn. L. Rev. 838 (1943); Williams, Public Charities Not Liable for Tort in Pennsylvania, 54 Dick. L. Rev. 6 (1949); Ball, The Liability of Charitable Institutions for Torts of Agents and Servants, 38 Ky. L.J. 105 (1949); Bobbe, Tort Liability of Hospitals in New York, 37 Cornell L.Q. 419 (1952); Note, Charities — Liability for Torts of Employees, 30 N.C.L. Rev. 67 (1951); Note, Tort Liability of Charitable Institution, 9 U. Pitt. L. Rev. 253 (1948); Note, Charitable Institutions — Immunity from Tort Liability, 4 De Paul L. Rev. 56 (1954); Note, Tort Immunity of Charities in Ohio, 4 W. Res. L. Rev. 348 (1953); Note, Is Charitable Immunity on the Way Out?, 7 S.C.L.Q. 443 (1955); 9 Brooklyn L. Rev. 78 (1939) (tort liability of charitable institutions in New York); Note, Status of the Law in New York Concerning Tort Liability of Hospitals, 25 Fordham L. Rev. 498 (1956); 18 Colum. L. Rev. 261 (1918); 22 id. 748 (1922); 8 Cornell L.Q. 146 (1923); 11 id. 62 (1925); 5 Md. L. Rev. 336 (1941); 18 Mich. L. Rev. 539 (1920); 19 id. 395 (1921); 7 N.Y.U.L.Q. Rev. 541 (1930); 2 S. Cal. L. Rev. 490 (1929); 77 U. Pa. L. Rev. 191 (1928); 48 Yale L.J. 81 (1938); Simeone, The Doctrine of Charitable Immunity, 5 St. Louis U.L.J. 357 (1959); Sister Ann Joachim, Immunity of Liability for Torts of Charitable Institutions, 39 B.U.L. Rev. 349 (1959); Note, A Survey of Charitable Hospital Immunity, 19 U. Pitt. L. Rev. 119 (1957); Note, Liability of Charitable Associations in Ohio, 8 W. Res. L. Rev. 194 (1957); Note, Tort Liability of the Trustee of a Charitable Trust: A Qualified Immunity, 44 Va. L. Rev. 1317 (1958); Note, The Immunity of Charitable Institutions from Tort Liability, 11 Baylor L. Rev. 86 (1959); Toth, Church Liability for Negligence, 11 Clev.-Mar. L. Rev. 119 (1962).

See Note, Liability of churches or other religious societies for torts causing personal injury or death, 124 A.L.R. 814 (1940); Note, Tort liability of private schools and institutions of higher learning, 160 id. 250 (1946); Note, Immunity of nongovernmental charity from liability for damages in tort, 25 A.L.R.2d 29 (1952); Note, Liability for injury or death due to physical condition of church premises, 80 A.L.R.2d 806 (1961); Note, Tort liability of public schools and institutions of higher learning, 86 A.L.R.2d 489 (1962); Note, Tort liability of public schools and institutions of higher learning for accidents occurring during use of premises and equipment for other than school purposes, 37 A.L.R.3d 712 (1971); Note, Tort liability of public schools and institutions of higher learning for injuries due to condition of grounds, walks, and playgrounds, 37 A.L.R.3d 738 (1971); Note, Immunity of private schools and institutions of higher learning from liability in tort, 38 A.L.R.3d 480 (1971); Annot., Tort immunity of nongovernmental charities — modern status, 25 A.L.R.4th 517 (1983).

We shall deal later with questions of conflict of laws as to charitable immunity. See §624.

Even though the charitable institution is immune from liability for the negligence of an employee, the employee himself is not immune.[10]

Injury caused by one who is not an employee. Even in states in which a charitable institution is held not to be exempt from liability in tort, it is not liable where the injury is not due to the fault of the board of management of the institution or of any of its employees, but is due to the fault of a person over whom the institution has no control.[11] Thus if a patient in a hospital is

---

As to the English law governing the liability of hospitals, see Speller, Law Relating to Hospitals (1947).

[10]*Maryland:* Wood v. Abell, 268 Md. 214, 300 A.2d 665 (1973).

Massachusetts: Mullins v. Pine Manor College, 389 Mass. 47, 449 N.E.2d 331 (1983).

Missouri: Schoen v. Kerner, 544 S.W.2d 43 (Mo. App. 1977).

[11]*England:* Hillyer v. St. Bartholomew's Hosp., [1909] 2 K.B. 820 (negligence of nurse acting under orders of operating surgeon); Gold v. Essex County Council, [1942] 2 K.B. 293 (negligence of radiographer), noted in 16 Austl. L.J. 79, 17 id. 82, 20 Can. B. Rev. 565, 58 Scot. L. Rev. 87.

Federal: Norland v. Washington Gen. Hosp., 461 F.2d 694 (8th Cir. 1972) (nurse subject to control of obstetrician; Arkansas law).

Arizona: Evans v. Bernhard, 23 Ariz. App. 413, 533 P.2d 721 (1975) (surgeon). Himes v. Particular Council of Pima County, 151 Ariz. 474, 728 P.2d 693 (Ariz. App. 1986) (council that coordinated work of local charities not liable for tort committed by servant of local charity).

Delaware: Vanaman v. Milford Memorial Hosp., 262 A.2d 263 (Del. Super. 1970) (hospital not liable for negligence of physicians not employed by it).

Iowa: Dickinson v. Mailliard, 175 N.W.2d 588 (Iowa 1970) (negligence of physicians in taking X-ray pictures).

Louisiana: Beck v. Lovell, 361 So. 2d 245 (La. App. 1978) (acts of surgeon).

Minnesota: Synnott v. Midway Hosp., 287 Minn. 270, 178 N.W.2d 211 (1970) (hospital nurse acting under direction of physician).

New York: Schloendorff v. New York Hosp., 211 N.Y. 125, 105 N.E. 92, 52 L.R.A. (N.S.) 505 (1914) (negligence of house physician and visiting physician); Fisher v. Sydenham Hosp., 176 Misc. 7, 26 N.Y.S.2d 389 (1941) (loss of patient's dentures through negligence of special nurse); Lee v. Glens Falls Hosp., 265 A.D. 607, 42 N.Y.S.2d 169 (1943), *aff'd,* 291 N.Y. 526, 50 N.E.2d 651 (1943) (where nurse negligently permitted patient to fall from bed, hospital held not liable on ground nurse not a servant of the hospital but employed to carry out physician's orders); Greenberg v. Society of the Hillside Hosp., 73 N.Y.S.2d 21 (1947), *aff'd mem.,* 273 A.D. 855, 77 N.Y.S.2d 142 (1948) (negligence of nurse and physician); Rainey v. Persse, 38 A.D.2d 785, 328

injured solely through the negligence of a physician or surgeon who is not an employee of the hospital, he cannot recover against the hospital. Similarly, a hospital is not liable for the negligence of a nurse in the hospital where the nurse is an employee of the patient and not of the hospital.

In a leading New York case[12] a woman sued a hospital,

N.Y.S.2d 165 (1972); Holzberg v. Flower and Fifth Avenue Hosps., 39 A.D.2d 526, 330 N.Y.S.2d 682 (1972) (anesthetist).

Ohio: Avellone v. St. John's Hosp., 165 Ohio St. 467, 135 N.E.2d 410 (1956) (holding hospital liable to patient for negligence of servant, overruling some of the earlier cases), noted in 5 Clev.-Mar. L. Rev. 118, 6 De Paul L. Rev. 176; Shutts v. Siehl, 109 Ohio App. 145, 164 N.E.2d 443 (1959) (hospital not liable for acts of nurse acting under authority of surgeon in charge of patient).

Pennsylvania: Casazza v. Sacred Heart Hosp., 12 D.&C.2d 456 (Pa. 1957) (hospital not liable for damage to neighboring property caused by contractor building nurses' home).

Washington: Canney v. Sisters of Charity of House of Providence, 15 Wash. 2d 325, 130 P.2d 899 (1942) (negligence of special nurse causing burns).

Canada: Staple v. City of Winnipeg, 5 D.L.R.2d 751 (Man. 1956) (negligence of operating surgeon); Johnston v. Wellesley Hosp., 17 D.L.R.3d 139 (Ont. 1970) (physician receiving no pay from the hospital).

In Stanhope v. Los Angeles College of Chiropractic, 54 Cal. App. 2d 141, 128 P.2d 705 (1942), it was held that even if an X-ray technician was not an employee of the hospital, the hospital is liable for his negligence if it represented to the patient that he was its employee.

See Rabasco v. New Rochelle Hosp. Assn., 266 A.D. 971, 44 N.Y.S.2d 293 (1943) (hospital liable for negligence of X-ray technician performing administrative act as servant of the hospital).

In Roe v. Minister of Health, [1954] 2 W.L.R. 915, noted in 70 Law Q. Rev. 305, the Court of Appeal took the view that a hospital would be liable for the negligence of an anesthetist.

In Baxter v. Morningside, 10 Wash. App. 893, 521 P.2d 946, 82 A.L.R.3d 1206 (1974), where a volunteer driver for a charitable corporation negligently injured the plaintiff in an automobile accident, it was held that the driver was an agent of the charitable corporation, and that it was liable.

In Mduba v. Benedictine Hosp., 52 A.D.2d 450, 384 N.Y.S.2d 527 (1976), it was held that even though a negligent physician was not an employee of the hospital in an emergency treatment, the hospital was liable because it held itself out as furnishing doctors.

See Note, Liability of charitable organization under respondeat superior doctrine for tort of unpaid volunteer, 82 A.L.R.3d 1213 (1978).

[12]Schloendorff v. New York Hosp., 211 N.Y. 125, 131, 132, 105 N.E. 92, 94 (1914).

alleging that the house physician discovered a lump that proved to be a fibroid tumor, and that he consulted the visiting physician who advised an operation, and that she consented to an examination but not to an operation, and that while she was under ether the operation was performed and that gangrene developed. This testimony was disputed, but the court held that even if it were true the hospital was not liable. Judge Cardozo said:

> The wrong was not that of the hospital; it was that of physicians, who were not the defendant's servants, but were pursuing an independent calling, a profession sanctioned by a solemn oath, and safeguarded by stringent penalties. If, in serving their patient, they violated her commands, the responsibility is not the defendant's; it is theirs. There is no distinction in that respect between the visiting and the resident physicians. Whether the hospital undertakes to procure a physician from afar, or to have one on the spot, its liability remains the same. . . .
>
> It is true, I think, of nurses as of physicians, that in treating a patient they are not acting as the servants of the hospital. The superintendent is a servant of the hospital; the assistant superintendents, the orderlies, and the other members of the administrative staff are servants of the hospital. But nurses are employed to

---

In Bing v. Thunig, 2 N.Y.2d 656, 143 N.E.2d 3 (1957), *rev'g* 1 A.D.2d 887, 147 N.Y.S.2d 358 (1956), noted in 9 Syracuse L. Rev. 123, the court (citing the text) held a hospital liable to a patient for injury sustained through the negligence of nurses, criticizing what was said by the court in Schloendorff v. New York Hospital.

In Blair v. New York Univ. College of Dentistry, 15 A.D.2d 211, 222 N.Y.S.2d 1 (1961), it was held that the negligence of a supervising dentist and a student dentist was imputable to the dental college.

In Fiorentino v. Wenger, 19 N.Y.2d 407, 227 N.E.2d 296, 280 N.Y.S.2d 373 (1967), it was held that a proprietary hospital was not liable to a patient for an operation by a physician not employed by it, unless it knew or should have known that there was lacking informed consent by the patient or that the operation was not permissible under existing standards.

See also Brown v. Moore, 247 F.2d 711, 69 A.L.R.2d 288 (3d Cir. 1957), *cert. denied,* 355 U.S. 882 (1957), in which the court held that under the law of Pennsylvania a proprietary hospital was liable to a patient for the negligence of its medical director, a neuropsychiatrist.

See Note, Liability of hospital or sanitarium for negligence of physician or surgeon, 69 A.L.R.2d 305 (1960).

carry out the orders of the physicians, to whose authority they are subject. The hospital undertakes to procure for the patient the services of a nurse. It does not undertake through the agency of nurses to render those services itself.

Where the institution is insured. Where a charitable institution is exempt from liability in tort, is it material that it has taken out a policy of liability insurance? In a number of cases it has been held that it is immaterial, and that there can be no recovery for the tort.[13] If the undertaking of the insurance company is merely

---

[13]*Federal:* Tomlinson v. Trustees of Univ. of Pennsylvania, 164 F. Supp. 353 (E.D. Pa. 1958), *appeal dismissed,* 266 F.2d 569 (3d Cir. 1959); Selkow v. City of Philadelphia, 201 F. Supp. 221 (E.D. Pa. 1962); Peters v. McCalla, 461 F. Supp. 14 (D.S.C. 1978) (South Carolina law).

Alabama: Thompson v. Druid City Hosp. Bd., 279 Ala. 314, 184 So. 2d 825 (1966) (city hospital).

California: Levy v. Superior Court, 74 Cal. App. 171, 239 P. 1100 (1925).

Connecticut: Edwards v. Grace Hosp. Soc., 130 Conn. 568, 36 A.2d 273 (1944); Cristini v. Griffin Hosp. 134 Conn. 282, 57 A.2d 262 (1948).

Illinois: Myers v. Young Men's Christian Assn., 316 Ill. App. 177, 44 N.E.2d 755 (1942), noted in 21 Chi.-Kent L. Rev. 256, 10 U. Chi. L. Rev. 211; Piper v. Epstein, 326 Ill. App. 400, 62 N.E.2d 139 (1945), noted in 24 Chi.-Kent L. Rev. 170, 266, 34 Ill. B.J. 173.

Kentucky: Williams' Admx. v. Church Home, 223 Ky. 355, 3 S.W.2d 753, 62 A.L.R. 721 (1928).

Massachusetts: Enman v. Trustees of Boston Univ., 270 Mass. 299, 170 N.E. 43 (1930), noted in 10 B.U.L. Rev. 396, 15 St. Louis L. Rev. 292; Higgins v. Emerson Hosp., 367 Mass. 714, 328 N.E.2d 488 (1975).

Michigan: De Groot v. Edison Inst., 306 Mich. 339, 10 N.W.2d 907 (1943); Sayers v. School Dist. No. 1, 366 Mich. 217, 114 N.W.2d 191 (1962) (government agency); Grant v. Cottage Hosp. Corp., 368 Mich. 77, 117 N.W.2d 90 (1962) (injury suffered prior to judicial repudiation of immunity); Podvin v. St. Joseph Hosp., 369 Mich. 65, 119 N.W.2d 108 (1963); Branum v. State, 5 Mich. App. 134, 145 N.W.2d 860 (1966), *semble* (governmental immunity).

Mississippi: Mississippi Baptist Hosp. v. Moore, 156 Miss. 676, 126 So. 465, 67 A.L.R. 1106 (1930).

Missouri: Dille v. St. Luke's Hosp., 355 Mo. 436, 196 S.W.2d 615 (1946); Krueger v. Schmiechen, 364 Mo. 568, 264 S.W.2d 311 (1954); Schulte v. Missionaries of La Salette Corp. of Missouri, 352 S.W.2d 636 (Mo. 1962), noted in 30 U. Kan. City L. Rev. 255; Bodard v. Culver-Stockton College, 471 S.W.2d 253 (Mo. 1971) (injury occurred prior to November 10, 1969; see n. 7 *supra*).

New Jersey: Fields v. Mountainside Hosp., 22 N.J. Misc. 72, 35 A.2d 701 (1944) (citing the text); Woods v. Overlook Hosp. Assn., 6 N.J. Super. 47, 69

to save the institution harmless from enforceable claims in tort against it, the company is not liable if the institution is not liable. But if the insurance company undertakes to save the institution harmless from claims in tort that would be enforceable apart from its claim to immunity as a charitable institution, it would seem that the victim of the tort should be permitted to recover against the institution to the extent to which the judgment would be satisfied by the insurance company. In such a case it has been held that there may be a recovery.[14] Here there is no

---

A.2d 742 (1949) (citing the text), noted in 1 Syracuse L. Rev. 503. Vitolo v. St. Peter's Church, 118 N.J. Super. 35, 285 A.2d 570 (1972).

New Mexico: Livingston v. Regents of N.M. College of Agric. & Mechanic Arts, 64 N.M. 306, 328 P.2d 78 (1958) (state institution).

North Carolina: Herndon v. Massey, 217 N.C. 610, 8 S.E.2d 914 (1940), noted in 19 N.C.L. Rev. 245.

Ohio: Emrick v. Pennsylvania R.R. Young Men's Christian Assn. of Crestline, 69 Ohio App. 353, 43 N.E.2d 733 (1942).

Pennsylvania: Siidekum v. Animal Rescue League, 353 Pa. 408, 45 A.2d 59 (1946).

South Carolina: Decker v. Bishop of Charleston, 247 S.C. 317, 147 S.E.2d 264 (1966).

Texas: Baptist Memorial Hosp. v. McTighe, 303 S.W.2d 446 (Tex. Civ. App. 1957); Watkins v. Southcrest Baptist Church, 399 S.W.2d 530 (Tex. 1966).

West Virginia: Fisher v. Ohio Valley Gen. Hosp. Assn., 137 W. Va. 723, 73 S.E.2d 667 (1952); Meade v. St. Francis Hosp. of Charleston, 137 W. Va. 834, 74 S.E.2d 405 (1953).

Wisconsin: Schau v. Morgan, 241 Wis. 334, 6 N.W.2d 212 (1942); Koenig v. Milwaukee Blood Center, 23 Wis. 2d 324, 127 N.W.2d 50 (1964).

[14]*Federal:* Stamos v. Standard Accident Ins. Co., 119 F. Supp. 245 (W.D. La. 1954); Edwards v. Kings Memorial Hosp. Assn., 118 F. Supp. 417 (E.D. Tenn. 1954); Tracy v. Davis, 123 F. Supp. 160 (E.D. Ill. 1954), noted in 33 Chi.-Kent L. Rev. 175.

Colorado: O'Connor v. Boulder Colorado Sanitarium Assn., 105 Colo. 259, 96 P.2d 835 (1939), noted in 20 B.U.L. Rev. 330, 53 Harv. L. Rev. 873, 24 Minn. L. Rev. 696, 16 Notre Dame Law. 126, 12 Rocky Mtn. L. Rev. 135, 7 U. Chi. L. Rev. 567, 3 U. Detroit L.J. 164, 1 Wash. & Lee L. Rev. 257.

Georgia: Cox v. De Jarnette, 104 Ga. App. 664, 123 S.E.2d 16 (1961); Morehouse College v. Russell, 219 Ga. 717, 135 S.E.2d 432 (1964), s.c. 109 Ga. App. 301, 136 S.E.2d 179 (1964); Young Men's Christian Assn. v. Bailey, 112 Ga. App. 684, 146 S.E.2d 324 (1965).

Illinois: Wendt v. Servite Fathers, 332 Ill. App. 618, 76 N.E.2d 342 (1947) (citing the text), noted in 26 Chi.-Kent L. Rev. 279, 36 Ill. B.J. 488, 43 Ill. L. Rev. 248, 16 U. Chi. L. Rev. 173, 1 Vand. L. Rev. 470, 5 Wash. & Lee L. Rev.

diversion of the assets from the charitable purposes for which they were given.

272; Moore v. Moyle, 405 Ill. 555, 92 N.E.2d 81 (1950), *rev'g* 335 Ill. App. 342, 82 N.E.2d 61 (1948), noted in 3 Baylor L. Rev. 83, 28 Chi.-Kent L. Rev. 268, 29 id. 107, 38 Ill. B.J. 187, 533, 39 id. 538, 40 id. 138, 45 Ill. L. Rev. 776, 1 Intra. L. Rev. (St. Louis U.) 168, 26 Notre Dame Law. 115, 23 Rocky Mtn. L. Rev. 352, 53 W. Va. L. Rev. 76; Tidwell v. Smith, 27 Ill. App. 2d 63, 169 N.E.2d 157 (1960); Darling v. Charleston Community Memorial Hosp., 33 Ill. 2d 326, 211 N.E.2d 253 (1965), *semble, aff'g* 50 Ill. App. 2d 253, 200 N.E.2d 149 (1964), *semble;* Johnson v. Girvin, 61 Ill. App. 2d 47, 208 N.E.2d 894 (1965).

Kentucky: Taylor v. Knox County Bd. of Educ., 292 Ky. 767, 167 S.W.2d 700, 145 A.L.R. 1333 (1942).

Louisiana: Lusk v. United States Fidelity & Guar. Co., 199 So. 666 (La. 1941); D'Antoni v. Sara Mayo Hosp., 144 So. 2d 643 (La. App. 1962); Hill v. Eye, Ear, Nose & Throat Hosp., 200 So. 2d 34 (La. 1967); Tyler v. Touro Infirmary, 223 So. 2d 148 (La. 1969) (insurance company directly liable where policy did not exclude liability for the negligence involved).

Tennessee: Vanderbilt Univ. v. Henderson, 23 Tenn. App. 135, 127 S.W.2d 284 (1938).

Texas: J. Weingarten, Inc. v. Sanchez, 228 S.W.2d 303 (Tex. Civ. App. 1950).

Wisconsin: Marshall v. Green Bay, 18 Wis. 2d 496, 118 N.W.2d 715 (1963) (governmental immunity).

In Hughes v. President & Directors of Georgetown College, 33 F. Supp. 867 (D.D.C. 1940), *aff'd sub nom.* President & Directors of Georgetown College v. Hughes, 76 App. D.C. 123, 130 F.2d 810 (1942), where recovery was allowed against a hospital, the court said that it was unnecessary to consider the fact that the hospital was insured. The case is noted in 23 B.U.L. Rev. 108, 12 Fordham L. Rev. 89, 6 U. Detroit L.J. 142, 11 U. Kan. City L. Rev. 228, 91 U. Pa. L. Rev. 571.

In Hill v. James Walker Memorial Hosp., 407 F.2d 1036 (4th Cir. 1969), it was held that although the decision in the *Rabon* case (cited in n. 7) did not apply to the liability of a hospital for negligence occurring prior to that decision, it applied where the hospital was insured.

Arkansas Stat. 1947, §66-3240, provides that an injured person shall have a direct cause of action against the liability insurance carrier of any organization not subject to suit for tort. The statute was held to be constitutional in Michael v. St. Paul Mercury Indem. Co., 92 F. Supp. 140 (W.D. Ark. 1950), noted in 6 Ark. L. Rev. 209. See McElroy v. Employers' Liab. Assurance Corp., 163 F. Supp. 193 (W.D. Ark. 1958); Ramsey v. American Auto. Ins. Co., 234 Ark. 1031, 356 S.W.2d 236 (1962).

In Maryland it was formerly provided by statute that the policy issued to cover the liability of any charitable institution for negligence or any other tort should contain a provision to the effect that the insurer should be estopped from asserting, as a defense to any claim covered by the policy, that such

Enjoining a tort. Even in states in which a charitable institution is held to be exempt from liability in tort to third persons, it is clear that a suit in equity can be maintained against the institution to enjoin a tort. Where the institution is so conducted as to constitute a nuisance to owners of neighboring property, they can enjoin the continuance of the nuisance.[15] Thus in a case

---

institution is immune from liability on the ground that it is a charitable institution. See Thomas v. Board of County Commrs., 200 Md. 554, 92 A.2d 452 (1952); Gorman v. St. Paul Fire & Marine Ins. Co., 210 Md. 1, 121 A.2d 812 (1956) (citing the text).

By Maryland Ann. Code 1957, art. 43, §556A, as enacted by Laws 1966, c. 673, it is provided that no hospital or related institution shall be immune from liability for tort on the ground that it is a charitable institution, but that if it is insured from such liability in an amount not less than $100,000, it shall not be liable for damages in excess of that amount.

By South Dakota Codified Laws 1967, §§27.19, 45.0202, governing bodies of any municipal corporation maintaining a hospital are permitted to contract for public liability insurance covering and protecting the employees and servants against liability for negligence.

By South Dakota Insurance Code, §58-23-3, it is provided that every policy issued to cover the liability of any charitable institution for tort shall contain a provision that the insurer shall be estopped from asserting charitable immunity as a defense.

West Virginia Code, §33-6-14a, as amended by Laws 1985, c. 105, and Laws 1986, 1st Extra Session, c. 24, provides that no policy of insurance shall be issued to a charitable corporation unless it shall contain a provision waiving the defense of charitable immunity, unless the provision is rejected in writing by the insured.

See Maine Rev. Stat. Ann., tit. 14, §158; Maryland, Ann. Code 1957, art. 43, §556A.

See Note, Charities: Liability Insurance without Liability, 2 U. Kan. L. Rev. 188 (1953).

See Note, Liability of indemnity insurance carried by government or political subdivision thereof, or by charitable institution, in respect of injury or damage as to which it is otherwise immune from liability, 145 A.L.R. 1336 (1943).

See Note, The Effect of Insurance on the Tort Immunity of a Governmental Subdivision, 34 Neb. L. Rev. 78 (1954).

[15]Deaconess Home & Hosp. v. Bontjes, 207 Ill. 553, 69 N.E. 748, 64 L.R.A. 215 (1904); Herr v. Central Ky. Lunatic Asylum, 97 Ky. 458, 30 S.W. 971, 53 Am. St. Rep. 414, 28 L.R.A. 394 (1895), 110 Ky. 282, 61 S.W. 283 (1901); Kestner v. Homeopathic Medical & Surgical Hosp., 245 Pa. 326, 91 A. 659, 52 L.R.A. (N.S.) 1032 (1914).

in Pennsylvania[16] the complainants were the owners of a house adjoining a hospital that maintained an operating room the windows of which faced the house at a distance of from 9 to 12 feet, with the result that the moans, shrieks, and groans of persons receiving surgical aid "were of such a character as to render wretched the lives of complainants, and of friends visiting them, and were such as to affect their nerves and impair their health." It further appeared that persons occupying rooms in the hospital were permitted to throw refuse across the fence and upon complainants' property. The court awarded an injunction, ordering the removal of the operating room to some other part of the building and restrained the defendant from permitting persons occupying rooms in the hospital to throw refuse matter upon complainants' property. In some cases it has been held that an action for damages can be maintained against the institution. Thus in *Love v. Nashville Agricultural and Normal Institute*[17] it was held that a charitable corporation was liable for so disposing of its sewage as to contaminate a spring of the plaintiff.

Negligence as a bar to recovery for services. Even in states in which, as in Massachusetts, the courts go to the extreme limit in exempting charitable institutions from liability for tort, a claim for injury resulting from negligence may be set up defensively. Thus in *Beverly Hospital v. Early*[18] it was held that where a patient was sued by a hospital for board, room, and attendance, the patient could defend by showing that owing to the negligence of the servants of the hospital his leg was burned so that it had to be amputated. The court said that although the patient could not hold the hospital liable for negligence, and could not plead

---

[16]Kestner v. Homeopathic Medical & Surgical Hosp., 245 Pa. 326, 91 A. 659 (1914).

[17]146 Tenn. 550, 243 S.W. 304, 23 A.L.R. 887 (1921), noted in 22 Colum. L. Rev. 748, 5 Tenn. L. Rev. 40.

In Jeffcoat v. Caine, 261 S.C. 75, 198 N.E.2d 258 (1973), a charitable hospital was held not immune from liability for an intentional tort, false imprisonment.

But in Crowley v. Bob Jones Univ., 268 S.C. 492, 234 S.E.2d 879 (1977), the court left open the question whether a university had immunity in the case of gross negligence or recklessness.

[18]292 Mass. 201, 197 N.E. 641, 100 A.L.R. 1338 (1935).

negligence by way of recoupment, he could avail himself of the negligence as showing that the services of the hospital were of no value.

Conflict of laws. We shall consider hereafter the question of the applicable law where the injury takes place in a state other than the state in which the charitable corporation is organized.[19]

§402.1. Proprietary institutions. As we have seen, an institution conducted for private profit is not a charitable institution.[1] The mere fact that fees are to be paid by the recipients of benefits does not prevent it from being charitable if the income is to be used only to maintain the institution or is to be applied to some other charitable purpose. But if the profits, if any, are to inure to the benefit of private individuals, the institution is not exempt from liability in tort.[2] It is not liable, of course, if it

[19]See §624.

§402.1. [1]See §376.

For cases holding that the institution was a charitable and not a proprietary institution, see Barrett v. Brooks Hosp., 338 Mass. 754, 157 N.E.2d 638 (1959) (charity patients not received); Killen v. Brazosport Memorial Hosp., 364 S.W.2d 411 (Tex. Civ. App. 1963) (reorganization of proprietary hospital).

[2]*Federal:* Radosevic v. Virginia Intermont College, 633 F. Supp. 1084 (W.D. Va. 1986).

Arkansas: See Crossett Health Center v. Croswell, 221 Ark. 874, 256 S.W.2d 548 (1953) (hospital established by a lumber company primarily for employees).

California: Bowman v. Southern Pac. Co., 55 Cal. App. 734, 204 P. 403 (1921).

Connecticut: Hawthorne v. Blythewood, 118 Conn. 617, 174 A. 81 (1934).

Indiana: Fowler v. Norways Sanatorium, 112 Ind. App. 347, 42 N.E.2d 415 (1942).

Massachusetts: Hall v. College of Physicians & Surgeons, 254 Mass. 95, 149 N.E. 675 (1925).

Missouri: Clark v. Faith Hosp. Assn., 472 S.W.2d 375 (Mo. 1971).

Nebraska: Malcolm v. Evangelical Lutheran Hosp. Assn., 107 Neb. 101, 185 N.W. 330 (1921).

New Jersey: Rafferzeder v. Raleigh Fitkin-Paul Morgan Memorial Hosp., 30 N.J. Super. 82, 103 A.2d 383 (1954), 33 N.J. Super. 19, 109 A.2d 296 (1954).

New York: Robertson v. Towns Hosp., 178 A.D. 285, 165 N.Y.S. 17 (1917); Hendrickson v. Hodkin, 276 N.Y. 252, 11 N.E.2d 899 (1937); Post v. Crown Heights Hosp., 173 Misc. 250, 17 N.Y.S.2d 409 (1940).

was not at fault. Thus it has been held that a hospital, though conducted for profit, is not liable for the negligence of a nurse not employed by the hospital but by the patient.[3]

Ohio: See Shaker Medical Center Hosp. v. Blue Cross of N.E. Ohio, 115 Ohio App. 497, 183 N.E.2d 628 (1962), holding hospital proprietary and not entitled to Blue Cross services.

Oregon: Ackerman v. Physicians & Surgeons Hosp., 207 Or. 646, 298 P.2d 1026 (1956).

Tennessee: Rural Educ. Assn. v. Bush, 42 Tenn. App. 34, 298 S.W.2d 761 (1957).

Virginia: Stuart Circle Hosp. Corp. v. Curry, 173 Va. 136, 3 S.E.2d 153, 124 A.L.R. 176 (1939).

Washington: Mueller v. Winston Bros. Co., 165 Wash. 130, 4 P.2d 854 (1931).

See 48 Yale L.J. 81 (1938).

In White v. Central Dispensary & Emergency Hosp., 69 App. D.C. 122, 99 F.2d 355, 119 A.L.R. 1002 (1938), it was held that a complaint in tort against a hospital is not demurrable although there is no allegation that the hospital was a proprietary institution, and that if it was a charitable institution, that should be alleged by the defendant as an affirmative defense.

In Mayberry v. Foster, 194 Okla. 205, 148 P.2d 983 (1944), where the defendant, a physician who owned a private hospital, sold it to a charitable association and thereafter the plaintiff was injured by falling down an elevator shaft, it was held that the plaintiff had not proved that the sale was a subterfuge to escape taxation.

In Cowan v. Eastern Racing Assn., 330 Mass. 135, 111 N.E.2d 752 (1953), the court said that a racing association was liable for a battery committed by its employees, even though at the time it was acting as agent of a charitable enterprise.

In Rivera v. Misericordia Hosp., 15 Wis. 2d 351, 112 N.W.2d 918 (1962), where an action was brought against a hospital, it was held that a demurrer to the complaint should not be sustained but that the hospital might set up in its answer the defense of charitable immunity.

See Note, Liability of private noncharitable hospital or sanitarium for improper care or treatment of patients, 124 A.L.R. 186 (1940); Note, Liability of owner or operator of private "rest home" or the like for injury or death of patron, 70 A.L.R.2d 366 (1960).

[3]Steinert v. Brunswick Home, 259 A.D. 1018, 20 N.Y.S.2d 459 (1940), *leave to appeal denied,* 260 A.D. 10, 22 N.Y.S.2d 822 (1940), *appeal denied,* 284 N.Y. 822, 31 N.E.2d 517 (1940); Bakal v. University Heights Sanitarium, 277 A.D. 572, 101 N.Y.S.2d 385 (1950), noted in 1 Catholic U.L. Rev. 165, 2 Syracuse L. Rev. 396.

In Fiorentino v. Wenger, 19 N.Y.2d 407, 227 N.E.2d 296, 280 N.Y.S.2d 373 (1967), it was held that a proprietary hospital was not liable to a patient for an operation by a physician not employed by it, unless it knew or should

Even in states in which, as in Massachusetts, the courts have gone far in exempting charitable institutions from liability in tort, it has been held that the institution is not exempt from liability incurred in the conduct of an enterprise for profit, even though the profits are to be applied only to charitable purposes. Thus in *Holder v. Massachusetts Horticultural Society*[4] it was held that where a charitable institution owned a building that it let to a tenant, it was liable to an employee for injuries caused by the negligence of the superintendent of the building. In *McKay v. Morgan Memorial Cooperative Industries & Stores*[5] a charitable institution organized to receive and dispose of secondhand goods and to apply the profits for the benefit of the poor conducted a store for the sale of the goods. A business visitor at the store fell through a trap door and was injured. It was held that the corporation was liable for the injury. The court drew a distinction between activities primarily commercial in character although carried on to obtain revenue to be used for charitable purposes, where the corporation is subject to liability, and activities carried on to accomplish directly the charitable purposes of the corporation, incidentally yielding revenue, where the corporation is not subject to liability. In other similar cases a charitable corporation has been held liable.[6] Thus a charitable

---

have known that there was lacking informed consent by the patient or that the operation was not permissible under existing standards.

[4]211 Mass. 370, 97 N.E. 630 (1912).

But a college in maintaining a dormitory is not engaged in a noncharitable activity, although the students pay rent for their rooms. Miller v. Concordia Teachers College, 296 F.2d 100 (8th Cir. 1961).

[5]272 Mass. 121, 172 N.E. 68 (1930).

See Mass. Ann. Laws, c. 231, §85K, as inserted by Laws 1971, c. 785.

See Reavey v. Guild of St. Agnes, 284 Mass. 300, 187 N.E. 557 (1933), *semble.*

But compare Carpenter v. Young Men's Christian Assn., 324 Mass. 365, 86 N.E.2d 634 (1949), holding a charitable corporation exempt although fees were charged, citing the text.

[6]*Federal:* Lichty v. Carbon County Agr. Assn., 31 F. Supp. 809 (M.D. Pa. 1940) (county agricultural association held liable for injuries to patron of county fair); Allison v. Mennonite Publications Bd., 123 F. Supp. 23 (W.D. Pa. 1954) (church publication house held liable for libel); Wertheimer v. Frank, 206 F. Supp. 681 (E.D. Pa. 1962) (Pennsylvania law as to public charity).

Federal: Kaltrider v. Young Men's Christian Assn., 457 F.2d 768 (6th Cir. 1972) (parking lot rented for profit; Ohio law).

corporation has been held liable to a person injured in an apart-

---

California: See Baker v. Board of Trustees of Leland Stanford Junior Univ., 133 Cal. App. 243, 23 P.2d 1071 (1933).

Georgia: Mack v. Big Bethel A.M.E. Church, 125 Ga. App. 304, 188 S.E.2d 915 (1972) (income-producing land).

Maine: Mendall v. Pleasant Mtn. Ski Dev., 159 Me. 285, 191 A.2d 633 (1963) (association of school principals whose source of revenue was receipts from games and not charitable donations).

Massachusetts: Moran v. Plymouth Rubber Co. Mut. Benefit Assn., 307 Mass. 444, 30 N.E.2d 238 (1940) (employees' association, even if charitable, liable to plaintiff injured by employee pushing lunch wagon from which food sold to members); Grueninger v. President & Fellows of Harvard College, 343 Mass. 338, 178 N.E.2d 917 (1961) (college held not immune from liability for negligence in medical treatment furnished by it for a fee under an insurance plan); Phipps v. Aptucxet Post, 7 Mass. App. 928, 389 N.E.2d 1042 (1979) (dances held by charitable corporation to pay expenses of its building).

Missouri: Blatt v. Geo. H. Nettleton Home for Aged Women, 365 Mo. 30, 275 S.W.2d 344 (1955) (charitable corporation held liable for injuries to invitee of tenant caused by negligent maintenance of common stairway in office building owned and operated by it), noted in 33 Chi.-Kent L. Rev. 349, 21 Mo. L. Rev. 97, 4 St. Louis U.L.J. 92.

New Jersey: Kirby v. Columbian Inst., 101 N.J. Super. 205, 243 A.2d 853 (1968) (operation of public bar and bowling alley).

North Carolina: Turnage v. New Bern Consistory No. 3, 215 N.C. 798, 3 S.E.2d 8 (1939) (Masonic lodge liable for slander in moving picture show, although proceeds given to crippled children's hospital).

Ohio: See Central Publishing House v. Flury, 25 Ohio App. 214, 157 N.E. 794 (1927), *aff'd,* 118 Ohio St. 154, 160 N.E. 679 (1928) (publishing house owned and operated by church); Blankenship v. Alter, 171 Ohio St. 65, 167 N.E.2d 922 (1960) (church conducting bingo game liable for injuries to player), noted in 22 Ohio St. L.J. 653.

Pennsylvania: Winnemore v. Philadelphia, 18 Pa. Super. 625 (1901) (building producing income that was applied to charitable purposes); Shenandoah Borough v. Philadelphia, 367 Pa. 180, 79 A.2d 433 (1951).

Tennessee: Gamble v. Vanderbilt Univ., 138 Tenn. 616, 200 S.W. 510, L.R.A. 1918C 875 (1917) (office building owned and operated by university); Baptist Memorial Hosp. v. Couillens, 176 Tenn. 300, 140 S.W.2d 1088 (1940) (hospital owning office building liable for tort; citing the text).

Texas: Armendarez v. Hotel Dieu, 145 S.W. 1030 (Tex. Civ. App. 1912) (hotel to raise funds for charitable work, held liable to employee for negligence of managing officers).

Canada: Les Dames de Notre Dame v. The King, [1952] 2 D.L.R. 386 (Can. S. Ct.) (religious corporation carrying on laundry business held taxable on that business).

But see *contra* Jackson v. Atlanta Goodwill Indus., 46 Ga. App. 425, 167

ment house conducted by it, on the ground that the conduct of the apartment house was not in itself a charitable undertaking.[7] A post of the American Legion, a charitable corporation, which operated a swing at a carnival at which a person was injured, was held to be subject to liability. It had on hand funds that would be used for the pleasure of the members. It was held that the injured person was entitled to a judgment under which he could reach these funds.[8]

So also although the institution is not conducted for profit, it is not a charitable institution where its purpose is merely to afford pleasure to the members or to promote their social interests.[9] An institution of this sort is not exempt from liability in tort.[10]

§402.2. Unincorporated charities.

In this treatise we are concerned with trusts rather than corporations; and in this chapter we are concerned more with charitable trusts than with charitable corporations. Where the question of exemption from liability in tort is concerned, cases involving charitable corporations are very numerous, but cases involving charitable trusts are rare. Ordinarily, where property is given to individual trustees for charitable purposes, the duties of the trustees are to

---

S.E. 702 (1933), *cert. denied,* 290 U.S. 625 (1933) (store of which proceeds devoted to charity); Cullen v. Schmit, 139 Ohio St. 194, 39 N.E.2d 146 (1942) (basement of church where religious articles were sold; profits to be used for religious purposes).

In Bakal v. University Heights Sanitarium, 277 A.D. 572, 101 N.Y.S.2d 385 (1950), *aff'd mem.,* 302 N.Y. 870, 100 N.E.2d 51 (1951), noted in 1 Catholic U.L. Rev. 165, 2 Syracuse L. Rev. 396, it was held that a proprietary hospital was not liable to a patient for burns caused by one of its nurses, because she was not acting as its servant.

[7]Pearlstein v. A. M. McGregor Home, 79 Ohio App. 526, 73 N.E.2d 106 (1947).

[8]Hammond Post No. 3, Am. Legion v. Willis, 179 Tenn. 226, 165 S.W.2d 78 (1942), noted in 2 Loyola L. Rev. 91.

[9]See §375.2.

[10]Chapin v. Holyoke Young Men's Christian Assn., 165 Mass. 280, 42 N.E. 1130 (1896); Bentley v. Hamden Post 88, 27 Conn. Supp. 56, 229 A.2d 32 (1967).

On the question whether a Young Men's Christian Association is a charitable organization, see §374.11.

make investments and to apply the income for charitable purposes. In cases like that no question of tort liability is likely to
arise. Where property is given for the purpose of conducting a
charitable undertaking, such as the establishment and maintenance of a medical or educational institution, the institution will
ordinarily be incorporated and not conducted by individual
trustees.

There are, however, a few cases in which the question of
liability in tort has arisen where the charitable institution is not
incorporated but is conducted by individual trustees who hold
title to the property. It seems clear that the same principles of
policy are applicable to charitable trusts as are applicable to
charitable corporations, although the technique involved may
be somewhat different. In the case of charitable trusts the situation is more nearly analogous to that of charitable corporations
than it is to that of private trusts.

So far as the right of the victim of the tort to reach the trust
estate is concerned, there are two possible obstacles to his recovery. The first obstacle lies in the policy exempting property
devoted to charity from tort liability. This policy is the same
whether the property is held by a charitable corporation or is
held by individual trustees. In the preceding sections we have
discussed this policy. To the extent to which the victim of the
tort is not permitted to reach property held by a charitable
corporation it cannot reach property held by individual trustees
for charitable purposes.[1] The second obstacle in the case of
charitable trusts lies in the fact that the courts have been reluctant to permit a direct claim against a trust estate. It is true that
even in the case of private trusts a tort creditor can hold the
trustees personally liable and if they are insolvent he can maintain a bill in equity to reach the trust estate if and to the extent
that the trustees are entitled to indemnity out of the trust estate.
It would seem proper, however, to permit a recovery from the
trust estate even though the trustees are not entitled to indemnity.[2] At any rate, in the case of charitable trusts it would seem
that the courts are less hesitant to permit a tort creditor to
enforce his claim against the trust estate directly even though

§402.2. [1]Burgess v. James, 73 Ga. App. 857, 38 S.E.2d 637 (1946).
[2]See §§264, 271A.2.

the trustees are not entitled to indemnity, except so far as public policy exempts the property from such claims. In the case of an unincorporated charity, suit may be brought against the trustees or against an officer as such and recovery allowed out of the trust estate.[3]

A further question arises as to the personal liability of the trustees. Undoubtedly, if the trustees are personally at fault they are personally liable.[4] This is true even in cases where the property of the trust is exempt from liability on grounds of public policy. Where the trustees are not personally at fault it has been held that they are not personally liable.[5] Thus in *Farrigan v.*

[3]See In re Pritt, 113 L.T. 136, 31 T.L.R. 299 (1915).

[4]*England:* Woodward v. Mayor of Hastings, [1944] 2 All E.R. 565, noted in 61 Law Q. Rev. 110, 198 Law T. 3, 199 id. 27, 61 Scot. L. Rev. 26.

Massachusetts: Pease v. Parsons, 273 Mass. 111, 173 N.E. 406 (1930).

Missouri: Schoen v. Kerner, 544 S.W.2d 43 (Mo. App. 1977).

By Georgia Code 1981, §51-1-20, it is provided that trustees and officers of nonprofit hospital organizations shall not be liable to a hospital or persons receiving benefits, in the absence of gross negligence or willful and wanton misconduct.

By West Virginia Code, §35-1-7, as amended by Laws 1969, c. 120, it is provided that trustees of a church shall not be personally liable for any tort in the absence of gross negligence, but may be sued as trustees.

By Iowa Code, §504.5, as inserted by Laws 1975, c. 235, it is provided that directors, officers, members, or other volunteers of a charitable corporation shall not be personally liable for any claim based on an act or omission of such persons performed in the reasonable discharge of their lawful corporate duties. See also §504A.10.

In the case of a charitable corporation, the members of the board of trustees or managers are personally liable in tort if they are personally at fault. Herman v. Board of Educ., 234 N.Y. 196, 137 N.E. 24, 24 A.L.R. 1065 (1922), noted in 8 Cornell L.Q. 248.

See Hawkins, The Personal Liability of Charity Trustees, 95 Law Q. Rev. 99 (1979).

[5]Farrigan v. Pevear, 193 Mass. 147, 78 N.E. 855, 7 L.R.A. (N.S.) 481, 118 Am. St. Rep. 484, 8 Ann. Cas. 1109 (1906); Pease v. Parsons, 273 Mass. 111, 173 N.E. 406 (1930).

In the case of a charitable corporation, the members of the board of trustees and the manager are not personally liable in tort if not personally at fault. Miller v. Concordia Teachers College, 296 F.2d 100 (8th Cir. 1961); Latell v. Walsh, 88 Ohio Abs. 81, 181 N.E.2d 729 (1961) (bishop and priest immune; citing Restatement of Trusts §402).

In Somers v. Osterheld, 335 Mass. 24, 138 N.E.2d 370 (1956), it was held that the superintendent of a state hospital was not personally liable for the

Pevear[6] the plaintiff brought an action of tort against the trustees
of an unincorporated institution for the education and maintenance of destitute boys, alleging that he was injured while in the
employ of the defendants. It appeared that the injury resulted
from the negligence of another employee who put the plaintiff
to work in an unsafe place, and that the defendants were not in
any way personally at fault. It was held that the defendants were
not personally liable. The court said that they did not have
"such a private pecuniary interest as lies at the foundation of the
doctrine of *respondeat superior.*" This ground for denying recovery is too broadly stated. As we have seen, the trustees of a
private trust are liable in tort for the negligence of their employees, although they have not pecuniary interest in the trust other
than their right to compensation.[7] The real basis for the decision, it is believed, is somewhat narrower; it is the desire of the
court to prevent the diversion to other ends of trust funds devoted to charitable purposes. It is the desire to protect the trust
estate rather than to protect the trustees. If the victim of the tort
were allowed to recover against the trustees, they in turn, not
being at fault, would be entitled to indemnity out of the trust
estate.

Where there are several trustees of a charitable trust, and
a tort liability arises in the administration of the trust, and some
of the trustees were at fault and others were not, the former but
not the latter are personally liable to the person injured.[8]

§403. Liability upon Contract

In general, the principles applicable to the liabilities of
trustees of a private trust to third persons upon contracts made
in the administration of the trust[1] are applicable to the trustees
of a charitable trust. The trustees are subject to personal liability
upon contracts made by them in the administration of the trust,

---

negligence of an employee of the hospital under the doctrine of respondeat
superior, unless he was himself at fault.

[6]193 Mass. 147, 151, 78 N.E. 855, 7 L.R.A. (N.S.) 481, 118 Am. St. Rep.
484, 8 Ann. Cas. 1109 (1906).

[7]See §264.

[8]Pease v. Parsons, 273 Mass. 111, 173 N.E. 406 (1930).

§403. [1]See §§262, 263.

unless by the terms of the contract it is provided that they shall not be personally liable.[2] If the contract was properly made in the administration of the trust, the trustees are entitled to indemnity out of the trust estate.[3] Where a contract with a third person is made by the trustees of a charitable trust, the third person can reach the trust property and apply it to the satisfaction of his claim at least to the same extent as in the case where the contract is made by the trustees of a private trust.[4] Where a contract is made by a charitable corporation by the officers of the corporation acting within the scope of their authority, the other party to the contract can maintain a suit against the charitable corporation.

Where a charitable corporation is exempt from liability in tort,[5] it has been held that a person who is damaged through the negligence of an employee of the corporation cannot maintain an action against the corporation for breach of contract on the basis that the corporation agreed to render proper service to him.[6] Thus in *Roosen v. Peter Bent Brigham Hospi-*

[2]Hawthorne v. Austin Organ Co., 71 F.2d 945 (4th Cir. 1934), *cert. denied sub nom.* Austin Organ Co. v. Hawthorne, 293 U.S. 623 (1934), noted in 48 Harv. L. Rev. 674, 19 Minn. L. Rev. 238, 21 Va. L. Rev. 706; Peeples v. Enochs, 170 Miss. 472, 153 So. 796 (1934).

[3]Bradbury v. Birchmore, 117 Mass. 569 (1875); Nelson v. Georgetown, 190 Mass. 225, 76 N.E. 606 (1906).

[4]See §§266-271A.2.

[5]See §402.

[6]*Federal:* Ellsworth v. Brattleboro Retreat, 68 F. Supp. 706 (D. Vt. 1946); Strauss v. Decatur Park Dist., 177 F. Supp. 881 (S.D. Ill. 1959) (municipal corporation); Miller v. Concordia Teachers College, 296 F.2d 100 (8th Cir. 1961).

Alabama: Green v. Hospital Bldg. Auth., 294 Ala. 467, 318 So. 2d 701 (1975).

Arkansas: Helton v. Sisters of Mercy of St. Joseph's Hosp., 234 Ark. 76, 351 S.W.2d 129 (1961), noted in 16 Ark. L. Rev. 289.

Connecticut: Talbot v. Waterbury Hosp. Corp., 22 Conn. Supp. 149, 164 A.2d 162 (1960).

Illinois: Wattman v. St. Luke's Hosp. Assn., 314 Ill. App. 244, 41 N.E.2d 314 (1942).

Kentucky: St. Walburg Monastery v. Feltner's Admr., 275 S.W.2d 784 (Ky. 1955).

Massachusetts: Roosen v. Peter Bent Brigham Hosp., 235 Mass. 66, 126 N.E. 392, 14 A.L.R. 563 (1920).

New Jersey: Fields v. Mountainside Hosp., 22 N.J. Misc. 72, 35 A.2d 701 (1944).

tal[7] a patient sued a hospital for injuries resulting from the negligence of a nurse. There was one count in tort, and another count alleged an oral contract for careful treatment. The court held that the plaintiff could not recover on either count, saying that because there was no liability in tort there was no liability in contract such as was alleged, because the whole matter related to the execution of a charitable enterprise and was governed by the same principles. In *Rudy v. Lakeside Hospital,*[8] where an employee of a hospital negligently lost jewels of a patient entrusted to him, it was held that the hospital was not liable in tort or for breach of contract. In *Lovich v. Salvation Army*[9] an inmate of a charitable home caught typhoid fever as a result of eating food prepared by a typhoid carrier. It was held that the home was not liable on an implied warranty of fitness of the food for consumption, if the authorities of the home were not negligent in employing the carrier. On the other hand, in *Ward v. St. Vincent's Hospital*[10] it was held that a hospital that contracted to furnish a patient with a competent nurse was liable for breach of contract if it did not exercise proper care in the selection of the nurse, and that the patient could include damages for injuries she suffered as a result of the negligence of the nurse. A charitable corporation is, of course, liable on ordinary contracts made by it.[11]

Texas: Goelz v. J. K. & Susie L. Wadley Research Inst. & Blood Bank, 350 S.W.2d 573 (Tex. Civ. App. 1961).

See Shivers v. Good Shepherd Hosp., 427 S.W.2d 104 (Tex. Civ. App. 1968) (hospital not liable for breach of warranty of suitability of drug).

In State ex rel. Sisters of St. Mary v. Campell, 511 S.W.2d 141 (Mo. App. 1974), in an action against a hospital for causing death, it was held that the plaintiffs could not recover in a contract action, and that the tort action was barred by the statute of limitations.

[7]235 Mass. 66, 126 N.E. 392, 14 A.L.R. 563 (1920).

[8]115 Ohio St. 539, 155 N.E. 126 (1926).

See also McEvoy v. Hartford Hosp., 22 Conn. Supp. 366, 173 A.2d 357 (1961).

[9]81 Ohio App. 317, 75 N.E.2d 459 (1947).

[10]39 A.D. 624, 57 N.Y.S. 784 (1899).

See also Armstrong v. Wesley Hosp., 170 Ill. App. 81 (1912); Roche v. St. John's Riverside Hosp., 96 Misc. 289, 160 N.Y.S. 401 (1916), *aff'd,* 176 A.D. 885, 161 N.Y.S. 1143 (1916).

[11]*Arkansas:* Arkansas Baptist College v. Wilson, 200 Ark. 1189 (unrep.), 138 S.W.2d 376 (1940) (contract by college to employ teacher).

Kansas: Schiffelbein v. Sisters of Charity of Leavenworth, 190 Kan. 278, 374 P.2d 42 (1962) (contract to employ plaintiff for life in consideration of forbearance to sue for injuries, although defendant immune from tort liability).

In Portland Section of Council of Jewish Women v. Sisters of Charity, 266 Or. 448, 513 P.2d 1183 (1973), the plaintiff, a charitable corporation, made a contract with the defendant, a hospital, under which the plaintiff paid $5000 in consideration of the defendant's agreement to furnish ward accommodations and services in perpetuity to one person at a time designated by the plaintiff. It was held that the contract was specifically enforceable, although the cost of such services had greatly risen. It was also held that the contract contemplated service only to needy persons.